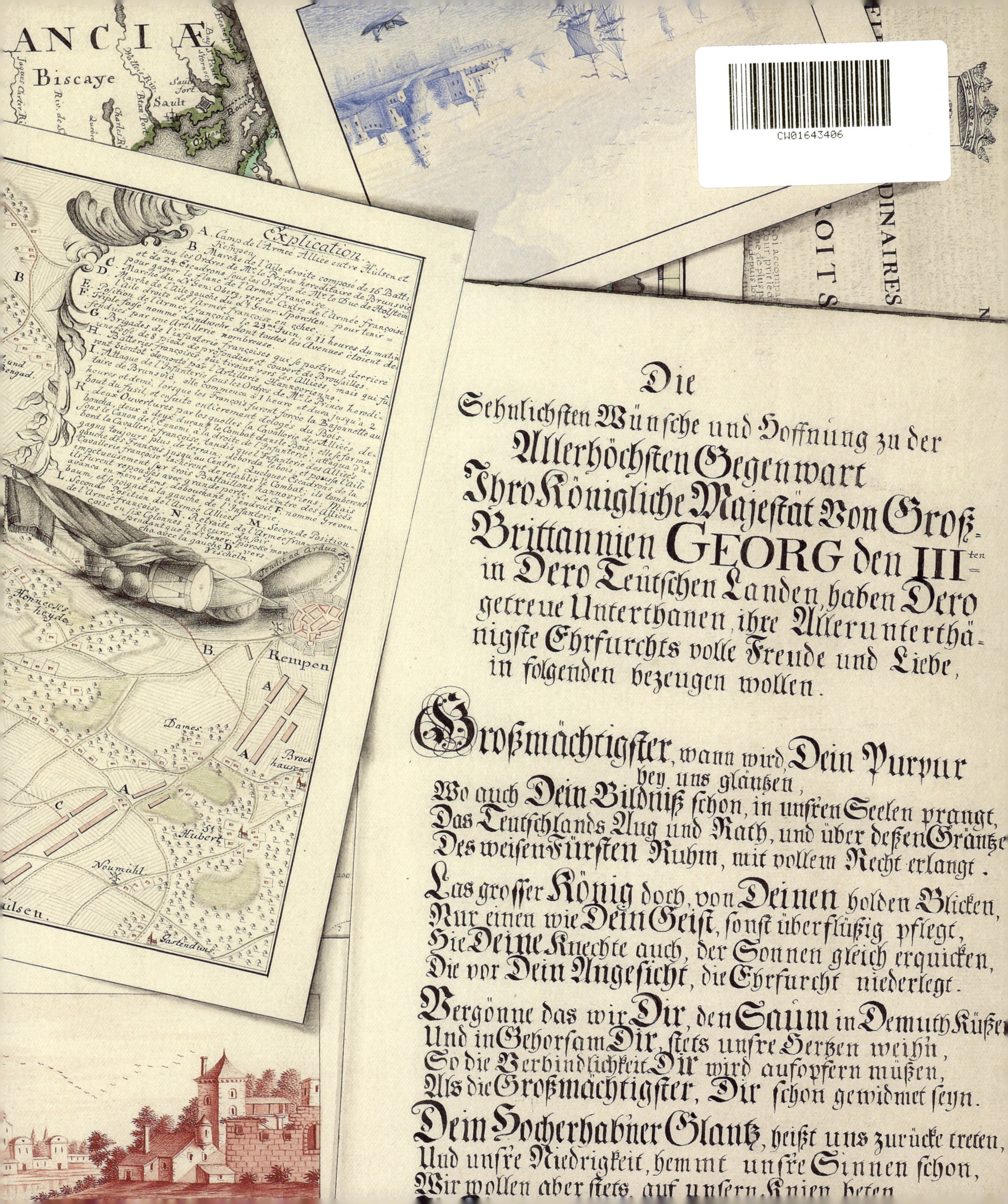

Die
Sehnlichsten Wünsche und Hoffnung zu der
Allerhöchsten Gegenwart
Ihro Königliche Majestät Von Groß-
Brittannien GEORG den III-ten
in Dero Teutschen Landen, haben Dero
getreue Unterthanen, ihre Allerunterthä-
nigste Ehrfurchts volle Freude und Liebe,
in folgenden bezeugen wollen.

Großmächtigster, wann wird Dein Purpur bey uns glänzen,
Wo auch Dein Bildniß schon, in unsren Seelen prangt,
Das Teutschlands Aug und Rath, und über deßen Gräntze
Des weisen Fürsten Ruhm, mit vollem Recht erlangt.

Las grosser König doch, von Deinen holden Blicken,
Nur einen wie Dein Geist, sonst überflüßig pflegt,
Die Deine Knechte auch, der Sonnen gleich erquicken,
Die vor Dein Angesicht, die Ehrfurcht niederlegt.

Vergönne das wir Dir, den Saum in Demuth küßen
Und in Gehorsam Dir, stets unsre Hertzen weihn,
So die Verbindlichkeit Dir wird aufopfern müßen,
Als die Großmächtigster, Dir schon gewidmet seyn.

Dein Hocherhabner Glantz, heißt uns zurücke treten,
Und unsre Niedrigkeit, hemmt unsre Sinnen schon,
Wir wollen aber stets, auf unsern Knien beten

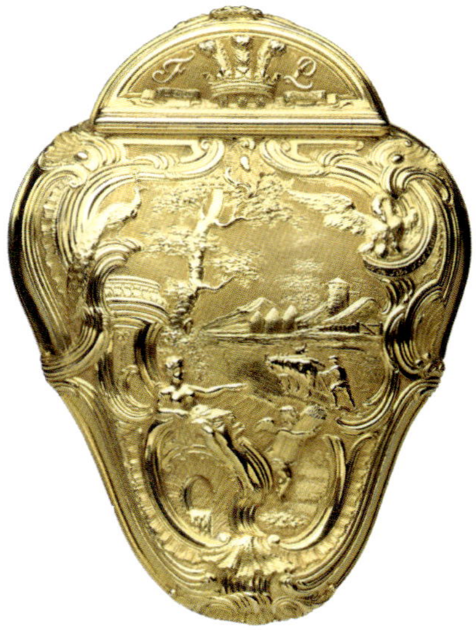

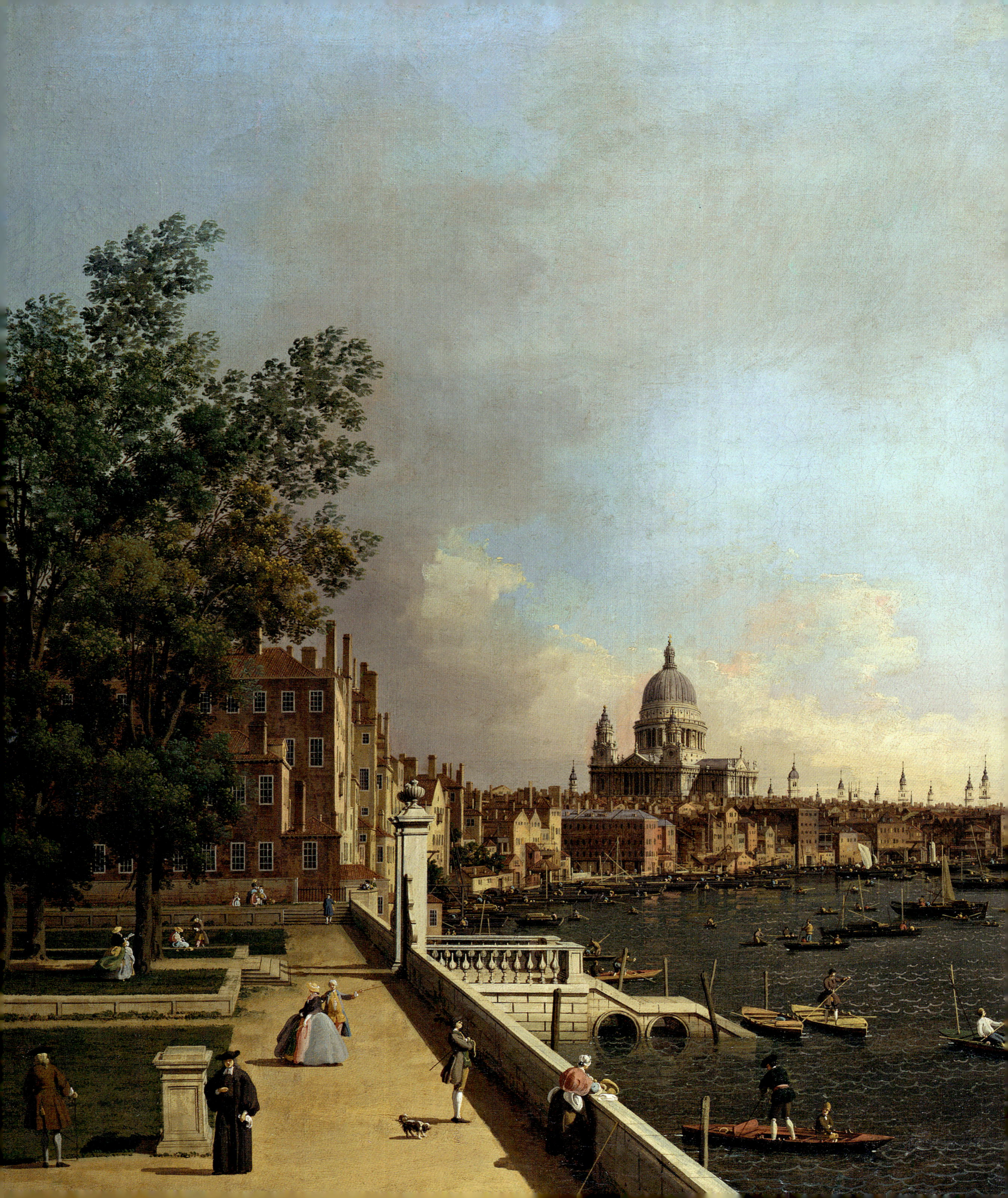

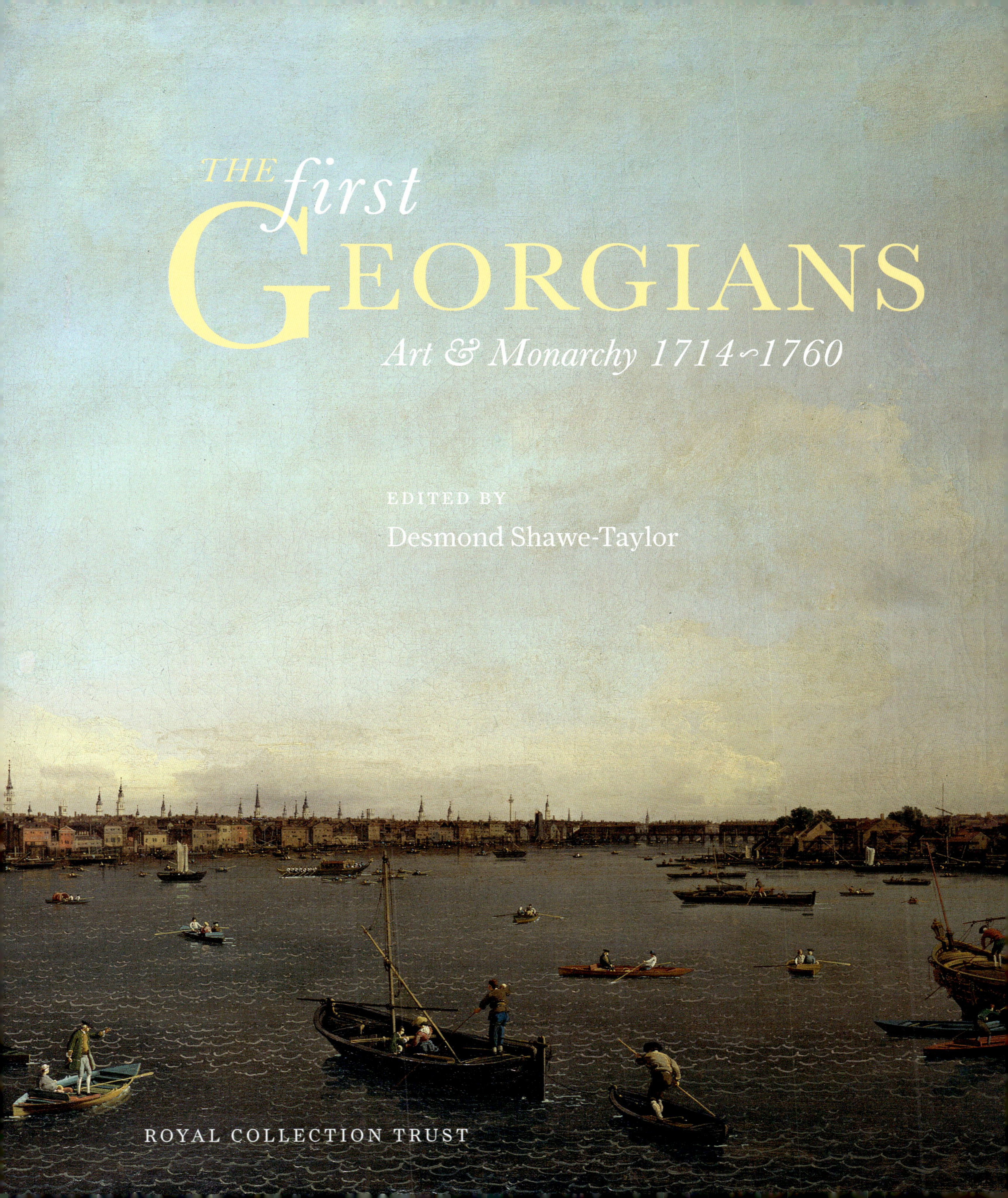

THE *first* GEORGIANS

Art & Monarchy 1714–1760

EDITED BY

Desmond Shawe-Taylor

ROYAL COLLECTION TRUST

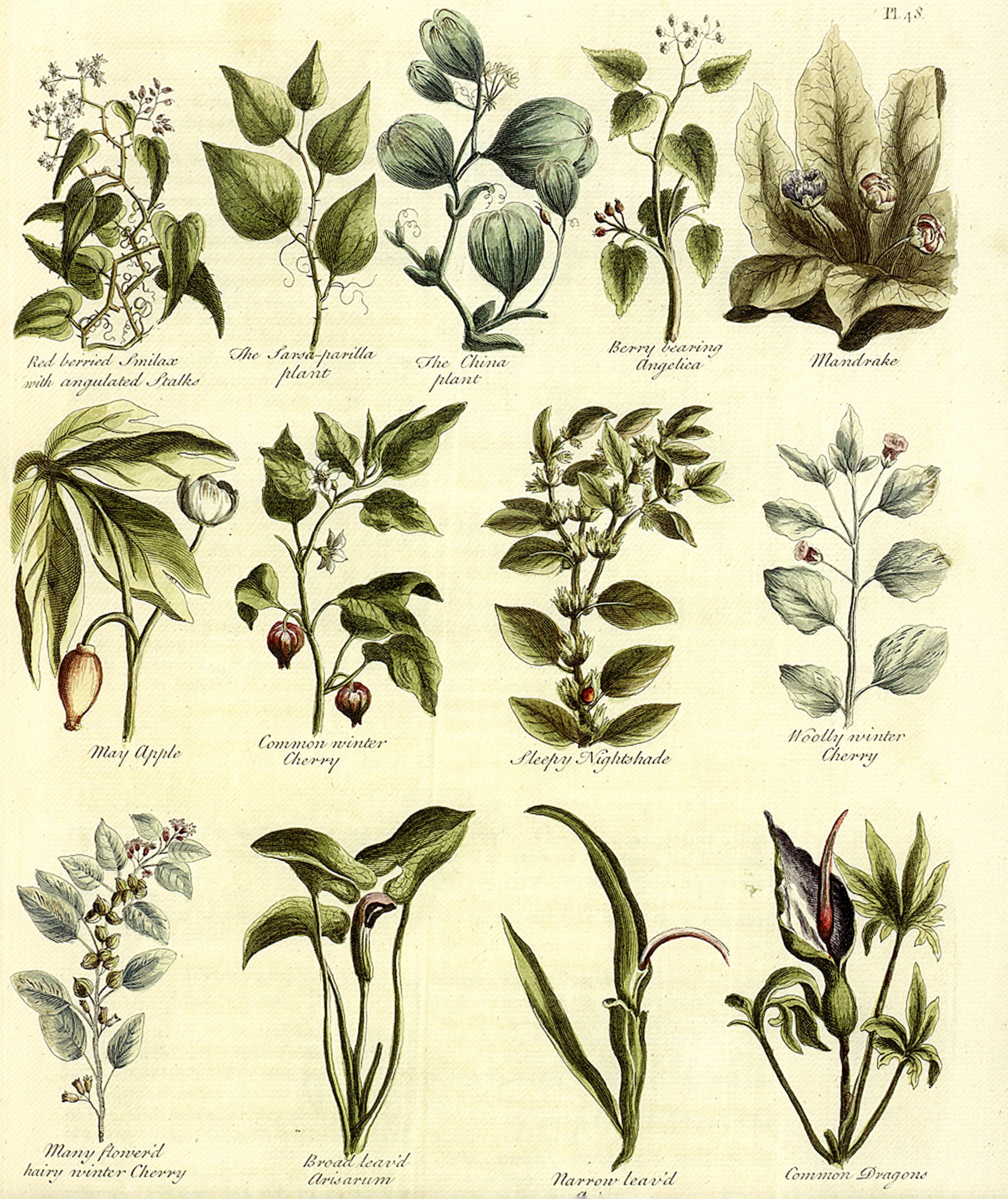
Pl. 48.
Red berried Smilax with angulated Stalks
The Sarsa-parilla plant
The China plant
Berry bearing Angelica
Mandrake
May Apple
Common winter Cherry
Sleepy Nightshade
Woolly winter Cherry
Many flower'd hairy winter Cherry
Broad leav'd Arisarum
Narrow leav'd
Common Dragons

Contents

Additional contributions to the catalogue by
ELIZABETH CLARK, JONATHAN MARSDEN, EMMA STUART

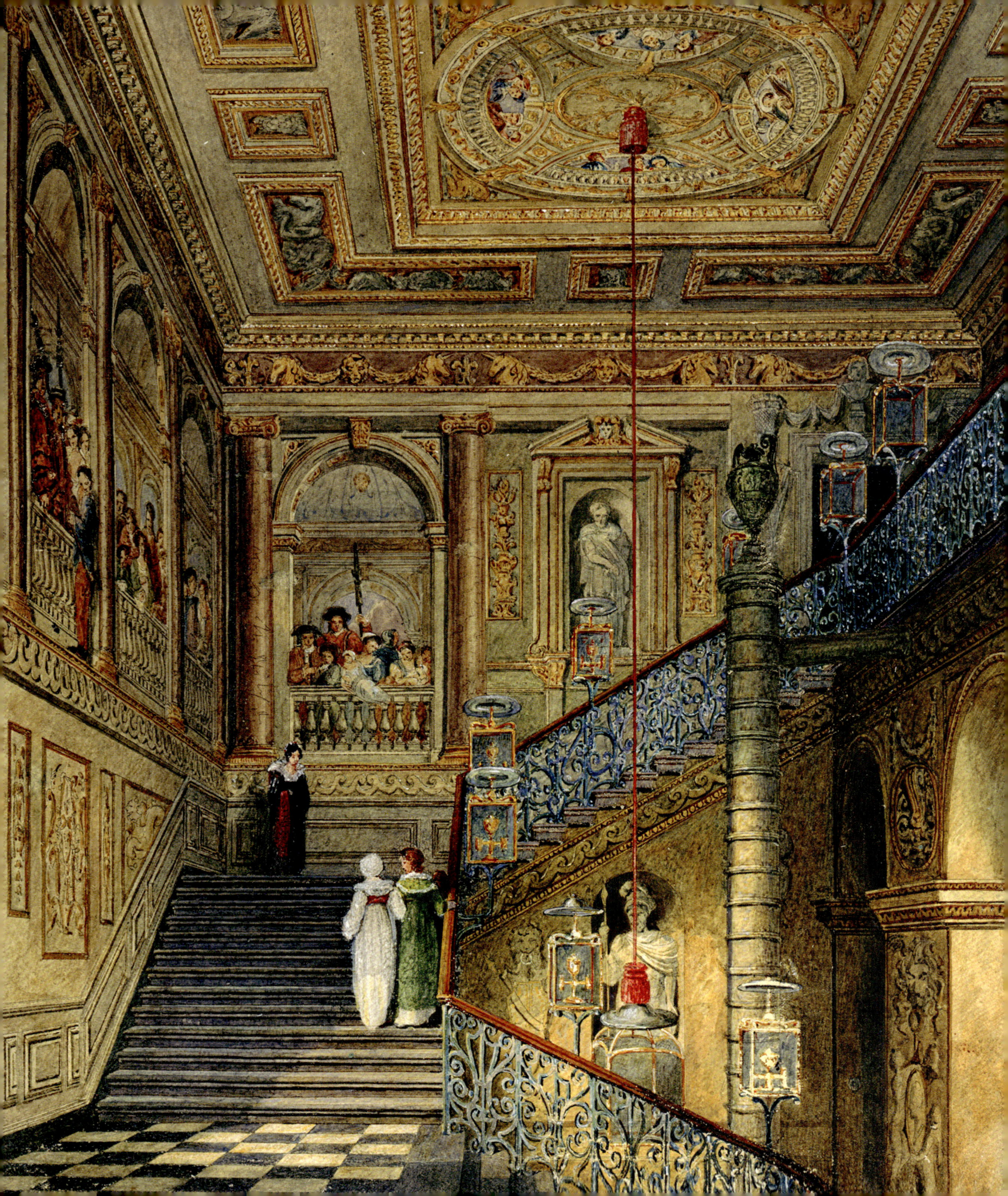

CLARENCE HOUSE

This year marks the three hundredth anniversary of the establishment of the Hanoverian dynasty on the British throne. A range of projects have been planned to celebrate the story of one of Europe's most successful ruling families. In Hanover itself a group of exhibitions tell the story of the 'Personal Union' between the crowns of Britain and Hanover, which lasted from 1714 until 1837. Historic Royal Palaces are redisplaying parts of Kensington Palace and Hampton Court to introduce the four reigns of the 'Georgian period'. An exhibition at the British Library covers the same time span. This Royal Collection Trust exhibition at the Queen's Gallery in London (and the BBC 4 series presented by Lucy Worsley which accompanies it) covers the reigns of George I and George II, from 1714 to 1760, in such a way as to complement the highly successful 2004 exhibition, *George III & Queen Charlotte*. In spite of their different perspectives and time-spans, all these projects agree in celebrating the audacity of the British constitutional experiment and the unique vitality of its culture during the eighteenth century.

The most eloquent apologist for early Georgian Britain was Voltaire, who was inspired by the liberty, religious tolerance and commercial enterprise he encountered. He praised the constitutional limitation on the powers of the monarch and the dynasty's acceptance of this new role. He particularly singled out Queen Caroline as a fellow champion of the enlightenment – an 'amiable philosopher on the throne'. This exhibition reflects the important role played by the Royal Family in the cultural life of the nation during these years. It also brings together objects made at this time but collected by later monarchs, who looked back on these reigns as a period of unique importance and the beginning of a lasting bond between King and country.

Exhibitions of this kind – showing the full range of the Royal Collection – require a particular investment of resources in conservation and scholarship, as well as logistical planning, display, promotion, interpretation and educational programming. As Chairman of the Royal Collection Trust, it gives me great pleasure to pay tribute to the professionalism of our staff, led in this endeavour by Desmond Shawe-Taylor, Surveyor of The Queen's Pictures, which has allowed us to look once again at the Collection, and at this seminal period in our history, with fresh eyes.

Charles

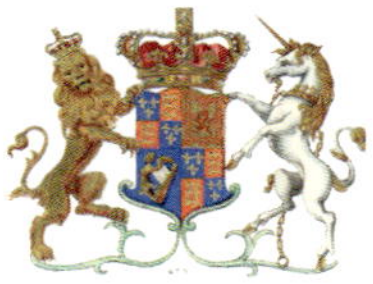
Charles I

I. THE PROTESTANT SUCCESSION: THE HOUSES OF STUART AND HANOVER

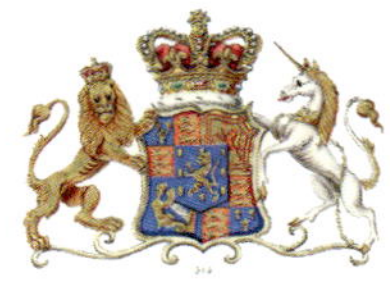
William III

JAMES I
King of England,
Scotland & Ireland
(1566–1625)

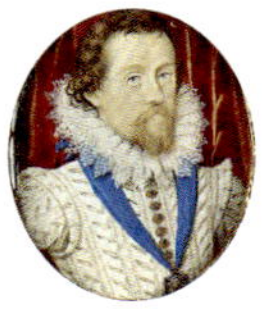

m.

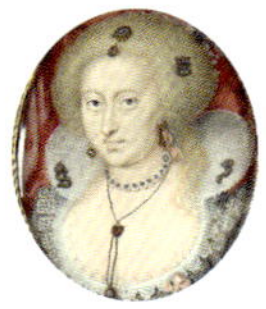

Anne (1574–1619)
d. of King Frederick II
King of Denmark
(Anne of Denmark)

Henrietta Maria
(1609–69)
d. of Henry IV,
King of France &
Navarre

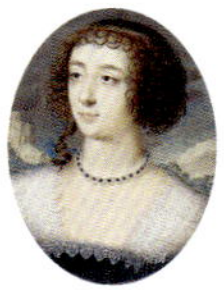

m.

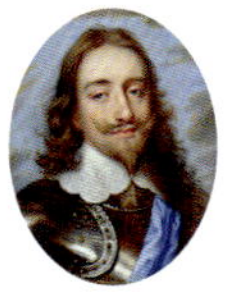

CHARLES I
King of England,
Scotland & Ireland
(1600–49)

Elizabeth
(1506–1662)
(Elizabeth of
Bohemia, The
Winter Queen)

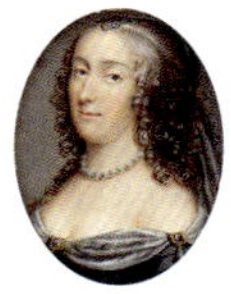

m.

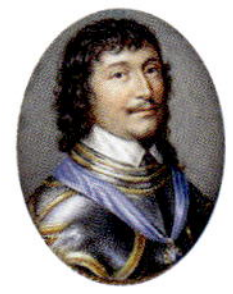

Frederick V,
Elector Palatine of
the Rhine, King of
Bohemia (1596–1632)
(The Winter King)

Sophia
(1630–1714)
(Electress
Sophia)

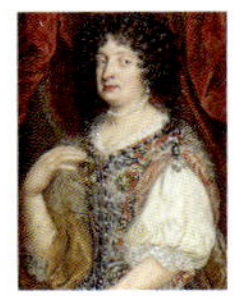

m.

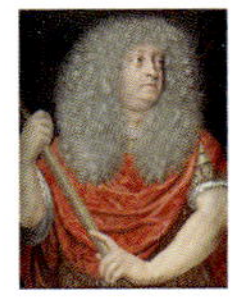

Ernest Augustus,
Prince Bishop of
Osnabrück, Elector
of Hanover
(1629–98)

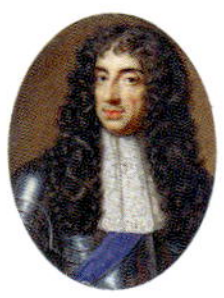

m.

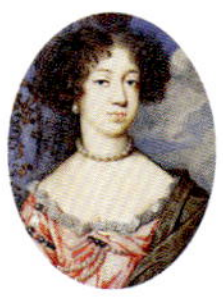

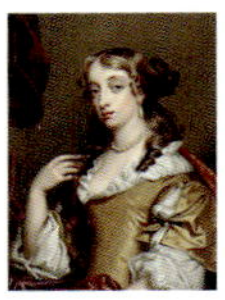

m. (1)

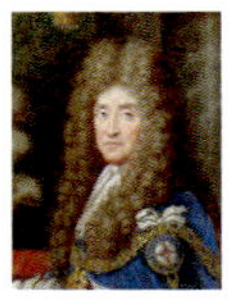

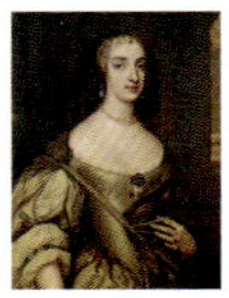

m.

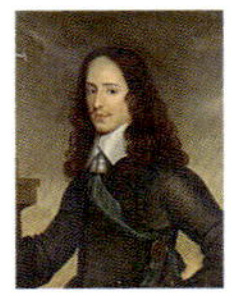

CHARLES II
King of England,
Scotland & Ireland
(1630–85)

Catherine (1638–1705)
d. of Joao IV,
King of Portugal
(Catherine of
Braganza)

Lady Anne Hyde
(1638–71)
d. of 1st Earl of
Clarendon

JAMES II
King of England,
Scotland & Ireland
(1633–1701)

Mary
(1631–60)
The Princess Royal

William II
Prince of Orange
(1626–50)

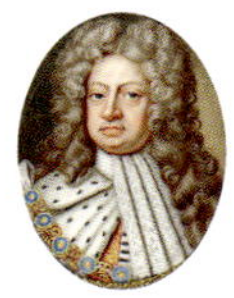

GEORGE I
(see The House of Hanover)

m. (2)

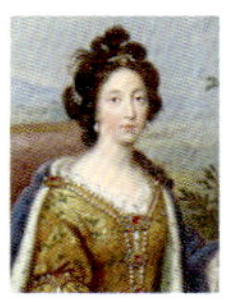

Mary (Beatrice)
of Modena
(1658–1718)
d. of Alfonso IV,
Duke of Modena

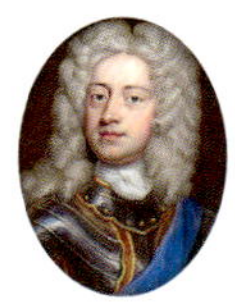

GEORGE II
(see The House of Hanover)

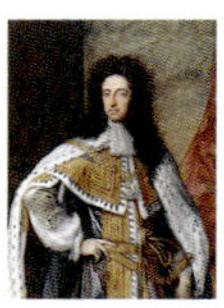

m.

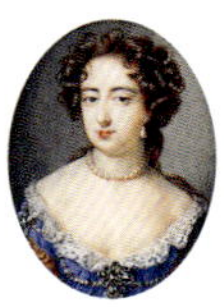

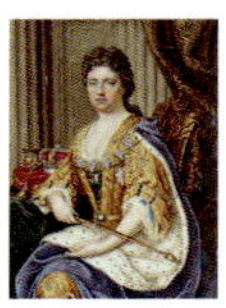

m.

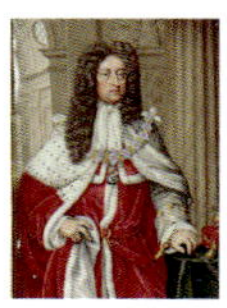

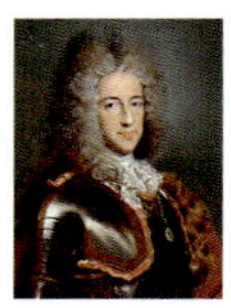

m.

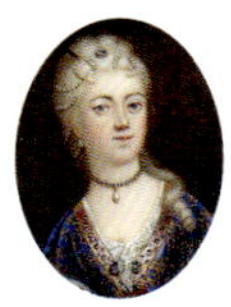

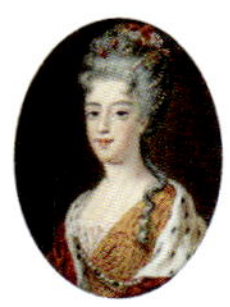

WILLIAM III
Joint King of
England,
Scotland & Ireland
(1650–1702)

MARY II
Joint Queen of
England,
Scotland & Ireland
(1662–94)

ANNE
Queen of England,
Scotland & Ireland
(1665–1714)

George
of Denmark
(1653–1708)

James Francis
Edward, Prince of
Wales (1688–1766)
('The Old
Pretender')

Clementina Sobieska
(1702–35), d. of Prince
Jakob Sobieska,
son of Jan III, King of
Poland

Maria
(1692–1712)

A son
(1687)
(stillborn)

William, Duke
of Gloucester
(1689–1700)

George
(b. & d. 1696)

A son
(1698)
(stillborn)

A daughter
(1684)
(stillborn)

Mary
(1685–7)

Anne
(1686–7)

Mary
(b. & d. 1690)

9 further
miscarried
or stillborn
children

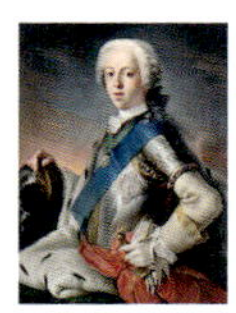

Charles Edward Stuart
(1720–88)
('The Young Pretender')

m.

Louise (1752–1824)
d. of Gustav Adolph, Prince
of Stolberg-Gedern

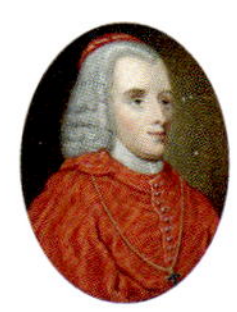

Henry Benedict,
Duke of York,
Cardinal York
(1725–1807)

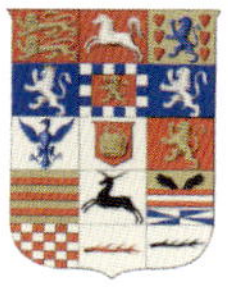
Brunswick-Lüneburg

II. THE HOUSE OF HANOVER AND ITS GERMAN RELATIONS

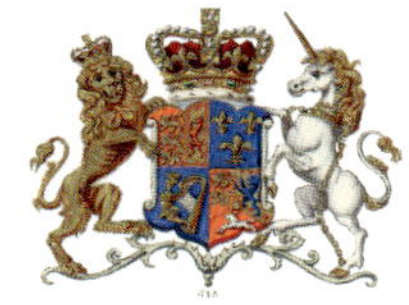
George I

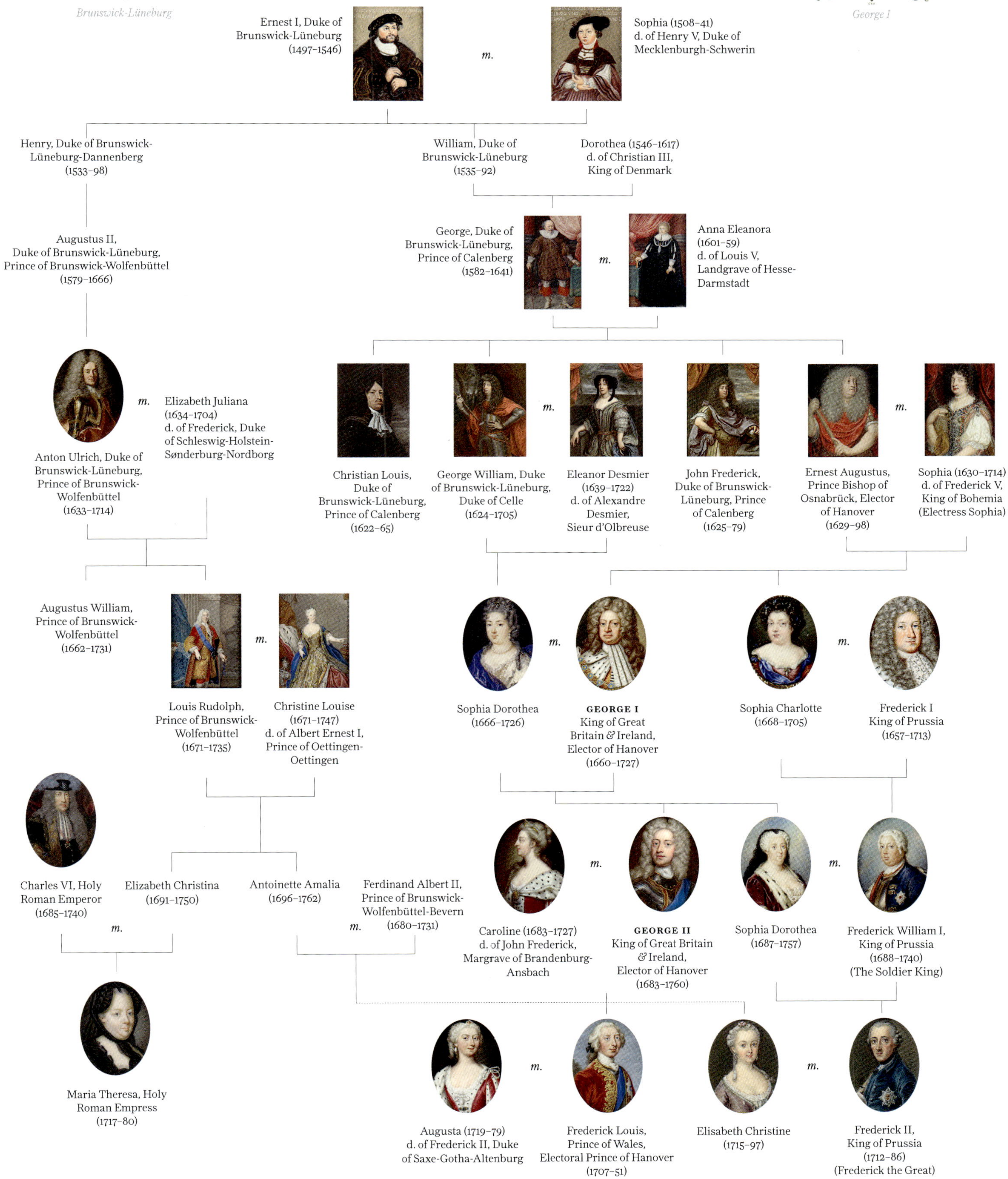

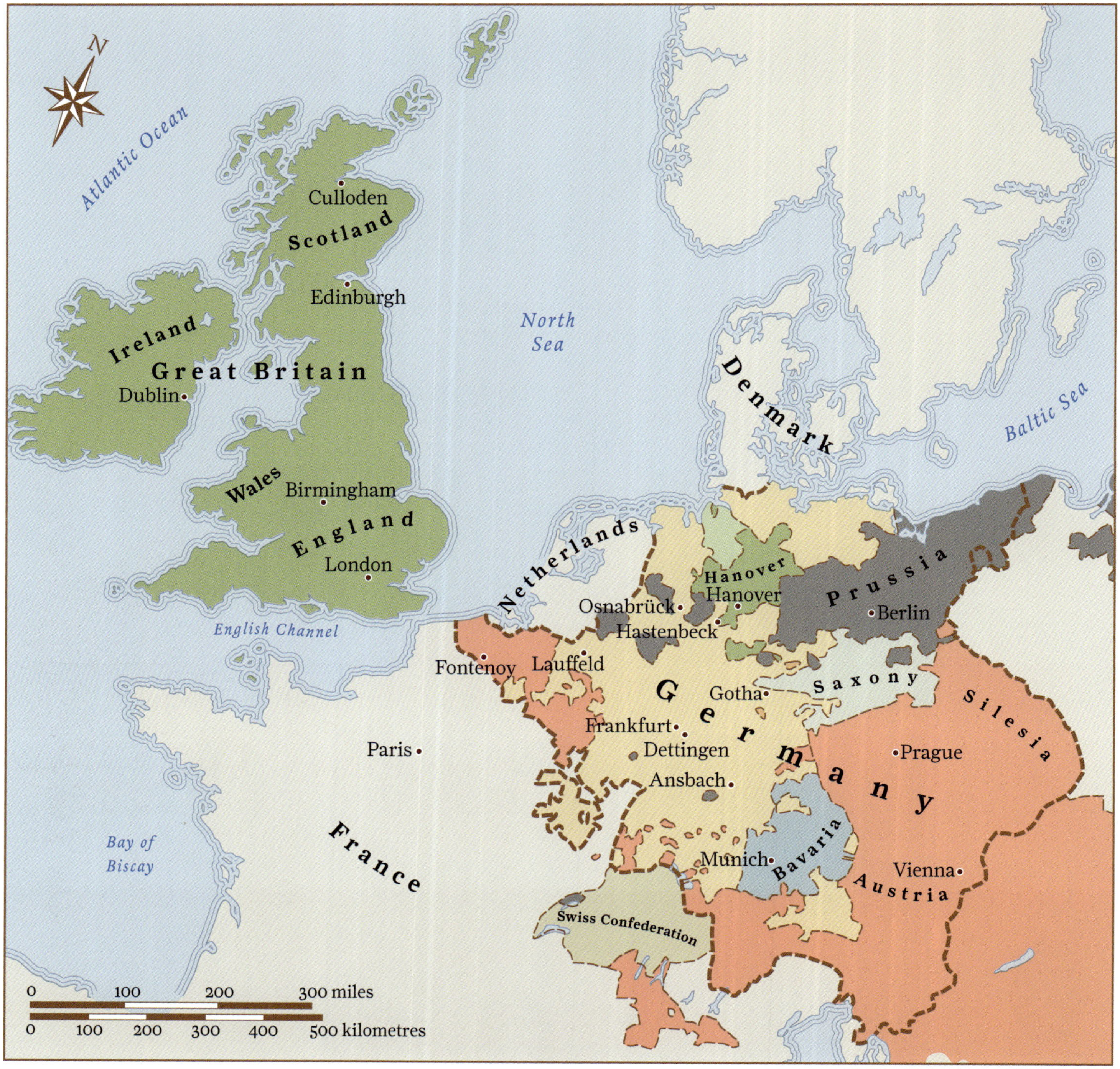

Europe 1714

Habsburg Lands

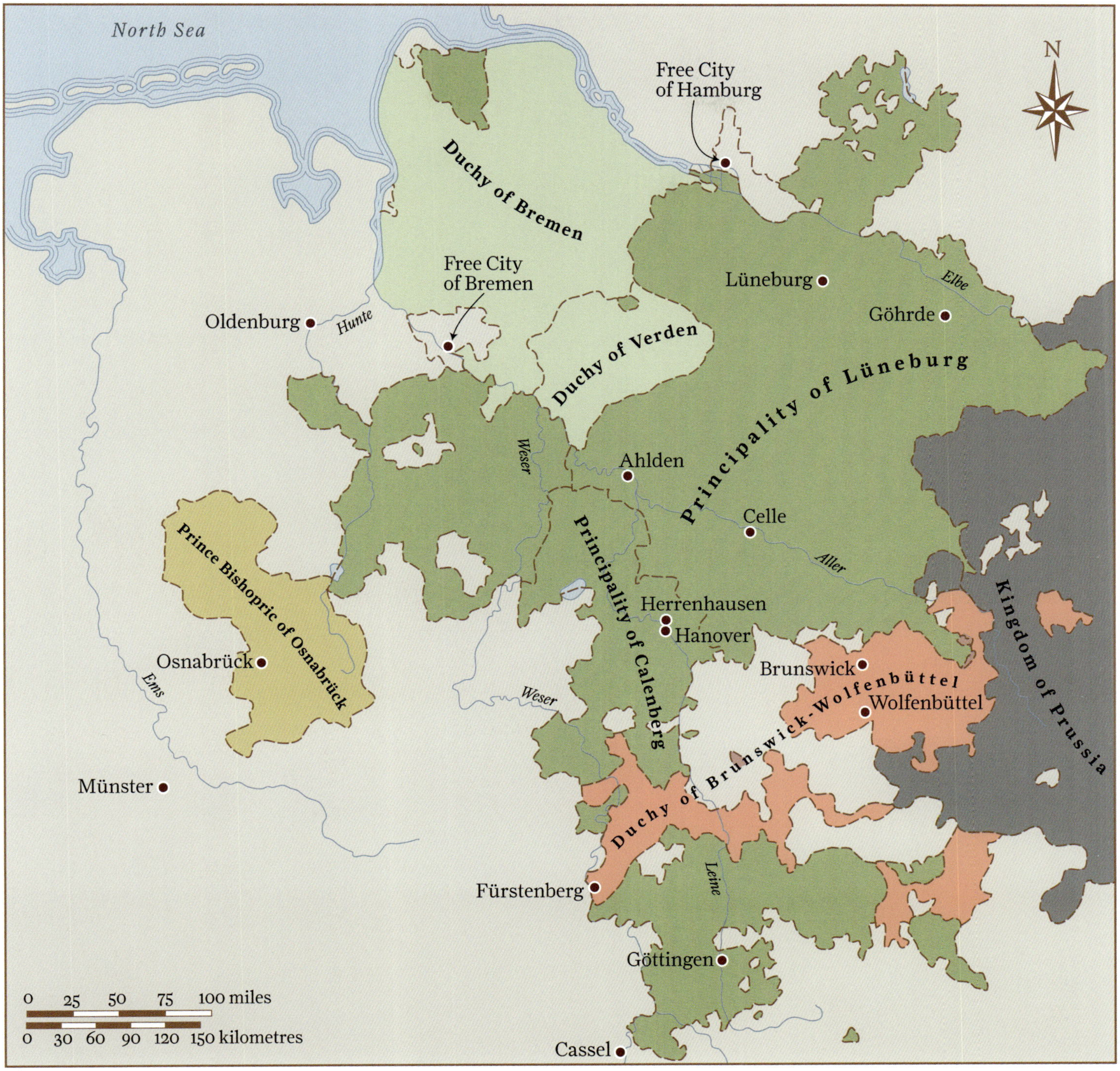

Hanover 1714

The Electorate of Hanover in 1714

Territories purchased by George I from the King of Denmark in 1715

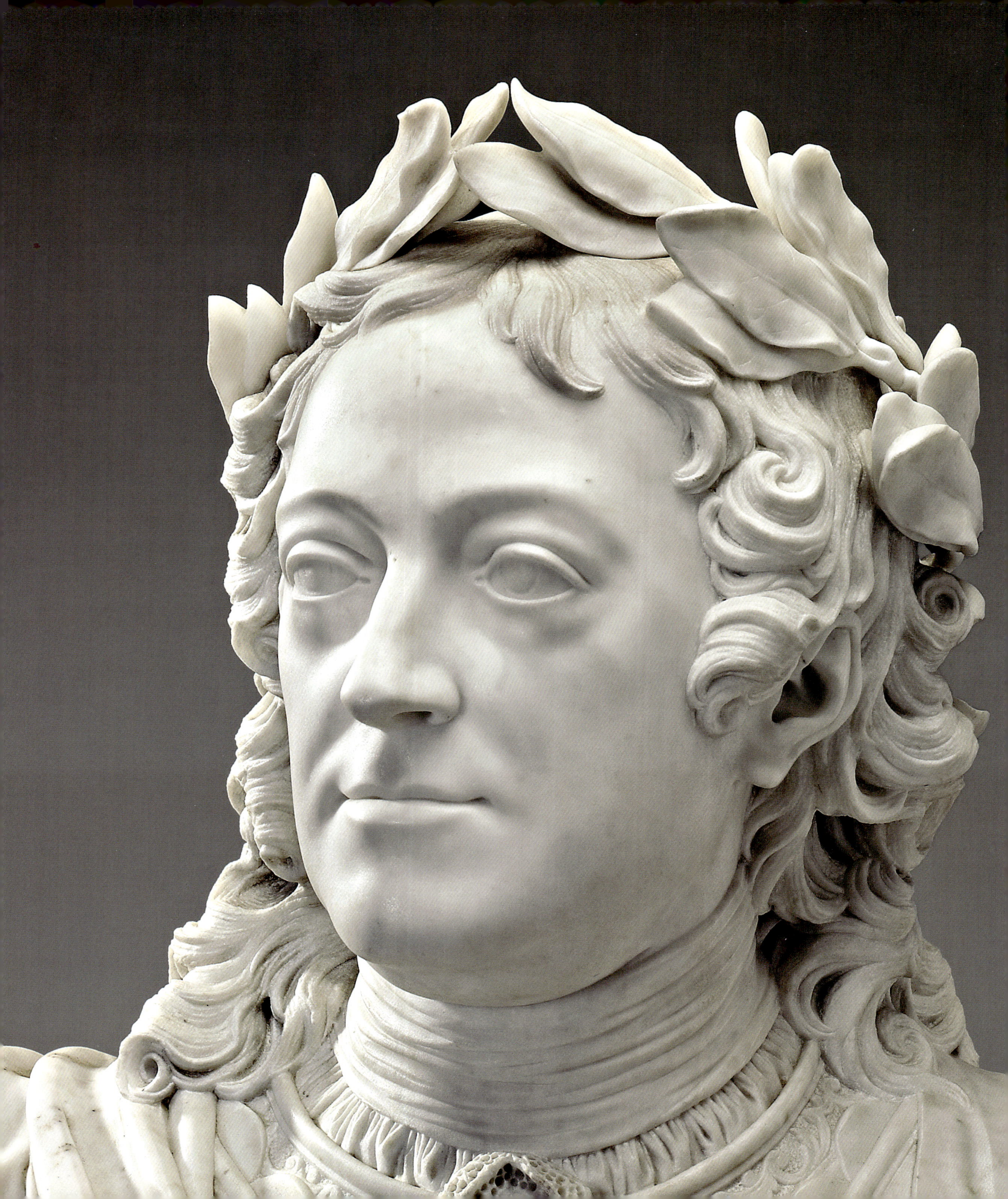

I

Ruling a Free Nation

DESMOND SHAWE-TAYLOR

Your Majesty will find in this Book bold impartial Truths, Morality unstain'd with Superstition, a Spirit of Liberty equally abhorrent of Rebellion, and of Tyranny; the Rights of Kings always asserted, and those of Mankind never laid aside. The same Spirit in which it is written, gave me the Confidence to offer it to the virtuous Consort of a King, who among so many crowned Heads enjoys, almost alone, the inestimable Honour of ruling a free Nation.

(Voltaire, dedication of his *Henriade* to Queen Caroline, 1728)[1]

THE FIRST GEORGE arrived in 1714. Georg Ludwig (1660–1727), Duke of Brunswick-Lüneburg, Elector of Hanover and member of the ancient Guelf dynasty, as George I of Great Britain and Ireland landed at Greenwich on 18 September 1714. The rather lack-lustre ceremony of that day was re-created in a more glorious form by James Thornhill on the walls of the Upper Hall at the Royal Hospital at Greenwich (fig. 1). Here the new King is shown in a triumphal car accompanied by Peace and Happiness, crowned by Eternity, announced by Fame and led by the figures of Truth, Justice, Religion and, most prominent of all, Liberty, with a Cap of Liberty on a staff and apparently flattening a figure of Rebellion.[2]

The new family are properly introduced on the end wall of the Upper Chamber (fig. 2), the position corresponding to the high altar of a church, as if they are the realisation of all the promises made in the other allegorical paintings in the Great Hall. A pyramid of allegories on clouds presents the idea of the return of the age of universal peace envisioned in Virgil's *Fourth Eclogue*, quoted on the frieze above: Stability sits above Astraea (Justice) and the Golden Age (an old man spilling coins). Below we see four Hanoverian generations, many of whose biographies appear below (nos 3–7). The Electress Sophia (see no. 3), with a castellated crown representing Cybele, the earth, is set back beneath the dome of St Paul's. Her son, George I (see no. 4), sits enthroned and receives a sceptre from Providence, which he prepares to plant all over the globe. His son, the Prince of Wales (later George II, see no. 5), stands to his left, with his grandson, Frederick (see no. 7), between them, affectionately resting his hand on his grandfather's knee. The Princess of Wales (later Queen Caroline; see no. 6) stands behind the King representing Prudence, with her sister-in-law, Sophia Dorothea, Queen of Prussia (1687–1757), who represents Concord. The younger children of the Prince and Princess of Wales, including William Augustus, Duke of Cumberland (see no. 40), sit on the steps, representing the various arts – Painting, Poetry and Music – which are tenderly nursed by Peace and Plenty. For all the extravagant allegorical flattery the new family seem down to earth, wholesomely domestic and reassuringly numerous (see nos. 9 and 15).

On the vault above them in the Upper Hall is an allegory of the apotheosis of Queen Anne (see no. 1); on the wall facing George's triumphant arrival is a depiction of the landing at Torbay of William III (see no. 8). The whole of the vault of the Great Hall is given over to an allegorical celebration of the reign of William and Mary and the

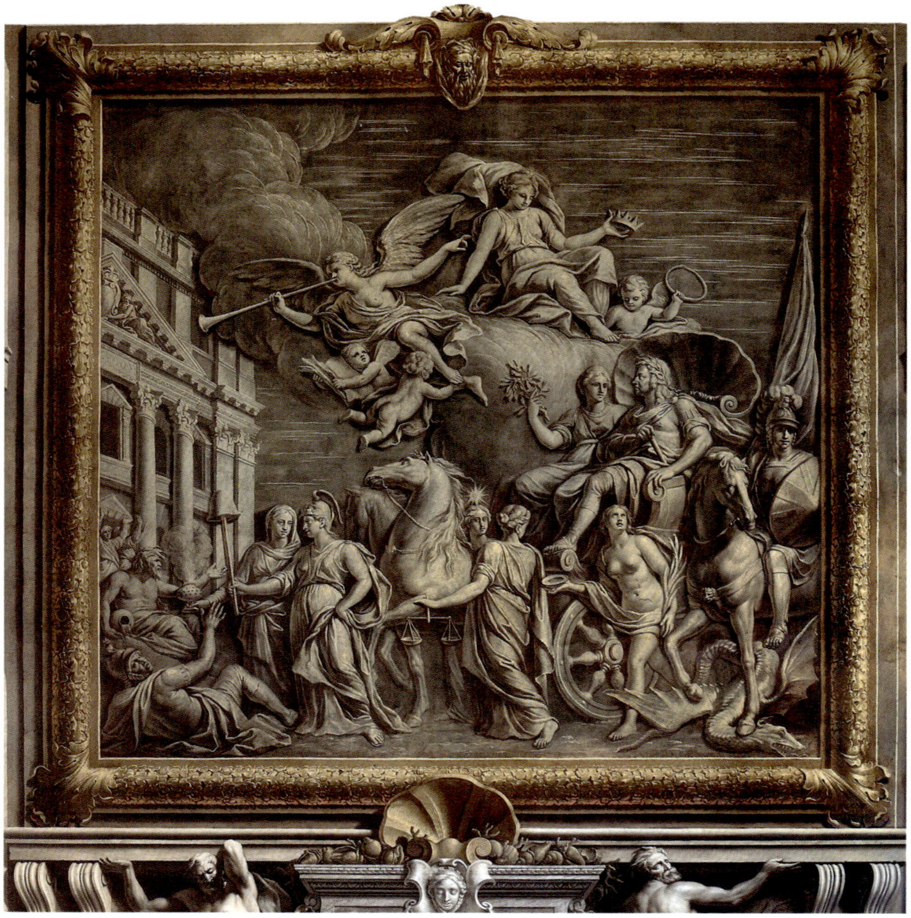

FIG. 1
Sir James Thornhill
The Triumphal Arrival of George I at Greenwich, 1725
Fresco
North Wall, Upper Hall, Old Royal College, Greenwich

ideals of the Glorious Revolution. This was not a royal commission, but one given by the Directors of the Naval Hospital for a room originally intended as a dining hall for wounded seamen. This is nonetheless the best expression of the ideals of the new dynasty and entirely typical in its members' attempt to associate themselves as seamlessly as possible with the Glorious Revolution of 1688 and the Stuart reigns which followed (see no. 8). The royal house might be different but the ideas were the same.

This tact draws attention to the contrast between the two foreign invaders. William's genealogical right was based on his Queen and co-ruler Mary II, who was James II's eldest daughter (see Genealogial Table, p. 8). The pair (or their supporters) disputed the legitimacy of the newly born Prince James, Mary's half-brother (see nos. 2 and 42), and claimed the throne from Mary's father, James II, on the grounds that his leaving the country represented an act of abdication.[3] William and Mary usurped the throne from an unpopular king in the type of royal family struggle which fills the pages of Shakespeare's history plays. By contrast George I ascended the throne after the death of the popular Queen Anne, whose twelve-year reign was one of the most successful in Britain's history. He had the flimsiest genealogical claim: fifty members of the European princely class had better. He was there because he was Protestant and the fifty were Catholic; he was chiefly there because the British people had found a way of choosing rather than being chosen. George's arrival was not a clandestine coup but an openly prepared and legally watertight process of succession-planning. The Act of Settlement of 1701 said that only a Protestant might wear the British crown and that

FIG. 2
Sir James Thornhill
The Family of George I, 1725
Fresco
West Wall, Upper Hall, Old
Royal College, Greenwich

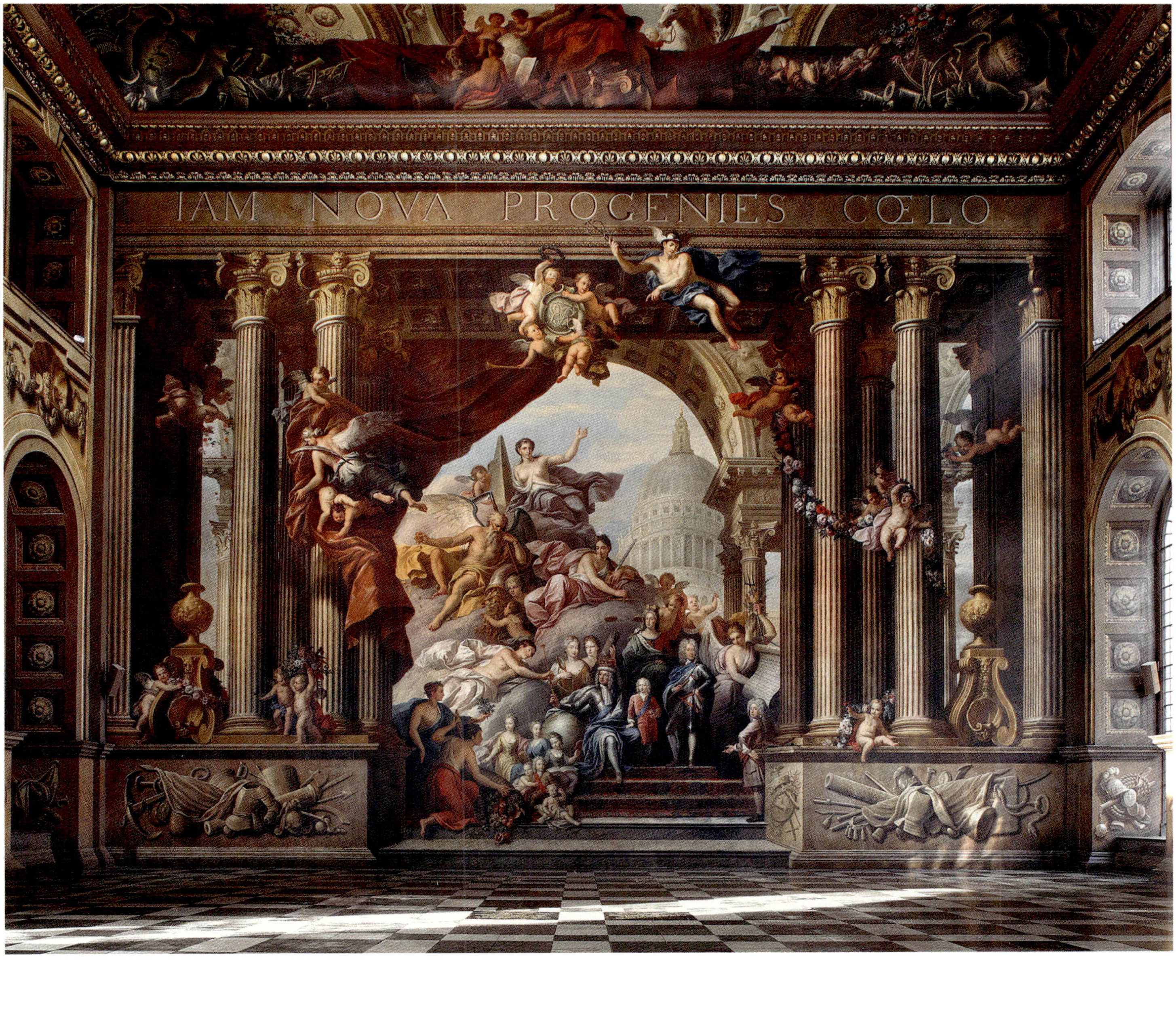

therefore the rightful claimant (upon the death of Queen Anne without issue) was Electress Sophia, the youngest daughter of James I's daughter, Elizabeth of Bohemia, and mother of George I (see Genealogical Table, p. 8). What the Act did not have to say, because it was obvious to all, was that it had the power to make a king. It demonstrated that ultimately the Act *was* the King.[4] It was for this reason that the Act of Settlement (and the mere fact of the Hanoverian succession) was described as a manifestation of the great tradition of British liberty, the second half of the Glorious Revolution and a sort of modern Magna Carta.[5] The Act of Union of 1707, bringing together the Scottish and English legislature, was driven by Parliament's desire to smooth the dynastic transition and can be seen as a momentous by-product of the Hanoverian succession.

The characteristic by which early Georgian Britain defined itself was liberty.[6] The power of the monarch was limited by a representative assembly. To us this immediately prompts the question 'how limited' and 'how representative', but at the time the situation could be confidently summed up by saying that 'the Kings of England are empowered to do their subjects as much good as they will, but that they are bound by laws which prevent them from doing harm'.[7] In 1713 *Cato, a Tragedy* by Joseph Addison (1672–1719) received its first performance; it told of the last days of the noblest champion of the Roman Republic, at whose suicide Rome itself was said to expire. Addison was urging his modern countrymen, who had driven out the tyrant James II, as the Romans had eliminated Julius Caesar, not to re-submit by calling James III back from his French exile, as the Romans had by accepting Augustus as their emperor.[8] The play was a triumph and became one of the century's liberty anthems: Voltaire wrote admiringly of it; George Washington had it performed to his troops at Valley Forge in 1778.[9] To understand its prestige we need to remember that its author could call himself without irony a 'Senator': Joseph Addison was the Member of Parliament for Malmesbury and Secretary of State for the Southern Department in 1717–8.[10] A play dealing with the effective demise of the Roman Senate emerged from a major European power which had awakened that most sacred of institutions from a hibernation of seventeen centuries.[11] Liberty for the early eighteenth century was less about wretches blinking into the light at the storming of the Bastille or Don Pizarro's prison and more about the senator class – elites of birth, wealth and talent – who could flourish in a society which protected property and allowed freedom of expression, worship and exchange.[12] These advantages were understood to be available for all, not least the many foreigners exiled in cosmopolitan London, like the Huguenot general who led George II's troops (no. 39) or the craftsmen who contributed so much to the manufacture of English luxury goods (see pp. 396–7). But the early Enlightenment found most glory in the veneration of exceptional individuals who could live in Britain without needing to conceal their stature by bowing and stooping. Goldsmith describes the British as Nature's elite:

With daring aims, irregularly great,
Pride in their port, defiance in their eye,
I see the lords of human kind pass by
Intent on high designs, a thoughtful band,
By forms unfashion'd, fresh from Nature's hand;

Fierce in their native hardiness of soul,
True to imagin'd right above controul,
While even the peasant boasts these rights to scan,
And learns to venerate himself as man.
(Goldsmith, *The Traveller or A Prospect of Society*, 1764, ll. 333–4)

This returns us to the comparison between William III and George I, because it was clearly easier to cast the great-grandson of the founder of the Dutch Republic (William the Silent; 1533–84) in the role of champion of liberty than an absolutist German prince with a wife locked up at home (see p. 33).[13] The response to this dilemma was (and to some extent remains) an attempt to minimise the significance of Hanover altogether: to adapt Pitt's words, what could a 'despicable Electorate' possibly offer a 'great, powerful and formidable kingdom'?[14] If what the Hanoverians brought to the table might seem threatening or alien then better to suggest that they brought nothing. Dullness is always reassuring. Some things should be said in defence to this approach. The establishment of a constitutional monarchy is surely of more significance than the character of any individual monarch. It is surely true to say that the epicentre of political and cultural life of Britain started to shift inexorably away from the court at this time.[15] These pages are full of private ventures, like the Chelsea porcelain factory (pp. 400–4) or Handel's opera company (pp. 380–2), which on the Continent would have enjoyed royal patronage. The list of commercial and philanthropic institutions founded during these years without royal patronage could be extended to include six London hospitals and the State of Georgia.[16] The first performance of the first national anthem – 'God save the King' – took place in 1745 not in St James's Palace or Westminster Abbey but a London theatre.[17] The Hanoverians themselves seem deliberately to have maintained a low profile – discreet and workmanlike in London and its surrounding residences, invisible elsewhere. None of these things, however, made the Hanoverians insignificant or actively hostile to the British constitutional project. Nor did they mean that significant proportions of the population were not to various degrees loyal to their new dynasty: the Swiss visitor Saussure was surprised at the respect shown him by George I's courtiers, noting that 'The English do not consider their king to be so very much above them that they dare not salute him, as in France, though they have a profound respect for him, are greatly attached to him, and are sincerely faithful to him'.[18] The range of objects described in these pages and the stories behind them reveal the part (even if only second fiddle) played by the first Georges in British culture and society of the period.

So what sort of culture and society did the first Georges find and rule over? The most important characteristic after the love of liberty, and obviously related to it, was fractiousness. What else could be expected of a period in which there were two rival British kings, one based in London and the other in Rome (see no. 3), both enjoying enthusiastic support (and enduring bitter hostility) throughout the period? The containment of the Jacobite threat was the business of the first thirty years of Hanoverian rule and is treated in Chapter III. The Stuart-Hanoverian dynastic struggle was expressed at home in the rivalry in Parliament of the Tory and Whig factions, the latter supporting the Hanoverian succession and not surprisingly therefore finding themselves in office for the duration of the first two reigns. Fractiousness did not, however, stop there: the Whig party split into two rival factions, the 'Patriots' and the 'Courtiers', defined by Lord Hervey as 'Whigs in place' and 'Whigs out of place'.[19] The Hanoverian family split in rather the same way: George II (while Prince of Wales) argued violently with his father, George I; Frederick, Prince of Wales, argued violently with his father, George II (see no. 17); the first three generations established a convention whereby successive Kings and Princes of Wales fought each other for at least the rest of the century. The Hanoverians did not invent filial impiety amongst princes, as the story of David and Absalom might demonstrate; what Britain provided was a public and political stage upon which it could be enacted. The impact lay not so much in the factions supported by the Princes of Wales, which in general came to nothing, but in the process by which the Prince was thereby lured away from the palace and the court and absorbed into the cultural life of the capital.[20] Much has been said of the way in which the British Royal Family became bourgeois during the nineteenth century; it had prepared itself during the eighteenth century by becoming aristocratic. Frederick, Prince of Wales, in particular presented himself as a fashionable man about town, becoming a member of the Saddlers' Company and the Freemasons, and forming several clubs of his own.[21] Frederick's bust (no. 7) was commissioned to adorn an aristocrat's 'Temple of Friendship' and to signal his leadership of the Patriot (or 'Whigs out of place') faction.[22]

A tangible expression of this tendency to go native can be found in the royal building projects (or their absence), described in Chapter II. The significant gap in royal patronage during this period was the failure to re-build Whitehall Palace, the London home of the monarchy, which had burned down in 1698 (see p. 54). At the same time very little architectural work was done at St James's Palace or Windsor Castle. From the moment in 1717 that George II (when Prince of Wales) was ejected from St James's Palace by his father and set up at Leicester House (see p. 56), significant acts of royal patronage tended to centre around residences more aristocratic than royal. The first Georges lavished attention on houses – Leicester House, Carlton House, the White House at Kew and Park Place – and palaces of domestic scale, like Kensington and Richmond. This trend continued into the next reign, when George III acquired the Queen's House (now Buckingham Palace) and the Prince of Wales (later George IV) created Europe's most magnificent town house at Carlton House. Unlike the inherited royal palaces these houses did not come complete with painting collections (except in the unusual case of Kew), which is why they (and the Princes of Wales who inhabited them) account for the lion's share of Old Master acquisitions. The fact that fourteen of the twenty paintings catalogued in Chapter VI were acquired by Frederick, Prince of Wales, reflects the duration of his exile from royal residences (from 1737 until his death in 1751) as well as his enthusiasm for the Old Masters.

There can be no greater contrast between this process of royal integration and the way in which Louis XIV had forced his nobility to quit Paris for Versailles. Louis had made a new aristocracy out of functionaries who owed everything to him, marginalising the ancient nobility with wealth and lineage. The families enriched by the early Hanoverians by contrast were from the landed aristocracy, with remarkably little patronage extended to mistresses, illegitimate children and favourites brought over from Germany. Neither the foreign dynasty nor the emergence of representative government did anything to undermine the power of the traditional landed class. This British aristocracy, so comfortably in possession of the field, differed from their Continental equivalents in their attitude to trade. They were happy to trade themselves and willing to accept merchants into their caste, providing they were wealthy enough.[23] Almost all the commercial enterprises of the period, at home and abroad, depended upon this enterprising caste of aristocratic merchants and merchant-aristocrats, whether it was the East India Company, which after the Battle of Plassey in 1757 became the effective ruler of half of India, or the Bridgewater Canal, which opened in 1761.[24] Voltaire explained how much more was contributed to the world by a merchant who enriched his country giving orders from his study to Surat and Cairo than by a powdered courtier who knows precisely at what time the King rises and retires.[25] Some of the most enduring emblems of Englishness were invented at this time, celebrating this intersection of gentlemen and businessman: Sir Andrew Freeport, the city merchant described in *The Spectator*, who referred to the sea as the 'British Common'; Swift's merchant captain, Gulliver, a giant amongst the petty courtiers of Lilliput; John Bull himself, the type of the independently minded English merchant, invented in 1712 by John Arbuthnot (1667–1735).[26]

Voltaire wrote enthusiastically about gentlemen with a head for business partly because he was one himself. He was first attracted to England by the copyright laws which made it worth his while to publish an English translation of his *Henriade*, a eulogy of Henri IV of France with many admiring remarks about his contemporary on the English throne, Elizabeth I.[27] The dedication to Queen Caroline is quoted above and shows the link made at this time between the philosophical study of history and the love of liberty, discussed in Chapter VII. The licensing of publications was operated throughout Europe in the Renaissance period as a system of royal censorship; it developed in England in the seventeenth century into a printer's monopoly, held by the Stationers' Company. When John Locke and others took up the cause in 1693 they turned it into a means of protecting the intellectual property of the author; the 'Act for the Encouragement of Learning', better known as the 'Statute of Anne', was passed in 5 April 1710.[28] This was the scribbler's Glorious Revolution.[29] Hogarth successfully campaigned for a law to cover printed imagery in the same way as printed text; the so-called 'Hogarth's Act' (see p. 140) was passed in 1735.[30] These laws made fortunes for writers like Pope and artists like Hogarth, and meant that there was a tangible financial expression to the veneration of genius which was such an important part of the period. Grub Street, the home of the struggling but alarmingly prolific professional writer, was another side of this freedom of opportunity.[31] Restless greedy scribblers were the literary manifestation of an early Georgian type – energetic and self-seeking opportunists, whether picture dealers, South Sea speculators, or place-seekers crowding the levees of the great (see no. 311). The descriptions and the images of these people come from the favourite genre of period – satire. Visual satire matched its literary equivalent; most aspects of British cultural life find themselves ridiculed in the prints of Hogarth described in Chapter IV.

All these things – satirical freedom, political factions, rampant new money – suggest a society spiralling out of control. The image is deliberately chosen because the new English science offered a rational for this disorder, suggesting that if properly observed things were 'spiralling *in* control'. According to Voltaire, the correct answer to the trite and frivolous question who was the greatest man who ever lived was Sir Isaac Newton (1642–1727).[32] Newton's discoveries occurred during the Restoration period and the foundation of the Royal Society in 1660 was owed to Charles II, but he lived into the Georgian period, when the honours bestowed upon him in life and death seemed to symbolise the fair-mindedness of a free society.[33] Newton's work, especially on gravity and the motion of the spheres, was also widely popularised.[34] Voltaire, for example, devoted many of his *Letters Concerning the English Nation* of 1733 to explaining English philosophy and Newton in particular. He introduces Newton by observing that the Frenchmen arriving in London finds philosophy, like everything else, very much changed, for he 'had left the World a *plenum*, and he now finds it a *vacuum*. At *Paris* the Universe is seen, compos'd of Vortices of subtile Matter; but nothing like it is seen in *London*.'[35] His readers need to know this because the emptiness of space allows heavenly bodies to continue for ever in their frictionless motion, without needing angels to push them. But there is a deeper point: space was previously believed to be full of aether, a heavenly atmosphere (Voltaire's 'Vortices of subtile Matter'); to the God-fearing aether is clearly a *good thing* and emptiness (that pre-creation state described in the second verse of the Bible) is clearly a *bad thing*. The great project which Newton concluded – building upon the discoveries of Copernicus (1473–1543), Tycho Brahe (1546–1601), Galileo (1564–1642), and Kepler (1571–1630) – had been bedevilled by the belief in good things and bad things – circles rather than ellipses, a fixed earth rather than a moving one, and so on.[36] Newton provided an explanation which went beyond such things. It was simple enough in broad outline for the layman to apprehend: if there is nothing to slow down a heavenly body then it needs only a gravitational force to make it continue indefinitely in an orbit rather than a straight line. The detail of his work lay outside the layman's comprehension but was enough to generate a healthy respect for a system of mathematics invented to explain gravitational forces not in circular but elliptical orbits (where they are continuously changing in strength and direction) and able to cover a universe where nothing is fixed (and the orbiting body exerts the same force on the orbited as vice versa). Without needing to get into this level of detail the thinking population of Europe learned never again to believe in the good things and bad things taught them by a Church they came to think of as 'Catholic and Absolutist'.[37] The stage was obviously set for a general clash of Science and Faith, but instead English scientists demonstrated their piety and Anglican clergyman their philosophy and reached an Enlightened concordat.[38] Newton's friend Roger Cotes wrote, 'The gates are now set open, and by the passage he has revealed we may freely enter into the knowledge of the hidden secrets and wonders of natural things ... and, which is the best and most valuable fruit of philosophy, be thence incited the more profoundly to reverence and adore the great Maker of all'.[39] There was a beneficent God – or at least a 'Great Architect of the Universe' – in Newton's emptiness.[40]

By the time Newton published his *Mathematical Principles of Natural Philosophy* (*Philosophiae naturalis principia mathematica*) in 1687 the ground rules for the new philosophy had been established. Leibniz explained in his *Confessio Naturae contra Atheistas* of 1668: 'we must agree with those contemporary philosophers who have revived Democritus and Epicurus and who Robert Boyle aptly calls corpuscular philosophers, such as Galileo, Bacon, Gassendi, Descartes, Hobbes, and Digby, [who argue] that in explaining corporeal phenomena, we must not unnecessarily resort to God or to any other incorporeal thing form, or quality'.[41] Newton provided a triumphant confirmation of the value of not resorting unnecessarily to God, which meant defusing the value-judgements in the parts in order to understand the beautiful regulation of the whole. This intellectual template could be applied to almost any aspect of life. John Locke employed it for his description of the workings of the human mind, rejecting innate beliefs and describing the empty vessel of a child acquiring understanding through sense-perception.[42] Thus Locke did for Original Sin what Newton did for aether. Money was another obvious evil which acquired a Newtonian pardon.[43] Daniel Defoe in his *Review* of 1706 noted that 'Nothing obeys the Course of Nature more exactly than Trade, Causes and Consequences follow as directly as Day and Night'.[44] Spending money on the sort of unnecessary trifles described in Chapter X was not profligacy but economic stimulation, as Bernard Mandeville explained in his 1714 work, *The Fable of the Bees: or, Private Vices, Public Benefits*.[45] This idea that 'getting and spending' was more about public benefit than private vice found its definitive expression with the publication in 1776 of Adam Smith's *Wealth of Nations*.[46] By this time the Bank of England had been founded, in 1694; the City of London had survived its first great crash, the South Sea Bubble of 1720, and had laid the financial foundations for the Industrial Revolution and the British Empire.[47] Personal interaction could be similarly methodised: David Hume (1711–76) described his *A Treatise of Human Nature* of 1739–40 as 'an attempt to introduce the experimental method of reasoning into Moral subjects'.[48] Pope similarly suggested that all human impulses were self-regulating in his influential hymn to cautious optimism, the *Essay on Man* of 1733:

> Two principles in human nature reign;
> Self-love, to urge, and reason, to restrain;
> Nor this a good, nor that a bad we call,
> Each works its end, to move and govern all
> (*Essay on Man*, Epistle II, 1733, ll. 53–6).

Sexual love also began to be called something neither good nor bad. The ideal of the romantic love match, encouraged by the social interaction in Assembly Rooms round the country, can be seen as an acknowledgement that such impulses required only right regulation, in this case not gravitational force but a maiden aunt.[49] This habit of thinking can be summed up in a single Newtonian phrase: something (love, money, greed, self-

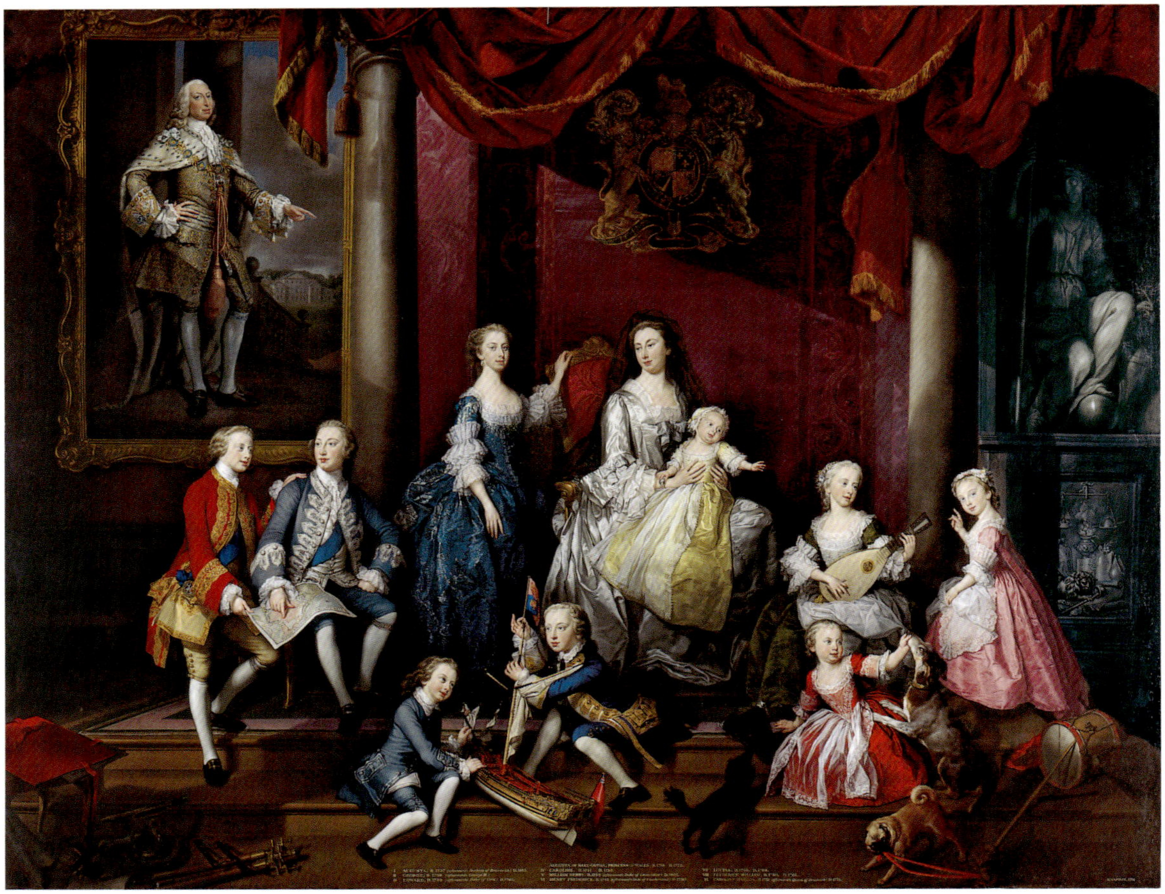

FIG. 3
George Knapton
The Family of Frederick, Prince of Wales, 1751
Oil on canvas
RCIN 405741

interest, whatever it may be) *makes the world go around*. The institution which to the Georgians most clearly expressed this Newtonian principle was the British Constitution itself, with the invisible force of the law regulating the opposing forces of the Crown and Parliament. In his *Commentaries on the Laws of England* of 1765–9, William Blackstone wrote that the King, Lords and Commons, 'like three distinct powers in mechanics, they jointly impel the machine of government in a direction different from what either, acting by itself, would have done; but at the same time a direction partaking of each, and formed out of all; a direction which constitutes the true line of the liberty and happiness of the community'.[50]

It is not far-fetched to suggest that such ideas impact upon visual culture. The informal garden (described in Chapter II) is intended to express an underlying order found in the whole of nature if we look beyond its irregular parts. Queen Caroline's Hermitage (see p. 270, fig. 73 and nos 145–9) was a temple to the god of the new settlement– the 'great Maker of all' – and a shrine to his high priests – pious scientists and philosophers, like Newton, Boyle and Locke, and philosophical divines, like Clarke and Wollaston. Knapton's 1751 group of Princess Augusta and her children (fig. 3) is a unique example of an attempt to suggest constitutional ideas in a life-sized royal portrait. It shows the late Prince of Wales as a portrait hanging on the wall, which is exactly balanced by a carved figure of Britannia, accompanied by an allegorical relief explaining the British constitution. The scales hold in balance the Crown and a Cap of Liberty; below a British lion guards another Cap of Liberty and lies upon the documents which secured it – the Magna Carta and Act of Settlement. The whole portrait then reads as a pair of scales with the Prince and the constitution held in balance.

The Princess sits enthroned on the fulcrum, as a guardian of these principles rather than claimant to the throne, and supervises her children.[51] It is the unsynchronised variety of their activities, driven by impulses of curiosity, affection and delight, which expresses the now familiar Newtonian message of unity in multiplicity. The heir to the throne is not singled out; the family are not united in grief for their recently deceased father; instead they play their improving games with cheerfulness and affection.

The short title for the habit of thinking described above is 'the Enlightenment', something which (in the opinion of Voltaire and many Continental philosophers) early Georgian Britain taught by precept and example.[52] A central tenet of Enlightened thinking is the refusal to accept the authority of any opinion without checking it against observation and unprejudiced reasoning.[53] The authority of Ptolemy did not deter Copernicus *et al.* from proving him wrong. This way of thinking transformed philosophy, science, politics, law and history, but what about literature and the fine arts? Was there a transformation in thinking about matters of taste? At the popular end of the spectrum forms were invented without reference to literary or artistic theory – the journalism of Addison and Steele, which in effect invented modern English prose style; the philosophical dialogues of Berkeley and Hume; Richardson's epistolary novels; Swift's moral fables; Gay's satirical 'rock opera' (no. 79); Hogarth's 'modern moral subjects' (nos 86 and 89) and so on.[54] These are genres which could only be invented by minds which Goldsmith might describe as 'by forms unfashioned, fresh from Nature's hand'. When it came to high art on the other hand, the early Georgians showed a very conventional side. Addison's *Cato*, like almost all such tragedies of the period, was written in the mould recommended by Aristotle and practised by Jean Racine (1639–99). Even at the time there was a consensus that works of this kind, were, as Dr Johnson put it (see p. 383), 'crush'd by rules, and weaken'd as refin'd'.[55] In many areas of culture the early Georgians had more respect for authority than at any other time in British history. Many of the aristocracy's new hobbies – Palladian architecture and interior decoration (discussed in Chapters II and V), Old Master collecting (discussed in Chapter VI), Italian opera (mentioned in Chapter IX) – came with theoretical instruction manuals in several languages, which were read and accepted without question or qualification. The best example of this sophisticated conformism can be seen in the training George III received in the 1750s from William Chambers, which enabled him to conceive and draw classical buildings, correct in every proportion and decorative detail (see fig. 51).[56]

The 'rules' were widely accepted because they were classical (and the Georgian elite identified with classical antiquity because of its rationality and love of liberty) and because they were universal.[57] The Enlightenment promoted a cultural interaction in Europe which led to a standardisation in arts, architecture, literature and even the languages themselves.[58] It is difficult to say if standardisation involves signing up to sensible conventions or submitting to stultifying conformity. For whatever reason, modern viewers find themselves admiring the depth of artistic understanding demonstrated by aristocratic and royal patrons and the tasteful coherence of their buildings and collections. At the same time they may lament the absence of a visual style which corresponds to the British Enlightenment in the way that observational realism seems so well to express the distinctive spirit of the Dutch Republic during its golden age.

There were assaults on this strand of conformity within early Georgian culture. According to Hogarth the English man of taste hung brown daubs on the walls of his jerry-built stucco box while listening to the warbling of eunuchs.[59] *The Analysis of Beauty* of 1753 (nos 94–5) offered an alternative approach to the visual arts which depended upon no precedent or authority. Though un-philosophical to a degree, the *Analysis* revolutionised thinking about art by discussing *variety* rather than beauty, suggesting the driving force of visual excitement might be as important as the restraining force of harmony or balance.[60] Allan Ramsay's *Dialogue upon Taste* of 1755 attacked the 'old religion of pictures' (as Hogarth called it) head on. According to Ramsay's spokesman, Colonel Freeman, to pronounce on matters of taste was as absurd as to suggest that one sauce for venison was 'better' than another.[61] The attempt to turn Roman forms into an absolute standard was not an ideal but a compromise, a 'mediocrity', merely 'a method that, although it might charm few, would disgust nobody'.[62] Ramsay's positive ideal was uncomplicated naturalism of a type which an uneducated (and therefore 'unprejudiced') person would instantly appreciate.[63] Every theory of art at this date was based on naturalism but Ramsay tried to isolate this from the 'acquired taste' of the connoisseur. There are some works in this exhibition which might be said to follow Ramsay's precepts – Thomas Sandby's topographical watercolours (no. 27); Canaletto's Thames views (nos 235–6) and Liotard's pastels (nos 242–4). These works have a freshness of empirical observation which seems to epitomise the Enlightenment; but they are the exception rather than the rule.

Another way in which Georgian England expressed its cultural independence was through the second most famous Englishman, that spanner-shaped genius Shakespeare. There was no folk superstition so outrageous that Shakespeare did not make it utterly credible; no word so coarsely Anglo-Saxon that he did not introduce into his noblest utterances; no rule of classical drama so basic that he did not disobey it in every play. And yet even Voltaire acknowledged the power of this creator of the English theatre, who 'boasted a strong, fruitful Genius: He was natural and sublime, but had not so much as a single Spark of good Taste, or knew one Rule of the Drama'.[64] Early Georgian theatre was dominated by heavily re-written revivals of Shakespeare: David Garrick (1717–79), in particular, made a career as the high priest of the cult of the Bard. Shakespeare was a central part of the fashion for antiquarianism during the period, described in Chapter VII, and seems to provide all the clues as to its popularity. He represented the Elizabethan age, so beloved of antiquarians, with its beautiful queen and devoted courtiers appearing so much more glamorous than the political machinations of a modern monarchy. His expressive, irregular and 'incorrect' language dazzled next to the dullness of modern verse, just like the 'barbaric' Gothic architecture of romantic ruins and fairy-tale castles when compared to the serviceable comfort of Palladianism. Most of all he represented the two great enemies of reason – passion and credulity. His typical hero is driven near to madness by some ungovernable passion and in this state finds himself visited by supernatural agents.[65] The revival of this fantastical spirit informs Queen Caroline's other garden structure at Richmond, Merlin's Cave, which featured (amongst other wax-work figures) Elizabeth of York and Queen Elizabeth consulting the magician.

We have already seen in Knapton's group portrait that the family of Frederick, Prince of Wales, was coached in the ethos of their adopted country (see no. 19). 'As I shall always rely on the affection of my people,' he wrote to a friend, 'I hope that they will place the same confidence in me, and be assured, that during my Reign I will never endeavour to extend the Power of the Crown, but should rather chuse that its influence should be lessened, than give any grounds of Jealousy to my subjects.'[66] In 1749 Frederick's children mounted a production of that set text of British Liberty, Addison's *Cato* (see above, p. 16). The young Prince George, later George III, recited a specially written prologue for the production which brought together many of the themes of this period – the emphasis on becoming English; the idea that liberty was somehow natural and that in England it belonged with the venerable traditions beloved of antiquarians, while also depending upon William III and the Glorious Revolution:

A boy in England born – in England bred;
Where freedom well becomes the earliest state,
For here the love of liberty's innate.
Yet more; before my eyes those heroes stand,
Whom the great William brought to bless this land,
To guard with pious care that gen'rous plan
Of power well bounded, which it first began.[67]

This declaration of intent is typical of George III's education and prepared for his celebrated pronouncement upon succeeding his grandfather, 'I glory in the name of Briton'. George III's reign was spent entirely in England and was characterised in its political engagement and in its artistic and scientific patronage by a kind of Addisonian high-mindedness. George III's son, the future George IV, exhibited the principles of action and reaction by entering opposition politics as enthusiastically as his grandfather when Prince of Wales had done. It hardly needs saying, however, that during the reign of George III the torch of liberty was lit elsewhere, and the pace began to be set in America and France. These developments set the British government, though by no means every subject, against their American and French counterparts.[68] The champions of republican liberty regarded the British constitutional balance of royal prerogative and parliamentary restraint as *ancien régime* befuddlement served up with characteristic Anglo-Saxon hypocrisy.[69] British apologists had always argued that their liberty was an ancient tradition rather than a modern invention. This line of argument became even more appealing when trying to distinguish the British constitution from that created from scratch in Revolutionary France.[70] According to Edmund Burke British liberty was a special inheritance rather than a right and there was in the British constitution a natural quality which meant that 'in what we improve we are never wholly new; in what we retain we are never wholly obsolete'.[71]

One consequence of this development was that the British lost those Continental admirers, like Voltaire, who provided so eloquent and such an influential articulation of its project. The exiles of the nineteenth century formed political systems based on avoiding Britain's horrors, not imitating its glories. Another lesser consequence was that the memory of the early Georgian period started to be viewed with special fondness by Englishmen who might have been appalled by its actuality. George IV, for example, collected many works by or attributed to Hogarth (see Chapter IV), including the portrait of *David Garrick and his Wife* (no. 257), which seems so neatly to epitomise the age but which could not be less royal in character. In 1814 the Prince Regent celebrated jointly the defeat of Napoleon (before the Hundred Days) and the centenary of the Hanoverian succession.[72] By this time the Jacobite treat had vanished and the French king had been restored; this was a moment when the fractious freedom of the age of Hogarth could be looked upon with an amused indulgence.[73] At this moment one of the most exciting (and fraught) eras in British cultural life began to settle, in the popular imagination, into an age of elegance and gentility. It is hoped that the tercentenary of the arrival of George I will provide an opportunity to add some light and shade to this pallid picture.

1

SIR GODFREY KNELLER, BT (1646–1723)

Queen Anne of Great Britain and Ireland (1665–1714) *c.*1702–4

Oil on canvas, 75.9 × 63.9 cm
RCIN 405614

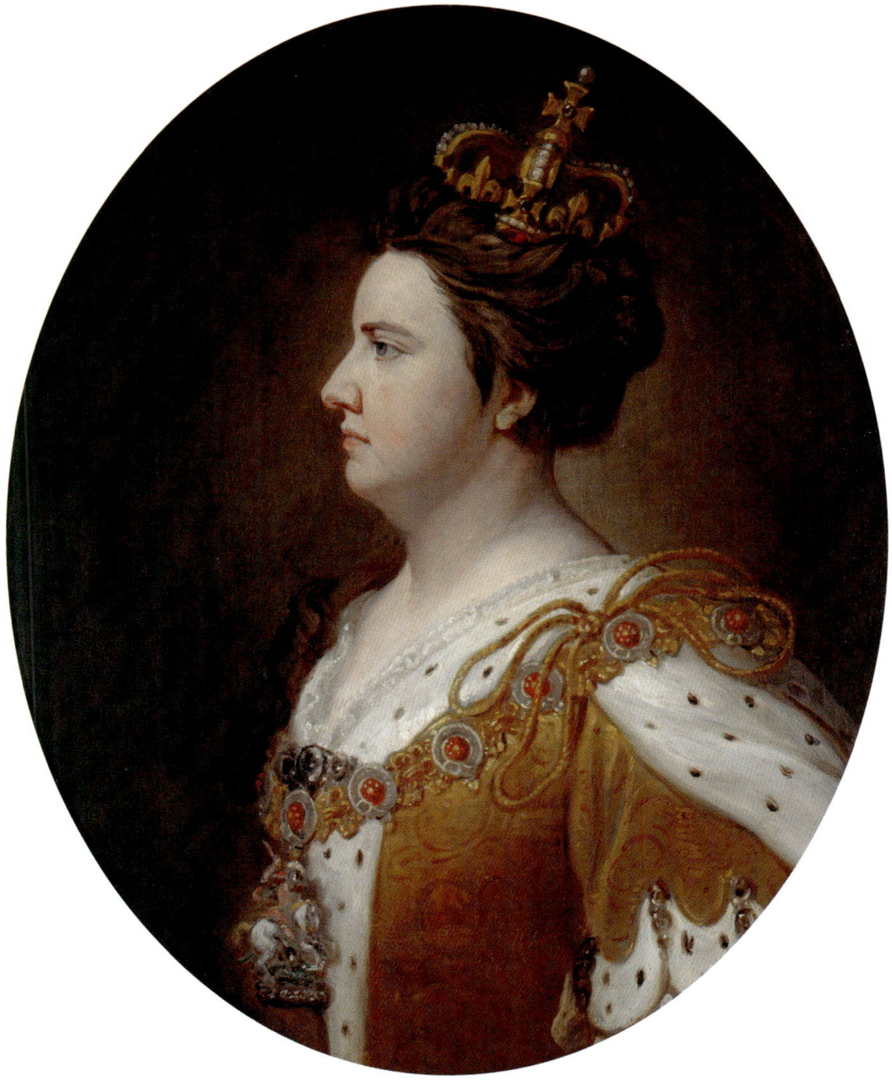

PROVENANCE Purchased by HM The Queen for the Royal Collection in 1953

LITERATURE Millar 1963, p. 144, no. 339

The second daughter of James II and Lady Anne Hyde, in 1702 Queen Anne succeeded her childless sister and brother-in-law Mary II and William III. She adopted the motto *semper eadem* ('always the same') from her great predecessor, Queen Elizabeth I; throughout the eighteenth century her reign was regarded as another Elizabethan age. The War of the Spanish Succession (1701–14) marked the emergence of the British army as a force to be reckoned with on the Continental stage for the first time since the reign of Henry VIII. Anne displayed her gratitude to John Churchill, Duke of Marlborough, for this achievement by presenting him with Blenheim Palace, a vast country seat erected as a monument to the nation.

In July 1683, Anne married Prince George of Denmark, son of Frederick III of Denmark and Anne Catherine of Brandenburg. The Queen endured seventeen pregnancies, only one of which produced a potential heir, William, Duke of Gloucester (1689–1700). His death in July 1700 at the age of eleven caused Parliament to institute the Act of Settlement.

Like Kneller's profile of George I (no. 4), the present image was created for the Royal Mint to produce new coinage and celebratory medals for Queen Anne's accession.[74]

Attired in a gold dress with an ermine-lined cloak attached to her shoulders, the Queen is depicted wearing a small crown and the collar-chain of the Order of the Garter. Queen Anne also commissioned Kneller to paint a full-length state portrait and a large history piece for the Long Gallery at Blenheim, showing the Queen presenting an allegory of Military Merit with the plans for the palace. Her dispute with the Duchess of Marlborough meant that this commission never proceeded beyond the stage of a oil sketch.[75]

Queen Anne was the last monarch to touch for the King's Evil, and her patients included Dr Johnson, who wore his touch-piece round his neck throughout his life.[76] This practice was abolished by George I, a Lutheran first and Anglican second, protector of Dissenters and enemy of every vestige of Popery.[77] WB

2

PIERRE MIGNARD (1612–1695)

The Family of James II 1694

Oil on canvas, 46.4 × 59.7 cm
RCIN 400966

PROVENANCE Presented to King Edward VII by the Marquis de Breteuil in 1894

LITERATURE *Kings and Queens* 1983, p. 70, no. 47; Boyer 1992, p. 110, no. 95

Following the Glorious Revolution of 1688, the Catholic King James II (1633–1701), his consort Mary of Modena (1673–1718) and their small son James Francis Edward (see no. 42), later recognised by the Jacobites as James III, were forced to leave England for France, where James's first cousin, Louis XIV, provided them with the old Château de Saint-Germain-en-Laye, situated between Paris and Versailles. The Stuart King resided here in great splendour and in close connection with the French court. Prepared to return to England in the same way that his brother Charles II had done in 1660, James II maintained as much as possible of the ceremonial that was specific to the English court at Whitehall.[78] Neither James II nor his son and grandson – the 'Old' and the 'Young Pretenders' – succeeded in regaining the British throne. Indeed the failure of the 1715 uprising (see pp. 91 and 98–101) and the death of Louis XIV in the same year weakened French support for their cause and obliged the Jacobite court to move to Rome. James III is buried in St Peter's.

Pierre Mignard depicts here what could have been Britain's alternative royal family.[79] Veritably enthroned on a *fauteuil Louis-quatorze*, James II is dressed in the full regalia of the Order of the Garter, of which he had been the Sovereign until his deposition. Queen Mary, also seated upright on an armchair, is wearing a yellow-gold dress embroidered with flowers, contrasting with an ermine-lined blue mantel pinned to her shoulders. At the centre of the picture, on a violet cushion, sits their two-year-old daughter Princess Louisa Maria (1692–1712), holding a delicate rose – a reference to the Royal Badge of England, which James II continued to use in exile. On the other side of the Queen stands her six-year-old son James, his torso encased in armour adorned with the blue Order of the Garter sash, pointing to a green velvet cushion upon which rest a small-scale Imperial eight-arched crown and sword. The painting alludes to the education of the aspirant Prince of Wales, who was being prepared to return to Britain in order to claim the Crown – which was clearly made to fit him.

This work is a finished oil-sketch for a much larger composition, now in a private collection, one of the last great works by Mignard. Appointed First Painter to King of France in 1690, the accomplished colourist died only few months after its completion. Unusually the sittings took place at different places and were witnessed by numerous courtiers, and on one occasion by Louis XIV himself. The canvas travelled from the artist's studio to Saint-Germain, then to Versailles and finally back to the studio, where the old and feeble painter put his finishing touches in November 1694.[80] WB

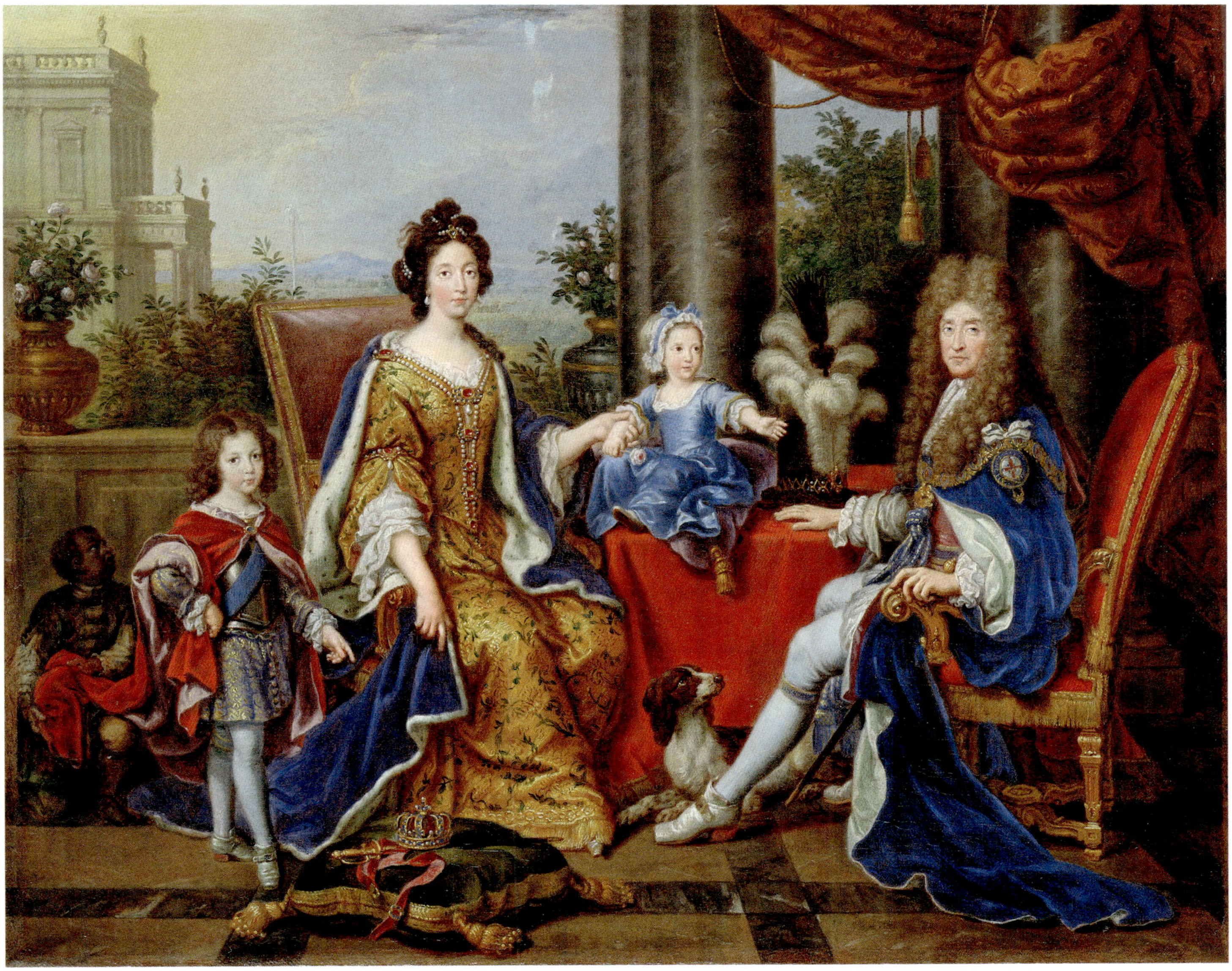

3

ATTRIBUTED TO NOËL III JOUVENET (ACTIVE IN HANOVER 1685–95, D. 1698)

Electress Sophia of Hanover (1630–1714) probably before 1692

Oil on canvas, 73.4 × 54.6 cm
RCIN 400944

PROVENANCE Purchased by Sir J.C. Robinson for Queen Victoria in 1885

Electress Sophia of Hanover was the youngest daughter of the Winter Queen, Elizabeth of Bohemia, the granddaughter of James I and the mother of George I (see Genealogical Table, p. 8). As neither William III and Mary II nor Queen Anne had produced progeny, the Act of Settlement of 1701 proclaimed her heiress presumptive to the British Crown. Electress Sophia died only two months before Queen Anne, though 35 years her senior, and thus narrowly missed her opportunity to become Queen herself.

A British visitor to Hanover in 1701, John Toland, gave an account of the elderly Electress's exceptional powers and their exceptional preservation:

> She has ever enjoy'd extraordinary Health, which keeps her still very vigorous, of a cheerful Countenance, and a merry Disposition. She step[s] as firm and erect as any young Lady, has not one Wrinkle in her Face which is still very agreeable, nor one Tooth out of her Head, and reads without Spectacles ... [she] has bin long admir'd by all the Learned World, as a Woman of incomparable Knowledge in Divinity, Philosophy, History, and the Subjects of all sorts of Books, of which she has read a prodigious quantity. She speaks five Languages so well, that by her Accent it might be a Dispute which of 'em was her first. They are Low-Dutch, German, French, Italian, and English, which last she speaks as truly and easily as any Native.[81]

Sophia was an avid patron of the arts and culture, and entertained a close relationship with the scientist-philosopher Gottfried Wilhelm Leibniz (see below, Chapter VII). Their regular walks through the gardens at Herrenhausen allowed for spirited intellectual exchanges. It was on one of those long promenades that Sophia was taken ill and she died shortly afterwards.

When acquired by Queen Victoria, this profile portrait was believed to represent Eléonore Desmier d'Olbreuse (1639–1722), Duchess of Celle, George I's mother-in-law; in fact it depicts his mother, Sophia, around the age of 60, prior to the elevation of the Dukedom of Brunswick-Lüneburg to the status of an Electorate in 1692. Portrayed wearing a black dress with an intricate lace collar and a pearl necklace, Sophia wears an ermine mantle draped around her back, signifying her princely status. The then duchess's renowned sense for the latest fashions is displayed through her French *frelange* hair dress. Sophia's cousin, Elizabeth Charlotte of the Palatinate, Duchess of Orléans (1652–1722), known as Liselotte, sent her very precise sketches from Paris with instructions how to attach the wire framework holding the hair and its adorning bows together.[82] Far from being an indicator of mourning, Sophia's black attire reflects her own personal taste in clothing. In 1684 she specifically ordered black dresses from her Hanoverian ambassador in Paris, Count Balati, for her to wear at the wedding of her daughter, Sophia Charlotte, with the Electoral Prince of Brandenburg.[83]

Throughout her life, Sophia of Hanover was often painted, even in old age, when there was a growing international interest in the woman that might wear the British crown.[84] This portrait may be the work of the French painter Noël III Jouvenet, active at the court of Hanover between *c.*1685 and *c.*1695, and brother of the celebrated Parisian artist Jean III Jouvenet. Noël III supplied cartoons for the so-called *Familientapeten* – a set a tapestries extolling the achievements of the Guelf dynasty – and he is believed to have decorated interiors at Herrenhausen.[85] The treatment of light and shade as well as of the flesh, the textiles and especially the lace proves very close to Jouvenet's contemporary portrait of Carl Philip of Hanover, younger brother of George I (University of Göttingen). Whilst slightly naïve in execution, the portrait displays great attention to detail and a lucid brushstroke, which contrast with the much looser hand of Andreas Scheitz (1655–1735), who equally captured Sophia as an elderly woman (Historisches Museum, Hanover). Although the Royal Collection portrait is similar to the profile by Johann Conrad Eichler, signed and dated 1707, he is excluded as its author, for he had been born only in 1688 and would not have been able to portray Sophia before 1692.[86] WB

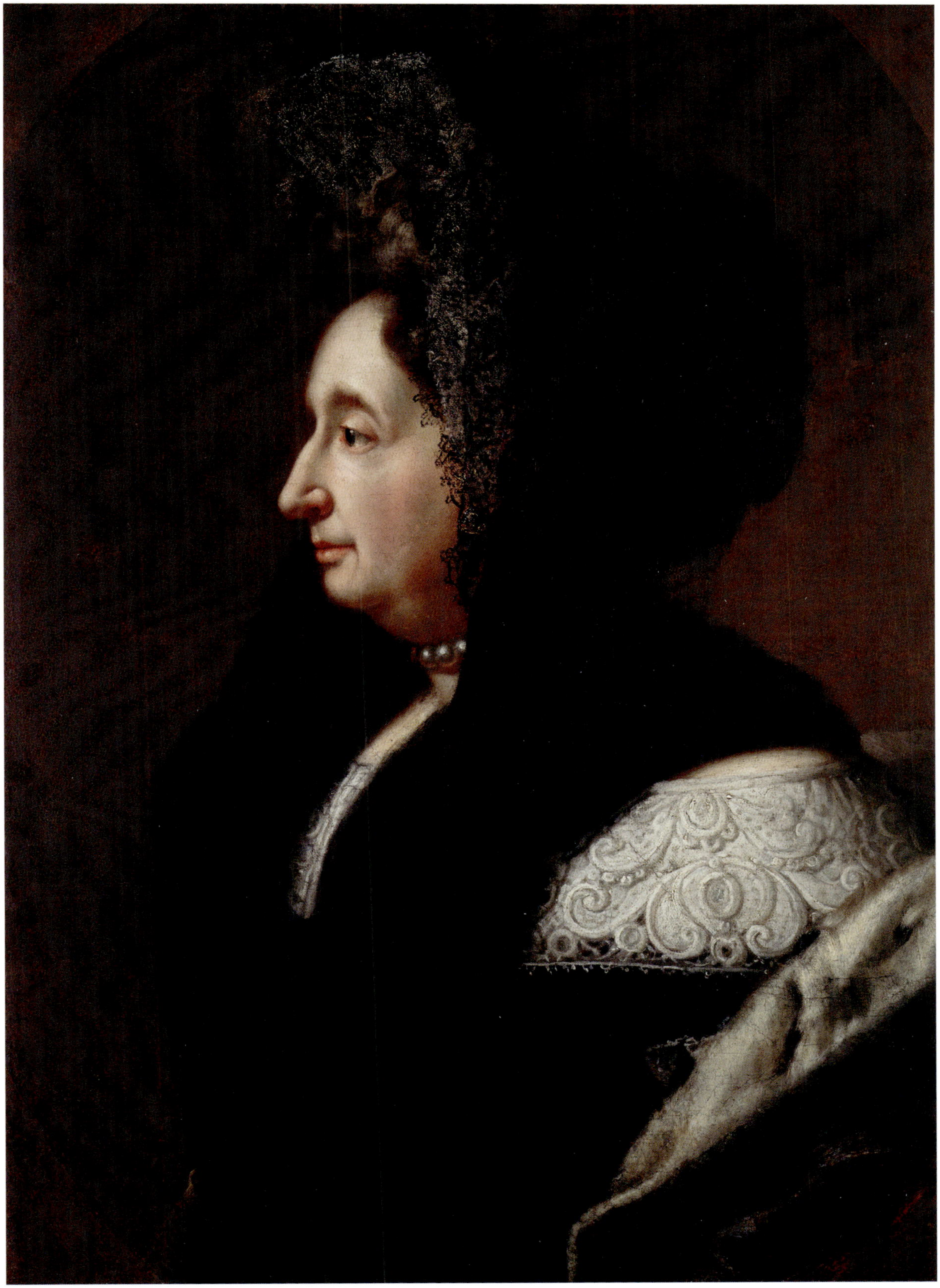

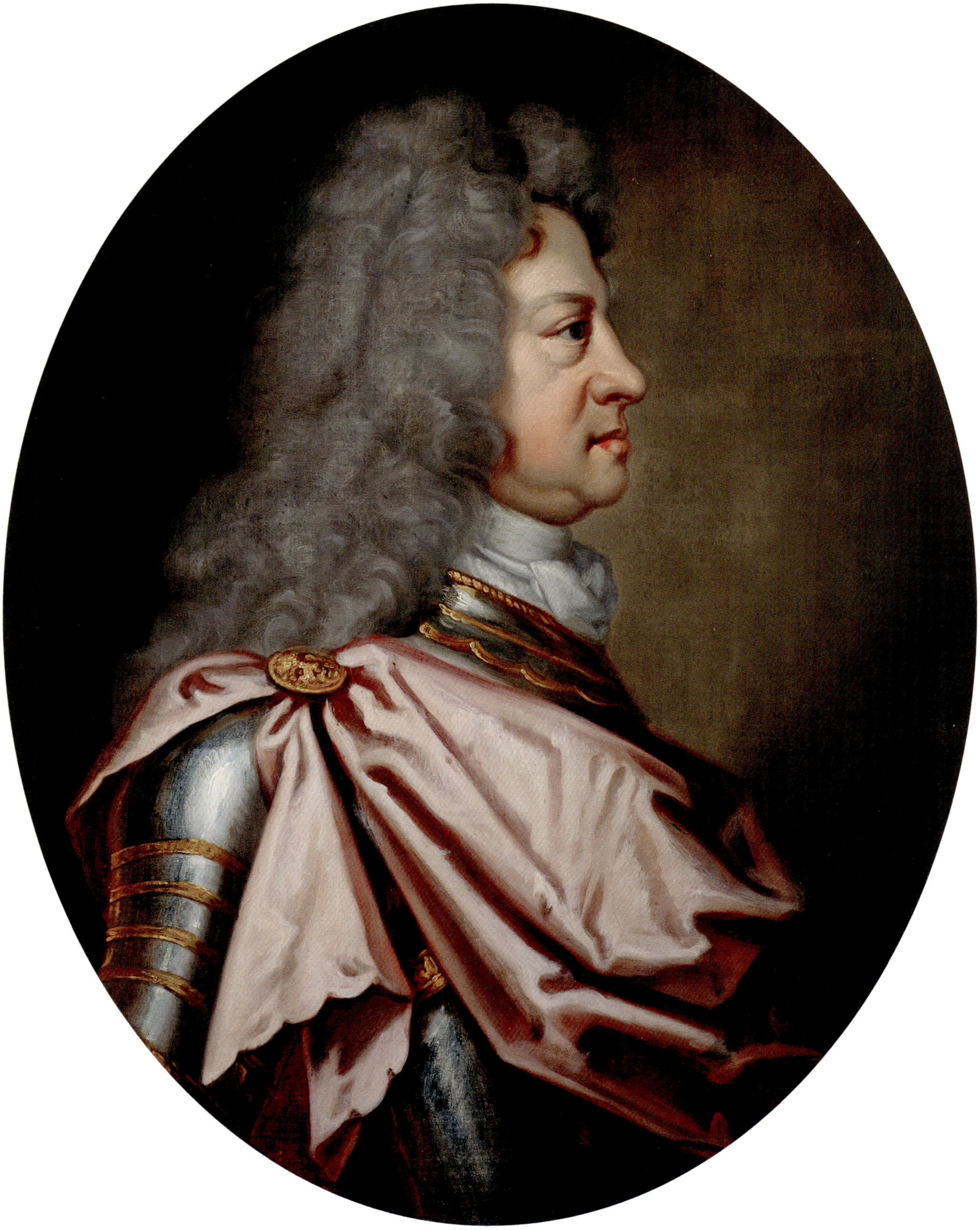

4

STUDIO OF SIR GODFREY KNELLER, BT (1646–1723)

George I, King of Great Britain and Ireland, Elector of Hanover (1660–1727) *c.*1715

Oil on canvas, 111 × 98 cm
RCIN 403401

PROVENANCE First recorded at Buckingham Palace in 1866

LITERATURE Millar 1963, p. 148, no. 39

George Louis of Brunswick-Lüneburg succeeded to the British throne on 1 August 1714, at the age of 54. Born in Hanover, the son of a minor German prince, George initially had limited prospects of reigning anywhere.[87] His rise was the result of the ambition of his father, Ernest Augustus, Duke of Brunswick-Lüneburg (1629–98), and the ancestry of his mother, Electress Sophia (see no. 3), granddaughter of James I. Since Ernest Augustus himself was but the youngest son of George, Duke of Calenberg (1582–1641), he had no entitlement to any of the Brunswick estates and instead, in 1662, was appointed Prince Bishop of Osnabrück. However, after two of his elder brothers, Christian Louis (1622–65) and John Frederick (1625–79), died without male issue, the estates were divided between the two remaining brothers: George William, Duke of Celle (1624–1705), inherited the principality of Lüneburg while Ernest Augustus became Duke of Calenberg and in 1679 took up residence in Hanover. This Brunswick inheritance was consolidated by the marriage in 1682 of the offspring of these two brothers: Ernest Augustus's son George Louis (George I), and George William's daughter Sophia Dorothea of Celle (1666–1726; see fig. 4 and no. 190). This meant that upon Duke George William's death in 1705 the principalities of Calenberg and Lüneburg were united, in an entity which came to be called 'Hanover'. Whilst territorially useful, the cousins' marriage came to a dramatic end with the exposure in 1694 of Sophia Dorothea's not so secret affair with Count Philip von Königsmarck (1665–94). Whilst her handsome lover was probably murdered, Sophia Dorothea was divorced from George, separated from her two children and imprisoned for life at Schloss Ahlden. These drastic measures, likely to have been orchestrated by Ernest Augustus, overshadowed George I's public image for the rest of his life and led to his estrangement from his son, the future George II, who was never to see his mother again.

The fortunes of the Hanoverian dynasty improved in other ways during these years: in 1692, Ernest Augustus was granted the rank of Prince Elector while the Act of Settlement of 1701 proclaimed Sophia heiress presumptive to the British throne. After succeeding his father as Elector in 1698, George Louis fought with distinction in the War of the Spanish Succession and was rewarded by a further expansion of Hanoverian territories. He succeeded to the British throne after his mother's death in June 1714 was closely followed by that of Queen Anne in August of that year. He arrived in England in September accompanied by his son, George Augustus, now Prince of Wales, his mistress Melusine von der Schulenburg (1667–1743) and his half-sister Baroness Sophia von Kielmansegg (1675–1725). The King barely knew his new kingdom, having visited it only once, for a few months in 1680 during the reign of Charles II. Although he had a basic knowledge of English, he preferred conversing in French, the lingua franca of European courts at this date. He regularly returned to his native Hanover, something much criticised by his British subjects. His greatest interests appear to have been hunting and the opera.

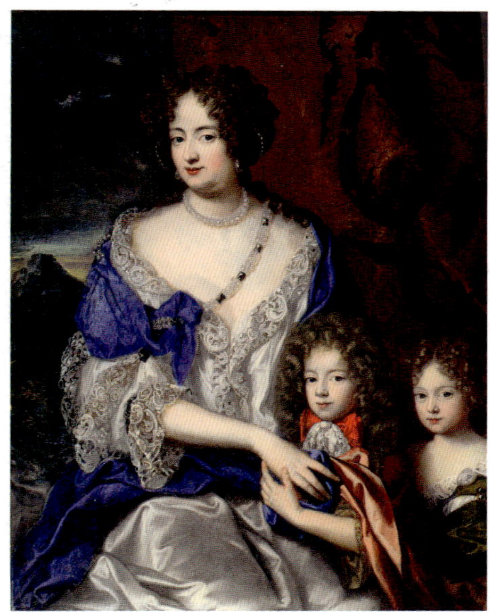

FIG. 4
Jacques Vaillant
*Sophia Dorothea of Celle with her children, George II and Sophia Dorothea of Prussia, c.*1692
Oil on canvas
Residenzschloss, Celle

The present portrait is one of several versions of Kneller's official profile for the coinage marking the beginning of the new reign, painted shortly after the King's arrival.[88] Like a Roman Emperor, the King wears a cape decoratively draped around his armour and is represented as 'Defender of the Faith', ready to champion, as he had in the past, the Protestant cause. WB

5 & 6

JOHN MICHAEL RYSBRACK (1693–1770)

George II of Great Britain and Ireland, Elector of Hanover (1683–1760) c.1739

Marble, 69.8 cm high
Incised on the left hand side of the bust: *RYSBRACK. F.*
RCIN 31322

Queen Caroline of Great Britain and Ireland, Electress of Hanover (1683–1760) c.1739

Marble, 71.5 cm high
RCIN 31317

PROVENANCE Commissioned by Queen Caroline

LITERATURE Esdaile 1932, pp. 41–2; Webb 1954, pp. 155–6, fig. 74; Whinney 1964, pp. 86–7; Kerslake 1977, I, p. 94; II, pl. 255

Ever since his early experience on the battlefield, George II appears to have projected himself a solider monarch. His bravery at the Battle of Oudenarde in 1708, where he fought the French alongside British troops lead by John Churchill, Duke of Marlborough, afforded him the nickname of 'Young Hanover Brave'. He was an able commander and the last British monarch to lead his troops into battle (see no. 46).

Nonetheless, in spite of his particular passion for military matters, recent scholarship has emphasised that George II was far from indifferent to politics. Though restricted by Parliament and therefore theoretically much less influential than in Hanover, the King appears to have sought more involvement and control over his government's decision-making.[89] Accounts of his personal character paint a picture of a stolid and punctilious man, passionate only in anger.[90] According to Horace Walpole, 'His motions ... were measured by etiquette and the clock. He visited [his mistress, the Countess of Suffolk] every evening at nine; but with such dull punctuality, that he frequently walked about his chamber for ten minutes with his watch in his hand, if the stated minute was not arrived.'[91]

George II's patronage of the arts was limited by Parliamentary control of the civil list allowance, with which he had to maintain his large family and court. Instead of spending on new palaces and paintings, George invested in ephemeral entertainment. In all their lavishness, spectacles such as his and Queen Caroline's coronation, as well as their daughter's weddings, aimed at making the Hanoverian dynasty's grandeur and power undisputed.[92] However, beyond these short-lived displays, he also established the University of Göttingen in 1734 – the first institution of its kind within Hanover – and supported the foundation of the British Museum in London in 1753.

Queen Caroline was born on 1/11 March 1683, under the name of Wilhelmina Charlotte Caroline of Brandenburg-Ansbach. Her native principality may have been one of the smallest of the Empire, but her family, the House of Hohenzollern, was one of Germany's most ancient and ambitious. Caroline's early life was overshadowed by the premature deaths of her parents, John Frederick, Margrave of Brandenburg-Ansbach (1654–86) and Eleonore of Saxe-Eisenach (1662–96), as well as of her stepfather, George IV, Elector of Saxony (1668–94). From the age of thirteen, the orphan Princess was raised in Berlin, at the court of Sophia Charlotte of Brandenburg, sister of George I. Caroline benefited greatly from the cultivated and intellectual circle of Sophia Charlotte and her mother, the Electress Sophia (see no. 3).

Her combination of wit and beauty (and the negligible political weight of Ansbach), made Caroline one of the most sought-after princesses on the European marriage market. Owing to her deep Protestant faith, she even declined the proposal of the most eligible yet Catholic candidate, the future Emperor Charles VI. This remarkable rejection would later be used in Britain to publicise the Queen's unfailing Protestantism.

Caroline first met the then Electoral Prince George Augustus of Hanover in June 1705, when he visited Ansbach incognito. George almost immediately sought his father's approval for the match, which he received soon afterwards.[93] George and Caroline's relationship appears to have been one of affection and interdependency. For all that her influence over the King triggered satire and mockery, he did not cease to rely on her advice and judgement. The Queen endured the presence of her husband's mistresses with serene tolerance. On her deathbed she thoughtfully advised him to remarry. The King's promise that he would limit himself to mistresses was met by the Queen's famous reply: '*Ah mon Dieu! Cela n'empêche pas*!'[94]

A woman of unusual erudition, Queen Caroline was qualified by some of her contemporaries as 'one of the most learned princesses in Europe'.[95] Chapter VII explores her interest in British history and culture, as well as the latest discoveries in medicine, the natural sciences and natural philosophy. Keen to emphasise her affiliation to the British monarchy in her patronage, the Queen even changed her name from Wilhelmina (as she was known in Germany) to Caroline in order to avoid the difficulty of its pronunciation for her English-speaking subjects.

George Vertue provides valuable information on the origin of the present two busts. In 1738 he noted that 'the KING ... sat to [Rysbrack] at Kensington twice. to have his picture modelled in Clay. the likeness much approvd on – and with a good Air. – also a Moddel of the Queen vastly like. Tho' not done from the life'.[96] The resulting terracotta models, which are signed and dated 1738, are also in the Royal Collection (RCIN 1411 and 1412). In 1739 Vertue recorded that 'two Marble Bustos the one of his present Majesty from a Model done from the life by Mr Rysbrack – and another busto of the late Majesty Q. Caroline both were erected in the New Library at St. James, Green Park'.[97] The busts probably stood in niches over the fireplaces at either end of the double-cube interior (see pp. 60–1 and 78), while Rysbrack's terracotta kings and queens (see nos 151–2) rested on high brackets along the side walls.

The two portraits, though properly a pair, are yet distinguished both by the fact that one was made posthumously and the other 'from the life', and by the costumes. The King wears the laurels of victory and is dressed in armour, albeit markedly old-fashioned in style. The Queen by contrast wears robes of State, with strings of pearls threaded through her hair and a high, jewelled diadem notable for its resemblance to those often portrayed on the goddess Juno. The likeness depends in almost every detail on her portrait in profile by the painter Joseph Highmore (no. 239), which must have been placed at the sculptor's disposal.

The King seems to have approved of his portrait, to judge from the fact that he gave a reduced version of it in ivory to his physician, the military surgeon Dr John Ranby.[98] A further terracotta version of Queen Caroline's bust (Amsterdam, Rijksmuseum) belonged to her daughter Anne, Princess Royal, and was recorded at the Stadholder's court in Leeuwarden in 1764.[99] JM & WB

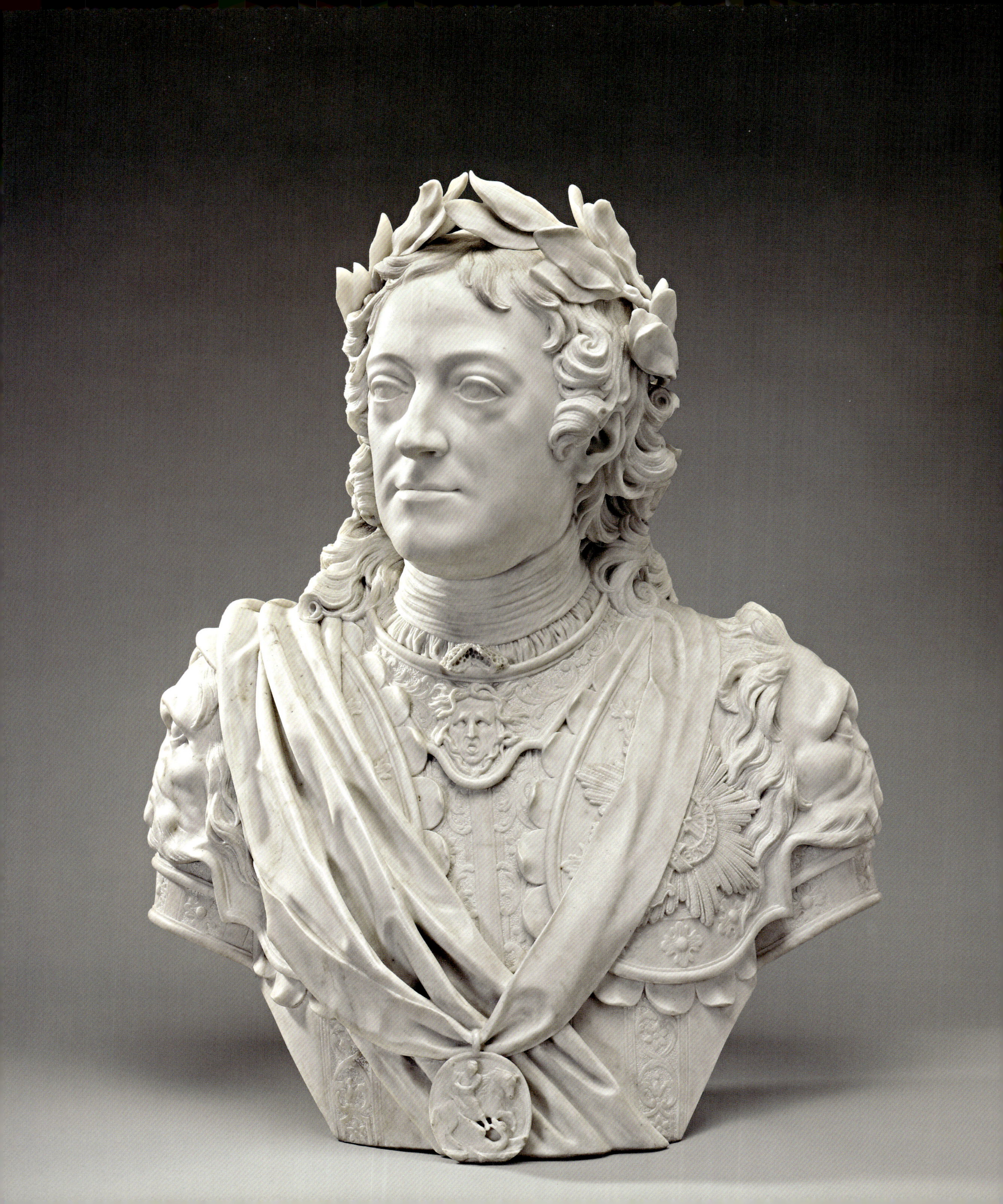

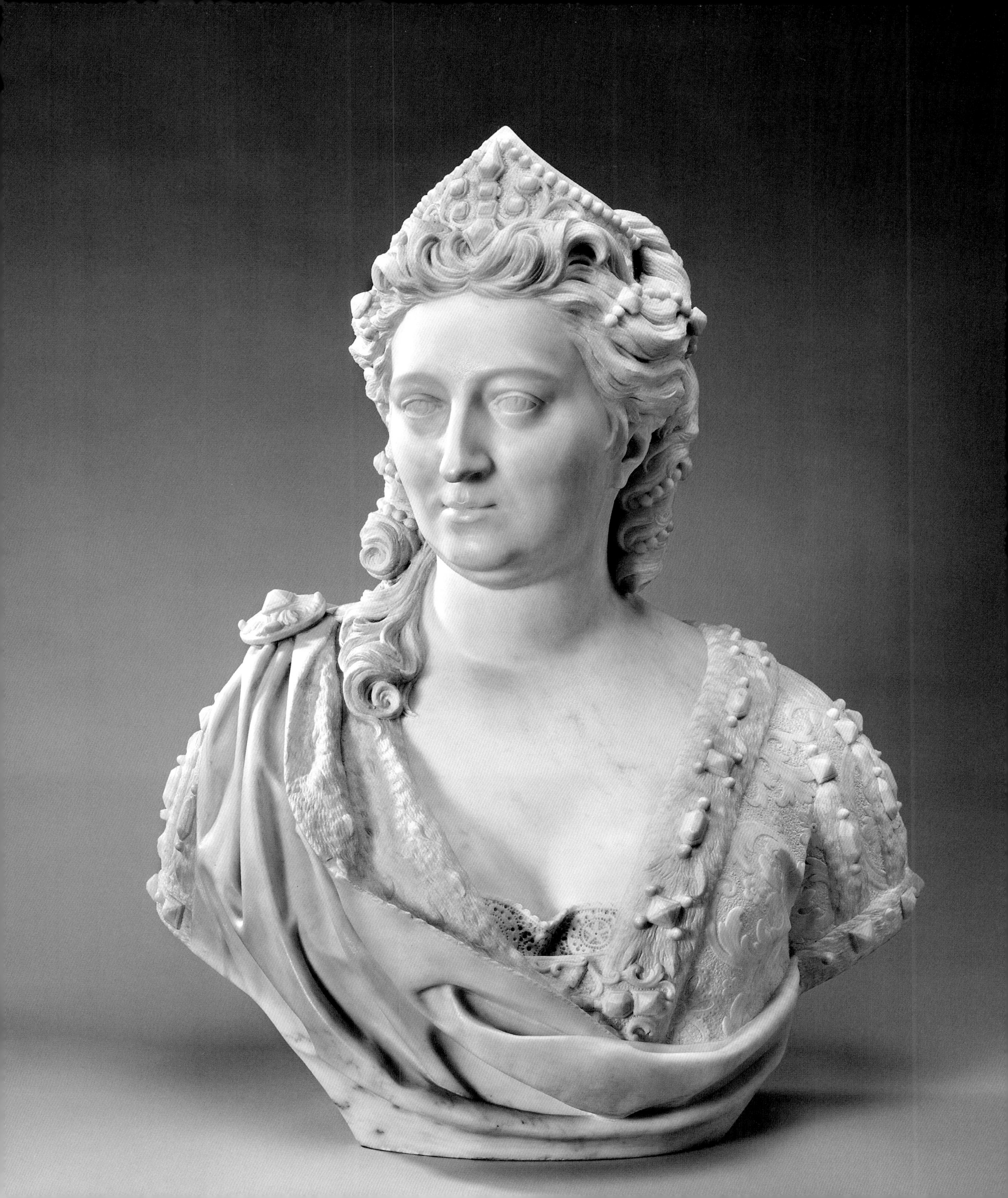

7

PETER SCHEEMAKERS (1691–1781)

Frederick, Prince of Wales, Electoral Prince of Hanover (1707–1751) c.1741

Marble, height incl. socle 81.0 cm
Socle incised: *F • P • of Wales*
RCIN 31169

PROVENANCE Commissioned by Richard Temple, Viscount Cobham; by descent to 2nd Duke of Buckinghamshire; sold Christie's, 15 August 1848; bought Rainey; 5th Earl Temple; by whom sold Sotheby's, London, 9 May 1941; bought by HM Queen Elizabeth

LITERATURE Esdaile 1932, pp. 41–2; Webb 1954, pp. 155–6, fig. 76; Whinney 1964, pp. 86–7; Kerslake 1977, vol. I, p. 84; Roscoe 1999, pp. 269 and 273, no. 177

Born in Hanover on 31 January/7 February 1707, Frederick Louis (Friedrich Ludwig), Prince of Wales, was seven years old when his grandfather George I, upon his accession to the British throne and consequent departure, appointed him his official representative in his German dominions. The young boy was separated from his parents, who were not only obliged to join the King to London and leave their son behind but also forbidden to return to Germany (until they acceded in 1727). Frederick was aged nine when he received Lady Mary Wortley Montagu in Hanover, who 'without flattery or partiality' described him as having 'all the accomplishments that it is possible to have at his age, with an air of sprightliness and understanding, and something so very engaging and easy in his behaviour, that he needs not the advantage of his rank to appear charming .... I was surprised at the quickness and politeness that appeared in every thing he said.'[100]

Lady Mary's admiration would not be shared by Frederick's parents, the future George II and Queen Caroline. The many years of separation and the strong influence George I is likely to have had on the young Prince on his regular visits to Hanover may have laid the foundation for the hostility between Frederick and his parents. George II's accession entailed great frustration for the Prince of Wales, who, until the age of 21, had played a leading role in Hanover and was now confined to a supporting one in London. Clearly favouring their second son, William, Duke of Cumberland, George II even considered breaking the Union between Britain and Hanover by making William heir to the insular kingdom and Frederick heir to the Continental electorate.[101]

Frederick's passion for music, the visual arts and architecture provided further scope for competition with his mother. His limited allowance also became a concern weighing on the relationship between him and his parents. Frederick hoped that an appropriate marriage would lead his father and Parliament to provide him with more generous funds. After much deliberation, Augusta of Saxe-Gotha-Altenburg (1719–72) was selected as a suitable bride.[102] The young Princess Augusta was introduced to George II on his sojourn to Hanover in 1735 and impressed him with her modesty and seeming naivety. The King clearly reasoned that she would be a harmless ally to his estranged son.

Augusta's education had ill prepared her to become to the consort of a potential future British monarch. Even after the engagement, her mother judged it unnecessary for her to learn English – assuming that, twenty years after the Hanoverian arrival, everyone in Britain would be speaking German.[103] However, after a difficult start at court, she demonstrated considerable skill and tact in establishing functional relations with the King and Queen while remaining loyal to her husband.[104] Especially after Queen Caroline's death in 1737, the couple's harmonious family life at Kew stood in contrast to that of the elderly king, living with his mistress Madame von Wallmoden.

Peter Scheemakers settled in London in around 1720, having completed an apprenticeship with his father in his native Antwerp. For the next three decades he produced a series of funerary monuments, of which seventeen survive in Westminster Abbey alone, and emerged as a serious rival to his more famous contemporaries, J.M. Rysbrack (nos 5–6) and L.-F. Roubiliac (nos 38, 39, 252 and 384). From 1728, Scheemakers spent three years in Rome, returning with numerous models after antique sculptures, intent on fostering a taste for the Roman style which is prominently displayed in his bust of Frederick, Prince of Wales.

The Prince was himself an important patron of Scheemakers. In around 1732 he commissioned two sets of small marble busts of Dryden, Milton, Shakespeare and Spenser, one for Carlton House and the other as a gift for Alexander Pope, intended for the poet's villa at Twickenham (see p. 390). Scheemakers is also said to have provided chimneypieces for Carlton House, a bas-relief in stucco for William Kent's garden pavilion there, and a set of four limestone term-pedestals to stand beside the pavilion, supplied in 1735 (see fig. 8).[105] No trace survives of the '4 Seasons with Pedestals' for which the prince paid Scheemakers in 1743 and which were sent to Lord Archibald Hamilton.[106]

Frederick is shown here in draped Roman armour, prominently displaying his Garter badge, and without a wig of the kind still worn by his father in Rysbrack's bust (no. 5). The bust was commissioned not by the prince himself but by the prominent Whig peer Richard Temple, Viscount Cobham (1675–1749) for the Temple of Friendship in the garden at Stowe in Buckinghamshire. Cobham had served as a general under Marlborough and devoted his retirement to politics. His opposition to the ministry of Robert Walpole was expressed in the 1730s and 1740s in a remarkable series of politically inspired buildings at Stowe. The Temple of Friendship was begun in 1737 after the Prince of Wales had visited Stowe in some state as Lord Cobham's guest. Designed by James Gibbs, the temple was no doubt intended to confirm the allegiance of Cobham's 'Patriot' faction with the Prince, in opposition to Walpole. Ten busts were commissioned to stand on pedestals and brackets around the walls, all with armorial socles identifying the sitters. Scheemakers was responsible for the first three, probably including the present bust and Lord Cobham's own portrait (London, Victoria and Albert Museum). The others represented members of Cobham's circle of Whig 'Patriots', including Earl Temple, the Earl of Marchmont, Earl Bathurst, Lord Gower, George Lyttleton, the Earl of Chesterfield, William Pitt the Elder and the Earl of Westmorland. Cobham's temple was completed in 1742, the year of Walpole's

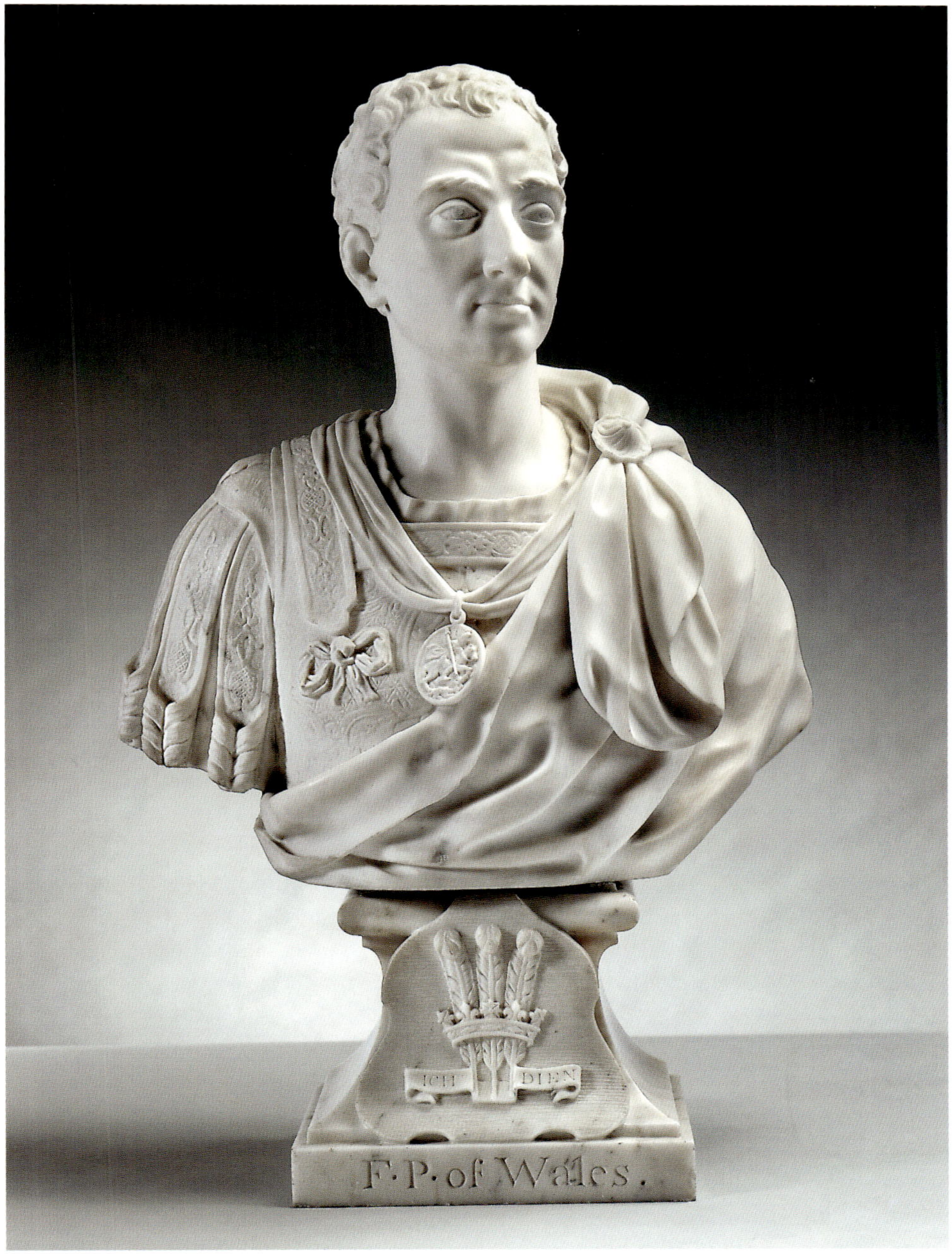

final resignation as Prime Minister. In the single rectangular interior of the temple the busts stood beneath a ceiling representing Britannia flanked by three inscriptions – 'the reign of Edward III'; 'the reign of Elizabeth I', and 'the reign of .....' (name obscured by drapery), from which Britannia averted her gaze, as if the current reign were unworthy of her. JM & WB

8

FRENCH OR FLEMISH

William III garlanded by Victory (1650–1702) early 18th century

Bronze group; pedestal of ebonised wood with gilt-bronze mounts, 90.2 cm high incl. pedestal); 54.6 cm high excl. pedestal

Cast inscriptions applied to the pedestal: 1) *ANGLIA LABORANTE / FIDE PERICLITANTE / VOTO PVBLICO / GUGLIELMVS III / ORAS APPVLIT / PROTECTOR RESTAVRAVIT / REX SVSTINVIT* (England in danger and Faith put to the test, by public wish William III landed on the coast, as Protector restored and as King maintained; 2) *BRITANNIA MAGNA PACATA / GVGLIELMVS SCOTIAM PETIT / REBELLES AD LEMERICAS ARCES / PROFLIGAT / AVXILIARIOS FVGAT / VICTOR REGNAT* (Great Britain pacified, William made for Ireland, drove the rebels into the citadel of Limerick, put their allies to flight and reigned as victor); 3) (twice) *HAEC · UNI SERVATA* (These things saved by one man)

RCIN 35463

PROVENANCE First recorded when sent from Kensington Palace in April 1812 for repair[107]

LITERATURE Volk 1966, pp. 74, 83; *Carlton House*, no. 33

Dressed in Roman armour but with a contemporary wig, William III is borne on a rearing horse over a prostrate enemy, while the winged figure of Victory descends to garland his head with laurels. This impressive bronze is one of approximately twenty known variants representing several European rulers and princes in almost exactly the same way, except for the heads, the costume and in some cases the prostrate figure. The majority represent Louis XIV; others the Elector Maximilian II Emanuel of Bavaria, Charles XII of Sweden and George I. This is the only one to portray William III, and to have a pedestal in this form. The reliefs probably depict William's landing at Torbay on 5 November 1688 and his victory over his father-in-law, James II, at the Battle of the Boyne on 1 July 1690.

The design of equestrian groups probably stems from a scheme by the Flemish-born sculptor Martin Desjardins for an monument to Louis XIV intended for Aix-en-Provence. Differences in quality between the various examples suggest that the groups were cast at different times and in different places, making use of models passed between founders, probably of Flemish origin, who collaborated with Desjardins in France. One example, representing Max Emanuel (Munich, Bayerisches Nationalmuseum), is signed by the Munich court sculptor Wilhelm de Groff and dated 1714, and a second, of Louis XIV (New York, private collection), bears the date 1707 and the signature of Roger Scabol, a founder who worked with Desjardins on several projects.

The origins of the William III bronze, which is one of the finest in the series, remain obscure. It is possible that it belonged to the King himself but it is more likely to have been created at some time after his death in 1702. In the second quarter of the eighteenth century the memory of William III was honoured in several prominent ways: in 1734–6 the cities of Hull, Bristol and Glasgow all erected large equestrian monuments to him (respectively by Scheemakers, Rysbrack and an unknown sculptor), all based loosely on the renowned statue of Louis XIV in Roman armour by François Girardon. In 1735 a bust of William (by Rysbrack, 1726) was included in the Temple of British Worthies at Stowe as having 'preserv'd the Liberty and Religion of Great Britain'. Although this political context might also have prompted the production of this bronze, the style of the mounts to the pedestal suggest an earlier date. Bronzes of this kind were rare in early eighteenth-century England and it may be significant that among the 'ancient and modern bronzes' sold by the auctioneer Langford on 23–5 February 1755 from the collection of a Mrs Kenyon was 'A fine equestrian figure in bronze of King William, on his coming to the Crown, triumphing over a figure representing tyranny'.[108] JM

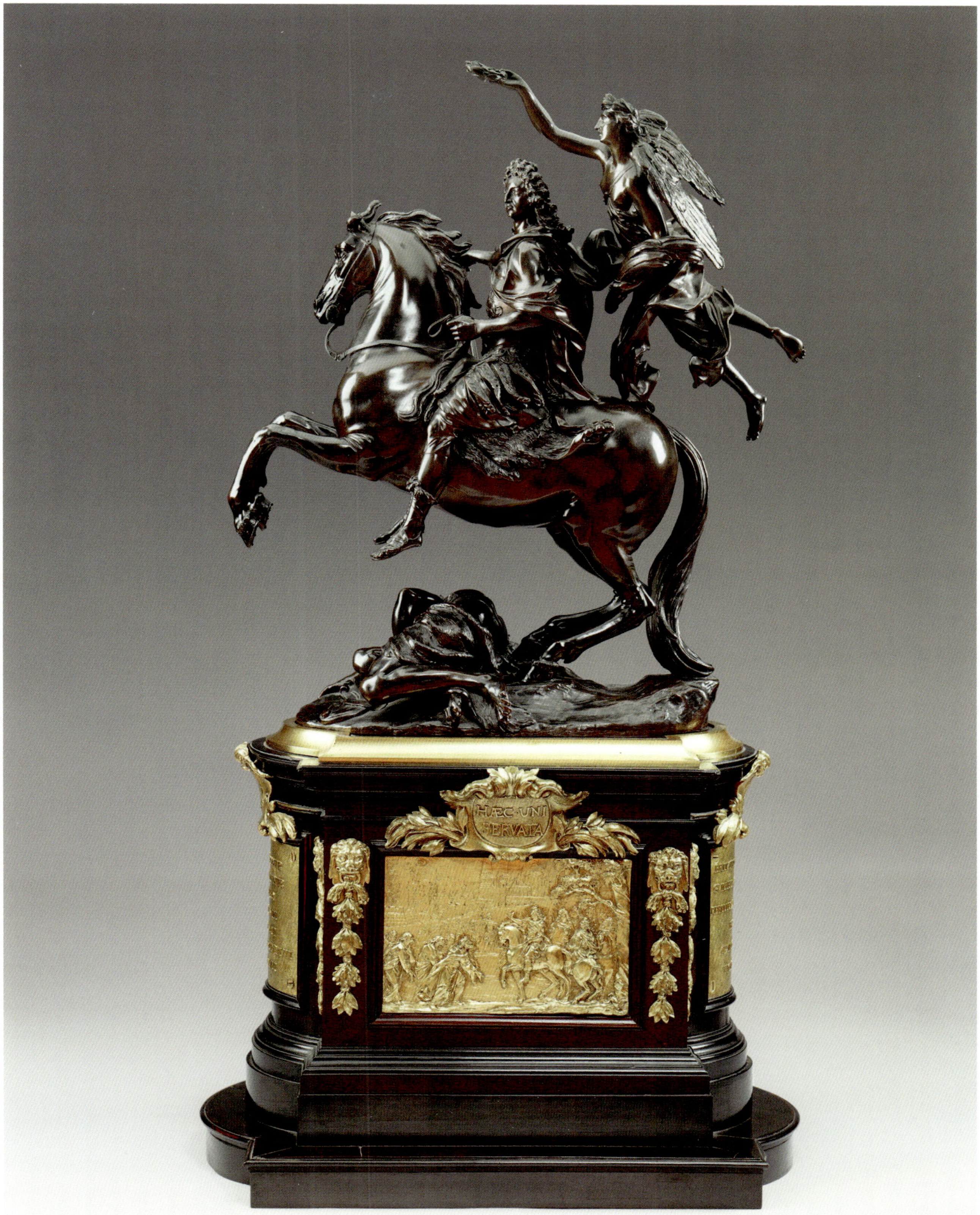
HÆC·UNI
SERVATA

9

JOHANN SEBASTIAN MÜLLER (1715–1792)
AFTER SAMUEL WALE (1721–1786)

The Hanoverian Succession 1752

Etching and engraving, 55.2 × 43.7 cm
RCIN 603772

PROVENANCE Royal Collection by *c.*1900

This print celebrates the Hanoverian succession to the British throne. It shows the reigning monarch, George II, and his consort, Queen Caroline, beneath a portrait of George I. Beneath the King and Queen are oval portraits of Frederick, Prince of Wales, and his wife, Augusta, Princess of Wales, and their children, Augusta, George, Edward, Elizabeth, William and Henry. To the left is a portrait of William, Duke of Cumberland. The portraits are surrounded by allegorical figures including Britannia, Plenty, Justice and Liberty (trampling on the Pope). To the bottom left are attributes indicating the virtues of the Hanoverians, among them a lute for music and a painter's palette for art. The inscription reinforces the print's promotion of the Hanoverian cause: 'To all true Britons, lovers of Liberty, and the present Succession, This Plate is Dedicated'.

The print is the work of the painter and illustrator Samuel Wale, known as the 'celebrated Wale', and the German engraver and botanist Johann Sebastian Müller, who had moved from Nuremberg to London in 1744.[109] It was first issued by subscription in 1748, priced at five shillings (fig. 5). This reissue of 1752 reflects the changes to the succession after the death of the heir to the throne, Frederick, Prince of Wales, in 1751. After Frederick's death, his son George became Prince of Wales, succeeding to the throne as George III in 1760. KH

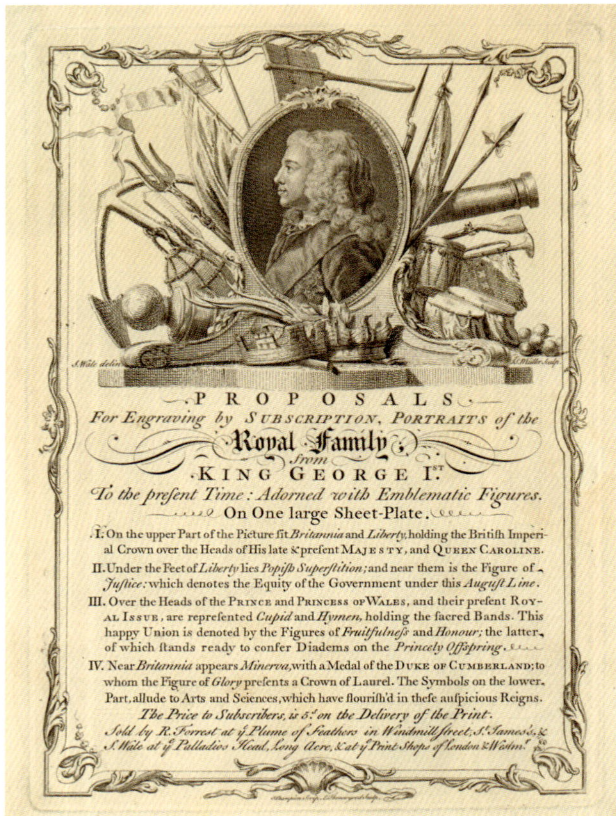

FIG. 5
Johann Sebastian Müller
Subscription ticket, *c.*1748
Etching and engraving
British Museum, London

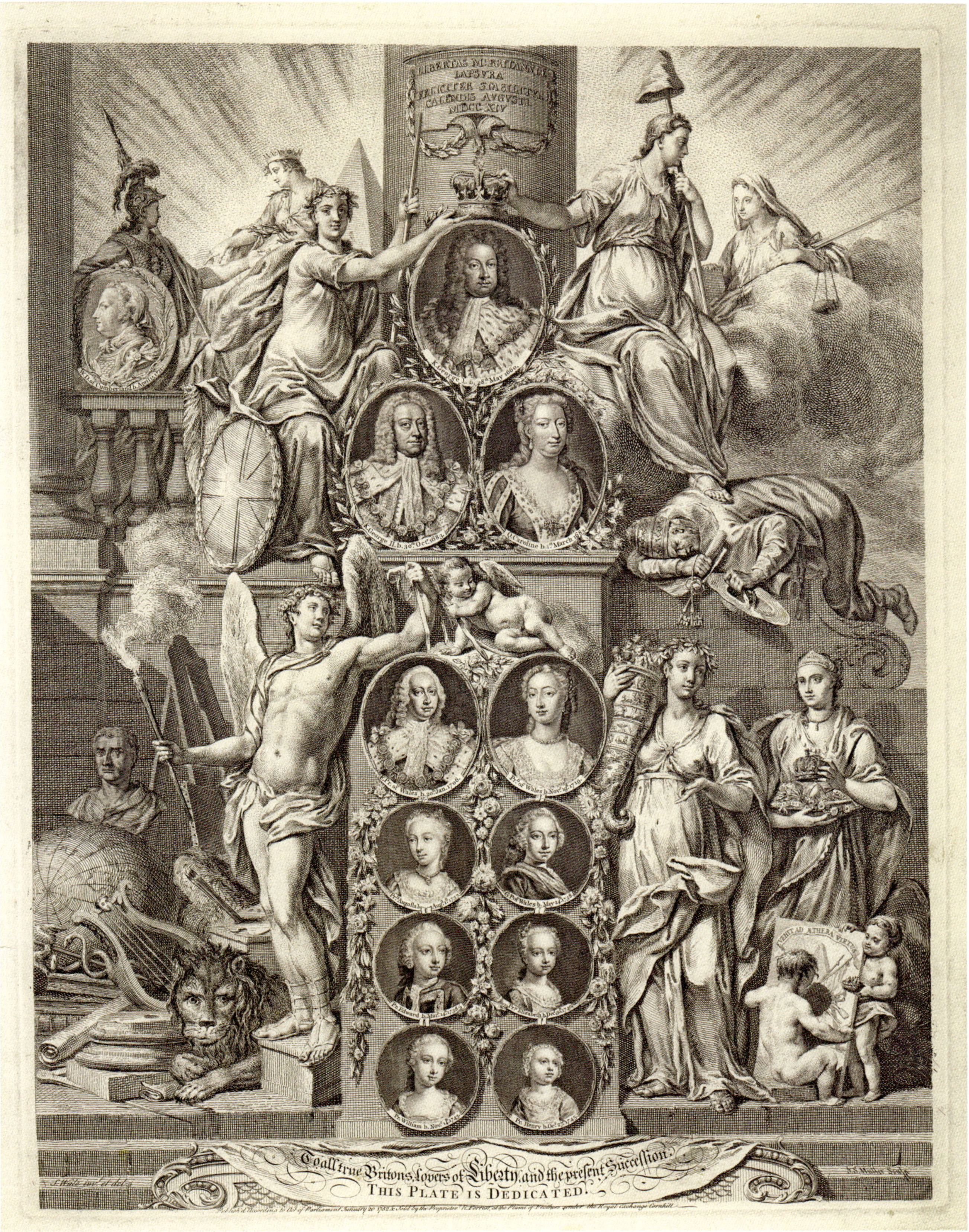

To all true Britons, Lovers of Liberty, and the present Succession.
THIS PLATE IS DEDICATED.
Pr. William b. Novr. 14 1743
Pr. Henry b. Octr. 27 1745

10

JOHN CROKER (1670–1741)

Medal commemorating the arrival of King George I in Britain

Copper, diameter 6.81 cm
RCIN 443198 and 443208

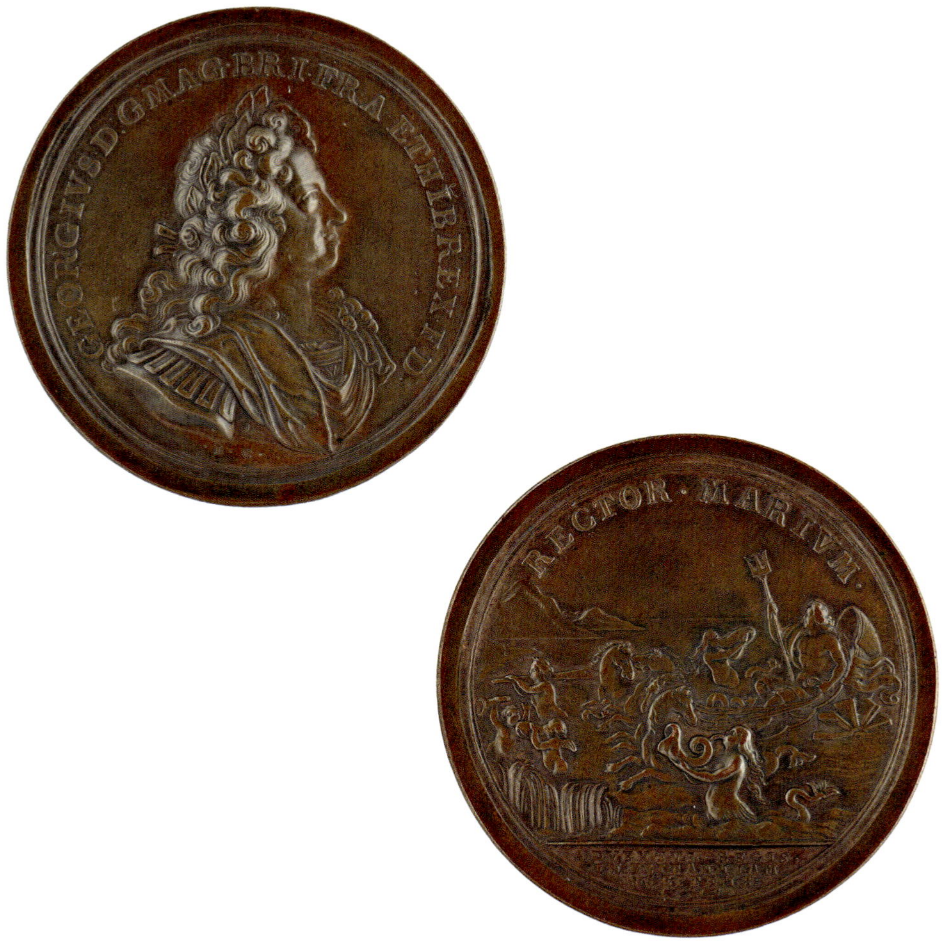

PROVENANCE (RCIN 443208) Acquired by Queen Mary

LITERATURE Hawkins 1885, II, p. 422/6; British Museum 1909–11, pl. CXXXIX/4

This medal was struck to commemorate the arrival of George I at Greenwich on 29 September 1714. His portrait is on the obverse, while on the reverse George I becomes Neptune with the motto *RECTOR MARIUM* (ruler of the seas) and seated in a marine chariot drawn by four horses and attended by Tritons and Nereids. John Croker, Chief Engraver of the Royal Mint since 1705, designed this and other official medals of the period, including those for the King's arrival in London on 1 October and his coronation on 31 October. He had also designed the coronation medal for Queen Anne and would do likewise for George II. ES

11

NICOLAUS SEELÄNDER (*c*.1683–1744)

Cliché of the obverse of a medal commemorating the coronation of George I

Silver, diameter 13.2 cm
RCIN 443200

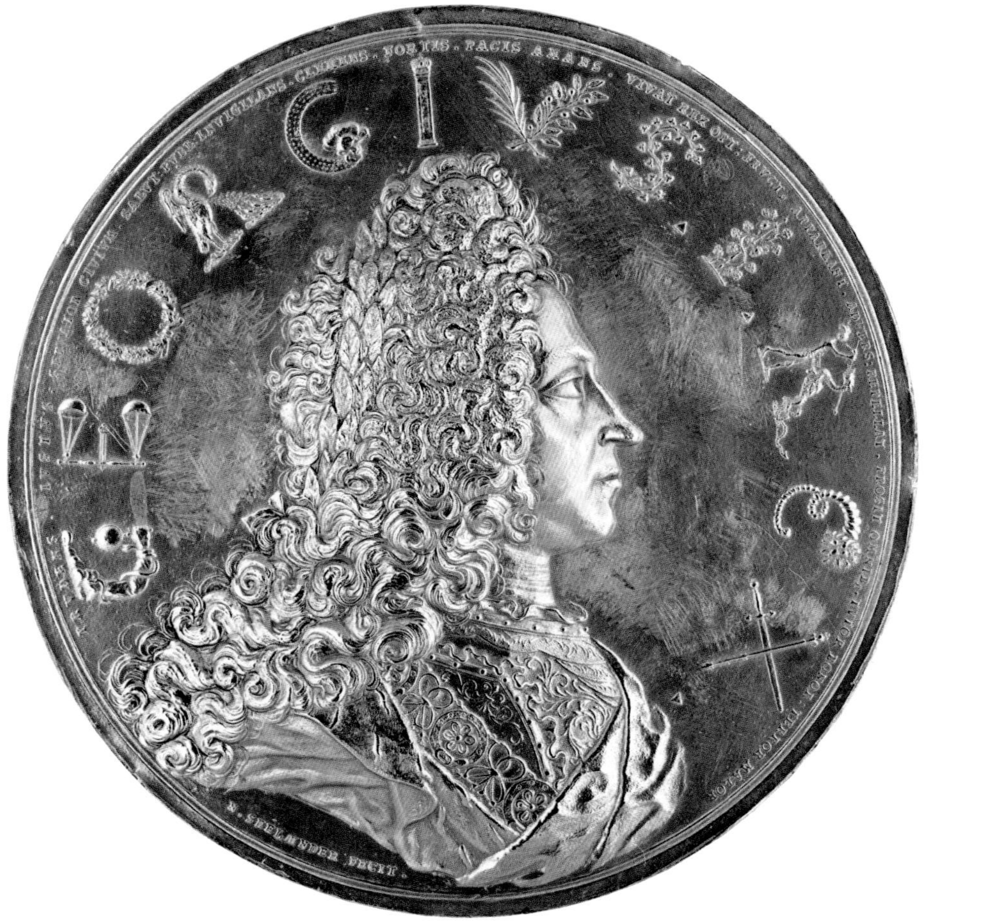

LITERATURE Hawkins 1885, II, pp. 426–7/15; British Museum 1909–11, pl. CXL/6

George I's coronation took place on 31 October 1714 (OS), about a month after his arrival in Britain. Several medals were issued to commemorate the occasion; this is one of the most elaborate, and probably the rarest. Nicolaus Seeländer later went on to become Chief Engraver to the Mint at Hanover. The reverse shows the King crowned by an angel and standing between Peace, Britannia, Justice and Genius (who holds the Electoral shield). The obverse (illustrated here) surrounds the King's head with the legend *GEORGIVS I REX*, each letter making a pictogram of one of the King's virtues, explained in Latin immediately outside it. The G illustrates an arm holding a mirror, emblem of Prudence, identified by *PRVDENS* (prudent). The E makes the scales of Justice, identified by *IVSTVS* (Just). The O is an oak wreath for *SERVATOR CIVIVM* (preserver of citizens); the R makes a pelican feeding its young with its own blood for *SALVT: PVBL. INVIGILANS* (watchful of the public safety); the second G illustrates a rainbow for *CLEMENS* (merciful); the I makes a pillar for *FORTIS* (strong); a palm and olive branch form the V for *PACIS AMANS* (lover of peace); the S is an ivy branch for *VIVAT REX OPT:* (long live the excellent King); another I is made from a spear supporting a vine for *FRVCT: APPAREANT* (may the fruits be manifest); the second R illustrates St George and the Dragon for *ADVERS: REPELLAT* (may he subdue his enemies); a cornucopia forms the second E for *PROSIT OMNIB.* (may he bring prosperity to all). The final letter, X, is made from a sceptre crossed with a sword and is explained by the words, *TVTOR BONOR. TERROR MALOR* (the defender of the good, the terror of the wicked). ES

12

JOHN CROKER (1670–1741)

Medal commemorating the Coronation of George II 1727 (O.S.)

Gold; silver, diameter 3.48 cm
RCIN 443219 (gold), 443220 (silver)

LITERATURE Hawkins 1885, II, p. 479/4; British Museum 1909–11, pl. CXLVIII/4

This medal was distributed at public expense during the Coronation ceremony on 22 October (NS), and was issued in gold, silver and copper. The reverse shows the King, seated on King Edward III's throne and holding the orb and sceptre, being crowned by Britannia, with the motto *VOLENTES PER POPULOS* (by a willing people), designed specifically to indicate a peaceful succession. The peaceful crowning of a second Hanoverian monarch, in direct succession from the first, indicated the growing solidity of the new royal house in Great Britain. The coronation took place at Westminster Abbey, and Handel's anthem *Zadok the Priest* was first sung on this occasion (see pp. 381–2). It has been sung at every subsequent coronation, traditionally during the anointing. ES

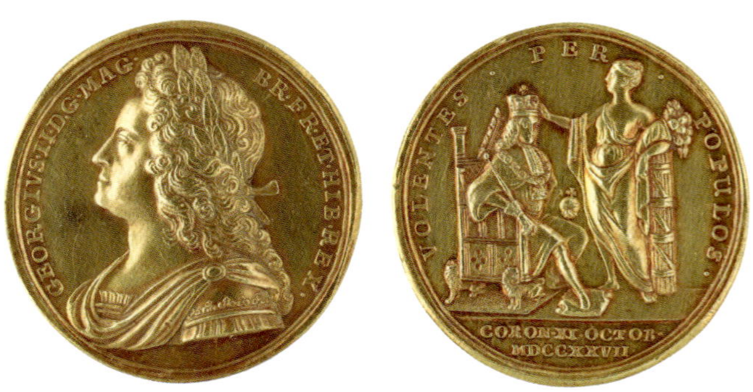

13

JOHN CROKER

Medal commemorating the Coronation of Queen Caroline 1727 (O.S.)

Gold; silver, diameter 3.48 cm
RCIN 443221 (gold), 443222 (silver)

LITERATURE Hawkins 1885, II, p. 480/8; British Museum 1909–11, pl. CXLVIII/12

To his medal commemorating George II's crowning Croker produced a companion medal for the Queen. On the reverse she is represented flanked by Britannia, with spear and shield, and by Religion, holding an open book, with the motto *HIC AMOR HAEC PATRIA* (this my affection, this my country) to demonstrate her loyalty to her new country and people. ES

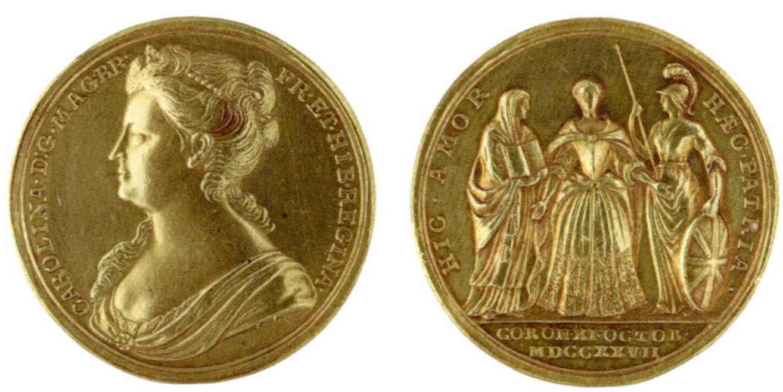

14

JOHN CROKER

Medal commemorating the revival of the Order of the Bath 1725

Silver; copper, diameter 4.65 cm
RCIN 443204 (silver), 443205 (copper)

LITERATURE Hawkins 1885, II, p. 463/75; British Museum 1909–11, pl. CXLVI/6; Risk 1972

'Whereas Our Royal Predecessors ... have, on occasion ... conferred ... that Degree of Knighthood which hath been denominated The Knighthood of the Bath; We ... hereby declare Our Royal Intention ... to erect the same into a regular Military Order ... called by the Name and Title of The Order of the Bath.'[110] Thus George I's Letters Patent of 18 May 1725 (OS) resurrected the Order, in abeyance since Charles II's time, and never previously so formalised. The official medal issued for the occasion celebrated the revival of an old Order and the knighting of the second son of the new: the reverse shows the four-year-old Prince William (later Duke of Cumberland) in his Bath robes, with the heading *SPES ALTERA* ('the other hope' – in other words, he was the second son, the back-up heir) and the motto, which in translation reads: 'The Order of the Bath revived and its decorations augmented, 1725. The Prince was the first Knight of the revived Order, which survives to this day'. ES

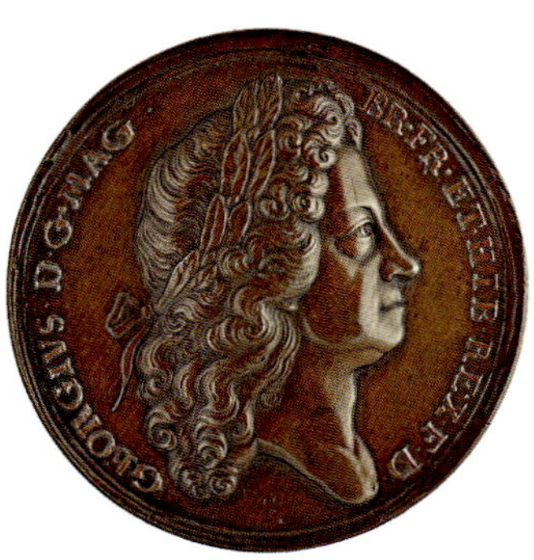

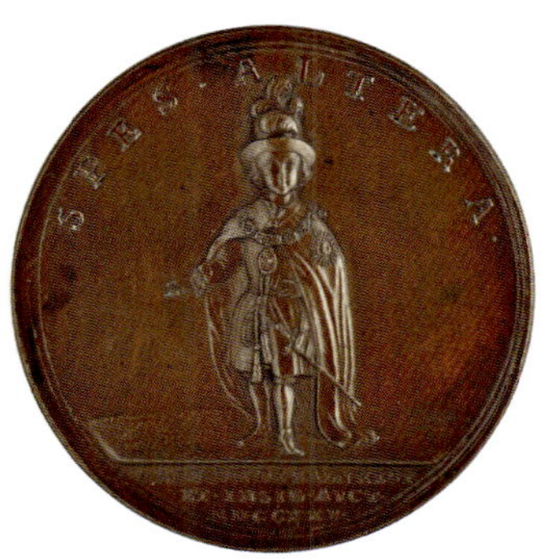

15

JOHN CROKER AND
JOHN SIGISMUND TANNER (*c*.1704–1775)

Medal commemorating the Royal Family 1732

Silver; pewter, diameter 6.9 cm
RCIN 443233 (silver), 440047 (pewter)

PROVENANCE (RCIN 443233) Acquired by Queen Mary; (RCIN 440047) presented to HM The Queen by Richard Hunter and Ida MacAlpine, 1974

LITERATURE Hawkins 1885, II, p. 500/47; British Museum 1909–11, pl. CLI/5

Croker and Tanner collaborated to produce this medal, intended for distribution to foreign royalty and to others in the favour of George II. It was issued in response to a medal produced in Italy in 1731 by the papal engraver Ottone Hamerani (1694–1768) depicting the two sons of James III, Charles Edward Stuart and Henry Benedict, on the occasion of Charles's eleventh birthday. The British response was clear enough, that George II was *de facto* King, and that he had a thriving family, including two heirs. The obverse, by Croker, shows George II and Queen Caroline; the reverse, by Tanner, shows busts of their seven children, with Frederick, Prince of Wales, in the centre, surrounded by the heads of William, Duke of Cumberland and the Princesses Anne, Amelia, Caroline, Maria and Louise. Tanner succeeded Croker as Chief Engraver of the Royal Mint upon Croker's death in 1741. ES

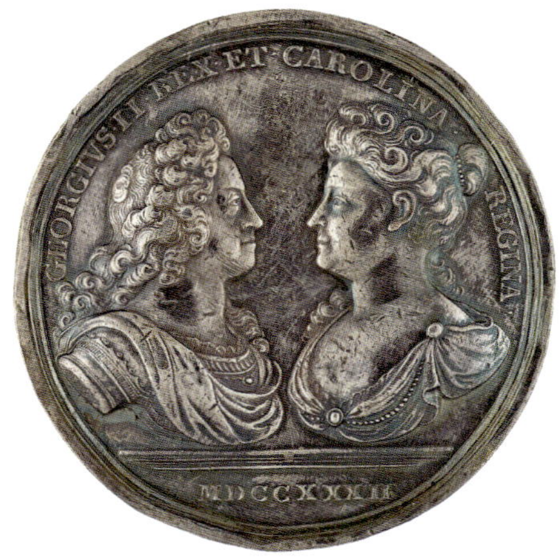

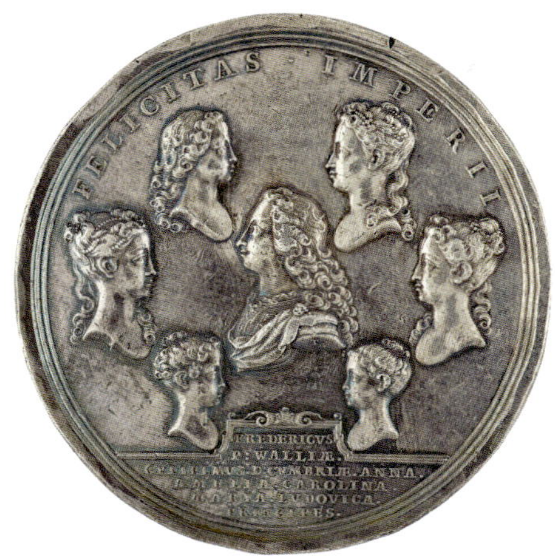

16

ADMIRALTY OFFICE, LONDON

A List of all the ships and vessells of his Maiesties Royal Navy, with their rates, numbers of men and guns in peace and war 1714/15

Manuscript in black ink, with key words in red or gold, in dark red sheepskin binding, with gold-tooling and gilt edges; crowned GR and GR reversed monogram in gold on both boards, 23.2 × 18.1 cm
RCIN 1081229
Open at p. 1

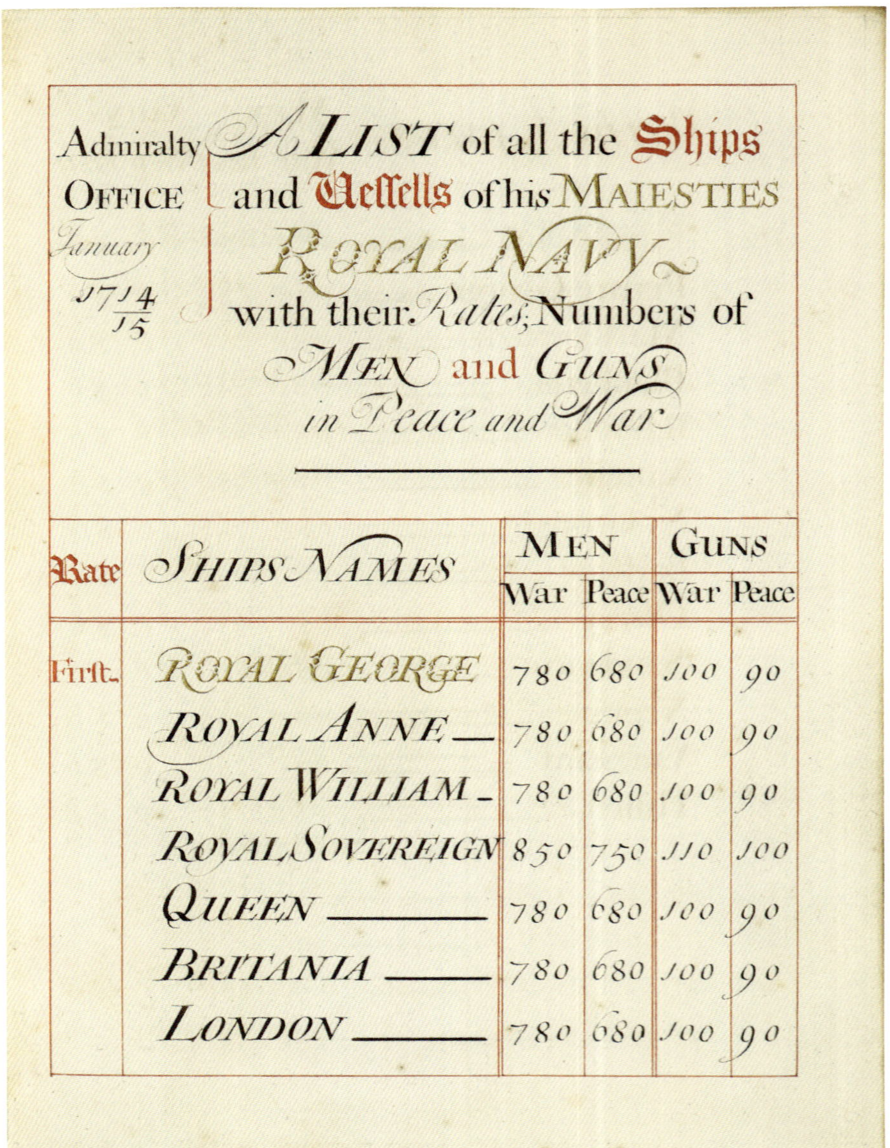

Admiralty Office January 1714/15

A LIST of all the Ships and Vessells of his MAIESTIES ROYAL NAVY with their Rates, Numbers of MEN and GUNS in Peace and War

Rate	Ships Names	Men		Guns	
		War	Peace	War	Peace
First.	Royal George	780	680	100	90
	Royal Anne	780	680	100	90
	Royal William	780	680	100	90
	Royal Sovereign	850	750	110	100
	Queen	780	680	100	90
	Britania	780	680	100	90
	London	780	680	100	90

PROVENANCE Compiled for George I; left royal ownership, mid-18th century; re-acquired by 1860

LITERATURE *Royal Treasures* 2002, p. 365; *Royal River* 2012, p. 241

Under William III (ruled 1689–1702) the creation of large navies in Britain had brought about a superiority at sea which can be regarded as being a key foundation of Britain's commercial confidence and wealth. George I took a close interest in military matters throughout his reign and, perhaps unconstitutionally, used the British navy to pursue his Hanoverian interests. Four months after the new King's arrival in Britain, this list showing the capabilities of the Royal Navy was drawn up for him. The date was expressed as January 1714/15, reflecting the discrepancy between the British and Continental calendars (see no. 176). The First- and Second-Rate lists of ships are headed in gold by the names *Royal George* and *Prince*. These ships were formerly called *Victory* and *Triumph*: they were renamed to honour the new Hanoverian dynasty. EC

17

FREDERICK, PRINCE OF WALES (1707–1751)

Letter regarding the writer's father 15 September 1737 (OS)

Manuscript, 22.7 × 18.7 cm (when folded)
RA/GEO/MAIN/54045

PROVENANCE Papers of Frederick, Prince of Wales

This letter from the 30-year-old Prince of Wales, probably written to Edward Seymour, later 8th Duke of Somerset, is clear evidence of Frederick's poor relationship with his father. The letter was sent with 'a short account of all that is pass'd relating to the Kings displeasure with me', which does not appear to have survived. Frederick was at this moment high in public favour after the birth of his daughter Augusta, but low in the King's esteem after insisting that the birth took place at St James's Palace even though the court was resident at Hampton Court. The Prince and his family were forced to quit St James's Palace, leaving (to cheering crowds) on 12 September 1737. This letter was written from Kew Palace shortly after the family had arrived there. It sought to win Seymour's support, expressing the prince's wish that his 'conduct will meet with an approbation so valuable as yours'. The Prince and King were uneasily reconciled in 1742. KH

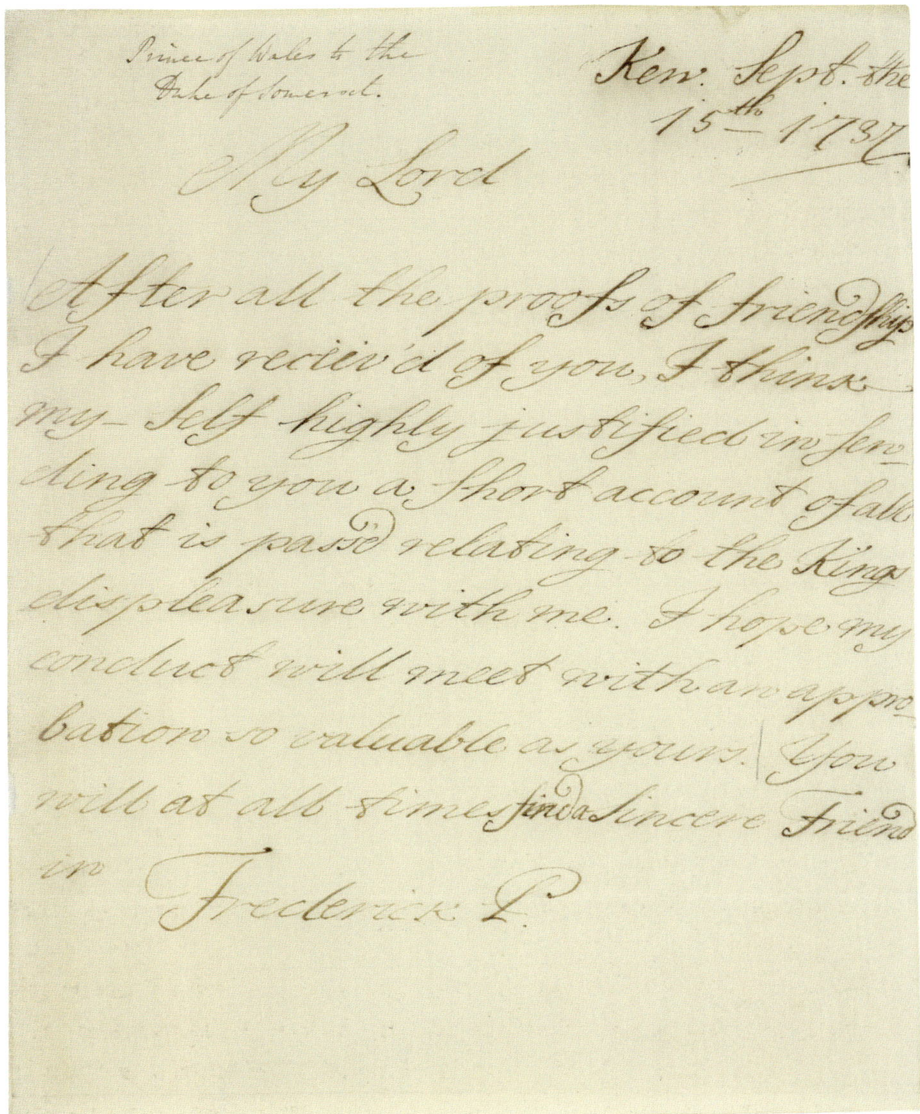
Prince of Wales to the Duke of Somerset.

Kew: Sept. the 15th 1737

My Lord

After all the proofs of friendship I have reciev'd of you, I think my-Self highly justified in sending to you a short account of all that is pass'd relating to the Kings displeasure with me. I hope my conduct will meet with an approbation so valuable as yours. You will at all times find a Sincere Friend in

Frederick P.

18

JOHN GROVE

Letter concerning vegetables to be grown at Kew c.1750

Manuscript, 22.3 × 18.3 cm

RA/GEO/MAIN/74193

PROVENANCE Papers of Sir George Lee of Hartwell

This undated letter, written by the Clerk of the Kitchen to an unidentified member of the Princess of Wales's household, accompanied a 'list of the roots & greens that are necessary for the use of Her Royal Highness's Tables, in the winter, & spring, which are the most expensive, and will conduce most to Her Interest to have them from her own garden'. The asparagus and French beans were to be grown in frames designed by John Dillman, a German gardener who was working at Kew before the Prince of Wales bought the lease and who continued there until his retirement in 1753.[111] Concerned with making economies for the Princess's household, Grove provides a breakdown of costs for food per month and notes that he will provide separate accounts for the feeding of the royal children and extra meals. The Prince and Princess of Wales had a noted interest in many aspects of horticulture, which they pursued in their gardens at Carlton House (also under the supervision of Dillman), Cliveden and Kew (see p. 304). KH

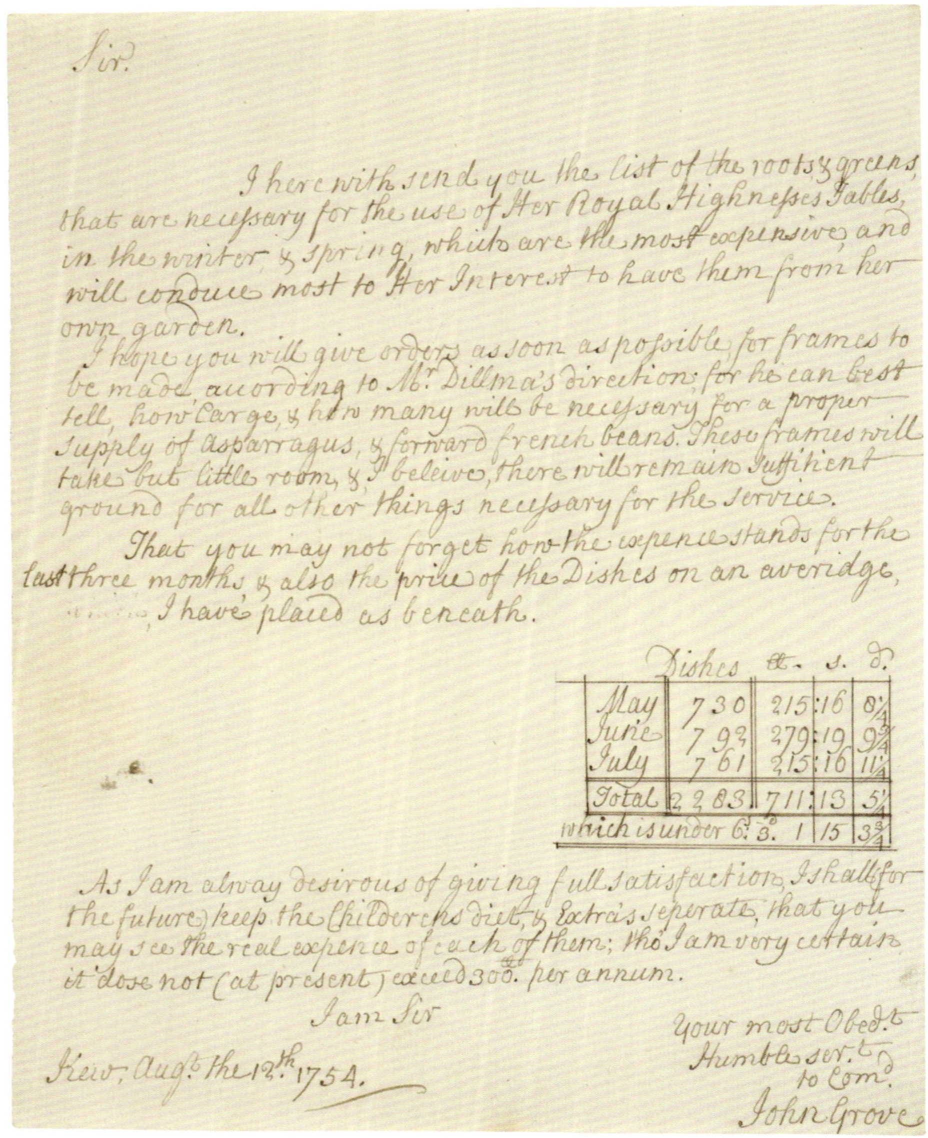
Sir.

I herewith send you the list of the roots & greens, that are necessary for the use of Her Royal Highnesses Tables, in the winter, & spring, which are the most expensive, and will conduce most to Her Interest to have them from her own garden.

I hope you will give orders as soon as possible for frames to be made according to Mr. Dillman's direction; for he can best tell, how large, & how many will be necessary for a proper supply of asparragus, & forward french beans. These frames will take but little room, & I beleive, there will remain sufficient ground for all other things necessary for the service.

That you may not forget how the expence stands for the last three months, & also the price of the Dishes on an averidge, I have placed as beneath.

	Dishes	£	s.	d.
May	730	215	16	8¼
June	792	279	19	9¾
July	761	215	16	11¼
Total	2283	711	13	5¼
which is under 6d.	3.	1	15	3¾

As I am alway desirous of giving full satisfaction, I shall for the future keep the Childrens diet, & Extra's seperate, that you may see the real expence of each of them; tho I am very certain it dose not (at present) exceed 300. per annum.

I am Sir

Kew, Augst. the 12th. 1754.

Your most Obedt. Humble servt. to Comd.

John Grove

Instructions for my Son George, drawn by my-Self, for His good, that of my Familys, and for that of His People, according to the Ideas of my Grand Father, and best Friend, George I.

19

FREDERICK, PRINCE OF WALES (1707–1751)

'Instructions for my Son George' 1749

Manuscript, 31.7 × 20.5 cm (when folded)
RA/GEO/MAIN/54227-32

PROVENANCE Papers of Sir Thomas Bootle

This manuscript was produced to instruct and guide the Prince of Wales's eldest son George (later George III). Written 'for His good, that of my Familys, and for that of His People, according to the Ideas of my Grand-Father, and best Friend, George I', the manuscript makes clear the Prince's dislike of his father, George II, whose own example is not cited. Dated 13 January 1749 (OS), the manuscript was clearly written by Prince Frederick to be used in the event of his death, since he notes that he will leave the instructions with his wife, Princess Augusta, 'who will read it to you from time to time and will give it to you when you come of age or when you get the Crown'. Other documents prepared by his advisors at the same time show the Prince was thinking hard about his own accession to the crown when the time came. The Prince urges his son, when King, 'to live with Oeconomy' (a precept the young Prince George appears to have taken to heart), and to work to reduce the national debt and ease the tax burden. He notes that true friends are hard to find and encourages his son to welcome disagreement as the sign of one who will tell him the truth rather than flatter. Interestingly, he suggests that Prince George should encourage his people to see him as 'an Englishman born and bred'. As the first British-born ruler in the Hanoverian line, Prince George had an advantage over his forebears who, born and raised in the Electorate, were regarded with suspicion by the British public. At the same time, the Prince should 'be allways kind' to the 'poor faithfull people' of Hanover. He alludes to George I's wish that the kingdom and Electorate should be divided, as impossible to rule together, 'and the latter Years have still more convinced me of the Wisdom of this Project'. The Prince, who is revealed in this document as a thoughtful and competent heir to the throne, never had the chance to act on his own advice, but assures his son here that 'I shall have no regret never to have wore the Crown, if you do but fill it worthily'. KH

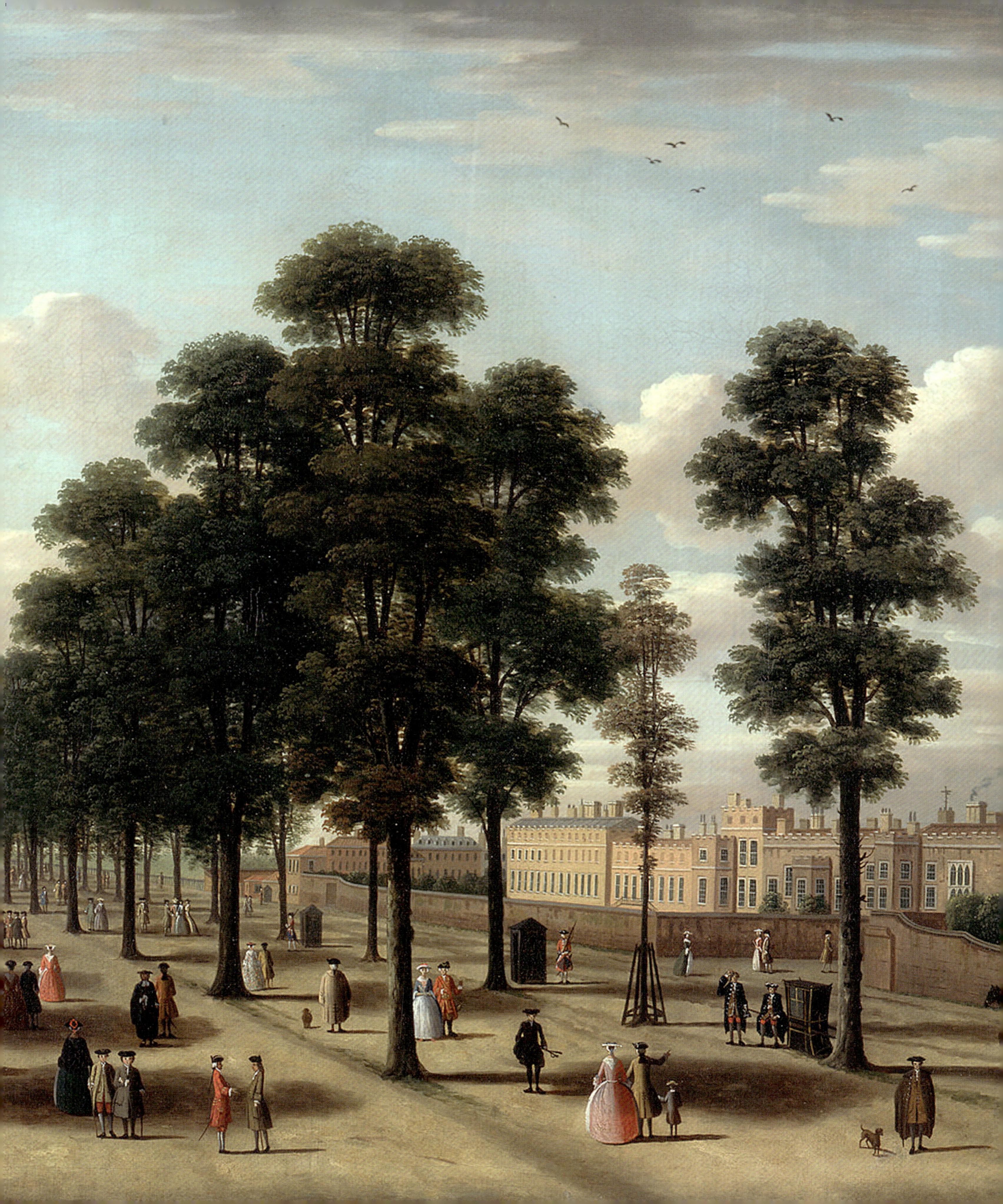

II

Houses, Palaces and Gardens
The First Georgians and Architecture

WOLF BURCHARD

IN 1728, Pierre Jacques Fougeroux, a French visitor to the newly established court of George II and Queen Caroline, described the royal couple's premises as a 'house upon which one has bestowed the most inappropriate name of Palace of St James'.[1] Clearly underwhelmed by the appearance of the relatively small and asymmetrical brick building (fig. 6), Fougeroux discerned that 'one must here disengage from the idea of Versailles and the grand palaces of the kings. One must step into the spirit of the English nation.'[2] Though condescending, these remarks characterise well the story of royal architectural patronage in early eighteenth-century Britain. In contrast to the situation in most other European countries, the prime patron was no longer the monarch but the aristocracy, rising tradesmen and rich public bodies.

History has given George I and George II a reputation for being rather oblivious of the field of architecture, which is something of an irony given that, together with George III, they lent their names to one of the most celebrated eras of British architecture – the Georgian period. It is presumably the comparative lack of exterior grandeur in their own palaces – both in Britain and Germany – that is responsible for their reputation. In reality both kings showed that they understood the value and importance of the promotion of architectural enterprises. Indeed, George I's appointment of William Kent at Kensington Palace represented a remarkable career boost for the former coach-painter, who rose to become one of the most prolific and acclaimed of all British architects.[3] George II and Queen Caroline were also active architectural patrons. Most of their building works may have been undertaken out of necessity, but their financial prudence and their great sensitivity for appropriate visual language as well as Caroline's affection for landscape gardens made them pioneers of early Enlightened architecture. Meanwhile the rival court of Frederick, Prince of Wales, whether at Kew, Carlton House or Leicester House, offered extraordinary artistic refinement as well as a more informal and intimate pattern of family life than that found in the palaces of the first two Georges. The inextricable link between elegance and informality was the foundation of George III's own family life at Buckingham House and Windsor in the second half of the century.

Early Georgian Architecture, 1714–1760

The outset of George I's reign saw the publication of the Scottish architect Colen Campbell's first volume of *Vitruvius Britannicus* (1715). Dedicated to the new sovereign,

DETAIL, FIG. 6

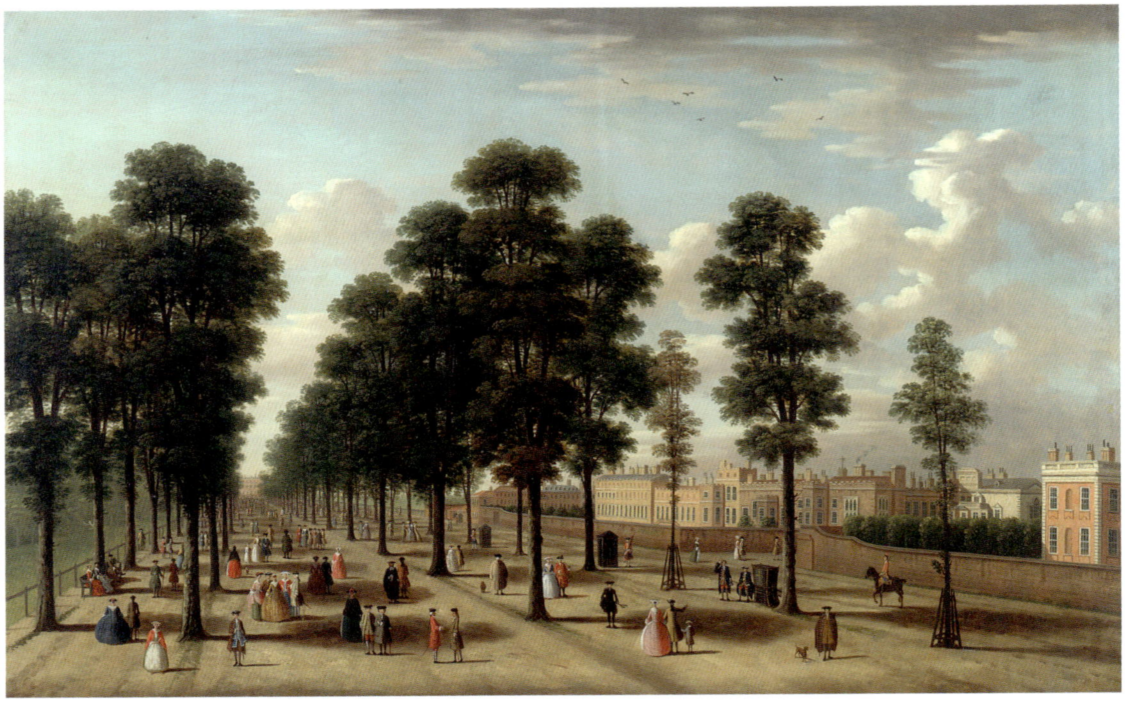

FIG. 6
British School
St James's Palace and the Mall, c.1740–50
Oil on canvas
Yale Centre for British Art

this architectural compendium aimed to demonstrate the high quality of modern building in Britain by reproducing numerous designs by Inigo Jones, Sir Christopher Wren and other leading architects. With great self-assurance, Campbell sought to display that, rather than being inferior, British architecture occasionally even surpassed that of its European neighbours. His introduction included a tribute to the 'restorers of architecture, which the fifteenth and sixteenth centuries produced in Italy' and 'above all the great Palladio ... whose ingenious labours [were to] eclipse many, and rival most of the Ancients'.[4] Yet on a par with his veneration for Andrea Palladio was Campbell's rejection of the 'absurdities' erected in seventeenth-century Italy. It was probably owing to the 'affected and licentious' output of Bernini and Borromini that Campbell believed the Italians to have forfeited their place as rightful heirs of the Ancients. Indeed he writes, 'the Italians ... have no better claim to [Antiquity] than they have to the purity of the Latin'.[5] For Campbell and his contemporaries, neo-Palladianism was the true heir of the ancients, since it demonstrated classical purity, taste and proportion and offered a counterbalance to the overblown and fanciful Catholic architecture seen in large parts of the Continent.

For all this architectural patriotism the simple fact remained that London lacked a proper royal palace. Whitehall Palace, the home of English monarchs since the time of Henry VIII, burned down in 1698, leaving only the Banqueting House standing. Colen Campbell began the second volume of the *Vitruvius Britannicus*, published in 1717, with five plates reproducing Inigo Jones's unexecuted scheme for Whitehall Palace (see fig. 7), no doubt to encourage George I to re-erect the palace or at least to build a new one more suited to his status. Neither William III nor Queen Anne had proved willing to undertake this task and in the event nor did the early Georgians. So it was that St James's Palace remained the official residence of the monarch throughout the eighteenth century.

St James's and Kensington Palace

George I and the future George II first set foot in St James's in September 1714 and it is likely that the two German

FIG. 7
Henry Hulsberg after Inigo Jones
Design for Whitehall Palace
published in Colen Campbell's
Vitruvius Britannicus, 1717
Engraving
British Museum, London

princes, like so many before them, were unimpressed by the exterior appearance of their new home.[6] Built by Henry VIII as a temporary residence for Anne Boleyn, the low and irregular elevation of the Tudor brick building must have looked mean in accommodation and obsolete in style.[7] Throughout the eighteenth century British and foreign visitors noted its inadequacy.[8] However, in spite of all criticism, the first two Georges refrained from either extensively enlarging their London palace or even replacing it by a more sumptuous structure.[9] Shortly after George I's arrival, Sir John Vanbrugh, then Comptroller of the King's Works, presented him with designs for a complete re-build of St James's in the fashion of Blenheim Palace (nos 22 and 23). The new King dismissed Vanbrugh's ambitious plans and asked the architect Nicholas Hawksmoor to build new stables instead.[10] Except for interior refurnishing (see Chapter V), George I kept St James's as it stood when he arrived. The State Apartments were largely preserved as they had been in Queen Anne's reign. The walls were adorned with crimson damask and tapestries; pictures were hung only over doors and fireplaces.[11] It was only in his private rooms that George allowed for soft furnishings of different colours, as well as rearrangements of the picture hang.[12]

The King was relatively old and shy when he arrived in Britain and particularly cautious whenever he had to perform on the public stage.[13] Accordingly, his artistic and architectural patronage was mostly confined to more private spaces, as reflected by his commissions for Kensington Palace. It may not have been a private residence *per se*, but its convenient location outside London, remote from the scrutiny of some of his more sceptical new subjects, appears to have afforded him the freedom he needed to promote the visual arts. The contrast between the palace's grand interiors and its distinctively plain, almost dull exterior embodies the King's astute balancing act in catering for the needs of his courtiers without offending the population as a whole.

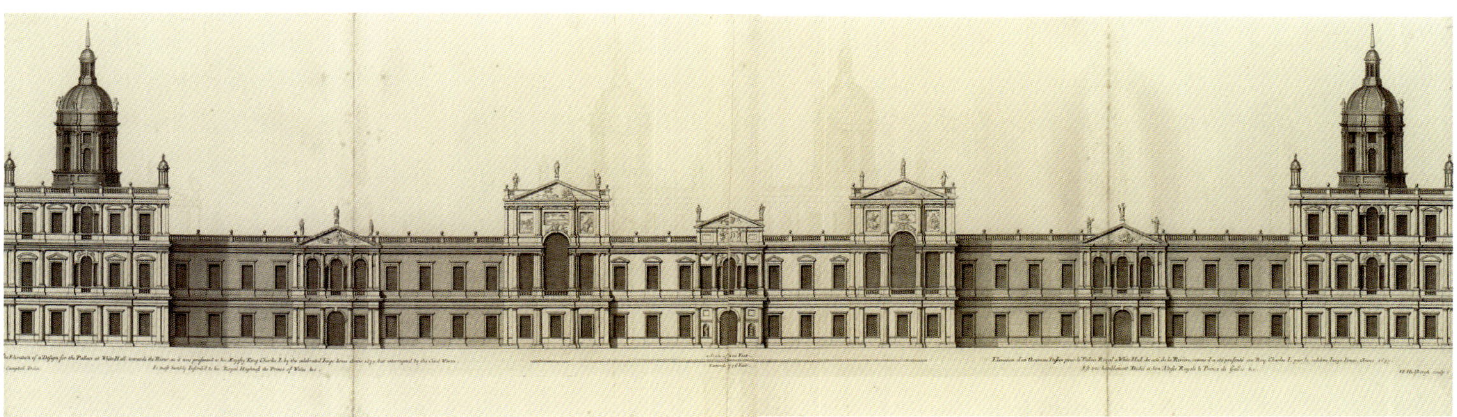

As early as 1718, George I had rooms refitted for his first stay at Kensington; the more significant building works, however, began in the early 1720s, when the centre of house was demolished to make way for a new suite of state rooms. In 1722, following the dismissal of Sir James Thornhill, William Kent was employed to adorn each of these new rooms by painting their ceilings and designing some of the wall decorations. Kent began with the so-called Cupola Room (no. 30), followed by the Great Drawing Room (no. 31), as well as the Presence and Privy Chambers (no. 32). His two later commissions, the King's Gallery and Staircase (no. 34), proved particularly successful with the King. Although Kent's interiors at Kensington may appear simple and occasionally slightly clumsy – especially when compared to his later works at Raynham, Houghton and Holkham – they represent an important shift in royal artistic and architectural patronage. Not only Thornhill, but an entire generation of architects had been excluded from the Kensington building site, resulting in a complete turnover of the architectural establishment. Since Vanbrugh, Hawksmoor and most especially the elderly Wren had dominated the scene during the previous reigns of William III and Queen Anne, their architecture was associated with the Stuart monarchy.[14]

Neo-Palladianism, in turn, was the style largely – though not exclusively – associated with the Whig Party, who had gained the King's favour as key supporters of the Hanoverian succession. Long before he came to the British throne, George I might have displayed some interest in Palladio when promoting Venetian-inspired architecture in his German dominions.[15] In Britain, however, where Palladianism had Whig connotations, he was more cautious, for fear of publically aligning himself with a particular political group. Therefore, externally – with the exception of a Venetian-style window – George's additions to Kensington Palace carefully blended with Wren's earlier works.

The Rival Courts at Leicester and Carlton House

In 1717 George I quarrelled with the Prince and Princess of Wales over the choice of godparent for their second son, Prince George William (1717–18), and expelled the couple from St James's Palace. They were obliged to rent accommodation from the Earl of Leicester at Leicester House. Far from undergoing a humbling exile, the Prince and Princess of Wales (who were always more at ease with English society than their sovereign) created a vibrant and colourful young court, in direct competition with that of the elderly King.[16] Leicester House was built between 1631 and 1635 and occupied roughly a quarter of today's Leicester Square (it was demolished in 1792); between 1717 and 1721 George and Caroline had it expansively refitted under the supervision of Colen Campbell.[17] Accounts of the interiors at Leicester House suggest that it was much more in keeping with contemporary ideas of elegance: its 'finely furnished' apartments were described as looking 'with a greater Air of Grandeur than the Royal Palace at St. James's'.[18]

George II's son, Frederick, Prince of Wales, was associated with three London town houses. On his first arrival in London in 1728 he lodged at Leicester House, then rented by his father. In the summer of 1737, he and his wife Augusta were banished from St James's Palace, where they were then living, just as George and

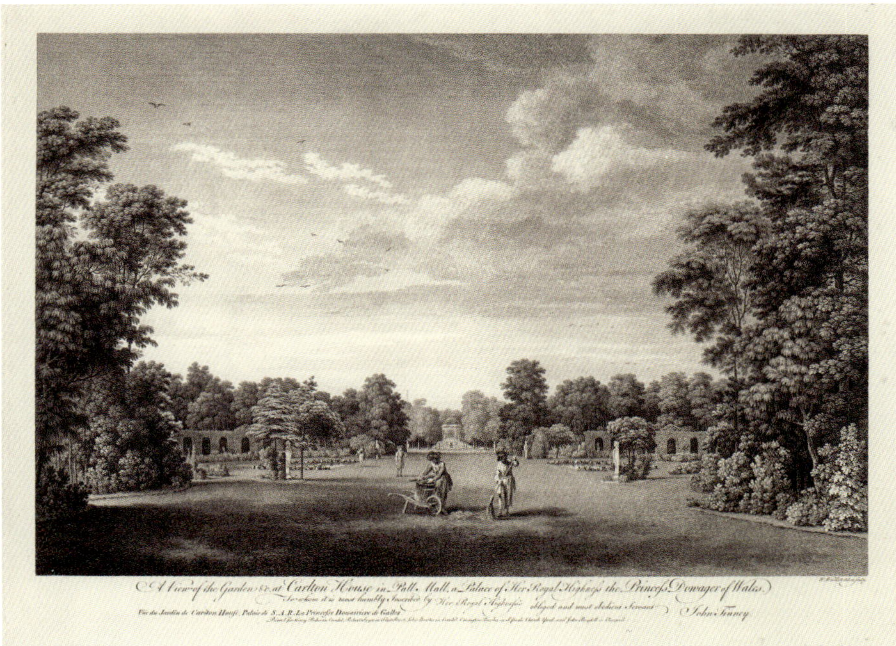

FIG. 8
After William Woollett
View of the gardens at Carlton House, 1760
Engraving
RCIN 702850

Caroline had been twenty years previously. Carlton House, which Frederick had purchased in 1732, could not accommodate his entire family so he leased Norfolk House, St James's Square. When that also proved too small he returned to Leicester House.[19] Carlton and Leicester House, both now lost, were transformed by Frederick into cultural and political centres to rival the court at St James's. It is testament to William Kent's reputation that Frederick chose to employ him on both, although he was also working for Queen Caroline at the time. Kent was first commissioned to create a small landscape garden for Carlton House (fig. 8). Visitors marvelled at his revolutionary 'natural' approach, so different from the ordered symmetry of the *jardin à la française*, the then dominant gardening style: 'There is a new taste in gardening just arisen, which has been practised with so great success at the Prince's garden in Town ... it has the appearance of beautiful nature, and without being told one would imagine art had not part in the finishing.'[20] At Leicester House, Kent was asked to remodel the interiors, creating lavish frameworks for the arrangement of Frederick's growing art collection.[21]

Visits to Hanover – the Palaces of George I's Parents

Both George I and George II returned to Hanover regularly, usually when Parliament was prorogued. Although criticised by large parts of the public, the kings' absence was of great political importance. As long as the Stuarts aspired to return to Britain, the right to the throne remained precarious for both Georges. The loyalty of their German subjects was therefore as essential to them as that of their British ones, as they might have to return to Hanover for good. Visits to the Continent also helped to promote diplomatic relations and consolidate political alliances between Britain, Hanover and other German principalities. The Hanoverians had numerous castles, palaces and hunting lodges in their German dominions, most of which have since been destroyed. The Georges usually resided in Hanover, either at their city palace, the Leineschloss, or at their suburban retreat Schloss Herrenhausen. Both bore the distinct architectural signature of George I's parents, Ernest Augustus and Sophia. Like that of St James's Palace, the external appearance of the Leineschloss would have been far from impressive to contemporaries (fig. 9). Internally, however, its state rooms were sumptuously decorated.

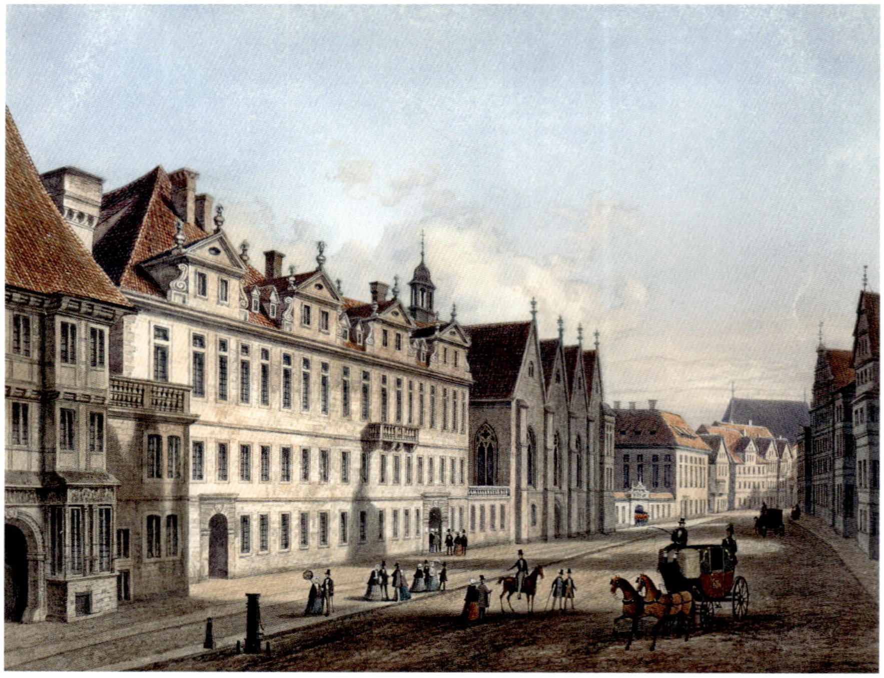

FIG. 9
Wilhelm Kretschmer
*The façade of the Leineschloss towards the city with the Electoral chapel in the background, c.*1825
Watercolour
Historisches Museum, Hanover

Its festivities even won the approval of the *Mercure Galant* – then Europe's most fashionable and supercilious magazine, published in Paris – where the court of George I's parents was singled out as 'one of the most refined courts of Germany'.[22]

On his first return to Hanover, in 1716, George I's suite included several British diplomats and courtiers. Amongst them were, visiting from Vienna, the ambassador Edward Wortley Montagu and his spirited wife, Lady Mary, who was dazzled by the French actors performing every night at the court theatre.[23] She was particularly impressed by the interiors of the Hanoverian palaces and surprised to find warm quarters and exotic fruits such as pineapples and oranges in spite of the cold December weather. The key to this luxury were stoves installed in plant-houses as well as domestic rooms, which proved more energy-efficient than open fireplaces; Lady Mary even ventured to import some to England.[24] The interiors of the Leineschloss had not always been as grand and comfortable as Lady Mary experienced them. They were mainly the product of Ernest Augustus's zeal to join the College of Electors – Germany's most prestigious club, holding the privilege of electing the Emperor. To underpin the legitimacy of this aspiration – eventually achieved in 1692 and confirmed by Emperor Joseph I in 1708 – Ernest Augustus needed to display his princely status on a prominent scale.[25] He had taken up residence at the Leineschloss in 1680, shortly after the death of his brother, Duke John Frederick, from whom he inherited the principality of Calenberg. Prior to this, Ernest Augustus had been Prince Bishop of Osnabrück, where, together with his wife Sophia, he had overseen the erection of a completely new palace with up-to-the-minute formal gardens (no. 20). The Leineschloss on the other hand was a rather gloomy timber-frame building – a former monastery, which the Catholic John Frederick had hoped to turn into some kind of Northern Escorial on a more modest scale.[26] Sophia found it particularly painful to trade her modern palace and gardens at Osnabrück for these dark and antiquated quarters and she explained in a letter to her brother Charles Louis, Elector Palatine: 'We are getting ready ... to reside in Hanover in a quite filthy and hideous house to leave one that is beautiful and comfortable, where there is a handsome garden. They somewhat reassure me with Herrenhausen.'[27]

Almost immediately after the ducal couple's arrival in Hanover, Ernest Augustus began improvements

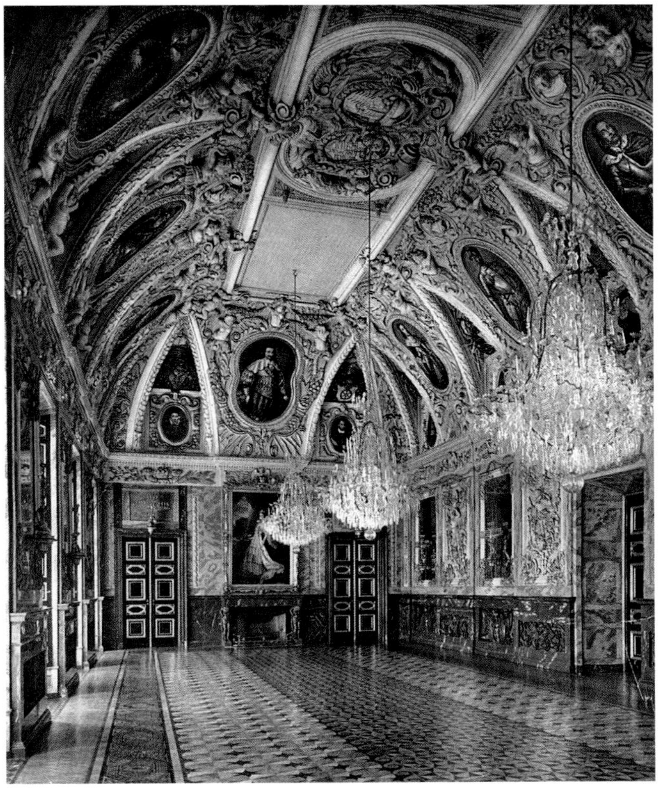

FIG. 10
The Rittersaal at the Leineschloss, c.1930
Historic photograph
Historisches Museum, Hanover

to the Leineschloss. Sophia's own involvement in the decoration of her new home was later noted – possibly with slight exaggeration – by John Toland, a British visitor to the electoral court in 1701–2: '[The Electress is] a great Worker ... and you cannot turn your self in the Palace without meeting som Monuments of her Industry, all the Chairs of the Presence-Chamber being wrought with her own Hands. The Ornaments of the Altar in the Electoral Chappel are all of her Work.'[28] Whilst Sophia's engagement with the practicalities of furniture-making may attest to her broad spectrum of cultural interests, the more substantial architectural works carried out at the Leineschloss were vital representational and political statements. Ernest Augustus's first great architectural venture was the erection of a vast new palace opera-house, seating 1300.[29] It was inaugurated in January 1689 with a rendition of *Enrico Leone* by Agostino Steffani.[30] This particular subject matter manifestly encapsulated the Duke's political ambitions: Henry the Lion, who had been Duke of Saxony and Bavaria, was the Guelfs' most prominent medieval ancestor. By the late seventeenth century both dukedoms had arisen to electorates and, according to Ernest Augustus, it was high time for the Dukes of Brunswick-Lüneburg to obtain the same privilege.[31] Moreover, Henry had been married to the Plantagenet Princess Matilda, daughter of Henry II of England. The opera stressed the Guelfs' legitimate status amongst the great European dynasties and emphasised their ancient connection with the English Crown, going far beyond Sophia's Stuart descent.

The Hanoverian's dynastic pre-eminence was central to Ernest Augustus's cultural and political endeavours, which is why he commissioned Gottfried Wilhelm Leibniz (1646–1716) to travel to Italy and research the genealogical links between the Houses of Guelf and Este.[32] Leibniz's findings materialised architecturally in the Leineschloss's Rittersaal – a banqueting hall erected between 1685 and 1688 to the designs of the Venetian architect Girolamo Sartorio (fig. 10). The vault's outstanding Baroque stucco work, carried out by Italian craftsmen, provided an abundant framework for 24 carefully selected ancestral portraits.[33] Ernest Augustus's and Sophia's own portraits were placed at each end of the room, whilst their coats-of-arms dominated the centre of ceiling. The equal prominence given to Sophia's arms is a testament to her importance as grand-daughter of James I. This heraldic statement was repeated at the so-called Galeriegebäude built for Sophia at Herrenhausen. It had originally been planned as an orangery, but then functioned as a ball room complete with lavish Baroque frescoes and stucco work (fig. 11).[34] The Venetian fresco painter Tommaso Giusti sought both to delight and exercise the eyes of

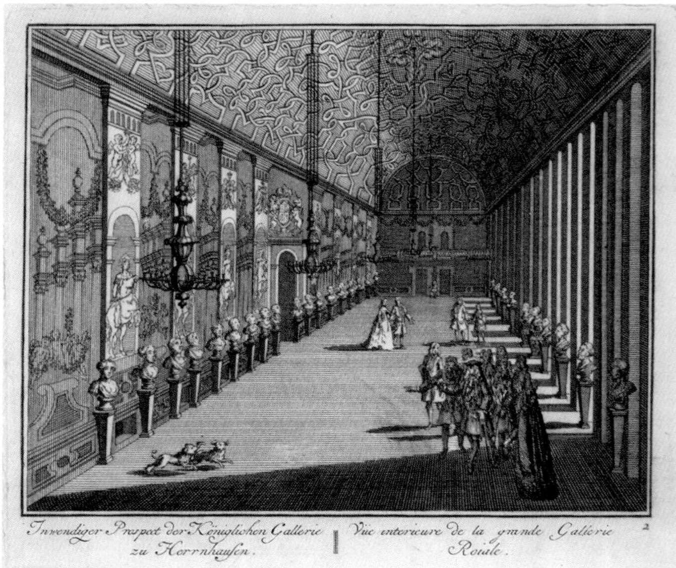

FIG. 11
Joost van Sasse
The Galeriegebäude at Herrenhausen, 1800
Engraving
Historisches Museum, Hanover

Hanoverian courtiers with a complex rendition of the *Aeneid*, surmounted by two huge electoral coats-of-arms – Sophia's and that of her husband. When he became King of Great Britain, George I expanded the gallery's decoration by lining up in it 28 busts of Roman Emperors which had previously belonged to Louis XIV of France.[35] The decoration of the Galeriegebäude was probably the first step of what Sophia hoped to be a broader scheme to enhance Herrenhausen. However, her hopes were never realised, as both her son and grandson settled for merely maintaining the palace rather than expanding it.

Appropriate Styles: Neo-Palladianism, Neo-Classicism and Neo-Gothick

As he ascended the British throne in June 1727, George II instantly made provisions for his large family to take up residence at St James's Palace in the autumn of the same year. Although the palace remained the monarchy's headquarters throughout his reign, George barely touched its fabric. His restraint may have reflected a desire to preserve, triggered by Queen Caroline's interest in Tudor architecture and antiquarianism and coupled with her sound understanding of public self-representation. Preserving the palace's humble yet distinctively English exterior not only displayed continuity, and therefore stability, to the outside world, but also financial responsibility.[36] Caroline's pioneering predilection for Tudor architecture manifested itself particularly at Hampton Court, where William Kent was commissioned to create new apartments for William, Duke of Cumberland at the east side of Clock Court.[37] Instead of breaking with the Tudor style, as Wren had done in the same courtyard, Kent emulated the palace's original sixteenth-century formal language (fig. 12). The new lodgings erected between *c.*1731 and 1734 thus constituted one of the earliest examples of Georgian Gothick revival style, anticipating Horace Walpole's Strawberry Hill by more than a decade.[38] While previous monarchs and architects may have exhibited a certain respect for the original Tudor structure by preserving and occasionally restoring some of its Gothic elements, Kent's enterprise meant much more than mere maintenance.[39] He created an entirely new wing, thoughtfully looking back at sixteenth-century English architecture and its romantic associations.[40]

Caroline's last and most important commission was her library at St James's Palace, again erected to the designs of William Kent, between 1736 and 1737 (no. 29).[41] It is in this space that her antiquarian interest as well as understanding of her British heritage culminated. The distinct neo-Palladianism of the interior announces this as an unmistakably British creation, in content and appearance. Both George and Caroline were well aware of the alternatives to Palladianism and more generally of the differences between British and Continental architectural vocabulary. Caroline, for instance, seems to have been

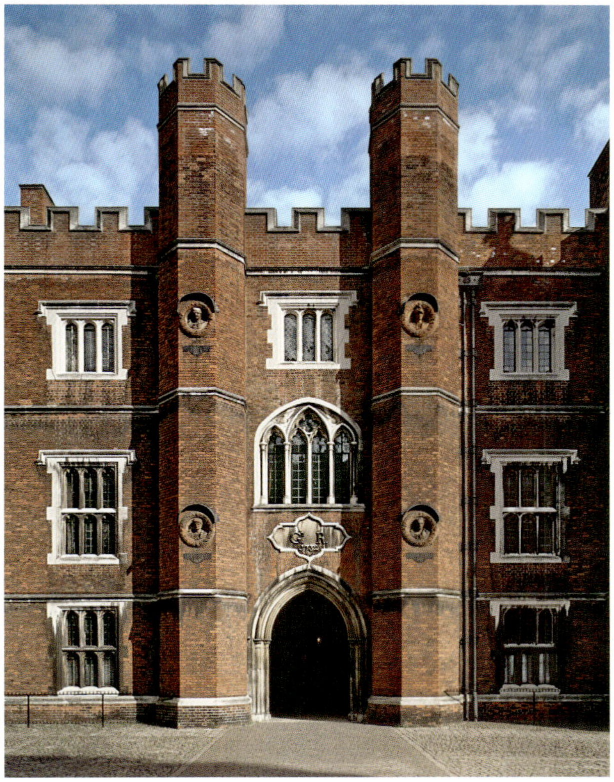

FIG. 12
William Kent's neo-Gothic entrance to the Duke of Cumberland's new apartments at Hampton Court

particularly interested in the urban development of her native city of Ansbach. In the spring of 1736, she asked her German chamberlain Julius Gottlieb Voit von Salzburg to provide her with Leopoldo Retti's designs for the remodelling of her nephew's city palace.[42] Retti's designs, neo-classical on the outside and rococo on the inside, remind us of the fact that the Margrave of Brandenburg-Ansbach – one of smallest German principalities – inhabited a metropolitan residence that was strikingly more palatial than St James's or Kensington Palace.

The growing influence of French neo-classicism in Germany also became evident in the rebuilding of a large wing of the Leineschloss destroyed by fire in April 1741, which George II was obliged to undertake without the advice of his late consort.[43] George gave the responsibility of organising and overseeing the re-building to his Electoral surveyor of works, Friedrich Karl von Hardenberg (1696–1763), and to the architect Johann Paul Heumann. On a diplomatic mission to Paris, Hardenberg showed Heumann's somewhat old-fashioned designs for the new wing to Jacques-François Blondel (1705–74), who later became the leading architect of the French Enlightenment.[44] Blondel made considerable alterations to the original plans, which were promptly approved by the King. Sober yet not severe, the Leineschloss's new wing could not conceal its French authorship – something that would have been inconceivable in Britain.

Formal and Informal Gardens

Although the Leineschloss was ceremonially more significant, Schloss Herrenhausen (fig. 13), just outside Hanover, was the favoured residence of George I and George II. Whilst not large, the palace contained outstanding pictures, sculptures and furniture. Moreover, the three-wing complex – which was much more in keeping with contemporary ideals of symmetry than the Leineschloss, St James's or indeed Kensington Palace – was embedded in a French formal garden of international renown. During the summer months, the gardens at Herrenhausen provided an ideal stage for concerts, fireworks and other court festivities.

The palace as such had been erected as a *maison de plaisance* to the designs of Hieronymo Sartorio for Duke John Frederick of Brunswick-Lüneburg in the 1670s, and was later enlarged for his brother Ernest Augustus.[45] It was a simple timber-framed construction covered in a layer of plaster emulating stone. The façades were adorned with stucco ornaments, which owing to inclement northern German weather conditions had hastily to be restored and replaced whenever its proprietors returned

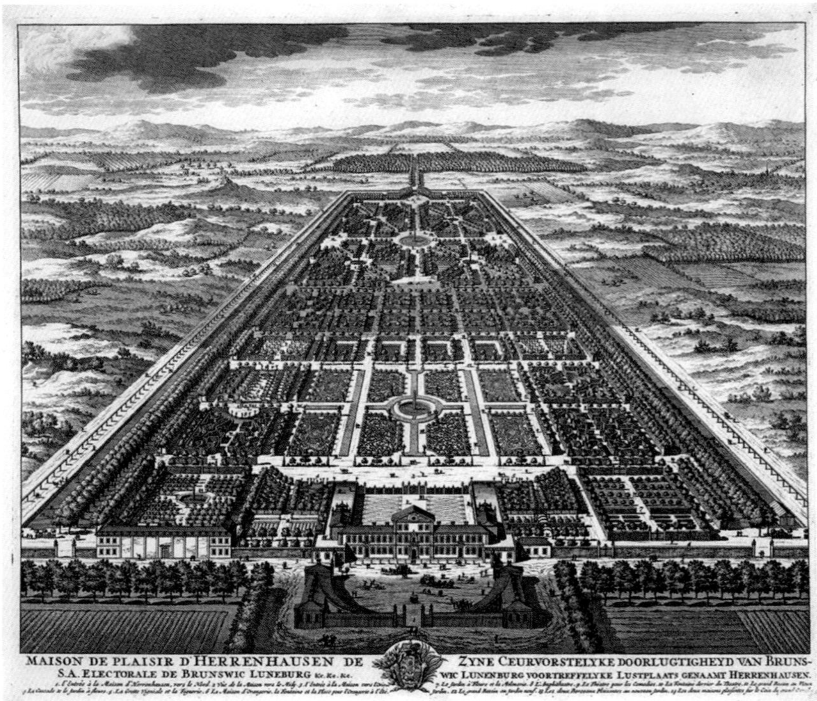

FIG. 13
Maison de Plaisir d'Herrenhausen de S.A. Electoral de Brunswic Luneburg &c., c.1740
Engraving
RCIN 704535

to Herrenhausen; the use of plaster rather than stone decorations therefore proved much less cost-effective than intended.[46] When Ernest Augustus died in 1698, Electress Sophia used the palace as a dower house.[47] Sophia had always preferred Herrenhausen to the Leineschloss; over the course of her life, she had seen many celebrated gardens in Italy, the Low Countries, France and of course Germany, and henceforth took great pleasure in improving and aggrandising the park at Herrenhausen.[48] However, the expanding gardens gradually appeared out of proportion in relation to the palace. Thus, after visiting the new residence and gardens of her daughter, Queen Sophia Charlotte of Prussia, Electress Sophia encouraged her son to follow this example and replace Herrenhausen by a more sumptuous structure.[49] Disregarding his mother's advice, George went for a thorough, yet economical refurbishment of the building, not a replacement. At the end of George I's reign, the architect Tobias Henry Reetz made one last attempt to instigate more substantial improvements to Herrenhausen, by supplying designs for a complete rebuilding of the palace in the rococo style. These designs were never executed.[50]

Instead of spending large sums on a palace that was primarily associated with his parents, George chose to focus on a different architectural project: a passionate huntsman, he commissioned the French architect Louis Rémy de la Fosse to build him an imposing hunting lodge at Göhrde, a large estate situated at the north-east corner of the Principality of Lüneburg (fig. 14). In 1705, George had inherited the principality from his uncle George, Duke of Celle, leading to a considerable expansion of the Electorate.[51] Certainly one of George I's most expensive architectural projects, Schloss Göhrde fell into disrepair after George II's last visit to Hanover and was demolished in 1827. An unusually high building, the three-wing lodge, erected primarily between 1706 and 1709 and displaying a distinctively French architectural language, must have looked like a Parisian *hôtel particulier* unexpectedly emerging from the woods surrounding it. Rather like the Stadholder William III's palace at Het Loo in the Low Countries, Göhrde was devised to entertain and impress foreign dignitaries. The numerous adjoining buildings, including stables for no less than 544 horses, testify to this function.[52] After his accession to the British throne,

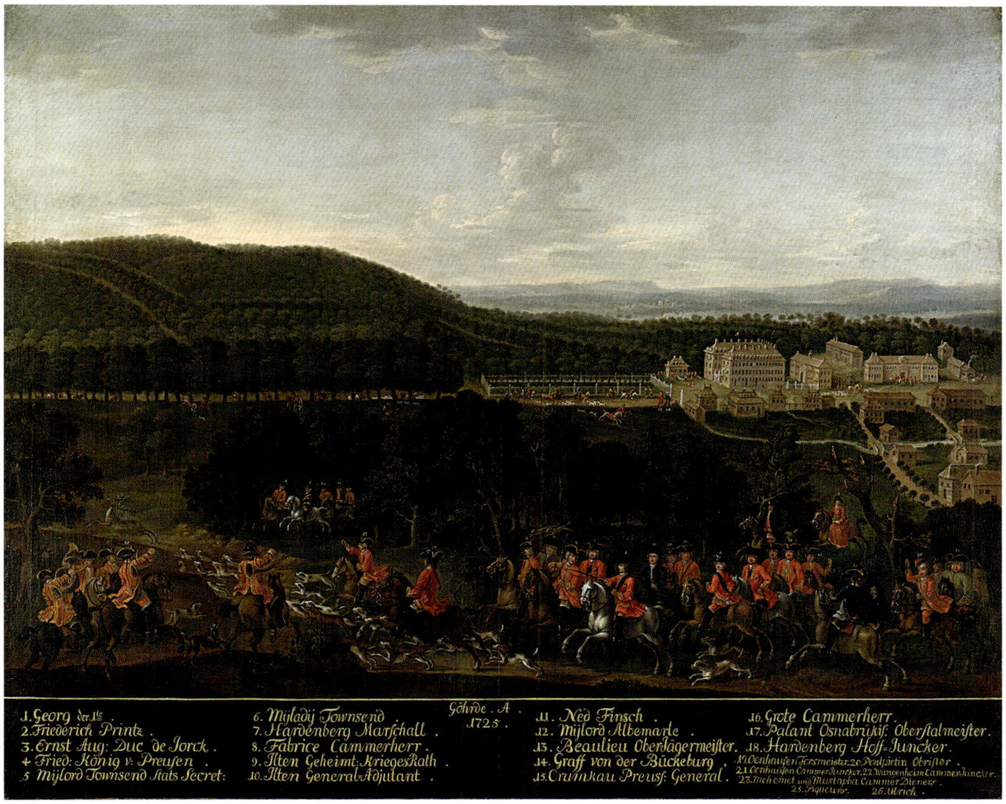

FIG. 14
German School
A Hunting Party at Göhrde, 1725
Oil on canvas
RCIN 404363

George I returned to Göhrde on each of his five sojourns in his homeland. His last visit took place in 1725 and is recorded in a picture in the Royal Collection featuring the palace in the background (fig. 14). The King is seen accompanied by his grandson Frederick, his brother Ernest Augustus, Duke of York, and his brother-in-law King Frederick I of Prussia as well as 23 English and German courtiers, constituting no more than the inner circle of a gigantic hunting party including more than 700 guests and 1000 horses accommodated at the palace and its environs.[53]

In spite of its grandeur, modernity and George I's personal affection for it, Schloss Göhrde was not intended to outshine Herrenhausen. After the decease of his mother, George I continued to preserve and improve the gardens there. Electress Sophia, who took such great pleasure in these gardens, was in fact taken fatally ill there, on one of her countless intellectual strolls during which she and Leibniz exchanged their philosophical, cultural and political ideas. Over the course of their most memorable promenade, they investigated the philosophical question of individuality. Simply put, Leibniz argued that, just as it was impossible to find two identical leaves in the hedges of Herrenhausen, it was equally impossible to find two identical individuals, or indeed to duplicate any other entity.[54] It may at first appear contradictory that a formal Baroque garden, associated with controlled order, would be an advocate of individuality. However, it was precisely that overall order that made the individuality of each of its components apparent to Leibniz.[55]

George I's own personal dialogue with Leibniz was of a more technologically practical nature. He gave him the assignment to oversee the construction of a fountain with a jet so high that it would be unrivalled by any other fountain in Europe. The motivation behind this project was twofold: first, the so-called Great Fountain was to show that, even if the gardens at Herrenhausen were inferior in size to those of other European monarchs,

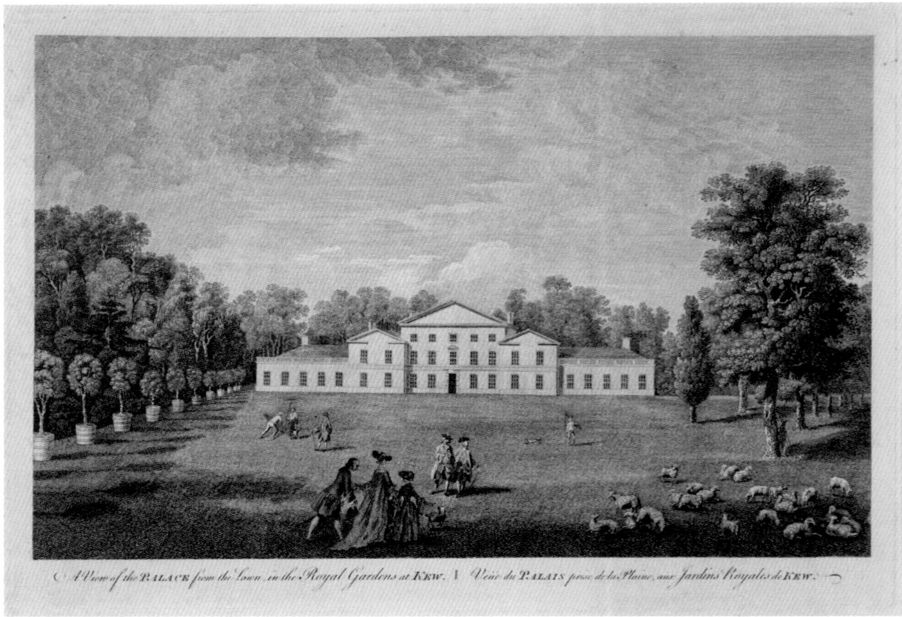

FIG. 15
William Woollett
The White House at Kew, c.1763
Etching and engraving
RCIN 702947a

they surpassed them in technical ingenuity; secondly, the fountain was to symbolise the resurrection of the House of Guelf, which had overcome the forces of gravity and turned from a second-rate princely family into one of Europe's most powerful dynasties.[56] How challenging it was to overcome these forces, both literally as well as metaphorically, revealed itself in the twenty years that it took to reach the desired height. The extraordinary physical tour de force was eventually accomplished by the Surveyor of Works William Benson (1682–1754), summoned to Hanover in 1717. It took Benson and his thirteen English engineers and workers four years to reach the height of 35 metres, making it the highest fountain in Europe. Beyond symbolising the rise of the Hanoverians, it also showed the personal ascent of George, who could look back at a most extraordinary career as a prince. Born the son of a minor duke (himself the fourth of five brothers), George had had almost no prospects of reigning even over a small principality, and had now advanced to become one of the most powerful monarchs in Europe.

After George I's death in 1727, George II returned to Hanover eleven times, his last visit in 1755.[57] During these visits, the gardens at Herrenhausen continued to play a central role in entertaining courtiers and foreign envoys. The new King did not alter the layout of the gardens, preserving them largely as they had been in the reign of his father, though endeavouring to make their maintenance more cost-effective. George II also invested in a range of new exotic plants, kept in the Galeriegebäude in the winter months, as well as expanding the fruit and vegetable gardens.[58] Hardenberg, who had been appointed surveyor of the Electoral gardens in 1735, was greatly interested in the most recent developments in landscape architecture. On his visit to England in 1744 he took the opportunity to see the great new gardens at Holkham Hall, and he was above all dazzled by the royal park at Richmond, laid out according the vision of the late Queen.[59]

Queen Caroline's passion for gardening puts her in the forefront of the British landscape movement, with major projects at Kensington (no. 24) and Richmond (no. 25). The latter in particular represented one of the archetypes of the early Enlightened landscape garden, which was to be emulated throughout Britain and abroad. As Prince and Princess of Wales, George and Caroline had acquired the Richmond estate as a private retreat in 1719.[60] As Queen, Caroline commissioned Charles Bridgeman (1690–1738), also working at Stowe and Rousham, to lay

FIG. 16
William Kent
Model of a design for a country palace for George II, 1735
Pearwood
RCIN 79398

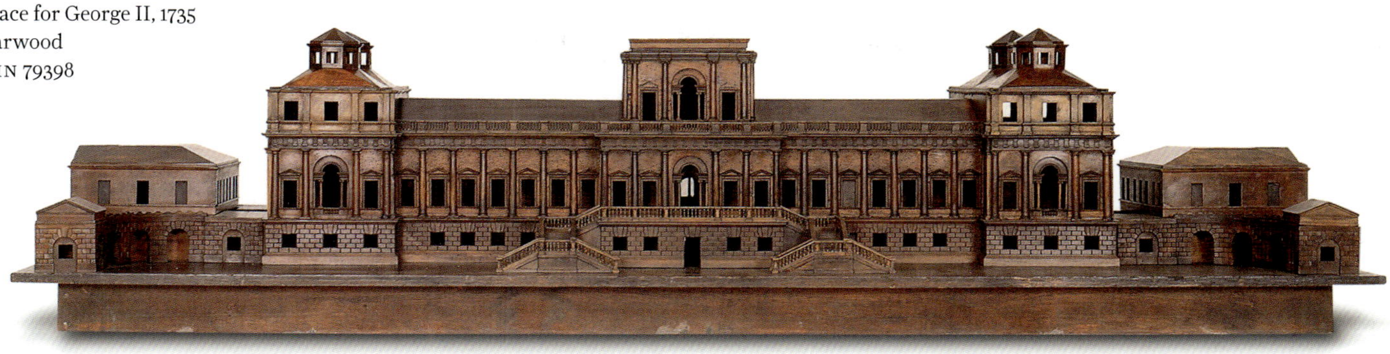

out the new gardens, complemented by follies designed by William Kent. The resulting landscape offered an idealised vision of nature imbued with cultural and dynastic messages. Kent conceived two curious edifices, the so-called Hermitage in 1730 (fig. 73) and Merlin's Cave in 1735. The Hermitage was a hybrid of a picturesque cottage and a temple devoted to five British scientists and theologians (nos 210–4). This specific choice of exclusively British thinkers not only encapsulated Caroline's belief in the interdependence between science and religion, but it also made very clear that she had entirely adopted the ideologies of her husband's kingdom. The presence of Newton and absence of Leibniz – the champion of the Hanoverian succession whom Caroline had met in person and had corresponded with until his death in 1716 – reflects her understanding of her role as consort to the King of Great Britain. Merlin's Cave, an even more peculiar Gothic folly, was yet another exercise to exhibit Caroline's attachment to the past of her adopted country. The group of five life-size wax figures, including Queen Elizabeth I and Merlin himself, illustrated the fulfilment of the magician's prophecy of the return of the ancient kings as effected by the Tudors.[61] Considering herself the rightful heir to the Tudors, Caroline strove to exhibit both her legitimacy as well as her profound knowledge of Britain's history and mythology.

At the same time as he was working for the Queen, Kent was also employed by Frederick, Prince of Wales, to remodel the White House at Kew (fig. 15), for which the architect is said to have created magnificent interiors.[62] In 1757, after the death of both Frederick and William Kent, Augusta chose William Chambers as her architect as well as architectural tutor to her son, the future George III (see fig. 51).[63] She commissioned Chambers to transform the gardens at Kew in such a way as to showcase a variety of non-European architectural styles, the centrepiece of which – a vast pagoda – constituted probably one of the boldest chinoiserie interpretations of the Rococo.[64]

Frederick and Augusta's family life at Kew departed from the rigidity of his parents' court to an even greater extent than it did at Carlton and Leicester House. The country home Kent had created for the Prince provided an appropriate framework for a more informal upbringing of George III and his siblings. This informality, which appears to have been largely facilitated by Kent, stood in pronounced contrast with the architect's solemn scheme for a huge neo-Palladian palace at Richmond intended for Frederick's parents, George and Caroline. Ambitious to the extreme, Kent's proposal would not materialise further than the formidable 1735 pearwood model preserved in the Royal Collection (fig. 16).[65] Many architects had tried to excite either George I or George II to erect a palace suitable to their status, but this scheme is certainly the most tangible of all these attempts.

The communication of continuity was the common denominator of early Hanoverian architectural patronage in Britain. This led to a curious upside-down situation: usually the aristocracy had to exhibit its ancient roots, while the monarch, whose lineage remained normally unquestioned, could experiment with new building fashions. With the arrival of the Georges this order was inverted. Whilst Sir Robert Walpole, Charles, Viscount Townshend, and others could build houses in an entirely new style, for everyone was aware of their ancient – British – identity, George I and George II had to preserve their old palaces in order to be associated with Britain and its previous monarchs. Fougeroux's comments about St James's Palace, quoted at the beginning, reflected the general surprise of foreign visitors as to the modesty of the monarchy's headquarters. The French, in particular, repeatedly showed their disdain towards British palaces, even before the Hanoverian succession. After Whitehall burned down, London guidebooks remembered it as 'one of the most famous Palaces in Christendom', whilst the French chronicler Louis de Dangeau observed that it was 'one of the nastiest houses in the world'.[66] The contrast between the architectural patronage of the early Georgian kings in Britain and that of absolutist princes on the Continent cannot be exaggerated. George I and George II grew up with this absolutist tradition and yet both did precisely what Fougeroux advised every foreigner to do when entering St James's Palace – to 'step into the spirit of the English nation'.[67]

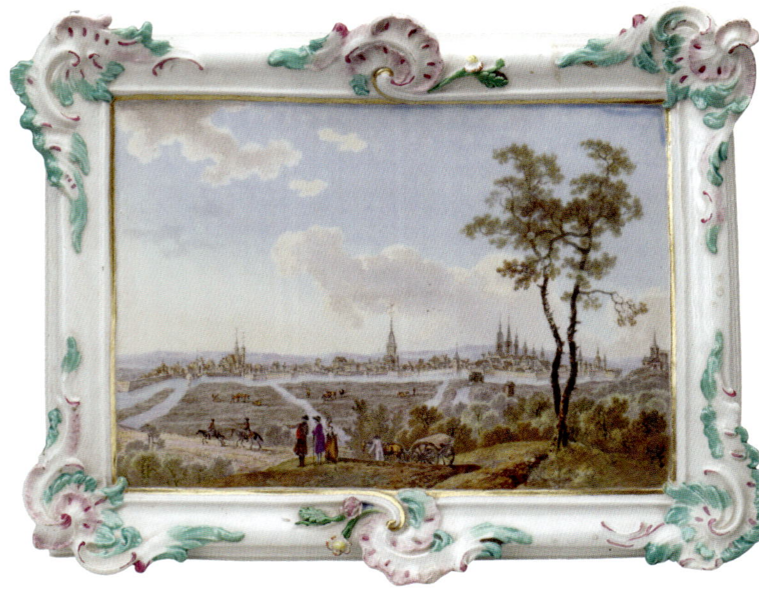

FIG. 17
Attributed to the Fürstenberg Porcelain Factory
View of the City of Osnabrück, c.1764–70
Hard-paste porcelain
RCIN 1203.1

20

FÜRSTENBERG PORCELAIN FACTORY

Porcelain plaque with view of Schloss Osnabrück c.1764–70

Hard-paste porcelain, 25.0 × 33.0 × 4.0 cm
RCIN 1203.2

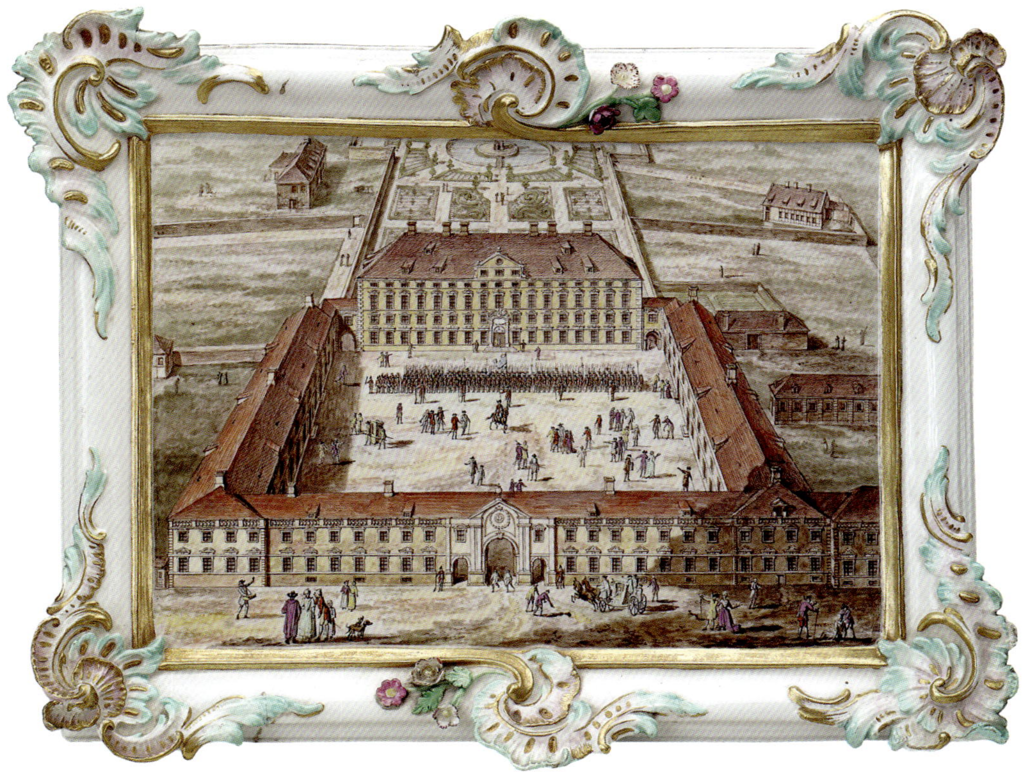

PROVENANCE Possibly presented to Frederick, Duke of York and Albany upon his appointment as Prince Bishop of Osnabrück in 1764

This unusually large porcelain plaque bears a fine and detailed bird's-eye view of Schloss Osnabrück, the favourite residence of Electress Sophia (then Duchess of Brunswick-Lüneburg), built between 1667 and 1673. Ernest Augustus having been appointed Prince Bishop of Osnabrück in 1662, George I spent his childhood in the picturesque city west of the Brunswick dominions and it was also here that he died, from a stroke, suffered on his strenuous journey from London to Hanover.

The extensive formal gardens – just about visible in the image's background – were a great merit of Osnabrück. Sophia had them carefully laid out by the French gardener Martin Charbonnier (d. 1720), who later also oversaw the aggrandisement of Herrenhausen.[68] An avid gardener, Sophia had travelled Europe to see the great horticultural achievements of her era. In 1679, she sojourned at Versailles under the name of Madame d'Osnabruc, paying a visit to her niece Elisabeth Charlotte, Duchess of Orléans. Although generally impressed by their layout, Sophia deemed the gardens at Versailles too artificial, out of scale and found fault in their lack of intimacy.[69]

Established in 1747 under the patronage of Charles I, Prince of Brunswick-Wolfenbüttel, the Fürstenberg Porcelain Manufactory aimed to rival those of Meissen and Vienna. The present plaque and its pair showing the skyline of Osnabrück (fig. 17) are indicative of this aspiration. The scale of the panel and the intricacy of its borders, adorned in imitation of rococo picture frames with shells and flowers highlighted in pink, gold and turquoise, testify to exceptional craftsmanship. Whereas other Fürstenberg tiles or plaques are usually framed in wood or use repetitive porcelain casts, the present framework and its ornaments appear to have been modelled individually.[70]

In 1764, George III's second son, Frederick, Duke of York, was granted the title of Prince Bishop of Osnabrück – he was only six months old. That same year, George III's eldest sister, Augusta, married the Hereditary Prince Charles William of Brunswick-Wolfenbüttel, heir to the founder of the Fürstenberg manufactory. Although arranged to achieve the reconciliation of the senior and junior lines of the House of Brunswick, the marriage was not a happy one. Augusta frequently returned to London, and it is conceivable that she commissioned the pair of Osnabrück plaques as present to her nephew to commemorate his new appointment. WB

21

JOHANNES KIP (1652/3–1722)

Veue et Perspective de la Ville de Londre, Westminster et Parc St Jacques c.1727

Etching, 100.1 × 208. 3 cm
RCIN 702207

PROVENANCE Royal Collection by *c.*1900
LITERATURE Coombs 1997; Hyde 2003

Johannes Kip's 'splendid' engraved panorama of London ('from Westminster to Limehouse') was begun in late 1715, when he advertised for subscriptions towards its production.[71] The completed work 'on 12 large Plates, 7 Foot long, and 5 Foot broad' was not ready until the summer of 1720, when it was issued with a dedication to Caroline of Ansbach, Princess of Wales.[72] It has plausibly been suggested that the delay in publication was due to the rift between George I and the Prince and Princess of Wales, who are shown riding in carriages at the bottom left of the print; they were reconciled with the King shortly afterwards.[73] The size of Kip's print, and its presentation, meant that it was issued mounted on canvas and rolls, probably to enable it to be displayed on a wall: in August 1716, the proprietor of the Great Print Shop, off St Martin's Lane (where Kip's panorama was also sold), advertised 'all sorts of large Maps coloured on Sticks and Rolls, ready done for Galleries or Halls'.[74]

Kip, an Amsterdam artist who had moved to London in 1686, specialised in highly detailed topographical engravings. With his compatriot Leonard Knyff, a painter, he produced a series of views of noble seats which were published as single-leaf engravings and as a bound volume, entitled *Britannia Illustrata*. The present prospect is his largest and most impressive engraving. Taken from the roof of Buckingham House, then owned by the Duke of Buckingham, the site of the present-day Buckingham Palace, it shows the view down the Mall to the River Thames, with the city of London to the left and Westminster, with the Abbey and Westminster Palace, to the right. St James's Palace, ranged around a series of courtyards, can be seen at centre left; the King's private apartments overlooking the formal gardens are clearly visible. Kip captures the dramatic curve of the river Thames before the building of Westminster Bridge (see nos 188 and 236), which makes the dome of St Paul's appear as if it were on the opposite bank.

Although Kip's view showed London in 1715, it remained popular, and the plates were printed for some years after 1720.[75] Small changes were made to the plate to reflect the changing city. The present impression has been amended to show the new tower of the church of St Martin-in-the-Fields, designed by James Gibbs and completed in 1724.[76] Like many of the later versions, the present print is missing the top four plates, which included the English title of the print and a dedication to the Princess of Wales. This omission may indicate that the present version dates from after the Princess's accession as Queen in 1727, although Joseph Smith appears to have been happy to publish all twelve plates in 1728.[77]
KH

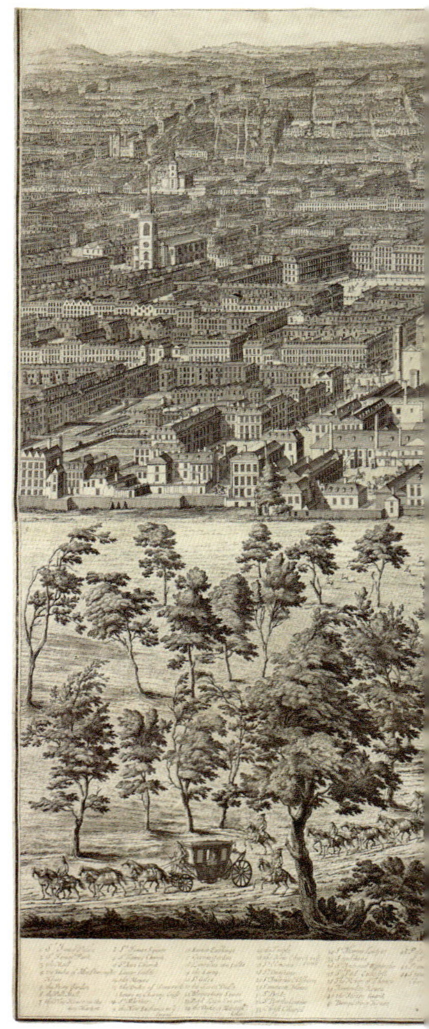

Photograph pre-conservation

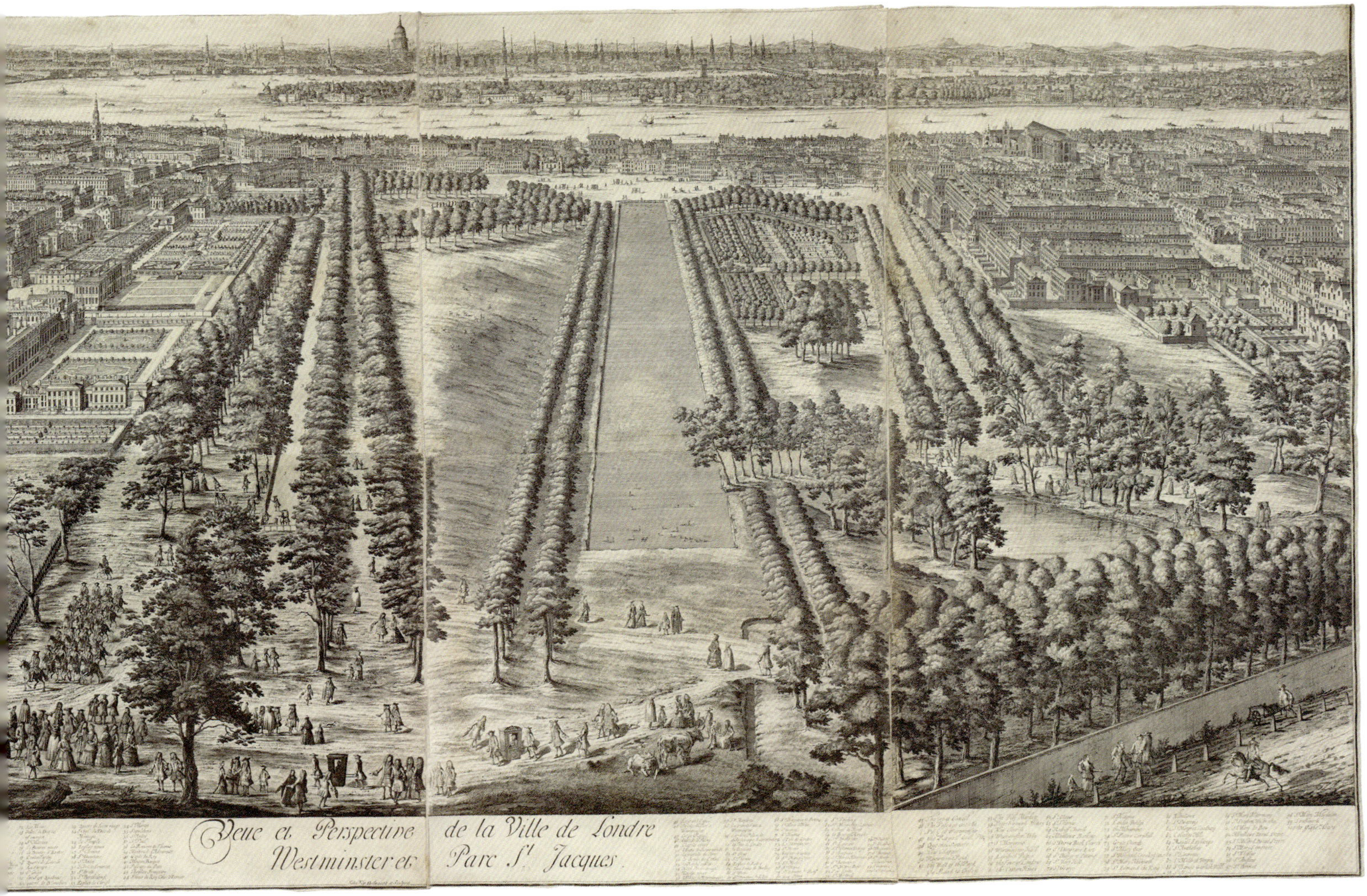
Veue et Perspective de la Ville de Londre
Westminster et Parc St. Jacques

22

SIR JOHN VANBRUGH (1664–1726)

Appartement pour le Roy. Adjoints à la vielle maison sur le dessein general 1714

Pen and ink, watercolour and wash with pencil, 35.7 × 45.0 cm
RCIN 926303

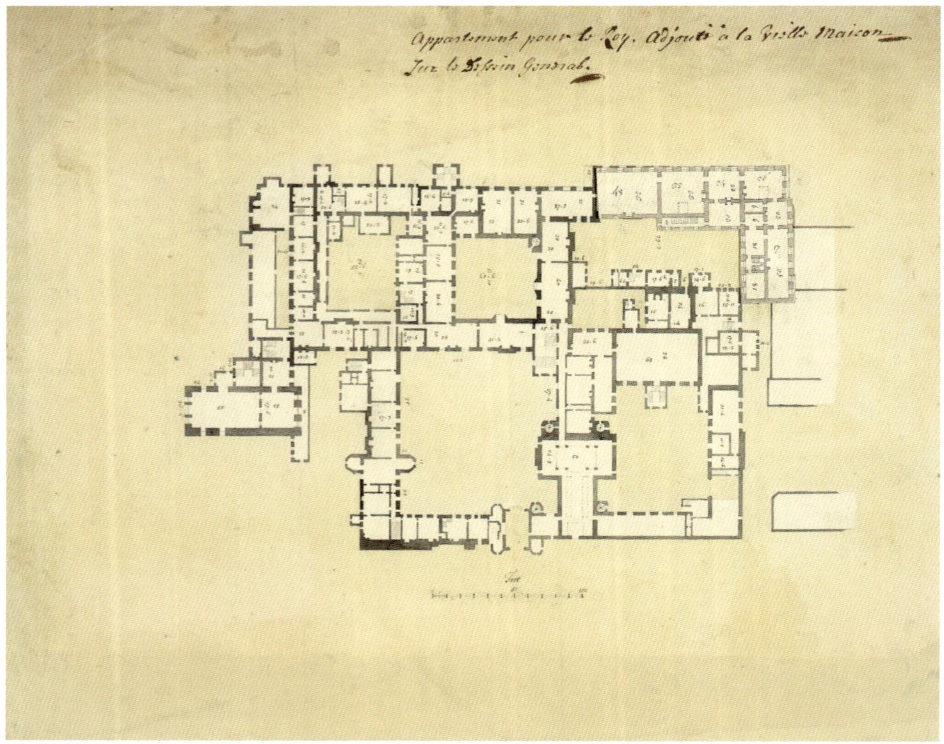

PROVENANCE Probably made for presentation to George I

St James's Palace was the principal London residence of George I and George II. This survey plan by Sir John Vanbrugh accurately records the building's 1714 layout and shows a proposed extension to the south range erected by Sir Christopher Wren for Queen Anne in 1702. Showing the palace's first floor, the so-called *piano nobile*, the design comprises the Chapel Royal, the Queen's Chapel, then known as the French Chapel, and the State Apartments, which Vanbrugh aspired to enlarge. It is one of a set of five architectural designs, the other four representing the proposed new building, two with English captions and two with French ones (RCIN 926299–302). The fact that one of Vanbrugh's designs inscribed in English is dated 1712 suggests that they were originally intended for Queen Anne. It is conceivable that the Queen rejected the plans, and that the architect then tried his luck once again with George I, presenting the same proposals only this time with French inscriptions. Unfortunately for Vanbrugh, the new monarch was no more interested in rebuilding the palace than was the old, though George I commissioned Nicholas Hawksmoor, who had collaborated with Vanbrugh at Blenheim, to erect him new stables. WB

23

SIR JOHN VANBRUGH

Les Deux Grands Appartements du dessin general adjointez au reste de la veille maison 1714

Pen and ink, watercolour and wash with pencil, 33.3 × 47.7 cm
RCIN 926302

PROVENANCE Probably made for presentation to George I

With this design, again inscribed in French specifically for George I, Vanbrugh offered a completely new south façade for St James's Palace, dominated by a giant portico towards the Mall. Whilst entirely replacing the State Apartments and the Royal Family's private quarters (in pink), the architect simultaneously aimed at preserving the most important historic elements of the palace, such as the Tudor Gate House, the Chapel Royal and Inigo Jones's Queen's Chapel (in grey). The symmetrical layout of the imposing new south range which Vanbrugh envisaged would have provided enough space to house the separate households of a king and queen or, in the case of the early Hanoverians, those of George I and his heirs, the future George II and his wife Caroline. Vanbrugh's scheme suggested the erection of a large new staircase leading up to what would presumably have been a Guard Chamber overlooking the Great Court. This opened on to two large halls, the second of which, featuring a striking colonnade, would have constituted the junction between the King's and the Prince of Wales's apartments. Both enfilades would have followed the conventional succession of State Rooms, starting with a Presence Chamber, followed by a Privy Chamber, State Bedchamber, a Closet and a Private Bedchamber. Vanbrugh also projected a third even more ambitious design for a complete replacement of St James's Palace (fig. 18). In addition to new State Apartments (in yellow), he proposed the building of a vast entrance gate to the north, as well as a new chapel to be mirrored by an opera house (in grey). Realising that the grandeur of the scheme might scare off any potential royal patron, Vanbrugh inscribed it 'A new Designe for St James's House, which may be Executed by Degrees'. Of this proposal there is no French language version in the Royal Collection, suggesting that Vanbrugh may have realised it was too ambitious for George I and never presented it. WB

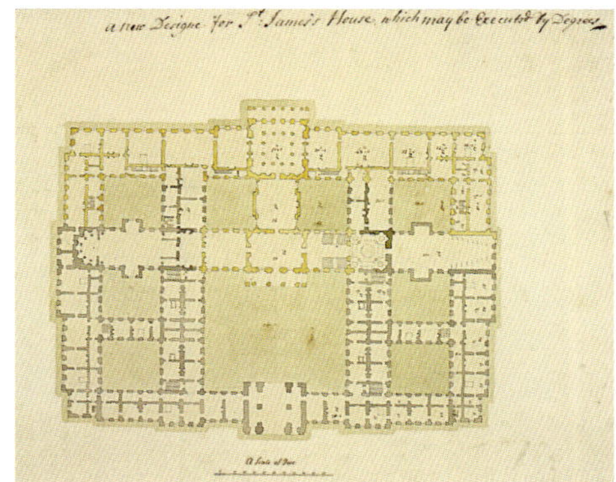

FIG. 18
Sir John Vanbrugh
A new Designe for St: James's House, which may be Executed by Degrees, *c.*1714
Pen and ink, watercolour and wash with pencil
RCIN 926301

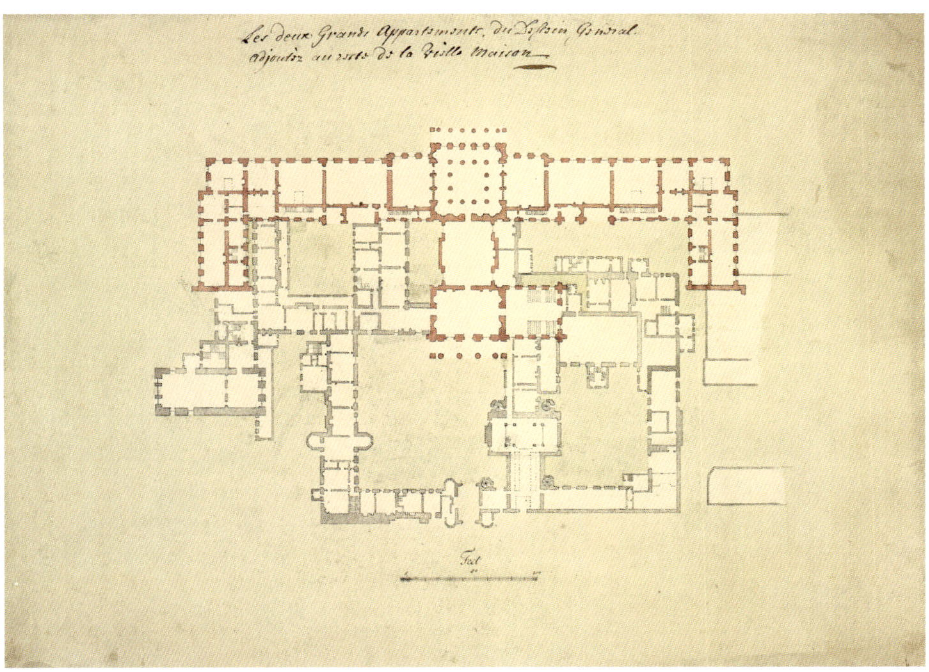

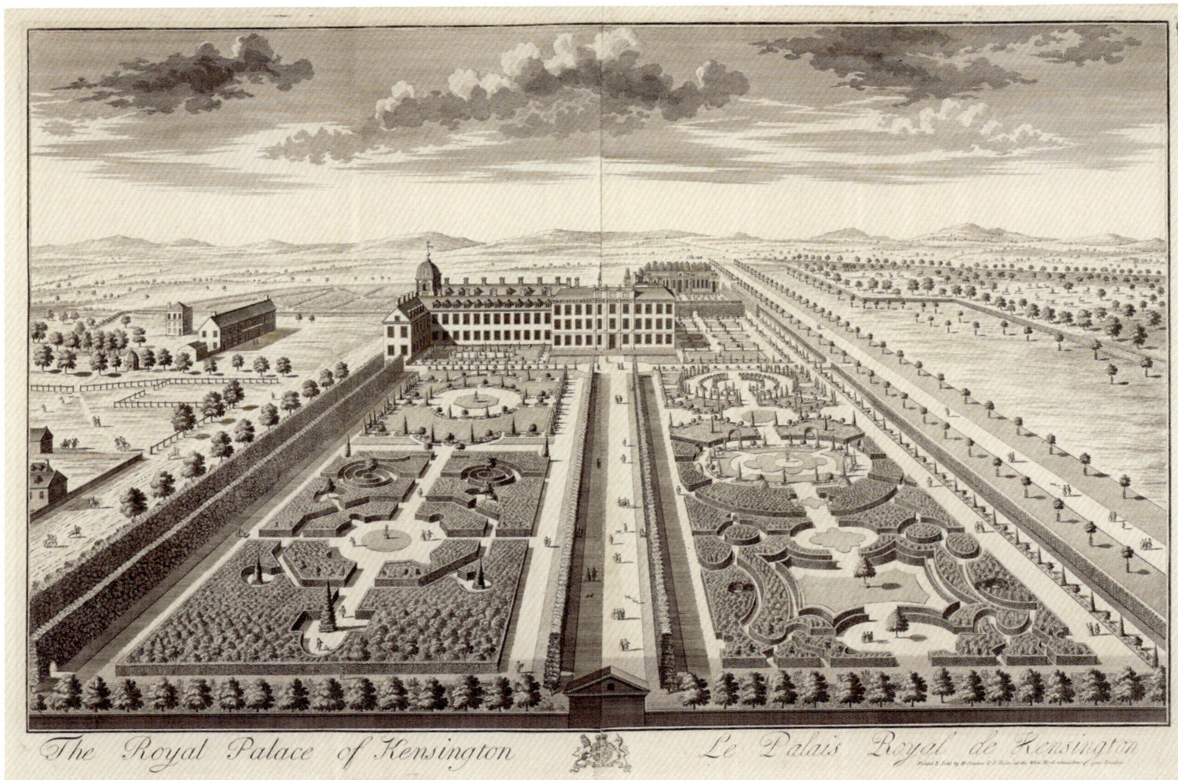

24

HENRY OVERTON (1676–1751) AND J. HOOLE (ACTIVE 1720S), PUBLISHERS

The Royal Palace of Kensington *c.*1720–30

Etching and engraving, 56.9 × 87.6 cm (plate); 58.2 × 90.2 cm (sheet)
RCIN 702920

PROVENANCE Royal Collection by *c.*1900

This large bird's-eye view of Kensington Palace depicts its south front and its topiary gardens as they looked at the very beginning of George I's reign. On his first visit to Kensington, the newly arrived Hanoverian King must have felt very much reminded of his gardens at Herrenhausen. Presumably because George I felt most at home at Kensington, he soon engaged in an ambitious architectural campaign to improve the palace's State Apartments.

The first formal gardens of bosquets and parterres were originally begun in the reign of William III and later enlarged by Queen Anne. Rivalling Louis XIV, William had even instructed the Earl of Portland, his ambassador in Paris, to convince the French King's gardener André Le Nôtre to come to England; Le Nôtre, however, turned the offer down.[78] A conservative gardener, George I kept the gardens at Kensington largely in the spirit he had found them, but he expanded them to allow for a zoological menagerie.[79]

More substantial alterations to the gardens took place after the King's death in 1727, when Queen Caroline employed the Royal Gardener, Charles Bridgeman, to improve the wider landscape surrounding the palace. George Bickham, in his 1741 description of Kensington Palace, praised the Queen and Bridgeman's joint efforts: 'The Gardens of this Palace, which are three Miles and a half in Circumference, are very fine, and have been much improved and enlarged since his present Majesty [George II] came to the Throne, under the Care and Management of the late ingenious Mr. Bridgeman. They are kept in the greatest Order, and in the Summer Time, when the Court is not there, are resorted to by a vast Concourse of the most polite Company.'[80] WB

25

JOHN ROCQUE (ACTIVE 1734–62), PUBLISHED BY JOHN BOWLES

Plan of the House, Gardens, Park, & Hermitage of their Majesties, at Richmond 1734

Etching and engraving, 58.1 × 91.1 cm
RCIN 702999

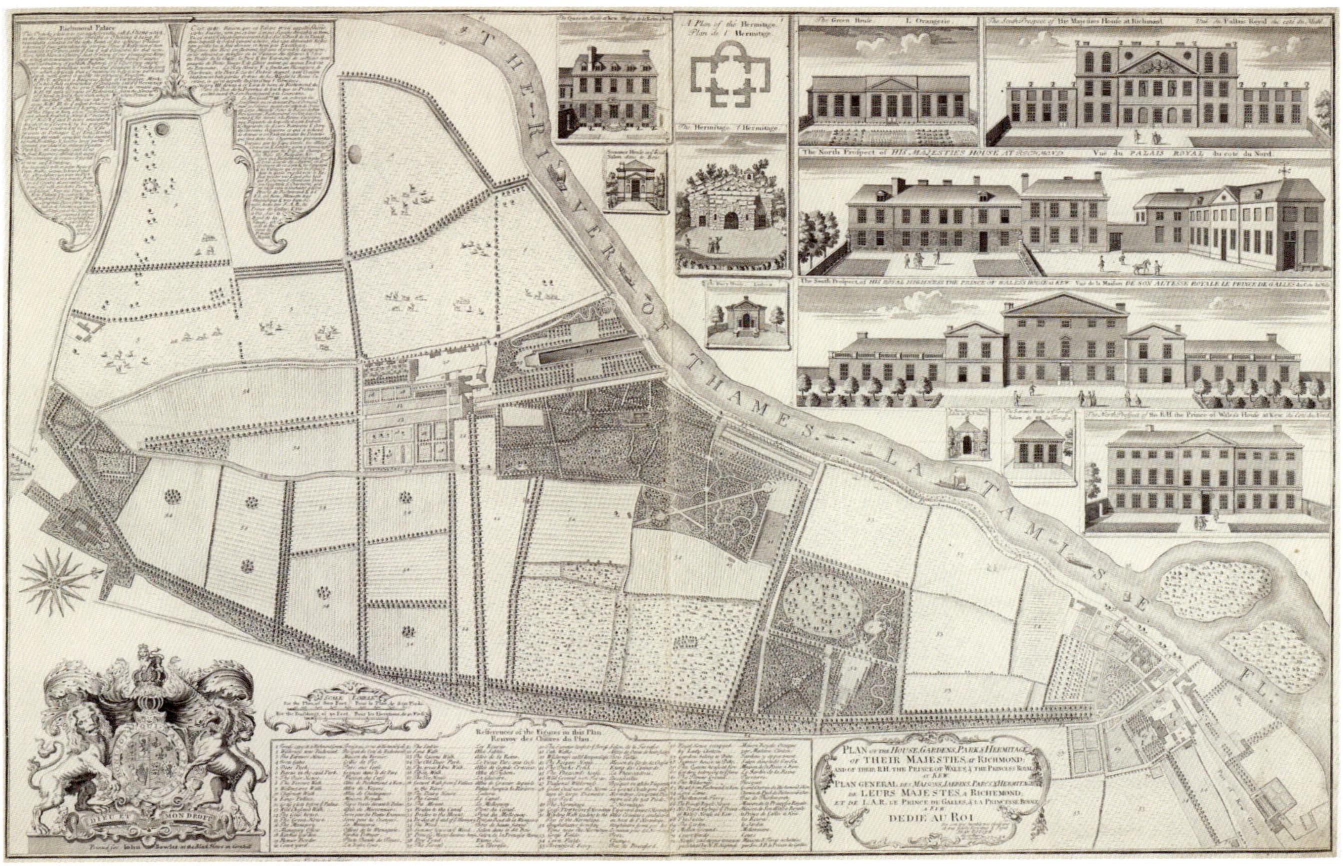

PROVENANCE Royal Collection by *c.*1900

When Queen Caroline received Richmond Lodge as a dower house upon George II's accession to the throne, she almost immediately engaged in the creation of one of the earliest English landscape gardens. Combining the ingenuity of both the Royal Gardener Charles Bridgeman and the architect William Kent, the Queen sought to remodel the grounds following examples of classical antiquity. Robert Castell's 1728 publication *The Villas of the Ancients Illustrated* is likely to have constituted a key source of inspiration for Bridgeman's and Kent's joint efforts.[81] Featuring a small array of follies, sculptures and temples, the picturesque landscape of hills, fields and forests was to reflect Queen Caroline's intellectual leanings as well as her strong affinity for the British nation.

This large map, by John Rocque, Topographer to the King, which is captioned both in French and English and dated 1734, not only provides us with a detailed layout of the estates of Richmond and Kew during the reign of George II but also gives several elevations of the now lost houses that the Hanoverians occupied – notably Richmond Lodge, acquired by George and Caroline in 1715 (see no. 26) and the slightly more imposing White House at Kew, erected by William Kent for Frederick, Prince of Wales, between 1731 and 1735 (fig. 15).[82] Rocque's print also shows the façade and plan of the Hermitage, a cottage-like temple dedicated to the achievements of British science and theology, which Caroline commissioned from Kent in 1730 (see nos 145–9 and fig. 73). WB

26

JEAN BAPTISTE CHATELAIN (1710–1758) AFTER MARCO RICCI (1676–1730), PUBLISHED BY JOSEPH GOUPY (1689–1769)

A Prospect of the Royal House at Richmond *c.*1740

Etching and engraving, 43.6 × 55.6 cm (plate); 46.0 × 57.8 cm (sheet)
RCIN 703015.a

PROVENANCE Royal Collection by *c.*1900

The Palace of Richmond, more commonly known as Richmond Lodge, came into the possession of George and Caroline, Prince and Princess of Wales in 1715, following the downfall of the Duke of Ormonde, known for his Jacobite leanings. In the capacity of Ranger of Richmond Park, Ormonde had leased the estate since the death of William III, and re-faced the south front of the Lodge, as visible in the background of this print.[83] Ormonde's new symmetrical, yet most peculiar façade with its triangular pediment flanked by circular windows masked a much older, irregular building, which would never have met the standards of the neo-Palladian architectural ideals that dominated the reigns of George I and George II. This impression of Richmond Lodge shows its unusual façade overlooking a large lawn occupied by several gardeners as well as members of polite society gathered at the palace's front gate.

The print is one of a pair of views of Richmond by the Huguenot printmaker Jean Baptiste Chatelain after a depiction by the Venetian painter Marco Ricci, and was published by Joseph Goupy. A French artist who had settled in London, Goupy was favoured by Frederick, Prince of Wales, to whom he gave art lessons.[84] A drawing of a similar view, by the Prince's topographer John Rocque, survives at the British Museum.[85]

Owing to its pleasant location, Queen Caroline developed a particular affection for Richmond Lodge – so much so that in the early 1730s both Sir Edward Lowett Pearce, Surveyor General of Ireland, and William Kent developed ambitious designs for a replacement of the lodge by a sumptuous new palace.[86] However, neither of the designs ever came into being. WB

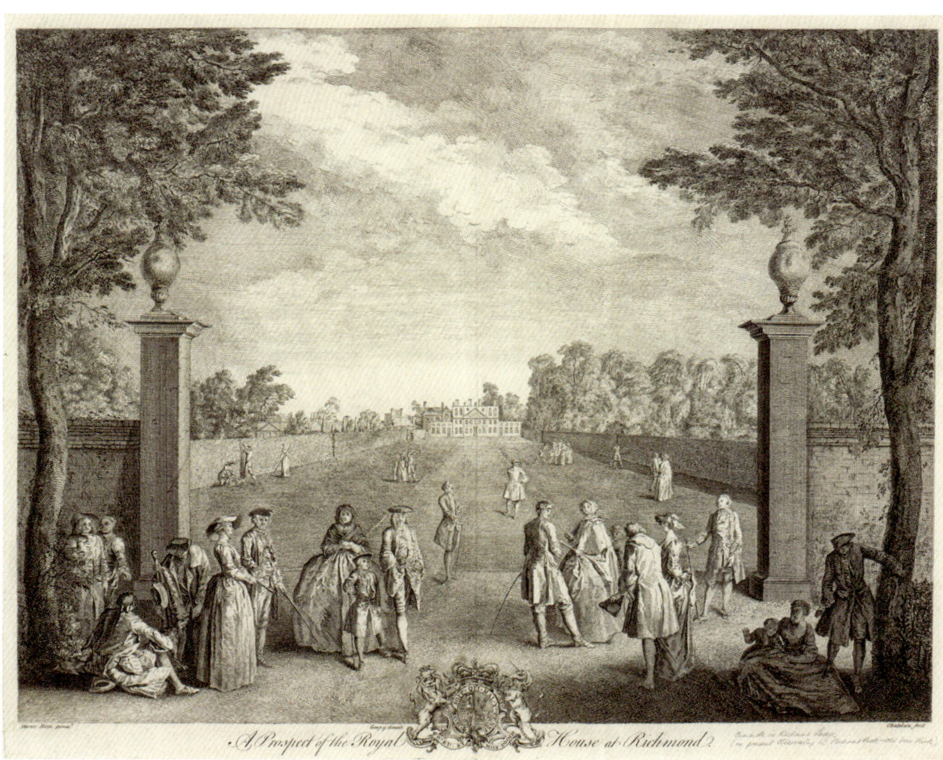

27

THOMAS SANDBY (1721–1798)

Windsor Great Park with Virginia Water, looking north c.1753–60

Watercolour and bodycolour over pencil with pen and ink, on two sheets of paper, unfinished, 43.7 × 111.3 cm
RCIN 914640

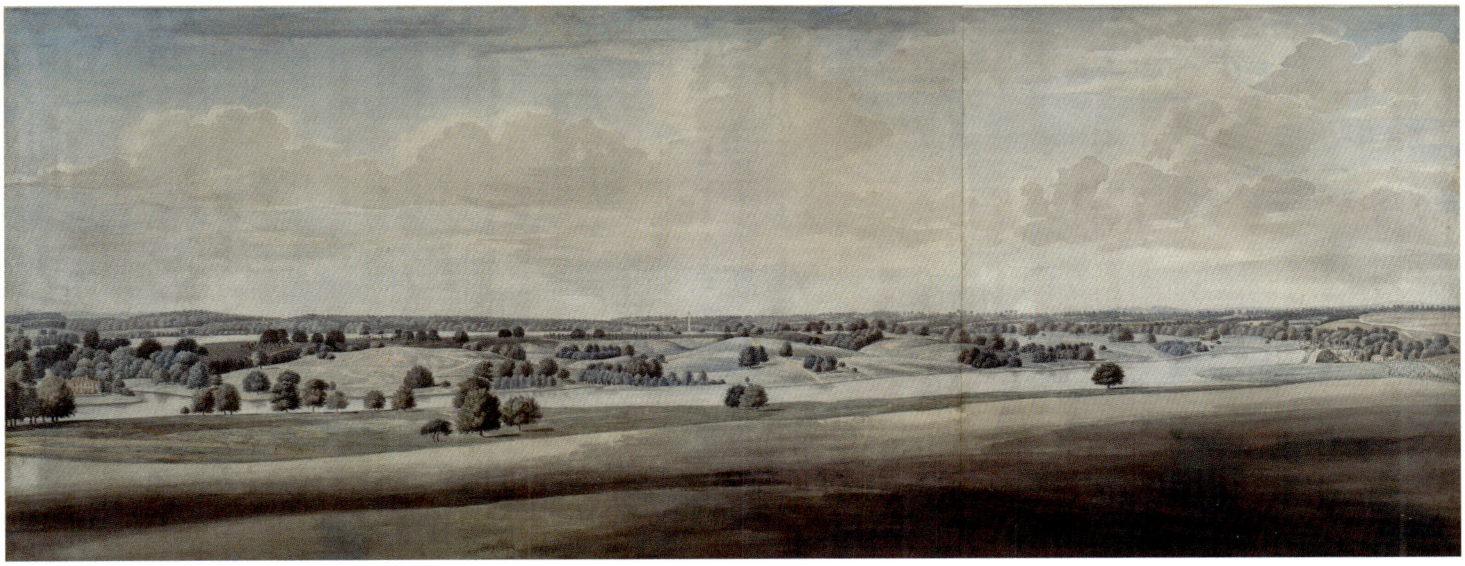

PROVENANCE Commissioned by William Augustus, Duke of Cumberland; King George III; by descent

LITERATURE Oppé 1947, no. 115

William Augustus, Duke of Cumberland, was appointed Ranger of the Great Park in 1746 and oversaw the relandscaping of the area, using his contacts in America to supply interesting trees, plants and seeds for his use as well as gathering specimens from European sources.[87] A further appointment as Keeper of Cranbourne Chase in 1751 gave him the use of Cranbourne Lodge. In 1753 the Duke created the artificial lake Virginia Water, which had a cascade at its eastern end. At the same time George II erected an obelisk in the Duke's honour. Both Virginia Water (with the cascade) and the obelisk can be seen in the present view, which shows the northern aspect from Fort Belvedere, a tower built by the Duke. Fort Belvedere was used as a tea house: shelves for books and china were recorded in 1754.[88]

Thomas Sandby was draughtsman to the Duke of Cumberland and was responsible for military drawings (see no. 49) as well as work in the Great Park. In 1764 he was appointed Deputy Ranger of the Great Park as well as the Duke's steward.[89] This watercolour is one of a set of six commissioned from Sandby by the Duke to show views in Windsor Great Park and Cranbourne Lodge. The six (of which five survive, all in the Royal Collection) were recorded hanging in the Duke's Dressing Room at the Great Lodge in the Park in 1765, shortly after their completion.[90] KH

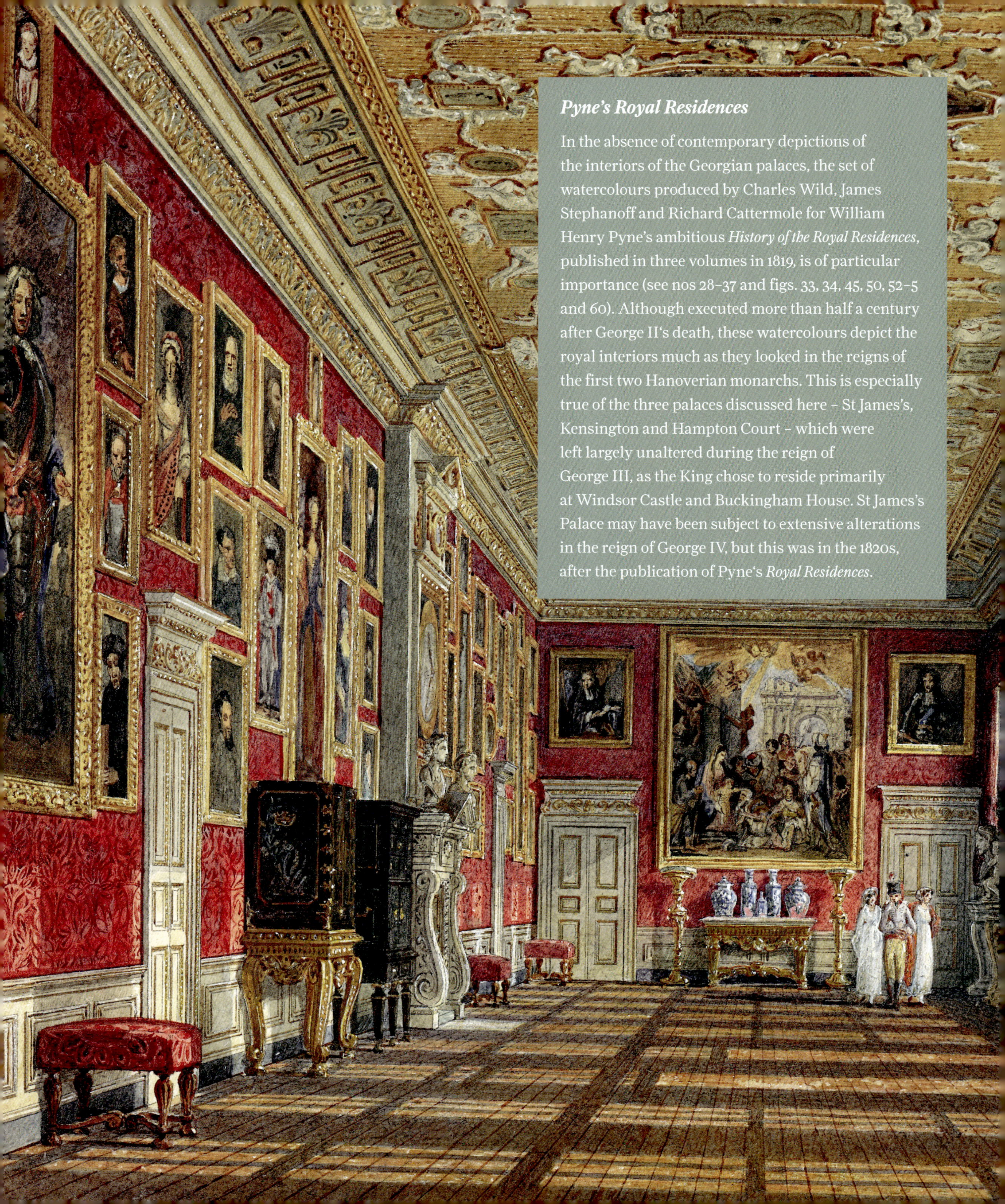

Pyne's Royal Residences

In the absence of contemporary depictions of the interiors of the Georgian palaces, the set of watercolours produced by Charles Wild, James Stephanoff and Richard Cattermole for William Henry Pyne's ambitious *History of the Royal Residences*, published in three volumes in 1819, is of particular importance (see nos 28–37 and figs. 33, 34, 45, 50, 52–5 and 60). Although executed more than half a century after George II's death, these watercolours depict the royal interiors much as they looked in the reigns of the first two Hanoverian monarchs. This is especially true of the three palaces discussed here – St James's, Kensington and Hampton Court – which were left largely unaltered during the reign of George III, as the King chose to reside primarily at Windsor Castle and Buckingham House. St James's Palace may have been subject to extensive alterations in the reign of George IV, but this was in the 1820s, after the publication of Pyne's *Royal Residences*.

28

JAMES STEPHANOFF (1789–1874)

The New Kitchen, St James's Palace *c.*1819

Watercolour and bodycolour, 20.5 × 25.3 cm
RCIN 922167

PROVENANCE Executed for Pyne's *Royal Residences*; probably acquired by George IV

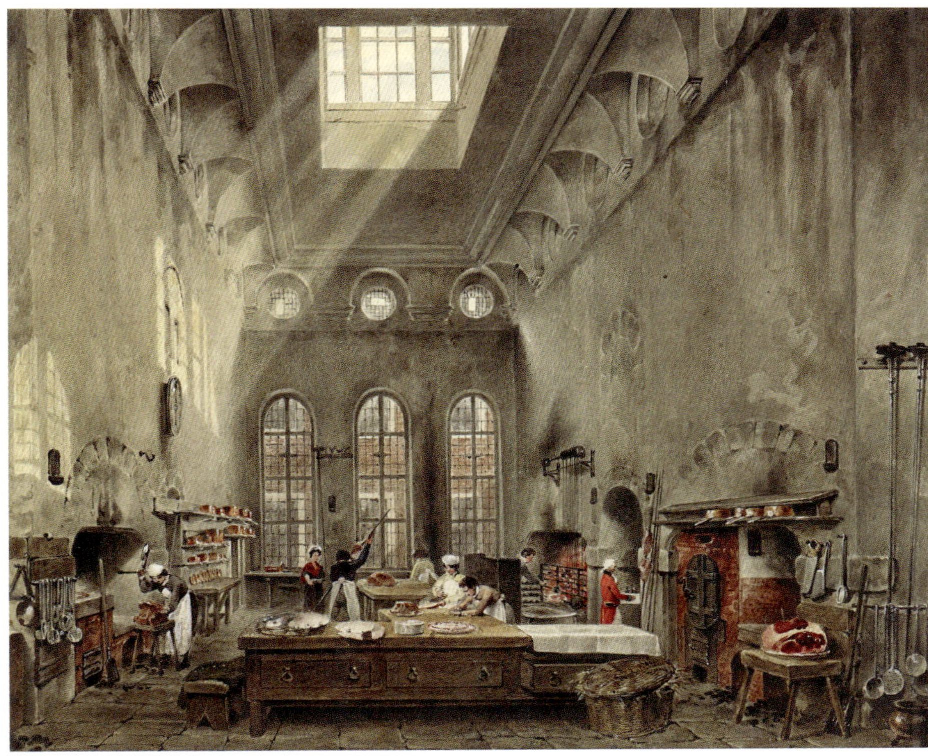

This watercolour by Stephanoff shows the inside of the so-called New Kitchen block, which Sir John Vanbrugh was commissioned to build at St James's Palace in 1717.[91] Shortly after the arrival of the Hanoverians, it had become apparent that the old kitchens at the palace's south-east corner were unable to cater for the needs of both the King's and the Prince of Wales's households.[92]

Vanbrugh's new kitchen comprised a two-storey-high cooking space, as captured by Stephanoff, flanked by smaller spaces housing pantries and sculleries. It was generously lit through a large skylight as well as tall windows on the north and south sides. The dispute between the King and the Prince of Wales meant that Prince George and Caroline were banished from St James's and did not benefit from this modern kitchen until their own accession in 1727.[93]

At the same time Vanbrugh was erecting the kitchen at St James's, his fiercest rivals, William Benson and Colen Campbell, were building the so-called German Kitchen for George I at Hampton Court. Whilst both kitchens shared a similar, practical layout, their exteriors were strikingly dissimilar. Benson and Campbell delivered a building which on the outside was more reminiscent of a neo-Palladian villa than a functional cooking space.[94] WB

29

CHARLES WILD (1781–1835)

The Queen's Library, St James's Palace c.1819

Pen and ink with watercolour and bodycolour, 20.0 × 25.1 cm
RCIN 922168

PROVENANCE Executed for Pyne's *Royal Residences*, probably acquired by George IV

The only significant architectural addition made to St James's Palace in the reign of George II was the library pavilion erected by William Kent for Queen Caroline between 1736 and 1737.[95] A woman of unusual erudition, the Queen owned a considerable collection of English, German and French books, originally scattered over several rooms between her private apartments and those of the King. Caroline never had a chance to arrange these books in her new library as she was taken ill when visiting the site in November 1737, and died soon afterwards.[96] Had the Queen lived, Kent's spectacular neo-Palladian interior might have become a place for stimulating intellectual debates.[97]

With this watercolour, Charles Wild captured the library shortly before the building was dismantled in 1825. John Michael Rysbrack's terracotta busts of medieval and Renaissance monarchs (nos. 151 and 152), visible on the wall-brackets, were commissioned by Queen Caroline as an allusion to the Hanoverians' dynastic roots and legitimacy.[98] According to Kent's designs, these busts were to be complemented by painted or plaster decoration in the coving, including portraits of British worthies, such as Newton and Locke. However, it remains unclear whether this part of the decoration was ever completed.[99] At either end of the room, Kent had placed large chimneypieces adorned with swags of flowers and small heraldic emblems taken from the Brandenburg-Ansbach coat of arms. This discreet reference to her own family subtly conveyed that for all her identification with British history, culture and science, it was the Queen's education at the courts of Prussia and Hanover that made her the early Enlightened monarch that she was. The library at St James's Palace was the pinnacle of Queen Caroline's patronage, an architectural materialisation of her broad interest in science and culture. WB

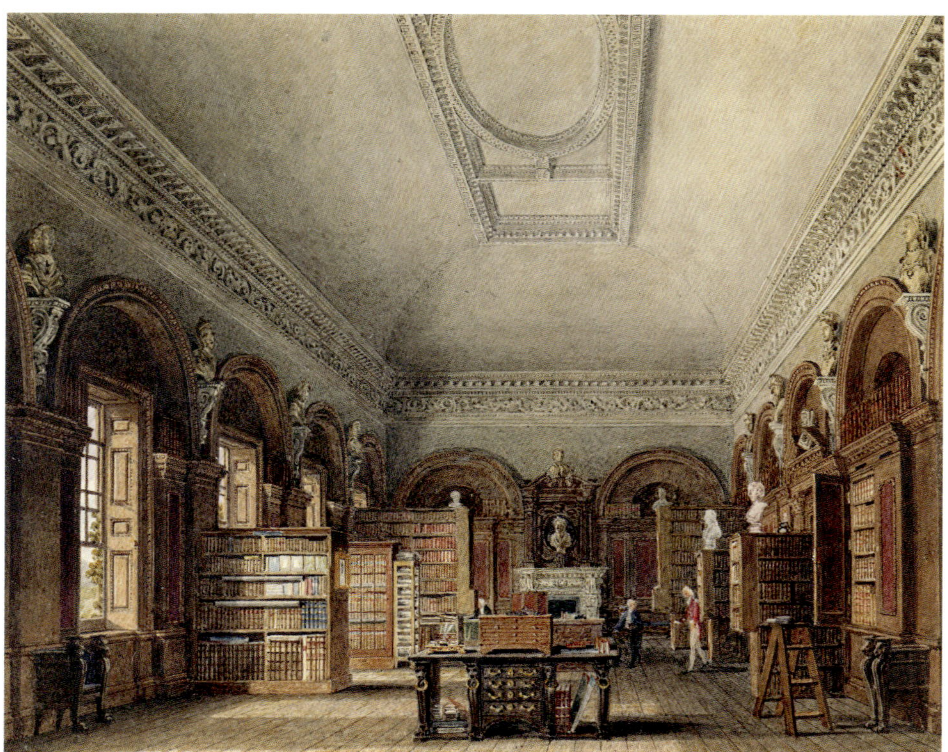

30

RICHARD CATTERMOLE (1795?–1858)

The Cupola Room, Kensington Palace *c.*1817

Pen and ink with watercolour and bodycolour, over pencil, 20.4 × 25.3 cm
RCIN 922156

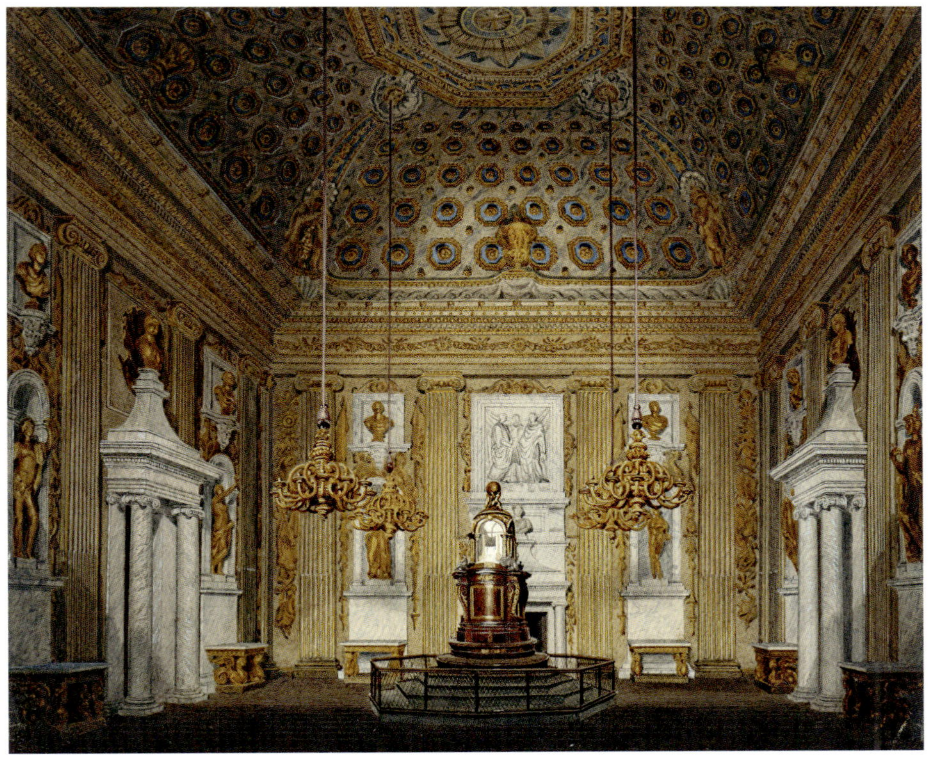

PROVENANCE Executed for Pyne's *Royal Residences*; probably acquired by George IV

The so-called Cupola Room – the earliest and certainly most exuberant addition made to Kensington Palace in the reign of George I – was the centrepiece of the suite of three new State Rooms decorated by William Kent between 1722 and 1725.[100] The commission went first to Sir James Thornhill in his capacity of the King's Sergeant Painter, who was to supply designs for the fictive coffered dome dominated by a large Garter Star. Thornhill was in favour, having just created a pictorial celebration of the Hanoverians' arrival in Britain at the Upper Hall at Greenwich (figs. 1–2), but his estimate was considered unreasonably high. Though at first approved, his proposal was subsequently dismissed in favour of Kent, whose alternative quotation proved considerably cheaper.[101] Kent first painted the ceiling – on the basis of Thornhill's own designs – and then decorated the walls with painted wooden pilasters and white marble niches housing gilt-lead statues of Roman deities (RCIN 1421–6) similar to the 27 figures the Elector Ernest Augustus had set up at the Gardens in Herrenhausen around 1690.[102]

The room was not an unqualified success: George Vertue observed that 'Niches of Marble & pedestals with statues, guilt with burnish'd gold ... makes a terrible glaring show, & truly gothic, according to the weakness of the conceptions of the Surveyors. & Controlours of the Kings. Works'.[103] WB

31

CHARLES WILD (1781–1835)

The Great Drawing Room, Kensington Palace c.1816

Pen and ink with watercolour and bodycolour, over pencil, 19.8 × 24.6 cm
RCIN 922157

PROVENANCE Executed for Pyne's *Royal Residences*; probably acquired by George IV

The Great Drawing Room was the second space Kent decorated at Kensington Palace.[104] His combination of crimson wall-hangings and gilt-wood frames, delivered to his own designs, found favour with George I and his court; it was repeated at the nearby King's Gallery and in the Saloon at Houghton Hall. Although the hang in Wild's early eighteenth-century watercolour does not correspond with that of the early Georgian period, it still conveys Kent's characteristic symmetry, which he attempted to accentuate with his neo-Palladian picture frames. At its centre, Kent adorned the ceiling with a scene of tragic liaison between Jupiter, king of the gods, and his mortal lover Semele. Though it was dismantled in the nineteenth century, a copy of Kent's original decoration has since been reintroduced into ceiling.

George II is often said to have shown no interest in the visual arts. An encounter which occurred precisely in the Great Drawing Room at Kensington suggests that in fact the King had distinct opinions regarding the art that surrounded him. On his return from Hanover in 1735, George II was infuriated to find that Queen Caroline had altered the Great Drawing Room's picture hang and done away with a *Venus and Cupid* after, then attributed to, Michelangelo (fig. 19). George II turned on Queen Caroline's favourite, Lord Hervey, who recorded the exchange: 'My Lord, I have a great respect for your taste in what you understand, but in pictures I beg leave to follow my own. I suppose you assisted the Queen with your fine advice when she was pulling my house to pieces and spoiling all my furniture. Thank God, at least she has left the walls standing!' Then, asking whether all the pictures, even the *Venus and Cupid*, should be put back in place, Hervey was met by the King's response: 'I like my fat Venus much better than anything you have given me instead for her.'[105] WB

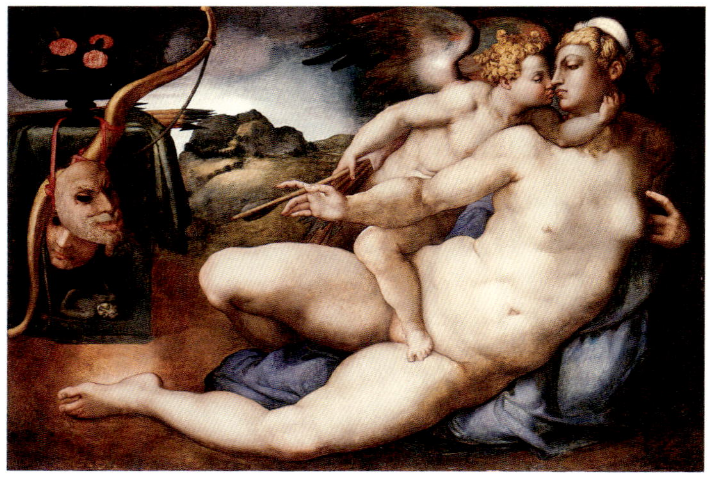

FIG. 19
Giorgio Vasari
after Michelangelo
Venus and Cupid, c.1543
Oil on panel
RCIN 405486

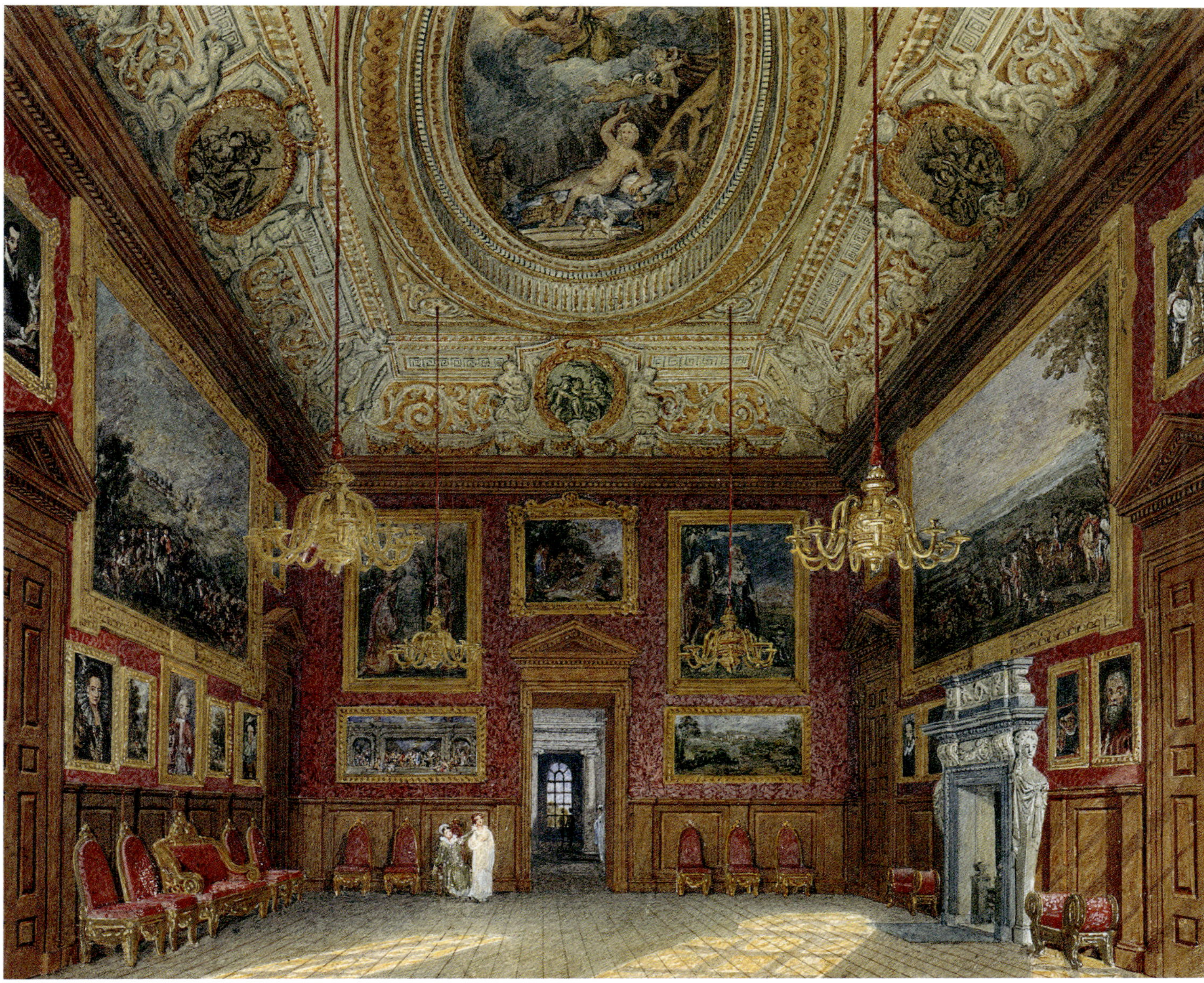

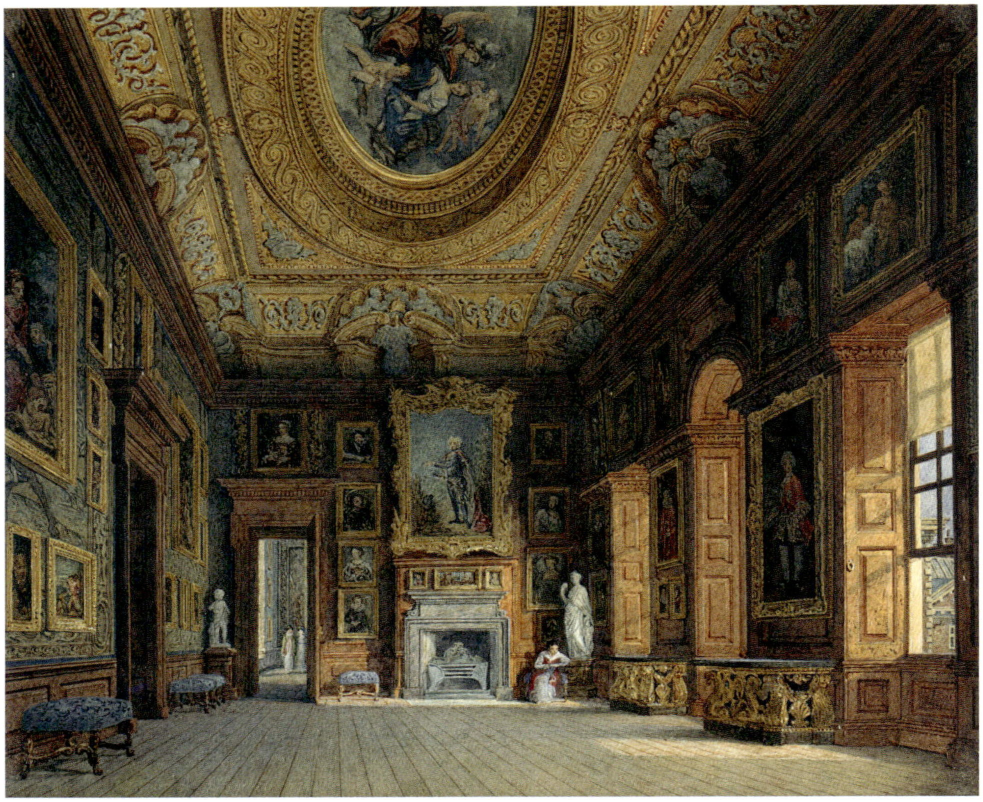

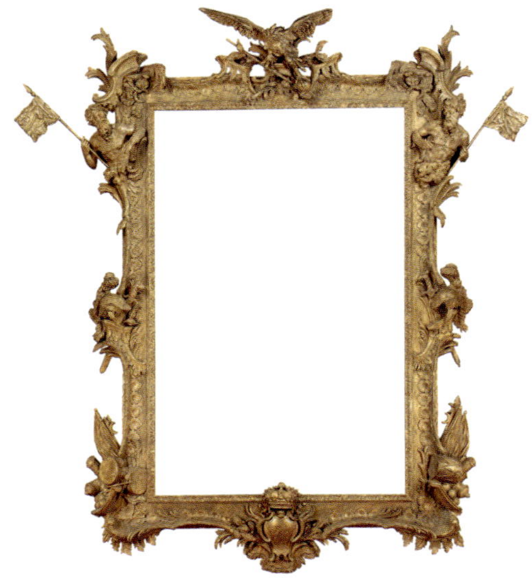

FIG. 20
Paul Petit
Gildwood frame for Pesne's portrait of Frederick the Great (no. 240), 1749
Private collection

32

CHARLES WILD (1781–1835)

Queen Caroline's Drawing Room (The Privy Chamber), Kensington Palace c.1816

Pen and ink with watercolour and bodycolour, over pencil, 20.3 × 25.0 cm
RCIN 922151

PROVENANCE Executed for Pyne's *Royal Residences*; probably acquired by George IV

During the reigns of George I and II, the interior depicted in this watercolour, which Pyne referred to as 'Queen Caroline's Drawing Room', actually functioned as the palace's Privy Chamber. Although it was built in 1718–19, it was not before 1723 that William Kent was commissioned to decorate its ceiling. Like that of the Great Drawing Room (no. 31), Kent's substantial golden framework contains the illusion of an oval aperture with his pictorial rendition of Mars and Minerva, deities of war and wisdom, surrounded by trophies of the Arts and Sciences.[106] The immediate juxtaposition of the figurative scenery and the decorative coving reveals Kent's strengths and weaknesses. His ornaments are inventive but his figures are gauche. Kent may have made the designs for the two intricately carved gilt-wood pier tables between the window bays, featuring a female mask attended by dolphins. A very similar pair of tables, although probably copied or at least considerably altered in the nineteenth century, survives in the Royal Collection (RCIN 21593.1–2).[107]

Overall, the dense picture hang, superimposed on to tapestries, as represented in the watercolour, does not correspond with that of either George I or George II, but of the late eighteenth century. In the reign of George I the walls were indeed covered with tapestries; George II replaced them with dynastic portraits of Henry VIII, James I, Charles I, William III and Queen Anne.[108] Antoine Pesne's full-length likeness of Frederick the Great (no. 240) over the chimney, now detached from its magnificent frame (fig. 20), was positioned there at a later stage. WB

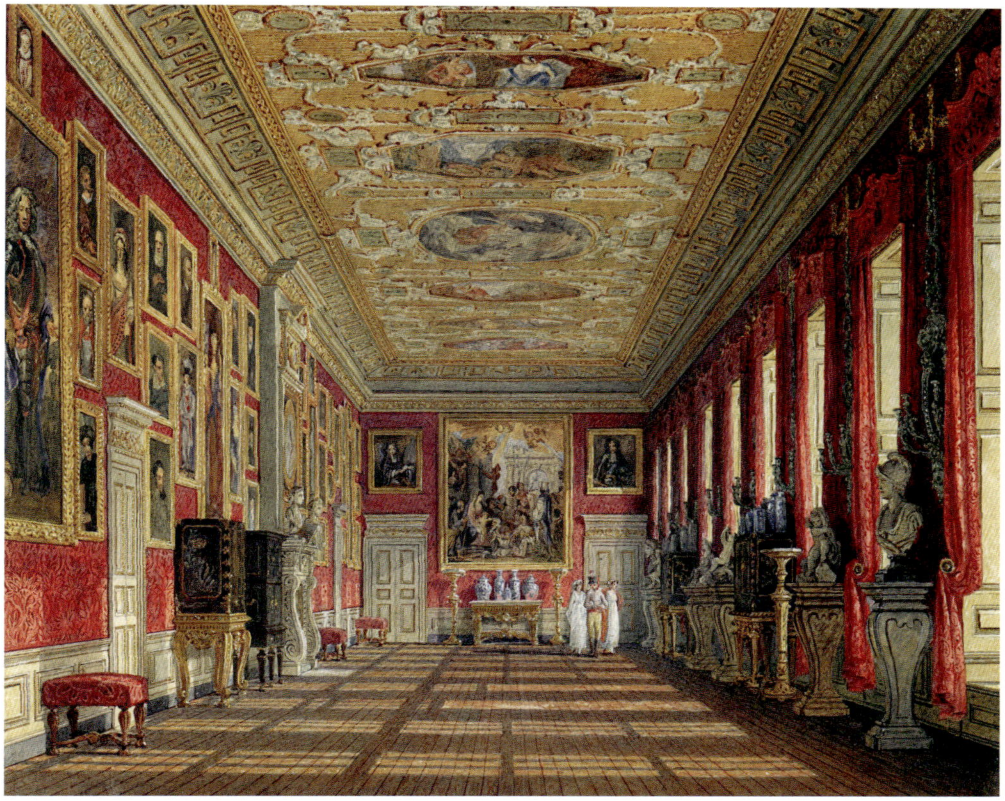

33

CHARLES WILD

The King's Gallery, Kensington Palace *c.*1816

Watercolour with touches of bodycolour over etched outlines, 19.8 × 25.0 cm
RCIN 922158

PROVENANCE Executed for Pyne's *Royal Residences*; probably acquired by George IV

William III had the King's Gallery erected as part of the extensive aggrandisement of Kensington Palace overseen by Sir Christopher Wren between 1694 and 1696.[109] From the beginning the gallery was designed as a space for the display of some of the finest paintings in the Royal Collection. John Evelyn visited it in April 1696 and noted that it contained 'all the best Pictures of all the Houses'.[110] In 1725, George I commissioned William Kent to redecorate the gallery in its entirety; it was completed in 1727, at the very end of his reign.[111] For the ceiling, Kent devised seven octagonal compartments telling the story of Ulysses from Homer's *Odyssey* – an English translation of which was published by Alexander Pope in 1726. Kent further supervised the gilding (carried out by Thornhill) and painting of newly designed door cases and of the wainscot, contrasting with the rich wall-hangings of crimson silk-damask. Finally, he designed a new chimneypiece containing William III's sundial as well as a *Madonna and Child* fresco then thought to be by Raphael (RCIN 408640).

The refurbishment campaign also comprised a rearrangement of the paintings. Considered too crowded, the hang was considerably thinned to make way for large, almost exclusively Italian Old Masters, for which Kent designed new frames. The walls thus gained a more structured look. Charles Wild's watercolour conveys a sense of the interior's appearance in the early Georgian era, but the picture hang dates from the reign of George III. In recent years the George I arrangement has been re-instated (fig. 65). WB

34

CHARLES WILD (1781–1835)

The Great Staircase, Kensington Palace 1819

Pen and ink with watercolour and bodycolour over etched outlines, 25.5 × 20.2 cm
RCIN 922149

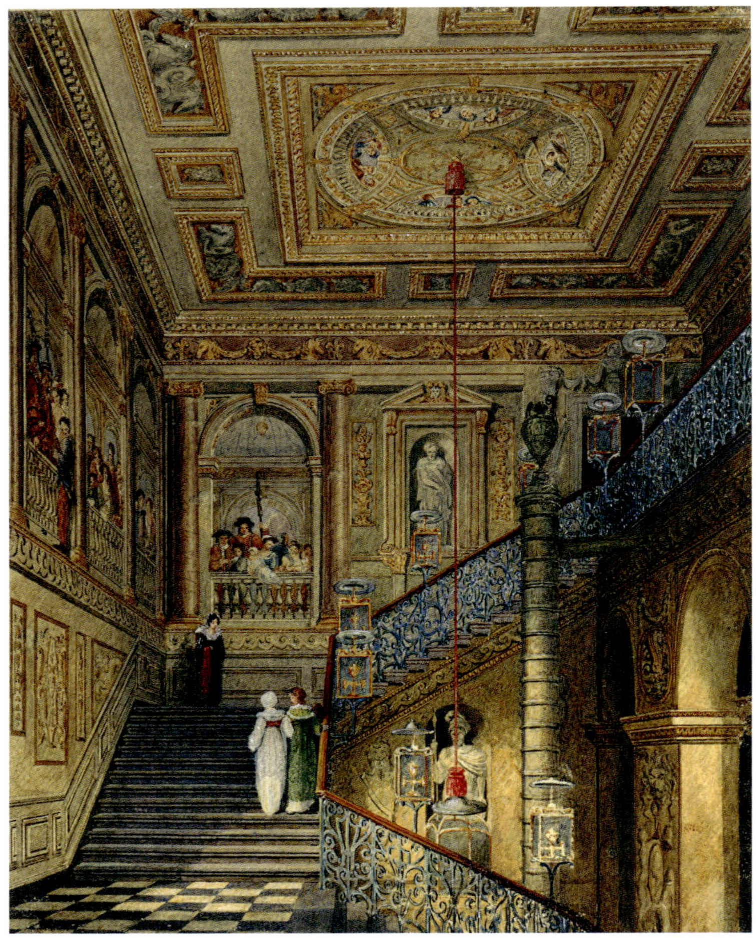

PROVENANCE Executed for Pyne's *Royal Residences*; probably acquired by George IV

This watercolour by Charles Wild depicts the Great Staircase at Kensington Palace erected to the designs of Sir Christopher Wren for King William III in 1696. The trompe-l'oeil decoration on canvas was undertaken by William Kent for George I between 1725 and 1727.[112] Kent created an illusionistic arcade under which he depicted members of the early Hanoverian court gathered behind a balustrade. As well as members of polite society, Kent also portrayed the King's dwarf Ulrich and his Turkish valets Mustapha and Mehemet as well as 'Peter the Wild Boy'.[113] Merry and unconventional, the selection of sitters enabled Kent to counterbalance the sobriety and weight of the fictive architectural framework; it was also a means by which the King could display his particular fondness for some of his less senior courtiers.[114] At the centre of the ceiling, Kent tried to create the illusion of a large dome with yet another balustrade from which other courtiers looked down into the staircase – one being the decorative painter himself. Unfortunately, the perspective as well as most of the portraits fail to convince their beholders.

Although manifestly inspired by Louis XIV's Ambassadors' Staircase at Versailles, which equally featured fictive loggias, Kent's decorative scheme departed from the Baroque tradition of late seventeenth-century royal staircases. Compared to the lavish stairs which Antonio Verrio adorned for Charles II at Windsor and William III at Hampton Court, both the iconography and the formal language of Kent's scheme prove more restrained and classical.[115] The uniformity and moderation of the painted architecture paired with the absence of any allegorical idealisation of the sovereign was perhaps more in keeping with George I's rational vision of kingship. WB

35

RICHARD CATTERMOLE (1795?–1858)

The Queen's Gallery, Hampton Court c.1818

Watercolour and bodycolour over pencil, 20.2 × 26.3 cm
RCIN 922135

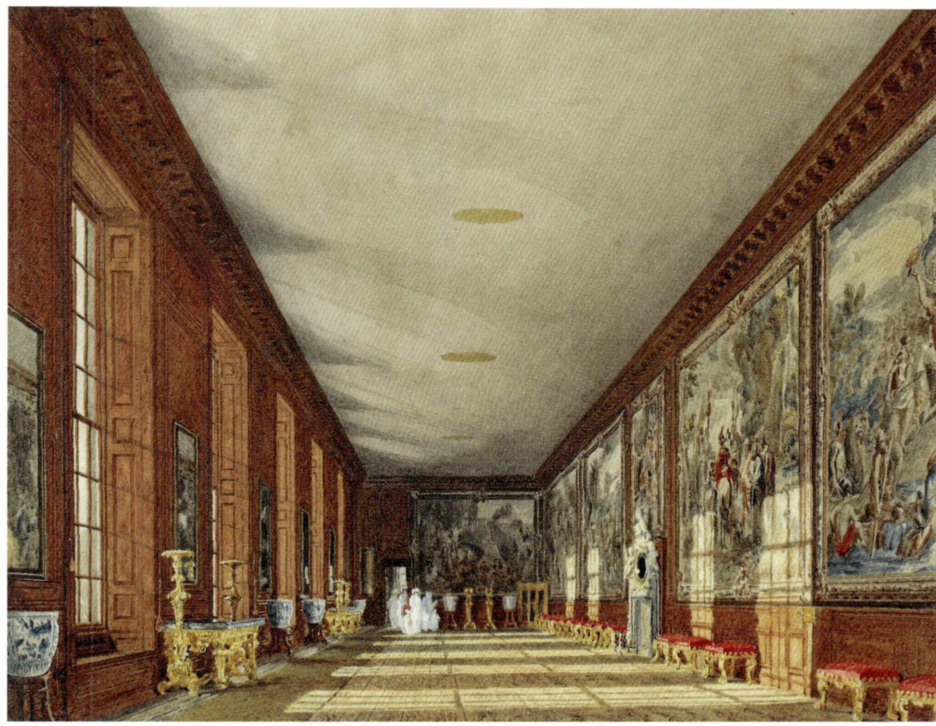

PROVENANCE Executed for Pyne's *Royal Residences*; probably acquired by George IV

In November 1714, little more than a month after he had arrived in London, George I visited Hampton Court for the first time and gave orders to have some of the State Apartments refurbished, and where necessary completed. It was not, however, until the summer of 1717 that he first held court at the palace.[116] The new King resided in the former apartments of William III and, in the absence of a queen, the Prince and Princess of Wales in those originally intended for Queen Mary II.

Cattermole's watercolour depicts a large set of stools acquired for the gallery by George II in 1737 from Henry Williams (no. 114), as well as a pair of carved gilt-wood candelabra stands supplied by Benjamin Goodison to Frederick, Prince of Wales in 1732–3 (no. 112). It remains uncertain when the gallery was hung with a set of seven tapestries representing *The History of Alexander the Great* (RCIN 1079.1–7) mostly after Charles Le Brun's designs from the mid-1660s.[116] According to George Bickham, the series had been acquired by General William Cadogan for George I and originated from the Brussels workshop of the accomplished Flemish weaver Judocus de Vos.[118] Although it was originally designed specifically for Louis XIV of France as a symbolic portrayal of his absolutist claim, Le Brun's *History of Alexander* also experienced great appreciation amongst other European princes and art collectors.[119] The first Alexander tapestries had been produced at the Gobelins manufactory outside Paris but, following the wide dissemination of the designs through prints, Flemish weavers such as de Vos began to create unauthorised copies.

George I acquired another set of art works associated with the King of France around the same time that he bought the tapestries. Shortly after Louis XIV's death in 1715, he commissioned his envoy in Paris to buy 28 busts of Roman Emperors from the French royal collection for his gallery at Herrenhausen (fig. 11).[120] It may at first appear peculiar that a British monarch would purchase art works so closely linked to the French crown. However, by the early eighteenth century the Alexander series appears to have been associated less with Louis XIV and much more with the artist Le Brun. WB

36

RICHARD CATTERMOLE (1795?–1858)

The Queen's State Bedchamber (Prince of Wales's Bedchamber), Hampton Court c.1816

Pen and ink with watercolour and bodycolour, 25.8 × 21.0 cm
RCIN 922134

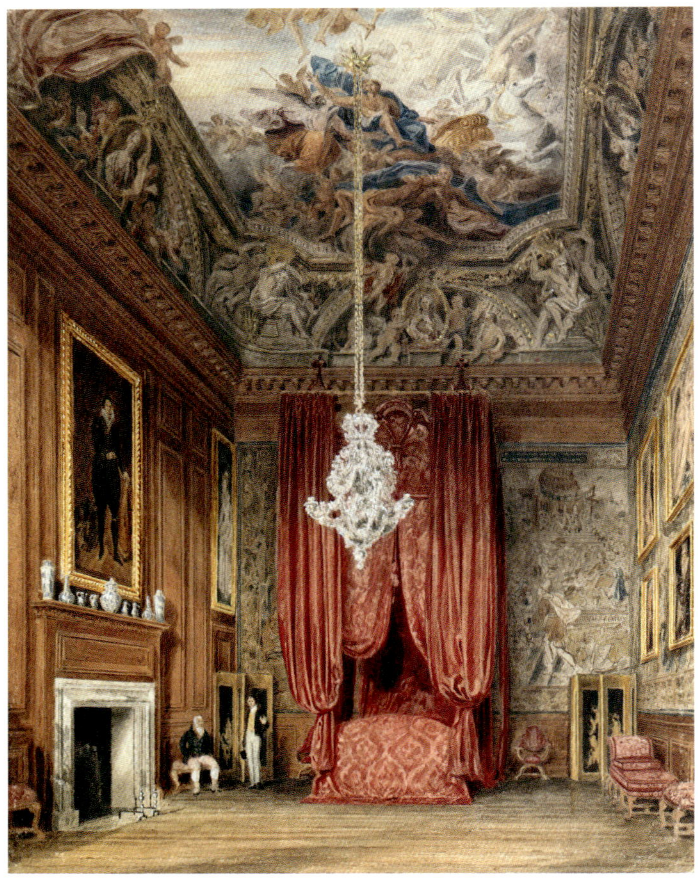

PROVENANCE Executed for Pyne's *Royal Residences*; probably acquired by George IV

This room is commonly known as Queen Mary's Bedchamber, although its decoration was not completed before 1715. Since George I came to Britain without a consort, the Queen's Apartments at Hampton Court, including this room, were used by his son and daughter-in-law George and Caroline. The couple commissioned the large State Bed with crimson silk-damask hangings as part of an impressive furnishing scheme. With an oak frame made by Richard Roberts, and upholstered by Thomas Phill and Jeremiah Fletcher, it was one of the most costly beds ordered through the Great Wardrobe in the first years of George I's reign.[121] Caroline continued to use it as Queen. The exuberant and remarkably Baroque ceiling decoration, a sketch for which is preserved in the Royal Collection (no. 37), constitutes one of Sir James Thornhill's last great artistic coups. Thornhill's unusual choice of subject, probably the Abduction of Cephalus, a dramatic and sensual story ending with adultery and death, may have been made to emphasise the unbreakable conjugal love between the Prince and Princess of Wales for whom the ceiling was painted.[122]

The State Bedchamber was of great ceremonial and symbolic importance. It was here that the so-called *levées* took place – gatherings attended by only the most influential courtiers and politicians – and it was the space where the survival of dynasty was ensured. The fulfilment of this task was recorded in the ceiling's coving. At each side, it featured roundel portraits of George I, the Prince and Princess of Wales, and their eight-year-old son Prince Frederick, who had remained in Germany as official representative of the Hanoverians.[123] Dynastic entitlement and continuity also determined the picture hang, which included Paul van Somer's portraits of King James I and his daughter Elizabeth of Bohemia, through whom the Hanoverians founded their claim to the British throne.[124] Both George I and George II displayed great awareness of the significance their respective bedchamber paintings conveyed. Whilst the father had a portrait of Charles VI (RCIN 404952) hung in his State Bedchamber at St James's Palace, to highlight his loyalty to the Emperor in his capacity of German Prince Elector, the son, in Hanover, displayed a portrait of his cherished mistress Amalie von Wallmoden.[125] WB

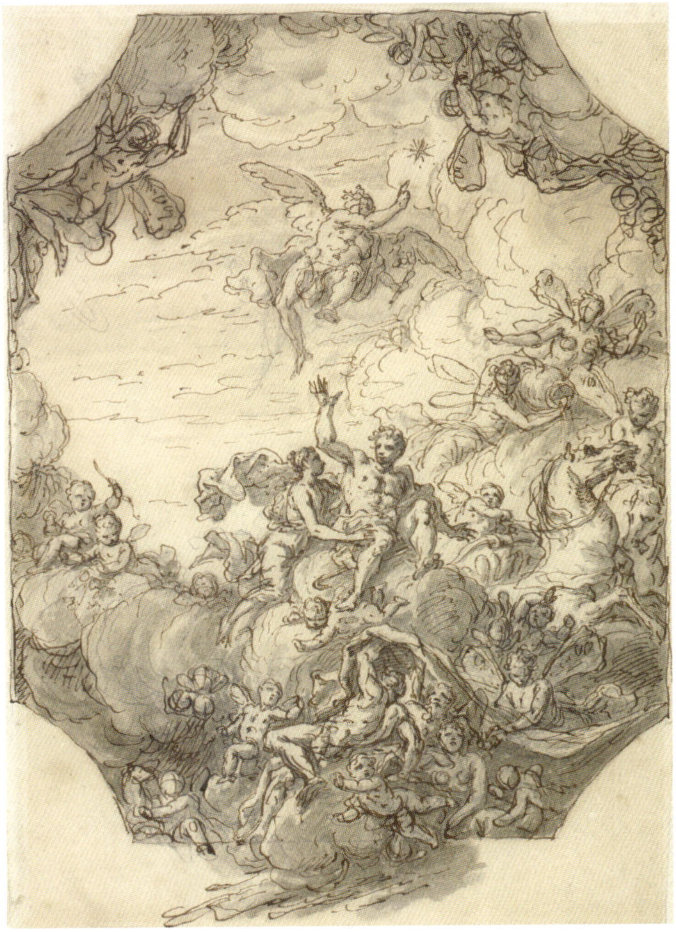

37

SIR JAMES THORNHILL (1675/6–1734)

***Design for the Prince of Wales's Bedchamber at Hampton Court** c.1715*

Pen and brown ink with grey wash over pencil, 27.1 × 19.4 cm
RCIN 917762

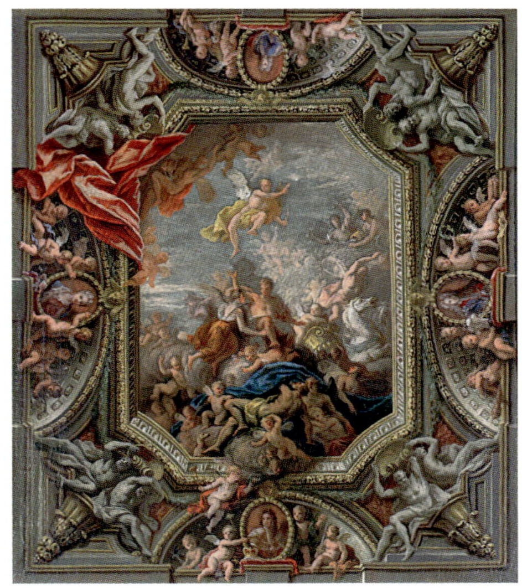

FIG. 21
Sir James Thornhill
Maquette for the Prince of Wales's Bedchamber, *c.*1715
Oil on canvas
Sir John Soane's Museum

PROVENANCE Acquired by HM The Queen in 1954

This fine sketch was drawn by the successful decorative painter Sir James Thornhill as a preliminary design for the Prince of Wales's Bedchamber at Hampton Court (no. 36). It shows an animated mythological scene centred around a youthful man and a winged woman towering on a lavish display of draperies, clouds and putti. Except for the arrangement of figures in the upper left corner, Thornhill followed the drawing almost exactly in the final painting. A larger and more detailed presentation oil sketch, comprising the roundel portraits of George I, George II, Queen Caroline and Frederick, Prince of Wales flanking the main scene, is preserved at the Sir John Soane's Museum (fig. 21). It records an intermediate stage between the drawing in the Royal Collection and the painted ceiling.

Whereas Thornhill regularly annotated his more complex decorative schemes, the present design lacks any indication of its obscure subject matter. Interpretations range from 'The rising of Aurora from the Ocean in a chariot drawn by white horses', 'Leucothoë restraining Apollo from entering his chariot' to the most recent reading, 'The Abduction of Cephalus', a subject Thornhill had explored in a similar fashion in 1710 at Hanbury Hall, Worcestershire.[126] The complex and dramatic storyline evolved from the repeated attempts of Eos (or Aurora), goddess of the dawn, to seduce the dashing Greek prince Cephalus, a story used in the Baroque era to exemplify the overwhelming power of love. WB

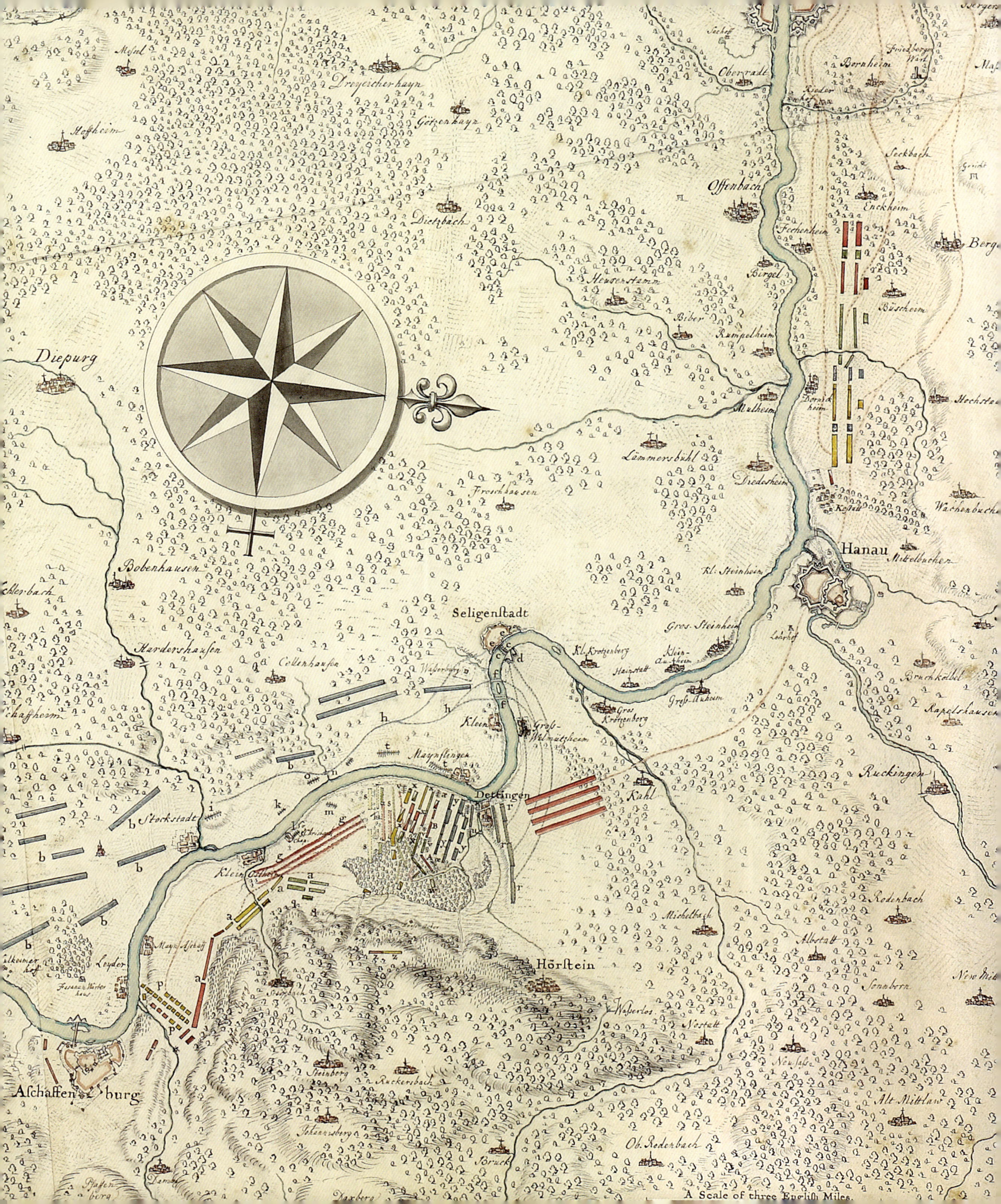
Mosel
Hoffheim
Dreyeicherhayn
Götzenhayn
Dietzbach
Offenbach
Oberradt
Bornheim
Seckbach
Enckheim
Fechenheim
Bergel
Heusenstamm
Biber
Rumpelheim
Bischeim
Diepurg
Mulheim
Lämmersbühl
Dredesheim
Froschhausen
Hanau
Mittelbuchen
Wachenbuchen
Hochstadt
Bobenhausen
Kl. Steinheim
Gros-Steinheim
Seligenstadt
Hardershausen
Collenhausen
Kl. Krotzenberg
Hainstatt
Klein-Auheim
Groß-Auheim
Gros Krotzenberg
Bruchköbel
Rapelshausen
Ruckingen
Klein
Mainflingen
Dettingen
Kahl
Stockstadt
Klein Ostheim
Hörstein
Michelbach
Albstatt
Rodenbach
Sonnborn
New Mitt
Waßerlos
Nostatt
Alt Mittlaw
Steinberg
Ruckersbach
Johannisberg
Aschaffenburg
Leyder
Mayn Aschaff
Oh. Rodenbach
Bruck
Daxberg
A Scale of three English Miles.

III

A 'Wondrous Game' The Early Georgians at War

KATE HEARD

Behold! the Wondrous Game behold!
See Kingdoms Stak'd in lieu of Gold,
The Greatest Game that E'er was play'd
The Greatest Betts that E'er was laid
(Caption to satirical print of 1757, fig. 22)

IN 1757, the fashionable London printseller Matthew Darly published a satire on the Seven Years' War, which could be purchased from his shop in the Strand for 6d (fig. 22). The opening lines of its rubric are quoted above. The etching captures the complicated nature of European alliances, showing the main protagonists as players in a cricket match. At the centre, Frederick II of Prussia holds a bat labelled 'Fortitude', and waits for Maria Theresa of Austria to bowl. While the Netherlands and Spain act as umpires, Louis XV of France fields and Elizabeth of Russia enters to help Maria Theresa. Augustus of Poland has been bowled out, while George II watches from the side-lines with a bat entitled 'Honour & Courage'. Each character has a speech bubble which explains their situation and allegiance, and a set of verses beneath further describes the stakes in 'the Greatest Game that E'er was play'd'.

George II is speaking to an unidentified companion, probably the Duke of Cumberland, saying 'Ah! Boy there was a time when I coud play with the best of them & I hope to have the best of the bett now'. George II is laying two bets (clearly visible in the foreground), one for England and one for Hanover. Between 1714 and 1760, George I and George II were heavily involved in European negotiations and conflicts, and their dual status often made for uncomfortable negotiations.[1] The politicians and public of Great Britain were nervous of being dragged into Hanover's concerns, hesitant about Hanover's traditional standing army and endlessly panicked about paying for the Hanoverian political agenda. Hanover, in return, was suspicious of Britain and her priorities on the international stage. The Hanoverian Friedrich Karl von Hardenberg explained to a French minister that 'I understood well that the King and Elector were physically the same person, but with respect to their territories they were motivated by quite different considerations'.[2]

While the electorate of Hanover's concerns focused on the expansionist policies of Prussia and Hanover's place amongst its neighbours in the Holy Roman Empire, Britain regarded France with the most apprehension. Although Britain was at various times allied with her during this period, France was thought to pose the greatest threat to British security and ambition, and (Protestant) British foreign policy was largely aimed at countering (Catholic) French power.[3] Distrust of France was so entrenched that, in 1715, Robert Walpole could use 'Frenchified' as a term of abuse for those he suspected of 'Treachery and Treason',

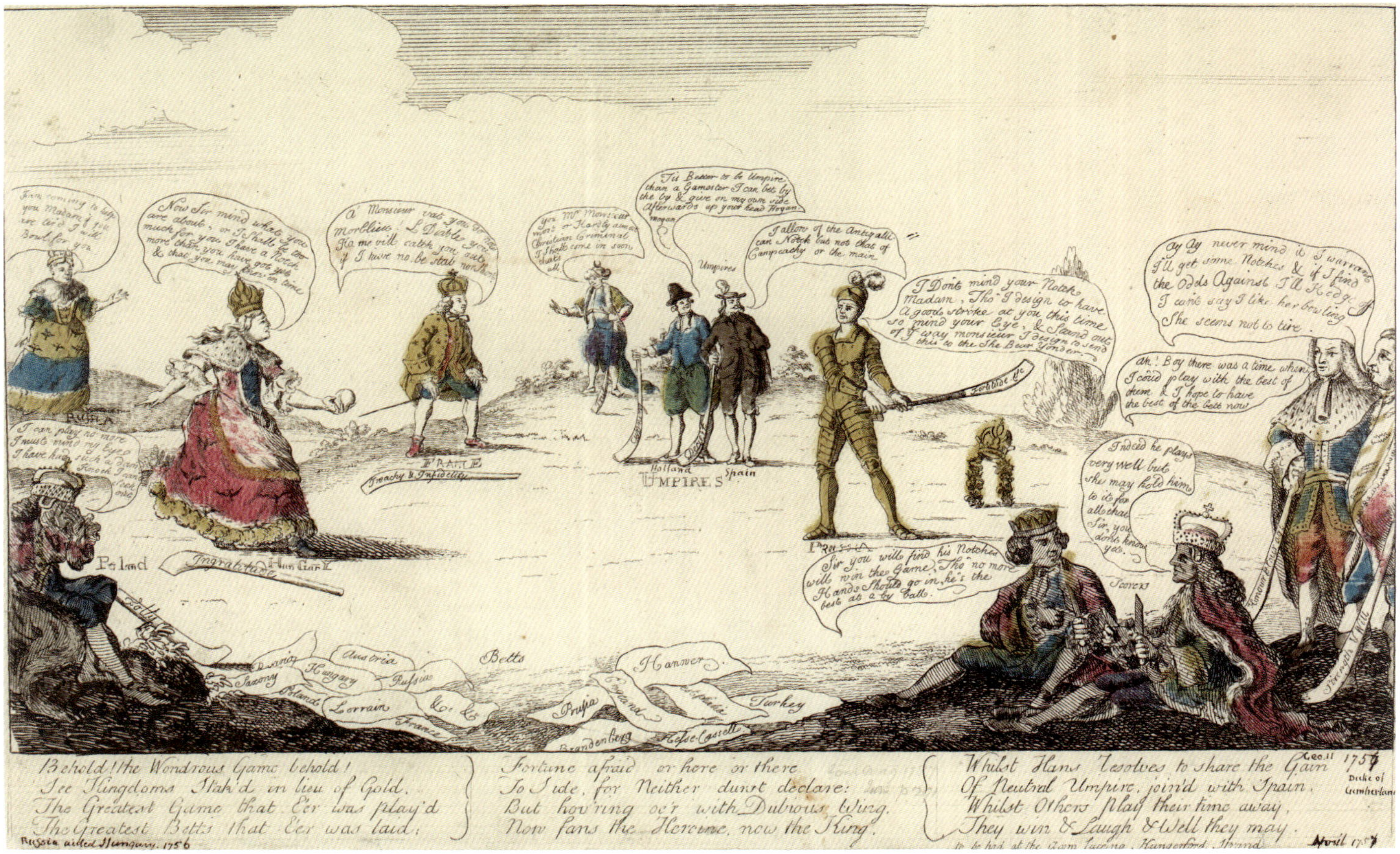

while French culture and imported goods were criticised by those who sought to protect British trade (see fig. 100).[4] Another cause of European unrest was hostility between France and Prussia – two great powers with conflicting military ambitions. The central conundrum of George I and George II's foreign policy was that their British crown encouraged them to ally with Prussia against France, while the electorship of Hanover required them to seek the support of France against Prussia.[5]

Military priorities were also different. The British Isles relied on naval strength for protection, and did not maintain a sizeable standing army, instead raising troops for specific campaigns.[6] Hanover protected its land borders by maintaining a significant permanent force. Suspicion of a standing army (thought to be a tool for the suppression of traditional liberties) was deeply entrenched in Britain, and the subject of heated debates in Parliament.[7] The early Georges were perceived as trying to introduce 'German' policies to the detriment of Britain. In 1717 the Jacobite sympathiser and MP William Shippen was imprisoned in the Tower of London for a speech in which he asserted that George I's policies 'seem rather calculated for the Meridian of Germany than of Great Britain. Tis the only Infelicity of his Majesty's Reign that He is unacquainted with our Language and Constitution; and tis therefore the more incumbent on his British Ministers to inform him, That our Government does not stand on the same foundations with his German Dominions which by Reason of their Situation are obliged to keep up Armies in Time of Peace.'[8] For many in Britain, 'Hanover' became a synonym for 'trouble': a (probably fictional) letter from one John Pately, said to have been a member of the cavalry at the Battle of Minden, claimed 'They tell us heer nought's in Vashion but *Hanoverins* in *Lundon*; if they did but zee the Place, and

FIG. 22
Matthew Darly
The Cricket Players of Europe, 1757
Etching with hand colouring
British Museum, London

now the Vokes that we vight for, they voud winder what made em vall in Love we't'.[9]

The lack of an adequately sized standing army, however, meant Britain had no permanent protection against invasion. The most likely invaders were supporters of the Stuart right to the throne, called 'Jacobites' (after *Jacobus*, the Latin for James). Their claimant was Prince James Francis Edward Stuart, 'James III' or 'The Old Pretender' depending upon allegiance – the Catholic son of James II, who had been exiled in France since a few months after his birth (no. 42). Closer in line to the throne than the electors of Hanover, he declared himself in 1714 'the only born Englishman now left of the Royal Family'.[10]

Supported by the French monarchy (which saw a handy means of riling its neighbour), 'James III' remained the centre of a rival court, which resisted Protestant rule in Britain (represented by his half-sisters Mary II and Queen Anne, and, from 1714, George I). His supporters encouraged risings in Britain and attempted a number of invasions in support of his claim to the throne. In 1715, Prince James landed in Scotland to join the Earl of Mar, who was leading a rising against George I (nos 42–4). In 1717 the Jacobite court moved to Rome, from where Prince James continued his attempts to unseat the Hanoverians. In 1719, Spain sponsored another Jacobite attempt on the crown, which was crushed by government forces under General Joseph Wightman at the Battle of Glen Shiel (no. 45). At the same time as he launched the Glen Shiel uprising, Prince James formed an alliance with the Sobieski family, heirs of John III of Poland (ruled 1674–96), through his marriage to Maria Clementina Sobieski (1702–35). The couple had two children, Prince Charles Edward Stuart (1720–88), the 'Young Pretender' (no. 54), and Prince Henry Benedict Stuart (1725–1807), both of whom maintained the Stuart claim after Prince James's death in 1766. Supporters of the Jacobite cause were not only an occasional threat from abroad: some British residents recognised no other sovereign.

The most serious threat from the Jacobites came in 1745, when Prince Charles Edward, acting on an offer of French aid, landed in Scotland. Meeting with substantial support, the Prince marched south, reaching Derby before he was forced to retreat (nos 54–67). The Jacobite advance was met with panic across the country: 'God knows what is to become of us', wrote the wife of the vicar of Dersingham in Norfolk, 'nor where we can go for to be sure they will be all over ye Country if they come here, we have Pack'd up our most valuable things to hide somwhere if they do come'.[11] Prince Charles Edward was defeated by the Duke of Cumberland at the Battle of Culloden in 1746 and his followers scattered or killed. Soon after a scheme was devised to map the terrain in which they might hide and launch subsequent attacks (no. 67).[12]

A scare of a different sort took place in the late 1750s, when it was thought that French troops were about to land on the south coast. According to the Scottish philosopher David Hume, 'The Panic is inconceivable. The People in the Country are hurrying up to Town: Those in the Town are hurrying down to the Country: No body thinks of Resistance. Every one believes the French, Popery, & the Pretender to be at their Heels.'[13] The troops from Hanover and Hesse-Kassel which were stationed in southern England to counter the threat were seen as part of the problem (no. 69). *The Monitor* warned that this was

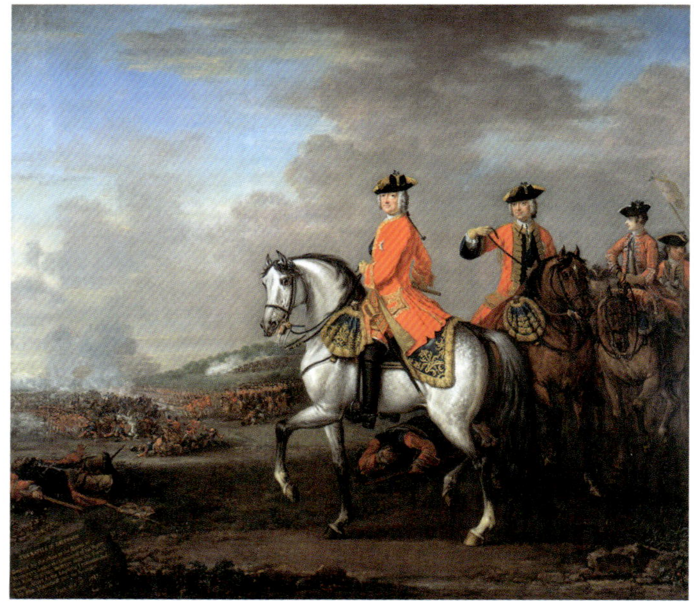

FIG. 23
John Wootton
King George II at the Battle of Dettingen, 1743
Oil on canvas
National Army Museum

'a design to render [His] Majesty absolute and to change the government into an oligarchy by the aid of a powerful standing army of natives, Hessians and Hanoverians'.[14] The imported troops were the object of much hostility, so much so that one observer thought that 'one effect this unexampled brutality may have, & I hope, will have since it has effectually prevented our ever having help from abroad in any extremity, [is] to put us upon keeping always a good standing force at home'.[15] A Militia Act was passed in 1757 to reform that body in England and Wales, though it resulted in prolonged riots.

Conflict with France was not merely conducted across the Channel, but travelled to North America and India. Here, the hunt for new trade routes and resources had driven imperial expansion, and Britain and France vied for overseas territory and local control. Battles fought at such places as the Monongahela River (no. 68), Quebec (no. 72) and Puducherry (no. 73) were a part of Franco-British rivalry, and the Seven Years' War, one aspect of which was the competition of the two powers across their overseas territories, has been described as the first world war.[16] The nature of the conflict meant that the Royal Navy, which had always played a key role in the island's defence, was of primary importance.

Over these debates, conflicts and crises presided a series of impressively capable military leaders.[17] George I had begun his distinguished military career at the age of fifteen, when he had won praise at the Battle of Conzbrücke (1675), while as Elector of Hanover he had successfully asserted the electorate's territorial claims by means of military threats and invasion.[18] The new King was, Daniel Defoe noted approvingly, 'as able to handle the scepter, and wield the Sword, as he is to wear the Crown'.[19] His son, George II, too, was a distinguished military leader, who had fought with great bravery at the Battle of Oudenarde (1708). He was the last British monarch to lead his troops into the field, at the Battle of Dettingen (no. 46), although he chose to wear the yellow sash of Hanover on the occasion – tactfully altered to the blue sash of Britain in John Wootton's depiction of the victory (fig. 23).[20] During George II's reign, the army became more professionalised, with competent career soldiers replacing those who held commissions obtained by purchase or inheritance (which had been described as an 'Evil Practice' by George I).[21]

George II's second son, William Augustus, Duke of Cumberland, fought for the first time at Dettingen and became one of the outstanding military leaders of the decade. A military enthusiast from an early age, Cumberland devoted his life to the army, which he led as Commander in Chief of forces abroad from 1745.[22] 'I fear this *blade* is so *sharp*,' wrote Lady Mary Hervey when Cumberland was sent to the Continent in 1747, 'that if we trust him out of our own scabbard, we shall not get peace.'[23] Cumberland was a noted strategist and oversaw important army reforms, laying down a set of

FIG.24
Anonymous British artist, 18th century
Prince George of Wales playing at soldiers, 1747
Pen with grey and brown ink and grey wash over pencil
RCIN 913932

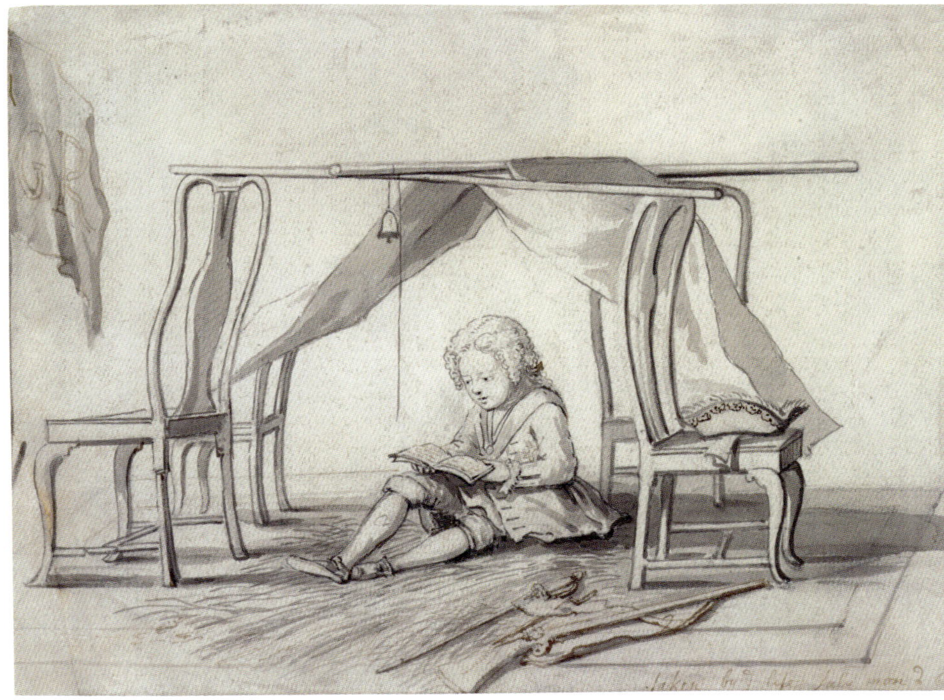

standing orders and insisting his troops practise drilling and hone their use of bayonets – a skill which was of vital importance to the defeat of Jacobite forces in 1746.[24] A volunteer in the British army in 1746, Michael Howard, recording the results of Cumberland's training, noted that the soldiers formed their ranks 'with Great Beauty of Discipline and Order'.[25]

Cumberland's enthusiasm for military matters led him to form a large and important collection of military maps and plans relating both to historic battles and to ones in which he had participated.[26] His collection is dominated by land campaigns during the period when he was commanding the army, and includes important documents of the suppression of the 1745–6 Jacobite rising, seen from the point of view of the victor rather than of the vanquished. On the Duke's death in 1765, the collection was inherited by his nephew George III, who, like all Hanoverians, had been introduced to military strategy in his nursery (fig. 24). The collection formed the basis of the King's Military Map Collection, which remains at Windsor Castle and which includes many of the works presented here.

The reign of George II ended on a military high, the '*annus mirabilis*' of 1759, with victories over France in arenas across the world, leading Horace Walpole to remark that the country's 'Bells are worn threadbare with ringing for victory'. While Sir Edward Hawke and Edward Boscawen led naval fleets to victory over the French at the Battles of Lagos and Quiberon Bay, Robert Clive and George Pocock defeated their French rivals in India and General James Wolfe overcame French challenges in Canada, his campaign culminating in the taking of Quebec (no. 72).

Despite the pessimism of their British subjects, the early Hanoverians were skilful and astute commanders, who managed to balance the concerns of their two territories to advantage, and who left their adopted country in a better military position than they had found it. Of course, the latter was partly an accident of timing – had George II died earlier or later his reign might not have concluded with such a ring of success. 'How very happy a death, and how luckily timed for him, was that of the late king!' wrote the elderly and ever perceptive Lady Mary Hervey, 'taken off at the most glorious period of his reign, shining with success and glory.'

38

LOUIS-FRANÇOIS ROUBILIAC (1702–1762)

George II (1683–1760) *c.*1760

Marble, height incl. socle 78.1 cm
Signed *L F / Roubiliac / inv.*[t]
RCIN 31614

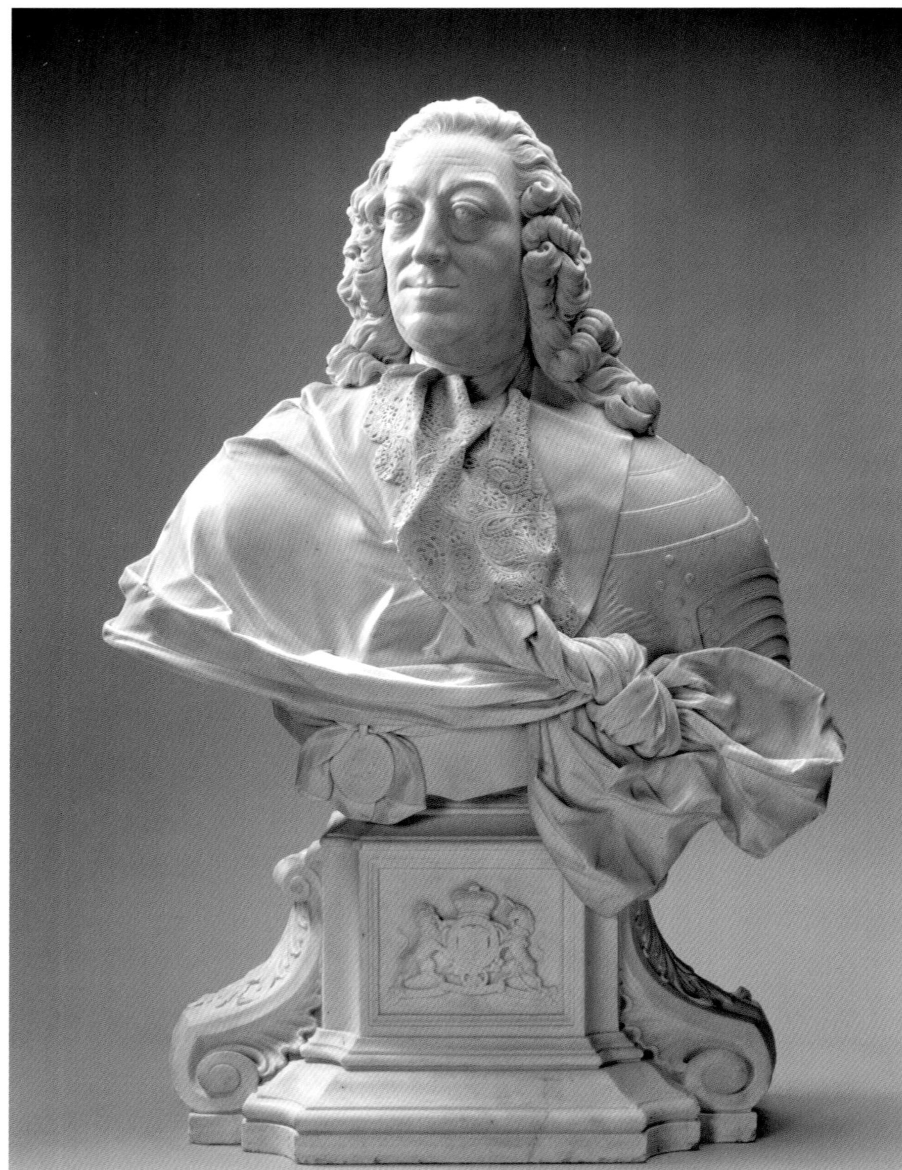

PROVENANCE John, 1st Earl Ligonier; by inheritance to Mrs Lloyd of Gloucester Place, London, by whom presented to George IV on 27 June 1817

LITERATURE Esdaile 1928, pp. 91–2, 184, pl. XXIV; R. Whitworth, *Field Marshal Lord Ligonier*, Oxford, 1958, p. 380; Whinney 1964, p. 112; Murdoch 1983, pp. 39–40; Kerslake 1977, vol. I, p. 94

Louis-François Roubiliac, a native of Lyon, learnt his art in Dresden with Balthasar Permoser (1651–1732) and in Paris with Nicolas Coustou (1658–1733). Disappointed by his failure to achieve first prize in the Prix de Rome he moved to London in 1730. Though not himself a Huguenot, he associated with the sizeable expatriate French community of artists and patrons in London, many of whose families had left France following the withdrawal in 1685 of the protection afforded to Protestants by Henri IV's Edict of Nantes. Roubiliac made an immediate impact on his craft in Britain and enjoyed a career of more than thirty years, winning fame for his funerary monuments and portrait busts. These two outstanding examples illustrate his ability to memorialise a character and to convince the viewer of the real presence of steel, cotton, hair, silk and fur where in fact there is only white marble.

It seems likely that both busts (nos 38 and 39) were commissioned by or for Lord Ligonier, probably in connection with his office as Commander in Chief of British forces from 1757 to 1759.[27] Ligonier was born at Castres in France to a Huguenot family that was forced to emigrate after 1685. He joined the British army in 1702 and was able

39

LOUIS-FRANÇOIS ROUBILIAC

John, 1st Earl Ligonier (1680–1770) c.1760

Marble, height incl. socle 70.5 cm
Signed *L.F. Roubiliac / sct ad*
RCIN 35256

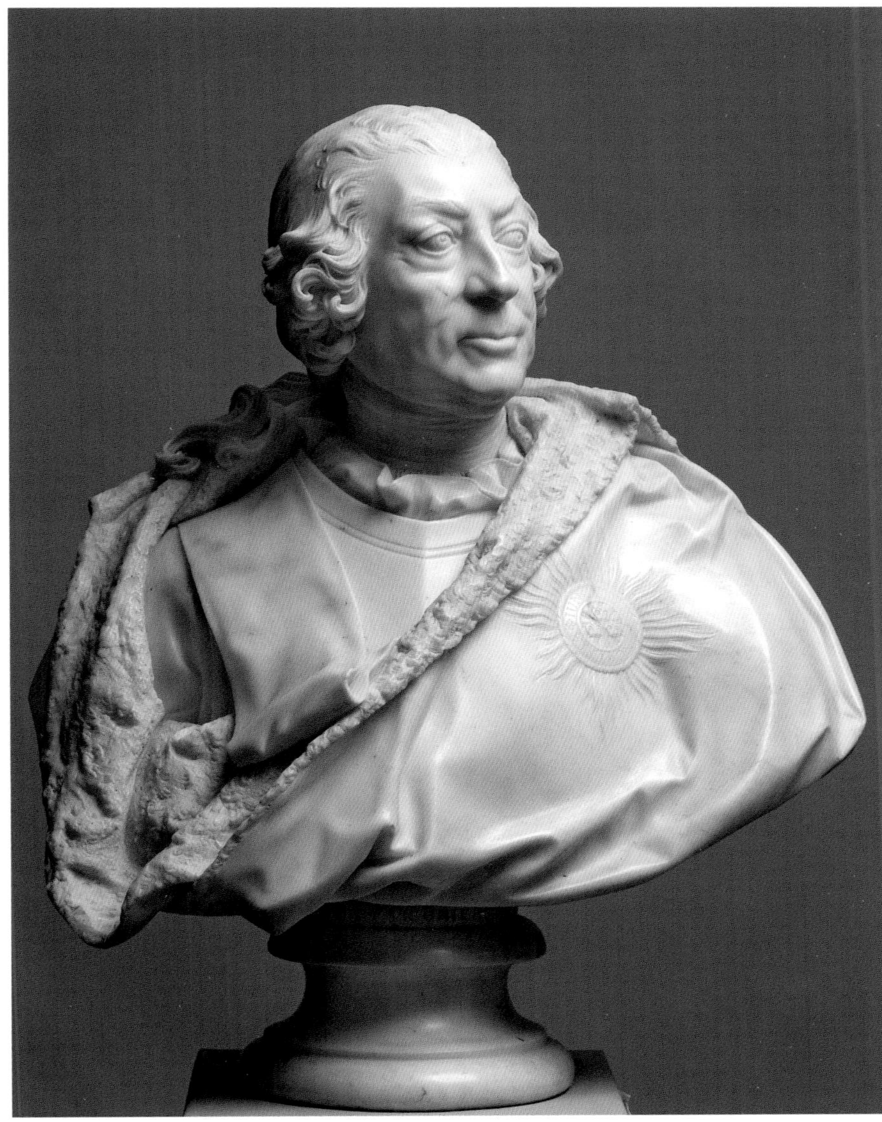

to purchase a captaincy by 1703, attaining the rank of Field Marshal in 1766 after a career of sixty years. He served under Marlborough at Blenheim, Ramillies, Oudenarde and Malplaquet, with the Duke of Cumberland in 1745, and ultimately as Master General of the Ordnance. He became a close confidant of George II, who invested him as a Knight of the Bath on the battlefield of Dettingen in 1743. Aggressive by instinct and humane as a commander, he has been called the most outstanding general in the British army between Marlborough and Wellington, and in his time he shared something of their fame, and a degree of notoriety from the 'harem' he kept at Downe Place at Cobham in Surrey.

The different forms of signature suggest that Roubiliac created his portrait of Ligonier from the life but not so that of the king, who may even have died before it was finished. The aged features of both men are fixed with unsparing realism, and those of the general, who with raised eyebrows seems to scan the horizon, perhaps across an extensive battlefield, are rendered with astonishing skill. The 76-year-old king's oyster eyes, protruding jaw and sagging skin made unpromising material for a portrait, and the eye is drawn, deliberately no doubt, to the astonishing knotted length of drapery that extends wantonly over the edge of the king's armour, conjured out of cold marble. In this markedly Baroque – and old-fashioned – portrait Roubiliac was surely setting out to surpass the works of Bernini, which he would have known both from his studies with Bernini's pupil Balthasar Permoser and from his time in Paris with Coustou. JM

40

JOHN WOOTTON (1682?–1764)

William Augustus, Duke of Cumberland (1721–1765) *c.*1745

Oil on canvas, 47.6 × 42.6 cm
RCIN 400695

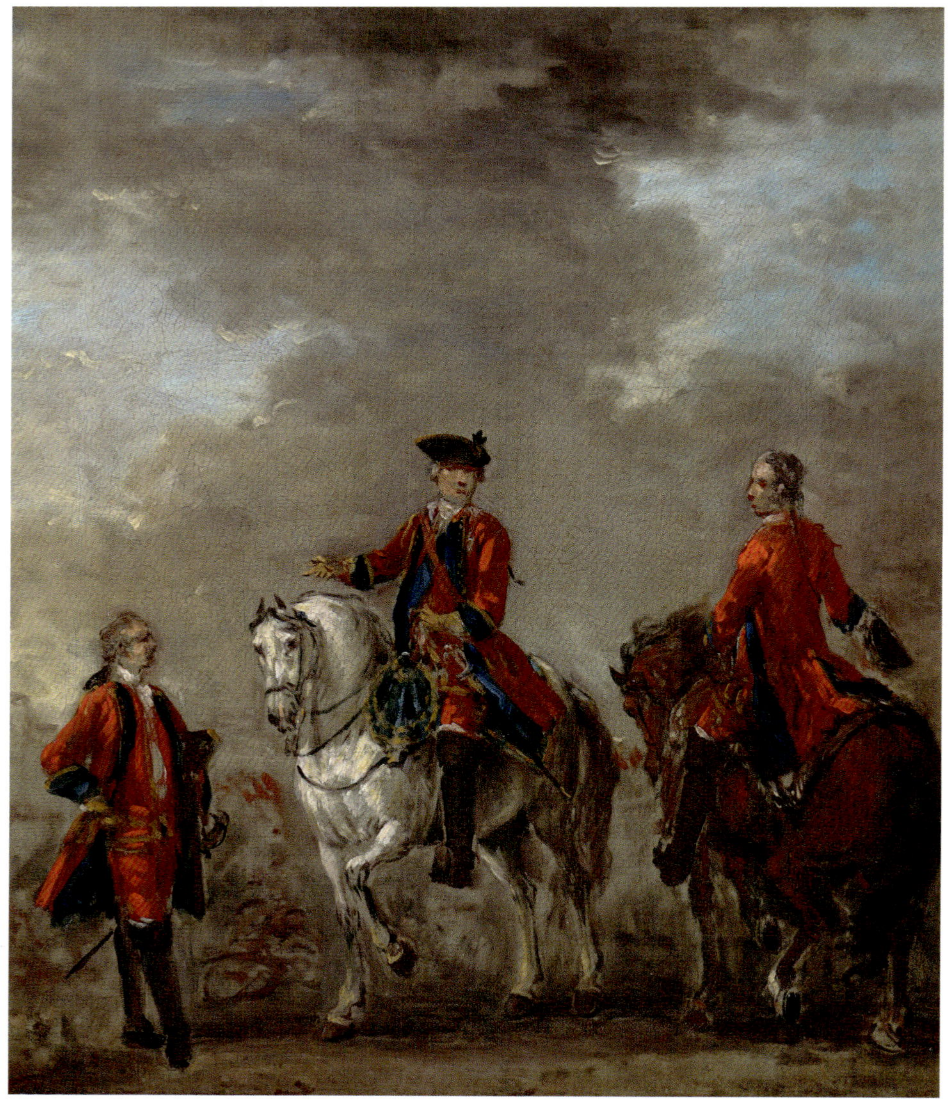

PROVENANCE Purchased by HM The Queen from Thomas Agnew & Sons in 1959

LITERATURE Millar 1963, p. 180, no. 544

This compositional sketch loosely relates to the full-length equestrian portrait commissioned by Frederick, Prince of Wales, to celebrate the Battle of Dettingen and completed in 1744 by Thomas Hudson (1701–79) and John Wootton (RCIN 407465). The Duke is shown similarly mounted and in a similar pose, wearing the frock uniform of the 1st Guards, with the star and riband of the Garter and an engagement visible in the background. It would seem that Wootton was here planning a different version of the 1744 composition, presumably also full-length but to include two senior officers with the Duke. The only composition surviving of this type is in the collection of the Duke of Argyll and is usually dated 1747; it depicts Lord Henry Campbell and Sir John Ligonier in attendance.[28]

This oil sketch shows Wootton at his best, lively in the handling of the brush and confidently capturing posture and movement. As so often happened at this time, an English artist was here working in a style substantially similar to that of his French rivals, in this case Charles Parrocel (1688–1752), who accompanied the French army confronting the Duke of Cumberland's forces during these years, 1744–45. DS-T

41

LUDWIG WIEDEMANN (1690–1754)

Pair of cannon 1749

Composite bronze and wrought iron, on a cast iron carriage
Length 115 cm; bore 9.525 cm
RCIN 67423.1-2

PROVENANCE Cast for William Augustus, Duke of Cumberland, 1749

LITERATURE ffoulkes 1937, p. 98; Carman 1955, pp. 47–8

Colonel Ludwig Wiedemann, originally from Augsburg, ran the foundry in Dresden best known for casting the *Goldener Reiter*, the gilt equestrian sculpture of Augustus II of Poland which stands in the city centre. According to Mary Endell he was given military honours by Augustus III for his invention of a new form of 'air-cannon'.[29] Wiedemann seems to have moved to England around 1747, bearing a patent for a new form of cannon, one of lighter weight than the standard field gun of the period. He managed to gain the ear of the Duke of Cumberland and with his patronage was able to cast cannon of various sizes at the World's End foundry in Chelsea.

During Easter 1749 Wiedemann's cannon were tested against those of the Master Founder of the Ordnance, Andreas Schalch. The test took place in Windsor Great Park before the Duke of Cumberland and the Master-General of Ordnance, John, 2nd Duke of Montagu (1690–1749). Each founder tested 24-, 12- and 6-pounder guns at a variety of ranges. However, according to the Ordnance Minutes of 4 April 1749, the test was not completed as one of Wiedemann's 6-pounder guns burst. Nevertheless, the cannon were retained – three being sent to Woolwich, and the rest remaining in Windsor.

In the 1770s the cannon at Woolwich were selected to be melted down. On inspection the guns were described as having a core of lead coated in brass. In the opinion of the Ordnance team the brass had too high a zinc content and this was the factor which had caused the failure in the 1749 test. In fact, recent radiography has revealed that the guns have a core of wrought iron staves, bound by lead-welded joints, and coated inside and out in brass. The brass is porous in texture and it may have been this rather than the zinc content which caused the difficulties. Nevertheless, the problematic creation of a wrought iron core, and the brass casting inside and out, remain a testament to Wiedemann's technical skill.

Wiedemann's experiments with different metal alloys were part of a long-running tradition to create a more mobile, lightweight artillery. The foundries of the Netherlands experimented with different metal alloy cores throughout the seventeenth century, and the founders working for Gustavus Adolphus in the 1620s even experimented with gun barrels formed from leather.[30] That Wiedemann's cannon were kept at Windsor suggests that the Duke of Cumberland, as a seasoned military leader, had a personal interest in these experiments. KJ

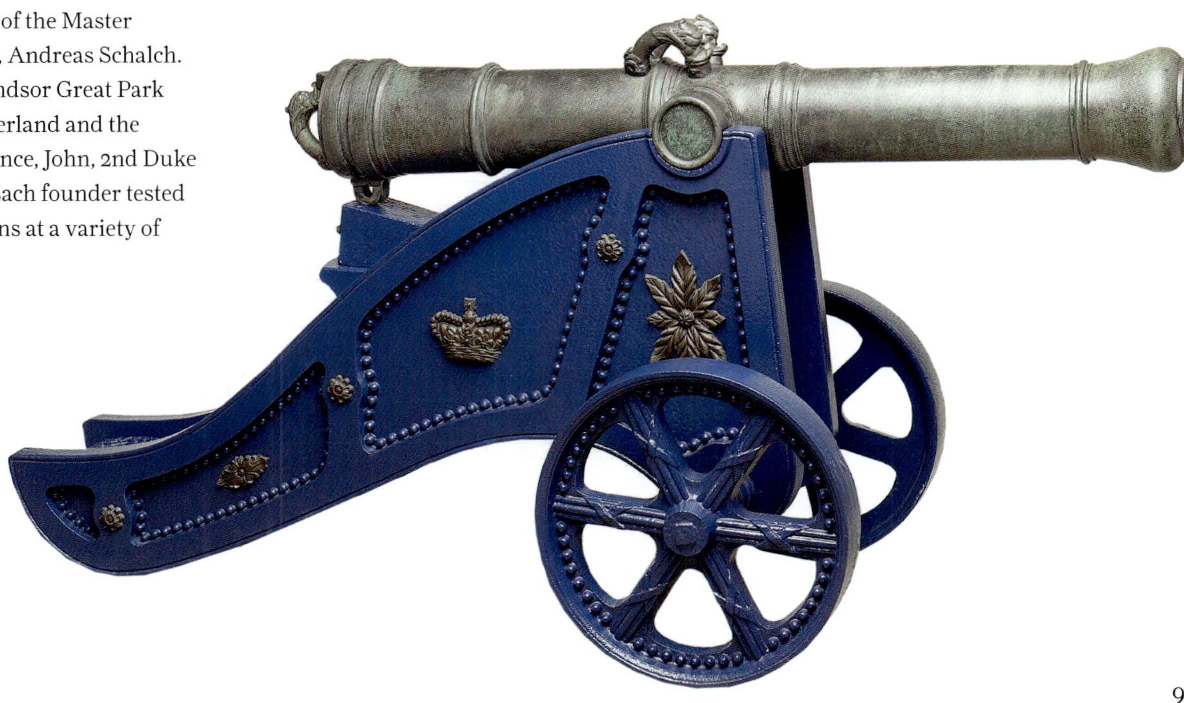

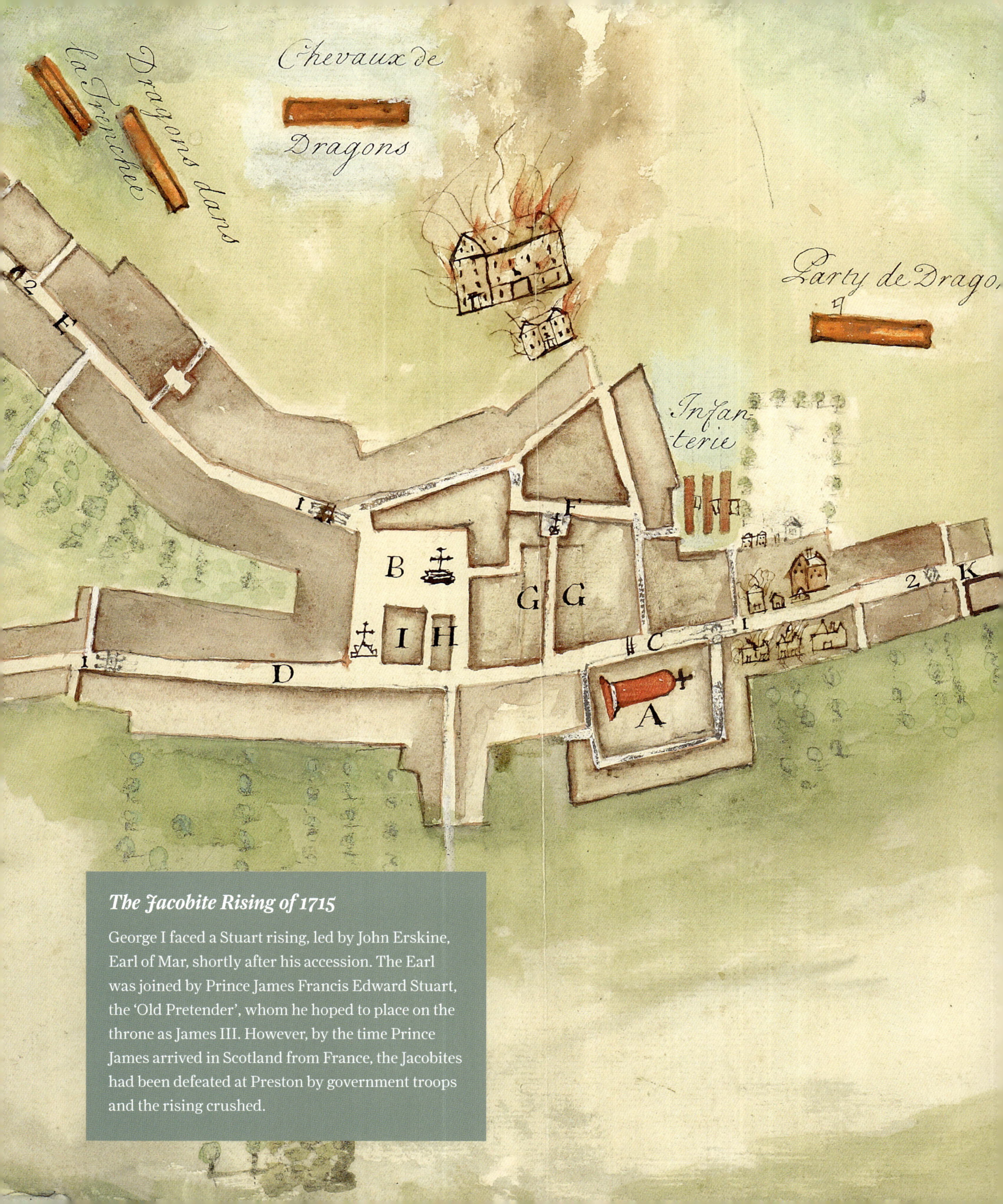

The Jacobite Rising of 1715

George I faced a Stuart rising, led by John Erskine, Earl of Mar, shortly after his accession. The Earl was joined by Prince James Francis Edward Stuart, the 'Old Pretender', whom he hoped to place on the throne as James III. However, by the time Prince James arrived in Scotland from France, the Jacobites had been defeated at Preston by government troops and the rising crushed.

42

FRANÇOIS CHEREAU (1680–1729)
AFTER ALEXIS-SIMON BELLE (1674–1734)

James III, King of Great Britain (1688–1766) 1712

Etching and engraving, 39.7 × 26.6 cm
RCIN 603524

PROVENANCE Perhaps the impression purchased by the Prince of Wales (later George IV) in 1807[31]

LITERATURE O'Donoghue 1908, no. 7; Kerslake 1977, p. 155; Sharp 1996, no. 129; *King over the Water* 2001, p. 49

This print, taken from a painting by the Jacobite portraitist Alexis-Simon Belle, shows the 'Old Pretender' as James III, King of Great Britain and rightful successor to James II. He is shown in martial dress, with a breastplate over his clothing, and wears the sash of the Jacobite Order of the Garter. His attire celebrates his military record: he had fought with honour at the Battles of Oudenarde (1708) and of Malplaquet (1709). Prince James was often represented in such costume, but in reality was said to cut a less impressive military figure: one of his supporters during the Jacobite rising of 1715 described the general disappointment at the Pretender's demeanour, noting that 'we saw nothing in him that looked like spirit'.[32]

The print is dedicated to Prince James by Belle, who styled himself 'Painter to His Britannic Majesty' ('*peintre de s.M. Brit*'). Belle also acted as the publisher of the print, which was issued from his premises in Paris. Engravings after Belle's portraits circulated in Britain, where they might be used as models for other painted portraits.[33] KH

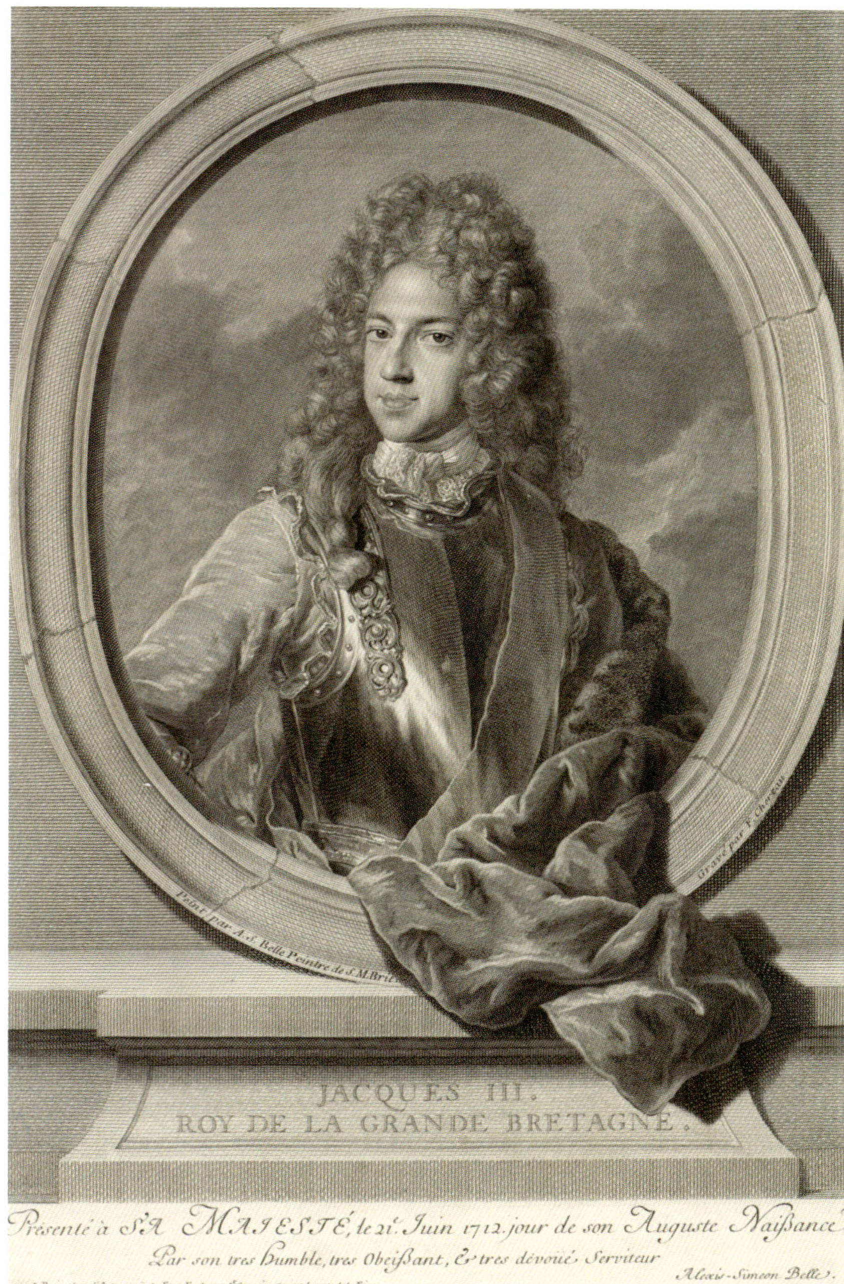

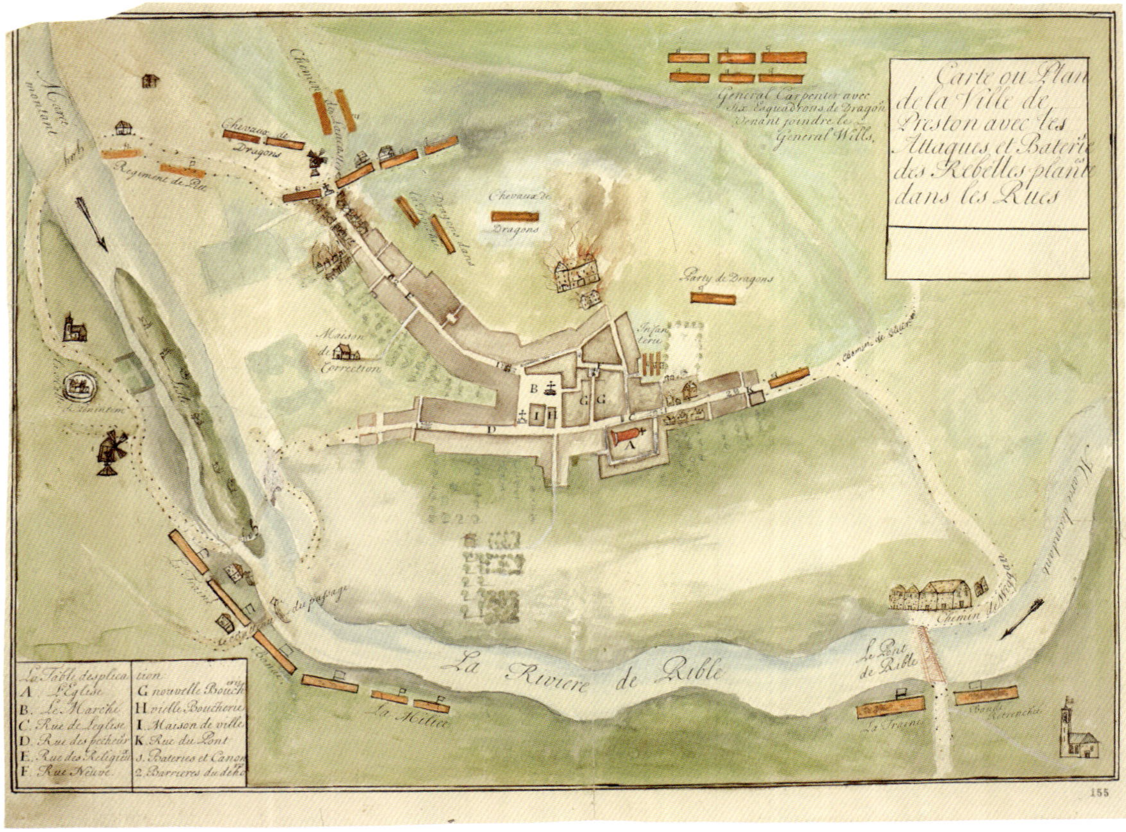

43

ANONYMOUS

Plan of the town of Preston showing the rebel positions 1715

Pen and ink with watercolour over pencil, 50.2 × 68.6 cm
Not to scale
RCIN 726092

PROVENANCE King's Military Map Collection[34]

LITERATURE Hodson forthcoming

In early November 1715, a Jacobite army of around 1400 men marched across the English/Scottish border, heading south and meeting little resistance as they passed through Penrith, Appleby, Kendal and Lancaster.[35] At Preston the Jacobite advance was stopped by an army led by Major-General Charles Wills. The Jacobite commander Thomas Forster barricaded the town as Wills attacked. The government troops were soon reinforced by cavalry which had travelled from Newcastle under Lieutenant-General George Carpenter.

The progress of the conflict and the fierce nature of the fighting are clearly shown in this plan of the battle. Wills and his men approached Preston across the River Ribble, using an unguarded bridge. Marching around the town they launched attacks from the east and north, burning houses as they went. The Jacobite forces held ground until the arrival of Carpenter with his cavalry shored up the government position. Internal disagreement further weakened the Jacobite ranks, who surrendered on 14 November.

This map may be by an amateur artist, and is not to scale or topographically accurate: the island in the river, for example, is shown to the west rather than the south of Preston. The draughtsman has included incidental detail such as rabbits on the island. The plan shows an earlier stage in the battle than the official version (no. 44), with Carpenter's men up to the far north-east on the approach to the town. KH

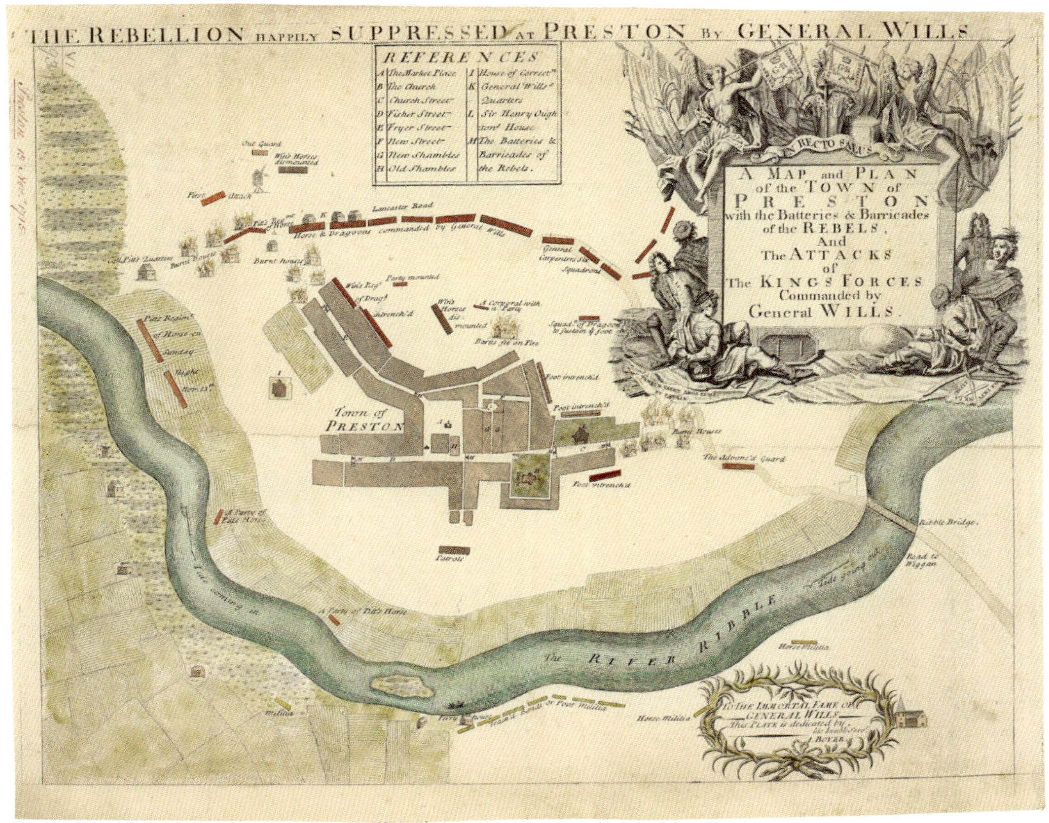

44

ABEL BOYER, DEDICATOR? (1667?–1729)

The Rebellion happily Suppressed at Preston by General Wills 1715

Etching and engraving with hand colouring, 38.3 × 48.2 cm
Not to scale
RCIN 726093

PROVENANCE King's Military Map Collection[36]

LITERATURE Hodson forthcoming

This is one of a number of printed souvenirs issued to celebrate the suppression of the rising at Preston. It is probably the map which was advertised for sale in the *Post Man* of 7 January 1716, priced at one shilling and available from P. Donnoyer in the Strand or Michael Hennekin in St Martin's Lane.[37] The map was accompanied by a sheet of letter press 'with an Account of the Victory obtained over the Rebels, and a List of the Principal Prisoners, in a printed Half Sheet pasted to the said Plan', which is missing from the present version, but which survives with the British Library impression.[38] The 'A. Boyer', whose name appears on the print may be Abel Boyer, a French writer and lexicographer resident in Britain from 1689 and a fierce advocate of the Hanoverian succession.

The plan shows the government forces ranged around the town, with Carpenter's six squadrons lined up alongside Wills's forces. As in the manuscript map (no. 43), a number of houses are shown burning: the people of Preston were thus punished for allowing the Jacobites to shelter in the town, such depictions serving as a warning to others in the path of the rising. The fictive plaque which surrounds the title is topped by winged Victories who blow their trumpets over subdued Jacobite prisoners.

Although this print celebrates Wills as the victor at Preston, it is clear that the government victory was as much due to the actions of Lieutenant-General George Carpenter, who arrived with reinforcements after Wills had suffered heavy losses. The fêting of Wills in the aftermath of Preston led to ill feeling between the two men, who came close to duelling over their disagreement.[39] KH

The Jacobite Rising of 1719

In 1719, George I faced another Jacobite rising. The Stuarts were encouraged and aided by Spain, which sought to weaken Britain in the wake of a series of treaties threatening Spanish interests in Italy and of Admiral Byng's decisive defeat of the Spanish navy in August 1718. It was intended that a main force led by James Butler, 2nd Duke of Ormonde, should land in the west of England. In the event the ships carrying this force were scattered by storms in the Bay of Biscay and Ormonde was forced to abandon his attempt. The only soldiers that landed belonged to a small diversionary force, bolstered by a contingent of Spanish infantrymen, which arrived on the north-west coast of Scotland and set up their headquarters in Eilean Donan Castle on Loch Alsh. They were ill prepared: the Marquis of Tullibardine, a Jacobite leader, noted afterwards that 'we came with hardly any thing that was really necessary for such an undertaking'.[40] They were joined by those who had continued the Jacobite resistance in Scotland, led by (among others) Lord George Murray and Rob Roy.

45

JOHN HENRY BASTIDE (*c.*1700–1770)

Plan of the Battle of Glen Shiel 1719

Pen and ink and brush with wash and watercolour, 51.4 × 67.8 cm
Scale approx. 1 : 2,460
RCIN 727016

PROVENANCE King's Military Map Collection[41]

LITERATURE Millar 1882–3; Sanford Terry 1905; Pollard 2009a; Hodson forthcoming

Travelling south-east from Eilean Donan, the Jacobites met government troops, commanded by General Joseph Wightman, at the Pass of Glen Shiel in the North West Highlands on 10 June 1719. Wightman attacked both flanks of the opposing troops with mortar fire and infantry advances, forcing the Jacobites back up the mountain, chased by a government regiment led by Colonel Clayton, and scattering a tenacious group of Spanish soldiers, who later surrendered.[42] The terrain was particularly challenging: Wightman described Glen Shiel as 'a considerable Pass' in a letter to the Duke of Roxburghe, while a contemporary account of the battle noted that the mountains 'fenced [the combatants] on both sides'.[43] Wightman's victory ended Jacobite, and Spanish, hopes of a serious challenge to the Hanoverian government in 1719.

Bastide's map combines a bird's-eye view of the valley with an elevation of the adjacent mountains, a device which captures the dizzying altitude at which parts of the battle were fought. He has represented the sections of the two forces as blocks, but also as individual figures engaged in conflict. General Wightman is portrayed mounted at the head of a company of dragoons, just to the north of the river Shiel. The mortars in front of him can be seen firing into the Spanish regiment's position, which is marked with an 'A'.

John Henry Bastide, an engineer, was present at the battle as a member of Colonel Montagu's regiment.[44] He made a number of plans of the battle, showing the engagement from different directions.[45] KH

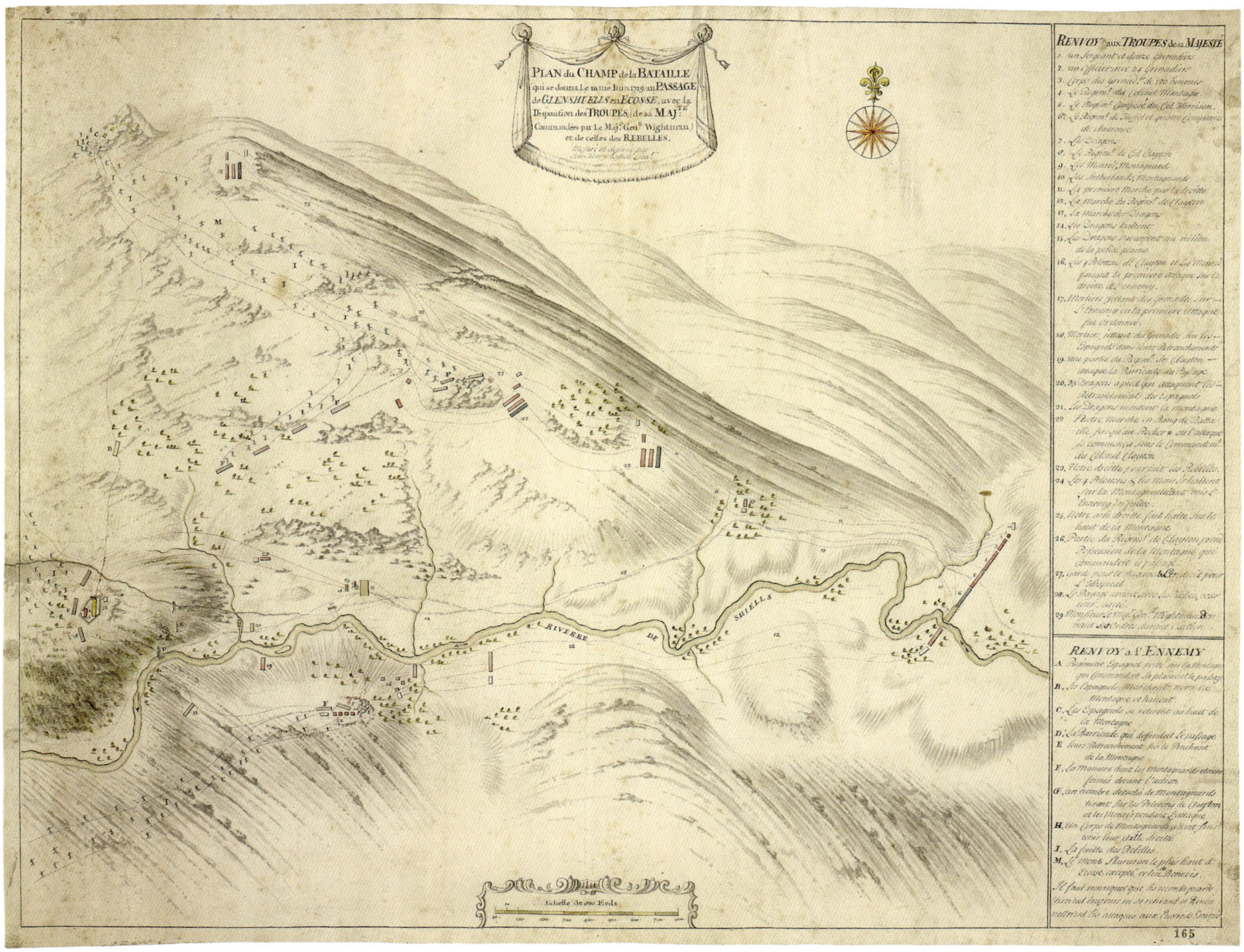
PLAN du CHAMP de la BATAILLE
qui se donna Le 10me Iuin 1719 au PASSAGE
de GLENSHIELS en ECOSSE, avec la
Disposition des TROUPES, (de sa MAJ.TE
Commandées par Le Maj.r Gen.l Wightman)
et de celles des REBELLES.
RIVIERE DE SHIELLS
Echelle de 100 Pieds
RENVOY aux TROUPES de sa MAJESTÉ
1 un Sergeant et douze Grenadiers
2. un Officier avec 24 Grenadiers
3. Corps des Grenad.rs de 120 hommes
4. Le Regim.t du Colonel Montagu
5. Le Regim.t Composé du Col. Harrison.
7. Les Dragons.
8. Le Regim.t de Col. Clayton
9. Les Monrés, Montagnards
10 Les Sutherlands, Montagnards
14. Les Dragons battent
15. Les Dragons s'avancent au milieu de la petite plaine
21. Les Dragons montent la montagne
23. Notre droitte poursuit les Rebelles.
25. Notre aile droitte fait halte sur le haut de la Montagne
RENVOY à l'ENNEMY
C. Les Espagnols se retirent au haut de la Montagne
D. La Barricade qui deffendoit le passage
E. leurs Retranchement sur le Penchant de la Montagne
H. Un Corps de Montagnards allant soutenir leur aile droitte
I. La fuitte des Rebelles.
M. Le Mont Skururan le plus haut d'Ecosse excepté celui de Benevis.
165

The War of the Austrian Succession 1740–48

In 1713 the Holy Roman Emperor Charles VI issued an edict called the 'Pragmatic Sanction', which, contrary to Salic law, allowed Habsburg possessions to be inherited by a woman. Upon his death in 1740 his daughter, Maria Theresa, was therefore able to inherit the throne. However, acceptance of the Sanction proved short-lived: three months after her accession Frederick II of Prussia capitalised on Maria Theresa's weak position by invading Silesia, which he had long coveted. Prussian expansionism was widely feared, particularly as Frederick had allied with France, which also stood to benefit from a diminuition of Habsburg power. In an attempt to halt the advance of this alliance, Britain, Hanover and the Dutch Republic came to Maria Theresa's aid, forming a 'Pragmatic Army' to fight for the Habsburg cause. The War of the Austrian Succession was to be the proving ground of the Duke of Cumberland, who first saw action at the Battle of Dettingen in 1743, then took command of the Pragmatic Army in early 1745 and distinguished himself in defeat at the Battle of Fontenoy in May of that year. After a brief return to Britain to face the Jacobite rising of 1745–6, Cumberland was back on the Continent from 1747 until peace was concluded in 1748.

46

ATTRIBUTED TO SCHULTZ (D. 1749)

A Plan of all the Marches and Incampments of the Army of the Allies commanded by His Majesty the King of Great Britain from the Battle of Dettingen to the End of the Campain, in the Year 1743 1743

Pen and ink with watercolour, 85.5 × 115.9 cm
Scale approx. 1 : 94,667
RCIN 728103

PROVENANCE King's Military Map Collection; probably prepared for William Augustus, Duke of Cumberland

LITERATURE Hodson forthcoming

On 27 June 1743, the Pragmatic Army, led by George II, met the French, commanded by the Marshal de Noailles, just outside the small village of Dettingen. The situation for the allies was dire: their supply routes had been blocked and they were in retreat, caught in a vulnerable position between two groups of French troops and in the range of hostile artillery fire. It would have been even worse had the duc de Gramont not made a tactical error in moving his troops and provoked an engagement before the French were fully in position. Against the odds, George II and his army broke the French lines, the King and his son, the Duke of Cumberland (who suffered a wound to his leg in the fighting), gaining much praise for their actions. Edward Stilman, a yeoman of cavalry, wrote that the King was 'as bold as a liont with his can[e] in one hand and his Sord in the other'.[46]

This large and elegant map, by one of the mapmakers on Cumberland's staff, possibly Schultz (see no. 48), was made as a record of the progress of the allied army during the campaign. It shows the Battle of Dettingen at the bottom right, with the French (in blue) blocking the allied progress to the north and west (north is oriented to the right of the sheet). The subsequent march of the army and its encampments are traced, with the nature of the terrain and key settlements clearly marked. The map is unfinished: space has been left for a 'Journal', an account of the campaign, which was never added.

The victory at Dettingen was so celebrated that the field of battle was soon the object of curious visitors. The Scottish philosopher David Hume described in March 1748 how he had 'walkd out & survey'd the Field of Battle, accompany'd with the Postmaster, who saw the Battle from his Windows. Good God, what an Escapade we made there!'[47] KH

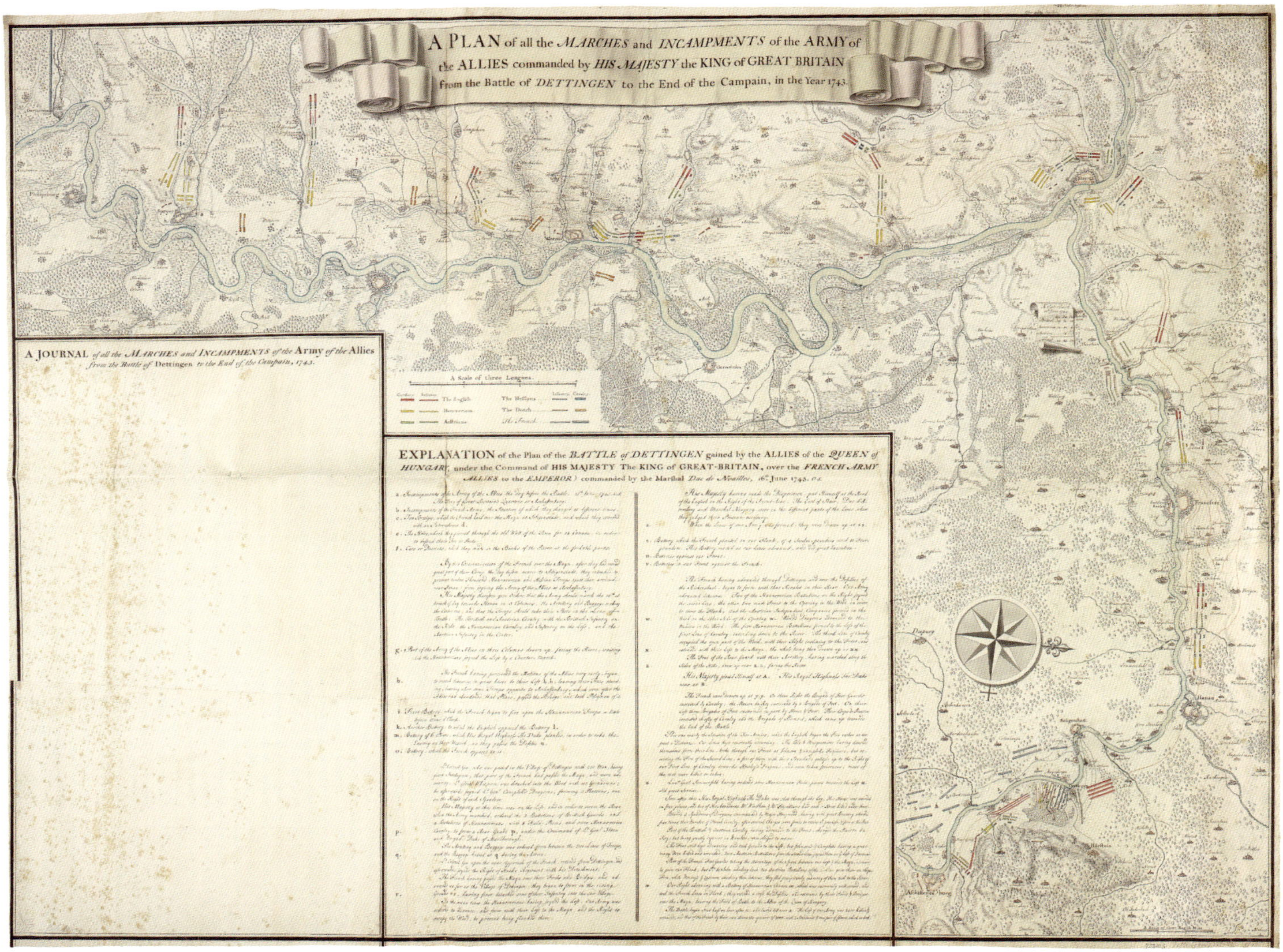
A PLAN of all the MARCHES and INCAMPMENTS of the ARMY of the ALLIES commanded by HIS MAJESTY the KING of GREAT BRITAIN from the Battle of DETTINGEN to the End of the Campaign, in the Year 1743.
A JOURNAL of all the MARCHES and INCAMPMENTS of the Army of the Allies from the Battle of Dettingen to the End of the Campaign, 1743.
A Scale of three Leagues
The English
Hanoverians
Austrians
The Hessians
The Dutch
The French
EXPLANATION of the Plan of the BATTLE of DETTINGEN gained by the ALLIES of the QUEEN of HUNGARY, under the Command of HIS MAJESTY The KING of GREAT-BRITAIN, over the FRENCH ARMY ALLIES to the EMPEROR; commanded by the Marshal Duc de Noailles, 16th June 1743.

47

MARY HARRIS

Receipt for mathematical instruments 1745

Manuscript, 21.3 × 18.0 cm
RA CP/MAIN/2/48

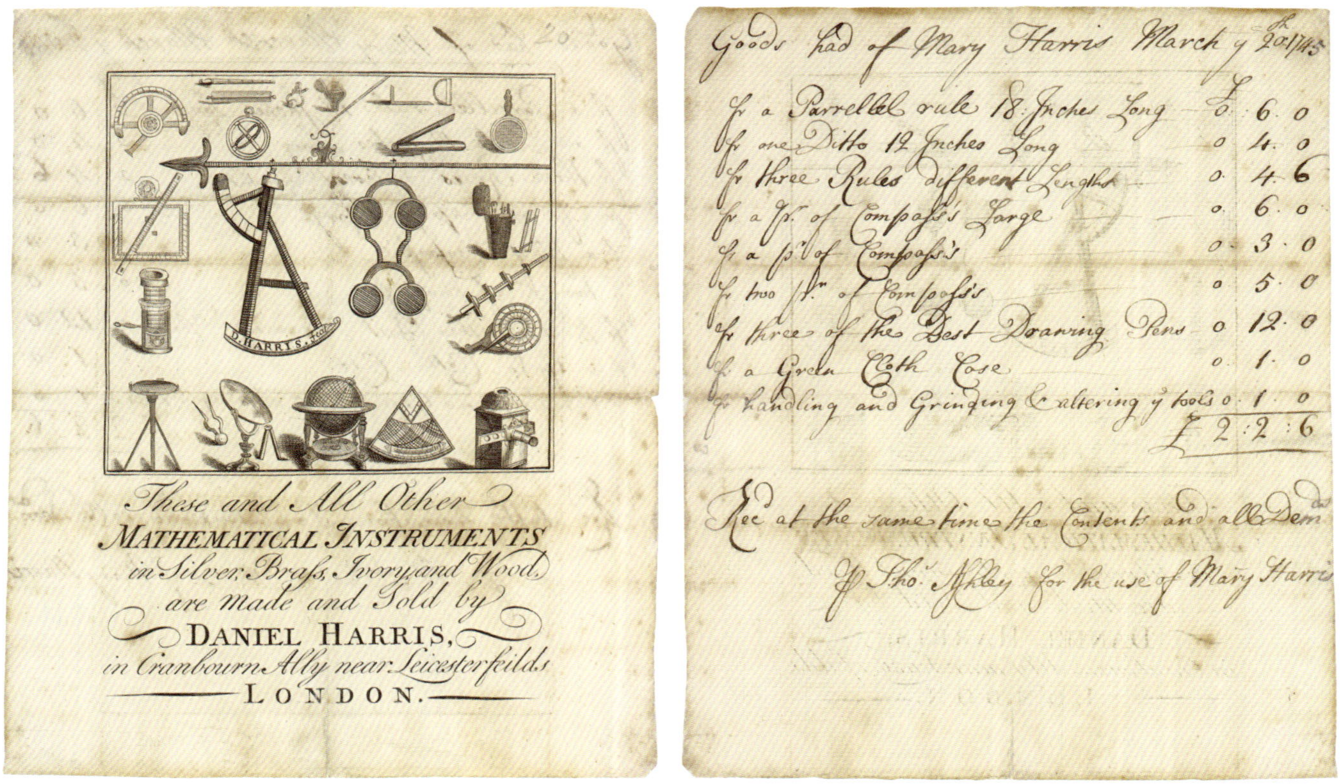
These and All Other
MATHEMATICAL INSTRUMENTS
in Silver, Brass, Ivory and Wood,
are made and Sold by
DANIEL HARRIS,
in Cranbourn Ally near Leicesterfeilds
LONDON.

Goods had of Mary Harris March ye 20th 1745

	£	s	d
for a Parrellel rule 18 Inches Long	0	6	0
for one Ditto 12 Inches Long	0	4	0
for three Rules different Lengths	0	4	6
for a pr of Compass's Large	0	6	0
for a pr of Compass's	0	3	0
for two prs of Compass's	0	5	0
for three of the Best Drawing Pens	0	12	0
for a Green Cloth Case	0	1	0
for handling and Grinding & altering ye tools	0	1	0
	£ 2	2	6

Recd at the same time the Contents and all Demands
pr Thos Ashley for the use of Mary Harris

PROVENANCE Papers of the Duke of Cumberland

This receipt for instruments purchased from Mary Harris is among the papers of the Duke of Cumberland. The objects acquired were basic mathematical instruments – two parallel rules, three rules, three compasses and three 'Best Drawing Pens'. They were altered to order, and were purchased with 'a Green Cloth Case' which was probably used to store them. They may have been acquired for the purposes of map and plan making. The bill is dated 20 March 1745 (NS 31 March 1745), just before Cumberland and his staff travelled to the Netherlands to pursue Britain's agenda in the War of the Austrian Succession.

The receipt is written on the back of the trade card of Daniel Harris, who offered 'Mathematical Instruments in Silver, Brass, Ivory and Wood' from his shop in Cranbourne Alley, London.[48] An example of his work is provided by a string-gnomon dial signed *D Harris A Londres*, now in Oxford.[49] That the goods were supplied by Mary rather than Daniel Harris may indicate that he had died and that the business was being carried on by his widow or daughter. Thomas Ashley, who made out the receipt, was running his own business as an instrument maker by 1749.[50] KH

48

SCHULTZ (D. 1749)

Encampments in the Netherlands 1745

Pen and ink with watercolour over pencil on tracing paper, 51.6 × 89.1 cm
Scale approx. 1 : 110,000
RCIN 729062

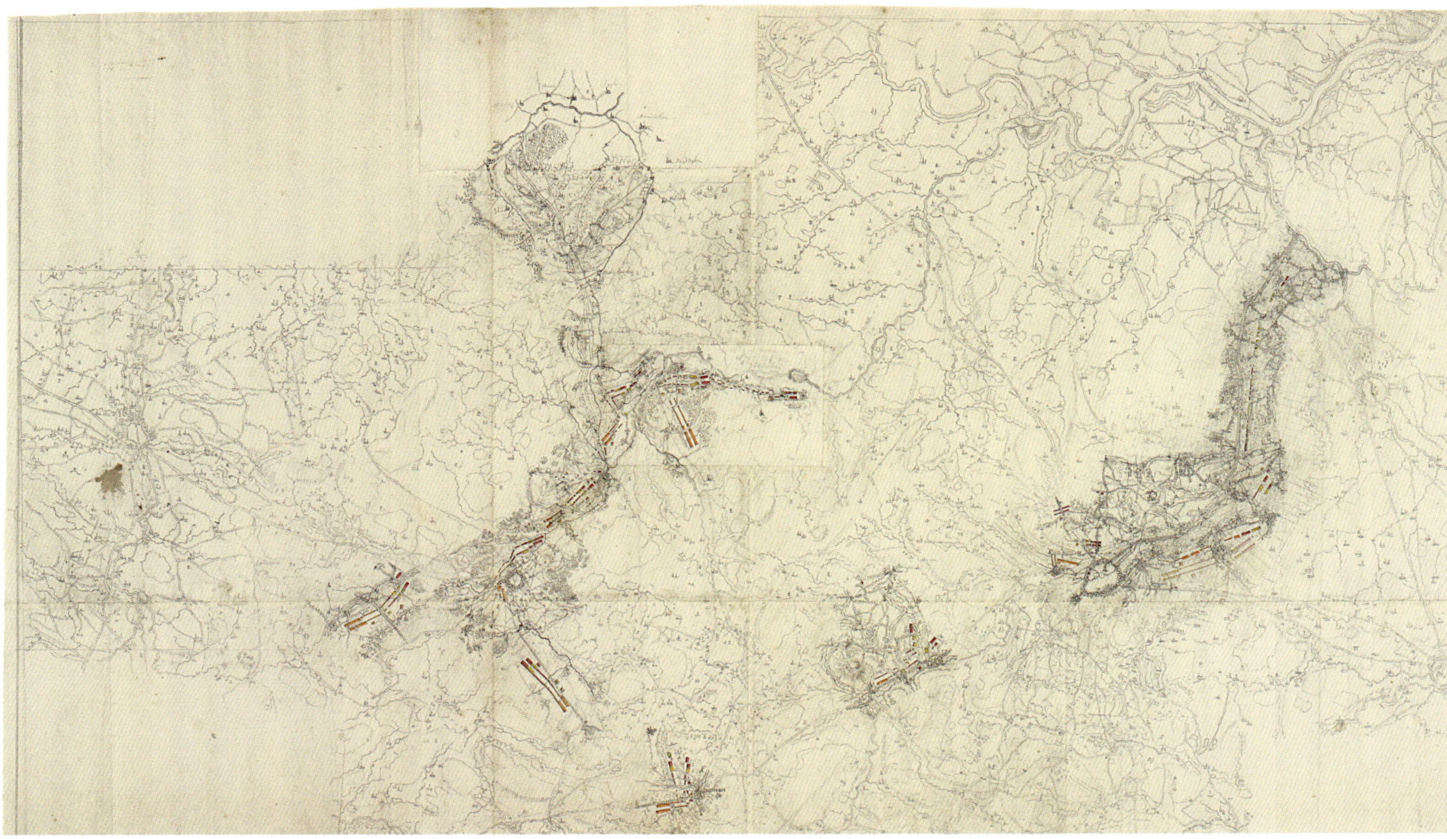

PROVENANCE King's Military Map Collection; probably prepared for William Augustus, Duke of Cumberland

LITERATURE Hodson forthcoming

This delicate drawing is based on a tracing taken from an earlier printed map of Brabant. It was made by Schultz (whose first name is not know), engineer to the Duke of Cumberland, who was with the Duke in 1745 (see also no. 46). Schultz worked up his tracing to give detail to the area in which the Duke and his troops were camped. Roads, woodland and towns are inked in, while the positions of the camps are given in colour.

The map shows camps placed just outside towns and villages for the comfort and hygiene of the personnel. An early commentator on the Continental campaigns of the mid 1740s noted that British troops were 'cantoned in the adjacent country, where they might lie comfortably, suffer nothing from the foulness of the air, nor from the nauseous stench that might be occasioned from a multitude; or, in other words, care was taken to preserve them from distempers, occasioned by contagion and infection .... The clean were separated from the unclean, and all were properly encamped'.[51] KH

49

THOMAS SANDBY (1721–1798)

A British Camp 1748

Pen and ink with watercolour over pencil,
24.5 × 132.0 cm
RCIN 914728

PROVENANCE Perhaps acquired by George IV; certainly Royal Collection by 1892[52]

LITERATURE Oppé 1947, no. 156

Thomas Sandby, who was employed as draughtsman to the Duke in 1746, was with Cumberland in Flanders in 1747–8, and made a number of meticulous drawings of the army camps, among them this watercolour. The army was based at Eindhoven on 5 July 1748, when Sandby signed and dated this work.

Cumberland ran his camps according to strict rules: sale of issued property and food was forbidden, as were gambling and women.[53] However, drinking appears to have been rife, staving off fear, boredom and homesickness. A witness to the British army in Flanders in 1744 noted 'the Recruits reeling about continually drunk with Gin brandy &c that they got at Bruges'.[54] KH

50

FRANÇOIS DE HANCKO (ACTIVE 1741–7)

Plan of the Battle of Fontenoy 1745

Pen and ink with watercolour over pencil, some outlines pricked for transfer, 54.5 × 29.3 cm
Scale approx. 1 : 20,000
RCIN 729094

PROVENANCE King's Military Map Collection; probably acquired by William Augustus, Duke of Cumberland

LITERATURE Hodson forthcoming

As Commander of the Pragmatic Army, the twenty-four-year-old Cumberland needed to regain the key town of Tournai, which had been besieged by the French forces under the Marshal de Saxe. The two armies met just outside the village of Fontenoy on 11 May 1745, on a site chosen by Saxe for its defensive strength. The French army was ranged across the top of a ridge, between redoubts placed in the villages of Antoine (on the banks of the Scheldt) and Fontenoy and in the forest of Barry. The Pragmatic Army was divided into two groups: the Dutch contingent fired on Fontenoy and the French troops from the left, while the British and Hanoverians, headed by Ligonier (see no. 39) advanced on the French army ranged across the ridge between Fontenoy and the Barry forest. To do so they were forced to advance up the slope, at the mercy of cannon fire from the French army in its advantageous position. Although the Pragmatic troops reached the top of the incline, they were pushed back by the fierce fighting and Cumberland was forced to retreat. After the battle, Ligonier wrote somewhat defensively to the Secretary of State, Lord Harrington, 'It was not a Rash measure, the Rising [sic] if possible [of] the Siege of Tournay was thought of such consequence that tho' the enemy was posted and much Superior in numbers, It was by His Royal Highness, the Marshall, as well as Prince Waldeck [the Dutch

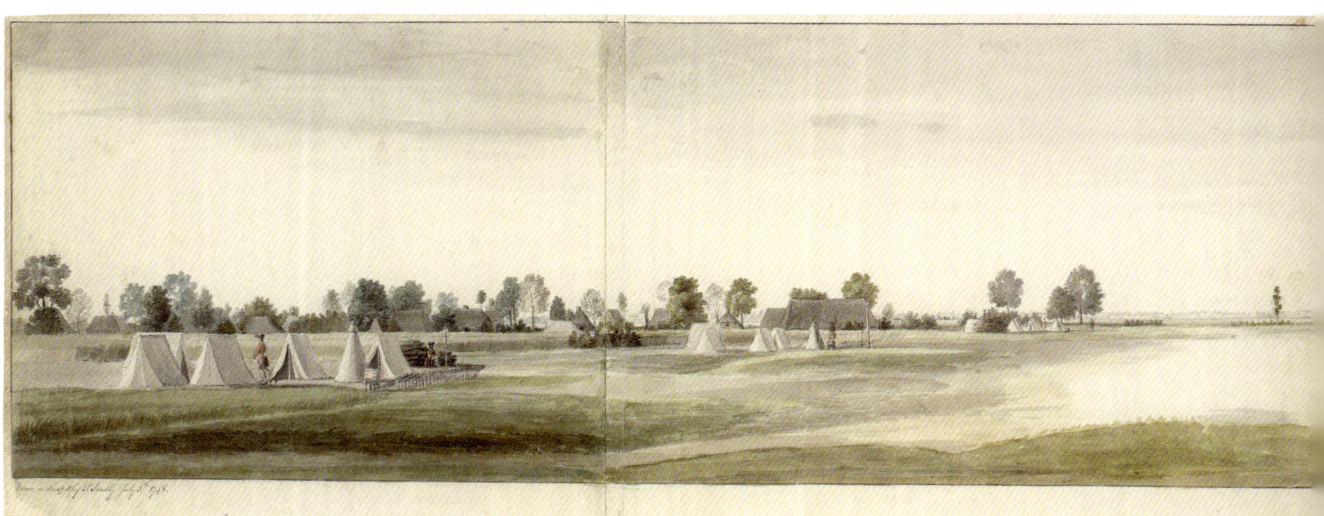

commander], resolved to Attempt the Relief'.[55] Despite the defeat Cumberland and Ligonier were both praised for their bravery during the battle.

This map, by François de Hancko, a German engineer in British service, shows the English in red, the Hanoverians in yellow, the Dutch in orange, the Austrians in green and the French in blue. Although a clear and detailed depiction of the progress of the fighting, it has no contours and does not therefore record the elevation of the ridge which gave the French their advantage. The positions of the French and British troops have been pricked with a pin to transfer them either from or to another sheet of paper. KH

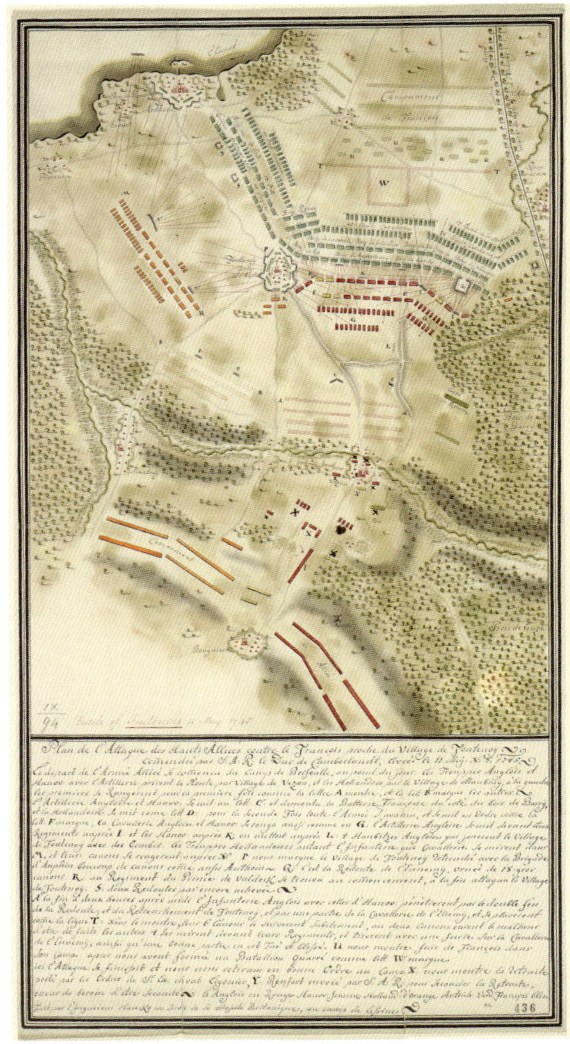

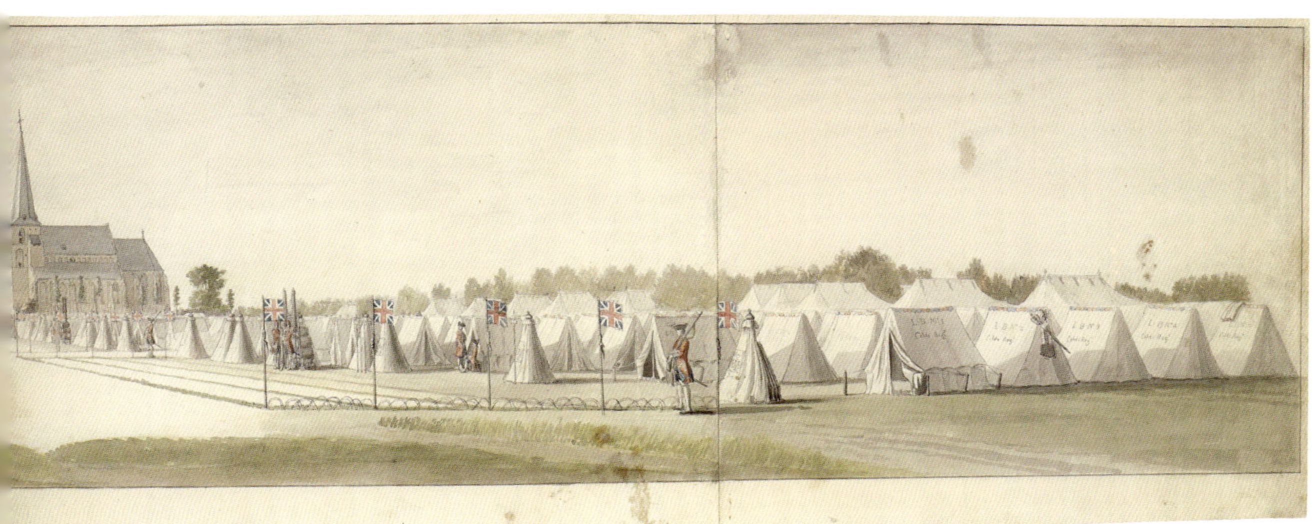

51

SCHULTZ (D. 1749)

A Circular View of the Horizon from the Steeple of the Church of DIEGHEM, with the Situation of the INCAMPMENTS of the Army of the ALLIES, Commanded by His Royal Highness the DUKE of CUMBERLAND. From the 14th July to the 2d of August, 1745, N.S. (The Head-Quarters at Dieghem & Saventhem) 1745

Pen and ink, diameter 27.0 cm
RCIN 729140

PROVENANCE King's Military Map Collection; probably made for William Augustus, Duke of Cumberland

LITERATURE *Flight and the Artistic Imagination* 2012, p. 43; Hodson forthcoming

After the victory at Fontenoy (no. 50), the French army worked its way north towards the port of Ostend, taking Tournai (which was surrendered by the allies on 9 June), Oudenarde and Ghent *en route*. Cumberland and his army were forced back to the east and ran the risk of being cut off from ports from which they could embark for Britain. The *Westminster Journal* noted that 'even *Hanover* and *Bremen* may be at last of some use to *England*, if it be only a way to bring home our troops'.[56]

This drawing records the position of Cumberland's troops from 14 July until 2 August, when they were based at Dieghem and Zaventem, just outside Brussels. At some point during this stay, Schultz, one of Cumberland's military draughtsmen, climbed the crossing tower of Dieghem church to survey the land around. One of the drawings he produced was this meticulous fish-eye panorama, including the church spire of Malines (Mechelen), the horizon and the allied encampments ranged along the bottom and top right of the circle. KH

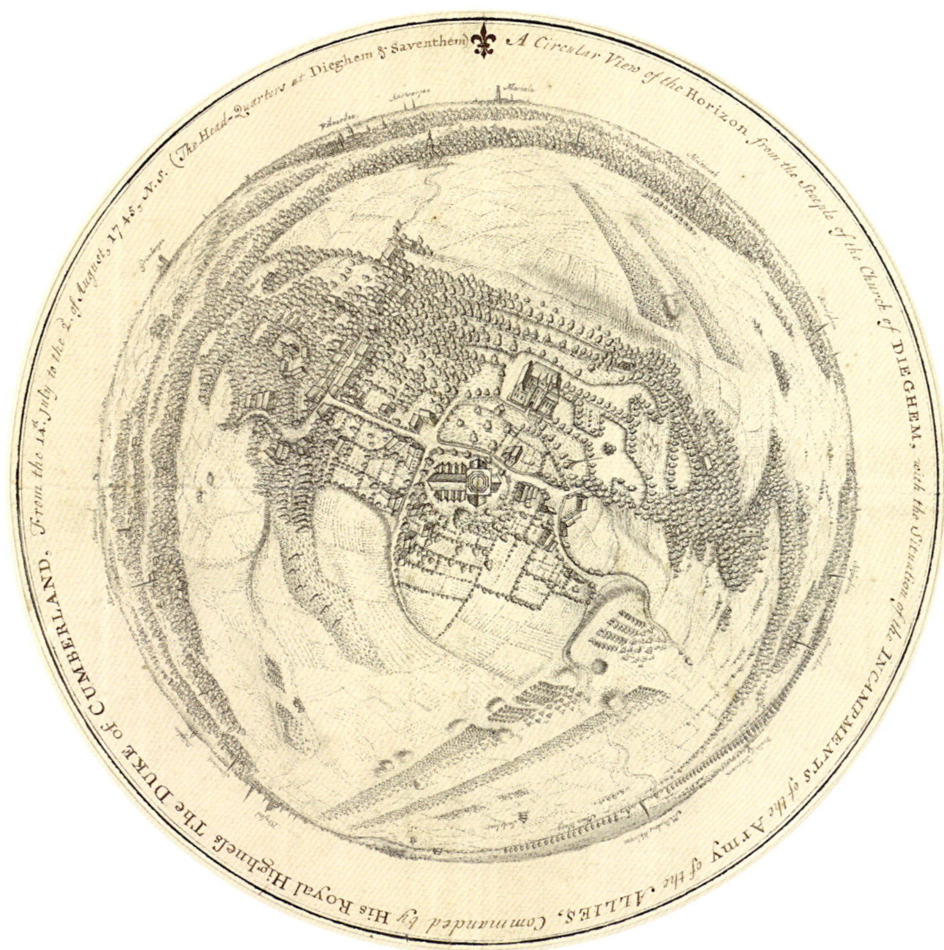

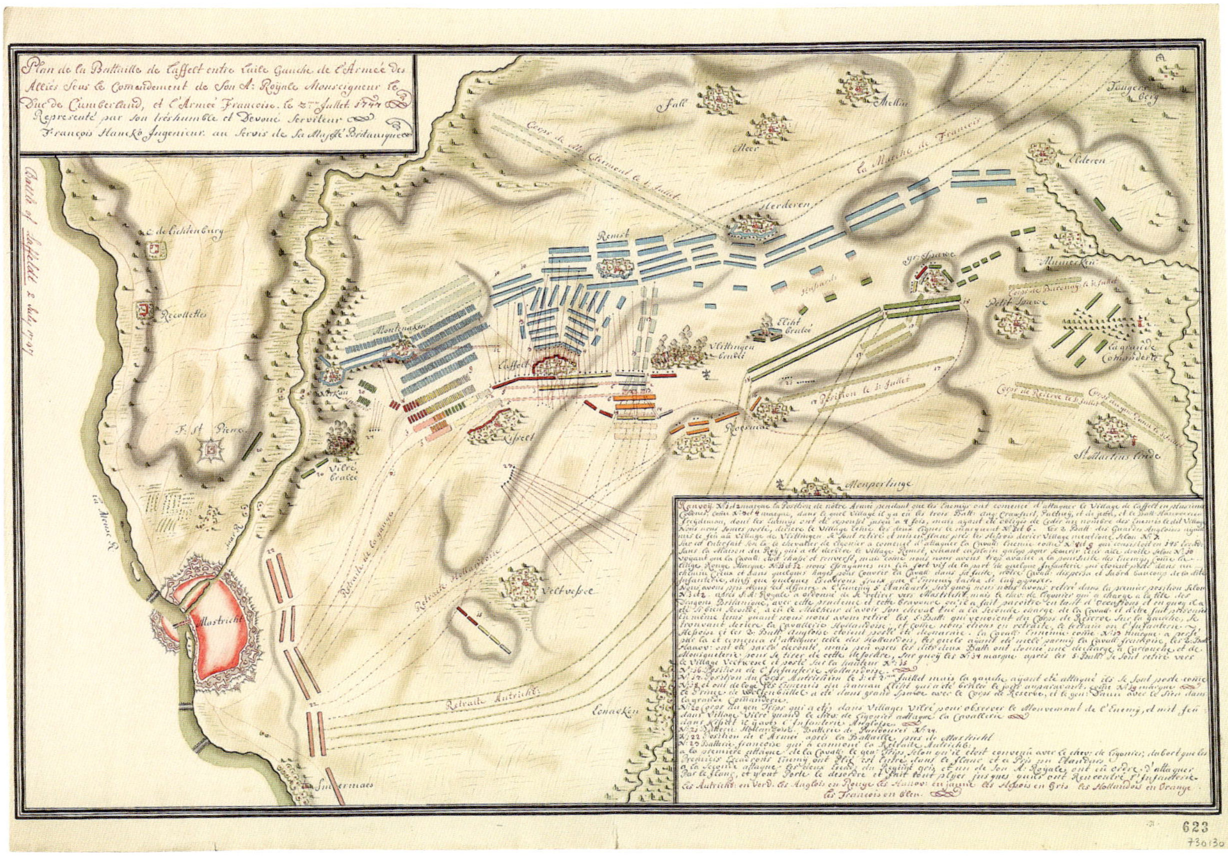

52

FRANÇOIS DE HANCKO (ACTIVE 1741–7)

Plan of the Battle of Laffeldt 1747

Pen and ink with watercolour over pencil, 36.4 × 53.1 cm
Scale 1 : 32,036 approx.
RCIN 730130

PROVENANCE King's Military Map Collection; probably acquired by William Augustus, Duke of Cumberland

LITERATURE Hodson forthcoming

On 2 July 1747, the Pragmatic Army met French forces under the Marshal de Saxe at the small village of Laffeldt. Cumberland's aim was to stop the French taking Maastricht, a strategic objective in France's attempts to invade Dutch territory. The French force was the larger and Saxe again proved to be Cumberland's strategic superior, attacking the allies with the full force of his troops. In Horace Walpole's assessment the duke 'behaved bravely as usual; but his prowess is so well established, that it grows time for him to exert other qualities of a general'.[57] The hero of the battle was Ligonier (no. 39), who launched a celebrated series of cavalry charges to protect the allied infantry, saving many lives, but resulting in his own capture. As a high-profile Huguenot fighting for the British, Ligonier risked execution for treason, but was spared by Louis XV.[58]

Hancko's meticulous map, which is oriented with south-west at the top, traces the course of the battle. Cumberland had attempted to block the French by setting fire to villages in their path – a fateful decision, as he was removing his own options for defensive positions: Hancko here shows the settlements burning amidst the fighting. After the defeat, the allied army retreated towards Maastricht, their post-engagement position marked '22' on Hancko's map. Cumberland's repeated attempts to preserve the city ended in failure: it was taken by the French in May 1748. KH

53

GEORGE VERTUE (1684–1756)

A Plan and Elevation of the Royal Fire-Works to be performed in St. James's Park, April the 27th, 1749, on Account of the General Peace signed at Aix la Chapelle, Octr 7 MDCCXLVIII 1749

Etching and engraving, 42.6 × 57.2 cm
RCIN 750427

LITERATURE Boorsch 2000, p. 34; *Handel* 1985, no. 199; Alexander 2008, no. 946

The Peace of Aix-la-Chapelle was concluded in October 1748 between France and Britain and signalled an end to hostilities between the two countries. By the terms of the treaty, Britain returned the key port and fortress of Louisburg (captured by the British in 1745) to the French in return for a cessation of French hostilities in Flanders. The loss of a strategic stronghold in North America was a small price to pay to prevent a French invasion and end a protracted war. Henry Pelham described the agreement as 'almost a miraculous deliverance for this country', and there was widespread rejoicing.[59]

The celebratory display of fireworks was overseen by the Board of Ordnance and supervised by Charles Frederick, 'Comptroller of His Majesty's Laboratory at Woolwich'. The display was designed by Giovanni Niccolò Servandoni, a respected architect and stage designer who had worked in Rome and Paris, and had undertaken projects in London for Frederick, Prince of Wales (fig. 25). Music was composed for the occasion by Handel and rehearsals were undertaken at Vauxhall Gardens, where the entrepreneur Jonathan Tyers had the equipment necessary for such an event.[60] George II was reportedly less enthusiastic and it was noted at court that he did not like fireworks.[61]

Vertue's engraving was commissioned by the Board of Ordnance, and was intended to be part of a set of official views marking the occasion. But the appearance of rival prints forced the project to be revised, and only this 'fine plate' (in Vertue's own words) was published. The fireworks, too, did not go according to plan: the right-hand wing of the temporary structure burned down in the middle of the performance, killing two people and prompting Servandoni to attack the Duke of Montagu with a sword. KH

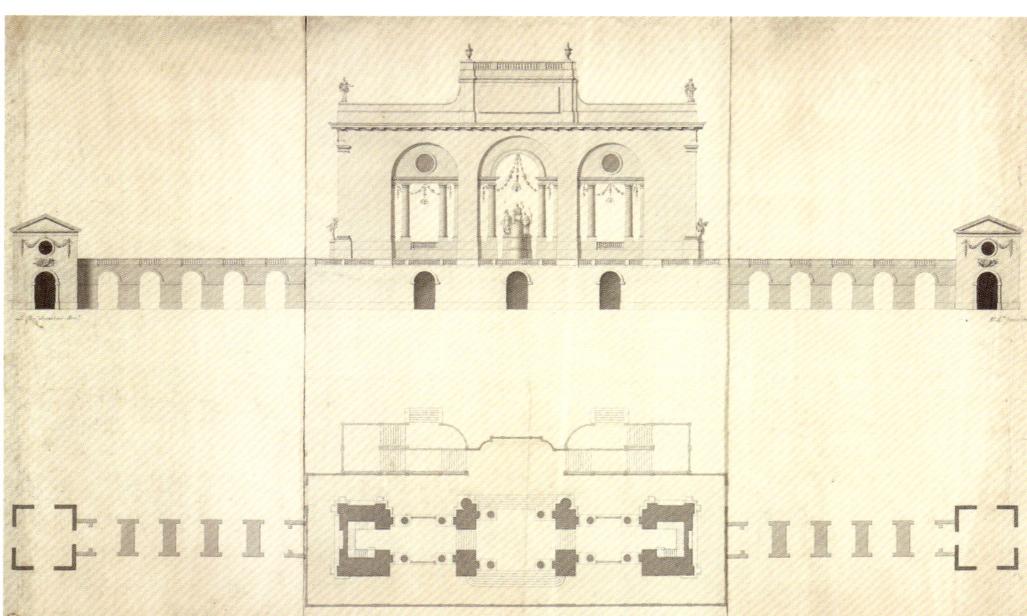

FIG. 25
William Jones after Giovanni Niccolò Servandoni
Plan and elevation of the structure designed for the Royal Firework display, 1749
Pen and ink and wash
RCIN 918982

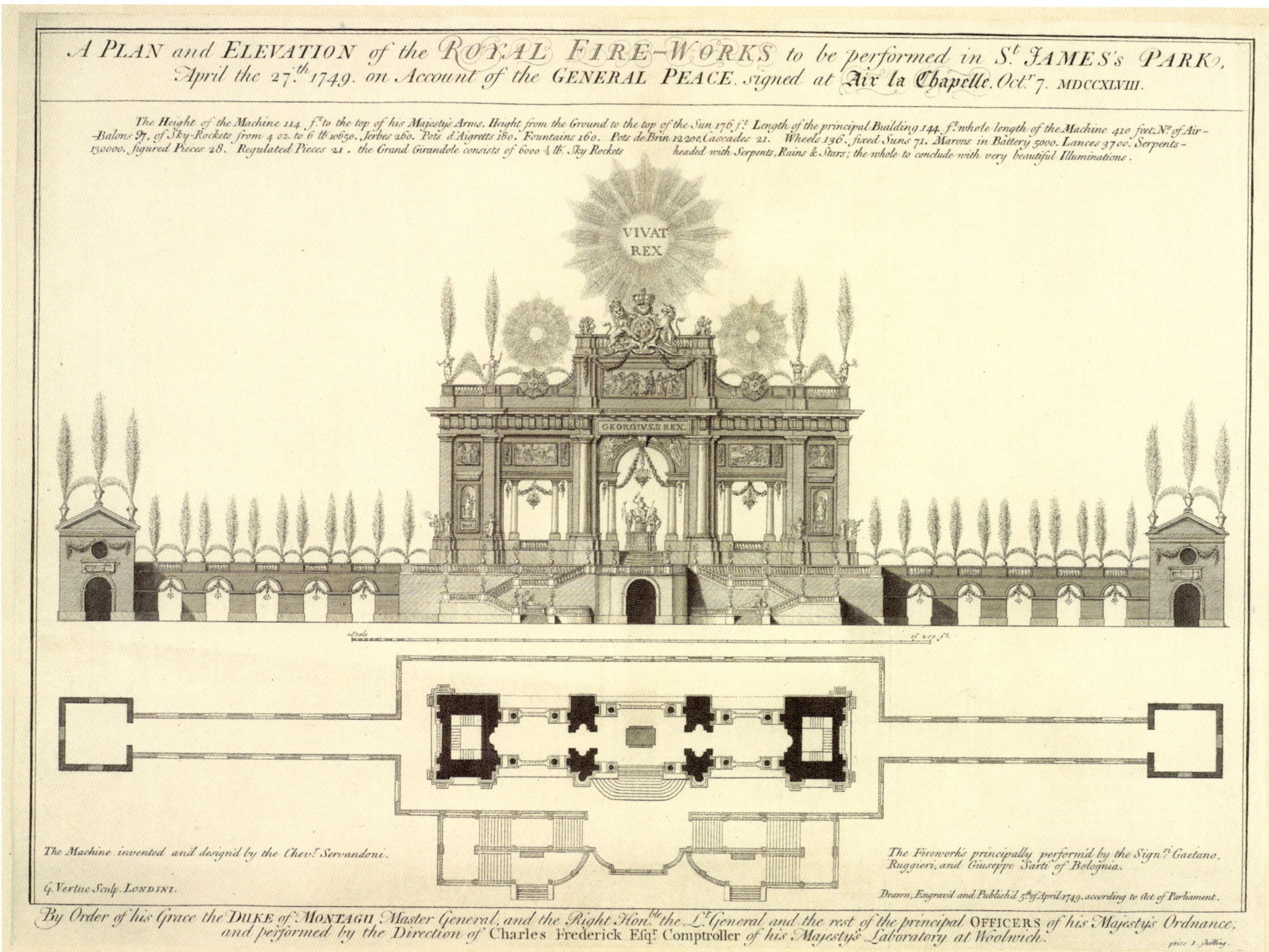
A PLAN and ELEVATION of the ROYAL FIRE-WORKS to be performed in St. JAMES's PARK,
April the 27th 1749. on Account of the GENERAL PEACE. signed at Aix la Chapelle. Octr. 7. MDCCXLVIII.
The Height of the Machine 114 ft. to the top of his Majesty's Arms. Height from the Ground to the top of the Sun 176 ft. Length of the principal Building 144 ft. whole length of the Machine 410 feet. No. of Air-Balons 87, of Sky-Rockets from 4 oz. to 6 lb 10650. Jerbes 260. Pots d'Aigretts 180. Fountains 160. Pots de Brin 12200. Cascades 21. Wheels 136. fixed Suns 71. Marons in Battery 5000. Lances 3700. Serpents 130000. figured Pieces 28. Regulated Pieces 21. the Grand Girandole consists of 6000 ½ lb. Sky Rockets headed with Serpents, Rains & Stars; the whole to conclude with very beautiful Illuminations.
VIVAT
REX
GEORGIVS.II.REX.
The Machine invented and design'd by the Chevr. Servandoni.
G. Vertue Sculp. LONDINI.
The Fireworks principally perform'd by the Signri. Gaetano Ruggieri, and Giuseppe Sarti of Bolognia.
Drawn, Engrav'd and Publish'd 5th of April 1749. according to Act of Parliament.
By Order of his Grace the DUKE of MONTAGU Master General, and the Right Honble. the Lt. General and the rest of the principal OFFICERS of his Majesty's Ordnance;
and performed by the Direction of Charles Frederick Esqr. Comptroller of his Majesty's Laboratory at Woolwich.
price 1 shilling.

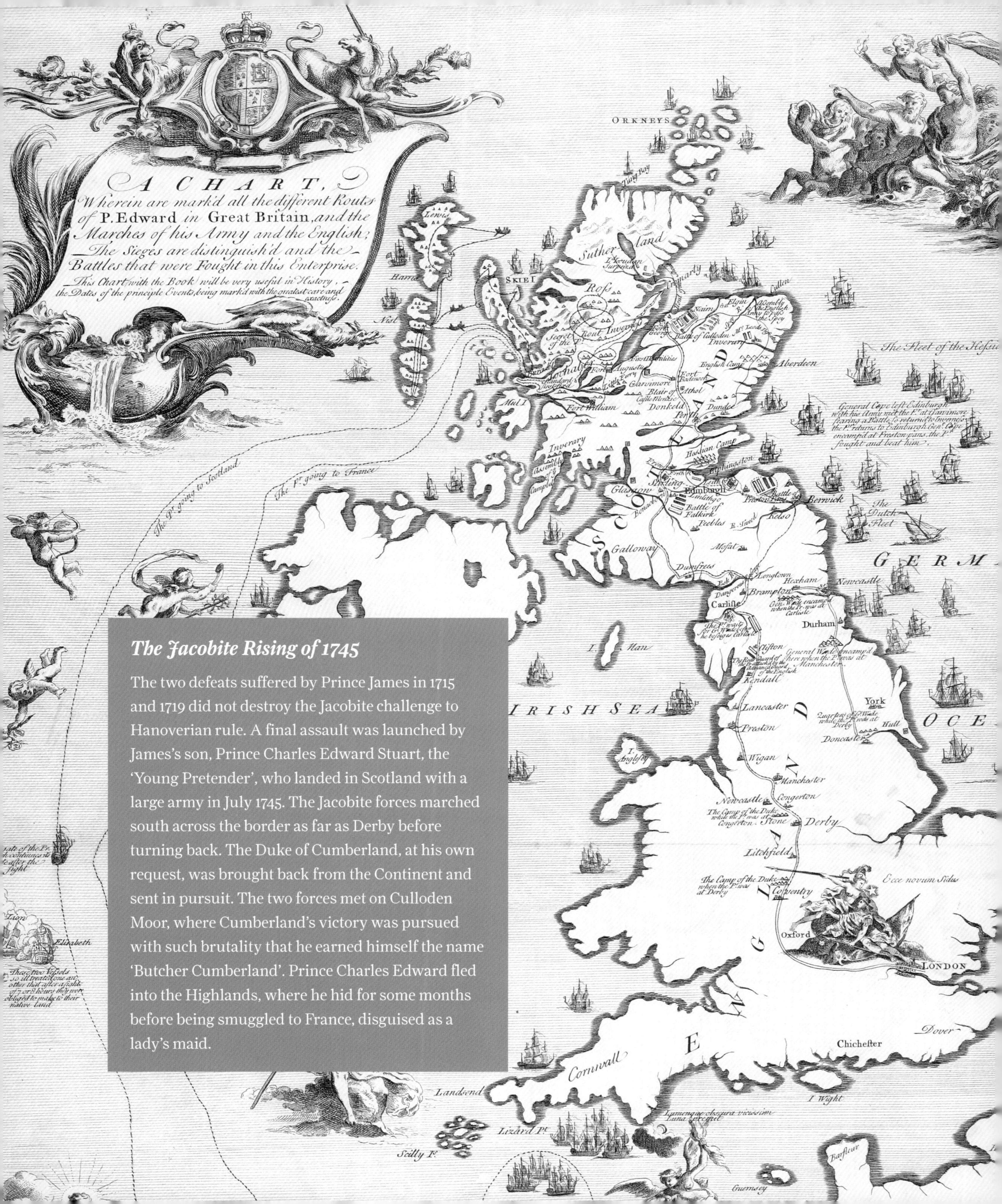

The Jacobite Rising of 1745

The two defeats suffered by Prince James in 1715 and 1719 did not destroy the Jacobite challenge to Hanoverian rule. A final assault was launched by James's son, Prince Charles Edward Stuart, the 'Young Pretender', who landed in Scotland with a large army in July 1745. The Jacobite forces marched south across the border as far as Derby before turning back. The Duke of Cumberland, at his own request, was brought back from the Continent and sent in pursuit. The two forces met on Culloden Moor, where Cumberland's victory was pursued with such brutality that he earned himself the name 'Butcher Cumberland'. Prince Charles Edward fled into the Highlands, where he hid for some months before being smuggled to France, disguised as a lady's maid.

54

JEAN DAULLÉ (1703–1763) AND JEAN GEORGES WILLE (1715–1808) AFTER GIORGIO DOMENICO DUPRÀ (1689–1770)

Prince Charles Edward Stuart (1720–1788) 1740

Etching and engraving,
42.5 × 29.6 cm (plate); 32.0 × 23.0 cm (sheet)
RCIN 603614

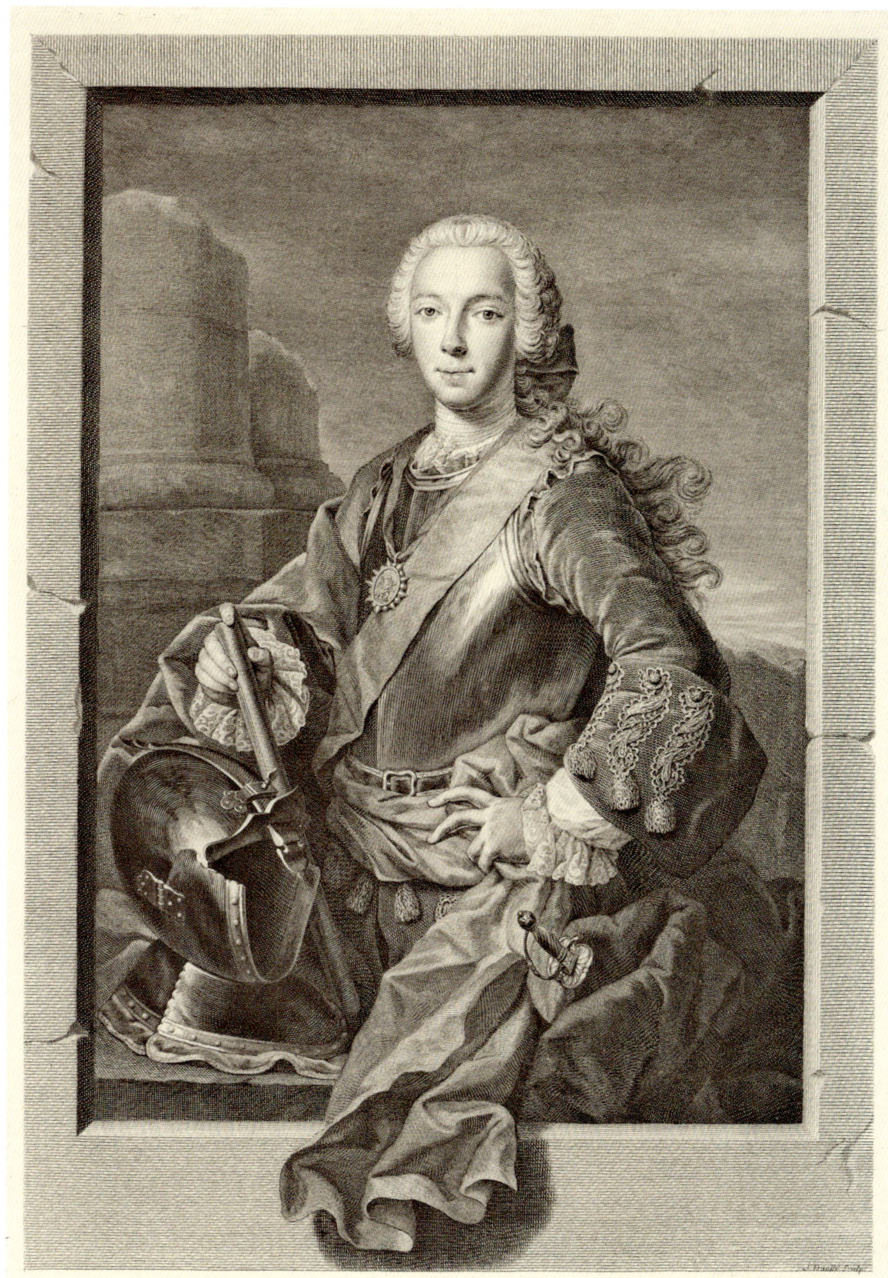

LITERATURE Sharp 1996, no. 209; *King over the Water* 2001, p. 80; Nicholson 2002, p. 49

This elegant image of Prince Charles Edward Stuart was the official print made after Domenico Duprà's 1740 portrait of the 'Young Pretender'. Duprà's portrait shows the Prince echoing the pose of his father in Alexis-Simon Belle's painting of 1712 (see no. 42) with one hand on his hip and the other resting on a helmet. Daullé's print, which was a pair with one of Charles's brother Prince Henry, was published in Paris, but intended for circulation among Jacobite supporters in Britain.[62] Daullé was royal engraver to Louis XV and produced numerous high-quality portrait engravings. He was responsible for the Prince's head, while his colleague Wille engraved the rest of the plate.[63] KH

55

WILLIAM EYRES (ACTIVE 1744–64)

Order of Battle at Prestonpans 1745

Pen and ink with watercolour, 37.2 × 43.5 cm
RCIN 729153

PROVENANCE King's Military Map Collection; probably acquired by William Augustus, Duke of Cumberland

LITERATURE Hodson forthcoming

On 21 September 1745, the Jacobite and government armies met just outside the village of Prestonpans, nine miles to the east of Edinburgh. General Sir John Cope, the commander of the government forces, had chosen the site for the engagement, which one of his aides de camp described as 'about an English Mile Square, where Both Dragoons and Foot Could Act; and very well Secur'd on all Sides to prevent any Surprize'.[64] Cope's position, shielded by ditches, marshy land, and the seashore, gave him a firm advantage: James Johnstone, aide de camp to the Jacobite commander Lord George Murray, noted that it 'was chosen with a great deal of skill. The more we examined it, the more we were convinced of the impossibility of attacking it; and we were all thrown into consternation, and at quite a loss what course to take'.[65]

This order of battle was drawn up by the engineer William Eyres, who contrasts the actual order of the government troops at the top with a second formation which, he notes, was 'intended, but not executed for want of gunners'. The explanation is given in the right-hand column that '[t]he Rebel Army outflank'd the Kings'. Eyres also records the 'many Officers, and Country Gentlemen who were Spectators' at the battle, reminding us that such engagements were often fought in front of an audience, curious or anxious about its outcome. KH

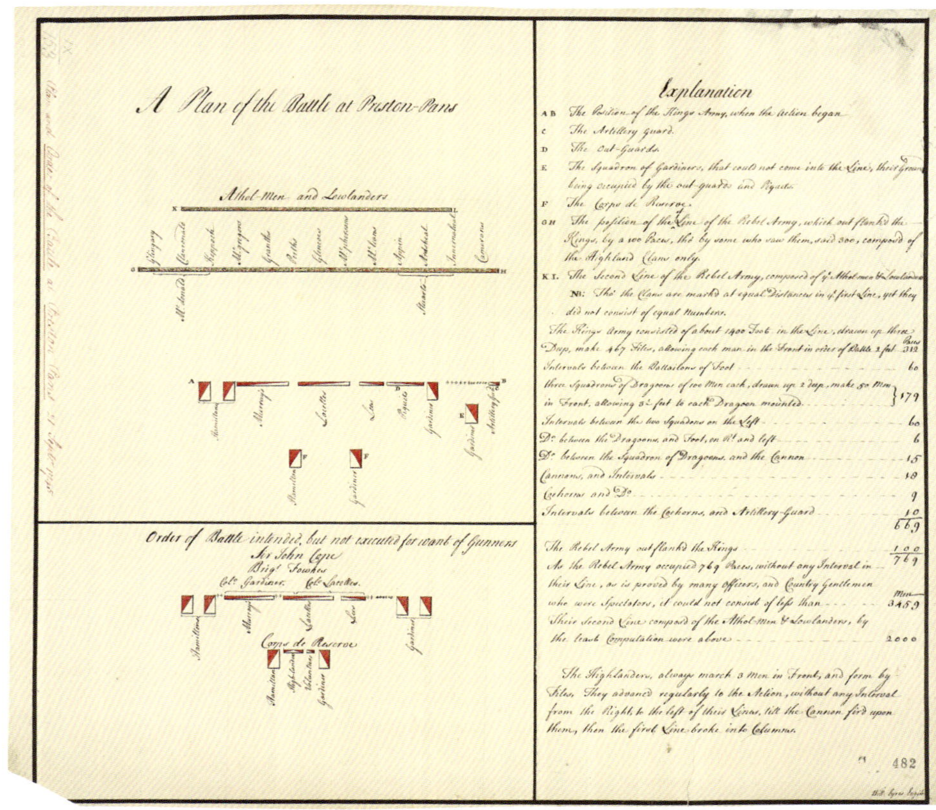

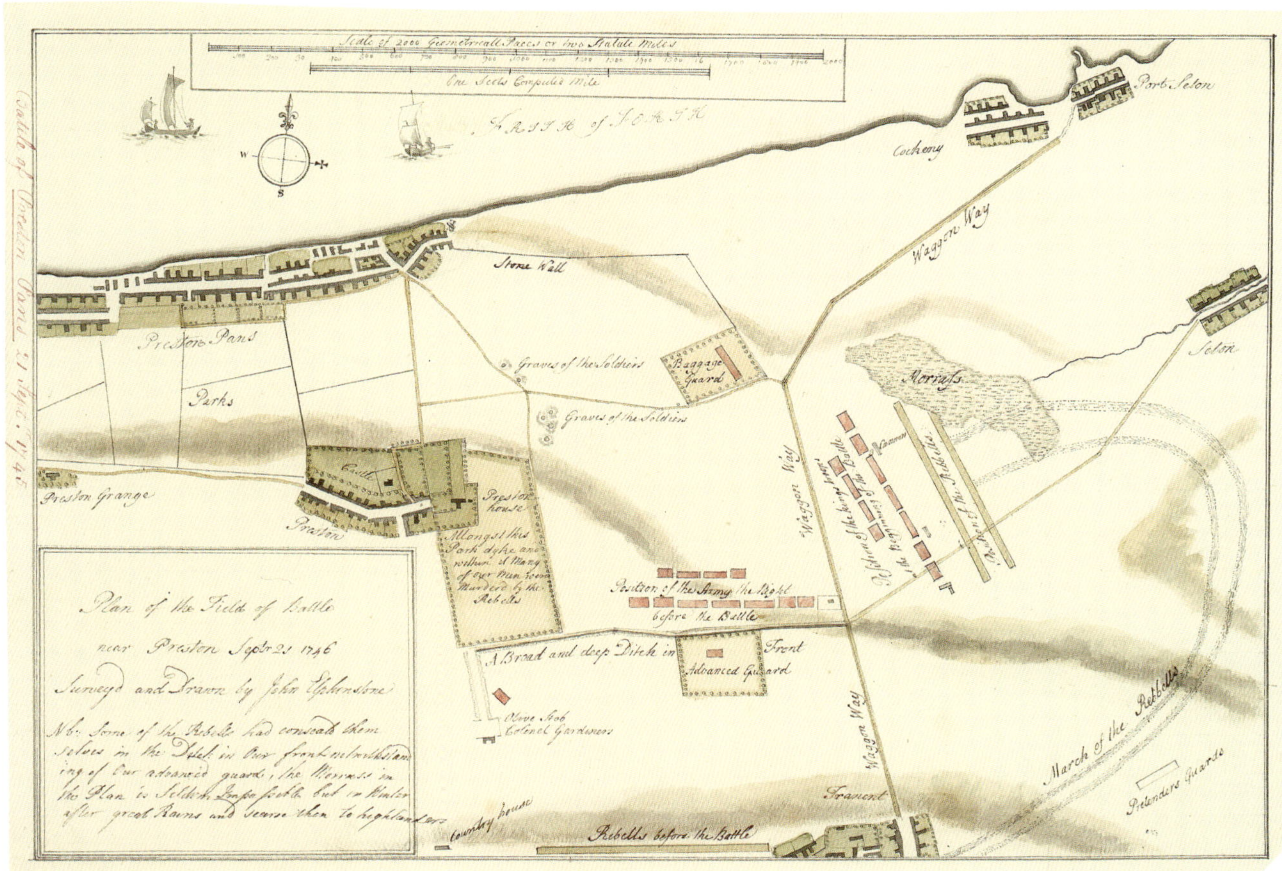

56

THE HON. JOHN ELPHINSTONE (1706–1753)

Plan of the Battle of Prestonpans 1745

Pen and ink with watercolour, 21.7 × 32.0 cm
Scale approx. 1 : 21,744
RCIN 729154

PROVENANCE King's Military Map Collection; probably acquired by William Augustus, Duke of Cumberland

LITERATURE Hodson forthcoming

Despite the favourable position of the its troops (see no. 55), the encounter at Prestonpans was a government debacle. The majority of those manning the government artillery, which had been intended to give cover to Cope's forces, fled as the Jacobite army charged. They took the gunpowder with them, meaning those who remained were unable to fire repeated rounds.[66] Other squadrons similarly failed to stand against the Jacobite charge, and Cope's army was forced to retreat to Berwick, across the border.

John Elphinstone was an engineer and cartographer, whose 1745 map of Scotland was the best source for its geography prior to the survey carried out under William Roy from 1747.[67] KH

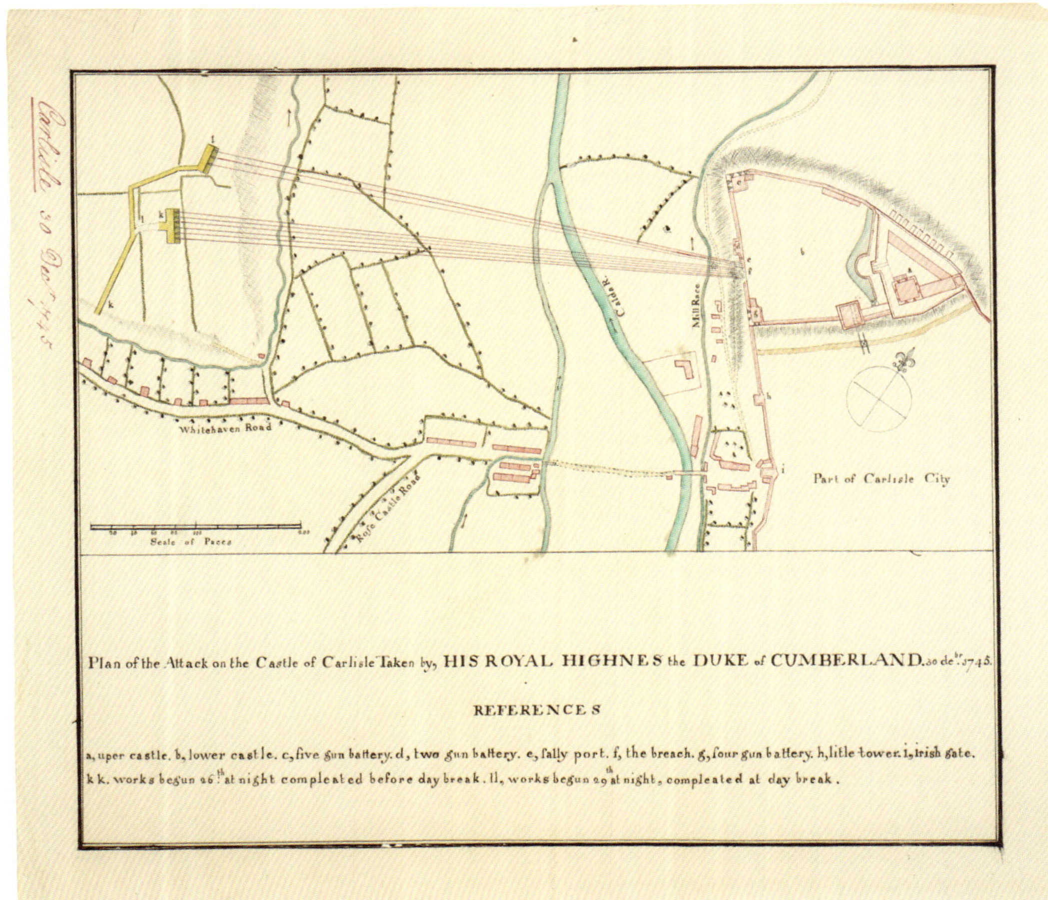

57

ANONYMOUS

Plan of the Attack on the Castle of Carlisle Taken by His Royal Highnes the Duke of Cumberland 1745

Pen and ink with watercolour, 31.4 × 36.6 cm
Scale approx. 1 : 2,087
RCIN 729160

PROVENANCE King's Military Map Collection; probably acquired by William Augustus, Duke of Cumberland

LITERATURE Hodson forthcoming

After the unexpected victory of the Jacobites at Prestonpans, Prince Charles Edward marched further south, crossing the English border on 8 November. He took the city of Carlisle seven days later, the inhabitants surrendering to his forces after a brief siege.[68] A key site in the defence of north-west England, with a castle dating back to the eleventh century, Carlisle had symbolic as well as military significance, and royal forces rushed to retake the town, which had been left defended by a small Jacobite garrison. Capitulation to the government forces was quick and Michael Hughes, a volunteer for the Duke of Cumberland, noted, '*Carlile Castle* would soon have been demolisht; but his Royal Highness did not think it prudent to destroy a good Castle for so worthless an Enemy; and therefore said he would entertain them with a few Cohorns [a portable mortar], which put them into such a Hurry and Fright, that a white Rag was immediately hung up, and a Messenger came to his Royal Highness in order to capitulate: But the Duke sent them Word, That to any Articles of Capitulation they were not intitled, as being Rebels and Traytors to His Majesty's Crown and Dignity'.[69] This plan shows the Cohorns bombarding the fort, causing a breach in its defensive wall. KH

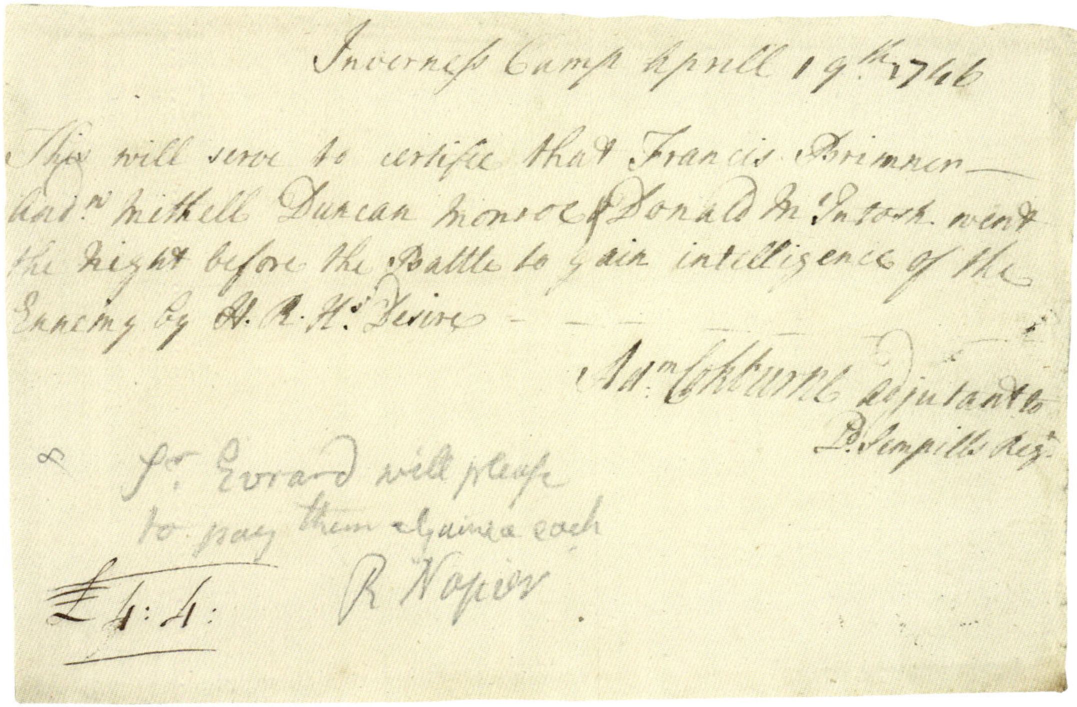
Inverness Camp Aprill 19th 1746

This will serve to certifie that Francis Brimner And^w Mitchell Duncan Monroe & Donald McIntosh went the Night before the Battle to gain intelligence of the Enemy by H.R.H.s Desire —

Ad^m Cokburne Adjutant to Ld Sempills Reg^t

Sr Evrard will please to pay them a Guinea each

£4:4: R Napier

58

Order for payment to spies 19 April 1746 (OS)

Manuscript, 9.5 × 14.5 cm
RA CP/MAIN/14/47

PROVENANCE Papers of William Augustus, Duke of Cumberland

Fear of espionage during the Jacobite rising was rife on both sides: a suspected Jacobite spy was hanged by Cumberland the night before the Battle of Culloden, although he won a reprieve and was brought down from the gallows alive.[70] But Cumberland also used spies, as is shown by this certificate, issued by Adam Cokburne, adjutant of Lord Sempill. Cokburne confirms that four men (Francis Brimner, Andrew Michell, Duncan Monroe and Donald McIntosh) had infiltrated the Jacobite camp in search of intelligence on the eve of Culloden. Payment was authorised by Robert Napier, Cumberland's Adjutant-General, and made by Sir Everard Fawkener, the Duke's personal secretary. KH

59

POSSIBLY IN THE HAND OF PRINCE WILLIAM AUGUSTUS, DUKE OF CUMBERLAND (1721–1765)

Draft order of battle at Culloden 1746

Pen and ink with some watercolour and pencil annotations, 37.5 × 30.5 cm
RCIN 730019

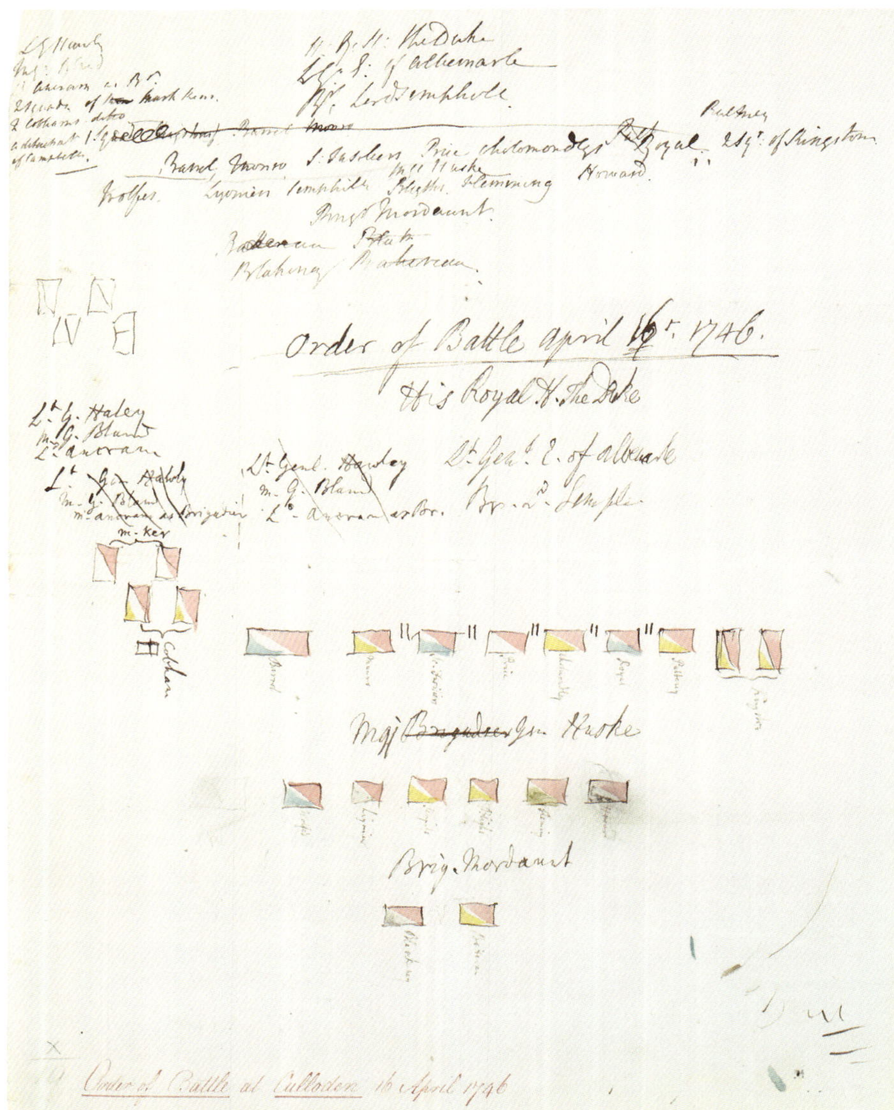

PROVENANCE King's Military Map Collection; previously owned by William Augustus, Duke of Cumberland

LITERATURE Hodson forthcoming

At the Battle of Culloden, the Duke of Cumberland was in command of an army of 6,400 foot and 2,400 mounted soldiers.[71] This rough draft shows him and his commanders adjusting these forces in the light of intelligence about the placement of the Jacobite troops. The colours of each section relate to the uniforms used: Ligonier's men, for example, wore red coats with buff facings while Barrell's men wore red coats with blue facings.

In contrast to Prince Charles Edward, who remained behind his front line (no. 60), Cumberland is here shown at the head of his troops along with the Earl of Albermarle and Lord Sempill. Also unlike the Prince, the Duke formed his front line of battalions interspersed with pairs of three-pounder cannon, which would do such damage to the Jacobite lines. Realising that more forces were required to the right of his lines, and nervous about movements undertaken by Lord George Murray, the Duke moved Pulteney's Regiment (13th Foot) forwards ('Pultney' can be seen inserted into the list at the top of the sheet of paper). This last-minute adjustment (so vividly recorded on this scrap of paper) testifies to the Duke's ability to adapt to his opponents' moves. KH

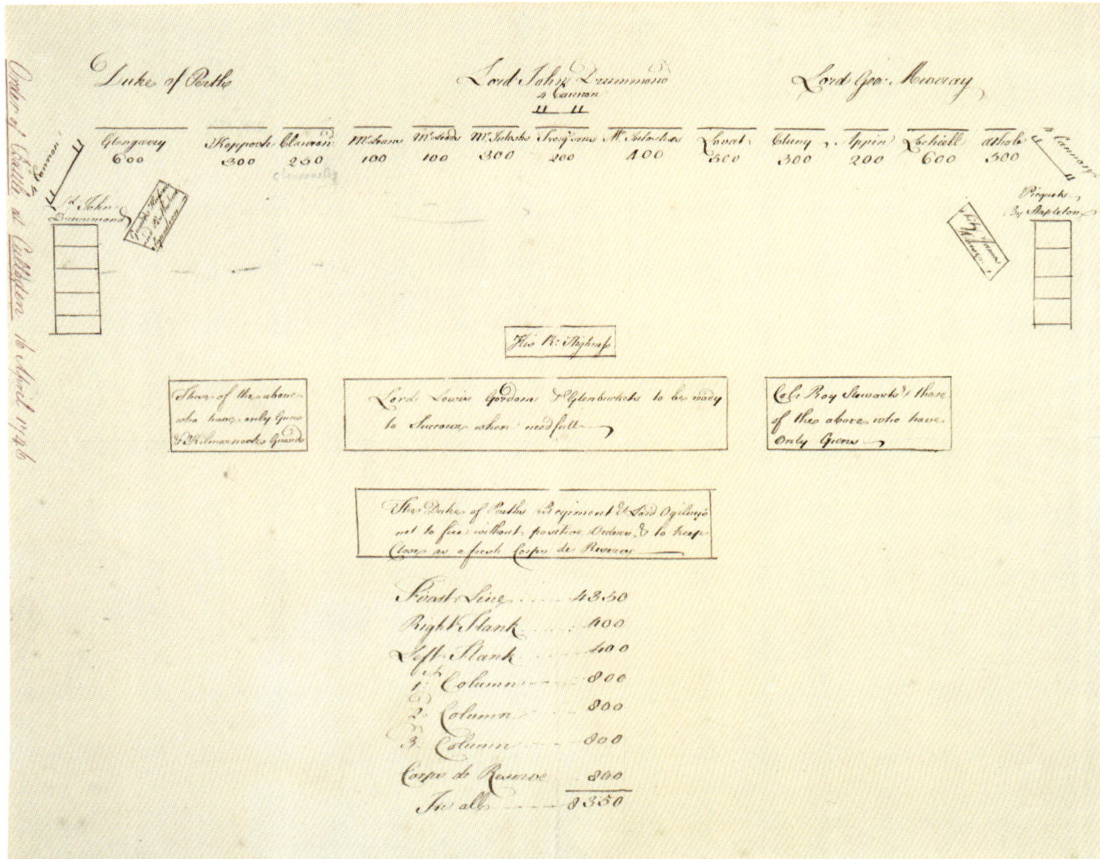

60

ATTRIBUTED TO THOMAS SANDBY (1721–1798)

Order of battle of the Jacobite forces at the Battle of Culloden 1746

Pen and ink with some annotations in pencil, 30.5 × 38.6 cm
RCIN 730021

PROVENANCE King's Military Map Collection; probably made for William Augustus, Duke of Cumberland

LITERATURE Hodson forthcoming

This order of battle shows the formation and strength of the Young Pretender's troops at Culloden. Princes Charles Edward chose to place 4,350 men in his front line as a tight formation, with four cannon each to left, right and centre. As Michael Hughes recalled, 'The Rebels had planted a Battery at the Side of a Stone Wall, but they soon left it; for our Cannon begun to play so very briskly upon them, and their lines were formed so thick and deep, that the Grapeshot made open Lanes quite through them, the Men dropping down by Wholesale'.[72]

The plan records not only the troop formations, but Prince Charles Edward's strategy, with certain regiments held back from the front line 'to succour when needfull'. A group were ordered 'not to fire without positive Orders, & to keep Close as a fresh Corps de Reserve'. The main hand may be that of Thomas Sandby, with pencil annotations by Schultz; both men worked for the Duke of Cumberland. KH

61

JAMES FARMER (1715–1773)

Two flintlock military pistols 1745

Walnut, steel, brass; length 50.0 cm; calibre: 1.42 cm
Marks: both engraved on the lock *FARMER 1745*; both marked on barrel and lock with proof marks of the Board of Ordnance; .1 marked on lock *XD / TI / 19* and *31* on barrel; .2 marked on lock *11 DRAGS* and *6/23* on brass escutcheon
RCIN 67008.1-2

PROVENANCE Supplied to the Board of Ordnance in 1745

These standard issue military pistols, which are similar but not an exact pair, were supplied to the Board of Ordnance in part by James Farmer, a Birmingham gun-maker who worked in London in the mid-century in partnership with his brother-in-law Samuel Galton. Typically for pistols of this type, each part was supplied separately and the parts were assembled at need. According to the engraved marks on the locks one of the two was supplied to the 10th Dragoons, the other to the 11th.

Neither regiment was known by these numbers until after 1751. In 1745 the 10th Dragoons were named after their commander, Field Marshall Richard Temple, 1st Viscount Cobham (1645–1749). At the outbreak of the 1745 rebellion, Cobham's Dragoons were serving in the War of Austrian Succession, under the command of the Duke of Cumberland, but as one of the few regiments of horse available they were despatched to Scotland to join the English forces. The 11th Dragoons were under the command of Lord Mark Kerr. The regiment had been formed in 1715 to fight at Prestonpans and had seen little action since, although one troop of the regiment had been involved in the Battle of Clifton Muir in 1745. In April 1746 they were pressed into action once more.

In drawing up his battle plans at Culloden, Cumberland selected the two regiments to protect the flanks of his front line: on the left he placed Kerr's Dragoons (the 11th), consisting of three squadrons, commanded by Lord Ancram, and on the right Cobham's Dragoons (the 10th), also consisting of three squadrons, under General Bland. However, Cumberland afterwards ordered the latter to the left, to aid in the intended attack upon the right flank of the Highlanders. The Jacobites had very little cavalry and their infantry charges were of little effect against the English lines. Kerr's Dragoons lost only three men in the battle. Cumberland's cavalry charged from both wings to crush the rebels in the middle, and were then commanded to pursue the defeated Jacobites and show 'no quarter'. The Dragoon regiments were involved in the subsequent putting down of isolated groups of rebels in the Highlands. KJ

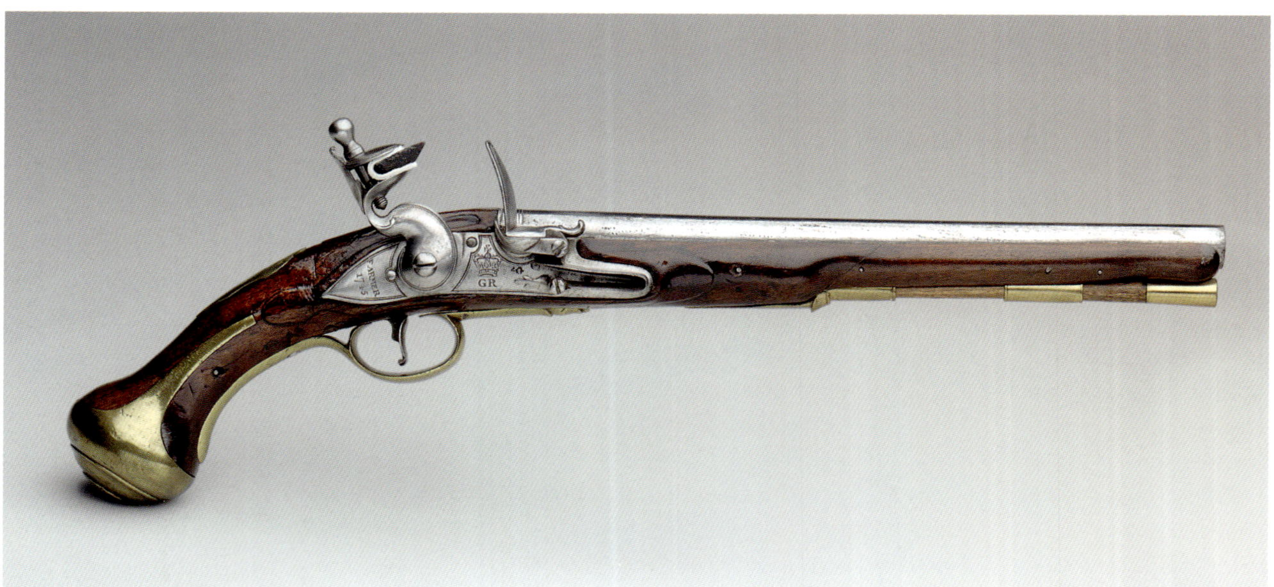

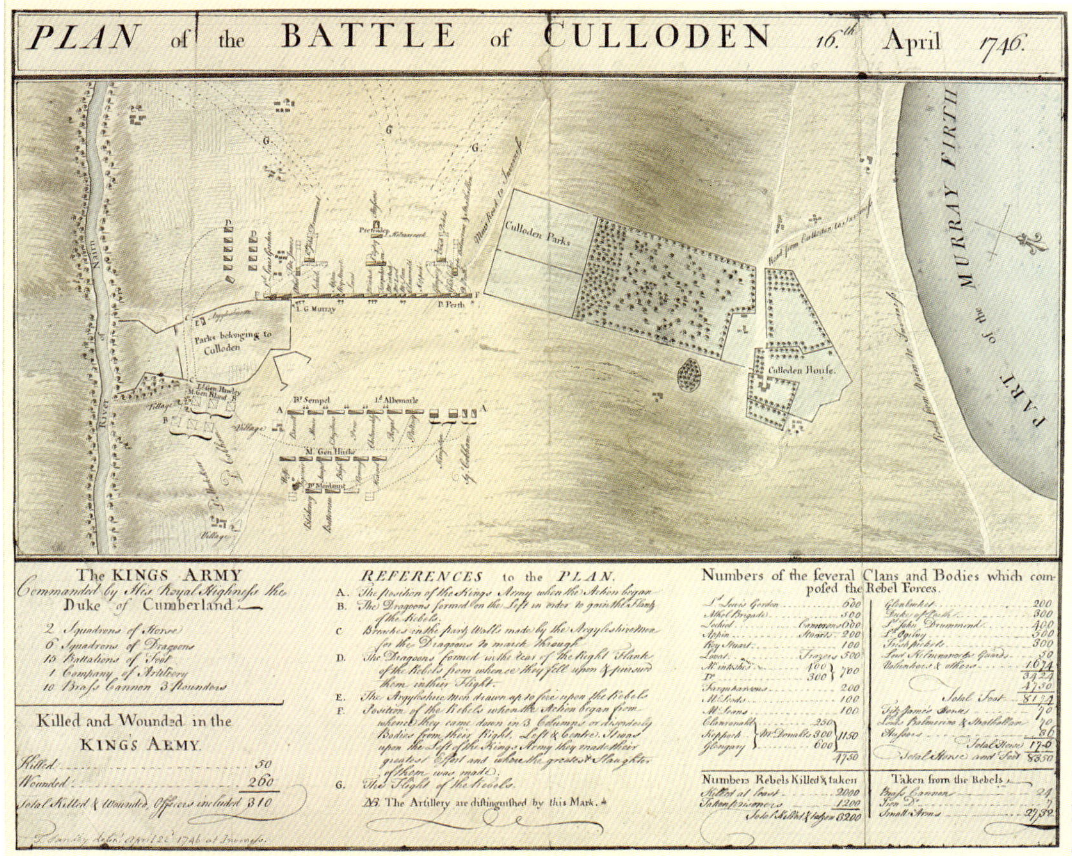

62

THOMAS SANDBY (1721–1798)

Plan of the Battle of Culloden 1746

Pen and ink with watercolour over pencil, 32.0 × 42.5 cm
Scale approx. 1 : 15,000
RCIN 917177

PROVENANCE King's Military Map Collection; probably made for William Augustus, Duke of Cumberland

LITERATURE Oppé 1947, no. 150; Pollard 2009b, pp. 34–35; Woosnam-Savage 2009, pp. 168–71; *Sandby* 2009–10, no. 4; Hodson forthcoming

This plan of the Battle of Culloden, made seven days after the engagement, shows the Jacobite forces ranged between the walls of the Culloden Park on the right and the Culwhiniac Parks on the left, which both provided protection, and restricted Jacobite movement. The government forces are ranged opposite, in the formation decided upon in the Duke of Cumberland's plan (no. 59), with the mounted regiments to the far left. Sandby also shows the vital action suggested by General Bland, and marked 'D' on the plan: the walls of the Culwhiniac Parks were breached and a brigade of government cavalry was thereby able to attack the enemy's right flank from behind.[73] The retreat routes of the Jacobite survivors are shown at the top of the plan and are marked 'G'. Other developments are not shown on the plan (perhaps in an attempt to keep it easy to read), but are described in the lettered references, which explains how the Jacobites 'came down in 3 Columns or disorderly Bodies from their Right, Left & Centres' and how the government cavalry 'fell upon & pursued' their defeated opponents.

Archaeological investigation of the battlefield site has shown that this drawing, probably made for Sandby's patron, the Duke of Cumberland, is highly accurate.[74] KH

63

THOMAS SANDBY (1721–1798)

Sketch of the field at the Battle of Culloden 1746

Pen and ink with watercolour over pencil, 29.4 × 53.2 cm
RCIN 914722

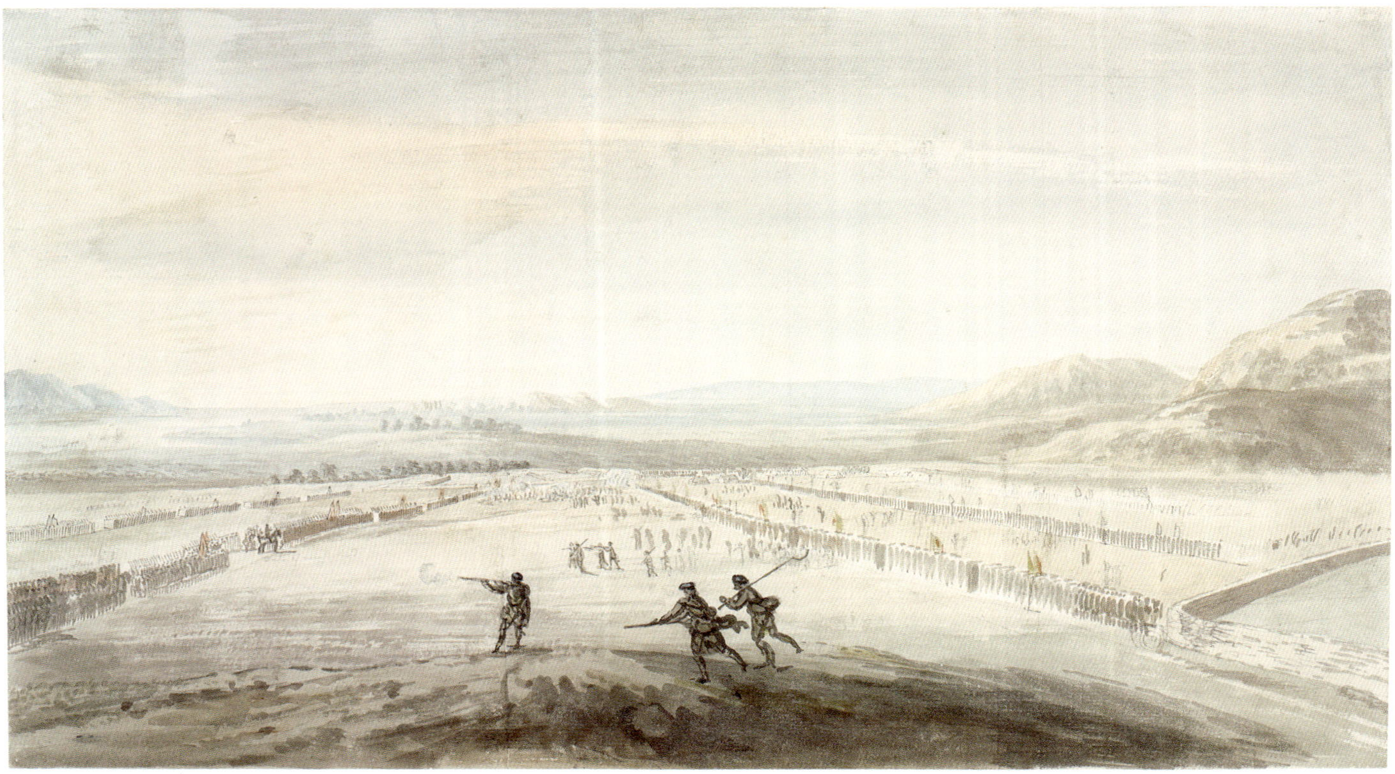

PROVENANCE Perhaps drawn for William Augustus, Duke of Cumberland

LITERATURE Oppé 1947, p. 151; *Royal Miscellany* 1990, no. 222; Woosnam-Savage 2009, pp. 171–2; *Sandby* 2009–10, no. 5; Hodson forthcoming

Sandby's watercolour of the view between the lines of troops, showing the charge of the Jacobites (from the right) gives a vivid impression of the battle. The Duke of Cumberland is shown mounted at the centre of his line of troops, facing the Jacobite advance. The walls of both enclosures can be seen and the mounted section in the left foreground has been named as 'Kingston's horse'.

The purpose of this elegant, but hurried, watercolour is unclear, and it may even be unfinished (labels written in pencil have not been erased or inked in). Although it claims to document the action at the battle, the topography is inconsistent, with the battle apparently viewed from the north and the landscape background, with the Murray Firth, from the south. KH

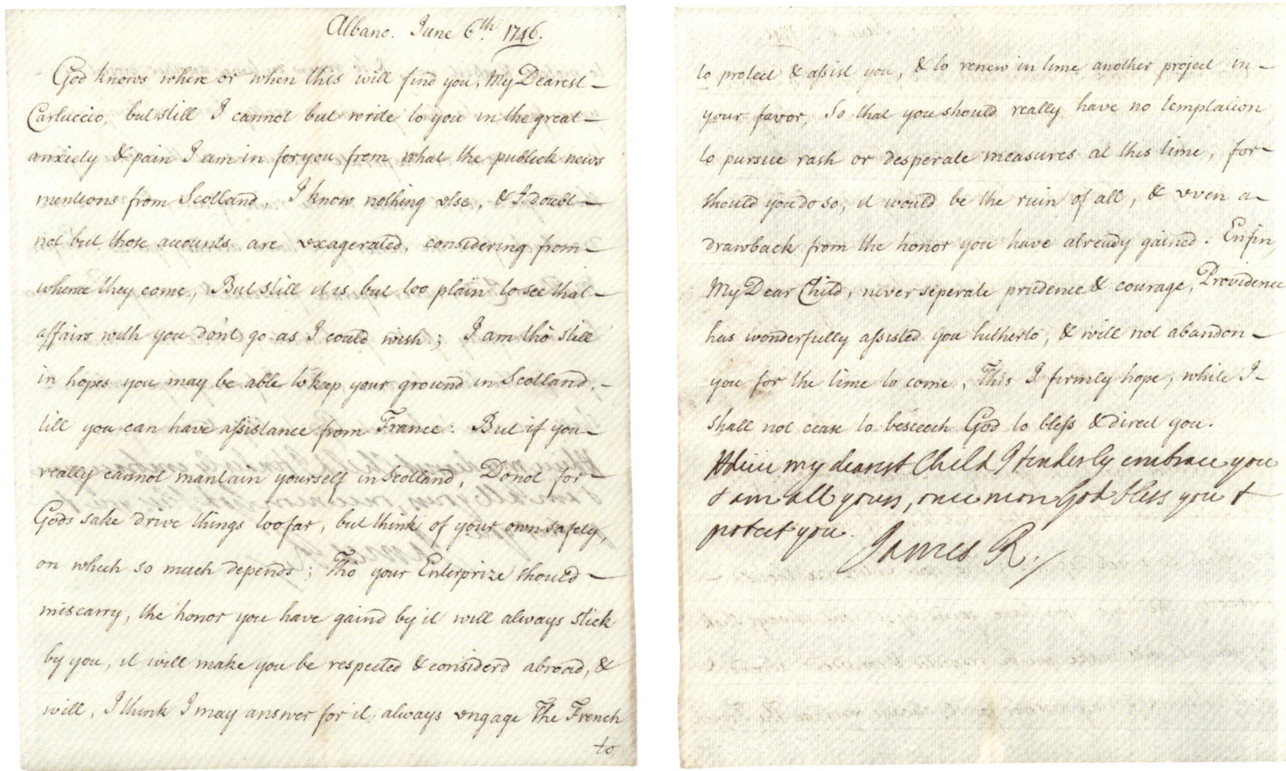
Albano. June 6th 1746.

God knows where or when this will find you, My Dearest Carluccio, but still I cannot but write to you in the great anxiety & pain I am in for you from what the publick news mentions from Scotland, I know nothing else, & I doubt not but those accounts are exagerated, considering from whence they come, But still it is but too plain to see that affairs with you dont go as I could wish; I am tho still in hopes you may be able to keep your ground in Scotland, till you can have assistance from France: But if you really cannot mantain yourself in Scotland, Do not for Gods sake drive things too far, but think of your own safety, on which so much depends; Tho your Enterprize should miscarry, the honor you have gaind by it will always stick by you, it will make you be respected & considerd abroad, & will, I think I may answer for it, always engage the French to

to protect & assist you, & to renew in time another project in your favor, So that you should really have no temptation to pursue rash or desperate measures at this time, for should you do so, it would be the ruin of all, & even a drawback from the honor you have already gained. Enfin My Dear Child, never seperate prudence & courage, Providence has wonderfully assisted you hitherto, & will not abandon you for the time to come, This I firmly hope, while I shall not cease to beseech God to bless & direct you.
Adieu my dearest Child I tenderly embrace you & am all yours, once more God bless you & protect you.
James R.

64

PRINCE JAMES FRANCIS EDWARD STUART (1688–1766)

Letter to Prince Charles Edward Stuart, from Albano 6 June 1746

Manuscript, 18.5 × 23.0 cm
RA SP/MAIN/275/26

PROVENANCE Papers of the Stuart family, acquired by George IV in 1813 and 1817

As Prince Charles Edward fought, Prince James worked hard to raise support for the Jacobite cause in Italy. Based in Rome and Albano, he sent regular anxious letters to his son asking for news of the campaign ('I can never let the French post part without writing to you,' he admitted).[75] But it was to be over six weeks after the battle that he was finally to hear of his son's defeat, which reached him via 'the publick news'. This letter, written with no knowledge that it would get to the Prince, laments the failure of the Jacobite rising and attempts to mollify what the Old Pretender knew would be his son's hurt and fury. He assured his son (then attempting to escape Scotland for France, and in hiding from government troops) that 'if you really cannot maintain yourself in Scotland, Do not for Gods sake drive things too far, but think of your own safety, on which so much depends; Tho your Enterprise should miscarry, the honor you have gained by it will always stick by you, it will make you be respected and considered abroad'. KH

65

RICHARD YEO (*c*.1720–1779)

Medal commemorating the Battle of Culloden 1746

Gold; silver, diameter 5.15 cm
RCIN 443227 (gold), 443228 (silver)

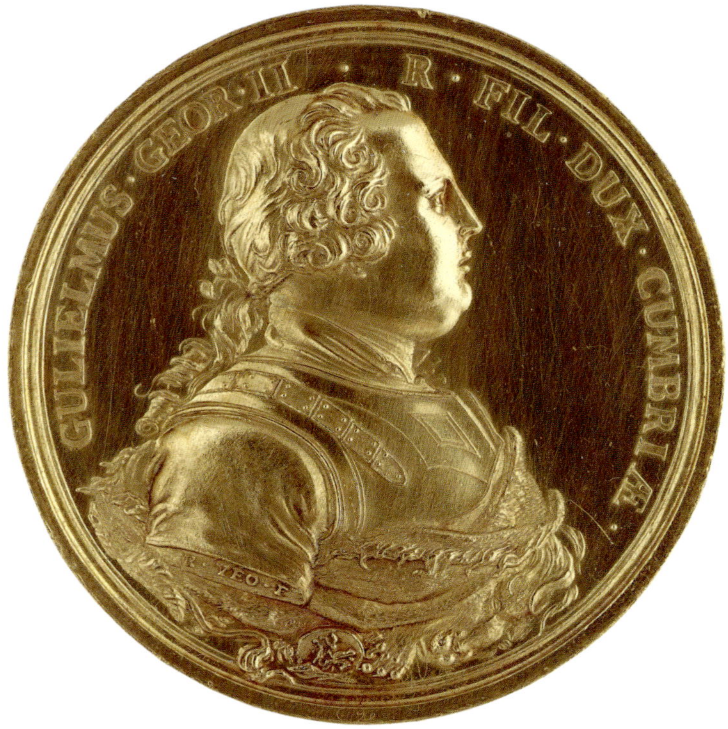

LITERATURE Cochran-Patrick 1884, p. 83, pl. XV/4; Hawkins 1885, vol. 2, p. 613, no. 278; British Museum 1909–11, pl. CLXVII/12

After the defeat of the Jacobite forces at Culloden, several medals commemorating the engagement were struck. This is probably the finest of them, designed by Richard Yeo, afterwards engraver to the Royal Mint, and successor to John Tanner as Chief Engraver in 1775. He was a member of the Society of Artists, and a founder member of the Royal Academy, with whom he exhibited 1769–70. He designed two medals for the Battle of Culloden: the first was designed to be worn, but this second was created for a collector's market, issued in gold, silver and copper. It was advertised in the *London Gazette*, 3–7 February 1747, and was available by subscription at one guinea for the silver and half a guinea for the copper. The gold was to be sold for two guineas more than the cost of the metal. The obverse showed a bust of the Duke of Cumberland, possibly modelled from life, with a lion's skin wrapped around him, and the reverse an image of Hercules trampling Discord, while raising Britannia. The inscription on the reverse emphasised the message – in translation, 'The rebels driven from England and defeated at Culloden, 16 April 1746'. The lion's skin may have been draped around the duke in order to identify him with the Hercules on the reverse, who is shown, following tradition, clad in the skin of the Nemean Lion (whom he killed in his first Labour). ES

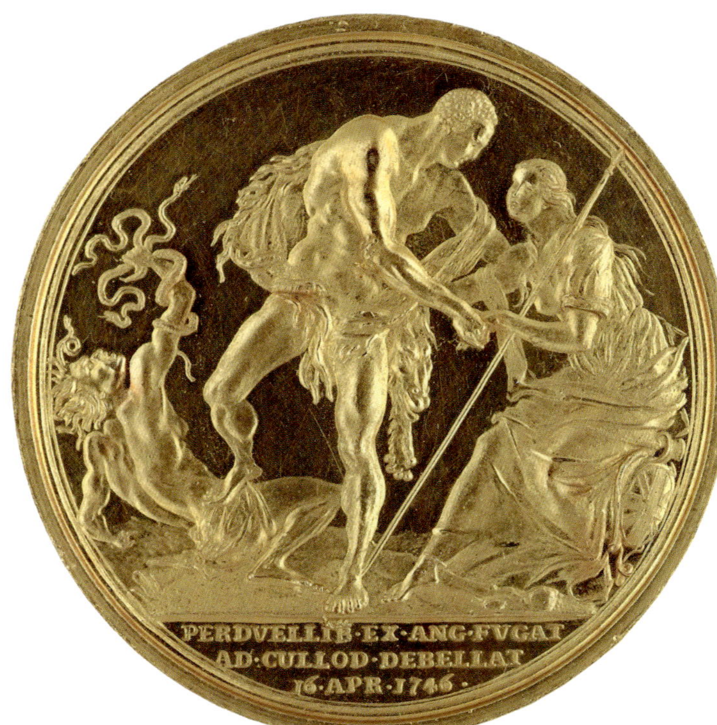

66

JAMES ALEXANDER GRANTE (ACTIVE 1745–6), CARTOGRAPHER

A Chart wherein are mark'd all the different Routs of P. Edward in Great Britain 1749

Engraving and etching, 64.2 × 41.2 cm (plate), 68.8 × 45.6 cm (sheet)
Scale approx. 1 : 2,429,198
RCIN 729135

PROVENANCE King's Military Map Collection[76]

LITERATURE Hodson forthcoming

This map of the Young Pretender's progress around Scotland and northern England in 1745–6 is based on a larger one by James A. Grante which was published in Paris in 1748. Grante, an Irish engineer, had fought for the French at Fontenoy before joining Prince Charles Edward in Scotland as Colonel of the Jacobite Artillery.[77] The map, which was accompanied by a description of the Stuart campaign, was dedicated to 'The Honest' (that is, Jacobite supporters) and shows Britannia invoking the Zephyrs to deliver the Prince to safety in France.

Although it was engraved in Edinburgh, an inscription on the map notes that it was to be 'sold in May's Buildings, Covent Garden'. No printseller's name is given, but it was probably distributed by the prolific George Bickham, an engraver and printseller with Jacobite sympathies. He was selling pro-Stuart prints and maps of Culloden in 1749, and appears to have been a member of the 'Oak Society', which raised money for the Young Pretender in 1750.[78] An impression of the map among the Secretary of State's papers in the National Archives suggests that its publication was the subject of government attention at the time.[79] KH

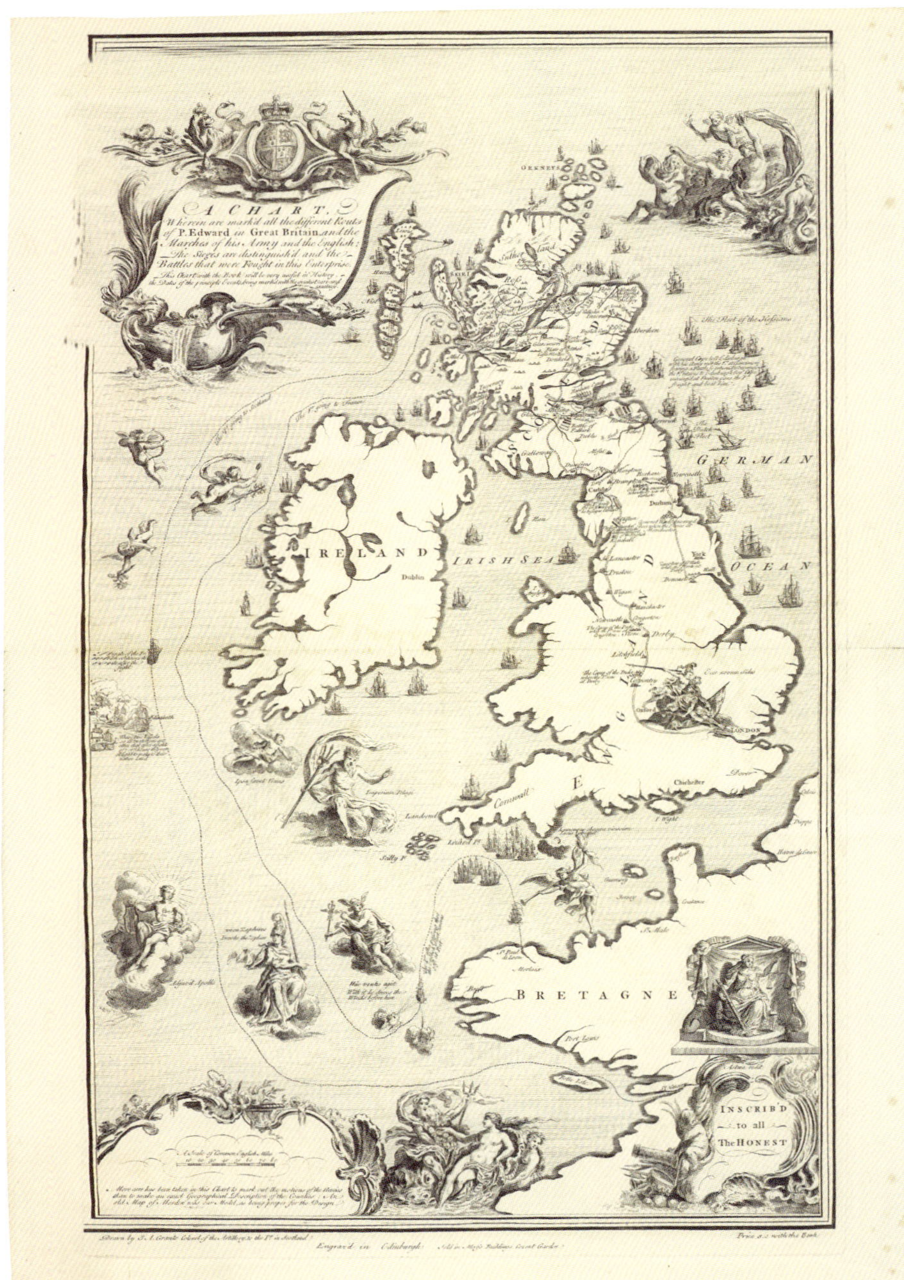

67

PAUL SANDBY (1731–1809)

Colonel David Watson (1713–1761) *c.*1750

Black and red chalks, 19.8 × 14.8 cm
RCIN 914405

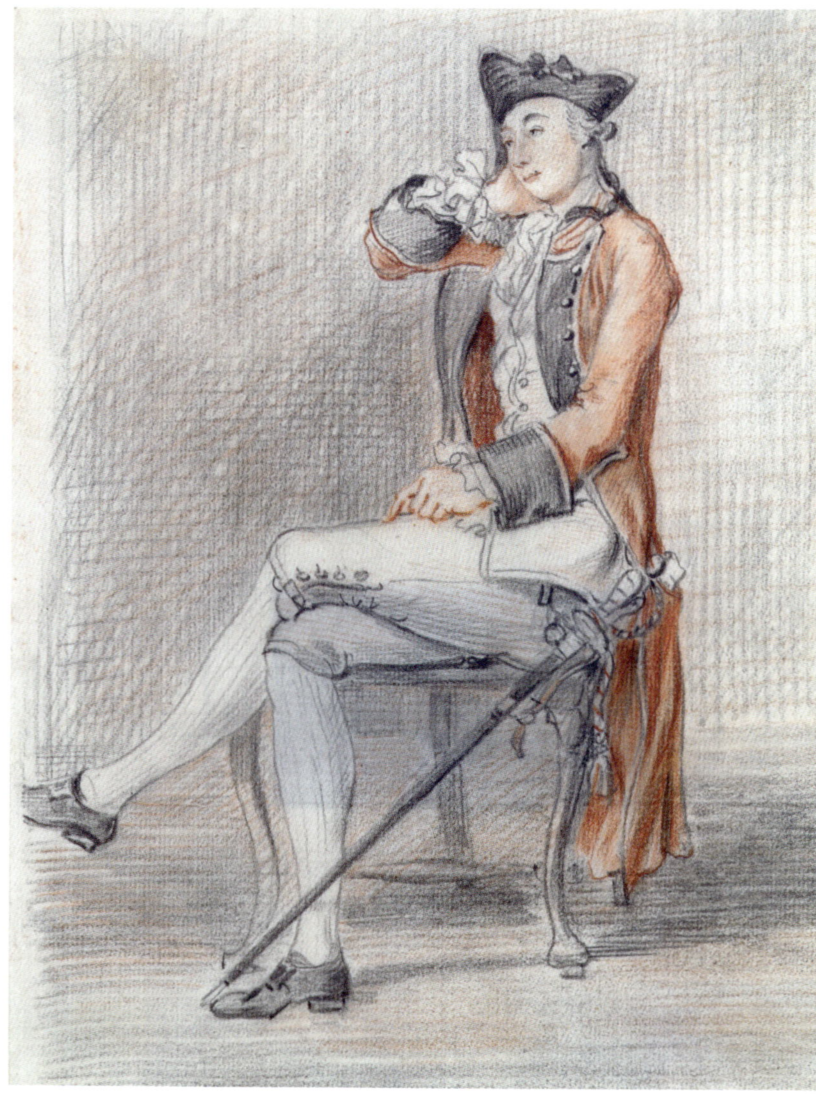

PROVENANCE Possibly among the group of figure studies acquired from Sir Francis Dyke Acland in 1930

LITERATURE Oppé 1947, no. 273

David Watson was born in Muirhouse in Scotland. He was an experienced soldier who had undertaken campaigns in northern Europe and Gibraltar, and who had a particular talent for engineering and surveying. After the Battle of Culloden, in which he had fought under the Duke of Cumberland, Watson proposed that a full survey of the Highlands be undertaken. He believed that ignorance of the terrain was hampering attempts to suppress the Jacobites, and that comprehensive maps of the area were necessary for victory. The idea was approved, and Watson headed the survey from its inception in 1747.

Paul Sandby was part of Watson's original survey team (though he was only sixteen at the time), as was the surveyor William Roy, who went on to found the Ordnance Survey. Sandby's chalk sketch shows his employer in formal dress, but in a relaxed pose, leaning back in a chair with his legs crossed. As well as constituting a record of Watson's appearance, the drawing forms an exercise in foreshortening and angles for the young artist, who has had to think carefully about the proportions of the figure and the position of the chair legs. In his use of coloured chalks, Sandby was looking to French artists such as Philippe Mercier (see no. 255). The drawing probably dates from the early 1750s, when Sandby was still working with the survey. Sandby made other sketches of his colleagues on the survey; a number of these survive, in the Royal Collection and in a sketchbook now in the National Gallery of Scotland. KH

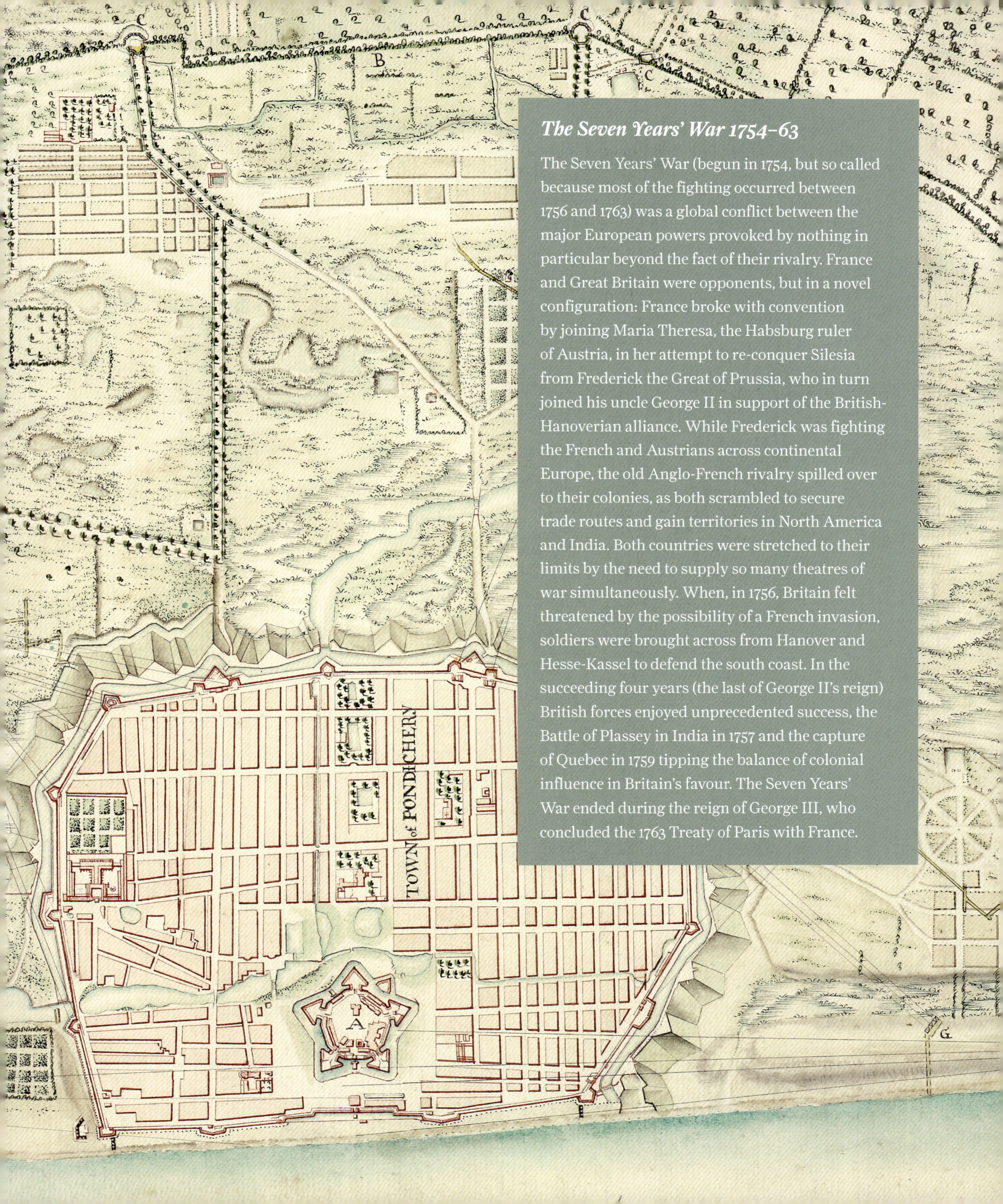

The Seven Years' War 1754–63

The Seven Years' War (begun in 1754, but so called because most of the fighting occurred between 1756 and 1763) was a global conflict between the major European powers provoked by nothing in particular beyond the fact of their rivalry. France and Great Britain were opponents, but in a novel configuration: France broke with convention by joining Maria Theresa, the Habsburg ruler of Austria, in her attempt to re-conquer Silesia from Frederick the Great of Prussia, who in turn joined his uncle George II in support of the British-Hanoverian alliance. While Frederick was fighting the French and Austrians across continental Europe, the old Anglo-French rivalry spilled over to their colonies, as both scrambled to secure trade routes and gain territories in North America and India. Both countries were stretched to their limits by the need to supply so many theatres of war simultaneously. When, in 1756, Britain felt threatened by the possibility of a French invasion, soldiers were brought across from Hanover and Hesse-Kassel to defend the south coast. In the succeeding four years (the last of George II's reign) British forces enjoyed unprecedented success, the Battle of Plassey in India in 1757 and the capture of Quebec in 1759 tipping the balance of colonial influence in Britain's favour. The Seven Years' War ended during the reign of George III, who concluded the 1763 Treaty of Paris with France.

68

ANONYMOUS

Map of Monongahela River 1755

Pen and ink, 38.7 × 24.7 cm
Scale approx. 1 : 1,003,290
RCIN 731063

PROVENANCE King's Military Map Collection; probably acquired by William Augustus, Duke of Cumberland

LITERATURE Hodson forthcoming

In December 1754, Edward Braddock, Lieutenant-General in the Coldstream Guards, was sent to take control of Fort Duquesne (now part of Pittsburgh) in the wake of setbacks suffered by troops commanded by George Washington (then an officer in the British army). The fort had recently been constructed by the French on disputed and strategically important land at the meeting point of the Monongahela and Allegheny Rivers. Braddock arrived at the British-held Fort Cumberland on 10 May, having gathered together around two thousand 'very indifferent men'.[80] Braddock and his force marched south towards Fort Duquesne, but were ambushed by French and indigenous forces about ten miles from the fort on 9 July. Around two thirds of Braddock's troops were killed, while Braddock himself was fatally wounded.

This map shows Braddock's difficult route from Fort Cumberland (at bottom right) to Fort Duquesne (where the rivers meet to form the Ohio River). The British expedition faced difficult terrain which varied between mountainous and boggy. The plan shows the course of the rivers, with a dotted line plotting the road usually taken between Fort Cumberland and Lake Erie, and two red lines showing the points at which Braddock and his men crossed and re-crossed the Monongahela – near where they were attacked and defeated. KH

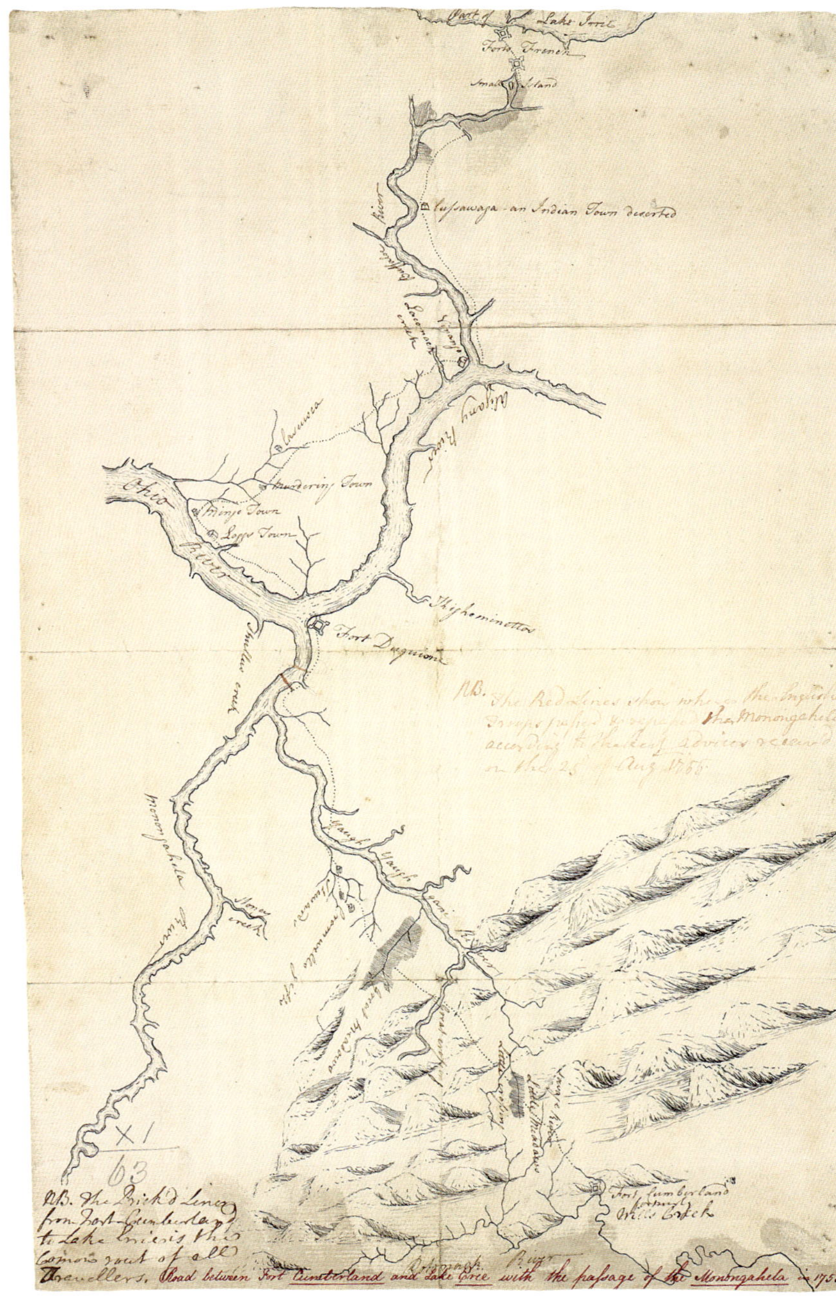

69

ATTRIBUTED TO WILLIAM ROY (1726–1790)

March Routes of the Eight Hessian Battalions 1756

Pen and ink with watercolour, 27.7 × 15.4 cm
Scale approx. 1 : 762,000
RCIN 731071

PROVENANCE King's Military Map Collection; previously in the map collection of Lt-General Robert Napier

LITERATURE Hodson forthcoming

The vast areas over which the Seven Years' War was fought stretched British resources to their limit. In May 1756 troops were brought to Britain from Hanover and Hesse-Kassel, and were stationed in southern England in case of French invasion. Their presence was not popular: the *London Evening Post* asked its readers to 'see if you can find one instance of a nation not being ruined, that called upon foreign forces for its defence'.[81]

This small, meticulous map traces the route taken through southern England by the eight battalions brought from Hesse-Kassel (twelve battalions travelled from Hanover). The same information is tabulated above. It is probably by William Roy, who was at the time one of a team tasked with surveying parts of southern England in response to the threat from France. KH

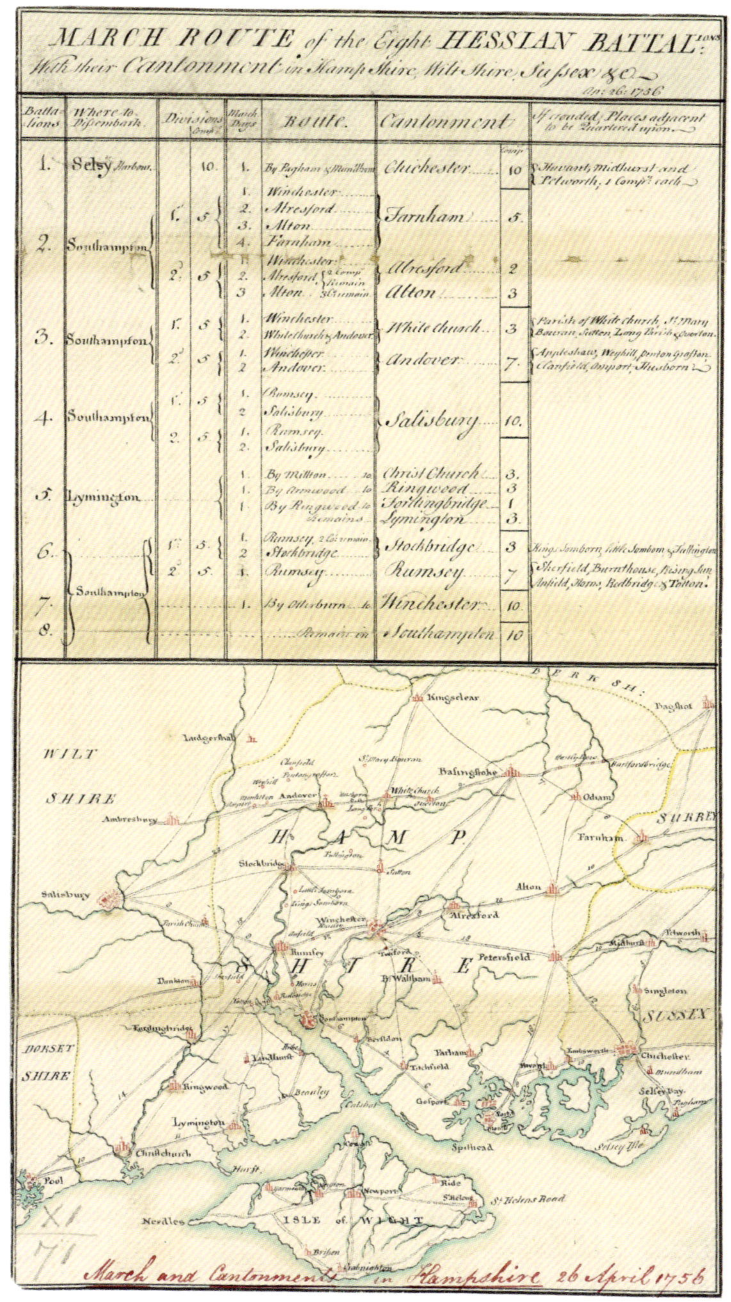

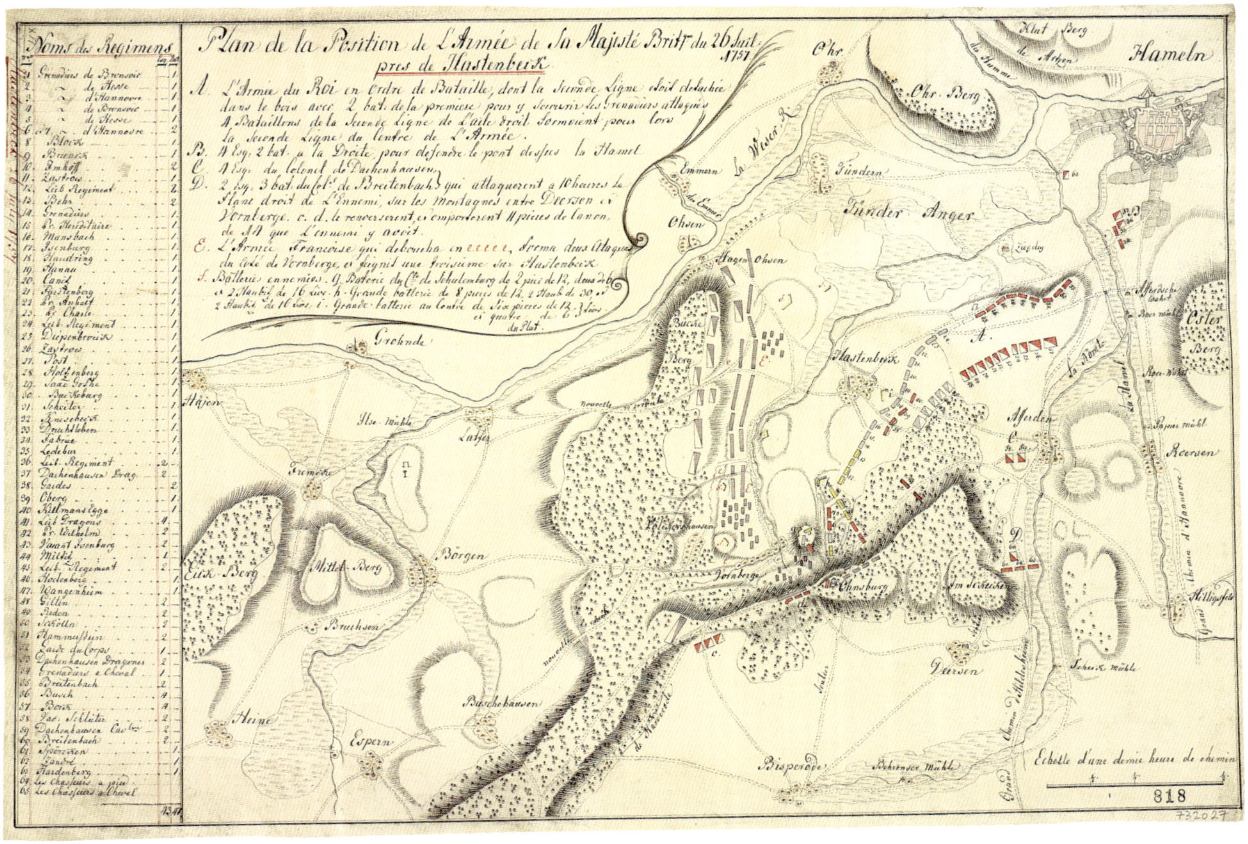

70

ATTRIBUTED TO GEORG JOSHUA DU PLAT (1722–1795)

Plan of the Battle of Hastenbeck 1757

Pen and ink with watercolour, 29.4 × 44.0 cm
Scale approx. 1 : 38,666
RCIN 732027

PROVENANCE King's Military Map Collection; acquired by William Augustus, Duke of Cumberland

LITERATURE Hodson forthcoming

The village of Hastenbeck lies near Hameln and was on the border of the Electorate of Hanover. The Battle of Hastenbeck took place on 26 July 1757 between an allied army (made up of troops from Britain, Hanover, Hesse-Kassel and Brunswick) and the French. At 60,000 men, the French army heavily outnumbered their opponents, who were only 35,000 strong, and the hilly, wooded terrain made planning and fighting difficult.[82] The battle was confusing for those in command, who could not see their troops, and Cumberland was forced to move back from the action by heavy artillery fire. It became clear that the allies could not win and Cumberland ordered a retreat. The defeat left the Electorate of Hanover unprotected against France, and 'the archives, the plate, the mint, nay and the fine set of horses belonging to the stables of Herenhausen' were moved for safety to England.[83] Cumberland subsequently signed a treaty of peace with France – the Convention of Kloster Zeven – which, as George II saw it, allowed the French 'to keep possession and ruin my dominion as long as they please'.[84]

This map, attributed to the Hanoverian military engineer Georg Joshua du Plat, shows the confusing terrain over which the battle was fought, with uneven ground and a fork of woodland trapping the armies. Du Plat was later responsible for surveying the electorate for George III.[85] KH

71

J.F.C. SCHILLING (ACTIVE 1730S–60S)

Medley drawing with a map of the Battle of Krefeld (1758) 1767

Pen and ink with watercolour
50.7 × 71.7 cm (trimmed irregularly)
RCIN 732063

PROVENANCE King's Military Map Collection; perhaps a gift to George III

LITERATURE Hodson forthcoming

Medley prints and drawings – trompe l'oeil compositions which took on the appearance of a scattering of ephemeral items – were popular artistic conceits in the early eighteenth century.[86] This German example takes the appearance of an assortment of prints, maps and official publications. Prominent among them is a plan of the Battle of Krefeld, fought between an allied army headed by Ferdinand, Duke of Brunswick, and the French, commanded by Louis de Bourbon. This partially obscures the map of New England which was published by Johann-Baptist Homann in or after 1716 (present-day southern Ontario and Quebec and New York State are visible). Schilling has slightly adapted Homann's map so that the words 'Nieu Jork' are visible to the left. Alongside are laid prints of land and seascapes, in red, blue and black, the popular Dutch-published gazette *Nouvelles Extraordinaires de Divers Endroits*, and an exhortation to George III to visit Hanover from the citizens of the Electorate. The borders of the sheet have been trimmed to the edges of each of the documents as if some spill over the edge of the striped paper or fabric on which they rest and the sheet of the *Nouvelles Extraordinaires* has been painted to suggest that text is showing through from the verso.

J.F.C. Schilling, who made this drawing at Stade in Hanover, was a captain in the Hanoverian army. A number of his plans, drawn from the 1730s to the 1760s, are included in George III's collection of topographical prints and drawings, now in the British Library. Schilling may be reproducing his own plan of the Battle of Krefeld. The battle took place in 1758, some years before the medley was drawn, and was a victory for the allied army, commanded by Ferdinand of Brunswick.

Medleys are sometimes regarded as programmatic in the choice of documents depicted. If the present drawing contains a message it is unclear, although it may be significant that the German material dominates and that the most prominent item is the appeal to George III, to whom the drawing may have been sent. KH

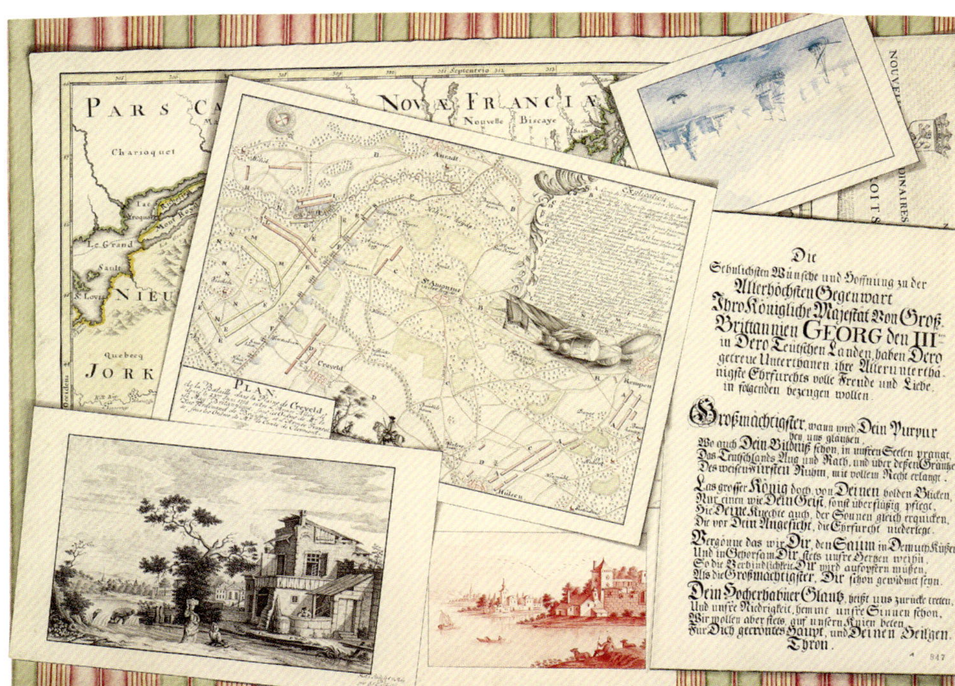

HUGH DEBBIEG (1731–1810)

Plan of encampment on the Île d'Orléans 1759

Pen and ink with watercolour, squared in pencil, 46.4 × 51.8 cm
Scale 1 : 96,000
RCIN 732103

PROVENANCE King's Military Map Collection; probably acquired by William Augustus, Duke of Cumberland

LITERATURE Hodson forthcoming

In 1759, as the British started to make gains over the French in North America, focus fell on Quebec City. This was the capital of New France, from which the French controlled the St Lawrence River. On 27 June, a British force under General James Wolfe landed on the Île d'Orléans, situated in the middle of the river, four miles from Quebec City. Here, they set up a camp from which, supported by the navy, they planned to attack the French stronghold, commanded by the Marquis de Montcalm. In the meantime, an army, under Major-General Jeffrey Amherst, was marching overland towards Quebec City from Lake Ontario.

Wolfe was later to write to William Pitt, Secretary of State, that '[i]t was absolutely necessary to possess these two points [the Île d'Orléans and the Point of Levi on the south bank] and to fortify them, because from either one or the other, the enemy might make it impossible for any ship to lie in the bason of Quebec, or even within two miles of it'.[87] The British hospitals and stores were placed on the island, and were secured with fortifications. Captain Hugh Debbieg's survey shows the layout of the encampment on the island, which would later serve as a hospital and store. The importance of the British navy to Wolfe's efforts is shown in Debbieg's recording of high and low water marks: to reach the island, British ships had navigated an uncharted river. Debbieg, an engineer who had worked on the survey of Scotland (no. 67), acted as General Wolfe's assistant Quartermaster General.[88] The pencil squares on his map suggest that it served as a model for a second plan or was copied from an earlier example.

From their camps on the island and the south bank, the British pursued a concerted campaign against the French, culminating in September with British victory (and Wolfe's death) at the Battle of the Plains of Abraham, after which Quebec surrendered. In Britain, there were 'very great rejoycings' at the news of the victory.[89] The loss of Quebec was a heavy blow for France, who ceded Canada to Britain by the Treaty of Paris in 1763. KH

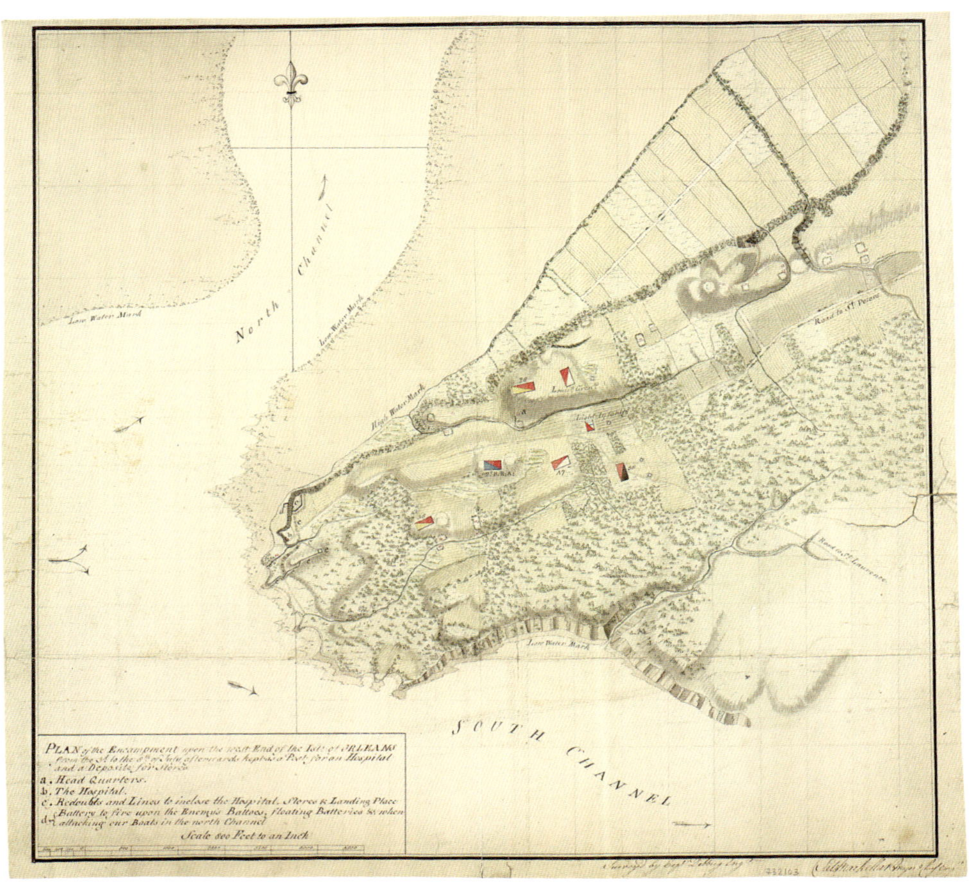

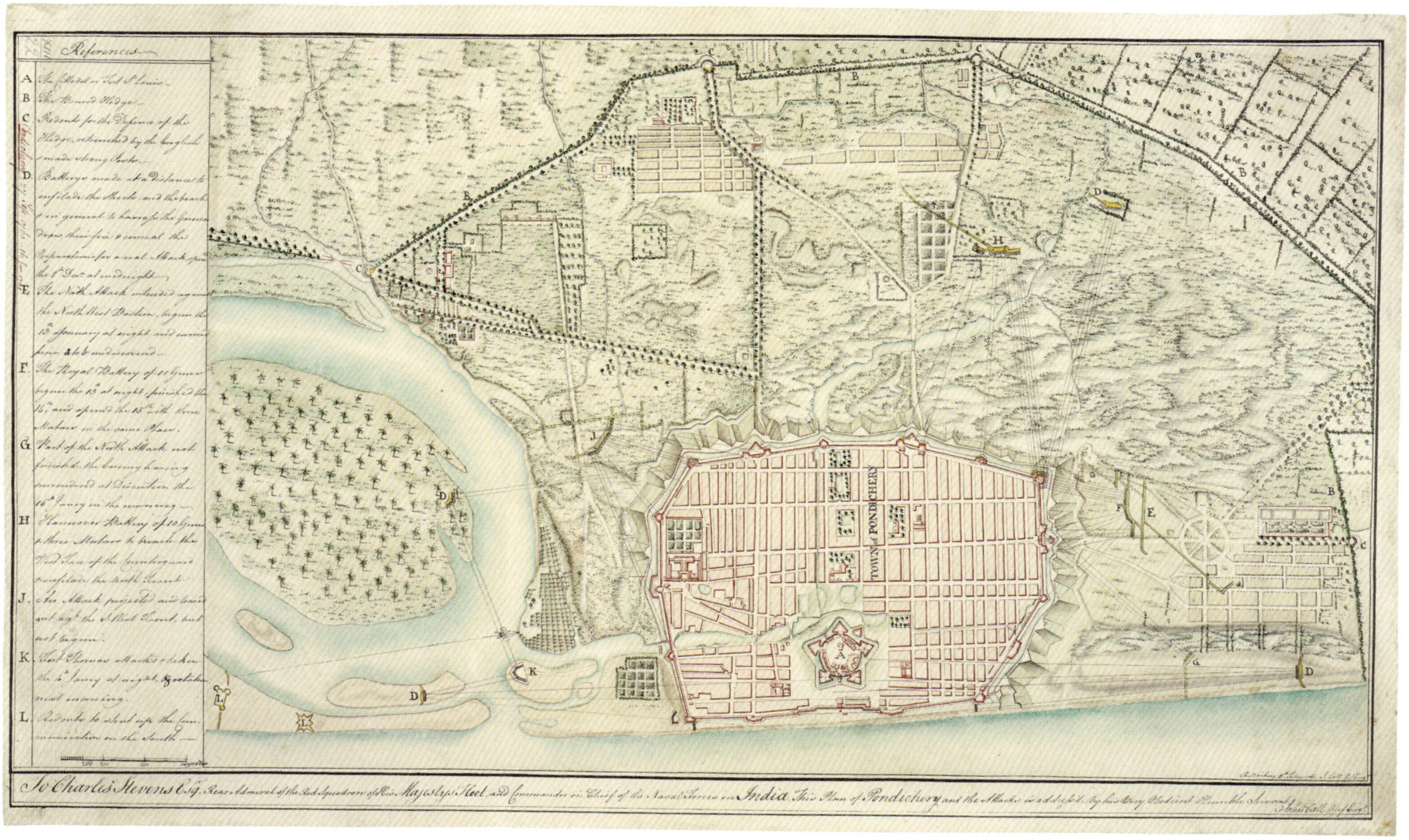

73

JOHN CALL (1732–1801)

Map of Pondicherry 1760–1

Pen and ink with watercolour, 33.9 × 57.6 cm
Scale approx. 1 : 10,550
RCIN 733022

PROVENANCE King's Military Map Collection[90]

LITERATURE Hodson forthcoming

In 1760, the British laid siege to Pondicherry (now Puducherry) in south-east India. The town was held by the French and was an important staging post for the French East India Company; the British had previously tried, and failed, to take it in 1748. After a prolonged siege, the town surrendered to the British in January 1761; Robert Orme noted that 'the surrender was inevitable, for at the scanty rate of the wretched provisions, to which the garrison had for some time been reduced, there did not remain sufficient to supply them two days more'.[91] The decision was taken to destroy the buildings and fortifications of the town to reduce its strategic value, and it was returned to France by treaty in 1763. Orme lamented that after a few months of British rule 'not a roof was left standing in this once fair and flourishing city'.[92]

This map shows the layout of the town and surrounding terrain. It was made by John Call, Chief Engineer for the British East India Company, whose plans and topographical views of India were used to illustrate Robert Orme's *History of the Military Transactions of the British Nation in Indostan* (1763–78). Call's plan was dedicated to Charles Stevens, who commanded British naval operations in the area, and shows Puducherry assailed from three sides by batteries of guns and mortars. KH

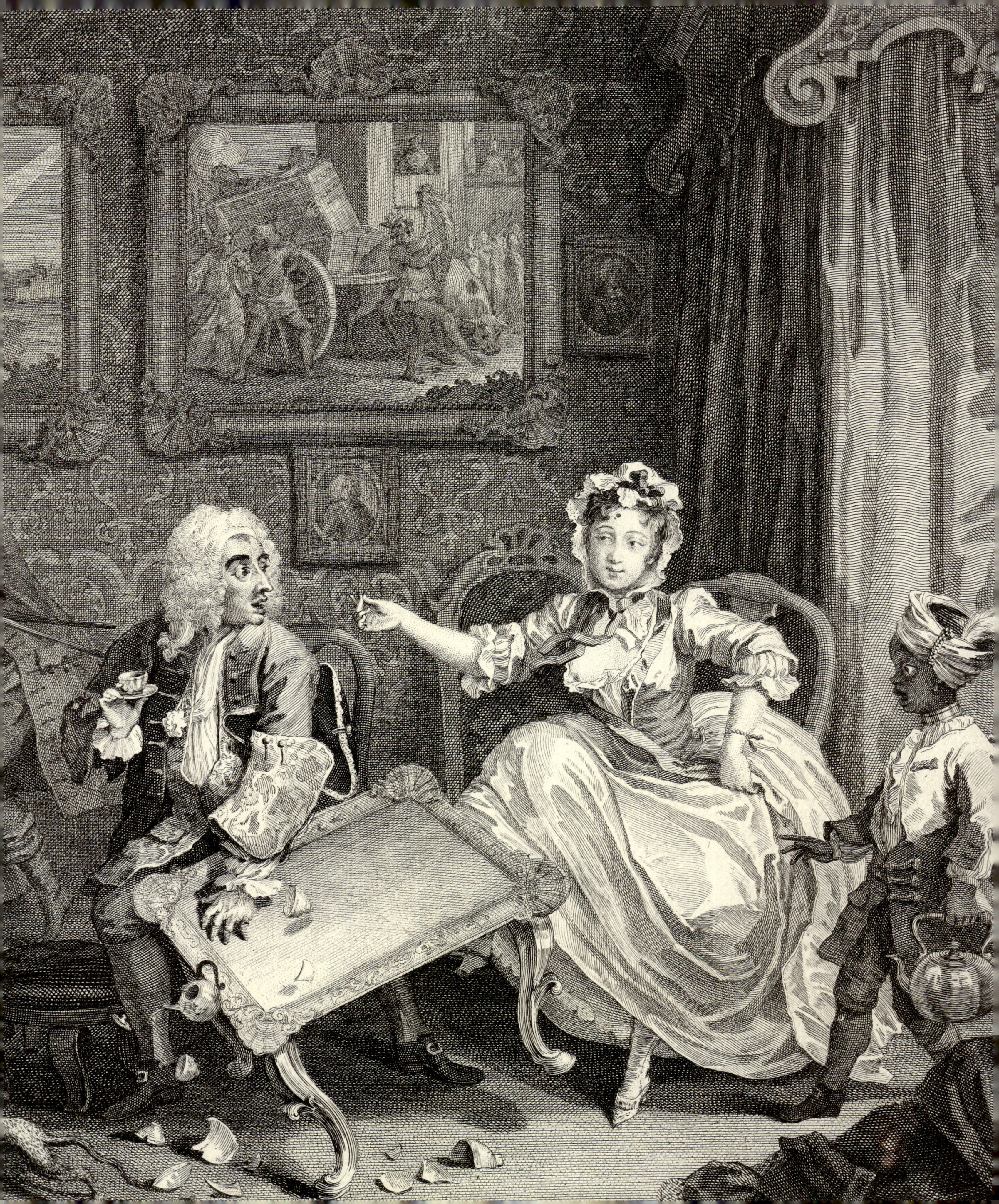

IV

'Prints should be priz'd as Authors should be read' Hogarth and Graphic Art

KATE HEARD

IN AUGUST 1714, when George I inherited the throne of Britain, a sixteen-year-old London boy was in the sixth month of his apprenticeship with Ellis Gamble (active 1712–33), a London silversmith. William Hogarth, the son of a schoolmaster and failed lexicographer, may have witnessed his new King's entry into London on 20 September. Six years later, in 1720, Hogarth left Gamble's employment, which he found 'too limited in every respect', and set himself up as an independent copper-plate engraver, undertaking small commissions such as shop cards, book illustrations and benefit tickets.[1] Under the Hanoverian dynasty, Hogarth achieved great success, becoming not only a prominent artist but a writer on art and a noted philanthropist. His rise, however, was almost entirely independent of the new royal family, which provided him with little patronage or support. Hogarth's career was made in the age of, but despite, the first Georges.[2] The Royal Collection contains an important group of Hogarth's works (paintings, drawings and prints), but they almost all reached the collection in later reigns. The breadth of the holding is sufficient to allow each of the artist's preoccupations to be explored, and many of these have a very direct bearing on the themes of this exhibition.

In 1720, Hogarth enrolled at a drawing school run by the engravers Louis Chéron (1660–1725) and John Vanderbank (see no. 238). When Chéron and Vanderbank's school collapsed in 1724, Hogarth ensured the continuation of its meetings at the house of Sir James Thornhill (1675/6–1734), a respected painter who became the young artist's father-in-law in 1729. Life drawings made by Hogarth at the meetings of the school show a confident draughtsman, working in bold strokes on large sheets of paper (no. 78). One of Hogarth's ambitions was to be taken seriously as a history painter, as his father-in-law had been. We can see in one case that an early academic study (no. 88) was recycled as a figure in Hogarth's *Pool of Bethesda*, a biblical subject painted in 1735 for St Bartholomew's Hospital. These drawings seemed to have joined the Royal Collection in the nineteenth century, presumably as valuable records of the career of a respected member of the British School.

Political satire forms a small part of Hogarth's output. The bursting of the South Sea Bubble in 1720 prompted a surge in moralistic satirical prints and Hogarth entered the market with his *The South Sea Scheme* of 1721 (no. 75). A subject which was to occupy him much more profoundly throughout his career was aesthetic judgement and fashionable taste. In 1724 he published *The Bad Taste of the Town*, sometimes known as *Masquerades and Operas* (no. 76), available for a shilling at a number of London printsellers,

FIG. 26
William Hogarth
Self-portrait (Gulielmus Hogarth), 1747
Etching and engraving
RCIN 811832

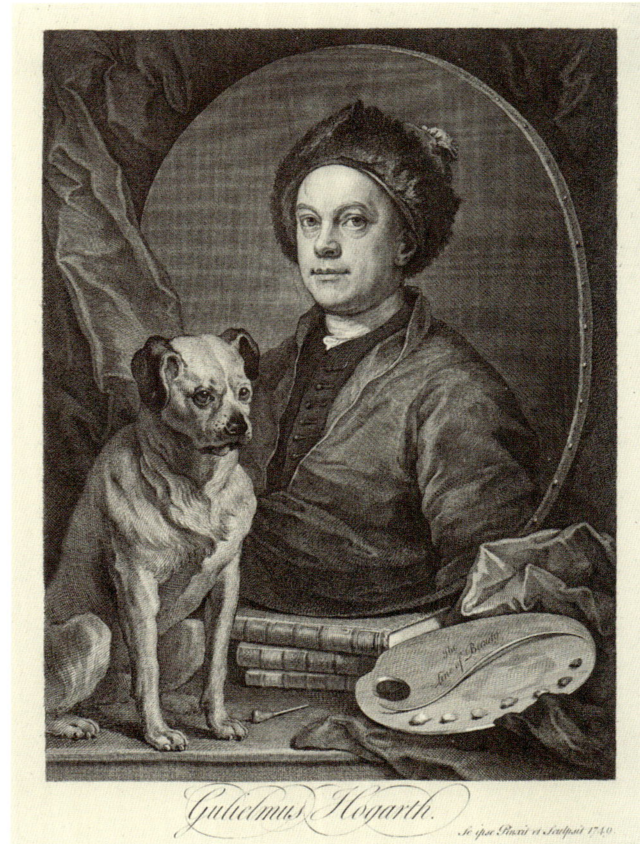

which satirised the pro-Italian taste of the elite circle surrounding the Earl of Burlington, among them William Kent. Kent had also attended the Vanderbank drawing school, and became Hogarth's implacable enemy when he undercut Thornhill in a bid for royal employment (see p. 79). But this print represents more than personal pique: Hogarth suggests that if serious culture is affected and exclusive, like the high-walled academy and nonsensical over-priced Italian opera advertised on the banner, then the public will fall prey to licentious trash. Hogarth explored this intersection of taste and morality notably in a new type of mini-treatise, the subscription ticket. These were sent as a receipt for down payments on Hogarth's print series and other works, and contain a germ of an idea – a sort of *amuse cerveau* – as to how that series might be enjoyed. *A Harlot's Progress* was announced in *Boys peeping at Nature* (nos 84 and 85), which played on the idea that the word 'nature' was often used in the period to describe intimate and indelicate matters while at the same time 'Nature' was seen as the proper study of all the arts. Hogarth's *Battle of the Pictures* of 1745 (no. 90) advertised an auction of his own original paintings and attacked the taste in Old Master painting of the time so acutely that we have borrowed the title for this section of the present exhibition (see Chapter VI). But Hogarth had already in his *Marriage à-la-Mode* of 1743–5 (no. 89) returned to and comprehensively demolished the 'Bad Taste of the Town' in architecture, furniture, painting and music. Hogarth clearly expected his audience to recognise the paintings or types of painting hanging on the walls. The moral was perhaps most powerfully driven home in scene four, where the Countess decorates her bedroom with pictures of Jupiter raping Ganymede and Io, the latter paired with a biblical subject, Lot and his Daughters. She listens to a castrato, collects Chinese porcelain and is planning a visit to a masquerade with her lover. If her taste is elegantly corrupting, that of her father is brutalising: the final scene shows his mean apartments decorated with crude Dutch *drolleries* (as they would have been called) in the manner of Adriaen Brouwer.

Hogarth's theories were not all negative. In 1745 he painted a self-portrait with a mysterious line on his palette entitled 'the line of beauty' (fig. 26). Hogarth's public had to wait until 1753 for this enigma to be resolved, with the publication of *The Analysis of Beauty*, a treatise which Hogarth wrote 'with a view of fixing the fluctuating IDEAS of TASTE' (nos 94–5). In this inflammatory and influential work, Hogarth aimed to demonstrate his ability as a theoretician, using words instead of images to treat a 'subject generally thought to be a matter of too high and

FIG. 27
William Hogarth
Characters and Caricatures (subscription ticket for *Marriage à-la-Mode*), 1743
Etching
RCIN 811714

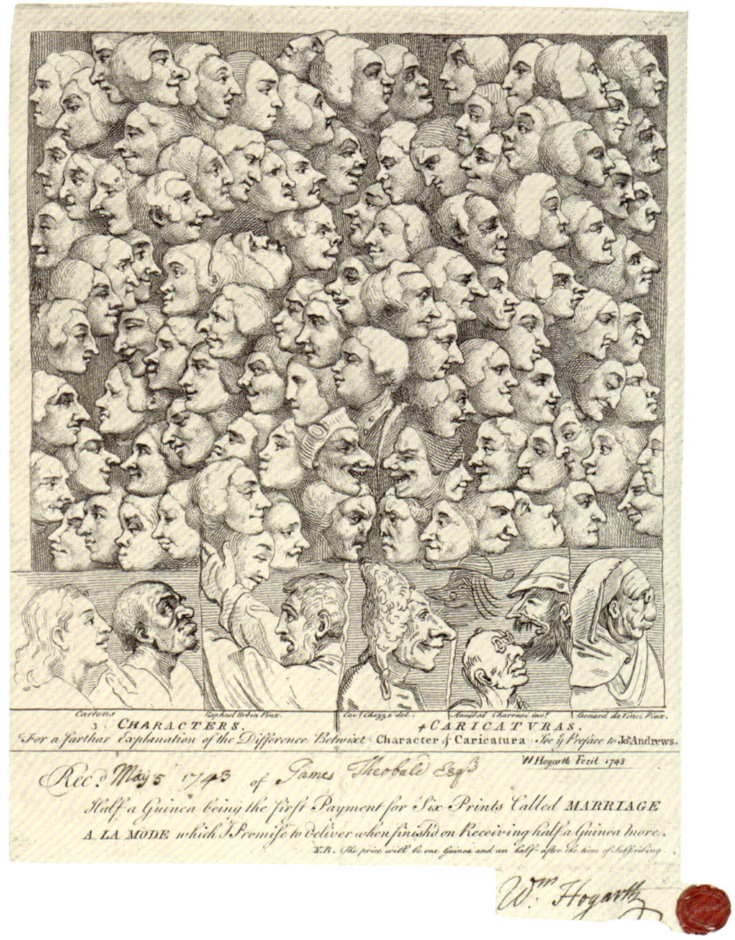

too delicate a nature to admit of any true or intelligible discussion' in a way which 'may overthrow several long received and thorough establish'd opinions'.[3] In it he argued for a new approach to composition, one which concentrated on line and form and particularly on the serpentine 'line of beauty', which he saw as the basis of ideal taste.[4]

Hogarth created *Characters and Caricaturas* of 1743 (fig. 27) as his subscription ticket for *Marriage à-la-Mode*. Here he referred to the recently published novel *Joseph Andrews*, in which the author, Henry Fielding, had claimed, 'He who should call the ingenious Hogarth a burlesque painter, would in my opinion do him very little honour'.[5] Hogarth had already alluded to this idea in his *Midnight Modern Conversation* (no. 87), in which he cautioned viewers 'not to find one meant Resemblance' in his work. Fielding and Hogarth believed that the business of art was to create generalised characters – not individuals – which were realistic and not mere caricatures. For Hogarth art had a moral purpose: it was neither personal slander nor Punch and Judy tomfoolery. Hogarth's satirical prints had a serious intention, a moral message which was revealed through the actions of the characters portrayed. It was this wish to warn and admonish which led him to produce the greatest, and most successful, of his prints – the groups of 'modern moral subjects' which began with *A Harlot's Progress* of 1732. *A Harlot's Progress*, like the moral subjects which followed, told a cautionary tale over a set of prints (in this case six). The story follows the young and innocent Moll Hackabout, who is corrupted on her arrival in London and becomes a prostitute before being imprisoned and dying of a venereal disease. Moll's story was presented by Hogarth without text, in prints so rich in symbols and motifs that the lively debate about their interpretation which began on the day of their publication continues today. Hogarth likened his work to a theatrical performance, his characters performing 'a Dumb shew' to tell their story. This analogy reminds us of a revolutionary development in literature, the emergence of novels describing the world from the point of view of the servant class – Defoe's *Moll Flanders* of 1722, Richardson's *Pamela* of 1740 and Henry Fielding's *Joseph Andrews* of 1742. In all these examples the heroes and heroines suffer from the canting 'virtue' of their betters as well as their vices, just as Moll Hackabout suffers equally from the vicious Colonel Charteris and the zealous magistrate Sir John Gonson, who occupy similar positions in scenes one and three.

Hogarth sold *A Harlot's Progress* by subscription, cleverly marketing it as a limited edition with restricted

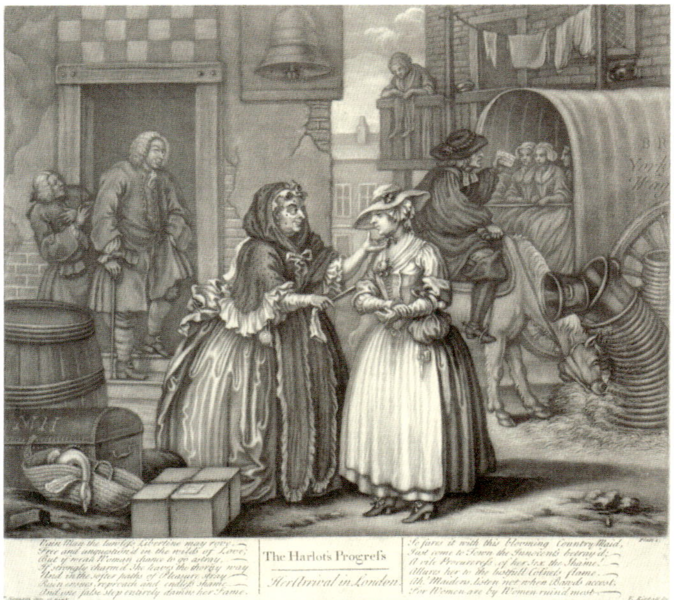

FIG. 28
Elisha Kirkall after
William Hogarth
The Harlot's Progress, scene 1, 1732
Mezzotint
RCIN 811518.a

availability, and it proved wildly popular, with 1,240 sets issued. Hogarth here encountered a problem. He had promised his subscribers that the edition would be limited, and that no further impressions would be produced. But in doing so he prevented himself from responding to the popularity of the series. Other publishers rushed to fill the gap, and within weeks pirated versions of Hogarth's original prints were available (fig. 28). Hogarth reacted by authorising a second version, which presented the story with three scenes to a sheet and with decorative borders, but he had lost the initiative. He sought to ensure that, in future, his work would be protected. In 1735 Parliament, largely in response to Hogarth's encouragement, passed an Act vesting fourteen years' copyright in printmakers who were named on their prints. This act, often known as 'Hogarth's Act', was important in the establishing of the status of printmakers as owners of their work.

Although Hogarth was angry at the copying of *A Harlot's Progress*, he must have realised that the proliferation of his designs increased his fame, making him by the mid-1730s a renowned artist, hailed not just as a printmaker but as 'an eminent history and conversation painter' by Joseph Mitchell.[6] He had been painting group portraits and theatrical scenes for some years, among them a scene from *The Beggars' Opera* (no. 79), and conversation pieces such as that of the Popple and Ashley families (fig. 29). Now, he became a sought-after portraitist, painting society figures such as Captain Thomas Coram, who had encouraged the establishment of the Foundling Hospital, an innovative children's home; Benjamin Hoadley, Bishop of Winchester; and the actor David Garrick (no. 257). He also undertook philanthropic work, becoming involved with the Foundling Hospital (to which he gave continued support) and donating paintings to St Bartholomew's Hospital.

Despite his success, Hogarth stumbled in his attempts to secure royal patronage. Having been rebuffed in the early 1730s, when a promised permission to paint members of the royal family was withdrawn (no. 245), Hogarth again faced rejection in 1750 owing to *The March to Finchley*, an oil painting depicting troops marching out to meet the forces of the 'Young Pretender' (no. 92). The engraving after the painting was dedicated to Frederick II of Prussia, an act which is said to have been a deliberate slight to George II, who had refused to purchase the painting, instead responding negatively to a viewing (although he was claimed to have requested some of Hogarth's prints as a result).[7] The story of the monarch's reaction is probably apocryphal, but Hogarth's disgruntlement is clear: he had recently been passed over for a royal appointment, and probably he dedicated the print to Frederick II in reaction to this failure. He would not receive royal recognition until 1757, when he was appointed Serjeant Painter to the ageing George II through the influence of the Duke of Devonshire.[8]

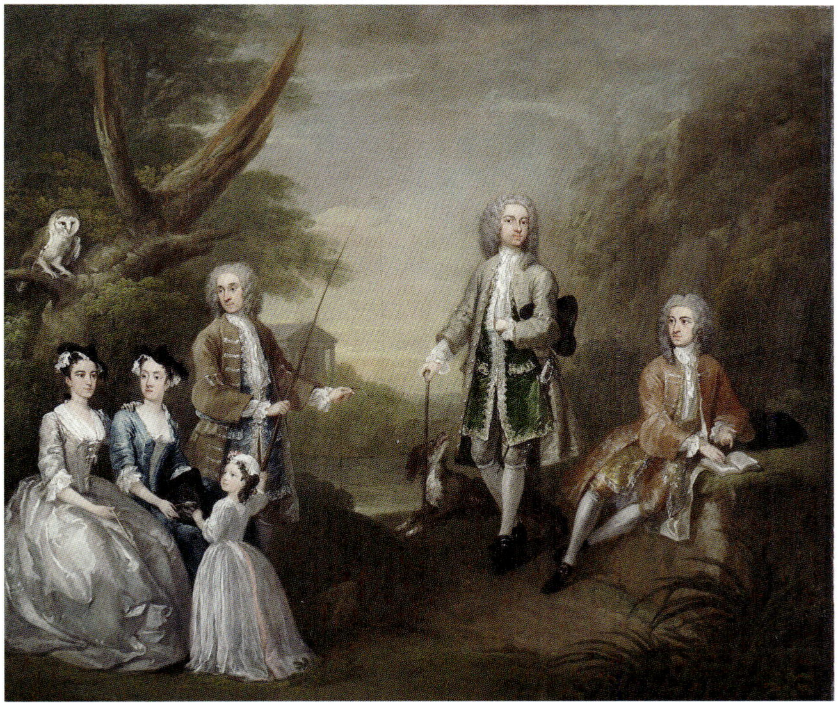

FIG. 29
William Hogarth
The Popple and Ashley Families, 1730
Oil on canvas
RCIN 400048

Although Hogarth became the most prominent printmaker of the age, there is little evidence that examples of his graphic art were collected by the early Hanoverians. It was said that, after the painting of *The March to Finchley* had been dismissed, Hogarth's 'collection of prints were sent for, and some of them bought at the common prices', but there is no record of these prints in the Royal Collection subsequently or any other evidence for collecting by George I or George II in this area.[9] George II owned a copy of *The Analysis of Beauty* (no. 94), which remains in the Royal Library, and which appears to have had the two illustrative plates bound in, but later removed.[10] But there is little evidence for print purchases by members of the Royal Family between 1714 and 1760, and most of the prints which are known to have been owned by the early Hanoverians are presentation copies from hopeful artists rather than purchases indicative of interest or taste.[11] Princess Augusta subscribed to a series of portrait prints of prominent figures.[12] Best documented is the print collection of Frederick, Prince of Wales, who is known to have owned a number of volumes of prints.[13] These were mainly reproductive prints after Old Master paintings, although printed views of Windsor Castle and contemporary portraits and religious prints are also recorded. Frederick also ordered Vertue to collect portrait prints of figures who might adorn his planned gardens at Kew, although this project was never realised.[14]

In the fifty years between his apprenticeship in 1714 and his death in 1764, Hogarth had risen from jobbing silver engraver to society's favourite printmaker, a leader of taste who broke down the boundaries between 'high' and 'comic' art. In the artist's own judgement, '[t]he three things that have brought abuse upon me' were his portrait paintings, *The Analysis of Beauty* and his prints.[15] But excellent examples of all three were in the Royal Collection within sixty years of Hogarth's death: the painted portrait of David Garrick and his wife (no. 257) was purchased by George IV, a volume of the *Analysis* was owned by George II, and the engraved works came into firm royal favour with the reign of George III, whose wife and daughters built a tea room pasted with the artist's engravings. Their collection forms the foundation in the present Royal Collection of works on paper by '[t]hat excellent moralist, the humorous Hogarth'.[16]

74

WILLIAM HOGARTH (1697–1764)

Hogarth's trade card 1720

Engraving, 7.7 × 10.2 cm (sheet)
RCIN 811305

PROVENANCE Royal Collection by 1845[17]

LITERATURE Paulson 1989, no. 3; *Hogarth* 2006–7, no. 14

Printed trade cards were a well-established means of advertising a business in the eighteenth century.[18] For the young Hogarth the trade card also acted as a means of showcasing his talent as an engraver. It demonstrated his ability to engrave different scripts, to delineate figures, and to furnish a variety of decorative devices – swags, putti, cartouches and frames – while the surface on which the figures stand is an example of the art of perspective. The putti in the upper border hold a print and a silver or gold covered cup, demonstrating Hogarth's skill as a metal engraver and a printmaker. Hogarth produced this card in April 1720, when he left an apprenticeship with the metal engraver Ellis Gamble to set up his own business. KH

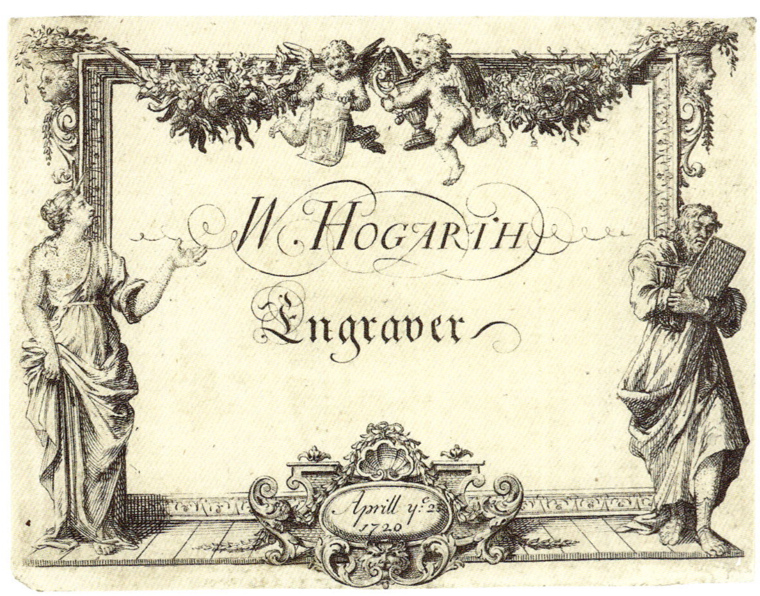

75

WILLIAM HOGARTH

The South Sea Scheme 1721

Etching and engraving, 26.2 × 33.0 cm (plate); 27.5 × 34.2 cm (sheet)
RCIN 811308

PROVENANCE Purchased by Queen Victoria at the H.P. Standly sale (Christie's, 14 April 1845, lot 1249)

LITERATURE Paulson 1989, no. 43

In this print, and the preparatory drawing for it (fig. 30), Hogarth offered a Bruegelian vision of London's downfall in the wake of the collapse of the South Sea Company in 1720. Large numbers of people seeking a swift return had invested in the Company, which produced copious promises but had few assets, and many were ruined by its bankruptcy. Jonathan Swift noted on 20 October 1720 that 'Conversation is full of nothing but South-sea, and the Ruin of the Kingdom, and scarcity of money'.[19]

Hogarth shows the base of the Monument, erected in London to commemorate the rebuilding of the city in the wake of the devastating Great Fire of London (1666). Before it, a carousel spins, parodying the man being tortured on a wheel in the foreground. To the right, another man is tied to a whipping post, his cloak held aside by a monkey so that his bare flesh can be whipped. A man with his arms raised is having his pockets picked. A sign at left notes that 'A Ten Thousand pound man [is] to be Raffled for', reflecting the wild speculative schemes which led to the financial collapse.

Hogarth's print was issued with an explanatory and moralising verse, which supplemented his picture of chaos in a city that was (as he inscribed on the Monument) destroyed 'by the South Sea in 1720'. Among the 'causes why in London, / So many Men are made, & undone', Hogarth

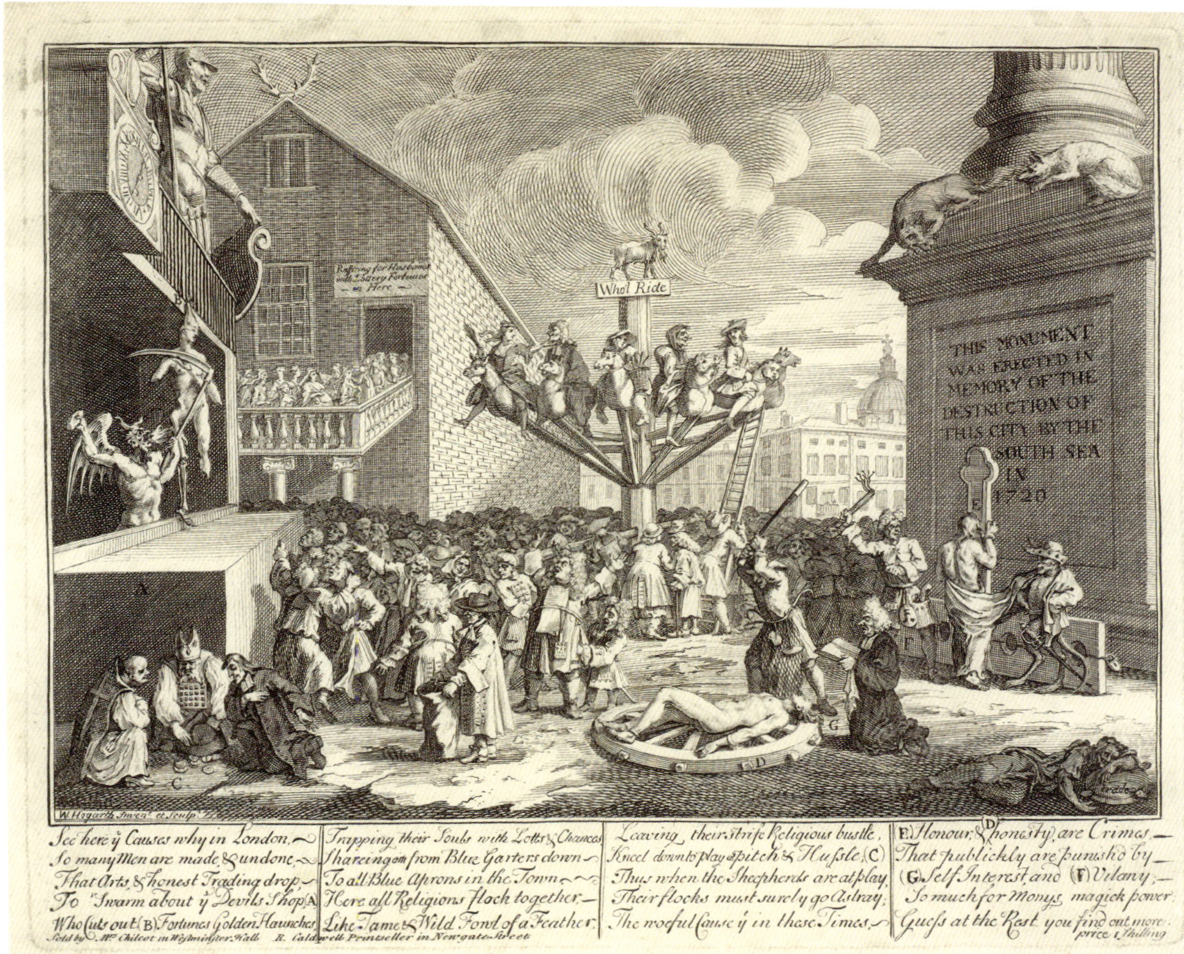

identified financial speculation on the part of churchmen (who are shown gambling in his picture) and the involvement of all levels of society 'from Blue Garters down / To all Blue Aprons in the Town'. The use of a merry-go-round to depict the chaos may have been inspired by an anonymous Dutch broadside, *Des Waerelds doen en doolen, Is maar een Mallemoolen* ('The World's actions and errors are but a merry-go-round'), which used the device to satirise foolish financial investments.[20] Hogarth's work was sold through the printsellers Mrs Chilcot (based in Westminster Hall) and Richard Caldwell (based in Newgate Street), who also stocked impressions of Hogarth's *The Lottery* (1724).
KH

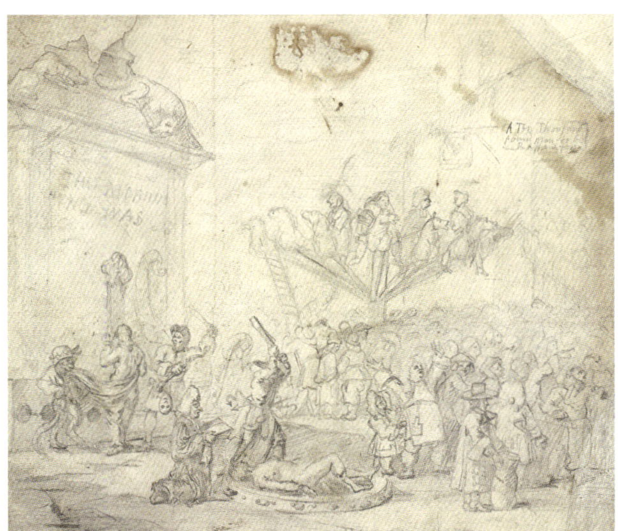

FIG. 30
William Hogarth
Study for *The South Sea Scheme*, 1721
Black chalk
RCIN 913479

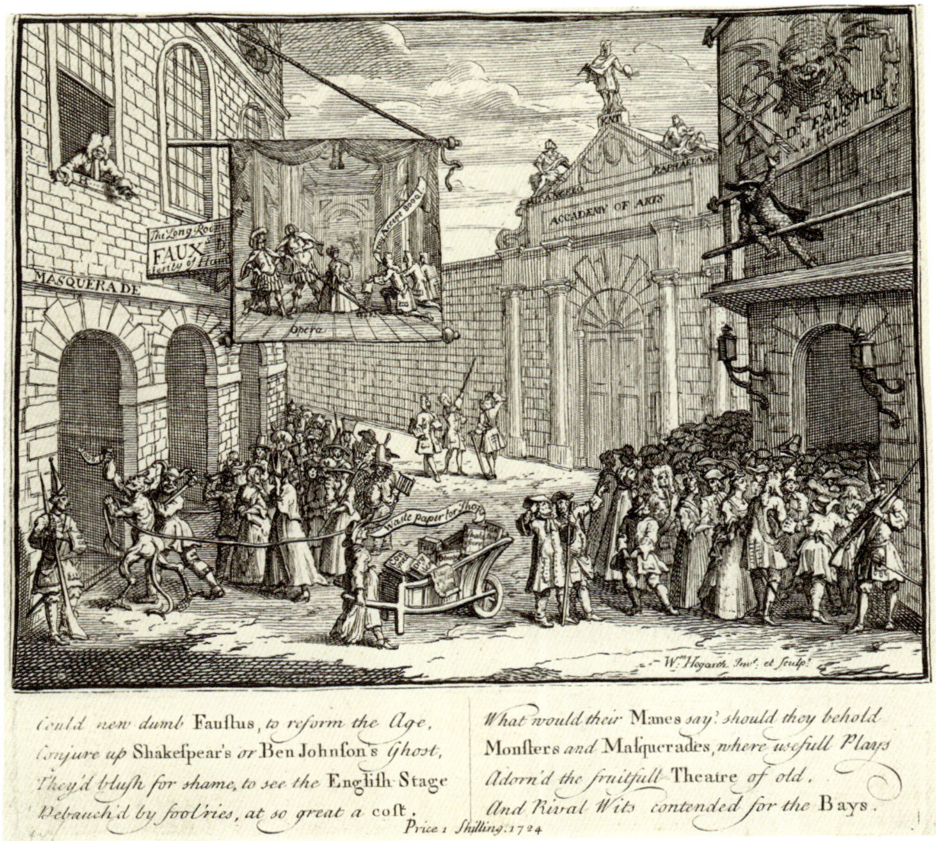

76

WILLIAM HOGARTH (1697–1764)

The Bad Taste of the Town 1724

Etching and engraving, 15.5 × 17.7 cm
RCIN 811358

PROVENANCE Purchased by Queen Victoria at the H.P. Standly sale (Christie's, 14 April 1845, lot 1150)

LITERATURE Paulson 1989, no. 44

This 'little Satyrical print' (as it was described in the *Daily Post*) was produced by Hogarth to ridicule the 'reigning follies' of fashionable London.[21] Hogarth loathed the fashion for foreign forms of art – Dutch prints and paintings, Italian opera and art – which he believed were encouraged at the expense of British talent. Hogarth was here entering the struggle over aesthetics between Sir James Thornhill and Lord Burlington's circle, which included Thornhill's great rival for commissions, the architect William Kent.[22]

At the centre of the print is a waste-paper hawker, whose barrow is filled with the great names of British literature – Shakespeare, Dryden, 'Congrav' [William Congreve], Addison and Otway. In the present impression, the reference to Pasquin (a figure associated with satire) on the paper hanging over the edge of the wheelbarrow has been scratched out – in subsequent impressions it would be replaced with Ben Jonson's name. To either side, crowds flock to entertainments in 'Bad Taste' – at Burlington House in Piccadilly (sarcastically nicknamed the 'Accademy of Arts' and presided over by William Kent, Michelangelo and Raphael in an allusion to the preference of the Burlington circle for Italianate design); a conjuring display by Isaac Fawkes (a popular magician whose name Hogarth renders as 'Faux', or false) and a masquerade (a series of which were currently being organised by Johann Jacob Heidegger from Switzerland, who can be seen looking out of the window). A group is being coralled into the masquerade by a rope held by a satyr and a fool. Italian opera is signified by a large hanging showing the fashionable Italian singers Francesca Cuzzoni, Senesino (Francesco Bernardi) and Gaetano Berenstadt, taken from an anonymous caricature of 1723 showing the three performing in Handel's *Flavio*. To the right, crowds can be seen around the entrance to the pantomime *The Necromancer; or, Harlequin Doctor Faustus*. The verses at the foot of the sheet were printed on a separate plate and another version of the print, also dated 1724, bears a different inscription. KH

77

ATTRIBUTED TO WILLIAM HOGARTH

Impression from a tankard belonging to the Clare Market Artists' Club 1724?

Engraving and etching, 11.0 × 16.5 cm
RCIN 812336

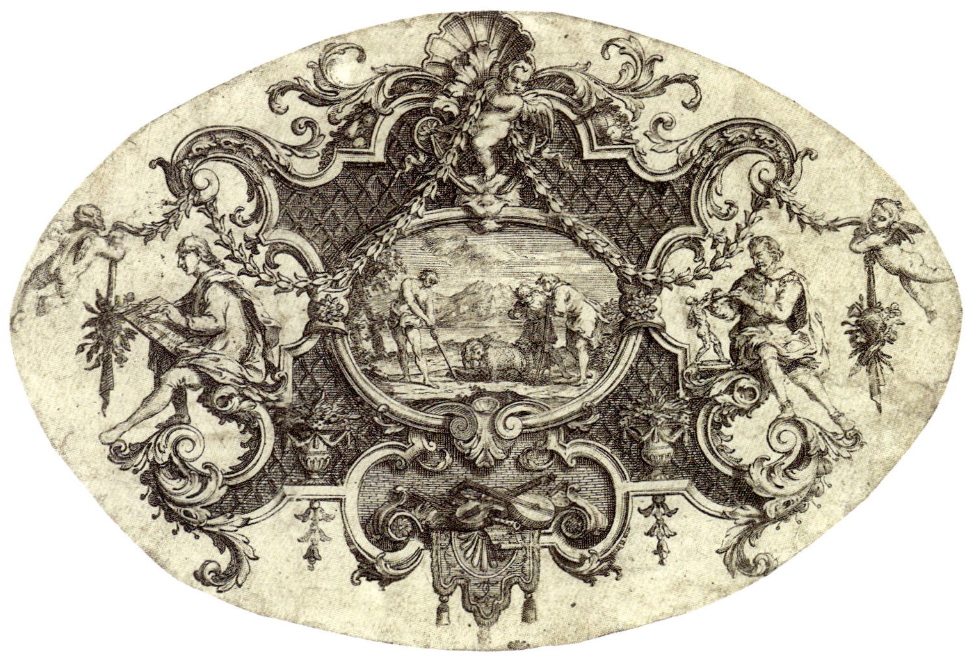

PROVENANCE Unidentified collector's mark (an oak leaf printed in black; not in Lugt); Royal Collection by 1845[23]

LITERATURE Paulson 1989, no. 25

The Clare Market Artists' Club met at the Bull's Head Tavern on the site of a meat and fish market which ran between Drury Lane and Lincoln's Inn Fields in London.[24] This rare print is said to have been taken from an engraving on a tankard made for the club by Hogarth, who trained as a metalwork engraver. It shows an elaborately decorated cartouche, flanked by a draughtsman and sculptor. Samuel Ireland (d. 1800), a printmaker who formed a fine collection of Hogarth's works and who owned this drawing in the mid 1790s (given to him by the painter Charles Catton), said that the central scene showed the biblical story of Laban and his Sheep, but it may instead show a more appropriate subject for an artists' club – the discovery of the young shepherd Giotto's talent, when he drew a perfect circle on the ground with a stick.[25] KH

78

WILLIAM HOGARTH (1697–1764)

A male nude holding a javelin *c.*1728

Black chalk with some white and red chalk on blue paper, 54.5 × 40.0 cm
RCIN 913488

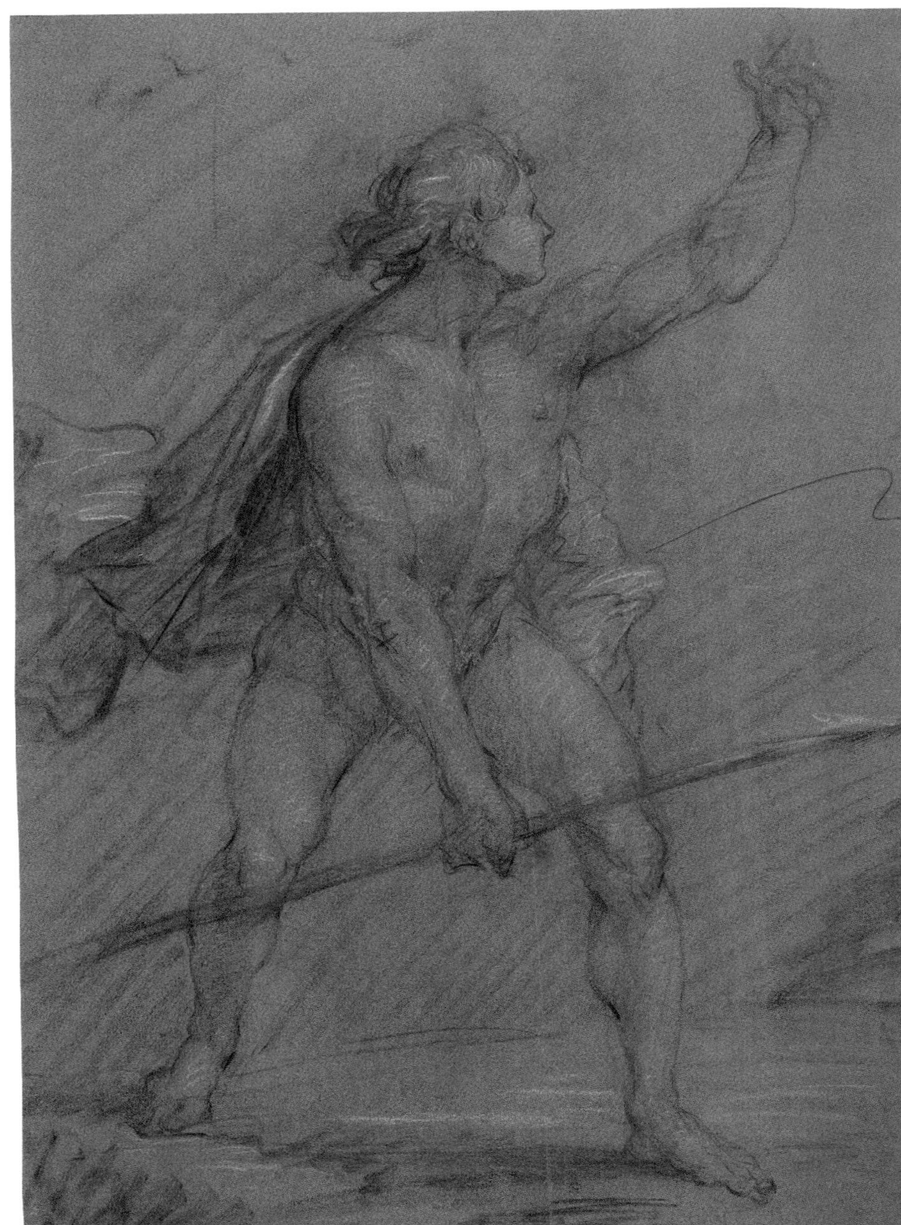

PROVENANCE Probably in the collection of Samuel Ireland; Royal Collection by 1833

LITERATURE Oppé 1948, no. 28; Oppé 1950, no. 348; *Hogarth* 1954, no. 52; *Hogarth* 1971–2, no. 96

This large drawing is a study from a life model, perhaps made at the St Martin's Lane Academy, where artists regularly gathered to draw and socialise from 1720. It is probably one of the group of drawings noted in Samuel Ireland's collection as being from 'Hogarth's sketchbook'. Although the drawing is executed in black chalk, Hogarth has used white to indicate the highlights and red chalk to indicate the curve of the figure's neck and for a line in the right background. The figure does not appear to have been used by Hogarth in any of his surviving paintings. KH

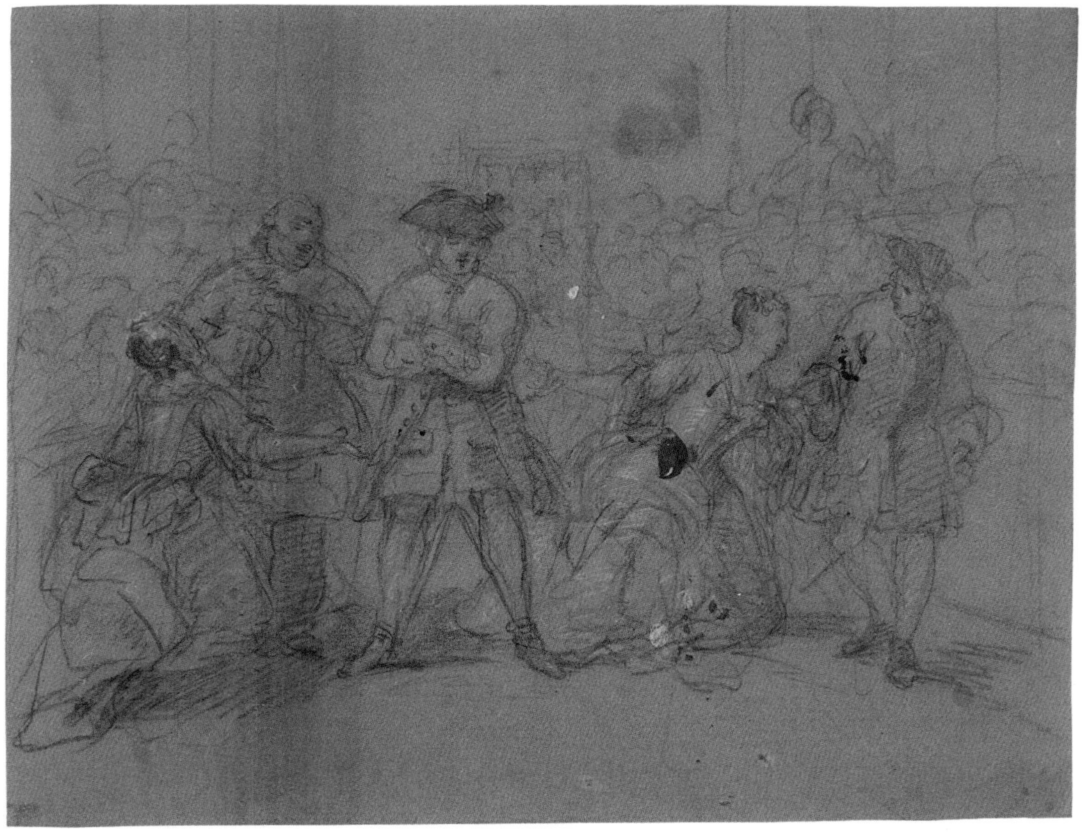

79

WILLIAM HOGARTH

Scene in 'The Beggar's Opera' *c.*1728–9

Black chalk with some white chalk on blue paper, some outlines pricked; splashed with oil paint, 37.3 × 49.2 cm
RCIN 913487

PROVENANCE Samuel Ireland (his sale 1797, lot 134); Royal Collection by 1833

LITERATURE Oppé 1948, no. 23; Oppé 1950, no. 344; *Hogarth* 1954, no. 53; *Hogarth* 1971–2, no. 44; *Master Drawings* 1986, no. 123; *Royal Treasures* 2002, no. 382

Hogarth painted two versions of this scene in *The Beggar's Opera*; this study is for the first, dated 1728.[26] Rendered fluently in black and white chalk on blue paper, the drawing is splashed with oil colours, suggesting that Hogarth continued to refer to it as he moved to working the theme on canvas.

The subject is taken from Act III, Scene 2, of John Gay's *Beggar's Opera*, which had first opened at Lincoln's Inn Fields at the end of January 1728, 'with such success,' the playwright noted, 'that the Playhouse hath been crouded every night'.[27] The highwayman Macheath (centre) is shown in the Newgate Prison with both his wife (Polly, to the right) and his mistress (Lucy, to the left) pleading with their fathers (responsible for Macheath's imprisonment) for his life. Boxes on stage held members of the audience, who can be seen surrounding the actors. It was from these seats that Charles Powlett, 3rd Duke of Bolton, saw and fell in love with Lavinia Fenton, the actress who played Polly Peachum. By July 1728 Gay was reporting that 'The D of Bolton ... hath run away with Polly Peachum, having settled 400l. a year upon her during pleasure'.[28] Although in his finished painting Hogarth portrayed Bolton staring at Lavinia Fenton, the audience is here only roughly sketched in. KH

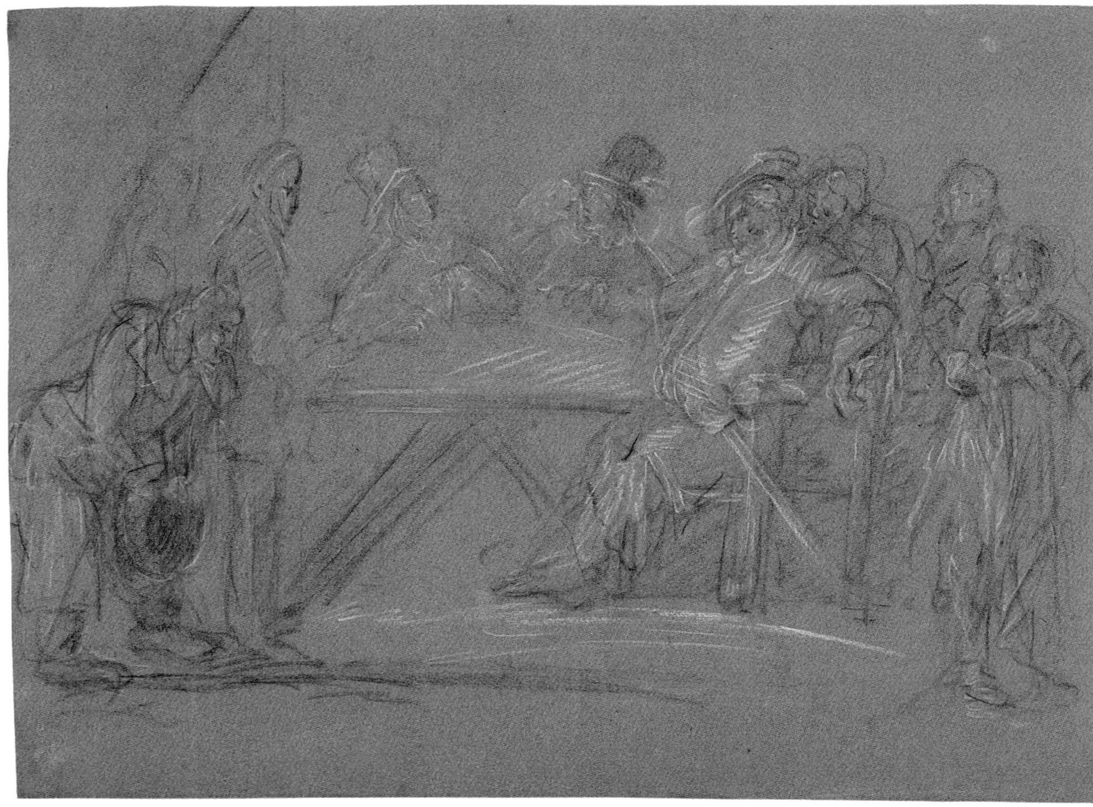

80

WILLIAM HOGARTH (1697–1764)

Falstaff examining his recruits 1730

Black and white chalk on blue paper, 38.9 × 54.0 cm
RCIN 913491

PROVENANCE Probably in the collection of Samuel Ireland; Royal Collection by 1833

LITERATURE Oppé 1948, no. 24; Oppé 1950, no. 345 *Hogarth* 1954, no. 51; *Hogarth* 1971–2, no. 43

Hogarth made this rapid drawing in preparation for an oil painting, once belonging to David Garrick and now in a private collection.[29] Falstaff exploits his position as a recruiting officer to allow suitable young men to bribe their way out of service, leaving him with a company of misfits (*Henry IV Part II*, Act III, Scene 2). Falstaff leans back in his chair facing two unimpressive recruits, while behind him more promising candidates edge away, one of them slipping money into his left hand. Hogarth may have seen the production of the play mounted at the Lincoln's Inn Fields Theatre in 1729–30, in which Falstaff was played by James Quin.[30] Here he records the arrangement of the figures on the stage, which he then worked up with other studies for the finished painting. He has modelled the outlines in black chalk and indicated the highlights in white chalk, a technique made possible by the rich blue colour of the prepared paper. KH

81

WILLIAM HOGARTH

Three figures *c.*1730

Black and white chalk on blue paper, 32.3 × 28.0 cm
RCIN 913489

PROVENANCE Probably purchased by the Prince of Wales (later George IV) at Samuel Ireland's sale, 1801 (lot 38, 'Three, Susanna and the Elders, in chalk taken from Hogarth's sketchbook')

LITERATURE Oppé 1948, no. 28; Oppé 1950, no. 347

This drawing was described as showing Susannah and the Elders in Samuel Ireland's sale catalogue. The central woman, however, is clothed and attended by a man and a woman and the drawing must depict a different scene, perhaps that of a procuress selling her charge's services. As in the drawings of *The Beggar's Opera* and of Falstaff, Hogarth worked in chalks on blue paper (which has mostly been darkened with rough chalk hatching), and the drawing is said to have been taken from his sketchbook. Like his drawing of Falstaff, this work serves to block in the position of the figures in black chalk and to work out the main highlights in white. KH

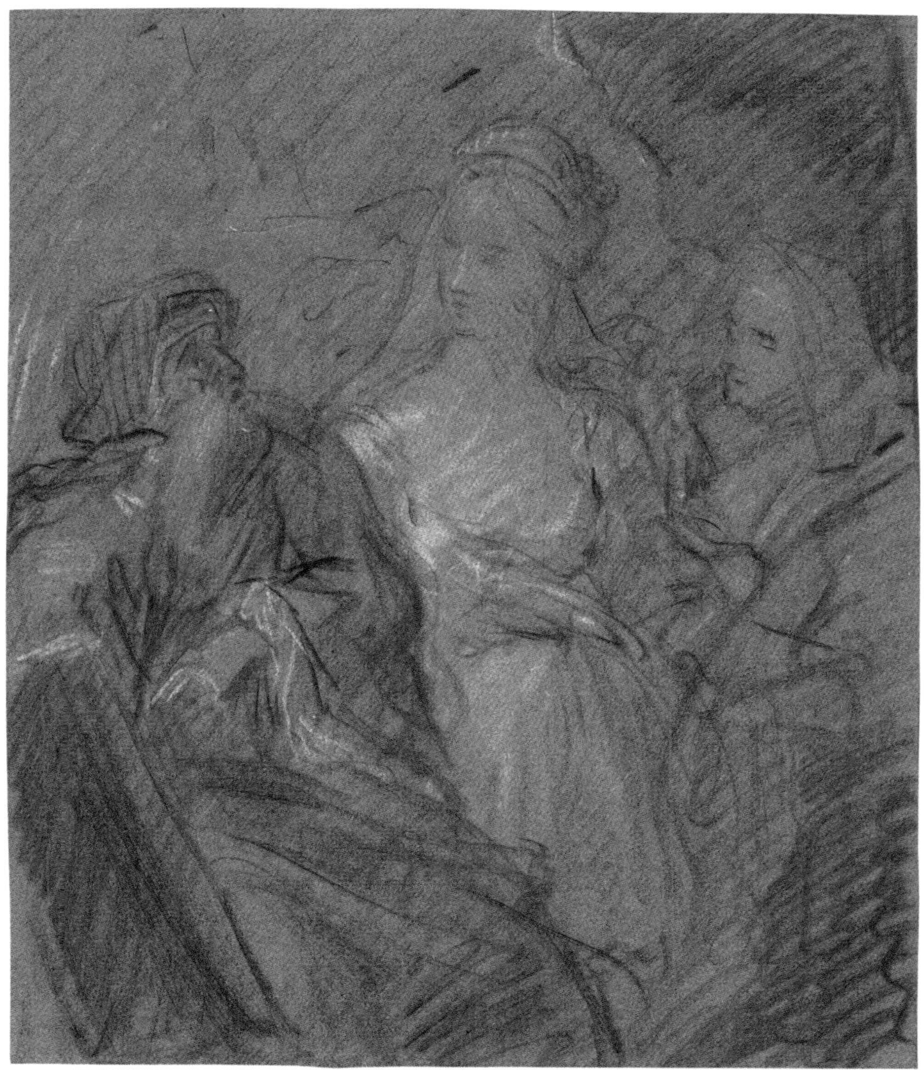

82

WILLIAM HOGARTH (1697–1764)

Two pairs of figures *c.*1730

Pen and ink with brown wash over pencil, 13.2 × 17.5 cm
RCIN 913478

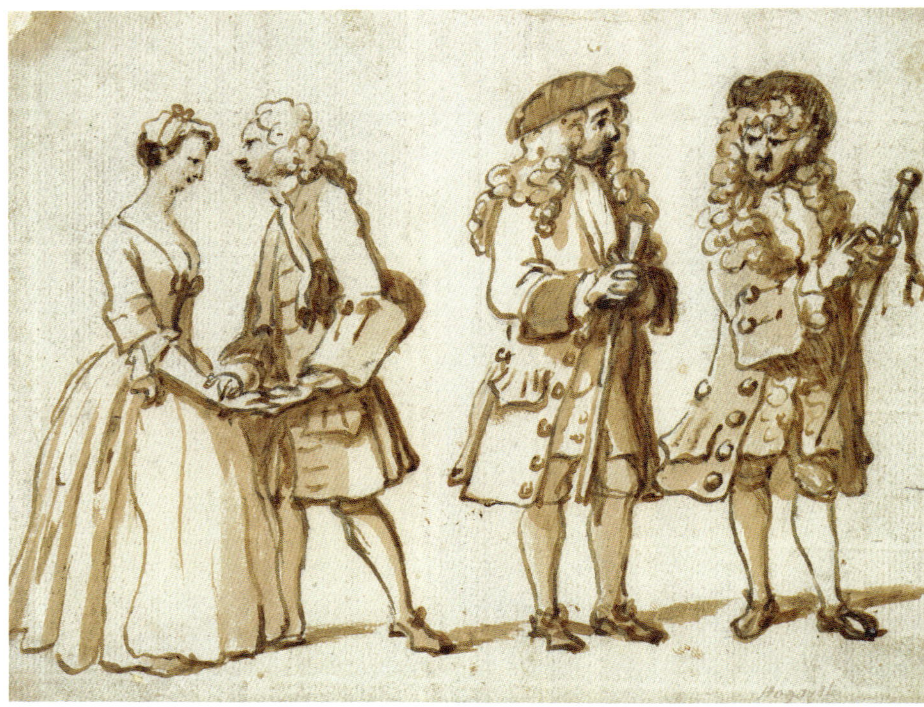

PROVENANCE Purchased by Queen Victoria at the H.P. Standly sale (Christie's, 14 April 1845, lot 1022)

LITERATURE Oppé 1948, no. 18; Oppé 1950, no. 340

These two pairs of figures are thought to be independent of one another: on the left a couple converse, on the right two bewigged figures stand in an attitude of disagreement. The pair on the left have been connected with an unfinished project, 'the happy marriage', two oil sketches for which are in the collection of Tate Britain, but their pose is not specific enough to indicate whether their relationship is happy or coercive. It has been suggested that the two male figures to the right are an early idea for the doctors in scene five of *A Harlot's Progress* (no. 86). Their disputing attitudes and contrasting appearances are certainly similar to those of the men in the print, but here one appears to gesticulate to a pair of forceps rather than a bottle and both are standing. KH

83

WILLIAM HOGARTH

***Dr Misaubin and Dr Ward** c.1730*

Pen and ink with wash over pencil, 10.2 × 15.4 cm
RCIN 913472

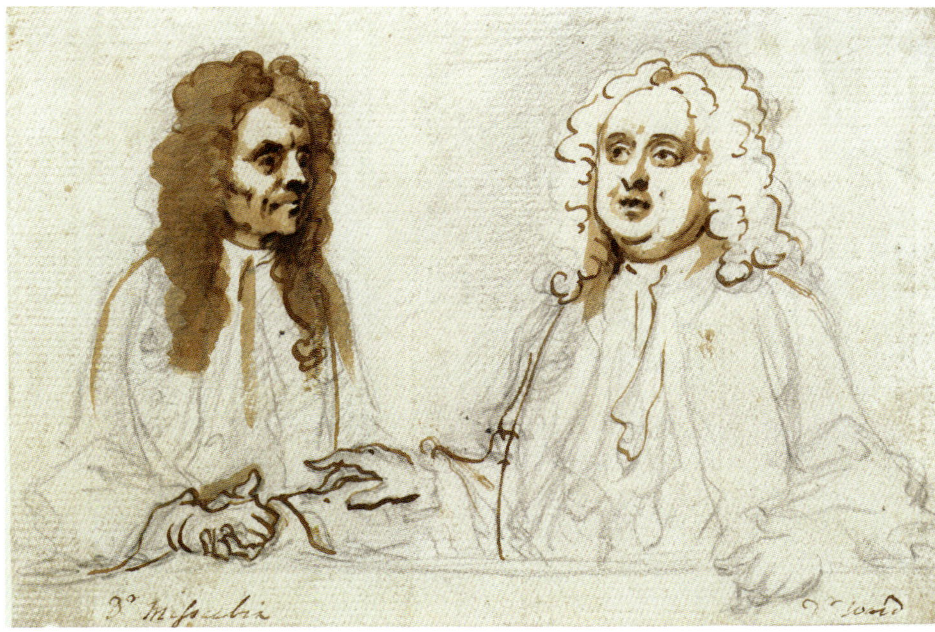

PROVENANCE Baker sale, from where acquired by H.P. Standly; purchased by Queen Victoria at the H.P. Standly sale (Christie's, 14 April 1845, lot 1022)

LITERATURE Oppé 1948, no. 19; Oppé 1950, no. 341

Unlike the drawing of four figures (no. 82), with which this work is probably contemporary, these two men appear to be portraits. The drawing is inscribed, though not in Hogarth's hand, with the names 'Dr Misaubin' and 'Dr Ward', identifications which were retained in the 1820s, when the drawing was engraved with this title by W.J. Smith. John Misaubin (1673–1734) was a French doctor who practised in London, and he appears looking similar in a satirical print by Arthur Pond.[31] The man on the right is probably Joshua Ward (1684/5–1761), a peddler of pills, although here Hogarth has not shown the birthmark on his right cheek which is apparent in other portraits. Ward was included in Hogarth's print the *Company of Undertakers* (1737) . Both Misaubin and Ward were regarded, especially by satirists, as quacks: Hogarth included them as such arguing over the treatment of the dying heroine in *A Harlot's Progress* (no. 86).[32] Joshua Ward was abroad from 1715 until 1734, the year of Misaubin's death, so the drawing must have been made during a short window in 1734 or is, more likely, an imagined interaction between the two men. KH

84

WILLIAM HOGARTH (1697–1764)

Boys peeping at Nature 1730

Pen and brush with ink and wash, over pencil, 12.2 × 13.3 cm
RCIN 913497

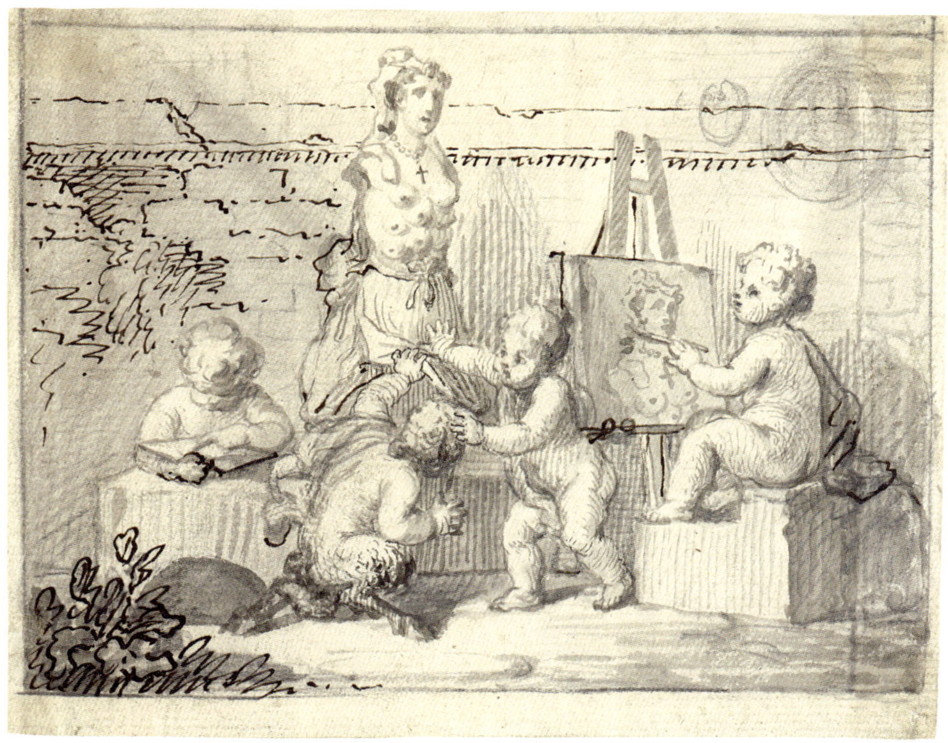

PROVENANCE Purchased by Queen Victoria at the H.P. Standly sale, Christie's, 14 April 1845, lot 1025

LITERATURE Oppé 1948, no. 22; Oppé 1950, no. 343; *Hogarth* 1971–2, no. 55; Clayton 2007, pp. 14–15

This drawing, a design for the subscription ticket for the *Harlot's Progress* series, shows two putti, one painting and one engraving, flanking a statue of the Ephesian Artemis (or Diana), a personification of Nature. A small satyr has lifted the skirt of the statue to peep underneath while a third putto tries to prevent him, pushing his head away with one hand and shielding the sculpture with the other. The painting putto uses the statue as his model, while the engraving putto ignores her completely.[33] This picture of childish amusement is also an artistic allegory: the satirist seeks to return to nature in his work and therefore must look at the seamier side of life, which the idealising artist has been taught to shun. The notion that art has the potential to reveal may reflect the moral message of *A Harlot's Progress*, which sought to shed light upon the consequences of a series of actions and choices.

Hogarth partially based his drawing on a painting of *Nature adorned by the Graces* by Peter Paul Rubens and Jan Brueghel, which shows three women decorating a statue of the Ephesian Artemis, while, below, Silenus is surrounded by a faun and three women. This painting was in the collection of Hogarth's father-in-law, Sir James Thornhill. Hogarth's satyr (which appears in a pose similar to the faun's in the Rubens-Bruegel painting) undoes the work done by the Graces by unadorning the statue.[34]

In his *Analysis of Beauty* of 1753 (no. 94), Hogarth criticised those painters that 'arrived at ... excellence in their works, by the mere dint of imitating with great exactness the beauties of nature, and by often copying and retaining strong ideas of graceful antique statues, which might sufficiently serve their purposes as painters, without their troubling themselves with a farther enquiry into the particular causes of the effects before them'. By peeping at nature, Hogarth's boys stretch beyond the confines of traditional artistic practice. KH

85

WILLIAM HOGARTH

Boys peeping at Nature 1730

Etching, 16.5 × 12.5 cm (sheet)
RCIN 811507

PROVENANCE Unidentified collector's mark (an oak leaf printed in black, not in Lugt); Royal Collection by 1845[35]

LITERATURE Paulson 1989, no. 120

Hogarth's etching, after the drawing in the Royal Collection (no. 84), was issued as a subscription ticket for his series *A Harlot's Progress*, which was completed in April 1732. In the printed version the artist has omitted the roughly sketched palette and portrait hanging on the wall behind the easel. Underneath the image is a receipt with a blank for the name of the subscriber, in this case filled in by the landscape painter George Lambert, for whom Hogarth also designed a bookplate.[36] Subscribers paid half a guinea on signing up to the project and half a guinea on its completion. Hogarth added inscriptions to his picture to illuminate his meaning – '*Antiquam exquirite Matrem*' ('seek out your ancient mother') from Virgil's *Aeneid*, and '*necesse est/ Indiciis monstrare recentibus abdita rerum,/ dabiturque Licentia Sumpta pudenter*' ('things not obvious must be presented in new terms . . . and licence is allowed if it is used with care') from Horace's *Ars Poetica*.[37] KH

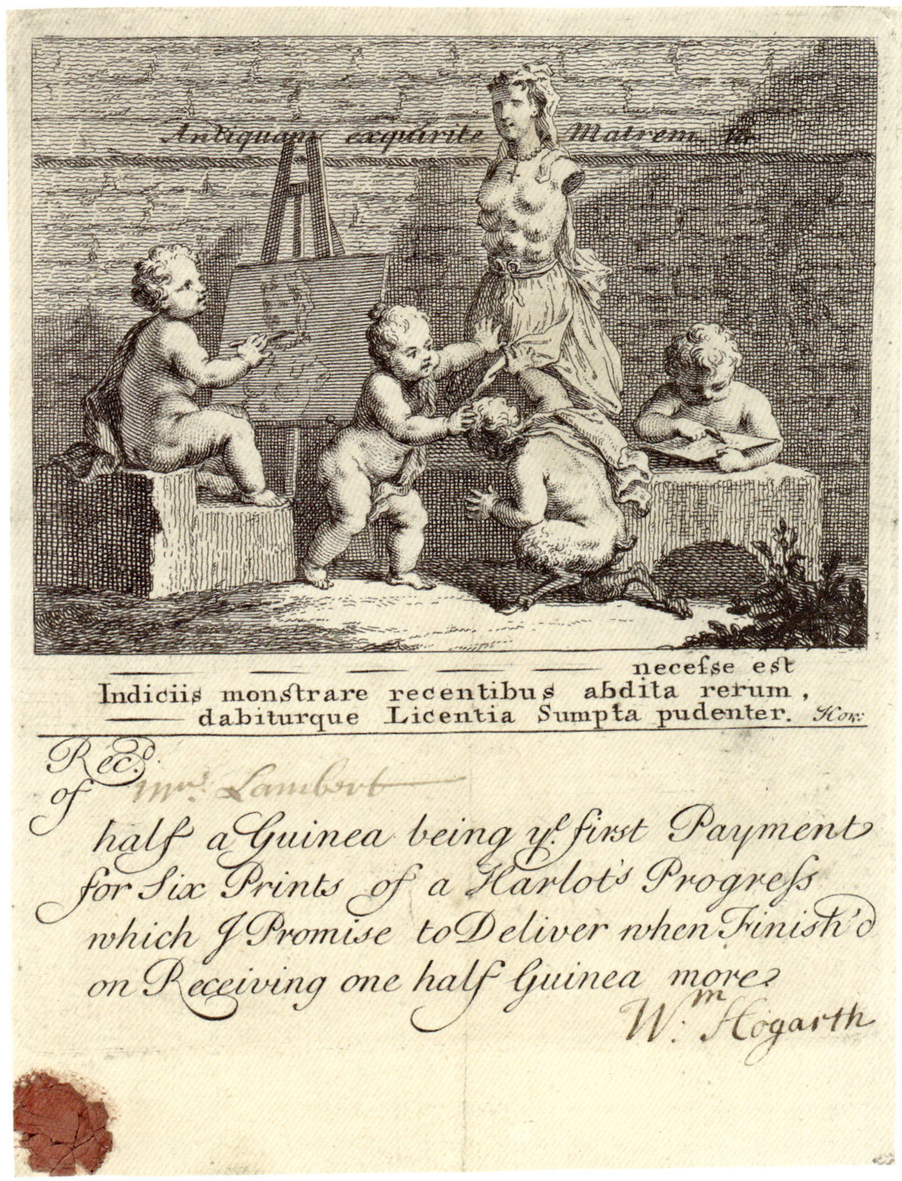

86

WILLIAM HOGARTH (1697–1764)

A Harlot's Progress 1732

Plate one
Etching and engraving, 31.7 × 39.0 cm (plate); 33.1 × 40.4 cm (sheet)
RCIN 812512.a

Plate two
Etching and engraving, 31.2 × 37.6 cm (plate); 32.7 × 39.2 cm (sheet)
RCIN 811512.b

Plate three
Etching and engraving, 32.0 × 38.8 cm (plate); 33.6 × 40.3 cm (sheet)
RCIN 811512.c

Plate four
Etching and engraving, 31.3 × 38.6 cm (plate); 33.1 × 40.0 cm (sheet)
RCIN 811512.d

Plate five
Etching and engraving, 31.9 × 39.0 cm (plate); 33.3 × 40.4 cm (sheet)
RCIN 811512.e

Plate six
Etching and engraving, 31.3 × 38.4 cm (plate); 32.8 × 39.8 cm (sheet)
RCIN 811512.f

PROVENANCE Perhaps the set listed in the inventory of prints at Buckingham House, *c.*1810;[38] alternatively, the set purchased by George IV when Prince of Wales from Colnaghi & Co., 6 March 1804;[39] certainly Royal Collection by 1845, when listed by John Glover[40]

LITERATURE Paulson 1989, nos 121–6

The six prints telling the cautionary story of *A Harlot's Progress* were published in April 1732, the first of Hogarth's 'modern moral subjects'. The scenes were to stand without accompanying text: 'my Picture was my Stage and men and women my actors who were by Means of certain Actions and expressions to exhibit a Dumb shew'.[41] Hogarth made the prints himself, noting in a newspaper announcement to his subscribers that he, 'being disappointed of the Assistance he proposed, is obliged to engrave them all himself, which will retard the Delivery of the Prints to the Subscribers about Two Months'.[42]

The *Progress* follows the fortunes of the young Moll Hackabout, recently arrived in London, who falls prey to Mother Needham, a real-life brothel-keeper in Park Place. The first print shows the meeting of Moll and Mother Needham; to the right, in a doorway, stands Colonel Francis Charteris, a notorious sexual predator, who died just before Hogarth finished his prints. In the second scene, Moll is seen as mistress to a wealthy Jewish lover, whom she has cuckolded with a younger man (seen stealing out of the doorway to the left). Her command of the situation is seen in the gesture she makes with her right hand – imperiously clicking her fingers – while kicking over a small table. The third print shows her in a reduced state, with bailiffs entering her dismal lodgings to arrest her as she drinks tea (in a parody of the tea table she overturned in the previous print). The fourth print shows her, gaunt and distressed, in Bridewell prison, beating hemp. By the fifth scene she is sick, shown dying before a fire, while her young son plays dangerously close to the flames, two doctors argue over her case and a woman rummages through a trunk of clothes to lower left. By the sixth and final print, Moll is dead, her coffin surrounded by a group of insincere mourners.

George Vertue noted that the series was extremely popular, with a large number of subscribers, and that 1,240 sets were printed. They were almost immediately pirated by other printsellers, who attempted to piggyback on a wave of popularity which led to the performance of an opera (*The Jew Decoy'd; or the Progress of a Harlot*) and a pantomime (*The Harlot's Progress: or, the Ridotto Al'Fresco: A Grotesque Pantomime Entertainment*).[43] The number of copies of the work prompted Hogarth to initiate the Engraving Copyright Act ('Hogarth's Act'), which protected an engraver's copyright over an image and which became law in June 1735.
KH

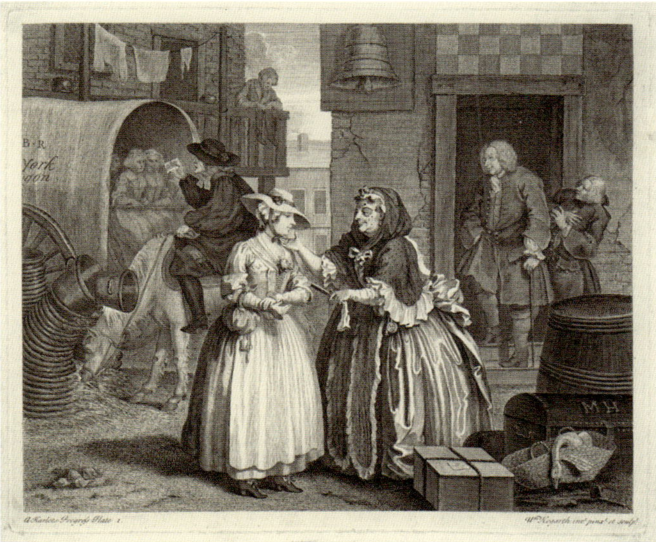
A Harlot's Progress Plate 1
Wm. Hogarth inv. pinx. et sculp.
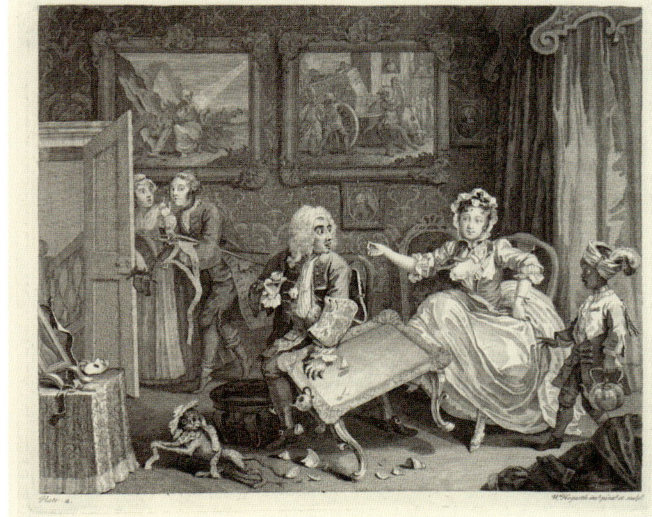
Plate 2
Wm. Hogarth inv. pinx. et sculp.
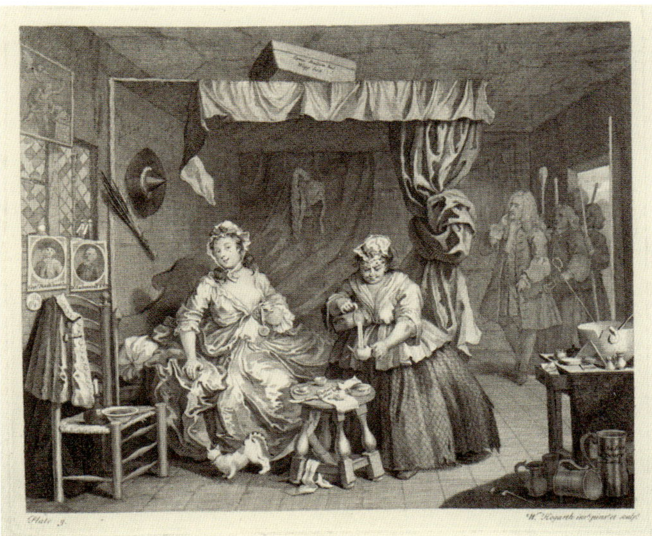
Plate 3
Wm. Hogarth inv. pinx. et sculp.
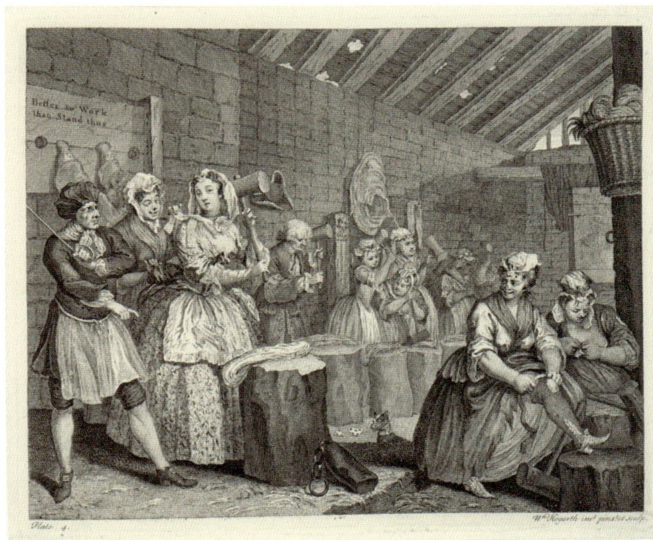
Better to Work
than Stand thus
Plate 4
Wm. Hogarth inv. pinx. et sculp.
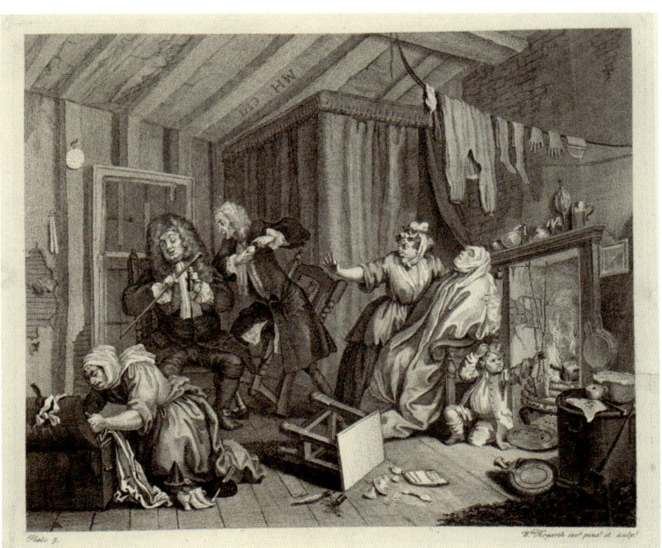
Plate 5
Wm. Hogarth inv. pinx. et sculp.
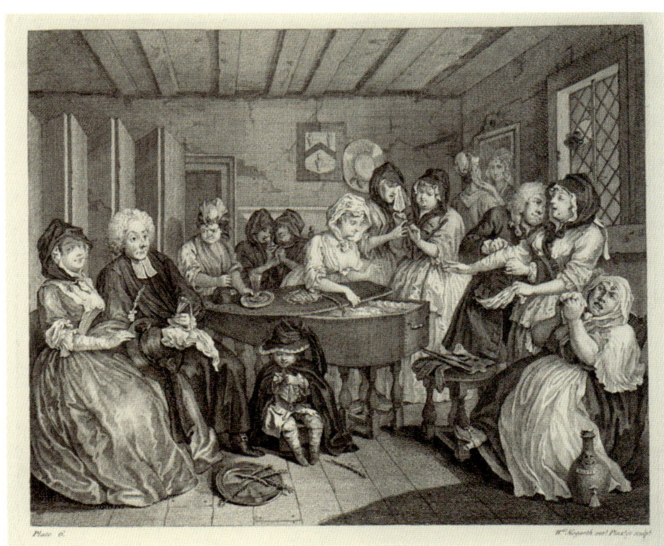
Plate 6
Wm. Hogarth inv. Pinx. et sculp.

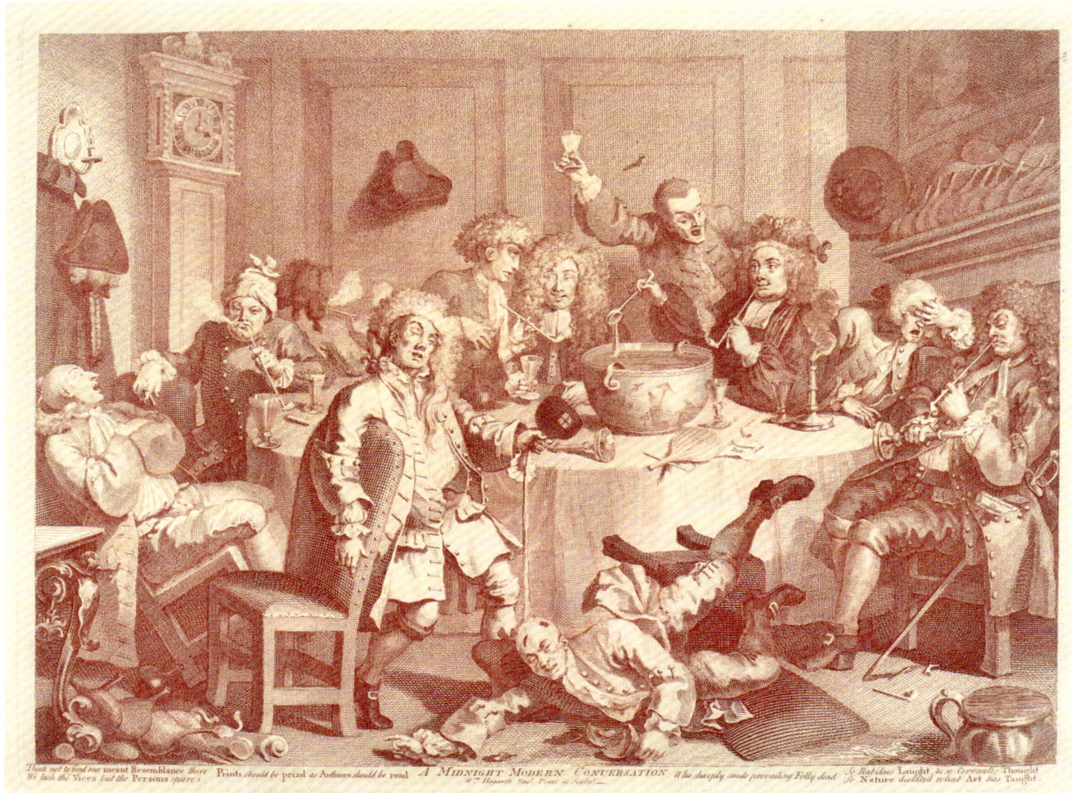

87

WILLIAM HOGARTH (1697–1764)

A Midnight Modern Conversation 1733

Etching and engraving, printed in red, 34.2 × 46.9 cm (plate); 35.9 × 48.4 cm (sheet)
RCIN 811532

PROVENANCE Royal Collection by 1845[44]

LITERATURE Paulson 1989, no. 128

Hogarth set his depiction of carousing drunks in the private room of a coffee house or tavern. The time is four in the morning and the drinkers are in advanced stages of inebriation, having enjoyed the contents of the (still full) punch bowl and of numerous bottles which litter the table and floor. As Hogarth's title makes clear his model, and object, is the conversation piece, which depicted groups of family or friends in decorous poses. This antithesis shows a group of men caught in a single, unposed, moment of chaos.

Although attempts have been made to identify the individual characters in the satire, Hogarth himself warned against such an approach. A rhyming couplet at the bottom of the print tells viewers that they should 'think not to find one meant Resemblance there/ We lash the Vices but the Persons spare'. The second line is adapted from one of Martial's epigrams (X, 33). Although prostitutes were known to frequent such institutions, the company is all male, and the vice is drunkenness rather than other libertine forms of behaviour. The message of the work is reinforced in the gestures of the man who has fallen over a chair in the foreground, whose outstretched hand points at a large pile of bottles, and of the standing man in the background, who raises his glass in a loud toast.

Hogarth's print was based upon a painting now in the Yale Center for British Art, and was published by subscription in March 1733. This impression, like a number which survive, has been printed in red, probably a nod to print connoisseurs who wished to gain ever more interesting impressions for their collection. Here Hogarth shows as much awareness of his market as he does of the follies of his day. KH

88

WILLIAM HOGARTH

A female nude *c.*1720–35

Black and white chalk on buff paper, 36.9 × 28.9 cm
RCIN 913482

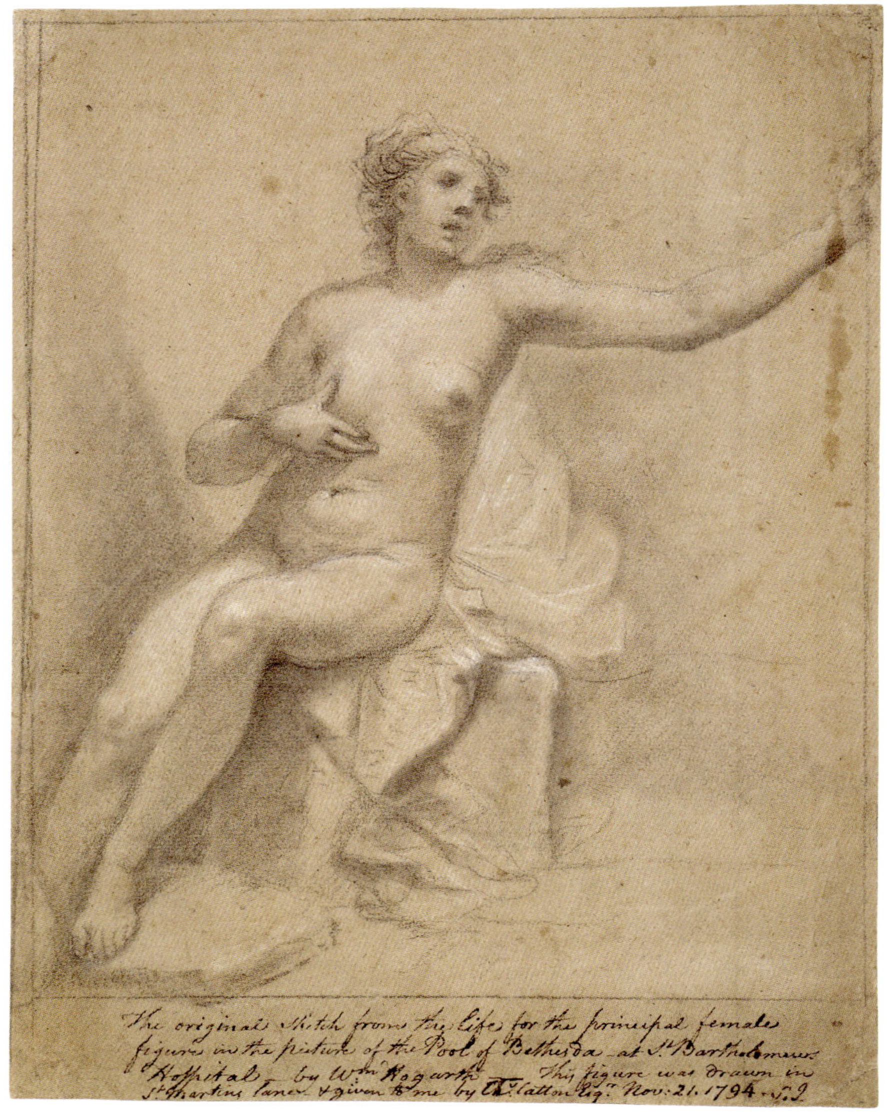

PROVENANCE Charles Catton; by whom given to Samuel Ireland, 21 November 1794; possibly his sales, London: Christie, Sharp and Harper, 6 May 1797, lot 135; part, or London: Leigh, Sotheby and Son, 7 May 1801, lot 308; part; probably acquired by George IV; Royal Collection by 1833

LITERATURE Oppé 1948, no. 25; *Holbein to Hockney* 2004 no. 56

The history of this drawing is given in an ink inscription at its foot by Samuel Ireland. As Ireland notes, this study of a woman with her left arm raised formed the basis of one of the figures in Hogarth's depiction of *The Pool of Bethesda* painted for St Bartholomew's Hospital in London in 1736. The painting depicted a group of invalids gathered around the pool with the miracle of Christ healing the paralytic at their centre, and was painted by Hogarth as a gift to the hospital, where it remains today.

Rather than making the study specifically for the painting, Hogarth seems to have used an existing drawing of a nude woman as the basis for the figure in the painting. The drawing probably shows a life model posing at the St Martin's Lane Academy. A similarly sized study of a nude woman reclining, also in black chalk on buff paper and also made at St Martin's Lane, is in the British Museum.[45] Hogarth's decision to use the drawing as the basis for the woman in the final painting may have been a late one: an oil sketch for the painting in the Manchester City Galleries shows the woman in a different pose, with her head turned to the left, and her left arm resting on the bed behind her. KH

89

AFTER WILLIAM HOGARTH

Marriage à-la-Mode 1743–5

GERARD JEAN BAPTISTE SCOTIN II (1698–AFTER 1755)

Plate one
38.4 × 46.5 cm (plate); 39.7 × 48.0 cm (sheet)
RCIN 811721.a

BERNARD BARON (*c.*1696–1762)

Plate two
38.0 × 46.3 cm (plate); 39.5 × 47.6 cm (sheet)
RCIN 811720.b

BERNARD BARON

Plate three
38.5 × 46.6 cm (plate); 39.7 × 48.0 cm (sheet)
RCIN 811723.b

SIMON FRANÇOIS RAVENET I (1706–1774)

Plate four
38.2 × 46.5 cm (plate); 39.6 × 47.9 cm (sheet)
RCIN 811723.c

SIMON FRANÇOIS RAVENET I

Plate five
38.2 × 46.5 cm (plate); 39.7 × 47.9 cm (sheet)
RCIN 811720.c

GERARD JEAN BAPTISTE SCOTIN II

Plate six
38.2 × 46.5 cm (plate); 39.5 × 47.2 cm (sheet)
RCIN 811723.d

PROVENANCE Perhaps the set listed in the inventory of prints at Buckingham House, *c.*1810;[46] certainly Royal Collection by 1845, when listed by John Glover[47]

LITERATURE Paulson 1989, nos 158–63

The set of six prints entitled *Marriage à-la-Mode* or 'fashionable marriage' was published by Hogarth in 1745, having been in planning since at least 1743. The prints are based on a set of paintings by Hogarth now in the National Gallery in London. By contrast to his previous printed sets, which he had engraved himself, here Hogarth oversaw the project, but employed French printmakers to make each of the plates. This, in itself, was treated as a selling point: in an early advertisement for the set, he explained his wish to have the prints 'engrav'd by the best Masters in Paris, after his own Paintings', and himself travelled to Paris in May 1743 to employ engravers. In doing so, Hogarth implied that his paintings were comparable to the works of the finest artists, which were eagerly being copied in reproductive prints by the sort of printmakers that he employed to work on the project. He noted in a later advertisement that he would engrave the heads of the figures himself 'for the better Preservation of the Characters and Expressions'.

Marriage à-la-Mode follows the fortunes of a young couple joined in a marriage of convenience which quickly unravels in the face of gambling, infidelity and greed. In the first scene, the marriage is arranged between their parents, who sit at opposite sides of a table. It is clear that the agreement is one of money for title: the father of the daughter is clearly wealthy, while the young man (Viscount Squanderfield) is heir to an earldom: his father holds a lengthy family tree, and sits in a room where everything is marked with coronets. The couple's fate is already implied in the attention paid by the lawyer Silvertongue to the young girl, and her fiancé's lack of interest in her. Boredom and debt has set in by the second scene, where the couple are shown slumped into chairs as a horrified steward leaves the room with a stack of bills. The third scene shows the young Earl Squanderfield (who has inherited his father's title) visiting the quack doctor Misaubin with a young mistress: they seek treatment for venereal disease. The earl is not the only one to be unfaithful: the fourth scene shows his wife arranging a rendezvous with Silvertongue. The fifth scene shows the results of a duel between the earl and the lawyer: the earl has been fatally wounded as Silvertongue climbs out of the window. In the final scene, the countess is seen dying: her young son (marked with the spot of venereal disease) is held up to her face, while a man removes the rings from her left hand. A sheet on the floor, with 'Counsellor Silvertongue's last dying speech' indicates that the lawyer has been executed.

Hogarth appears to have planned a sequel to the *Marriage*, which was never finished. Two surviving oil studies which show scenes from a happy marriage are probably related to this scheme.[48] KH

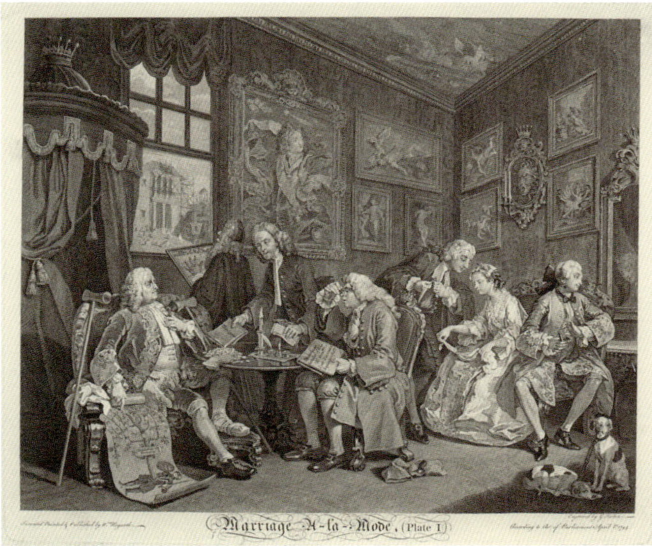
Marriage A-la-Mode, (Plate I)

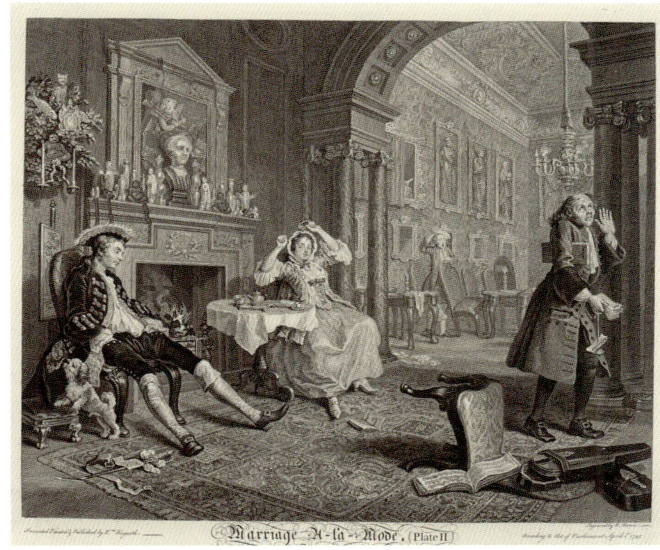
Marriage A-la-Mode, (Plate II)

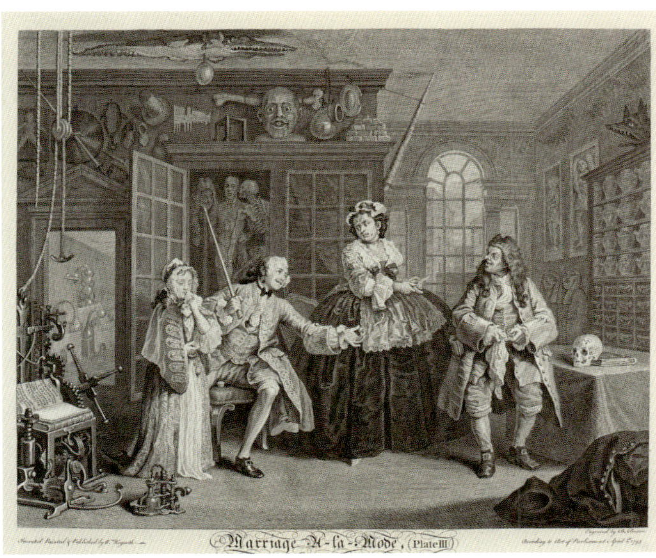
Marriage A-la-Mode, (Plate III)

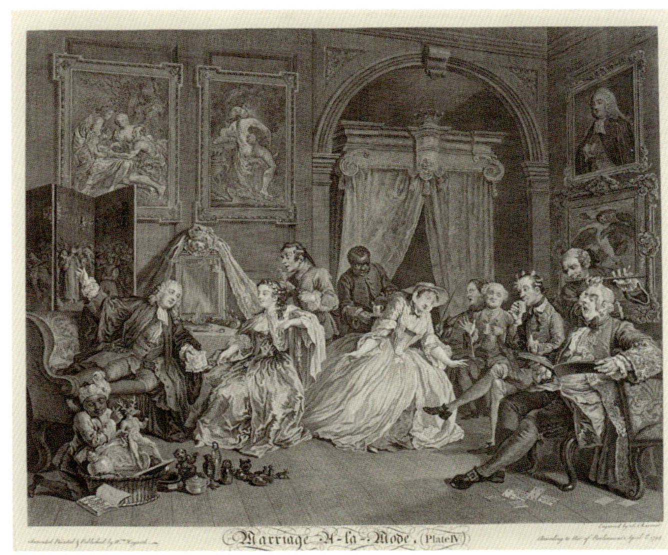
Marriage A-la-Mode, (Plate IV)

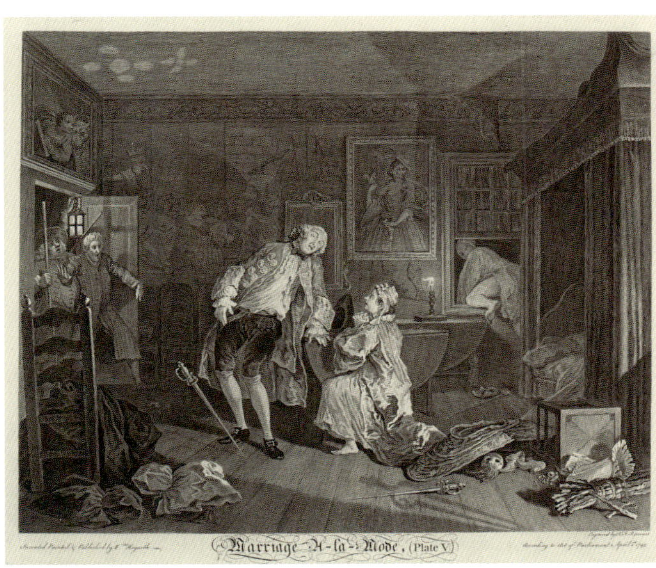
Marriage A-la-Mode, (Plate V)

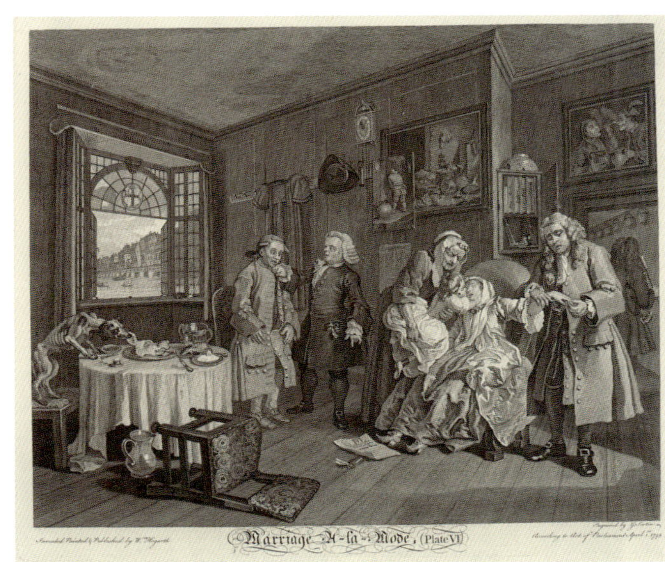
Marriage A-la-Mode, (Plate VI)

90

WILLIAM HOGARTH (1697–1764)

The Battle of the Pictures 1745

Etching, 20.3 × 22.2 cm (sheet); 19.8 × 21.2 cm (plate)
RCIN 811767

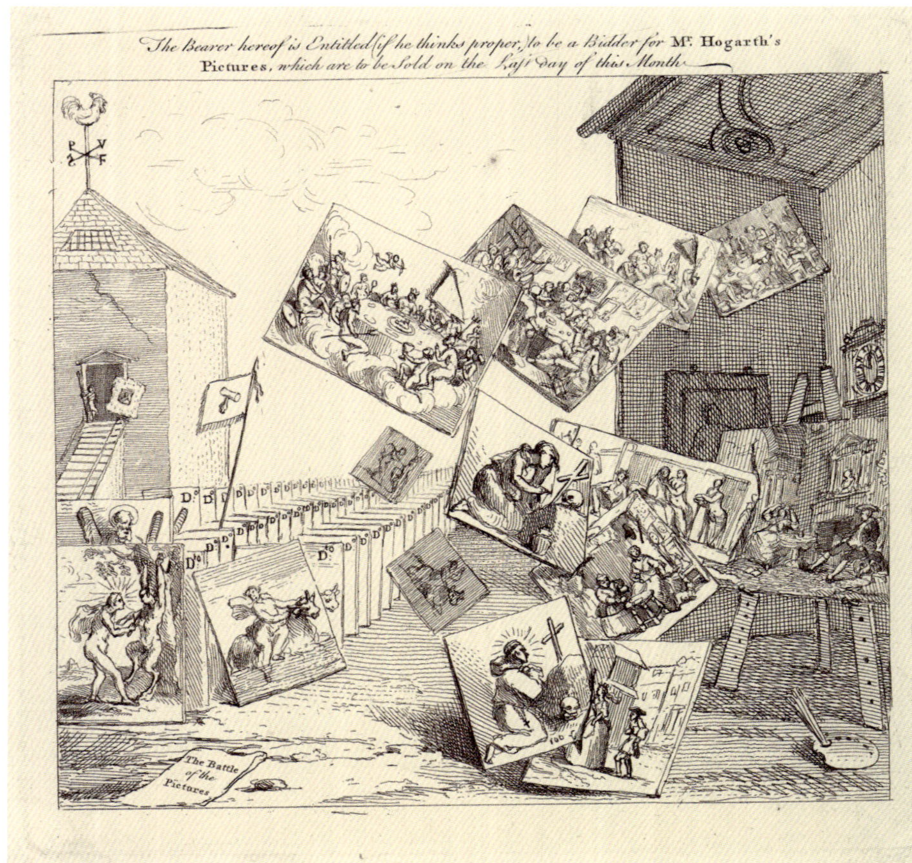

PROVENANCE Royal Collection by 1845[49]

LITERATURE Paulson 1989, no. 157

In February 1745, Hogarth sold by auction many of the oil paintings on which his successful prints had been based. Entrance to and bidding at the auction was by ticket, as usual decorated with a witty Hogarth picture. Here, Old Master paintings are shown marching into battle with Hogarth's own works: the second scene of *Marriage à-la-Mode* is under attack on its easel from the Aldobrandini *Wedding* (an ancient fresco now in the Vatican Museum, which was known through printed and painted copies) while *A Midnight Modern Conversation* sails above, competing with a Bacchanalian scene. Hogarth's open studio contrasts with the auction house on the left, which is entered by a grand staircase and has a large crack appearing in its wall. The clock at the back of the studio shows the time creeping towards midday, when Hogarth's auction was to start. Hogarth's title, inscribed on a sheet at the bottom of the picture, is a reference to Jonathan Swift's *Battle of the Books* (1705), which describes a contest between ancient and modern authors set in the King's Library.
KH

91

WILLIAM HOGARTH

The proportions of Garrick and Quin 1746

Pen and brown ink over pencil, 22.6 × 18.5 cm
RCIN 913477

PROVENANCE Collection of J.P. Kemble; his sale, (10th day), lot 76; purchased from Colnaghi & Co. for £15 15s by George IV[50]

LITERATURE Oppé 1948, no. 39; Oppé 1950, no. 351

This letter from Hogarth was sent to one 'TH', an unidentified member of a literary society in Norwich. In it Hogarth contrasts the figures of James Quin and David Garrick, both popular actors, who in 1746 were performing together in *The Fair Penitent*. Hogarth knew and had painted both actors. Garrick was tall and thin, while Quin was famously short and fat. Hogarth proposes an experiment to study the perception of proportion: 'Let the figures be doubled down so as to be seen but one at once, then let it be ask'd which represents the Tallest man'. The question appears to have arisen in reaction to a print of Garrick, which Hogarth describes overleaf as taken from a painting of Garrick as Richard III 'painted from Mr Garrick, as big as the life'. This letter may be Hogarth's response to criticism levelled at the print after his painting of Garrick in that role, which had been published on 20 June 1746.

Hogarth's sketch was published in facsimile by the London-based Robert Laurie and James Whittle in 1797, by which time society was in the grip of 'Hogarthomania'.[51] A facsimile after the full letter was published in 1808. KH

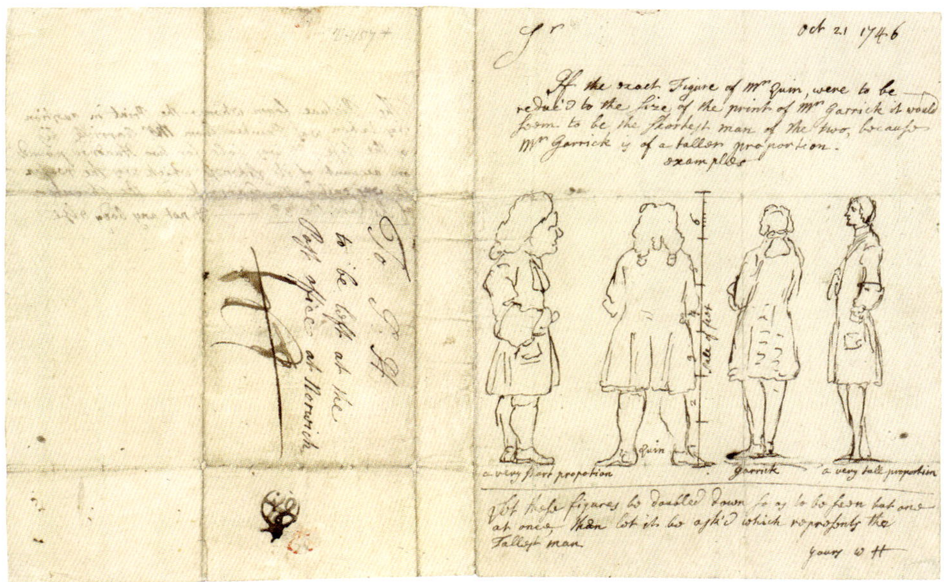

Sr Oct 21 1746

If the exact Figure of Mr Quin, were to be reduc'd to the size of the print of Mr Garrick it would seem to be the shortest man of the two, because Mr Garrick is of a taller proportion.

examples

Let these figures be doubled down so as to be seen but one at once, then let it be ask'd which represents the Tallest man

yours W H

The Picture from whence the Print in question was taken, was Painted from Mr Garrick big as the life, & was sold for two Hundred pounds on account of its Likeness which was the reason it was call'd Mr Garrick in the Character of Richard the 3d —— & not any body else

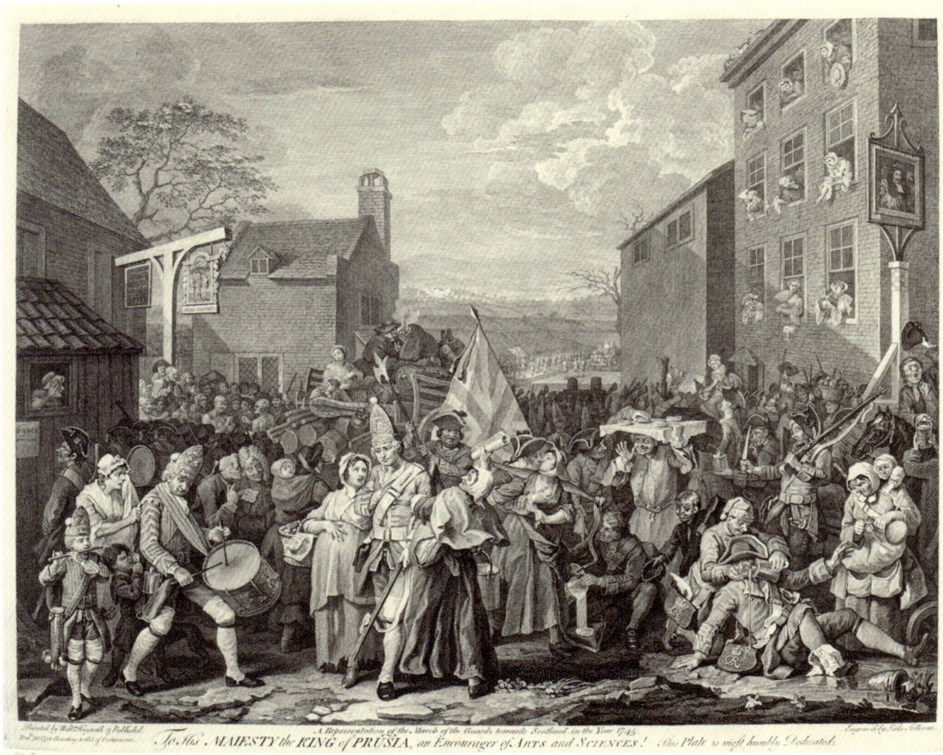

92

LUKE SULLIVAN (1705–1771) AFTER WILLIAM HOGARTH

The March to Finchley 1750

Etching and engraving, 43.0 × 55.4 cm (plate); 44.0 × 56.4 cm (sheet)
RCIN 811901

PROVENANCE Unidentified collector's mark (an oak leaf printed in black; not in Lugt); Royal Collection by 1845[52]

LITERATURE Paulson 1989, no. 184; *Hogarth* 2006, p. 84

This print, which was engraved by Luke Sullivan after a painting by Hogarth, was made available by subscription. Subscribers were encouraged to pay an extra three shillings to enter a lottery to win the original painting. When subscriptions closed, 1,843 people had entered, and Hogarth increased the figure to 2,010 by giving a further 167 tickets free to the Foundling Hospital, which won the draw. The Foundling Museum reacquired the painting in 2002.[53]

Hogarth's picture is set in 1745 and shows the Guards marching out of London to counter the Jacobite rising led by the 'Young Pretender'. The scene is set at the Tottenham Court Road turnpike, and is one of chaos, highlighted further by the order of the troops who march into the distance. Women and children cling to the departing soldiers, a man has collapsed, drunk and dishevelled, in a puddle and the standing soldier in the foreground is assailed by a woman who carries a print of the Duke of Cumberland and another who attacks him with a copy of the *Jacobite's Journal* (in reality a pro-Hanoverian publication, but probably here intended to signify her sympathy to the Jacobite cause).[54] The inn sign to the far right shows King Charles (II) – a popular pub name, but also a reminder of the threat of the Pretender, who aspired to be the next King Charles. This early state bears the publication date 30 December 1750, subsequently changed to 31 when it was found that 30 was a Sunday.

The *March to Finchley* was famously dedicated to Frederick II of Prussia: Hogarth's riposte, it was said, for the unfavourable reaction of George II to his work. On being shown the painting, the king is said to have grumbled, 'Does the fellow mean to laugh at my guards?… [H]e deserves to be picketed for his insolence! Take this trumpery out of my sight.'[55] A letter of 1765, from an anonymous correspondent who claimed to be a friend of Hogarth, also claimed that the painting had been shown to George II, who declined to buy it, but, after it had been returned to the artist 'his collection of prints were sent for, and some of them bought at the common prices'.[56] The truth is hard to discern, but the dedication of a print depicting the defence of the Hanoverian regime to a foreign ruler cannot have been anything but an expression of disgruntlement at the patronage opportunities available at the British court, and it may be relevant that Hogarth had not been given the position of Painter in Ordinary, granted by the King to John Shackleton (d. 1767) in March 1749.[57] KH

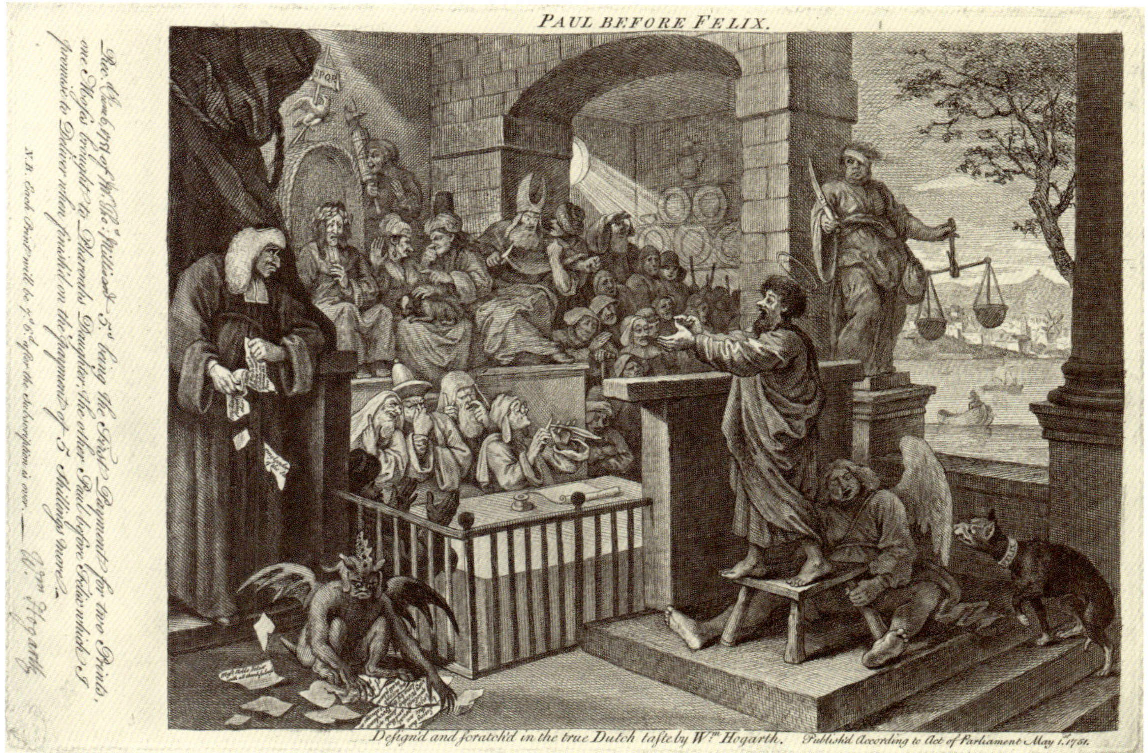

93

WILLIAM HOGARTH (1697–1764)

Paul before Felix Burlesqu'd 1751

Etching and engraving with mezzotint tone, 26.1 × 40.0 cm (plate); 26.6 × 40.5 cm (sheet)
RCIN 811923

PROVENANCE Perhaps the impression listed in the inventory of prints at Buckingham House, *c.*1810;[58] certainly Royal Collection by 1845, when listed by John Glover[59]

LITERATURE Paulson 1989, no. 191

Paul before Felix Burlesqu'd was issued as a subscription ticket for Hogarth's pair of biblical prints *Paul before Felix* and *Moses brought to Pharaoh's Daughter*. The image, which was captioned 'Design'd and scratch'd in the true Dutch taste', laid out Hogarth's dislike of the Dutch art which was being imported in great volume, and of the connoisseurs who purchased such work at the expense of home-grown talent. A number of the spectators in this print are dressed in the Dutch style. In the same year as *Paul before Felix Burlesqu'd* was published, the celebrated collectors Samuel Harding and Thomas Hudson had been duped by Hogarth's friend the painter Benjamin Wilson into believing prints Wilson himself had made were the works of Rembrandt.

Hogarth based the image on one of the prints for which it recorded a subscription, *Paul before Felix*, which itself was based on an oil painting of that subject painted by Hogarth for Lincoln's Inn. The scene shows the moment when Paul defends himself before the judge Felix against the accusations laid forth by the lawyer Tertullus.[60] The ticket parodies the original, showing a motley band of judges and lawyers pulling faces as they listen to a diminutive Paul make his case. Justice looks from behind her blindfold and a little demon reassembles the sheets of paper torn by Turtullus behind him.

The print proved so popular on its issue in 1751 that Hogarth began to issue it as a separate print, and to use *Boys peeping at Nature* (no. 85) as the subscription ticket for the two biblical scenes. This impression is an early state, when the print was still being used as a subscription ticket, made out in this case to Thomas Millisant, who has not been identified. KH

94

WILLIAM HOGARTH (1697–1764)

The Analysis of Beauty 1753

Printed on paper, red leather binding with gold tooling; arms of George II stamped on both boards, 26.3 × 21.3 × 2.4 cm

RCIN 1151343

PROVENANCE Probably acquired by George II

The Analysis of Beauty, written by Hogarth and published in 1753, sets out the artist's ideas on taste and artistic practice. The text is defensive in tone, written partly in response to criticism of Hogarth's work, and partly anticipating criticism of the text itself. A key theme is the role of the curved 'line of beauty', which Hogarth had introduced into the frontispiece to his engraved works in 1745 as a teaser: 'no Egyptian hieroglyphic ever amused more than it did for a time; painters and sculptors came to me to know the meaning of it, being as much puzzled with it as other people'.[61] Hogarth's treatise met with a hostile reaction from a number of commentators, among them Joshua Reynolds and Paul Sandby, but this copy, which bears the stamped arms associated with books owned by George II, was clearly acquired for the Royal Library soon after publication. However controversial, the text had a broad circulation.[62] KH

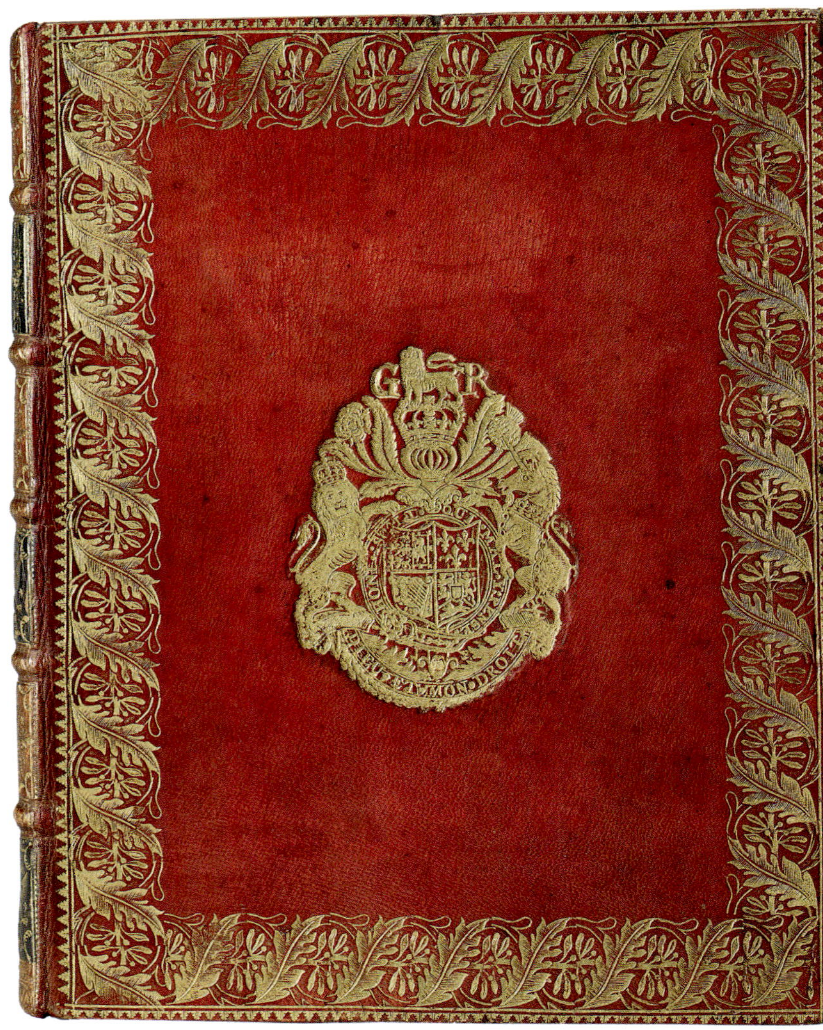

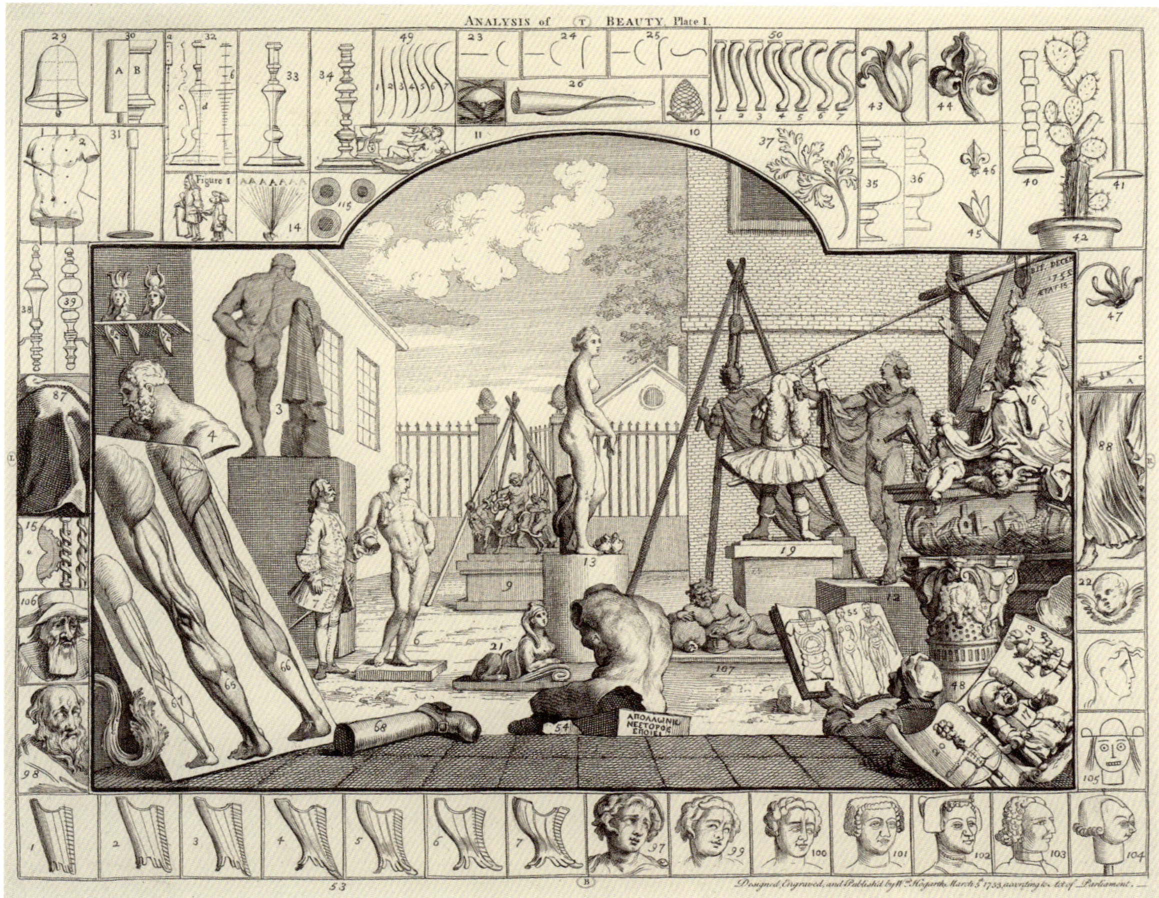

95

WILLIAM HOGARTH

The Analysis of Beauty, plate one 1753

Etching and engraving, 38.6 × 49.7 cm (plate); 59.6 × 51.0 cm (sheet)
RCIN 811944.a

PROVENANCE Perhaps the impression purchased by George IV, when Prince of Wales, from Colnaghi & Co., 5 March 1804;[63] certainly Royal Collection by 1845, when listed by John Glover[64]

LITERATURE Paulson 1989, no. 195

This print, one of a pair of plates, was produced by Hogarth to explain his tract *The Analysis of Beauty*, published in March 1753. The *Analysis* intended to consider objects 'in a new Light, both as to Colour and Form' and the two prints were 'to point out to the reader what sorts of objects he is to look for and examine in nature, or in the works of the greatest masters'.[65] Hogarth's prints could be used decoratively as well as instructively: in the same advertisement, he promised they would be 'fit to Frame for Furniture'.[66]

The first plate of the *Analysis* shows John Cheere's statuary yard, full of sculpture, diagrams and figures. Cheere's premises were near Hyde Park Corner, and contained lead and plaster versions of sculpture for interior and garden decoration. Although Hogarth thought his prints could be framed and hung on a wall, the central image, and its border of smaller diagrams, is full of numbered references to the text alongside which it was supposed to be viewed. No. 20, directly centre in the top border of the image, shows the line which Hogarth believed to be the basis of beauty. The figure on a pedestal seen from behind (numbered 19) is the actor Quin, who appears in a similar stance in Hogarth's letter on proportion (no. 91). The second plate shows a line of dancers, who change from elegant to clumsy as the composition moves from left to right. KH

V

Furniture and Interiors in the Royal Palaces 1714–1760

RUFUS BIRD

AT THE BEGINNING of the reign of George I the embroiderer Stephen Toulouze was paid 'For taking out of the 4 Corners of a Crimson Velvet Covering of a Barge four A's and Embroidering instead of them four G's £2.5.0'.[1] Updating rather than replacing, perhaps valuing continuity, certainly liking to save money – all these things are typical of George I's approach to furnishing his new residences. Here we explore the transformation in British furniture in royal interiors during the first half of the eighteenth century. We will try to establish the degree to which the early Georgians furnished their palaces in a recognisably British style.

The evolution of styles in furniture and interiors across the reigns of the first two Georges was connected, perhaps for the first time, to the development of architectural ideas. It was also linked to changes in State and Court business. These years witnessed the creation and furnishing of some of the last formal Baroque royal apartments, yet the theory, design and practice followed by architects and designers in royal service from the accession of George I until approximately mid-century could be said to be in some ways revolutionary – marked by the gradual migration from France as the primary centre of influence to Italy. In the context of political thought the developments were considered radical, and, when seen beside the furnishing projects of William III and Mary II, the programme of decoration was visually distinct. More profound and less obvious was the development of the treatment of the exterior and the interior as a unity. Houghton Hall in Norfolk is one of the very few complete examples of this form of 'total furnishing' created during the period; the royal equivalents at New Lodge, Richmond, and the White House at Kew have not survived intact.

Crucial to early Georgian royal furnishing was the relationship between the routine processes of procurement and the emergence of new ideas in architecture and design. Royal furnishing was delivered in the period by the Great Wardrobe, a department funded by the government using an address book of reliable craftsmen. The artist who did most to transform taste in the visual arts during the period was William Kent. The relationship between Kent and the Wardrobe can be seen played out in the important royal campaigns at Hampton Court and Kensington. It must also be seen in the wider context of furniture design in Britain during the period and the theories which underpinned building programmes and inevitably informed their interiors.

FIG. 31
Thomas Hudson
John, 2nd Duke of Montagu, c.1740
Oil on canvas
The Duke of Buccleuch and Queensberry

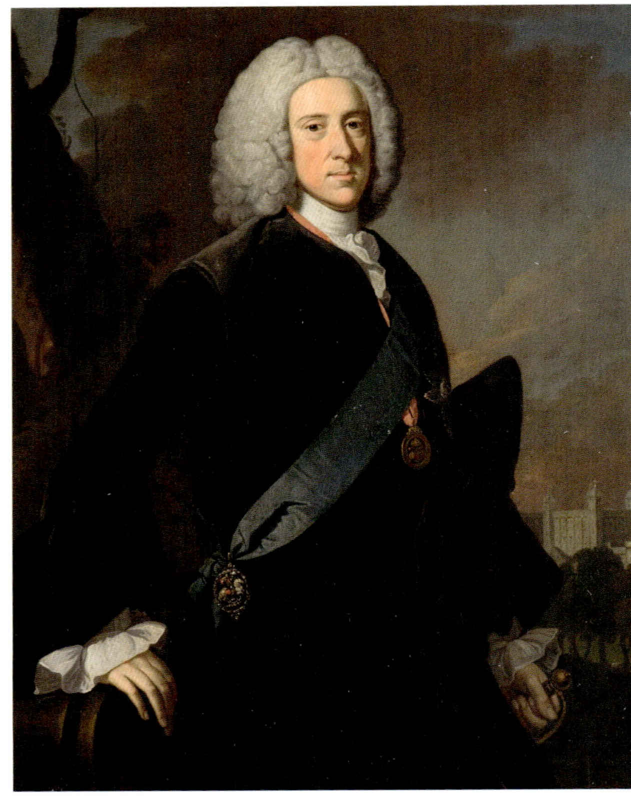

The Great Wardrobe

For the most part, the way the royal palaces looked to a visitor at Court in the eighteenth century was determined by what was ordered by the Great Wardrobe.[2] The Mastership of the Great Wardrobe, a profitable sinecure (and the only office in the Royal Household which could be retained for life), was held from 1689 to 1709 by Ralph, 1st Duke of Montagu, and from 1709 to 1750 by his son John, 2nd Duke of Montagu (fig. 31).[3] General decisions on the type and form of decoration – the quantity and type of furniture to be supplied, the colour of the wall hangings, and so on – were the responsibility of the Lord Chamberlain.[4] He, in consultation with the King and other senior members of the household, would issue a warrant to supply particular pieces. The responsibility for delivering the goods resided with the Great Wardrobe, and the Master of the Great Wardrobe selected the craftsmen.

Chief in the hierarchy of craftsmen during the period, in terms of both importance and cost, was the upholsterer. During George I's reign the warrants were sent to the partnership of Thomas Phill and Jeremiah Fletcher. After his death in 1723 Fletcher was succeeded in the partnership by his widow, Rebecca, and it continued until Phill's death in 1729, when John Gilbert became the preferred upholsterer. However, he died the same year and was succeeded by his widow, Sarah.[5] Between 1736 and her death in 1741, Sarah Gilbert entered into a partnership with William Reason; and after a short-lived partnership with Sarah Lowys, from 1744 onwards Reason continued alone as upholsterer to the Great Wardrobe. Often the fabrics were sourced from a mercer and several names recur during George I's reign, including John Johnson & Co., Richard Chamberlayne & Co. and Anthony Freeman. In 1726, Freeman supplied a total of 855 yards of crimson Genoa damask for the Great Gallery at Kensington.[6] The upholsterer carried out the job of covering chairs, stools and settees, of making curtains and covering cornices, and of upholstering the beds. For example, in the period Michaelmas 1725 to Michaelmas 1726, Thomas Phill charged £26 'for making the crimson Damask Hangings lined with Linnen & laced with crimson Arras Lace' for the Great Gallery at Kensington Palace.[7] A third supplier was the 'laceman': he supplied *passementerie*, gimp and other trimmings. Again at the Great Gallery, William Weeks supplied '827 yds¼ of broad crimson in grain silk arras lace binding £103.8.1½', for the crimson damask hangings, window curtains, chairs and stools.[8]

If at the beginning of the eighteenth century the upholsterer reigned supreme, by the end of George II's reign this primacy was challenged by a new type of practitioner, the 'upholder'. Upholders could deliver a complete package of furnishing to a newly built house, from the dining-table and chairs to the door handles and doors themselves and the mouldings along the dado rail. These large workshops were established as a convenient destination for the newly wealthy land-owning class building large houses. The heyday of these businesses came during the latter part of the eighteenth century, although their roots are found in the traditional specialised trades of cabinet-maker and joiner. While the distinction between 'cabinet-maker' (maker of tables, stands, chests, mirrors etc.) and 'joiner' (maker of chairs, stools, settees and beds) persisted in the first part of the eighteenth century, these boundaries disappeared with the arrival in the 1750s and 1760s of the new, much larger firms of upholders, such as Chippendale & Rannie, Mayhew & Ince, Vile & Cobb, Whittle & Norman, France & Bradburn and the father and son team of William & John Linnell.[9] It was Vile & Cobb who supplied furniture to George III and Queen Charlotte in the following reign, until 1763, when they were succeeded by France & Bradburn. The Great Wardrobe was discontinued in 1782.

The creators of furniture (i.e. cabinet-makers and joiners) who earlier filled the pages of the Great Wardrobe's accounts were the joiners Richard Roberts (accounts recorded between 1714 and 1729) and Henry Williams (accounts recorded between 1729 and 1758), and the cabinet-makers James Moore and John Gumley, a partnership formed in 1714 which was employed for almost the entire reign of George I.[10] John Gumley was the glazier and concerned himself with the supply of mirrors, Moore was the gilder and cabinet-maker. James Moore died in October 1726 and John Gumley in 1728. Gumley's widow, Elizabeth, continued the firm by entering into a partnership with William Turing. The Great Wardrobe accused this new partnership of overcharging and from 1729 turned instead to James Moore's former apprentice Benjamin Goodison.[11] While the cast of suppliers to the Royal Household and their specific roles were, for this period, largely unchanging, the role of the joiner seems gradually to have evolved. For instance, during the reign of George I, Richard Roberts supplied all the beds and seat furniture, but none of it was gilded. His skill was in the provision of an elegant, functional but essentially basic frame, on which upholstery could draw the eye.[12] His successor, Henry Williams, continued to supply large quantities of seat furniture to the palaces (at all levels of the Household). Meanwhile the cabinet-maker Benjamin Goodison continued in the footsteps of his master and predecessor James Moore, supplying giltwood tables, mirrors, stands and the like. Gradually the orders began to overlap: for instance, both joiner and cabinet-maker supplied gaming tables and, perhaps most significantly, both supplied giltwood furniture.

Prior to the 1720s, there was little gilded furniture outside the royal palaces and it was generally reserved for the principal rooms of the State Apartment.[13] From the 1720s until the accession of George III, gilded furniture, especially against a background of silk or tapestry wall-hangings, was regarded as the richest possible furnishing.[14] The next step down was the partly gilded scheme, in which carved polished wood was embellished with some gilding, usually on the raised surfaces, which allowed the interplay of light and dark. This scheme was often combined with a matching upholstery and wall-hanging scheme in 'caffoy' (a wool-pile fabric often with a silk-ground weave) or 'moquette' (the same but with a linen-ground weave) used in principal rooms to imitate silk velvets: the 'lesser' textile employed at the opening of the sequence of rooms in an apartment alluded to the riches to come. The adjoining, superior spaces (usually a Drawing Room, Bedchamber and Closet) were hung with progressively richer textiles, in ascending order – silk damask, silk velvet, tissue and tapestry. While there was a distinct hierarchy of materials ranging from tapestry, figured velvet and tissue all the way down to the humbler cotton, linen, dimity, calico and worsteds (with harateen, cheney, moreen, paragon and serge somewhere in between), a simpler hierarchy existed in the treatment of carved or polished wood.[15] Treatments in silver (rare) and gold (widespread) are recorded, with the former less popular due to its liability to tarnish, even following the customary application of a protective lacquer, sometimes tinted yellow to provide a silvery-gold surface. In 1727 Gumley & Moore supplied 'For The Great Gallary at Kensington' 'Six oval sconces silver'd at £8 each £48', while Gumley & Turing supplied '2 very large carved & gilt frames for Marble Slabbs at £40 each £80'.[16] These were accompanied by a pair of stands each (no. 104). For almost all gilded furniture of the period, the surface (prepared to receive the gold leaf) was either carved directly in wood (more durable and expensive) or into gesso (less durable but cheaper). Carved gesso allowed considerable freedom of expression and a higher degree of elaboration in design than was possible in wood. Gesso was most common around 1700 but gradually fell out of use as workshops moved towards carving in wood and by mid-century had virtually disappeared. During the period of transition the two techniques were often combined. Gilding conceals this distinction but it is possible to tell that the candle-stands no. 103 are entirely carved in gesso, while nos 112 and 113 are entirely carved in wood and the side-tables nos 108 and 109 combine both techniques: the bases are in carved wood and the tops in gesso.

During the eighteenth century, furniture intended for the richest interiors was water-gilded, a process which included preparing the ground with a white gesso (a chalky mix of whiting and water), which was brushed on to the surface as thinly as possible, especially where there was carving. On top of this was applied a yellow or red (and sometimes both) layer of clay: this was usually a very thin coloured ground. On top of this was laid a weak size made from a mix of water and a little animal glue which, for a fairly short time and in reasonably warm conditions, provided a sticky surface for exceptionally thin layers of gold leaf, which were carefully brushed on. Once all the gold was applied, a distinction was made between areas (often flat and smooth) to be given a bright burnish and those to be left unburnished or even toned down. Sometimes the red clay preparation layer is found on areas intended to be burnished and the yellow clay under unburnished areas. The alternative, cheaper (and quicker) treatment was oil gilding. In this process, the gesso layer was treated with a size made with linseed oil to provide a sticky surface for the gold (which remained sticky for longer than in the water-gilding process). In this case the surface did not take burnishing and was therefore of an even and generally slightly duller complexion. During the eighteenth century, oil-gilding was generally used for surfaces where the richness of the carving was paramount and which did not require elaborate burnishing.[17]

The Principal Residences, St James's Palace and Windsor Castle

The important furnishing campaigns during the early Georgian period took place at Hampton Court and Kensington Palace and are discussed below (pp. 198–211). However, neither of these palaces was considered to be on a par with the two residences of paramount historical and ceremonial significance to the British monarchy, St James's Palace and Windsor Castle. It is worth briefly examining the Great Wardrobe's impact in these two spaces, though nothing made in this period survives in either. From 1714 to 1760, the payments in the Wardrobe accounts for St James's Palace far exceed those for Hampton Court, Kensington Palace and Windsor Castle together. Across both reigns, there was a steady stream of replacement, refurnishing and movement of objects. Many of the activities of the family are clearly visible in the accounts: for example, the Wardrobe accounts record payments in 1733 to the upholsterer Sarah Gilbert for the decoration of the 'French Chapel' at St James's Palace for the marriage of Anne, Princess Royal to William, Prince of Orange, which took place the following year.[18]

In the various apartments at St James's, there was a seemingly never-ending flow of furniture and materials. In the State Apartments, the dominant colour for upholstery was crimson, either in velvet or silk damask, although in 1725 César de Saussure noted rooms there 'hung with beautiful old tapestries'.[19] In the private apartments the previous year's colour might go out to be replaced by the fashionable colour of that year, only to be replaced again the following year. There were large quantities of chairs, of varying levels of quality and charged accordingly. Some were clearly made at speed and perhaps designed for a short life.[20] After the intense furnishing activity at St James's Palace during the first few years of George I's reign, the furnishing of other palaces (and yachts) begins to appear in the accounts – Kensington Palace and Hampton Court in particular. But work at St James's continued, whereas the accounts for Kensington and Hampton Court are mostly restricted to fairly short but intense periods.

At Windsor Castle, the situation was one of preservation and renewal. Although little visited by the courts of George I and George II, Windsor was important not least for its considerable antiquity: a new building programme there could have sent just the wrong sort of message, whereas studied veneration of the ancient building and its contents ensured the right degree of respect by the new dynasty, lately arrived from Hanover. A certain amount of refurnishing and repair was carried on at Windsor through both reigns, but the best picture to be gained of the interiors at Windsor can be gleaned from two contemporary sources, George Bickham's *Deliciae Britannicae*, 1742, and J. Pote's *History & Antiquities of Windsor Castle*, 1749. Both descriptions suggest that furnishing was carried out with an eye to stability and continuity. Such was the case with the State Bed ordered by Queen Anne just before her death in 1714 (fig. 32) and placed in the Queen's Bedchamber. Its magnificence, grandeur, cost and association with the last (Protestant) Stuart monarch were no doubt significant. The King's Presence Chamber included some of the seventeenth-century silver furniture: 'Under a fine Pier-Glass there is a large Silver Table, beautifully engraved; as also two Silver Stands, neatly engraved'. There were certainly other silver tables there (RCIN 35301, 35302, 35298; fig. 33).[21] In late 1727 or early

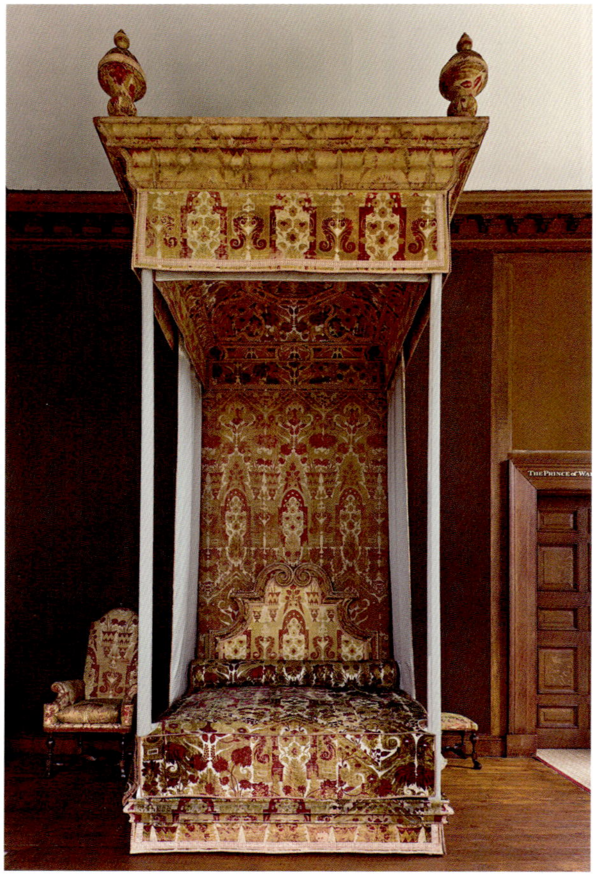

FIG. 32
Richard Roberts and
Hamden Reeve
Queen Anne's State Bed (shown without foot curtains), *c.*1714–15
Hampton Court Palace,
Historic Royal Palaces
RCIN 1112

1728 Gumley & Turing made for use at Windsor '3 setts of leather Covers lined with Flannel for the Silver Tables and Stands in their Maties [Majesties'] Appartments £15'.[22] Most of the principal rooms were lined with tapestries and of course paintings, many of which were hung during the reign of Charles II or Queen Anne.[23] In Queen Elizabeth's Gallery, Pote mentions 'a curious Amber casket presented by the King of Prussia to Queen Caroline' and this is complemented (in the China Closet) with another amber casket 'presented to Q. Anne by Doctor Robinson, Bishop of London, and Plenipotentiary to the Congress of Utrecht'.[24] In the King's Bedchamber were a 'Bed and Curtains ... all of blue Damask, richly trimm'd with gold fringe. There are Silver Sconces regularly dispos'd all

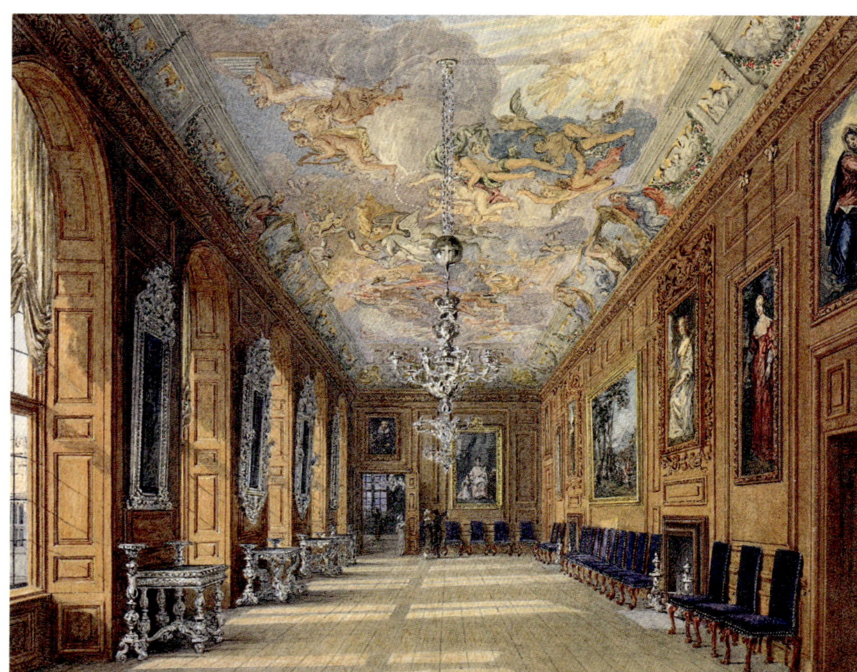

FIG. 33
Charles Wild
The Queen's Ballroom, Windsor Castle, 1817
Watercolour with touches of bodycolour, over pencil
RCIN 922101

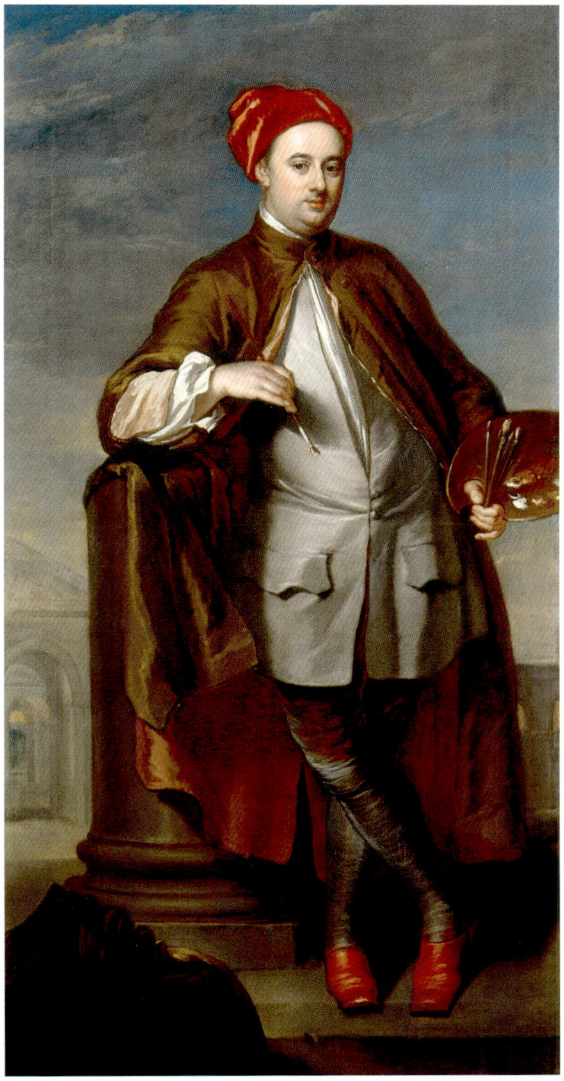

FIG. 34
William Aikman
William Kent, *c*.1723–5
Oil on canvas
National Portrait Gallery, London

round the Room. Over the Chimney are plac'd three curious Marble Busts; and the Tapestry Hangings are a Representation of the well-known story of Hero and Leander.' The description suggests a fairly old-fashioned interior, which might have been familiar to Charles II, although it must be said that in 1715 the upholsterers Phill & Fletcher invoiced the Wardrobe 'scouring & dying 194 yrds of blue Damask £9.14.0' from 'A Blue Damask Bedd window Curtains and Chairs that were brought from Windsor'.[25] Blue was a rare colour for use as hangings in a State apartment, the usual colour being crimson, followed by green. The association of blue with the Garter may have been behind its selection for the King's Bedchamber.

William Kent: Architecture and Interior Decoration

While the Great Wardrobe provided the royal palaces with furnishings, the Office of Works carried out alterations and general maintenance to the palaces. As will be seen, the influence of this Office may have extended into the workshops patronised by the Great Wardrobe. William Kent (fig. 34), appointed Master Carpenter to the Board of Works in 1726 and Deputy Surveyor in 1735, was involved in almost every royal building project from the 1720s until his death in 1748.[26] His approach to architecture, design and interior decoration is the prinipal key to the change in direction of the presentation of interiors during this period.

Kent's ten-year sojourn in Italy, from 1709 to 1719, was profoundly influential on his later work and provided him with a virtually endless source of inspiration. A missionary zeal can be detected in the letters he wrote to Burrell Massingberd of Ormesby, Lincolnshire, his patron and financial supporter during his time in Italy. He was determined to immerse himself in Italian art of all kinds and of all ages, the better to return to England to reform the artistic flabbiness he considered prevalent there.[27] He was clearly thinking ahead to his time back in England when he wrote to Massingberd from Rome on 18 December 1718, 'I lay what little money I have in prints and stucco figurs [sic] as heads & feet &c. which will be of great use to me when I cannot see ye antiques .... I now am to make a study of ornements yt will be proper to adorne about my paintings if [I] can introduce this Italian gusto into England'.[28] In spite of his clearly immersive experience in Italian culture, mostly spent in the workshop of the Roman painter Giovanni Battista Chiari (1654–1727), he strove for originality and independence of thought.[29]

FIG. 35
Jonathan Richardson
Richard Boyle, 3rd Earl of Burlington and 4th Earl of Cork, 1717–19
Oil on canvas
National Portrait Gallery, London

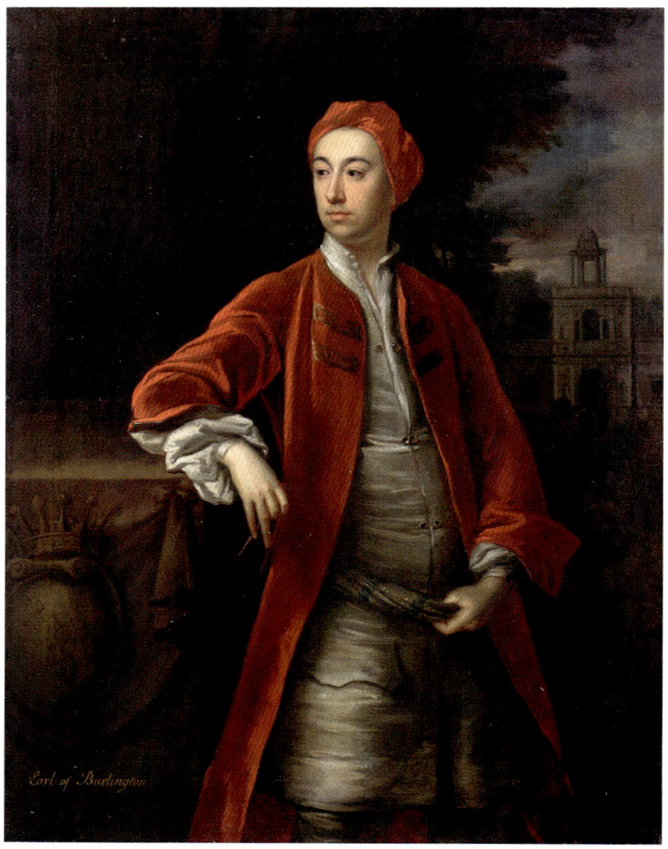

In Italy Kent met Thomas Coke, later 1st Earl of Leicester (1697–1759), a generous supporter who from 1734 involved Kent in the rebuilding of his country seat, Holkham Hall. On 3 April 1717, whilst in Rome, he met Thomas Hewett (1656–1726), who later became Surveyor-General of the King's Works (from 1719 to 1726) and Kent's employer at Kensington Palace.[30] The most important contact Kent made in Italy was with Richard Boyle, 3rd Earl of Burlington (1694–1753; fig. 35), with whom he travelled there. Both Burlington and Kent were determined to reform architecture and the decorative arts in Britain by shaking off the influence of France. French taste had been the fashion in the second half of the seventeenth century, encouraged by designers such as Daniel Marot (1661–1752), who had worked for Louis XIV as well as William III and Queen Anne. In spite of Britain's political opposition to France from 1689, it remained a dominant influence in the decorative arts throughout Europe.

A Revolution?

The theoretical framework laid down in the early years of the eighteenth-century by Anthony Ashley-Cooper, 3rd Earl of Shaftesbury (1671–1713), provided the seeds of a new national style. In his *Letter Concerning the Art or Science of Design* of 1712 he suggested the creation of a British national taste and style based on the spirit of national freedom.[31] That freedom was upheld by the same body (i.e. Parliament) which had intervened to ensure a Protestant succession and as a direct consequence the Elector of Hanover now also reigned as King of Great Britain. Three years earlier, in *Soliloquy: or Advice to an Author*, Shaftesbury had suggested a theory of cause and effect between the liberty of the people and the flourishing of arts and sciences.[32] In 1710 he was able to write, 'We [in Britain] are now in an Age when Liberty is once again in the Ascendant'.

But what was the style to be? It was Lord Burlington who took on Shaftesbury's challenge of creating a national style, which Burlington considered should be rooted in ancient Rome. A formal syntax aligning Britain with

FIG. 36
Robert van Voerst after
Sir Anthony Van Dyck
Inigo Jones, *c.*1632–5
Print
RIBA British Architectural
Library

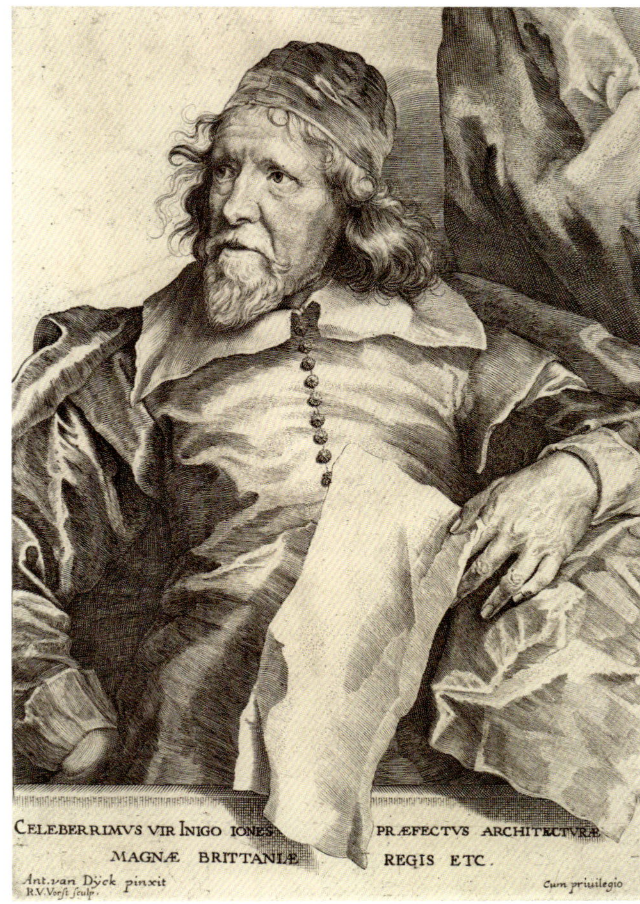

Rome, evoking ancient virtue and liberty, would set Britain apart from the prevailing dominant court style in Europe, the style promoted in France under the illiberal, absolutist rule of Louis XIV.[33]

It became Burlington's life's work to revive and bring to Britain the spirit of Andrea Palladio and Inigo Jones (fig. 36). Palladio had revived ancient Roman architecture in Italy in the sixteenth century; Inigo Jones had brought this style to Britain as court architect to Charles I in the seventeenth century, but this project, court-based as it was, had been cut short by the Civil War and the execution of the King. The heritage of Inigo Jones, however, provided the thread of continuity and reference for British architecture. Burlington and the architect Colen Campbell would continue his vital work in the establishment of a distinctive British style in the first half of the eighteenth century. Burlington encouraged a new generation of architects and patrons into a body of neo-Palladians, more or less united behind the architectural principles found in Vitruvius's treatise *De architectura* (first century BC), Alberti's *De re aedificatoria* (*c.*1450) and Palladio's *Quattro Libri dell'Architettura* (1570).[34]

However, only at the new apartment at Kensington Palace could it be said that a major royal project was carried out in full support of this new style. The King's Gallery, with its painted ceiling (by Kent, of 1725) incorporating a background of simulated mosaic, based on examples by Raphael and Peruzzi, was unprecedented in England (no. 33 and fig. 65); and the fictive coffering of the Cupola Room and the matching painted wall decoration (no. 30), all by Kent, were a bold evocation of ancient Roman architecture. The ceilings in the Presence Chamber, Council Chamber and King's Bedchamber were all inspired by ancient Roman *grottesche*, once more evoked in the background of the fictive loggia of Kent's mural decoration on the King's Staircase (no. 34 and fig. 37), itself based on Giovanni da Udine's wall decorations in the Vatican Logge. At the ancient palaces of Hampton Court, Windsor Castle and St James's, by contrast, tapestries dominated, hung from cornice to floor over oak panelling.

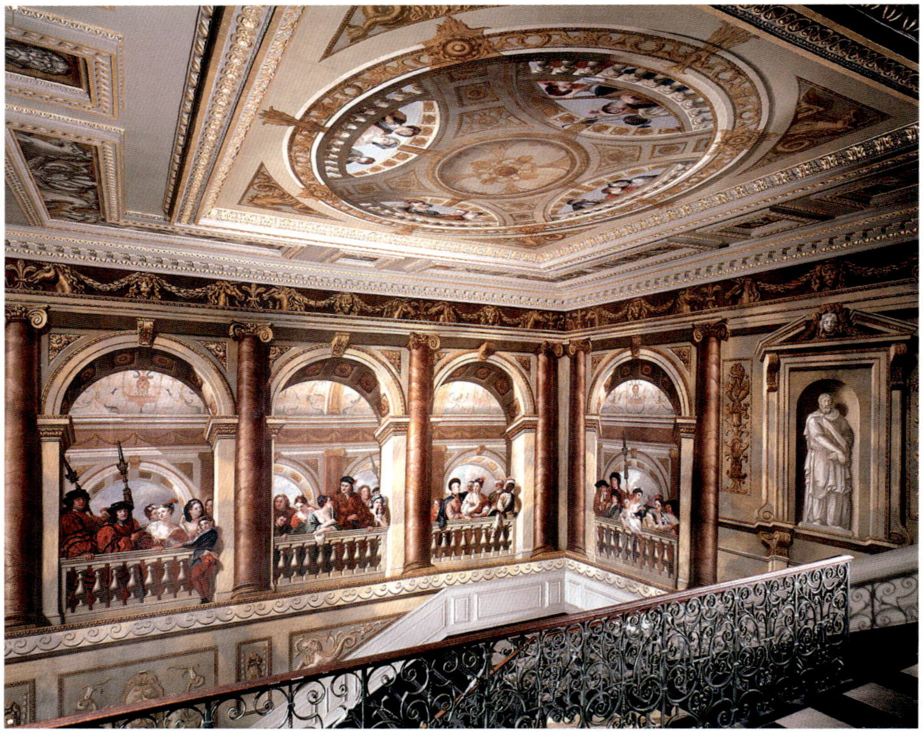

FIG. 37
William Kent
The King's Staircase, 1725–7,
Kensington Palace,
Historic Royal Palaces

In the Great Gallery and elsewhere at Kensington, the walls were hung from cornice to dado in crimson silk damask, while the mouldings and chimneybreasts were painted white with gilt highlights.

The furniture supplied for the palaces did not, for the earlier part of George I's reign, fall to a member of Burlington's improving Italophiles. If anything, John, Duke of Montagu, Master of the Great Wardrobe, was a Francophile. The gilt-gesso furniture (probably) made for Kensington was created in a firmly established tradition, one perfected by the French *émigré* cabinet-makers Jean, René and Thomas Pelletier.[35] Tables with all-over decoration in raised gesso, subsequently water-gilded, provided a spectacular and glittering surface and consciously emulated the silver furniture of the second half of the seventeenth-century (fig. 38). The Pelletier family had been introduced to the court of William III by Ralph, 1st Duke of Montagu, when Master of the Great Wardrobe. In general the surviving designs for furniture of George I's reign employed a decorative language rooted in seventeenth-century France. Tables and mirrors by Moore & Gumley seem to draw on a latent French Baroque concept of design, as seen in the widely disseminated published designs by Jean and Pierre Le Pautre,[36] rather than a sixteenth-century Italian source, as promoted by Burlington and Kent. It was the multi-talented Kent who, after his appointment as architect at Hampton Court in 1731, harmonised the furnishings with the architecture. Kent almost certainly influenced the design of new furniture in the 1730s at Hampton Court, as he had already done so successfully at Houghton Hall.[37] Kent's approach was to look to architecture and its theory, as well as to contemporary Italian furniture designs such as those published in Rome by Giovanni Giardini in *Disegni diversi*, 1714 (fig. 39) – neither conceded much to function or practicality.[38] The Abbé de Montfaucon's highly influential handbook of Roman source material, *Antiquité Expliquée*, translated by David Humphreys into English as *Antiquity Explained and represented in Sculpture*, 1721–25,[39] provided a vocabulary in keeping with Palladian architectural designs. Many other pattern books were also available and played an important part in the dissemination of designs

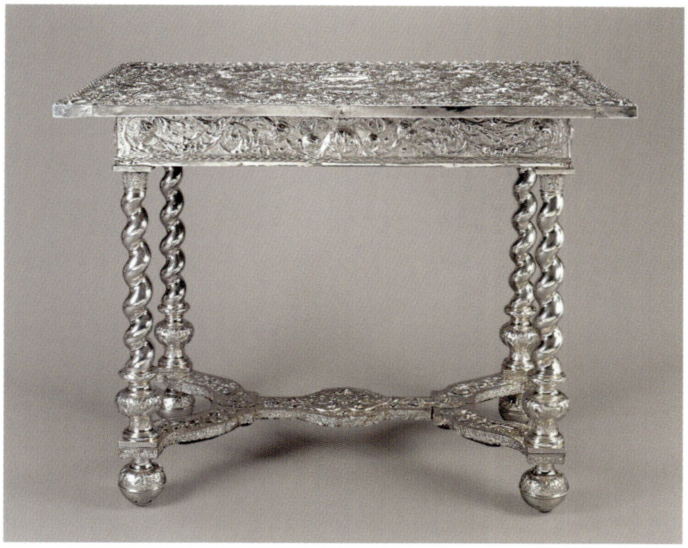

FIG. 38
English, *c.*1670
Table
Embossed silver on oak
RCIN 35299

throughout the period, especially French-inspired rococo patterns, which were widely distributed in the 1730s. By the mid-1750s, the pattern books had given way to trade catalogues of fashionable designs published by the large firms of cabinet-makers or upholders such as Thomas Chippendale and Mayhew & Ince.[40]

With the exception of the new apartment at Kensington Palace and Mary II's apartment when completed at Hampton Court, the interiors of the British royal residences remained largely as they appeared during the previous two reigns, with concomitant replacement fabric and plenty of new furniture. As both George I and George II were reluctant to build a completely new palace, in spite of the shortcomings of St James's and the growing clamour for a new royal palace, it was only at Kensington that a novel programme of decoration was attempted.

The court and the various palaces in which it operated provided a venue for state function and a theatre for acting out political ambition. The stage sets which provided the backdrop were the refurnished palaces, spaces which survive intact in very few instances. Nonetheless we have to suppose that the monarchical culture promoted by the first two Georges through the medium of furnishing would not have been untouched by contemporary theoretical considerations in architecture as well as by the

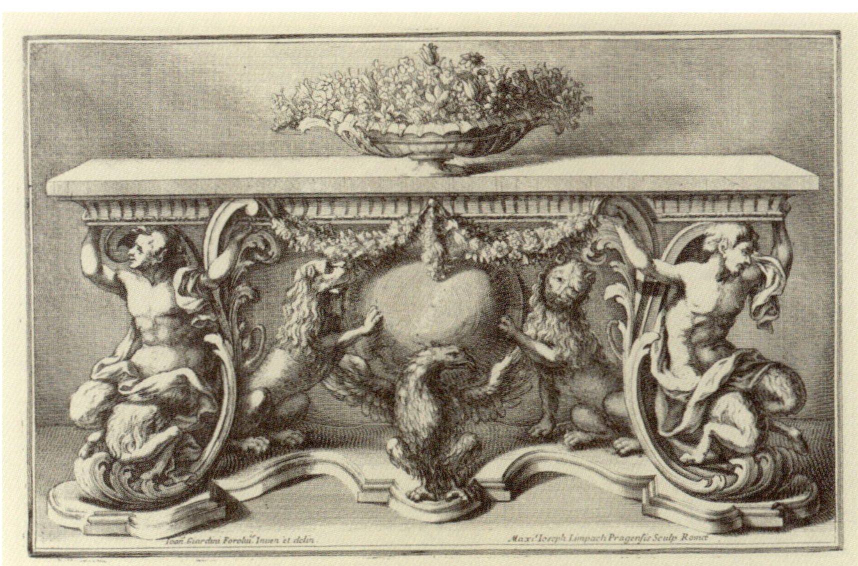

FIG. 39
Maximilian Joseph Limpach
after Giovanni Giardini
Design for a console table, from
Giovanni Giardini, *Disegni diversi*,
Rome, 1714, plate 55
Engraving
Bard Graduate Center Library,
New York

FIG. 40
Richard Cattermole
The Queen's State Bedchamber, Hampton Court Palace, c.1816
Watercolour and bodycolour
RCIN 922134

FIG. 41
The Queen's State Bedchamber,
Hampton Court Palace,
Historic Royal Palaces

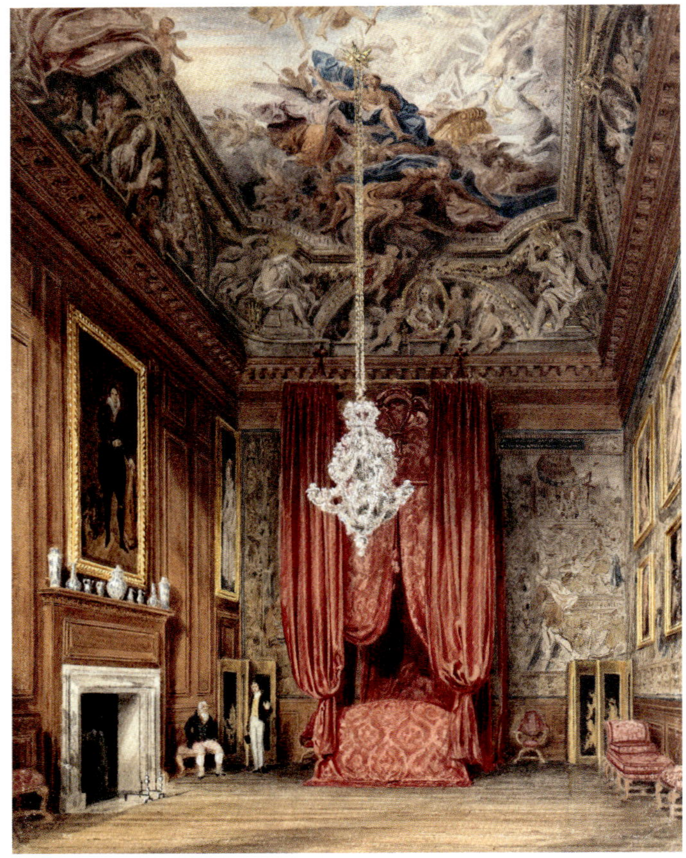

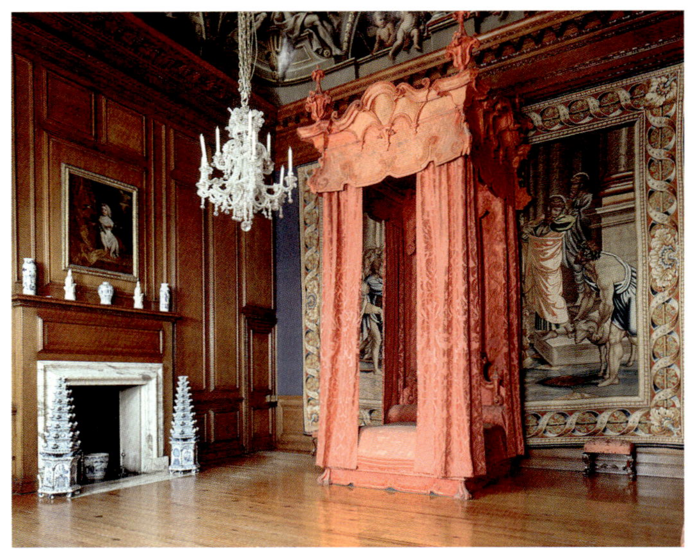

completely new building projects undertaken by members of the nobility (the prime examples are Houghton Hall and Holkham Hall, both in Norfolk). George I's cautious acceptance of the new style introduced by Burlington, Kent and Surveyor-General Hewett at Kensington and continued by George II and his son Frederick, Prince of Wales, suggests that they were, to a limited degree, sponsors of this new, national style. Its Romano-Italianate and Jonesian references were highly suggestive to the Hanoverians, and evoked notions of ancient Rome, liberty, as well as encouraging dynastic links with the Stuarts.

The Reign of George I: Hampton Court Palace

Like Kensington, Hampton Court was used as a summer palace. Kensington, being nearer to the seat of government, enjoyed lengthy summer visits lasting from May to October; Hampton Court played host to the court intermittently and usually for shorter spells. In fact George I paid only two visits, the first being a short visit in November 1714, when he decided to embark on the completion of Queen Mary II's apartments, left unfinished by William III after her death in 1694. The Prince and Princess of Wales visited during the summer of 1716 and, according to Dudley Ryder, dined 'every day in public at Hampton Court and all sorts of people have free admission to see them even of the lowest sort of rank'.[41] The King's next visit fell during the summer of 1717, from 10 June to 13 November, and was followed immediately by the estrangement between the King and the Prince of Wales. While both George I and George II were content to leave intact the King's (i.e. William III's)

FIG. 42
Richard Roberts
Armchair, 1715
Walnut, crimson silk damask
RCIN 1088

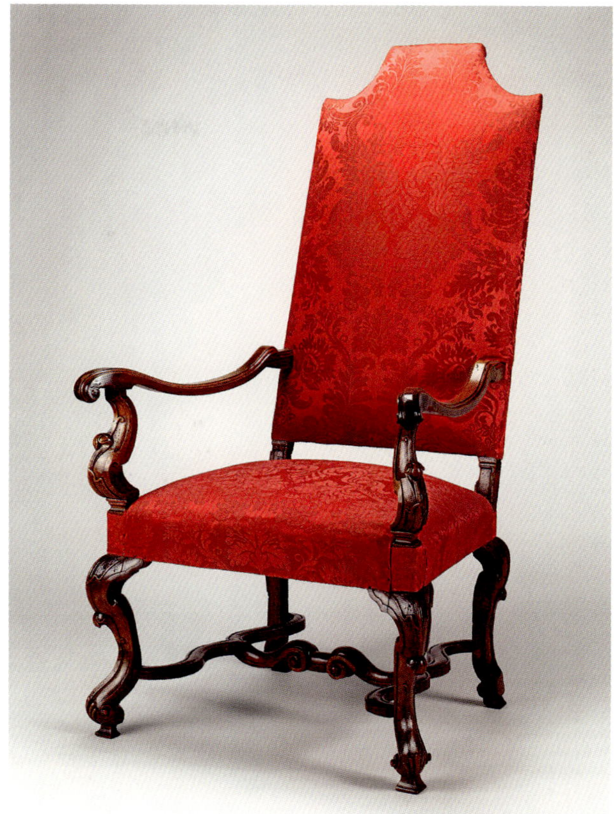

Apartment, and to make use of it as such, the business of furnishing Hampton Court took place largely in the Prince and Princess of Wales's apartment, which was Queen Mary's former apartment. Here, the sequence of rooms commenced with the Queen's Guard Chamber, followed by the Presence Chamber and Public Dining Room or Ballroom along one axis, completed by Vanbrugh in 1715–16. Next, along Wren's East Front, came the Audience Chamber, Withdrawing Room, Bedchamber, Gallery and Closet. The Wardrobe accounts detail the furnishings of the rooms in some detail. On the approval of the Duke of Montagu given on 15 September 1715, Moore & Gumley supplied a mirror or pier glass each in the Privy Chamber, Drawing Room (see no. 98), Bedchamber, Dining Room, Closet, Little Bedchamber and the Princess's Dressing Room. Each mirror was given precise measurements and each had a table to go beneath it 'finely carved and gilt' and matching pairs of stands. In the Bedchamber, the table and stands were supplied with 'Indian' (i.e. lacquer) tops. The mirror for the Drawing Room cost £156 (the highest price) and the tables cost between £34.10.0 and £50.[42] The Bedchamber, the most important room in the apartment, was fitted out with a new state bed; the frame (a 'Bedstead all oak ... £35') was supplied by Richard Roberts in 1715 and was covered in crimson silk damask provided by the mercers John Johnson & Co., who supplied '439 yds ½ of rich Crimson Damask at 23s ... £505.8.6'; the bed was upholstered by Thomas Phill & Jeremiah Fletcher 'Making up the Crimson Damask Bedd all Compleate' (figs. 40 and 41).[43] Accompanying the bed was a pair of armchairs (see fig. 42) and eighteen stools (see no. 97), supplied by the same combination of joiner and upholsterer, who supplied chairs and canopies of state for the adjoining rooms.[44] The King and Prince and Princess of Wales made use of a presence chamber and each was supplied with a 'state frame' (canopy), a state chair and stools of varying quantities as well as window cornices – all of which were made by the joiner Richard Roberts.[45]

The Bedchamber, parallelled at St James's, was the *locus classicus* for establishing dynastic links: it symbolised the heart of the monarchy and, more than in any other space, it allowed the Hanoverians to re-state their connection with the early Stuarts, which by association implied continuity and antiquity.[46] The Bedchamber was lined with tapestries, the richest form of hanging, and also served to emphasise the antiquity of the new dynasty. At Hampton Court and St James's Palace John Robinson, linen draper, was charged in 1715 with lining a number of tapestries which were presumably taken from store, and the tapestry weaver, John Vanderbank, was called upon to restore many of the same to bring them into service.[47]

96

Lacquer cabinet JAPANESE, LATE 17TH CENTURY
Stand ATTRIBUTED TO THOMAS AND RENÉ PELLETIER (ACTIVE 1702–12)

Cabinet-on-stand *c.*1705

Black and gold lacquer, gilded and gessoed pine, brass, 188 × 112.5 × 61 cm
Cabinet RCIN 35274, stand RCIN 31186

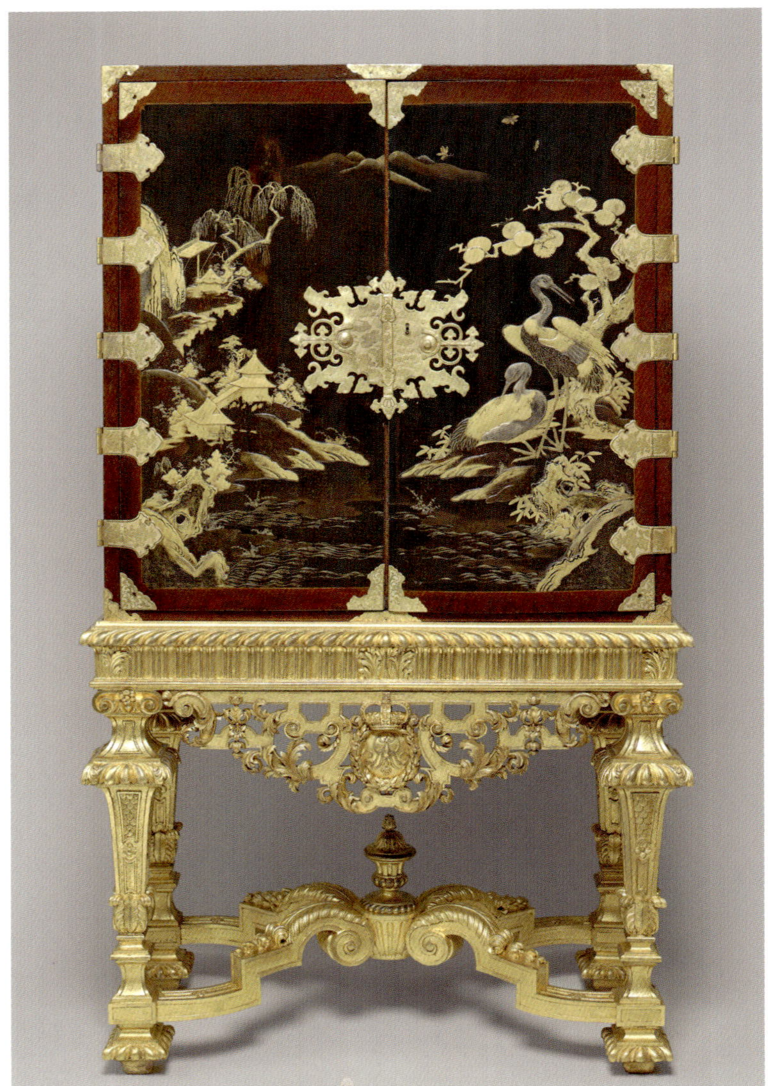

PROVENANCE First recorded in the King's Writing Closet at Hampton Court, *c.*1819, but possibly supplied to Queen Anne, *c.*1703, for the Gallery, Kensington Palace

LITERATURE Murdoch 1998, pp. 364–5, fig. 6

During the early eighteenth century lacquer was an important and luxurious element of furnishing a state apartment: it was usually reserved for the most important of spaces. On account of its expense, fragility and exotic quality it signified luxury and high status. This lacquer cabinet was certainly brought from Japan in the cargo of an East Indiaman ship either of the British East India Company or of the Dutch East India Company. At this date, the Japanese restricted international trade to the Dutch and Chinese through their port at Decima Island in Nagasaki Bay. The giltwood stand was made to fit as a support for the cabinet and was possibly made by Thomas and René Pelletier, French émigré cabinet-makers. Alternatively, it may have been supplied in 1703–4 by Gerrit Jensen, cabinet-maker to the Great Wardrobe during Queen Anne's reign.[48] The cabinet and its stand probably furnished the Gallery at Kensington Palace during her reign, and remained *in situ* as a highly valued object during subsequent reigns. The earliest record is in a watercolour of *c.*1819 by Richard Cattermole of the King's Writing Room, Hampton Court (RCIN 922133).

From the beginning of George I's reign lacquer was used in both state and private apartments. In 1715 Gerrit Jensen supplied 'a large Indian cabinet' at a cost of £30 for the Bedchamber of the Princess of Wales's Apartment at St James's Palace.[49] Several lacquer screens were supplied for various locations, and notably in 1715 two 'Indian screen[s]' (one with four leaves and another with three leaves) were supplied for the Countess of Kielmansegg's apartment at St James's Palace.[50] RB

97

RICHARD ROBERTS (ACTIVE 1714–29)

Two stools 1715

Walnut, beech, crimson silk damask, 50 × 64 × 47.5 cm
RCIN 1089.8 and .11

PROVENANCE Supplied to George I, for the Prince and Princess of Wales's State Bedchamber, Hampton Court Palace, in 1715

LITERATURE Rutherford 1927, pp. 80, 83

Eighteen of these stools (of which sixteen survive) were supplied for the use of the Prince and Princess of Wales in their State Apartments at Hampton Court, probably for the Bedchamber, the most important space in the sequence of the State Apartments. They came with a pair of armchairs (see fig. 42), which would have been placed either side of the bed and brought forward to the end of the bed for the Prince and Princess of Wales's use during an audience. The set was supplied by the cabinet-maker to the Great Wardrobe, Richard Roberts, who also supplied the oak frame for the centre-piece of the ensemble, the State Bed (RCIN 1086). Roberts's bill for the stools reads:

> For His Royal Highness the Prince of Wales Bedchamber at Hampton Court .... For 18 square Stools Frames of Walnuttree finely carved and pollished £40.10.0.[51]

The stools are covered in modern crimson silk damask. The original fabric was supplied by one of the mercers, John Johnson or Richard Chamberlayne.[52] The original *passementerie* or trimmings were supplied by William Weeks, laceman, and upholstered by Thomas Phill and Jeremiah Fletcher.[53] The design of the stool is relatively advanced, showing early use of the cabriole or scrolled leg. Seat furniture of the previous reign featured legs of S-scrolled form, which developed from the 'horsebone' shape favoured during the reign of William III and Mary II.[54] RB

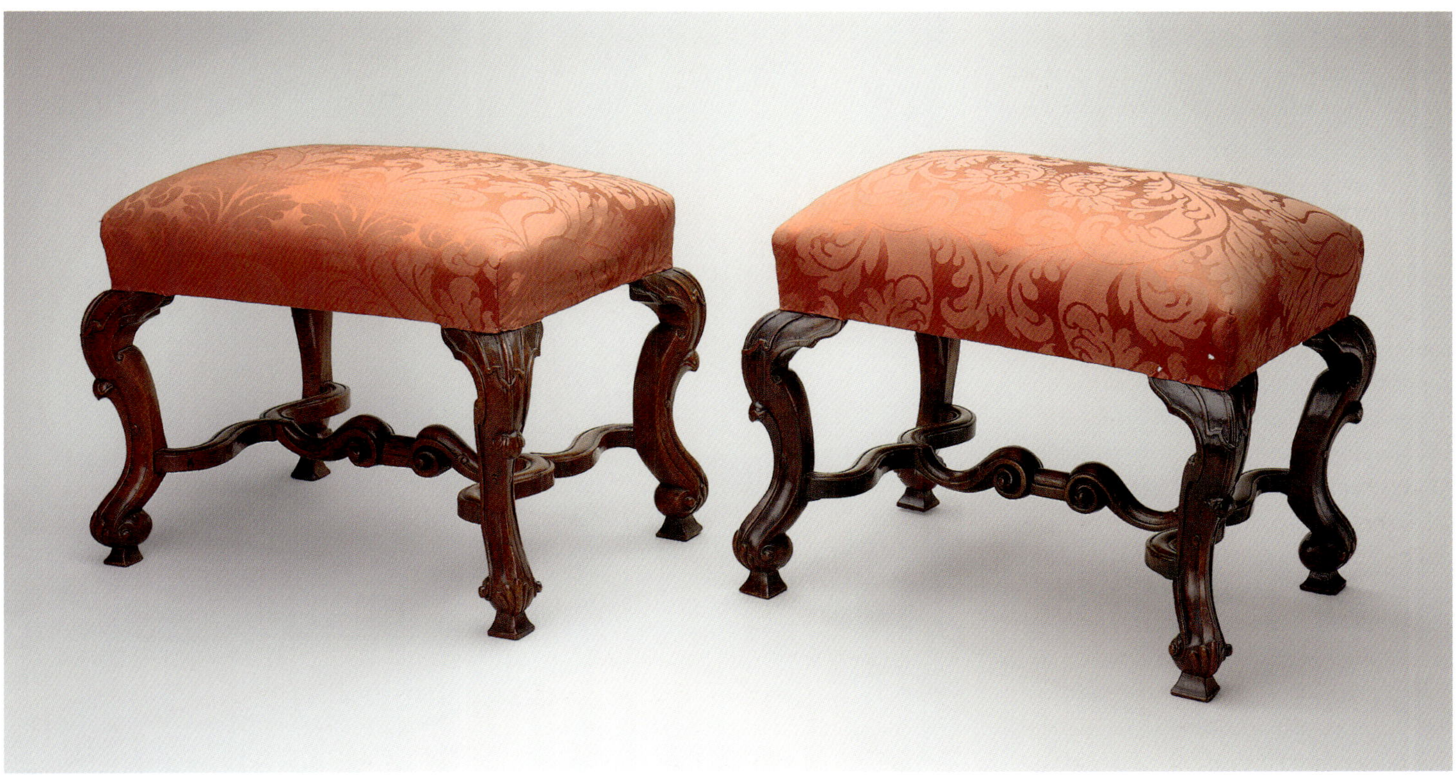

98

JOHN GUMLEY (1672–1729)

Pier glass or mirror 1715

Gilded and gessoed pine, bevelled mirror glass, 300 × 138 cm
Marks: strip with gilt-gesso lettering *GUMLEY*; inscribed in chalk on the reverse *1821/ Wales* [?]/ *Painter* and *9 Chamberlain* ... [?]/ *9 Chamberlain* ... / *R Jenkins / A Sturgess* [?] and *Hung March 16th 19000* [sic]
RCIN 1090

PROVENANCE Probably supplied to George I for the Prince and Princess of Wales's Drawing Room, Hampton Court Palace, 1715

LITERATURE Edwards and Jourdain 1944, pp. 21, 89 and 91, figs. 10 and 13; Edwards 1964, p. 658, fig. 1; Bowett 2009, p. 290–1, fig. 6:47

This pier glass is almost certainly one of three supplied for the Prince and Princess of Wales's State Apartment at Hampton Court in 1715. The invoices from Moore & Gumley include three large mirrors that in size and kind match approximately three surviving mirrors (RCIN 1090, 1104 and 1105).[55] They were for the three principal State Rooms – Privy Chamber, Drawing Room and Bedchamber. The Drawing Room mirror was described in the account from Moore & Gumley: 'For a large Glass in a Glass Frame and Ffestoon finely done with carved and gilt work Cont[aining] 11 Foot 10 Inch ½ by 4 foot 9 Inch ½ £156'.[56] This account describes a frame 'containing' a plate of specific dimensions (362 × 146 cm) which correspond to the inner plate of no. 98.[57] Given the high cost of mirror plate, it made sense to measure the plate dimensions in this way as evidence of the expense. The mirror was supplied by John Gumley, business partner to James Moore: his name appears in raised lettering on a strip of gilt-gesso on one upright.

The design of the mirror depends on French prototypes. A concession to the classical orders is made in the use of a Corinthian capital atop each upright, each of which is glazed, silvered and bevelled. The size of the mirror emphasises the large scale of the expensive central plate (replaced in 1958). RB

99

RICHARD ROBERTS (ACTIVE 1714–29)

Chair 1717

Walnut and *petit point* needlework, 117.5 × 55 × 58 cm
RCIN 1071.5 and .7

PROVENANCE Possibly supplied to George I for his Dining Room at Hampton Court Palace in 1717

LITERATURE Macquoid 1905, p. 190, fig. 168; Edwards and Jourdain 1955, pp. 39 and 10; Wood 2008, I, p. 9, n. 62, fig. 8; Bowett 2009, p. 164, fig. 4:40

Ten chairs of the type shown (two exhibited) seem to be the surviving remnants of the eighteen supplied for George I's Dining Room at Hampton Court. They can be associated with the following account for 'Richard Roberts, Joyner' [to the Great Wardrobe] for the period Michaelmas 1717–Michaelmas 1718:

> For 18 Chairs made of the best Walnuttree bended backs finely carved and pollisht and silk lace Seats for his maties [=Majesty's] Dining Room ... £36.0.0.[58]

Although Roberts supplied a great number of chairs during the early years of George I's reign, when this style was in vogue, this is the only account which incorporates three elements seen here – the curved back, carving, and upholstered seats. The term 'bended back' probably refers to the Chinese-inspired form of narrow upright seat-back or splat, which curves into the small of the back: such forms of Far Eastern invention were (confusingly) often referred to as 'Indian'.[59] Though the chairs have replacement rails, they betray no trace of alternative caned or matted seats.

The design of the back reflects chair patterns popularised by Daniel Marot, designer at the court of William III, though the use of the cabriole leg is forward-looking. The *petit point* needlework seat covers were probably made in the mid-eighteenth century and may have been applied later, when the chair rails were replaced. Three of the chairs are inscribed in pencil on the inside of the rear seat-rail 'E C Gunn', which presumably refers to a restorer or upholsterer. RB

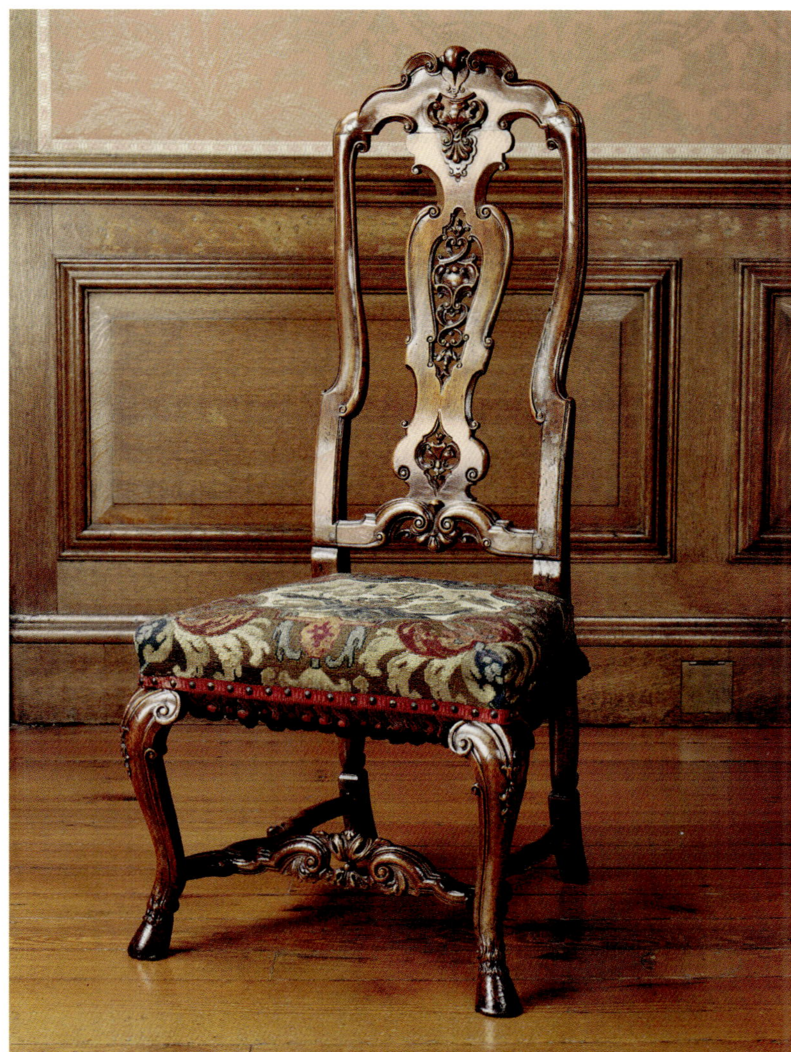

Of the palaces used and furnished by the royal family during the period, Kensington is the one with the most furniture and sculpture surviving today.[60] The apartments at the palace were described by César de Saussure during his visit to London in 1725 as 'convenient and in good taste'.[61] The furnishings were made or acquired expressly for the purpose of furnishing George I's new apartments, although it was characteristic of the new King that no new furniture was ordered until the building project was well underway. This was not before 1720, when furniture was ordered most probably for his private apartment.[62] It was not until 1724 that furniture was ordered for the refurbished State Apartment and then only for the Cupola Room, Privy Chamber, Drawing Room, Presence Chamber, Council Chamber and State Bedchamber. Of the new rooms, only the Great Gallery remained unfurnished. Crimson silk damask dominated throughout, both hung on the walls and covering the seat furniture, although the Great Closet was hung with embroideries and the State Bedchamber with seven pieces of old tapestry said to represent *The Children of Israel*.[63]

Although the walls of the Bedchamber were hung with tapestry, the State Bed, according to George Bickham's description of it in the early 1740s, was in crimson damask, just as it had been when ordered from Richard Roberts in 1724.[64] Each of the new rooms, with the exception of the Cupola Room, was supplied with one or two 'armed chairs'. The Presence Chamber was supplied with a new Chair of State covered in crimson damask, while the covering for the Canopy of State which survived from the previous reign was changed from velvet to damask in 1724, presumably to match the chair and the rest of the apartment. Each room also contained a varying number of stools and sometimes also 'fforms' (benches). Kent's Cupola Room marks the beginning of a new style, designed as it was to imitate a Roman coffered ceiling, with pilasters and niches containing gilded statues and, over the chimneypiece, a *basso relievo* or low relief (by Rysbrack, beginning a partnership which would endure).[65] Kent's intention was to evoke a Roman *tablinum*[66] complete with low relief panel (also by Rysbrack) directly copied from a surviving antique model in the Palazzo Sacchetti, Rome.[67] In the heart of the royal palace of the new dynasty, this was a powerful statement of intent – to bring a new self-consciously antique Roman style to Britain. This new 'ancient' style was continued in the ceiling decorations Kent executed for the Presence, Council and Bed Chambers in the antique 'grotesque' style, of which George Vertue, a firm supporter of Thornhill and his Tory backers, wrote disapprovingly – 'the Ceiling in Imitation of the Antient Roman Subterranen Ornaments. Poor stuff.'[68] Kent's work, which runs through the new State Apartments at Kensington to varying degrees, was not restricted to the ceilings: in the King's Gallery and the Drawing Room, Kent applied to the Treasury for an additional payment of £50 'for drawing the Sides of the Drawing Room with all the pictures sketcht in Proper Colours designing and drawing the mouldings and ornaments for all the picture frames, glasses etc.', and similarly 'for drawing the Gallery with all the pictures sketcht in Proper Colours the frames drawn with their ornaments at large for the sconces, glasses etc'.[69] Kent was duly paid for the extra work which he claimed he had done, suggesting that his involvement extended beyond

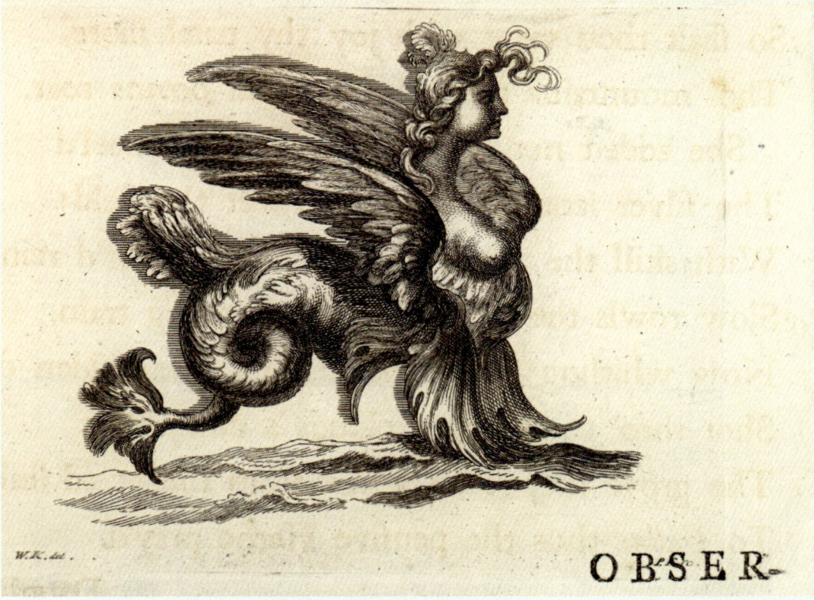

FIG. 43
Paul Fourdrinier
after William Kent
Tailpiece depicting a winged mermaid, from Alexander Pope, *The Odyssey*, 1725–26, vol. 2, Book 6, p. 87
British Library, inv. 12270.k.8

simply painting the ceilings to designing the frames and arranging the paintings. It is possible that he was also involved in the design of some of the pier tables, designed in an antique Roman style contrasting to other furniture supplied for the apartment: descriptions in the Wardrobe accounts read as if they were designed by Kent.[70] In the Cube or Cupola Room, his first project there, he was responsible for the ceiling and wall decoration while the appearance of six 'sphynx tables' in the Wardrobe accounts (for Gumley & Moore) suggests that Kent's classicizing influence may have found its way into Moore's workshop: whether this was at Kent's, the King's, or the Surveyor of the Office of Work's behest is not clear. The 'sphynx' tables have been tentatively identified with the six giltwood pier tables visible in the watercolour of the Cupola Room by George Cattermole for Pyne's *Royal Residences* taken in 1817 (no. 31), where they were described (by W. H. Pyne) as having been designed by Kent himself.[71] Judging by tables emanating from Gumley & Moore's workshop at the same date and for the same location (see no. 103), such a radical change in design could reasonably be attributed to Kent's influence (fig. 43).

The creation of the new State Apartment at Kensington was finally completed barely a month before George I's death at Osnabrück in June 1727. The Great or King's Gallery was the final room to be completed, and perhaps the room in which Kent's influence is most apparent: the combination of white and gold paintwork with crimson damask hangings was first employed in a British royal palace in the Great Gallery at Kensington. While Kent painted the ceiling in his Roman manner, with figures in imitation of plaster and fictive gold tesserae in the background, all derived from ceilings of Roman palaces with which Kent would have been familiar, the older, ousted Sir James Thornhill provided only the gilding. Along the window wall were four pedestals in *alabastro onice* surmounted by figures of the four seasons (no. 105) by the Roman sculptor Camillo Rusconi (1658–1728), which can still be seen in the King's Gallery in Charles Wild's 1816 watercolour (no. 33). Kent must first have seen these in the collection of the Marchese Pallavicini in the Palazzo all'Orso in Rome, which he visited in 1715 and 1716, and may have encouraged their acquisition for Kensington.[72] An even more concrete example of the encouragement of Italian art within the royal sphere is seen in Burlington's presentation to George II around 1730 of Soldani's bronze *bas relief* series of *The Four Seasons*, executed in 1715 (no. 106).

100

RICHARD ROBERTS (ACTIVE 1714–29)

Two stools *c.*1725

Walnut, beech, crimson silk damask, 49 × 61 × 45 cm
RCIN 1005.1 and .2

PROVENANCE Supplied to George I, possibly for the Great Gallery, Kensington Palace, 1726

On account of their leg design (see no. 97), these stools, of which thirteen survive, are likely to be associated with an order from the 1720s, rather than with the earlier furnishing campaign at Hampton Court. They may be connected with the twenty supplied by Richard Roberts for the Great Gallery at Kensington, invoiced on 9 January 1726: 'For 20 wallnut tree Square stool frames finely carv'd and pollish'd £45'.

The apartment at Hampton Court was furnished by 1717, when George I held his first court there, while that at Kensington was completed in 1727, only months before his death. It is also possible that these stools were supplied for use at St James's Palace, where quantities of furniture (especially seat furniture) were delivered throughout the early Georgian period.

Both stools in the exhibition display a top cover of splendid crimson damask, probably supplied for a late seventeenth-century stool or chair and applied here at a much later date.
RB

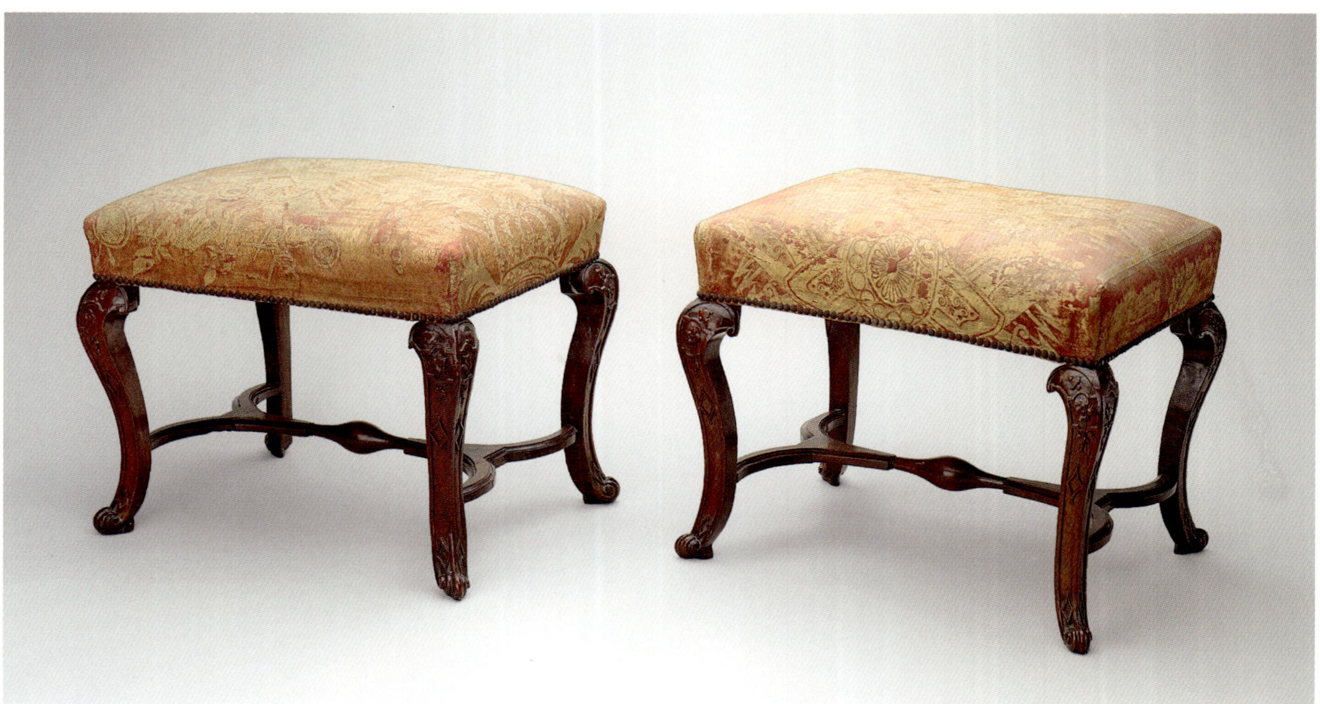

101

JAMES MOORE (*c.*1670–1726)

Pier table and pair of stands *c.*1720

Gilded and gessoed walnut and oak, (table) 84 × 124 × 57 cm; (stands) 123 × 52 cm
Marks: the tops incised *Moore*
Pier table RCIN 1102, stands RCIN1101.1-2

PROVENANCE Supplied to George I, probably for the 'Pillar Room' in the private apartments at Kensington Palace

LITERATURE Macquoid and Edwards 1927, III, p. 260, fig. 22 (table), p. 143, figs. 11 and 11A (stands); Edwards and Jourdain 1944, pp. 23, 95, figs. 21–22 (table), pp. 23, 96–97, figs. 23, 25 (stands); Bowett 2005, pp. 39 and 46, fig. 5 (table), fig. 4 (stands)

This remarkable design of table and matching stands was clearly inspired by contemporary Chinese furniture design in its rectilinear, clear outlines.[73] Its applied decoration on the other hand, which is both carved in wood and applied in gesso, is purely classical, with the Greek-key pattern on the table running across the frieze, down the legs and across the arched supports. The same pattern occurs on the stands, running over all four faces of the support. The table features a roundel in the centre of the frame and a larger version in the centre of the top, each containing the cipher GR (*Georgius Rex*) for the King encircled by the Garter and motto of the Order surmounted by a king's crown. The decoration of the top is surrounded by symmetrical arrangements of scrolling foliage. This motif is also employed on the top of the candle-stand or torchere.

The table and stands may be those associated with a bill of 1722: 'For Two large gilt Tables & two pair of Stands Suitable wth Leather Covers for the Pillar Room ... £50.0.0'.[74] If this identification is correct, the second table and pair of stands have not survived. RB

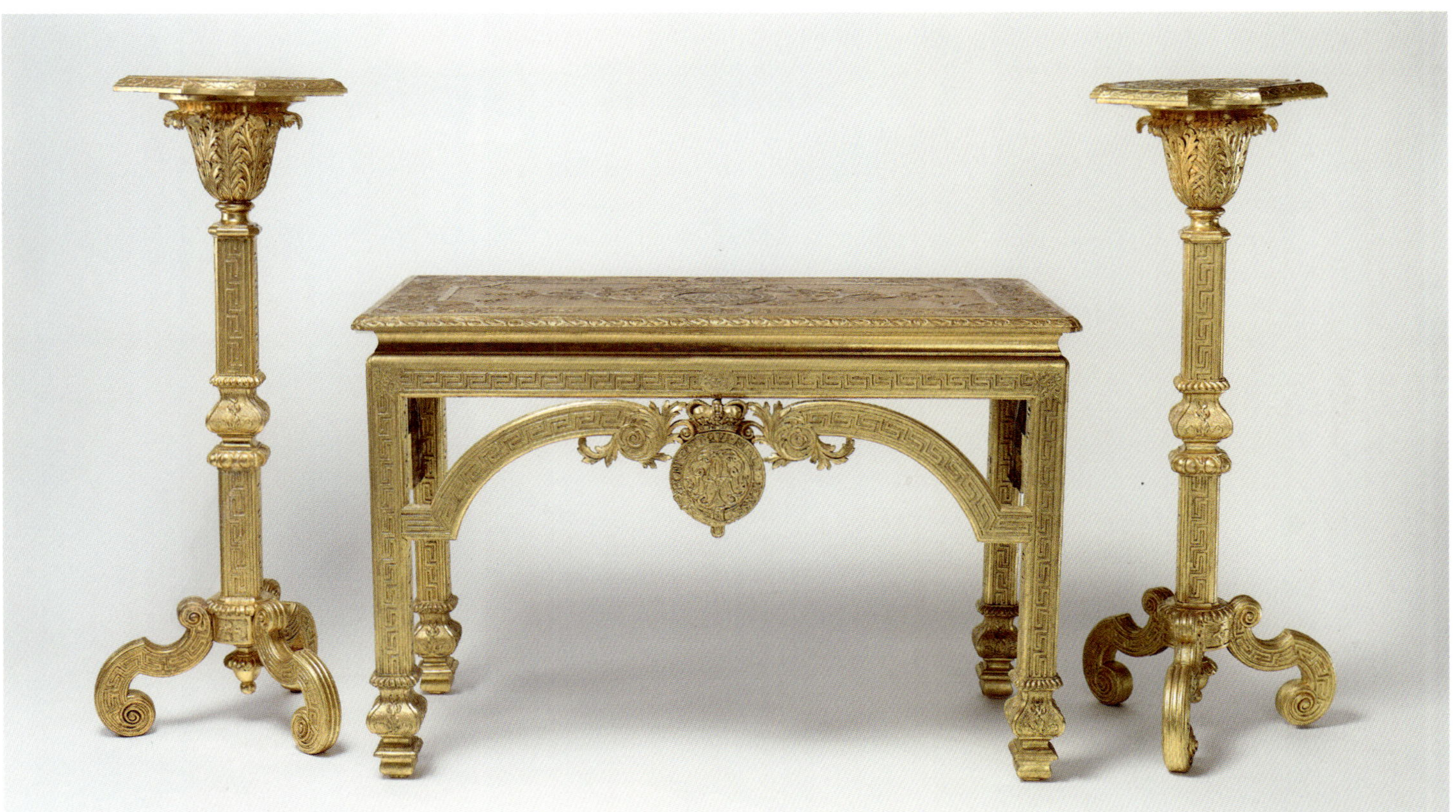

102

JAMES MOORE (*c*.1670–1726)

Pier table 1723–4

Gilded and gessoed oak and pine, 85 × 142.5 × 68 cm
Marks: the top incised *MOORE*; inscribed on the back rail in pencil *com on 10 of agoust* [sic]
RCIN 596

PROVENANCE Supplied to George I, probably for the Drawing Room, Kensington Palace, 1723–24

LITERATURE Smith 1931, p. 197, figs. 226–7; Edwards and Jourdain 1944, pp. 23 and 92, fig. 16; Harris, de Bellaigue and Millar 1968, p. 109; Bowett 2005, p. 46, fig. 13

This table, perhaps originally one of a pair, was supplied through the Great Wardrobe by the royal cabinet-makers James Moore and John Gumley probably for the Drawing Room at Kensington Palace.[75] The bill from Gumley & Moore for the period Michaelmas (29 September) 1723 to Michaelmas 1724 includes 'For 2 fine gold table frames @ 36 each £72.0.0'.[76] These were accompanied by a pair of large mirrors costing £120 each, four stands costing £18 each and four chandeliers costing £60 each.

The table consists of a rectangular top with elaborately cut gesso, centred by George I's cypher GR (*Georgius Rex*), encircled by the Garter and motto of the Order surmounted by a crown. The central motif is encircled by laurel and outside this, covering almost the entire field, are C scrolls, some placed adjacent to one another, others placed back to back. This seemingly random arrangement is in fact rigidly composed in two halves: each half of the table is centred on a lozenge, with the C scrolls framing the compartment. The formality of the arrangement is relieved by interspersed foliage of acanthus, floral sprays and, in each corner, the rose of England and thistle of Scotland. The top is supported on a frame with a deep coved frieze, with arcades each enclosing three acanthus husks. The apron, attached to the lower edge of the frieze, is composed of three elements: the larger central cartouche repeats the design in the centre of the top, namely the royal cypher encircled by the Garter and the motto of the Order and sprigs of laurel surmounted by a crown; and the panels at either side, of confronted C scrolls, enclose the rose and thistle. The four legs are square in section and taper, but feature a bulbous heading, perhaps intended to evoke a classical capital; the legs are joined together just above the feet by a stretcher carved with strapwork formed of semi-circles at each end tied by a bar with a lozenge in the centre. Every surface is covered either with punched gesso or with carving, and sometimes a combination of both techniques. A section of the strapwork on the top is prominently incised *MOORE*, an unusual practice for a furniture-maker at this date, although Moore's partner, the mirror-maker John Gumley, added his name to a giltwood strip on a pier glass at Hampton Court (no. 98) and also signed a pair of pier glasses now at Chatsworth.[77] The all-over gilded treatment may have been intended to mimic the effect of seventeenth-century silver furniture. RB

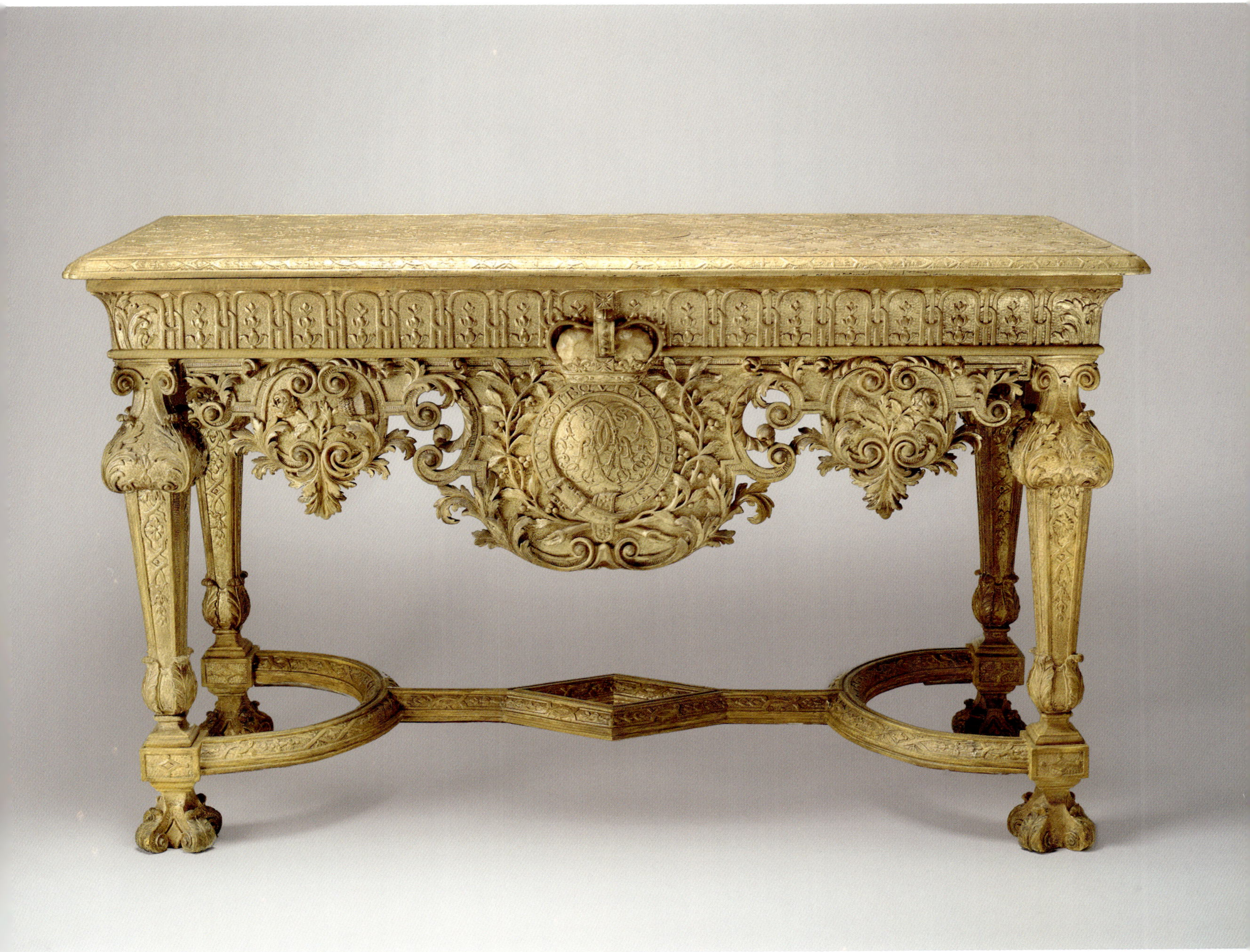

103

JAMES MOORE (*c*.1670–1726)

Pier table and pair of candle-stands 1723–24

Gilded and gessoed oak, pine and lime, 86 × 150.5 × 59 cm (table); 143.0 × 59 cm (candle-stands)
Marks: the edge of the top of each stand incised *MOORE*
Pier table RCIN 597.2, candle-stands RCIN 1087.1-2

PROVENANCE Probably made for George I for the Privy Chamber, Kensington Palace, 1723–24

LITERATURE (Pier table) Smith 1931, fig. 228, p. 197; *Royal Treasures* 2002, no. 81; Bowett 2005, pp. 44–5, fig. 12; (candle-stands) Edwards and Jourdain 1944, pp. 96–7, figs. 24 and 27; Bowett 2005, pp. 44–5, fig. 11; *Royal Treasures* 2002, no. 82

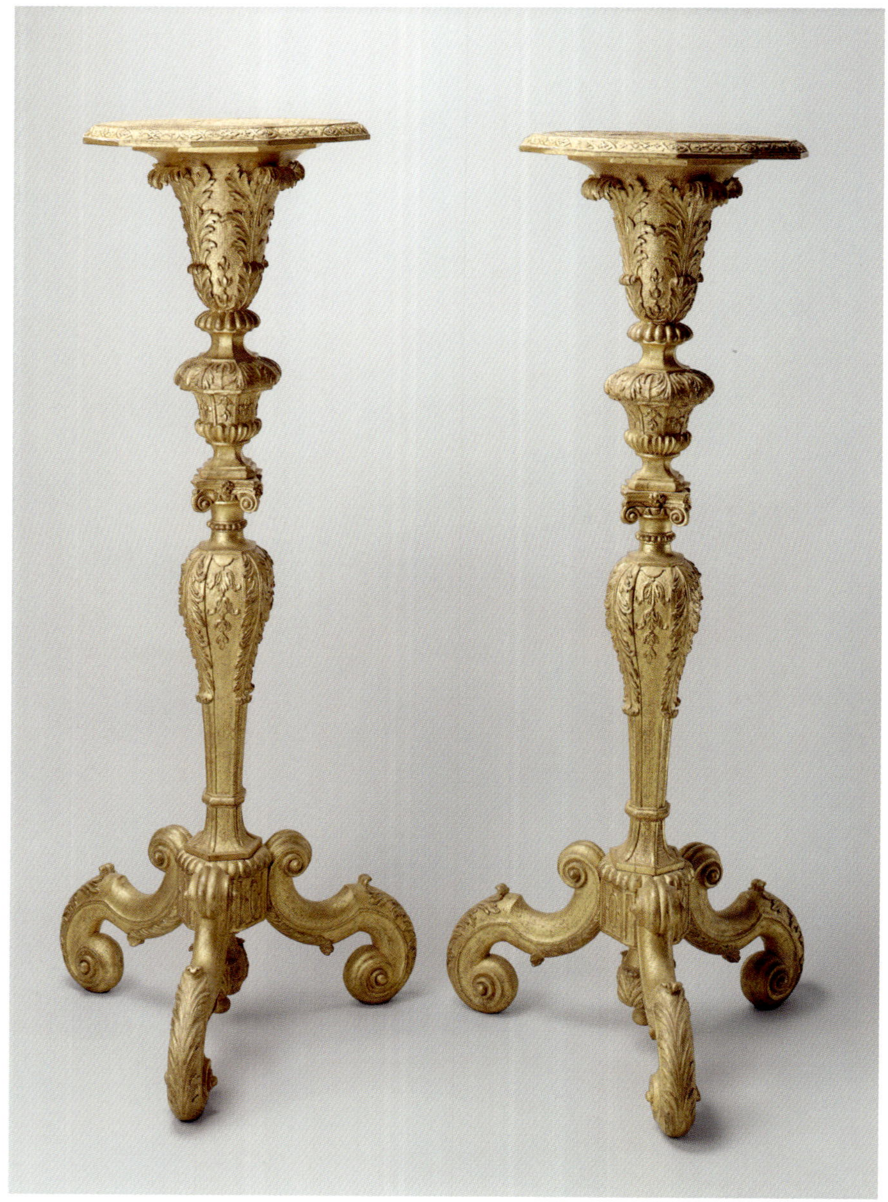

Although described as being made by Moore and Gumley, it was probably Moore who was responsible for this table (one of a pair) and its matching stands. Gumley probably made the pair of mirrors which were to hang directly above each table (which do not survive). They were perhaps those destined for the Privy Chamber, Kensington Palace, and recorded in the period Michaelmas (29 September) 1723 to Michaelmas 1724 in the Wardrobe accounts as '2 very fine large Table frames at £36 each ... £72'. The tables were supplied with '2 very large Hanging Glasses at £120 each ... £240' and '4 large Stands gilt at £18 each ... £72'.[78] Their design depends on scrolling foliage and strapwork patterns (see detail p. 166) similar to those found in the highly influential designs published by Daniel Marot at the beginning of the eighteenth century.[79] Marot's designs mark the last flowering of a highly elaborate Franco-Dutch Baroque style, favoured by William III. In the example of the candle-stands, the S-shaped (sometimes called 'horsebone') legs are suggestive of chair legs made during the 1690s and early 1700s.[80] This influence is all the more remarkable given the 'Italianising' role played by William Kent in the creation of the new State Apartments at Kensington Palace in the 1720s. RB

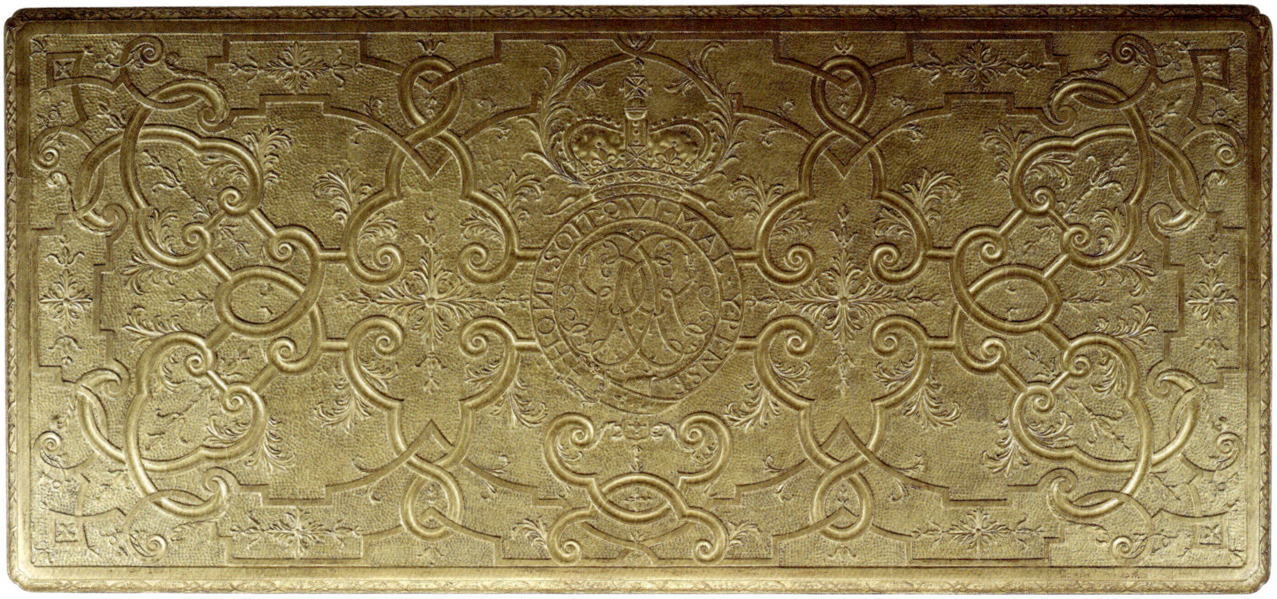

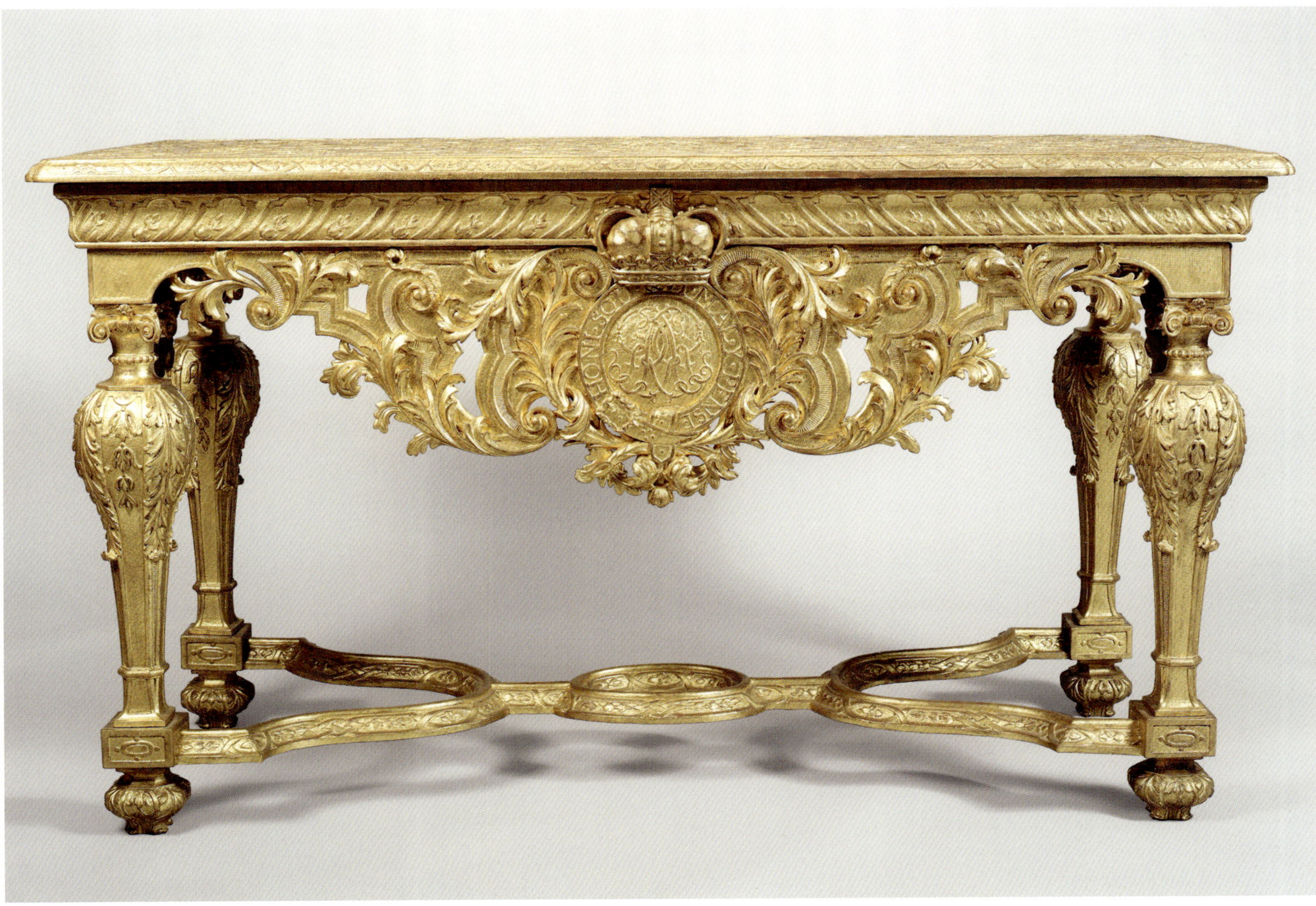

104

JOHN GUMLEY (1672–1729) AND WILLIAM TURING (ACTIVE 1714–30)

Side table and pair of candle-stands 1727

Table: gilded and gessoed oak and pine, *bleu turquin* marble, 86.5 × 152.5 × 75.5 cm
Candle-stands: gilded and gessoed walnut and pine, white marble, 154 × 60.5 cm
Table RCIN 21599, candle-stands RCIN 33389.1-2

PROVENANCE Made for George I for the Great [i.e. King's] Gallery, Kensington Palace, 1727

LITERATURE Laking 1905, p. 36, pl. 16; Edwards and Jourdain 1944, p. 94, fig. 19 (table only); Bowett 2005, pp. 43–44, fig. 9

A warrant to furnish the King's or Great Gallery at Kensington was issued in early 1727 and an order for a pair of tables and four matching stands was placed with John Gumley and William Turing, the latter succeeding Moore in the partnership after Moore's sudden death in October 1726. The Gumley & Turing invoice also describes the leather baize-lined covers created to protect the pieces when not in use:

> 'For 2 very large carved & gilt frames for Marble Slabbs at £40 each, £80.0.0.
> for 4 fine large carved & gilt Stands for Marble Tops at £18 each, £72.0.0
> for 6 Leather Covers lined wth Bayz to cover ye Tables & Stands to the Ground, £19.0.0 ...
> Montagu [signed] Nov 8th 1727'.[81]

All four stands but only one table survive in the Royal Collection; the matching table is in the Cincinnati Museum of Art, no. 1990.50, with a brocatelle marble top. The original arrangement would have included a mirror over each table.

The Great Gallery was completed at the end of May 1727. The King, however, died at Osnabrück on 11 June and never saw the work. It is not known if the tables were ever installed there. The earliest depiction of the Gallery, Charles Wild's watercolour of 1816 (no. 28), shows three of the four stands but neither of the tables or mirrors. One table may be that shown, at Windsor, in Charles Wild's 1816 watercolour of the King's Bedchamber, where its frame and distinctive stretcher seem to be recognisable.[82] Lacking from the present table, however, is the large carved apron which probably included the royal arms, in common with other tables supplied at this period for Kensington (see nos 101–3). RB

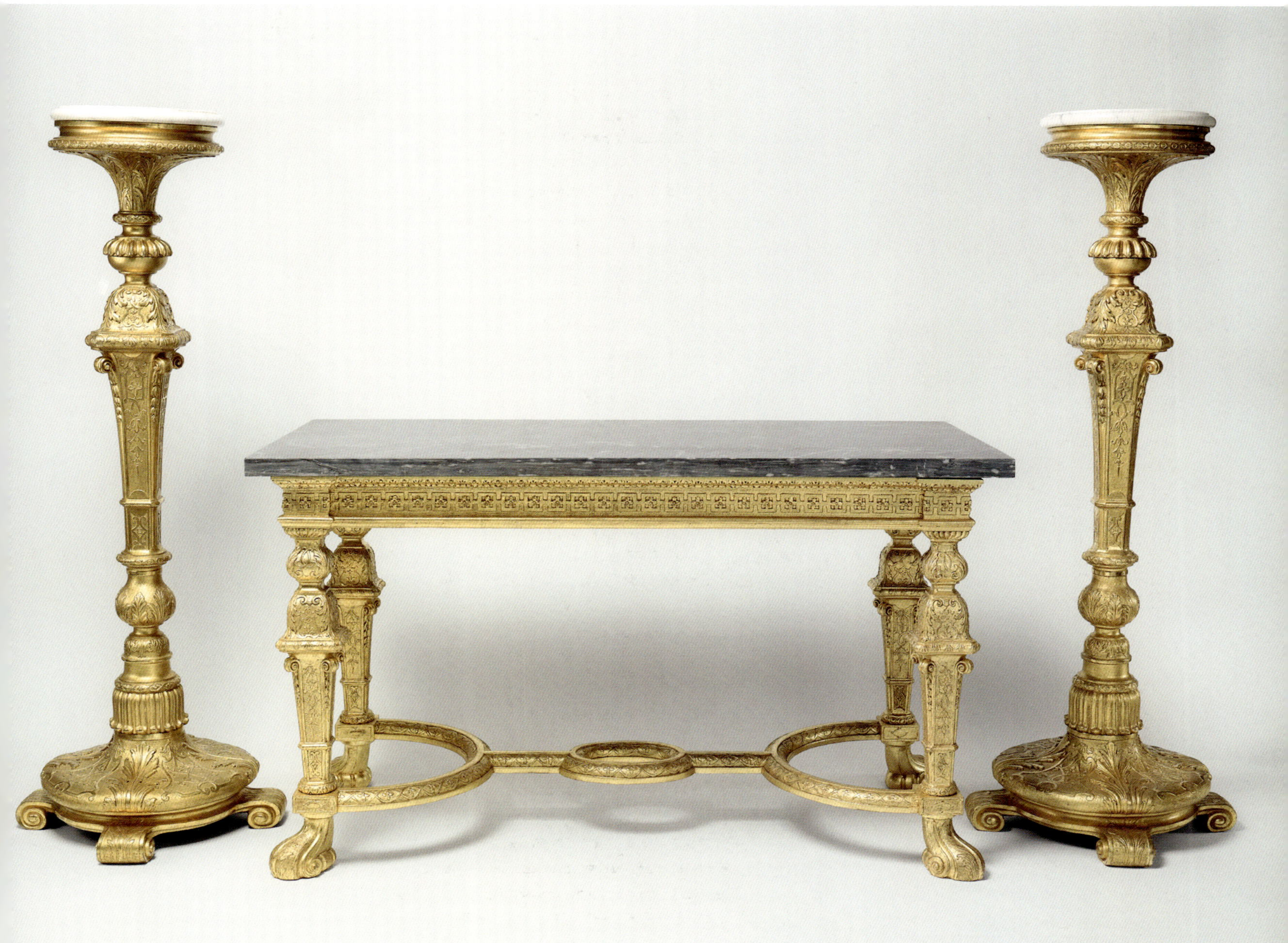

105

CAMILLO RUSCONI (1658–1728)

The Four Seasons *c.*1700

Marble

(a) ***Spring***

74.3 × 71.4 × 45 cm
RCIN 71426

(b) ***Summer***

74.9 × 52.7 × 43 cm
RCIN 71427

(c) ***Autumn***

76.2 × 59.7 × 44 cm
RCIN 71424

(d) ***Winter***

73 × 70.5 × 45 cm
RCIN 71425

ITALIAN *c.*1700

Four pedestals

Limestone, veneered with onyx marble (*alabastro onice*), 123 × 59.5 × 59 cm
RCIN 35322.1-.4

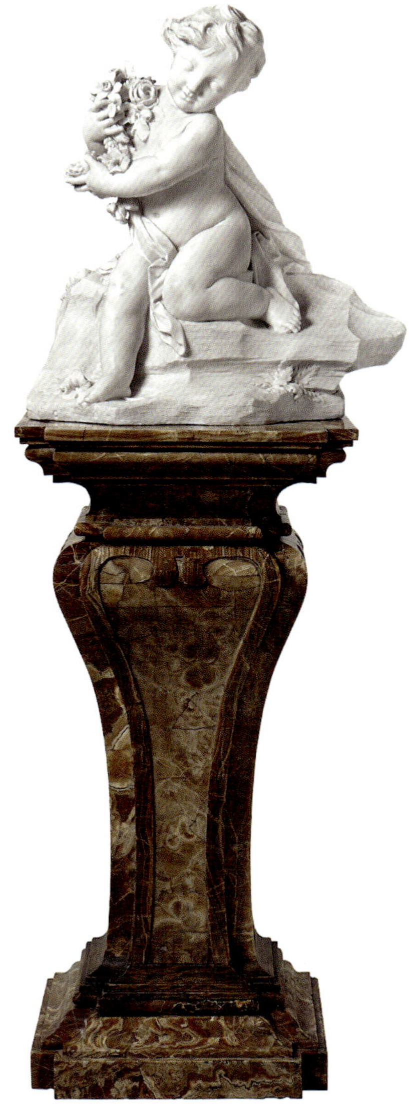

PROVENANCE Marchese Nicolò Maria Pallavicini (1650–1714), Rome; George II, London, probably by 1732; Kensington Palace, by 1750 (MS Inventory [OM30], p. 6); Windsor Castle, from 1828

LITERATURE Enggass 1976, pp. 92–3; Rudolph 1995, p. 224; Martin 2000, esp. pp. 58–66; *Royal Treasures* 2002, no. 98 (pedestals only)

These four spirited groups are rare examples of Roman Baroque sculpture in the Royal Collection. They were among the first works in marble by Camillo Rusconi, who set up independently in Rome in 1686 following the death of his master, Ercole Ferrata (1610–86). Rusconi's early output was confined to figurative tomb sculpture, mainly in stucco, but in the late 1690s he was asked to model a figure of a boy with a bunch of grapes for the Marchese Nicolò Maria Pallavicini. With the encouragement of Carlo Maratti (see no. 127) and the approval of their patron, the single figure was carved in marble and joined by representations of the other three *Seasons*, which were placed on their onyx pedestals in the Marchese's gallery. Representations of the seasons were a common adornment of Italian Baroque palaces and gardens, but few examples show the expressive liveliness of Rusconi's groups. Not content dutifully to identify each figure merely with the time-honoured attributes, Rusconi uses action, pose and gesture to characterise each Season, for example *Winter* draws a cape about him. The groups were evidently popular and often copied at full scale or in miniature during the course of the eighteenth century.

Pallavicini died in 1714 and the contents of the Palazzo all'Orso were gradually dispersed. From descriptions and drawings of the *Four Seasons* it is clear that they remained at the palace until at least 1723. The biographer Baldinucci relates that by around 1730 the four groups had been:

> ... sold to some Englishmen, who brought them to London and sold them to King George ... for 4,000 *scudi*; [the King] placed them in his Royal Gallery, where ... they are admired by all connoisseurs.[83]

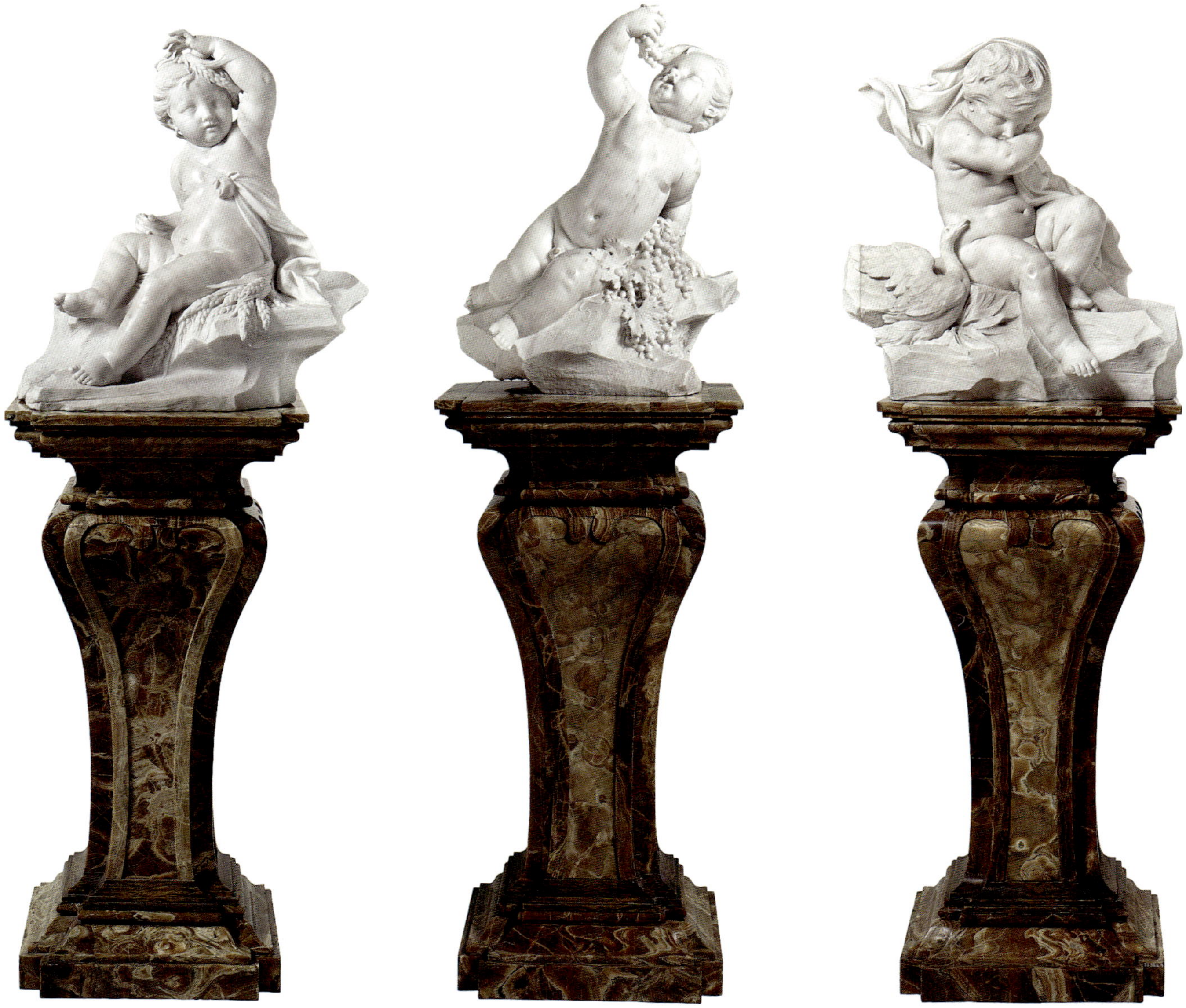

The timing of the acquisition suggests a connection with the work undertaken by William Kent at Kensington between 1725 and 1727, specifically for the King's Gallery, where the four groups appear (with their pedestals) in Charles Wild's view of the Gallery (no. 36).

The purchase of the groups by George I for his gallery at Kensington has parallels in the formation of contemporary English collections such as that of the 1st Earl of Leicester at Holkham Hall in Norfolk, where William Kent was also architect. The appeal of these emblems of nature to George I can also be understood by reference to his early life in the Electorate, where his mother had laid out elaborate gardens (notably at Herrenhausen) heavily populated by marble sculptures.

The skilled maker of the veneered pedestals is not known, but they seem to have been intended to support the Rusconi groups. The sophisticated way in which the veneers are applied to the curved surfaces of the pedestals is almost without parallel.[84] JM

106

MASSIMILIANO SOLDANI-BENZI (1656–1740)

The Four Seasons 1715

Bronze reliefs

(a) *Spring*

47.7 × 66.3 cm
At the extreme lower left is a ribbon inscribed: *MAXIMILIANVS.SOLDANI.BENZI./ NOBILIS. FLORENTINVS. FAC. ANNO. 1715*
RCIN 21932.1

(b) *Summer*

48.2 × 66.3 cm
At the extreme lower left is a ribbon inscribed: *MAXIMILIANVS.SOLDANI. BENZI./ NOBILIS. FLOR.FACIEBAT.ANNO.1715*
RCIN 21932.2

(c) *Autumn*

47.7 × 66.3 cm
At the extreme lower right is a ribbon inscribed: *MAXIMILIANVS. SOLDANI. BENZI./ NOBILIS. FLOR. FACIEBAT.ANN. 1715*
RCIN 21932.3

(d) *Winter*

48.5 × 66 cm
At the extreme lower left is a ribbon inscribed: *MAXIMILIANVS.SOLDANI.BENZI./ NOBILIS. FLORENTINVS.FAC.ANNO./ 1715* (Vulcan's shield is inscribed: *UNUM/ OMNIA CONTRA/ TELA*.)
RCIN 21932.4

PROVENANCE *Summer* and *Autumn* purchased from the artist in Florence in February 1715 by Richard Boyle, 3rd Earl of Burlington (1694–1753); *Spring* and *Winter* commissioned at the same time but delivered subsequently; all four reliefs presented by Burlington to George II

LITERATURE Fortnum 1876, p. CXXXV; Weihrauch 1956, p. 176; Lankheit 1962, pp. 133, 233; Friedman 1988, p. 844; Avery 1994, pp. 14–16, figs 7–8; Clark 1995, pp. 257–8; Avery 1998, pp. 27–50

The medallist and sculptor Massimiliano Soldani-Benzi dominated Florentine sculpture in the late Baroque period, working throughout his life for the ruling Medici family. The origin of these superb reliefs can be found in a commission of 1708 from Crown Prince Ferdinando de' Medici, heir to Cosimo III, Grand Duke of Tuscany, for two reliefs representing *Summer* and *Autumn*, intended for presentation to the Crown Prince's brother-in-law, John William, Elector Palatine. These two were soon joined by reliefs representing *Spring* and *Winter*, completed in 1711.

The reliefs were composed in clay, and the models then used to make piece-moulds from which the bronzes would eventually be cast by the lost-wax process. The clay models were fired for the purpose of preservation and remain in the Palazzo Pitti, Florence, in their original glazed frames. When first completed in bronze, the reliefs would have had a golden surface, imparted by powdered haematite suspended in an oil varnish.[85] Soldani's technique was designed to enable further casts to be made, and through adjustments at the wax stage he could add armorials or mottos specific to the patron concerned. In April 1715 the 21-year-old Lord Burlington visited Soldani's studio during his Grand Tour, and purchased casts of the *Summer* and *Autumn* reliefs for £125 each, leaving a commission for *Spring* and *Winter*.[86] These were embellished with Burlington's arms and short verse inscriptions from Virgil's *Aeneid*, one of which (on *Spring*) substitutes 'Burlingtonus' for 'Marcellus'.

In a manuscript addition to George Vertue's 1758 description of Queen Caroline's Closet at Kensington, Horace Walpole noted, 'In the King's Bedchamber ... some Bronze pictures, presented to George 2^{d} by Ld Burlington'.[87] Vertue himself had earlier noted, at the sale of the 2nd Earl of Radnor's possessions at his house in St James's Square in 1723, 'four fine pieces in Brass guilt with gold. being alto relievo's by Max: Soldani. 1715/ many figures raised quite out from the flatt'.[88] This reference, likely to refer to the *Four Seasons*, is puzzling, as no other evidence has come to light for the existence of a third complete set.

If we accept Walpole's word, the gift seems most likely to have taken place between 1730, when Burlington was invested as a Knight of the Garter, and 1733, when he resigned all his public positions in protest at being passed over for one of the higher offices of State.[89]

The first set of casts made for the Elector (Munich, Bayerisches Nationalmuseum) were displayed in ebony and gilt bronze frames and hung alongside the paintings in the gallery at the electoral palace in Düsseldorf.[90] It is not known how the present set was first framed, but in 1814, when they were still kept at Kensington Palace, they were described as having 'black frames'.[91] JM

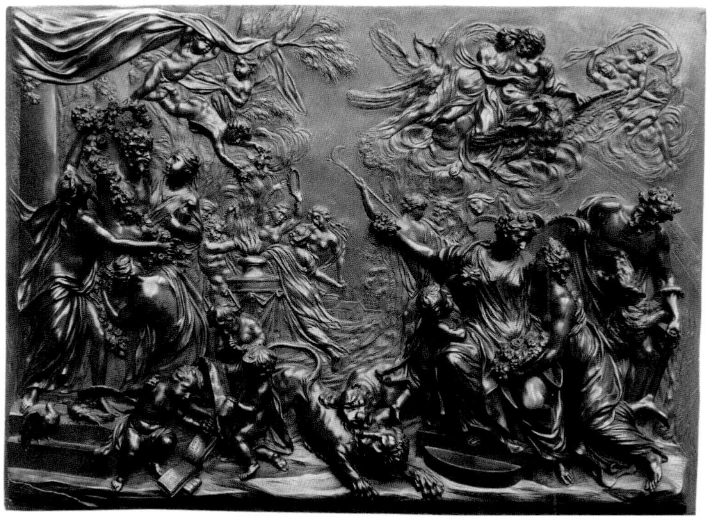
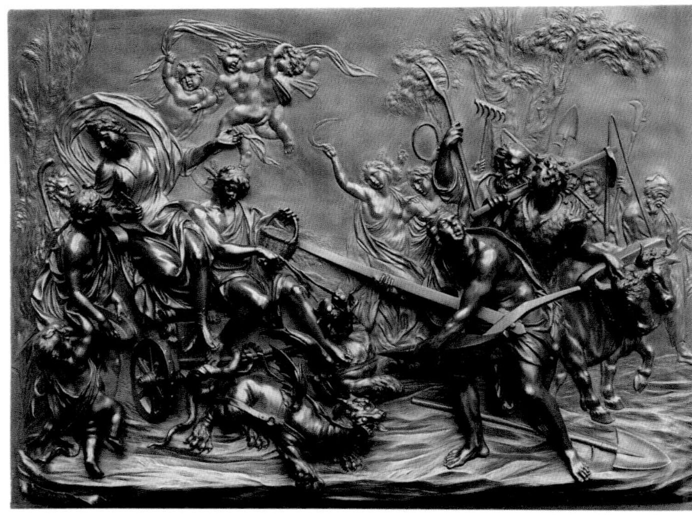
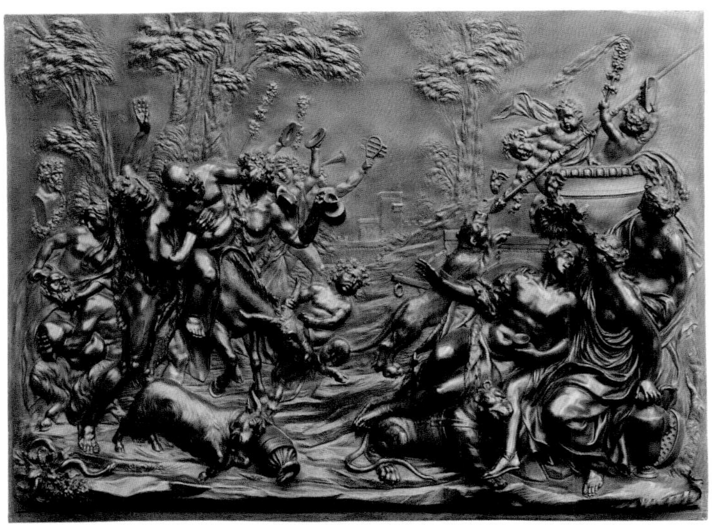
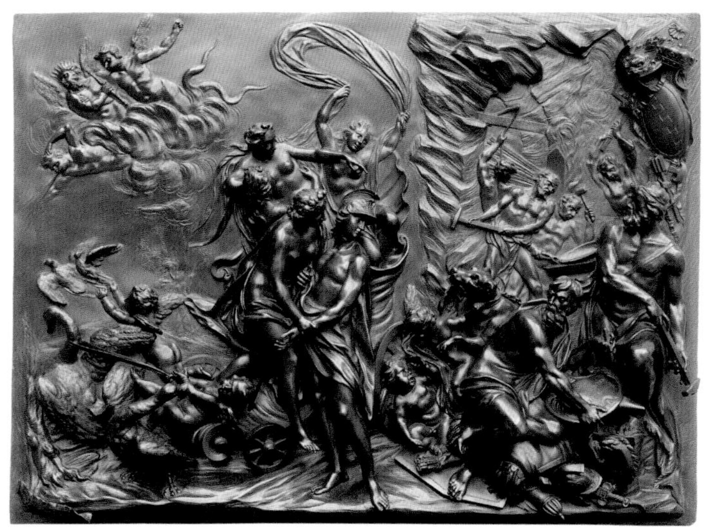

Reign of George II and Frederick, Prince of Wales

Kensington in the Reign of George II

Kensington Palace was much used in George II's reign and the furniture ordered for it tended to reflect the requirements of the occupants. In contrast with the single and elderly George I, the younger George II and his consort Queen Caroline brought with them not only their own households but also the growing entourages attached to their children, fast approaching marriageable age.[92] As the State Apartments were largely complete, for the most part these were left untouched. The picture was rather different in the private apartments, where considerable orders were placed in the early years of the reign. The largest order belongs to a warrant dated 9 June 1732, which covered hundreds of individual items, almost all destined for the apartments of the royal children, and amounted to an estimated £6,810.[93] The mid-1730s continued the familiar rhythm of summer court visits, reflected in the orders for new furnishings. Fashion played a part too: in June 1736 an order suggests a revival in the interest in lacquer furniture, such as screens and cabinets (see no. 95), in this case for Augusta of Saxe-Gotha, the new Princess of Wales. However, the succession of orders could not continue indefinitely and just as the requirement for new furniture had increased at the beginning of the new reign so it dried up after Queen Caroline's death in 1737. The reduction in orders was compounded by the estrangement between the King and the Prince of Wales, who after 1738 never returned to Kensington. The 1740s has been described as 'one of the most disappointing decades in the furnishing history of Kensington Palace', characterised by occasional bulk orders for basic and plainly functional furniture.[94] A change in the use of materials comes in the mid-1750s with the new fashion for patterned paper, printed linens and cottons: these were hung in the royal children's bedrooms. Even though the monarch was ageing, through the 1750s the orders came thick and fast and the final order in 1759–60 was sizeable.[95] Furniture from the private apartments from this period is still to be identified.[96]

Frederick, Prince of Wales

If the monarch or consort required furnishings conforming to a certain level of appropriateness in their state apartments, the Prince of Wales was at greater liberty to follow fashion or his own taste. When Frederick arrived in Britain from Hanover in 1727 on the accession of his father, George II, he was initially on good terms with his parents, and apartments at St James's, Hampton Court and Kensington were created for him. However, he was able to marry Augusta of Saxe-Gotha only in 1736, after his sister, Princess Anne, had been married to William IV, Prince of Orange, the future Stadholder of the Netherlands, in 1734. This was perceived by Frederick as favouritism and contributed to the growing enmity between father and son. Notwithstanding these issues, which came to a head in 1737, lavish apartments were created for Augusta reflecting her status as Princess of Wales, and the northern part of Kensington Palace was altered and extended in order to accommodate Frederick and Augusta's growing family.

It is difficult to reconstruct the flavour of the apartments created for the Prince and Princess of Wales as very little that can be certainly associated with these spaces survives. However, nos 107–111 can be linked with some certainty to accounts for the furnishing of the Prince of Wales's apartments, probably at Hampton Court, for

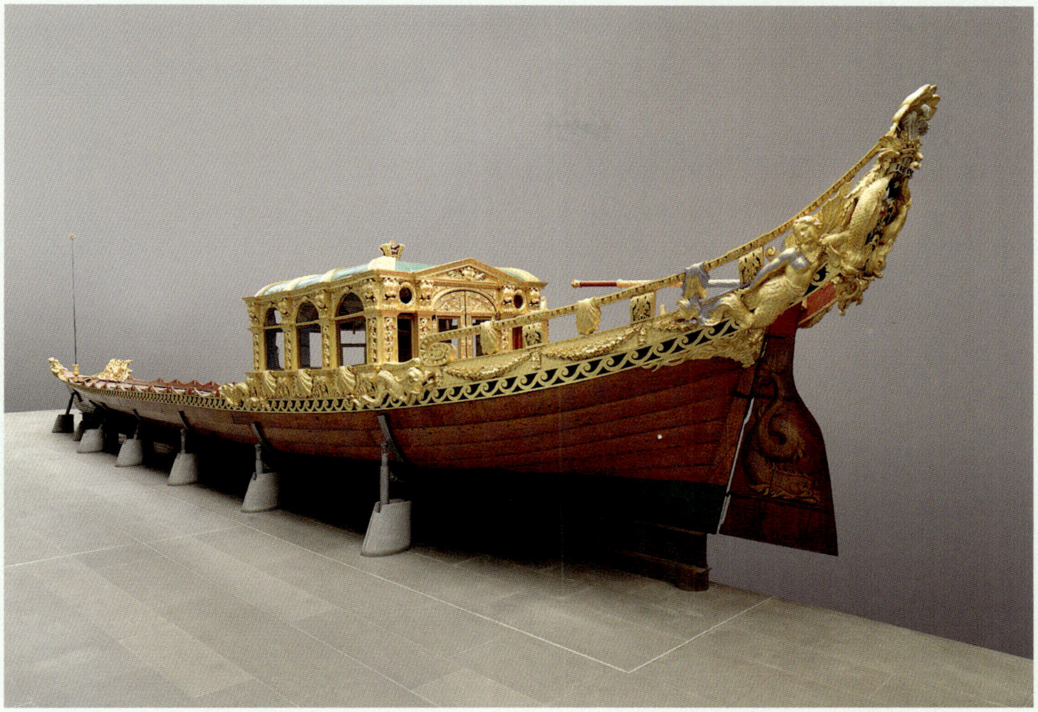

FIG. 44
Designed by William Kent, shipwright John Hall, carver James Richards, gilder Paul Petit
The Prince of Wales's Royal Barge, 1732
Giltwood, oak, iron
On loan to the National Maritime Museum, Greenwich, RCIN 69797

the most part prior to his marriage to Augusta. These surviving pieces from the 1730s, perhaps coincidentally, make extensive use of a classical vocabulary of design and decoration. The mirrors (nos 110–11) employ a Vitruvian scroll and egg-and-dart border at the edge of the frame; the table (no. 107) displays a guilloche carving on the outer face of the leg combined with a fluted frieze: the scrolled profile of the leg is derived from a Roman 'truss', an architectural ornament employed in the design of ancient temples. The gilt-gesso tables (nos 108–9) make use of similar classical ornamentation. This classicizing of ornamentation in furniture design was probably in part due to the involvement of the architect William Kent, who wished to introduce the Italian 'gusto' into England in the years after his return from Italy in 1719. Frederick is likely to have encountered Kent first in the 1730s, and thereafter made use of his talents for his own projects, continuing to patronise him after the division with his parents. Kent meanwhile managed to work satisfactorily for the King and Queen as well. Earlier, in 1732, Frederick had commissioned Kent to design a magnificent barge (fig. 44), with carving by Kent's favoured carver, James Richards, and gilding by Paul Petit, while the barge itself was built by the shipwright John Hall.[9] The barge is an extraordinary hybrid assemblage of styles which combine successfully in a work which is entirely of its time. Frederick is often associated with the rococo style and he certainly favoured the fantastical creations in silver by craftsmen fully versed in that style (see no. 312). However, like other patrons of the 1730s and 1740s, Frederick happily combined various styles and never confined himself to a single one. Even that temple to the Rococo, Chesterfield House, designed by Isaac Ware, a high priest of neo-Palladianism, combined a variety of styles, including a restrained classical dining-room, while the drawing-room was a rococo masterpiece. Ironically it was Ware who, in *A Complete Body of Architecture* of 1756, railed against the Rococo, a style firmly associated with France. Ware's British audience in the later 1750s was likely to have appreciated such anti-French sentiments owing to the resumption of hostilities against France in 1756 which marked the beginning of the Seven Years' War.[98]

107

ATTRIBUTED TO BENJAMIN GOODISON (*c*.1700–1767)

Side table *c*.1730–7

Oak, burr-walnut, walnut and pine, 84 × 115 × 60.5 cm
RCIN 1195

PROVENANCE Probably supplied for George II or Frederick, Prince of Wales, in the 1730s

LITERATURE Macquoid and Edwards 1927, III, p. 259, fig. 20

While it is difficult to associate this table with a specific entry in one of the Great Wardrobe accounts, in style it conforms closely to furniture made for the royal palaces in the 1730s, in particular to furniture supplied by Benjamin Goodison (see nos 108–9), which was designed in a robust classical manner. Between 1729 and 1760, warrants for new furniture were sent by the Wardrobe to Benjamin Goodison. In 1721 the passing of the Naval Stores Act removed import duties on timber brought from British colonies and stimulated widespread use of mahogany.[99] The Wardrobe accounts reveal that mahogany was generally employed for utilitarian furniture such as gaming-tables, dining-tables, circular tables with a 'claw' foot or base, while walnut continued to be reserved for higher-quality pieces. Even so, it was unusual for a piece made at this period which relied on carved detail to be executed in walnut, especially when mahogany was freely available. This table may be an instance of the higher status of walnut as a timber compared to mahogany, a situation which reversed in the middle years of the eighteenth century. The simple scrolled outline of the legs and their carved elements derive firmly from classical sources.[100] These sources were familiar to William Kent and the design of this table may be attributed to him. Walnut (and mahogany) furniture such as this was probably intended for use in the private apartments of George II or Frederick, Prince of Wales; by contrast the furniture used in the State Apartment would have been entirely gilded (with the possible exception of some functional chairs and stools such as no. 97 and fig. 42). RB

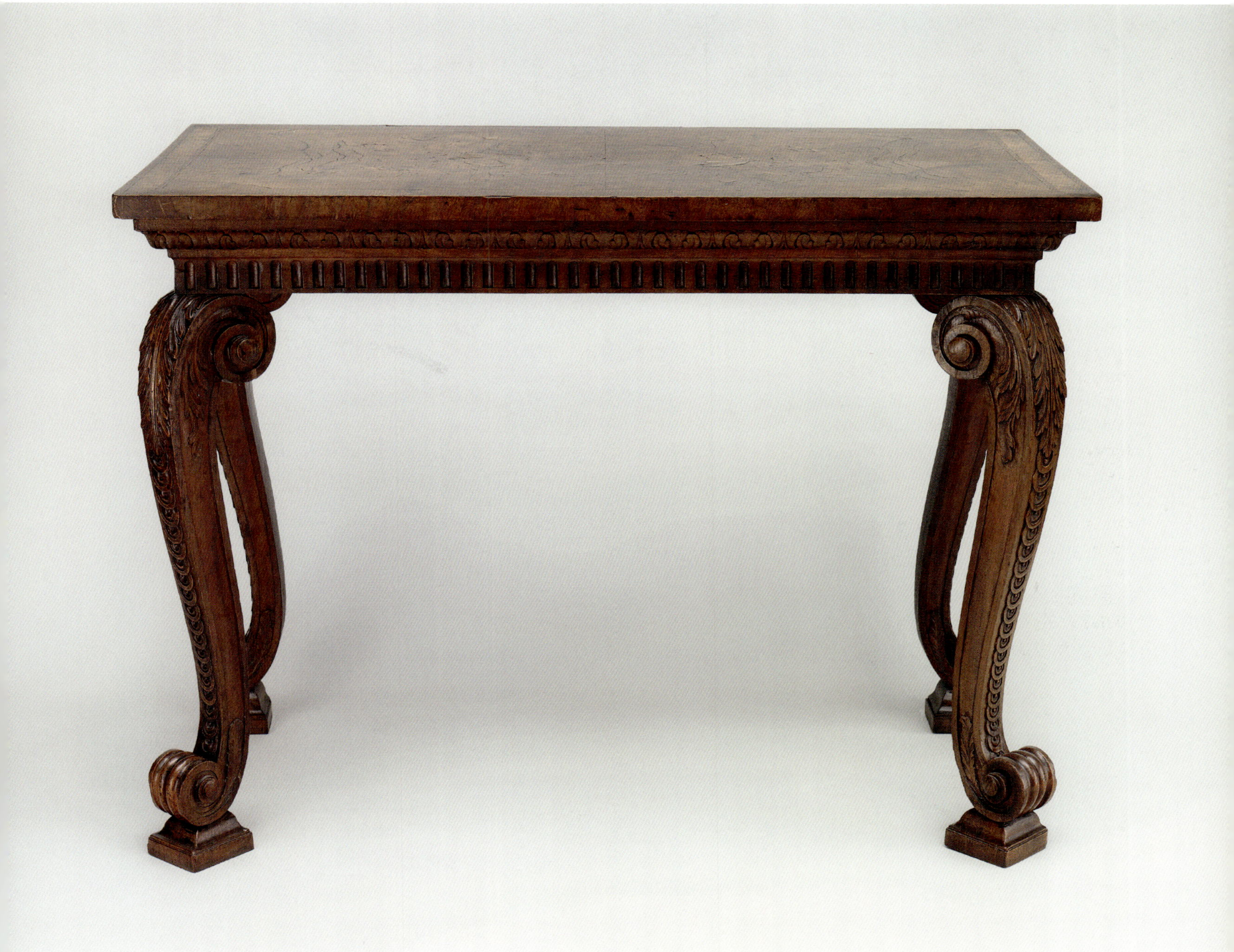

108 & 109

ATTRIBUTED TO BENJAMIN GOODISON (*c.*1700–1767)

Two side tables *c.*1730

Gilded and gessoed oak and pine, (no. 108) 82 × 112 × 65 cm; (no. 109) 79 × 119 × 70 cm
RCIN 35267 and RCIN 35268

PROVENANCE Probably supplied to George II or Frederick, Prince of Wales, *c.*1730

LITERATURE Laking 1905, p. 40, pl. 18 (no. 108) and p. 41 (no. 109)

Between 1729 and 1760, Benjamin Goodison supplied a number of tables, probably of this general design, to the King and to the Prince of Wales. Unfortunately it is not possible to identify them in the accounts with any degree of precision. Their design suggests they were made in the earlier part of Goodison's period working for the Wardrobe. No. 108 makes use of the distinctive out-scrolled upper part of the leg, a *leitmotif* employed by Goodison's master, James Moore, on tables at Blenheim Palace and elsewhere in the period leading up to 1715.

This seemingly rather old-fashioned pattern of leg is combined with a rich classical vocabulary: the frieze is carved with a Vitruvian scroll and centred by a lion mask, from which depend oak-leaf swags; the legs themselves are carved with fish-scales. The design of no. 109 is close to that of a table with a similar profile of leg supplied for Frederick, Prince of Wales, also inlaid with circular guilloche mouldings (no. 107). Here, however, the design is expressed with a fully developed classical vocabulary of decoration: the frieze is carved with a Vitruvian scroll above a central female mask, flanked on either side by drapery swags; the side panels of the legs are carved with fish-scales. The tops of both tables are executed in gilt-gesso, a usage in decline from the mid-1720s. Thereafter marble slabs, which would serve to emphasise the classicizing or 'antique' nature of furniture, were more usual.

Both these tables are visible in Wild's 1816 watercolour of the Queen's Drawing Room at Windsor (fig. 45), supporting two of George III's ship models. Subsequently (perhaps as early as George IV's reign) both were moved to the Queen's Audience Chamber, where they continued to serve as stands, this time for two lacquer cabinets.[101]
RB

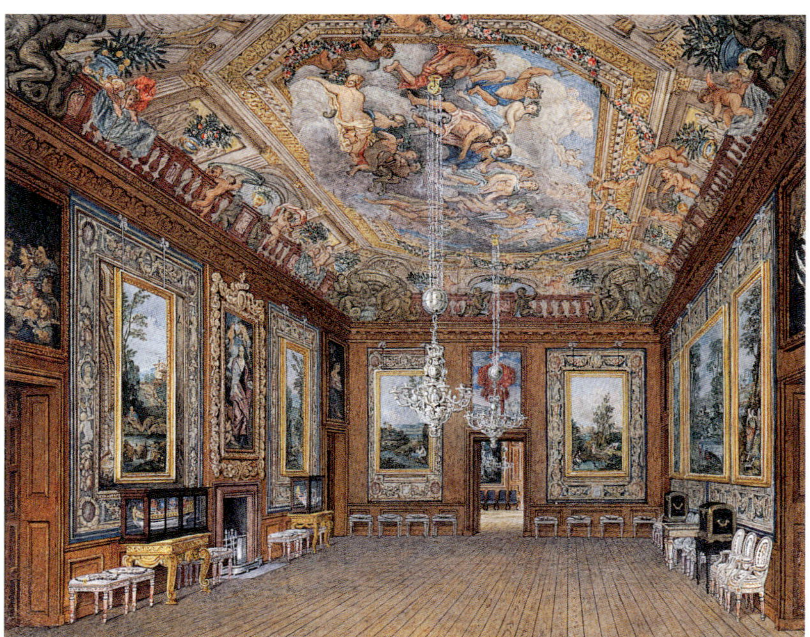

FIG. 45
Charles Wild
The Queen's Drawing Room, Windsor Castle, 1816
Watercolour with touches of bodycolour, over pencil
RCIN 922102

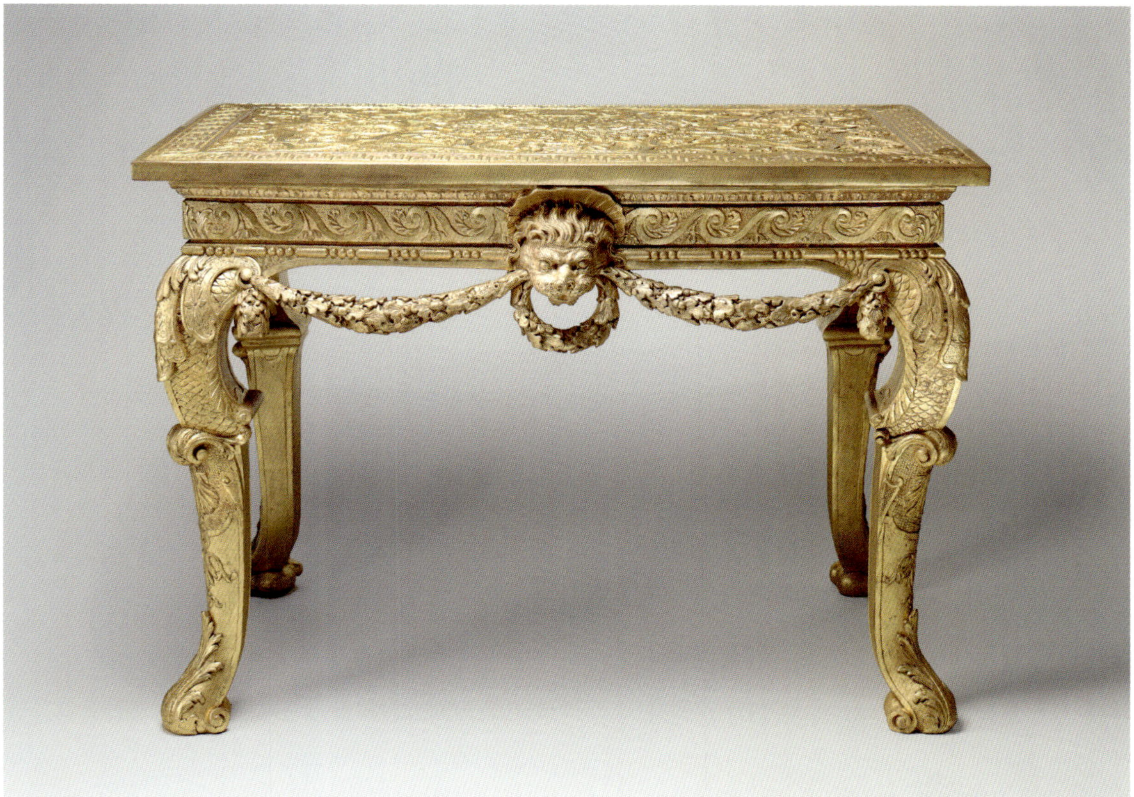

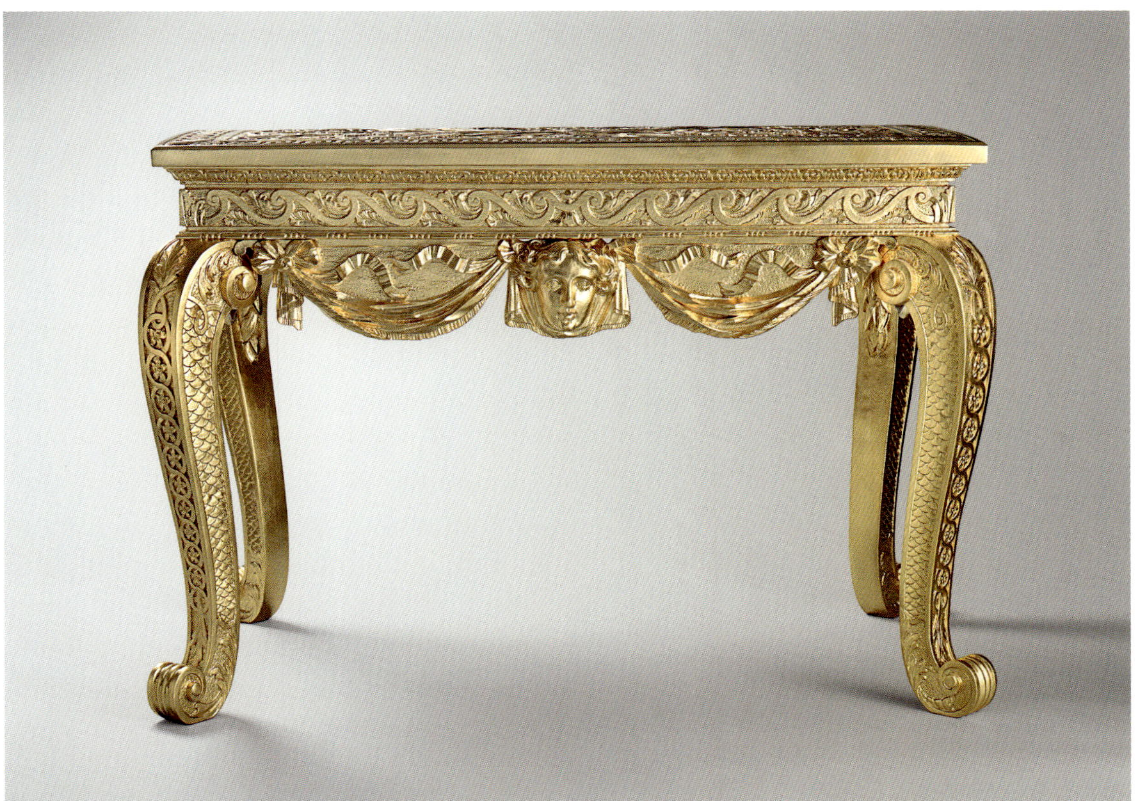

Hampton Court

Hampton Court received greater attention during the reign of George II, when the apartment given over to the former Prince and Princess of Wales was put to use as the Queen's apartment and some new, updated furniture was brought in. The most dramatic change in the State Apartment came in the Queen's Withdrawing Room, where Queen Caroline's dislike of Thornhill and Verrio's wall paintings celebrating Prince George of Denmark, consort of Queen Anne, caused her to move into it Mantegna's *Triumphs of Caesar* following their displacement from the Triumph Gallery by the Alexander tapestry series (see no. 114). Around the nine canvases was hung green silk damask supplied by Mathew Vernon and made by Sarah Gilbert with trimmings supplied by William Weeks, the laceman.[102] The Drawing Room and Triumph Gallery were provided with new seat furniture made by the joiner Henry Williams (see nos 114–6), probably designed by William Kent, at that time working on new apartments at Hampton Court. Given Kent's involvement in the overall design of a room, including the ceiling, cornice, chimneypiece and doorcases as well as the furniture, it would seem probable that he had a hand in their design. He was certainly responsible for the design of the new apartment for the Duke of Cumberland, second son of the King and Queen, carried out in the early 1730s (see fig. II.7): hitherto we have seen Kent associated with the classical style but here he turned his hand to Gothic, a style he had been working in for the Hon. Henry Pelham at nearby Esher Place. It was Sir Robert Walpole who insisted on the use of Gothic as the style for the Cumberland Suite, situated along the east side of Clock Court, and occupying a part of the gatehouse.[103] Once more the selection of an ancient, this time British, style placed the emphasis on continuity in the context of its location and antiquity in the choice of its decoration. Decoration of a different sort was also within Kent's capabilities: in 1734 he was commissioned to redecorate the Queen's Stair and did so in a firmly classical, proto-Italianate style, which celebrated contemporary British sea-power in its nautical allusions and depictions of Neptune, tridents and dolphins. He also, in placing on the stair the large painting by Gerrit van Honthorst of *The Presentation of the Liberal Arts to Apollo and Diana* with Charles I as Apollo and Queen Henrietta Maria as Diana (fig. 46),[104] aligned George II and Queen Caroline with the greatest British collector of paintings, a Stuart King and forebear with whom the Hanoverians sought publicly to ensure their proximity. Other apartments at Hampton Court were fitted out at the same time, including that for Frederick, Prince of Wales. Frederick's apartment, in contrast to his younger brother William, Duke of Cumberland's, were in the Wren-designed building, at the opposite corner to the Queen's Closet. These rooms were fitted out in a classical idiom, with furniture by Benjamin Goodison, and may have included the mirrors (nos 110–11); the two pairs of stands, probably for adjoining rooms (nos 112–3); the walnut table (no. 107) and possibly the two gilt-gesso tables (nos 108, 109).

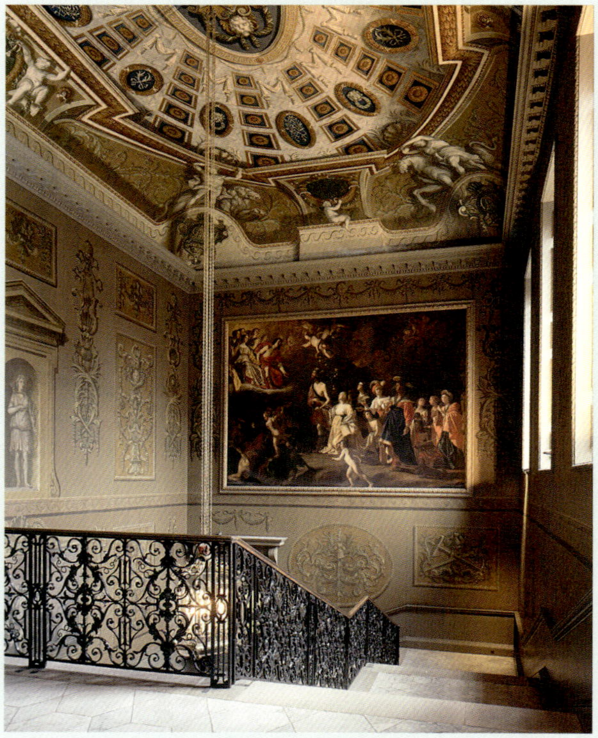

FIG. 46
The Queen's Staircase, Hampton Court Palace, Historic Royal Palaces

110 & 111

ATTRIBUTED TO BENJAMIN GOODISON (*c.*1700–1767)

Two mirrors 1732–3

Gilded and gessoed pine, mirror glass, brass, (no. 110) 105.5 × 69 cm; (no. 111) 104 × 69.5 cm
Inscribed in chalk on the reverse (no. 110) *No 3*, the frame incised *III*
RCIN 1304.1 and RCIN 1164

PROVENANCE Supplied to Frederick, Prince of Wales, in 1732–3, probably for Hampton Court Palace

LITERATURE Edwards and Jourdain 1944, p. 103, fig. 37; Edwards 1964, p. 363, fig. 37; *Princes as Patrons* 1998, no. 53; Bowett 2009, p. 282, fig. 6:31

At least ten 'sconces' (mirrors with candle-branches) were supplied for Frederick, Prince of Wales, at Kew and Hampton Court in the 1730s by the cabinet-maker to the Great Wardrobe, Benjamin Goodison. These two mirrors belong to a number of this general pattern, some with candle-branches, which survive at Hampton Court Palace and which can be connected with this commission. One of them (no. 110) can be seen hanging on the right-hand wall in Mercier's depiction of Frederick's lodgings (no. 255). Matching surviving pieces with the imprecise entries in the Great Wardrobe accounts is more difficult.[105] The Prince of Wales feathers are employed as a decorative device on no. 110 in the place of the shell motif found on no. 111. The design of these mirrors reflects the neo-Palladian style of architecture introduced by William Kent, Master Carpenter of the Office of Board of Works and architect overseeing refurbishments at Hampton Court during the 1730s. RB

112 & 113

ATTRIBUTED TO BENJAMIN GOODISON (*c.*1700–1767)

Two pairs of candle-stands 1732–3

Gilded and gessoed pine, portor marble, 146 × 41.5 × 41.5 cm
RCIN 1231.1-2 and RCIN 1232.1-2

PROVENANCE Supplied for Frederick, Prince of Wales's apartments at Hampton Court Palace, 1732–3

LITERATURE (no. 112) Edwards and Jourdain 1944, pp. 104, 264, fig. 39; *Princes as Patrons* 1998, no. 52; (no. 113) Macquoid and Edwards 1927, III, p. 153, fig. 1

Both pairs of stands are probably those described in Benjamin Goodison's Wardrobe Account as '4 Stands carved & gilt Term fashion'. All four together cost £42. The following entry in the accounts details '4 Girandoles to carry 4 Candles Each' at a cost of £17, which were probably intended to be placed on the top of each stand.[106] These 'Girandoles' (or candelabra) have not been traced, although designs (by Kent) for candelabra were published by J. Vardy in *Some Designs of Mr. Inigo Jones and Mr. Wm. Kent*, 1744, pls. 18 and 24; fig. 47).

Benjamin Goodison's role as cabinet-maker to the Great Wardrobe and to the Household of the Prince of Wales is neatly parallelled by that in architecture of William Kent. However, although Kent's involvement at Hampton Court from 1731 as architect to the Board of Works meant that he oversaw the designs of both the interiors and the furniture, documentary evidence of a direct link between Kent and Goodison is lacking.
RB

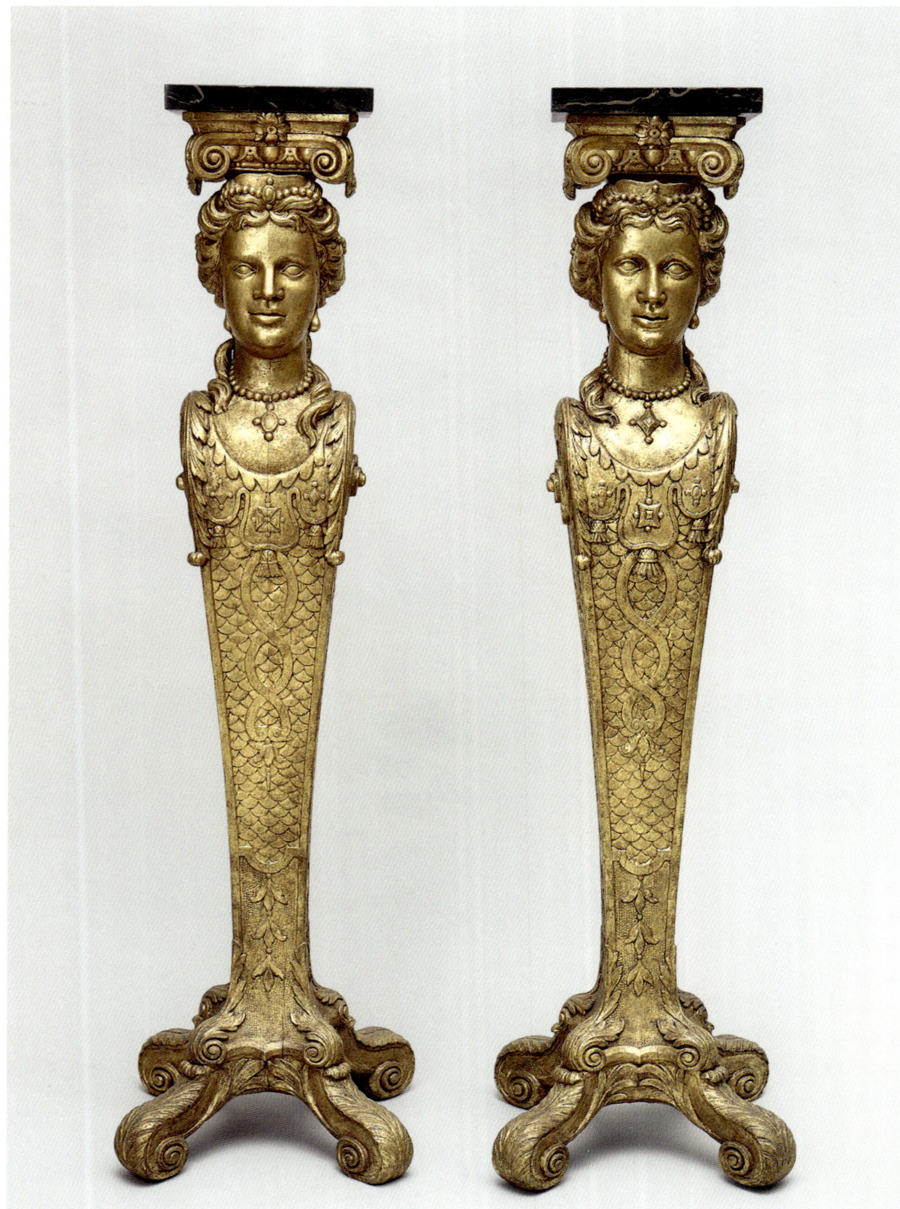

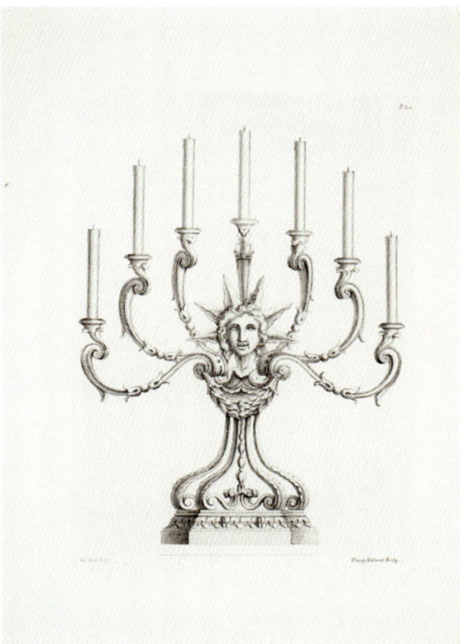

FIG. 47
William Kent
Design for a candelabrum,
plate 24 in *Some Designs of Mr. Inigo Jones and Mr. Wm. Kent*, 1744
RCIN 1150776

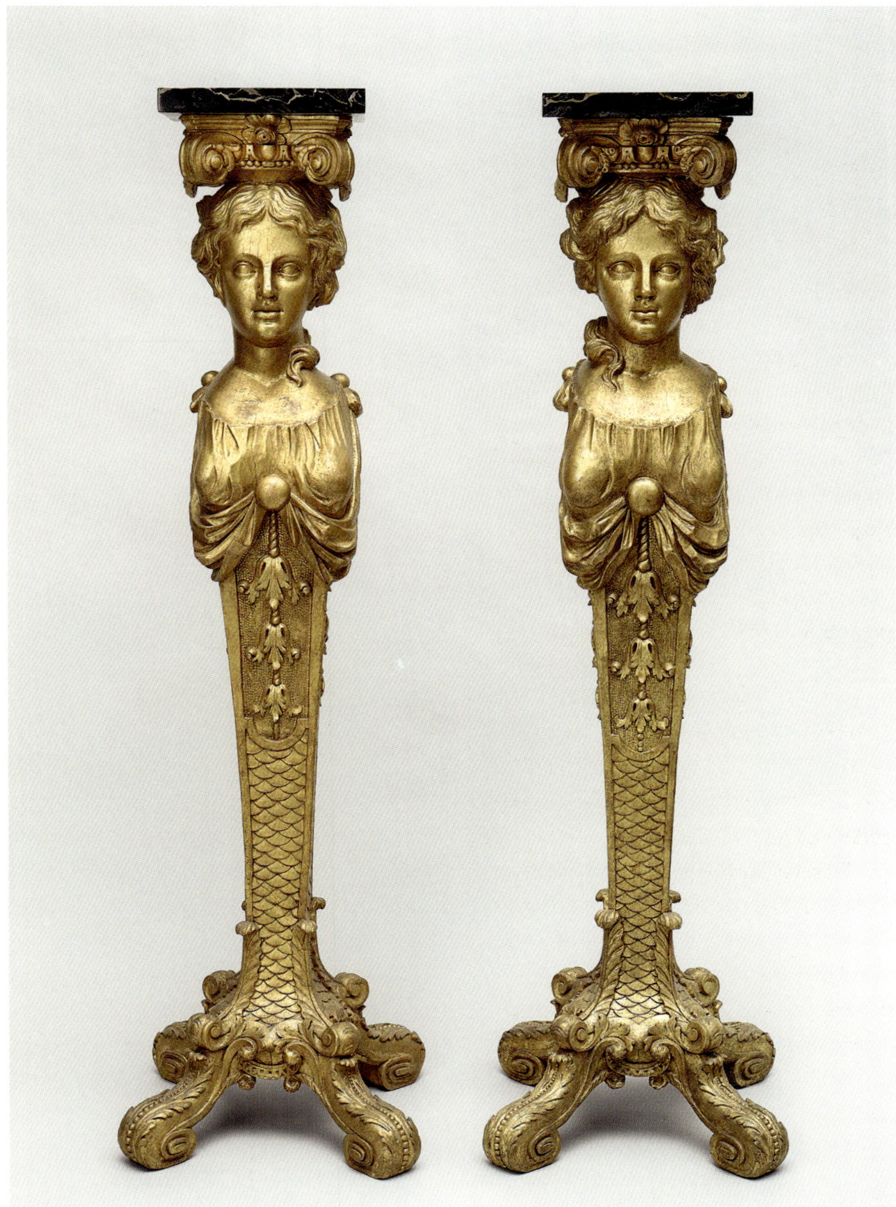

114

HENRY WILLIAMS (1717–1758)

Two stools 1737

Gilded and gessoed pine, beech, green silk damask, 50 × 69 × 48.5 cm
Label: *For the Triumph Gallery/ at Hampton Court*
RCIN 1242.2 and .8

PROVENANCE Supplied to George II for the Triumph Gallery (i.e. the Queen's Gallery), Hampton Court Palace, 1737

LITERATURE Macquoid and Edwards 1927, III, p. 169, fig. 39; Edwards and Jourdain 1955, p. 68, fig. 162; Wood 2008, I, pp. 16 and 18, figs. 20–22

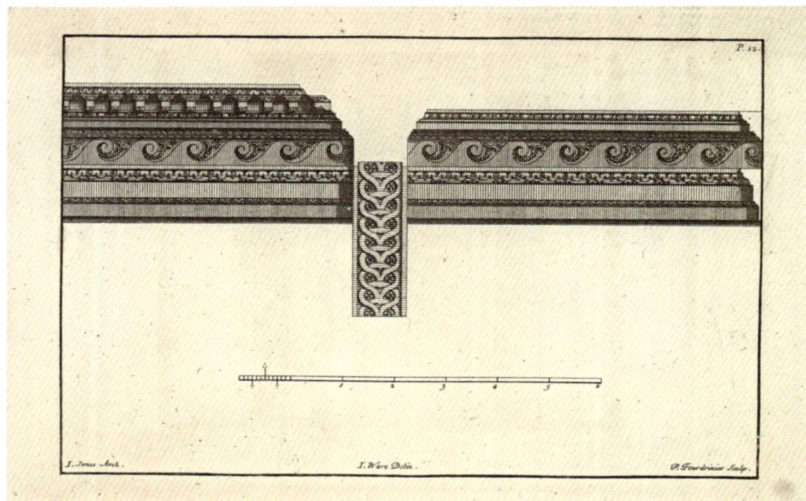

FIG. 48
After Inigo Jones
'Vitruvian' scroll, from a design for a ceiling, from Isaac Ware, *Designs of Inigo Jones and others*, 1738, plate 12
British Library

Eighteen stools of this pattern (of which seventeen survive), along with four 'large settee frames' (presumably of the same general pattern but untraced), were supplied in 1737 for Hampton Court by the cabinet-maker Henry Williams. They were described in Williams's account as '18 sq stool frames richly carved and gilt ... £99.0.0.' The upholstery was supplied by Sarah Gilbert, who charged 'For The Triumph Gallery there [i.e. Hampton Court] ... for stuffing up & covering with green Damask trim'd with Lace and adorn'd with gilt nails, 4 large Settees, and 18 square Stools, and for Canvas, Girthwebb, curled Hair and sewing silk &c. us'd £63.8.0'.[107] Gilbert also charged 'for 8000 Gilt Nails to trim the sd settees & stools £9.12.0' and 'for Strong paper & making cases for Ditto £2.2.0'.[108] William Weeks, laceman, supplied the *passementerie* for the settees, but the 18 stools are not mentioned specifically: 'For 168 yds of green Arras binding Lace at 11s yd £7.14.0'.[109]

The warrant from the Great Wardrobe for their making (i.e. the commission) notes that they were intended for the 'Triumph Gallery', as the Queen's Gallery at Hampton Court was called from the presence there of Mantegna's *Triumphs of Caesar*. These paintings had been moved, probably in 1737 but not before 1725, to the Queen's Withdrawing Room (see no. 35) and their place taken in the Queen's Gallery by a set of tapestries of *The Triumphs of Alexander the Great*, reputedly acquired by William, 1st Earl Cadogan, during his Embassy to the States General in 1716.[110]

The design of the stools combines elements that would have been familiar to the previous reign's cabinet-maker, James Moore, notably the scrolled upper leg bisecting the corner. This device was used by Moore on furniture supplied for the Duchess of Marlborough at Blenheim Place in the 1710s.[111] If this feature seems old-fashioned on these stools (it was first employed by Moore approximately twenty years earlier), the overall effect is of a design rooted in classical vocabulary. The stools include several Palladian *leitmotifs* and these perhaps indicate the involvement of William Kent, who had taken over the role of refurbishing Hampton Court in 1731. The 'Vitruvian' or wave scroll which wraps around the seat rails is combined with Roman acanthus leaves carved on the out-scrolling legs (see fig. 48). Unusually, the Vitruvian scroll is fitted on top of the damask, which is applied to an 'outer' seat frame or rail. This contains a beech drop-on frame which supports the upholstered seat.[112] RB

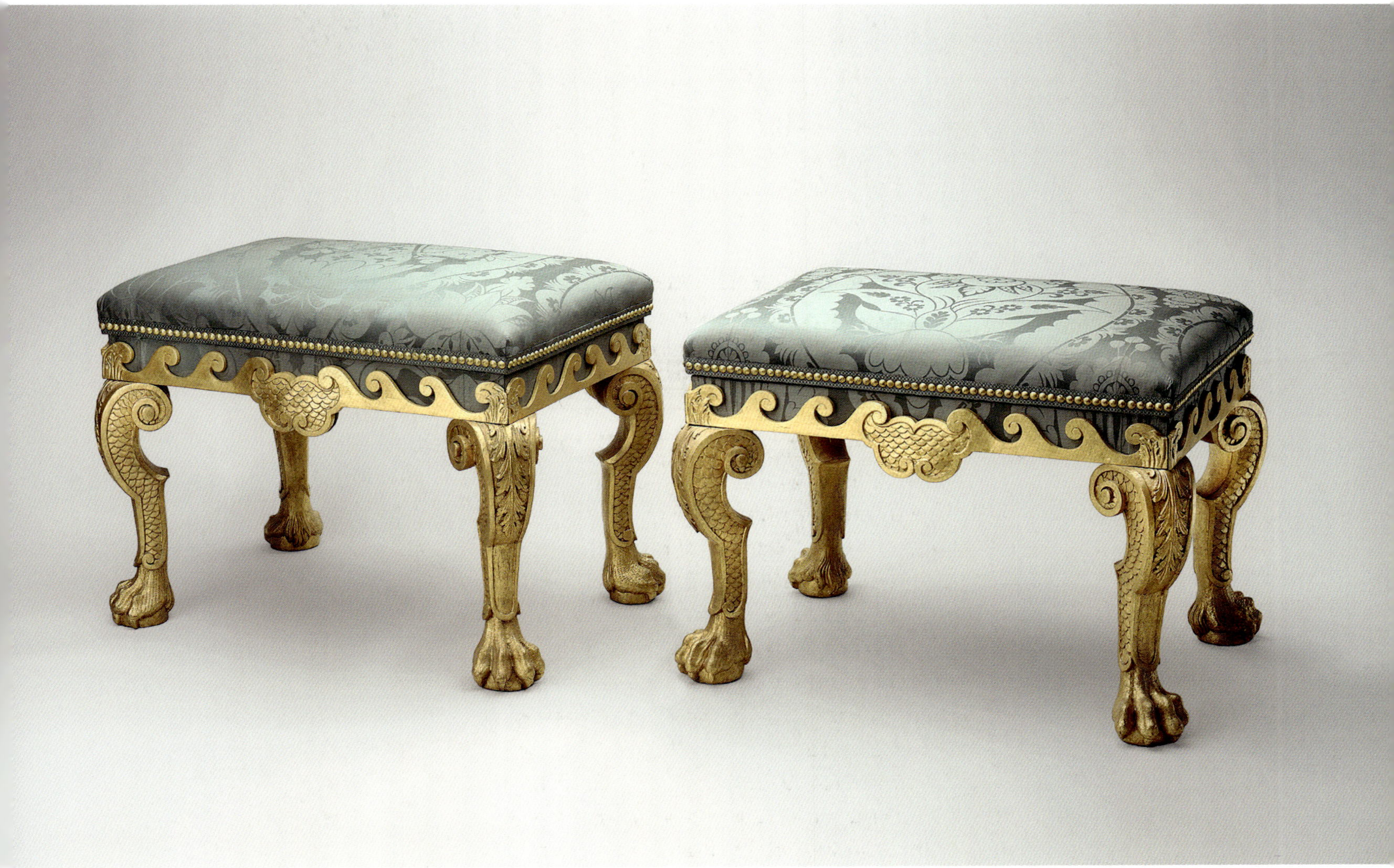

115 & 116

HENRY WILLIAMS (1717–1758)

Pair of armchairs and two stools 1737

Armchairs: gilded and gessoed beech, pine, oak and walnut, green silk damask, 128.5 × 77.5 × 74 cm
Stools: gilded and gessoed pine, green silk damask, 52 × 66.5 × 53 cm
Inscribed on the reverse of the removable back-frame (or chassis) of one armchair
H Bartlett Feb y 1830 Recovered Kingston Surrey
RCIN 31178.1-2 and RCIN 1230.4 and 7

PROVENANCE Supplied to George II for the Queen's Withdrawing Room, Hampton Court Palace, 1737

LITERATURE Macquoid and Edwards 1927, III, p. 170, fig. 40 (armchairs only); Edwards and Jourdain 1955, p. 68, fig. 161 (stools) and p. 179, fig. 163 (armchairs)

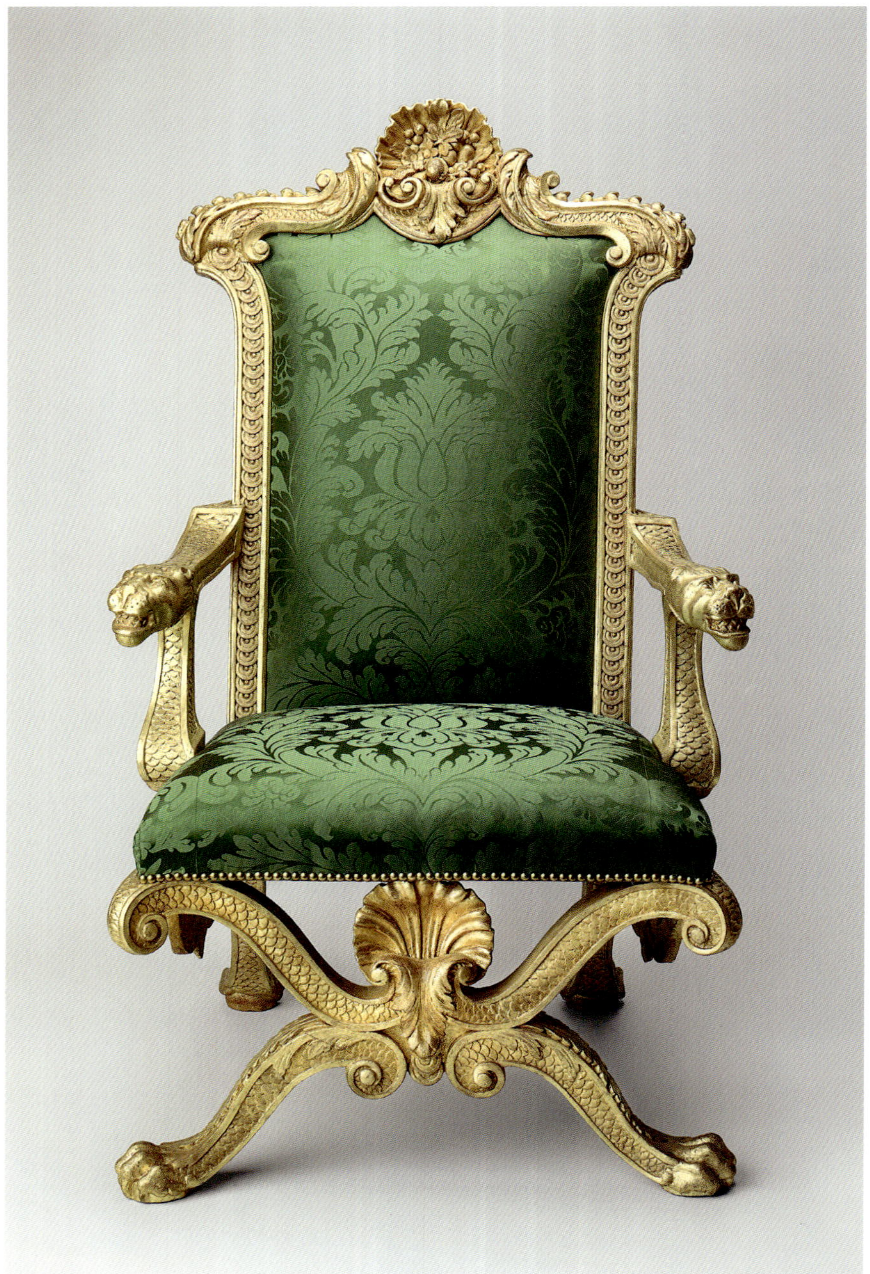

In 1737 Henry Williams supplied two armchairs (no. 115; only one shown) and 24 matching stools (no. 116; one shown; two exhibited) for the Queen's Withdrawing Room, Hampton Court. His invoice reads:

> For the Queen's Withdraw^g Room at
> Ditto [i.e. Hampton Court]
> For 3 very large Window Cornishes
> finely carved £18.0.0.
> For 2 Large Arm Chair frames finely
> carved & Gilt £32.0.0.
> For 24 Square stool frames suitable
> £192.0.0.[113]

Today, there are twenty-three stools of this pattern in the Royal Collection, divided between Hampton Court Palace and the Palace of Holyroodhouse.[114] A number survive in other collections.[115]

The X-frame design was probably a vestigial manifestation of a sixteenth-century English or Italian throne chair.[116] Though not strictly thrones, the armchairs (no. 115) were designed to have a similar significance – representing the King and Queen in the room. In practice there was no requirement for seating in a drawing room as the King and Queen circulated among their guests and the assembled company were obliged to remain standing in the royal presence.

Though it was made by Henry Williams, the designer of this set of seat furniture was almost certainly William Kent, the architect responsible for the refurbishments of the State Apartments at Hampton Court in the late 1730s. Comparison of the backs of the armchairs with those of the saloon chairs at Houghton Hall, Norfolk, strengthens this attribution.[117] Kent may have considered the form as he included a sketch of a stool in a drawing of the marriage of the Princess Royal and the Prince of Orange in 1734 (fig. 49).

The 'Green genoa damask' to cover the seat furniture was supplied by the mercer Mathew Vernon at a cost of 16s 6d per yard.[118] Sarah Gilbert, upholsterer, was paid, according to the same account book, 'for stuffing up & covering with green Damask 2 Arm Chairs and 24 square stools, and for Materials us'd £34.10.0'.[119] William Weeks, laceman, responsible for *passementerie*, supplied a quantity of such material for the edgings of the soft furnishings in the room, which included the wall hangings, curtains and cornices, as well as the chairs and stools.[120] This last document is especially interesting as Mantegna's *Triumphs of Caesar* had recently been moved from the Queen's Gallery into the Queen's Withdrawing Room (see no. 114), where these canvases were used, along with the green damask, to cover up Thornhill's wall paintings of Queen Anne and Prince George of Denmark. RB

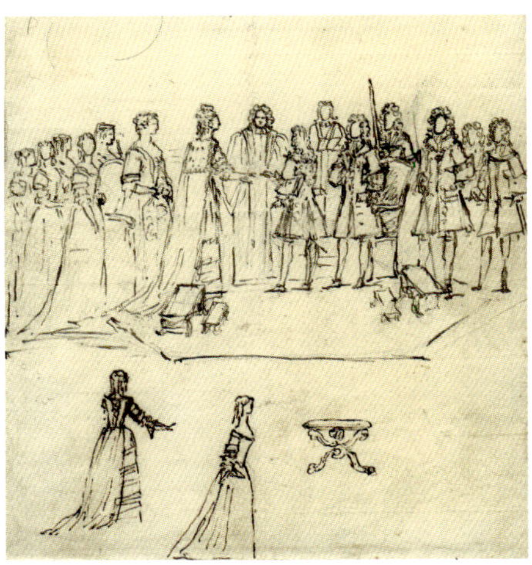

FIG. 49
William Kent
The Marriage of William, Prince of Orange and Anne, Princess Royal, at St James's Palace (including a sketch of an X-frame stool), 1734
Pencil, pen and ink
British Museum, inv. 1927,0721.1

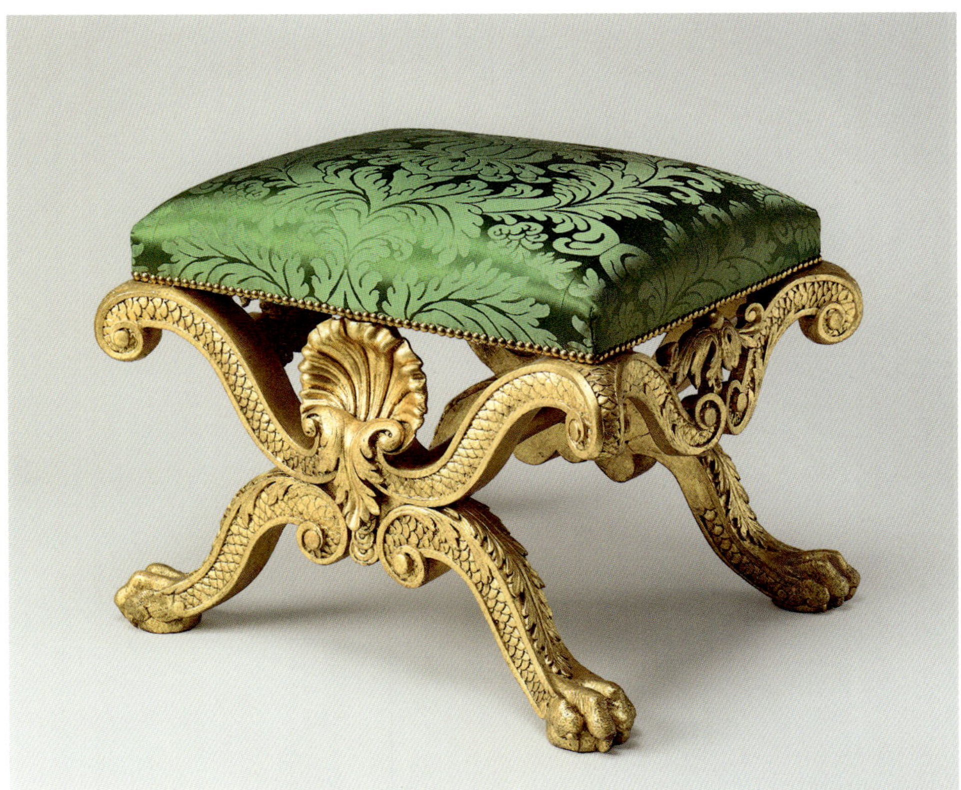

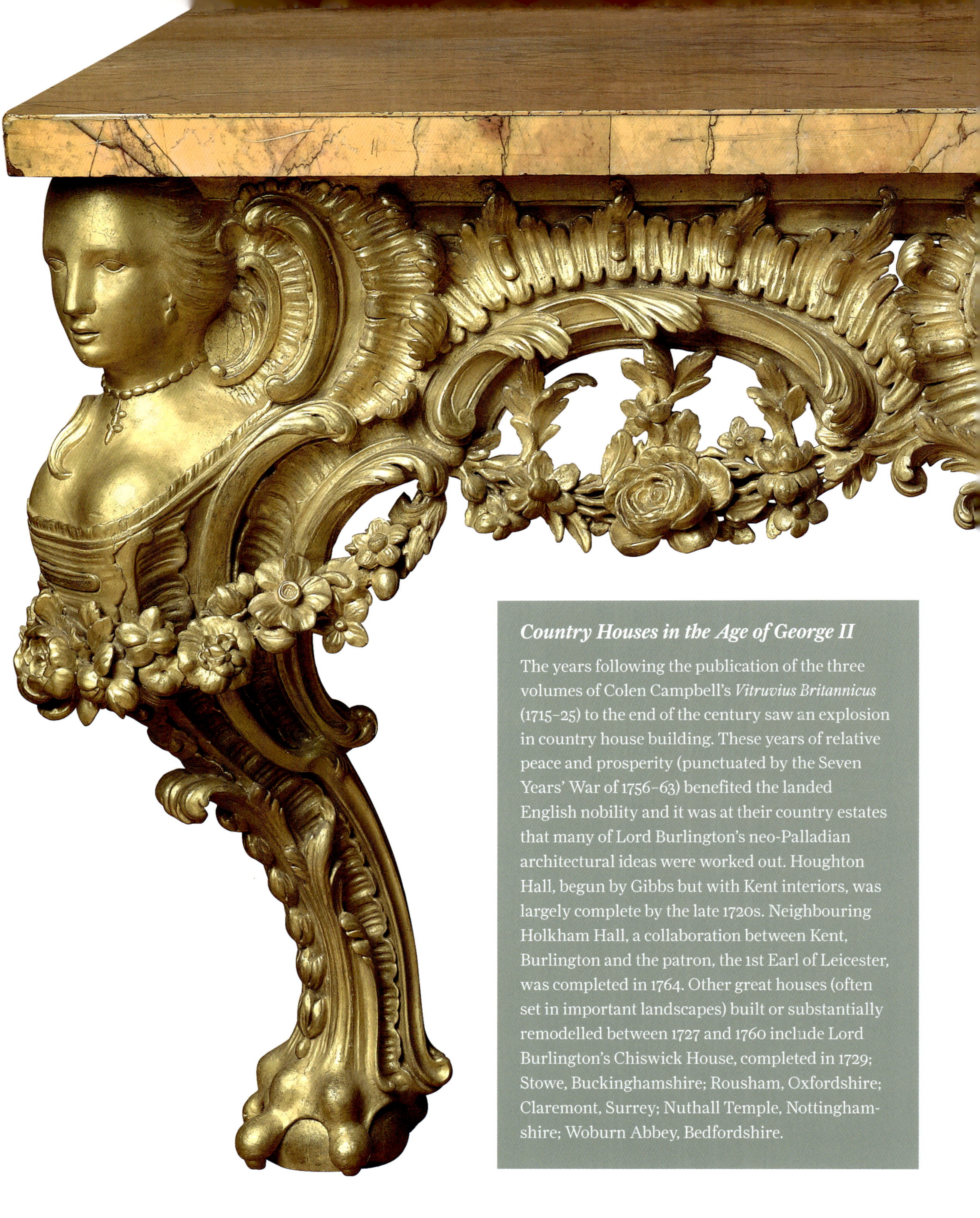

Country Houses in the Age of George II

The years following the publication of the three volumes of Colen Campbell's *Vitruvius Britannicus* (1715–25) to the end of the century saw an explosion in country house building. These years of relative peace and prosperity (punctuated by the Seven Years' War of 1756–63) benefited the landed English nobility and it was at their country estates that many of Lord Burlington's neo-Palladian architectural ideas were worked out. Houghton Hall, begun by Gibbs but with Kent interiors, was largely complete by the late 1720s. Neighbouring Holkham Hall, a collaboration between Kent, Burlington and the patron, the 1st Earl of Leicester, was completed in 1764. Other great houses (often set in important landscapes) built or substantially remodelled between 1727 and 1760 include Lord Burlington's Chiswick House, completed in 1729; Stowe, Buckinghamshire; Rousham, Oxfordshire; Claremont, Surrey; Nuthall Temple, Nottinghamshire; Woburn Abbey, Bedfordshire.

117

ATTRIBUTED TO BENJAMIN GOODISON (*c.*1700–1767)

Pair of chests *c.*1730

Partly gilded mahogany, marble, brass, 94.5 × 104.5 × 56.6 cm
RCIN 4649.1-2

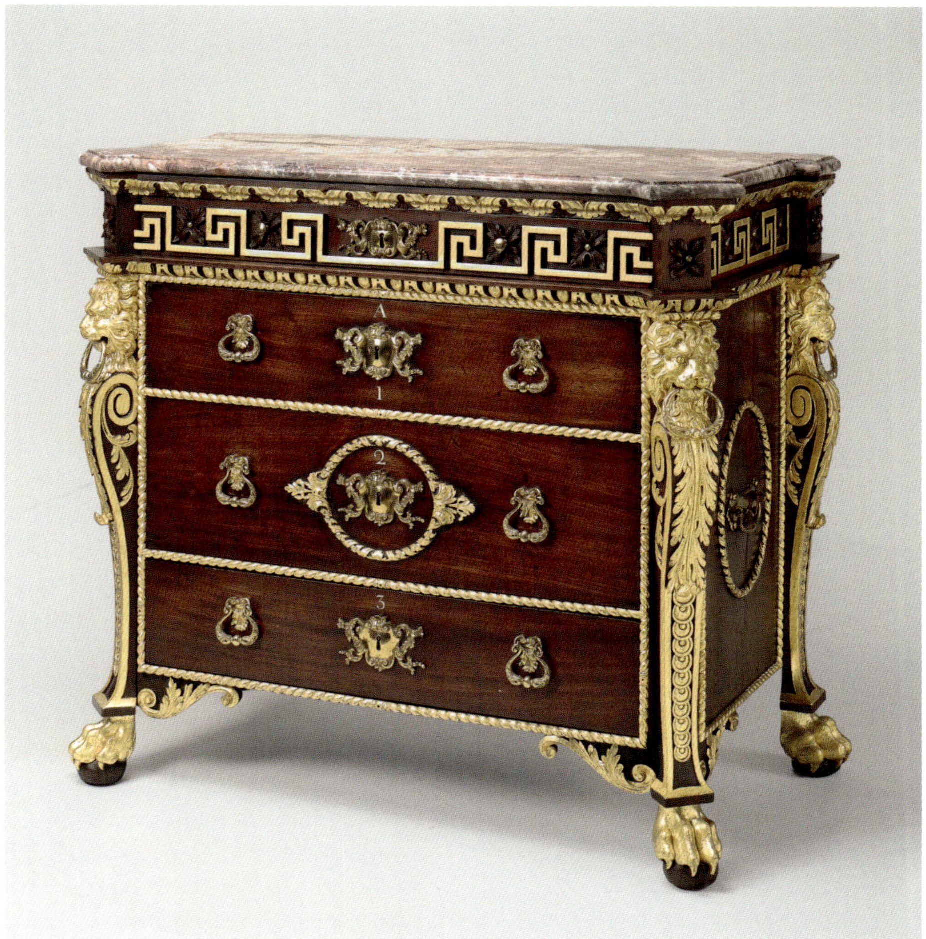

PROVENANCE Supplied to Sir Thomas Robinson (d. 1777), Rokeby Hall, Yorkshire, *c.* 1730; sold in 1769 to John Sawrey Morritt (included in the sale of Rokeby Hall); by descent in the Morritt family at Rokeby; bought by HM Queen Mary from Mallett, London, 1930

LITERATURE *Country Life* 1930, p. 898, fig. 1; Beard 1977, p. 483

The pair of chests (only one shown) was probably supplied around 1730 for Sir Thomas Robinson's house at Rokeby, designed by himself and proclaimed ready for furniture in 1731.[121] Robinson was influenced by Lord Burlington's neo-Palladianism. It is likely that the chests were made by Benjamin Goodison (active 1719–67), a cabinet-maker much employed by Burlington's circle, who perhaps executed Robinson's own design. This would have been entirely characteristic of Robinson, as he designed bookcases for use at Rokeby and generally took as much care over the major elements of the interior as of the exterior of the house.[122]

These chests may be attributed to Goodison on the basis of characteristics shared with a library table at Boughton House, Northamptonshire, supplied by Goodison to John, 2nd Duke of Montagu around 1737–41, though they may possibly have been altered from larger fitted library furnishings.[123] The side handles are engraved with the arms of John Bacon Sawrey Morritt (1771–1845). RB

118

Design ATTRIBUTED TO GIOVANNI BATTISTA BORRA (1712–1786), possibly carved by JEAN ANTOINE CUENOT (D. 1762)

Two pier tables *c.*1755

Gilded and gessoed pine, marble veneered on stone composition, each of two 87 × 184 × 94.5 cm
RCIN 35272.1-2

PROVENANCE Presumably supplied to Richard Grenville, 2nd Earl Temple (1711–1779), Stowe, Buckinghamshire; sold at the Stowe sale, 15 August–7 October 1848, H.R. Forster auctioneers, lots 818, 819; P.D. Pauncefort Duncombe, Esq.; Sir Everard Pauncefort Duncombe, Bt, Great Brickhill Manor, sold Geo. Wigley & Sons Auctioneers, 10–17 November 1919, lot 919; the Earl of Harewood, Chesterfield House, sold Sotheby's, 7 April 1932, lot 266; HM Queen Mary

LITERATURE Seeley 1817, p. 57; edn 1832, p. 71; edn 1838, p. 69; FitzGerald 1973, fig. 19, p. 582

The two tables (only one shown) are designed in a modified Italianate style, entirely in keeping with the Baroque Roman spirit which William Kent imported to Britain following his ten years' sojourn in Italy at the beginning of the century. However, their design is also close to those published by Batty Langley in his *City and Country Builder's and Workman's Treasury of Designs*, 1739, plate CXLIV. In fact their design holds a place between the earlier French-inspired designs of Langley and the similarly French-inspired designs of Chippendale and his contemporaries published in the 1750s.

The tables were possibly designed for the State Bedchamber at Stowe by the Piedmontese architect G.B. Borra, who was employed by Lord Temple to oversee the completion of the State Apartment at Stowe from 1752 to 1764. According to the 1769 guidebook, Borra was responsible for the designs of the ceiling and State Bed (now in the Lady Lever Art Gallery, Port Sunlight).[124] It is not certain how far his influence spread to other furnishings. Jean Cuenot had worked with Borra as a specialist carver at Norfolk House, St James's Square, London, and may have been involved in producing similar elaborate carving at Stowe.[125] The earliest guide to Stowe, published in 1756, describes in the State Bedchamber 'Two Marble Tables'; what are presumably the same tables are described in the 1769 and 1773 editions as 'Two Marble Tables of *Giallo Antico*'. The Bedchamber was altered significantly in the 1770s, reducing the window bays from three to two and consequently reducing the two window piers to one. It is therefore not surprising to discover in the 1777 guide that the tables had migrated elsewhere: one table of '*Giallo Antico*' is recorded in the Dressing Room next door. By the time of the 1817 guidebook, however, the tables, if indeed they are the same, have re-emerged in the State Music Room, where they remained until their sale in 1848. RB

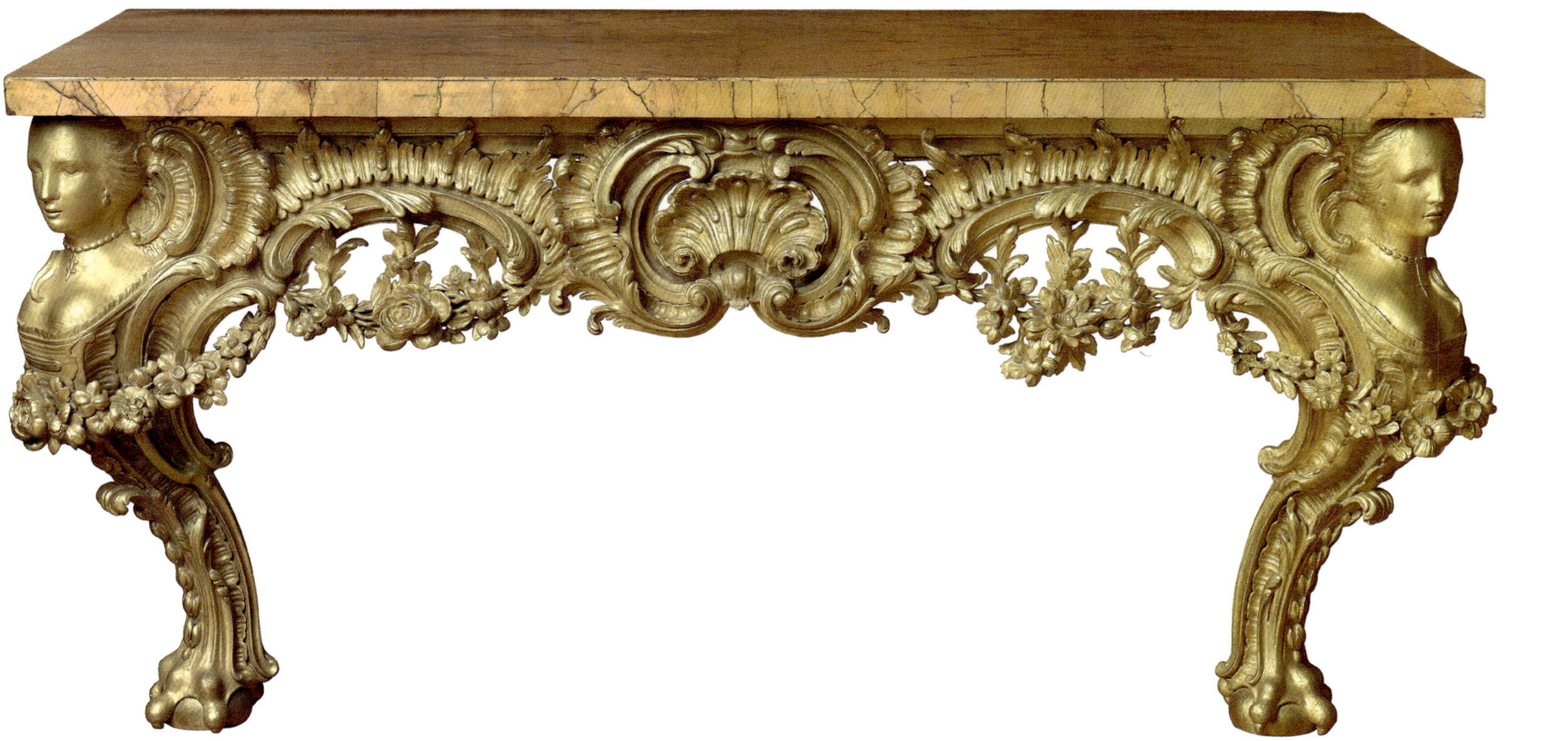

119

POSSIBLY BY BENJAMIN GOODISON (*c.*1700–1767)

Two side chairs *c.*1730

Gilded and gessoed walnut, crimson silk damask, each of two 104 × 59 cm
RCIN 33392.4 and .7

PROVENANCE W.R. Hearst, St Donat's Castle, sold Christie's, 18 May 1939, lot 52; Frank Partridge; bought by HM Queen Elizabeth The Queen Mother

LITERATURE Rieder 1978, pp. 9ff.

The exhibited pair of chairs (only one shown) belongs to an extended set of seat-furniture, now numbering at least 30 side chairs and three settees (a pair in the Royal Collection and one in the Metropolitan Museum of Art, New York). Of these, only a small number are of eighteenth-century manufacture and can be linked to the famous sale of the contents of Stowe House, Buckinghamshire, in 1848, though nothing of them is mentioned in the 1839 inventory of that house.[126] Their attribution has been the subject of much discussion. The name James Moore was suggested by analogy with his pair of tables with carved aprons executed for Stowe between 1714 and 1718.[127] The set has also been dated to the 1730s, after Moore's death in 1726.[128] The attribution proposed here to Moore's apprentice and successor, Benjamin Goodison, is based on the similarity to a pair of tables formerly on loan to the National Trust at Upton House, Warwickshire, which have recently been connected with Goodison.[129] Such elaborate surface decoration in gilt-gesso is a technique frequently found on furniture made before 1730 (see nos 94, 96, 99–102); however, the overall profile of the chair frame is common to walnut or mahogany chairs from the 1720s and 1730s. All-over gilt-gesso surface treatment was clearly impractical for a chair and seems to have been restricted mostly to tables, mirrors and candle-stands. RB

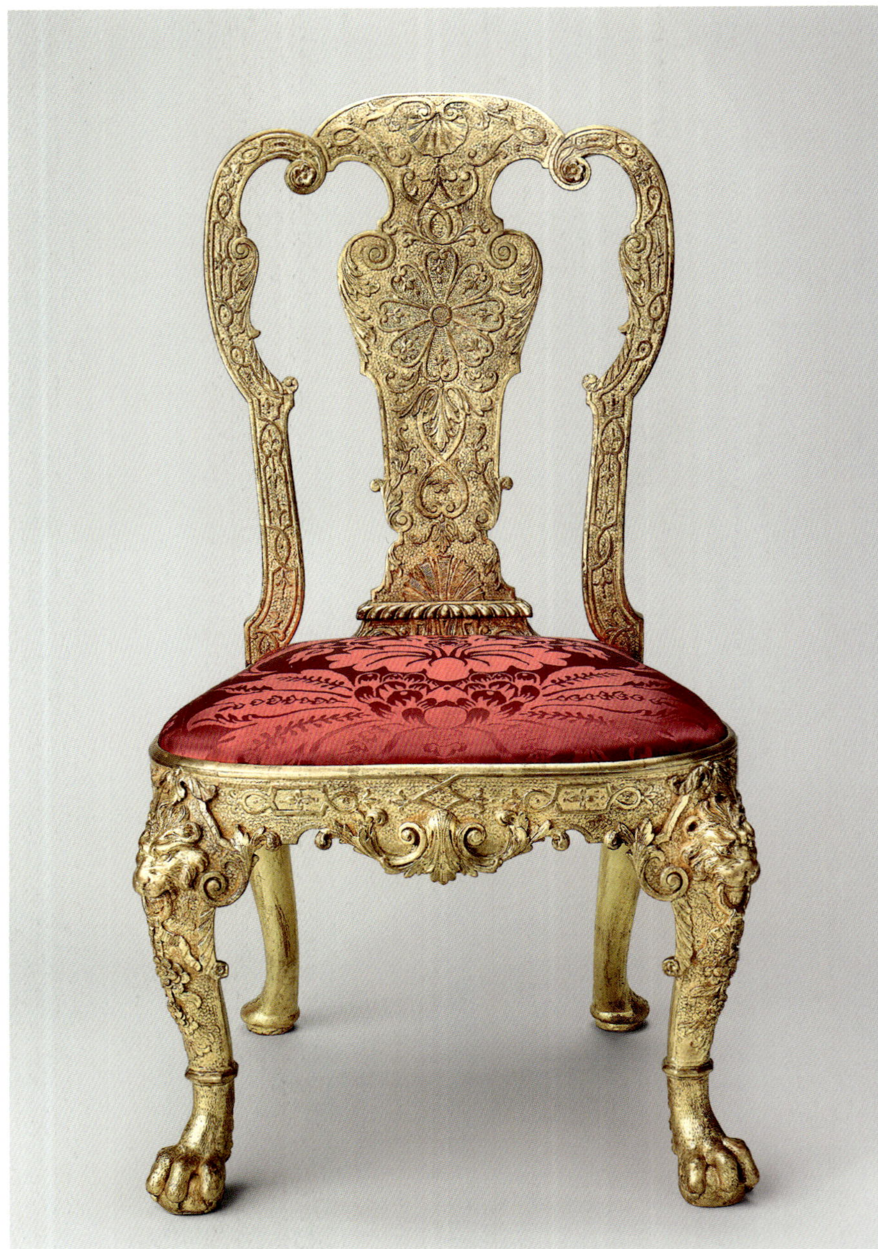

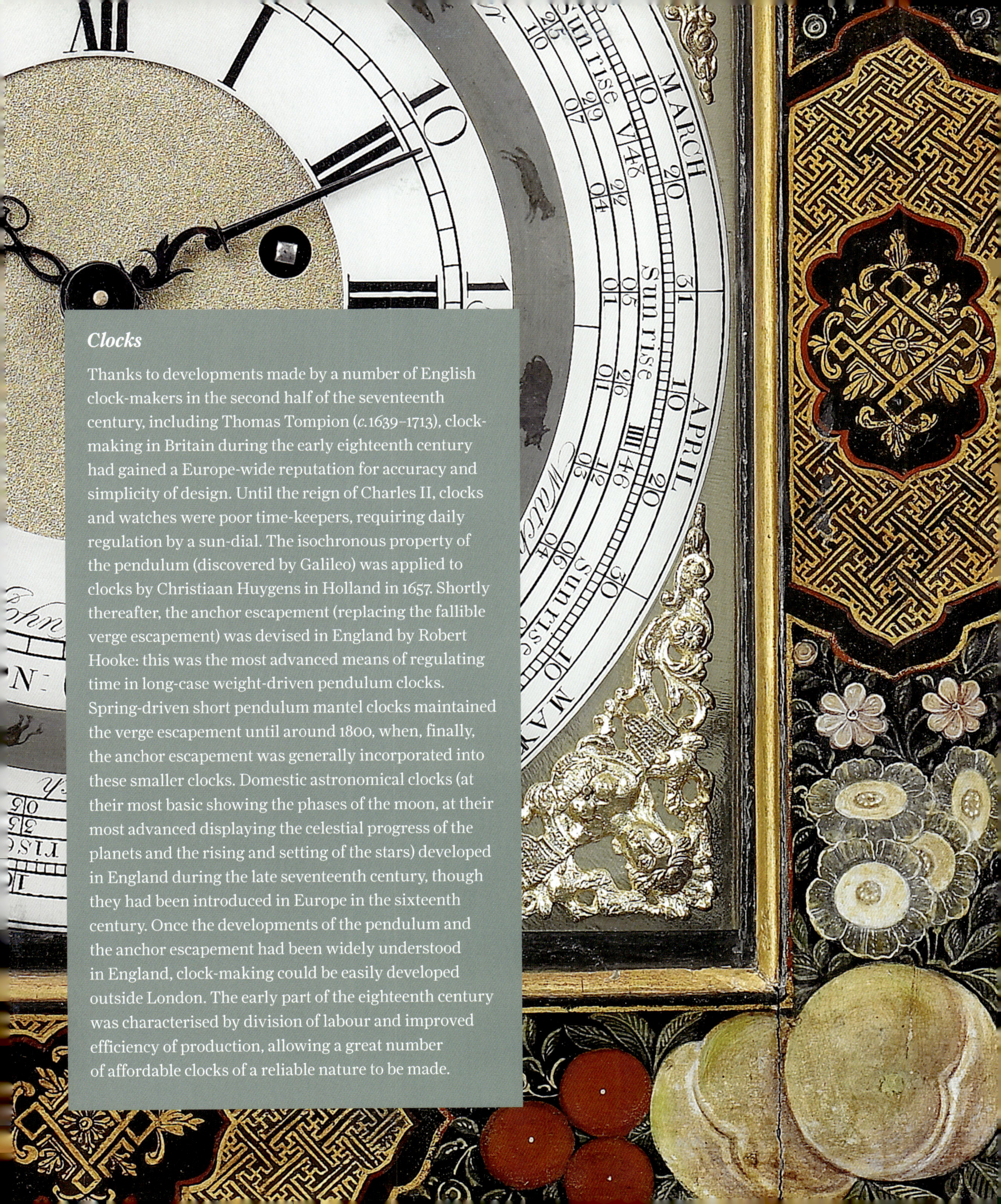

Clocks

Thanks to developments made by a number of English clock-makers in the second half of the seventeenth century, including Thomas Tompion (*c.*1639–1713), clock-making in Britain during the early eighteenth century had gained a Europe-wide reputation for accuracy and simplicity of design. Until the reign of Charles II, clocks and watches were poor time-keepers, requiring daily regulation by a sun-dial. The isochronous property of the pendulum (discovered by Galileo) was applied to clocks by Christiaan Huygens in Holland in 1657. Shortly thereafter, the anchor escapement (replacing the fallible verge escapement) was devised in England by Robert Hooke: this was the most advanced means of regulating time in long-case weight-driven pendulum clocks. Spring-driven short pendulum mantel clocks maintained the verge escapement until around 1800, when, finally, the anchor escapement was generally incorporated into these smaller clocks. Domestic astronomical clocks (at their most basic showing the phases of the moon, at their most advanced displaying the celestial progress of the planets and the rising and setting of the stars) developed in England during the late seventeenth century, though they had been introduced in Europe in the sixteenth century. Once the developments of the pendulum and the anchor escapement had been widely understood in England, clock-making could be easily developed outside London. The early part of the eighteenth century was characterised by division of labour and improved efficiency of production, allowing a great number of affordable clocks of a reliable nature to be made.

120

MELCHIOR BAUMGARTNER (1621–1686)
AND CHARLES CLAY (D. 1740)

The Temple and Oracle of Apollo

The gilt-bronze statuette early 17th century; the casket 1664; the clock, organ and mahogany case *c.*1740
Gilt bronze, rock crystal, silver gilt, enamel, mahogany, ebony
St George and the Dragon 17.5 × 29.5 × 14.8 cm; casket 191.5 × 91 × 76 cm; organ 113 × 91 × 76 cm
RCIN 30037

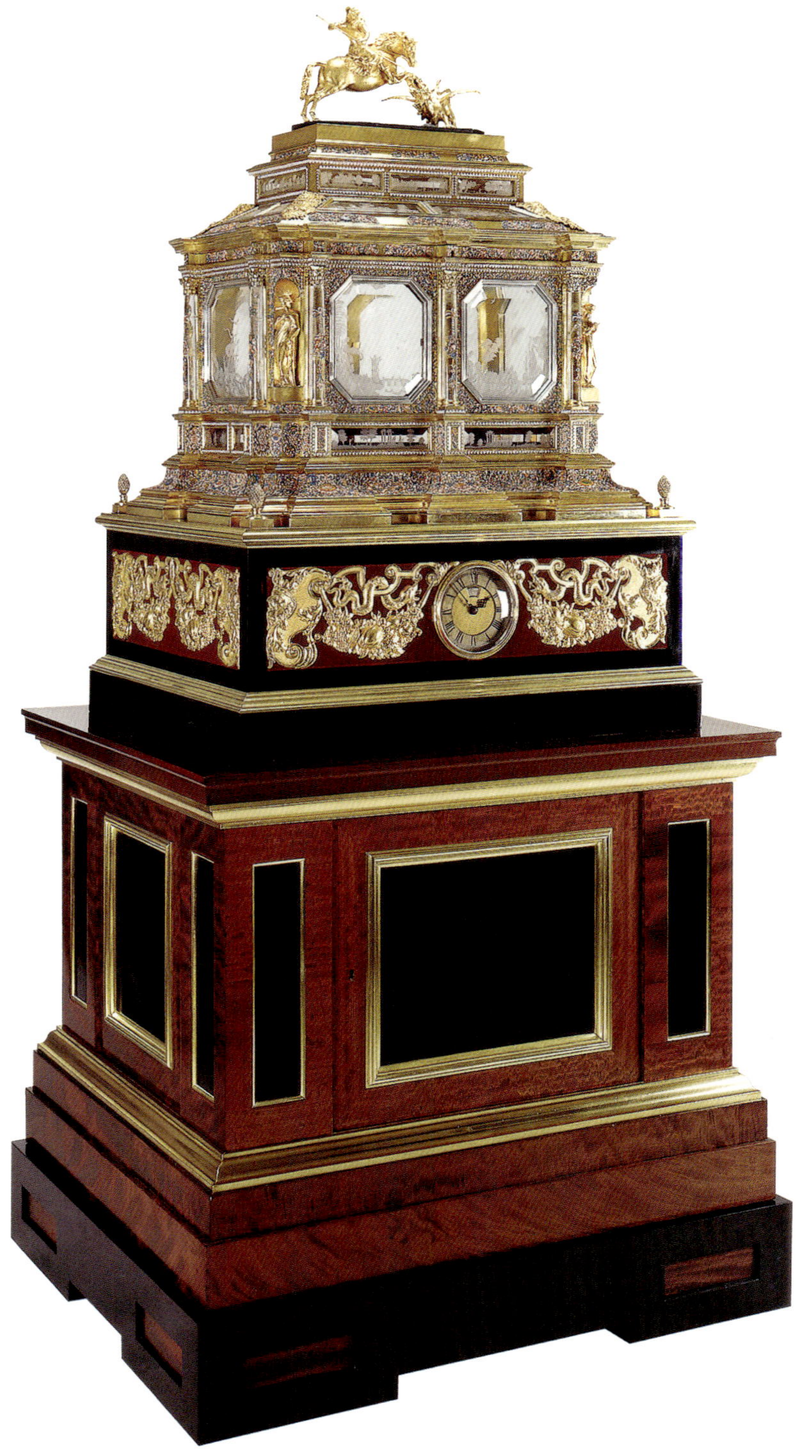

PROVENANCE Acquired either by Frederick, Prince of Wales, *c.*1743–50, or by Augusta, Princess of Wales, 1759

LITERATURE Haspels 1987, p. 187; Roberts 1995, pp. 58-59; Gwynn 1997; *Princes as Patrons* 1998, no. 51

This complex piece, combining several generations of additions, was largely the creation of the enterprising and ambitious clockmaker Charles Clay. In 1723 Clay secured the post of Clockmaker to His Majesty's Board of Works and he provided the turret clock for St James's Palace. He died in 1740.

The piece makes its focal point a rock-crystal casket by the Augsburg goldsmith Melchior Baumgartner, whose inscription (in German) is found on a panel inside the lid 'I Master Melchior Baumgartner have made this casket in Augsburg and covered it with silver in the year 1664'. Also incorporated in the casket are 40 panels of rock crystal, engraved with land- and sea-scapes, the six principal panels of canted rectangular form and with bevelled edges. The panels depict figures and houses in landscapes, while each side panel depicts a shipping scene, one during a calm, the other during a storm. The panels are divided by rock-crystal columns with Corinthian capitals in silver-gilt. Almost all remaining areas are decorated by exquisite applied enamelled and silver-gilt mounts of fruiting swags and floral trails. At each angle in a shell-headed niche is a gilt-bronze figure of a classical goddess. Below the casket is a stepped pedestal containing both a clock and an organ, which plays ten melodies, all but two of which correspond to settings composed by Handel.

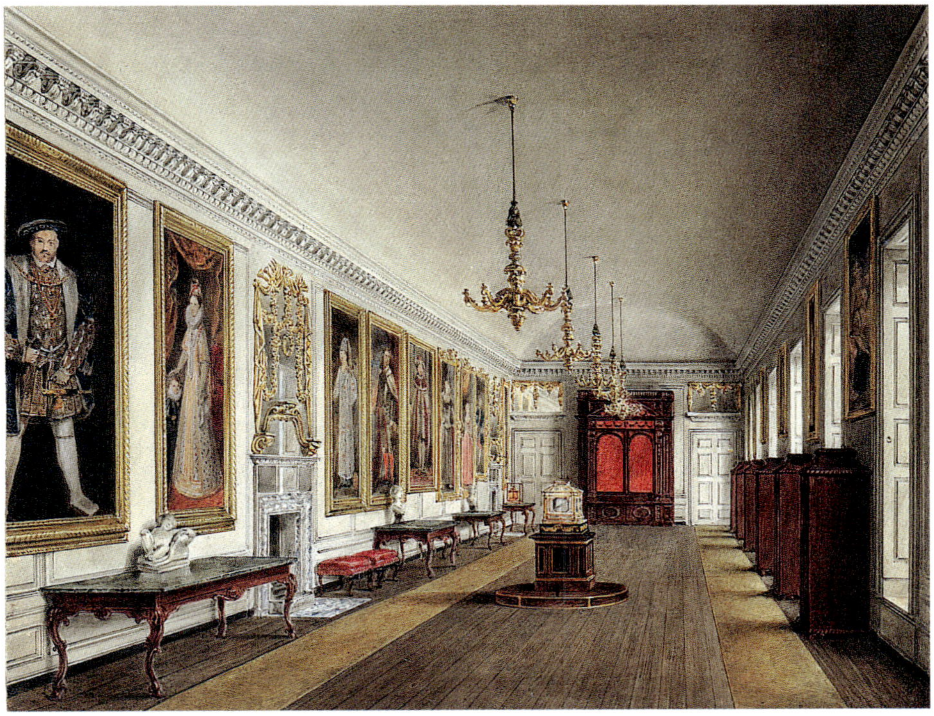

FIG. 50
James Stephanoff
The Queen's Gallery, Kensington Palace, 1819
Watercolour over pencil
RCIN 922155

The early history of the Augsburg casket is unknown, although Baumgartner is known to have supplied similarly elaborate pieces to the Bavarian and Brunswick courts.[130] The piece is first noted in a London newspaper advertisement of 20 November 1741, in which Sarah Clay, widow of the clockmaker Charles Clay, announced the exhibition at Cecil Street, off the Strand, of 'the most curious and valuable of all the Pieces of Clock Work which her late husband left behind', *The Temple and Oracle of Apollo*, and charging 1s per person to view.[131] The entire ensemble is described in splendid language as it appears today (less the group of St George and the Dragon and the eponymous figure of Apollo, now lost). This announcement suggests that it was through the agency of the maker/entrepreneur Charles Clay (or his widow's) that the casket, clock-work and organ were assembled into their present spectacular form.

Besides Clay's post in the Office of Works, he was a familiar figure to Frederick, Prince of Wales: he had created a magnificent four-sided musical clock, *The Temple of the Four Grand Monarchies of the World* (RCIN 1418), completed by John Pyke in 1743 and acquired for Augusta, Princess of Wales. By the early nineteenth century it was recorded in watercolours published by W.H. Pyne in the Cupola Room at Kensington Palace (see no. 30), where it remains today. Also at Kensington, in the Queen's Gallery (fig. 50), was the present organ clock. How the latter arrived there is not clear, although the most likely route is through Frederick, Prince of Wales, or his widow, Augusta, either of whom might have acquired the organ-clock immediately following its advertisement in 1743. An alternative possibility involves an inconclusive bill of sale of 1759 to Augusta, Princess of Wales from George Pyke noting 'an Organ Clock in a Black Case with Glass Columns', priced at £94 10s.[132] John and George Pyke (father and son) continued Clay's business of elaborate musical clock-making after 1740. RB

121

JOHN PYKE (ACTIVE 1710–62)

Table clock *c.*1740

Painted, japanned and gilded pine, partly overlaid with paper cut-outs, gilt brass, 142.5 × 67 × 49 cm
RCIN 30421

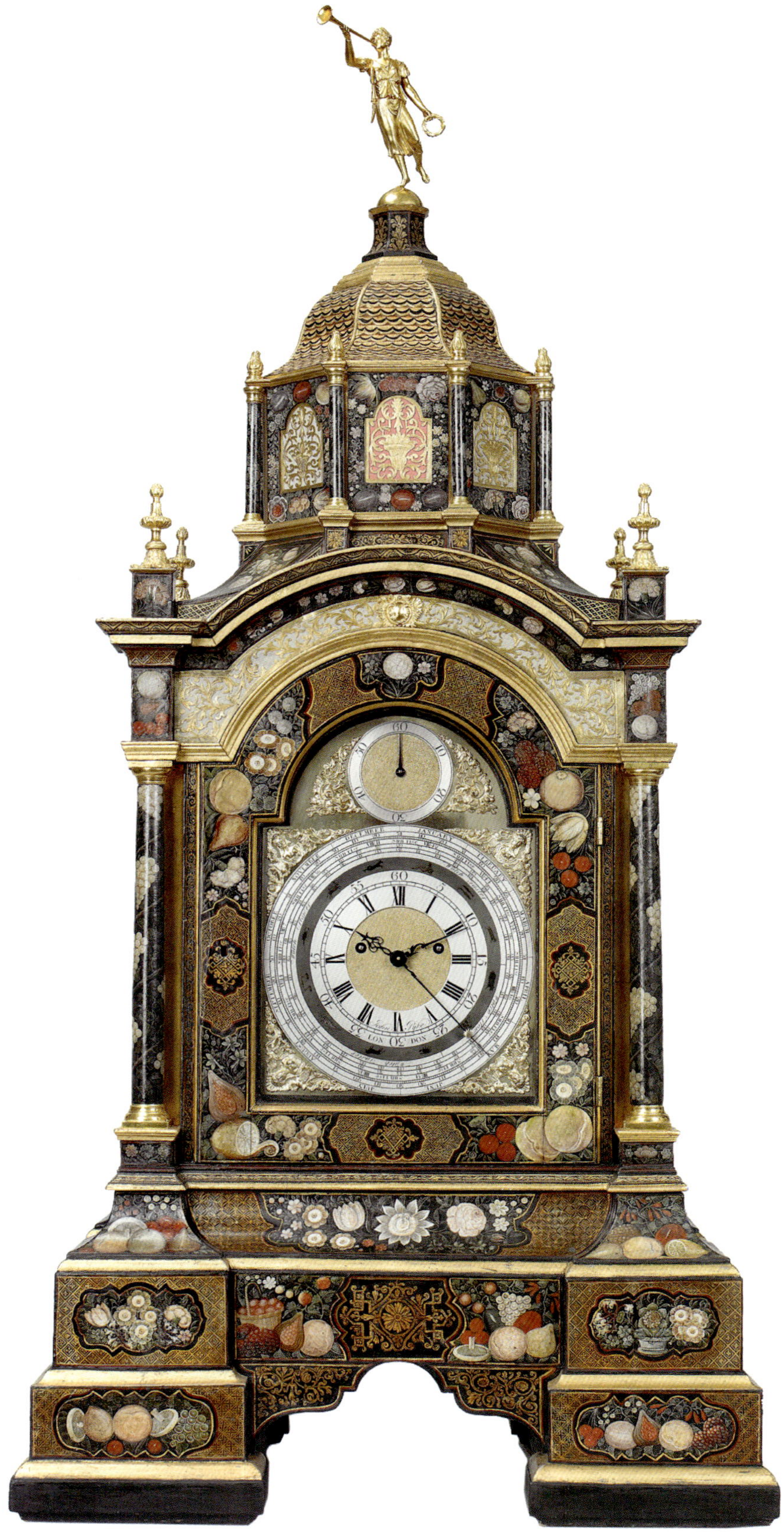

PROVENANCE Bought by HM The Queen, 1960

LITERATURE Jagger 1983, p. 84, fig. 112

This magnificent, large-scale clock was possibly fitted originally with a musical mechanism. The pierced side panels and corresponding panels in the domed upper part were perhaps intended to allow sound to emerge. John Pyke was a clockmaker who enjoyed complex mechanisms combined with music-playing machinery. He was responsible for the completion of Charles Clay's musical clock, *The Temple of the Four Grand Monarchies of the World* (RCIN 1418), at Kensington Palace, but now lacking its musical mechanism. Pyke was apprenticed in 1710, admitted to the Freedom of the Clockmakers' Company in 1720 and died in 1762. His son George was also a clockmaker with an interest in musical and automaton clocks.

The surface of the clock is decorated in a particular fashion which loosely imitates the lacquered creations of the Far East that were popular in Britain in the late seventeenth and first half of the eighteenth century. The panels of fruit and flowers were pre-painted on to paper and cut to size before application to the clock case. However, the gilded trellis panels were decorated directly on to the clock's surface. Today the clock has a dark green surface but was originally a dark blue, the blue having discoloured as a result of the many layers of varnish applied, not all of which could be removed during conservation as the original gilding was applied over the varnish. RB

122

BENJAMIN GRAY (1676–1764) AND
FRANÇOIS-JUSTIN VULLIAMY (1712–1798)

Bracket clock *c.*1750

Ebonised wood, gilt and silvered metal, blued steel, 49 × 27 × 17 cm
RCIN 2872

PROVENANCE Supplied to George II

LITERATURE Jagger 1983, p. 87, fig. 117; Clifford Smith 1931, p. 299

This bracket clock is characteristic of a type of English clock produced in considerable numbers in Britain during the first half of the eighteenth century. Benjamin Gray was in royal service from 1742, when he was appointed Watchmaker in Ordinary. In the following year he entered into a partnership with François-Justin Vulliamy, which lasted until Gray's death at the great age of 88 in 1764. Thereafter Vulliamy, younger by some 36 years, took on the business as sole proprietor. Vulliamy came from the Swiss canton of Vaud to Paris and from there to London to increase his knowledge of horology, in particular the development of the cylinder escapement. The partnership's premises at no. 74 (later re-numbered 68) Pall Mall, where they moved in 1752, remained the headquarters of the family firm of Vulliamy for a further three generations. Over this later period the firm was to experience considerable royal patronage, especially from George IV. RB

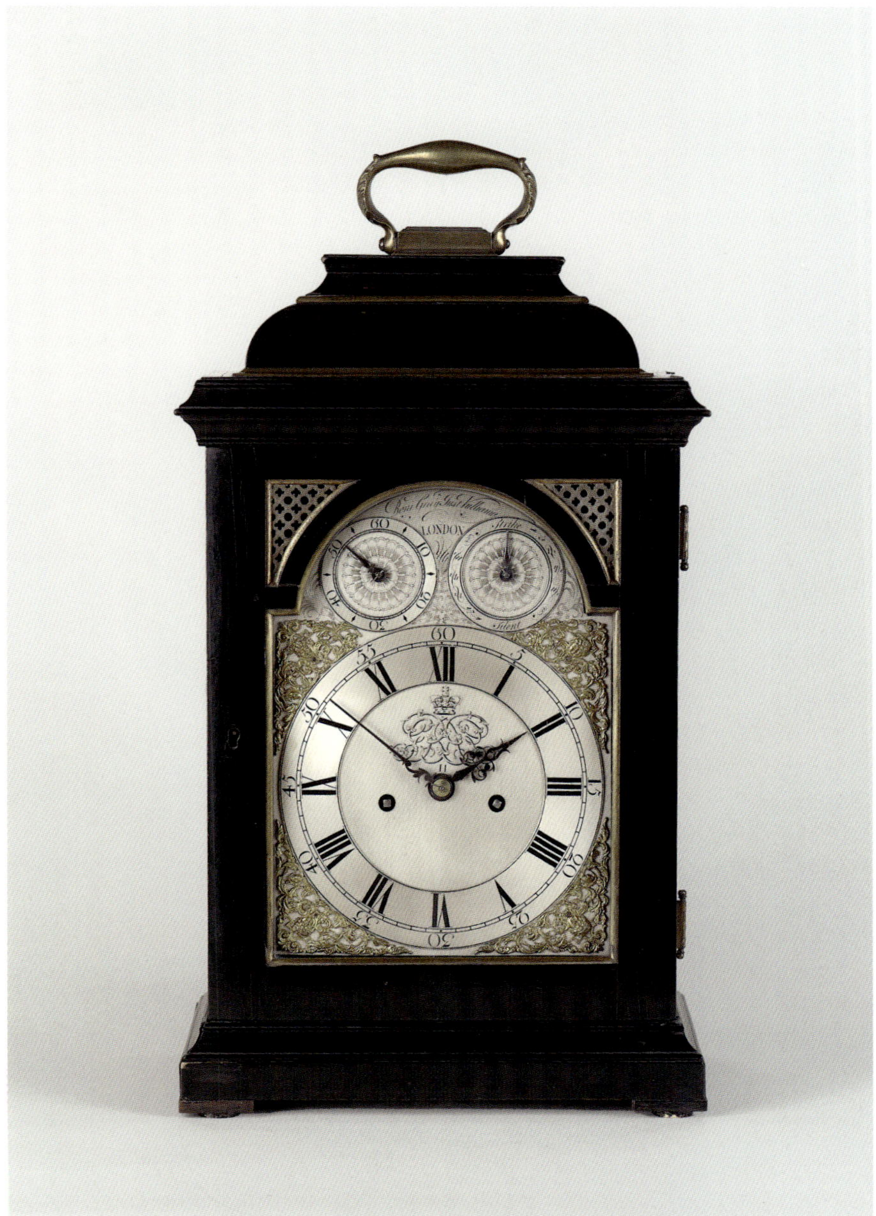

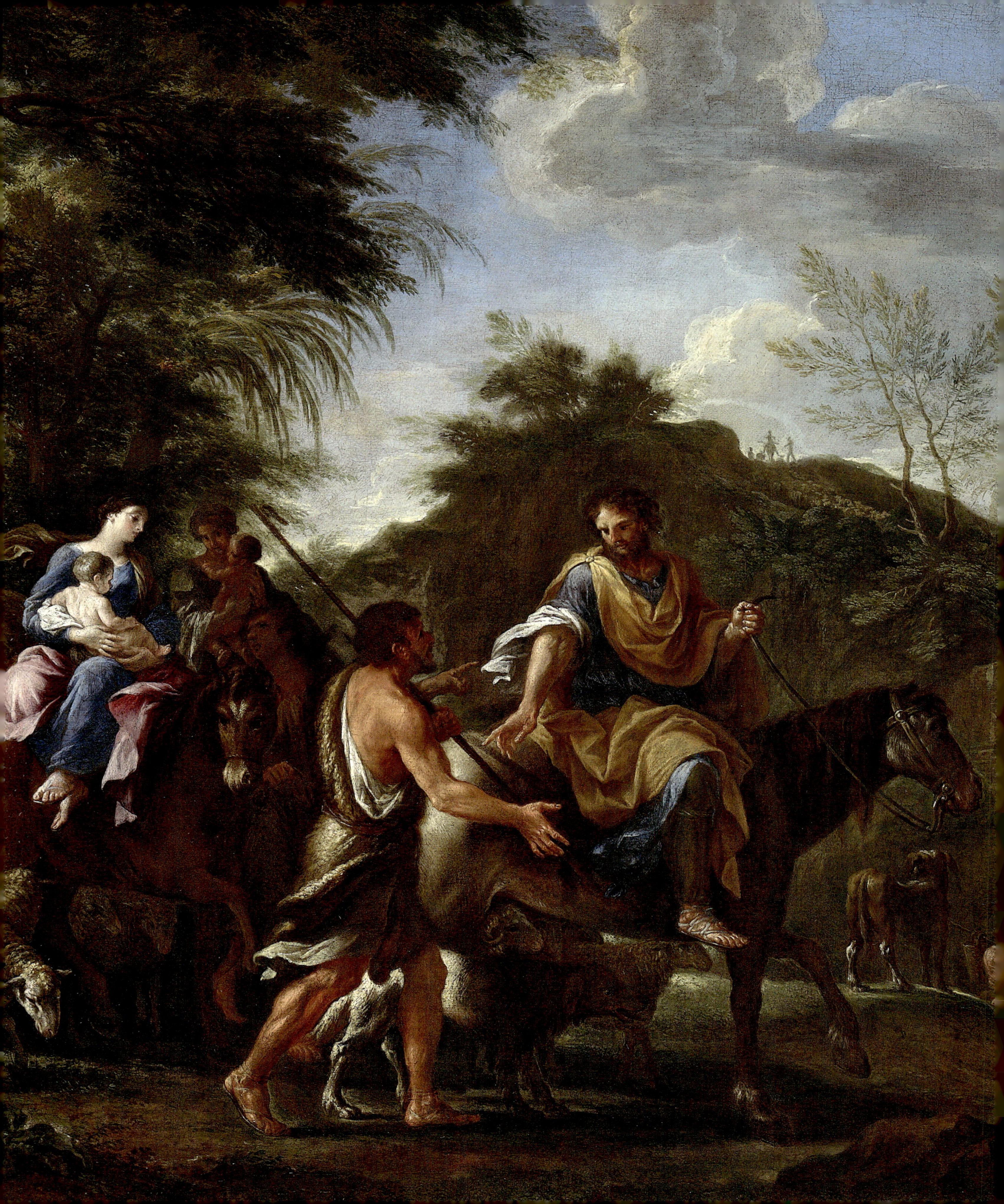

VI

The 'Battle of the Pictures'

DESMOND SHAWE-TAYLOR

IN 1744 HOGARTH PLANNED to auction nineteen of his original oil paintings. The admission ticket he designed for the event (no. 90) exposed the greatest threat to this venture and the livelihood of living British artists in general – the Old Masters. Hogarth's *Battle of the Pictures* was not the only occasion he took to proclaim that Old Master paintings imported into England were mawkish and repetitive, that 'picture-jobbers' were con-men and English noblemen gullible fashion-victims.[1] Hogarth was certainly right to point out that the early eighteenth century was the great age of Old Master importation and that the principal collectors came from the aristocracy. The collection formed for Houghton Hall by Sir Robert Walpole was more splendid and representative of the taste of the period than the royal acquisitions discussed in this chapter.[2] Indeed George II ridiculed Queen Caroline for barging into the houses of her subjects in order to see pictures.[3] But what was the taste that she sought there? What characterised the choice, framing and display of what is sometimes called for convenience 'country-house collecting'? These questions are best answered by separating the two functions of Old Master paintings – decorating rooms and improving minds.[4]

We have seen the transformation of royal interiors during these years and the way in which the display of tapestries survived, rather like court dress, as something grand and old-fashioned (p. 85). When these interiors were systematically recorded for Pyne's *Royal Residences* of 1819 (nos 28–36), some, like the Queen's Drawing Room at Windsor (see fig. 45), retained an ensemble from the seventeenth century, with Verrio's illusionistic ceiling painting and an oak-panelled wall entirely covered with tapestries between its dado and cornice (see also nos 35–6). Paintings originally fitted into such a scheme only over the doors and the fireplace, though by 1817 they were also hung over the tapestries. We have also seen how illusionistic wall-paintings by Verrio and Thornhill fell out of favour (see p. 204), to be replaced by simple silk wall-covering and a tactical arrangement of framed Old Masters – the sort of scheme for which Kent claimed payment at Kensington (see p. 184). An ideal version of this modern style can be seen in one of the many architectural drawings executed by Prince George (later George III) under the supervision of William Chambers in the late 1750s (fig. 51), which shows a section of an imaginary villa with a saloon boasting a beautifully symmetrical arrangement of imaginary paintings in Kentian frames.[5]

The actual interiors created for George III demonstrate something very similar. In the King's Drawing Room at Windsor (fig. 52), the wall zone has been covered with a

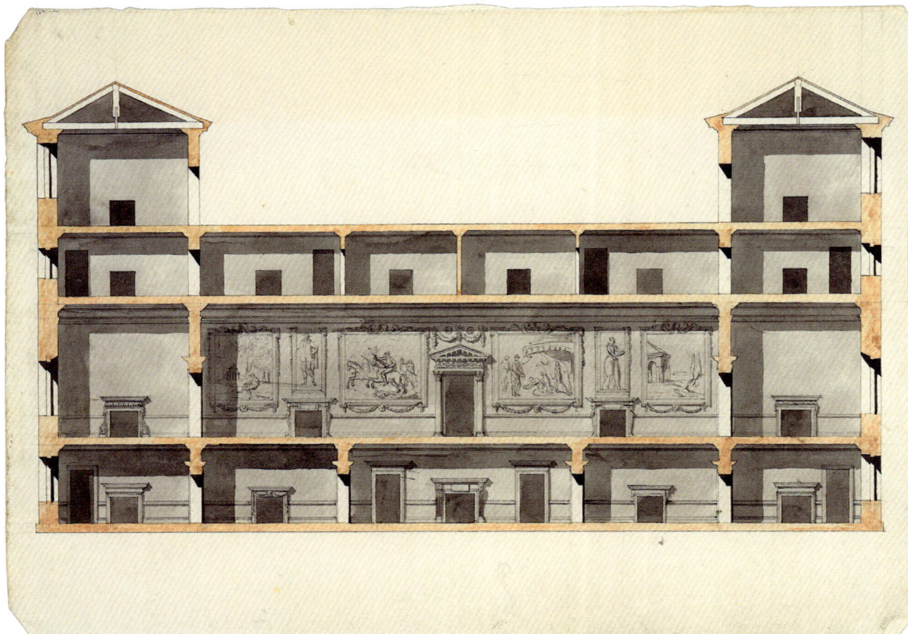

FIG. 51
Prince George (later George III)
Cross-section showing the interior of an imaginary villa
Watercolour
RCIN 981542

blue-grey silk, while Old Master paintings have become the dominant decoration of the room. The state rooms on the first floor of the Queen's House (now Buckingham Palace) – the Crimson Drawing Room (fig. 53), the Second Drawing Room or Queen's 'Warm Room' (fig. 54) and Blue Velvet Room (fig. 55) – were created in 1762–76 for Queen Charlotte by George III and his architects William Chambers and Robert Adam.[6] The arrangement of paintings dates from these years but in many respects preserves the taste of the first half of the eighteenth century, containing many highlights from the collection of George III's father, Frederick, Prince of Wales. The vaults have become plain or lightly decorated in the 'Pompeian' style; the dado and cornice remain and the central field of the wall is covered with a single silk zone. This wall area is articulated by spaced paintings treated with the same architectural gravity as windows or doors: the paintings follow a sort of 'fenestration' as well as belonging in roughly coherent groups from the point of view of the story of art.

Clearly this system requires picture frames to play a more significant role than hitherto. In a famous exchange of 1735, recorded by Lord Hervey (see no. 32), George II demanded the return of his 'gigantic fat Venus' (see fig. 19) and other paintings to the Great Drawing Room at Kensington, though he knew 'that all the frames of the removed pictures [were] cut or enlarged to fit their successors'.[7] This makes it clear that the frames stayed in the Drawing Room while their contents were shipped in and out. Early Georgian frames fall into three types, all seen in the King's Drawing Room at Windsor (fig. 52) and all of which in their surrounds to a lesser or greater extent follow the tripartite arrangement of a classical entablature with architrave, frieze and cornice.[8] The 'architrave' or 'Kentian' can be seen in an example by William Kent himself, surrounding no. 137, while no. 138 has a frame of similar design attributed to Benjamin Goodison.[9] The forms of the classical entablature are closely followed – a narrow leaf-and-tongue moulding to recreate an architrave at the 'sight edge'; variations on a Greek-key pattern in the frieze set above 'sanding' (rough texture under the gilding to suggest the effect of uncut stone, often used in actual friezes); and chunky egg-and-dart mouldings to recreate an architectural cornice at the outer edge.

The next most common and most architectural frame is named after the dominant Italian painter of the later seventeenth century, Carlo Maratta (see below, no. 127).

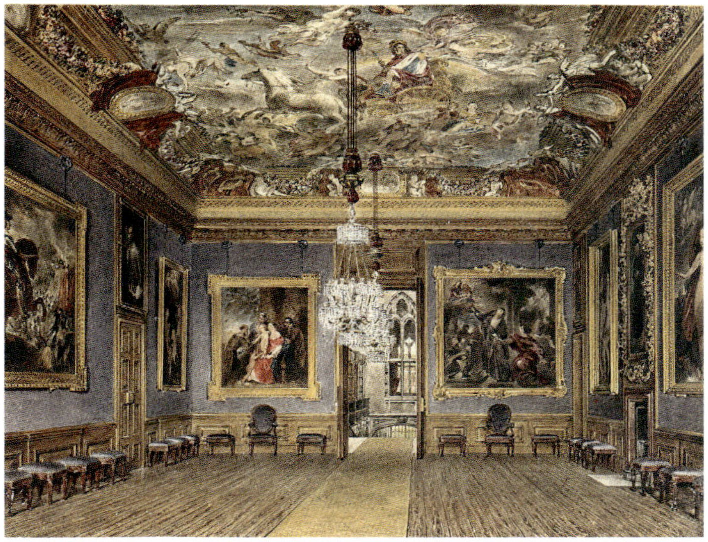

FIG. 52
James Stephanoff
The King's Drawing Room, Windsor Castle, 1815–9, for Pyne's *Royal Residences*
Watercolour
RCIN 922107

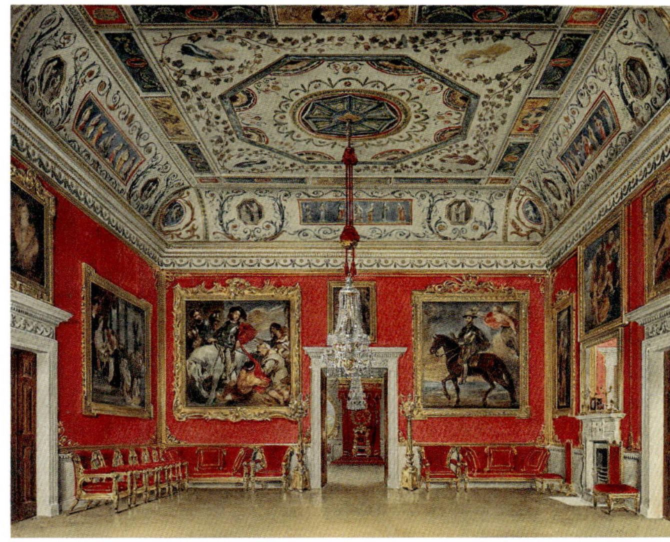

FIG. 53
James Stephanoff
The Crimson Drawing Room, Buckingham House, 1817, for Pyne's *Royal Residences*
Watercolour
RCIN 922142

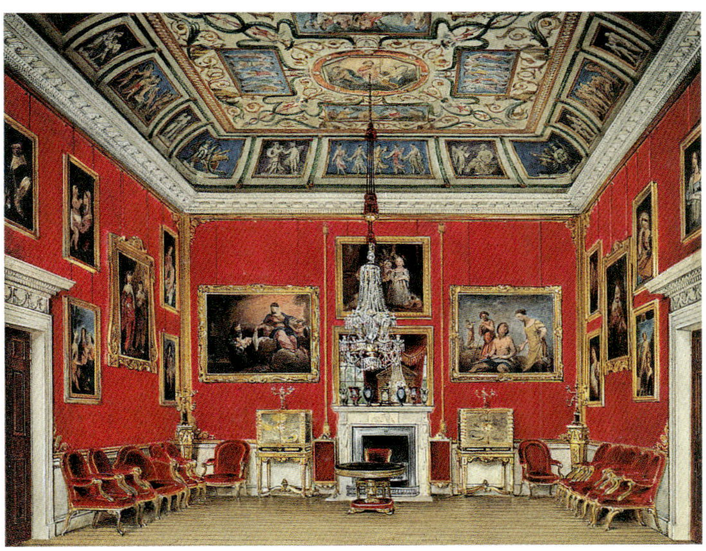

FIG. 54
James Stephanoff
The Second Drawing Room, Buckingham House, 1818, for Pyne's *Royal Residences*
Watercolour
RCIN 922143

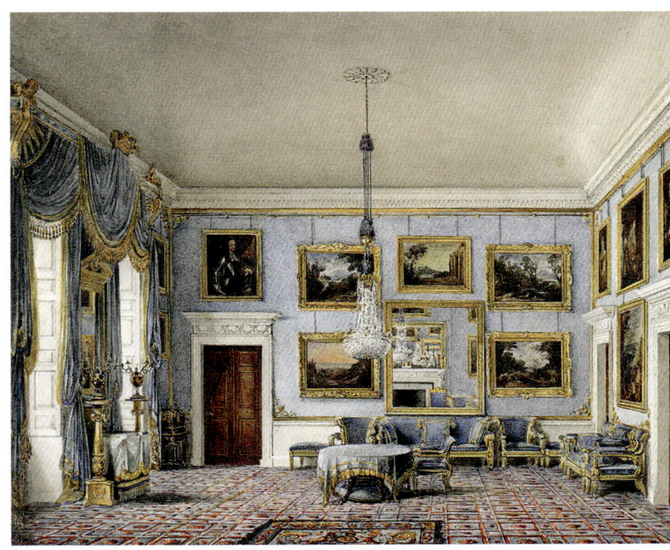

FIG. 55
Charles Wild
The Blue Velvet Room , Buckingham House, 1817, for Pyne's *Royal Residences*
Watercolour
RCIN 922144

The 'Maratta' frame made for Amigoni's portrait of 1735–6 (no. 256) shows this characteristic form. It, too, is a version of a classical cornice but softened and more moulded. In particular the frieze zone is replaced with a large semi-circular concave moulding called a 'cavetto'. There is usually a narrow moulding, often a ribbon-and-stick, separating the cavetto from the outer edge, and something similar to articulate the sight edge. A leaf-and-tongue moulding is usually incorporated, either at the sight edge or (as in this case) filling the void of the cavetto. This type was used for modern works, as in this case, and for the Old Masters, though these frames in the Royal Collection were often embellished out of all recognition by George IV.

The final type of frame follows the French style of the early eighteenth century. All the examples here (seen framing nos 125, 131–5 and 141) were created for Frederick, Prince of Wales, probably by English makers.[10] French-style frames are more fanciful and varied in design than others of the period, but they are built upon the same tripartite foundations – a leaf-and-tongue architrave at the sight edge, a narrow sanded frieze, and a large cornice of S-shaped or cyma profile at the outside. The gilding of this cornice zone is cross-hatched to create a shadowy effect and elaborate decoration is applied – strapwork, floral motifs and C-scrolls. The final element applied here is the cartouche, a fancifully shaped form reminiscent of a shell or a coat of arms. Sometimes four are introduced to round off the corners of the frame; sometimes eight, one at each corner and one in the centre of each side. In this latter case the frame acquires a swinging outline, as if made up of volutes (see no. 131). This applied decoration of scrolls and cartouches gives the French-style frame the character of a dish rather than an architectural element (see no. 20).

The Royal Collection contained works in sets, like the Mantegna *Triumphs of Caesar* or Raphael tapestry cartoons, which could be relied upon to create symmetrical interiors (see fig. 60). The effect could be achieved by commissioning copies of Old Master paintings, which could be arranged as sets of matching sizes, as must have occurred with the 25 copies by Joseph Goupy recorded in 1749 in Princess Augusta's Dressing Room at Leicester House (all now lost with the exception of RCIN 407565).[11] Pyne's interiors, on the other hand, show such frames in a generally symmetrical and coherent arrangement, surrounding works not acquired or commissioned as a group but in ones and twos, the twos often 'marriages of convenience' rather than works actually created as a pair. To get Old Master purchases to compose in this way is a complicated business, something George Vertue obviously appreciated when he visited Leicester House in 1749 and admired a room full of Rubens and Teniers landscapes 'in Gold frames uniform. and finely designd & Carvd – most elegantly'.[12] The King's Gallery at Kensington Palace (fig. 65) preserves this opportunistic uniformity of spacing and framing devised by William Kent for George I.

We know how the Georgians liked to arrange paintings but what sort of painting did they like? To answer this we must appreciate that British collectors of this period bought into Old Master artistic theory as enthusiastically as they bought Old Master paintings; they were connoisseurs, they had 'taste', carefully and systematically formed. This artistic theory originated in Italy and became codified by the later seventeenth century, particularly with the foundation of the French Academy in Paris and

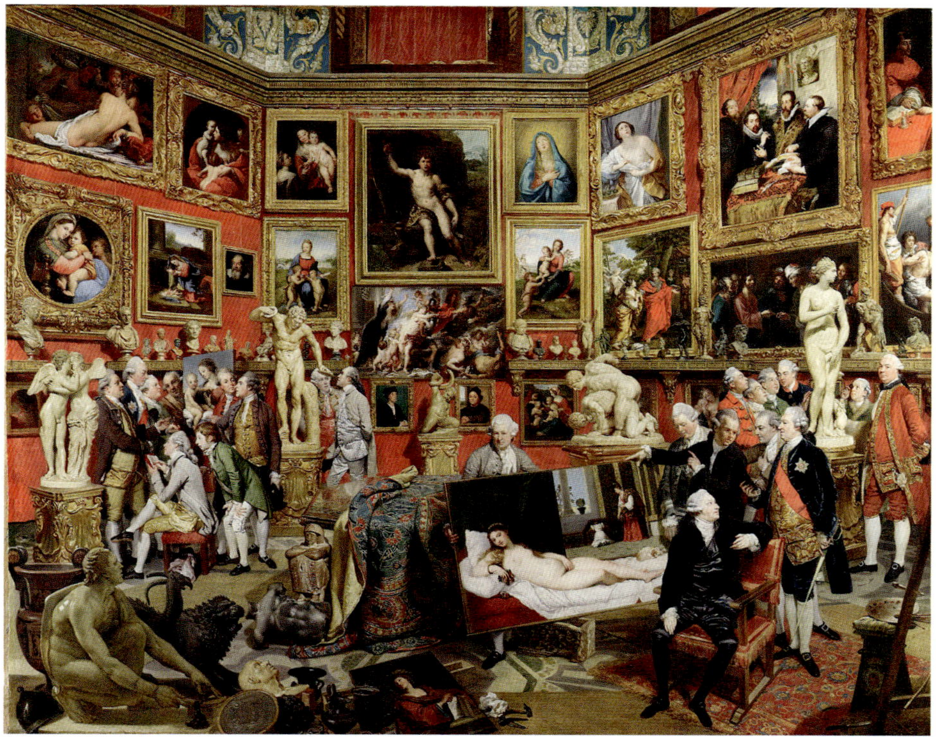

FIG. 56
Johan Zoffany
The Tribuna of the Uffizi, 1772–7
Oil on canvas
RCIN 406183

in Rome.[13] These academic ideas of art were disseminated throughout Europe by means of translations, adaptations and plagiarising of Italian source material. In England the works of Du Fresnoy and Roger de Piles were translated from French, while Jonathan Richardson and eventually Sir Joshua Reynolds wrote original English artistic theory following the same model.[14] Meanwhile the same absorbed assumptions inform judgements jotted down by Vertue, Horace Walpole and many other collectors of the period. As noted above (p. 23), there was more conformity than one might have expected from such an irreverent and dynamic society. Reynolds advised students of the Royal Academy: 'With respect to the pictures that you are to choose for your models, I could wish that you would take the world's opinion rather than your own'.[15]

Reynolds's advice reminds us that the understanding of art has changed over the years. We see the story of art as one of conflict and contrast; they saw it as one of continuity and conformity. We admire individuality; they admired the ability to perform some universal, unchanging core-activity.[16] This idea of continuity and a 'core curriculum' led to the formation of a 'canon'. Vasari and his many imitators wrote prescriptive treatises about painting, but then described so many lives and admired so many works that it seemed in practice as if they praised indiscriminately (providing only that the artist came from their home town).[17] This approach changed with Giovanni Pietro Bellori, whose lives of modern artists (*Le Vite de' Pittori, Scultori et Architetti Moderni*), published in 1672, followed a theoretic tract with the lives of only twelve exemplary artists, the author explaining exactly what about them was to be admired and what avoided.[18] Bellori's fastidiousness makes it especially significant that his three final lives, published posthumously in 1732 – of Guido Reni, Andrea Sacchi and Carlo Maratta – contain unqualified adulation.[19] Bellori's conception of the selective and critical biography contributed to a much narrower or more discerning taste during the following century. This section attempts to check off the royal acquisition of Old Masters against this canon.

The most famous at-a-glance summation of eighteenth-century taste is Zoffany's *Tribuna of the Uffizi* (fig. 56), which

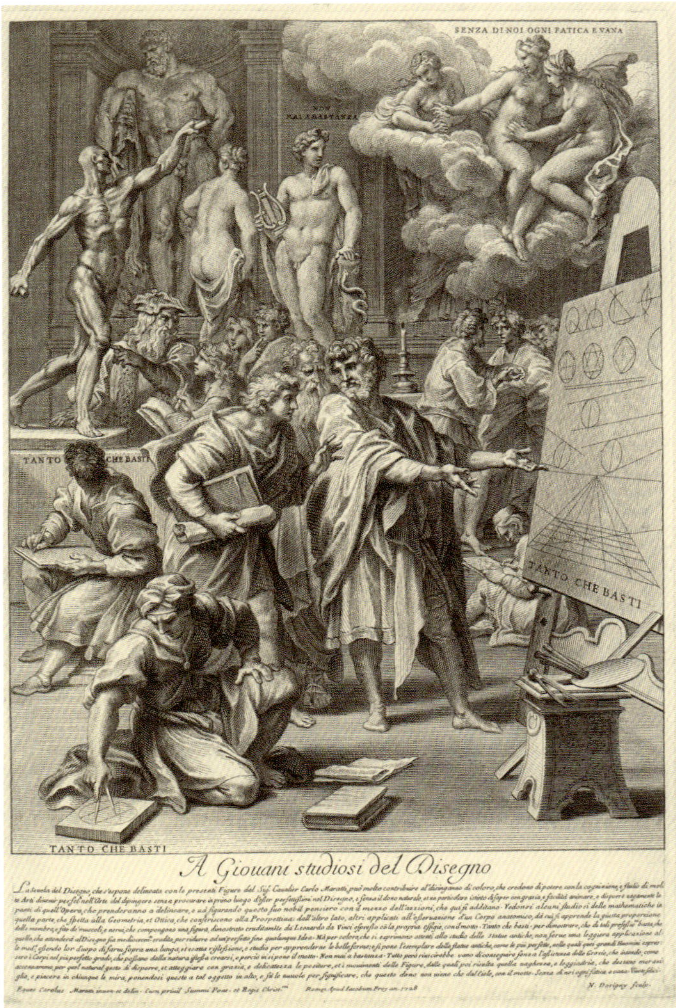

FIG. 57
After Carlo Maratta
A Giovani studiosi del Disegno, 1728
Engraving
RCIN 807743

sees Renaissance painting in the context of its ultimate inspiration, the sculpture of classical antiquity. Zoffany improvises on the arrangement of paintings but in reality and in his rendering there is no ambiguity about the dominant tradition.[20] Raphael's *St John* hangs centrally, pointing upwards, surrounded immediately by other Raphaels (all Madonnas) and by the works of Guido Reni; on the flanking walls appear works by Correggio, Annibale Carracci and Pietro da Cortona. Lord Cowper appears in the scene trying to sell George III the one type of painting he lacks, a Raphael *Madonna* (now in the National Gallery of Art, Washington). Though begun in 1772, the *Tribuna* reflects the taste of the first as well as the second half of the century. This taste considered painting to have begun and ended with Raphael and his admirers: earlier paintings (Botticelli or Giotto) were banished altogether; later paintings generally reflect his influence.[21] It was thought that Raphael excelled in everything but in particular in the depiction of divine beauty; in this respect he inspired the great tradition of painting passing through the Carracci to Guido Reni and, to a lesser extent, to Baroque painters such as Pietro da Cortona and Rubens.

Horace Walpole was celebrating this tradition when he wrote in 1752 of the Old Master paintings at Houghton: 'In short, in my opinion, all the qualities of a perfect Painter, never met but in RAPHAEL, GUIDO, and ANNIBAL CARACCI'.[22] Only one other artist attracted this sort of adulation at this time and that was Carlo Maratta (see no. 127), the most recent exponent of this tradition. One of the rooms at Houghton was 'the Carlo Maratta Room' after the artist, who, according to Horace Walpole, 'added Grace, Beauty and Lightness, to the Majesty, Dignity, and Solemnity' of his predecessors.[23] In his life of Maratta, Bellori reproduces (with explanation) his Raphael-like print of an idealised working academy (fig. 57), which offers the most succinct summary of the ideas behind the creation and reception of works in this section.[24] Against each part of the artist's curriculum – perspective, anatomy, geometry – Maratta writes 'as much as may be necessary' ('*tanto che basti*'), while against the study of antique statues he writes 'never enough' ('*non mai abbastanza*'), for, Bellori explains, 'in good statues is found the model and the perfection of painting, along with the proper imitation [of examples] drawn from nature'.[25] While the Antique teaches you to recognise Beauty in Nature, something else is needed to recreate it – the divine gift of 'Grace'. In the sky the three Graces sit above an inscription which reads, 'Without us all labour is in vain' ('*Senza di noi ogni fatica e vana*'). The rubric to an engraving after Guido Reni by Robert Strange suggests that these ideas had become absorbed in England, referring as it does to those 'Delicate refined expressions reserved for the pencil of the famous Guido, that incomparable artist, who is justly termed the Painter of both Grace and Sentiment'.[26]

This overarching conception determined the choice of paintings acquired by the early Georgians, but it can be loosely subdivided into three. The dominant tradition can be seen in the sought-after painters of 'Grace and Sentiment', beginning with Raphael's Madonnas and ending with Maratta (see nos 123–8). Another related tradition, surprisingly absent from Zoffany's *Tribuna*, begins with Raphael's more severe narratives and leads to figure paintings and landscapes by Nicolas Poussin, and artists influenced by him (see nos 129–35). A third tradition, clearly expressed in the *Tribuna*, continues to reflect the influence of Raphael but includes Venetian painting and results in the more colourful and sensual painting of Rubens and Van Dyck (see nos 136–42). These three traditions reflect the development of the Italian Renaissance ideal in three parts of Europe – Italy, France and the Low Countries.

The Painter of Grace and Sentiment

The royal residence which came closest to expressing early Georgian taste was Leicester House, the home of Frederick, Prince of Wales, which once housed at least half of the paintings in this section.[27] The clearest insight into contemporary taste is found in the Princess's Dressing Room, entirely hung, as mentioned above, with Goupy's copies after the Old Masters.[28] The freedom of the copyist allowed an ideal hang, featuring Raphael (the Tapestry Cartoons and a *Holy Family*), four Guido Reni (including *Aurora*, *Bacchus and Ariadne* and *The Toilet of Venus*), and figural works by Annibale Carracci, Andrea Sacchi, Titian, Van Dyck and Salvator Rosa, as well as seven landscapes – by Rosa, Claude, Filippo Lauri, Rubens, Pietro da Cortona, Nicolas Poussin and Titian. The nearest space to this including original works was the Prince's Closet (also called 'Dressing Room'). George Vertue's diary for July 1749 describes his visit; after seeing various rooms he is welcomed into the 'Prince's Closet' by the Prince himself:

> well says the Prince I have sent for you here to let you see some that I mostly value. then pointing to a peice of St Peter holding in his Armes the child Jesus. painted by Guido [now attributed to Carlo Maratta, RCIN 402881] how do you think or like that picture of Guido a peice most admirable. surely – I said. then turning to another of the same Great Master being a Lucretia at half figure [probably *Cleopatra*, no. 126]. so beautifull strong clear & Natural. of the finest taste of that skillfullest artist Guido – I much admired – two paintings of Andra del Sarto [no. 123 and fig. 58] for the design & rarity much to be admired so many others of sublime Masters antient and scarse none modern nor none very large in this closset but most pieces of great value & esteemation.[29]

A 1749 manuscript catalogue of pictures at Leicester House and Vertue's subsequent visit tells us that, in addition to the four paintings identified above (nos 123,

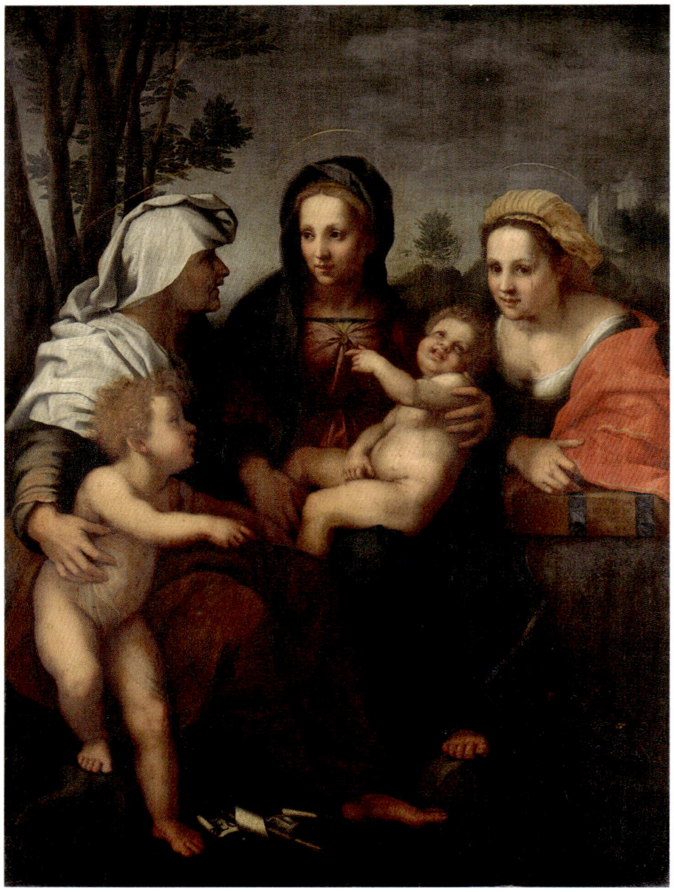

FIG. 58
After Andrea del Sarto
The Holy Family with St Catherine, *c.*1600
Oil on panel
RCIN 402820

126, fig. 58 and RCIN 402881), this space included nos 125 and 140 along with other works by Maratta (RCIN 404954) Bassano, Albani, Lauri, Luca Giordano and Carlo Cignani, self-portraits by Murillo (now in the National Gallery), Annibale and Ludovico Carracci, and a portrait by Rubens said to depict Ben Jonson.[30]

Even in the eighteenth century some recoiled from the excess of 'grace and sentiment' seen in this group of paintings (particularly no. 126). Hogarth's *Battle of the Pictures* (no. 90) contains rows of prettily penitent saints all in the Reni mode. He was especially angered by the £404 paid in 1758 for the mawkish *Sigismunda*, then attributed to Correggio and now to Francesco Furini, at the sale of the collection of the diplomat Sir Luke Schaub (1690–1758).[31] Schaub was a particular friend of Frederick, Prince of Wales and described by Vertue as his 'prime minister conaisseur in pictures'.[32] Maratta's reputation in particular started to look vulnerable as the century progressed. Horace Walpole thought that he has 'unluckily been one of the Destroyers of painting, by introducing that very light Stile of Colouring, which in less skilful Hands has developed into glare and tawdry'.[33] In his fifth *Discourse* of 1772 Reynolds delivers a weightier verdict:

> in my opinion, [Carlo Maratta] had no great vigour of mind or strength of original genius. He rarely seizes the imagination by exhibiting the higher excellencies, nor does he captivate us with that originality which attends the painter who thinks for himself. He knew and practised all the rules of art, and from a composition of Raffaelle, Carracci, and Guido, made up a style, of which the only fault was, that it had no manifest defects and no striking beauties; and that the principles of his composition are never blended together, so as to form one unified body, original in its kind, or excellent in any view.[34]

Reynolds's mild rebuke became outright condemnation during the nineteenth century, especially from the Pre-Raphaelites, who derived their name from a desire to retrace the stream of Italian painting to beyond the point when it had become polluted by the 'Raphaelism' seen in this group of works.[35]

123

WORKSHOP OF ANDREA DEL SARTO (1486–1530)

The Virgin and Child with St John c.1515

Oil on panel, 100.3 × 74.7 cm
RCIN 406113

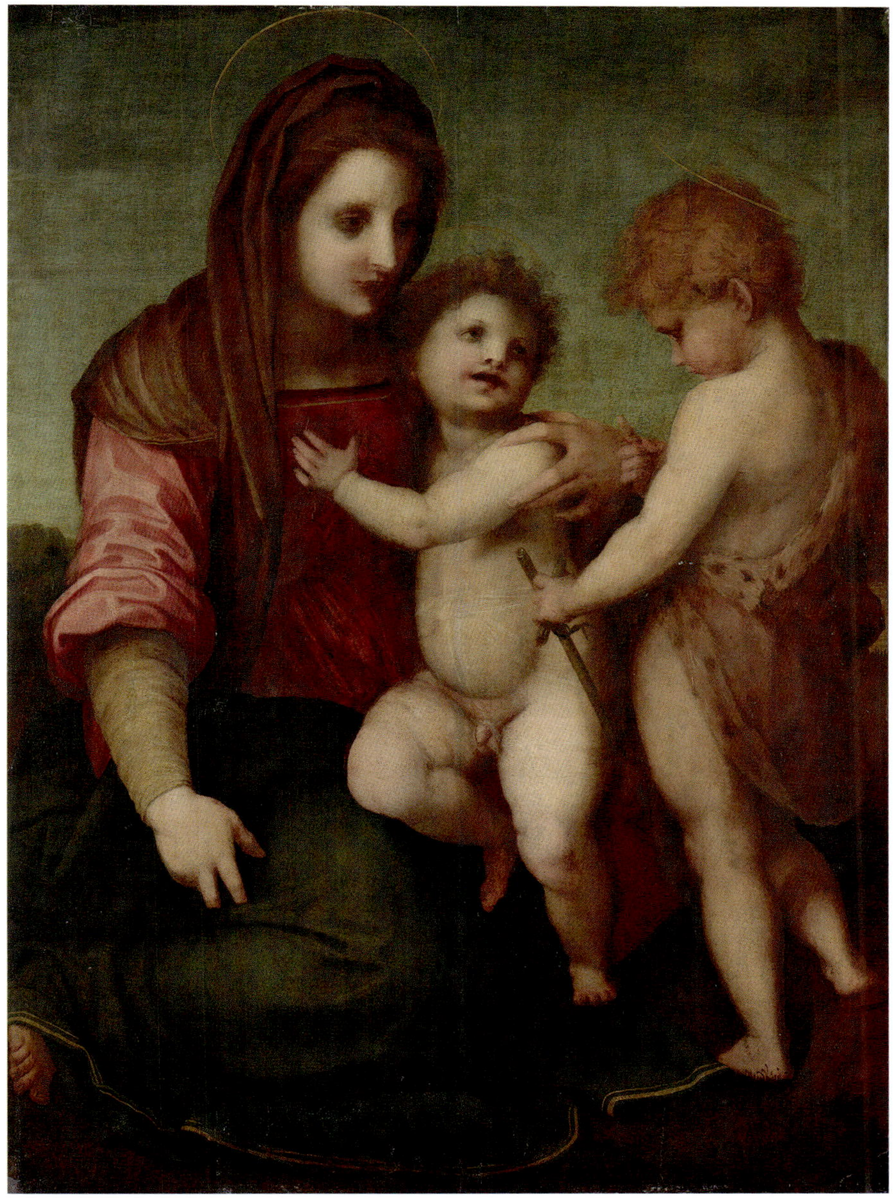

Photograph pre-conservation

PROVENANCE Acquired by Frederick, Prince of Wales

LITERATURE Shearman 1983, pp. 11–2, no. 5; Rorschach 1993, p. 66, no. 86

Horace Walpole records a long conversation on painting with Frederick, Prince of Wales, during which the Prince admitted to a special affection for the works of Andrea del Sarto.[36] Del Sarto probably represented an acceptable replacement for the largest gap in the Royal Collection at this time, a Raphael *Madonna* (see above, p. 228). This painting and a 'Holy Family' (almost certainly fig. 58) were recorded in 1749 at Leicester House in the Prince's Closet (see above, p. 229).[37] Though on poplar panels of similar dimensions these works were not created as a pair and must have been brought together by a dealer, collector or Frederick himself in a way which was entirely typical of the age of the symmetrical 'country house' hang. In Pyne's *Royal Residences* they can be seen still treated as a pair in the Second Drawing Room at Buckingham House (fig. 54, lower tier, left-hand wall), in a beautifully spaced and symmetrical hang and in the prestigious company of Van Dyck, Guido Cagnacci, Guercino and Carlo Maratta.[38]

Modern scholarship regards the works less enthusiastically than Frederick did: *The Holy Family with St Catherine* (fig. 58), a copy of the Tallard *Madonna* (Hermitage, St Petersburg), is believed to date from *c.*1600, while this *Virgin and Child with St John* is one of many versions considered to have issued from del Sarto's studio. John Shearman wrote that 'in spite of the executant's obvious freedom to improvise, the picture remains a dull, inexpressive and technically rather naïve work'.[39] Recent conservation has revealed more of that 'freedom to improvise' and has removed at least some of the suggestion of dullness in the execution. DS-T

124

ATTRIBUTED TO PONTORMO (1494–1556)
(JACOPO CARRUCCI DA PONTORMO)

The Virgin and Child *c.*1530–35

Oil on panel, 122.0 × 102.2 cm
RCIN 406117

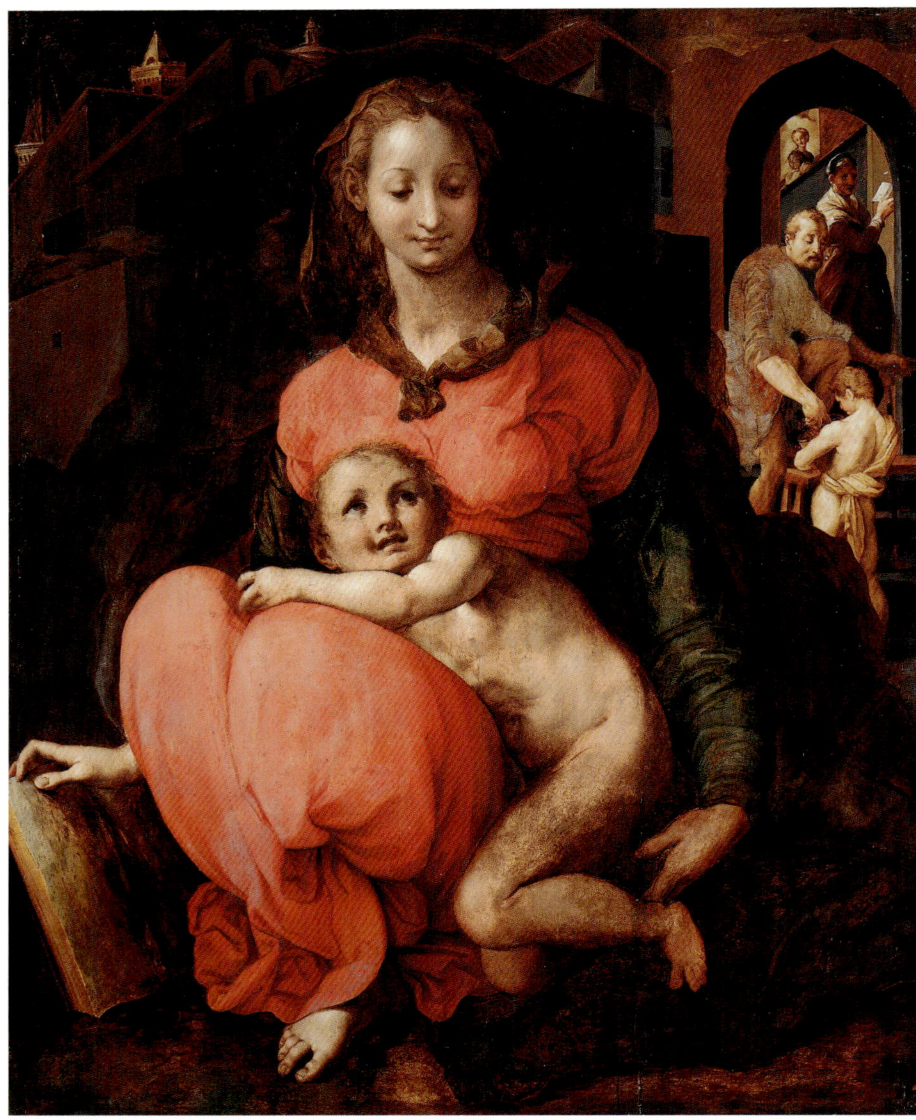

PROVENANCE First recorded in the Royal Collection in 1818

LITERATURE Shearman 1983, pp. 201–4, no. 211; Costamagna 1994, no. 73; *Art of Italy* 2007, pp. 65–7, no. 6

This panel is first recorded in the Royal Collection (in 1818) as a good 'early work' of Andrea del Sarto; it was then hanging in Queen Caroline's Bedroom at Kensington Palace with a large selection of Old Masters, mostly acquired in the Stuart or early Georgian period.[40] This company suggests that it was a work inherited by George III, probably from his father, rather than one he purchased himself.[41]

The composition, known as the 'Madonna of the Book', exists in 25 versions, many of high quality but none generally accepted as the unique original. It seems that Pontormo's studio produced many, if not most, of the versions with the active participation of the artist himself. No. 124 is a work of high quality, painted with the freedom and confidence of a master rather than a copyist.[42] In some ways recent scholarship has come closer to the eighteenth-century approach, when many versions of a composition were accepted as autograph.

The painting would seem to illustrate the education of the Christ Child, who appears twice – learning from the book his mother holds in the foreground and from his father in the carpenter's workshop in the middle ground. The Virgin's mother, St Anne, holds another book underneath the arch, further alluding to the theme of education through the generations. DS-T

125

BENVENUTI TESI, CALLED IL GAROFALO (*c*.1476–1559)

The Holy Family 1533

Oil on panel, 42.5 × 55.4 cm
RCIN 406923

PROVENANCE Recorded in 1749 at Leicester House in the collection of Frederick, Prince of Wales

LITERATURE Shearman 1983, pp. 110–1, no. 110; Rorschach 1993, p. 61, no. 35; *Art of Italy* 2007, pp. 126–7, no. 33

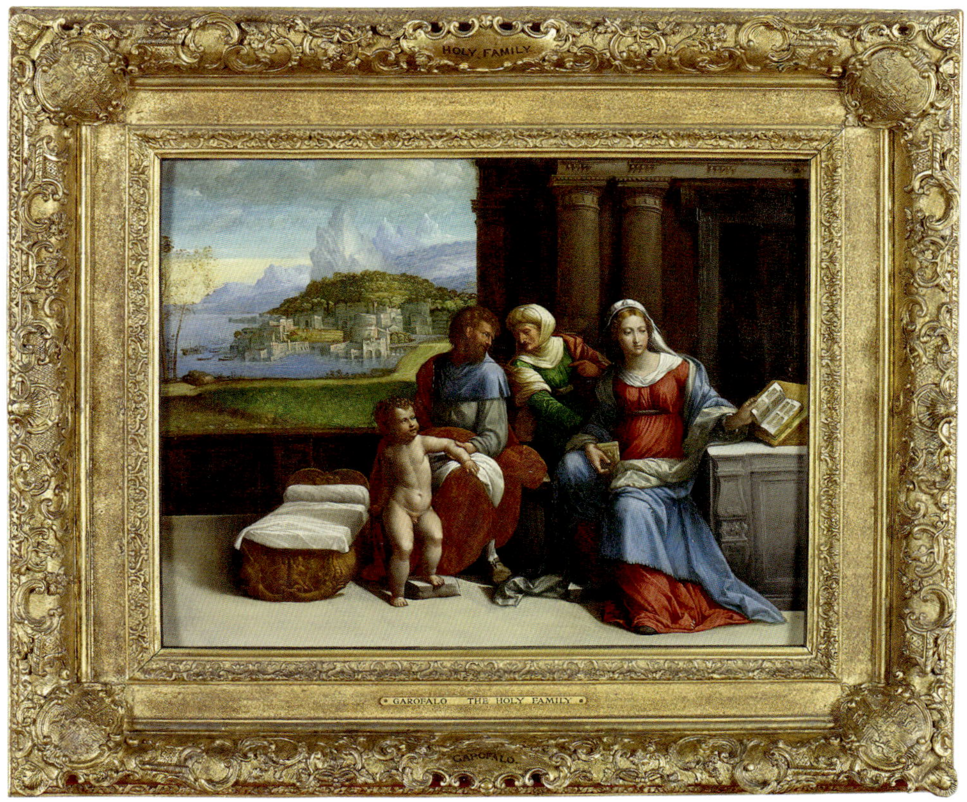

This panel is signed and dated on the reverse with far more information than is usual for this period: *'fu compito A di 2 mazo 1533./G.R.F.L'* ('completed on the 2 May 1533. G[a]R[o]F[a]L[o]'. A relatively late work, no. 125 shows a moment in Garofalo's work, and Ferrarese painting in general, when awareness of modern trends in Roman painting, in particular the work of Raphael and Giulio Romano, was grafted on to a local tradition. Characteristically Ferrarese is the bright colour, sharp detail and the expressive landscape. The nearest equivalent to such a vivid use of sunlight with a hint of impending storm can be found in Giorgione's *Tempesta* of 1506–8 (Accademia, Venice). The influence of Roman painting can be seen in the archaeological correctness of the classical architecture and furnishings of the room and the sculptural forms of the drapery and compact figure group.

There is little indication of any awareness of Ferrarese Renaissance painting in mid-eighteenth-century Britain and the excellent examples which joined the Royal Collection in the Stuart period do not appear or are misattributed in the inventories of the next century.[43] No. 125, on the other hand, was correctly identified by Vertue as a 'Garofolo' in 1749, hanging in the best company possible in the Prince's Closet at Leicester House; it retained its ranking and attribution in 1819 when hanging with nos 126 and 128 in the King's Dressing Room at Windsor.[44] Part of the painting's success may be due to its signature, which allowed an artist off the normal eighteenth-century menu to be identified with some confidence. It may have been valued not so much for the distinctive Ferrarese landscape, which fascinates us, but as an available substitute for early Raphael. The signature would have allowed Frederick or Vertue to look up Garofalo in Vasari, where they would have found their Raphael-centred aesthetic prejudices endorsed. Vasari relates that in 1505 Garofalo travelled to Rome and was almost struck by despair 'by seeing the grace and vivacity that the pictures of Raffaello revealed, and the depth in the design of Michelagnolo. Wherefore he cursed the manners of Lombardy, and that which he had learned with so much study and effort at Mantua ... he resolved, since there was no help for it, that he would unlearn it all.'[45] DS-T

126

GUIDO RENI (1575–1642)

Cleopatra with the Asp c.1628

Oil on canvas, 114.2 × 95.0 cm
RCIN 405338

PROVENANCE Recorded in 1749 at Leicester House in the collection of Frederick, Prince of Wales

LITERATURE Levey 1991, pp. 123–4, no. 576; Rorschach 1993, p. 65, no. 72; *Art of Italy* 2007, pp. 286–7, no. 99

Guido Reni was monotonously revered, from the moment he first made his name around 1600 until the late nineteenth century, as the keystone of the great tradition of Raphael. Charles I owned a set of four 'Labours of Hercules' (now in the Louvre) and his Queen, Henrietta Maria, specially commissioned a ceiling painting by Reni depicting Bacchus and Ariadne, which never arrived.[46] In the eighteenth century the Hanoverians replaced these losses with a group of works (many now considered to be studio) including the *Toilet of Venus* and *Perseus and Andromeda* acquired by George I in 1723 and given to the National Gallery by William IV in 1836 (National Gallery, nos 90 and 87) and this painting, acquired some time before 1749 by Frederick, Prince of Wales.[47] George I's two paintings were hung in pride of place in the Great Drawing Room at Kensington Palace and can later be seen, still treated as a pair, in the King's Drawing Room at Windsor (fig. 52, right wall).[48] No. 126 hung in the Prince of Wales's Closet, the inner sanctum of the picture hang at Leicester House described above (p. 229). Pyne's *Royal Residences* of 1819 shows this picture in the King's Dressing Room at Windsor as part of a hang with two Raphael School *Holy Families* and many examples of works from the Raphaelesque tradition by Garofalo (no. 125), Annibale Carracci, Guido Reni, Guercino, Carlo Dolci and Filippo Lauri (no. 128).[49] It is probably no accident that Charles I's Renis were of heroic, manly subjects while the eighteenth-century batch were generally tender, feminine and imbued with pathos.[50] No. 126 provides an epitome of this group and in general of the cult of the 'Divine Guido'.

During his own lifetime Reni's genius was particularly identified with images of suffering female beauty – Magdalens, Lucretias and Cleopatras – usually presented as single figures, half or full length. No. 126 was probably commissioned by a Venetian merchant called Boselli, through the agency of fellow Venetian Palma Giovane, as part of a 'half-length' competition between four artists – Palma Giovane himself, Reni, Niccolò Renieri (1591–1667) and Guercino. The fact that Palma Giovane won was put down to Venetian chauvinism by Reni's Bolognese biographer, Carlo Cesare Malvasia.[51]
The three major works joining the Royal Collection during the eighteenth century might similarly be seen as programmatic essays in beauty and pathos – *The Toilet of Venus* representing 'Beauty Adorned', *Andromeda* 'Beauty in Distress' and *Cleopatra*, 'Dying Beauty'. There are parallels with operatic arias of the period, where the dying words of Cleopatra, Lucretia or Dido would provide a vehicle for the prima donna of the moment (see p. 381). Beauty in the period was associated with weakness or timidity and so a beautiful woman was believed to look her best when threatened.[52] Keats expresses a similar idea when describing the refined sensation of Melancholy, that 'dwells with Beauty – Beauty that must die' (*Ode to Melancholy*, 1819, l. 21).

Reservations were expressed about this aspect of Reni's art during his lifetime, when it was noted that in the most important attributes of painting, action and emotion, he was surpassed by Domenichino (1581–1641).[53] In his fifth *Discourse* Reynolds discussed the contradiction between the serenity of beauty and the distortion of passion. In his opinion 'Guido, from want of choice in adapting his subject to his ideas and his powers, or from attempting to preserve beauty where it could not be preserved, has in this respect succeeded very ill. His figures are often engaged in subjects that required great expression: yet his Judith and Holofernes, the daughter of Herodias with the Baptist's head, the Andromeda, and some even of the Mothers of the Innocents, have little more expression than his Venus attired by the Graces.'[54] It is very likely that the *Andromeda* and *Venus* mentioned here are George I's purchases, then at Windsor and now in the National Gallery. DS-T

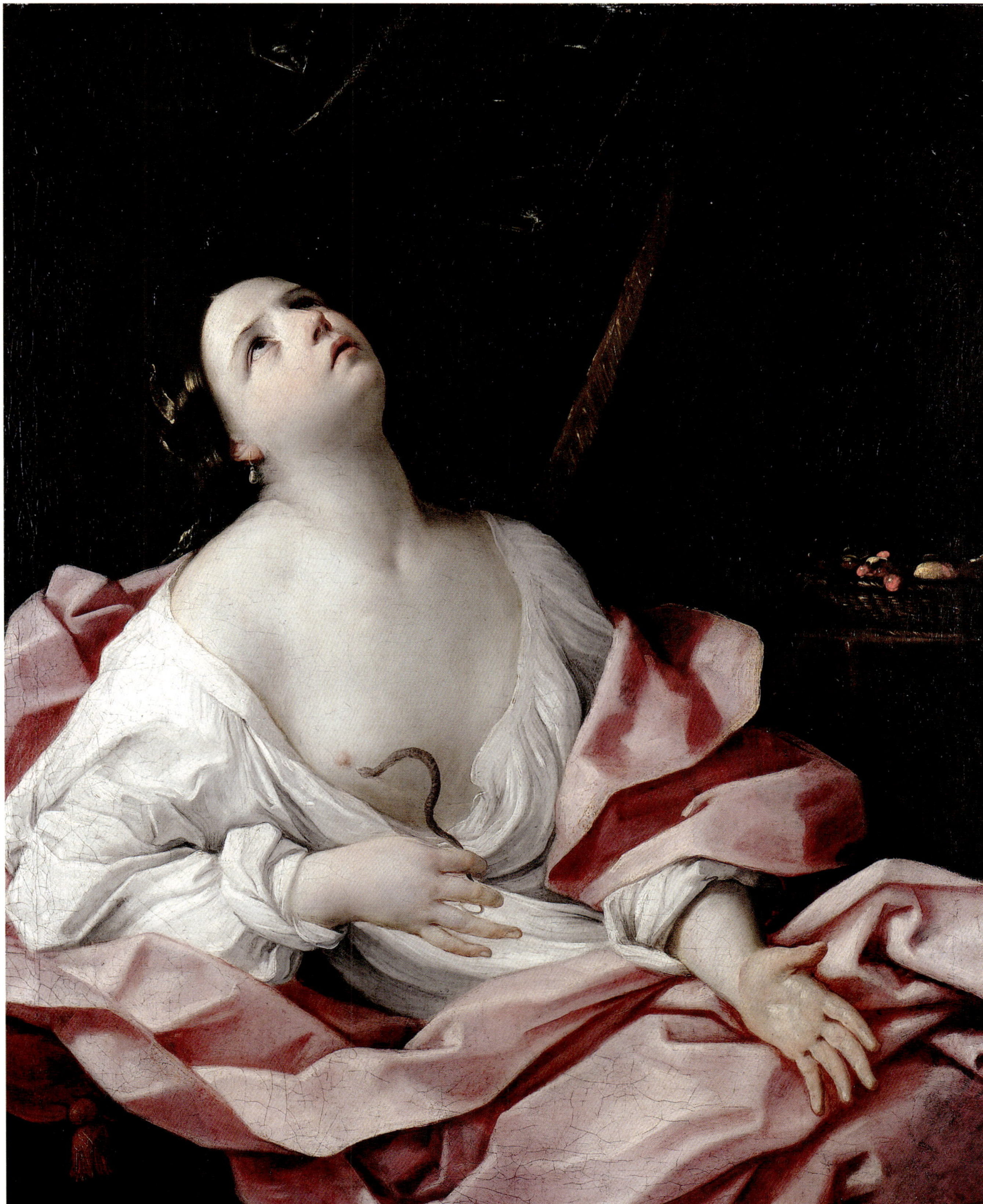

127

CARLO MARATTA (1625–1713)

The Annunciation *c.*1660

Oil on copper, 68 × 50 cm
RCIN 405633

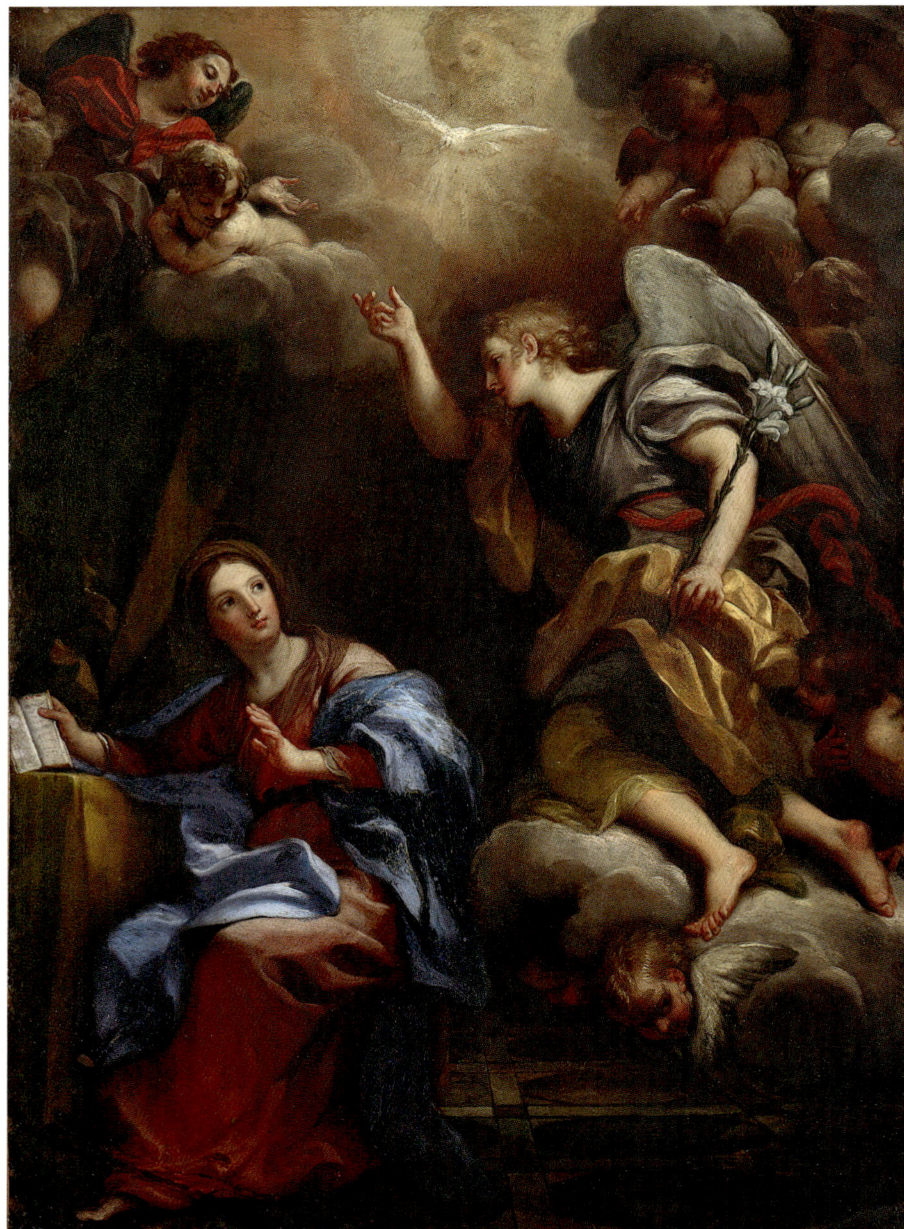
Photograph pre-conservation

PROVENANCE Probably the 'Salutation painted on copper' recorded by George Vertue in Queen Caroline's Closet, Kensington Palace (Vertue 1743, item 81)

LITERATURE Levey 1991, p. 109, no. 539

Carlo Maratta was regarded in Georgian Britain as the most recent exponent of the great tradition of Raphael. Important works by him were acquired. In 1748 Frederick, Prince of Wales, bought from Mr Edwin the huge *Vision of St Stanislas Kostka* (RCIN 405693) of *c.*1680, which was in the Second Drawing Room at Buckingham House (see fig. 54, on the left of the central wall) along with Maratta's *St Joseph* (but then attributed to Reni) and some of the best Van Dycks of the collection.[55] Frederick further purchased Maratta's *Christ Child within a Garland of Flowers* (RCIN 404954), which hung in his Closet at Leicester House and later in the Crimson Drawing Room at Buckingham House.[56] And in pride of place, in Queen Caroline's Picture Closet (fig. 78, item 81), was this *Annunciation*.[57]

The bland, smooth and classical features of the Virgin and angels derive from Maratta's apprenticeship with Andrea Sacchi, but the diagonal, crowded composition and the way the drapery billows and flutters suggests that Maratta had looked at Sacchi's arch rival, Pietro da Cortona. Bellori hated so intensely those artists, like Bernini and Cortona, that we call 'Baroque' he could not bring himself even to mention their names in his *Vite*. By the eighteenth century, however, there was no awareness of this conflict between classicism and Baroque; both were treated as a part of a single Raphaelesque tradition.[58] DS-T

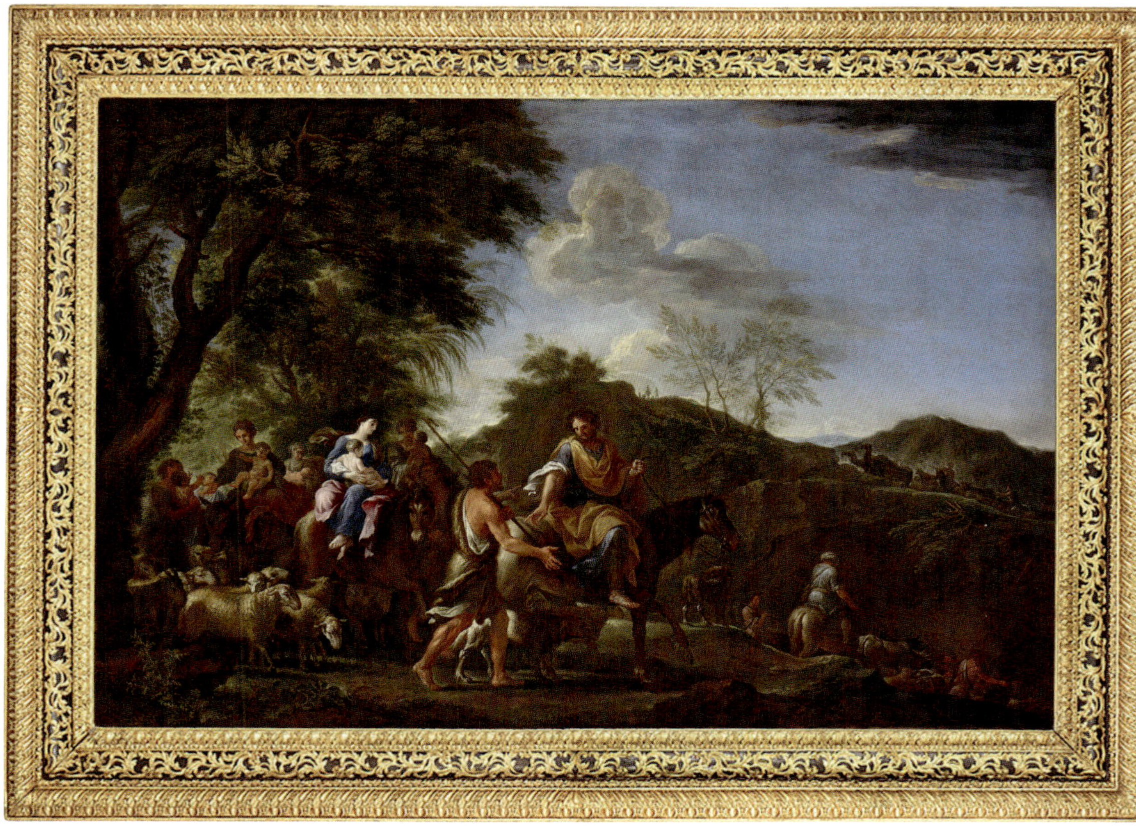

128

FILIPPO LAURI (1623–1694)

Jacob fleeing from Laban 1686

Oil on canvas, 93.3 × 142.0 cm
RCIN 406356

PROVENANCE Painted for Marchese Niccolò Maria Pallavicini (1650–1714); acquired by Frederick, Prince of Wales, in 1747–9

LITERATURE Pascoli 1730–6, II, p. 140; Levey 1991, pp. 103–9, no. 531; Rorschach 1993, p. 62, no. 47

Artistic life in Rome towards the end of the seventeenth century was more fluid than the theorists allowed, particular in the collecting of landscape painting. Though regarded (with some justification) as a speciality of foreigners working in Rome (see nos 131–5), there was a native Italian tradition of setting religious and mythological scenes in landscapes, seen particularly in the work of Francesco Albani (1578–1660). Lauri was born in Rome of a Flemish father, Balthasar Lauwers, and made a successful career working in this tradition for the Roman nobility, while sending examples to France, Spain, Holland, Germany and England.[59] Like Albani, he was much admired in early Georgian England: Queen Caroline bought one (in 1729), as did Sir Robert Walpole.[60] Frederick had two paintings by Lauri listed at Leicester House in 1749, a *Nativity* and this painting, described as 'Jacob's Journey into Egypt' and hanging in the '2nd Room' with landscapes by Titian, Claude and Gaspard Dughet (see below, p. 240).[61] It later appears in Pyne's *Royal Residences* of 1819, with nos 125 and 126, in the King's Dressing Room at Windsor.[62]

This painting was executed in 1686 for the Marchese Pallavicini.[63] It depicts the moment at which Jacob escapes from his father-in-law, Laban, with his wives, children, camels and herds (Genesis 31: 17–18). The subject allows for a contrast between a wild terrain, with a suggestion of a long, strung-out caravan, painted in the style of Salvator Rosa, and foreground groups, reminding the viewer of depictions of the Flight into Egypt, in the style of Maratta and his contemporaries.

This painting has one of the most magnificent frames in the Royal Collection. Obviously created in Italy, presumably like the painting for the Marchese Pallavicini in 1686, it is as finely carved in wood (rather than gesso) as any piece of furniture. An elaborate version of the 'Maratta' type (see pp. 224–6), this frame reveals the underlying tripartite division of a classical entablature, the frieze zone emphasised by the dark background against which the fine, gilded foliage stands out. This Roman frame differs in profile from English ones of the next generation (seen elsewhere in this section) in being much flatter as well as finer. DS-T

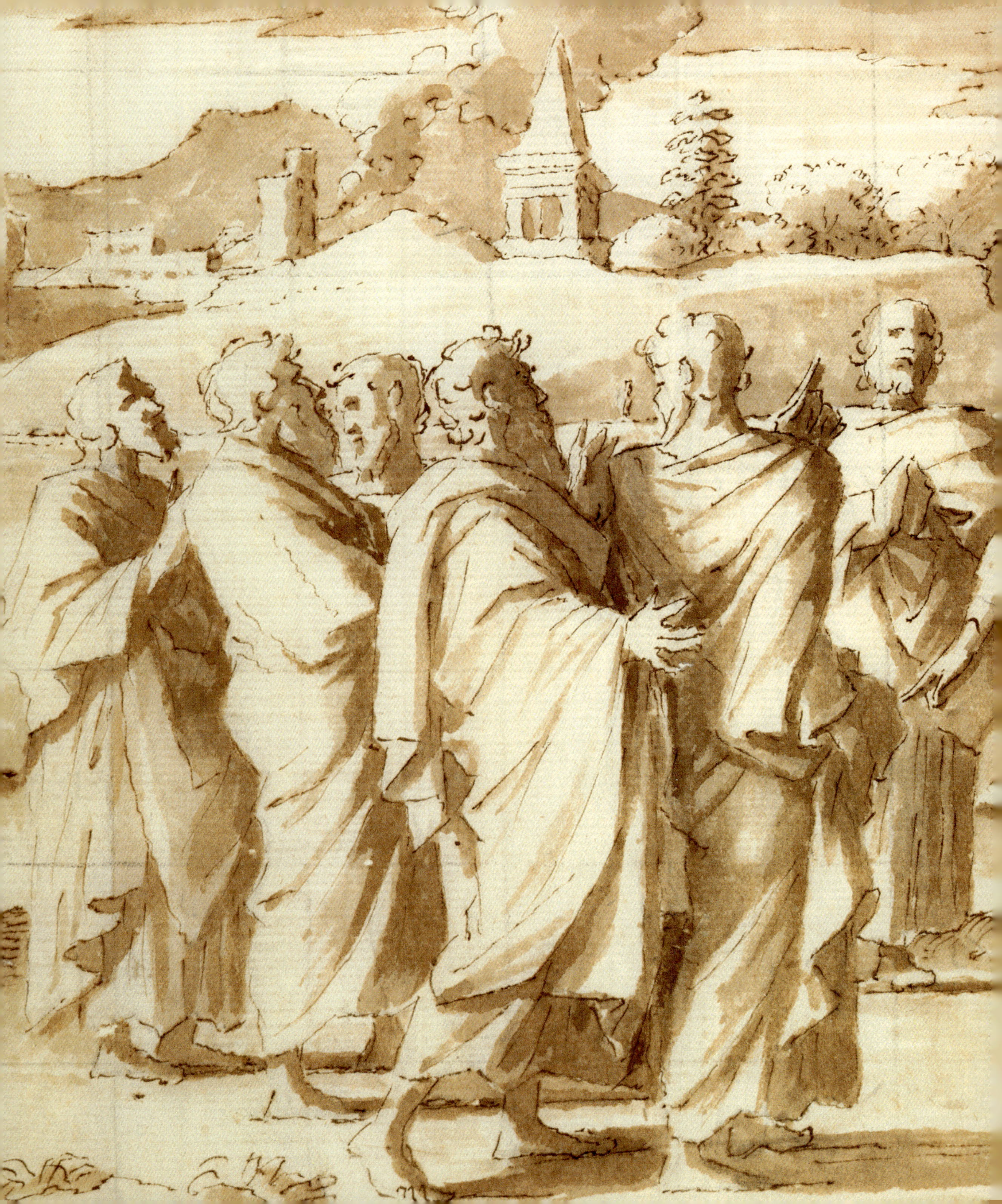

Both Nicolas Poussin (1593/4–1665) and Eustache Le Sueur (see no. 129) were described in the eighteenth century as the 'French Raphael'.[64] In his *Fourth Discourse* of 1771 Reynolds remarked that the 'best of the French School, Poussin, Le Sueur, and Le Brun, have formed themselves upon these models [Roman, Florentine and Bolognese], and consequently may be said, though Frenchmen, to be a colony from the Roman School'.[65] The meaning of Reynolds's words is vividly conveyed by a drawing, executed in Rome by another French-speaking artist, Claude Lorrain, showing an artist on a make-shift scaffolding sketching antiquities (fig. 59). The works in this section were produced by this colony.

The genius of Raphael was understood in the seventeenth and eighteenth centuries to have two aspects, the feminine grace of the Madonnas (discussed above) and the manly action and expression of the Tapestry Cartoons (fig. 60). This second aspect was also believed to have been revived by the Carracci, but thereafter it was 'taken forward' by Annibale's leading pupil during his Roman years, Domenichino. This tradition of heroic narrative was adopted by Nicolas Poussin and made into the official style of the French Academy by its first President, Charles Le Brun (1619–90). This was also the official style of English history painting (so far as such a thing existed): Thornhill's scenes of the life of St Paul in the dome of St Paul's Cathedral were clearly intended as a tribute to Raphael's Cartoons; the neo-classical paintings of Gavin Hamilton and Benjamin West first created in Rome during the 1760s take their inspiration from Poussin.[66]

History painting – the poetic depiction of pagan gods, Christian saints and classical heroes – was believed at

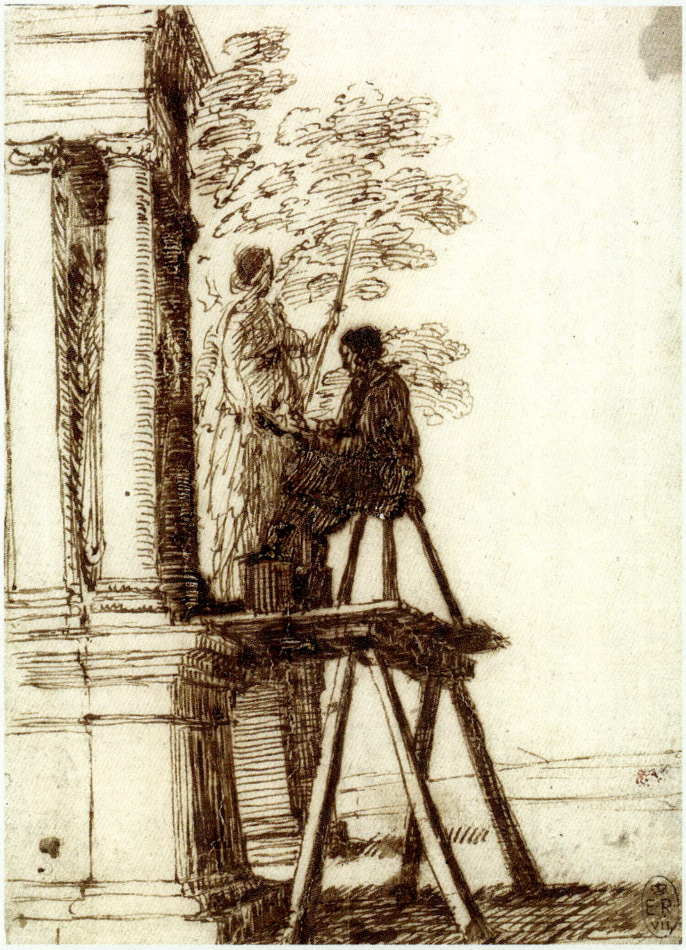

FIG. 59
Claude Gellée, called le Lorrain
An artist drawing a statue, c.1640
Pen and wash, brown ink
RCIN 913092
Acquired by George III in 1762

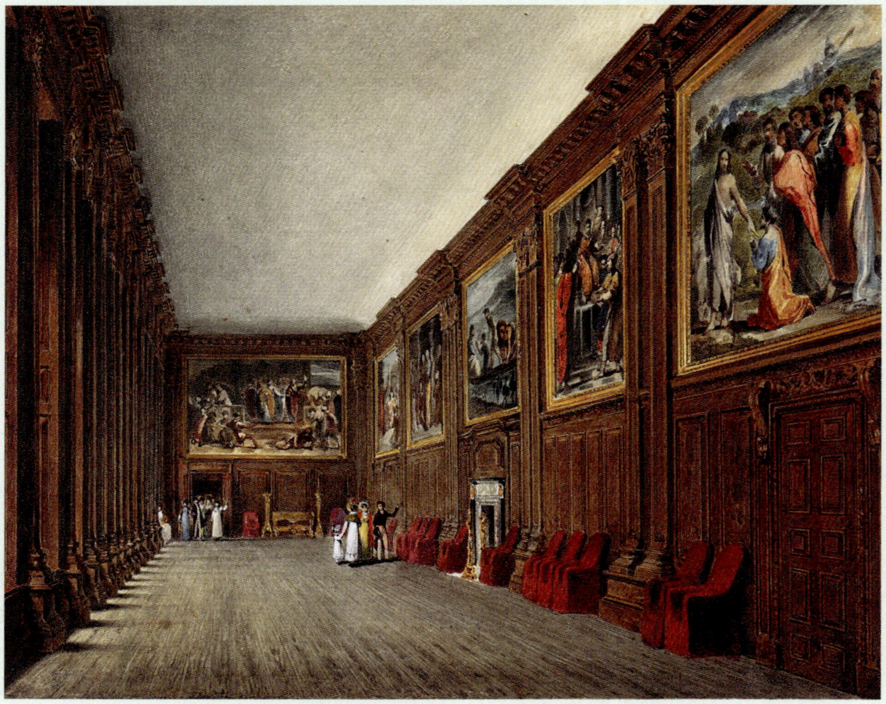

FIG. 60
James Stephanoff
The Cartoon Gallery, Hampton Court, 1818, for Pyne's *Royal Residences*
Watercolour
RCIN 922136

this time to be the highest vocation of the artist. With Domenichino and Poussin landscape painting began to share in this prestige.[67] They created a structured and intellectual form of landscape painting, in which lucid spaces and archaeologically accurate architecture supported the heroic narratives. It is interesting that George III's ideal picture hang (fig. 51) flanks heroic narratives with contemplative landscapes of similar scale and significance. Many of the paintings in this section are first mentioned by George Vertue in 1748 at Leicester House, the home of Frederick, Prince of Wales, in an arrangement which combines 'ancient learning' with landscape painting. Vertue records in the 'next room, or second room – paintings Landskips by Gaspar & Nicolas poussin figures – 4 of them large & fine. – over the chimney. a painting of antient learned men & by Le Seur – a capital picture – a large Landskape by Titian – several noble paintings by Cortona a Battle by Philip Lauro – a most excellent & capital picture – 2 Claud Lorains – and other Italian masters.'[68] An inventory of Leicester House dated September 1749 describes this same hang, confirming that nos 128, 129 and 133 were certainly in this room, and in all probability nos 132, 134 and 135 as well.[69] This group of landscape paintings re-appear in the Blue Velvet Room at Buckingham House in 1819.[70] Charles Wild's watercolour (fig. 55) gives us the earliest impression of how such a 'landscape room' might have looked: Claude's *View of Tivoli* (no. 132) hangs opposite Gaspard Dughet's *Landscape* (RCIN 404647); below, a pair of Dughets (nos 134 and 135) flank Claude's *Landscape with Temple* (RCIN 404690; now thought to be by an imitator). Rubens's *Summer* and *Winter* (RCIN 401416 and 401417) are visible hanging one above the other on the right-hand wall. Dughet's *Jonah* (no. 133) and Claude's *Harbour Scene* (no. 131) were hanging in the room on the fourth wall, not visible in the watercolour. Seventeenth-century portraits by Van Dyck, Lely and others fill the over-door spaces.[71]

The most important groups of Old Master drawings collected during the reigns of George I and George II also emanate from what might be called the 'Poussin circle' in Rome.[72] One album was put together by Cardinal Camillo Massimi, a friend and patron of Poussin and Claude,

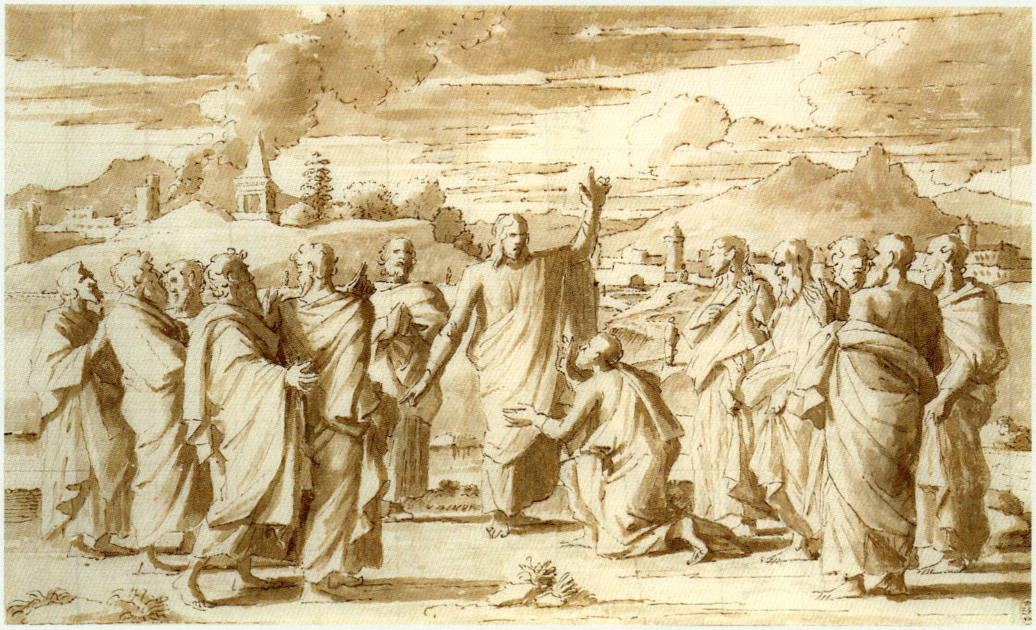

FIG. 61
Nicolas Poussin
Ordination, 1647
Pen and brown ink
RCIN 911899

and acquired after his death by Dr Richard Mead, who sold or gave it to Frederick, Prince of Wales, some time before 1750.[73] Also relevant is the acquisition in 1762 by the young George III of the drawing collection of Cardinal Alessandro Albani, effected through the agency of James Adam (perhaps directed by Lord Bute), which contained Carlo Maratta's drawing collection and that of the great Roman seventeenth-century antiquarian Cassiano dal Pozzo.[74] Dal Pozzo was the most inspiring pedant in the history of art. He represented the classical learning and systematic archaeology of the period, while at the same time befriending, patronising and influencing artists of every type, including Bernini, Pietro da Cortona, Poussin and Claude. In short, in some twenty years between the early 1740s and 1762 Frederick and his eldest son had put together one the world's most important collection of drawings relating to seventeenth-century Roman archaeology and landscape painting. The drawings illustrated here as comparatives show how close a relationship existed between them and the paintings in this section. As an example, Poussin's preparatory drawing (fig. 61) for his *Ordination* of 1747 (National Gallery of Scotland), acquired by Frederick, Prince of Wales, shows the link between heroic figure painting in the tradition of Raphael and classical landscape painting, with distances measured out by classical architecture.[75]

The Georgians' favourite landscape painter was Claude, whose work was always considered more delightful and simply beautiful than that of his sterner contemporary Nicolas Poussin. But even Claude landscapes seem to have been advanced under this classical and intellectual banner in eighteenth-century England. Claude was described by Horace Walpole as 'the Raphael of Landscape-Painting'.[76] Reynolds explained in 1771 that Claude found beauty not by 'taking nature as he found it' but by compiling landscapes out of 'various drafts' made 'from various beautiful scenes and prospects', a practice 'founded upon the same principle as that by which the Historical Painter acquires perfect form'.[77]

129

EUSTACHE LE SUEUR (1616–1655)

Caligula depositing the Ashes of his Mother and Brother in the Tomb of his Ancestors 1647

Oil on canvas, 161.3 × 122.3 cm
RCIN 404983

PROVENANCE Acquired by Frederick, Prince of Wales, by 1749

LITERATURE *Queen's Pictures* 1991, p. 134, no. 43; Rorschach 1993, pp. 62–3, no. 50; Mérot 2000, pp. 228–9, no. 77; *Eustache Le Sueur* 2000, p. 111, no. 29

Le Sueur was a pupil of Simon Vouet (1590–1649) who was much commended in the literature of the seventeenth century for deserting the style of his teacher in favour of that of Nicolas Poussin and Raphael, though he never made the trip to Italy.[78] Le Sueur's reputation reached its zenith in the eighteenth century, when he was regarded as the 'French Raphael': Charles de Brosse wrote in 1739–40, 'Le Sueur our French Raphael, were he to colour as well as he invents and draws, would he not be as much the 'Divine Le Sueur' as the other is the 'Divine Raphael'?'[79] The fact that Frederick, Prince of Wales, hung this painting of 'antient learned men' in the most prestigious place (over the mantel) in his room of French painting at Leicester House (see above, p. 240) suggests that he was well aware of the prestige which the artist enjoyed in Paris at this time.

This work was painted in 1647 for Claude de Guénégaud for his hôtel in the Marais (since destroyed) as one of a pair. The other painting, known only through preparatory drawings,[80] depicted the rare and edifying story of Lucius Albinus: when escaping from the sack of Rome by the Gauls, Lucius encountered the Vestal Virgins carrying their sacred flame; immediately he ordered his wife and children out of his chariot in order to make way for this public rather than personal treasure.[81] The story of no. 129 is similarly rare and comes from Suetonius' *Life* of Caligula, who began his reign on a wave of popularity and relief at the death of his predecessor, Tiberius. Caligula particularly impressed the Roman people by the piety with which he returned to Rome the ashes of his brothers and mother, exiled and murdered by Tiberius. After the ashes had been brought to Ostia and thence up the Tiber to Rome he 'arranged that the most distinguished knights available should carry them to the Mausoleum, about noon, when the streets were at their busiest'.[82] This scene is obviously set in a graveyard with, to the right, the Pyramid of Gaius Cestius, a familiar Roman funereal landmark (see fig. 62). Caligula is shown seated to the right with a laurel crown and baton of office. He gestures towards an elderly priest, who is in the act of placing one urn into one of the arches in the base of a sarcophagus, revealed by removing the slab of marble at his feet. A second urn rests on a tripod table at which kneels an acolyte. To the right, another priest looks on while, to the left, a group of soldiers strain forward to pay their respects with their standards and lances seen against the sky. Part of Caligula's appeal was that he was said to be 'born in a barracks'. Suetonius relates that as a child he wore the miniature uniform of a private soldier, including the *caliga*, or half-boot, from which he gained his nick-name 'Caligula' (little boot) and which he wears here. All this gave him a special hold on the affections of the common soldier.[83]

These subjects must have been chosen by Claude de Guénégaud with good reason; to us they remain puzzling, for, while Lucius Albinus was unquestionably virtuous,

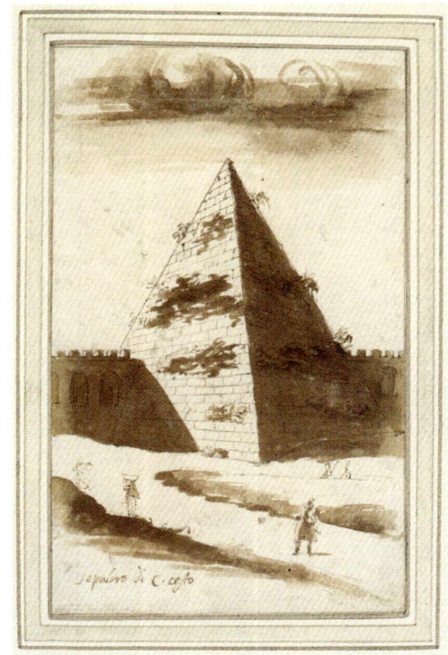

FIG. 62
Giovanni Antonio Dosio
The Pyramid of Gaius Cestius
Pen and wash, brown ink
RCIN 910794
Acquired by George III in 1762

Caligula turned out to be an infamous monster. Perhaps we are to recognise an angry petulance in Caligula's expression, which allows us to read dramatic irony in what is otherwise a conventional image of piety. Perhaps there is a contrast intended between the plebeian Lucius himself lifting his children off his chariot for the public good and the patrician Caligula ordering another to bear his mother's urn for the sake of public relations. The British owners of this painting clearly understood its meaning, though with slight errors of identification. The Leicester House inventory of 1749 describes the episode as the funeral of Caligula's father Germanicus rather than of his mother Agrippina.[84] Boydell's print of the painting, dated 1765 and dedicated to its owner, the Princess Dowager of Wales, describes it as 'Nero depositing the ashes of Britannicus', referring to the story of another psychopathic emperor, this time honouring the ashes of his noble stepbrother, Britannicus, whom he had himself poisoned.[85] DS-T

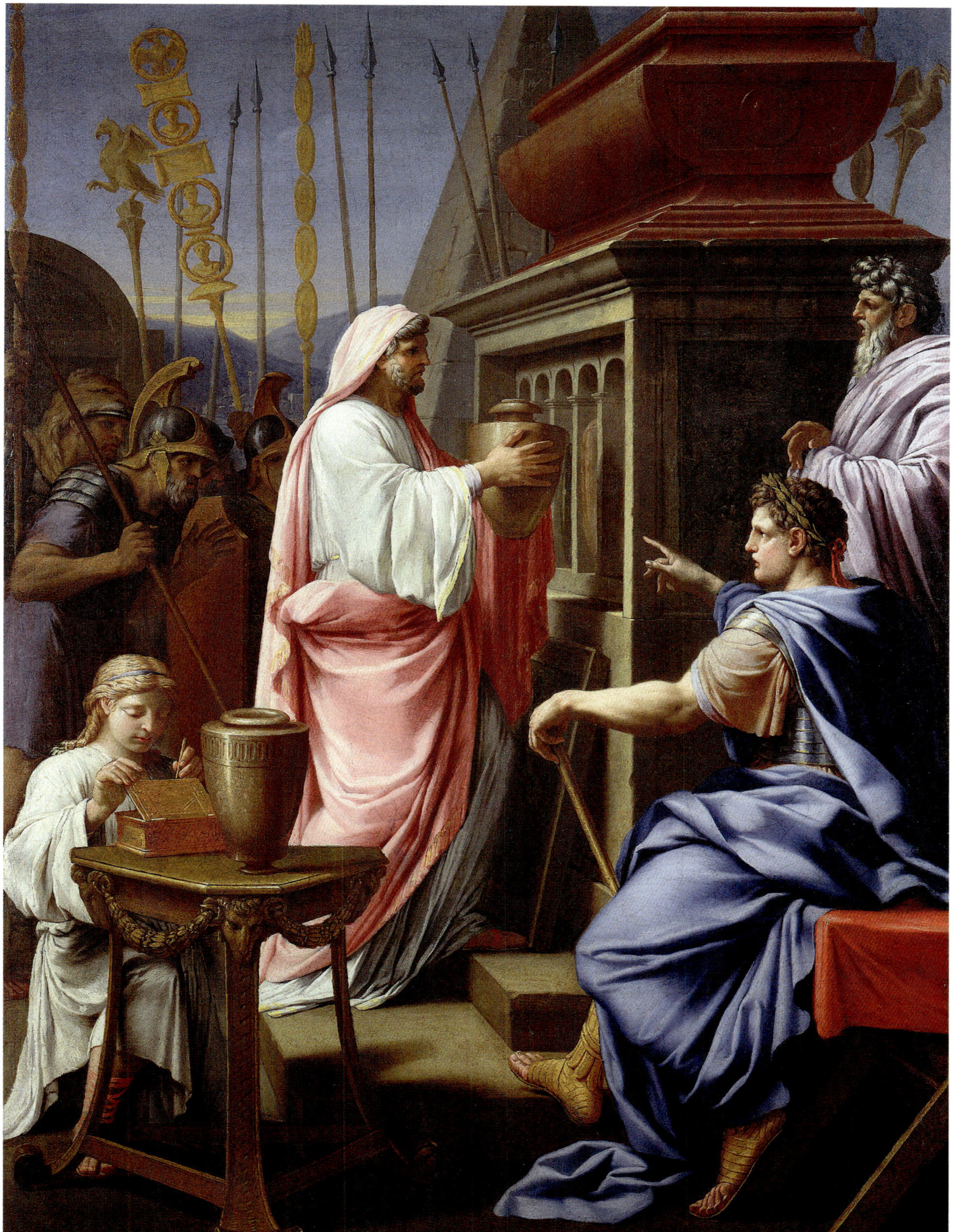

130

TROPHIME BIGOT (1579–1650)

Christ in the Carpenter's Shop *c.*1630

Oil on canvas, 99.0 × 135.8 cm
RCIN 404753

PROVENANCE First recorded in the collection of George III; perhaps acquired by Frederick, Prince of Wales

LITERATURE Wright 1985, p. 140

Bigot was a Provençal artist, the author of several signed altarpieces for Arles and Aix, who is documented in Rome between 1620 and 1634: he may also have been the creator of a coherent group of Caravaggesque scenes (once attributed to the 'Candlelight Master') of which this is a fine example.[86] None of this would have concerned the original royal purchaser of no. 130, whether Frederick, Prince of Wales, or his son George III, for the work is first recorded (in a 'Passage at Kensington Palace' in 1819) as 'G. della Notte. An Old Man and Boy by Lamplight ... Very good'.[87]

Gherardo della Notte is the Italians' name for Gerrit van Honthorst, who spent some years in Rome (1616–20) immediately before Bigot arrived. Both artists spent their Roman years looking at the work of Caravaggio. Writers on art in the seventeenth and eighteenth centuries generally disapproved of Caravaggio, though not with entirely blind prejudice: they liked his realism, hated his unvarnished ugliness and disapproved of his habit of masking bad drawing with dark shadows.[88] There was certainly enough interest in Caravaggesque tenebrist realism throughout this period for the work of slightly softer-edged followers, like Honthorst, to be collected. Honthorst had another advantage for the Georgians: he had worked in London for Charles I in 1628 and contributed many important portraits to the Royal Collection.[89]

No. 130 is a good example of what in the eighteenth century would have been regarded as the acceptable face of Caravaggism, with an old, un-idealised face providing a contrast with a young and beautiful one and with everyday objects providing immediacy and verisimilitude.[90] Joseph hacks at a piece of wood with a chisel, which conceals the flame of an oil lamp being filled by the Christ Child. The two chisels visible in the painting, the jar marked '*olio*' and the metal lamp with linked rods attached to hang it from the wall are all recognisably early seventeenth-century objects. In a way characteristic of Caravaggio the story has been re-told in modern dress and was believed in 1819 to depict merely an 'Old Man and Boy' (see above). Of course it is much more than this, as Bigot has made it seem that the Christ Child is the source of the light, not the hidden flame, reminding us that He is the 'Light of the World'. DS-T

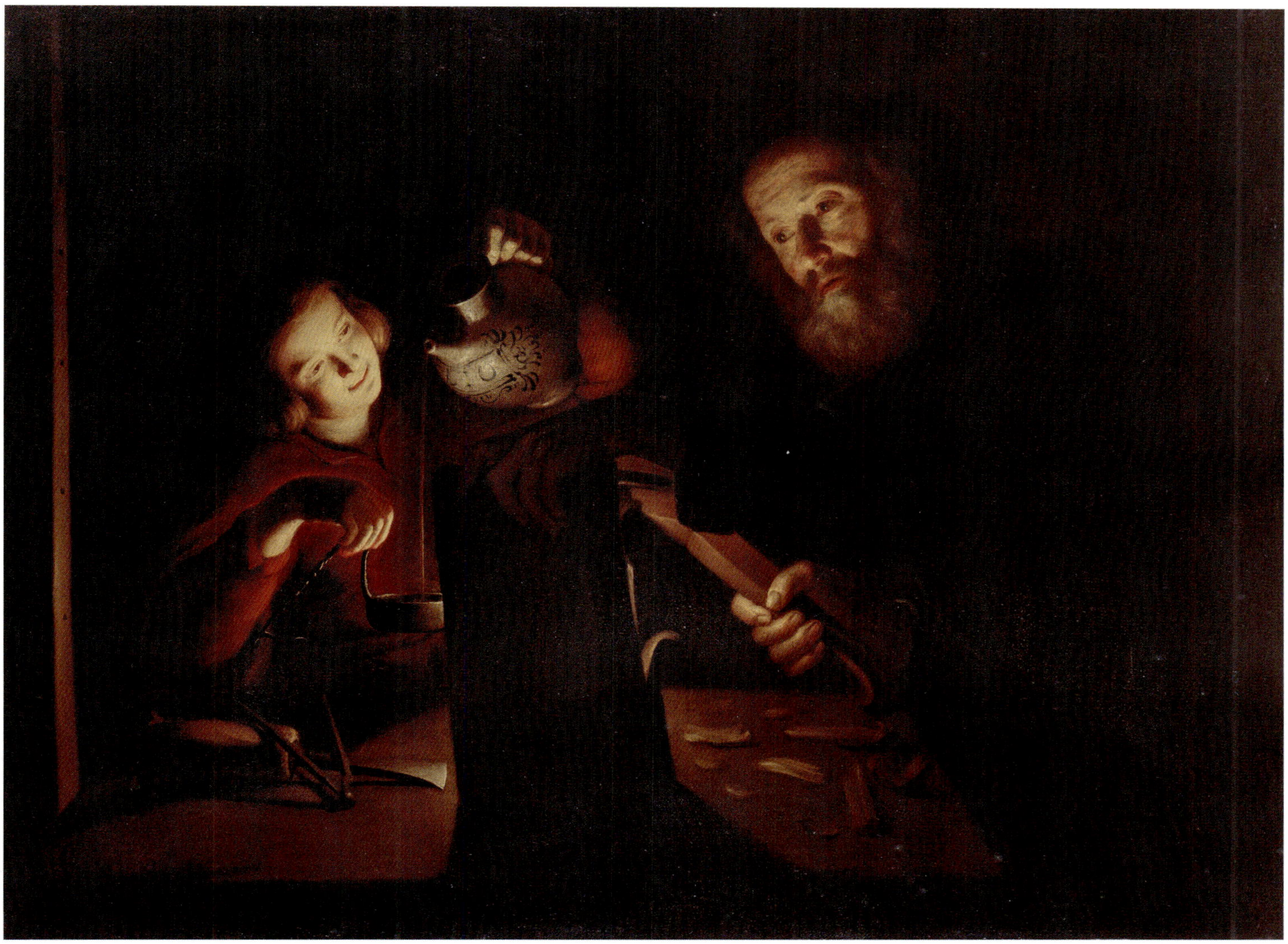

131

CLAUDE GELLÉE, CALLED LE LORRAIN (1600/4–1682)

Harbour Scene at Sunset 1643

Oil on canvas, 74.3 × 99.4 cm
RCIN 401382

PROVENANCE Probably in the collection Frederick, Prince of Wales, by 1748

LITERATURE Roethlisberger 1961, no. LV19; *Queen's Pictures* 1991, p. 132, no. 42; Rorschach 1993, p. 59, no. 18; *Dutch Landscapes* 2010, no. 30

From early in his career Claude sold landscapes for very high prices to kings, popes and the cream of the French and Italian nobility. So successful was he that he started recording each of his compositions in his 'Book of Truth' (*Liber Veritatis*) to prevent the circulation of forgeries.[91] The English did not discover Claude, but their passion for his works was the single most remarkable aspect of Georgian taste.[92]

This landscape, though possibly mentioned at Leicester House (see above, p. 240), is first catalogued unambiguously in 1819 in the Blue Room at Buckingham House (on the wall not shown in fig. 55), where it is described as 'The perfection of the Master, and in as perfect preservation as when it came from the easel of the Painter'.[93] Such enthusiasm is certainly justified. This port scene has a precision of detail and brilliance of colour which Claude seems to have reserved for his most important patrons. Unfortunately the provenance of the painting is not known as it is not recorded in the *Liber Veritatis*; instead it seems to be a reprise with variations of Claude's LV 19 of 1637.[94] The fleur-de-lys on the ship's mast to the upper left suggests that he may have undertaken it at the instigation of a member of the French royal family.

Claude's port seems to be loosely inspired by the bay of Naples: the towers in the water are reminiscent of the Castel dell'Ovo and the distant mountain a sort of Vesuvius. However, architecture has been imported from Rome to dignify the scene: the towers resemble attenuated versions of the Castel Sant'Angelo; the pyramid of Gaius Cestius (see fig. 62) can be seen in the background and the Arch of the Argentarii takes pride of place in the right foreground. All these landmarks were recorded in drawings which joined the collection in these years (see fig. 63, acquired by George III in 1762).[95] Frederick and his English contemporaries particularly seized upon this sort of archaeological detail as an indication of shared learning and a stimulus for reflection.[96] One detail suggests that Claude and his original patrons thought in the same way: the temple to the right of the pyramid (apparently an invention of Claude's) contains the clearly recognisable figure of *Fortuna*, a naked woman with flying drapery balancing on an orb. What better goddess to preside over this scene, where wealth, luxury and life itself are dependent upon the hazards of the sea?

The frame provided for this painting, presumably by Frederick, Prince of Wales, justifies the term 'rococo'. The main body of the frame is entirely replaced by bundles of reeds, bending like volutes, which link up the eight cartouches, while fictive flowers grow freely over the surface. The curious membrane – shell-like in form and resembling seaweed in substance – is a typical example of rococo fantasy. DS-T

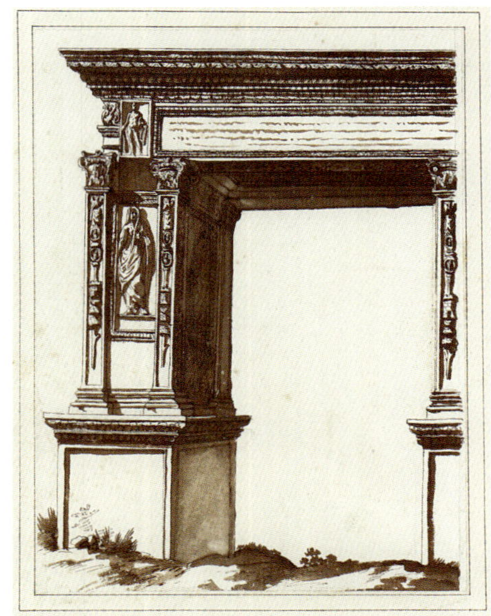

FIG. 63
Circle of Poussin
The Arch of the Argentarii, 1620s
Pen and brown ink
RCIN 908237

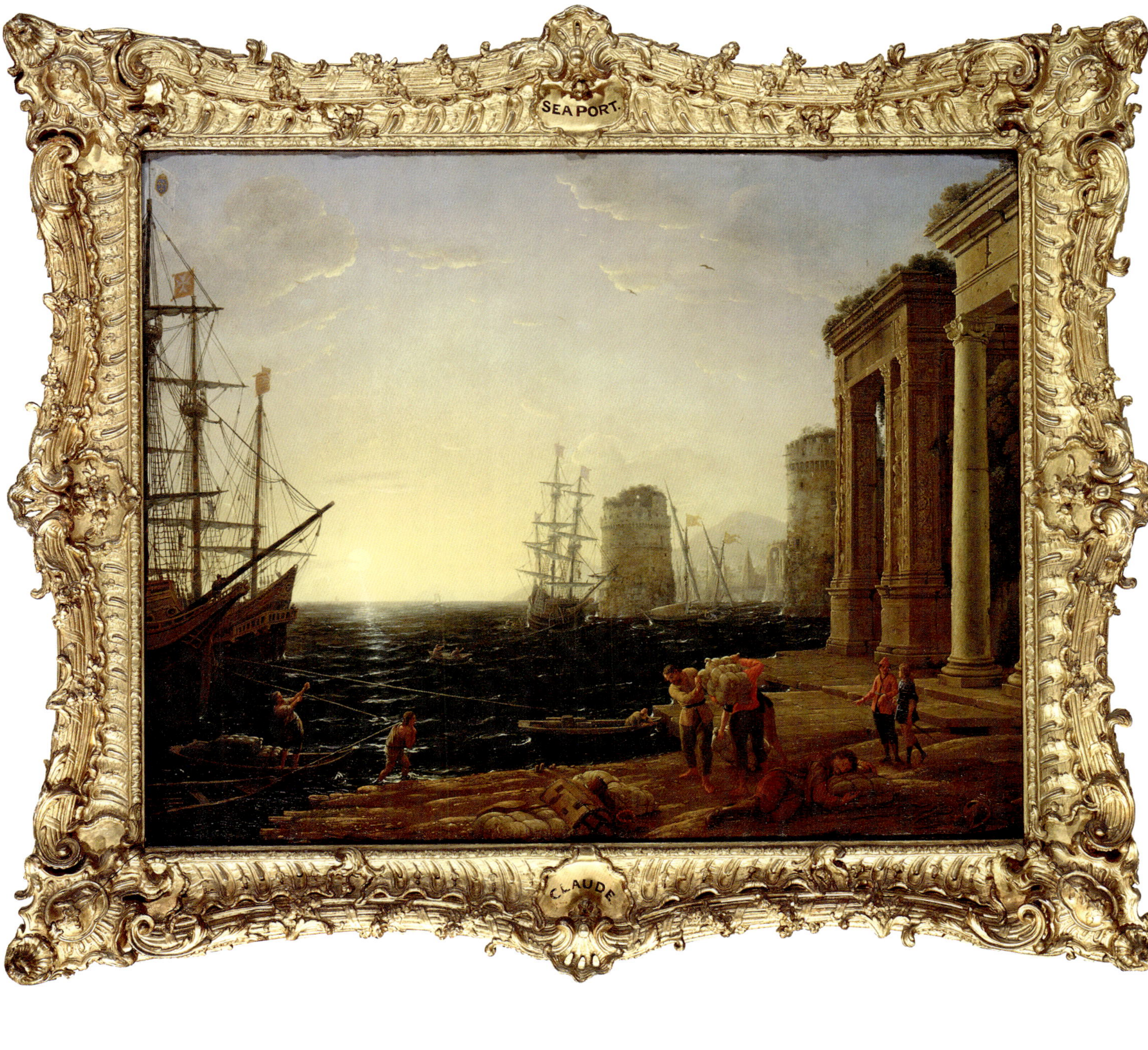
SEA PORT.
CLAUDE

132

CLAUDE GELLÉE, CALLED LE LORRAIN (1600/4–1682)

View of the Roman Campagna from Tivoli 1645

Oil on canvas, 98.2 × 131.2 cm
RCIN 404688

PROVENANCE Painted for Michael Passart; purchased by Frederick, Prince of Wales, by 1748

LITERATURE Roethlisberger 1961, LV 89; Kitson 1978 no. 89; Rorschach 1993, p. 60, no. 21; Chomer 2000, no. 44; *Royal Treasures* 2002, pp. 83–4, no. 12

This landscape is probably the 'Evening' listed in the 1749 inventory of Leicester House, hanging next to 'Morning' (RCIN 404690), both by Claude; it is probably one of the Claude's seen there by Vertue (see above, p. 240).[97] It is first catalogued unambiguously in 1819 in the Blue Room at Buckingham House and is visible in Wild's watercolour view of the room (fig. 55), making a group with three Dughets (nos 134–5 and RCIN 404647).[98] It was then identified as a 'View of Rome from Tivoli', which is surely correct, though it is not possible to identify the spot where the view was taken. There is a cascade to the left and the dome of St Peter's visible on the horizon.

Tivoli was Europe's first beauty spot. It possessed every element sought by Grand Tourists – two cascades with wild and picturesque rocks; a gentle distant panorama of Rome and the surrounding *campagna*; the ruin of the circular Temple of Vesta; and, nearby, the excavations of the Villa of the Emperor Hadrian and the Renaissance gardens of the Villa d'Este. To the left of no. 132 can be seen a distinct pattern of buildings at Tivoli: at the extreme left a line of roofs ending in a tower, which is the modern town; beyond and lower down this same shape is replicated in the arches of the ruins of the so-called 'Villa of Maecenas'. A reconstruction of this same building (RCIN 910387) joined the Royal Collection with the Cassiano dal Pozzo material mentioned above.[99] This still-extant structure is now thought to be the 'Temple of Victorious Hercules' and seems less romantic than it did when believed to be a beautifully sited villa belonging to the most famous patron of the arts in history. It is not difficult to imagine the reaction of a classically educated Englishman contemplating the ruins of terraces upon which Horace and Virgil might have sat.

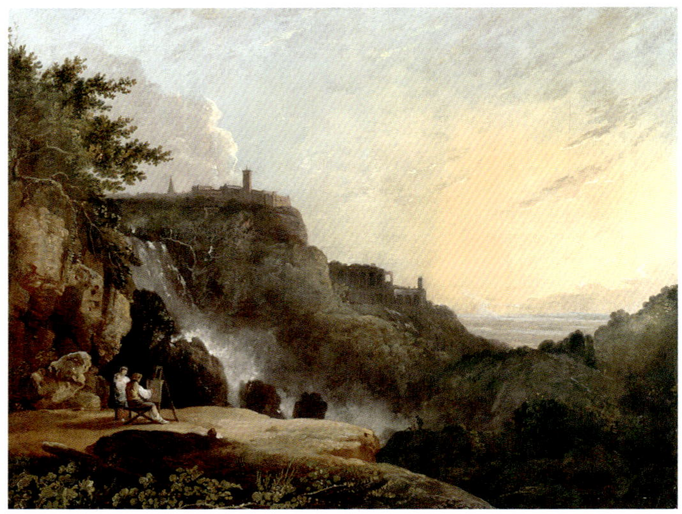

FIG. 64
Richard Wilson
View of Tivoli, 1752
Oil on canvas
Dulwich Picture Gallery

Soon after Frederick acquired this painting British artists began to explore the same terrain. Richard's Wilson's depiction of Tivoli (fig. 64), usually dated 1752, shows the standard accompaniment for any beauty-spot – an artist at his easel. A drawing by Wilson depicting the Villa of Maecenas from below rather than above is inscribed with the date April 1754, and the company – Viscount Bolingbroke (1734–87) and the Earls of Pembroke (1734–94), Essex (1732–99) and Thanet (1733–86) – all of whom 'dined and spend the Day together on the Spot under a Large Tree'.[100]

It is often suggested that the English projected a more elegiac meaning onto Claude's scenes than originally intended. But Claude's patron would surely have been familiar with the fame of Maecenas, and might he not also have seen some moral in the rhyming forms of ancient villa and modern Tivoli, as the sun sets over the 'Eternal City'?
DS-T

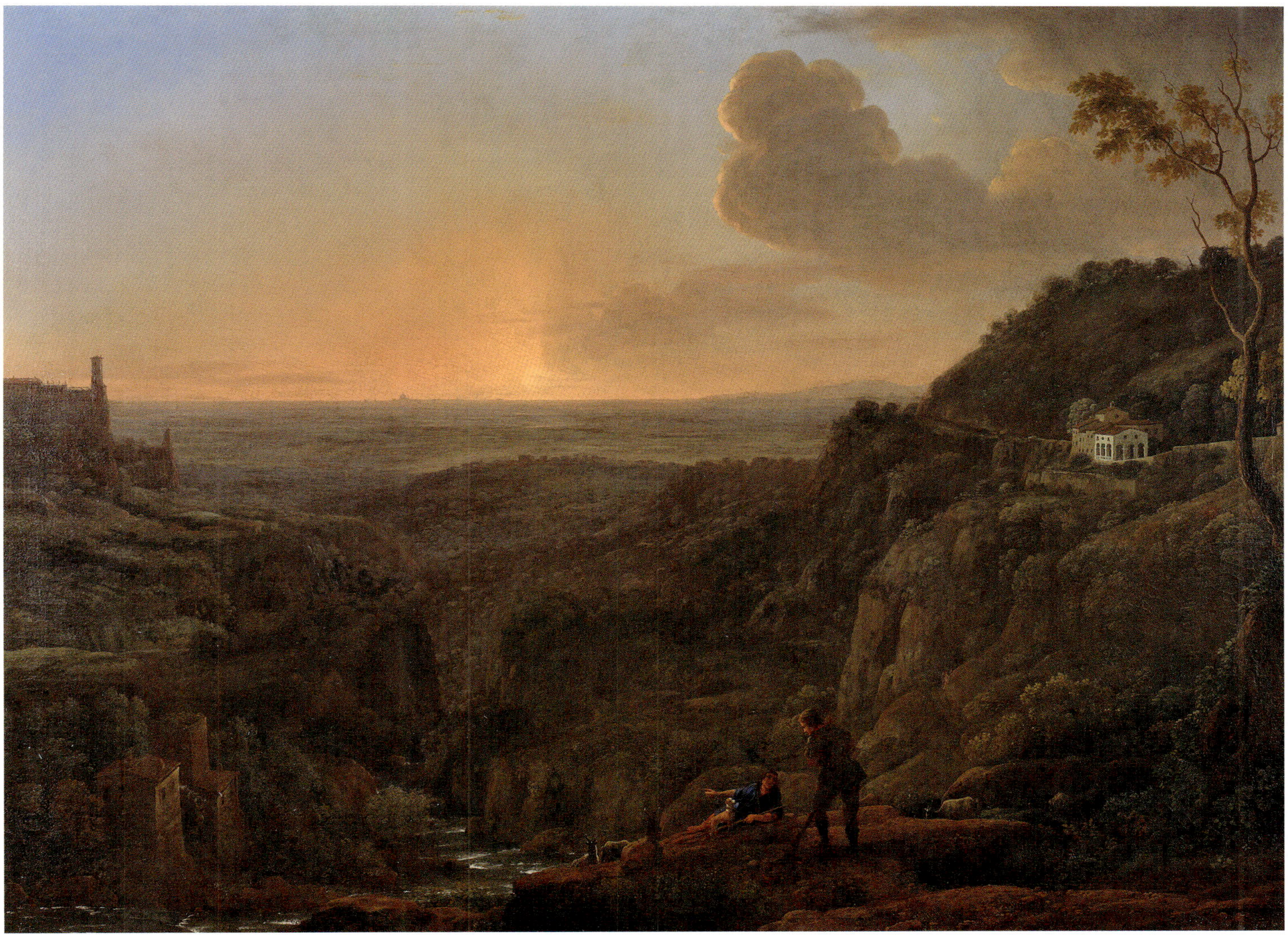

133

GASPARD DUGHET (1615–1675)

Seascape with Jonah and the Whale c.1653–4

Oil on canvas, 97.8 × 136.1 cm
RCIN 405355

PROVENANCE Painted for the Marchese Niccolò Maria Pallavicini; acquired by Humphrey Edwin and from him *c.*1745 by Frederick, Prince of Wales

LITERATURE Passavant 1836, I, pp. 111–2; Walpole 1752, p. 94; *Gaspard Dughet* 1980, pp. 38–9, no. 6; Boisclair 1986, no. 127; Rorschach 1993, pp. 60–1, no. 31

Soon after Nicolas Poussin's arrival in Rome in 1624 he was nursed through an illness by a French cook named Jacques Dughet. Poussin ended up marrying Jacques's daughter, Ann Marie in 1630, employing one son, Jean, as a secretary (and later guardian of his legacy) and training another, Gaspard, as a painter.[101] Gaspard Dughet not only adopted his brother-in-law's style of landscape but also his name. This canny marketing ploy paid off especially during the eighteenth century, when collectors had need of symmetrical wall-fillers and yet a relatively small pool of acceptable Old Master 'names' from which to find them. The very high proportion of paintings sold in this period attributed jointly to both Nicolas and Gaspard Poussin – two artists that modern scholars believe never collaborated – suggests that the art market was happy to exploit this blurred distinction.[102]

No. 133 had just such a joint attribution. It is described in the Leicester House inventory of 1749 as a collaboration of Gaspard and Nicolas Poussin, an attribution repeated in the print after the painting made in 1748 by François Vivares.[103] The work hung in the Blue Room at Buckingham House (though not visible in fig. 55), where it is described as Gaspard Poussin's masterpiece, for 'power of execution, for conception and for force of effect, unquestionably the finest work known of this Master'.[104]

The subject comes from the first chapter of the Book of Jonah: a great storm can only be assuaged if the jinxed man leaves the ship; Jonah offers himself and is thrown overboard, where he is swallowed by a great fish; he spends three days praying within the belly of the fish before God commands it to vomit him up on dry land. The subject had a profound religious significance as a premonition of the sacrifice of Christ, which is why in 1588 Paul Bril was commissioned to paint a fresco of the subject for the Scala Santa – the model for this composition.[105] Dughet also uses the subject as an opportunity to paint chaos and catastrophe, which would have been seen in a more religious light in his day. His inspiration lies in the work of Nicolas Poussin, which is probably why the joint authorship was first suggested. Poussin was admired for matching weather conditions and human tragedies, as he did with his *Pyramus and Thisbe* of 1651 (Alte Pinakothek, Munich), which was in England by 1750 and widely known through a Vivares print. Poussin's biographer Félibien explained how he represented the most extraordinary effects of nature, however difficult, 'accompanying his landscapes with stories or with suitable actions; as in this case which is stormy weather he has found a sad and lugubrious subject'.[106] For English collectors it was especially this ability which gave landscape a role in 'history painting'. For exhibition in 1760, Richard Wilson painted his *Destruction of the Children of Niobe*, in which a Dughet-like storm is similarly employed to express the idea of an angry god.[107]

In 1757 Edmund Burke published his *Philosophical Inquiry into the Origin of Our Ideas of the Sublime and Beautiful*, in which he attempted to describe the attraction in art of scenes which in life we would shun. He listed particular attributes of fearful or 'sublime' subjects, all of which can be seen in this painting – darkness, vacuity, 'sad and fuscous colours' and a 'rudeness of work', which 'excludes the idea of art and contrivance' (Part II, Sections VI, XII and XVI). DS-T

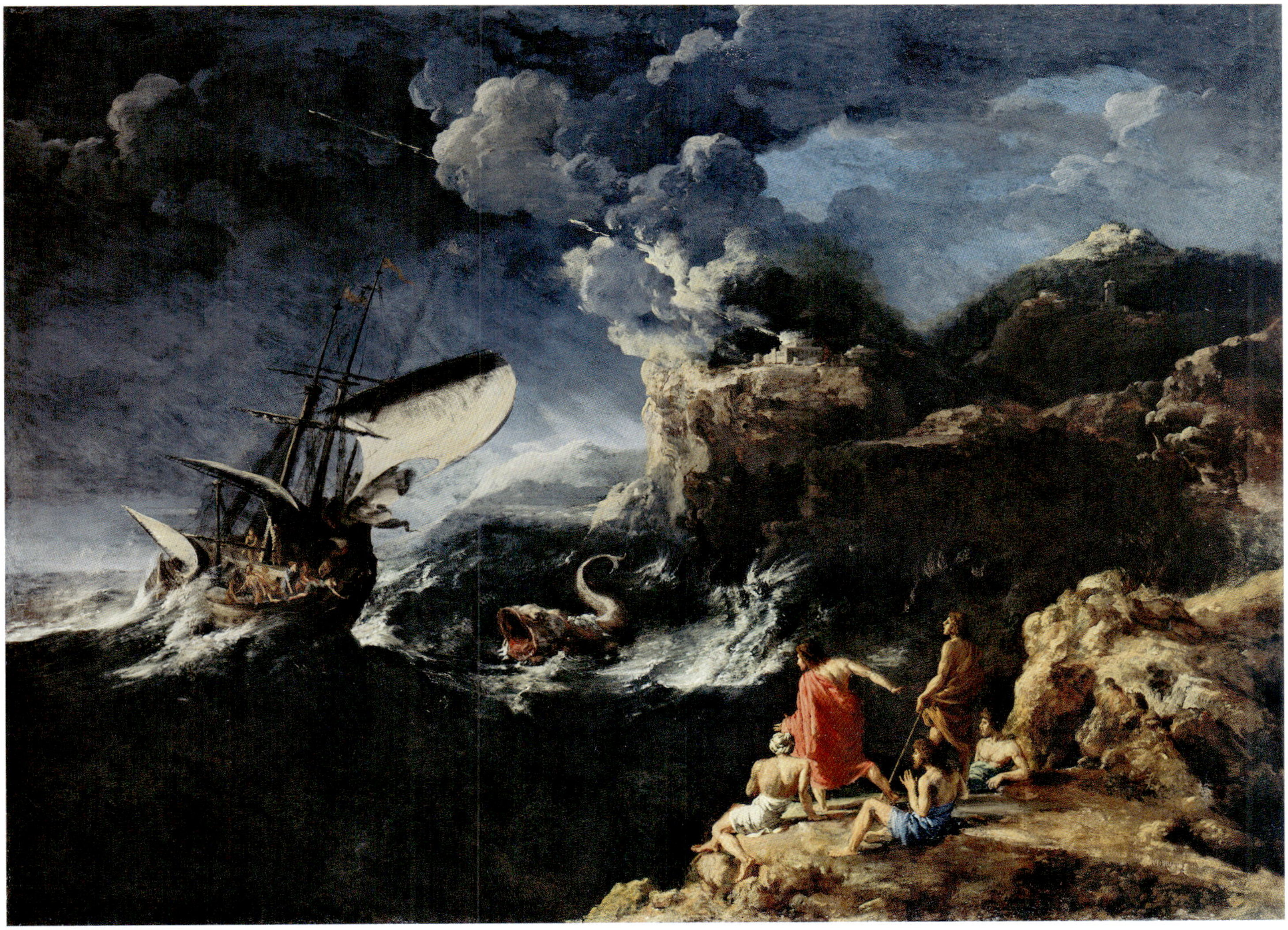

134 & 135

GASPARD DUGHET (1615–1675)

Landscape with Figures beside a Waterfall c.1653–4

Oil on canvas, 100.0 × 139.8 cm
RCIN 405320

Landscape with Figures by a Pool c.1670–5

Oil on canvas, 97.1 × 133.3 cm
RCIN 405318

PROVENANCE Acquired by Frederick, Prince of Wales, before 1749

LITERATURE Passavant I, p. 112; *Gaspard Dughet* 1980, pp. 37–8, no. 5 (no. 134) and no. 21 (no. 135); Boisclair 1986, no. 120 (no. 134) and no. 310 (no. 135)

The advantage of Gaspard Dughet for Georgian collectors was that he painted a large quantity of works and employed standard sizes, which meant that he produced excellent wall fillers.[108] These two landscapes were certainly not painted as a pair – no. 134 dates from the early 1650s and no. 135 from the 1670s – but they had become one by 1819, when they can be seen hanging on either side of a Claude landscape in the Blue Room at Buckingham House (fig. 55).[109] It is probable that they were among the paintings seen by Vertue hanging in Leicester House in 1749; their matching frames of this period would suggest that they had already found each other at this date.

No. 134 relates to Nicolas Poussin's mood landscapes, like his *Man frightened by a Snake* of 1648 (National Gallery). Dughet uses the same sombre palate – a hot red earth colour ground clashing with the green grass and heavy slate-blue sky. There is here the suggestion of a narrative in the piping boy and the shepherd hurrying off to the right – an arrangement similar to one of Claude's favoured subjects, Mercury stealing the herds of Admetus.

Dughet's landscapes were especially admired for the touch of the paintbrush: another landscape (RCIN 404647) was described in the inventory of 1819 as painted 'with the force and spirit of Salvator Rosa'.[110] This may be seen in both these landscapes in the way in which dry paint is thickly applied, almost dragged, over a coarse weave of canvas, producing frayed edges – a technique derived from Titian. The roughness of the paint paradoxically produces a soft effect on the eye, especially when seen from a distance. Such application favours the rough terrain, the rocks and the waterfalls depicted here. In the eighteenth century this style of landscape (and paint application) was called 'Picturesque' and represented a category of landscape distinct from the sublime and the beautiful.[111] DS-T

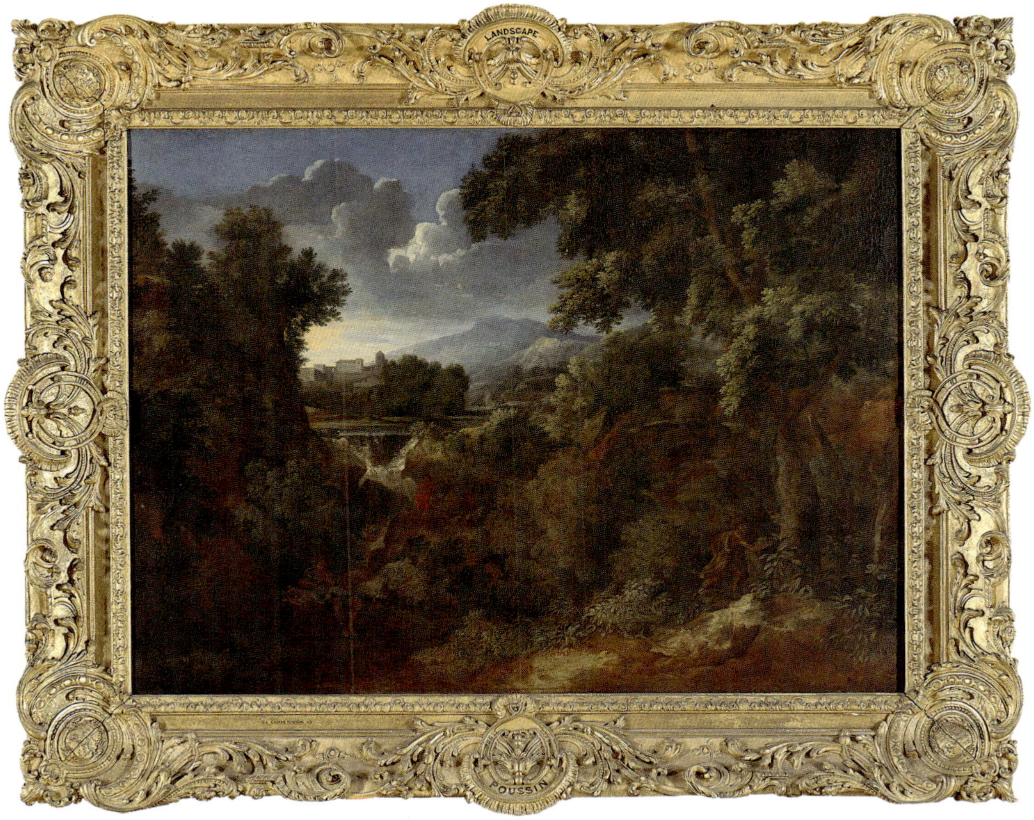
LANDSCAPE
POUSSIN

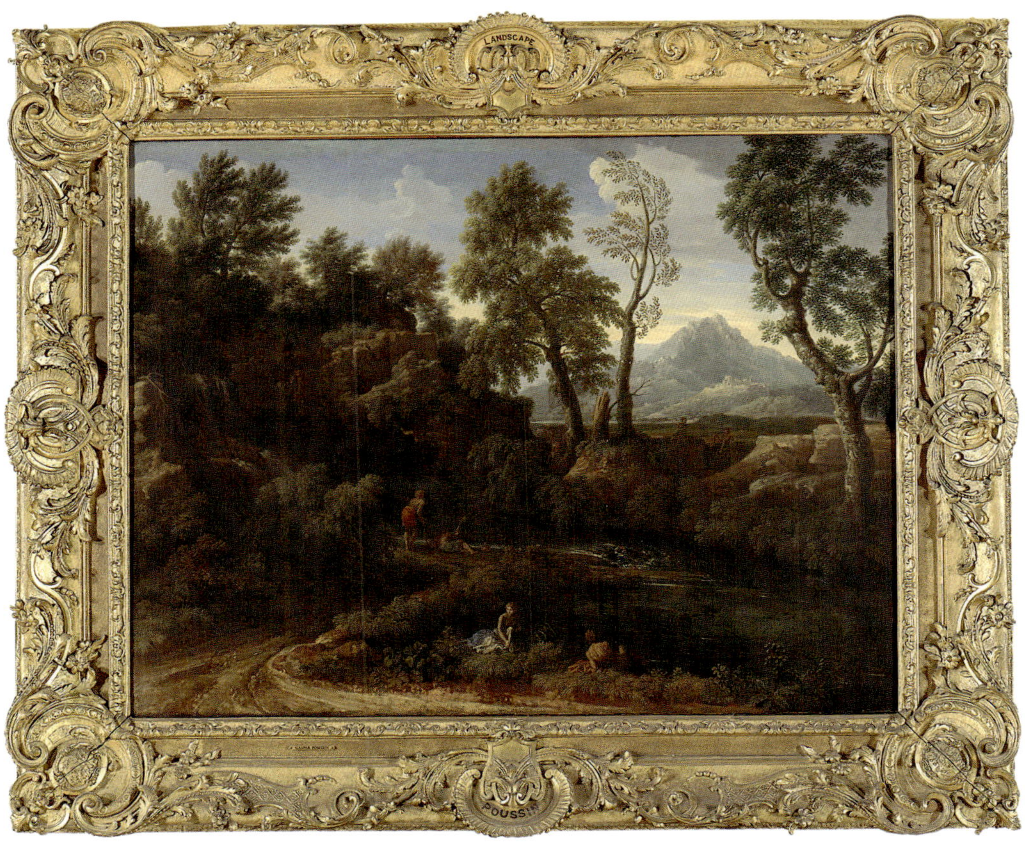
LANDSCAPE
POUSSIN

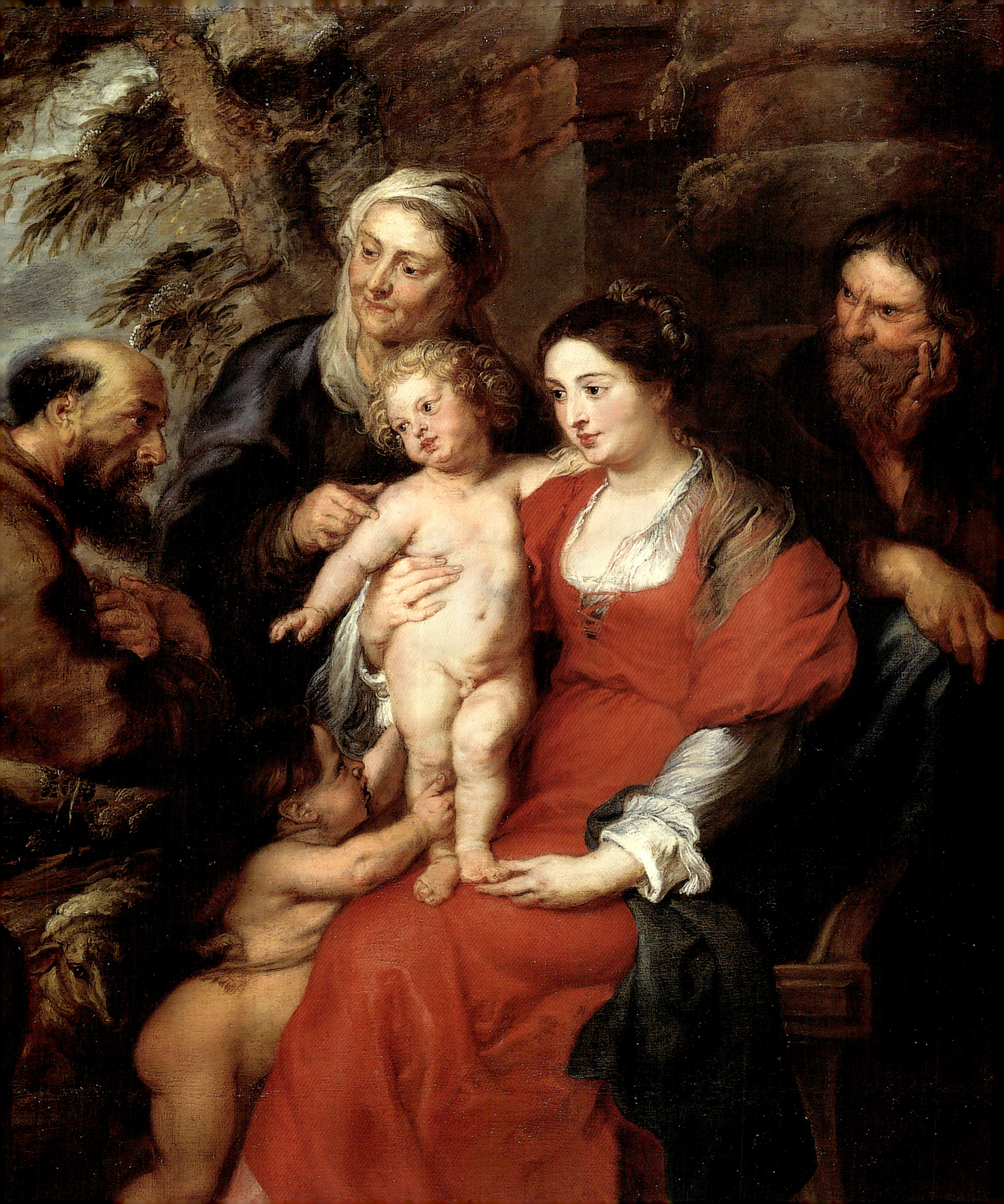

Venetian painting hardly features amongst royal acquisitions in the Georgian period. The frequent references in the 1750 inventory of Kensington Palace to prominently hung paintings by Giorgione, Titian, Veronese, Bassano, Tintoretto, Paris Bordone, 'Old' and 'Young' Palma, suggest that the Hanoverians admired Venetian painting well enough, but that their needs were satisfied by the riches they had inherited from the Stuarts.[112] The King's Gallery at Kensington is today hung according to the scheme William Kent devised in 1727 for George I, with most of the paintings surrounded by frames of his design (fig. 65). The hang is dominated by large Venetian paintings, in particular two Tintorettos from Mantua (RCIN 407247 and 405476), though interspersed with some Correggios.[113] At either end Kent hung the huge Van Dycks, the 'Great Piece' (RCIN 405353) and the equestrian portrait of Charles I (RCIN 405322), both now replaced by copies. (Both dominating pairs – the Tintorettos [RCIN 407247 and 405476] and the large Van Dycks [RCIN 405353 and 405322] – were given stardardised dimensions by adding strips to the top of the smaller of the two.)[114] Thus the King's Gallery featured a magnificent image of Charles I amongst the magnificence of his collection. Kent's other spectacular arrangement at Kensington was in the Great Drawing Room, where paintings believed to be by Titian, Bassano and Veronese were hung with Michelangelo's 'fat Venus' (fig. 19; see under no. 31) and the pair of Guido Renis (see under no. 126).[115] Queen Caroline's disruption of these paintings greatly annoyed George II (see p. 80). In pride of place in the Great Drawing Room over the mantel Kent hung Rubens's *Holy Family* (no. 137), which Vertue described as having a 'brilliance superior to all the rest'.

The prominence given to Van Dyck in the King's Gallery and to Rubens in the Great Drawing Room suggests something which was accepted wisdom in the period, namely that these two artists represented a continuation of the tradition of Venetian painting. The Hanoverians inherited fine paintings by Rubens and Van Dyck as well as by their Venetian masters, but in this case they were evidently eager for more. Two huge Rubens paintings were bought by George I from the famous Scottish economist John Law (1671–1729) after his return to England in 1723 (nos 136 and 137). Four canvases of a similar scale in the Rubens-Van Dyck orbit were acquired by Frederick, Prince of Wales, and are recorded hanging the 3rd Room at Leicester House in 1749 – no. 138; Rubens, *Philip II* (RCIN 404392); Rubens, *The Family of Sir Balthasar Gerbier* (RCIN 405415, then thought to be a collaboration with Van Dyck); and Van Dyck, *St Martin dividing his Cloak* (RCIN 405878, then thought to be by Rubens).[116] Three of these four hung together in the Crimson Drawing Room at Buckingham House (fig. 53). Frederick, Prince of Wales, also acquired a famous pair of Rubens landscapes (RCIN 401416, 401417), which hung at Leicester House in 1749 and later joined the Poussins and Claudes in the Blue Velvet Room at Buckingham House (they appear one above the other on the right of fig. 55).[117] After various moves all eight paintings mentioned above were brought together by William IV in the King's Drawing Room at Windsor, thereafter known as the 'Rubens Room' (fig. 66).[118] Frederick, Prince of Wales, also acquired five portraits by Van Dyck, nos 139 and 140 and an unidentified *Lady* (RCIN 404399), *Beatrice de Cusance* (RCIN 404404) and *Man*

DETAIL, NO. 137

FIG. 65
The King's Gallery, Kensington Palace, Historic Royal Palaces

(RCIN 407188). In the reign of William IV these all joined Van Dycks belonging to Charles I in the Queen's Ball Room at Windsor to make the 'Van Dyck Room'.[119]

The prestige of Van Dyck and Rubens depended upon more than their love of Venetian art: they were also touched by Raphael. George Vertue even thought that it was Rubens who had brought Raphael's tapestries to England, which explained why one could see connections between them and the old man in his *St Martin and the Beggar* (RCIN 405878).[120] During this period Rubens and Van Dyck were the most inspiring and yet (especially Rubens) troublesome artists within the canon. Bellori includes both in his twelve lives, a great honour for non-Italians, and praises both for their colour: Rubens 'took to Flanders the good Venetian colouring', while Van Dyck 'succeeds more delicately in flesh colours [even than Rubens], and approaches more towards Titian's colouring'.[121] On the other hand Bellori concludes his life of Rubens with the damning judgement that he admired Raphael and the Antique but did not imitate either.[122] This mixed message was turned into unqualified enthusiasm by the 'Rubenists' in the French Academy. Their most eloquent spokesman, Roger de Piles, proposed somewhat heretically that Rubens was as great an artist as Raphael, able to match him in composition and expression, on the same lap for drawing and clearly his superior in colour.[123]

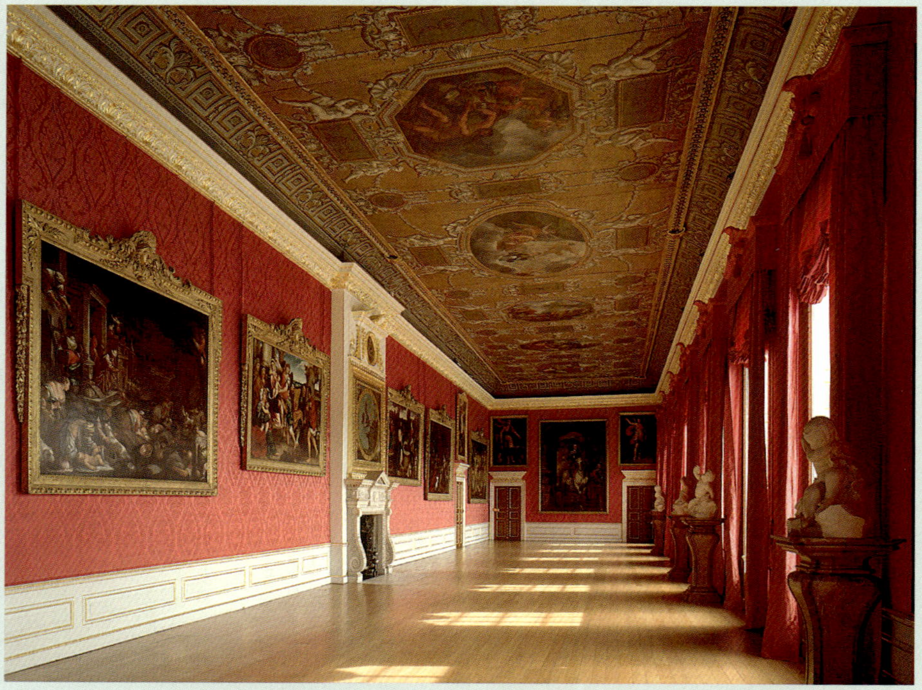

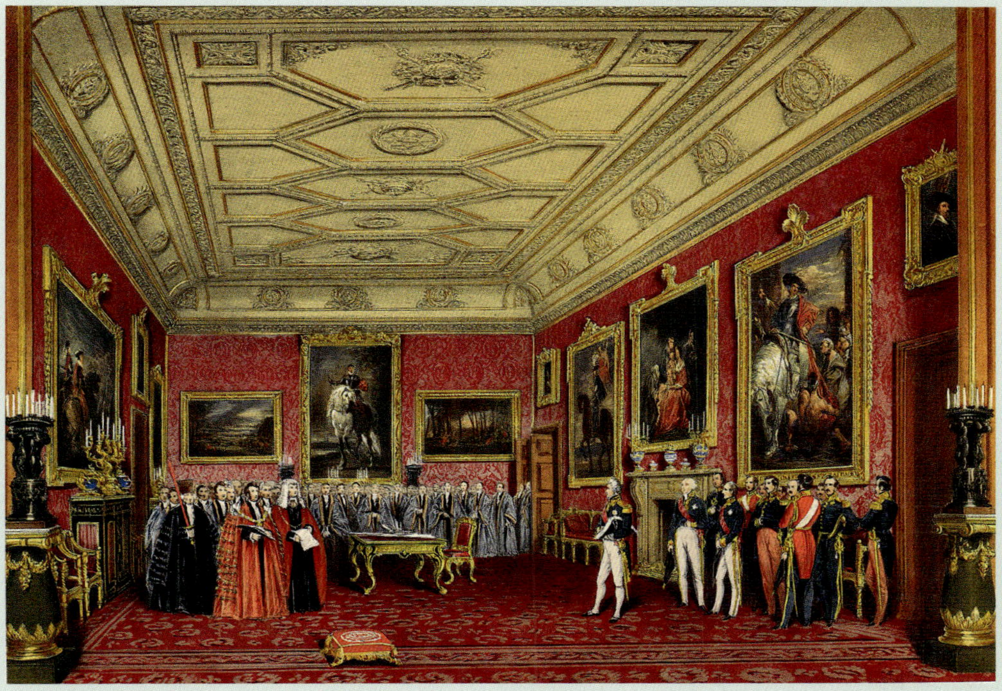

FIG. 66
After Joseph Nash
The City of London addressing Louis Philippe in the 'Rubens Room' at Windsor Castle, 1844
RCIN 750908.c

Rubens and Van Dyck also appealed to the Hanoverian arrivals because both had worked in England and both had been knighted by Charles I. In the absence of a recognisable native tradition such visiting artists were understandably seized upon as part of the 'English School'. The story of portrait painting in Britain was dominated for two centuries by the example of Van Dyck (with occasional glances at Rubens), as can be seen in the works of Lely, Kneller, Reynolds, Gainsborough and Lawrence. Rubens and Van Dyck were part of English history as well as English painting – Rubens had worked as a diplomat, Van Dyck had portrayed every significant player in the Caroline court. This makes it especially remarkable that of the six huge Rubensian paintings acquired during these years, three depict the enemies of the British crown or the Protestant cause which put the Hanoverians on the British throne. No. 136 was believed throughout this period to depict the blackest villain of Protestant mythology, Fernando Alvarez de Toledo, 3rd Duke of Alba (1507–82). No. 138 depicts the Battle of Nördlingen, the worst Protestant defeat during the Thirty Years' War. Frederick, Prince of Wales, also owned Rubens's portrait of Philip II of Spain (RCIN 404392) – the man who launched the Armada – and another image of the Duke of Alba, attributed to Titian.[124] The three paintings from Rubens and his studio (nos 136, 138 and RCIN 404392) are magnificent statements of confident power executed by the most famous propagandist in the history of art, one that had celebrated the reign of James I on the Whitehall Banqueting House ceiling in similar terms.[125] It is possible that they were acquired without thought for their subjects, but this would seem out of keeping with the antiquarian enthusiasm with which the collection was enhanced and re-displayed at this date, discussed in Chapter VII. This fascination with glorified enemies may have operated as an intimidating reminder of the perennial Catholic threat: Dukes of Alba could still be governing a united Spanish Netherlands, and descendants of Philip and Mary could be on the English throne.[126] On the other hand it may be that these paintings were themselves trophies of victory. The fact that British money could outbid Spanish or imperial loyalty may somehow have suggested to the Georgians that Britain was left in possession of the field of battle.

136

SIR PETER PAUL RUBENS (1577–1640)

Don Rodrigo Calderón (1576–1621) on Horseback 1612–5

Oil on canvas, 304.8 × 216.5 cm

RCIN 404393

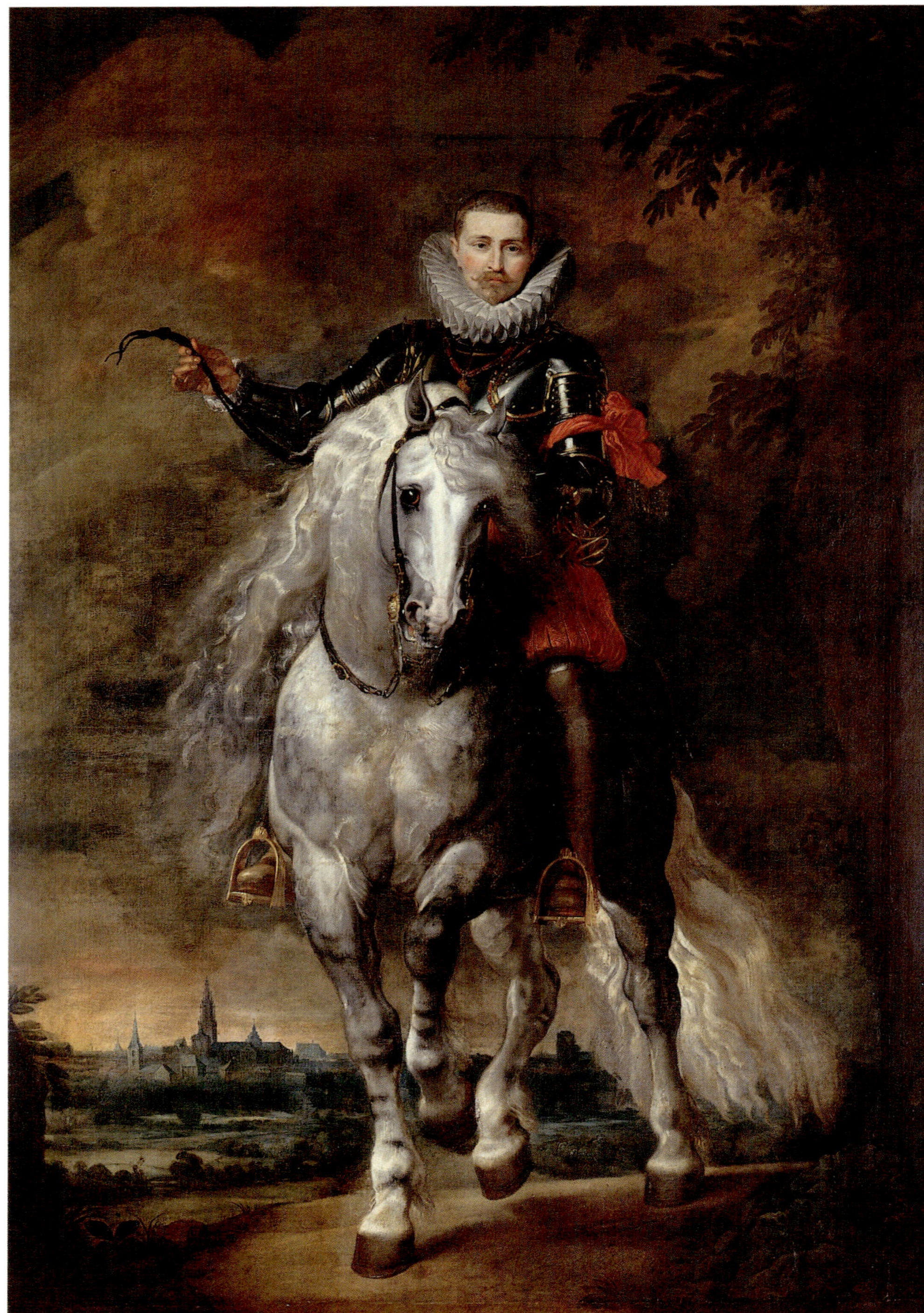

Photograph pre-conservation

PROVENANCE Purchased by George I from John Law in 1723

LITERATURE Millar 1977, p. 90; White 2007, pp. 236–41, no. 66

This painting and the next (no. 137) were bought by George I as part of a group of six pictures from 'Mr Laws' (presumably John Law) in 1723 and both were hugely extended soon after their purchase.[127] British eighteenth-century collectors often commissioned artists to add uneventful passages of 'background' to their Old Masters. The most obvious reason for doing this was to create pairs, as described above (p. 255), referring to the large Tintorettos (RCIN 407247 and 405476) and Van Dycks (RCIN 405322 and 405322) in the King's Gallery, Kensington Palace, but there seems also to have been a general desire to increase the proportion of background relative to incident. Whatever the reason, attitudes towards the Old Masters seem astonishingly casual by our standards.

The original canvas size of no. 136 is uncertain but it may have been barely larger that the surviving section, still now clearly visible to the naked eye and measuring *c.*265 × 190 cm.[128] This would have made the work very close in scale as in composition to Rubens's *Duke of Lerma* (fig. 67), measuring 283 × 200 cm, with the same dramatic effect of a figure seeming to burst out of a constraining frame. In George I's collection this canvas was extended on all sides: two late eighteenth-century inventories give measurements of *c.*370 × 272 cm, some 105 cm higher and 80 cm wider than the surviving bit of original canvas.[129] This seems to have been done to match it with Van Dyck's equestrian portrait of Charles I (RCIN 405322, measuring 368 × 270 cm), another work inspired by Rubens's *Duke of Lerma*. No. 136 was first mentioned in the collection by Horace Walpole on 2 June 1748, hanging at Kensington Palace on the 'staircase by the gallery', while the two huge Van Dycks hung in the Gallery itself.[130] By 1819 these three paintings, then of identical size, were brought together in the Queen's Presence Chamber at Windsor, where they can be seen in Charles Wild's watercolour of 1817 (RCIN 922099).

No. 136 was further transformed in preparation for the creation of the 'Rubens Room' at Windsor Castle in the 1830s (fig. 66). Someone seems to have admired the pairing of Van Dyck's *St Martin* (RCIN 405878) and Rubens's *Philip II* (RCIN 404392) in the Crimson Drawing Room at Buckingham House (fig. 53), while at the same time lamenting the asymmetry of their frames. As a result their frames were simply swapped: Van Dyck's *St Martin* received the William Kent-designed architrave frame from no. 136 (seen in Wild's watercolour, RCIN 922099), so that it and *Philip II* could hang in matching frames on either side of the mantle in the Rubens Room (where they hang to this day). No. 136 was then left with the extraordinary rococo frame originally designed for the *St Martin*. The unique character of the frame did not matter in this case because it was chosen to occupy the centre of a wall, opposite the window in the Rubens Room. This hanging position prompted the decision to reduce its size, taking off some of the additions which had only recently been added (some 40 cm off the height and 25 cm off the width), presumably in order to make room for the two Rubens landscapes on its either side (see fig. 66).

Eighteenth-century references to this painting consistently describe it as a portrait of the 'Duke of Alba' (Fernando Alvarez de Toledo, 3rd Duke of Alba, 1507–82; see above, p. 257); Rubens executed posthumous portraits so this is not an impossible idea.[131] Recent scholarship, however, has identified the sitter as Don Rodrigo Calderón, a less controversial representative of the Spanish government who visited the Spanish Netherlands in 1612, which is why a view of Antwerp appears in the background. Infrared images taken during recent conservation work (fig. 68) reveal several pentiments. The sitter originally wore a hat with a feather and rested his right hand on top of a general's baton of command. DS-T

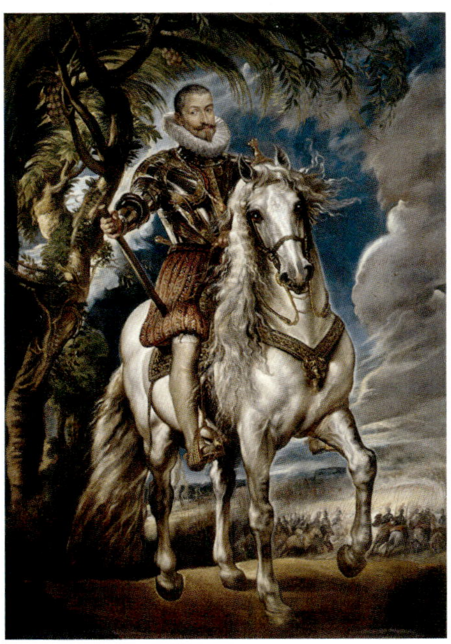

FIG. 67
Peter Paul Rubens
Equestrian Portrait of the Duke of Lerma, 1603
Oil on canvas
Prado, Madrid

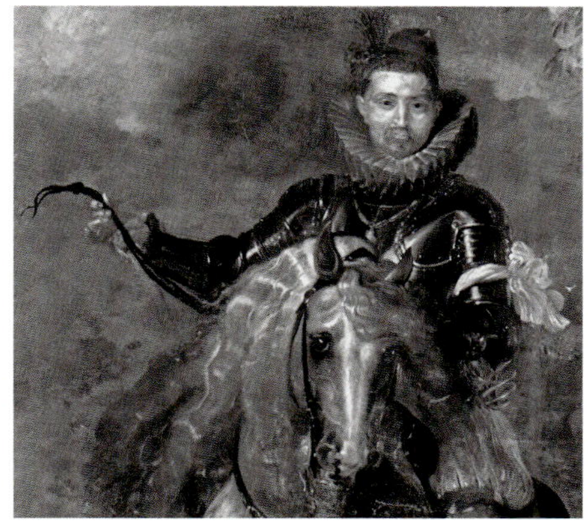

FIG. 68
Infrared reflectograph of no. 136

137

SIR PETER PAUL RUBENS (1577–1640)

The Holy Family with St Francis 1620–30

Oil on canvas, 191.5 × 214.0 cm
RCIN 407674

PROVENANCE Purchased by George I from John Law in 1723

LITERATURE Millar 1977, p. 90; *The Queen's Pictures* 1991, p. 126, no. 39; White 2007, pp. 187–95, no. 59

This painting was hung by George I over the mantel in the Great Drawing Room at Kensington, having gained a 60 cm extension at its top to make it worthy of this altar-like position (see p. 255 above). It was then in the King's Drawing Room at Windsor (with no. 138), where it can be seen in its full Georgian height in 1819 (fig. 52). The painting remained in this room when it became the 'Rubens Room', though moving to the coveted over-mantle position (fig. 66). In this case all the eighteenth-century additions have since been removed or concealed, leaving Rubens's original.[132]

No painting by Rubens allows us to understand the Janus character of his reputation more clearly. Bellori mentions that Rubens admired Raphael; this work is clearly intended to be an essay in the sweet tenderness of Raphael's Holy Families, in particular recalling *The Holy Family of Francis I* (Louvre) of 1518, which Rubens could have seen in the French royal collection (fig. 69).[133] On the other hand the painting has qualities actively discouraged by the Academy. Rubens's bodies have a blushing, flesh-and-blood wobbliness which makes those of his contemporary Guido Reni look like statues. For Vertue this painting 'has a brilliance superior to all the rest [in the Great Drawing Room] a pencill. fire. harmony &c. most ravishing tho' the others are of a finer taste in another way'.[134] 'Brilliance' probably means freshness of realism as well as the use of luminous and vivid colour; 'fire' and 'pencil' refer to a liveliness in the handling of the brush (then called a 'pencil'); 'harmony' refers to the way in which all the colours of a painting are made to relate to each other.[135] For what blushing does to the body sunlight does to landscape, suffusing it with colour, in this case a spectrum from red-brown to blue-grey, giving it the character of a living thing.[136] It was these characteristics of sensuality, atmosphere and vivid, breathing realism that inspired artists on the margins of the Academy, like Watteau and Delacroix. DS-T

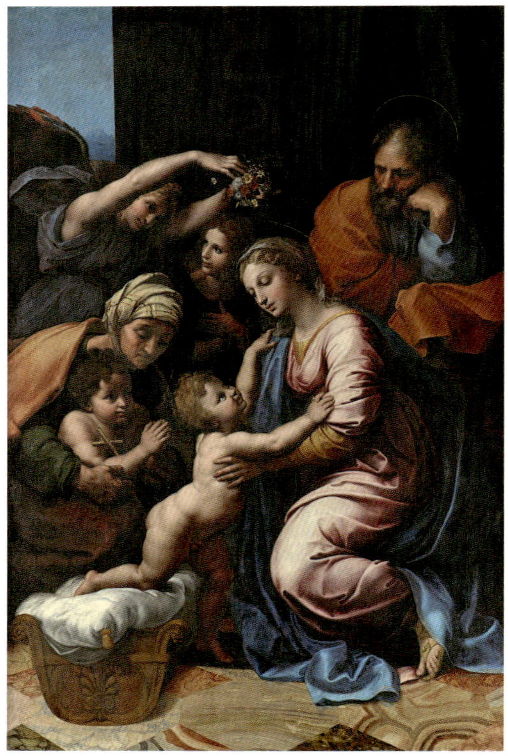

FIG. 69
Raphael
The Holy Family of Francis I, 1518
Oil on canvas
Musée du Louvre, Paris

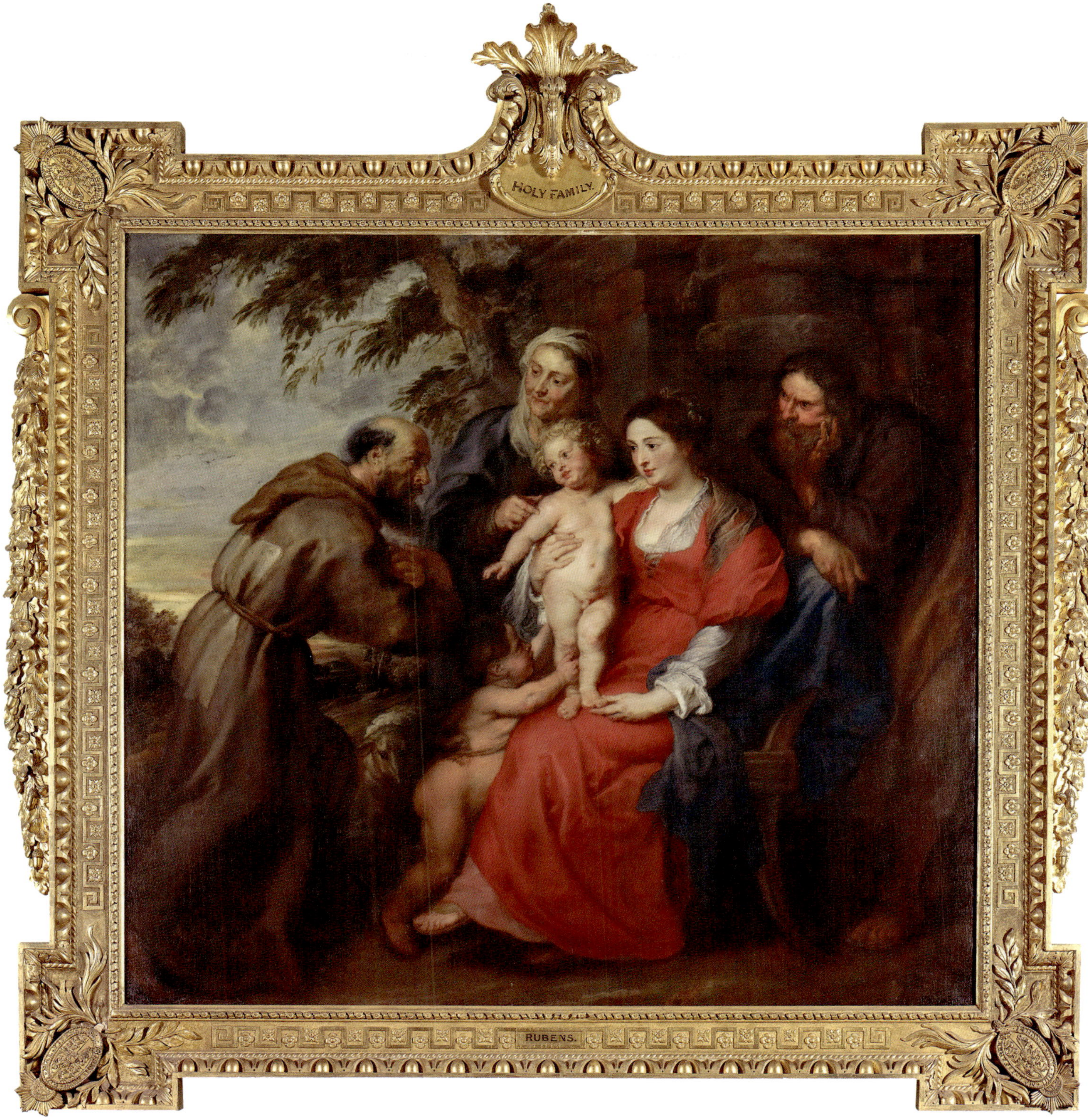
HOLY FAMILY.
RUBENS.

138

JAN VAN DER HOECKE (1611–1651) AFTER RUBENS

The Battle of Nördlingen 1634

Oil on canvas, 242.0 × 339.6 cm
RCIN 400100

PROVENANCE Acquired by Frederick, Prince of Wales

LITERATURE Martin 1972, no. 37; Rorschach 1993, p. 66, no. 80; White 2007, pp. 120–4, no. 34

Cardinal-Infante Ferdinand (1609–41), the younger brother of Philip IV of Spain, was appointed Governor of the Spanish Netherlands in 1633. On his way to take up office he joined forces with his cousin, Ferdinand, King of Hungary, at the head of the combined Spanish and Imperial army, and on 2 September 1634 inflicted a crushing defeat on the Swedish at the Battle of Nördlingen. Upon his arrival in the Low Countries the citizens of Antwerp planned a 'joyous entry', the ceremony with which all new governors took possessions of the loyal cities under their rule. The decorations for this entry, which took place on 17 April 1635, were conceived by Jan Gaspar Gevaerts and Nicholas Rockox and executed by Rubens and his studio; they consisted of temporary arches and other forms of road-side decoration, all recorded in an illustrated volume entitled *Pompa Introitus Ferdinandi* (Antwerp 1642). No. 138, depicting the victory at Nördlingen, appeared on the centre of the 'Arch of Ferdinand' in the Lange Nieuwstraat. The documents tell us that Jan van den Hoecke was commissioned in November 1634 to execute a canvas based on Rubens's oil sketches, the work being completed in January 1635.[137]

As part of a temporary structure to be seen out of doors and from a distance, this canvas is necessarily broadly painted, but shows the great skill with which Rubens's design individualises the heroes (one light-against-dark, the other dark-against-light) and generalises the foot-soldiers, so that we can see the broad pattern of the engagement.

The subject of this painting was correctly identified by Vertue when he saw it at Leicester House in July 1750, when it was attributed to Rubens (as it remained until the late nineteenth century).[138] The peculiar meaning of a battle scene depicting an imperial victory (see p. 257 above) must be seen in relation to the huge pair of battle scenes painted in 1742 for Frederick and hanging on the stairs at Leicester House, depicting the sieges of Lille and Tournay (RCIN 407182 and 407184), two imperial victories of 1708 and 1709, this time won with their new British allies.[139] It is impossible to say what contrast or comparison Frederick intended. This painting was subsequently moved to the King's Drawing Room, where it appears in 1819 (fig. 52); it remained in this same position when this room became the 'Rubens Room' (fig. 66). DS-T

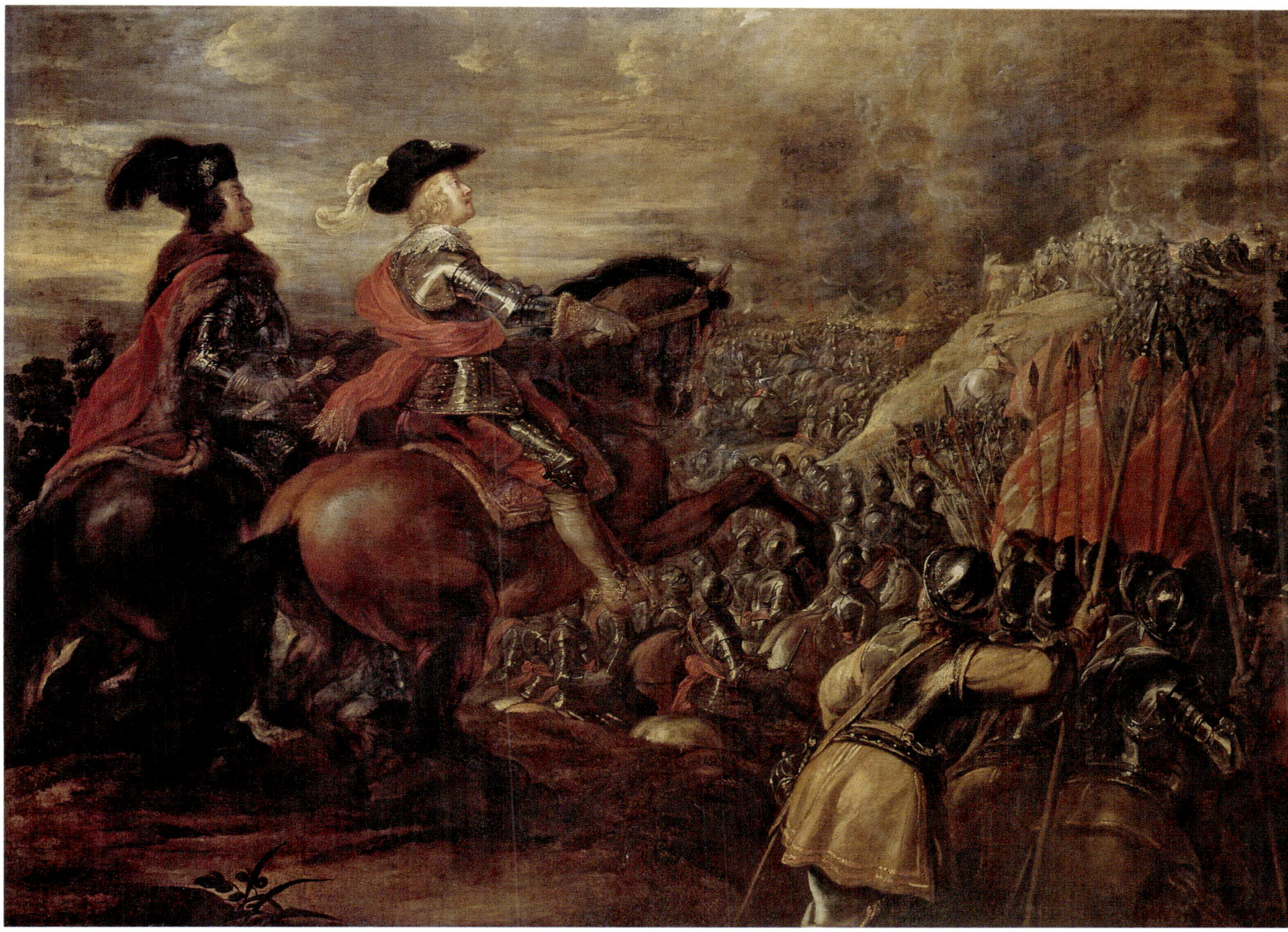

Photograph pre-conservation

139

SIR ANTHONY VAN DYCK

Portrait of a Man c.1630

Oil on canvas, 70.9 × 59.3 cm
RCIN 406036

PROVENANCE Probably acquired by Frederick, Prince of Wales

LITERATURE Millar 1963, p. 109, no. 187; Barnes 2004, p. 415, no. 111.A.31

There were two Van Dycks of unidentified men in Frederick's collection, both documented as having been cleaned by September 1747 – a 'Gentm Half Length' and a 'Mans Head'.[140] The former is almost certainly RCIN 404085, and the painting here is probably the latter, and may also be the 'head' by Van Dyck recorded in the '3rd Room' at Leicester House in the 1749 inventory.[141]

This is one of several Van Dyck heads of *c.*1630 which are loosely finished, many of them, like this one, set in a fictive oval frame by a later hand; it has been suggested that they may have been from-the-life studies for Van Dyck's most prestigious commission, the group portrait of 23 Brussels city councillors, destroyed in 1695.[142] DS-T

140

SIR ANTHONY VAN DYCK (1599–1640)

Thomas Killigrew (1612–1683) with an Unidentified Man 1638

Oil on canvas, 132.9 × 144.1 cm
RCIN 407426

PROVENANCE Acquired by Frederick, Prince of Wales, before 1747

LITERATURE Millar 1963, p. 101, no. 156; Rorschach 1993, p. 70, no. 120; *Van Dyck* 1999, no. 95; Barnes 2004, p. 542, no. IV.146; *Van Dyck & Britain* 2009, p. 112, no. 47

This is one of an important group of paintings which belonged to George Bagnall and were seen by Lord Egremont at his house in Soho Square on 3 February 1729.[143] Frederick, Prince of Wales, acquired the present work from Bagnall along with Van Dyck's *St Martin* (RCIN 405878), two Jan Breughel coppers (RCIN 405513, 405514) and a group of paintings by David Teniers, including no. 141. When Vertue visited Leicester House in July 1749 he saw two 'Gent. in conversation by Vandyke Killigrew. & Carew poets' hanging over the chimney of the '3rd Room', which was otherwise hung with 'several whole length portraits ladies by Vandyke'.[144] In September 1749 the painting is recorded in the Prince's Dressing Room as depicting Killigrew and 'Webb the Architect', that is Inigo Jones's assistant John Webb (1611–72).[145]

One of the figures here has always been recognised as the poet Thomas Killigrew

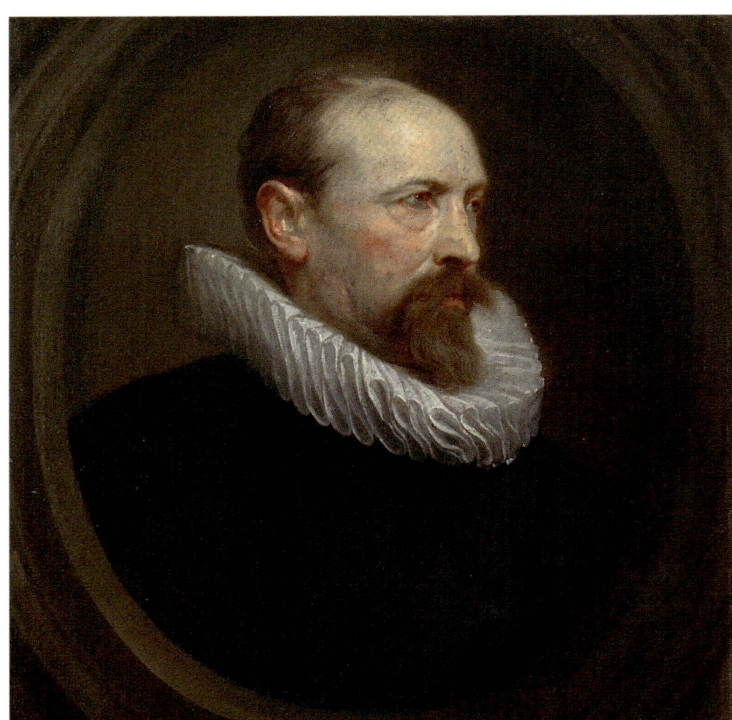

Photograph pre-conservation

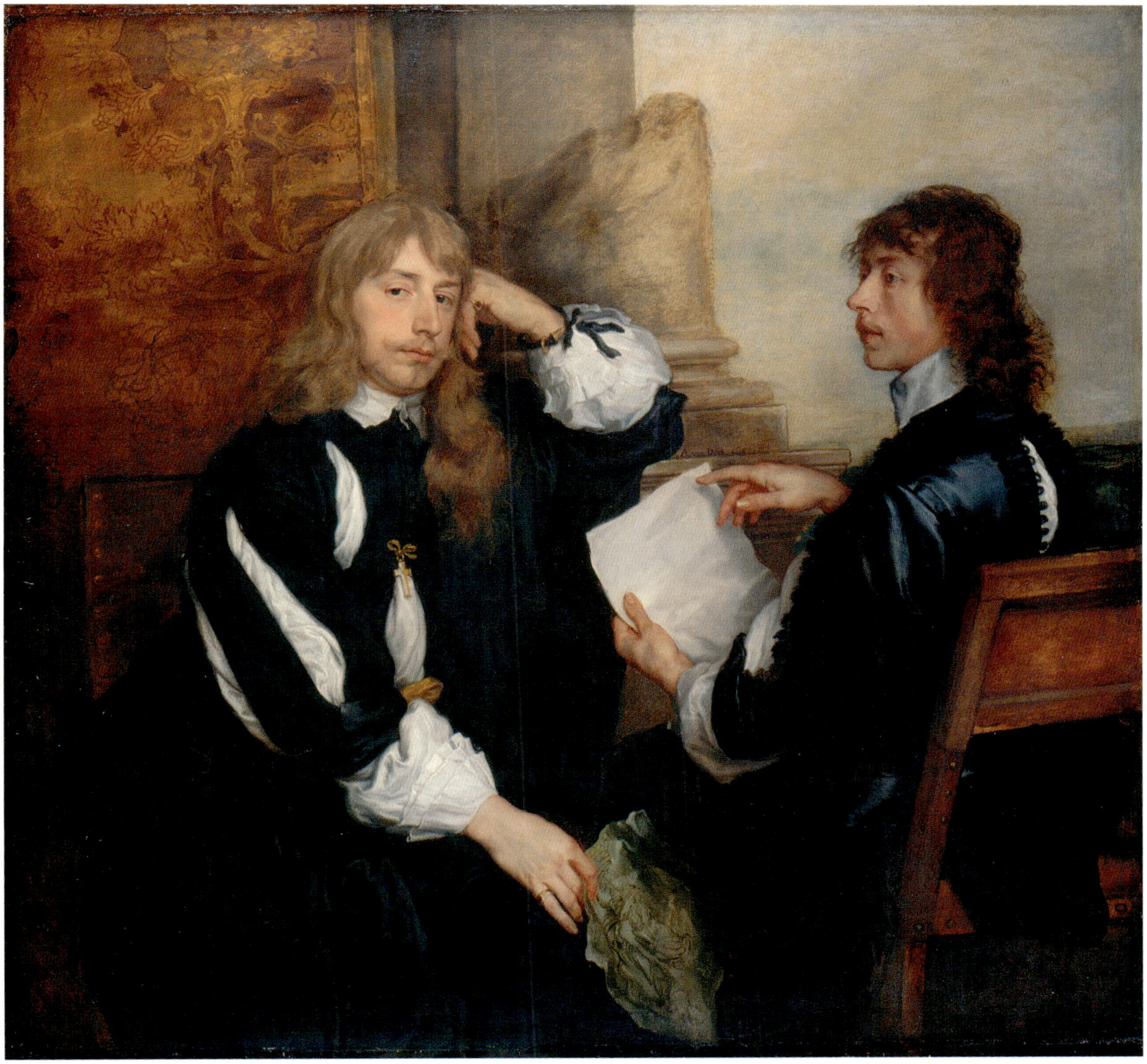

(1612–83); the other has never been satisfactorily identified. The compiler of the 1749 inventory thought that the subjects were a poet and an architect, presumably receiving the commission for the monument depicted in the drawing. George Vertue thought the painting depicted two poets and referred to a song about jealousy written by Thomas Carew (1595–1640) at Killigrew's request and arising from a dispute between Killigrew and his wife.[146] More recently the painting has been interpreted as presenting Killigrew in mourning for his wife, Cecilia, who died on 1 January 1638; he adopts a melancholy pose, wears his wedding ring on a black ribbon, sits in front of a broken column and holds a tomb design in his right hand.[147] His unidentified companion – a friend or secretary – holds a blank piece of paper, as if waiting for Killigrew to dictate an inscription or elegy for his late wife. If we were to add a speech bubble it might read: 'Let the page remain blank; my grief is too profound for words!'

This is a portrait about love and friendship, appreciated then as now for its expressive gestures and enigmatic meaning. Frederick may have believed, like Vertue, that he had a portrait of two 'Cavalier' poets, rather than one, and may have appreciated an image of Thomas Killigrew, whose loyalty to the Stuart cause was as important as his reputation as a poet, dramatist and theatrical manager.[148] William Sheppard's celebrated portrait of 1650 was well known through the engraving by William Faithorne of 1664 (NPG 3795 and D19236); it shows Killigrew in Venice representing the exiled Charles II and includes an image of the late King, Charles I, in the background. DS-T

141

DAVID TENIERS (1610–1690)

Interior of a Farmhouse with Figures ('The Jealous Husband') *c.*1660

Oil on canvas, 71.6 × 87.4 cm
RCIN 405342

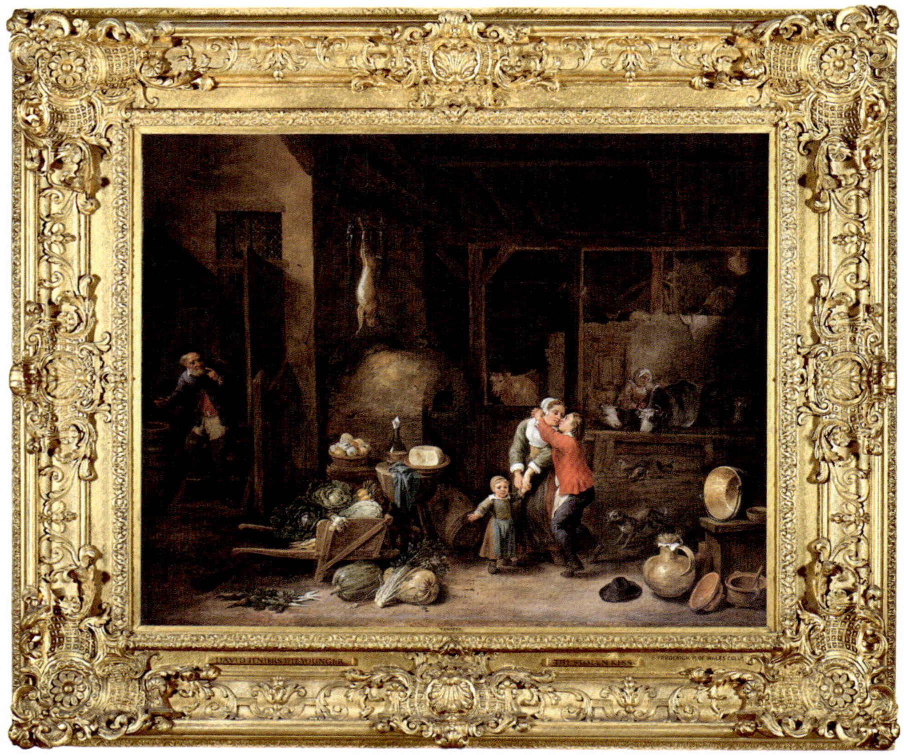

PROVENANCE Bought by Frederick, Prince of Wales, from George Bagnall

LITERATURE Rorschach 1993, p. 67, no. 92; White 2007, pp. 338–9, no. 107; *Bruegel to Rubens* 2008, no. 45

When it came to the painting of the Low Countries, eighteenth-century collectors distinguished between the dignity of Rubens and Van Dyck on the one hand and the crudity of low-life painters on the other. Attitudes to this type of painting changed slowly during the eighteenth century – in theory despised throughout the period, in practice examples of it became more and more sought after by collectors. This trend culminated in George IV's acquisition, between 1800 and 1830, of an incomparable group of seventeenth-century Dutch and Flemish landscapes and genre paintings.[149] Previous royal collectors had been slow starters in this area, with very few Dutch paintings joining the collection during the reigns of George I and George II.[150]

The exception to this rule was Frederick, Prince of Wales, who acquired an important and coherent group of landscape and peasant scenes by Flemish artists. Central to this group was a pair of rustic landscapes by Rubens, *Winter* (RCIN 401417) and *Summer* (RCIN 401416), which by 1749 were hanging in the anti-chamber at Leicester House along with four 'times of day' by David Teniers (RCIN 404775–404778), all six paintings in splendid frames made for them by Benjamin Goodison.[151] The four Teniers belonged with an important group of paintings acquired from George Bagnall, which also included a magnificent pair of Jan Breughel landscapes (RCIN 405513, 405514) and this genre scene.[152] Rubens, Teniers and Jan Breughel seemed to belong together: Teniers was Jan Breughel's son-in-law and a friend of Rubens's, and all three artists (in their landscape and genre painting) followed in the respected tradition of the great Pieter Bruegel the Elder.[153] Teniers, like Jan Breughel and Rubens, was a court artist who ended his career as a nobleman living on a country estate.[154] These interconnections serve to explain why the landscapes and peasant scenes of Teniers and Breughel enjoyed so much more prestige in the early eighteenth century than anything by their Dutch contemporaries.[155] These are broad comedies of peasant life created by gentlemen.

Names and connections definitely helped in the making of artists' reputations at this time but ultimately the works were admired for themselves – in this case for the extraordinary precision of detail, the liveliness of Teniers's touch and the rustic comedy. A print by Thomas Major after the painting, published in 1750, tells us that the painting then hung in the Prince of Wales's collection at Carlton House and calls it 'The Jealous Husband'.[156]

No. 141 was splendidly re-framed by Frederick, though the documents referring to the repairing of the frame by Paul Petit in 1749 provide no evidence as to who supplied it in the first place.[157] DS-T

142

FRANS HALS (*c*.1580–1666)

Portrait of a Man 1630

Oil on canvas, 116.6 × 90.1 cm

RCIN 405349

PROVENANCE First recorded in the Royal Collection in 1795 (Geo. III, Buck Ho.)

LITERATURE White 1982, pp. 43–4, no. 56; Rorschach 1993, p. 61, no. 39; *Royal Treasures* 2002, p. 81, no. 9

Some time around 1740 a print was published purporting to be a Van Dyck portrait of Frans Hals, an artist often thought of as a late nineteenth-century discovery.[158] The royal inventories of 1818 and 1819 record three paintings by 'Frank Halls'.[159] Two are very close to Hals's style, though now attributed to Jan Molenaer (RCIN 405487) and Judith Leyster (RCIN 404807); both came from the Consul Smith collection, where they were both described in 1762 as by Jacob Jordaens.[160] The third is this portrait, which must be an eighteenth-century acquisition but what it was bought as and by whom cannot be determined. In 1819 it was hanging in the 'Garden Room' within the King's Apartments on the ground floor of Buckingham House, and described as 'Excellent'.[161] The other paintings in the room include works attributed (mostly correctly) to Titian, Rubens, Van Dyck, Honthorst, Velázquez, Jan Wyck and Simon Verelst.[162] The arrangement at Buckingham House tends to reflect the taste of the beginning of George III's reign (the 1760s), even if recorded at its end. It seems that the qualities of Hals's work were appreciated throughout the century and that his name was known, even if it took time to associate the name with the right paintings.

The brilliance of Hals's brushwork, which inspired Manet to produce his tribute painting, *Le Bon Bock* of 1873 (Philadelphia Museum of Art), was also admired in the eighteenth century. Connoisseurs of the period sought out brushwork (or 'pencilling' as they called it) and deplored a 'dry' or 'laboured' finish.[163] To our eyes Frans Hals and Van Dyck are opposites, the one using exciting but abrupt handling to describe brashly confident merchants, the other conveying aristocratic languor with a fluid and elegant brush. Reynolds on the other hand saw them as comparable: 'In the works of Frank Halls, the portrait-painter may observe the composition of a face, the features well put together, as the painters express it; from whence proceeds that strong-marked character of individual nature, which is so remarkable in his portraits, and is not found in an equal degree in any other painter. If he had joined to this most difficult part of the art, a patience in finishing what he had so correctly planned, he might justly have claimed the place which Vandyck, all things considered, so justly holds as the first of portrait-painters.'[164] DS-T

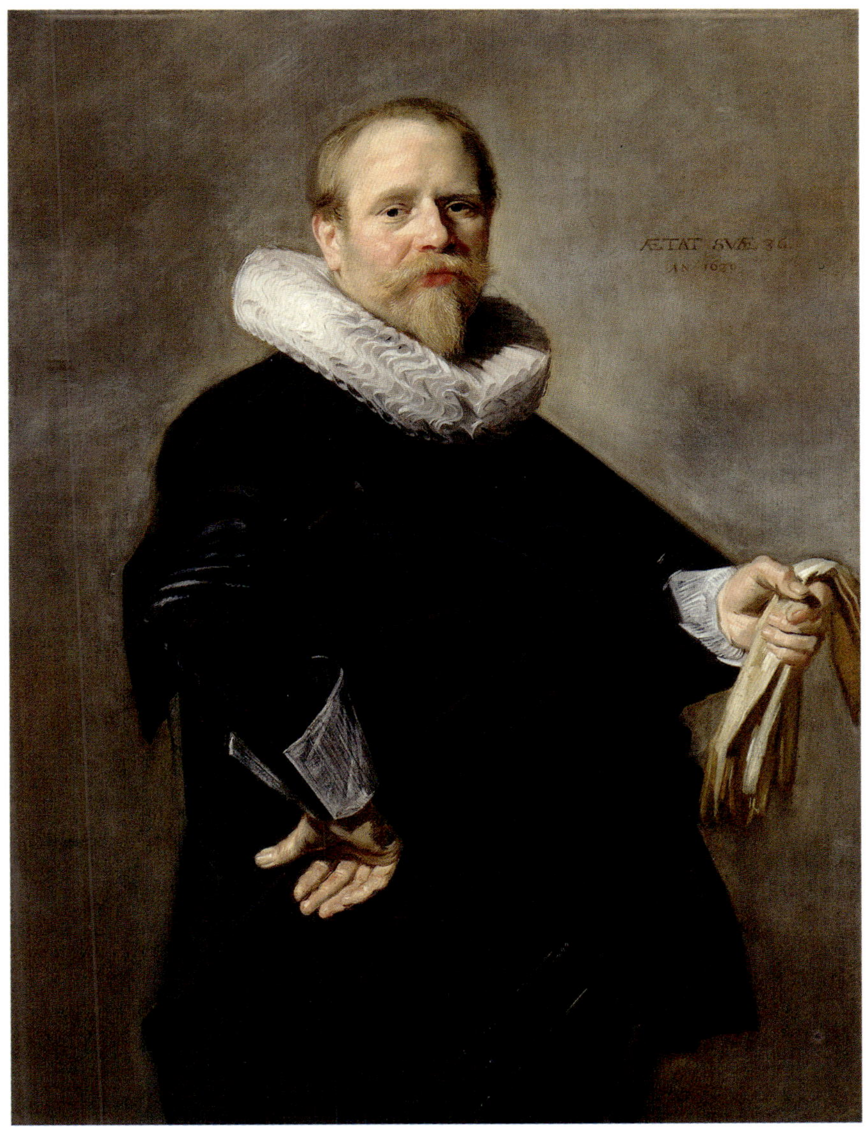

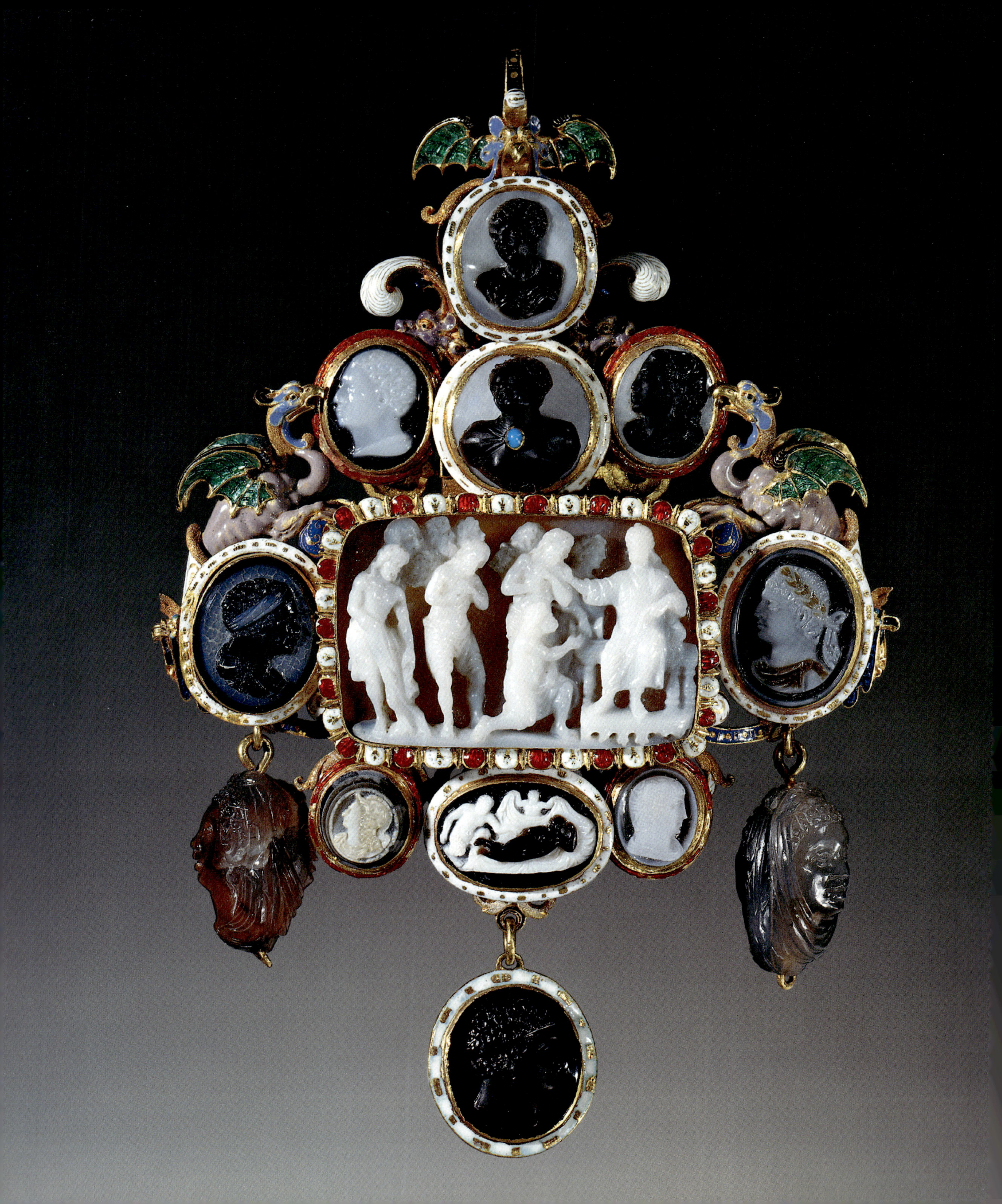

VII

'An Amiable Philosopher on the Throne' Queen Caroline and the Encouragement of Learning

KATHRYN JONES AND DESMOND SHAWE-TAYLOR

It must be confess'd that this Princess, abstracted from her Crown and Titles, was born to encourage the whole Circle of Arts, and to do good to Mankind. She appears as an amiable Philosopher on the Throne, having never let slip one Opportunity of improving the great Talents she receiv'd from Nature, nor of exerting her Beneficence.[1]
(Voltaire about Queen Caroline in *Letters Concerning the English Nation* of 1733)

VOLTAIRE'S EXTRAVAGANT PRAISE of Queen Caroline was prompted by her decision to have her children inoculated, thus lending support to this new practice, observed by Lady Mary Wortley Montagu (1689–1762) in Turkey, when she accompanied her husband there in 1716–8.[2] It was generally agreed that Queen Caroline was the most intellectual member of the Hanoverian dynasty. The idea was less appreciatively expressed by George II, who 'often rebuked her for dabbling in all that lettered nonsense (as he termed it), called her a pedant, and said she loved to spend her time more like a school-mistress than a queen'.[3] Voltaire's English phrase 'amiable philosopher' imprecisely renders the French '*aimable philosophe*'. '*Aimable*' probably has some sense of being well-intentioned as well as agreeable, and '*philosophe*' means much more than merely 'philosopher'. A *philosophe* was one who had signed up to the new project of unprejudiced enquiry, which it was believed would transform all branches of learning. Philosophy was not a room in the mansion of learning but a torch which illuminated all of the rooms. It is for this reason that the 'encyclopedia' was of such central importance to the Enlightenment: the *Cyclopaedia; or, An Universal Dictionary of Arts and Sciences* was published by Ephraim Chambers (*c.*1680–1740) in 1728 and the more famous *Encyclopédie* by Denis Diderot (1713–84) in 1751–76.[4]

The Hanoverians did not need to come to England to learn this as their intellectual formation had taken place under the tutelage of the outstanding philosopher Gottfried Wilhelm Leibniz (1646–1716). From 1676 until his death, Leibniz served as court councillor and librarian to successive rulers of Hanover, crescendoing in title – Duke John Frederick, Elector Ernest Augustus and King George I. In 1680 Leibniz was commissioned by Ernest Augustus (though work continued under George I) to research the history of the Guelf dynasty, which, he established in the archives of Modena, was connected with the ancient Este family (see p. 59). This work, though never completed, produced the result that in 1692 the Emperor Leopold I awarded to the dukedom of Brunswick-Lüneburg and Calenberg (Hanover) title to the ninth electorate. During his time in Hanoverian service Leibniz formed especially close friendships with the Electress Sophia, whom he saw regularly in Hanover from 1680 until her death in 1714, and Sophia Charlotte, Electress of Brandenburg and sister of George I, whom he came to know through correspondence and frequent visits to Berlin after 1698. In 1704, when staying for six months in Lietzenburg with Sophia Charlotte, Leibniz met Princess Wilhelmine Caroline of Ansbach, the future Queen Caroline, with whom he corresponded for the rest of his life. Leibniz made important contributions to most branches of learning – philosophy, theology, mathematics, physics, law and history. His activity was crucial for the spread of Enlightenment science on the Continent: in 1700 he became president of the newly founded Society of Sciences in Berlin and, in 1712, Privy Councillor as well as scientific advisor to Tsar Peter the Great.

The relationship Leibniz had with England was a complex one. He was disappointed not to have had the opportunity to spend more time in London and especially not to have been brought over with the new King in 1714. His reputation in England meanwhile suffered from his dispute with Newton over the invention of calculus, which Queen Caroline tried to moderate but which made her apparently reluctant to honour him in her new country. Differential calculus (called 'real analysis' in the USA) deals with complex curves (and phenomena which can be so represented). To take a Newtonian example, a body dropped in space will accelerate because of the Earth's gravitational force, but that acceleration will also increase as the object approaches the Earth and the gravitational force becomes stronger. It would not be difficult to estimate how far this object would fall in a given time. It is more difficult to represent this calculation precisely, either on a graph or algebraically, so that it can be used in more general proofs and demonstrations. Newton and Leibniz found that thinking of the curve as a flight of tiny steps allowed them to do this. They could then turn the flight of steps back into a curve by imagining that each step was infinitely small. This process they called 'infinitesimal' calculus. Newton and Leibniz invented it independently, but unfortunately nobody – least of all Newton's admirers – was prepared to grant this. Particularly after his death, and before Newton's, Leibniz was openly accused of plagiarism. He achieved some retrospective vindication when his system of notation was finally validated by mathematicians in the twentieth century.[5]

Though not honoured as he might have been in England, Leibniz had offered his various princely pupils an enthusiastic endorsement of the new mechanical explanation of matter (as represented by the Royal Society), seen as part of a larger, essentially theological, conception of existence (see p. 21). The attempt to reconcile science with faith also exercised English thinkers, in particular Robert Boyle (1627–91), who endowed a series of lectures at the Royal Society dedicated to defending Christianity against the teachings of 'atheists, deists, pagans' and of other religions. This is why his bust (no. 148) was given such a special prominence in Queen Caroline's Hermitage and why two clergymen joined company considered even at the time a little out of their orbit. Samuel Clarke (no. 149) delivered the Boyle Lectures in 1704 and tried throughout his life to apply philosophical or scientific reason to matters of morality and faith.[6] William Wollaston (see no. 145) published *Religion of Nature Delineated* in 1724, arguing that religion can be read from Nature and the revelations of the incarnation were merely confirming what the observation of Nature taught.[7] Leibniz did not appear in Queen Caroline's Hermitage perhaps out of tact and perhaps because he did not belong within its precise argument about the way English freethinkers could maintain faith in what was a notoriously godless country.[8] But Leibniz had prepared the ground at least in the minds of the Hanoverians by offering an approach to every aspect of learning and political life which was well-informed, open-minded and optimistic.[9] The Hanoverian royal family did not bring the new science to England any more than they brought new ideas of liberty, but they participated openly and fully in both, which made them the most Enlightened monarchs of their age. This fact is one of Leibniz's many achievements.

The most important aspect of philosophical learning for the early Georgians was history. During the reigns of George I and George II a number of histories of their new dominions were published, including histories of England – by Paul de Rapin Thoyras (printed in The Hague in 1715 and translated into English in 1724), John Oldmixon (from 1729), Thomas Carte (1747), David Hume (1754–61) and Tobias Smollett (1757–65) – and a history of Scotland, in Gaelic, by Robert Lindsay published in 1728. In 1716 the Society of Ancient Britons was founded, with a particular interest in the history of the Welsh, in honour of the new Prince and Princess of Wales. Queen Caroline's library contained a number of sixteenth-century tomes on history, including Francis Bacon's work on Henry VII, Thomas More on Edward V and Richard II, and William Camden on Queen Elizabeth.[10]

Realising the importance of Leibniz's work in re-elevating the Guelf dynasty within the Empire, the Hanoverians were anxious also to show their connections with English royal lines, to justify their claim to the British throne. The family tree by Müller (no. 9) was drawn up in the tradition of kings tracing their roots back to Charlemagne – common among the princely families of Germany, although in this case it was the foundation of a new dynasty that was emphasised. George I is crowned by Britannia, and supported by his sons, grandsons and great-grandsons. George II owned a complete series of medals by Dassier depicting the monarchs from William I up to and including himself, with many of the images drawn from Rapin's *History of England*. Leibniz's history had demonstrated to the Hanoverians the propaganda value of such publications, but the history written by their British supporters needed to establish the lineage not just of their blood but also of the idea of liberty and constitutional government – as Rapin's work did.

The Huguenot nobleman Paul de Rapin, sieur of Thoyras (1661–1725), had settled in the Dutch Republic after the Revocation of the Edict of Nantes in 1685 and accompanied William III to England in 1688, fighting at the Battle of the Boyne. Not unexpectedly, his *Histoire d'Angleterre* is a celebration of the Protestant cause and the ideals of the Glorious Revolution. Its dedication to George I observes 'that the constant union of the Sovereign with his Parliament, is the most solid foundation for the glory of the Prince and the welfare of the Subjects'. Rapin's thesis, and that of all Whig historians, was that the English owed their love of liberty to their Saxon roots, and that the foundations of constitutionalism were laid in the Anglo-Saxon period. Trouble started when James I and Charles I attempted to impose an alien Gallic absolutism in defiance of these 'ancient liberties'.[11] Rapin's work appeared in many English editions and almost became the official account of the nation's history, in spite of David Hume's attempt to defend James's reputation in his *History of England* of 1754–61.

Rapin's was one of the first books read by Thomas Jefferson (1743–1826), who used the Saxon argument to great effect against George III in his *Summary View of the Rights of British America* of 1774.[12] The quintessential Anglo-Saxon was King Alfred, famed for his wisdom and justice. In 1723 Richard Blackmore wrote his *Alfred, an Epick Poem in twelve books*, and a few years later James Thomson (1700–48) and David Mallet (*c*.1705–65) created a new play entitled simply *Alfred*. This was first performed in 1740, in a specially constructed garden theatre at Cliveden for Frederick, Prince of Wales, with music by Thomas Arne (1710–78), and included the first performance of 'Rule Britannia'.[13]

Another favourite of Georgian antiquarians was Edward, the Black Prince, though as a Norman his virtues were more chivalric than constitutional. His life was feted in a play by William Shirley, first staged in 1750 with Garrick in the leading role, although, as Mrs Delany pointed out, it was 'rather a dull play; but the story, or rather incident, is so interesting'.[14] It can be no coincidence that Alfred and the Black Prince were the two figures selected by Frederick, Prince of Wales, as marble sculptures, possibly to adorn his garden at Carlton House.[15] By 1742 the busts were mounted on brackets in St George's Hall, Windsor Castle, home of that ultimate embodiment of chivalry, the Order of the Garter. Each of Frederick's busts was inscribed with the heroic characteristics of the sitter: the Black Prince was a great leader, who tempered military prowess with moderation and clemency; Alfred was quite simply the 'founder of the English Commonwealth and Liberty'.

The most popular period of history for early Georgian historians and antiquarians stretched from the accession of Henry VIII to the Civil War. Queen Elizabeth I in particular seems to have been something of a role model for the Electress Sophia and Queen Caroline. Leibniz wrote to Queen Caroline from Vienna on 16 December 1716, when she was Electoral Princess of Hanover: 'I pray God to grant you the same measure of years as the Electress [Sophia] enjoys, and the same good health. And I pray also that you may one day enjoy the title of Queen of England so well worn by Queen Elizabeth, which you so highly merit.'[16] The Princess replied from Hanover on 27 December 1713: 'I accept the comparison which you draw, though all too flattering, between me and Queen Elizabeth as a good omen. Like Elizabeth, the Electress's rights are denied her by a jealous sister with a bad temper [Queen Anne], and she will never be sure of the English crown until her accession to the throne.'[17]

Thomas Birch's *Memoirs of the Reign of Queen Elizabeth* was published in 1754. The sixteenth and early seventeenth centuries were also celebrated as a golden age of English literature: Spenser's *Faerie Queene* was reissued in 1725, while Horace Walpole's *Catalogue of Royal and Noble Authors of England*, published in 1758, lists a dozen noble sonneteers from Elizabethan times. Shakespeare acquired cult status during the early Georgian period: in 1740 Scheemakers's monument was erected in Westminster Abbey to a design by William Kent, and in 1769 a special jubilee was organised by David Garrick in his honour at Stratford.[18] As well as the full canon of Shakespearean histories, plays relating the stories of Sir Walter Raleigh, James I, Charles I, Thomas Overbury and the Earl of Essex also appeared on the stage during the early eighteenth century. The interest in this period must have had some influence over Queen Caroline, who acquired, remounted and commissioned a group of cameos portraying Henry VIII, Edward VI, Philip II of Spain and Elizabeth I (nos 158–61). Similarly Frederick, Prince of Wales, purchased a group of Richard Mead's sixteenth-century miniatures of Tudor subjects (nos 221–6), including a portrait believed to depict the epitome of the Elizabethan courtier-poet, Sir Philip Sidney (no. 221). The Prince's London home, Leicester House, contained a painting tantalisingly described as by Rubens and of Ben Jonson (see p. 230 above).

History was not just about dynasties and abstract ideas – it also had what would now be called 'human interest'. The early Georgian period saw a flourishing interest in the English past, as Mary Delany noted in a letter to her sister in February 1758: 'Such great characters as Henry the Fourth and his minister are so often the subject of conversation that one wishes to be well acquainted with them, and bear a part in the conversation'.[19] Portraits and personal effects became sought after as the illustration to the many character sketches and full biographies offered by history. In 1716 Mary Cowper, Lady in Waiting to Caroline when Princess of Wales, described the meeting of the collector Sir John Germaine and her mistress, which took place over two evenings, during which the Princess examined his historic artefacts. Germaine had acquired the collection of Henry Mordaunt, 2nd Earl of Peterborough (1621–97), which included seals and reliefs and 'amongst other Things, he showed us the Dagger of King Henry VIII, which he always wore and is pictured with'.[20] The small group of antiquarians who collected around Queen Caroline included Horace Walpole, Dr Richard Mead, the King's physician, Sir Andrew Fountaine, first tutor to the young Duke of Cumberland, and her Mistress of the Robes, Lady Sundon. Caroline also delighted in Lord Egmont's collection of 'printed heads', a group of 40 folio albums filled with prints of historic figures, borrowing them from him more than once. In April 1735 she commented to him that 'there is a particular satisfaction to see the portraits of eminent persons dead and gone but melancholy that such great actions are forgotten and that their glory remains in a sheet of paper'.[21]

There was a strong element of the fanciful in early Georgian antiquarianism, as can be seen in the person of Horace Walpole (1717–97), historical biographer, collector, builder in the Gothic style and author of a supernatural historical romance (what we would call a 'horror story').[22] Among the historical works mentioned above there are as many plays as scholarly studies, and their bias was as often in tales of chivalry or mayhem as in tracing the routes of constitutional government. This is a time when the Society of Antiquaries was founded (in 1717) and when ruins were explored, but also a time when Gothic architecture was fancifully revived (see p. 60) and when the fashionable world dressed up in 'Van Dyck' costume.[23] Even modern resorts, like Bath, exploited their antiquity, claiming to be founded by the mythic King Bladud, which prompted its principal architect John Wood (1704–54) to survey Stonehenge and base his elegant modern terraces on its mystic proportions.[24] Old poetry was dug up, as in the *Reliques of Ancient Poetry* collected by Thomas Percy (1729–1811) and published in 1765.[25] New poetry began to be written in imitation of old styles, like Thomas Gray's *The Bard. A Pindaric Ode* of 1757 and James Macpherson's *Fragments of Ancient Poetry Collected in the Highlands and translated from the Galic or Erse*

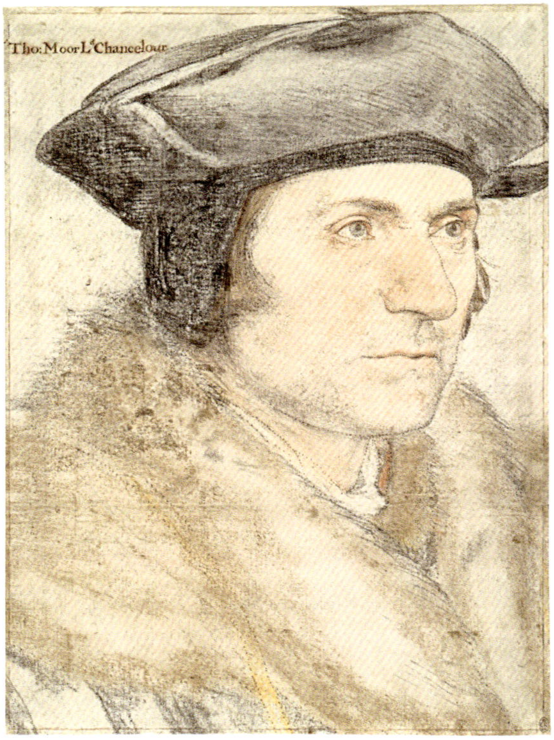

FIG. 70
Hans Holbein the Younger
Sir Thomas More, *c.*1526–7
Black and coloured chalks
RCIN 912268
One of the many Holbein drawings hung by Queen Caroline in her Picture Closet (see fig. 77, item 6)

Language of 1760 (the first appearance of the 'Ossian Poet'). Gray's poem was about a foreign invader, Edward I, who slaughtered all the Welsh bards in order to destroy the soul of his conquered subjects. It is surely possible that the whimsical antiquarianism of the early Georgian period was an attempt to preserve the English soul after the Hanoverian invasion. The 'Bard' in this case was of course Shakespeare, conveniently born near the centre of England, who wrote about every age, even treating the story of Bladud's son Leir, in a style which owed more to English folk songs than the classics.

Historical Portraiture

The antiquarian interests of the early Georgians manifested themselves most obviously in the collection of portraits. Here it is difficult to disentangle the artistic and historical interest. We have seen historical portraits as part of the story of Old Master collecting: Frederick, Prince of Wales, believed he had a portrait of two Cavalier poets, Thomas Killigrew and Thomas Carew (no. 140); Zoffany believed (correctly in the first two cases) that his *Tribuna* (fig. 56) contained images of Galileo, Sir Richard Southwell and Martin Luther.[26] Holbein was believed to have painted these last two portraits, and did do Richard Southwell's. A mixture of sound connoisseurship and optimistic fantasy was typical of the Georgian revival of Holbein.

Holbein was the first painter of stature to work in England and one of the greatest ever to do so, making him a favourite for English antiquarians and connoisseurs of the eighteenth century. The fact of his having been a successful German immigrant must have further increased his appeal for the Hanoverians. The 'discovery' of his portrait drawings was part of the inspiration for Queen Caroline's Picture Closet at Kensington (see pp. 321–2 and figs. 70, 77–80). According to George Vertue, the drawings came to light in 1727 in a little-used bureau in Kensington Palace. The Queen set about extracting the images from their albums, framing them individually and hanging them at Richmond Lodge. There they were seen by Lord Egmont in 1735, when he described 'in the Queen's closet the famous collection of Holbein's heads of eminent persons in King Henry 8th reign. They are 63 in number, upon half sheets of paper, and seem the sketches made for his portraits in oil.'[27] Vertue later recorded that they had been moved to Kensington and the number had extended to 93, suggesting that Caroline had added to the collection herself. Knowing of her interest, Horace Walpole gave Queen Caroline a pair of portraits thought to be of Holbein and his wife by the artist himself (figs. 71 and 72), which she hung in the Closet with the Holbein drawings (see fig. 78, items 94–5). The portraits are now believed to be by Hans Brosamer (*c.*1495–*c.*1554) of an unknown couple.[28]

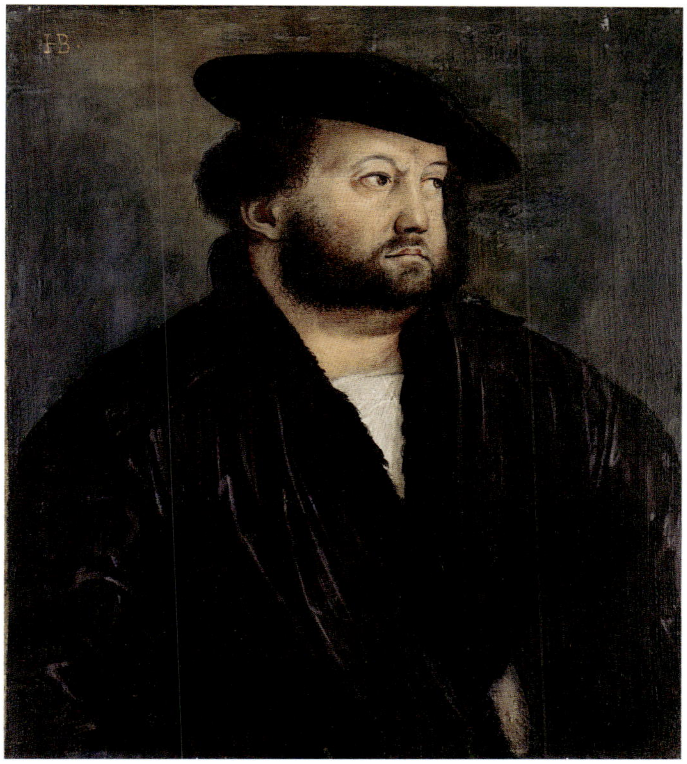

FIG. 71
Attributed to Hans Brosamer
Portrait of a man, c.1522–7
Oil on canvas
RCIN 402867
Given to Queen Caroline as a self-portrait by Holbein

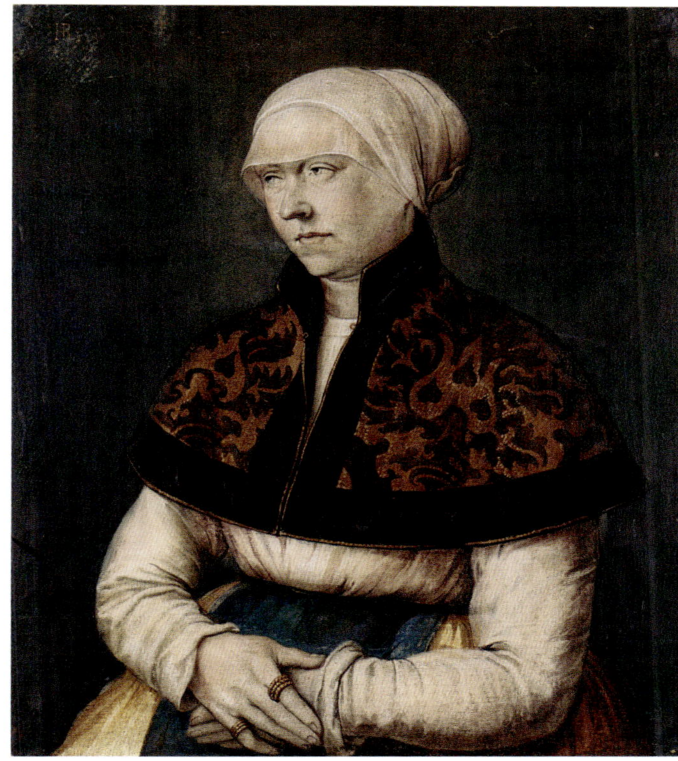

FIG. 72
Attributed to Hans Brosamer
Portrait of a woman, c.1522–7
Oil on canvas
RCIN 402866
Given to Queen Caroline as a portrait of his wife by Holbein

No paintings by Holbein survived in the Royal Collection from his time as court painter to Henry VIII. The Whitehall Mural had been destroyed as recently as 1698 by the fire in the palace. Its appearance was preserved in a painting by Remigius van Leemput (RCIN 405750), which Vertue copied in watercolour in 1737 at Queen Caroline's behest (RCIN 452658). The Holbein paintings inherited by the Hanoverians had all joined the collection during the seventeenth century, most of them acquired by Charles I.

The greatest collector of Holbein during this earlier period had been Thomas Howard, Earl of Arundel (1585–1646), who once owned the group of drawings in the Royal Collection, as well as the portrait of Derich Born (RCIN 405681), almost certainly given to him by Charles I and subsequently restored to royal ownership.[29] The portraits of Sir Henry Guildford and Thomas Howard (nos 144 and 145) were also in Arundel's collection (this time by inheritance) and must have appealed as historic documents as well as works of art. The same winning combination of art and history may have prompted members of the royal family to acquire them in the 1730s and 1740s, though not as a pair, which is why their early Georgian frames do not match. *Guildford* (no. 144) was bought by George II or Queen Caroline probably from the estate of Arundel's descendant, William, Earl of Stafford, who died in 1734.[30] *Howard* (no. 145) was bought by Frederick, Prince of Wales, having spent some years in an unknown collection in Amsterdam.[31] The two portraits were first hung as a pair in the twentieth century.

143

HANS HOLBEIN THE YOUNGER (1497/8–1543)

Sir Henry Guildford (1489–1532) 1527

Oil on panel, 82.7 × 66.4 cm
Inscribed at a later date: *Anno. D: MCCCCCXXVII. / Etatis. Suae. .xl ix* (Year 1527 / His Age 49)
RCIN 400046

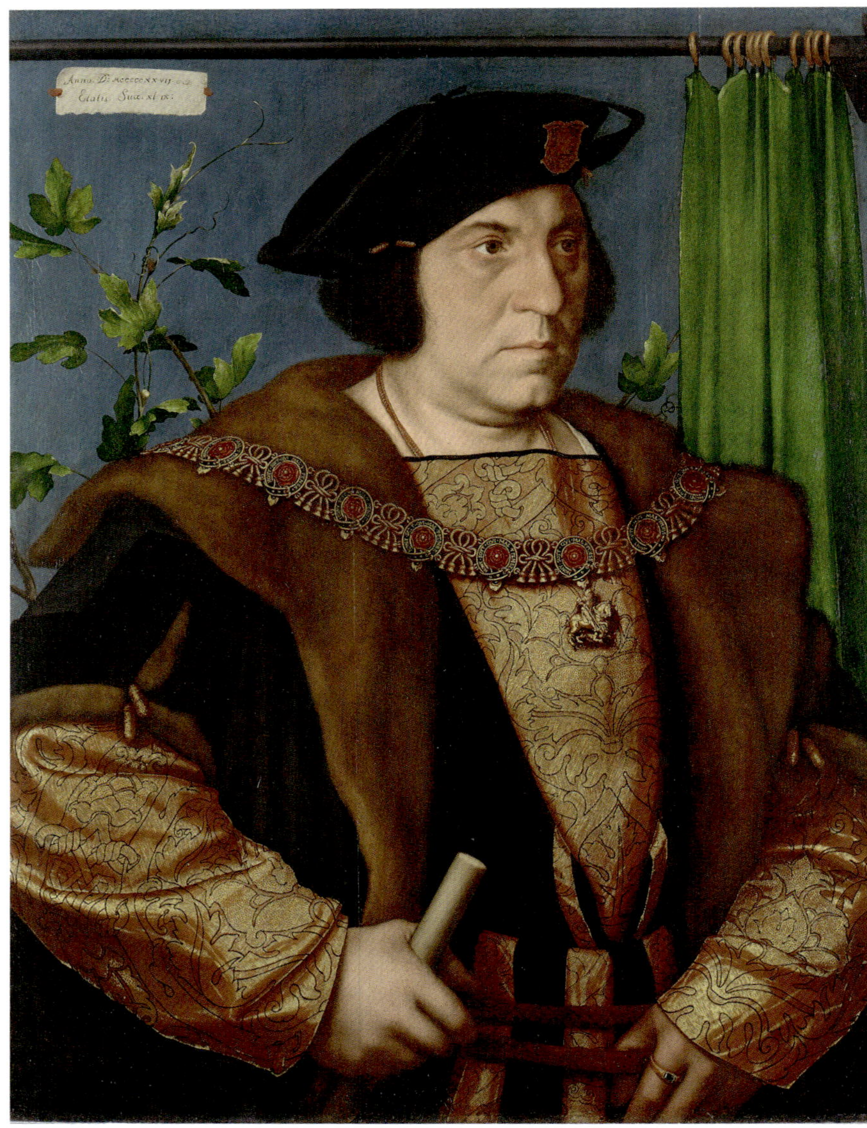

PROVENANCE Thomas Howard, Earl of Arundel; purchased from his heirs by George II or Queen Caroline *c.*1734

LITERATURE Millar 1963, pp. 58–9, no. 28; *Northern Renaissance* 2011, p. 162, no. 71

Sir Henry Guildford (1489–1532), one of Henry VIII's closest friends, was appointed Esquire of the Body at the King's accession in 1509 and then Master of Revels. After a brief interlude he returned as Comptroller of the Royal Household and remained in post until his death in 1532.

Guildford and Holbein almost certainly worked together in the planning of revels at Greenwich in 1527. This portrait and that of Guildford's wife Mary (now in the St Louis Art Museum) were commissioned by the sitter at this time – one of the first such commissions given to Holbein in England; both the preparatory drawing (RCIN 912266) and the finished oil painting survive. Guildford holds the white staff of office of the Comptroller of the Household, and a hat badge showing a clock and geometrical instruments. He stands against a deep blue background, decorated with the twisting vine found in a number of Holbein's portraits. Above his head is a curtain and rail which also occurs in the companion portrait (St Louis Art Museum) in such a way as to suggest, when the portraits are hung together, that husband and wife inhabit the same space. DS-T

144

HANS HOLBEIN THE YOUNGER

Thomas Howard, Duke of Norfolk (1473–1554) 1539

Oil on panel, 80.1 × 61.4 cm
RCIN 404439

PROVENANCE Thomas Howard, Earl of Arundel; bought from his heirs by Frederick, Prince of Wales, before 1750 (by descent)

LITERATURE Millar 1963, pp. 59–60, no. 30; Millar 1977, p. 97; *Northern Renaissance* 2011, p. 178, no. 80

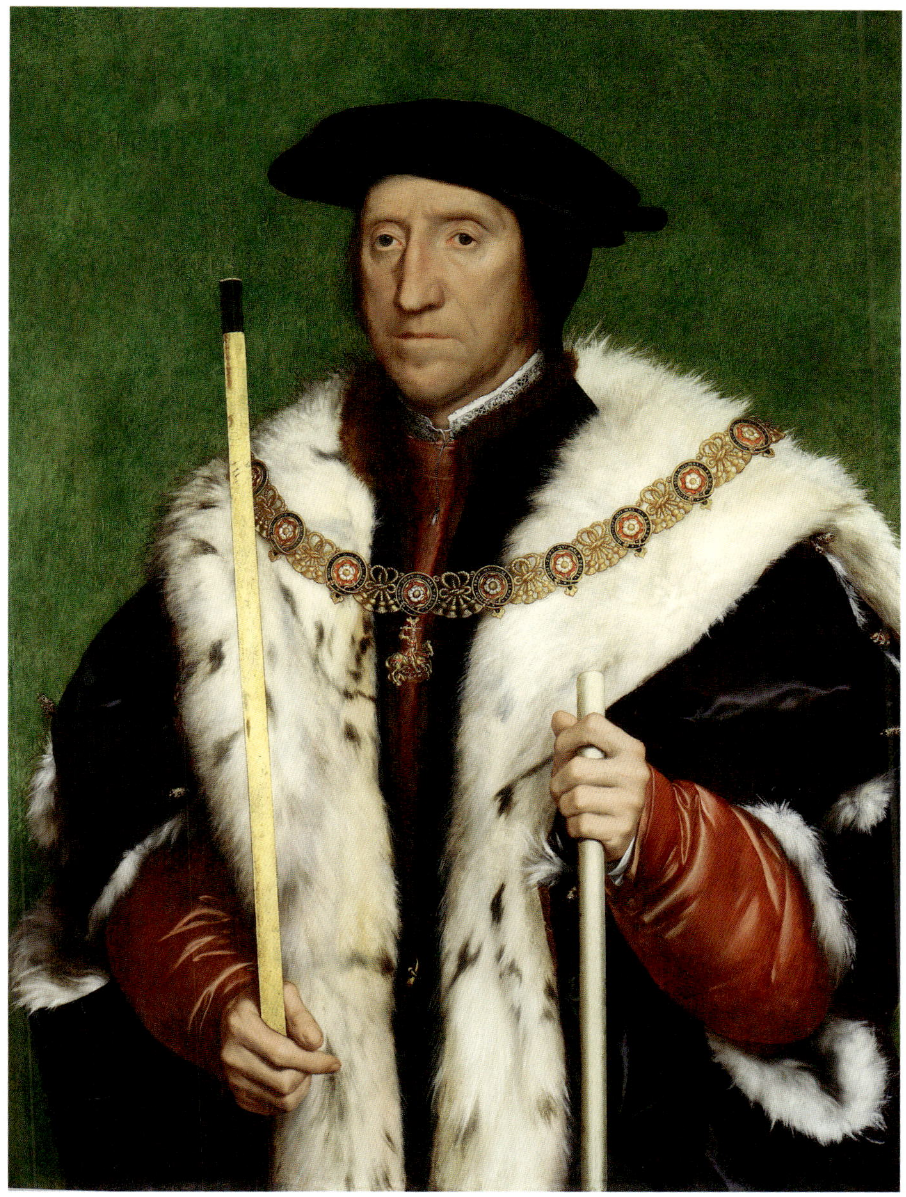

Thomas Howard, 3rd Duke of Norfolk, was one of the most powerful nobles in the country. His first wife was Anne of York, the sister of Henry VII's Queen, Elizabeth of York. He was uncle to Anne Boleyn, Henry VIII's second wife, and to Katherine Howard, Henry's fifth wife. He was godfather to Prince Edward and married his daughter Mary to Henry's illegitimate son Henry Fitzroy, Duke of Richmond. He was made a Knight of the Garter in April 1510, Lord High Treasurer in 1522 and Earl Marshal in 1533. In 1546, however, he and his son, the poet Earl of Surrey, were imprisoned for high treason. His son was executed but the Duke escaped because the King died the night before his appointed day of execution. He was imprisoned for six years, released by Queen Mary in 1553 and died the following year.

The three-quarter-length format is rare in Holbein's work and the sitters in the few other examples that exist held the highest positions at court. The format gave the Duke a more imposing presence than in reality, since he was described by the Venetian ambassador as 'small and spare in person'. Richly dressed, Norfolk holds the gold baton of Earl Marshal and the white staff of Lord High Treasurer, and wears the Order of the Garter. DS-T

Pantheons

As a means of declaring their intellectual allegiances, both Queen Caroline and Frederick, Prince of Wales, resorted to the creating of buildings dedicated to those they admired. These were arrangements of portraits and other artefacts, planned and housed in such a way as to create places where particular ideas were contemplated or worshipped. In some landscape gardens, such as Stowe, the word 'temple' was employed to make explicit this sense of a unifying ideal (see no. 7). Queen Caroline did not use this word but she created several pantheons of the same kind. Sometimes they were not completely separable from the arrangement of works of art within a sequence of rooms, as for example with the portraits within the Queen's Gallery in Kensington Palace. In other cases there is a clear separation between the sanctuary and the surrounding spaces, as can be seen in the three major projects for which Queen Caroline is remembered – the Library at St James's Palace (nos 150–2), the Picture Closet at Kensington (nos 153–5) and the Hermitage in Richmond (fig. 73 and nos 25 and 145–9).

The Hermitage and Merlin's Cave

Holding much in common with other contemporary commissions for a 'Temple of British Worthies', such as that created by Lord Cobham at Stowe, Caroline's Hermitage housed five busts by Guelfi of English heroes of science and philosophy – Sir Isaac Newton, John Locke, Samuel Clarke, William Wollaston and Robert Boyle (nos 145–9), whose works the Queen held dear to her heart. Close by the Hermitage stood another building, named Merlin's Cave, described by Horace Walpole:

> The building in question was designed by Kent and was by no means a cave but a thatched house .... At one end were six waxen figures large as life: Merlin and his secretary writing at a table and two female personages standing on one hand and two on the other, representing the Queen of Henry VII, Queen Elizabeth, and two characters out of Ariosto, who celebrated the House of Este, from which the House of Brunswick descended. This unintelligible puppet-show of which Stephen Duck, the thresher-poet, patronised by Queen Caroline, was Librarian, was demolished in the present reign.[32]

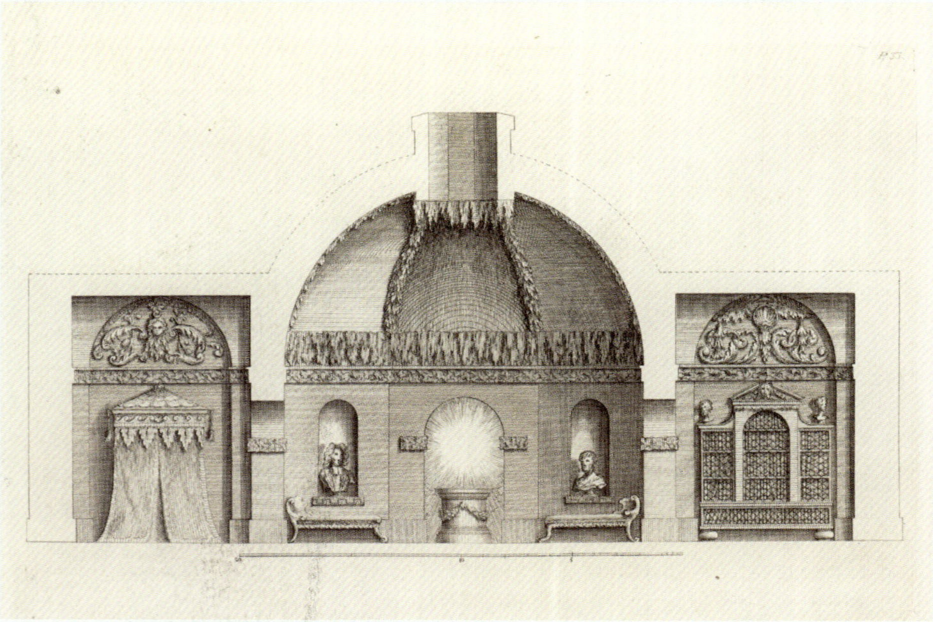

FIG. 73
A section of the Hermitage, plate 33 in *Some Designs of Mr Inigo Jones and Mr Wm Kent*, 1744
RCIN 1150776

145–9

GIOVANNI BATTISTA GUELFI (1690/1–1736)

Five busts of learned men 1730–3

Marble

The Hon. Robert Boyle (1627–1691)

Height excl. socle 62.86 cm
RCIN 1393

John Locke (1632–1704)

Height excl. socle 58.75 cm
RCIN 1395

Sir Isaac Newton (1642–1727)

Height excl. socle 60 cm
RCIN 1392

William Wollaston (1659–1724)

Height excl. socle 62.23 cm
RCIN 1390

Dr Samuel Clarke (1675–1729)

Height excl. socle 59.7 cm
RCIN 1394

PROVENANCE Commissioned by Queen Caroline in 1731 for her new Hermitage at Richmond Palace; probably completed in 1732

LITERATURE Webb 1954, pp. 147–54, figs 67, 69, 70; Giometti 1999, pp. 26–43; Porter 2000, p. 32; Keynes 2005, pp. 77–9; Marschner 2006, pp. 36–48

Although essentially a private commission for the grounds of a royal palace, the Hermitage designed for Queen Caroline by William Kent and constructed at Richmond in 1731–2 achieved immediate fame through the contemporary press because of the 'royal honour' it afforded to the memory of these five 'Men of *Learning* and *publick Virtue*'.[33] Queen Caroline seems to have been the first in the country to have erected a building which was chiefly intended for portrait sculptures of 'great men', and the fact that they were near-contemporary British men of thought rather than ancient men of arms lent further novelty to the scheme. The Hermitage stood for only twenty years but its appearance can be well understood from drawings and contemporary accounts. It was set into a hillside and the single external façade was formed of rough masonry so as to resemble that of an ancient, semi-ruined structure. This concealed an ample interior divided into three main spaces (fig. 73). A small vestibule led into an octagonal hall, where four of these busts – Newton, Locke, Clarke and Wollaston – were placed in niches. The bust of Boyle had a place of special honour, on a circular altar, his head surrounded by a radiating sun.

In 1731 George Vertue noted that 'Sig^{r} Guelphi' had received an order for four busts for Richmond.[34] G.B. Guelfi, who was probably born in Rome, spent some time in the workshop of Camillo Rusconi (see no. 105). It was in Rome that Guelfi encountered William Kent, who was to be his link with English clients such as Thomas Fermor, 2nd Baron Leominster, for whom the artist was working in 1721 on the restoration of ancient sculptures from the Arundel collection. His commission for the Richmond project may have come via Lord Burlington, for whom Kent and Guelfi had recently been working. The busts are all posthumous, obliging the sculptor to make use of engraved likenesses for his models. An initial account for four sculptures was paid in September 1732.[35] The bust of Boyle was paid for separately as part of an account which included the restoration of an antique statue of Venus.[36]

As a celebratory memorial to scientific 'worthies', the Hermitage can be distinguished from contemporary endeavours such as Lord Cobham's 'Temple of British Worthies' at Stowe, also designed by Kent and completed in 1734–5, where Newton and Locke stood with figures from the more distant past. The favour accorded to Robert Boyle, whose bust stood at the centre, somewhat higher than the others and with a radiating sun behind his head, may be taken to represent the Queen's estimation of the chemist, physicist, philosopher and founder member of the Royal Society. All five men were concerned with questions of physics and metaphysics, with the application of human reason – itself seen as a divine gift – in support of the fundamental Christian beliefs.

Boyle's position at the centre of the group divided the others into two pairs: to one

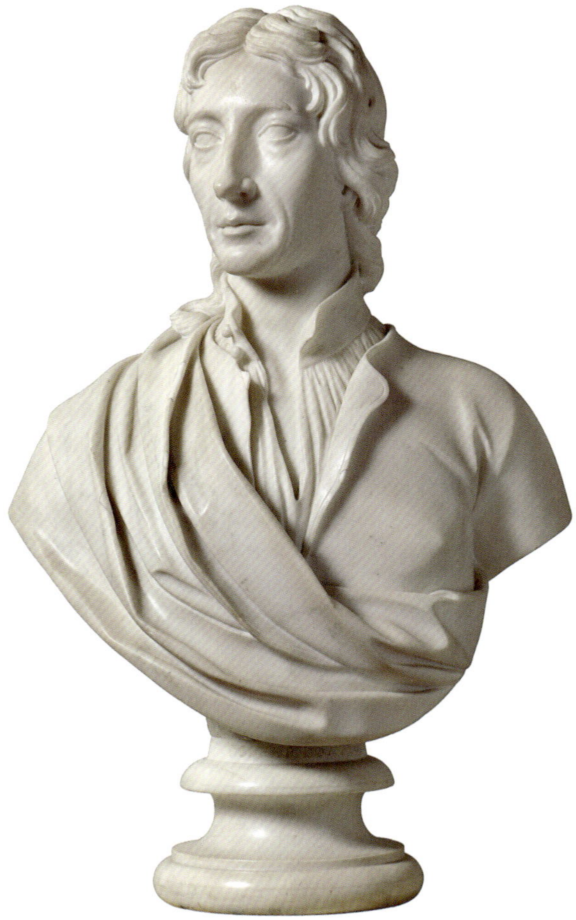

The Hon. Robert Boyle

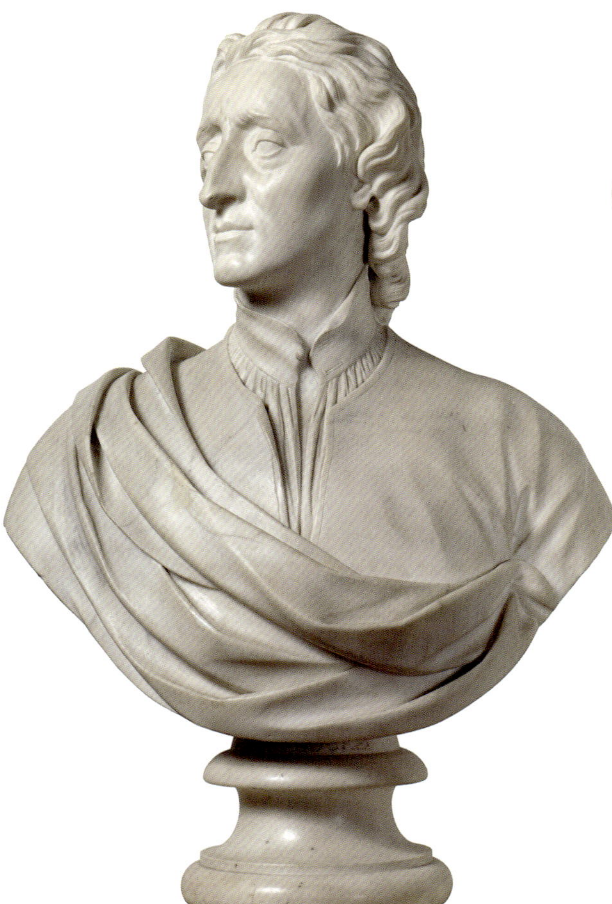

John Locke

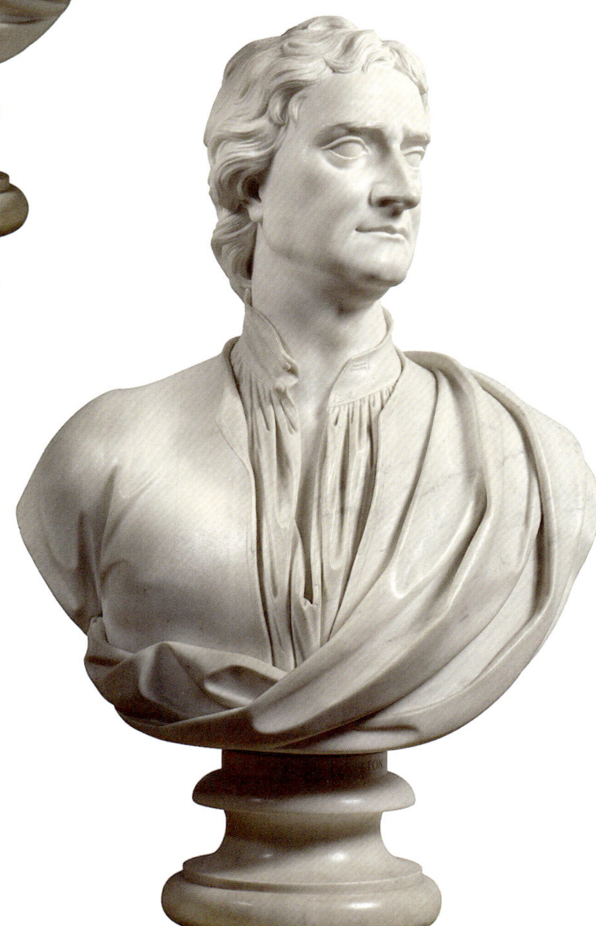

Sir Isaac Newton

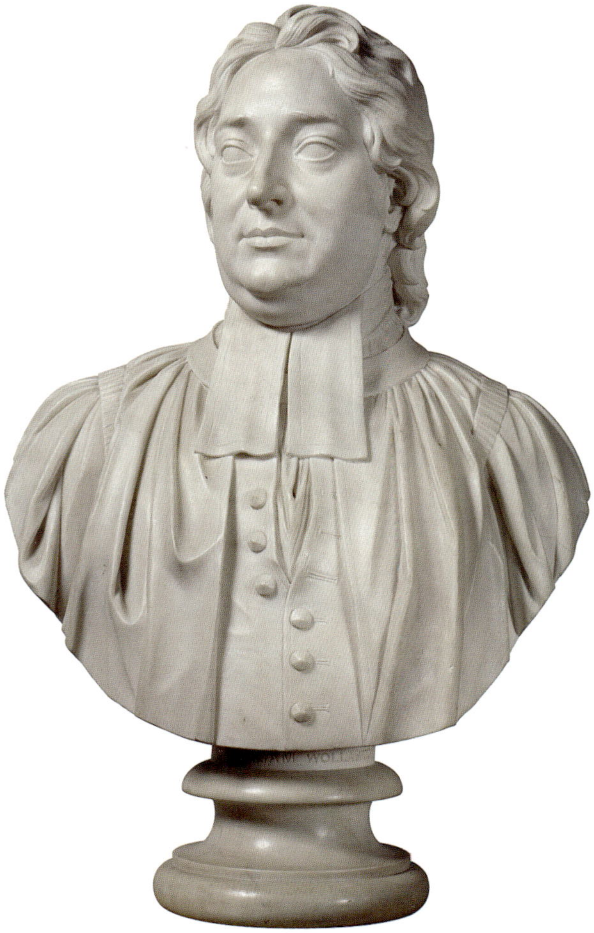

William Wollaston

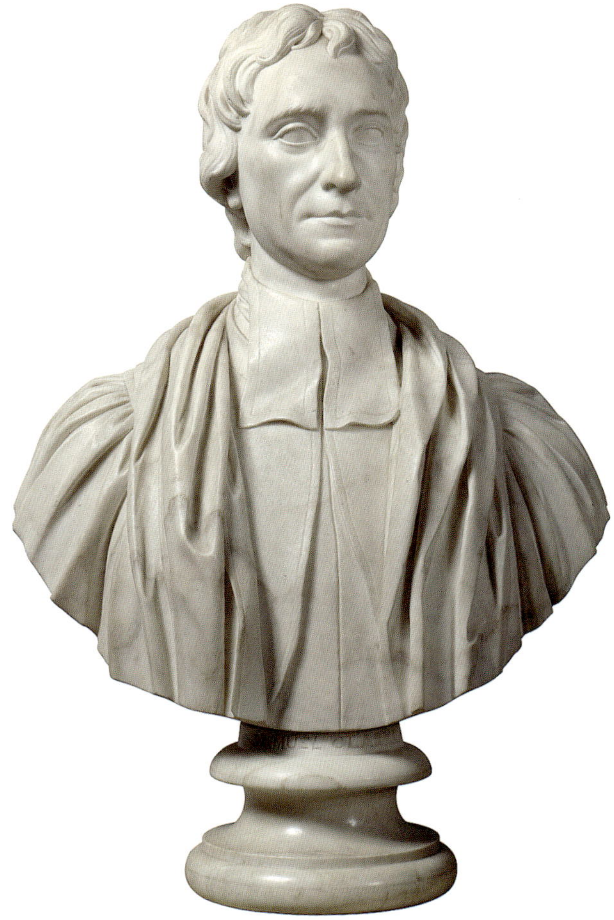

Dr Samuel Clarke

side stood Sir Isaac Newton, whom Queen Caroline when Princess of Wales had entertained at St James's in 1716 and who 'shew'd the World was *philosophically* and *mathematically* made; and that it could be *framed* and *held together* by none but an *infinitely Wise* and *Almighty* architect'.[37] Next to Newton stood John Locke, who was championed for his knowledge of 'the *Powers* and *Operations* of the Mind', and whose *Essay Concerning Humane Understanding* (1689) was judged 'the best Book of *Logic* in the World'.[38]

The metaphysician Samuel Clarke, a correspondent of Leibniz, had presented Caroline with copies of his books shortly after her arrival in England as Princess of Wales in 1714, and she, having read them swiftly, declared 'Dr Clarke shall be one of my favourites; his writings are the finest things in the world'.[39] His bust was paired at Richmond with that of his disciple William Wollaston, author of the widely circulated *The Religion of Nature Delineated* (1724).

In April 1733 the *Gentleman's Magazine* announced a competition for verses on the subject of the Hermitage and its occupants, and in successive numbers of the magazine the (with few exceptions) anonymous authors competed in praise of Queen Caroline's achievement. A common theme was her having favoured British philosophers over those of her native German lands, notably Leibniz.

Locke, Newton, Clarke and Wollaston were, the magazine declared, 'the *Glory* of their *Country*, and stamp'd a Dignity on human Nature .... These great and worthy Men the Queen *hath delighted to honour*, and is the first crown'd Head in the World, who had *uncommon Virtue* enough to *immortalize* Men so absolutely in the Interests of Mankind, that all their *political Principles* were cultivated for their Good .... When her Majesty *consecrated* these dead Heroes, she *built herself a Temple* in the *Hearts* of the People of *England*'.[40] JM

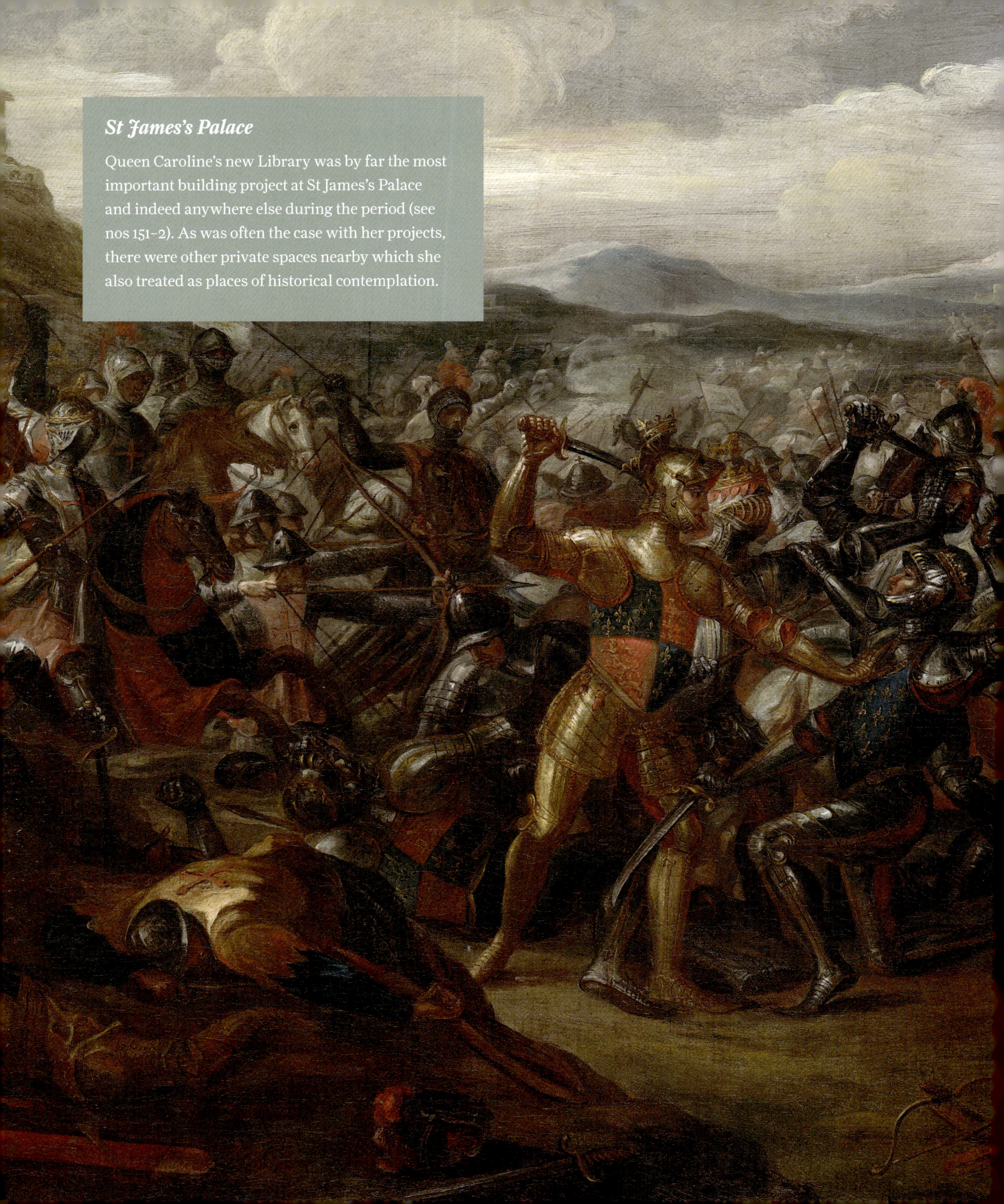

St James's Palace

Queen Caroline's new Library was by far the most important building project at St James's Palace and indeed anywhere else during the period (see nos 151–2). As was often the case with her projects, there were other private spaces nearby which she also treated as places of historical contemplation.

150

WILLIAM KENT (*c*.1685–1748)

The Battle of Agincourt *c*.1729

Oil on canvas, 82.0 × 122.2 cm
Signed: *Wm Kent Pinxt.*
RCIN 402901

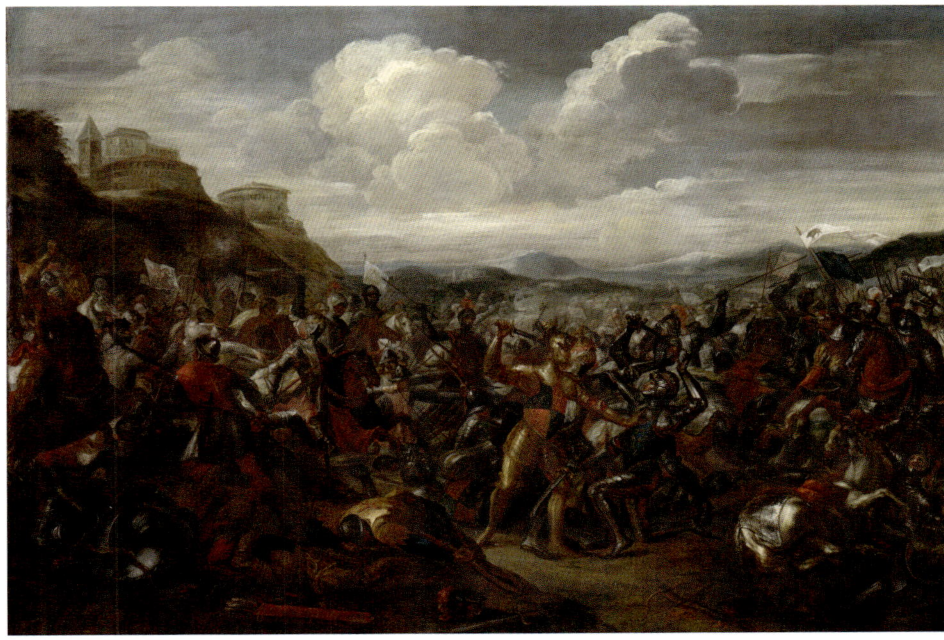

PROVENANCE Probably painted for Queen Caroline

LITERATURE Millar 1963, p. 171, no. 505

This is one of a set of three scenes from the life of Henry V (RCIN 402898 and 402900–1, both 76 × 60 cm), presumably executed for Queen Caroline and seen by Horace Walpole in her Dressing Room at St James's Palace in 1758.[41] One of the paintings is dated 1729 and all three were probably among the 'pictures' for which Queen Caroline paid Kent in 1730 and 1731; the three magnificent frames were probably those for which William Waters received payment at the same time.[42]

The largest of the scenes, this was presumably first hung as the centrepiece, flanked by the other two, both half the width and slightly less in height, making a triptych arrangement. The other scenes show Henry V meeting the French queen (RCIN 402898) and marrying her daughter, Catherine of Valois (RCIN 402900). This central scene depicts Henry V in the thick of his most famous victory, at the Battle of Agincourt in 1415. The three are examples of picturesque, inaccurate and slightly triumphalist antiquarianism, loosely evoking Shakespeare's famous play, though surprisingly this was not an especial favourite during the period.[43] The arrangement of the three would also seem to be an illustration of Dryden's words 'None but the brave deserve the fair' (*Alexander's Feast*, 1697, l. 16), surely intending to suggest an analogy between medieval and modern royal romances. Like Henry V, George II fought the French and won a beautiful and accomplished princess, though not strictly in that order. His courtship and marriage to Caroline of Ansbach occurred in 1705; after the succession was assured by the birth of his son Frederick, in 1707, he was permitted to risk his life serving in the armed forces, which he did with distinction in 1708 at the Battle of Oudenarde. The subject of love and war may also be intended to suggest by analogy that a magnanimous hero wins the love of the people he conquers as well as that of his royal bride, something which might also have been intended to apply to the Hanoverians.

Kent's limitations as a painter are clearly seen in this work. The arrangement is obvious, the drawing absent and the handling bland and nerveless. DS-T

151

JOHN MICHAEL RYSBRACK (1693–1770)

Edward, Prince of Wales, the Black Prince (1330–1376) *c.*1737

Painted terracotta, 64.5 cm high
RCIN 37067

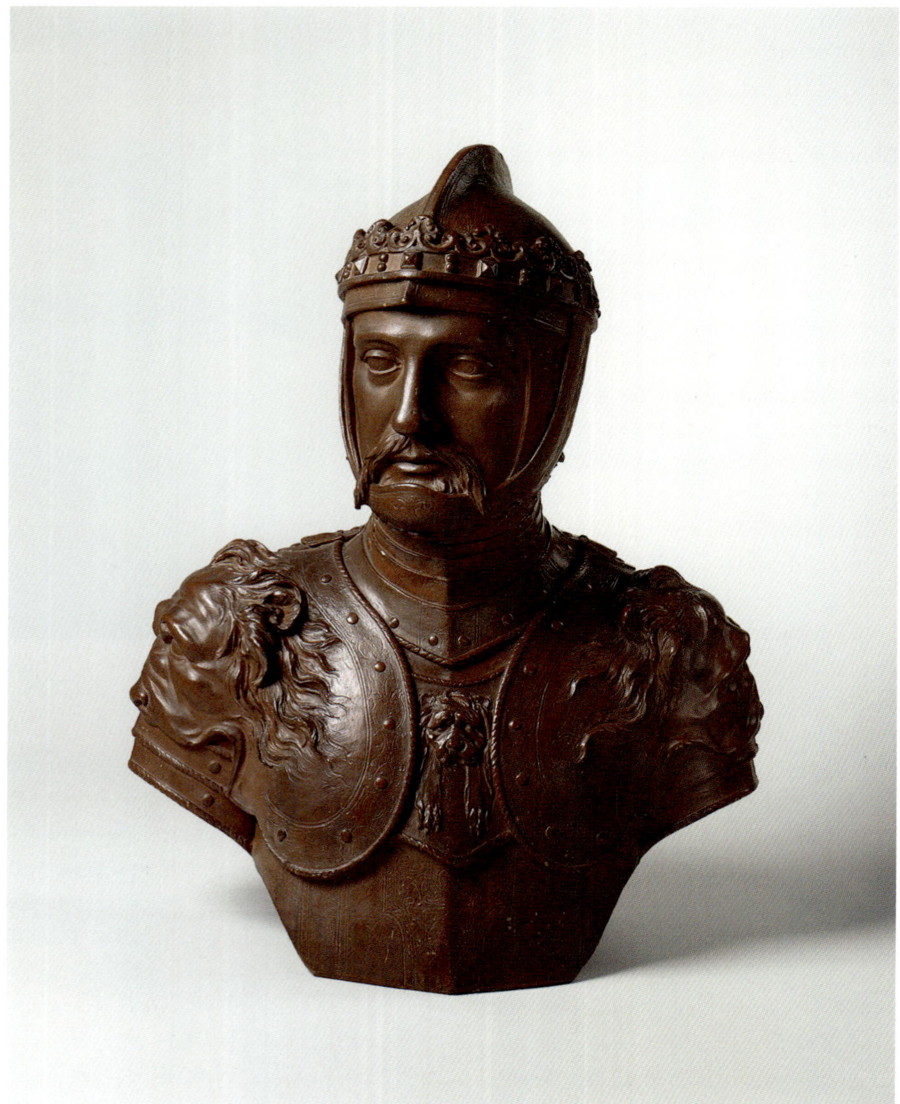

PROVENANCE Commissioned by Queen Caroline for her Library at St James's Palace

LITERATURE Webb 1954, pp. 145–6; Eustace 1998, pp. 31–40

George Vertue recorded a visit by Queen Caroline on 10 June 1735 to Rysbrack's studio, where she was able to see 'the Busts of Marble of Kings & Queens done lately by him to adorn some palace'.[44] An article in the *Gentleman's Magazine* a few weeks later noted that 'Her Majesty has ordered Mr Risbrack to make the Bustos in Marble of all the Kings of England from William the Conqueror, in order to be placed in her New Building in the Gardens at Richmond'.[45] Important as these early sources are, neither is completely accurate, for the series does not seem to have reached the marble stage, and there is no other contemporary reference to a series of kings at Richmond. These terracottas were in fact modelled for Queen Caroline's Library at St James's Palace (see p. 78). Whilst it may have been intended that the busts should then be carved in marble, the commission was annulled by the Queen's death in November 1737. On 23 January 1738 Isaac Ware as Secretary of the Board of Works wrote to Rysbrack: 'I am ordered ... to acquaint You that [the Commissioners of Works] will Allow you the Price you have Charged them for the Busto's in the Queens Library, but expect you will send them to the Office (there to be Lodged) the Models of the faces you made for Working after'.[46] It seems that the terracottas themselves were displayed in the Library, where they can be

152

JOHN MICHAEL RYSBRACK

Edward VI (1537–1553) 1738

Painted terracotta, 56.5 cm high
Incised in the clay on the central support: *Michael Rysbrack / 1738*
RCIN 53346

seen in Charles Wild's watercolour (no. 29). The others in the series represented Alfred, Edward III, Philippa of Hainault, Henry V, Catherine of Valois, Henry VII, Elizabeth of York, Elizabeth I and Henry Stuart, Prince of Wales.

Rysbrack's starting point for his likenesses may have been the imaginary portraits engraved by his friend and promoter George Vertue for Rapin Thoyras's *Histoire d'Angleterre*, published in English in 1724 (see p. 271), but these images left to the sculptor's own imagination some of the details of costume and armour. JM

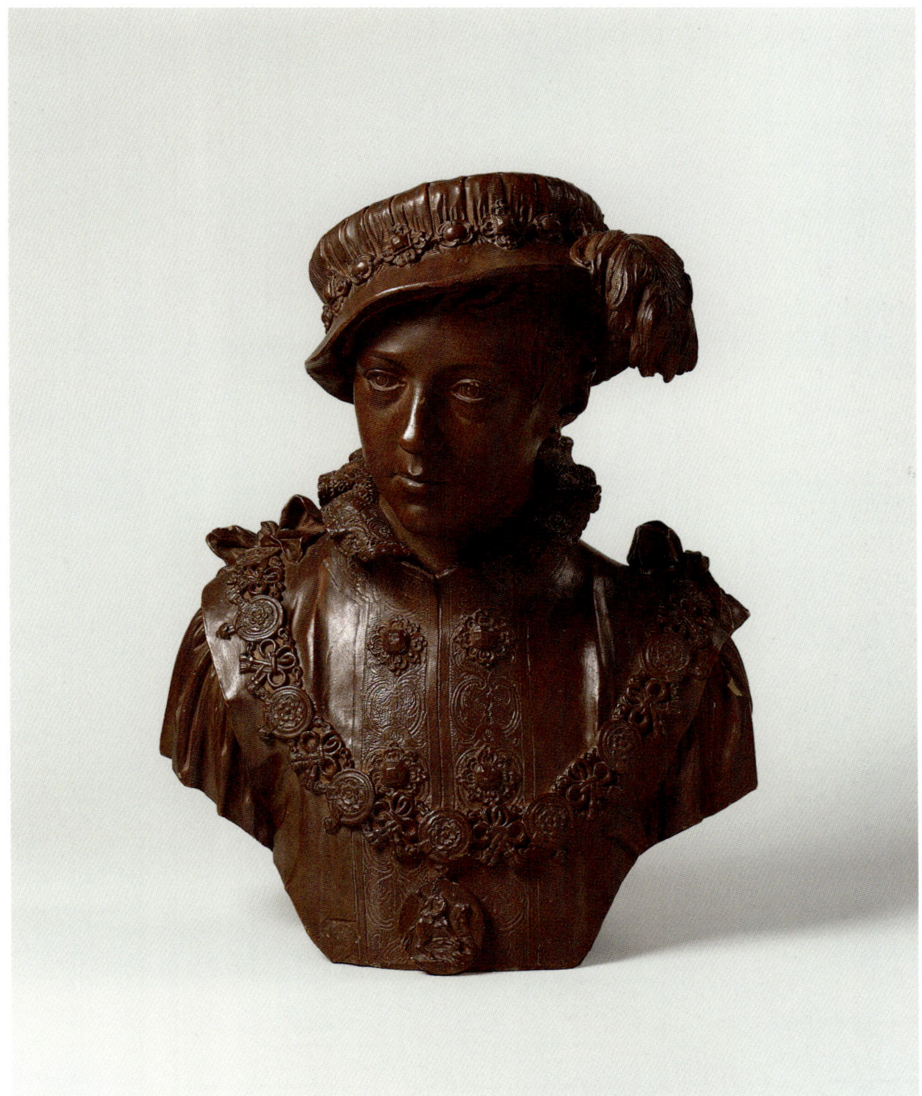

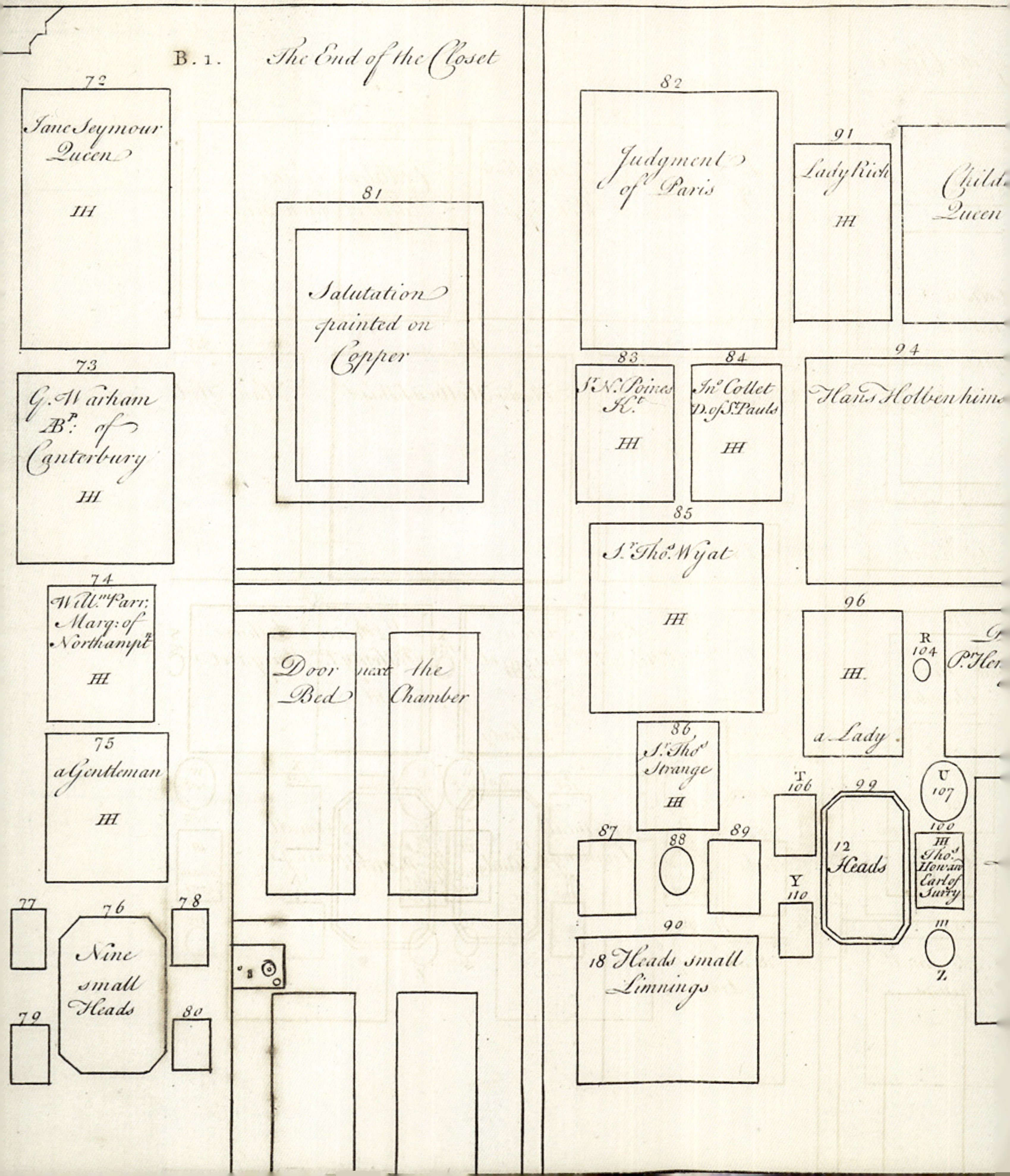
B. 1.
The End of the Closet
72
Jane Seymour Queen
HH
73
G. Warham Æp: of Canterbury
HH
74
Will.m Parr: Marq: of Northampt.n
HH
75
a Gentleman
HH
76
Nine small Heads
77
78
79
80
81
Salutation painted on Copper
Door next the Bed
Chamber
82
Judgment of Paris
83
S.r N. Poines K.t
HH
84
Jn.o Collet D. of S.t Pauls
HH
85
S.r Tho.s Wyat
HH
86
S.r Tho.s Strange
HH
87
88
89
90
18 Heads small Limnings
91
Lady Rich
HH
94
Hans Holben hims
96
HH
a Lady
99
12 Heads
100
HH
Tho.s Howard Earl of Surry
R
104
T
106
U
107
Y
110
111
Z
Quee

Kensington Private Apartments

The Picture Closet and the associated cabinet rooms at Kensington Palace reflected many of Queen Caroline's personal interests in microcosm, showing not only her fascination with art, but also with genealogy and history of the royal houses of Europe, with the collecting of a *Wunderkammer* (or 'cabinet of curiosities') and the classification of it, and with the education of her children.[47] To house her collections, Caroline made use of several spaces. The Picture Closet, prominently situated in the midst of the State Apartments, between the King's Drawing Room, the State Bedchamber and the King's Gallery, was largely for the display of the history of the houses of Europe. The exact layout of the hang of Picture Closet is known from four plans (see figs. 77–80) drawn by George Vertue and appended to the inventory of the contents which he compiled in September 1743. This was produced at 'the Queen's command', although by the time it was printed Queen Caroline had been dead for seven years.[48] The plans show a room tightly packed with small pictures, drawings and miniatures, interspersed with ivory carvings and waxes, stone bas reliefs and even an embroidered silk picture of Charles I.

In the private apartments was the so-called 'Little Library'. The centrepiece of this was, according to Walpole, a 'fine genealogical book on vellum of all the pedigrees of the Kings of England with their portraits and arms illuminated, drawn I think for Queen Elizabeth'.[49] The library also housed a number of volumes from Charles I's library. Alongside it were two cabinet rooms, used for the display of Queen Caroline's most precious objects, and two lists of these survive: the 'Curiositys & Medals in the Cabinet of His Majesty's Library', drawn up some time before 1755 by Mrs Purcell, seamstress and confidante to the Queen,[50] and Horace Walpole's hand-written list of 1763, appended to his copy of Vertue's catalogue of the Picture Closet, now in the Royal Collection (RCIN 1112557). Purcell and Walpole detail the cameos, intaglios, gemstones, seals, rings and medals held in the cabinet rooms. They also catalogue a group of exotic curiosities and treasures. This group of objects was entirely inspired by the *Wunderkammer* of the European courts which Caroline knew from her youth – particularly the renowned Grünes Gewölbe in Dresden, and Electress Sophia's cabinet in Herrenhausen.[51]

Vertue described these rooms, and in particular the Picture Closet, as 'the greatest store of portraits of the English'.[52] It was genealogy that was Caroline's particular love, and her Picture Closet and cabinet rooms were designed not only to show off the works of Holbein but to support her interest in the lines of the kings of Europe. According to various influential sixteenth-century treatises concerning the formation of museological collections, particularly that of Samuel Quiccheberg, the ideal was to include a painting or sculpture series which celebrated the pedigree of the collector. This was demonstrated in a number of princely courts in Europe – particularly that at Ambras Castle in Austria, where Archduke Ferdinand II created a collection of more than a thousand images delineating the history of his dynasty.

Nurtured in the courts of Ansbach, Dresden and Berlin, and above all in Hanover, Caroline had shown a fascination with genealogy throughout her life. As a young bride at Herrenhausen she had complemented Leibniz's history of the House of Guelf by constructing genealogical tables and researching the pedigrees of various other European dynasties. Although there was a certain tradition for displaying dynastic series in British palaces, the only surviving example was Jacob de Wet's run of Scottish kings in the gallery of the Palace of Holyroodhouse. At Queen Caroline's instigation, therefore, many of the portraits throughout the royal residences were rehung in coherent groups, but it was at Kensington that her energies were focused on creating dynastic series. In a contemporary source it is recorded that the Queen 'begged' for a set of panel paintings from Charles Cornwallis, 1st Earl Cornwallis (1700–62), so that she might display a more complete series of monarchs (see nos 153 and 154).[53] These were recorded in 1818 as hanging at Kensington. In the cabinet rooms, Walpole recorded more than a thousand medals – among them a full series of Roman Emperors of which Queen Caroline was particularly proud.

DETAIL, FIG. 78

153 & 154

BRITISH SCHOOL

Edward III (1312–1377) and *Richard II (1367–1400)* *c*.1600

Oil on panel, 57.2 × 44.0 cm; 57.9 × 43.7 cm
RCIN 404740 and RCIN 404748

PROVENANCE Acquired by Queen Caroline from Lord Cornwallis

LITERATURE Millar 1963, p. 49, nos 1 and 3

The Hanoverians did not inherit a comprehensive collection of portraits of English kings and queens upon their arrival in 1714. The only portraits of medieval monarchs then in the collection were six panels depicting Henry V, Henry VI, Edward IV and his Queen, Richard III and Elizabeth of York. Tudor monarchs were better represented but even here the legacy was disappointing. Queen Caroline supplemented this meagre supply with a group of fifteen panels (of roughly the same dimensions), most if not all acquired from Earl Cornwallis, perhaps in 1721–2, when he was Groom of the Bedchamber. In this way she added some duplicates and some important new names – Henry IV, Henry VII and his mother Lady Margaret Beaufort (fig. 74), as well as the present two, of Edward III and Richard II. The Cornwallis purchase also included, from the Tudor period, Henry VIII and two of his wives, Catherine of Aragon and Anne Boleyn, and Edward VI and Mary I. Queen Caroline hung the entire set in the Dressing Room of her private apartments at Kensington, near the Picture Closet.[54] Queen Caroline probably wanted as many English kings as she could obtain, but she must have sought some more assiduously than others and none more than these two. Edward III was a model warrior king and the essential ancestor of any claimant to the throne during the Wars of the Roses. The reign of his son, Richard II, represented a moment of stillness before the anarchy of civil war, as well as the first great age of English letters. The play of that name begins Shakespeare's great cycle which treats English history in an unbroken sequence up to the accession of Henry VII. Queen Caroline may have seen a parallel between the Wars of the Roses and the ongoing dynastic struggle between the houses of Hanover and Stuart. This makes the portrait of Margaret Beaufort especially interesting, as the mother of Henry VII provides such a perfect historical anti-type to the Electress Sophia, mother of George I. Like Sophia, Margaret Beaufort was renowned for her learning and accredited with the creation of two Cambridge Colleges, Christ's and St John's. Like George I, Henry VII followed a shaky claim to the throne with a stable occupation of it, his reign marking one of the fresh starts of English history.

Dendrochonology reveals that the tree which supplied the panel for the portrait of Henry VII (RCIN 404743) was felled some time soon after 1580, the date of its last ring. This means that it would have become a panel ready to be painted around 1600.[55] At least eight panels, including *Edward III* and *Richard II* (and RCIN 403045, 404196, 404740, 404744 and 404745), are sufficiently close in style to suggest that they belong to the same group. This set, created long after their sitters' deaths by a journeyman painter, are based on images in Westminster Abbey, among them the tomb of Edward III and the famous full-length painting of Richard II. DS-T

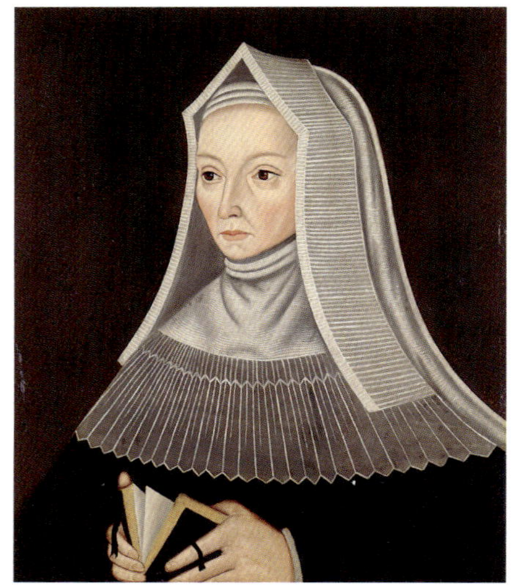

FIG. 74
British School
Lady Margaret Beaufort, Countess of Richmond
Oil on panel
RCIN 404749

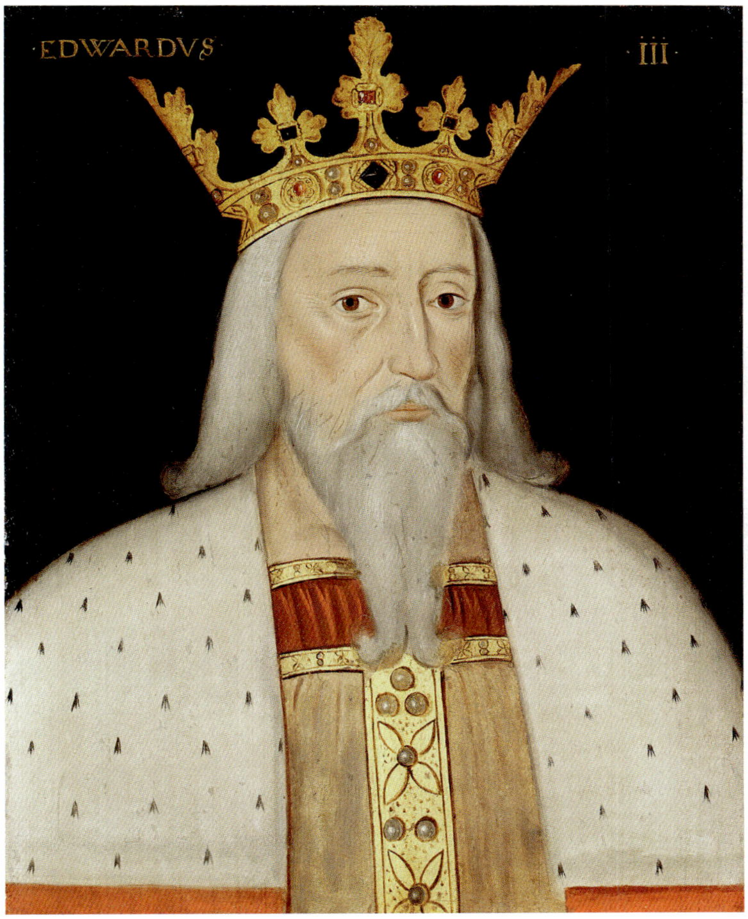
·EDWARDVS
·III·

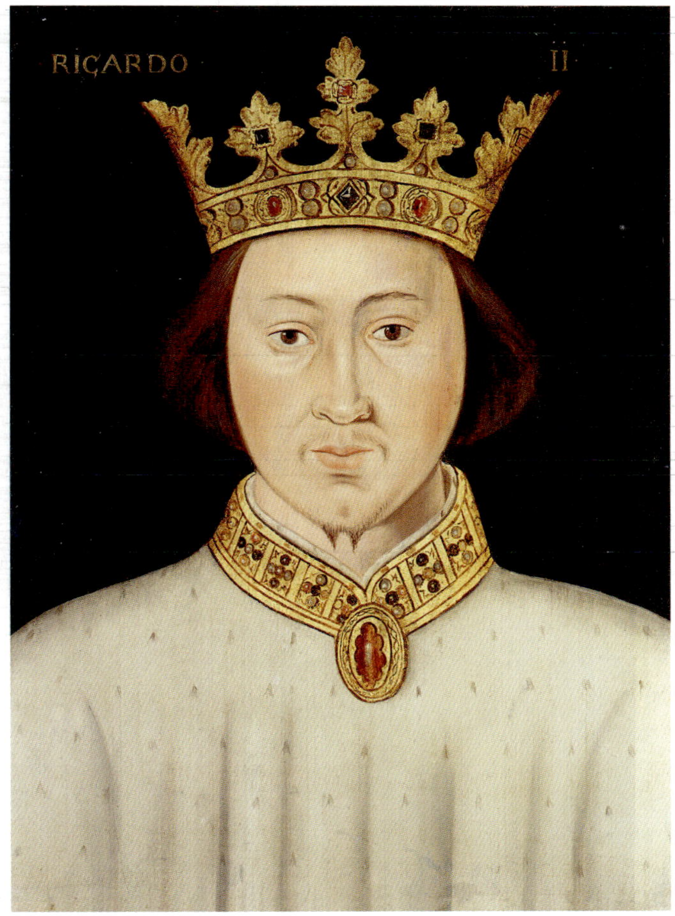
RIÇARDO
II

Queen Caroline's Wunderkammer

The inventories compiled by Mrs Purcell and Horace Walpole of Caroline's cabinet rooms listed not only her historic cameos and intaglios, medals, rings and seals but also a range of *Wunderkammer* works such as boxes, cups, salts and other vessels wrought from rock crystal, agate, aventurine, lapis lazuli, serpentine, amber, enamel, gold and pearls. Alongside these were natural objects such as branches of coral, bezoar stones, nuggets of metal ores, a 'unicorn's horn', and a mounted humming bird. These objects were displayed together with a small collection of weapons, described as Turkish and Indian, and the large group of medals owned by the Queen.

The elements of a collection of this type were described by Francis Bacon as seeking 'in small compass a model of universal nature made private'.[56] The idea was to reflect the wider world and include not only animal, vegetable and mineral objects drawn directly from nature but also works of art wrought by man, scientific instruments and ethnographic items. Such cabinets of curiosities were popular on the Continent throughout the sixteenth and seventeenth centuries, but were waning by the time Caroline set about her scheme. The Queen, however, was beginning an entirely new venture. There is little evidence for earlier cabinets of curiosities within the royal collections, although Charles I certainly had a cabinet of artworks which contained medals and sculpture, and a number of the cameos in Kensington cabinets were inherited by Caroline (nos 162–4). The Queen's *Wunderkammer* was far more extensive, however, and was developed with the encouragement of Sir Hans Sloane (1660–1753), whose own remarkable collection was housed in his home in Chelsea, which was first opened to the public in 1742. This collection later formed the basis for the British Museum, founded in 1753, and the Natural History Museum.

Queen Caroline's *Wunderkammer* was, by contrast, almost entirely private, compiled purely for her own delight and for the education of her children. It was supplemented by a group of books held in the 'Little Library', which included, according to Walpole's list, 'a large and fine collection of Atlas's' and 'the Editions of the King of France's Cabinet'. The Saxon tradition of collecting as a princely virtue seems to have been maintained by Caroline and continued by Frederick and Augusta. The brief mention by Vertue of Frederick's Closet at Carlton House shows that he was similarly interested in objects of historical curiosity, while Princess Augusta appears to have been a collector of medals, an interest she inherited from her father, Frederick II of Saxe-Gotha-Altenburg. After her death a memo to Lord North on the dispersal of her collections includes a note that 'when Lord Rochford, with Lord Boston & Mr Legrand had by the King's orders examined the Princess's cabinets, they took from them ... not only the Papers ... but particularly a quantity of medals'.[57] The core of Queen Caroline's collection remained undisturbed at Kensington Palace until the early nineteenth century, when much of it was sent to join George IV's *Wunderkammer* at Windsor Castle.

155

NORTH ITALIAN

The Adoration of the Magi

Cameo: 16th century; mount: *c.*1700
Onyx, silver gilt, 3.4 × 6.5 × 1.5 cm
RCIN 65175

PROVENANCE Probably acquired by Queen Caroline; first recorded in an inventory compiled before 1755 (BM.Add.Ms 20101)

LITERATURE Aschengreen Piacenti and Boardman 2008, no. 210

A virtuoso piece of carving, this cameo exploits the layers of the onyx to their full, adding a sense of space and perspective to the scene by fading into the darker layers or by leaving areas such as the star in very high relief. A sense of movement is added to the robes of the Magi and their retinue, which have been carved in an almost painterly fashion. The cameo was first recorded in an inventory drawn up by Mrs Purcell some time between the death of the Queen in 1737 and her own death in 1755. It demonstrates Queen Caroline's sophisticated taste in cameos, which must have been nurtured in the court of her stepfather, the Elector John George IV (ruled 1668–94), in Dresden, where the *Schatzkammer* collection was held in the Grünes Gewölbe. Caroline also spent much of her youth in Charlottenburg, the home of her guardian Sophia Charlotte (1668–1705), which housed another renowned treasury of works of art. It is likely that Caroline was also aware of the significant collection of cameos and antiquities brought together at Salzdahlum, the residence of Anton Ulrich of Brunswick-Wolfenbüttel (1633–1714). KJ

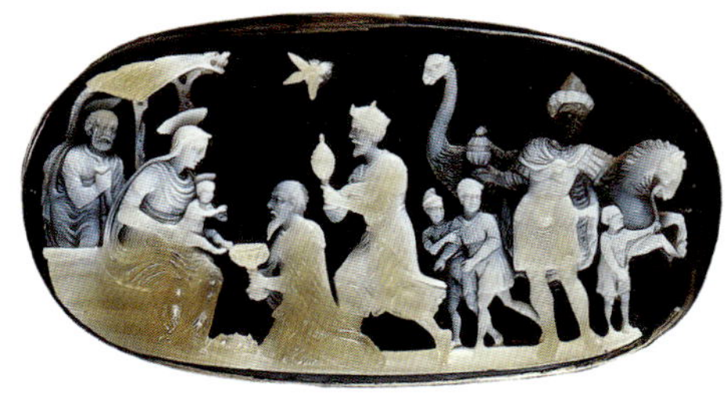

156

FRENCH

Pendant with thirteen cameos

Cameos: early 17th century; mounts: 18th century
Gold, émail en ronde bosse, émail champlevé, sardonyx, turquoise, black and white onyx, sard, brown and grey agate, black and grey agate, niccolo, 13.0 × 8.9 cm
RCIN 65256

PROVENANCE Probably acquired by Queen Caroline; first recorded in an inventory compiled before 1755 (BM.Add.Ms 20101)

LITERATURE Aschengreen Piacenti and Boardman 2008, no. 286

This jewel is identifiable as the 'hanging Jewell of onexes containing 12 heads and a piece of figures in the middle' listed by Mrs Purcell before 1755. The original jewel was possibly studded with gems rather than mounted with cameos and its tabernacle form suggests it may have been a religious piece. The central scene shows Joseph with his brothers, rather confusingly surrounded by cameo heads of Roman emperors, which, together with the somewhat crude mounting, suggests that the piece was assembled in the eighteenth century, possibly using part of an earlier mount made in the Paris workshops of the jeweller Jean Vangrol.[58] This piece may have been one of the gifts sent to Caroline by Elisabeth Charlotte of the Palatinate, widow of the Duke of Orléans, commonly known as Liselotte. Caroline and Liselotte were in frequent correspondence between 1715 and 1722, and exchanged a number of gifts, including, according to one letter, a present of 'engraved stones'.[59]

The idea of assembling such pieces in a group may have been inspired by the work of the goldsmith and jeweller Johann Melchior Dinglinger (1664–1731), who mounted a number of cameos in this style for the Elector Augustus II at the Saxon court in Dresden. Augustus's brother John George IV had married Queen Caroline's widowed mother Eleonore of Saxe-Eisenach in 1692. KJ

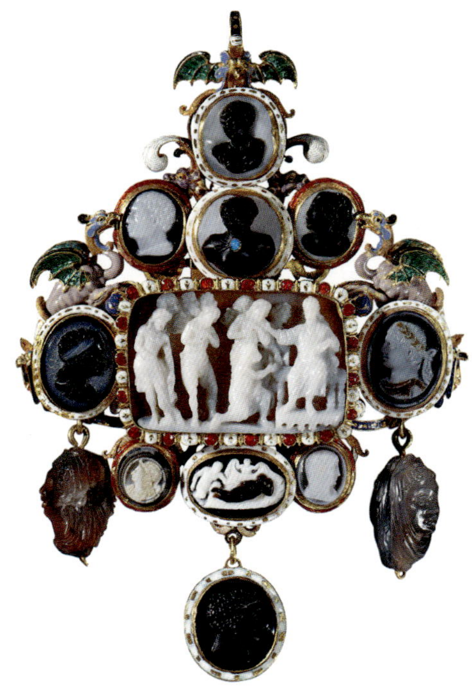

157

NORTH ITALY

Hercules

Bust: 2nd half 16th century;
socle: late 19th/early 20th century
Saxon agate, gilt metal, 5.7 × 3.8 × 3.0 cm
RCIN 65740

PROVENANCE Probably acquired by Queen Caroline; first documented in the Royal Collection in 1763

LITERATURE Aschengreen Piacenti and Boardman 2008, no. 32

Queen Caroline's taste for hardstone carving was expressed at Kensington not only through the cameo and intaglio collection but also through a 'crystal' bust of Charles I, which surmounted one of the cabinets, and this exuberant example of stone-cutting, which was housed in one of the drawers below. In his notes on Vertue's inventory of 1763, Horace Walpole described it as a 'fine bust of Commodus with the lions skin', and in the following year the bust was among a number of gems and curiosities sent to George III.[60] Small-scale busts of this kind were typically made by Milanese craftsmen in the grand ducal workshops of Florence to decorate cabinets and other pieces of furniture. KJ

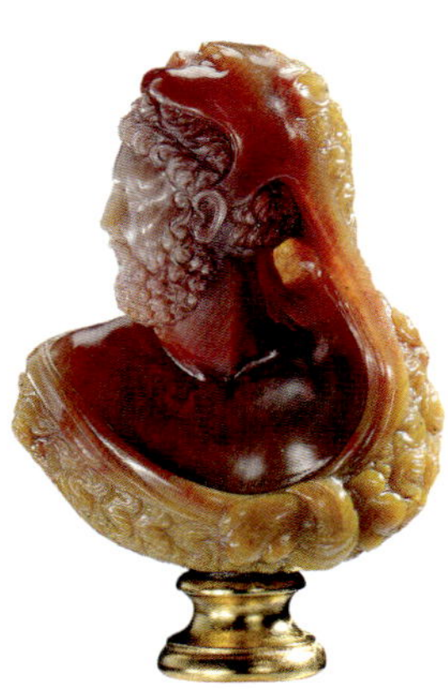

158

POSSIBLY ITALIAN

Henry VIII and Prince Edward

1st half 18th century
Sardonyx, gold, 5.7 × 7.8 cm
RCIN 65189

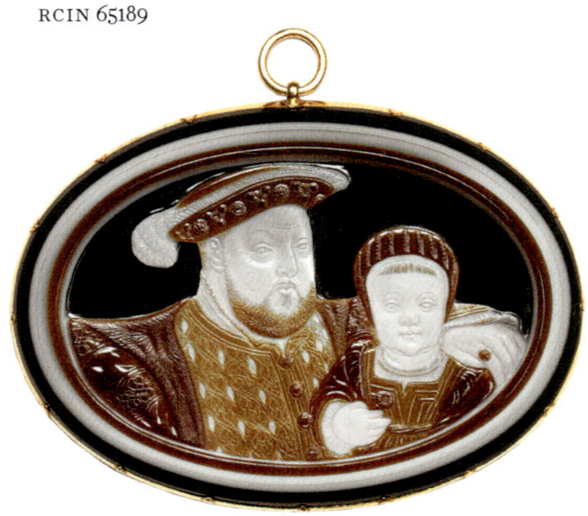

PROVENANCE Probably acquired by Queen Caroline; first documented in the Royal Collection in 1763

LITERATURE Aschengreen Piacenti and Boardman 2008, no. 245

For many years this piece was considered to be authentically sixteenth-century and a number of contemporary stone-cutters were suggested. Walpole, for example, in his annotations to Vertue's inventory of the Picture Closet, suggested it was the work of Valerio Belli (*c*.1468–1553/5) after Holbein. However, the unusual pose of Henry VIII placing his hand affectionately on his son's shoulder is wholly uncharacteristic for the period, and no double-portrait prototype of the pair is known. It is more likely that the cameo was an eighteenth-century work, reflecting Queen Caroline's interest in Holbein's Whitehall Mural (see p. 275).

On the reverse is an intaglio of the same subject so that when seen by candlelight the figures have greater depth and subtlety. This might explain the rather sketchily carved features of the two sitters, which in turn seem to relate the work to the portrait of Henry VIII (no. 159). KJ

159

ENGLISH

Henry VIII *c*.1730

Sardonyx, gold, 4.0 × 3.8 cm
RCIN 65190

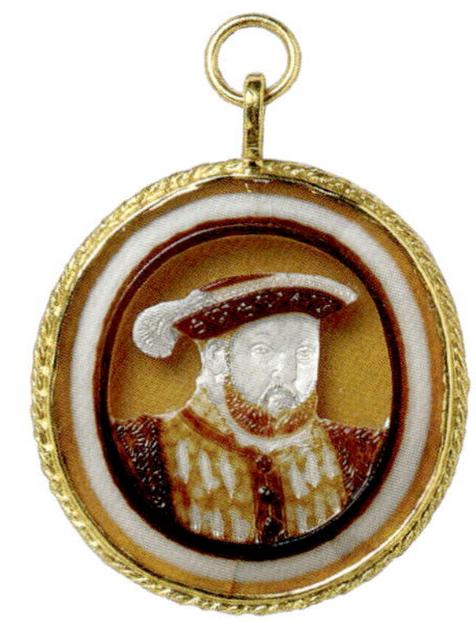

PROVENANCE Probably acquired by Queen Caroline; first documented in the Royal Collection in 1764

LITERATURE Aschengreen Piacenti and Boardman 2008, no. 212

The treatment of the face and the type of stone used in this cameo show a close relationship with no. 158, suggesting a similar eighteenth-century date of creation. Moreover, the image is related to a medal of Henry VIII by the Swiss medallist Jean Dassier (1676–1763), which was struck in 1731. Dassier produced a full set of medals of the kings and queens of England in chronological sequence from William the Conqueror to the reigning monarch, George II, to whom he presented the series. Many of the images had no known precedent to follow and so Dassier used the imaginary engravings by F.M. la Cave which illustrated Rapin Thoyras's *History of England* printed in The Hague in 1724 (see p. 271). KJ

160 & 161

ENGLISH

Elizabeth I

Cameo: *c.*1575–85; mount: early 18th century
Sardonyx, gold, 6.7 × 5.5 cm
RCIN 65186

ENGLISH

Elizabeth I

Cameo: *c.*1575; mount: late 16th century
Sardonyx, gold, enamel, 4.0 × 3.2 cm
RCIN 65187

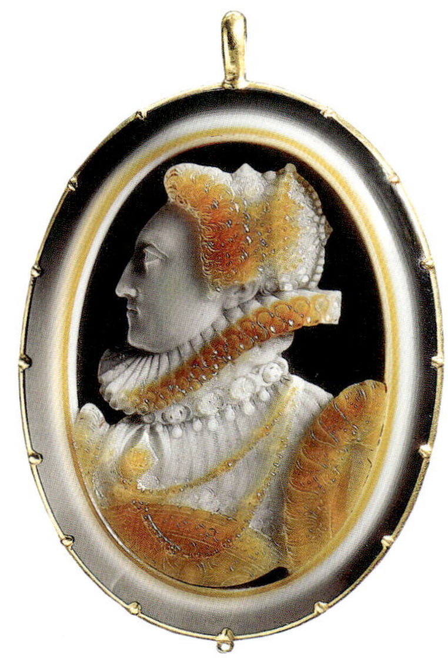

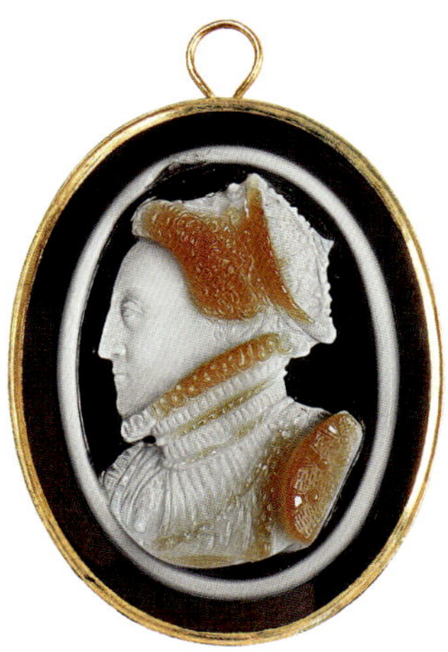

PROVENANCE Probably acquired by Queen Caroline; first recorded at Kensington Palace in 1763

LITERATURE Aschengreen Piacenti and Boardman 2008, no. 231 & 230

Among the objects catalogued by Horace Walpole in 1763 were 'great numbers of cameos and intaglios, few good'; Walpole selected two cameos of Elizabeth I as of especial quality, attributing them to the Italian cutter Valerio Belli (*c.*1468–1553/5), or 'Vincentino', as he was called in the eighteenth century. This attribution seems to have derived from John Evelyn, who in 1653 commented that he had seen a head of Elizabeth I, 'in a rare sardonyx, cut by a famous Italian', adding that Belli 'had been in England at the time of Queen Elizabeth' and had created the cameo for the musician Jerome Laniere (d. 1657).[61] Evelyn, who later commented that the cameo was 'now in his Majesty's cabinet', had met Laniere, who assured him that the image 'was exceedingly like her'.[62] The attribution is impossible – Belli died in 1553/5 – but it was retained by Walpole, perhaps because Belli was one of the few stone-cutters whose career is treated in Vasari's *Lives*. The larger cameo (no. 160), particularly admired by Walpole, appears to be one of a group of cameos produced to be presented to foreign monarchs, ambassadors and courtiers, although neither the workshop nor the chief engraver has yet been identified with certainty. The gold mount is early eighteenth-century in date and was probably added when the piece was acquired by Queen Caroline.

Elizabeth I appeared twice more among the portraits catalogued by Vertue and Walpole at Kensington. A ring with an image of Elizabeth, also attributed to Belli, was listed among the items presented to George III on the death of Princess Augusta in 1764.[63] Vertue also noted a portrait of 'Elizabeth in Chinese dress', which he attributed to Holbein, although it was given by Walpole to 'Zucchero' (Federico Zuccaro, *c.*1540/1–1609). This was probably the portrait which hung in the Queen's Dressing Room (RCIN 403451), in which Queen Elizabeth is portrayed prominently displaying a cameo. KJ

162

FRENCH?

James I

Cameo: *c.*1590; mount: 18th century
Onyx, gold, 1.9 × 1.7 cm
RCIN 65191

PROVENANCE Charles I (?); first documented in the Royal Collection in 1660; remounted, probably for Queen Caroline.

LITERATURE Aschengreen Piacenti and Boardman 2008, no. 217

163

FRENCH?

Philip II of Spain

Cameo: 2nd half 16th century; mount: 17th century
Onyx, gold, 1.9 × 1.7 cm
RCIN 65199

PROVENANCE Charles I (?); first documented in the Royal Collection in 1660

LITERATURE Aschengreen Piacenti and Boardman 2008, no. 215

164

ATTRIBUTED TO JACOPO NIZOLLA DA TREZZO (*c.*1515–1589)

Philip II of Spain

Cameo: 2nd half 16th century; mount: 18th century
Sardonyx, gold, 4.5 × 3.3 cm
RCIN 65201

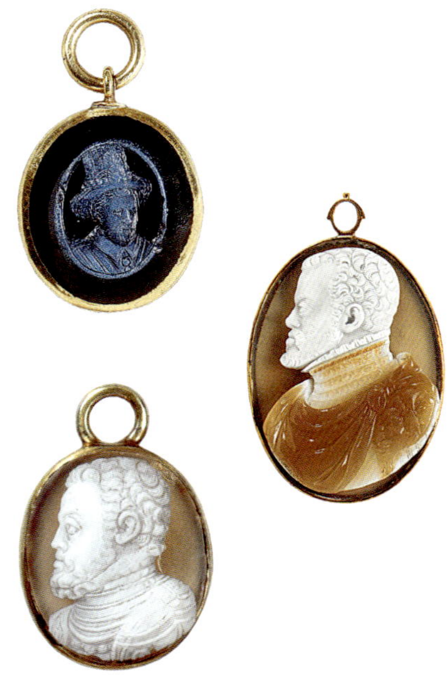

PROVENANCE Charles I (?); first documented in the Royal Collection in 1660; remounted, probably for Queen Caroline

LITERATURE Aschengreen Piacenti and Boardman 2008, no. 214

All three of these cameos may be identified in an inventory of Charles I's collection, compiled retrospectively at the Restoration in 1660.[64] Two of the group appear to have been remounted in the eighteenth century; it is not clear whether the cameos left the collection and were re-acquired by Queen Caroline or whether she simply ordered new mounts when the objects were placed in the cabinet rooms at Kensington. All three appear in Walpole's notes of 1763, where he records '2 of Philip 2' and '2 heads of James 1st cameos'. The second image of James I does not survive in the Royal Collection.

The cameos are testament to Caroline's interest in the courts of Europe. Among the other princes represented in the gem collection were cameos of Mary, Queen of Scots, Henri IV of France, and Emperor Leopold I, cut in amethyst. In turn these were supplemented by coins, including a full set of English monarchs from William I onwards, waxes of numerous German princes and of Pope Benedict XIV, a bas relief of Emperor Maximilian and Mary of Burgundy and a woven silk picture of Charles I. KJ

165 & 166

CAMEOS: ITALIAN; MOUNTS ATTRIBUTED TO JEAN VANGROL (D. 1640)

Two sets of eight cameos

Cameos: late 16th century, mounts: *c.*1640 with 18th-century additions
Onyx, gold, enamel

RCIN 65763 1.8 × 2.3 cm
RCIN 65764 1.9 × 2.4 cm
RCIN 65765 1.9 × 2.3 cm
RCIN 65766 1.7 × 2.3 cm
RCIN 65767 2.1 × 2.5 cm
RCIN 65768 1.9 × 2.2 cm
RCIN 65769 1.9 × 2.3 cm
RCIN 65770 1.8 × 2.2 cm

RCIN 65746 1.9 × 2.4 cm
RCIN 65747 1.8 × 2.2 cm
RCIN 65748 2 × 2.3 cm
RCIN 65749 1.1 × 1.6 cm
RCIN 65750 1.9 × 2.2 cm
RCIN 65751 2 × 2.3 cm
RCIN 65752 2 × 2.2 cm
RCIN 65753 2 × 2.3 cm

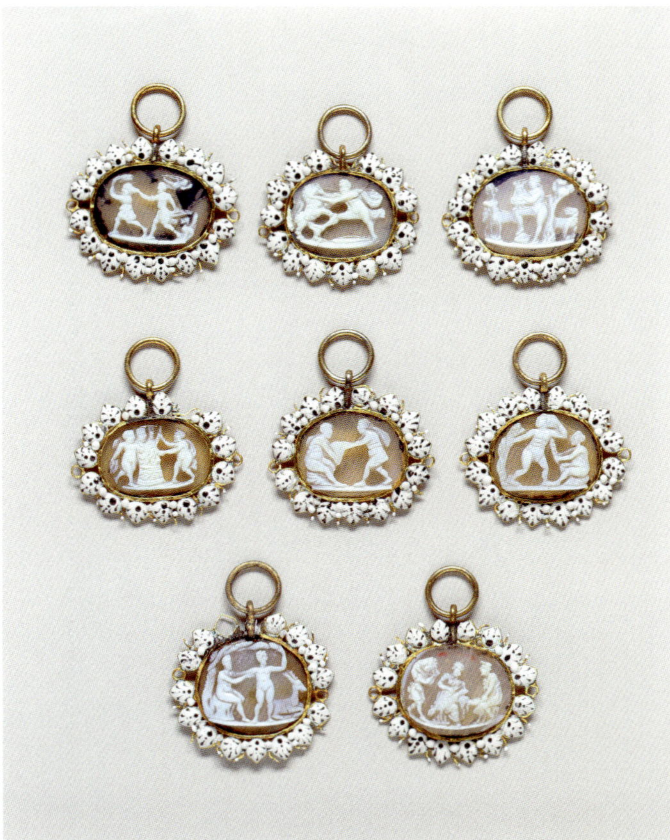

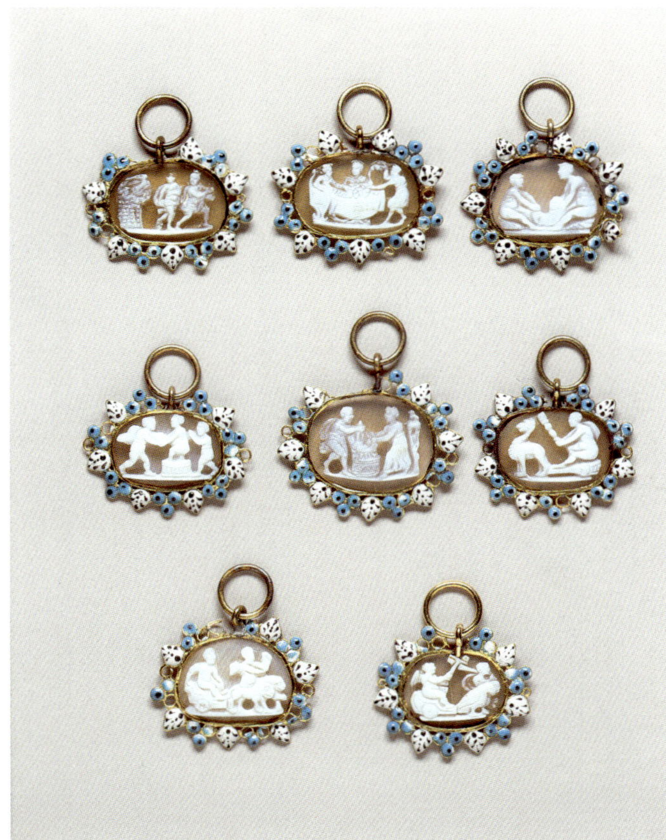

PROVENANCE Probably acquired by Queen Caroline; first recorded in the Royal Collection in 1763

LITERATURE Aschengreen Piacenti and Boardman 2008, nos 206 and 205

These small gems showing a variety of mythological and classical genre scenes were typically cut to be mounted into hardstone vases or gold and enamelled cups and bowls. They were produced in large numbers in the Milanese hardstone workshops of the sixteenth century. Their French seventeenth-century enamel mounts include lateral loops, however, which indicate that these were intended to be worn, either strung on a necklace or as other dress ornaments. Certainly in 1763, when Walpole made his additions to the Vertue inventory of the cabinet rooms, he noted 'many cameos, small set in enamel as if designed for buttons'. KJ

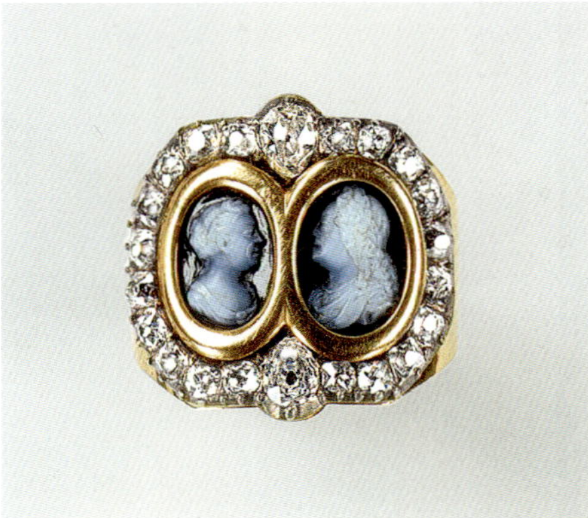

167

ENGLISH

Ring with cameos of George II and Queen Caroline

Cameos: *c.*1730; ring: early 19th century
Onyx, gold, diamonds in silver settings, enamel, 1.9 × 1.9 × 2.2 cm
Reverse of the bezel marked with the motto of the Order of the Garter (*Honi Soit Qui Mal Y Pense*) in blue enamel
RCIN 65422

PROVENANCE Belonged to King Edward VII; presented to King George V and Queen Mary by Queen Alexandra in 1910

LITERATURE Aschengreen Piacenti and Boardman 2008, no. 247

Although these cameos were reset in the early nineteenth century, they were probably executed in England before the death of Queen Caroline. The portraits derive from John Croker's medal of 1732, although the images have been reversed, suggesting the cutter was working from a printed source. The 1732 medal, which shows the royal couple's children on the reverse (see no. 15), is thought to have been issued in response to a medal of James Francis Stuart which showed his two sons on the reverse. It is possible that these cameos were created at the same time as Croker's work. KJ

168–71

ISAAC GOSSET (1713–1799)

George I (1660–1727) c.1760

George II (1683–1760) c.1760

Frederick, Prince of Wales (1707–1751) c.1760

Augusta, Princess of Wales (1719–1772) c.1760

Wax, with ebonised frame, respectively 17.6 × 15.2 × 2.2 cm; 18.4 × 15.3 × 2.5 cm; 14.4 × 12.0 × 2.2 cm; 22.7 × 20.3 × 3.7 cm
RCIN 37131, 37119, 37111 and 37070

PROVENANCE Possibly from the collection of George III

Vertue described the skill of the 'Ingenious Isaac Gosset' as 'so universally approved on for likeness' that he dedicated a section in his notebooks to wax carving, which he considered a growing industry.[65] Gosset was from a Huguenot family which had fled to Jersey after the Revocation of the Edict of Nantes. The family later moved to London and Isaac learned wax modelling and frame carving from his uncle Matthew. His wax production was prolific and covered both classical and contemporary figures. Gosset's renown arose from the fact that, unlike most contemporary wax modellers, he worked from life, and at speed, apparently producing a portrait in under an hour. Gosset also created a secret recipe for tinting his wax to appear like old ivory. His waxes were highly fashionable and were sold at four guineas a piece for an original portrait or one guinea for a copy. Vertue noted that Gosset 'had the honour of the King sitting to him'. He also created portraits of Frederick, Augusta, William, Duke of Cumberland and the young George III as well as 'great numbers of persons of Quality and persons of distinction – Learned and others'.

Queen Caroline is known to have commissioned various works from Gosset, and may even have granted him a pension.[66] The Picture Closet at Kensington displayed numerous waxes, framed both singly and in groups of up to sixteen figures. Some Vertue catalogued as historic and contemporary princes but most remained unidentified. KJ

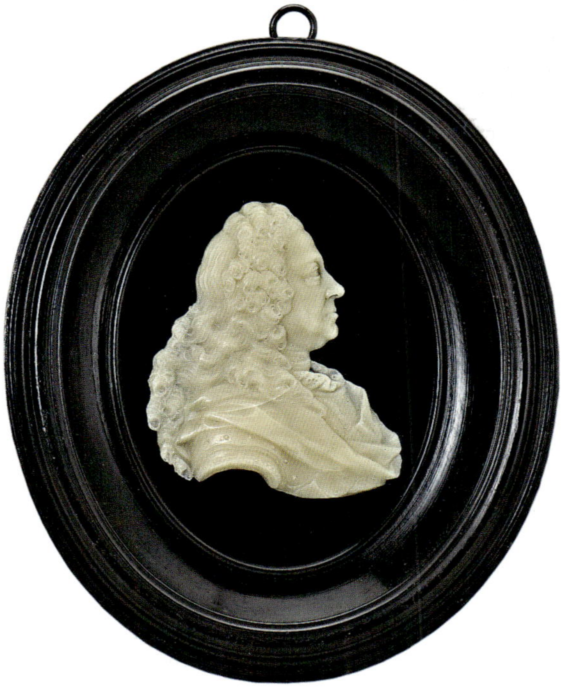

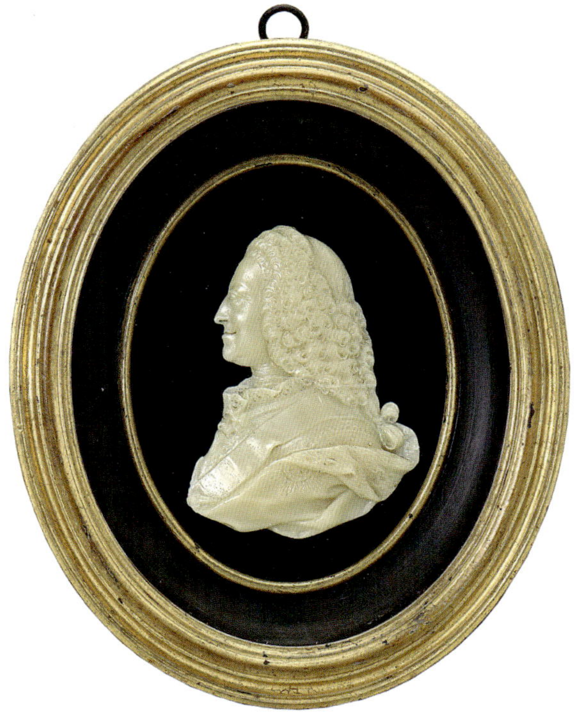

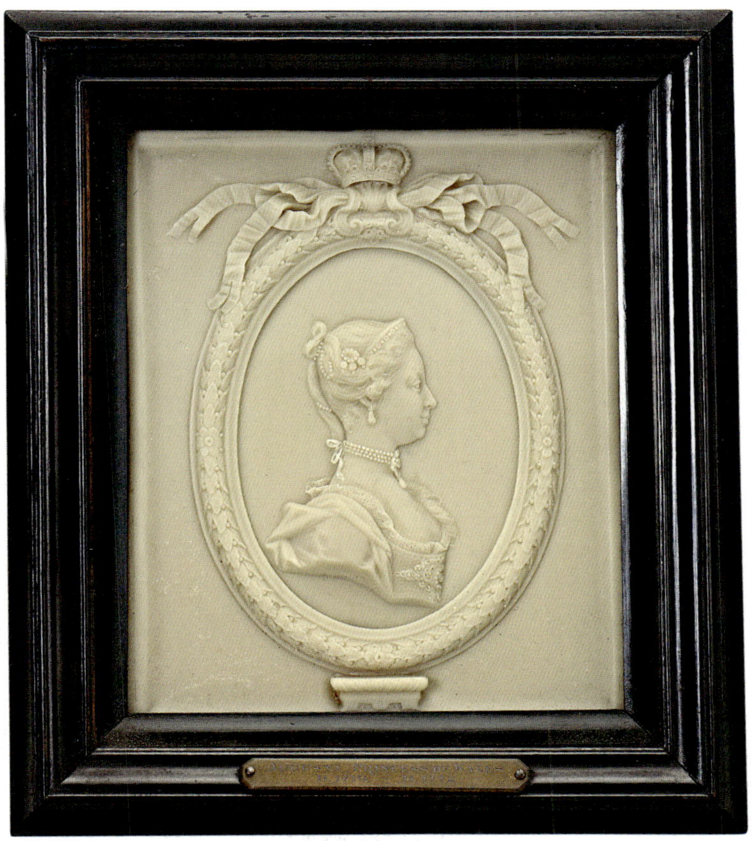

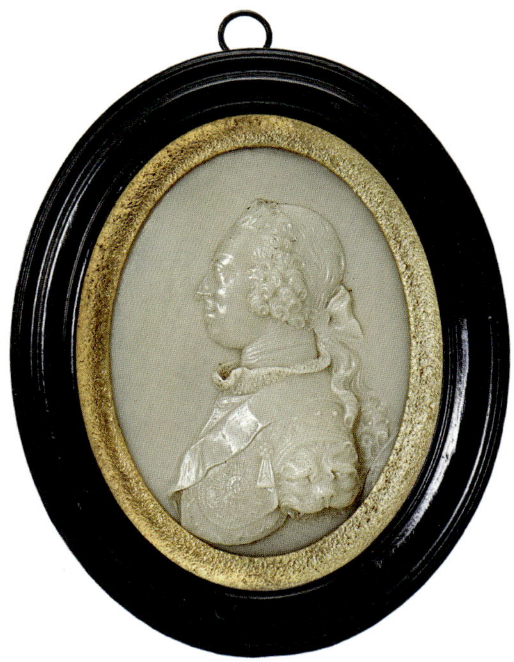

172–3

ATTRIBUTED TO GASPAR VAN DER HAGEN (D. 1769)

Pair of portrait reliefs of William IV of Orange and Anne, Princess Royal c.1735

Ivory, each 12.3 × 9.5 × 2.2 cm
Marks: (1) in ink on reverse: *Anne. Daughr of George the 2nd / born 1709 Married 1734 / William Charles Henry / prince of Orange* (2) in ink on reverse: *William Charles Henry / prince of Orange & Stadtholder / married Anne Daughr of George 2nd*
RCIN 70166.1-2

PROVENANCE Acquired by Queen Mary in 1932

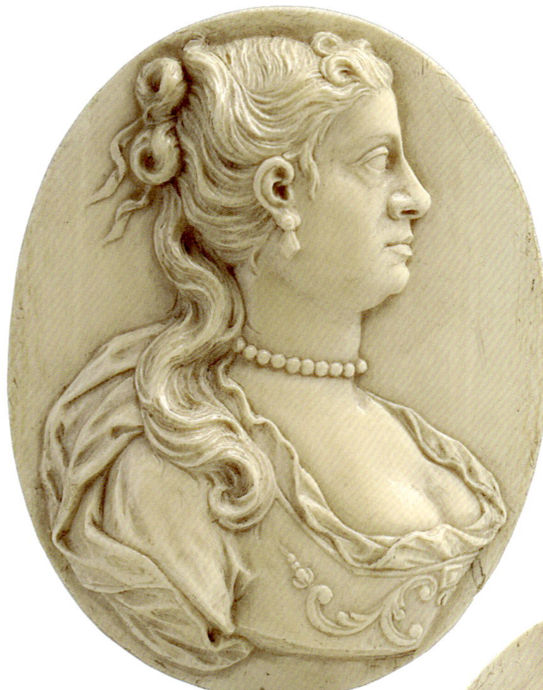

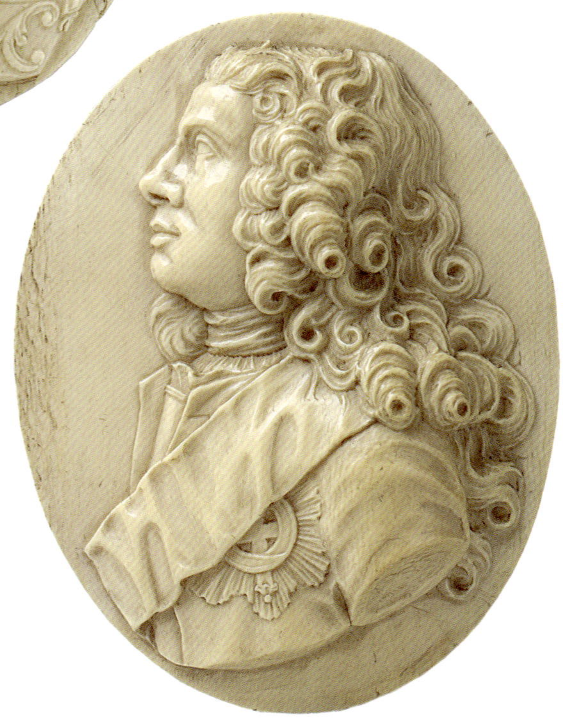

This pair of plaques was presumably made to commemorate the wedding of Princess Anne and William of Orange in 1734. The source is a double oval portrait of the royal couple after Philippe Mercier (1689–1760), which was widely circulated in a number of printed impressions in both Paris and London.

Gaspar van der Hagen, a Flemish artist, was an assistant to the sculptor John Michael Rysbrack (1694–1770). In 1747 Vertue noted 'Mr Vander Hagen. Sculptor works for Mr Rysbrack. has done several heads portraits in Ivory.—very well. but not meeting with propper encouragement did not continue'.[67] The only known work by van der Hagen is a marble relief of Hercules (Yale Center for British Art, New Haven). Some ivories have been attributed to him, however, on the basis of Vertue's remarks and a comparison with Rysbrack's style. These include a number of profile plaques, among them one of George II, and a small bust of William, Duke of Cumberland (Victoria and Albert Museum, London).

The Picture Closet at Kensington contained several ivory relief carvings, including a number of Bacchanalian scenes and two portrait profiles, of which Vertue does not list the sitters. KJ

174

WILLIAM AUGUSTUS, DUKE OF CUMBERLAND (1721–1765)

Emperor Vespasian 1731

Boxwood with an ebonised frame, 9.1 × 8.4 × 1.0 cm
Marks: front inscribed: *VESPASIEN.XI*
Reverse inscribed: *This medal was turned by His Royal Highness William Duke of Cumberland at Barn-Elms the 27th day of August 1731*
RCIN 70396

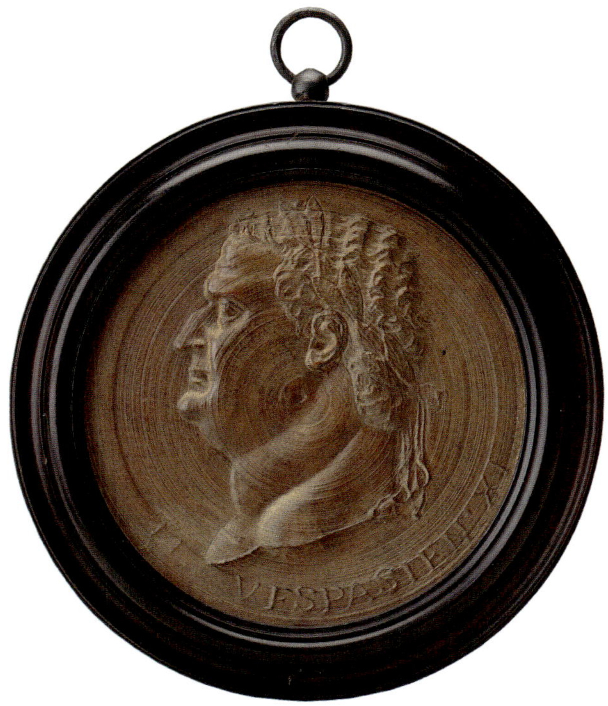

PROVENANCE Made by William, Duke of Cumberland, 27 August 1731

The skill of turning materials on a lathe had been considered a princely art since the sixteenth century, and was part of the education of both boys and girls in the royal houses of Europe. Turned ivory objects were often surmounted by complex polyhedra and were part of the education of geometry and mathematics. At the courts of Dresden, Copenhagen and Vienna the creation of turned pieces was particularly prolific, but Louis XV was also taught the art, as were Queen Caroline's children. An anonymous obituary of Anne, Princess Royal, noted that under the tutelage of the artist Kramer she 'progressed quite far in the turning of ivory and amber'.[68] A bill from John Bradburn records that a wheel-turning lathe was supplied to Augusta, Dowager Princess of Wales, in 1769 at a cost of £22 13s.[69] George III certainly learned the skill, as at least two boxes by his hand survive, one in the Royal Collection (RCIN 65779) and the other in the Anton Ulrich Collection Brunswick. A note on the reverse of this piece states that it was created by William, Duke of Cumberland, at the age of ten, and was turned at Barn Elms, the home of Cumberland's governor Stephen Poyntz (1685–1750). KJ

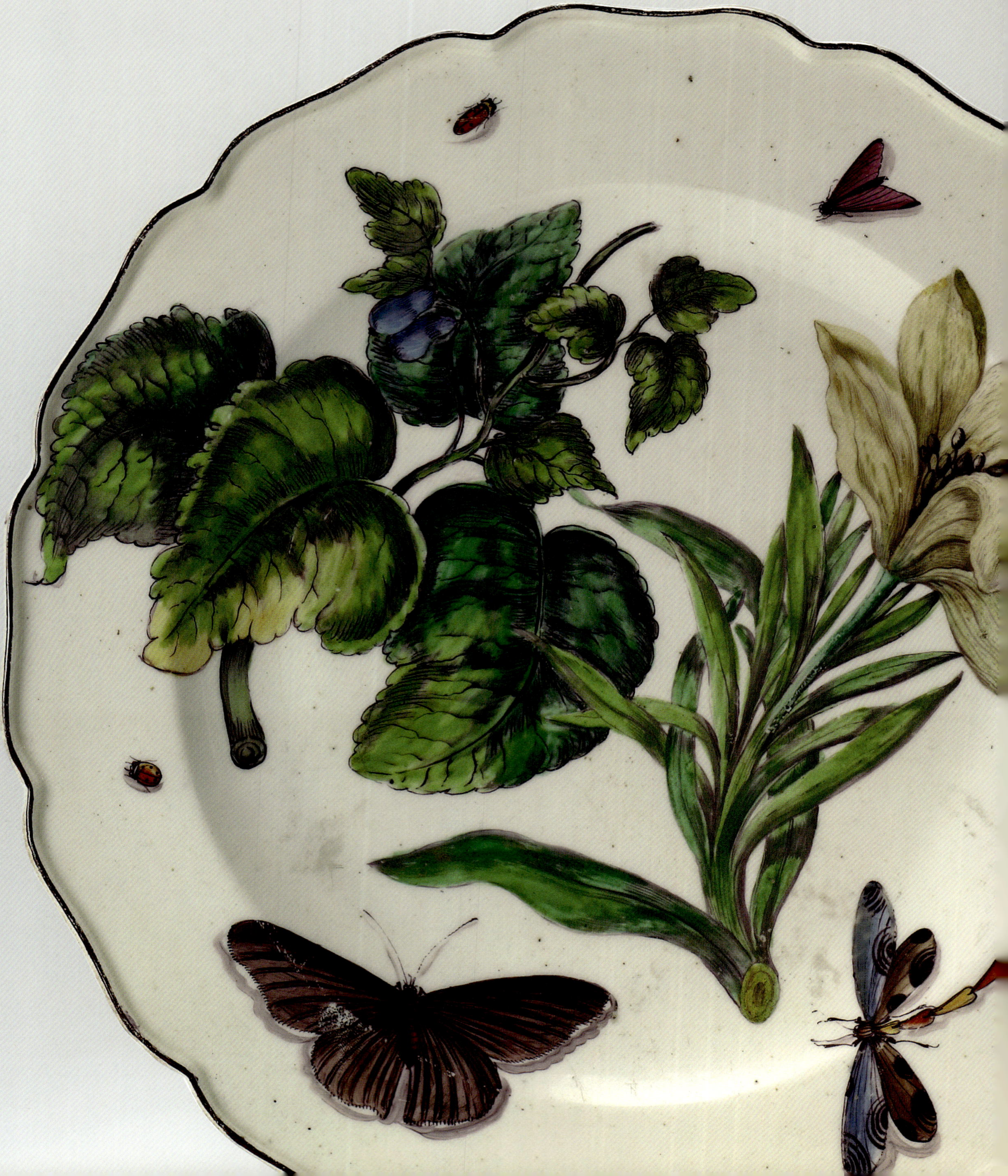

FIG. 75
Sir James Thornhill
John Flamsteed, 1725
Detail of the vault, Great Hall,
Old Royal College, Greenwich

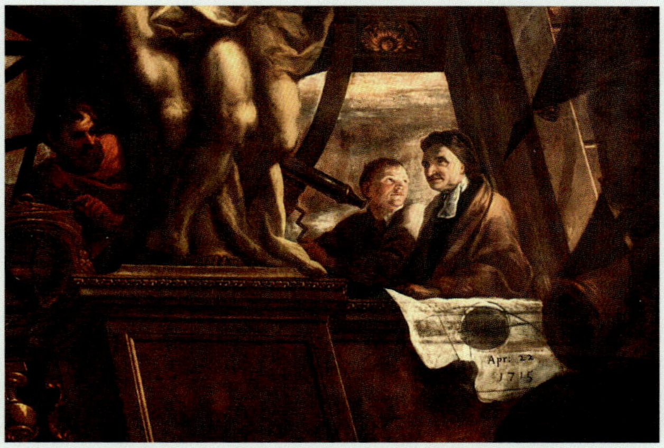

Science in Early Georgian Britain

In view of the European importance of the Royal Society, the progress made in science in this period was less dramatic than that made in the previous century and the involvement of the royal family was peripheral. Advances generally came not so much in new theoretical discoveries but in the practical application of those already made. The single most significant advance was the introduction of innoculation, courageously supported by Queen Caroline, who had her own children innoculated, thereby drawing the praise of Voltaire which heads this chapter.[70]

The greater understanding of the Earth's atmosphere and the behaviour of gases achieved by Newton and Boyle led to the development in 1712 by Thomas Newcomen (1663–1729) of the atmospheric steam engine.[71] This worked by filling a large cylinder with steam, which replaced the air; as the water vapour condensed a vacuum was created in the cylinder, drawing the piston down. The idea of a cylinder with a piston driven by pressure differential has proved enduring, although since Newcomen's time the cylinder's cubic capacity has generally reduced and the rate of iteration of the pressure changes within it has increased.

The precision with which Newton and the Greenwich astonomers could predict the movement of heavenly bodies was a matter of particular pride. In the Great Hall at Greenwich, James Thornhill included a date, 22 April 1715 – not that of the painting but of an eclipse predicted by the Astronomer Royal, John Flamsteed (1646–1719), whose portrait appears immediately above (fig. 75). This confidence in the accuracy and efficacy of the new astronomy lay behind the longitude contest (see no. 175).[72] It is possible to measure the north-south position (latitude) of a ship at sea by measuring the angle between the horizon and the stars; it is not possible to do the same for the east-west position (longitude), as the world is constantly spinning in this direction – unless of course you know the time. The solution to this problem was to create an accurate watch, but this was not exactly what the commission had in mind, which is why John Harrison (1692–1776) had to wait until 1773 to obtain his long-overdue reward. The idea of the practical application of astronomy also led to the reform of the calendar (see no. 176). The spinning of the earth is not in precise synchronisation with its orbit round the sun. A calendar cannot deal with fractions of a day and so needs periodically to miss or gain one in order to keep dates and seasons in step – in other words so that the longest day always falls on 21 June. The Julian calendar, used throughout medieval Europe, had some such adjustments but was vastly improved by the Gregorian calendar (named after Pope Gregory XIII) introduced in 1582. Britain had stayed with the Julian calendar, which meant that the longest day in 1700 fell on 10 June and would have fallen on 8 June in 2014 had not matters been taken in hand. Fortunately it was decided to convert to the Gregorian calender in 1752 by declaring 3 September to be 14 September, eliminating eleven days. It was embarrassing for a nation which prided itself on its astonomy to be caught acknowledging (with grudging tardiness) the superiority of a papal invention. At the same time it was decided that the New Year should begin on 1 January rather than on 25 March.

175

JOHN FLAMSTEED (1646–1719)

Atlas Coelestis London: [s.n.], 1729

Printed on paper, red sheep binding with decorative gold tooling, small crown motifs, Queen Victoria's bookplate inside front board, 54.1 × 42.0 cm
RCIN 1059272
Open at the constellation Virgo

PROVENANCE Acquired by 1780; in George III's Cumberland Lodge Library

LITERATURE Willmoth 1997

The Royal Observatory at Greenwich was founded in 1675 by Charles II, and John Flamsteed, a self-taught astronomer well respected by the scientific community, was appointed the first Astronomer Royal in 1675, 'for rectifieing the Tables of the motions of the Heavens, and the places of the fixed stars, so as to find out the so much desired Longitude of places for the perfecteing the Art of Navigation'.[73] He began to collect data for a new star catalogue, the *Historia Coelestis Britannica*, compiled entirely from telescopic observations of nearly 3,000 stars visible from Greenwich. After a controversial edition was published in 1712 by Edmund Halley (against Flamsteed's wishes; indeed he managed to collect and burn 300 copies) the final three-volume version was published posthumously by his widow in 1725, followed by this atlas in 1729. It was the largest and most accurate star atlas that had ever been published, and contained two planispheres designed by Abraham Sharp, one of Flamsteed's protégés in the Royal Observatory, and 25 maps of the constellations, engraved after designs by James Thornhill, the Baroque English history painter. Flamsteed's atlas was intended to improve upon its predecessors, particularly the 1603 *Uranometria* of Johann Bayer (whose charts presented the constellations from both the back and the front), in its accuracy and consistency of presentation.

The constellation Virgo (the Virgin) is the second largest in the sky after Hydra, whose sinuous back can just be seen at the bottom of the plate. Classical astronomers identified her with Demeter/Ceres, the Greek/Roman goddess of wheat and agriculture; in the Middle Ages she was traditionally identified with the Virgin Mary. ES

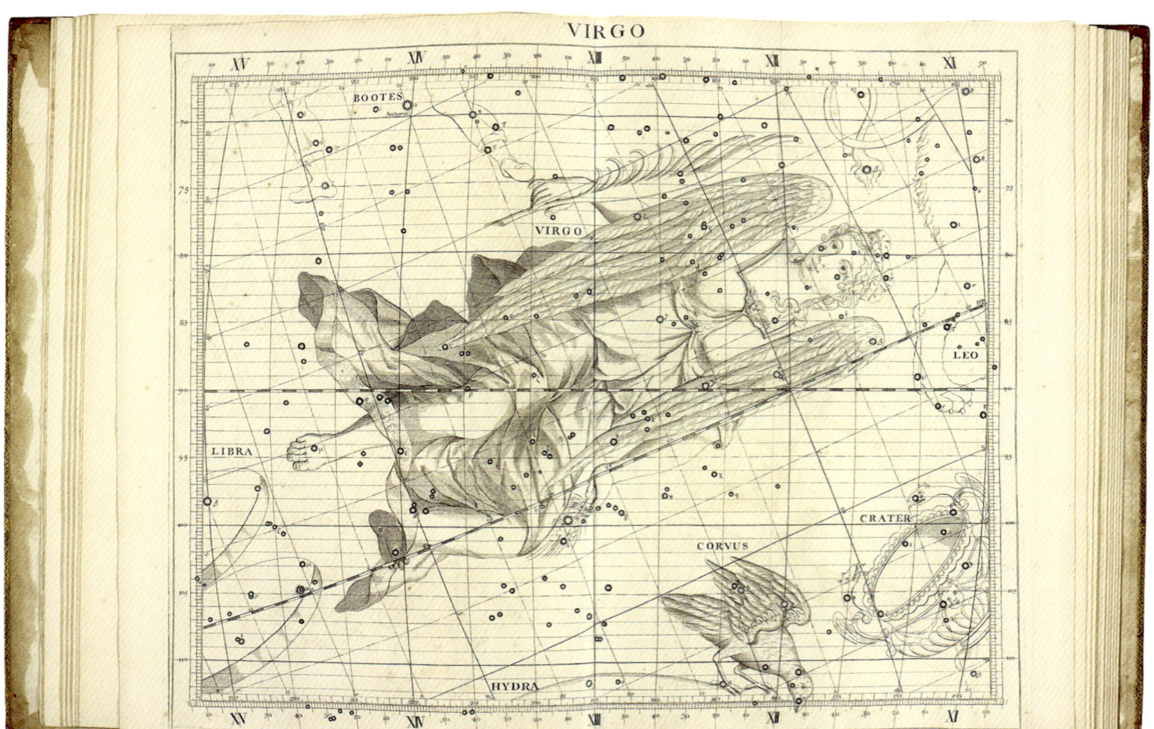

176

ROBERT TAILFER (1710–*c*.1736); GEORGE BICKHAM, ENGRAVER (*c*.1684–1758)

True and Correct Tables of Time: Calculated from the Old Stile for 784 years … and for the New Stile … By R.T. half-pay Officer London: [s.n.], 1736

Printed on paper, black sheep binding, extensively gold tooled and with the arms of Frederick, Prince of Wales, on both boards, bookplate of Queen Elizabeth II verso flyleaf, 21.7 × 13.4 cm
RCIN 1082352
Open at frontispiece and title page

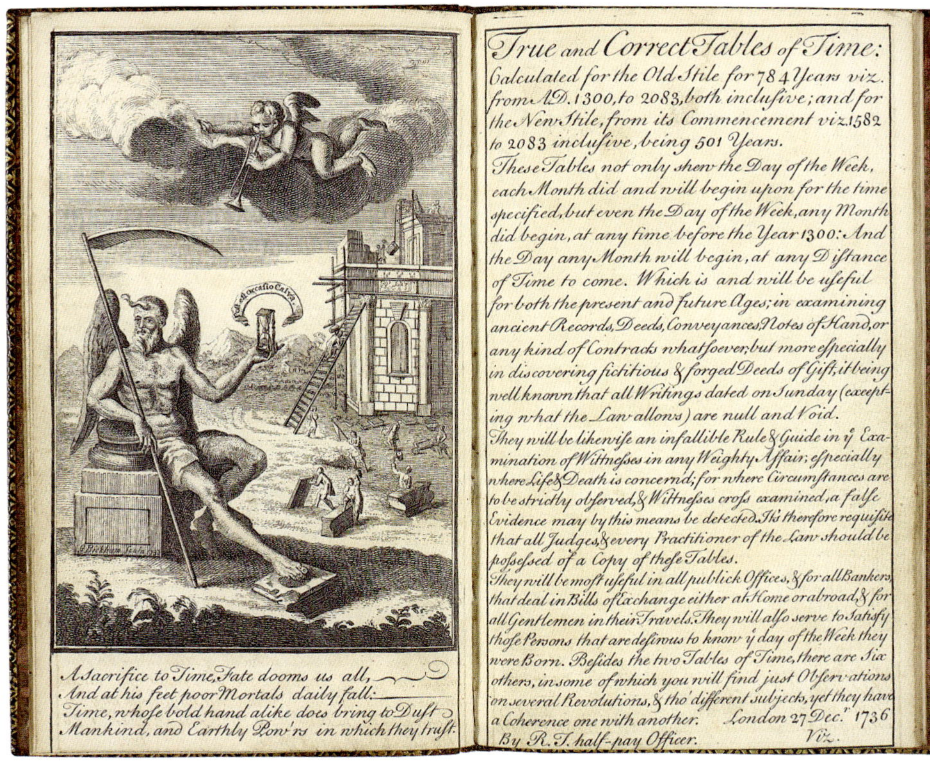

PROVENANCE Bound for Frederick, Prince of Wales; owned by G. de Chaville, 1841; acquired by Queen Elizabeth II from G. Michelmore & Co., London, 14 October 1953 (lot 101, £200)

LITERATURE Poole 1995

The True and Correct Tables of Time was written to ease translation between the old-style Julian calendar and the more accurate Gregorian calendar. The adjustment in 1752 caused two short years – 1751 lasted only from 25 March to 31 December, in order for 1752 to start on 1 January, and eleven days, 3–13 September 1752, were sacrificed to bring the British calendar in line with the rest of Gregorian Europe. This reputedly caused great consternation, as the public cried 'Give us our eleven days!'

Robert Tailfer, being a naval officer, would have been more conversant than most with the confusions arising from two different dating systems. His work enabled the reader to find out the Julian date for any day between 1300 and 2083 and the Gregorian date for any day between 1582 and 2083. The whole book was engraved by George Bickham the Elder. Tailfer's impulse was not an isolated one. The 1730s saw several attempts to encourage calendar reform, notably in the *Gentleman's Magazine*, where its editor Sylvanus Urban fulminated upon the discrepancies between the various start dates for the New Year: 'I find myself often perplexed with the notorious Disagreement in Dates from Christmas to Lady-Day by almost every English Historian; and should therefore rejoice to see this uncertain Epocha … reduced to a regular and certain Standard'.[74] ES

Zoology, Botany and the Foundation of Kew Gardens

The point of the new philosophy was not to know but to know how to ask. This is why Francis Bacon (1561–1626) was revered alongside the great scientists of the seventeenth century. For Voltaire he was the 'Father of experimental Philosophy', his *Novum scientiarum organum* the 'Scaffold with which the new Philosophy was rais'd'.[75] Bacon described the process of observation and experimentation with no particular outcome envisaged. Nowhere is this patient accumulation of observed data better seen than in the zoological and botanical researches of the first half of the eighteenth century. This was the period during which colonial expansion exposed European scientists to a new world of flora and fauna. This was also the time that Carolus Linnaeus (1707–78) set out the classification system which is the foundation of modern botany. If one were to list royal projects of lasting significance from these years there would probably be two – the founding of the Royal Botanical gardens at Kew in 1759 and the education of George III (see no. 187), who succeeded to the throne in 1760 with an unprecedented range of interests and a concern to further the cause of British science and technology (see nos 177–8, 180–2 and 185–6). Both these achievements should be credited to Princess Augusta and her maligned Scottish mentor John Stuart, 3rd Earl of Bute (1713–92). It is at Kew that one sees the realisation of the promise of the dynasty and a re-living of the conversations between Leibniz and the Electress Sophia in the gardens of Herrenhausen at the turn of the previous century.[76]

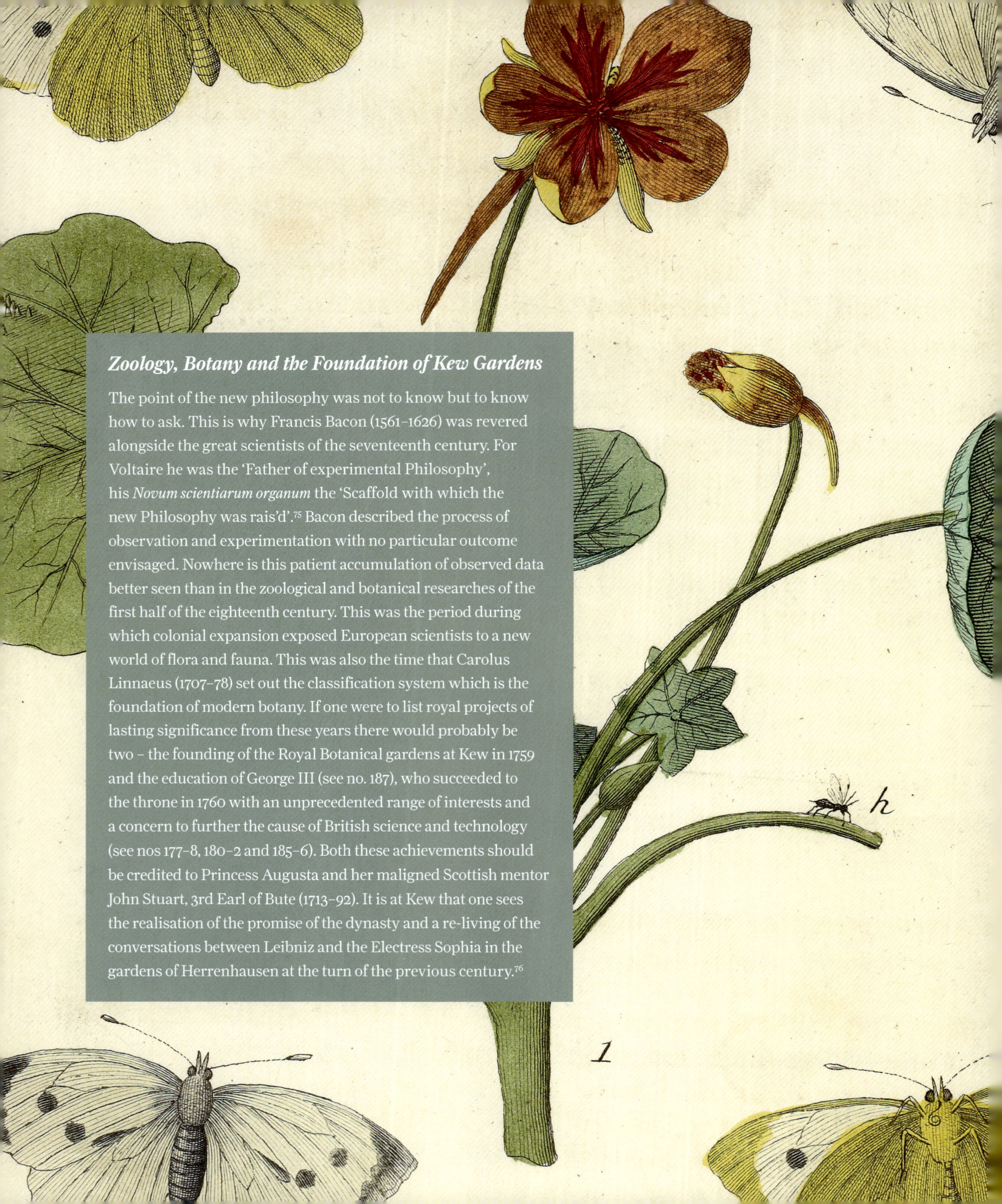

177

MARK CATESBY (1683–1749)

The swallow-tail hawk *c*.1722–26

Brush and ink with watercolour and bodycolour, 37.4 × 26.3 cm
Inscribed in brown ink: *Swallow tail Hawk / Accipiter Minor caude forcipator / 4*
RCIN 924817

PROVENANCE Thomas Cadell; from whom bought by George III, 1768

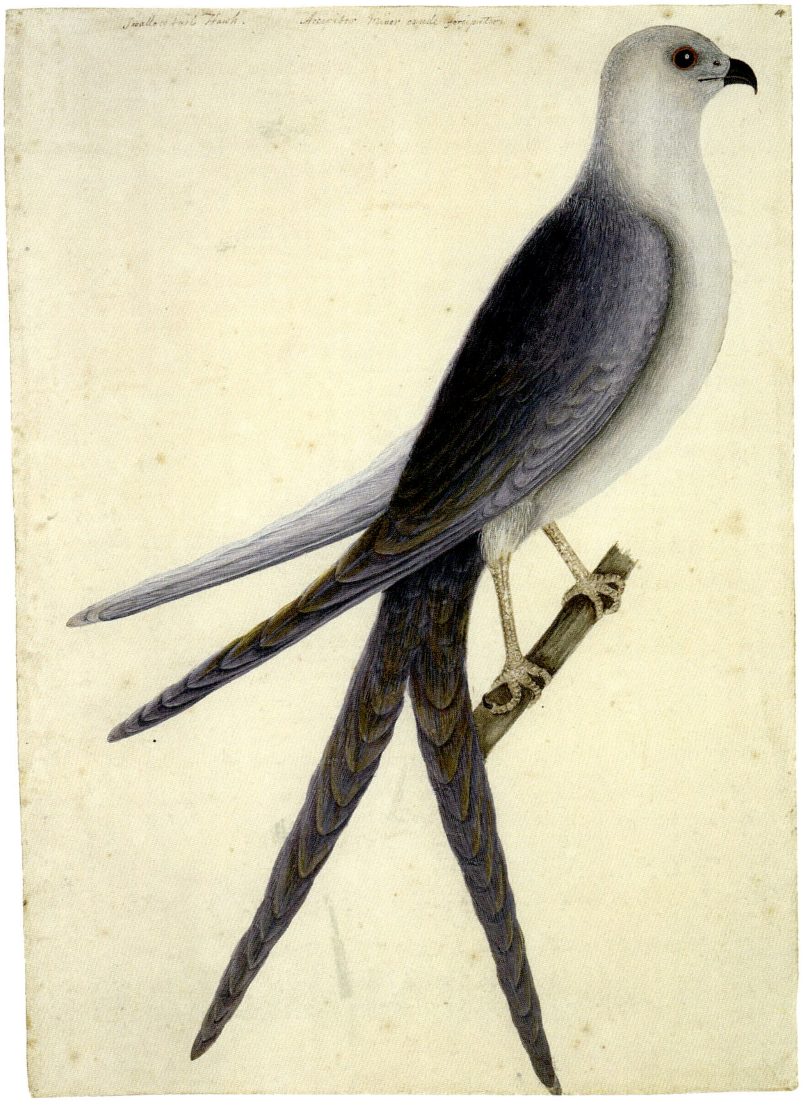

Mark Catesby was interested in 'Plants, and other Productions in Nature' from an early age, and at the age of thirty was given the opportunity to travel to the east coast of America with his sister Elizabeth, who had married a doctor who practised in Williamsburg, Virginia.[77] Catesby spent seven years in Virginia collecting specimens and seeds for London buyers before returning to Britain. In London his drawings of birds and plants met with praise and a group of benefactors paid for his travel to Carolina in 1722. Catesby developed a systematic means of travelling around the country, ensuring that he was in different places at different seasons to maximise the variety of flora and fauna he could encounter. He made numerous drawings of plants, reptiles, mammals, fish and birds, working hard to ensure that his depictions were as helpful for an understanding of the subject as possible. He later explained, 'As I was not bred a Painter I hope some faults in Perspective and other Niceties may be more readily excused, for I humbly conceive Plants, and other Things done in a Flat, tho' exact manner, may serve the Purpose of Natural History, better in some Measure than in a more bold and Painter like Way'. On his return to Britain, his drawings were reproduced in *The Natural History of Caroline, Florida and the Bahama Islands*, which appeared in a series of volumes between 1729 and 1747. The first volume was dedicated to Queen Caroline (noting her 'great Goodness in encouraging all sorts of Learning'), the second to Augusta, Princess of Wales. The original drawings for the volumes, which had been in the possession of Catesby's widow until her death, were purchased by George III from the London bookseller Thomas Cadell in 1768.

This drawing was the basis for plate 4 in the first volume of the *Natural History*. Catesby noted of the swallow-tail hawk that 'they continue long on the wing, catching, as they fly, Beetles, Flies and other Insects, from trees and bushes. They are said to prey upon Lizards and other Serpents; which has given them (by some) the name of Snake-Hawk. I believe they are Birds of passage, not having seen any of them in winter.' Catesby's thoughts on migration, based on his careful observation of bird habits during his travels, were delivered in an important lecture at the Royal Society in 1747. KH

178

MARK CATESBY (1683–1749)

The nuthatch, the small nuthatch and the highland willow oak *c.*1722–26

Brush and brown ink with watercolour and bodycolour and some scratching out, 37.0 × 26.7 cm
Inscribed in brown ink: *Small Nuthatch / Sitta capite fusco / Nuthatch / Sitta capite nigro / Highland Willow Oak / Quercus humilior salicis folio breviore / 22*
RCIN 924835

PROVENANCE Thomas Cadell; from whom bought by George III, 1768

In this drawing, which was the basis for plate 22 in the first volume of the *Natural History* (see no. 177), Catesby brings together a white-breasted nuthatch and a brown-headed nuthatch on a stump of highland willow oak (bluejack oak). Nuthatches, which feed on insects, are typically found on trees, and Catesby would draw an ivory-billed woodpecker, a bird with similar characteristics, on another such stump. As usual, Catesby's composition is concerned with showing the distinctive traits of the birds he depicts: nuthatches are known for their ability to navigate tree trunks with their heads towards the ground, as shown here. Catesby noted of his subjects that 'the back claw is remarkably bigger and longer than the rest, which seems necessary to support their body in creeping down as well as up Trees, in which action they are usually seen pecking their food (which are Insects) from the chinks or crevices of the Bark'. Like many of the birds Catesby painted, the nuthatches were probably studied from life. As he later noted of his ornithological pictures: 'I painted them while alive (except a very few) and gave them their Gestures peculiar to every kind of Bird'.[78] Catesby's work on North American birds would be an important source for Carl Linnaeus's 1758 system of taxonomy. KH

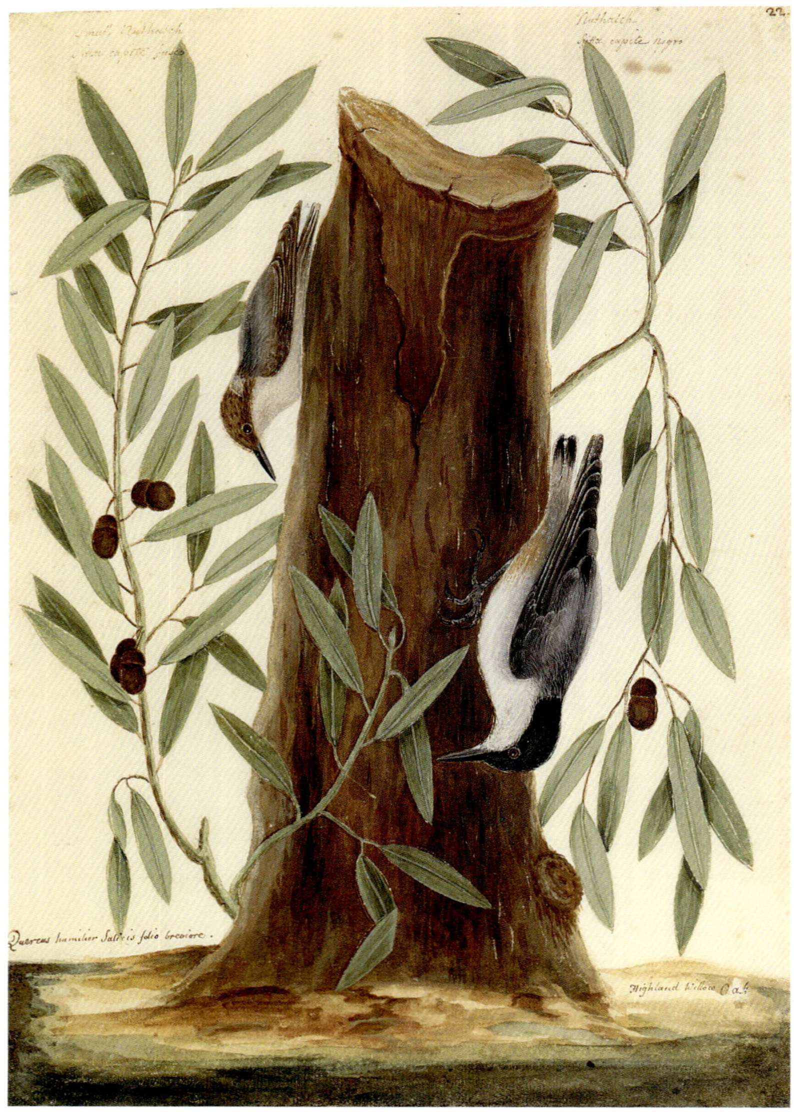

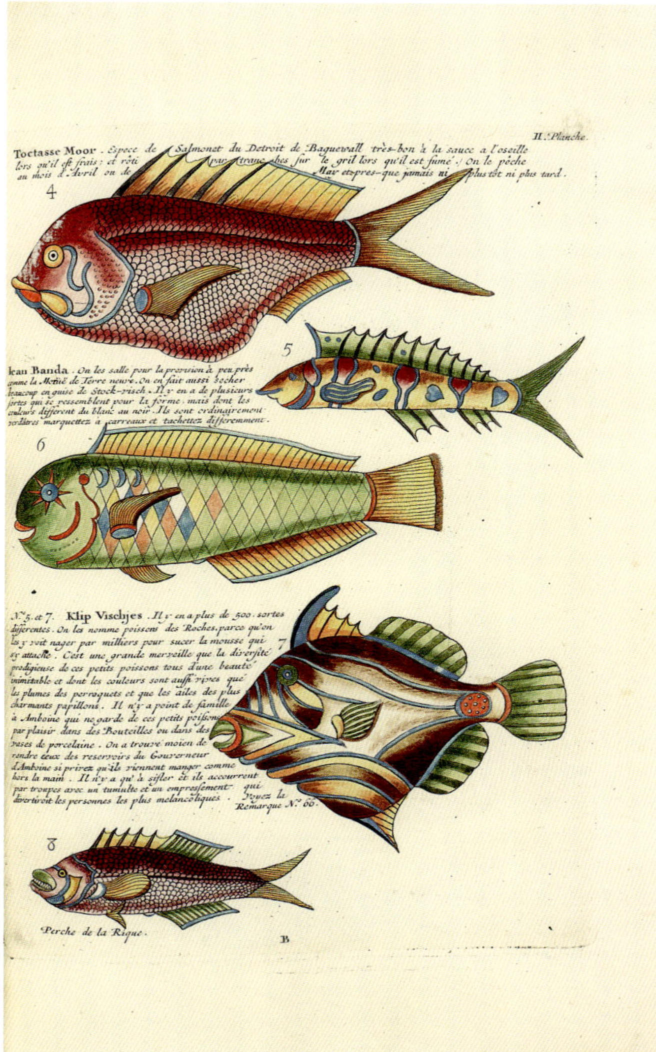

179

LOUIS RENARD (*c*.1678–1746)

Poissons, ecrevisses et crabes de diverses couleurs et figures extraordinaires, que l'on trouve autour des Isles Moluques et sur les côtes des Terres Australes Amsterdam: Reincier & Josué Ottens, 1754, 2nd edn, 2 volumes in 1

Printed on paper, hand-coloured illustrations, brown calf binding, rebacked; arms of John Stuart, 3rd Earl of Bute (1712–92) on both boards, Queen Victoria's bookplate inside front board, 41.4 × 27.3 cm

RCIN 1057042

Open at plate II, Toctasse Moor and others

PROVENANCE Dedicated to George I (included from the 1st edn); owned by John Stuart, 3rd Earl of Bute; Sotheby's, London, 5 May 1794 (lot 975, £1 15s); acquired for the Royal Library by 1860

LITERATURE Pietsch 1995

This extraordinary work purports to show marine life from the East Indies at a time when the natural wildlife of that area was virtually unknown in Europe. Renard, both a publisher and a spy for the British Crown, produced the work in 1719 in an edition of 100 copies; this second edition, also of about 100 copies, was made up after his death based on 36 unsold sets of pages from the first edition and the original copper plates.

The work consisted of two books, with 100 plates and 460 hand-coloured engravings. The first part is fairly realistic, the second far more fanciful. The illustrations were supposedly based on drawings by Samuel Fallours (active 1703–20) belonging to Baltazar Coyett, Governor of Ambon and Banda (1694–1706), and to Mr Van der Stael, Governor of the Molucca Islands. It has been noted, however, that a volume of painted drawings in the Sloane collection (British Library, Add. Mss 5268), presented to Hans Sloane by Renard, has a much greater similarity in order and style to Renard's second part than does the Van der Stael set.[79] Thus the Sloane set is actually far more likely to have been the model used by Renard's engraver.

The extravagance of his drawings clearly concerned Renard, for the preface contains several affidavits asserting the accuracy of the colouring and depiction. The descriptive text on the plates tends towards the anecdotal and culinary, rather than the scientific. The plate shown here, for example, contains Toctasse Moor (no. 4), which is very good in a garlic sauce when it is fresh, and roasted in slices on a grill when it is smoked. The colourful Klip Fish (no. 5 and 7; Little Rockfish) is so pretty that everyone in Ambon keeps some in a glass bottle or in a vase, the better to admire them. ES

180

ELEAZAR ALBIN (D. 1742?)
WILLIAM DERHAM (1657–1735)

A Natural History of English Insects: illustrated with a hundred Copper Plates, curiously engraved from the Life, and exactly coloured by the Author ... : to which are added large notes and many curious observations by W. Derham London: William Innys, 1749 [new edn]

Printed on paper, hand-coloured illustrations, mottled brown calf binding, Queen Victoria's bookplate inside front board, 30.0 × 24.5 cm
RCIN 1057018
Open at plate 1, the caterpillar (dedicated to the Princess of Wales)

PROVENANCE Dedicated to Caroline, Princess of Wales; acquired by 1780; in George III's Cumberland Lodge Library

LITERATURE Albin 1713; Albin 1720

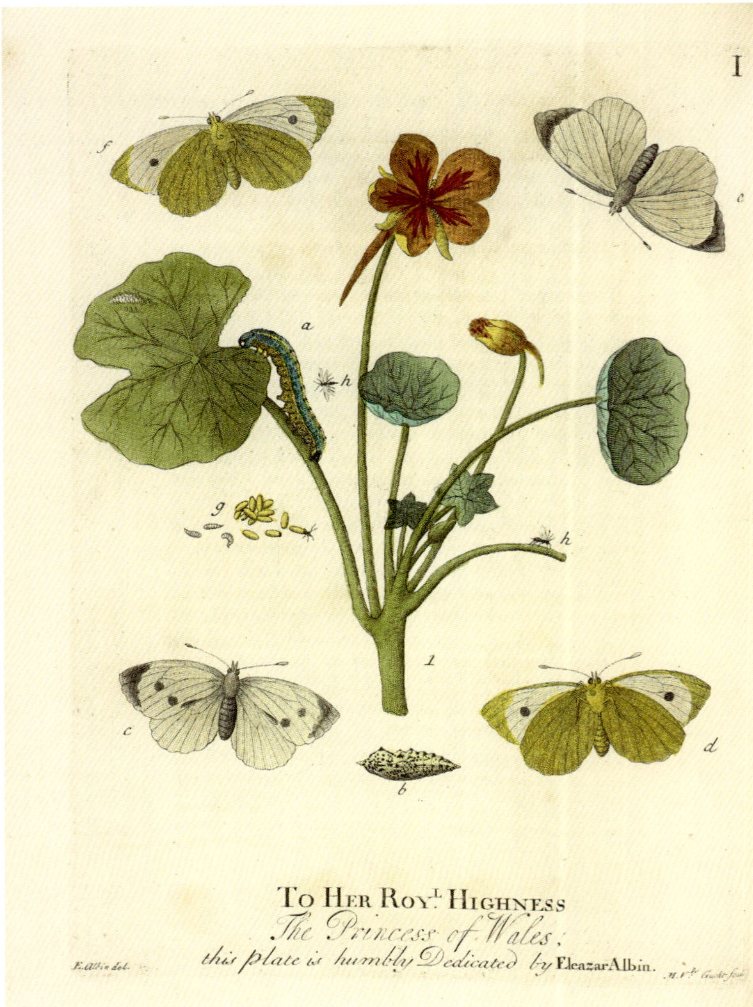

Little is known of Albin's early life, though he was probably born in Germany to a family named Weiss. By 1708 he had changed his surname to Albin and was living in London with his family. His profession of art teacher led him to the close observation of the natural world, reinforced by painting work which he undertook for the naturalist Joseph Dandridge (1665–1747), who collected insects and observed their metamorphosis from egg to fly. He also drew natural history subjects for Sir Hans Sloane, before gaining the patronage of the Dowager Duchess of Beaufort, who encouraged him to compose the present work. An advertisement went out in about 1713 entitled *Proposals for printing by subscription a natural history of English insects*, but the first edition did not materialise until 1720, owing chiefly to the early death of the Dowager Beaufort and the slow rate of subscriptions.

Albin prided himself on his visual accuracy, stating in his introduction that his drawings were copied after life, unlike those of other illustrators, who 'either did not look often enough at their Pattern, or affected to make the Picture outdo Nature'.[80] The work was published with black and white copper plates, which could be coloured on request by the author. His description of the cabbage white (seen here) includes all stages of its life cycle, from caterpillar via chrysalis to butterfly, what they like to eat, and how to control them. Albin's publication was supported by his circle of patrons and colleagues – members of the Beaufort family, Joseph Dandridge and Hans Sloane – as well as by Caroline, Princess of Wales, to whom the work was dedicated. William Derham, the editor, was a Fellow of the Royal Society, and the first to measure the speed of sound with reasonable accuracy. ES

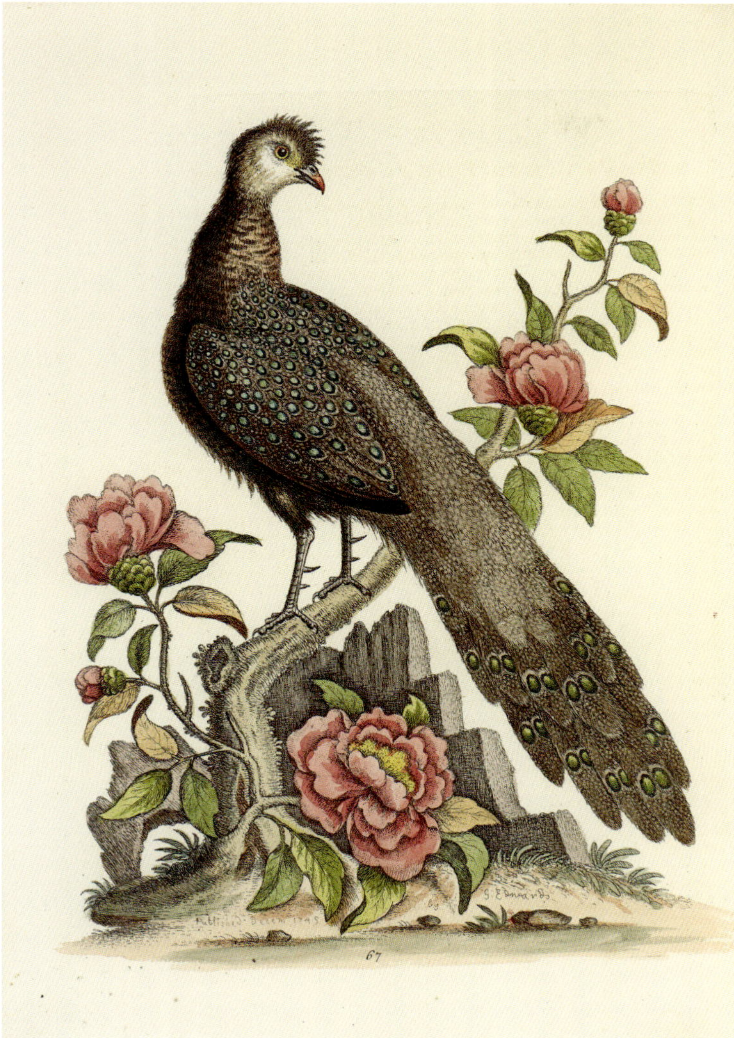

181

GEORGE EDWARDS (1694–1773)

A Natural history of uncommon birds, and of some other rare and undescribed animals ... exhibited in two hundred and ten copper-plates, from designs copied immediately from nature ... ; [pts 1-2]

London: George Edwards, 1743–47 (1750)

Printed on paper, hand-coloured illustrations, mottled brown calf binding, rebacked; Queen Victoria's bookplate inside front board; George III's bookplate verso additional title page, 30.4 × 24.8 cm
RCIN 1057008
Open at plate 67, the peacock pheasant from China

PROVENANCE Acquired by 1780; in George III's Cumberland Lodge Library

LITERATURE Stuart Mason 1992

Edwards began studying natural history, especially birds, after an unsuccessful career as a businessman, 'applying himself to drawing and colouring such animals as fell under his notice', including foreign specimens brought into the Port of London by ship.[81] Edwards' chief aim was to 'achieve a natural and accurate portrayal', though often from stuffed specimens; with no clear idea of suitable backgrounds he would perch smaller birds on a lichen-covered branch, or give them a general backdrop of water (for the water birds) or vegetation.[82] His work drew many admirers from the rich and learned, but his chief patron was Sir Hans Sloane.

Edwards was a naturalist as well as an artist, and thus tried to depict birds as accurately as possible, unlike some of his predecessors. He was taught to etch by Mark Catesby, and produced his own plates for publication, which he then coloured personally or supervised others at the work, in order to preserve colour accuracy:

> I do not purpose to part with any of the Prints uncolour'd while I live, lest they should be afterwards colour'd by unskilful People .... A Copy carefully and exactly colour'd from the original Drawings, will be deposited in the Library of the College of Physicians ... which may serve as a Standard to refer to and compare with ... in case the Plates should outlive me.[83]

This copy includes an engraved frontispiece entitled *Ornithologia nova*, a tribute to Francis Willughby's *Ornithologia* (1676). It also includes the title page of 1751, showing the Copley Medal, awarded to Edwards by the Royal Society in 1750. This medal, instigated in 1731, is the oldest and most prestigious award of the Royal Society for outstanding achievement in the physical and biological sciences. ES

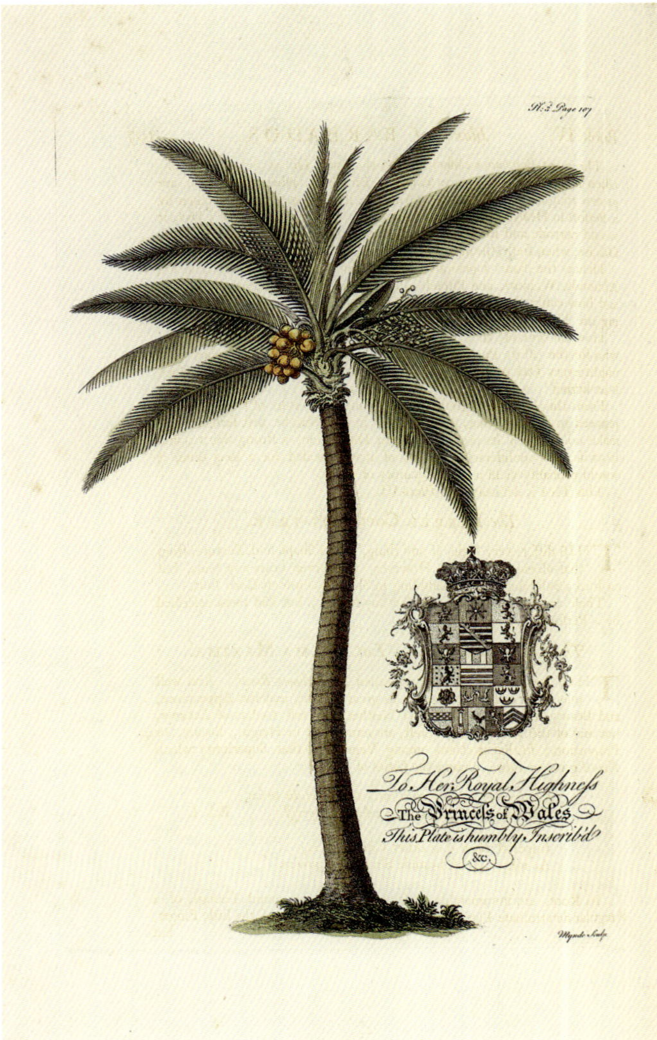

182

GRIFFITH HUGHES (1707–*c*.1758)

The Natural History of Barbados

London: Griffith Hughes, 1750

Printed on paper, hand-coloured illustrations, red sheep binding with green inlay in floral patterns, arms of Frederick, Prince of Wales, on both boards, Queen Victoria's bookplate inside front board, 42.5 × 28.2 cm
RCIN 1081286
Open at plate 3, the 'coco nut-tree', dedicated to Augusta, Princess of Wales

PROVENANCE Bound for Frederick, Prince of Wales; in George III's Cumberland Lodge Library from *c.*1780

LITERATURE Stearns 1948

Griffith Hughes was appointed rector of St Lucy's Barbados in 1736, where his prolonged stay (until at least 1748) gave him the opportunity to carry out research into the natural history of the island. During a visit to England in 1743 he made the acquaintance of many of the leading scientists of the day, including Sir Hans Sloane (who had visited the area in 1687–8 when physician to the Duke of Albemarle, Governor of Jamaica), and promoted his idea of a publication based upon his research. Georg Dionysius Ehret, the renowned botanical artist (see nos 183, 184), made plates for the publication (his name appears on twelve of the 29), Thomas Jefferys, Geographer to the Prince of Wales, engraved a map of the island, and the whole was paid for by an impressive list of subscribers. The King, the Prince and Princess of Wales and the Duke of Cumberland head the list, while the Prince, Princess and Duke each received the dedication of one of the hand-coloured plates. As a mark of support from the scientific community Hughes was made a Fellow of the Royal Society in 1748, and received both a BA and an MA from St John's, Oxford (his old college). Philip Miller, Ehret's brother-in-law and head of the Chelsea Physic Garden 1722–70 (see no. 184), wrote 'Explanatory Notes of all Botanical and Technical Terms made use of in the foregoing Work'. On publication the work was described as lacking accuracy and scholarship, but Hughes had achieved a number of firsts, including the description of a grapefruit, which he called 'The Forbidden Fruit', and the coining of the phrase 'yellow fever'. His observations throughout were based upon personal or reliable witness: 'This I can with Truth say, that I have not represented one single Fact, which I did not either see myself, or had from Persons of known Veracity'.[84] ES

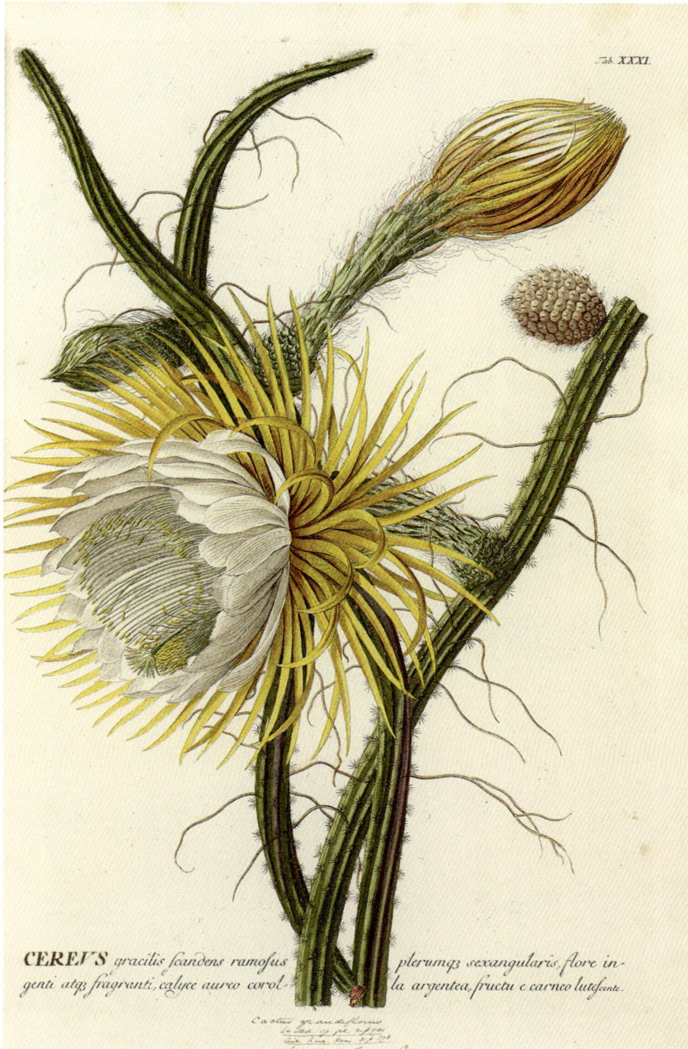

183

CHRISTOPH JACOB TREW (1695–1769), AUTHOR
GEORG DIONYSIUS EHRET (1708–1770), ARTIST
JOHANN JACOB HAID (1704–1767), ENGRAVER

Plantae selectae quarum imagines ad exemplaria naturalia Londini in hortis curiosorum nutrita ...

Nuremberg, 1750–73

Printed on paper, hand-coloured illustrations, brown calf binding, Queen Victoria's bookplate inside front board, 51.8 × 38.0 cm
RCIN 1052133
Open at plate 31, Cereus (cactus)

PROVENANCE Acquired by William IV, 1830–37

LITERATURE Calmann 1977, pp. 95–8

Ehret (see also no. 184) was a German botanist, best known for his illustrations. His first major sale was through Christoph Jacob Trew, a doctor and botanist in Nuremberg, who became his patron, and used many of Ehret's botanical illustrations in his own work. He even named a genus of plants after the artist – *Ehretia*, flowering plants of the borage family –for revealing in his drawing its peculiar character for the first time. The 1730s saw Ehret travel to Britain, where he was introduced to Sir Hans Sloane and to Philip Miller; he also spent time in the Netherlands in the garden of George Clifford, a Director of the Dutch East India Company, where Ehret met Carl Linnaeus, then Clifford's botanical curator, who was working towards his own new system of botanical categorisation.

While Ehret's early drawings were made on both paper and vellum, his preferred media for finished work became bodycolour (opaque watercolour) on vellum, influenced by time spent in Paris at the Jardin des Plantes in 1734. His drawings for *Plantae selectae* had been acquired over a number of years by Trew, who then entrusted them to Johann Jacob Heid, an engraver in Augsburg, to be prepared for publication. (Trew's collection of drawings for *Plantae selectae* are now chiefly housed in the University Library of Erlangen, Bavaria.) The images that Trew chose to publish were those from plants recently introduced or then unknown to the public – such as the banana and pineapple, neither of which had been tasted in Europe at that time – and the Cereus cactus (shown here; also known as the Queen of the Night, the Night-blooming cactus and Moon cereus), which only blooms by night, the flowers usually wilting by morning. ES

184

CHELSEA PORCELAIN MANUFACTORY (*c*.1745–69)

Set of plates *c*.1755

Soft-paste porcelain, 22.3 cm diameter (average) and 31.6 cm diameter (average)
RCIN 102350, 102351, 102354, 102359, 102344 and 102347

PROVENANCE Purchased by HM Queen Elizabeth The Queen Mother

In July 1758 an announcement of a sale of Chelsea porcelain in Dublin listed a service decorated 'in curious plants, with Table Plates, Soup Plates and Dessert Plates enamelled from Sir Hans Sloan's plants'. This distinguished it from the usual Chelsea wares decorated with so-called 'Indian' or chinoiserie flowers. Instead these were botanically accurate illustrations, the designs being based on the plants growing in the Chelsea Physic Garden, which was in the immediate neighbourhood of the porcelain factory, on the banks of the Thames. Sir Hans Sloane, a president of the Royal Society and resident of Chelsea, had purchased the land in which the garden had been founded in the 1720s, granting a lease in perpetuity to the Society of Apothecaries. The garden allowed apprentice apothecaries to identify medicinally useful plants, but it also had a sheltered aspect, which meant that more exotic specimens could survive there. The Society appointed Philip Miller (1691–1771), a renowned gardener, as curator of the Physic Garden in 1722.

Miller published a number of works aimed at gardeners and in 1756 he produced a work entitled 'Figures of Plants'. This contained a collection of 300 illustrations of specimens drawn from the Physic Garden. The illustrations were the work of German artist Georg Dionysius Ehret (1708–70), who visited England in 1734 and lodged with Miller. His first visit lasted only a year, but he later returned and remained in England, marrying Miller's sister-in-law Susanna Kennet.

In the tradition of medieval herbals, Ehret's illustrations often combined a number of plants in one plate. He usually included cross-sections of the specimens, as well as the insects relevant to the pollination of the plant. A number of Ehret's illustrations relate directly to decorations on Chelsea wares – including the insects and the cross-section diagrams, albeit adapted in layout to fit the shape of the porcelain works. However, many of the other porcelain decorations do not appear to have a source in Ehret and it may be that the artists were working directly from the plants in the Physic Gardens, itself. Sir Hans Sloane died in 1753 but the porcelain factory's continued use of his name was clearly a marketing ploy to lend an intellectual appeal to their wares. KJ

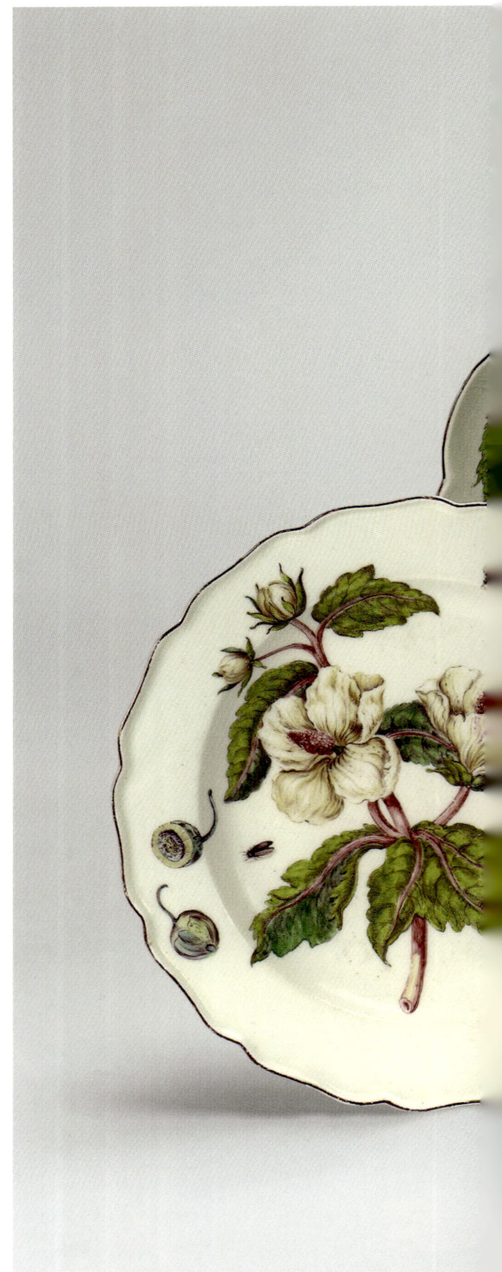

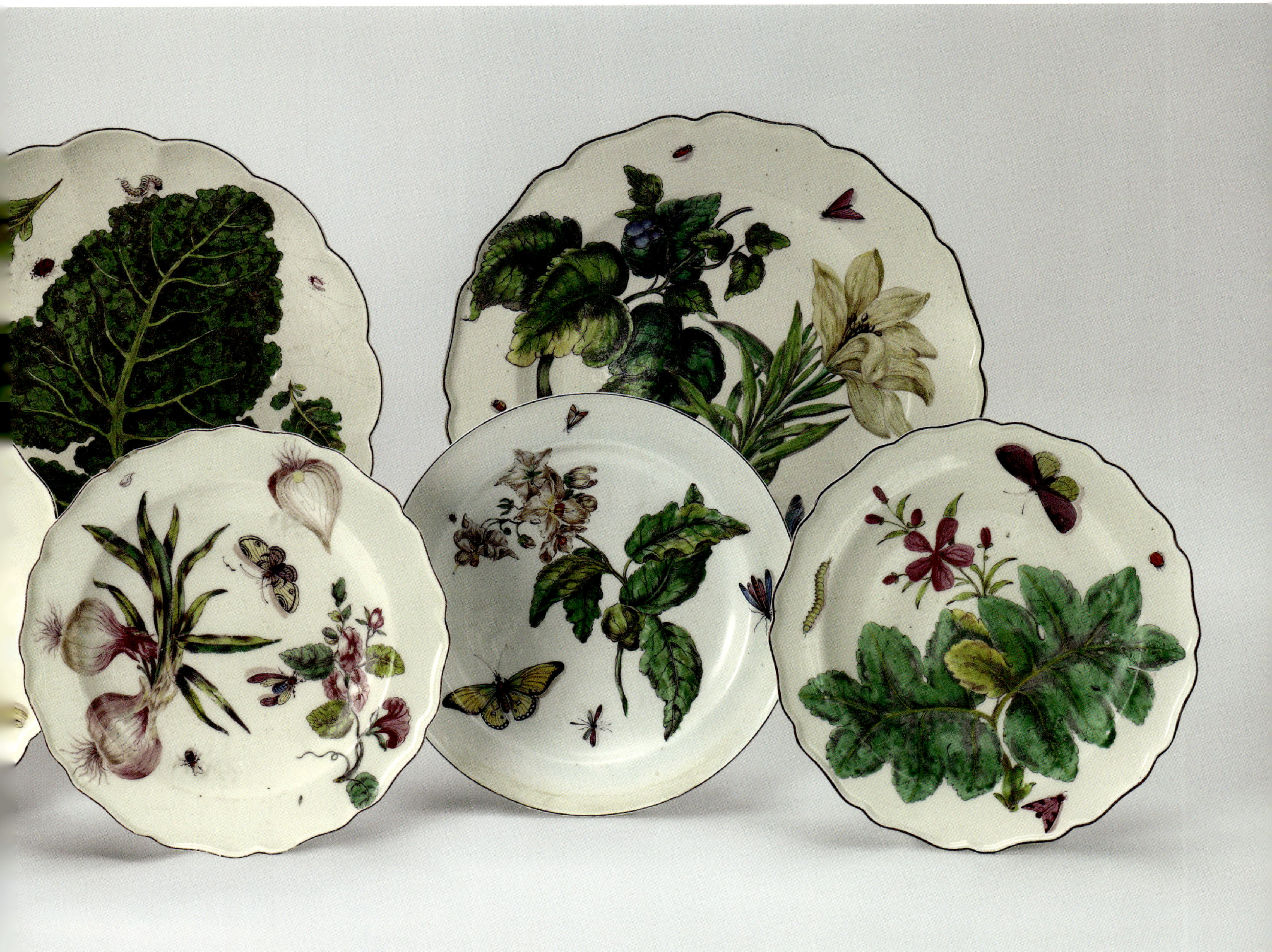

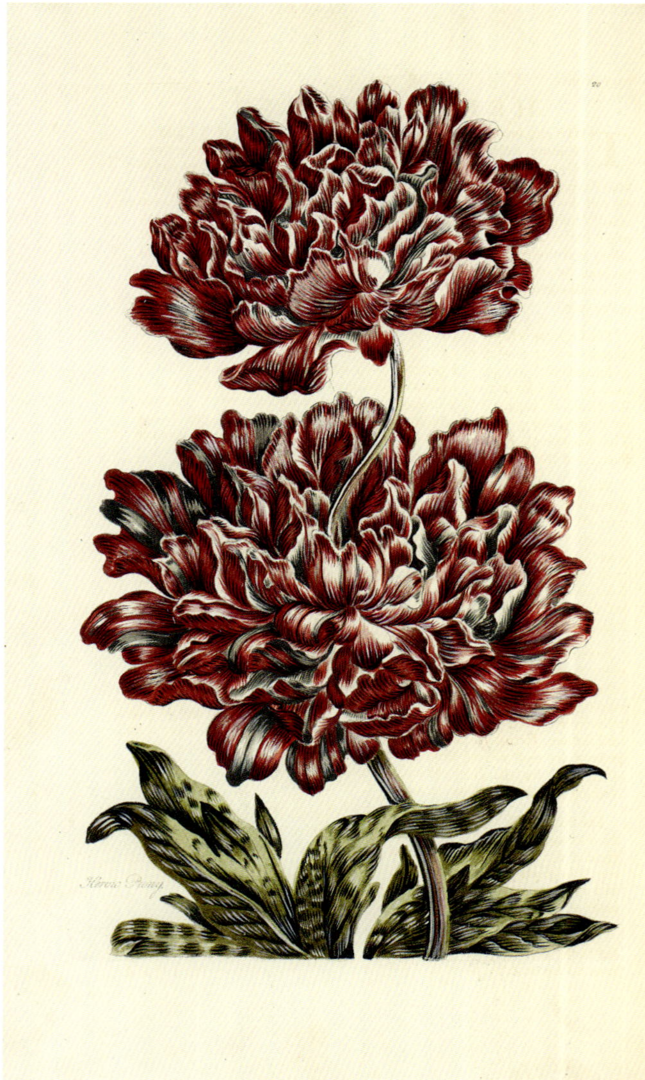

185

JOHN HILL (1716?–1775)

Exotic botany, illustrated in thirty-five figures of curious and elegant plants, explaining the sexual system, and tending to give some new lights into the vegetable philosophy London: John Hill, 1759

Printed on paper, hand-coloured plates, bound in brown mottled calf, rebacked, with George III's arms on both boards, 47.1 × 30.5 cm
RCIN 1052135
Open at the Heroic Piony [sic]

PROVENANCE Dedicated to Hugh Percy, Earl of Northumberland (c.1714–86); acquired by George III

LITERATURE Wordruff 1920

Little is known of John Hill's life before the 1730s. At various times he was an apothecary, an actor, and a gossip columnist. Through his study of botany he became acquainted with various members of London's scientific community, including Sir Hans Sloane, and was employed by the Duke of Richmond and Lord Petre to arrange their gardens and collections of dried plants. John Stuart, Earl of Bute, later became his patron, and in 1761 obtained for him the post of gardener in the newly established botanical gardens at Kensington Palace (previously the residence of George II). Dr Johnson observed of him to George III that 'if he would have been contented to tell the world no more than he knew, he might have been a very considerable man'.[85]

Hill's exotic plants, such as this (otherwise unidentified) 'heroic piony', a native of Senegal, were new to Europe, the majority being raised in the hothouses of his patron, Lord Northumberland, and engraved from life. His introduction describes his technique of reconstituting dried specimens by macerating them in warm water:

The Plant was laid in a China Dish, and Water was poured upon it, nearly as much as the Cavity would hold; another Dish, somewhat smaller, was turn'd down upon this, and the Edges were cemented with common Paste spread upon brown Paper. This was set upon a Pot half full of cold water, and placed over a gentle Fire .... The Plant, however, rumpled up in drying, expands and takes the natural Form it had when fresh. Even the minutest Parts appear distinctly. The Specimen is destroyed by this Operation, but it shews itself, for the Time, in full Perfection.[86] ES

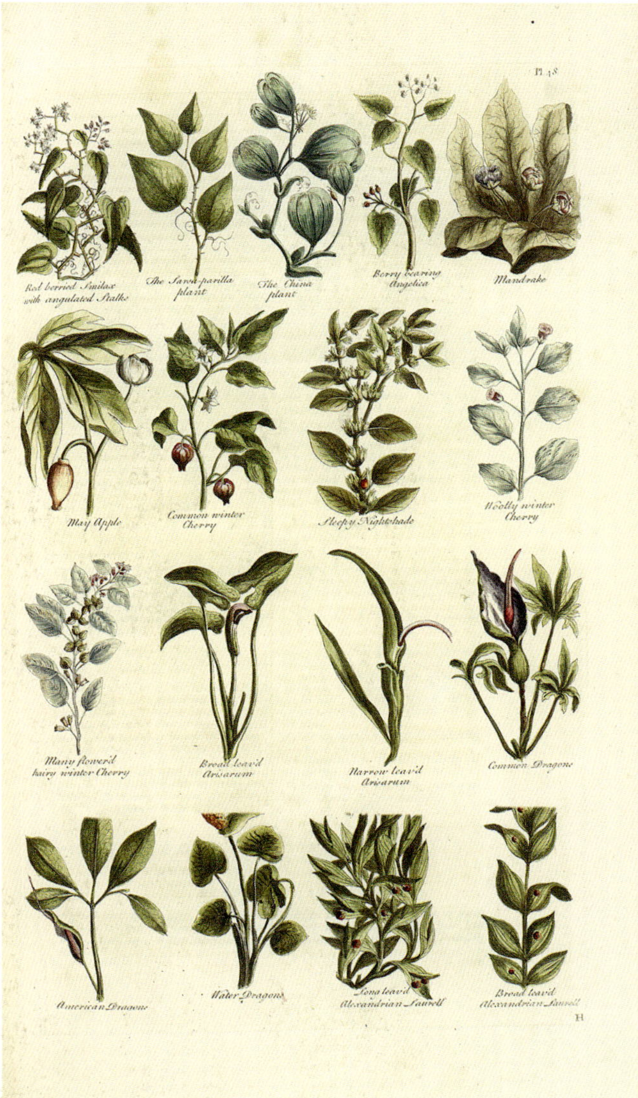

186

JOHN HILL (1716?–1775)

The British Herbal: an history of plants and trees, natives of Britain, cultivated for use or raised for beauty London: Osborne & Shipton, 1756

Printed on paper, with hand-coloured plates, half bound in brown pig, rebacked, bookplate of King George V, 47.8 × 31.0 cm
RCIN 1052134
Open at plate 48, including the mandrake, sleepy nightshade and arisarum

PROVENANCE Dedicated to Hugh Percy, Earl of Northumberland (c.1714-86); acquired by George III

LITERATURE Stern 1967, Wordruff 1920

Hill's *British Herbal* grew out of his earlier work, *The Useful Family Herbal* (1754), which gave instructions for gathering and preserving roots, flowers and herbs, recipes of medicines and other useful household applications of herbal lore. Hill's *British Herbal* provided an authoritative work for the amateur plant lover, with an interest in plants for both medical and ornamental purposes, but with little technical knowledge. He continued to use the older names and taxonomies, rather than the new methods of categorising pioneered by Carolus Linnaeus (see p. 304): a frequent comment in the work is 'Linnaeus places this ...', usually followed by Hill's own, different, opinion. Linnaeus's colleague Peter Collinson wrote to him in May 1756: 'Dr. Hill is publishing a history of plants, of which I send you a specimen. As he proceeds through the genuses, he criticizes your method, but not like the foul-mouthed Germans. He treats you like an Englishman, with decency and good manners.'[87] Hill had evidently some sympathy with Linnaeus's views. In his earlier work, *A General Natural History, or New and Accurate descriptions of the Animals, Vegetables and Minerals of the Different Parts of the World* (1748–52), his volume on plants was of particular importance since it introduced the British public to the Linnaean system of plant classification two years before Linnaeus published his own *Species Plantarum*.
ES

187

GEORGE III (1738–1820) WHEN PRINCE OF WALES

Geometrical study with a house and a tree c.1756

Pen and ink over pencil, with wash, 23.5 × 14.5 cm
RCIN 980282

Study of a spiral with buildings c.1756

Pen and ink over pencil, with wash, 21.9 × 13.4 cm
RCIN 980288

PROVENANCE Drawn by the Prince as geometrical exercises; discovered by Queen Charlotte around 1813 and placed in a portfolio in her library at Frogmore (Pyne 1819, III, p. 8); in the library at Buckingham House by 1828, when transferred to the library at Windsor Castle (Inventory A, p. 172)

LITERATURE Oppé 1950, no. 3; Roberts 1987, pp. 58–9

These drawings are two of 38 such sheets drawn by the young Prince of Wales as part of his education in draughtsmanship and geometry. In each case, a geometrical study has been drawn at the top of a sheet of paper, and a wash drawing of a house or landscape added underneath. The geometrical studies are based on the examples in Sebastien le Clerc's geometrical textbook *Pratique de la Géometrie*, 1688.[88]

Technical drawing was considered an important skill for the young Prince, allowing him to understand subjects such as military fortification and architecture, as well as being a fashionable accomplishment for young boys. Between 1751 and 1756, a 'Master of Fortification and Drawing' was paid £100 a year to teach Prince George and his brother Prince Edward. In 1756 the architect Joshua Kirby was the Princes' drawing master and may have overseen these examples.

The Prince became a talented draughtsman, with a lifelong love of architectural drawing.[89] Such juvenile studies as these are lucky survivals, owing their continued existence to Queen Charlotte's careful curating of her own library collections and to her devotion to her husband, who was incapacitated by the time she found and preserved these drawings. KH

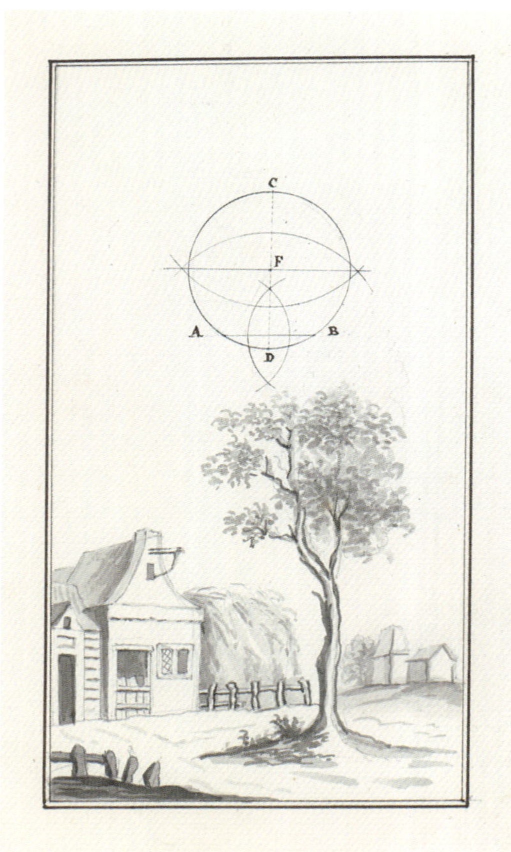

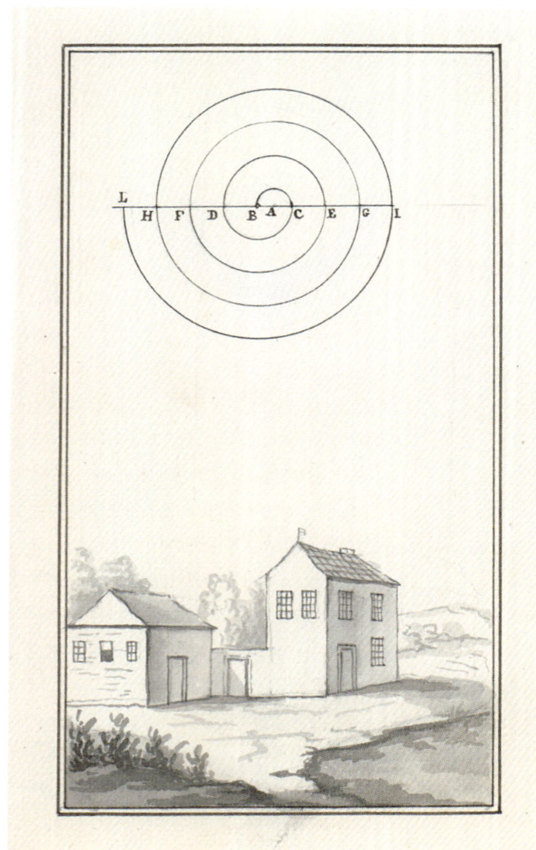

188

JOHN SIGISMUND TANNER (*c.*1704–1775)

Jernegan's Lottery Medal 1736

Silver, diameter 3.9 cm
RCIN 443231

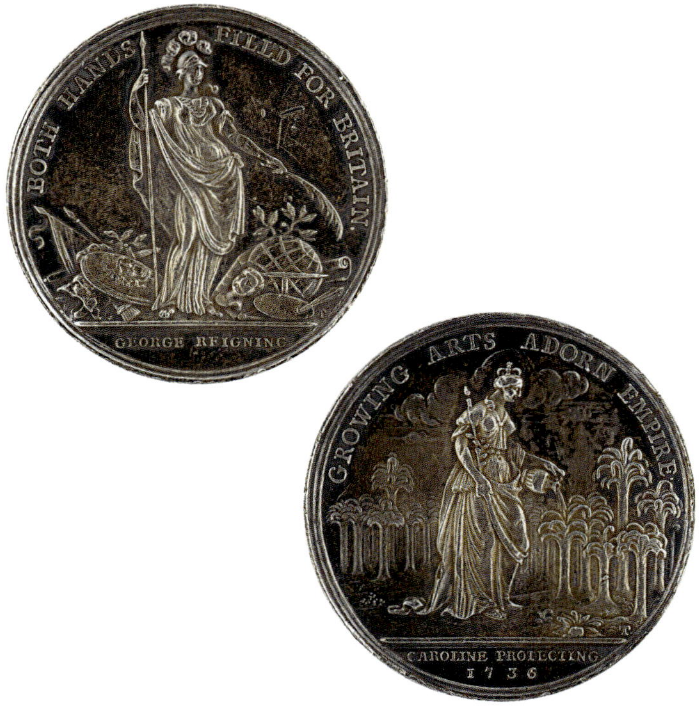

LITERATURE Hawkins 1885, II, pp. 517–2; British Museum 1909–11, pl. CLIII/5; Knight 1842

'On the 2nd of March, 1735 ... one Henry Jernegan, goldsmith, petitioned the House, stating that he had made a silver cistern, that had been acknowledged by all persons of skill ... to excel whatever of the kind had been attempted in this kingdom'.[90] Jernegan had commissioned his cistern in 1734–5 as the largest ever wine cooler, to be decorated with Bacchanalian scenes, but having failed to dispose of it, offered it as prize in a lottery; funds from the sale of tickets would go towards the rebuilding of Westminster Bridge. Lottery tickets cost five or six shillings, and each ticket holder was also given a silver medal, valued at about three shillings. About 30,000 tickets were sold and much money was raised for the bridge works. The medal was designed by H.F. Gravelot and cut by John Tanner of the Mint. The obverse depicts Minerva with spear and palm branch standing between a pile of arms and emblems of the arts and sciences; the motto reads *BOTH HANDS FILLED FOR BRITAIN*. The reverse shows Queen Caroline watering a grove of young palm trees, referring to her well-known love of botany, as well as the nurturing of 'green shoots' of knowledge. The motto reads *GROWING ARTS ADORN EMPIRE*. The original cooler is now in the Hermitage Museum, St Petersburg. ES

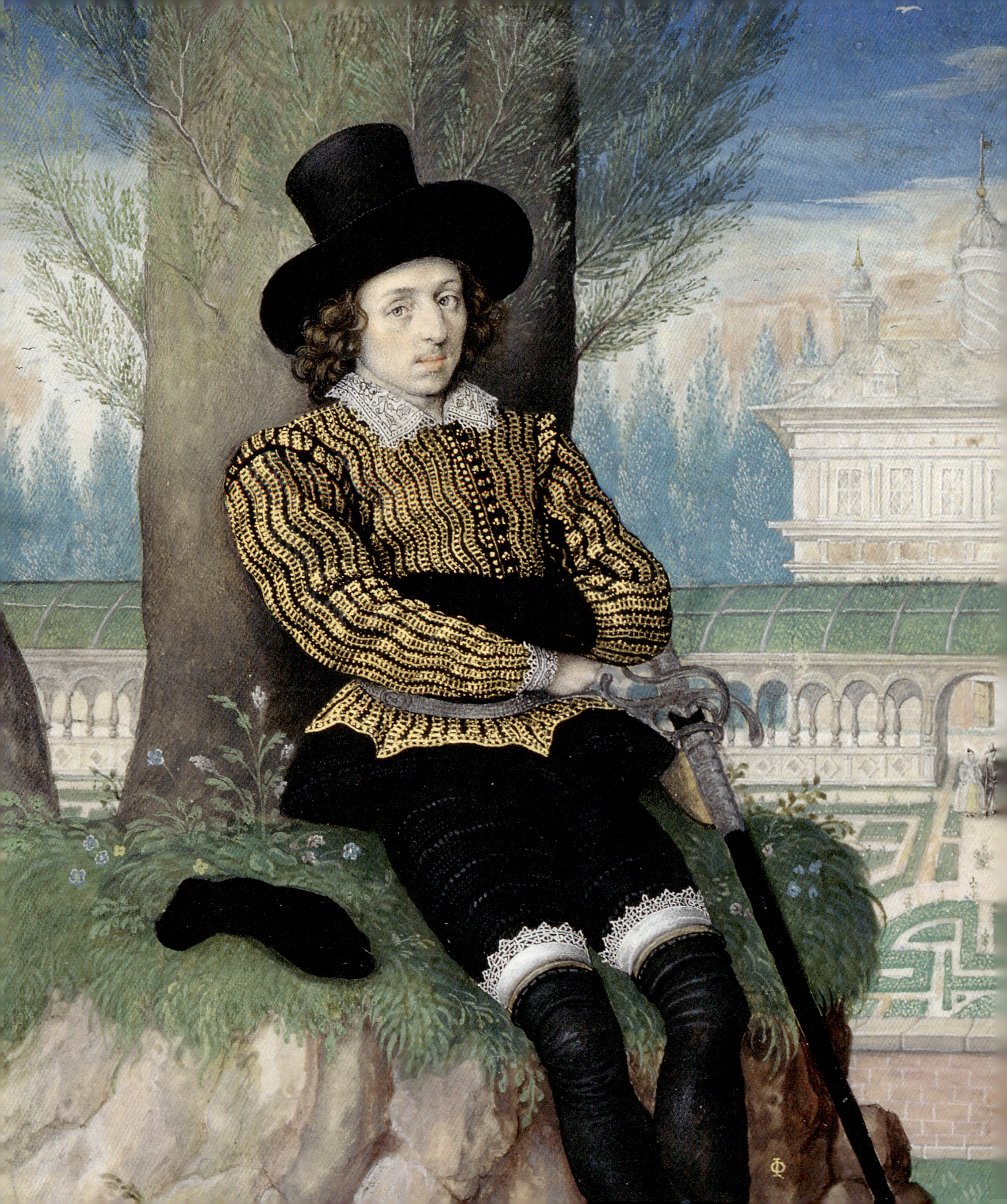

VIII

'Curious Limnings' Portrait Miniatures in the Early Georgian Period

VANESSA REMINGTON

Patronage of Miniaturists by the Early Hanoverians

Since the accession of James I in 1603, the Stuarts had proved adept at exploiting the portrait miniature art-form as a tool with which to support their authority when on the throne, and to press their claims to the throne when deposed. Charles II, before the Restoration, and later James II and his descendants in exile at St Germain-en-Laye and then in Rome, used portrait miniatures as a means to foster and reward loyalty amongst their dispersed supporters. When George I ascended to the throne in 1714, it might have been expected that he and his successors, more even than their Stuart predecessors, would resort to this small but effective art-form as a means to curry favour with members of the court in London and to distribute the royal image widely and at low cost. Instead, the patronage of portrait miniaturists by George I was a relatively passive business, marked by the appointment very late in George I's reign of the leading miniature painter Bernard Lens (1682–1740) as his Painter in Enamel. George II was a much more engaged patron, but he too ignored the value of the portrait miniature as a propaganda tool and instead commissioned miniatures as personal treasures, cherished items of sentimental value to be retained within the family rather than distributed more widely. In his will of 1751, George II made a specific bequest of 'the Ruby and Brilliant Rings given me by the Queen, and the Queen's, my Pictures and others made by Zinck, and all things contained in the same Box' to whichever should be the longest lived of his two daughters, Amelia and Caroline.[1]

The portrait miniature patronage of the early Hanoverians was significant not so much in the use to which they put miniatures but the type of miniature they commissioned. In 1714, the favoured medium for working on a miniature scale in England was watercolour on vellum. This technique had remained predominant throughout the seventeenth century despite its obvious shortcomings, including the vulnerability of miniatures to fading when subject to light exposure. In Europe, however, Henri Toutin (1614–83) of Paris had used the technique of enamelling to produce portrait miniatures for the first time in the 1630s. The application of pigments consisting of metal oxides to a metal base through fusion in a furnace was a process fraught with technical difficulties; mistakes could not be corrected, and with each firing came the risk of the metal plaque cracking. Nonetheless, the benefits were sufficient to ensure that the technique took hold and spread throughout Europe, with enamellists from Geneva, such as Jean Petitot (1607–91), taking the lead in

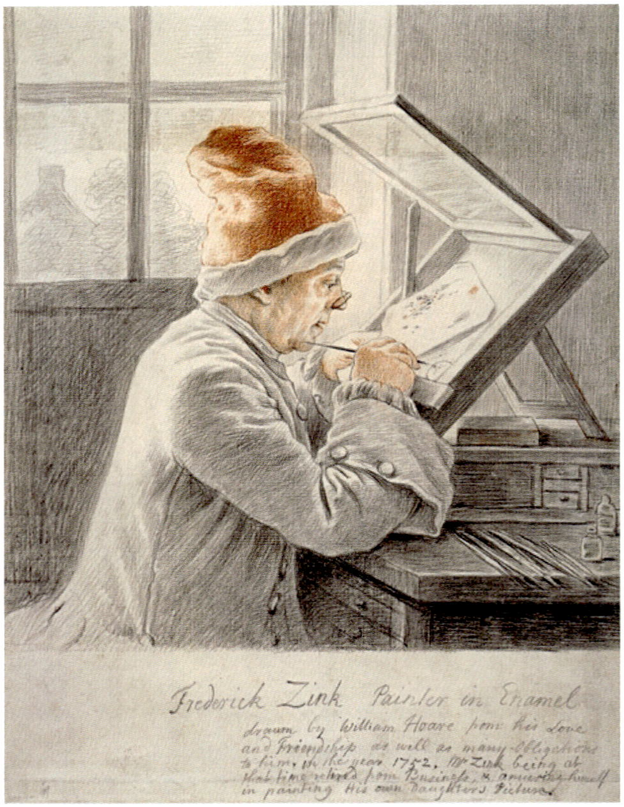

FIG. 76
William Hoare
Christian Friedrich Zincke, 1752
Black and red chalk drawing
British Museum, London

spreading the popularity of these glossy, durable new portrait miniatures. In England the enamel technique was practised only intermittently during the seventeenth century, and then only by foreign artists. Jean Petitot worked at the court of Charles I until the outbreak of the Civil War, but spent most of his long career in the service of Louis XIV. His son Jean Petitot the Younger (1653–1702) returned briefly to the English court from 1677 to 1682. The Swedish enamellist Charles Boit (1662–1727) was the first artist to hold the title of Court Enamellist, securing this appointment in the service of William III in 1696 and continuing to work for Queen Anne. Boit experienced recurrent technical difficulties in his work, and eventually fled to France to escape the debts he had incurred, leaving his pupil Christian Frederick Zincke to flourish in his place (fig. 76). Zincke had come to London from Dresden and was perfectly placed to succeed with the Hanoverian monarchy, partly because he spoke German and also because he had learned his trade in a country where the art of enamelling was particularly strong in the seventeenth and early eighteenth centuries. The courts of the Electors of Brandenburg, later Kings of Prussia, in Berlin and Potsdam, the court of the Electors of Saxony, in Dresden, and the court of the Electors Palatine, in Dusseldorf, were particularly enthusiastic sponsors of the art-form.

Zincke, who arrived in London in 1706, is not known to have returned to Germany until 1733. He became a naturalised British citizen by Act of Parliament in 1720, and single-mindedly established a long and extremely successful career as an enamellist, underwritten by the continuous and enthusiastic patronage of George II, Queen Caroline and Frederick, Prince of Wales. By 1740 he was capable of underwriting a loan of over £2250, evidence of prosperity previously unheard of for an enamel painter in Britain.[2] By his zealous and continuous practice of the art, supported by royal patronage, Zincke achieved what no other artist had done before him, and brought enamel painting into the mainstream of the English portrait miniature tradition.

The Display of Miniatures

On his accession, George I inherited a collection of just over fifty miniatures. The collection had been diminished by the sale of works from the Royal Collection after the execution of Charles I in 1649 but still featured examples by Hans Holbein the Younger (1497/8–1543), Nicholas Hilliard (1547–1619), François Clouet (*c.*1520–72), John Hoskins (*c.*1590–1665) and Samuel Cooper (1608?–72). Many of the most important were located in two cases

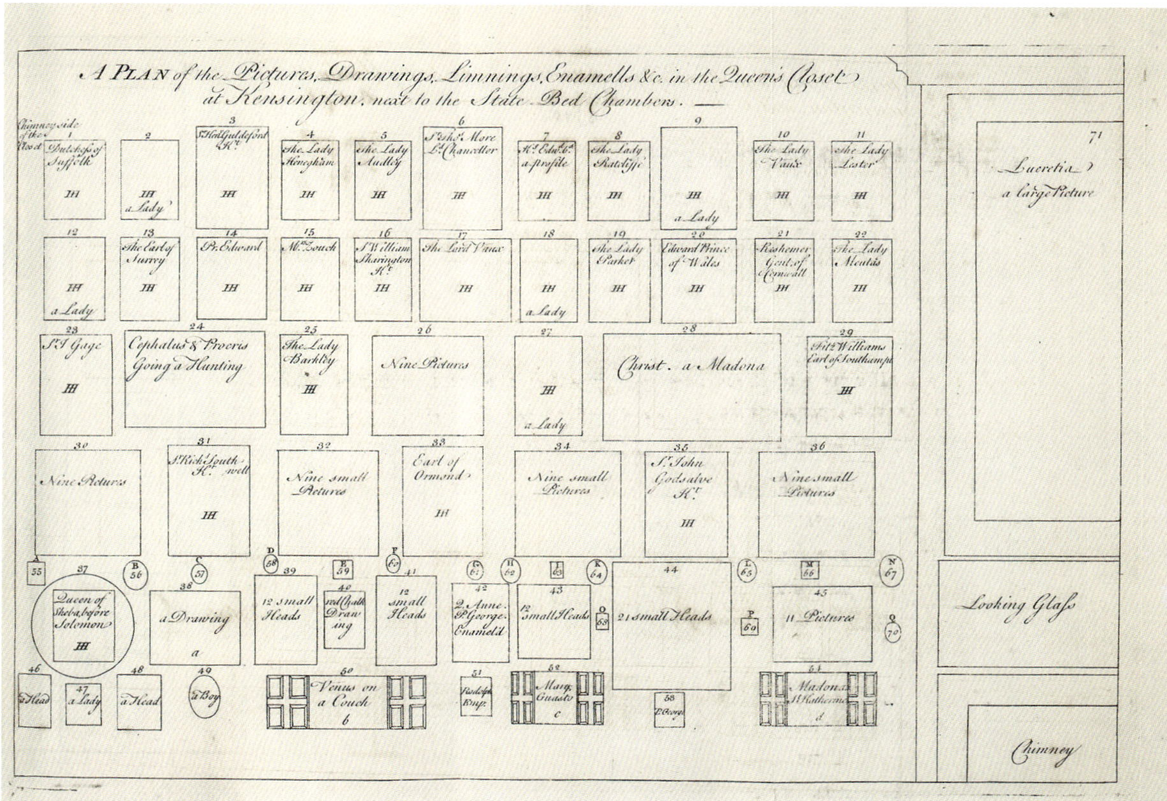

FIG. 77
George Vertue
Hanging plan
of the chimney
wall (opposite the
windows) of Queen
Caroline's Picture
Closet, Kensington
Palace, 1743
RCIN 1112554

in the King's Drawing Room at Kensington Palace, with others housed in a press in the Lower Closet at Hampton Court, and with some miniatures hanging on the walls of individual residences. The cases at Kensington were inventoried in a manuscript recording George I's collection at Kensington in 1723.[3] Despite the quality of the remaining miniatures, the collection as a whole seems to have been fragmented and somewhat neglected until the intervention of Queen Caroline. On the Queen's instructions the miniatures were brought together in the mid-1730s and united with drawings and oil paintings in her Picture Closet at Kensington Palace to form a cogent display which she was concerned to document and record.

The exact layout of the rooms is known from four hanging plans (figs. 77–80) drawn by George Vertue and appended to the inventory which he compiled in September 1743. This was produced at 'the Queen's command', although by the time it was printed Queen Caroline had been dead for seven years.[4] George Vertue's inventory of the Picture Closet, together with his surviving drawings, reveals a room which was densely hung with particular prominence accorded to the set of portrait drawings by Hans Holbein the Younger (see p. 274). Integrated between small paintings and portrait drawings are groups of miniatures framed together in groups of up to twenty. These were recorded as 'limnings', using the original term for small-scale portraits painted in watercolour that later became known as miniatures. Individual miniatures, itemised in Vertue's inventory, were hung in small spaces between the larger pictures.

The chimney wall (fig. 77) was hung with a particularly dense hang of drawings by Hans Holbein the Younger on the upper tiers. These included his portraits *Katherine, Duchess of Suffolk* (item 1; RCIN 912194), *Sir Henry Guildford* (item 3; RCIN 912266), *Elizabeth, Lady Audley* (item 5; RCIN 912191), *Sir Thomas More* (item 6; FIG. 70) and *Sir John Godsalve* (item 35; RCIN 912265). The eye-level tiers below integrated smaller miniatures and limnings, including

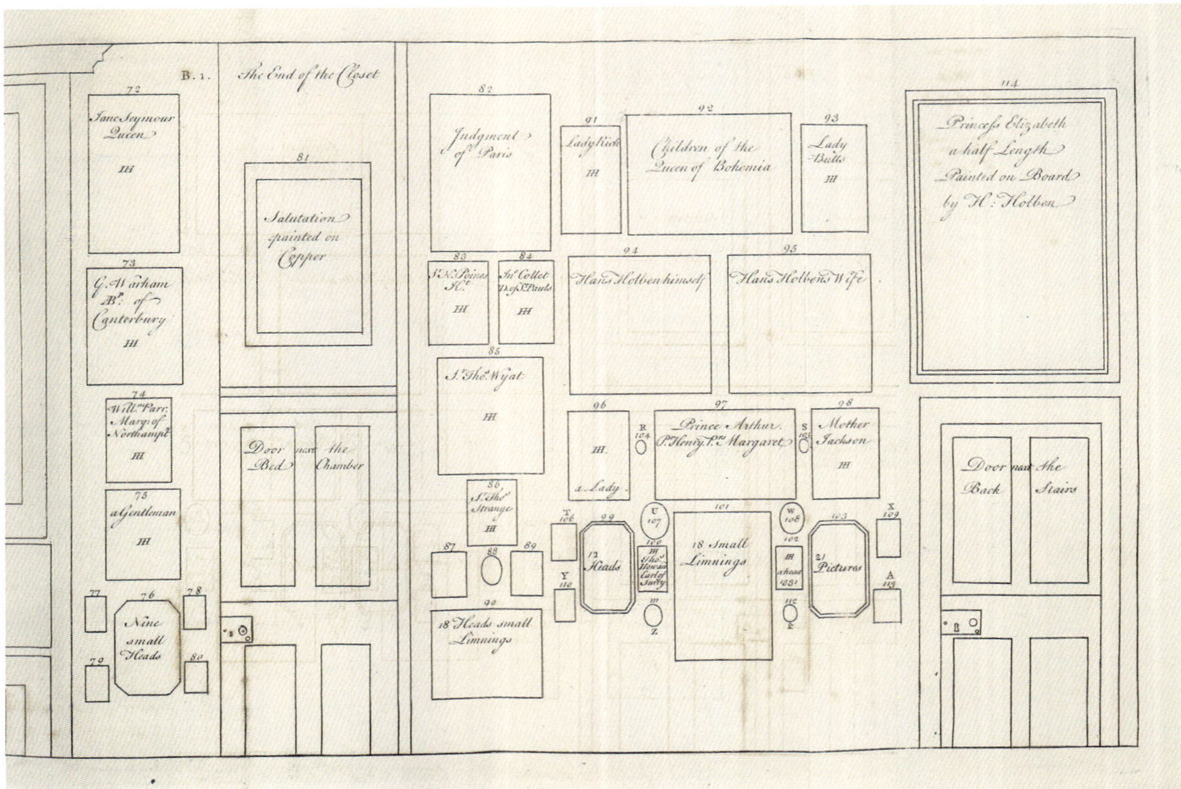

FIG. 78
George Vertue
Hanging plan
of the end wall
(opposite the
entrance) of
Queen Caroline's
Picture Closet,
Kensington
Palace, 1743
RCIN 1112554

Holbein's limned copy on vellum of '*Solomon and the Queen of Sheba*' (item 37; RCIN 912188) and three limned copies after Old Master paintings by Peter Oliver (1594?–1647) – *Venus* after Titian (item 50; no longer in the Royal Collection); the *Allegory of the Marchese d'Avalos* after Titian, copied by Peter Oliver in 1629 (item 52; RCIN 452459) and Titian's *Madonna with St John and St Katherine* (item 54; RCIN 452436).

Components of the series of miniatures by the Brunswick-Lunebürg court miniaturist (see nos 195–8) also appeared on this wall; those of *Ernest of Celle, Duke of Brunswick-Lunebürg*, and *Sophia, Duchess of Brunswick-Lunebürg* (nos 195–6) can confidently be identified amongst a group of nine miniatures framed together as item 26. They were amongst 88 miniatures of the Hanoverians' forebears which were brought together by Queen Caroline, mounted in frames of nine including one landscape in each (fig. 77, 79–80, items 26, 30, 32, 34, 36, 139, 141, 158–9, 173 and 203). Two thirds of this dynastic assembly remain in the Royal Collection, although the landscapes cannot now be identified. On the lowest tier, four frames housed groups of miniatures which were clearly smaller in scale than the Brunswick set, and were in different media. Some were specified as enamels by Vertue; others were encased in jewelled settings. Both British and European subjects were represented in the same framed sets, although many of the subjects were not identified by Vertue. As item 44, for example, were 21 small heads, of which only two were identified by George Vertue – as 'The Emperor and Empress of Germany'. Interspersed in the gaps above and below this tier were single oval miniatures such as several from Samuel Cooper's set of unfinished sketches of *Catherine of Braganza* (item 62; RCIN 420644), *Frances Theresa Stuart, Duchess of Richmond* (item 64; RCIN 420085) and *Barbara Villiers, Duchess of Cleveland* (item 65; RCIN 420109).

The end wall (fig. 78) repeated the arrangement of Holbein drawings interspersed with oil paintings and

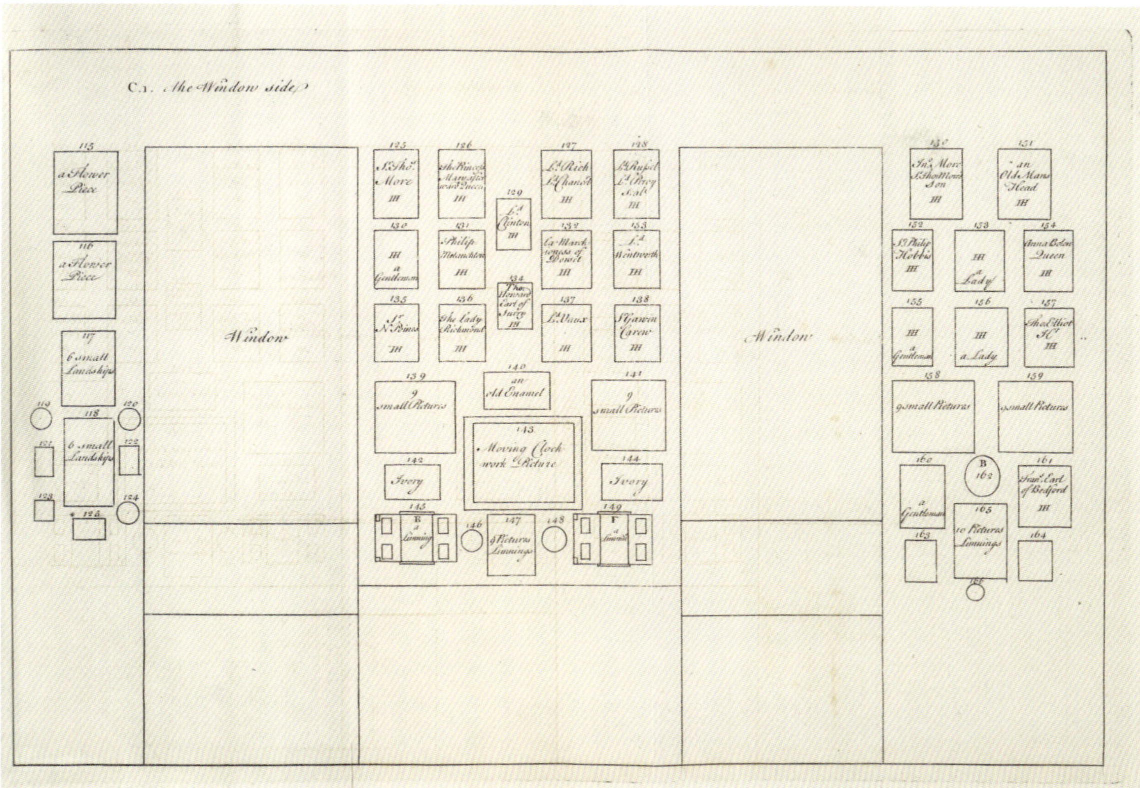

FIG. 79
George Vertue
Hanging plan
of the window
wall of Queen
Caroline's
Picture Closet,
Kensington
Palace, 1743
RCIN 1112554

miniatures. A 'Salutation' (item 81, probably no. 127) hung over the door to the bedchamber, opposite the panel of Elizabeth I (item 114, RCIN 404444) now attributed to William Scrots (active 1537–53). 'Hans Holbein himself' and his wife (items 94–5) are the portraits now attributed to Brosamer (figs. 71–2). Immediately above them hung the 'Children of the Queen of Bohemia' (item 92, RCIN 403558), the elder siblings of the Electress Sophia and thus a reminder of the origin of the Hanoverian claim to the British throne; beneath them (item 97) hung Jan Gossaert's *Children of Christian II, King of Denmark* (RCIN 405782), then identified as the children of Henry VII. Queen Caroline may have re-acquired this painting, which was recorded in the inventories of Charles I but not those of Charles II. On the lower tier hung miniatures from the historical collection; Vertue lists as item 88 'a small oval frame, containing five small heads, King James the First and his Queen, Prince Henry and Princess Elizabeth, and Prince Charles with the arms in the middle'.[5] Item 103 contained 21 oval miniatures, both historic and contemporary, including miniatures of James I and Anne of Denmark, of the King and Queen of Bohemia, probably by Nicholas Hilliard and Isaac Oliver, along with miniatures of the Princesses Anne, Caroline and Louise, possibly enamels by Zincke (no. 213).

The window wall (fig. 79) contains 'Flower pieces' by Maria van Oosterwyck (1630-93, items 113-4, RCIN 405625–6), the only examples of still lives found in the Closet. Item 143 in the centre of the wall is an untraceable 'Moving Clockwork Picture', presumably a mechanical curiosity of the sort beloved of the seventeenth-century *virtuoso*, but otherwise absent from this particular display.[6] 'Nine small pictures' in 'a square gold frame' (item 139) probably included nos. 193–4 and miniatures remaining in the Royal Collection portraying Frederick III, King of Denmark and his consort Sophia Amalia, *c.*1670–80; item 159 contained nos. 199–202 in the same arrangement.[7] Limnings by Peter Oliver were chosen for the lower tier

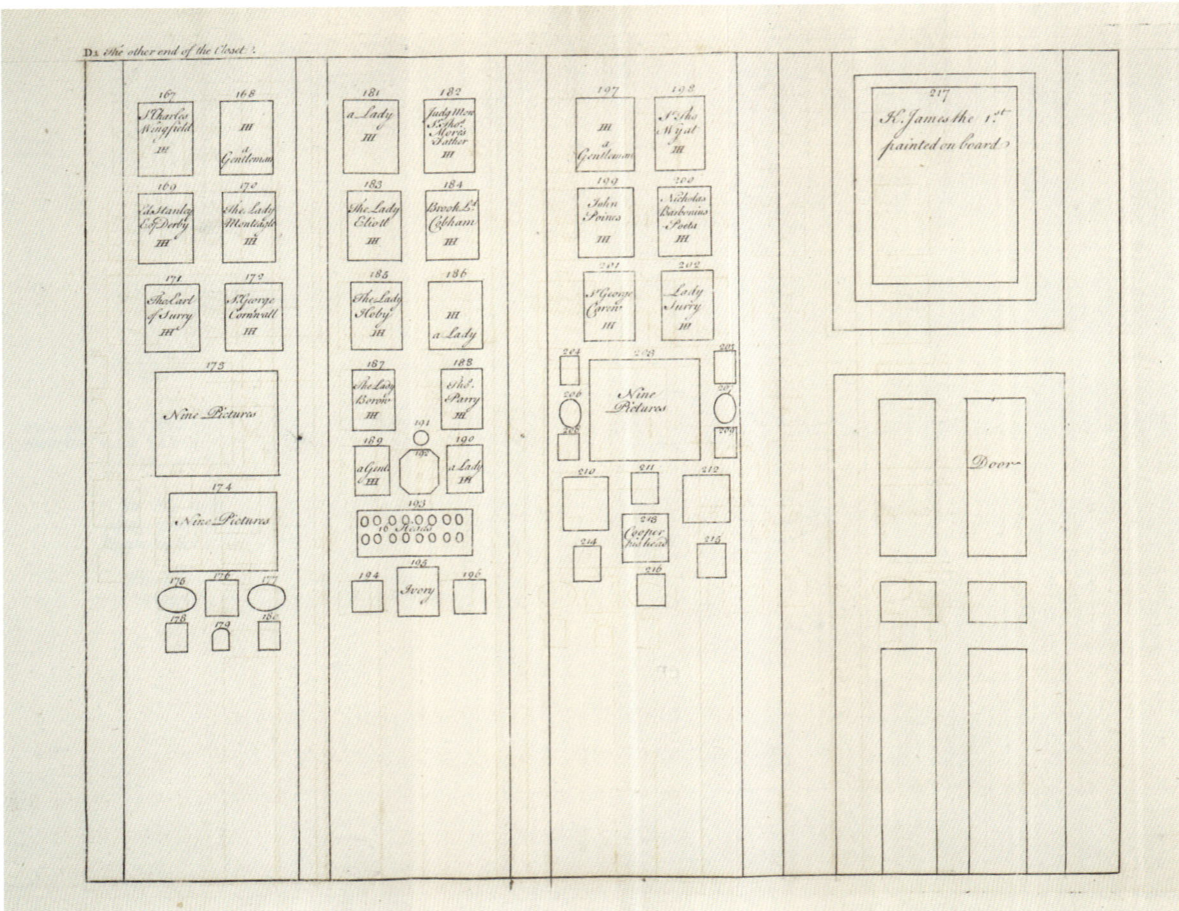

FIG. 80
George Vertue
George Vertue
Hanging plan of the entrance wall of Queen Caroline's Picture Closet, Kensington Palace, 1743
RCIN 1112554

on this wall, too, with two copies after Correggio, *Venus and Cupid* (item 145; RCIN 452457) and *Venus and Mercury teaching Cupid to read* (item 149; RCIN 452458). These were at this stage still framed in the hinged cases described in the 1639 inventory of Charles I's collection by Abraham van der Doort, with closing outer flaps.

The pattern was similar for the entrance wall (fig. 80), with a dense hang of Holbein drawings above several tiers of smaller-scale miniatures. The ovals constituting item 193 were not miniatures but a series of wax heads of princes of Germany, Denmark and Poland; carved ivory profiles of Queen Anne and Prince George of Denmark could be found immediately beneath. A drawing in crayons of Samuel Cooper, described as a self-portrait but now attributed to John Hoskins the Younger (1607/8–72) is listed by Vertue on the last section of the final wall (item 213, now Victoria and Albert Museum, inv. Dyce 91).[8]

The display in Queen Caroline's Picture Closet followed the model of the Stuart cabinet room, epitomised by Charles I's Cabinet Room at Whitehall Palace, recorded in Abraham Van der Doort's inventory of 1639, which emulated the Italian Renaissance *studiolo*, a small room designed to display paintings, sculpture, drawings, antiquities and rarities in close proximity. Charles I's Cabinet Room had been dismantled when his goods were sold, but a similar Stuart closet furnished with miniatures survived at Ham House. An inventory of the Green Closet at Ham House, compiled in 1728 shortly before Queen Caroline created her own closet at Kensington in the 1730s, lists 60 paintings, of which 30 were described as small.[9] The appearance and historical focus of Queen Caroline's displays in the Picture Closet at Kensington Palace

FIG. 81
Allan Ramsay
Richard Mead, 1740
Oil on canvas
National Portrait Gallery, London

may also have been influenced by the new breed of eighteenth-century collectors exemplified by Dr Richard Mead (1673–1754), physician to George II from 1727 (fig. 81). The appearance for the first time in English of the term 'connoisseur' in 1719 coincided with a period in which collecting patterns and interests shifted. Instead of collections of miniatures representing the accumulated aristocratic patronage of several generations, they were now acquired piecemeal by middle-class antiquarians like Mead. The bibliophile, antiquarian and art collector displayed his exceptional collections in a gallery in the garden of his house on Great Ormond Street, where he entertained scholars and friends. The reputation of his collection of miniatures was such that, when Mead died, Horace Walpole lamented: 'Dr Meade is dead & his collection is going to be sold – I fear I have not virtue enough to resist his miniatures – I shall be ruined'.[10] Some of the miniatures belonging to Dr Mead, which had been so coveted by Walpole, were acquired by Frederick, Prince of Wales (nos 221–5), and added to the 'Curious limnings and valuable pictures &c.' which he kept in his Closet at Carlton House.[11] Frederick may have planned to enrich his own collection to rival his mother's displays in the Closet at Kensington, but, whatever his long-term intentions, his aims were frustrated by his early death in 1751 and the assimilation of his goods into the Royal Collection.

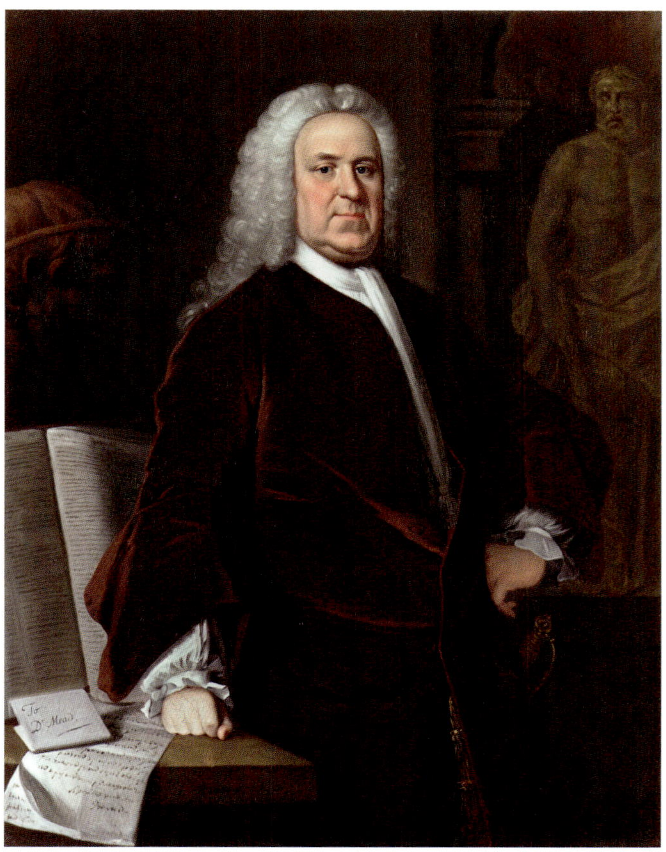

189

BERNARD LENS (1682–1740)

George I (1660–1727) *c.*1714–20

Watercolour on ivory, 36 × 31 mm
RCIN 420179

PROVENANCE First recorded in the Royal Collection in 1844 (*List* 1844, p. 16)

LITERATURE Walker 1992, no. 6

Bernard Lens held the title 'Painter in Enamel' to George I from 1723 and continued in office as 'Painter in Enamel and Cabinet Painter' to George II on a salary of £200, yet he produced very few miniatures for his royal patrons. Although he stands as a key figure in the development of the art of miniature painting in England (see also no. 192), his main contribution to the arts at the early Georgian court was made not as a miniaturist but in his capacity as drawing master to Princesses Mary and Louise.

Bernard Lens was in many ways an innovator; he was the first artist in England to popularise the practice of painting miniatures on ivory rather than vellum and he revived the seventeenth-century tradition of making limned copies in watercolour on vellum or ivory of Old Master paintings. It is therefore surprising to find that Lens's only portraits of George I in the Royal Collection are copies based on prototypes by Sir Godfrey Kneller, in this case the image of *c.*1715 used for the coinage (see no. 4). VR

190

ANONYMOUS, GERMAN SCHOOL, *c.*1690–95

Sophia Dorothea of Celle, Consort of George I (1668–1726)

Watercolour on vellum, 6.2 × 4.9 cm
RCIN 420940

LITERATURE Cust 1910, no. 4/12; Reynolds 1999, no. 270

This late seventeenth-century miniature depicts Sophia Dorothea of Celle, consort of George I and mother of George II and Queen Sophia Dorothea of Prussia. Sophia Dorothea of Celle was the daughter of George William, Duke of Brunswick, and his French wife, Eléonore Desmier d'Olbreuse. Arranged solely to achieve territorial ambitions, Sophia Dorothea's marriage to George was an unhappy one. It ended tragically with the exposure of her affair with Count Philip von Königsmarck (see p. 33). Not only were the couple divorced, but Sophia Dorothea was sent to Schloss Ahlden, where she was forced to remain, separated from her children, for the rest of her life. She died in 1726 after 32 years of imprisonment without ever having set foot in England or having been acknowledged Queen Consort. WB

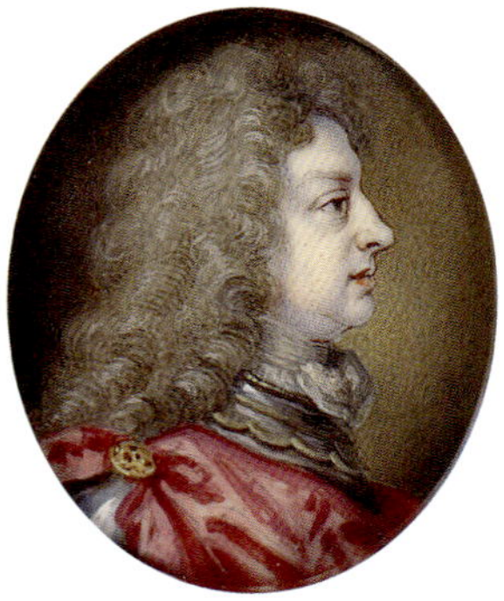

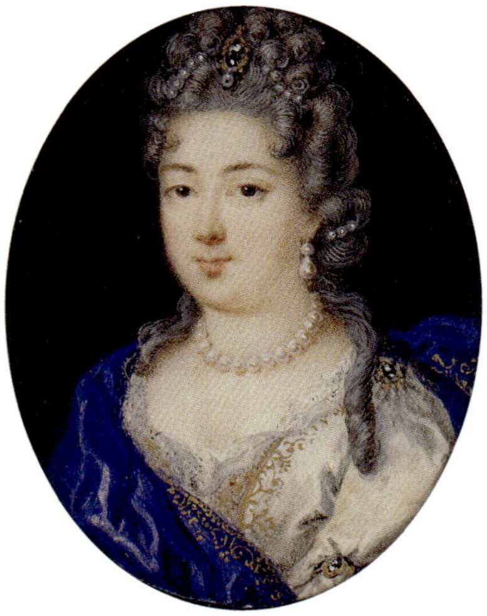

191

ATTRIBUTED TO LUDOLF LAFONTAINE (1704–1774)

George I (1660–1727) *c.*1727–35

Watercolour on ivory, 73 × 58 mm
RCIN 420655

PROVENANCE First recorded in the Royal Collection in 1870 (RL 1870 5.A.1)

LITERATURE Walker 1992, no. 110; Lavender 1993, no. 69

Although the commission of a miniature portrait of George I during the later part of his reign would naturally have fallen to his Painter in Enamel, Bernard Lens (see no. 189) this particular miniature does not bear the hallmarks of Lens's style. It is closely related to the three-quarter-length oil portrait by Georg Wilhelm Lafontaine (1680–1745) in the Royal Collection (RCIN 405247), which probably dates from *c.*1725–7. The miniature may have been painted by Georg Wilhelm's son, Ludolf Lafontaine, who was born in Celle in 1704, was trained by his father in both oil and miniature painting, and worked in both England and Holland. He would have had access to the original oil painting in his father's studio but could conceivably have used the line engraving of 1733 by G.W. Monguibert. In 1734 Ludolf became court painter in Brunswick, where he stayed until his death in 1774.

The pared-down nature of the miniature, which omits the royal regalia seen in the oil portrait, and exchanges the Banqueting House for a plain drab background, emphasises the simplicity of presentation of the monarch. George I appears here in the sympathetic guise of an English gentleman. VR

192

BERNARD LENS

Princess Louise (1724–1751) 1739

Watercolour on ivory, 47 × 39 mm
Signed and dated: *BL 1739* and inscribed on the backing card: *B. Lens Fecit/ad vivum 1739*
RCIN 420180

PROVENANCE Probably in the Royal Collection since it was painted; first recorded in the inventories in 1851 (*Miniatures* 1851, no. 27)

LITERATURE Walker 1992, no. 7

Bernard Lens was the son of an engraver and the grandson of an enameller, and is likely to have trained at the drawing school established by his father in St Paul's Churchyard, London, in 1697, the first commercial establishment of its kind. By 1707 he was described in a letter written by George Tollet to Robert Harley, father of Edward Harley, 2nd Earl of Oxford, as: 'very able and the best master we have in London'.[12] As drawing master to Princess Mary, Princess Louise and William, Duke of Cumberland, Lens would have had the opportunity to paint their portraits from life. He would also have had access to the historic miniatures in the Royal Collection which had, by the mid-1730s, been assembled in Queen Caroline's Closet at Kensington Palace (fig. 77–80). In producing this miniature of Princess Louise, Lens adopted a deliberately anachronistic approach, reverting to the blue background which was characteristic of the work of Nicholas Hilliard (1547–1619) and the early work of Isaac Oliver (d. 1617) at the Elizabethan and Jacobean courts (see no. 223). He may have been influenced specifically by Isaac Oliver's miniature of Princess Elizabeth, later Queen of Bohemia (RCIN 420031), which shows the sitter at the slightly younger age of fourteen, and shares with the present piece a delicacy of handling which is most evident in the flowers worn in the subjects' hair. VR

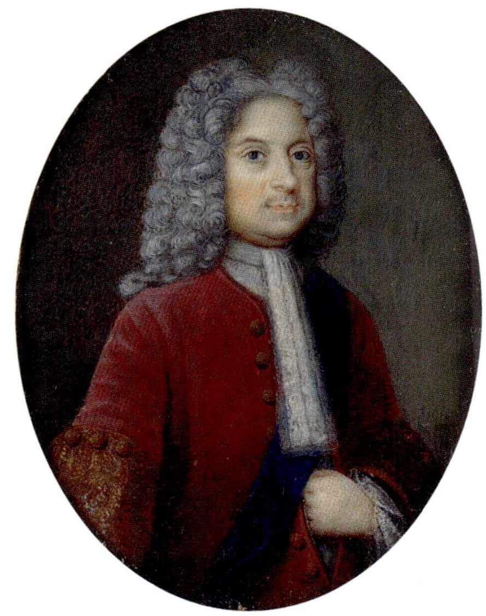

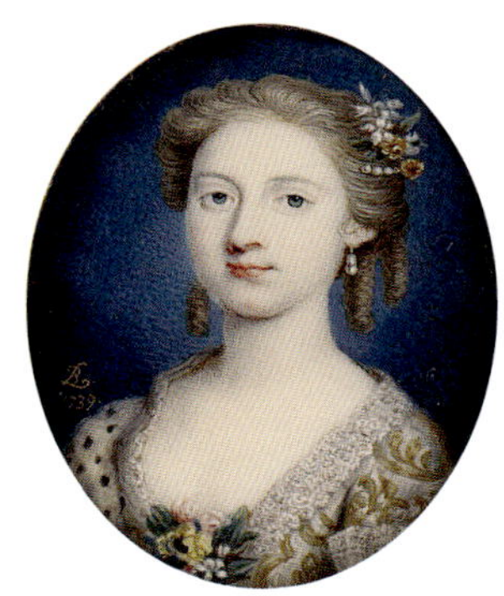

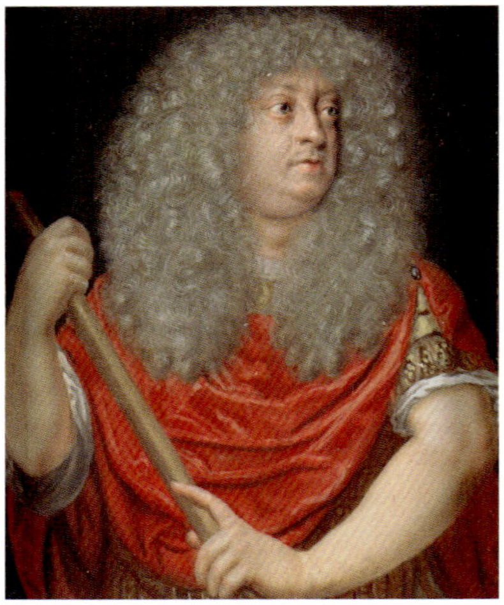

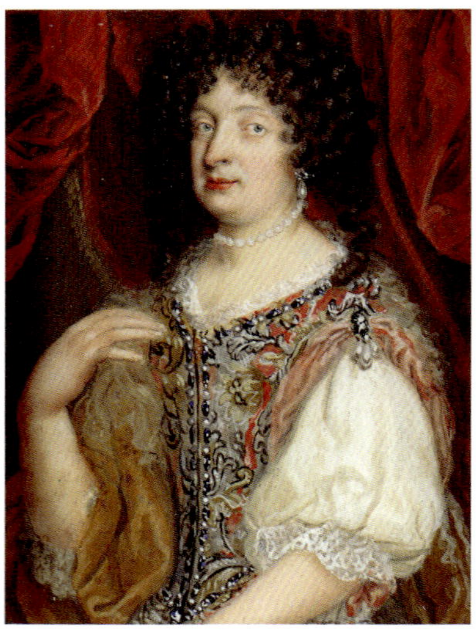

193 & 194

JEAN MICHELIN (1623–1696)

Ernest Augustus, Elector of Hanover (1629–1698) c.1670

Watercolour on vellum, 70 × 58 mm
Inscribed in ink on the gessoed reverse: *No. 33 Erneste Auguste Duc de Broun: et de Luneboug Eveque d'Osenbruc*
RCIN 420624

Sophia, Electress of Hanover (1630–1714) c.1670

Watercolour on vellum, 70 × 55 mm
Inscribed in ink on the gessoed reverse: *No. 34 Sophie Duchesse de Brown: et de Luneb: nee Princesse Palatine.*
RCIN 420627

PROVENANCE (Cat. 193) first recorded in Queen Caroline's Closet, Kensington Palace in 1743, item 139/4; (cat. 194): probably hung in Queen Caroline's Closet at Kensington Palace, although not identified by name in George Vertue's inventory, 1743, p. 21 item 139/4; first recorded with certainty in the Royal Collection in 1870 (RL 1870 21.E.3)

LITERATURE Reynolds 1999, nos 256–7

These miniatures of the Elector and Electress of Hanover (see pp. 30–33) date from c. 1670 and are rare examples of the work of Jean Michelin, who is said to have been born in Langres, France, and died in Jersey. He became a member of the Académie Royale in 1668 and worked for the Hanoverian court from 1668 until 1686. The miniatures featured among a group of 88 representing German and other families first recorded in Queen Caroline's Closet at Kensington Palace in 1743 by George Vertue (fig. 79, item 139). Vertue failed to identify the Elector in the inventory, but the miniature of Ernest Augustus can be distinguished as 'A Gentleman in red drapery, with a truncheon in both hands'. This form of presentation as a Roman general was one which the Dukes of Brunswick often chose for their portrayal in full-scale oil portraits. The presence of the Elector and Electress in the Hanoverian gallery of portraits represented in Queen Caroline's closet can be explained by their importance as the immediate forebears of George I. However, the Electress Sophia was also known personally to the young Caroline of Ansbach, as the older woman spent much time at the court of her daughter Sophia Charlotte, Electress of Brandenburg, and Queen of Prussia, where Caroline lived after the death of her own mother in 1696 (see pp. 269–70). As a widely travelled, knowledgeable and cultured woman, the Electress was an influential model on the future Queen Caroline. VR

195–8

GERMAN SCHOOL, 16TH CENTURY (THE BRUNSWICK-LÜNEBURG COURT MINIATURIST)

Ernest of Celle, Duke of Brunswick-Lüneburg (1497–1546) c.1595

Watercolour on vellum, 69 × 56 mm
Inscribed at the top in white: *ERNESTUS: HERZOG: BRANS.UND LUNEBURG.*
RCIN 420435

Sophia, Duchess of Brunswick-Lüneburg (1508–1541) c.1595

Watercolour on vellum, 69 × 56 mm
Inscribed at the top in white: *SOPHIA GEBORN HERZO: ZU MECHELBURG UND HERZO: ZU BRAUN : UND LUN*
RCIN 420436

William the Younger, Duke of Brunswick-Lüneburg (1535–1592) c.1595

Watercolour on vellum, 70 × 56 mm
Inscribed at the top in white: *WILHELM DER JÜNGER HERZOG ZU BRAUNS: UND LUNEB:*
RCIN 420439

George, Duke of Brunswick-Lüneburg-Calenberg (1582–1641) c.1595

Watercolour on vellum, 70 × 55 mm
Inscribed at the top in white: *GEORGE HERZOG ZU BRAUNSCHWIG: UND LUNEBERG*
RCIN 420445

PROVENANCE First recorded in the Royal Collection in Queen Caroline's Closet, Kensington Palace, by George Vertue in 1743 (Vertue 1743, p. 3, item 26 1/3/?4 and p. 5 item 34/6))

LITERATURE Reynolds 1999, nos 185–6, 189, 195

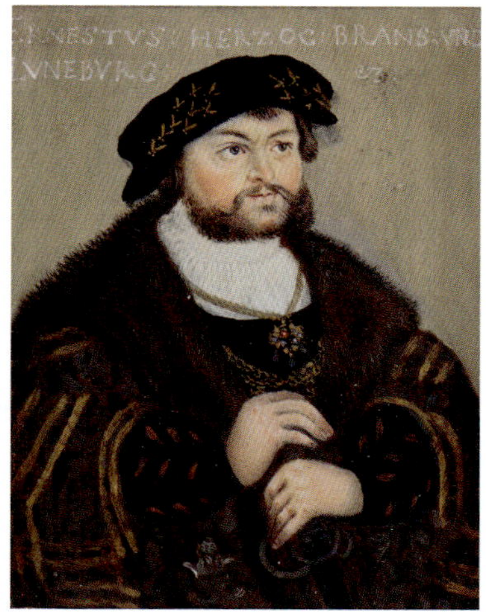

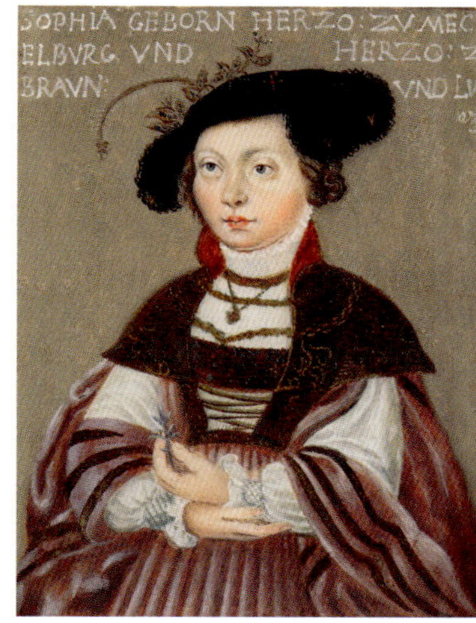

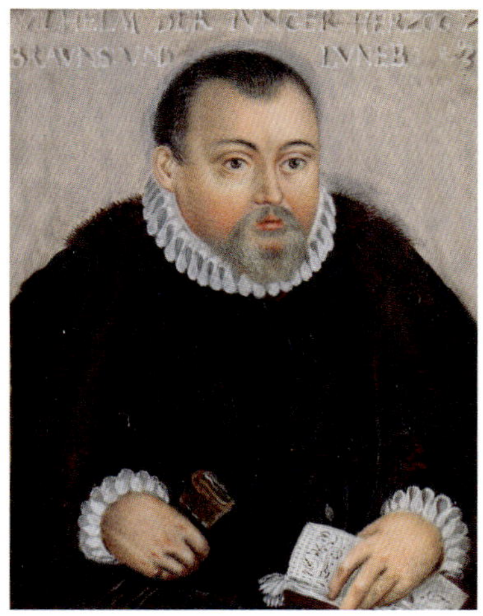

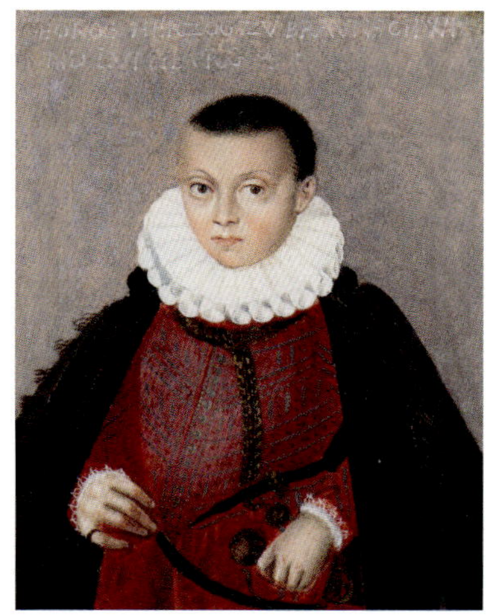

This group of four miniatures form part of a set of 49 similar portraits of German and other forebears of the Hanoverian dynasty which were first recorded hanging in Queen Caroline's Closet by George Vertue in 1743 (fig. 77, items 26 and 34). The set can be dated to the years between 1593 and 1597 and consistency of technique and style indicates that it is the work of a single as yet unidentified miniature painter, working in the tradition of German court portraiture established by Lucas Cranach (1472–1553) at the court of the Elector of Saxony at Wittemberg.

The central figure in the set is William IV the Younger, Duke of Brunswick-Lüneburg, great-grandfather of George I, who is depicted with his fifteen children and with the consorts of his daughters. George, the sixth son of William the Younger, is seen here at about the age of thirteen. Two of his sons, George William, Duke of Celle, and Ernest Augustus, Elector of Hanover, were the grandfathers of George II.

Ernest I, Duke of Brunswick-Lüneburg-Celle, was the son of Henry, Duke of Brunswick-Lüneburg, whom he succeeded in 1521. In 1528 Ernest married Sophia, daughter of Henry III, Duke of Mecklenburg-Schwerin. Ernest I's support for the Reformation and introduction of the Protestant religion into his territories ultimately secured the British throne for his Protestant descendant George I.
VR

199–202

UNKNOWN ARTIST, GERMAN SCHOOL?, 17TH OR EARLY 18TH CENTURY

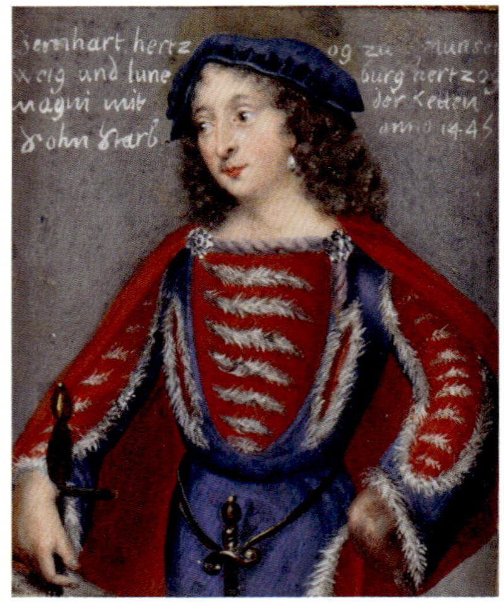

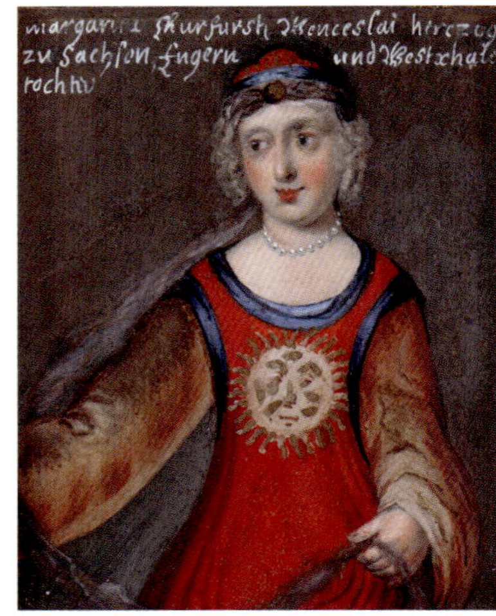

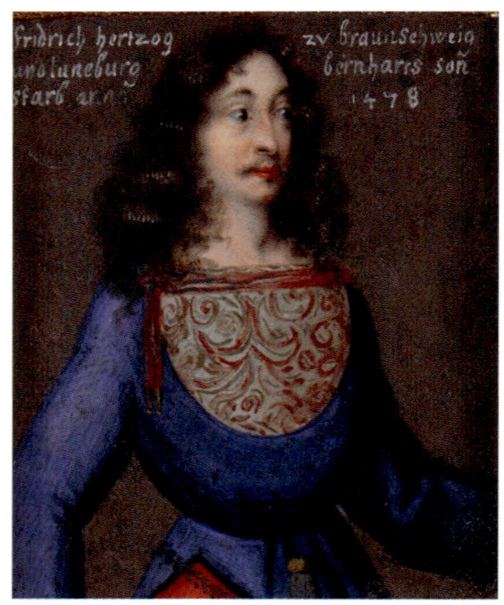

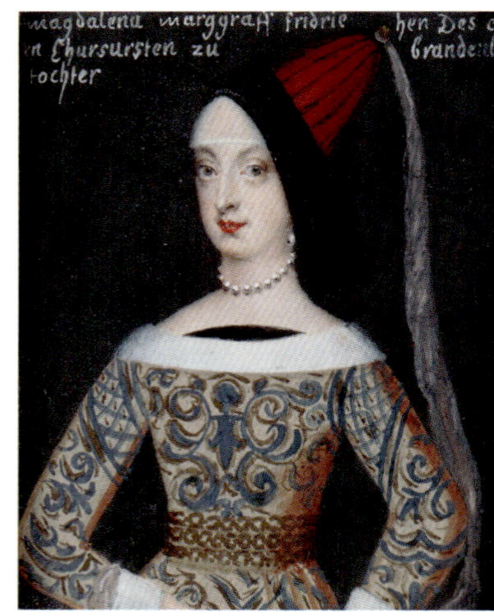

Bernard I, Duke of Brunswick-Lüneburg (d. 1434)

Watercolour on vellum, 70 × 59 mm
Inscribed at the top in white: *Bernhardt hertzog zu [Br]aunswchweig und luneburg hertzog Magni mit der Ketten Sohn Starb anno 1445*
RCIN 420423

Margareta, Duchess of Brunswick-Lüneburg (d. 1418)

Watercolour on vellum, 70 × 59 mm
Inscribed at the top in white: *Margarita Churfurst Wenceslai hertzogin zu Sachsen* [?] *fugern und West* [...] *alen tochter*
RCIN 420424

Frederick the Pious, Duke of Brunswick-Lüneburg (d. 1478)

Watercolour on vellum, 70 × 59 mm
Inscribed at the top in white: *Fridrich hertzog zu braunschweig und luneburg bernhards son starb anno 1478*
RCIN 420427

Magdalena, wife of Frederick the Pious, Duke of Brunswick-Lüneburg (d. 1454)

Watercolour on vellum, 70 × 59 mm
Inscribed at the top in white: *magdalena marggraff fridrichen Des ersten Churfursten zu brandenburg tochter*
RCIN 420428

PROVENANCE First recorded in the Royal Collection in Queen Caroline's Closet, Kensington Palace, by George Vertue in 1743 (Vertue 1743, p. 24 item 159 1/3/4/6)

LITERATURE Reynolds 1999, nos 239–40, 243–4

This group of four portraits are from a set of eight similar miniatures which form a retrospective extension to the series of 49 miniatures of the rulers of Brunswick-Lüneburg and their wives dating from *c.* 1595 also in the Royal Collection (nos 195–8). This secondary group of eight miniatures consists of fanciful portraits of fifteenth-century Dukes of Brunswick-Lüneburg and their consorts. They are embellished with inscriptions in Gothic script indicating a romantic view of the historic past and are later in date than the larger, original group. The set has previously been thought to date from the seventeenth century when the production of ancestral portrait sets in oil was common. However, the impetus to enlarge the original group of 49 miniatures may well have come when they were hung prominently in Queen Caroline's Closet at Kensington Palace in the mid-1730s (fig. 79, item 159). It is conceivable that the eight additional miniatures were produced on the instructions of Queen Caroline by an English miniaturist capable of emulating the naïve sixteenth-century style of the Brunswick-Lüneburg Court Miniaturist. VR

203

FOLLOWER OF CHRISTIAN FREDERICK ZINCKE

George I (1660–1727)

Enamel, 46 × 37 mm
RCIN 421779

PROVENANCE First recorded in the Royal Collection in 1858 (*List* 1858.97)

LITERATURE Walker 1992, no. 73

There is no surviving miniature of George I in the Royal Collection that was taken from life. Like other portrait miniatures produced by Bernard Lens (no. 189) and Ludolf Lafontaine (no. 191), this enamel derives from an oil painting and its production would not have required any additional sittings from the King. Portrait miniatures were first developed in the sixteenth century to be distributed as intimate and prestigious gifts within the upper echelons of court circles. The absence of any portraits of George I in this genre painted from life is therefore sufficiently unusual to support the notion that the monarch was resistant to having his portrait painted at all. This miniature is based in reverse on the official State Portrait of George I by Sir Godfrey Kneller (Houghton Hall, Norfolk; see further no. 189) and shows the King wearing State Robes with the collar of the Order of the Garter. It does not display the finesse characteristic of the technique of Christian Frederick Zincke (1684?–1767), who was already well established as an enamellist at the Stuart court by the time of George I's accession in 1714, and has been ascribed to a follower of the artist. VR

204

CHRISTIAN FREDERICK ZINCKE (1684?–1767)

George II (1683–1760) when Prince of Wales 1717

Enamel, 46 × 37 mm
Signed and dated on the reverse: *C F Zincke fecit / 1717*
RCIN 421777

PROVENANCE First recorded in the Royal Collection in 1858 (*List* 1858. 101)

LITERATURE Walker, 1992, no. 27

This is the earliest of the many surviving enamels of George II that Christian Frederick Zincke produced in the course of his long career at the early Hanoverian court in London. The head derives from Sir Godfrey Kneller's State Portrait of 1716 (no. 237); other versions of Kneller's 1716 State Portrait were produced in enamel by Zincke at this time, and he continued to use it as a source even after the Prince of Wales's accession as George II in 1727.

This enamel was not, however, George II's earliest commission of a miniature portrait. Whilst still resident in Hanover, he and Princess, later Queen, Caroline, were painted from life by the Geneva miniaturist Benjamin Arlaud (active 1701–17), possibly at the time of their marriage in 1705 (RCIN 420964 and 420182). Benjamin and his younger brother Jacques-Antoine Arlaud (1668–1746) were closely associated with the exiled Stuarts at St-Germain-en-Laye and painted a number of miniatures of Prince James Francis Stuart (see nos. 2 and 42) which formed part of a programme of 'focused propaganda to keep their loyal supporters close' and were instrumental in the dissemination of the Stuart claim to the throne.[13] VR

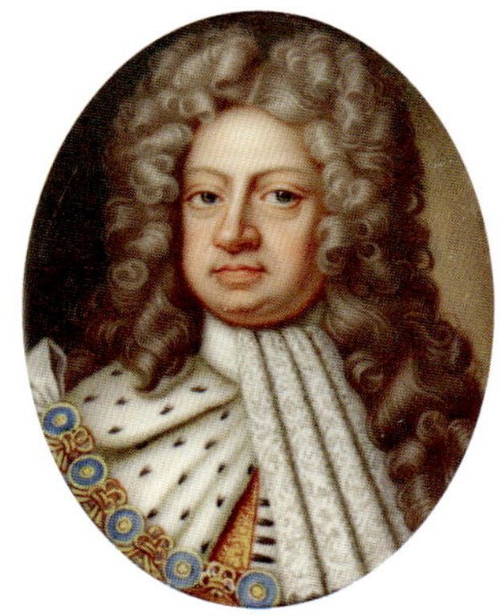

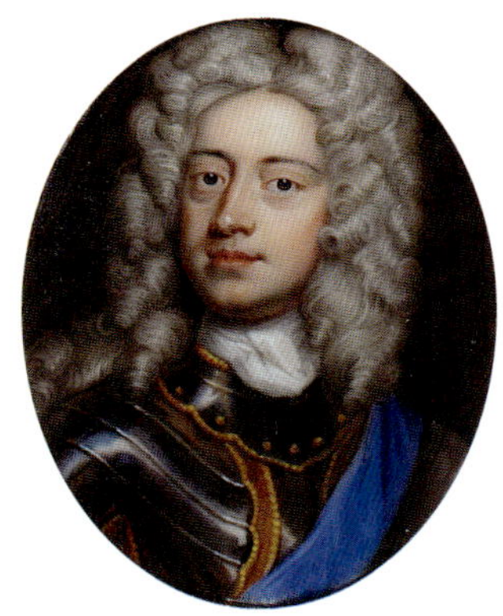

205

CHRISTIAN FREDERICK ZINCKE

Queen Caroline (1683–1737) c.1727

Enamel, 44 × 37 mm
RCIN 421800

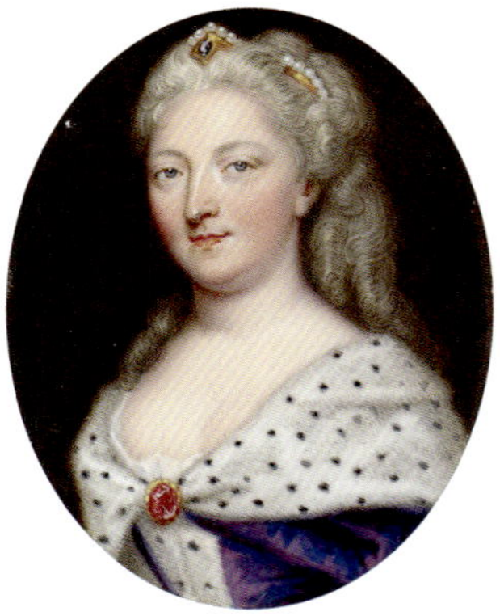

PROVENANCE Probably in the Royal Collection since it was first painted; first recorded in the Royal Collection in 1877 (*Enamels*, 1877, I. 183)

LITERATURE Walker, 1992, no. 37

Queen Caroline is shown here in Robes of State and an ermine cloak as in no. 215, and this miniature must also therefore date from around the time of the coronation in 1727. A number of versions of both types exist, including a variant of the present enamel in the Gilbert Collection. Both no. 205 and the enamel in the Gilbert collection were probably among 'the vast collection of miniatures and enamels of the family of George 2nd by Zincke' seen by Horace Walpole at Buckingham House in 1783.[14]

A variant of the present enamel shows the Queen bare-breasted, without any of the accoutrements of her regal status (fig. 82). This may have been intended as an intimate image of the Queen for the King alone, or perhaps was designed to be viewed more widely as an image of Caroline as matriarch as well as consort. In either case, this and the other miniatures by Zincke in this group constitute an important part of Caroline of Ansbach's iconography. VR

206–8

CHRISTIAN FREDERICK ZINCKE (1684?–1767)

Frederick, Prince of Wales (1707–1751) c.1714

Anne, Princess Royal, later Princess of Orange (1709–1759) c.1714

Princess Amelia (1711–1786) c.1714

Enamel, each 34 × 27 mm
RCIN 421804, 421805 and 421806

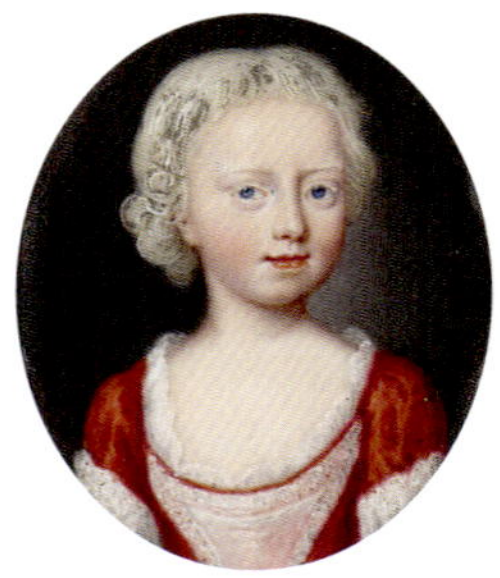

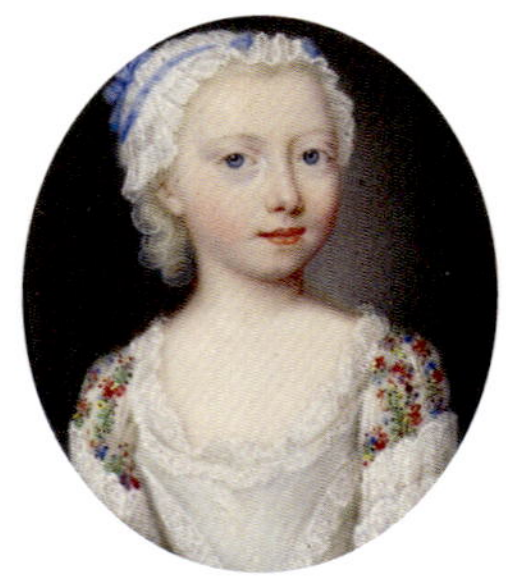

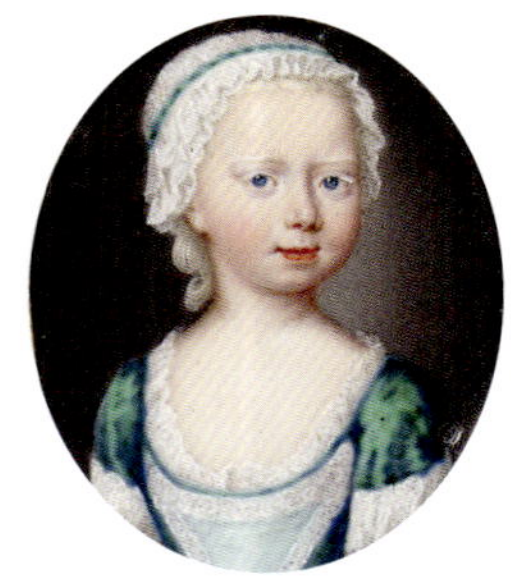

PROVENANCE Probably in the Royal Collection since they were first painted; first recorded in the Royal Collection in 1858 (*List* 1858, no. 141)

LITERATURE Walker 1992, nos 39, 47, 53

This group of three miniatures of Frederick, Prince of Wales, Anne, Princess Royal, and Princess Amelia constitutes an early example of Christian Frederick Zincke's work. It shows the children as they would have appeared in about 1714, when the Prince of Wales was about seven, the Princess Royal four or five and Princess Amelia three or four years old. Unlike his two younger sisters, Frederick was not brought to England by his parents on the occasion of his grandfather's coronation in 1714, and, unless Zincke made a previously unrecorded visit to Hanover, this miniature cannot have been painted from life. It must derive from an oil painting brought to London by the Prince's parents, but no longer recorded. The group was probably commissioned by George II and Queen Caroline when Prince and Princess of Wales and is the first expression of their interest in commissioning series of miniatures of family members. Systematic registers of family portraits in miniature had not been completed in this way since Isaac Oliver produced miniatures of the three children of James I and Anne of Denmark a hundred years earlier. It would not be repeated in so comprehensive a fashion until Queen Victoria commissioned Sir William Ross and Annie Dixon to paint her children in miniature between 1845 and 1857. VR

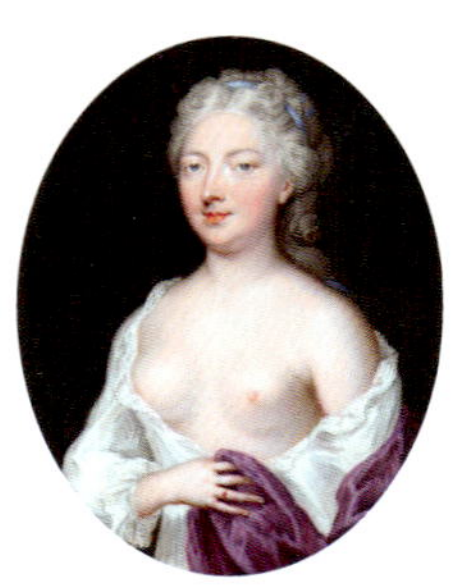

FIG. 82
Christian Frederick Zincke
Queen Caroline, c.1731
Enamel
Museum Schloss Fasanerie, Eichenzell

209–211

CHRISTIAN FREDERICK ZINCKE

Anne, Princess Royal, later Princess of Orange (1709–1759) c.1730

Princess Amelia (1711–1786) c.1730

Princess Caroline (1713–1756) c.1730

Enamel, 71 × 58 mm; 76 × 60 mm; 72 × 56 mm
RCIN 421797, 421822 and 421798

PROVENANCE Probably in the Royal Collection since they were first painted; first recorded in the Royal Collection in 1877 (*Enamels* 1877, I. 172; I. 173; I. 195)

LITERATURE Walker 1992, nos 49, 55, 57

Although Bernard Lens (see nos 189, 192) held the title of Painter in Enamel to George I and continued in office under George II, in reality it was the German miniaturist Christian Frederick Zincke who, George Vertue noted in 1731, was 'employ'd at Court to paint all the Princes [Princesses?] of the Royal Family'.[15] This series of enamels of the three eldest daughters of George II and Queen Caroline dates from 1729–30, when the artist was exceptionally busy with royal commissions. This particular group may have been initiated by sittings recorded by George Vertue: '1729.1730 The Princess Royal sat for her picture to Mr Zinke. and afterwards The other 2 sisters sat to him for their pictures. only heads. pretty large.'[16] Zincke's first effort at portraying Princess Amelia had been poorly received; this enamel was perhaps an attempt by Zincke to improve on his version. Princess Amelia later established her own extensive collection of Zincke's work, which was displayed at her home, Gunnersbury Park, in Ealing, Middlesex, and which Horace Walpole described when he related that she 'has many portraits of the royal family by him [Zincke] of a larger than usual size'.[17] VR

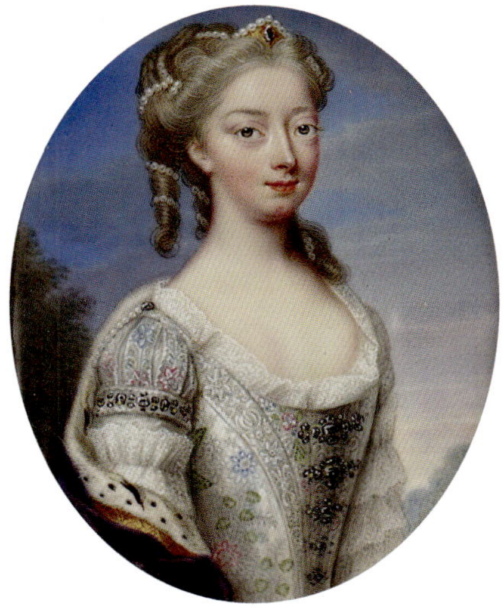

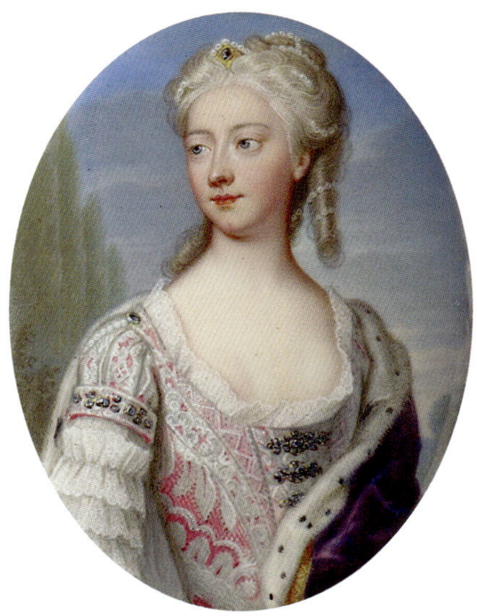

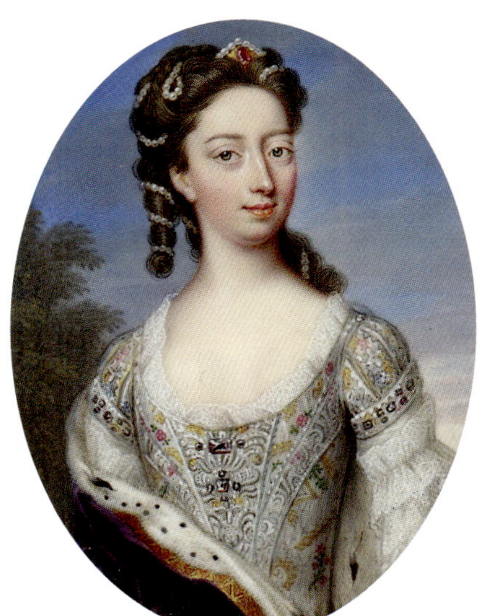

212

ENGLISH

Anne, Princess Royal (1709–1759) c.1730

Onyx, parcel-gilt silver, Burmese rubies, old mine-cut diamonds, 5.0 × 4.0 cm
RCIN 65243

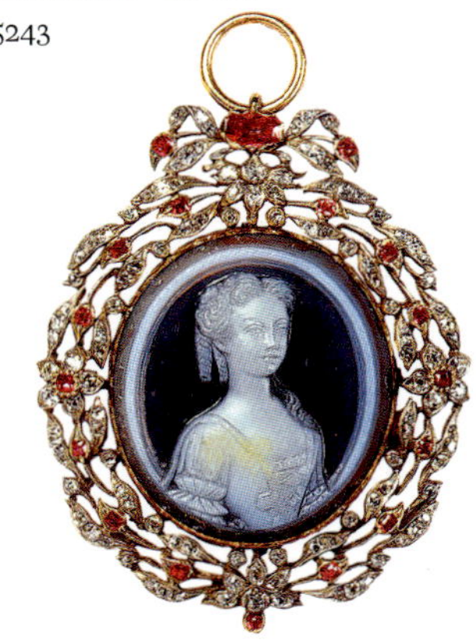

PROVENANCE Probably commissioned by Queen Caroline; first documented in the Royal Collection in 1872

LITERATURE Aschengreen Piacenti and Boardman 2008, no. 236

The majority of the cameos listed in the inventories of the Kensington Closet were either antique or historic portraits, and many of them were unmounted. However, at least one contemporary portrait was created, probably for the Queen, although no specific note of it is made in the inventories. The source appears to have been a miniature by Zincke (no. 209), one of the group commissioned by George II in 1730, and thought to be painted *ad vivum*. Two smaller versions of the same miniature are also in the Royal Collection. Unusually Zincke's image was not published and it may be that the gem-cutter had access to one of the miniatures. This suggests that the cameo was a direct royal commission. Unlike most of Queen Caroline's gems this example has been elaborately set in a jewelled mount for wearing, again suggesting a more personal involvement. It is possible that the work was commissioned at the time of the Princess's marriage to William IV of Orange, in 1734. KJ

213

CHRISTIAN FREDERICK ZINCKE (1684?–1767)

Anne, Princess Royal, later Princess of Orange (1707–1759) c.1727

Enamel, 70 × 55 mm
RCIN 421816

PROVENANCE Possibly the miniature of the 'Princess Royal' first recorded by George Vertue in Queen Caroline's Closet at Kensington Palace in 1743 (Vertue 1743, item 103/5; see fig. 78)

LITERATURE Walker 1992, no. 48

Anne, the second child and eldest daughter of George Augustus, Electoral Prince of Hanover, later George II, and Caroline of Brandenburg-Ansbach, was born in Hanover on 2 November 1709, and was brought to England with her mother and sisters in September 1714 on the occasion of her grandfather's succession to the British throne. The number of miniatures of the young Princess painted by Christian Frederick Zincke can be explained by the inflated status that Anne enjoyed as the eldest child of the Prince and Princess of Wales resident at the English court in the absence of her elder brother, Frederick, who remained in Hanover as the senior representative of the Electoral family. Her education was the subject of intense interest and as early as 1714 Mary, Countess Cowper, wrote that 'Princess Anne speaks, reads and writes German and French to Perfection, knows a great deal of History and Geography, speaks English very prettily and dances very well'.[18] She was later taught painting by Philip Mercier and music by Handel (see pp. 381–2).

In this strikingly informal portrait, however, she is shown without any indication either of her royal status or of her varied accomplishments, and she carries only a simple chaplet of flowers. Although the Princess Royal was a prominent figure at court in her youth, she spent very little time in England after her marriage in 1734 to William IV, Prince of Orange-Nassau (1711–51). VR

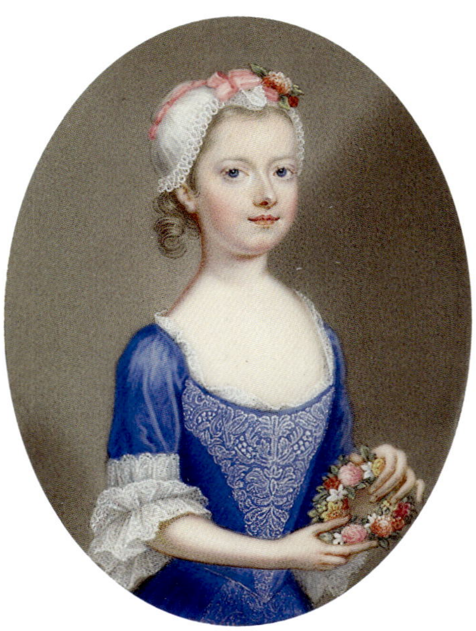

214

CHRISTIAN FREDERICK ZINCKE

George II (1683–1760) c.1727

Enamel, 75 × 59 mm
RCIN 421796

PROVENANCE Probably in the Royal Collection since it was first painted; first recorded in the Royal Collection in 1858 (*List* 1858, no. 141)

LITERATURE Walker 1992, no. 28; *Masterpieces in Little* 1996, no. 45

No other work in the Royal Collection demonstrates Christian Frederick Zincke's command over his demanding medium as effectively as this richly coloured and meticulously finished enamel. The technique required successive applications of metal oxide paints to a concave metal base layer. Repeated firings in a kiln were needed because each colour had a different melting point and would fuse with the enamel base at a separate temperature. It was still a relatively new technique at the point when this miniature was painted, having been introduced to England and applied to portrait miniatures for the first time less than a century earlier.

The image was adapted by Zincke from a portrait of George II when Prince of Wales dating from 1716 (no. 237). Zincke, already the leading enamellist at court, was increasingly favoured by George II after his accession, and the King was stated to have found his works 'beautifull and like'.[19] The highly stippled flesh tones, richness of colouring and attention to detail, particularly in the rendering of costume details such as the lace steinkirk and the collar of the Order of the Garter, distinguish Zincke's work from the more pedestrian output of followers such as Jean André Rouquet (1701–1758). VR

215

CHRISTIAN FREDERICK ZINCKE

Queen Caroline (1683–1737) 1727

Enamel, 70 × 54 mm
Signed and dated on the reverse: *Carolina Regina/ Magn: Britan:/ C F: Zincke. Fecit/ 1727* (initials in monogram)
RCIN 421820

PROVENANCE Probably in the Royal Collection since it was first painted; first recorded in the Royal Collection in 1858 (*List* 1858, no. 103)

LITERATURE Walker 1992, no. 35

Dated 1727, Zincke's enamel of Queen Caroline in profile accords closely with John Croker's coronation medal (no. 13). The classical robes in the medal, however, have been exchanged for coronation robes and an ermine cloak fastened with a gold Medusa brooch of a kind much favoured by the Queen (see no. 216). Some form of collaboration seems likely between the distinguished medallist and the enamellist, Christian Frederick Zincke, who had trained as a goldsmith before turning to the art of miniature painting in the first decade of the eighteenth century.

The close affinity between the medal and the miniature suggests a degree of accuracy in Zincke's representation of the 44-year-old Queen's features. However, Zincke was notorious for flattering his subjects, and this tendency was satirised by Edward Young in 1734 in his poem *Love of Fame* and again in the *Gentleman's Magazine* in 1740.[20] The criticisms levelled at Zincke did little to diminish his popularity and evidence suggests that the 'pretty good Fortune' with which George Vertue credited the artist by 1731 had grown considerably by 1740.[21] The effect of the royal family's patronage of Zincke was undoubtedly to secure his reputation and financial security until his retirement in 1746. VR

216

ITALIAN?, MOUNT ATTRIBUTED TO JEAN VANGROL (D. 1640)

Medusa

Cameo: 16th century; mount: *c.*1640
Onyx, enamel, gold, 2.6 × 2.4 cm
RCIN 65609

PROVENANCE First recorded in the Royal Collection in 1872

LITERATURE Aschengreen Piacenti and Boardman 2008, no. 49

Christian Zincke's miniature of Queen Caroline in coronation robes (no. 215) shows a large gold brooch at her breast portraying the head of Medusa, framed with either diamonds or white enamel. Although no such brooch is mentioned in the accounts of the coronation, nor painted in any other portraits of the Queen, the head of Medusa was typically depicted on the aegis of Minerva and the brooch may therefore have been an invocation by the artist of this association.

Several cameos carved with heads of Medusa remain in the Royal Collection, although it is not possible to trace them in the inventories of Queen Caroline's collection. However, the pre-1755 list drawn up by Mrs Purcell notes a group of stones 'set in gold and enamelled'. No description is made of the subject matter of the gems but she may have been referring to a number of cameos with similar mounts which have been attributed to the Parisian jeweller Jean Vangrol or his workshop.[22] Two other groups of cameos with mounts attributed to Vangrol were certainly in Caroline's collection (see nos 165 and 166), and the jewel mounted with several cameos (no. 156) may also have been a product of his workshop. It is possible that Queen Caroline received this group of French-mounted gems from Liselotte (see no. 156). KJ

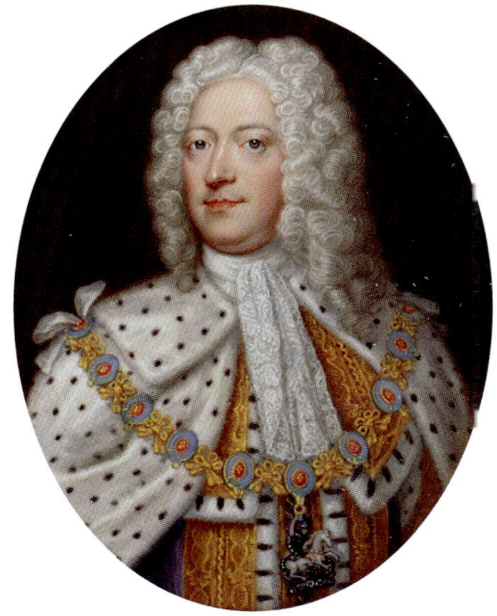

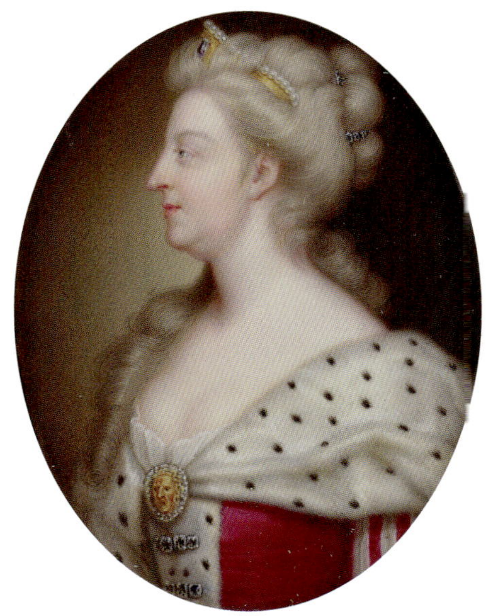

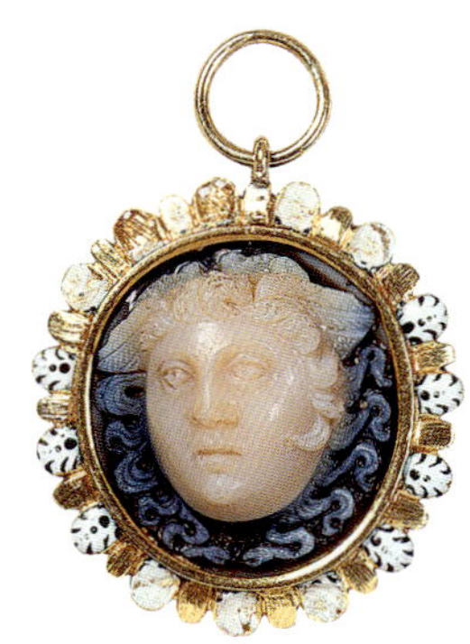

217 & 218

CHRISTIAN FREDERICK ZINCKE (1684?–1767)

William, Duke of Cumberland (1721–1765) *c.*1730

Princess Mary (1723–1771) *c.*1731

Enamel, 74 × 56 mm; 73 × 57mm
RCIN 421824, RCIN 421825

PROVENANCE Probably in the Royal Collection since it was first painted in *c.* 1730; first recorded in the inventories in 1877 (*Enamels* 1877, I. 196 and 197)

LITERATURE Walker 1992, nos 61 and 59

William, Duke of Cumberland, second son of George II and Queen Caroline, is depicted soon after his installation as a Knight of the Order of the Garter in June 1730 (see no. 40). At this period the artist, Christian Frederick Zincke, was employed to fulfil numerous royal commissions at court, including a group of miniatures of the Prince's older sisters, the Princesses Anne, Amelia and Caroline (see nos 207–9). This enamel is similar in composition and scale and appears to have been conceived as part of the group. Notably absent from the group is Frederick, Prince of Wales, who sat for the artist, but not apparently in connection with this series of family portraits, and it is significant that it was the younger William who was instead included.

Prince William was born in England and raised with his parents at court in London, unlike his brother, Frederick, who remained in Hanover. As the only son of the Prince and Princess of Wales resident at court, William was highly favoured and the Garter, which he wears here, was only the last in a succession of honours already received by the Prince before the age of ten. At four years old, he had been made a companion of the Knight of the Bath; in 1726 he was elevated to the peerage with the title Duke of Cumberland and in 1727 he was given a prominent role at his parents' coronation, from which his older brother Frederick, Prince of Wales, was excluded. The boy seen in the miniature on the brink of maturity was given his own household and an allowance of £6,000 within a year, confirming his elevated status at court even after the arrival of his elder brother in December 1728.

Princess Mary was the fourth daughter and eighth child of George II and Queen Caroline. Her age of about nine years old in this enamel miniature by Christian Frederick Zincke suggests that it must have been painted in *c.*1731, slightly later than the group of three enamels of her elder sisters, Anne, Amelia and Caroline, painted by the same artist *c.*1730 (nos 207–9). The similarity in their composition suggests that this enamel was intended to be displayed with the others in this group.

As a young woman, Princess Mary was described as 'a lover of reading, and far more solicitous to improve the mind than to adorn the body'.[23] Aged seventeen, she was married to Prince Friedrich of Hesse-Cassel (1720–85), but separated from him in 1755. She spent her later years in Hanau, where she acted as regent for her eldest surviving son, Wilhelm, who became reigning Count of Hanau in 1760.
VR

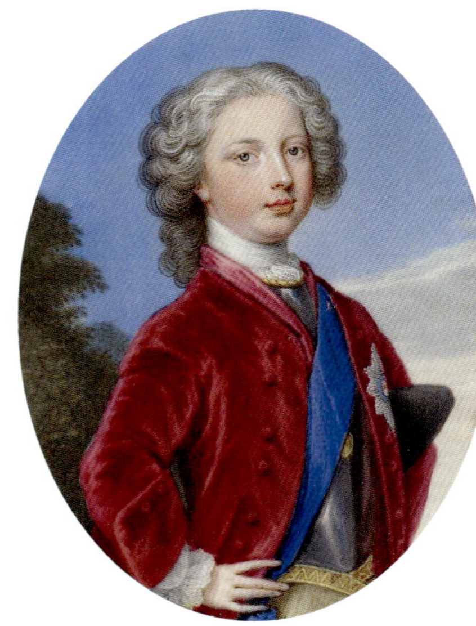

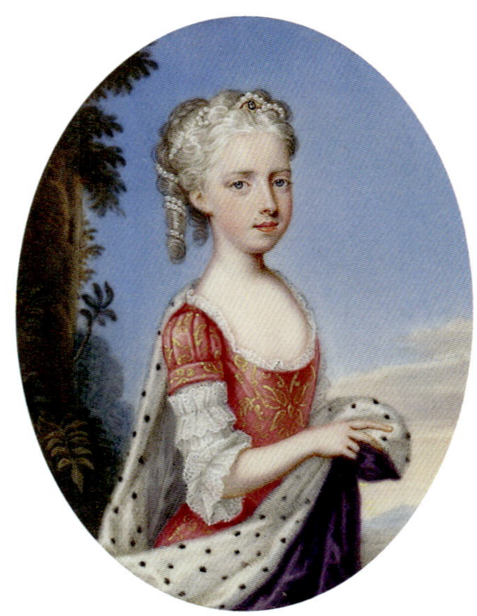

219

CHRISTIAN FREDERICK ZINCKE

Princess Caroline (1713–1756) *c.*1740

Enamel, 75 × 57 mm
RCIN 421818

PROVENANCE First recorded in the Royal Collection in 1858 incorrectly identified as Marie Josephine de Saxe, Dauphine de France (*List* 1858, no. 197)

LITERATURE Walker 1992, no. 56

Princess Caroline, the third daughter of George II and Queen Caroline, is shown here some ten years older than in Christian Frederick Zincke's earlier enamel (no. 211) of her dating from *c.*1730. Although many of his early miniatures were copies based on oil paintings, this enamel miniature does not conform to any known source and appears to have been painted from life. It shows the Princess wearing a dark hood over a fur tippet, and was probably painted after the death of her mother, Queen Caroline, in 1737. It is a relatively late work by Christian Frederick Zincke, painted at a point when the artist's failing eyesight induced him to put up his prices to as much as 30 guineas, and before he was forced to give up his practice altogether in 1746.

The enamel was previously identified as Princess Amelia, Caroline's older sister, but the appearance of the sitter conforms more closely to that of Princess Caroline, who was described by a contemporary as having 'very dark hair', by contrast to the flaxen-haired Princess Amelia.[24] Her appearance here is similar to that in a line engraving after Jacopo Amigoni dating to *c.*1735. Caroline's appearance in later life is not recorded as she suffered deteriorating ill-health, and led a secluded life in retirement at her apartments at St James's Palace. VR

220

CHRISTIAN FREDERICK ZINCKE

Frederick, Prince of Wales (1707–51) *c.*1743–51

Enamel, 44 × 37mm
RCIN 421829

PROVENANCE Probably in the collection of Frederick, Prince of Wales; first recorded in the Royal Collection in 1858 (*List* 1858, no. 114)

LITERATURE Walker 1992, no. 42

Frederick, Prince of Wales, was first painted by Christian Frederick Zincke as a child in *c.*1714. The frequency with which Zincke was employed at court accelerated in the late 1720s, but formal recognition of Zincke's success came in the form of an appointment not as 'Painter in Enamel' to the King but as 'Cabinet Painter' to the Prince of Wales in October 1732. In an unusual reversal of the normal balance of patronage between artist and patron, Zincke's services seem to have been the subject of competition between George II and his son, fuelled no doubt by the antipathy between the two. 'The King,' Vertue recorded, was 'so well pleasd with Mr Zincks works that he bespoke many Copies of his picture. & at the same time before the Queen (being present) he said I should like that you would imploy all your time in pictures for me I will take them all.'[25] The King's efforts to monopolise Zincke's services were unsuccessful, and both Frederick, Prince of Wales, and Princess Amelia acquired significant collections of enamels by the artist. Frederick, Prince of Wales, displayed his miniatures at Carlton House, acquired in 1732, and also at Leicester House, where £1.8.0 was paid for 'Cutting the wainscot to receive 4 oval panels wth Minnature Pictures'.[26] Many of Frederick's miniatures, possibly including the present enamel, were absorbed into the Royal Collection on the death in 1772 of his widow, Augusta. VR

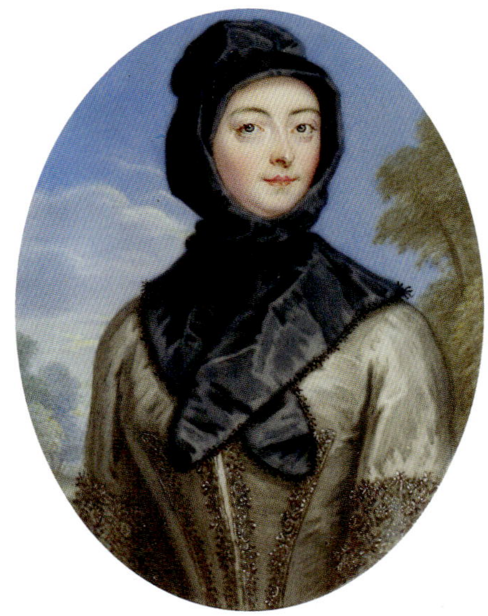

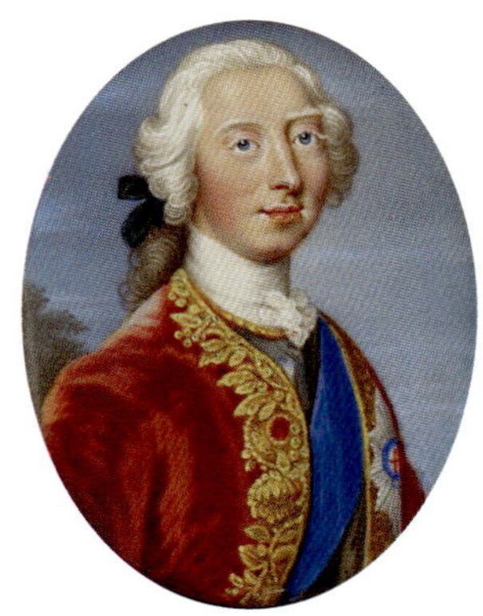

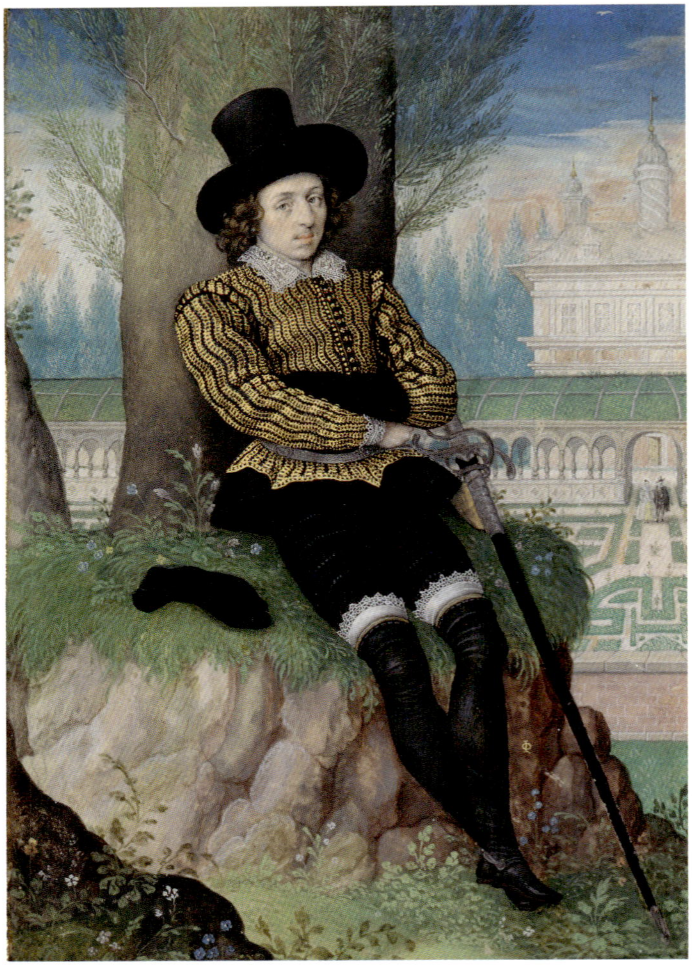

221

ISAAC OLIVER (*c*.1565–1617)

Portrait of a Young Man *c*.1590–5

Watercolour on vellum, 124 × 89 mm
RCIN 420639

PROVENANCE 'Mr Correy' by *c*.1725; Dr Richard Mead (1673–1754); bought by Frederick, Prince of Wales, between 1745 and 1751

LITERATURE Reynolds 1999, no. 50

One of the most beguiling and enigmatic of all Tudor images, and one of only a limited number of full-length sixteenth-century cabinet miniatures still in existence, Isaac Oliver's *Portrait of a Young Man* is one of the most significant Hanoverian acquisitions in any medium. This was the first of a group of five important Tudor and Stuart miniatures acquired by Frederick, Prince of Wales, from the collection of the renowned connoisseur Dr Richard Mead (see p. 325).

Dating from the early 1590s, it is an early work by Isaac Oliver, but was never surpassed by him in the course of a successful career as a miniaturist at the court of James I and Anne of Denmark. Oliver came to London from Rouen in 1568 as a Huguenot refugee, and learnt the art of miniature painting from Nicholas Hilliard (1547–1619). However, Oliver's technique, which involved the application of a fine stipple with the point of the brush to create areas of pronounced shadow, was at variance with Hilliard's approach, which entailed modelling the features of his sitters with small, hatched, parallel strokes to suggest depth but minimise shadowing. It was not so much Oliver's sophisticated technique which persuaded Frederick, Prince of Wales, to acquire this miniature from the collection of Dr Mead, but rather the romantic, historic associations of the subject, which was believed at the time to be Sir Philip Sidney (1554–86).

This identification depended in part on the interpretation of the building and formal gardens in the background as those of Wilton House in Wiltshire, the home of Sir Philip Sidney's sister Mary, Countess of Pembroke, notwithstanding the fact that the famous gardens at Wilton were designed after Sidney's death and for his nephew, Philip Herbert, 4th Earl of Pembroke, by Isaac de Caus (1590–1648). The elaborate background is now known to be based on an engraving in the architectural pattern book, *Artis Perspectivae ... multigenis Fontibus Liber Primus* by Hans Vredeman de Vries (1568) and more recent scholarship has focused on the figure not as a specific portrait but as the personification of Melancholy, a fashionable state of mind associated with scholarly isolation in the late-sixteenth and early-seventeenth centuries. VR

222

UNKNOWN ARTIST,
16TH CENTURY?

Portrait of a Man *c.*1530–5

Watercolour on card, 76 × 65 mm
RCIN 420042

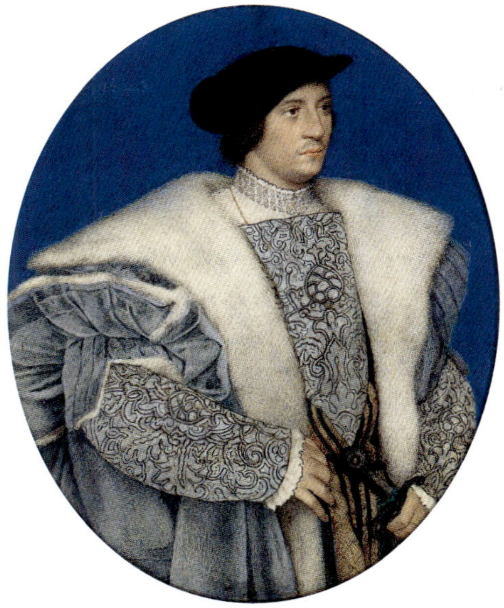

PROVENANCE Possibly Dr Richard Mead (1673–1754) and then Frederick, Prince of Wales; first recorded in the Royal Collection *c.*1837 (*Old List c.*1837, no. 43)

LITERATURE Reynolds 1999, no. 10

This miniature was first recorded in 1740 in George Vertue's Notebooks as 'another Curious Limning. Sd. to [be] by H. Holbens. – the picture of Henry Guldeford. (when young.) Comptrolor – to K. Hen.'.[27] The context of Vertue's statement suggests that the miniature was then in the collection of Dr Richard Mead, and this is borne out by the survival of its original gilt locket, which is similar to those preserved with other miniatures from Mead's collection. The locket bears an inscription identifying the sitter as Sir Henry Guildford and the artist as Holbein, and Frederick, Prince of Wales, doubtless believed that, in acquiring this work of art, he was adding to his own collection of miniatures a rare example by Hans Holbein. The sitter seems to have been identified as Guildford by comparison with Holbein's famous portrait (no. 143), which similarly shows a powerful, well-dressed courtier in an assertive, four-square posture. However, the man in this miniature, which is datable on grounds of style to the 1530s, is considerably younger than Guildford appears to be in his portrait of 1527 (when he was 38), and its technique shows a less skilful hand than Holbein's.

The art of miniature painting was still in its infancy during the first quarter of the sixteenth century. Although certain other artists are recorded as practitioners, little is known of their work. John Shute (d. 1563) and John Bettes (active 1545–59; d. 1570?), for example, are named by Richard Haydocke in his *Tracte containing the Artes of curious Paintinge Caruinge & Building* (1598) as limners, but their work in miniature has yet to be distinguished. VR

223

ISAAC OLIVER

Portrait of the Artist *c.*1590

Watercolour on vellum, 45 × 37 mm
Signed: *I.O.* in monogram centre right
RCIN 420034

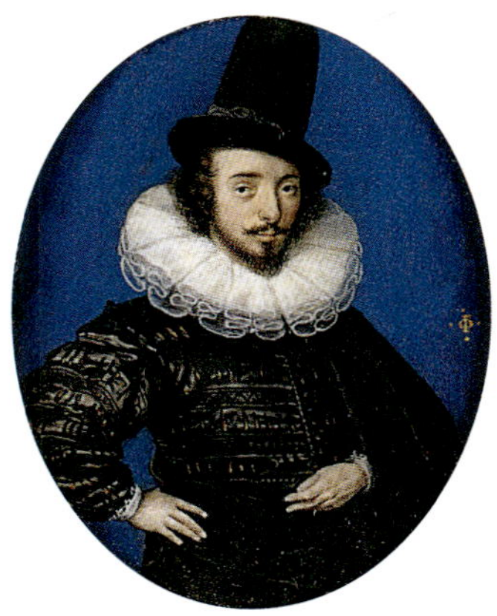

PROVENANCE Dr Richard Mead; from whom bought by Frederick, Prince of Wales, between 1745 and 1751

LITERATURE Reynolds 1999, no. 48

This confident self-portrait by the young miniature-painter Isaac Oliver is one of five exceptional miniatures by the artist acquired by Frederick, Prince of Wales, from the collector Dr Richard Mead in the late 1740s. The Prince of Wales had already built up a collection of miniatures of repute; his addition of such a strong representation of works by Isaac Oliver suggests that Oliver's work was of particular interest to him.

The quality of the miniature alone would have recommended its purchase to the Prince of Wales. An early work of *c.*1590, it adopts the three-quarter-length format, with the subject's hand on his right hip, reminiscent of full-scale Flemish portraiture, and rare in miniatures of the period. Although he was trained by Nicholas Hilliard, Isaac Oliver's style was dependent on European influences that were alien to Hilliard's work. His willingness to absorb visual references from Italian Renaissance art in particular made his work appealing to James I's consort, Queen Anne of Denmark, and to Henry Frederick, Prince of Wales, for whose household he worked from 1608–12. As a collector who favoured Italian, French and Flemish art of the seventeenth century, Frederick, Prince of Wales, may have seen a parallel between his own cosmopolitan tastes and those of his predecessor Henry Frederick, reflected in Henry's patronage of Isaac Oliver. VR

224

ISAAC OLIVER (1565?–1617)

Henry Frederick, Prince of Wales (1594–1612) c.1612

Watercolour on vellum, 77 × 56 mm
Signed on the right in gold: *I.O.* in monogram
RCIN 420057

PROVENANCE Dr Richard Mead; from whom bought by Frederick, Prince of Wales, between 1745 and 1751

LITERATURE Reynolds 1999, no. 56

Isaac Oliver's outstanding contribution to royal iconography was undoubtedly the large cabinet-miniature of Henry Frederick, Prince of Wales, of *c.*1612 (RCIN 420058) showing the warrior prince in armour, standing in front of a tented military encampment. The present miniature is one of many signed, reduced versions in existence; some may have been completed during the Prince's lifetime, but many are likely to have been produced posthumously.

George Vertue recorded the present miniature 'amongst Dr. Meads limnings one very curious of P. Henry. eldest son of K.J. first'.[28] In 1738, it was engraved in reverse while still in Dr Mead's collection by Jacob Houbraken for Thomas Birch's *Heads of Illustrious Persons of Great Britain* (1743), and soon afterwards it was purchased by Frederick, Prince of Wales, for his collection of miniatures. Its attraction for the Prince may have been heightened by the absence from the Royal Collection at this period of the larger cabinet miniature by Oliver. That left the Royal Collection at an unknown point in the early eighteenth century and was not re-acquired until 1807. VR

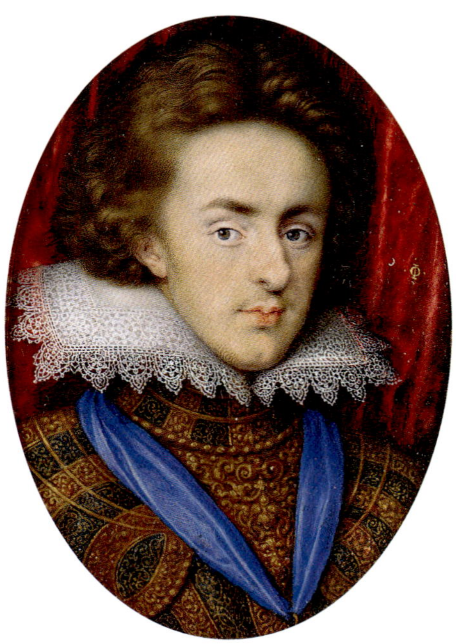

225

PETER OLIVER (1594?–1647)

Portrait of the Artist c.1620–5

Watercolour on vellum, 76 × 61 mm
RCIN 420029

PROVENANCE Dr Richard Mead; from whom bought by Frederick, Prince of Wales, between 1745 and 1751

LITERATURE Reynolds 1999, no. 74

One of a group of six miniatures acquired by Frederick, Prince of Wales, from Dr Richard Mead, this self-portrait by Peter Oliver serves as an interesting counterpoint to the self-portrait by the artist's father, Isaac Oliver, which is also among the group (no. 223). At the time of its purchase, the miniature was believed to be a portrait of the dramatist Ben Jonson (1572–1637), and the original locket, preserved with the miniature, retains this identification. The current identification can

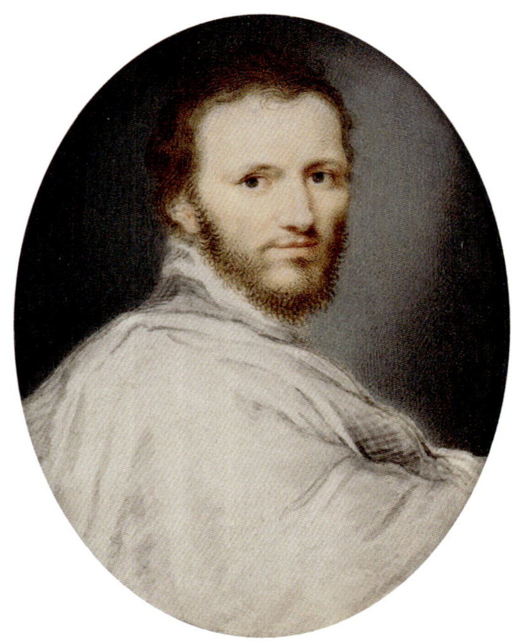

be sustained with reference to authenticated portraits of Peter Oliver, such as the oil painting by Adriaen Hanneman in the Royal Collection (RCIN 405518). As an image of Ben Jonson the miniature would joined the lost painting allegedly of Jonson attributed to Rubens (see p. 230), and illuminates the Prince of Wales's interest in collecting portraits of literary and historical characters, a predilection which he shared with his mother, Caroline of Ansbach.

In acquiring this work for his collection, Frederick unwittingly added to the Royal Collection an important and revealing work by the early seventeenth-century miniature painter whose versatile and accomplished output has often been overshadowed by his father's reputation. This relaxed and informal portrait, composed as though at the easel, marks a departure from the constraint of Isaac Oliver's *Self-Portrait* of *c.*1590, and prefigures the more flamboyant self-portraiture of artists such as Van Dyck in the following decade which fit clearly within the Baroque idiom. VR

226

ATTRIBUTED TO NICHOLAS DIXON (1660–1708)

*Mary II (1662–1694) c.*1685–94

Watercolour on vellum, 71 × 58 mm
RCIN 420147

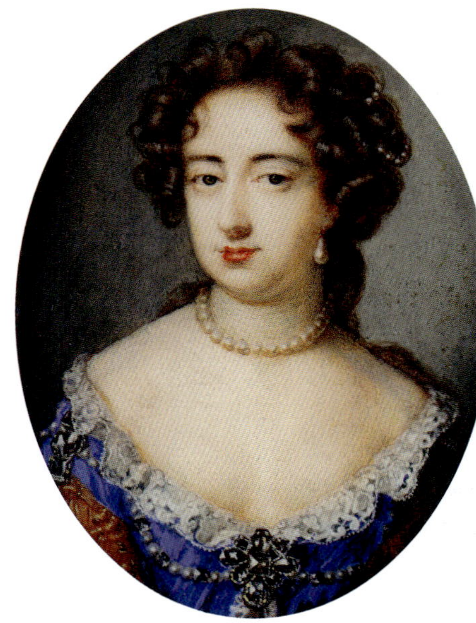

PROVENANCE Possibly purchased by Philippe Mercier for Frederick, Prince of Wales, in June 1735; first recorded with certainty in the Royal Collection *c.*1837 (*Old List*, *c.*1837, no. 29)

LITERATURE Reynolds 1999, no. 156

This miniature was not painted from life, but derives from a standard portrait of Mary II painted by William Wissing (1656–1687) at the command of her father, James II, in 1685 (RCIN 404449). The miniature is one of six acquired from the physician Dr Richard Mead by Frederick, Prince of Wales, in the late 1740s, and reflects the Prince's interest in historical portraiture.

Nicholas Dixon (active *c.*1660–after 1708) has been suggested as the artist responsible for this miniature. Dixon, who was appointed Limner to Charles II in 1673, also held the post of Keeper of the King's Picture Closet. His work is characterised by a tendency to reddish-brown in the flesh tones, and by exaggerated almond-shaped eyes, rather in the manner of Sir Peter Lely. Neither of these traits are exhibited here, and the attribution to Dixon remains open to question. VR

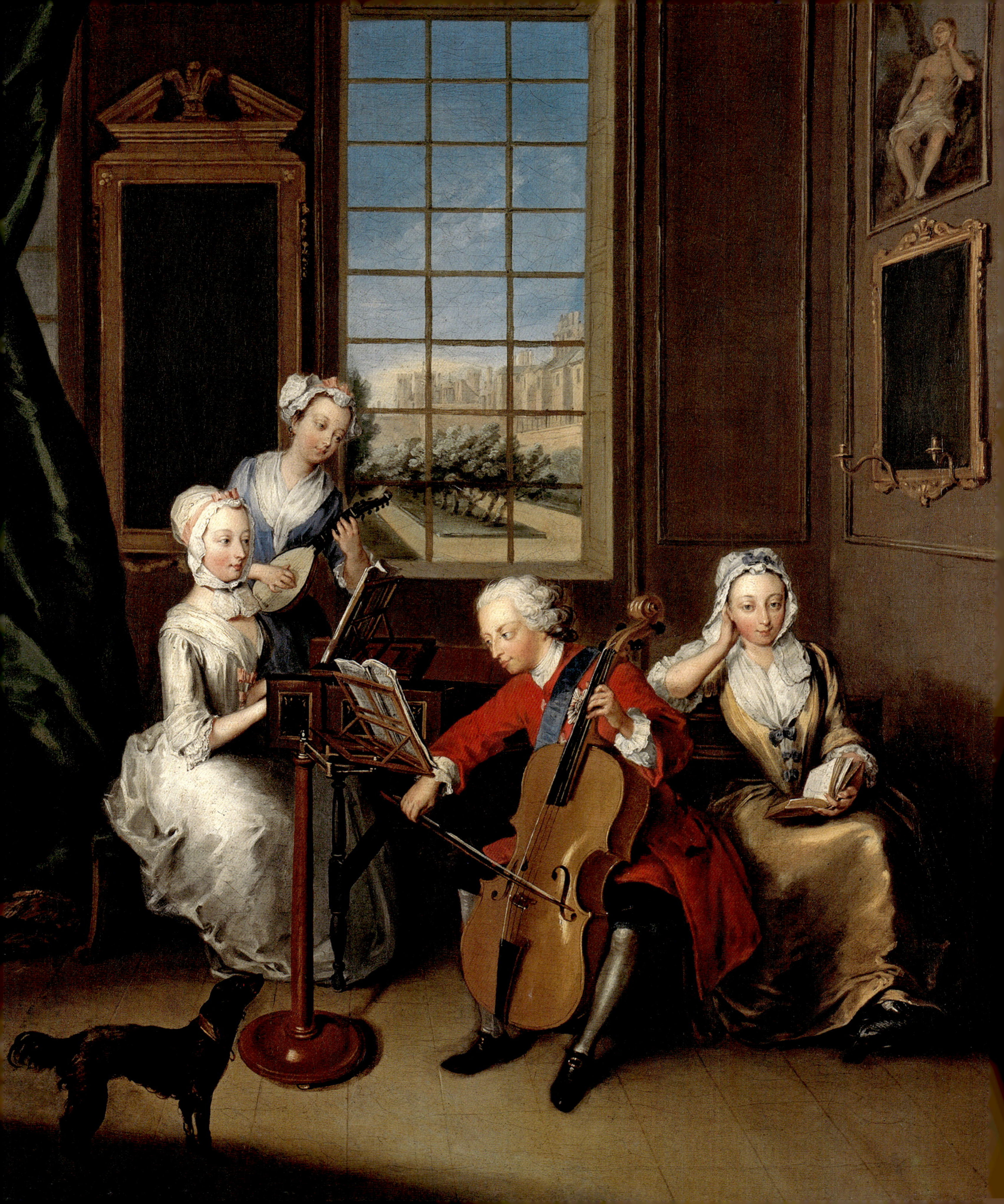

IX

'An Honour to our Nation' The Rise of a British School

DESMOND SHAWE-TAYLOR

ONE FIGURE on the west wall of the Upper Hall at Greenwich (fig. 2) so far unmentioned is the man standing to the right at the foot of the steps pointing to the King. This is a self-portrait of the artist, Sir James Thornhill (see no. 227). In the Great Hall and Upper Hall at Greenwich, between 1715 and 1725, Thornhill created the most ambitious piece of painted decoration in England, described by Richard Steele as 'a great and noble design' and 'an Honour to our Nation'.[1] Thornhill completed the ceiling decorations begun at Hampton Court by the Neapolitan artist Antonio Verrio (1636/9–1707) in competition with Sebastiano Ricci (see nos. 36–7); he was awarded the task of decorating the dome of St Paul's Cathedral in competition with Giovanni Antonio Pellegrini (see nos 227–31).[2] He was also commissioned to decorate George I's State Coach (no. 227). Thornhill dignified the art of painting: he was born to an aristocratic family; he became a Member of Parliament; he was made History Painter to George I in 1718 and knighted in 1720.

Thornhill's only rival in esteem was his friend Sir Godfrey Kneller (no. 237, fig. 85). Both artists worked, with others mentioned in this chapter, to lay the academic foundations of a British school of painting: Kneller directed an academy of painting and drawing at Great Queen Street in London between 1711 and 1716, at which point Thornhill took over until 1720. In 1720 John Vanderbank (no. 238) and Louis Chéron (1660–1725) established the St Martin's Lane Academy, which lasted until 1724. An academy of the same name was re-established by Hogarth in 1735 as a sort of artists' cooperative, using equipment from Thornhill's studio (see p. 137).[3] In 1749 George Vertue visited Frederick, Prince of Wales, in a 'Pavillion in his Garden' (see fig. 8), 'where I had the Honour to converse for some time, more than an hour – here he spoke much concerning the settlement of an Accademy for drawing & painting – and about paintings & famous Artists in England formerly – about the Cartons of Raphael Urbin. the paintings of Rubens in the banquetting house at Whitehall'.[4] In 1755 the St Martin's Lane artists started making plans for a formal academy, which resulted in the foundation of the Society of Artists in 1759.[5] In the early years of the reign of George I an observer might have predicted a great future for British painting and for the traditions represented by Thornhill and Kneller. The reality turned out rather differently. The abrupt end to Thornhill's royal career in 1722, when his scheme for Kensington Palace was rejected in favour of William Kent's, has already been noted (pp. 56 and 79).

DETAIL, NO. 255

Kent's work at Kensington took interior decoration away from the Baroque illusionism of Greenwich and, in spite of the anecdotal charm of the staircase (no. 34), did nothing to foster a native tradition of painting. Thornhill meanwhile retired to Hampton Court in disgust and painted versions of Raphael's Tapestry Cartoons.[6] Kneller's reputation experienced a similar reversal after his death, as portrait painting followed fashions imported from abroad.

It is difficult to discover a coherent pattern in the paintings commissioned by the early Georgian patrons. They did not apparently encourage a native school, nor did they persuade any notable immigrant talent to put down roots.[7] This chapter looks at the various disparate strands of modern painting they did encourage – Venetian decorative and landscape painting (nos 228–36), portrait painting by Continentals (nos 237–44) and English conversation pieces and landscapes (nos 245–51). The chapter ends with a glance at the association between the arts – music, poetry, drama, painting and sculpture – which did so much to raise the status of the British artist (nos 252–7). Leibniz observed that many things fall well which are badly thrown. Something like this might be said of British painting, which was so unsystematically encouraged and yet which offered so much by the end of George II's reign – the flourishing careers of Allan Ramsay (1713–84), Richard Wilson (1714–82), Joshua Reynolds (1723–92) and Thomas Gainsborough (1727–88), and in 1760 the first public exhibitions of contemporary art organised by the Society of Arts.[8]

Italian Artists in London

Italians remained important for British art for at least a half century after the death of Verrio in his Hampton Court lodgings in 1707. Many of the most important Italian artists of the first half of the eighteenth century worked in England. Antonio Bellucci (1654–1726) visited in the first decades of the century. Pellegrini (nos 228–31) spent the years 1708–13 in England, visiting at the instigation of the Earl of Manchester. Sebastiano Ricci and his nephew Marco Ricci (no. 232) were in London from 1712 to 1716; the Venetian state imposed a special tax to profit from the sterling they brought home.[9] Amigoni (no. 256) worked in England from 1730 to 1739, brought home a fortune and was said to have advised Canaletto (nos 235–6) to make the visit, which he did in 1747.[10] By this time several Italian portrait painters had settled permanently in London, including Andrea Soldi (1703–71), here from 1736 until his death, and Andrea Casali (1705–84), here from 1741 to 1766. Italian artists were still a significant force during the reign of George III, contributing four of the 29 founder members of the Royal Academy in 1768 – Francesco Bartolozzi (1725–1815), Agostino Carlini (*c.*1718–90), Giovanni Battista Cipriani (1727–85) and Francesco Zuccarelli (1702–88; nos 233–4).

Most of these artists were Venetians, who had always been especially cosmopolitan, but economic circumstances in Italy in the later seventeenth century made the export market increasingly significant for Italian artists. It is interesting that Italian art, and in particular Venetian, became much more adaptable at the same time. Artists continued to trade on the Italian tradition and the values of the academy (discussed in Chapter VI); in Venice there was a special reverence for the work of Veronese, who provided the model for the resurgence of Venetian painting in this period.[11] At the same time Venetian painters became aware of alternative styles, especially those employed by Northern artists working in Italy. We have seen how landscape painting was practised in Rome by Northern artists, like Filippo Lauri (no. 128), Nicolas Poussin, Gaspard Dughet (nos 133–5) and Claude Lorrain (nos 131–2), often using architecture as a cipher for human history. The Venetians of the eighteenth century developed this idea to produce caprices (see nos 233–4), which were more obviously fanciful and more crowded with allusive architectural fragments. These caprices were also much more decorative than conventional landscapes, in their brighter colours, flatter design and concentration of incident, which made them such a sought-after element in the interiors of the period. The best example of such an interior was the dining room at Goodwood, where in 1747 Vertue recorded the interior ensemble with ten caprices depicting emblematic monuments to British worthies, procured in 1722–30 for Charles, 2nd Duke of Richmond (1701–50) by the Irish impresario Owen McSwiney (1676–1754), and painted by the leading Venetian artists of the day, each work a collaboration involving two or more artists.[12] Marco Ricci's *Tomb of Newton* (RCIN 400585), which belonged to Consul Smith, was a more modest example of the same genre. Topographical view-painting was another speciality first practised in Italy by Northern artists. When Gaspar van Wittel (1653–1736), known in Italy as 'Gaspare Vanvitelli', first arrived in Rome in 1675 all the landscape painters there were from Northern Europe. By the 1730s his style of meticulous and atmospheric view painting was practised by a succession of native Venetians – Luca Carlevarijs (1663–1730), Canaletto (nos 235–6), Michele Marieschi (1710–43) and Francesco Guardi (1712–93).

The patron who did most to encourage the English market for Venetian artistic exports was Joseph Smith (*c.*1674–1770), the British Consul in Venice from 1744, who in the 1730s also set up the Pasquali Press, a publishing house with a huge range of titles, including an Italian translation of Ephraim Chambers's *Cyclopaedia* (see p. 269).[13] Smith started to form his collection of contemporary Venetian art in the early 1720s and acted as an agent for Canaletto in his dealing with other English clients. The Consul Smith collection was acquired *en bloc* in 1762 by George III; it represents the single most important episode in the patronage of that reign. Works from this collection are included below (nos 232–6) because in many cases they have particular English elements and because Smith himself is such an important player in British patronage of the early eighteenth century.

227

SIR JAMES THORNHILL (1675/6–1734)

Panel for a Royal State Coach: Britannia receiving Homage from the Four Continents *c.*1718

Oil on panel, 58.1 × 60.5 cm
RCIN 407518

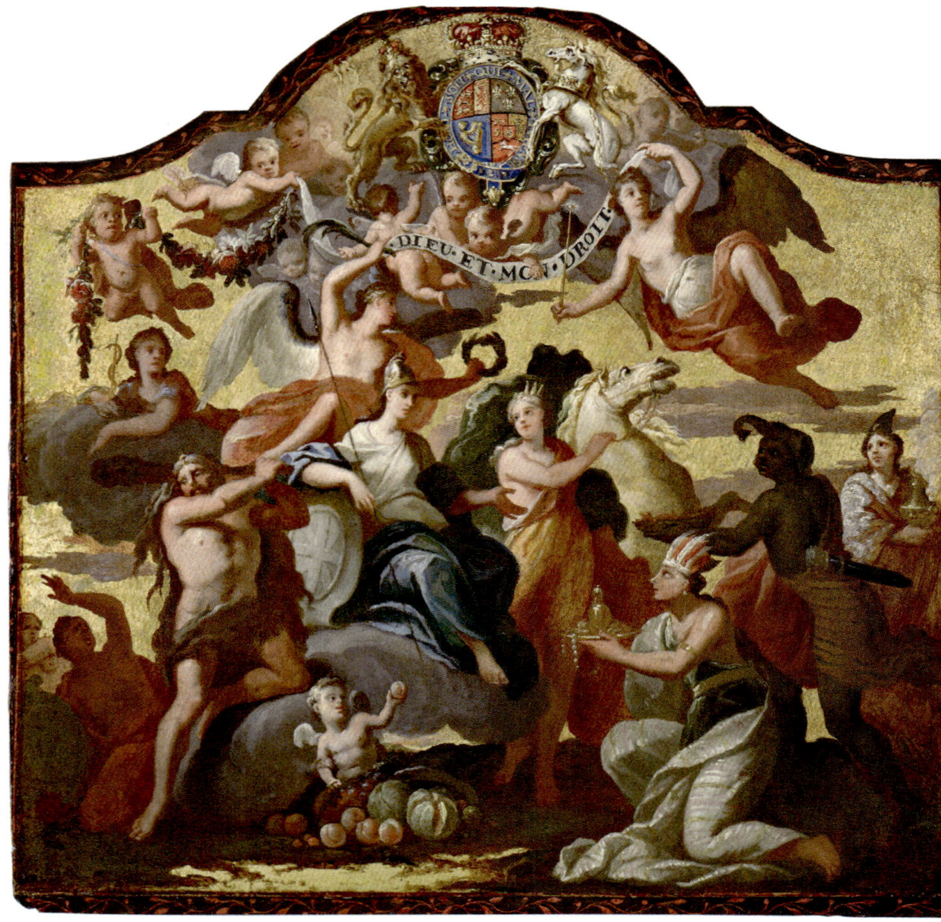

PROVENANCE Probably painted for the State Coach of George I; presented to HM The Queen in 1960

This panel for George I's State Coach probably dates from 1718, the year in which Thornhill was appointed History Painter to George I. It is one of many of similar format and dimensions which survive. There are two in the Victoria and Albert Museum, two in the Dorset County Museum, Dorchester, and two in the Yale Center for British Art, New Haven.[14] George III's State Coach of 1762 (RCIN 5000048) gives some idea of how these painted panels might have fitted into the design of the vehicle as a whole, though until we are certain of how many panels there originally were we can only guess at the arrangement. This panel is a conventional allegorical celebration of virtuous power, stamped with the royal coat of arms. Britannia, surrounded by allegories of Victory, Fame, Peace, Commerce and Providence (with the sceptre and divine eye), receives the homage of the Four Continents – Europe, America, Africa and Asia (with a spicy incense burner) – while Hercules fights off their opponents. Europe's traditional attribute of the horse here refers also to the heraldic emblem of Hanover.

Thornhill's work is brilliant and efficient. It is freely painted and resembles an oil sketch, since that is all the image-resolution a moving coach requires. The gold-leaf background provides the light of a sunrise while integrating with the gold of the surrounding coach. In view of its quality it is surprising how little English art of this type exists and how soon imported artists reclaimed this area of the market. George III's State Coach had its similar decorative allegorical panels painted by Giovanni Battista Cipriani (1727–85), a Florentine who worked in London from 1755 until his death and was a founder member of the Royal Academy. DS-T

228–31

GIOVANNI ANTONIO PELLEGRINI (1675–1741)

Apollo *c.*1710

Oil on canvas, 165.8 × 66.0 cm
RCIN 405478

Daphne *c.*1710

Oil on canvas, 164.8 × 65.0
RCIN 405498;

Bacchus *c.*1710

Oil on canvas, 164.2 × 71.5 cm
RCIN 405483

Ariadne *c.*1710

Oil on canvas, 165.7 × 73.4 cm
RCIN 405482

PROVENANCE From a set of fourteen decorative canvases, probably acquired by Frederick, Prince of Wales; first certainly recorded in 1818 in the Cube Room at Kensington Palace (as by Sebastiano Ricci and Carlo Cignani)

LITERATURE Levey 1991, pp. 118–21, nos 563, 564, 569 and 570

These four paintings come from a set of fourteen, consisting of twelve mythological subjects and a pair of smaller decorative scenes with cupids (RCIN 405479 and 405495), which would seem to have been planned as a group, and were probably commissioned for an English mansion during one of Pellegrini's stays in this country (1708–13 and 1719). Mercier's conversation piece of 1733 (no. 255) clearly includes Pellegrini's *Endymion* from this series (RCIN 405481), which suggests that by this time all fourteen were in the possession of Frederick, Prince of Wales. Though the setting for Frederick's music party remains uncertain and may even be imaginary, Mercier provides our only evidence as to intended arrangement of Pellegrini's canvases. The *Endymion* hangs high above a mirror and is set into the panelling of the room, with a thin framing moulding of the same profile as that used throughout. The canvases are of standard sizes: all twelve mythological figures are of the same height (*c.*165 cm); eight are *c.*65 cm wide; nos 230 and 231 are *c.*72 cm wide, while *Pan* and *Syrinx* (RCIN 405487 and 405484) are *c.*87 cm wide. It is common to see rooms decorated with panels of standard height and various widths – indeed, Mercier's room (no. 255) shows exactly that, though it does not seem big enough to contain another thirteen canvases. It is possible that the Pellegrinis were taken from another scheme, perhaps in a house originally leased by a member of the Royal Family; Frederick does seem to have acquired permanently groups of paintings which belonged in houses which he leased temporarily.[15]

The four paintings included here fall into two narratives – 'Apollo and Daphne' and 'Bacchus and Ariadne'. The same could be said for the pairs depicting 'Diana and Endymion' and 'Pan and Syrinx' from the same series (RCIN 406086 and 405481; 405486 and 405484). The four remaining Olympian gods pair off more loosely as 'Mars and Venus' and 'Mercury and Juno' (RCIN 405496 and 405485; 405480 and 405497).[16] The narrative links between the pairs are quite half-hearted: Apollo here starts towards Daphne, but Bacchus pays very little attention to his lover. The series looks more like an animated version of the sets of Olympian gods presented as statues (either real or painted) set in niches around the interiors of the period (see no. 30). The colours are bright, the tones light and the handling loose and sketchy, all suggesting that Pellegrini was emulating the broad and festive effect of Veronese's interior decoration.
DS-T

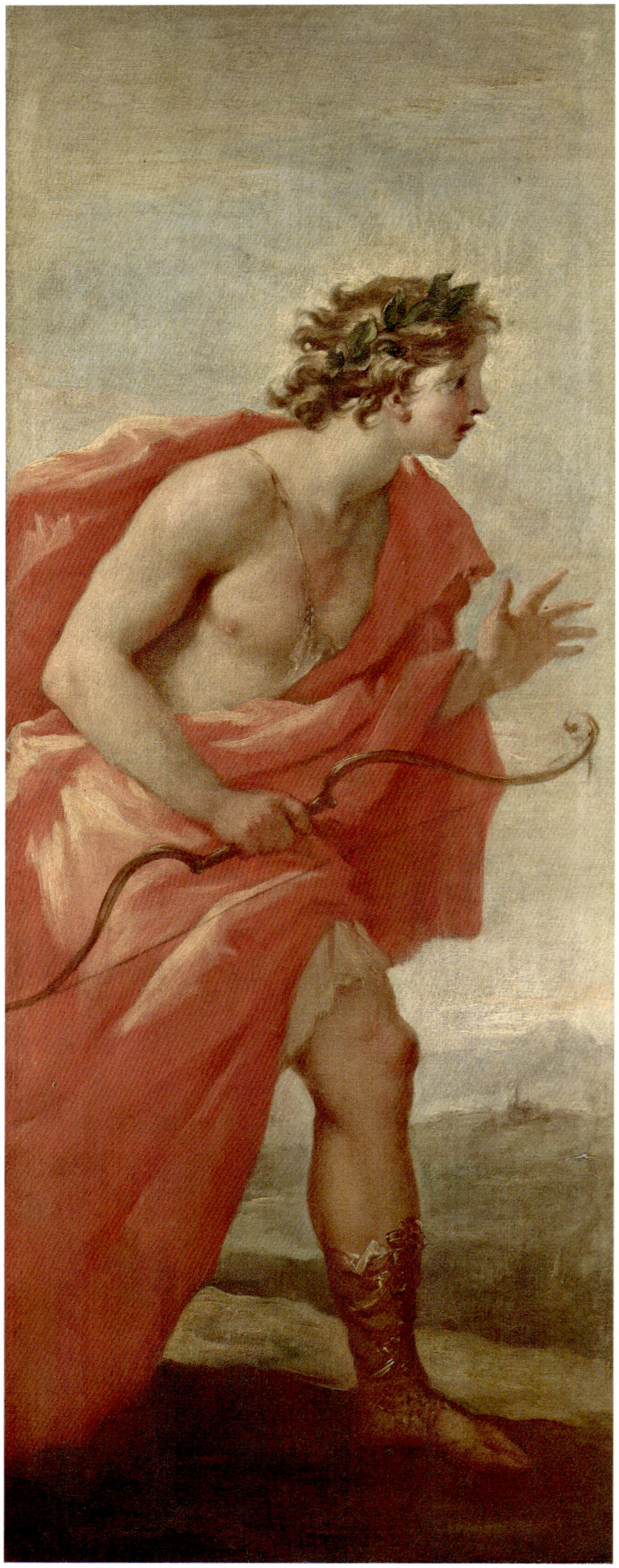

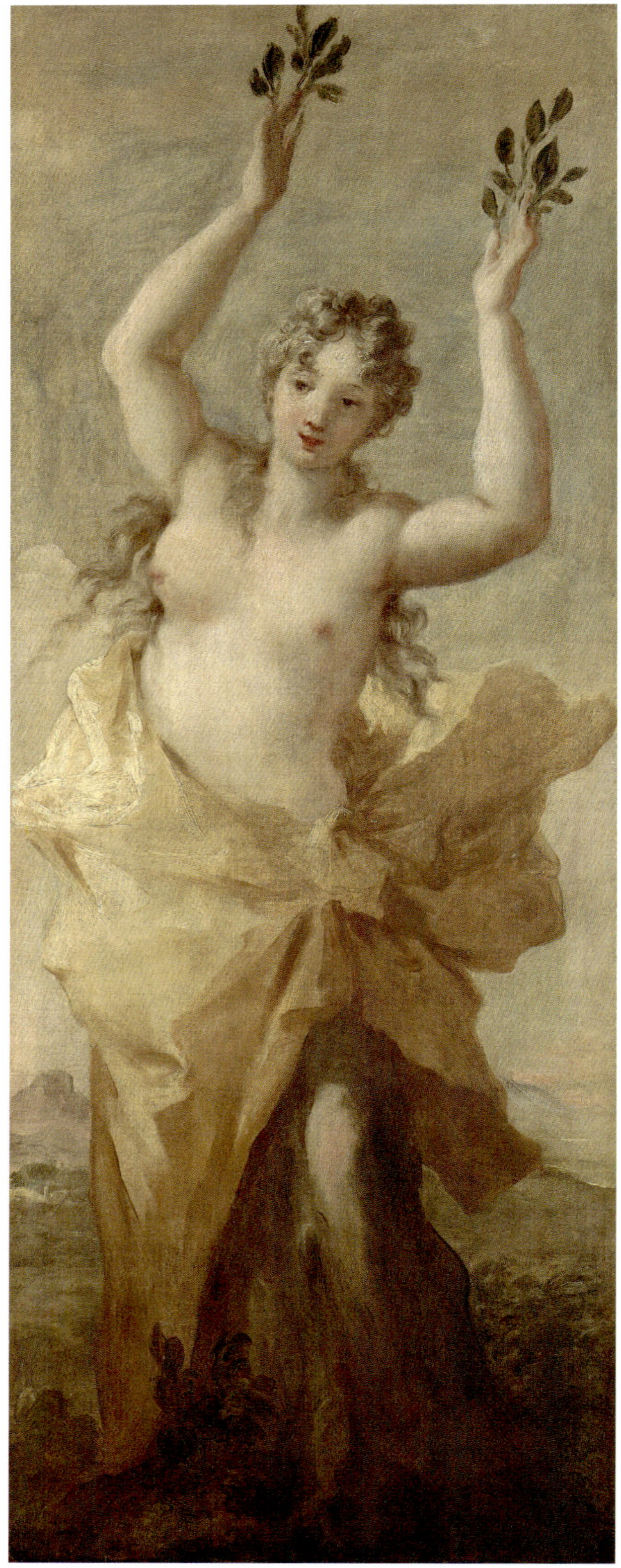

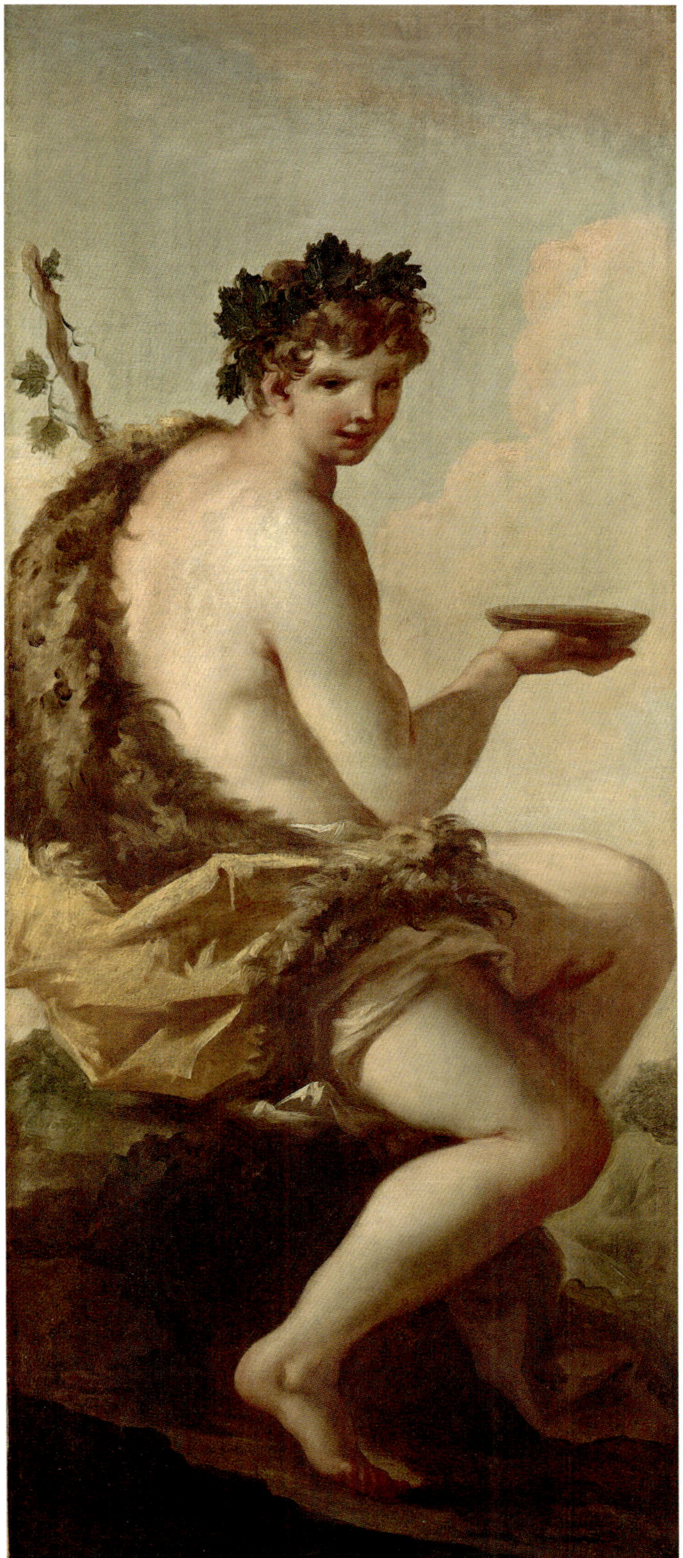

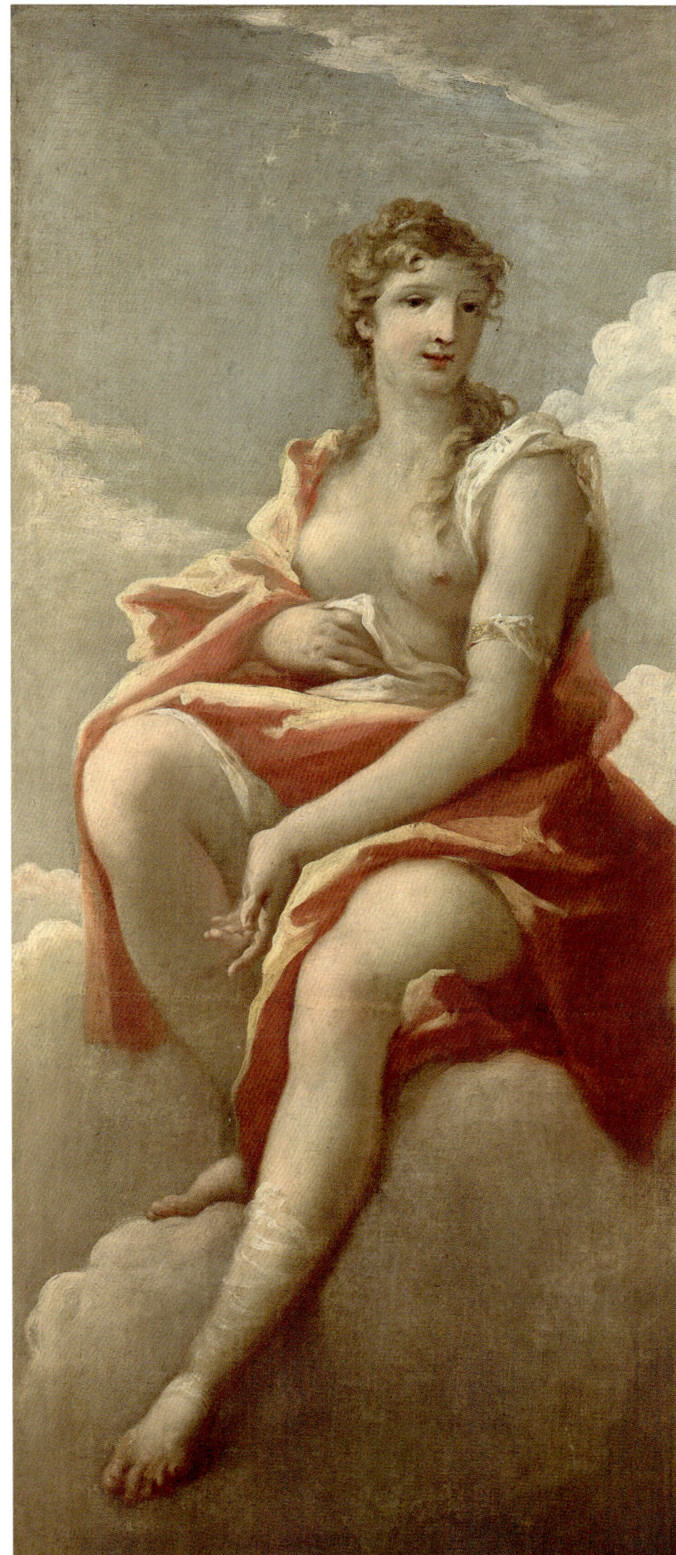

232

SEBASTIANO RICCI (1659–1734) WITH MARCO RICCI (1676–1730)

Moses striking the Rock *c.*1718

Oil on canvas, 99.3 × 134.9 cm
RCIN 402899

PROVENANCE Acquired by Joseph Smith and bought from him in 1762 by George III

LITERATURE Daniels 1976, p. 47, no. 145; Levey 1991, pp. 139–40, no. 623

Sebastiano Ricci trained with Federico Cervelli (*c.*1625–1700) in Venice; he worked throughout Italy before making several visits to Germany, where he was recorded in 1702, and England, where he spent the years 1712–6. In 1715 he was given the prestigious commission by George I to decorate the apse of the chapel of Chelsea Hospital with a fresco of the Resurrection of Christ.[17] Sebastiano first came to England apparently at the instigation of his nephew and pupil Marco. Uncle and nephew often collaborated, Marco providing the architectural or landscape backgrounds for Sebastiano's large canvases and Sebastiano providing figures for Marco's small landscapes.

This work is probably an oil sketch for a large painting executed in 1718–20 for the church of Santi Cosma e Damiano in Venice and now in the Accademia.[18] Exodus (17: 1–7 and 20: 1–13) tells how in the desert the Israelites were saved by Moses striking a rock and causing it to gush fresh water. The group high on the rock to the right includes Aaron sacrificing to Jehovah, while the white-cloaked man in the right middle-ground, accompanied by a soldier and addressing his people, seems to be Moses. This figure becomes more prominent in the finished painting. The emphasis given to a rugged landscape peopled by a varied crowd derives from Poussin's treatment of the Book of Exodus, in particular his *Israelites gathering Manna* (Louvre), a painting which was regarded as the model for judicious and inventive multi-figure narrative.[19] This openness to French as well as native influences is typical of Venetian painting in the early eighteenth century. Sebastiano Ricci shows that he too can distinguish between different ages (an elderly woman bottom right contrasted with a mother and children bottom left); different actions (scooping water with hands or bowls, carrying vessels of various sizes) and different temperaments (the greedy and the sharing). The woman in blue and white, crouching and turning upwards, appears to be offering a bowl of water to the soldier, so that he may feed two children who clutch at his side. A preparatory sketch for the same group (RCIN 907014) shows the soldier filling her bowl from a larger vessel. In this way Sebastiano Ricci subtly alters the meaning, making this central woman, like the mother to the lower left and the man to the lower right, into an emblem of Charity.

Marco Ricci executed the landscape and has similarly contrasted the blasted trunk to the right with the flourishing trees to the left, which seem instantly to have benefited from the stream winding around them. The application of the paint has a twisting capricious brilliance which is typical of both Riccis' work, especially in a sketch, and of Venetian art in general. DS-T

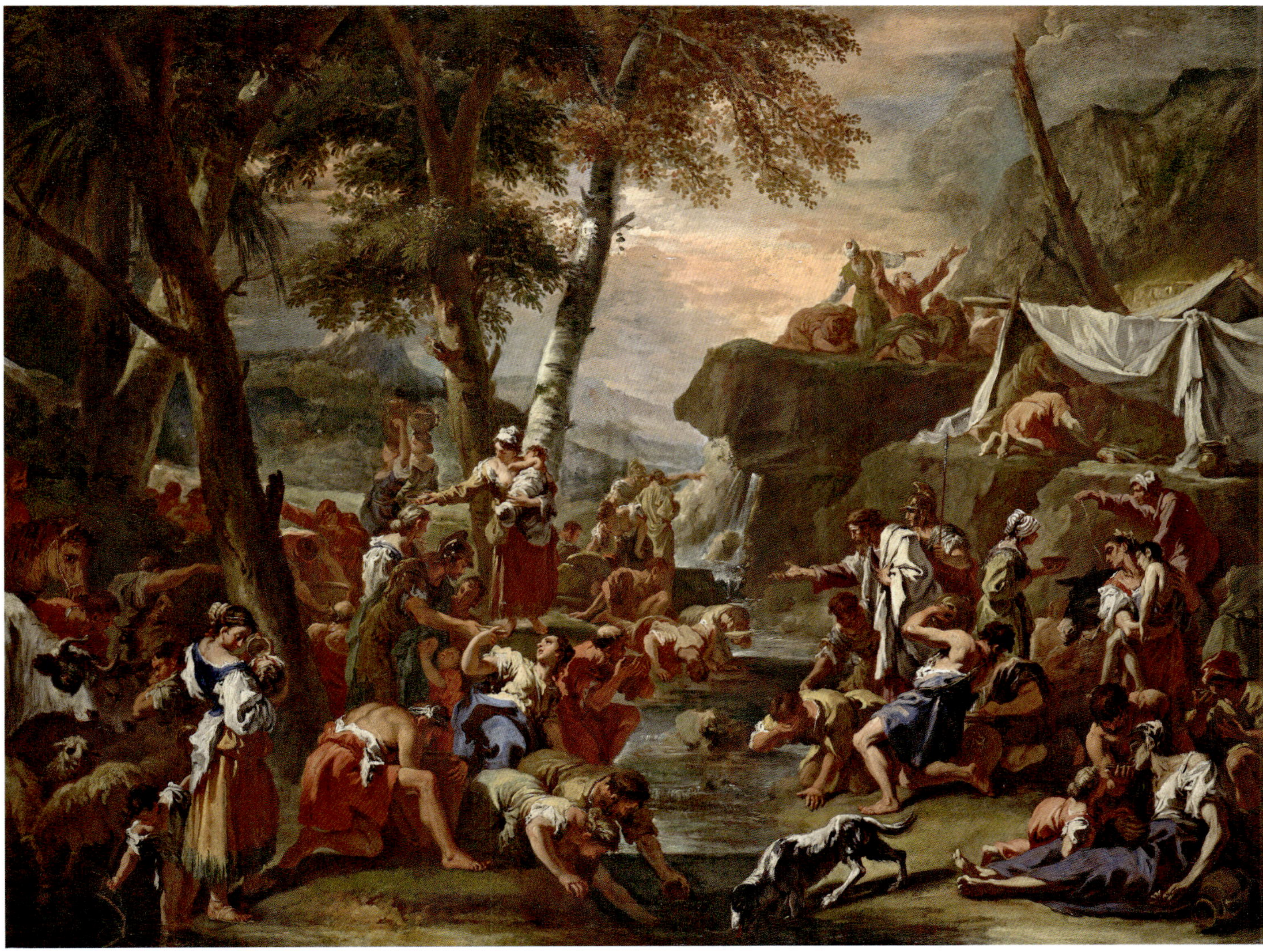

233–4

ANTONIO VISENTINI (1688–1782) WITH FRANCESCO ZUCCARELLI (1702–1788)

Landscape with a View of Mereworth Castle, Kent signed and dated 1746

Oil on canvas, 82.7 × 131.5 cm
RCIN 400687

Landscape with a Triumphal Arch to George II signed and dated 1746

Oil on canvas, 81.5 × 132.0 cm
Both paintings inscribed: *Visentini et Zuccarelli / Fecerunt Venetiis 1746.*
RCIN 400561

PROVENANCE Commissioned by Joseph Smith and bought from him in 1762 by George III

LITERATURE Blunt 1958, pp. 283–4; *Paintings from Windsor Castle* 1990, p. 118; Levey 1991, pp. 164–5, nos 672, 675; *George III* 2004, pp. 177–8, no. 153

Antonio Visentini's association with Consul Smith began around 1717 and led to his production in 1735 of a set of engravings after Canaletto's series of views of the Grand Canal in Smith's collection and to a role as principal illustrator for Smith's Pasquali Press. He made several albums of engravings of architectural masterpieces in Venice and elsewhere and composed several anti-Baroque treatises, including *Osservazioni di Antonio Visentini sopra gli Errori degli Architetti*.[20] Visentini supplied designs for Smith's palace on the Grand Canal and his villa at Mogliano Veneto on the mainland (fig. 83).[21] Like so many British aristocrats of this period Smith was an enthusiastic Palladian: in 1768 Smith's Pasquali Press published a facsimile reprint of Palladio's architectural treatise, *Quattro Libri dell'Architettura*.[22] Smith's admiration for Palladio also found expression in two groups of architectural caprices, both clearly intended as over-doors. In 1743–4 he commissioned a series from Canaletto, probably intended for his palace on the Grand Canal, in which famous Venetian buildings, many by Palladio (including his unexecuted scheme for the Rialto Bridge), appear in fanciful urban settings and combinations.[23] In 1746 he commissioned a series of eleven from Visentini, intended for his villa at Mogliano (fig. 83), in which famous English Palladian buildings appear in Italianate landscapes. The present two paintings come from this second set, of which six more survive in the Royal Collection.[24] Visentini supplied the architecture and Zuccarelli the figures and landscape. The choice of English architecture is strictly Palladian, paying tribute to Inigo Jones, the first importer of the style, through his Whitehall Banqueting House, Somerset House and Lindsay House (RCIN 400993, 404063 and 407285), as well as to the more recent group of Palladians who had transformed English architecture during the previous thirty years.

Mereworth Castle in Kent, depicted in no. 233, was a direct copy of Andrea Palladio's Villa Rotonda near Vicenza; it was designed by Colen Campbell for John Fane, later 7th Earl of Westmorland (1685–1762), and completed in 1723. The surrounding landscape is imaginary as are the figures, including scholarly admirers of the architecture and indigent dependants upon the generosity of its owner. The statues of Minerva and Hercules on the pediment do not appear at Mereworth as built and are typical of the type of symbolic embellishment expected of caprices.

The English Palladian style of architecture is often connected with Whig, Hanoverian constitutional ideology. In no. 234 the connection is made explicit by the inclusion of an imaginary triumphal arch celebrating

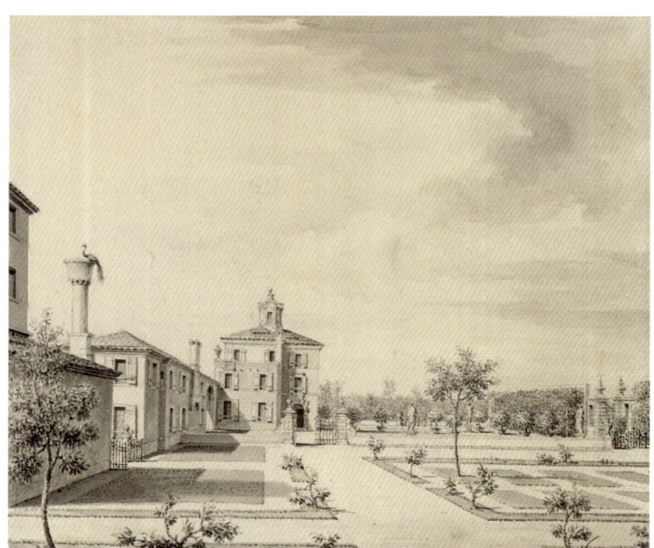

FIG. 83
Antonio Visentini
Consul Smith's Villa at Mogliano, c.1747
Black chalk and grey wash
RCIN 907704

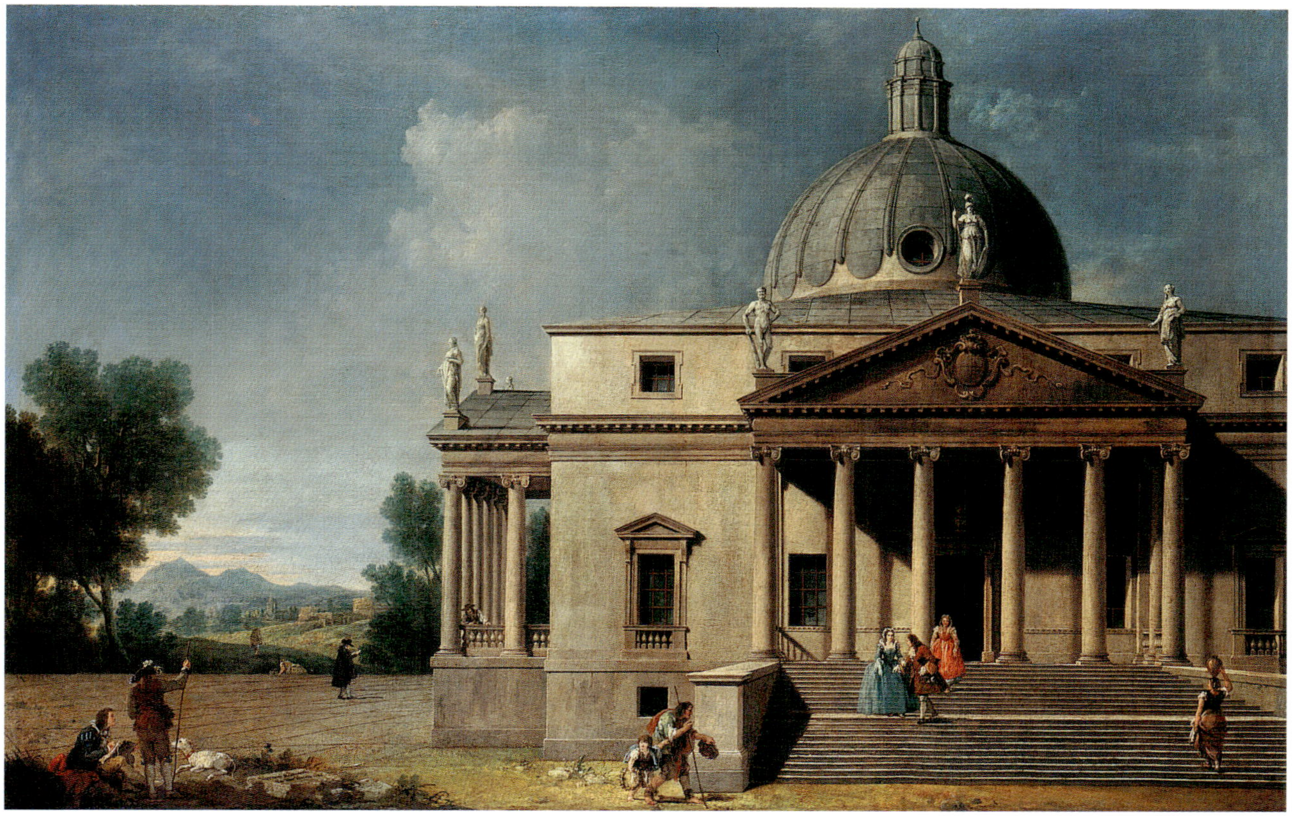

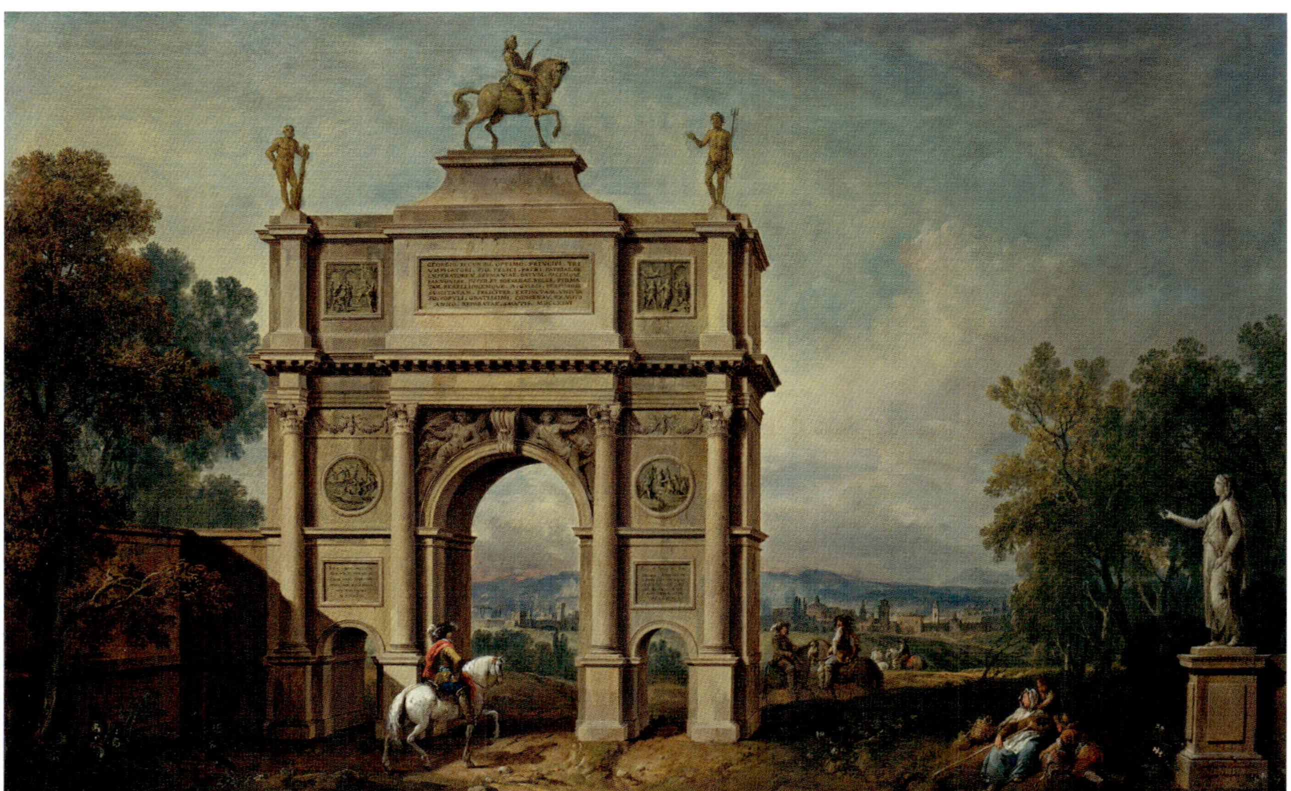

the victory of George II over his Stuart rivals to the throne. Consul Smith was the only British diplomatic presence in the Italian peninsular as James III held court in Rome as the acknowledged British King (see no. 3). It is in this context that this triumphant expression of allegiance to the 'London' (as opposed to 'Roman') King on the part of the British Consul should be understood.

Visentini's painting shows a triumphal arch surmounted by an equestrian statue of George II, flanked by statues of Hercules and Neptune; on the right is an unidentified female figure on a plinth. The arch is inscribed: *GEORGIO. SECVNDO. OPTIMO PRINCIPI TRI/VMPHATORI. PIO FELICI PATRI PATRIAE OB/ IMPERATOREM GERMANIAE DATVM PACEMQVE/ PANNONIAE INTER ET BORVSSIAE REGES FIRMA/TAM REBELLIONEMQVE A GALLIS PERFIDIOSE/ SVSCITATAM FELICITER EXTINCTAM VNIVER/ SO POPVLI GRATISSIMI CONSENSV EX VOTO/ ANNO REPARATAE. SALVTIS. MDCCXLVI.* ([This arch is dedicated] to George II, best, triumphant and pious prince, happy father of his country, on account of [to celebrate] an Emperor granted to Germany, peace established between the Kings of Prussia and Hungary, and the happy destruction of a rebellion stirred up by the perfidious French, by universal consent of a most grateful public in fulfilment of a vow in the year of our Lord 1746).

The date would suggest that the Battle of Culloden in 1746 was the most immediate caused for celebration, but the remainder of the inscription puts this re-establishment of the Hanoverians on the British throne in the context of a European network of allies. DS-T

Terrace of Somerset House

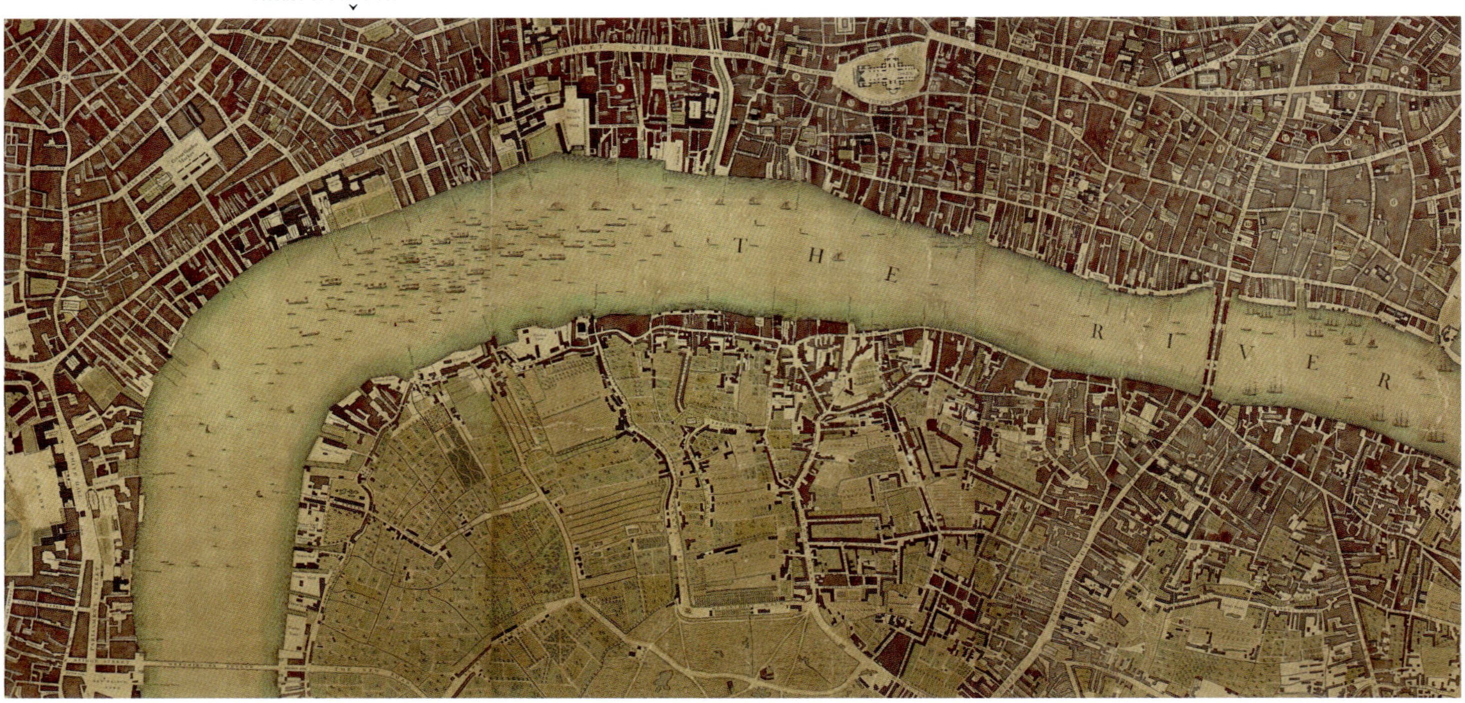

235 & 236

GIOVANNI ANTONIO CANAL, CALLED CANALETTO (1697–1768)

London: the Thames from Somerset House Terrace towards the City *c.*1750

Oil on canvas, 108.3 × 188.6 cm
RCIN 400504

London: the Thames from Somerset House Terrace towards Westminster *c.*1750

Oil on canvas, 107.9 × 188.5 cm
RCIN 400506

PROVENANCE The pair commissioned by Joseph Smith and bought from him in 1762 by George III

LITERATURE Levey 1991, pp. 18–9, nos 374–5; *Canaletto in England* 2006, pp. 60–9, nos 5–10

Canaletto's landscapes are more varied than at first appears. Some are magnificent assemblages, often involving a bird's-eye view; some, like this pair of Thames views, convey the illusion of actually standing within a scene. These two landscapes may be located on a map of the same spot at the same date (fig. 84). Together they make a panoramic view of over 180 degrees, though with a gap of some 50 degrees between the two scenes. Both views are taken from a slightly elevated position from opposite ends of the terrace of Somerset House (the left-hand bank of green on the north bank of the river indicated in fig. 84), so as to show its entire length twice. But it is surely Canaletto's intention to suggest that we see these two views from the same position and that this is what any visitor to the terrace of Somerset House would experience. These views were originally recorded in two drawings, one of which survives (Courtauld Gallery) and both of which were copied by Canaletto or in his studio (RCIN 907559 and 907560).[25] The drawings were used to generate an earlier pair of paintings (now in the Yale Center for British Art) and were re-used for this pair, which were painted for Consul Smith probably in Venice, while Canaletto briefly returned there in 1750–1.[26]

Imaginary landscapes allow the viewer to float above a landscape and see much more than would be possible in reality; they allow the artist to exaggerate the scale of significant features. Real single-viewpoint landscapes by comparison can seem dull and empty – so much sky and foreground, the interesting incidents so small, distant and obscured. On the other hand they convey so vivid a sensation of being in the landscape that every other element in the scene – the light, space and atmosphere – suddenly make themselves felt. It is tempting to suggest that this style of landscape is especially suited to places, like London, the monuments of which had become familiar by this date; the purpose of a landscape of this type is not to re-create London but to put the viewer in it.

The terrace of Somerset House was chosen by Canaletto because it was the best viewing platform and conveyed the elegance of modern England, which was such an important part of his subject matter. In this case the water-steps designed by Inigo Jones provide that same celebration of the Palladian tradition within English architecture as nos 233 and 234. This position also allows Canaletto to contrast the two parts of London, the old City dominated by St Paul's and the new fashionable Westminster and West End dominated by the Abbey.

Prints made after these views are entitled 'A West View of London with the Bridge' and 'A North East View of Westminster with the New Bridge'.[27] This would suggest that the meaning of the scene is encapsulated by the contrast between the old London Bridge, with its houses which were demolished in 1757, barely visible downstream in no. 235, and the new Westminster Bridge in no. 236, which opened in 1750 (see no. 188) and featured in so many London views at this time.[28] Also part of modern London was York Building Waterworks, which supplied thousands of houses with water by means of a steam engine (see p. 301) which ensured that the obelisk-shaped tower to the right of no. 236 was always full to the top, thus maintaining the pressure within the system.[29]

Canaletto also expresses the same distinction in the boats he includes, with freighters seen downstream and ferry-men, like gondoliers, serving their fashionable clientele upstream. Two splendid noblemen's barges appear in the scene (compare fig. 44), one almost mobbed by tiny boats, presumably those of traders hawking fresh produce. The same concentration of pleasure boats can be seen in Rocque's map (fig. 84). DS-T

FIG. 84
Detail of Rocque's map showing the Thames at Somerset House
RCIN 1028005

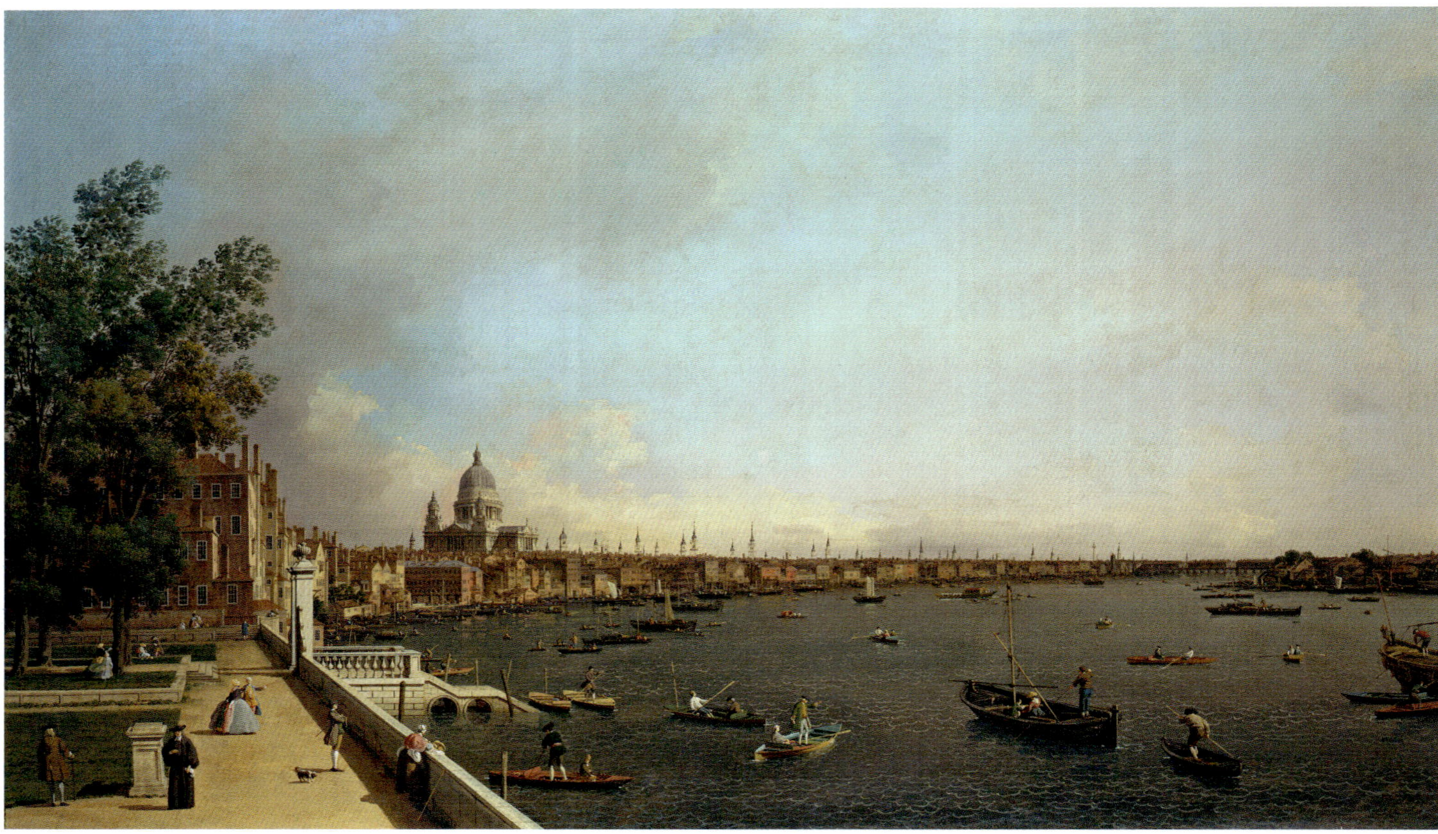

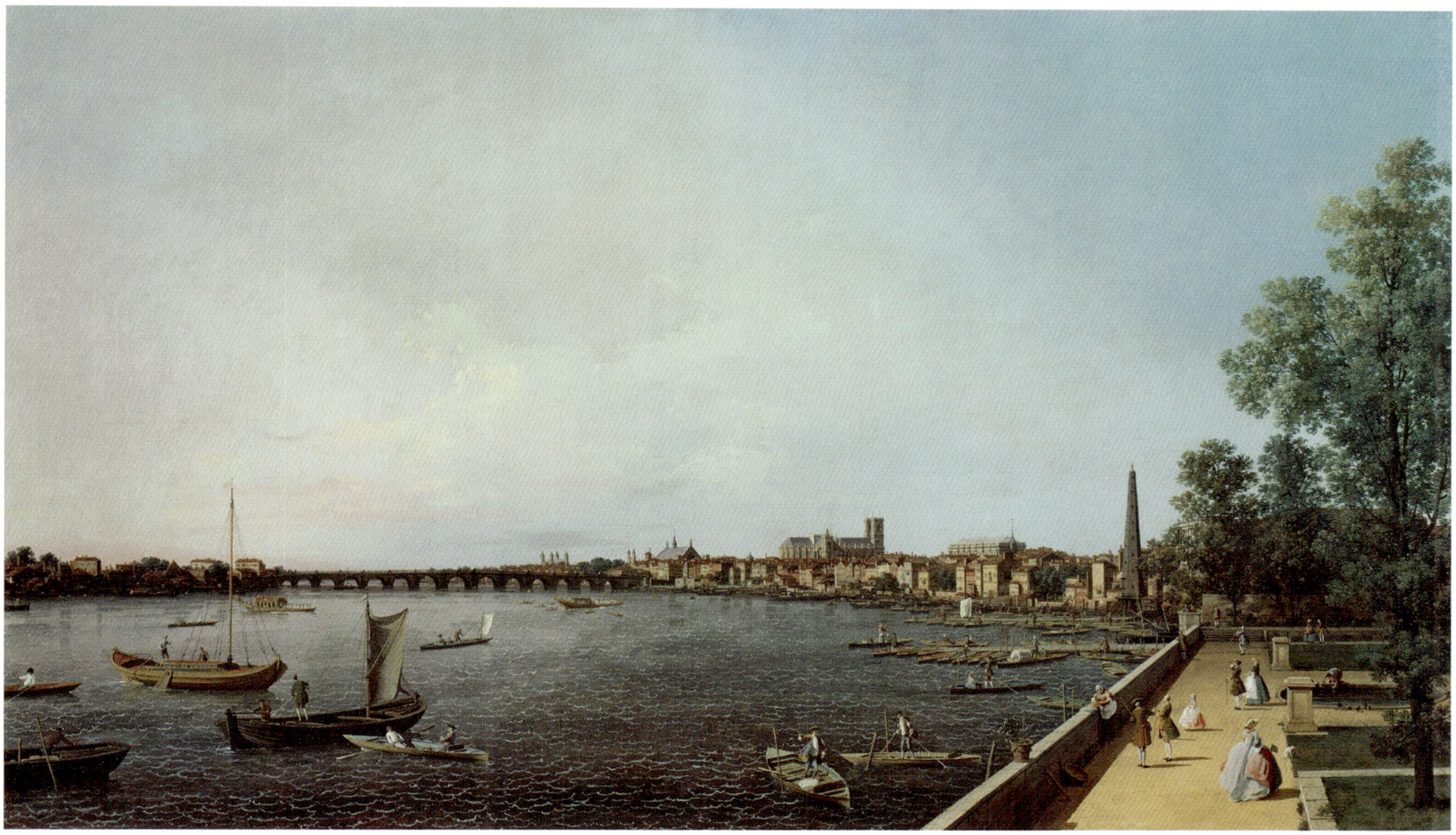

At the time of George I's arrival British portrait painting was considered to be safely entrusted to another German, Godfrey Kneller. Kneller was born in Lübeck, studied in Amsterdam with Rembrandt and his pupil Ferdinand Bol, and had set up in London as a fashionable portrait painter by 1676.[30] Kneller painted seven British monarchs – Charles II, James II, William III, Mary II, Anne, George I and George II. At Lely's death in 1680 he took over his post as Principal Painter to the Crown and in 1715 was the first artist to be made a Baronet (the next was John Everett Millais in 1885). Between 1711 and 1716 he directed an academy of painting and drawing at Great Queen Street in London and retired to Whitton Hall near Twickenham.[31] Kneller was a member of the Kit Cat Club, the most important assemblage of Whig noblemen, politicians and writers, and painted the membership in a distinctive medium-length format (36 by 28 inches) in a group of works now in the National Portrait Gallery.[32] His self-portrait shows the artist wearing a medal with the head of William III and a view of Whitton Hall in the background (fig. 85). Kneller represented the continuation of the tradition of Van Dyck and Lely, which was regarded as the English style of painting (see p. 257); his simple, bold, painterly approach, arrangement of the elements of the painting into strong clumps and direct presentation of the sitter seemed to sum up the characteristics of English bluff manliness.[33] Before the Hanoverians arrived Kneller had painted all the Englishmen admired by lovers of liberty and learning – Locke, Newton, Addison, William Congreve (1670–1729), Robert Walpole (1676–1745) – in this clubbable, democratic fashion.[34]

It was generally agreed after Kneller's death in 1723 that none of his pupils were up to the task of maintaining his English style of painting and that manly directness could, after a while, become monstrous dullness.[35] In the second half of the century commentators began to discuss the 'Augustan Age' of English letters and 'lowest

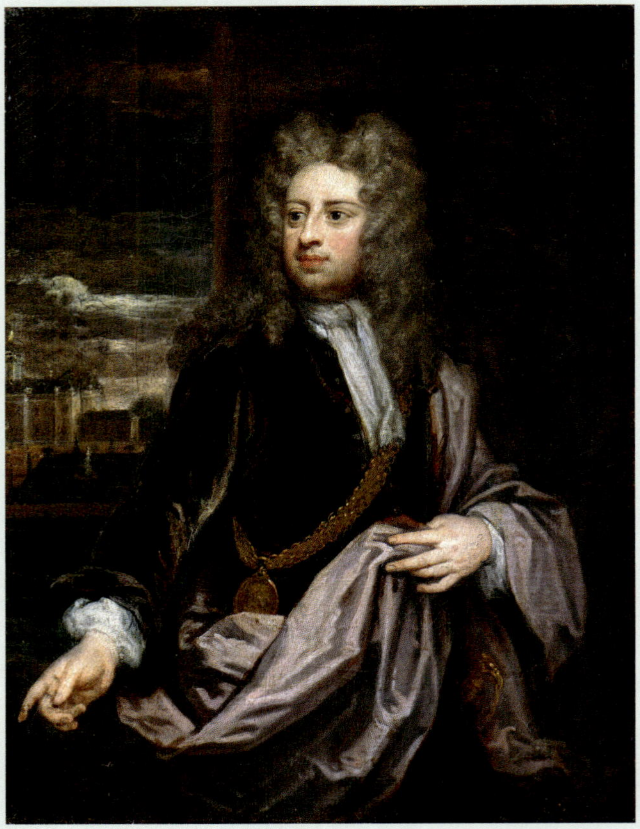

FIG. 85
Sir Godfrey Kneller Bt
Self-Portrait, *c.*1706–11
Oil on canvas
National Portrait Gallery, London

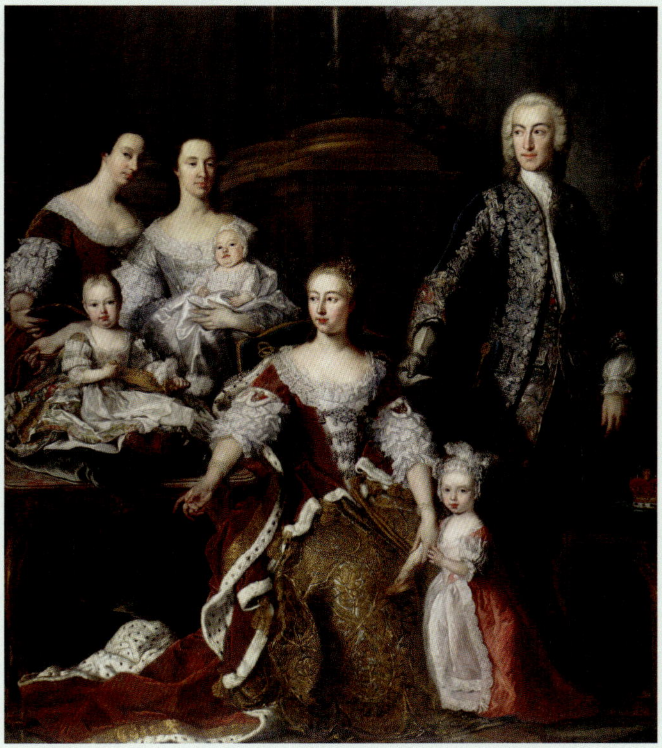

FIG. 86
Jean-Baptiste Van Loo
Augusta, Princess of Wales, with Members of her Family and Household, 1739
Oil on canvas
RCIN 403502

ebb' of English painting, moving towards a consensus that Addison represented the former and Kneller (and his followers) the latter.[36] Abbé Le Blanc, a French visitor to England during the years 1737 to 1744, found that portrait painters were 'more numerous and worse in London than ever they have been', creating portraits any dozen of which might be mistaken 'for twelve copies of the same original'.[37] The lack of royal encouragement was noted by a Swiss artist, Jean André Rouquet (1701–58), who worked in London during the years 1722–52, when there was only one pensioned painter – the unworthy John Shackleton (d. 1767).[38] In fact it was precisely during these years that the native face-mongers came under attack from Continental rivals, most of whom offered a French style of portraiture. The first element of the offer was a proficiency and subtlety of technique (far exceeding that of the locals), whether in the brilliant crispness of oil paint or the softness of pastels. The French style also implied a quality of design and taste which was fundamentally different from the school of Kneller – brighter coloured, more precisely finished, sharper in the detail and drawn with a complex patterning of forms, especially in the drapery, which loosely corresponded to the twisting forms of the Rococo. If the English wished to denigrate this style they called it 'fluttering'.[39] The 1701 portrait of Louis XIV by Hyacinthe Rigaud (1659–1743) now in the Louvre set the standard for the French style, which maintained its authority as the defining image of absolute monarchy throughout Europe and throughout the period covered here. Rigaud's manner was also perpetuated by Nicolas de Largillière (1656–1746), who, in his family portraits, added Watteau's elegant, casual and romantic interaction between the figures, creating a fusion between the group portrait and the *scène galante*. The artist who had most impact on the English market was Jean-Baptiste Van Loo (1684–1745), who arrived in 1737 and, according to Hogarth, 'with his grandeur and puffing monopolised all the people of fashion in the kingdom'.[40] This must have included the Prince and Princess of Wales, who visited his studio in 1738 and 'staid there to see him paint with great satisfaction'.[41] In 1739 they commissioned a group portrait of the Princess with her household (fig. 86), apparently to hang in her Dressing Room at Kew, where in 1761 it was seen by Horace Walpole along with Barthélemy du Pan's *Children of Frederick, Prince of Wales* (no. 241).[42] This work is clearly in the crisp French manner, which does not contrast with the work of contemporary English artists, like Joseph Highmore (no. 239), only because they too had defected to the French style.[43] When the Scot Allan Ramsay started to establish himself in London in 1740 he does not seem to have concerned himself with English rivals, boasting instead that he had 'put all your Vanlois [Van Loo] and Soldis [Andrea Soldi] and Roscos

[Cavaliere Rusca, 1696?–1769] to flight and now play the first fiddle myself'.[44]

Two other Continental artists (not mentioned by Ramsay) visited England during these years and made an obvious impact in royal circles: Antoine Pesne (no. 240) and Barthélemy du Pan (no. 241). Antoine Pesne was born in Paris, son of the portrait painter Thomas Pesne, with whom he studied as well as with his uncle, Charles de la Fosse (1636–1716). After having won the Prix de Rome in 1703 he visited Italy a few years later, in 1707, especially studying Venetian Old Masters and contemporary painters such as Andrea Celesti (1637–1712). His portraits of German visitors to Venice brought about an invitation to the court in Berlin, where he arrived in 1710 and spent the rest of his career, becoming Court Painter and Director of the Royal Academy. Pesne's early biographers, Abraham Humbert and Joachim Martin Falbe, describe a journey to London, probably in 1723, during which he painted a now lost portrait of the Prince of Wales (later George II); he soon returned to Berlin, as 'there was little taste for his work in London'.[45] Another biography, by Matthias Oesterreich, published in 1761, mentions that, especially in his later work, Pesne imitated Rembrandt and Lancret.[46] These contrasting artists give an excellent idea of the unique quality of Pesne's work: its mood derives from the poetic elegance of Watteau and Nicolas Lancret (1690-1743), while in its technique it employs a thicker, more encrusted surface which a generation of eighteenth-century French artists learned from Rembrandt. Du Pan was a Swiss portrait painter who first came to England in 1743, perhaps thinking to replace Van Loo, who had left in 1742. He seems to have worked in England until 1750, when he is briefly recorded in Dublin; he returned to Geneva in 1751.

Pastel portraiture was another Continental import of the early eighteenth century.[47] The medium may have derived in part from a growing interest in collecting Old Master drawings (many executed in coloured chalks) and from the idea that drawing was a more direct expression of the mind of the artist than painting. It is no accident that Queen Caroline 'discovered' Holbein's coloured chalk drawings (see p. 321) at exactly the time that pastel portraiture took hold in England. The technique offered an informal and direct vision of a sitter which seemed to clean off the thick, dark varnish of convention which had accumulated on top of oil painting. Pastels are light in tone and bright in colour; they allow for an animated relationship with a sitter. They were also connected with a new and more direct type of realism. In Allan Ramsay's *Dialogue on Taste* of 1755, Colonel Freeman suggests to Lord Modish that the fairest way to judge a painting would be to eavesdrop on the reactions of one of his 'tenant's daughters': 'I will venture to lay a wager that she shall be struck with your picture by La Tour [the pastellist Maurice Quentin de La Tour (1704–88)], and no less with the view of your seat by Lambert [George Lambert (1700–65)], and shall, fifty to one, express her approbation by saying, "They are *vastly natural*". When she had said this, she has shewn that she knew the proper standard by which her approbation was to be directed, as much, at least, as she would have done, if she had got Aristotle to heart and all his commentators.'[48] This tradition of Enlightened common sense is maintained in the work and writing of another pastellist, Jean-Étienne Liotard (1702–89), whose *Traité des Principes et des Règles de la Peinture*

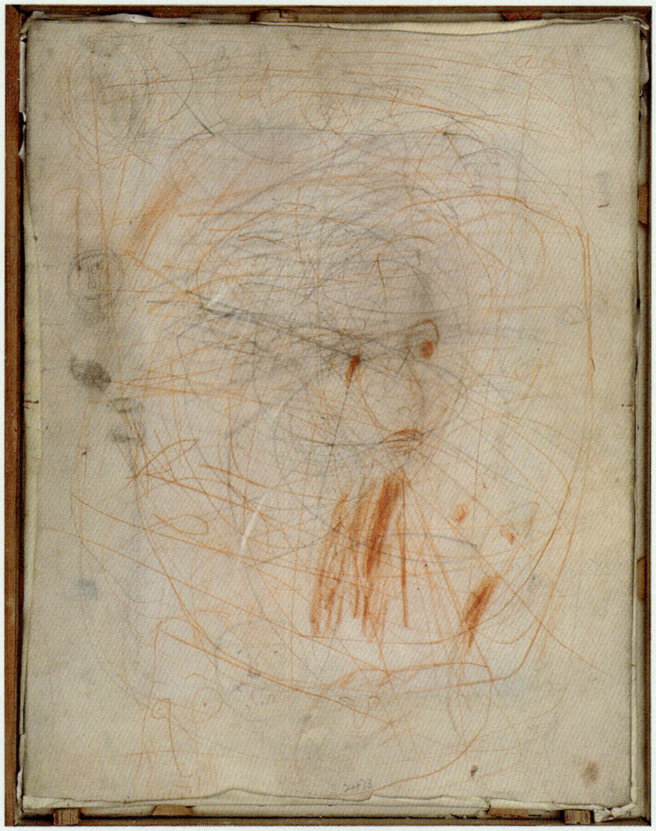

FIG. 87
Unknown child
Drawings, *c*.1754
Red chalk on vellum
Mounted on the reverse of the stretcher of Liotard's *Edward Augustus, Duke of York*
RCIN 400901

FIG. 88
Jean-Étienne Liotard
Self-portrait, *c*.1740
Enamel
RCIN 421436

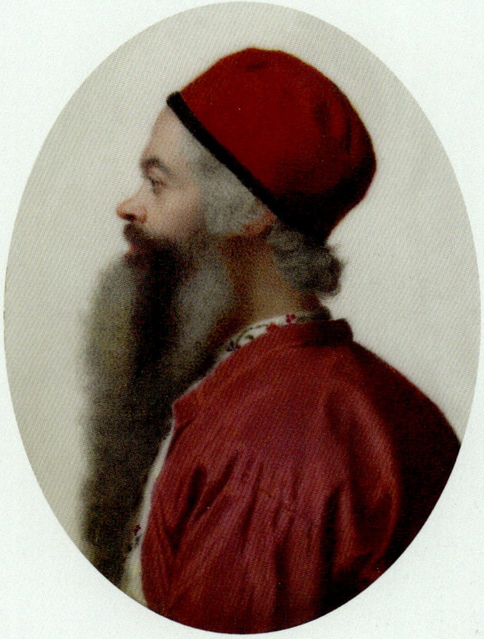

of 1781 is one of the least hackneyed works of its kind in the history of art. Recent reframing of the Liotard portrait of Prince Edward (RCIN 400901) has revealed a child's chalk drawing on a piece of vellum tacked on to the reverse of the stretcher (fig. 87). These doodles seem to depict a bearded man, which was exactly how Liotard himself appeared at this date (fig. 88). It would seem that as he was drawing the young Princess and Princesses he invited them to draw him, turning a portrait sitting from a chore to a game. This may have been his way of capturing the childish directness see in his portrait of Princess Louisa Anne (no. 244). It is also revealing that the favourite portrait painter of the young George III was Allan Ramsay, whose work at this time had acquired a softness and simple naturalism from his study of French pastel portraiture.[49]

237

SIR GODFREY KNELLER BT (1646–1723)

George II (1683–1760) as Prince of Wales
signed and dated 1716

Oil on canvas, 239.2 × 148.4 cm
RCIN 406073

PROVENANCE Presumably painted for the sitter

LITERATURE Millar 1963, pp. 144–5, no. 343

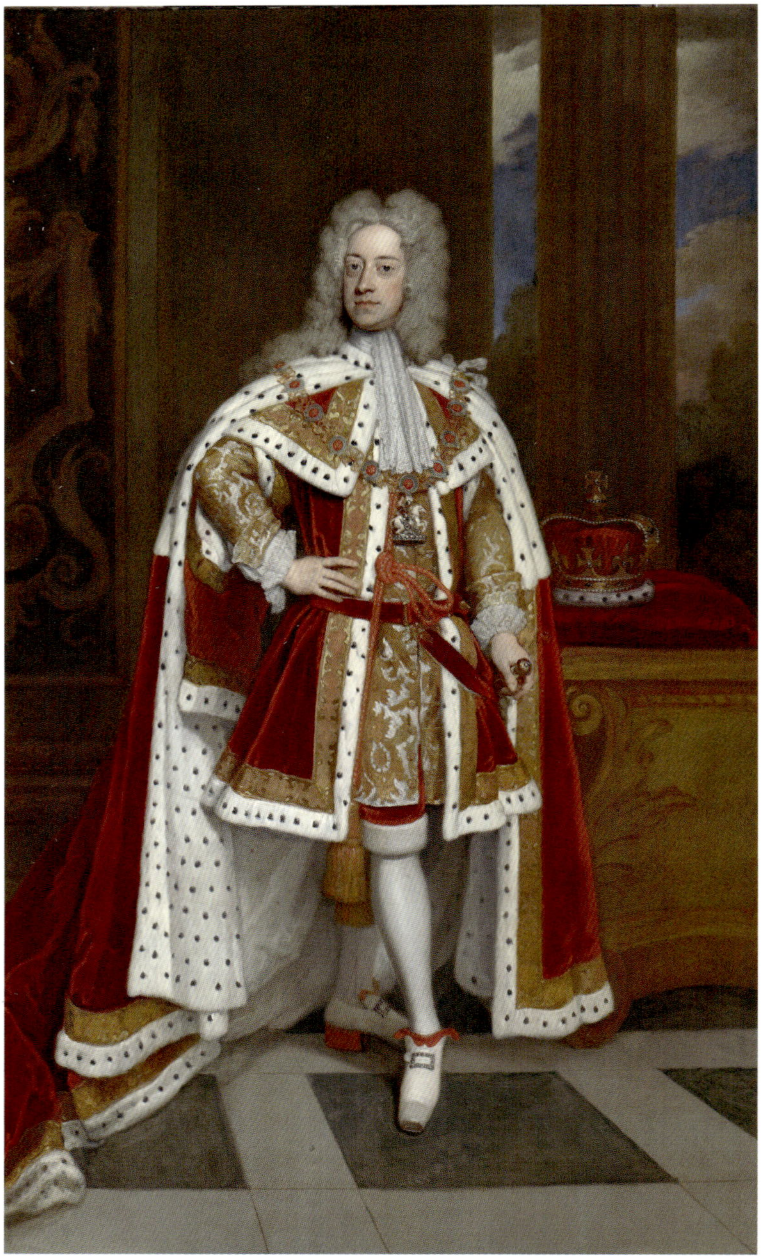

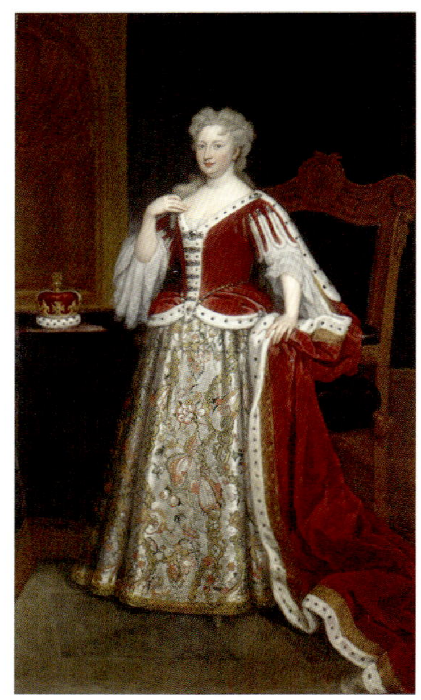

FIG. 89
Sir Godfrey Kneller Bt
Queen Caroline as Princess of Wales, 1716
Oil on canvas
RCIN 405313

This is one of a pair of portraits of the Prince and Princess of Wales (fig. 89) dated 1716 and probably painted during the six months (July–December 1716) when George I was in Hanover and his son acted as 'Guardian and Lieutenant of the Realm'. The sitter is shown in the most formal style possible, wearing State Robes with his prince's crown on the table to the right and the collar of the Garter round his neck. As always with full-length portraits of this date the setting is imaginary and intended to convey the grandeur of a classical palace of exactly the type which did not exist at this time in England.

With costumes of this splendour it is difficult to speak of simplicity, but in comparison with Rigaud's portrait of Louis XIV (Louvre) this appears decidedly matter-of-fact. These qualities were surely deliberate and calculated to endear the recently arrived Hanoverians to their new subjects. However, Kneller was seventy years old when he executed this portrait; it is not surprising that in execution it feels so stolid and workmanlike. DS-T

238

JOHN VANDERBANK (1694–1739)

George I (1660–1760) 1726

Oil on canvas, 316.0 × 240.4 cm
Signed: *J. Vanderbank. Fecit / 1726*
RCIN 404412

PROVENANCE Presented to King George V and Queen Mary in 1932

LITERATURE Collins Baker 1937, p. 298; Millar 1963, p. 169, no. 499

Vanderbank was born in London, the son of a Huguenot tapestry weaver from Paris who owned the Soho Tapestry Manufactory and was chief arras maker to the Crown from 1689 until his death in 1717. Vanderbank junior studied with Kneller and briefly set up his own academy (see p. 343). According to George Vertue, only 'irregular living' prevented him from distinguishing himself above all his contemporaries.[50] This is faint praise, as 'his contemporaries' were dull indeed, made up of names such as Jonathan Richardson I (1665–1745), who trained John Riley (1646–91); Charles Jervas (*c*.1675–1739) and Bartholomew Dandridge (1691–1754), both of whom, like Vanderbank, were pupils of Kneller.

This equestrian portrait was painted for a loyal subject, probably William, Viscount Bateman (1695–1744), rather than the King, but is clearly influenced by Michael Dahl's portrait of Prince George from the previous reign (RCIN 405895, then hanging at Windsor) and Van Dyck's equestrian *Charles I* (then in the collection of the Duke of Marlborough, now in the National Gallery). The King is shown mounted on a dun horse, wearing the riband and star of the Order of the Garter, holding his baton as British commander with his Household Cavalry behind. DS-T

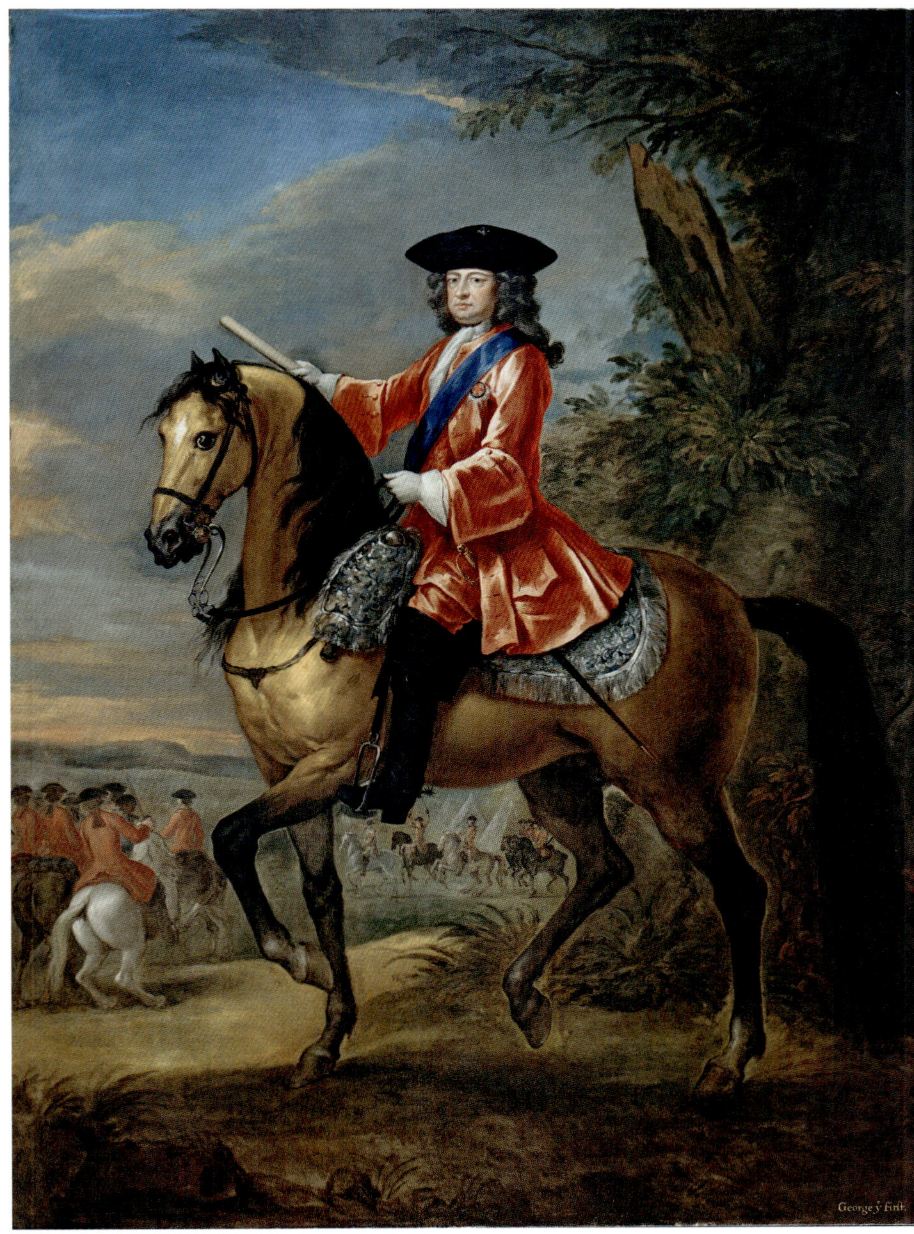

239

JOSEPH HIGHMORE (1692–1780)

Queen Caroline (1683–1737) *c.*1735

Oil on canvas, 75.1 × 61.8 cm
RCIN 406035

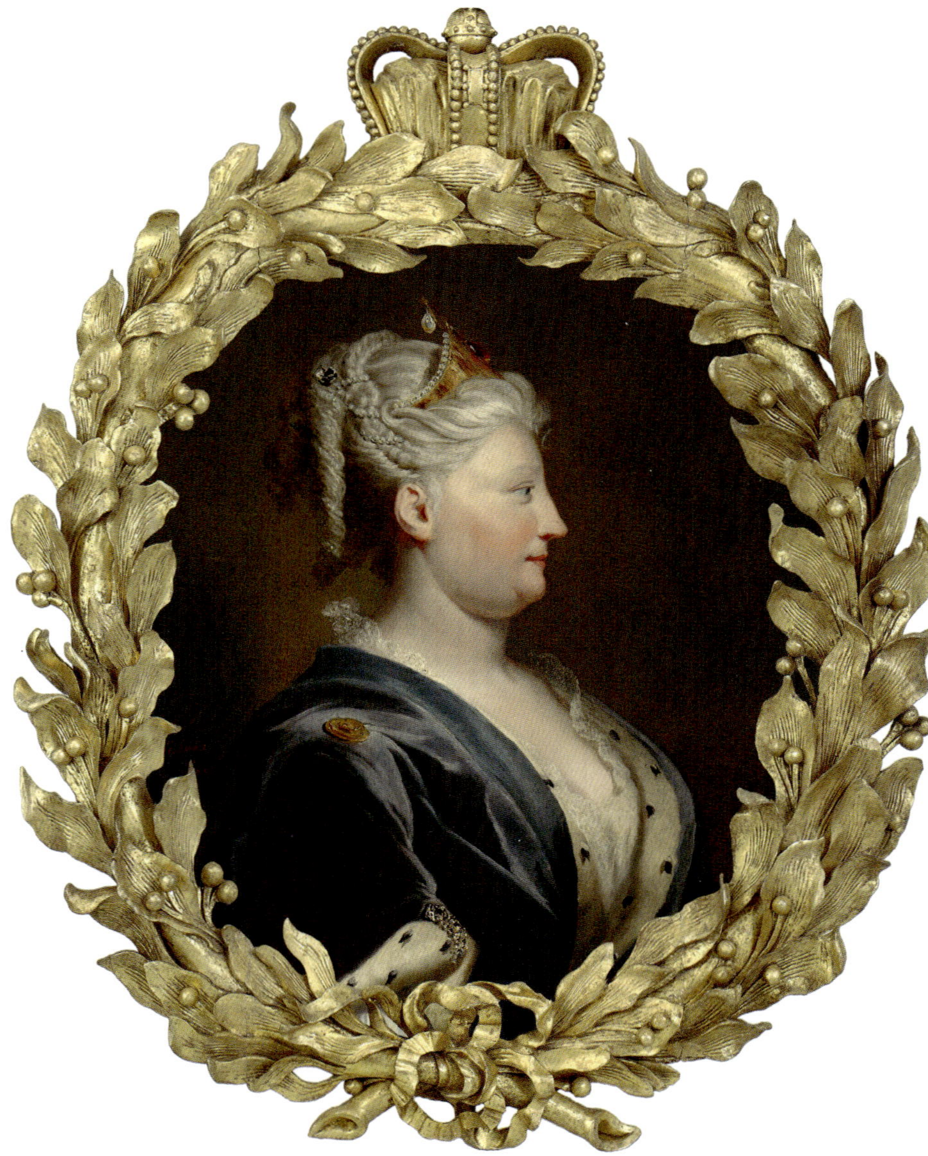

PROVENANCE Probably acquired by George IV for Carlton House, where first recorded in 1816

LITERATURE Millar 1963, p. 173, no. 518

Probably painted around 1735, Highmore's profile portrait depicts the fifty-year-old Queen dressed in a loose gown lined with an ermine collar. Her hair is coiffed around a jewelled diadem and interlaced with a string of pearls. It is uncertain if Highmore obtained a sitting from the Queen; we know for certain from Vertue that his request was on one occasion denied.[51] The artist's obituary, which lists a portrait of the Queen, emphasised his ability to 'take a likeness by memory as well as by sitting'. The companion image of George II was destroyed by fire in 1824 but appears in Charles Wild's watercolour of the West Ante Room at Carlton House (RCIN 922175) and in an engraving by John Tinney (fig. 90).[52] DS-T

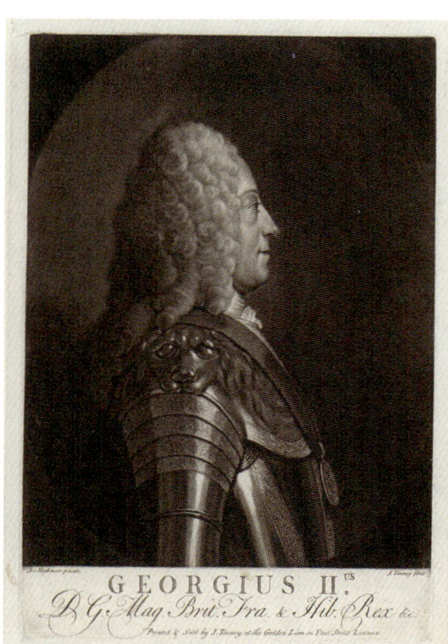

FIG. 90
John Tinney after Joseph Highmore
George II
Mezzotint
RCIN 603870

240

ANTOINE PESNE

Frederick II 'The Great', King of Prussia (1712–1786) 1740S

Oil on canvas, 265.8 × 177.7 cm
RCIN 406797

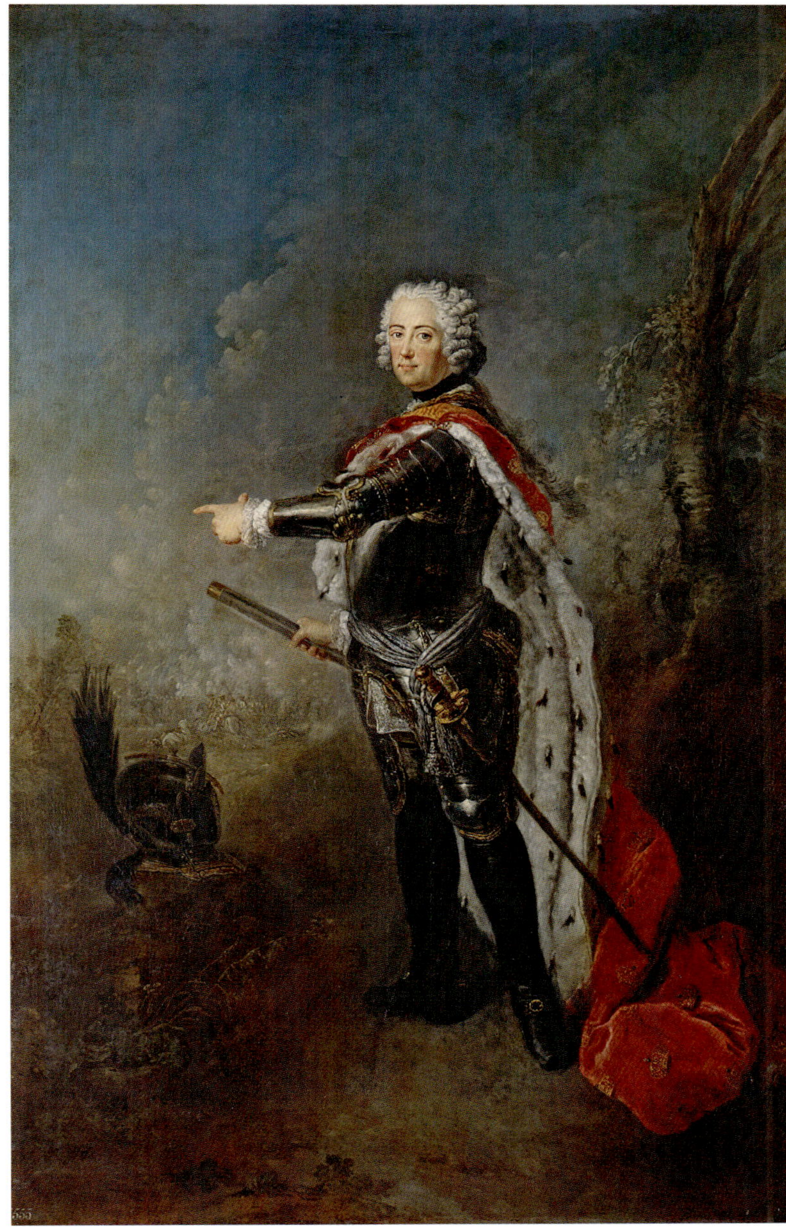

PROVENANCE Presumably acquired by Frederick, Prince of Wales

LITERATURE Börsch-Supan 1986, pp. 31–2

This large full-length portrait of Frederick the Great was presented by the sitter to Frederick, Prince of Wales in January 1748. The King of Prussia wrote to his first cousin:

> Monsieur my brother. I send you my portrait, as you have wished; I would hope it were the truthful translator of my thoughts, it would certainly say to Your Royal Highness everything that my heart feels for Him; it will show you that the ties of blood outlast both distance and time, that nothing can suppress this voice of nature.

Frederick had received the Prince of Wales's request a little more than a year earlier, in December 1746, and granted it, on condition that he received his cousin's portrait in return: this seems to have reached him in August 1749.[53]

Frederick II was the Prince of Wales's cousin through both his mother Sophia Dorothea, George II's sister, as well as through his grandmother Sophia Charlotte, who was George I's sister. Both Fredericks almost became brothers-in-law, for the Prince of Wales hoped to marry the King of Prussia's sister Wilhelmina. However, these negotiations were stopped by George II.

The painting of Frederick the Great is otherwise first recorded in the Privy Chamber at Kensington Palace in the inventory of 1818; it appears in Charles Wild's watercolour (no. 32) hanging in pride of place over the mantle.[54] The magnificent frame for the painting (fig. 20) can be identified as the one provided in 1749 by Paul Petit for the Prince of Wales, described in his accounts as 'richly carved with a Eagle and septer at Top with two Saveges Supporters Standards in their hand and Trophies of warr'; it must have left the collection in the early twentieth century and was only recently rediscovered.[55]

The first version of Pesne's composition was of the head and shoulders of the sitter as Crown Prince dated 1739 (Gemäldegalerie, Berlin), employed subsequently for many autograph and studio replicas. The present version sets the figure at full length in armour with a battle raging in the background. The distinctive qualities of Pesne's art are clearly visible in the brilliantly frothy indistinctness of the background and the sharp clarity of the figure, both elements painted with a strong, impasto touch. WB

241

BARTHÉLEMY DU PAN (1712–63)

The Children of Frederick, Prince of Wales signed and dated 1746

Oil on canvas, 245.0 × 368.8 cm
RCIN 403400

PROVENANCE Painted for Frederick, Prince of Wales

LITERATURE Collins Baker 1937, p. 71; Millar 1963, pp. 188–9, no. 572; Rorschach 1990, pp. 12 and 64; Vivian 2006, p. 414

In 1747 Frederick, Prince of Wales, paid £100 for this group portrait of his six eldest children; the painting was first recorded in 1761 hanging in his widow's Dressing Room at Kew Palace, where it was seen by Horace Walpole.[56] The huge size of the work suggests that it was originally intended for a great hall or drawing room; it may be connected with du Pan's two full-length portraits of the children's parents, Frederick and Augusta, Prince and Princess of Wales, of *c.*1745 in the Ulster Museum.[57]

This is a version of the French-style idyll, often called a *fête champêtre* or *fête galante*, invented by Watteau in the 1710s and much imitated during the next three decades by artists such as Lancret, Pater (fig. 92) and de Troy. These scenes seemed to combine an appreciation of finest nuance of high-life chic with a suggestion of the Earthly Paradise. Not surprisingly their influence spilled over into portraiture and can be seen in the idyllic pastoral and mythological portraits of Nicolas de Largillière (*Marquise de Gueydan as Flora*, 1730, Musée Granet), Jean-Marc Nattier (*Louise-Anne de Bourbon-Conde*, 1731, formerly with Stair Sainty Gallery, London) and Antoine Pesne (*Marianne Cochois Dancing*, 1745, Schloss Charlottenburg). Du Pan's work fits comfortably into this tradition, unusual only in its scale: such paintings are usually life size when including one or two figures and otherwise on the much smaller scale seen, for example, in Mercier's conversation pieces (see no. 255). Du Pan has absorbed from French portraiture the brilliant colours in the figures and foreground details and the softer, frothier treatment of the landscape, seeming to move in and out of focus in the background.

There may be some British elements to this scene, like the landscape sensibility with its picturesque exploitation of the margins between woodland, farmed land and an informal park with a temple. This has been identified by John Harris as the one designed by William Kent in 1734 for the garden of Carlton House (see fig. 8), though it is surely transposed here into an imaginary parkland setting.[58] The fact that such a scene involves royal children arranged with so little subordination is probably uniquely British. The archery contest which brings them together may allude to the common folk myth that a king earns his throne through such a contest rather than (or as well as) by hereditary right. In this case Prince George (the future George III) has just won, striking the popinjay with his arrow while his brother, Prince Edward, loads his flintlock. Princess Augusta, holding the baby Prince Henry, points to the winner and Prince William (still young enough to be in skirts) holds out his wreath of victory. To the left Princess Elizabeth drives a pretty carriage drawn by dogs and decorated with billing doves, which suggests it is dedicated to Venus, goddess of love. The scene has a sporting vigour that reminds us that belief in the benefit for children of exercise, fresh air and freedom predate the writings of Jean-Jacques Rousseau.

Prince George wears the uniform of the Royal Company of Archers, which had been fixed as early as 1713 and included the Stuart tartan.[59] Like all British regimental tartan this escaped the ban on Scottish national dress which followed the Jacobite Rising of 1745 (see pp. 114–27), but its inclusion is still surprising in a painting executed in the same year as the Battle of Culloden. This would seem an early example of the process by which Scottish identity became something manly and romantic, rather than threatening and rebellious. DS-T

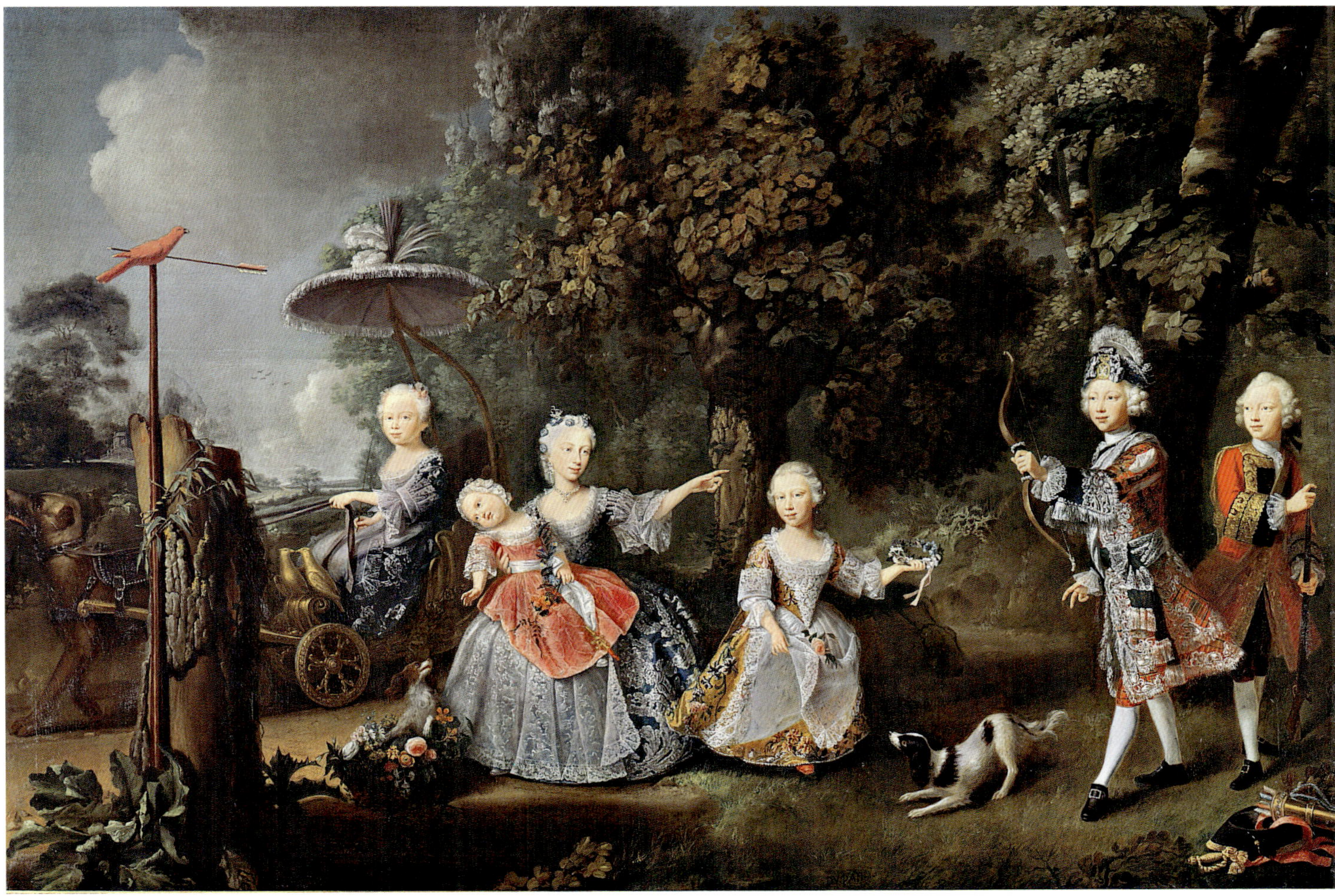

242–4

JEAN-ÉTIENNE LIOTARD (1702–89)

George, Prince of Wales (1738–1820), later George III 1754

Pastel on vellum, 40.6 × 29.8 cm
RCIN 400897

Princess Elizabeth Caroline (1740–1759) 1754

Pastel on vellum, 39.4 × 30.2 cm
RCIN 400902

Princess Louisa Anne (1749–1768) 1754

Pastel on vellum, 40.0 × 30.5
RCIN 400900

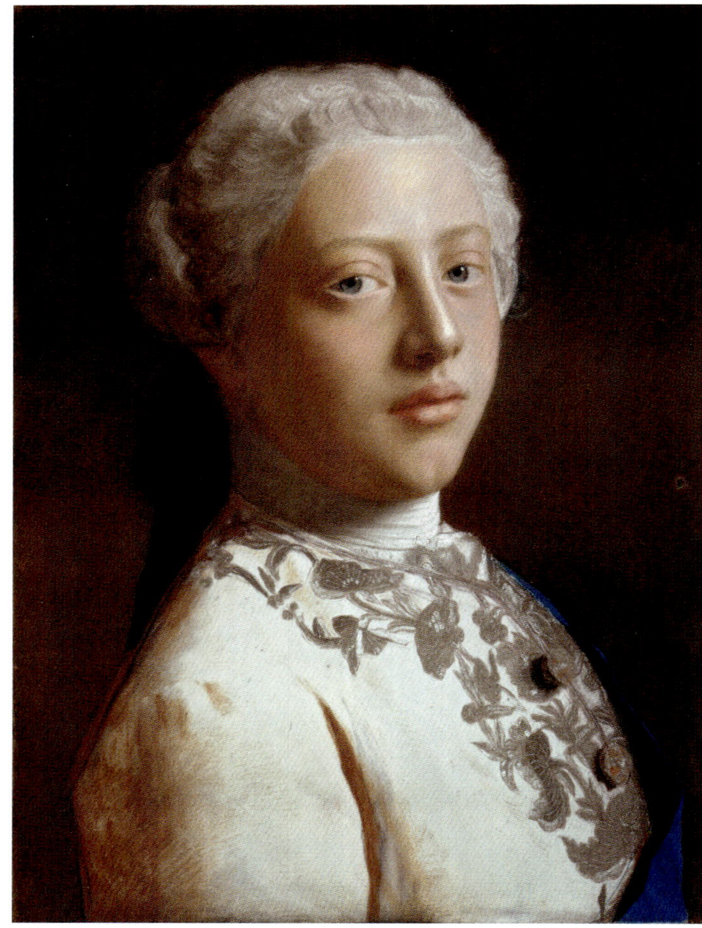

PROVENANCE From a set of eleven commissioned by Augusta, Princess of Wales in 1754

LITERATURE Millar 1963, pp. 190–1, nos 581, 583 and 586; *George III* 2004, pp. 23–4, no. 1

Liotard was a well-established and cosmopolitan figure by the time he received Augusta's commission. Born in Geneva, he had worked in Paris, Italy, Constantinople and Vienna. In the 1740s he had been commissioned to produce portraits of the Empress Maria Theresa in Vienna, and then in 1749, having been introduced at the French court, portraits of Louis XV and his five daughters. In 1754, during Liotard's two-year stay in England, Augusta, Princess of Wales, commissioned a pair of pastel portraits of herself and her late husband (on paper) and a series of her nine children (on vellum), of which these three form part.

Liotard is here working within a limited format and yet we can see a freshness of realism which can make his work stand out from his contemporaries. The structure of the forms is established with power as well as softness; pastel is an offshoot of drawing, which at this date was a discipline primarily aimed at establishing sculptural volume, and only secondarily adding qualities of texture, light and surface detail. What sets Liotard apart is his ability to find some trick of expression which establishes some real sense of encounter with his sitters. Here the challenge lies in conveying the fact that these Princes and Princesses, though wrapped in every attribute of the adult world, are still children. Princess Louisa Anne (no. 244) stares out at us with an authentic expression of childish vacancy which no other artist of this date would have observed. Liotard's success was also ascribed to the length of his beard and to the appeal of the Turkish dress he affected to the 'English love of singularity'.[60] DS-T

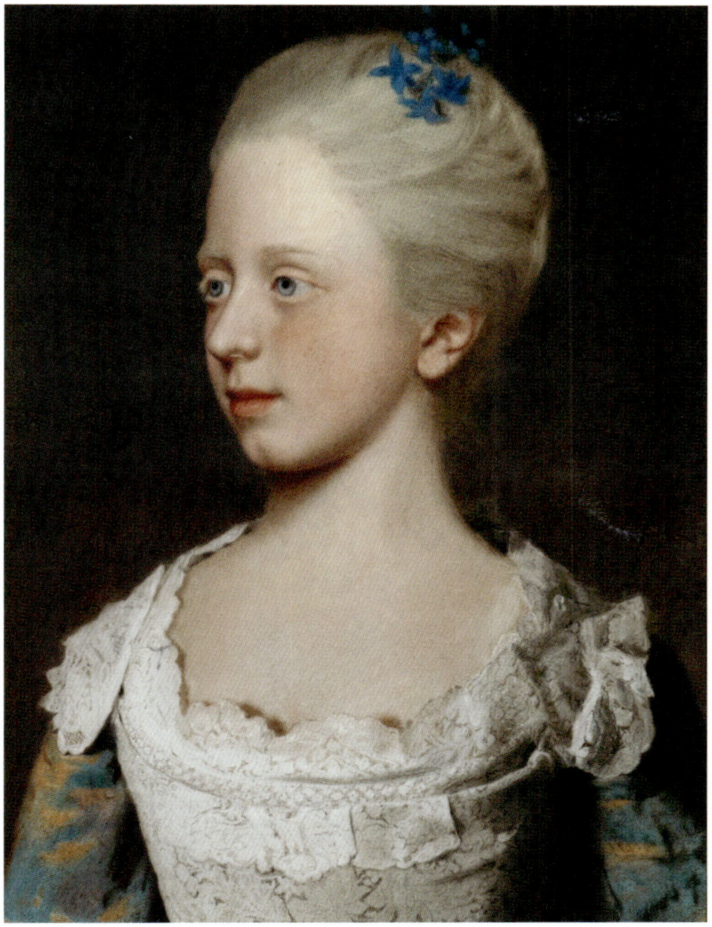

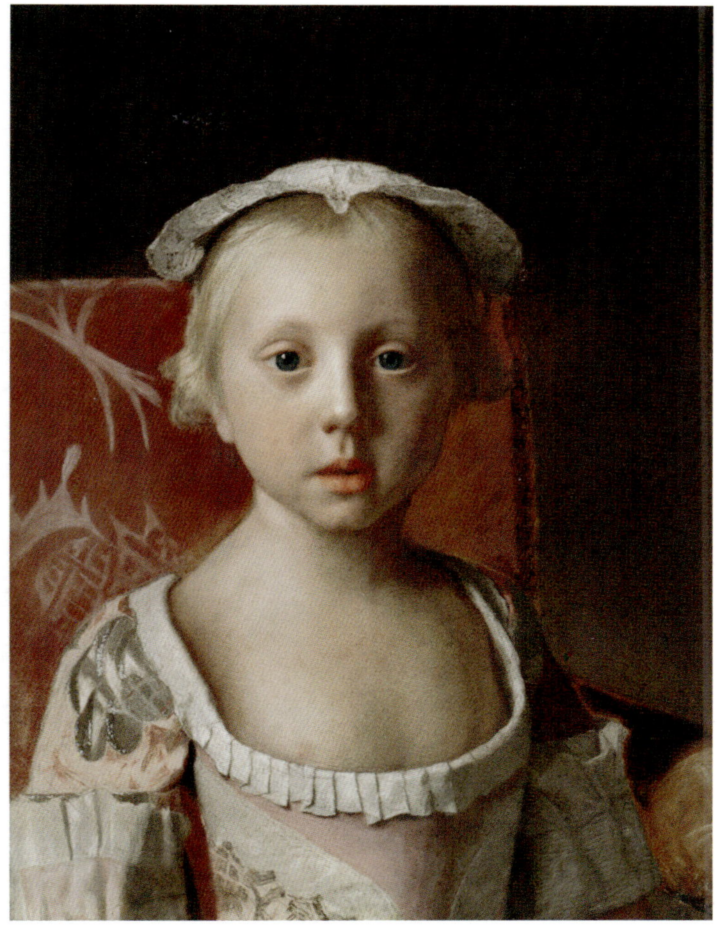

John Wootton (nos 246–50) was Thornhill's contemporary and friend and part of the circle of artists patronised by Queen Anne's chief minister, Edward Harley, 1st Earl of Oxford (1661–1724); he is shown as part of this company of Virtuosi in Thornhill's preparatory drawing of the 1720s (formerly Art Institute of Chicago), presumably intended for the decoration of a vault, perhaps at Wimpole Hall.[61] By this date Wootton had become an established practitioner in a variety of genres – battles, sporting scenes and classical landscapes – and was in his fifties by the 1730s, when he started working for the Hanoverians.[62] It does not come naturally to us today to bracket Wootton and Hogarth together, but both artists collaborated in 1734 on a group hunting portrait of Frederick, Prince of Wales, and his friends (fig. 91) at a time when their careers would not have seemed so divergent.[63] Hogarth was a pupil in Thornhill's private academy and subsequently married his daughter; he took his father-in-law's part in his confrontation with William Kent, an artist he repeatedly attacked in his early prints (see no. 76). A decade later he himself suffered in the same way at the same hands: having secured Queen Caroline's permission to record the wedding in 1734 of Princess Anne and William of Orange Hogarth found himself chased off by William Kent, anxious that his own image of the event should enjoy a monopoly.[64] George Vertue, our source for the story, also claims that Kent ensured that nothing came of the royal group portrait for which Hogarth had made a first draft (no. 245). In 1757, by way of delayed consolation, Hogarth was appointed Serjeant-Painter to George II (see p. 140) – at the end of a career apparently pursued with no other object than to disqualify him from such a position.[65]

English though these artists were, the type of commission they sought from the aristocracy and royal family – for hunting or battle scenes and group portraits – belonged to fashionable Continental genres. Wootton was trained by the Dutch battle painter John Wyck (1652–1700), and could be described with reasonable justice as an English Jean Baptiste Oudry (1686–1755).[55] Wootton's group portraits, like those of Hogarth, represent a response to exactly the same tradition of the French *scène galante*

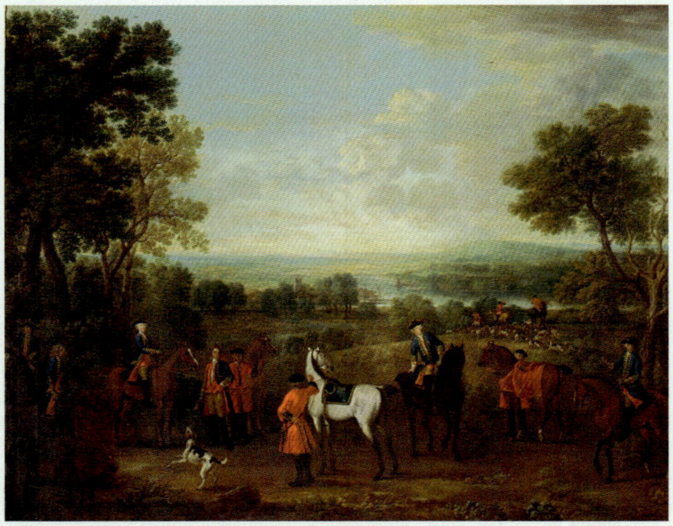

FIG. 91
William Hogarth and John Wootton
Frederick, Prince of Wales, hunting at Windsor, 1734
Oil on canvas
RCIN 401000
Painted for the Great Hall at the White House, Kew

FIG. 92
Jean-Baptiste Joseph Pater
Fête champêtre with a flute player,
1720–36
Oil on canvas
RCIN 400673

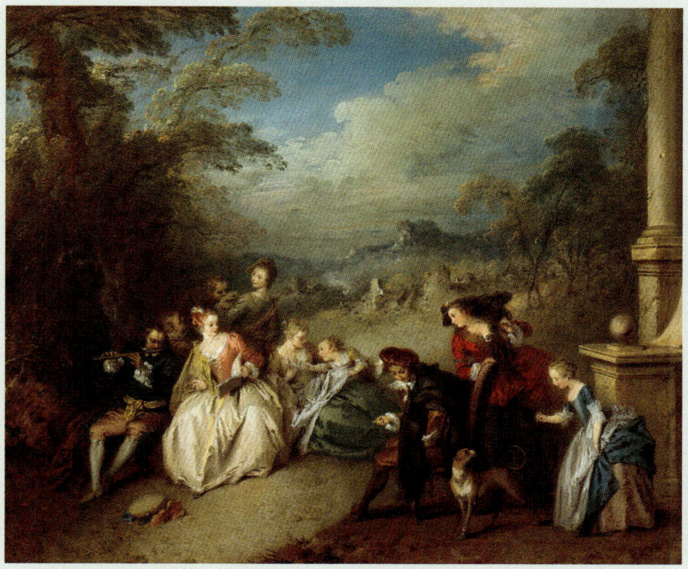

discussed above in relation to life-sized portraiture (pp. 359 and 366), as can be seen by comparisons with the work of Watteau, Mercier, Jean François de Troy and any number of French and Flemish artists of the early eighteenth century. This was what Frederick, Prince of Wales, liked. He was the acquirer of Mercier's group portrait (no. 255), gallant scenes by Jean-Baptiste Joseph Pater (1695–1736), first recorded in his collection in 1757 (fig. 92), as well as elegant French-style portraits (no. 241).[67] The Prince seemed to be following the precedent established in the early years of the century in commissioning from Wootton the subject matter of an Oudry or de Troy, while perhaps expecting a distinctive English flavour in their execution. Though Wootton was well regarded in one respect his works seems to have been treated as of coarser stuff than that of his French rivals mentioned above. His ambitious hunting scenes of the early 1730s at Althorp and Badminton hang in entrance halls, spaces for general access, furnished with hard surfaces (marble floors and wooden chairs) and austere decoration – spaces ideally suited to this type of broad-cloth English painting, which would not be acceptable in silk-furnished drawing rooms or closets.[68] As all the residences of Frederick, Prince of Wales, have been destroyed or transformed it is difficult to reconstruct this type of visual decorum, so obvious at Badminton or Althorp. However it is suggestive that one of Frederick's earliest and most ambitious English commissions, the hunting scene upon which Hogarth and Wootton collaborated in 1734 (fig. 91), was first recorded in the Great Hall at Kew Palace.[69] It can be assumed that the Gallery at Kew (original location for nos 246–7) and the Staircase at Leicester House, where Wootton's two huge siege views (RCIN 407182 and 407184) hung, were similarly generally accessed and austerely furnished spaces.

Wootton and Hogarth also worked in a different artistic milieu from their French contemporaries, one in which Old Master collecting played a relatively more significant part. Hogarth spent his career fighting this; Wootton on the other hand modelled his style on exactly those artists his patrons were acquiring at the time that they employed him. There are echoes of Rubens and Claude in his work, but the landscapist he most closely imitated was Gaspard Dughet, whose popularity at this time has already been discussed (see nos 133–5). In 1746 Wootton even painted a replica of one of Frederick's Dughets (no. 133) to provide an overmantle for the Library at Blenheim.[70] Wootton learned from Dughet a heavy dark tonality and thick rough touch as well as the techniques of structuring the terraces of a landscape. John Constable's damning verdict was that Wootton placed his country gentlemen in 'Italian landscapes resembling Gaspar Poussin [Dughet], except in truth and force'.[71] These words remind us how completely Wootton's reputation was effaced by the generation of Richard Wilson (1714–82) and George Stubbs (1724–1806) and how difficult it is to see his work of this period – the first English landscapes – with fresh eyes.

245

WILLIAM HOGARTH (1697–1764)

The Family of George II *c.*1731–2

Oil on canvas, 63.8 × 76.4 cm
RCIN 401358

PROVENANCE Purchased by HM The Queen in 1955

LITERATURE Vertue III, p. 68; Millar 1963, p. 184, no. 559; *Conversation Piece* 2009, pp. 80–1, no. 14

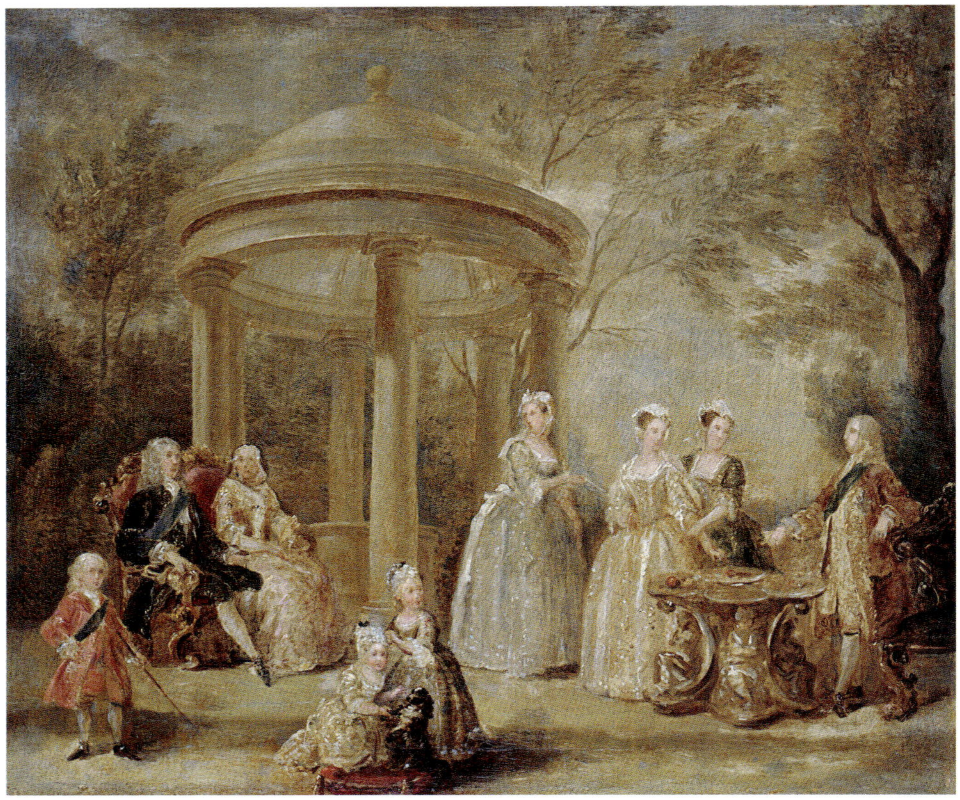

This is one of two oil sketches (the other is in the National Gallery of Ireland) for a commission which never materialised. Vertue claimed that Hogarth had been ordered to start work on it before being elbowed out of royal favour by William Kent; it may be that Hogarth produced the sketches as an (in the event) unsuccessful sales pitch. Either way they are all we have to reconstruct what might have been Hogarth's intention for the finished work.

The setting is the first distinctive aspect of Hogarth's image: for this is a landscape garden, recognised as the place where the new English ideas could be most clearly expressed, with a temple (without statue or dedication) almost upstaging the enthroned royal couple. In the National Gallery of Ireland version the garden is replaced with a palatial arcade and the throne acquires a splendid baldachin topped by a crown. The present sketch seems to depict the monarch on one side, his heir on the other (leaning on an armless throne), in a setting dominated by a temple to some unnamed concept. If this is where Hogarth's intention led then the missing concept would seem to be the idea of liberty and a constitution.

Hogarth also introduces some interest with the subsidiary characters: the two younger Princesses teach a dog to shake hands, a common detail in Dutch painting symbolising children's 'aptitude to learn'. The enigmatic episode to the right (exactly replicated in the National Gallery of Ireland oil sketch) centres around a stone garden ornament of four sides, with four shallow dishes set above four allegorical figures. Someone has placed fruit or flowers in three of the dishes, which Frederick, Prince of Wales, shows to his three eldest sisters, Anne, Amelia and Caroline. Are we to assume that in choosing a fruit or flower they will choose a virtue particularly appropriate to themselves – a kind of win-win Judgement of Paris? DS-T

246 & 247

JOHN WOOTTON (1682?–1764)

The Death of the Stag signed and dated 1737

The Return from the Chase signed and dated 1737

Oil on canvas, 198.1 × 200.8 cm; 199.0 × 192.6 cm
RCIN 407815 and RCIN 407814

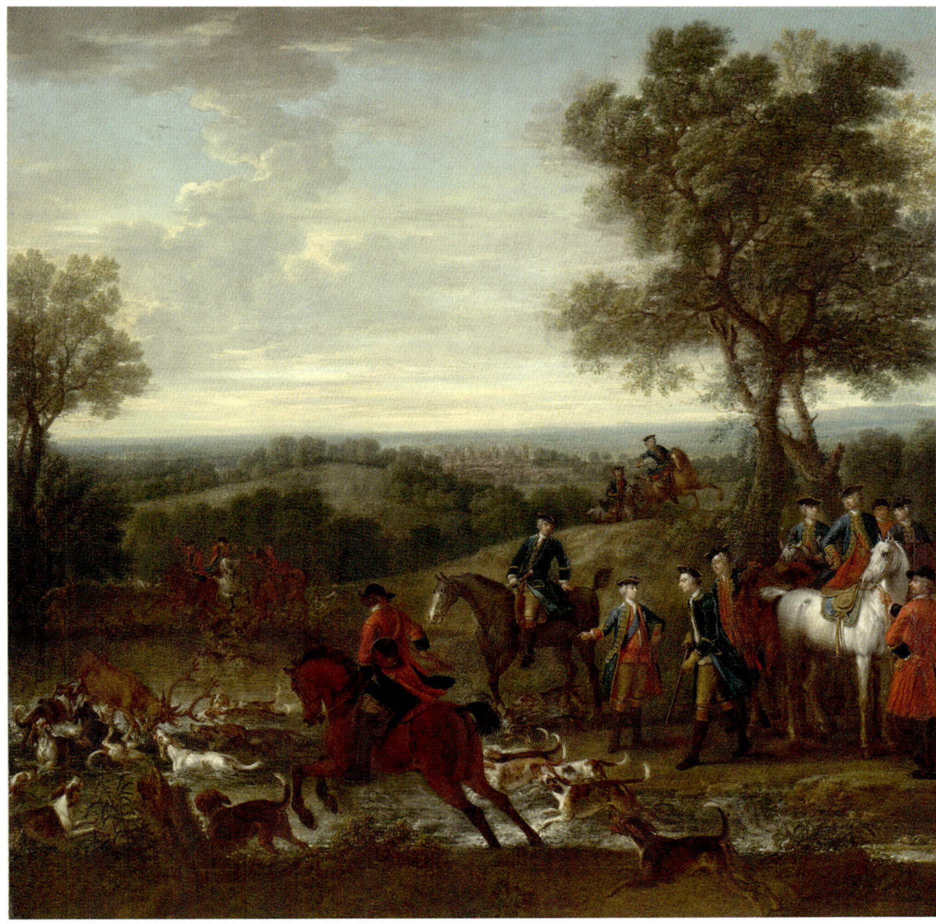

PROVENANCE First recorded on either side of the fire in the Gallery at Kew

LITERATURE Millar 1963, pp. 180–1, nos 545–6

In 1738 Frederick, Prince of Wales, paid 200 guineas for this pair of hunting scenes, both of which are dated to a year earlier; the frames may be those for which John Boson was paid £24 5s in 1739. The paintings were recorded in 1763 by William Chambers hanging in the Gallery at the White House at Kew. Chambers also lists the courtiers accompanying the Prince, who himself can be seen wearing his own hunting uniform standing slightly to the right of centre at the *Death* and riding centrally in a red coat and Garter star in the *Return*.[72] Based on Chambers's names the following courtiers would seem to appear in both scenes: Colonel Bloodworth, Master of the Prince's Horse, dressed in the uniform of a Ranger of the Great Park (on horseback in the centre of the *Death*, hat in hand below the castle in the *Return*); John Spencer (1708–46), Ranger of Windsor Great Park, in uniform (moving to put the stag out of its misery in the first scene and standing by a horse at the extreme left of the second); Charles Spencer, 3rd Duke of Marlborough (1706–58), Lord Steward of the Prince's Household (in the group to the right of the *Death* and on horseback, directly facing the viewer, in the *Return*). The *Death* also includes in the group to the right Charles Calvert, Lord Baltimore (1699–1751), Gentleman of the Bedchamber; William Villiers, 3rd Earl of Jersey (d. 1769), Lord of the Bedchamber; and Henry Herbert, 1st Earl of Powis (1703–72), Treasurer to the Prince. The *Return* includes Colonel Schutz,

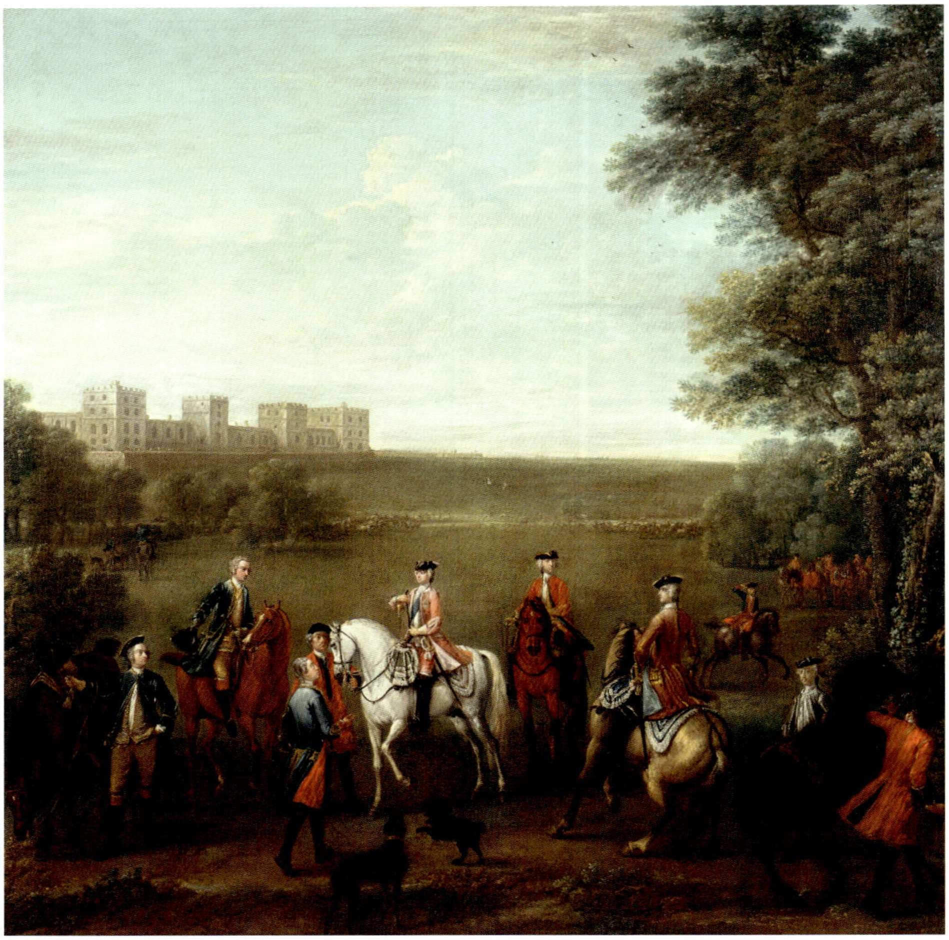

Master of the Robes (walking towards the Prince); Henry Brydges, 2nd Duke of Chandos (1708–71), Lord of the Bedchamber (seen in profile on horseback) and Lord Boston (1707–75), Chamberlain to the Princess of Wales (behind his horse).

The events take place in the Great Park at Windsor with the town and castle visible in the background of the first scene, while the *Return* takes place in the Home Park immediately below the west front of the castle. This is a traditional style of royal hunt within dedicated parkland at the invitation of the owner (in this case the Prince), with stag as quarry. The business of the hunt is left to the liveried huntsmen, who manage the dogs and the horn-players, whose job it is to announce by different calls the exact progress of the hunt. The Prince's companions, who wear a different livery – of companions rather than of servants – essentially follow the hunt in a series of gallops and gatherings. The *Death* (no. 246) expresses the contrast of function (possibly unconsciously) by placing all the huntsmen who participate on the left side of the composition, around a swirl of animals, and all the courtiers as onlookers on the right. Such hunts were happening throughout Europe, including Hanover, as can be seen by the anonymous painting of a royal hunt at Goehrde (fig. 14). This day spent in stately rides and parties to the accompaniment of many harmonious horn calls (of a type which feature in innumerable musical compositions of the era) could not be more different from the new fashion for fox-hunting invented at this time. In 1753 Hugo Meynell (1735–1808) took over as Master of Fox Hounds of the Quorn and developed the concept of the membership hunt which chased foxes across open land, variously owned and not specifically set aside for the purpose.[73] Meynell was a Member of Parliament and the nature of this association (a loosely aristocratic club) and this activity (a dare-devil chase across hedges and ditches, to the accompaniment of a single shrill bugle note) perfectly expressed the modern face of Georgian society. DS-T

248–50

JOHN WOOTTON (1682?–1764)

Landscape with a View of Park Place, Henley-on-Thames *c.*1742

Oil on canvas, 89.5 × 153.5 cm
RCIN 406898

Landscape with a View of Henley-on-Thames *c.*1742

Oil on canvas, 101.0 × 156.0 cm
RCIN 400507

Landscape with a Distant View of Henley-on-Thames *c.*1742

Oil on canvas, 101.0 × 153.2 cm
RCIN 400505

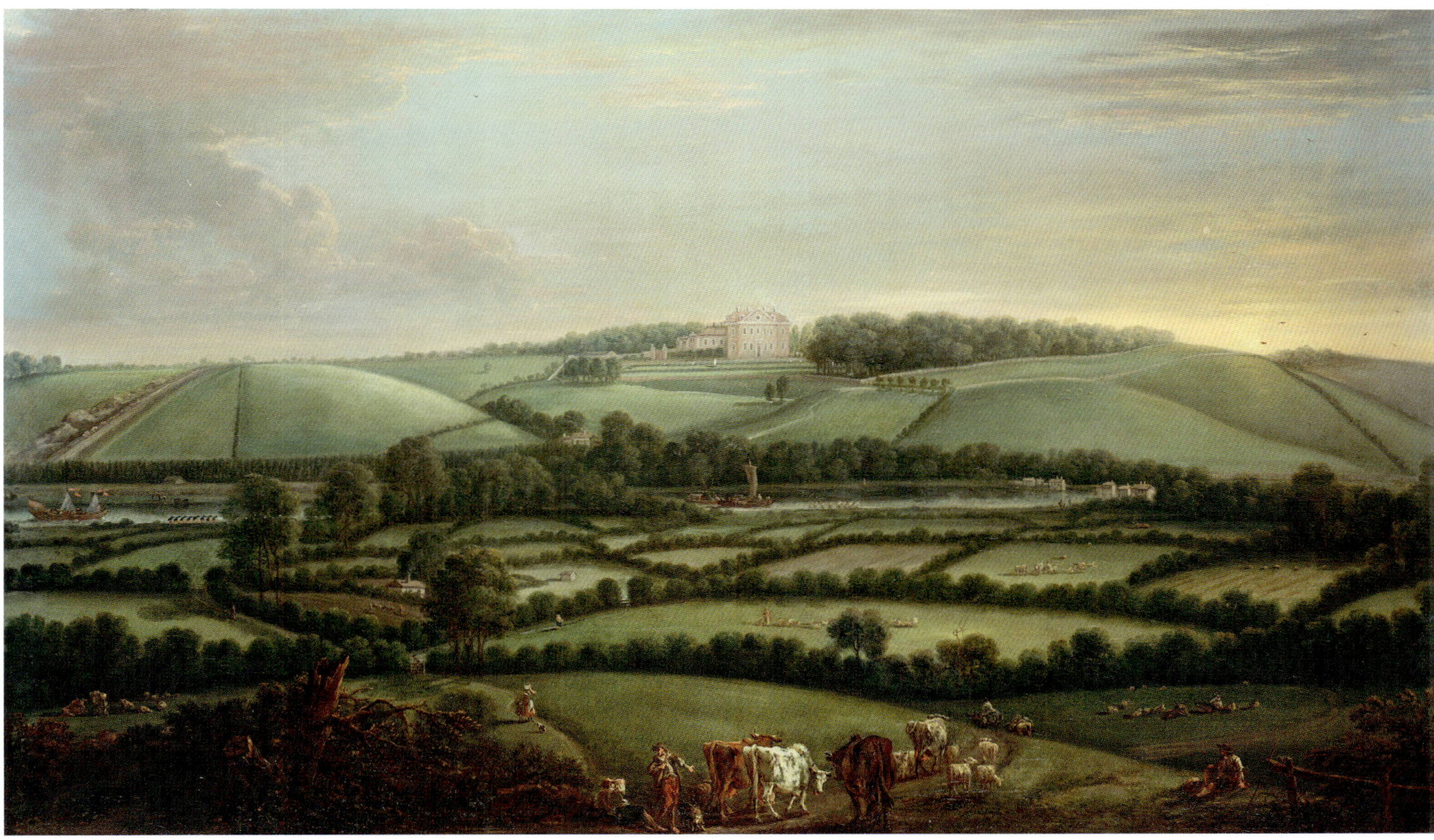

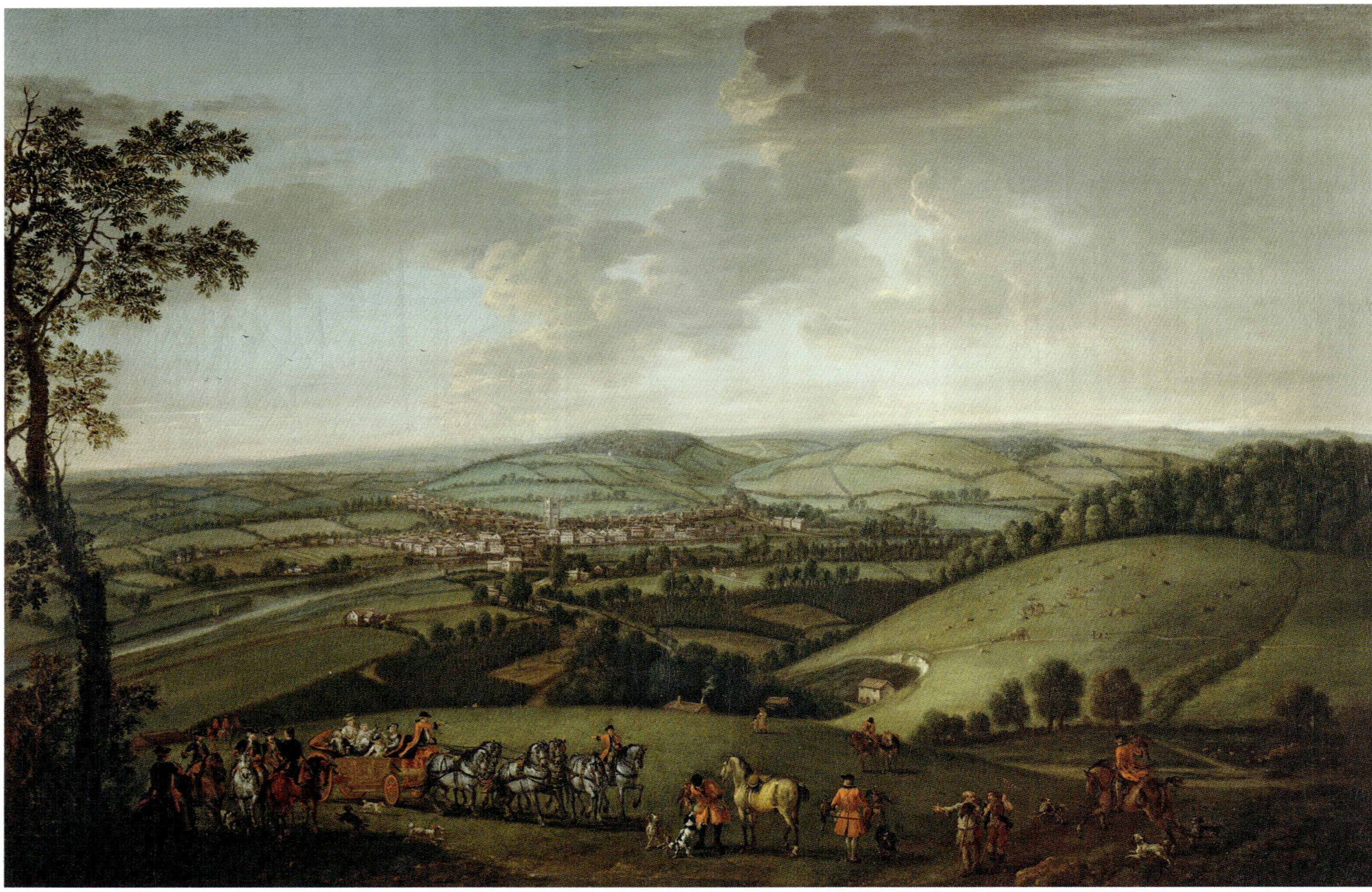

PROVENANCE Painted for Lady Archibald Hamilton; presumably acquired by Frederick, Prince of Wales; seen by Horace Walpole in Buckingham Palace; at Kensington Palace in 1818

LITERATURE Millar 1963, p. 181, nos 548–50; Harris 1979, nos 244–6; *Paintings from Windsor Castle* 1990, pp. 120–3, nos 53–4

In 1719 Lord Archibald Hamilton bought Park Place near Henley and built a country house, replaced in the late nineteenth century with the one which still survives. Lady Hamilton's friend, Frederick, Prince of Wales, acquired or leased the original house in 1738.[74] According to Horace Walpole these three landscapes were painted for Lady Hamilton when she had Park Place 'or after she sold it to the late Prince, who is walking with the Princess and her in one of them'.[75] Given the probable date of the paintings (1742–3) the latter is the most likely option.

It is not immediately obvious how these three should be grouped, but the painting of the house itself (no. 248) is clearly of primary significance. This shows the view from the Henley-Reading road with Henley just off to the left and the house directly opposite. This image seems to suggest a progress from the near (west) side of the river with its working farmland – rustic foreground figures, cottages, patchwork of small fields, hedgerows and paths – past the working river to the wide sweeping park and woodland surrounding the country house itself. The presence of the royal owner is suggested by the royal barge pulled by eight men in livery at the extreme left.

The vantage point for the other two paintings comes from the east side of the river, no. 249 lying directly in front of the house and no. 250 perhaps over the brow of the hill to the right of no. 248. They show the same elements in inverse order – with the foreground dominated by the elegant company of royalty, nobility and liveried servants progressing through the parkland laid out for this purpose. In no. 250 a noble walking party, attended by mounted grooms, is led by the Prince of Wales, with children playing with dogs before them; in no. 249, which perhaps reflects the view from the

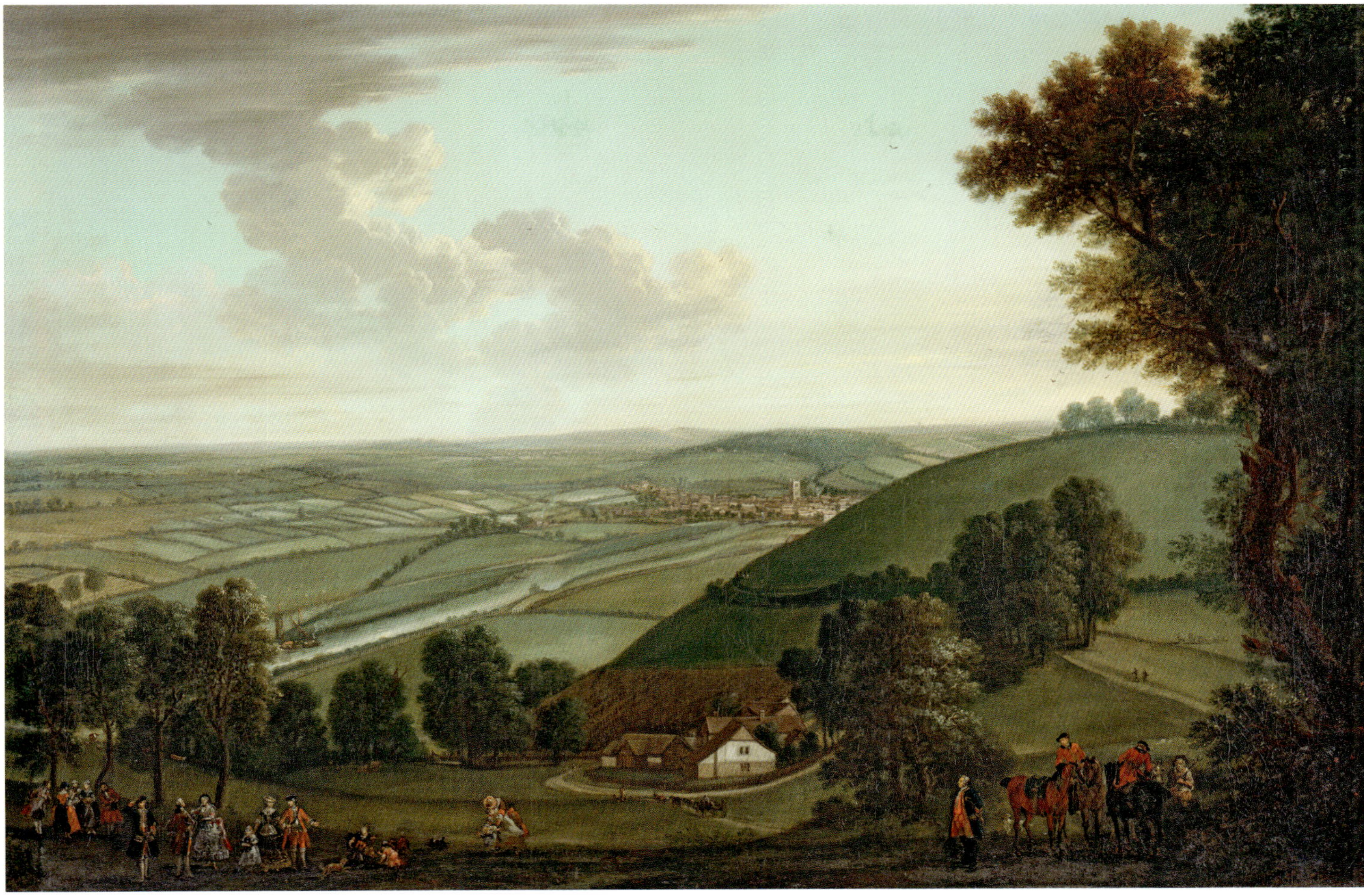

house itself, the Prince and his guests ride out, on horseback or in a carriage, attended by huntsmen with hawks. For all this now familiar conversational elegance, considerable emphasis is given to the working landscape within and beyond the park, with cottages and haymakers on the near side, as well as the obviously farmed landscape on the far side of the river. Henley was an important trading town at this date, which had also featured in several Jan Siberechts landscapes; one of 1698 (River and Rowing Museum, Henley) makes a similar play of the labour and prosperity of land and river. The Hanoverians were not adventurous travellers; Henley may have seemed to them like the gateway to the dark interior of their new lands. DS-T

251

BRITISH SCHOOL

***St James's Park and the Mall** c.1745*

Oil on canvas, 103.5 × 138.5 cm,
RCIN 405954

PROVENANCE Acquired by George IV

LITERATURE Millar 1963, pp. 195–6, no. 617; *Manners and Morals* 1987, p. 132, no. 114; *Queen's Pictures* 1994, p. 74, no. 20; *Conversation Piece* 2009, pp. 94–5, no. 18

George IV acquired this painting as a Hogarth, valued it at a handsome 100 guineas, and hung it in the Blue Velvet Closet at Carlton House amongst some of his finest Dutch masters, a rare honour for an English painting.[76] The painting is clearly inspired by Hogarth but is certainly not by him; various names have been suggested but no consensus has formed round any them, nor is it certainly by a British as opposed to a visiting artist. It can be confidently dated by the presence of Hawksmoor's towers added to Westminster Abbey in 1745 and of Frederick, Prince of Wales, who died in 1751.

St James's Park was laid out by Charles II in the formal French style with avenues of trees and a long rectangular canal (see no. 21 and fig. 6). This scene is viewed looking back towards Whitehall Palace down the oblique avenue of trees. To the right is the quadruple avenue of trees with a wide aperture down the middle, containing a surface of crushed cockle-shells. This area was originally created (though at this date no longer used) for a game resembling croquet, called pall-mall, which was why this road is still called 'the Mall'.

This royal park was open to the public and became a favourite resort. Of the Mall in particular a Swiss visitor wrote, 'Fashionable society comes to walk here in summer, from 7 to 10 in the evening, and in winter from 1 to 3 o'clock ... a great number attend, some to see, other to be seen, and others to seek their fortunes; for many priestesses of Venus are to be found here, some of them magnificently attired, all on the look-out to catch some inexperienced young fellow'.[77] Strictly speaking the artist here shows the sun low in the east, but seems to have intended the scene as a summer's evening, with the foliage merging with the dark of the sky. Other accounts tell of cows and deer in the fields around the park, while a visitor in 1765 especially appreciated the availability of udder-fresh cow's milk, seen here served in the lower left-hand corner apparently 'with all the cleanliness peculiar to the English, in little mugs at a penny a mug'.[78] All visitors stressed the way in which at St James's and other fashionable resorts in the capital there was an 'astonishing medley' of people of 'all ranks and conditions.[79]

This painting is a rare example, outside Hogarth's oeuvre, of a comic painting, describing modern life with a mixture of satire and enjoyment, as in the novels of Fielding and Sterne. The satire resides in affected high life and crude low life: on the one hand foppish postures and salutations of exaggerated insincerity; on the other women adjusting garters; men and dogs answering the call; couples kissing and chased off in the background when caught at worse. The enjoyment resides in people-watching, the sense that London is full of the glamour and variety of the world – soldiers and sailors of various nations, priests of various faiths, 'priestesses of Venus' and members of the beau monde, dressed in the height of fashion. This group is dominated by the clearly identifiable figure of Frederick, Prince of Wales, speaking to a fellow Garter Knight in the centre of the composition. Immediately behind us in this painting lies Carlton House, the Prince's London residence with its splendid private garden (fig. 8). He has left it in order to rub shoulders with his future subjects and the world in general. Frederick's mother, Queen Caroline, despised such habits of ingratiation: 'popularity always makes me sick', she is reported to have said in 1736, 'but Fretz's popularity makes me vomit.'[80] It clearly does not have this effect on the artist, for whatever the satirical elements of this scene they do not to implicate this effortlessly courteous principal figure. DS-T

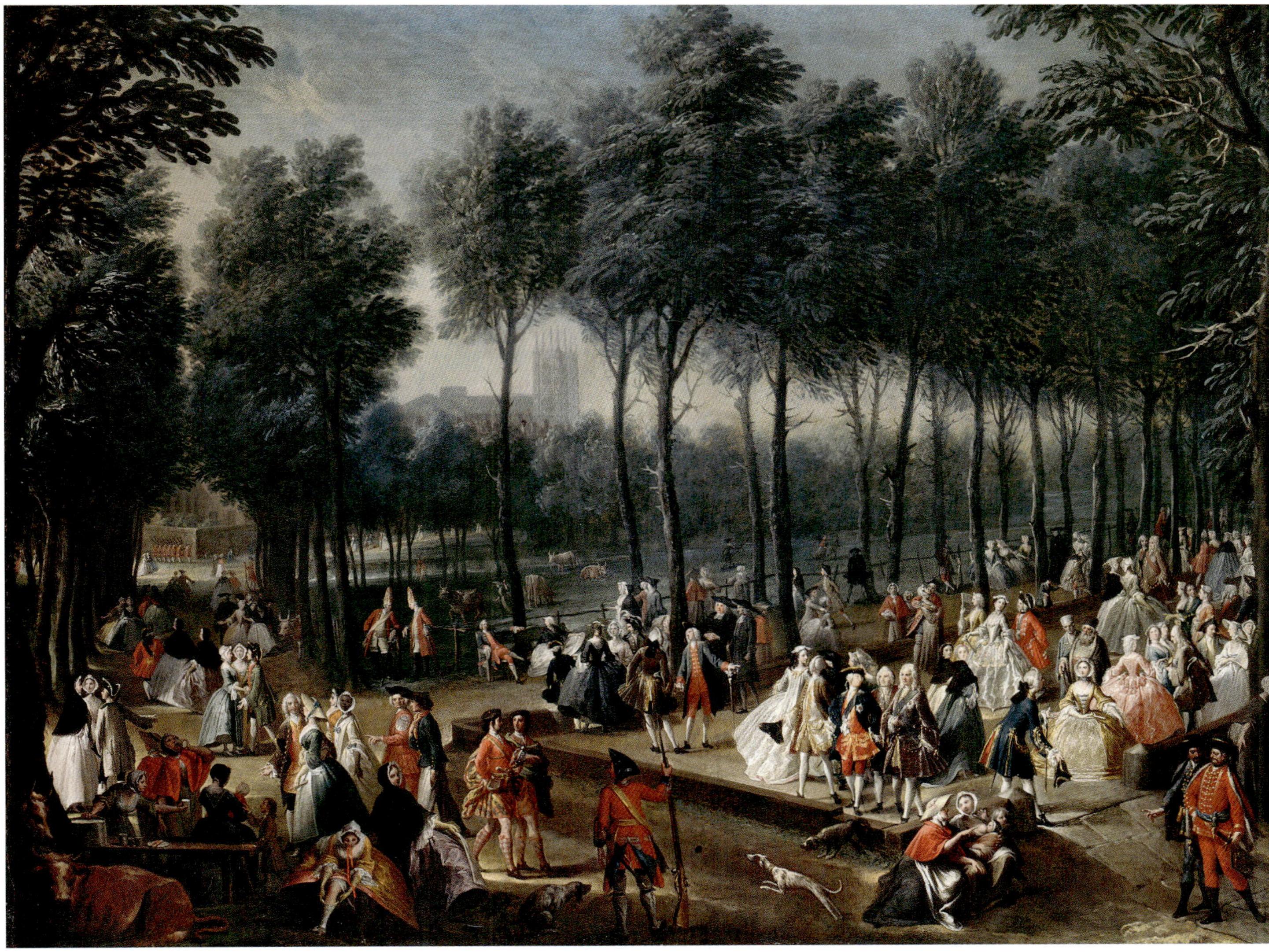

Hogarth's *Bad Taste of the Town* (no. 76) is one of many documents to the close association made at this time between all the 'sister arts'. As it happens in this print Hogarth considers that they are all going to hell in the same handcart. There are evidently two distinct errors – the pretentious exclusivity of the Royal Academy and Italian opera, and the crass popularism of Heidegger's pantomimes and masquerades. Meanwhile the art of Nature, represented by Congreve, Shakespeare, Otway and Dryden, is wheeled off for scrap paper. Masquerades were public fancy-dress parties of the kind which increasingly took place at London's public pleasure gardens, Vauxhall (fig.93) and Ranelagh.[81] For Hogarth and other moralists such places and such entertainments were an opportunity for licentiousness.[82] Pantomimes were very ragged assemblages of scenes, songs and acrobatics, with spectacular displays of stage machinery. Italian opera was at this date delivered by a Royal Academy of Music and Hogarth evidently connected it with the risk of a Royal Academy of Painting, which might be, as here, walled off from the outside world and dedicated to the adulation of William Kent. Hogarth clearly saw a conspiracy delivering all high-brow impostures – Palladian architecture, academic painting, Old Master dealing and Italian opera.

It is true that Italian opera belonged with these theoretically rigid Continental forms, which the English met on their Grand Tours and imported with enthusiasm, with little thought to their relation to any native genius or traditions. The librettos of Italian operas were cast in the mode of classical drama, seen in English tragedies of the period which have not stood the test of time. The stories, whether classical or biblical, tended to involve a small cast of noble characters in some dilemma of love and honour. What movement there is in the plot takes place during

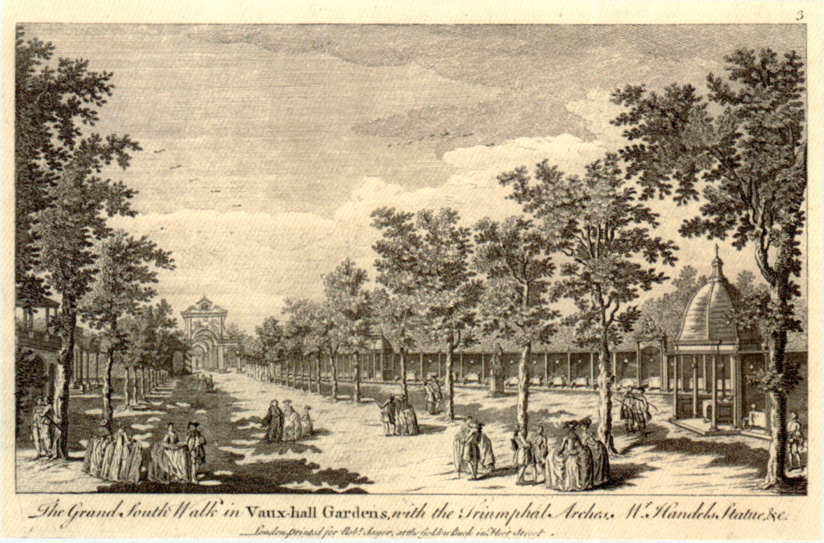

FIG. 93
Robert Sayer
The Grand South Walk in Vauxhall Gardens, c.1750–5
British Museum, London

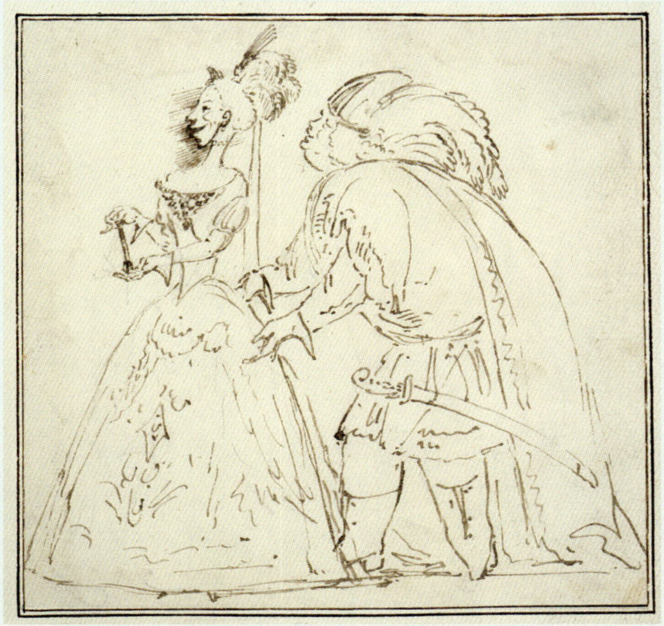

FIG. 94
Marco Ricci
Caricature of two opera singers, possibly Senesino and Faustina
Pen and ink
RCIN 907290

recitatives, allowing plenty of space for the characters to reflect upon their states of mind in long *da capo* arias, so called because they conclude with a undeveloped repetition of the opening melody 'from the top' (*da capo*). This formula allowed composers to explore single identified emotional states – jealousy, rage, love – in the same schematic way that painters had been taught to depict them.[83] There is a parallel with the affecting single figures of Guido Reni or Carlo Maratta – the dying Cleopatras or ecstatic St Cecilias (see no. 126). This formula allowed singers to demonstrate their technical mastery unimpeded by dramatic business. The most prized voices were those of castrati, who by all accounts could produce notes in the soprano range of astonishing force, purity and flexibility. These castrati were paid extravagant sums and were described as gangling and corpulent at the same time, with a distinctive wobbling gait, ridiculed in Marco Ricci's caricatures (fig. 94) and Hogarth's print (no. 76). The composers, musicians, singers and impresarios of opera in London were generally Continental and the works were performed in Italian. No wonder for Hogarth the whole venture was an unnatural foreign assault upon the rich and gullible.

Before we allow Hogarth the last word it should be remembered that the leading composer of Italian opera in London at this date was the greatest ever to work in England, George Frideric Handel (1685–1759).[84] For all their stilted conventions his Italian operas are still firmly in the repertoire. German visitors, who could be as enthusiastic as the French in running down English culture for never producing 'any great painters, sculptors, engravers, musicians or other artists of outstanding merit', often illustrated their point with the examples of their fellow countrymen, Kneller and Handel.[85] While Kneller's presence had nothing to do with the new German dynasty, Handel's had everything to do with it and represents the Hanoverians' most valuable cultural import. Having studied in Germany and Italy, in June 1710 Handel accepted a post as *Kapellmeister* at the court in Hanover and in the same year came to England, where he settled in 1712. Though he worked for Queen Anne and subsequently found himself dismissed from his Hanoverian post in 1713, recent research has suggested that he remained in favour with George I and may even have been sent as an emissary at a time when members of the new dynasty were forbidden from visiting their future kingdom.[86] Upon his succession George I continued the pension granted to Handel by Queen Anne; he and other members of the royal family employed him in many positions, including as music teacher to the highly talented Princess Anne.[87] The list of works commissioned by or in honour of members of the royal family includes the music for the coronation of George II, still used for this purpose, the Dettingen *Te Deum*, the *Water Music*, the *Music for the Royal Fireworks* (celebrating the Peace of Aix-la-Chapelle of 1749), and at least two oratorios written to commemorate William, Duke of Cumberland's victory at Culloden, *Judas*

Maccabeus and *Joshua*. George I was also a key supporter of the Royal Academy of Music, which delivered the Italian opera seasons at the King's Theatre, Haymarket, from its foundation in 1719 until its collapse amid financial difficulties in 1728/9. The next generations of the royal family were also significant patrons of composers of opera and of opera houses.[88]

Even with this level of commitment there was a fundamental difference between opera in London and in Hanover, and in every other European capital. Opera in Hanover was private and princely: it took place in a theatre within the Leineschloss (built in 1689; see above, Chapter II), staffed by members of the Elector's household and at the behest of the Elector (though members of the public were permitted to attend). Whoever may have backed Handel's London productions they took place in a venue – the King's Theatre, Haymarket – as public then as it is has been ever since. Handel's popularity with this public received its most astonishing testament in 1738, when Jonathan Tyers erected a statue of the composer in his pleasure gardens at Vauxhall (figs 93 and 95), where his *Water Music* (1717) and *Music for the Royal Fireworks* (1749) were first performed, and where incidentally Frederick, Prince of Wales, as ground landlord, had his own supper box.[89] Roubiliac's marble, the only such monument to a living composer in Europe's history, is typical of the early Georgian image of creative genius in its amiable informality, suggesting that someone of Handel's gifts may take up Apollo's lyre along with their cap and slippers and produce a masterpiece by their fireside. The terracotta model for Roubiliac's statue (Fitzwilliam Museum, Cambridge) belonged to Thomas Hudson, whose portrait of the composer (no. 253) has something of the same informality.[90]

This episode of commemoration conveys the honour paid to music, but we should also remember the help it offered to the visual arts. Handel was one of many geniuses of the period who were depicted often (in prints as well as paintings and sculpture) and whose celebrity contributed hugely to the fame of their depicters. It was by painting the actor Theophilus Cibber (1703–58) in 1737 that Van Loo first made his name in England, though he had 'no importunate invitations from any Nobleman'.[91] Alexander Pope (1688–1744) was another tireless promoter of the visual arts, and was painted and sculpted more than any English poet before or since. Voltaire remarked approvingly of the number of portraits of Pope he saw in aristocratic houses.[92] Pope fulfilled his side of the bargain by inviting the artist to share his stage. In his *Epistle to Charles Jervas* he suggested that the acts of writing and painting could only benefit each other as could the comparable appreciation of the classics and the Old Masters:

> Smit with the love of sister-arts we came,
> And met congenial, mingling flame with flame;
> Like friendly colours found them both unite,
> And each from each contract new strength and light.
> (Pope, *Epistle to Mr Jervas*, 1715)

The greatest champion of sister arts in the mid-eighteenth century was David Garrick (no. 257). Everyone agreed that he revolutionised the stage: Richard Cumberland later described the moment he first beheld 'little Garrick, then young and light and alive in every muscle and in every feature, came bounding on the stage

.... Heavens, what a transition! It seemed as if a whole century had been stepped over in the changing of a single scene.'[93] Garrick loved to be painted and drew the best out of artists, incidentally providing exactly the celebrity which ensured that this best was not lost to the world. Garrick also provides a link between the age of Hogarth and that of Zoffany, Reynolds and Gainsborough, all three of whom were his friends and immortalisers.

The mention of Garrick brings us back to Hogarth's *Bad Taste of the Town* (no. 76), which laments the neglect of the classics of the English theatre. Hogarth was probably exaggerating in 1724, but after Garrick's sensational debut as Richard III at Lincoln's Inn Fields in 1742, which launched a career developing the cult of Shakespeare, nobody could complain that serious theatre was neglected. However, even in this venture Garrick borrowed much of the popularism of Heidegger's pantomimes: he substantially re-wrote Shakespeare's plays; after the conclusion of a tragedy, however draining, a farce would be presented to round off the evening. Theatrical managers at this date (along with novelists and print-makers) were anxious to explain that they served a patron as exacting as any monarch – the public.[94] However, it was generally believed that, given the chance and within reason, this many-headed patron would choose works of art and literature which were natural, sensible and virtuous. Contemporaries would have seen the transition in Handel's work from extravagant operas in Italian to sensible oratorios in English as a manifestation of this principle.[95] These ideas are most aptly expressed in the Prologue which Samuel Johnson wrote for David Garrick at the opening in 1747 of the Theatre Royal, Drury Lane, under his management – another example of fellow artists sticking up for each other. After a brief history of the English stage, from Shakespeare's 'unresisted passion' to the obscenity of the Restoration era, Johnson comes to the present age, where he sees the same choice between high-brow tedium and popular trash as Hogarth:

Then crush'd by rules, and weaken'd as refin'd,
For years the pow'r of tragedy declin'd;
From bard, to bard, the frigid caution crept,
Till Declamation roar'd, while Passion slept.
Yet still did Virtue deign the stage to tread,
Philosophy remain'd though Nature fled.
But forc'd at length her ancient reign to quit,
She saw great Faustus lay the ghost of wit:
Exulting folly hail'd the joyous day,
And pantomime, and song, confirm'd her sway
(Samuel Johnson, *Prologue at the Opening of the Theatre-Royal, Drury Lane*, 1747, 4th Stanza)

For the future Garrick and Johnson promise nothing, instead they tell the audience that the matter is in their hands:

Then prompt no more the follies you decry,
As tyrants doom their tools of guilt to die;
'Tis yours this night to bid the reign commence
Of rescu'd Nature, and reviving Sense;
To chase the charms of Sound, the pomp of Show,
For useful Mirth and salutary Woe;
Bid scenic Virtue form the rising age,
And Truth diffuse her radiance from the stage
(Samuel Johnson, *Prologue at the Opening of the Theatre-Royal, Drury Lane*, 1747, 7th and final Stanza).

252

LOUIS-FRANÇOIS ROUBILIAC (1702–1762)

George Frideric Handel (1685–1759) 1739

Marble, 71 cm high
Incised at the back: *HANDEL / AETATIS SUAE- 54× / MDCCXXXIX* and on the vertical edge on the proper right side of the support: *ROUBILIAC.F.*
RCIN 35255

PROVENANCE Given by the sitter to John Christopher Smith (1683–1763); his son, also John Christopher Smith (1712–1795); by whom given to George III, *c.*1772–4

LITERATURE Esdaile 1928, pp. 51, pl. 10; Whinney 1964, pp. 103–4; Kerslake 1977, vol. I, pp. 127, 130; vol. II, fig. 321.

Roubiliac made four portraits of Handel, of which the first, the famous statue of the seated figure with Apollo's lyre, commissioned for Vauxhall Gardens and completed in 1738 (fig. 95), established the sculptor's reputation. The last was the composer's monument in Westminster Abbey.

Roubiliac's marble portraits present us with the persona of the inspired genius rather than the prosperous gentleman who appears in contemporary paintings by artists such as Thomas Hudson (see no. 253). In this bust, Handel is dressed well but in indoor garb of the kind worn in private, perhaps even while composing. The lop-sided, tasselled cap, carved with miraculous softness, and the disarranged coat are hallmarks of a sculptor intent on displaying every illusionistic trick, but also suggest a man careless of the material world, his mind on higher things. It should be remembered that the bust was intended for the composer's own home, not for any official setting.

By the time he sat for the portrait, Handel had enjoyed considerable success in London. He had composed more than forty operas and the great series of oratorios on Old Testament themes was already well under way. Having provided the music for George II's coronation in 1727, at the time he was sitting for this bust he was at work on the funeral anthem for Queen Caroline. In the previous year, 1737, he had suffered some kind of disorder or 'palsy', perhaps a minor stroke, arising no doubt in part from overwork, and he had been obliged to retire first to Tunbridge and then Aix-la-Chapelle to take the waters. Despite this, and the onset of blindness in the last ten years of his life, the bust depicts Handel with many of his greatest successes, including *Messiah*, still ahead of him.

John Christopher Smith the Younger, son of Handel's manager and principal copyist, was one of the composer's favourite pupils. Smith the Younger inherited many of Handel's possessions that had first been left to his father. They included '... my large Harpsichord, my little House Organ, my Musick Books, and five hundred Pounds sterl:' and probably also this bust. Smith the Younger was appointed music teacher to Princess Augusta, widow of Frederick, Prince of Wales. According to one source, 'The Princess ... derived so much satisfaction and improvement from his instructions, that she was often heard to say, that in her advanced age, she had acquired a new taste for music'.[96] It was Smith the Younger who presented the bust, the harpsichord and the 'Musick Books' (the composer's manuscripts) to George III. These last were presented to the British Library by HM The Queen in 1957. JM

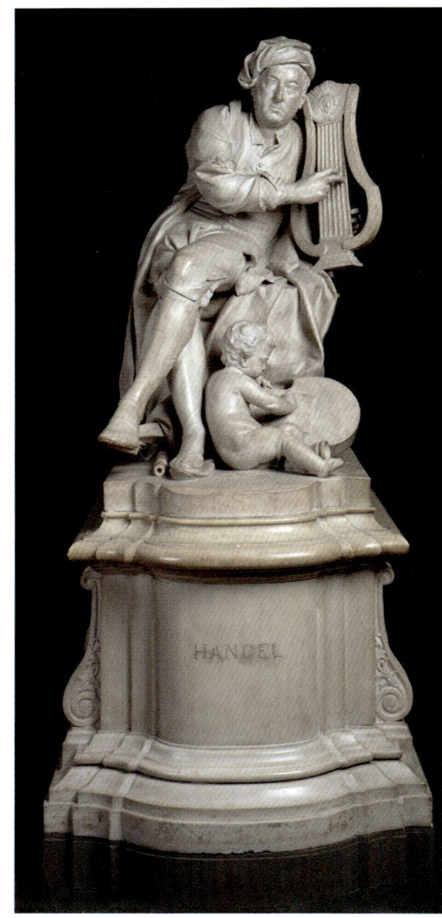

FIG. 95
Louis François Roubiliac
George Frederick Handel, 1738
Marble
Victoria and Albert Museum

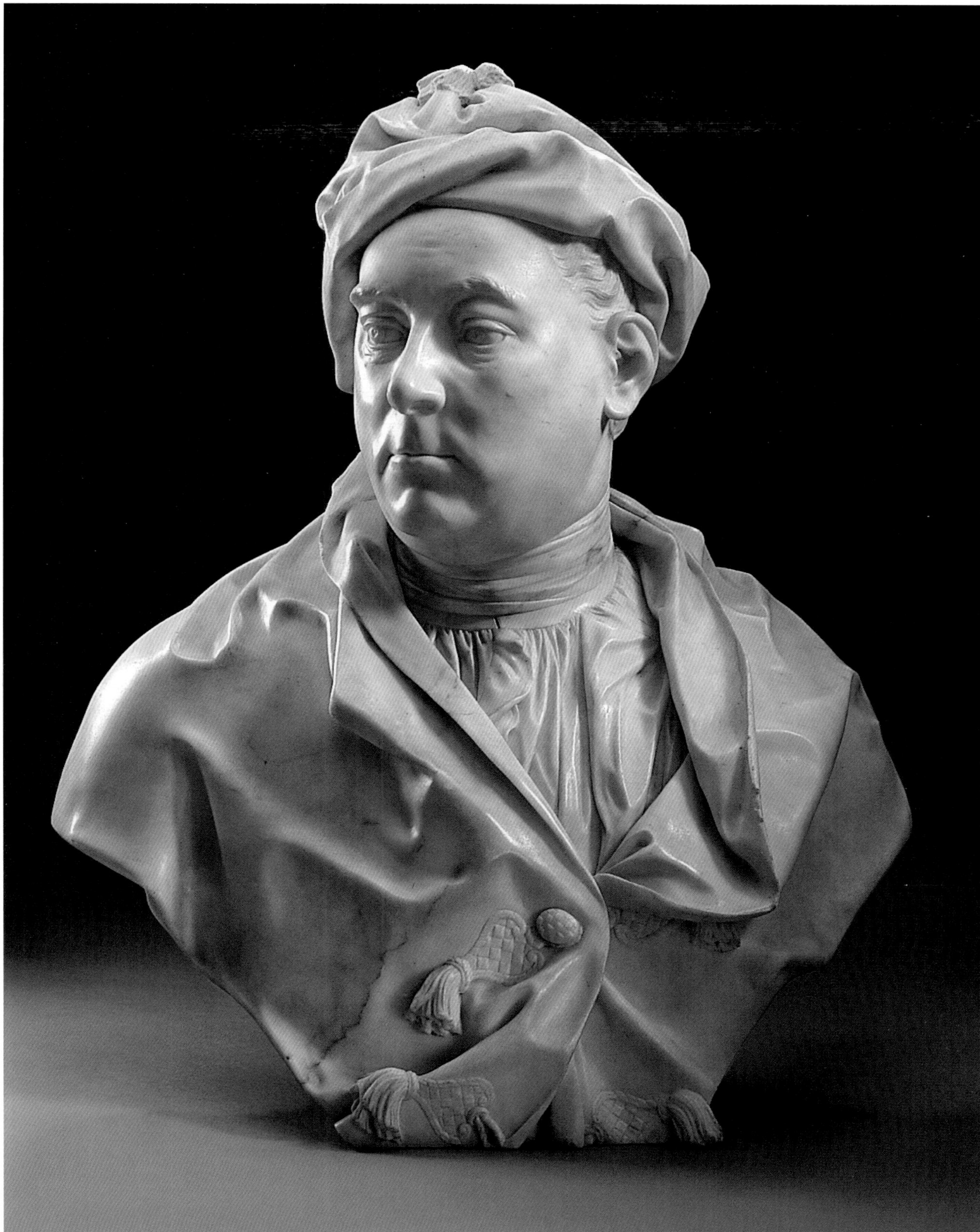

253

THOMAS HUDSON (1701–1779)

George Frideric Handel (1685–1759) 1756

Oil on canvas, 76.8 × 63.8 cm
RCIN 400960

PROVENANCE First recorded in the Royal Collection during the reign of Queen Victoria

LITERATURE Millar 1963, pp. 183–4, no. 556

This is an oil sketch for Hudson's famous full-length portrait of 1756, painted for Handel's librettist, Charles Jennens, and now in the National Portrait Gallery. Though the sketch represents a near definitive state of the composition there were subsequent changes: the grand staircase in the background to the right was replaced by a balcony open to the sky; the pile of books under the table (suggesting a profusion of previous compositions) was covered by the curtain; a cane was put in the composers right hand (not as inappropriate as one might think, as conductors beat time with their canes at this date); the score open on the table became *Messiah*, the most famous work upon which Jennens and Handel collaborated. DS-T

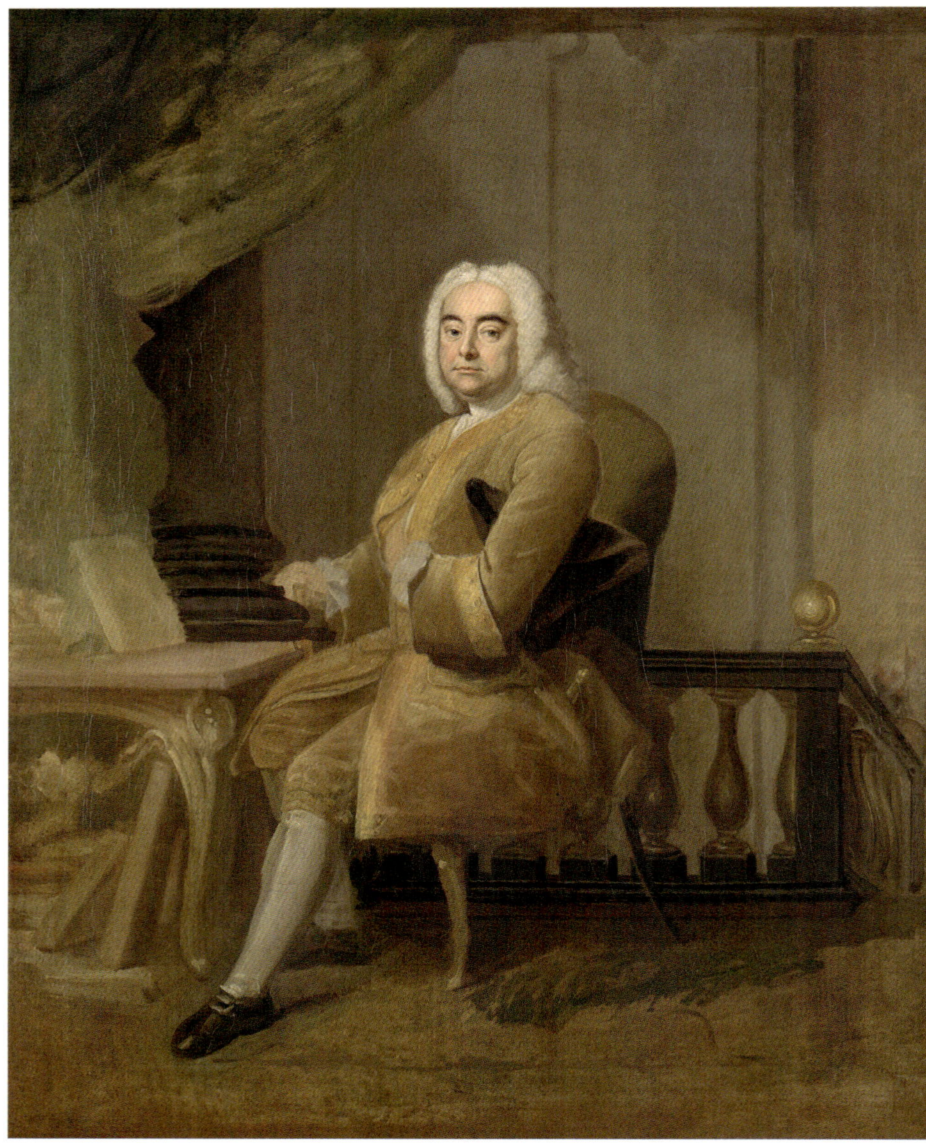

Photograph pre-conservation

254

BURKAT SHUDI (1702–1773)

Two-manual harpsichord 1740

Burr-walnut veneered case with walnut cross-banding, oak, pine, 96.0 × 95.0 × 246.0 cm
Signed in pen on the upper name batten *Burkat Shudi fecit Londini*; inscribed in pencil on the upper surface of the lever of the lowest note of the lower manual *94 f 1740*
RCIN 11896

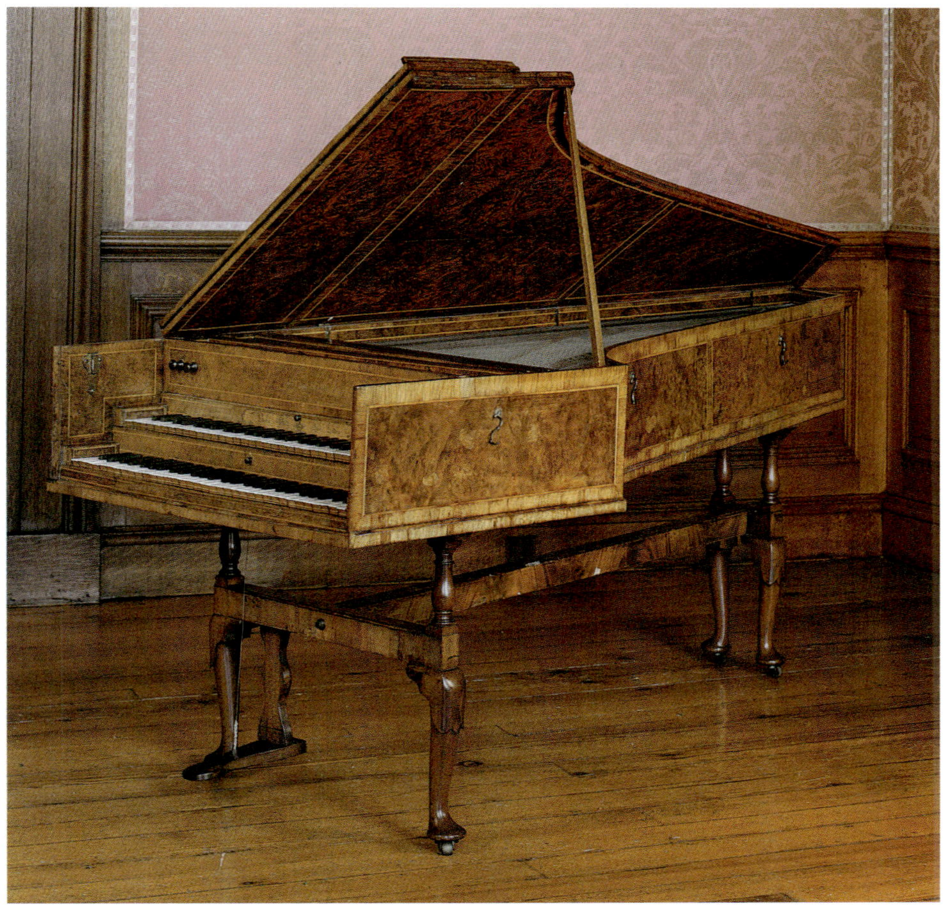

PROVENANCE Possibly commissioned or purchased by Frederick, Prince of Wales; first recorded at Buckingham Palace in 1825.

LITERATURE Dale 1913, p. 40; Boalch 1995, p. 614; *George III and Queen Charlotte* 2004, no. 262

Frederick, Prince of Wales, was an accomplished musician, playing several instruments, and patronising composers such as Thomas Arne, from whom he commissioned the English masque *Alfred*. Musical instruments are listed in the various houses in which he lived and a harpsichord with a black and gilt-painted case features in the painting by Mercier (no. 255) showing Frederick playing the cello, accompanied by two of his sisters, Anne and Caroline, while a third sister, Amelia, reads a volume of Milton's poems. The Swiss-born Burkat Tschudi arrived in London in 1718 and anglicised his name to Shudi. By 1729 he was making considerable numbers of instruments. His son-in-law John Broadwood carried on the business after his death.

This instrument was originally much larger: it was formerly a claviorgan, part-harpischord, part-chamber organ, of which today only the harpsichord element survives. Shudi is known to have made such instruments in partnership with the organ-builder John Snetzler (1710–85).

Shudi was employed by Frederick, Prince of Wales: in 1751 he was paid for 'Tuning of Harpsichord at Carlton House & Spinnet at Leicester House, [and] Kew' as well as providing the previous year 'a new Spinnet for Lady Augusta £8 10s' and 'a New Spinnett for HRH Prince George £8 10s'.[97] RB

255

PHILIPPE MERCIER (1689–1760)

'The Music Party': Frederick, Prince of Wales, with his Three Eldest Sisters 1733

Oil on canvas, 79.4 × 57.8 cm
RCIN 402414

PROVENANCE Probably painted for Frederick, Prince of Wales

LITERATURE Millar 1963, pp. 174–5, no. 522; *Conversation Piece* 2009, pp. 82–4, no. 15

Philippe Mercier was a pupil of Antoine Pesne (see no. 240) in Berlin; he came to England in 1716 and, from 1729, served as painter and librarian to Frederick, Prince of Wales.[98] This is usually considered to be the prototype of this composition, which exists in several versions, the others (National Trust and National Portrait Gallery) set out of doors with the Dutch House at Kew in the background. The interior here appears to be real, as it includes recognisable works – a mirror supplied in 1733 by Benjamin Goodison (no. 110) and *Endymion* by Giovanni Antonio Pellegrini (RCIN 405481, one of the same set as nos 233–4) – but it and the view out of the window have not yet been convincingly identified.

The Prince of Wales is shown playing the cello in what is probably a sonata, with his sisters providing the accompaniment - Princess Anne (1709–59) at the harpsichord and Princess Caroline (1713–57) on the mandora (a type of lute). The work in question would probably be scored for keyboard and cello, which would allow Princess Caroline to add chords or double the higher notes of the harpsichord. The important thing from the point of view of the scene is that the Prince of Wales is the soloist rather than the provider of a continuo bass accompaniment. The youngest sibling, Princess Amelia (1711–86), sits leaning back on the harpsichord case, looks up from a volume of Milton's poems and listens with pleasure to the music, as does the adoring spaniel.

The activity here (music) and the genre of painting used to depict it (the conversation piece) both work to create the impression that dynastic relationships are in some way natural. Frederick is given prominence not because he is the heir, but because be is the most talented musician; the duties of accompaniment and the deference of willing audience are not insisted upon but cheerfully granted. Music provides the appropriate metaphors of loving harmony and merited, understated pre-eminence.

However carefully the principle of primogeniture is articulated this image must have struck contemporaries as daringly informal and domestic. The setting is elegant but not luxurious; in the other versions (NPG and National Trust) the Dutch House at Kew provides a surprisingly old-fashioned background to the idyllic glade in which the musicians sit. In all versions the princesses are dressed, in Aileen Ribeiro's words, 'with an almost bourgeois sobriety', with 'closed gowns' fastened across the bodice, covering a white linen kerchief round the neck and wearing plain caps with lappets, one pinned up, one hanging down and the last fastened under the chin.[99]

Cultivation of the arts was generally considered to be an important part of royal and aristocratic life, but there was a distinction between activities like poetry, which were suitable for all classes, and those, like instrumental performance, which should be left to the hired professional. Exception to this rule was made for ladies, for whom music was a desirable accomplishment: Princess Anne, for example, was an excellent keyboard player, who had been taught by Handel.[100] On the other hand in 1737 Lord Hervey affected to be shocked by the sight of Frederick 'seated close to an open window of his apartment [at Kensington Palace], with his violoncello between his legs, singing French and Italian songs to his own playing for an hour or two together, whilst his audience was composed of all the underling servants and rabble of the palace.'[101] DS-T

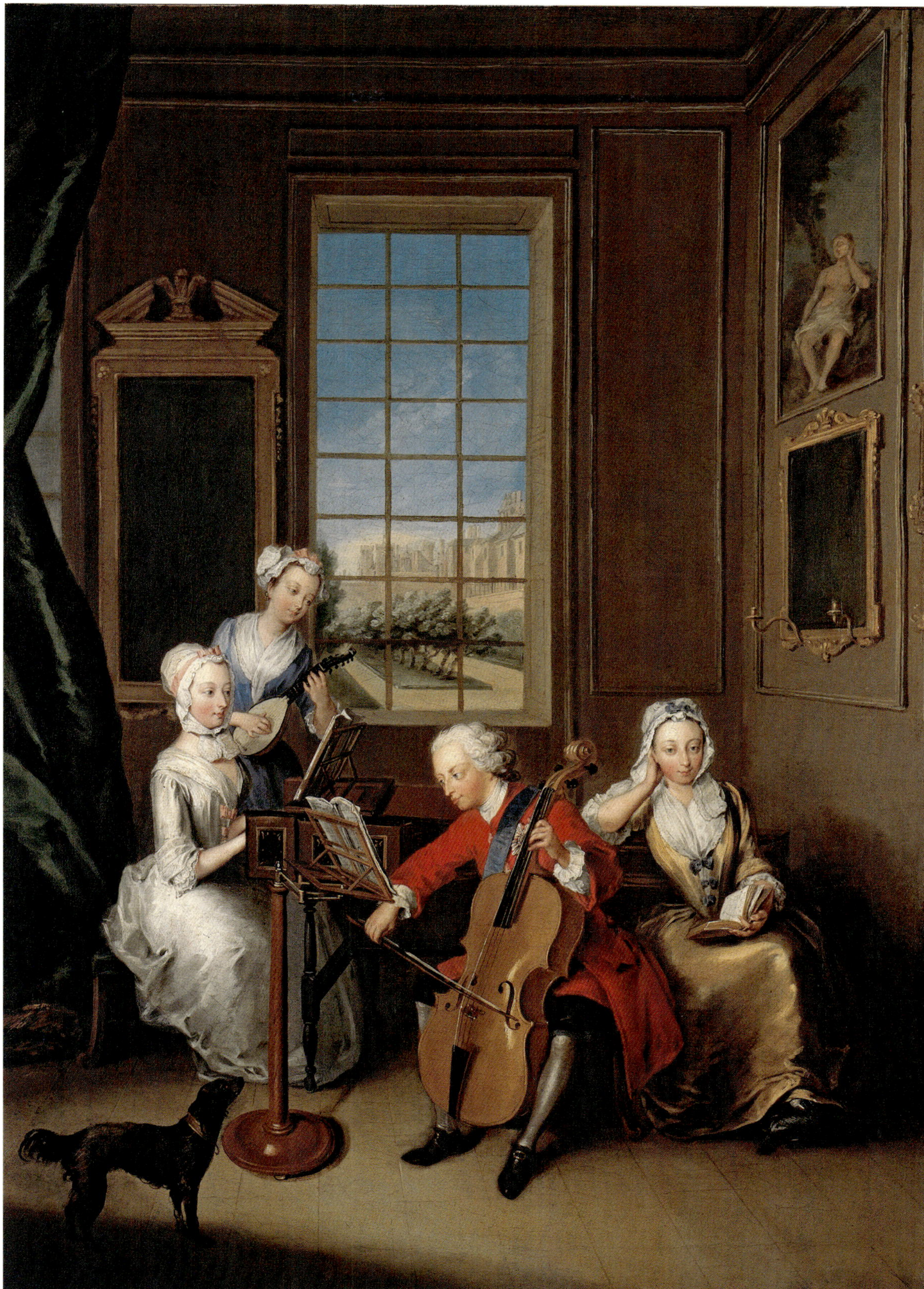

256

JACOPO AMIGONI (1682–1752)

Frederick, Prince of Wales (1707–1751), with a Copy of Pope's Translation of Homer ;1735–6

Oil on canvas, 128.3 × 106.7 cm
RCIN 401500

PROVENANCE Painted for George Bubb Dodington; acquired for the Royal Collection by George IV; first recorded at Carlton House in 1816

LITERATURE Millar 1963, pp. 175–6, no. 526

Alexander Pope is one of the defining intellects of the early Georgian era, through his poetry, friendships and garden design. In one respect he was most unsuited to this role: as a Catholic Tory, his early work, in particular *Windsor-Forest* (1713), celebrated the golden age of the reign of Queen Anne. The Hanoverian succession turned him into a virulent satirist attacking the dullness of the monarchs, referred to by him as Dunce the first and Dunce the second (*The Dunciad*, 1728, I, l. 6), and the demonic and unscrupulous energy of those advanced by their arrival. His only good words were for those driven into opposition or retirement by the new regime, men who exhibited every virtue of good sense, good heart, learning and taste.[102] He clearly counted himself among their number, creating his own retreat in his famous villa at Twickenham, complete with poet's grotto and pioneering informal garden.

In other respects Pope was part of the 'World' (in particular the commercial world) which he so abhorred: he bought his aristocratic independence through sales. The copyright act of 1711 provided the legal playing field and his translations of Homer's *Iliad* and *Odyssey* were the works which made him rich.[103] Pope knew the sort of people who might be literary patrons but he did not need them as such. Or, as he put it: 'Above a patron, though I condescend/ Sometimes to call a minister my friend' (*Epistle to Dr Arbuthnot*, 1735, ll. 265–6). He condescended also to call a member of the royal family his friend, after Frederick, Prince of Wales, had visited him at Twickenham in 1729.[104] In 1735 the Prince gave Pope a set of marble portraits by Scheemakers for his library, depicting Spenser, Shakespeare, Milton and Dryden.[105] This episode (and a desire to emulate his mother's Hermitage) was probably the inspiration for Frederick's 1750 scheme to create a Parnassus in the gardens at Kew with 40 busts of geniuses, ancient and modern, competing in pairs – Shakespeare versus Aeschylus, Newton versus Archimedes, and so on.[106]

This portrait was painted for the Prince's friend George Bubb Dodington (1691–1762), who paid forty guineas for it in 1736. The commission came soon after Dodington, in 1734, had fallen out of favour so dramatically that the Prince blocked up the gate which gave access from Dodington's house in Pall Mall to the garden of Carlton House (fig. 8).[107] Perhaps intended as a peace offering, the portrait depicts the Prince at the time of his friendship with Alexander Pope and with a copy of his translation of Homer in his hand. It is conceived in the informal manner associated with portraits of Pope; the unbuttoned cuffs are particularly prominent. Flying above the sitter and introduced by a wave of his left hand are two allegorical cherubs, Poetry crowned with laurel and bearing a lyre and Eternity holding a snake biting its tail. It seems to be Eternity who flies up in homage, offering his attribute as a prize to Poetry. The cherubs have a light, ironic character typical of the French Rococo and of the 'sylphs', invented by Pope for his *Rape of the Lock* of 1714, a mock-heroic depiction of fashionable idleness. The mythological depiction of inspiration recalls Andrea Sacchi's *Apollo crowning the Singer Pasqualini* (Metropolitan Museum, New York), a copy of which (by Joseph Goupy) hung in Princess Augusta's Dressing Room at Leicester House.[108]

In any other country at this date such a portrait would celebrate a patron. Frederick presents himself simply as a royal admirer of poetry. He has attributes of rank – the crown on the table and the Garter sash. Perhaps more importantly he wears a breastplate, indicating that he still hopes to achieve in the battlefield the type of fame which it is the business of Homers to make permanent.

Amigoni's Venetian experience seems to inform this portrait, with its thickly applied paint, brilliantly fluttering patterns of drapery and light pastel colours reminiscent of the work of Rosalba Carriera. Amigoni is the sort of artist Pope himself should have patronised, with the confidence to translate poetic ideas into successful compositions, as he had presumably done in a lost ceiling for John Rich at the Covent Garden theatre depicting the Muses crowning Shakespeare with laurels.[109] The allegorical business has a particular softness and delicacy, the way in which the figures blend into the background being an effect learned from pastels drawn on to grey paper. DS-T

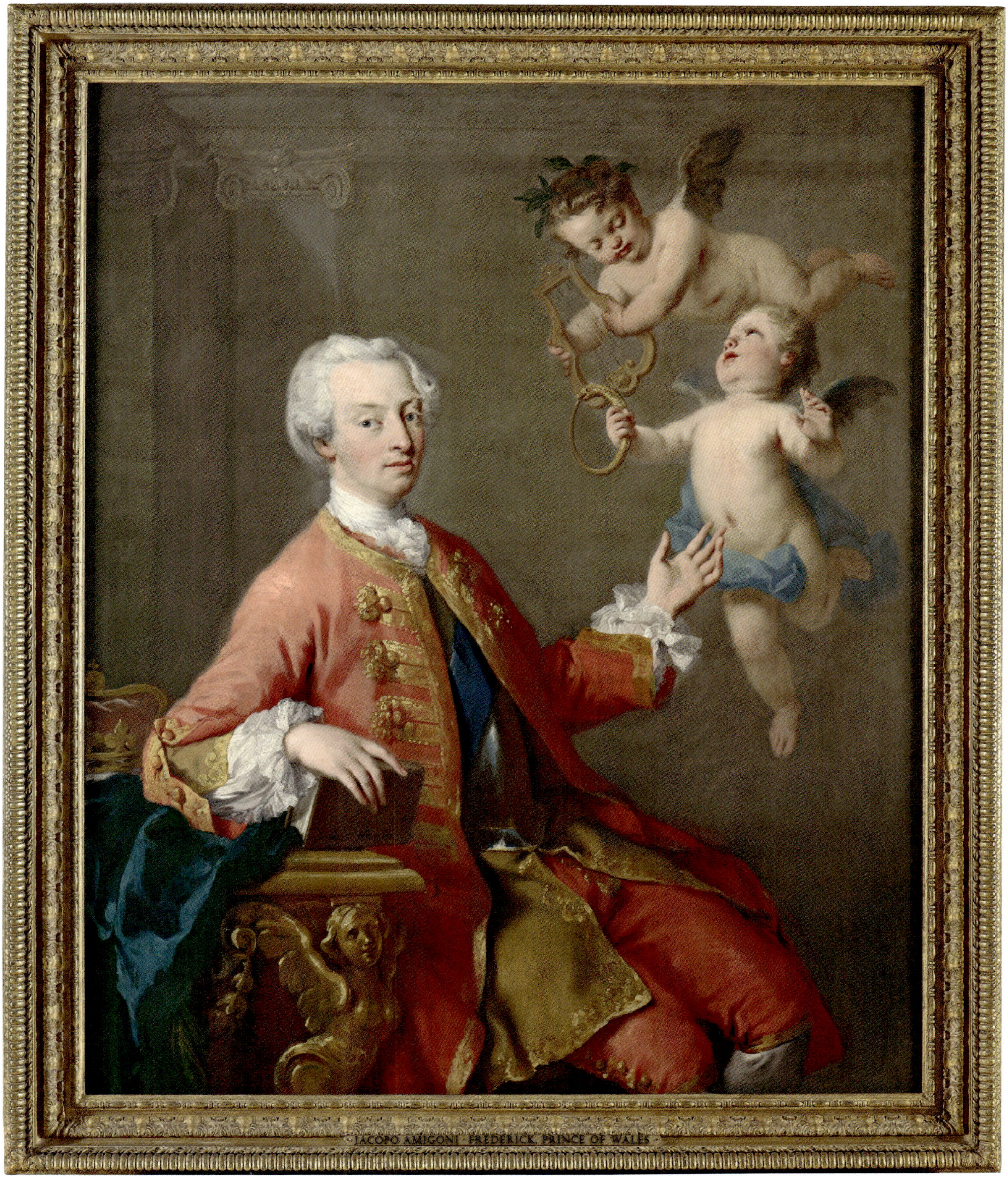
· JACOPO AMIGONI · FREDERICK, PRINCE OF WALES ·

257

WILLIAM HOGARTH (1697–1764)

David Garrick (1717–1779) and his wife, Eva-Maria Veigel (1724–1822) 1757–64

Oil on canvas, 132.6 × 104.2 cm
Signed and dated: *W Hogarth / [p]inxt 1757*, and inscribed (on the book above the desk) *SHAKE/SPEARE* and (on the paper on which Garrick writes) *The Prologue to/ Taste*
RCIN 405682

PROVENANCE Painted for the sitter but refused; given by Hogarth's widow to Garrick's, sold by her in 1823 and purchased soon after by George IV

LITERATURE Millar 1963, p. 185, no. 560; *Royal Treasures* 2002, p. 90, no. 18; *Hogarth* 2006, p. 224, no. 117

George IV clearly valued this painting, literally at 150 guineas and more generally as part of the inauguration hang of the Grand Corridor in Windsor Castle.[110] It continues to resonate as one of the most important images of Georgian Britain.

As a social document the portrait shows the arrival of what might now be called a celebrity or media couple. Actor-managers had made fortunes before the eighteenth century: Shakespeare retired comfortably and Edward Alleyn magnificently. David Garrick (1717–79) at the time of this portrait (in his fortieth year) had already combined financial success as an actor-manager – which had enabled him to buy a Thames-side villa at Hampton in 1753 – with international celebrity.[111] His success in part derived from his ability to present himself as Shakespeare's personal champion, which is why in this portrait he sits upon a holy relic of Bardolatry – the chair designed for him by Hogarth and made out of the wood of the mulberry tree supposedly planted by Shakespeare in Stratford (fig. 96).[112] Like many performers of the period Garrick was partly foreign, being born into a Huguenot family who had come to London from Bordeaux in the 1680s. In 1749 he married another sensational import on the London stage, the Viennese dancer Eva-Maria Veigel, known as Violette. The couple are here painted by their friend and Thames Valley neighbour, Hogarth, another self-made, self-promoting celebrity, though this time English to a fault. The sittings did not go as well as these circumstances suggest they should: there is evidence in the paint surface that Hogarth scored through the eyes, presumably to make changes, and the work remained in the artist's possession at his death in 1764.[113]

The iconography of the portrait is also characteristic of the age in its sly use of emblematic language. The scene can be read as a domestic incident: Mrs Garrick steals up behind her husband to snatch his pen as he sits at work on a prelude to *Taste*, Samuel Foote's farce of 1753. She also reminds us of a Muse guiding the pen of the writer. This is exactly what Horace Walpole meant when he commended Hogarth for avoiding the 'trite poverty of allegory. If he had an emblematic thought, he expressed it with wit, rather than by a symbol'.[114] Amigoni's portrait (no. 256) provides a good example of the former; Hogarth's of the latter. Many other signs are used to convey the characteristic image of the creative genius in this period – the smiling expressions, sparkling eyes, the complicit engagement with the audience and the finger pointing upwards towards the ultimate source of all inspiration.[115] There also seems to be some meaning intended in the extremely equal distribution of canvas between man and wife. Like Tolstoy, Hogarth was much concerned with the subject of happy and unhappy marriages. In his *Marriage à-la-Mode* (no. 89) he applied strict justice in allowing each partner an equal share of blame and suffering; in this portrait of a happy marriage he similarly granted equal weighting.[116]

In style this portrait demonstrates Hogarth's acknowledgement that if he wished to represent English painting he had to compete with the French style which dominated European portrait painting at this time. This portrait invites comparison with the work of Antoine Pesne (no. 240), du Pan (no. 241) and Jean-Baptiste Van Loo (fig. 86) as well as Amigoni (no. 256). Hogarth preserves a clumpy robust touch which is peculiarly his own, but in its fresh colour, light tone, fluttering patterns, fine details and gallant mood this is as cosmopolitan and Continental as the two sitters. DS-T

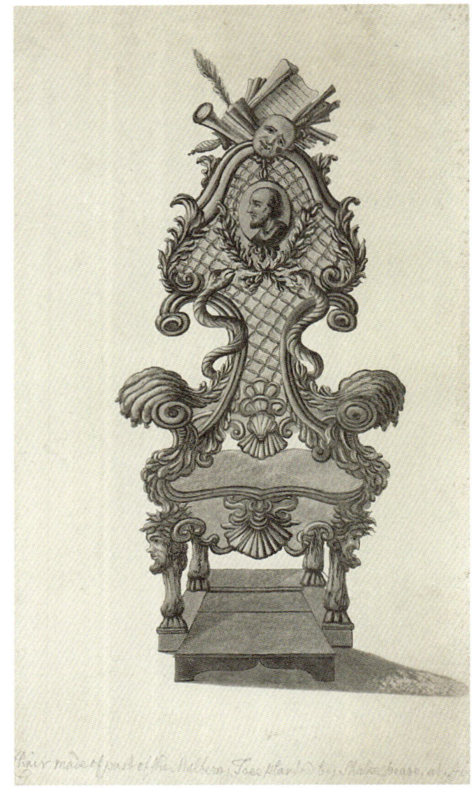

FIG. 96
Anonymous, *Garrick's Chair, made from the wood of the mulberry tree planted by Shakespeare*
Engraving
RCIN 661745

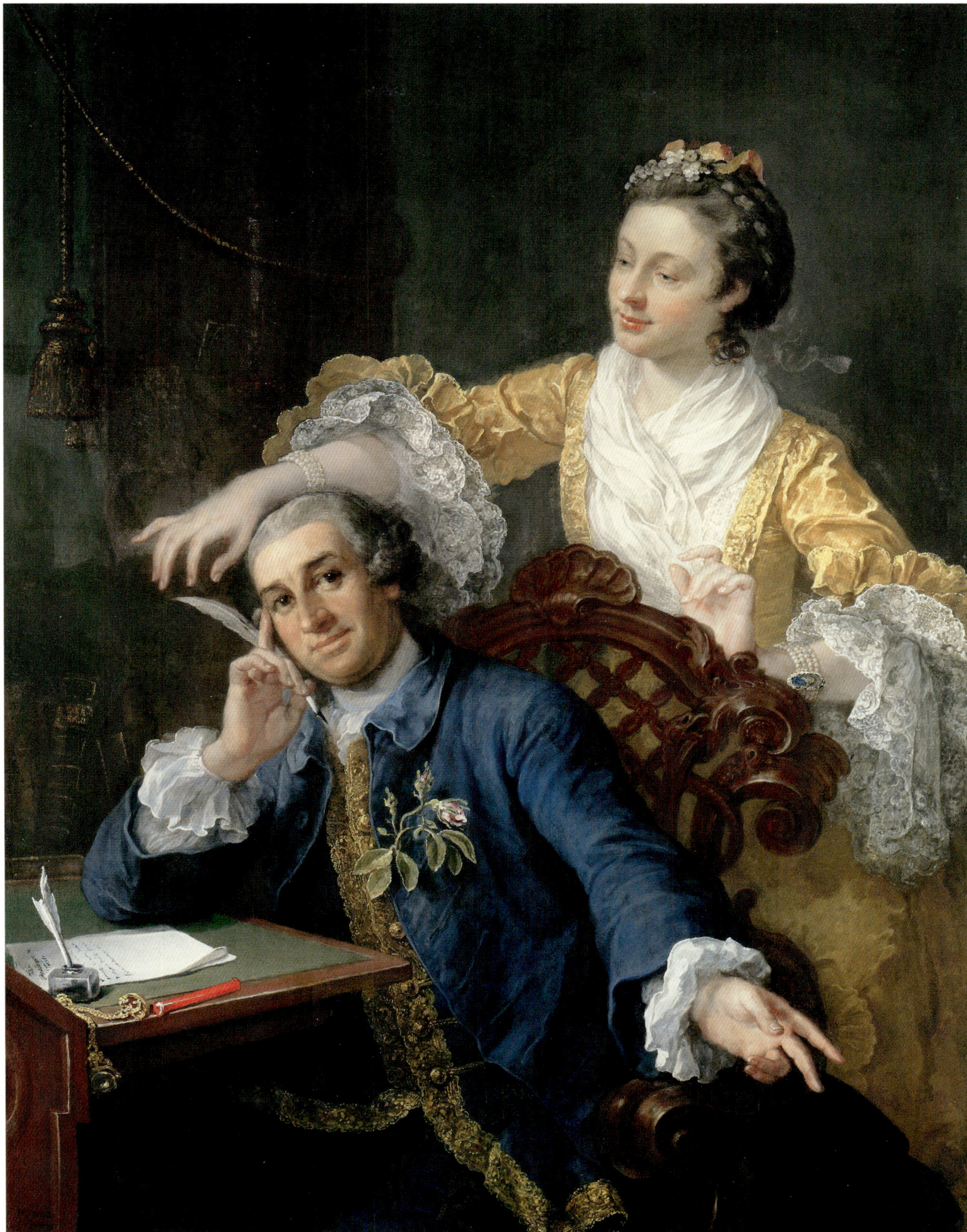

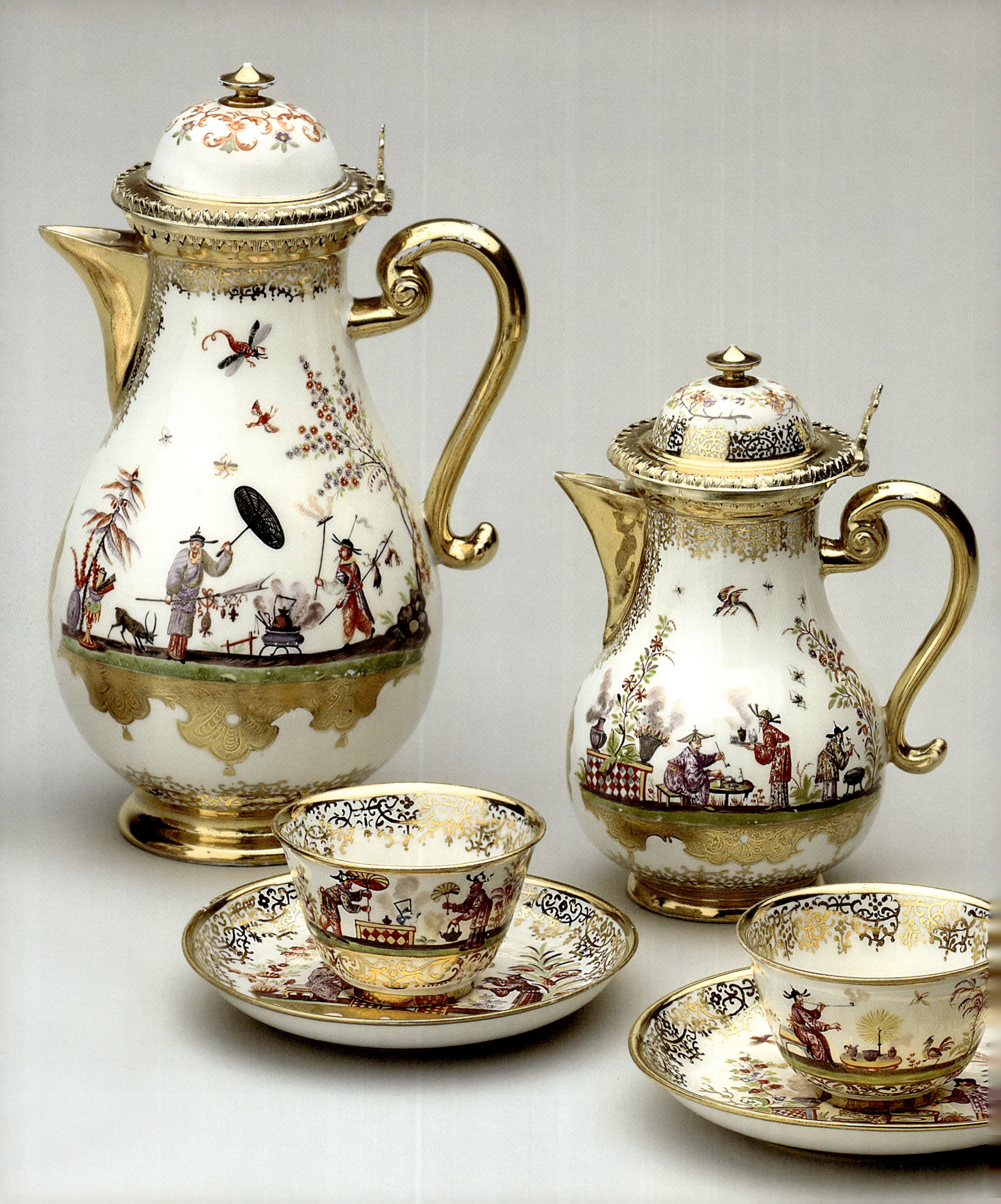

X

The 'Irresistible Tide of Luxury'

KATHRYN JONES

WRITERS DESCRIBING THEIR TOURS through Britain in the early Georgian period emphasised the enterprise and industry of the general population. In Bristol in 1722 John Macky noted, 'here is nothing but Hurry, Carts driving along with Merchandizes, and People running about with cloudy looks and busy Faces'.[1] At the end of the reign of George II, Smollett recorded 'commerce and manufacture flourished again, to such a degree of increase as had never been known in the island'.[2] This was a nation on the eve of industrial revolution; the creation of woollen cloth remained its principal output, but new inventions and industries were emerging. In 1733 John Kay took out a patent for a flying shuttle, and ten years later a factory in Northampton employed five roller spinning machines, invented by Lewis Paul and John Wyatt, each working 50 spindles. Newcomen's steam engine (see p. 301) was put into practice in 1712, and in the 1750s at Coalbrookdale new blast furnaces were created (fig. 97). Daniel Defoe noted in Derby 'a curiosity of a very extraordinary Nature', three Italian engines for making organzine, or warp threads, for silk weaving, 'by which Invention one Hand will twist as much Silk as before could be done by Fifty and that in a much truer and better Manner'.[3] Defoe's *Tour of Great Britain* of 1724–7 made much of the new trade routes and navigable waterways available to transport merchandise around the country, and the rapid growth of the trading and manufacturing cities such as Liverpool, Birmingham, Sheffield, Newcastle and Glasgow. Voltaire observed in 1733 that 'Posterity will very probably be surprised to hear that an island whose only produce is a little lead, tin, fuller's-earth, and coarse wool, should become so powerful by its commerce, as to be able to send, in 1723, three fleets at the same time to three different and far distanced parts of the globe'.[4]

In 1748 George II was called upon to ransom a crew of British prisoners captured by the Barbary corsairs and sold into slavery. To pay off the Dey of Algiers, the King sent broad cloth, brocade, silver tabby, damask, Holland, cambric, 'a gold repeating-watch, four silver watches, twenty pounds of tea, three hundred loaves of sugar, five fusées, five pair of pistols, an escritoire, two clocks and a box of toys'.[5] This list makes clear the exports of which the nation was particularly proud – its cloth, renowned since medieval times, remained at the top of the list, but supplemented by its famed watches, clocks and guns, as well as goods imported by

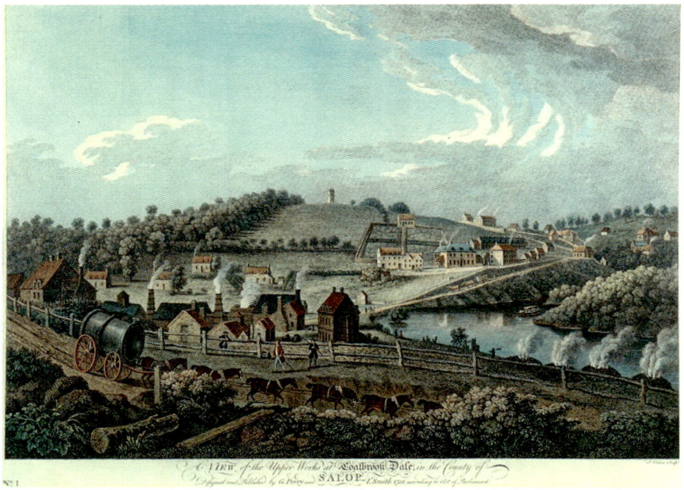

FIG. 97
Published by G. Perry and T. Smith
View of the Upper Works at Coalbrookdale, 1758
Coloured lithograph
Shrewsbury Museums Service

the East India and South Sea companies such as sugar and tea. The 'toys' refer not to children's playthings but to what Johnson's Dictionary defined as 'a thing of more show than use, a petty commodity, a trifle'. Toys were assorted smaller luxury items, the 'sword-hilts, screws, buttons, buckles and innumerable other works ... of great Perfection', which Macky describes being manufactured in and around Birmingham and exported throughout Europe.[6]

The Influence of the Huguenots

Smollett recognised that the growth of commerce and manufacture in England led to 'an irresistible tide of luxury and excess'.[7] The service of the leisured classes with new luxuries drove the commercial activity of the period. This class ensured the success of coffee houses, gaming haunts, pleasure gardens, assembly rooms and theatrical entertainments, and it supported the flourishing trade of newsprint and novels and the manufacture of every sort of fashionable accessory, often in the latest styles from France. This manufacture was heavily stimulated by the influx of Huguenot (Protestant) refugees from France, following the Revocation of the Edict of Nantes in 1685. The Huguenot community in London remained close-knit, even in the second generation, the residents centred around Spitalfields and Soho, standing as godparents for each others' children and employing apprentices and journeymen from each others' families. Hogarth depicted this sober community departing the French church in Soho in his image *Noon* (fig. 98). Among the industries which flourished under their influence were silk weaving, watch-making, gunsmithing, goldsmithing and ivory and wax-carving. Engraving was particularly noted and Vertue describes the engravers who 'With others who have settled here that make quite a different figure in lineal Arts in every branch near equal to any neighbouring nation at present as far as is accounted by those who have been a broad in most places – so it appears by report –'.[8] The London craftsmen showed a measure of resentment at the influx of foreign talent. In 1725 a remonstrance was issued to the Attorney-General asking that goldsmiths who were not freemen of the Goldsmiths' Company should not be allowed to submit plate for assay.

Nevertheless the Huguenots managed on the whole to integrate themselves quietly into British life and little, if any, distinction appears to have been made by their patrons. Seven of the founders of the Bank of England, for example, were Huguenot merchants. John Chardin, the son of a Huguenot jeweller, was created a baronet by George I and was one of Frederick's circle of friends (see no. 309). The King employed the Margas family, originally from Rouen, as subordinate goldsmiths and Lewis Mettayer, of Breton extraction, frequently supplied ambassadorial plate (see no. 271). The Prince of Wales's plate included works by a number of first- and second-generation Huguenots,

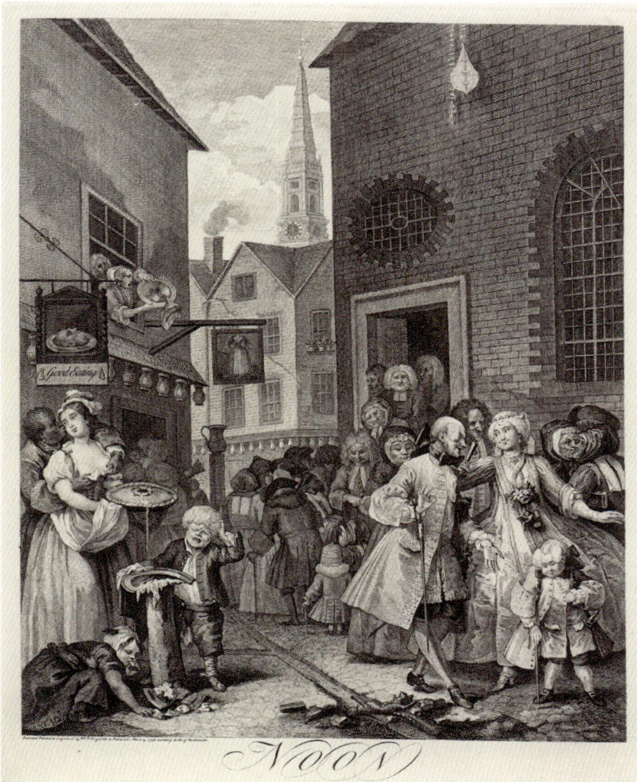

FIG. 98
After William Hogarth
The Four Times of Day: Noon, 1738
Etching
RCIN 811620.b

including Paul Crespin (no. 273), Paul de Lamerie (no. 275), and Lewis Pantin (no. 277), as well as Mary Pantin and Aymé Vedeau (no. 272). As Saussure recorded, the Huguenot craftsmen brought new techniques, new styles and new forms, but these were rapidly absorbed and adapted by their English counterparts:

> The artisans of England are renowned, and justly so, because they finish their works to perfection. They do not invent very much, but they perfect what the French and Germans have invented. They excel in clockmaking, joinery, saddlery and all sorts of works of iron and steel, which they finish better than anywhere else .... It is certain that Louis XIV did them a good turn in chasing the Protestants out of his kingdom. A large number of French artisans sought refuge in this island, where they established several manufactories.[9]

Invention and innovation

The growth of the luxury market was also inspired by the demand for new types of fashionable products. The successful creation of porcelain in Germany in 1709 led to competition throughout the rest of Europe to follow suit. In England a version of white porcelain was demonstrated at the Royal Society in 1743 by a Frenchman, Thomas Briand. When the first director of the Chelsea Porcelain Manufactory, Nicholas Sprimont (1716–71), wrote his *Case of the Undertaker of the Chelsea Manufacture of Porcelain Ware* in *c*.1752, he described meeting a chemist – possibly Briand – with whom he explored the creation of soft-paste porcelain in England.[10] Like all the early British porcelain factories the enterprise was run by craftsmen and entrepreneurs with no royal patronage. Chelsea was supported by Sir Everard Fawkener (see no. 259), while the Bow manufactory was founded by an Irish painter, Thomas Frye, and a glass merchant named Edward Heylyn. A short-lived factory was established in Vauxhall in the 1750s under Nicholas Crisp, a merchant, and the potter John Saunders. Similar ventures sprang up throughout England in the 1750s – at Bristol, Longton in Staffordshire, Worcester, Liverpool and Lowestoft. All were on a small scale and the rate of production was limited and precarious. As Samuel Richardson later noted, the Bow factory failed through 'want of capital in the undertakers or the more prosperous endeavours of similar establishments'.[11] Sprimont's document was a plea to the government to limit the import of foreign porcelains into England so that these newly founded ventures could survive. By contrast, in France Louis XV stepped in to support the factory at Vincennes, and in

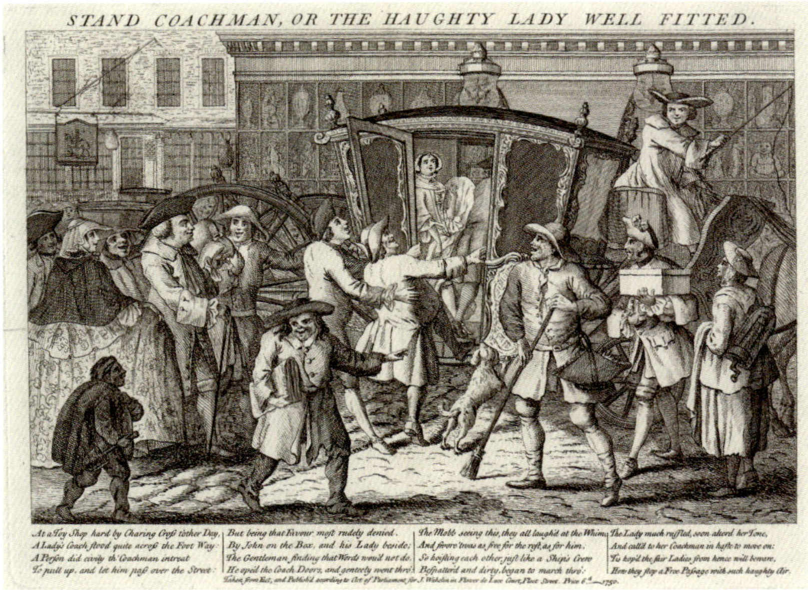

FIG. 99
Published by J. Wakelin
Stand Coachman, or the Haughty Lady well fitted, 1750
Etching
British Museum, London
The toy-shop of Mary Deards and Paul Chevenix on Suffolk Street near Charing Cross is shown in the background

Germany each principality owned and patronised its own factory. Nevertheless Chelsea flourished enough to create its own distinctive style, and it is possible that it received at least one royal commission in this period (no. 258).

Saussure's assessment that English craftsmen were not inventive must surely be disproved by the advances in horology in the period. John Harrison's experiments in marine chronometers took place from the 1730s onwards, while Thomas Grignion improved the cylinder escapement (no. 310). The growth of the sport of shooting throughout the century led to a number of experiments with the form and firing mechanisms of guns – these included innovations such as the rifled barrel, safety catches, barrels that could be rotated, four-barrelled carbines and detachable cartridges for pre-loading shot (nos 278–84). Gun-makers also experimented with materials (no. 284), and with the length and weight of their guns (no. 281).

Snuff-taking in this period became hugely fashionable for both men and women, creating a demand for snuff boxes, made in a variety of exotic and costly materials, and a range of sizes, styles and colours to accessorize the most modish clothes of the day (nos 285, 289, 290, 292–7). It is no coincidence that in the first image of Hogarth's *Marriage à-la-Mode* sequence (no. 89), the foppish young Viscount Squander is shown gazing vacantly into a mirror while taking snuff from a gold box. The creation of each box involved a huge number of craftsmen and specialist chasers, enamellers or jewellers and each workshop could sustain only a limited output. In 1738 Frederick, Prince of Wales, purchased a number of snuff boxes from the shop of Paul Bertrand, where a single item cost as much as £70.[12]

Buying luxury goods

London was described in this period as 'the most commercial of all the towns of Europe, and her trade is carried to all parts of the known world'.[13] The prime retail areas for luxury items were on Bond Street, and around the Strand, Pall Mall and St James's. Charles Gouyn's shop for 'girl-in-a-swing' porcelain, for example, was established in the 1740s in St James's, while César de Saussure, a Swiss visitor in 1725, recorded, 'Amongst others there is a jewellery shop opposite St Paul's which is probably the biggest and best in Europe. It is impossible not to admire the fine workmanship and curiosities which are displayed here.'[14]

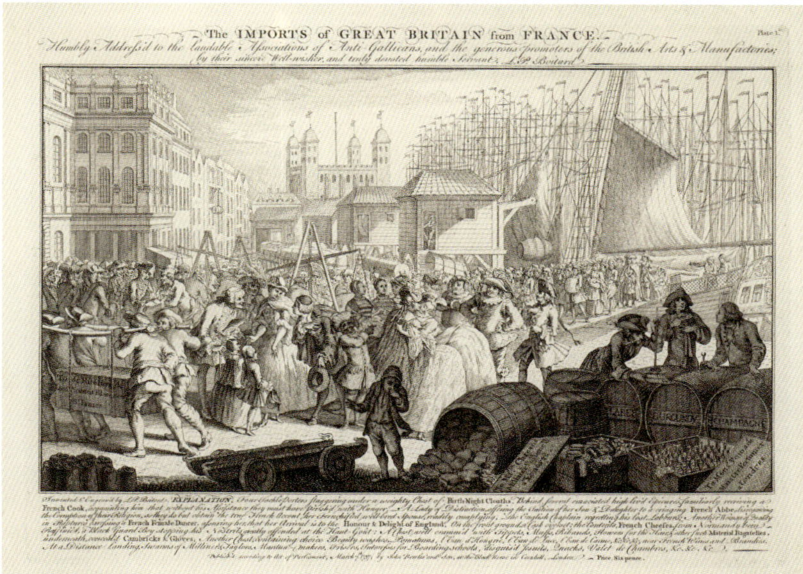

FIG. 100
Louis Philippe Boitard
Imports of Great Britain from France, c.1757
Etching
British Museum, London

This period saw the flourishing of an eighteenth-century phenomenon – the toy-shop (for the definition of 'toy' see above, p. 396). These specialist shops clustered in the most fashionable areas of London or the spa-towns of Bath, Tunbridge Wells and Scarborough. Toy-shops sold a huge range of items – not only snuff boxes and etuis, but also dress accessories such as watches, fans, jewellery or buckles, items of porcelain, glass or silver, waxes and models, stationery, prints, books, scientific instruments, tickets for concerts, and other small fripperies.[15] Most toy-men were not themselves makers although they sometimes described themselves as jewellers or goldsmiths. The best known toy-shop in London was run by Paul Chevenix and his wife, Mary Deards, at the Golden Door, on the corner of Pall Mall and Suffolk Street, near Charing Cross (fig. 99). Horace Walpole considered Chevenix's shop one of the sights of London, and it was from Mary Deards that he purchased the lease for Strawberry Hill. In Bath, Paul Bertrand ran a fashionable toy-shop close to the Abbey, where, in October 1738, Frederick, Prince of Wales, spent over £700 in a single visit.[16] His purchases, which ranged from 15 shillings for a silver corkscrew to expensive snuff boxes set with brilliants, included luxury items such as etuis and plate, but also buckles, smelling-salt bottles, a clock and two watches and, it appears, antique porcelain ('2 Old white Cups and Silver gilt sawcers' [and] 'a pair of old China candlesticks') (see nos 300–8).

Many of these items did not originate in England. These baubles and trinkets were identified with 'Frenchifying' – described by Johnson as 'to infect with the manner of France; to make a coxcomb'. In a satirical print of 1757 (fig. 100) entitled *The Imports of Great Britain from France*, Louis Philippe Boitard (*c.*1733-67) pointed out the hypocrisy of the English who employed French cooks in their kitchens, French Catholic abbés to educate their children and consumed French food and French fashions by the shipload. The print was aimed at the Anti-Gallican Society, which had been founded in 1745 'to extend the commerce of England and discourage the introduction of French modes and oppose the importation of French commodities'.

Nevertheless Bernard Mandeville in his *Fable of the Bees* of 1705 believed that the consumption of luxury goods stimulated the British economy, employing, he claimed, 'a million of the Poor', while Defoe noted in 1727 that 'London consumes all, circulates all, exports all, and at last pays for all, and this greatness and wealth of the City is the Soul of the Commerce to all the Nation'.[17]

258

CHELSEA PORCELAIN MANUFACTORY (*c.*1745–69)

Dessert service 1752–6

Soft-paste porcelain, each piece marked with a red anchor mark
Plates: 3.1 × 23.9 × 23.9 cm
Oval dish: 4.2 × 32.3 × 26.1 cm
Oval dish: 4 × 36.2 × 29.1 cm
RCIN 58781, 58784, 58785

PROVENANCE Possibly commissioned by William, Duke of Cumberland; first recorded in the Royal Collection in 1857

Although the Chelsea Porcelain Manufactory was never under royal patronage, and was set up and run independently by entrepreneurs and financiers, one member of the royal family was associated with the factory. In a letter of 1751 from Sir Charles Hanbury-Williams, ambassador to Dresden, to Henry Holland, the Duke of Cumberland is mentioned as a patron: 'I find also that the Duke is a great encourager of the Chelsea China and has bespoke a set for his own Table'.[18] It is possible that the service described in the letter was this one, which bears the red anchor mark of *c.*1752–8.

This service was one of the first from Chelsea to employ this shape of plate, probably based on a silver prototype with a scalloped rim interspersed by shaped reserves, here painted with fruits and insects. The shape was used again by Chelsea for the so-called 'Duke of Cambridge' service – in fact a service thought to have been created for William, Duke of Gloucester, brother of George III (1742–1805), and later bequeathed to Adolphus, Duke of Cambridge (1774–1850).[19] The 'Duke of Cambridge' service also bears a similar style of decoration – employing vibrant colours, in a limited palette – and of subject matter, of English fruits and small insects. It seems that the two services are closely related, and rather rare outputs for the Chelsea manufactory. In the *Daily Advertiser* of 1750 Chelsea announced that the forthcoming spring sale would 'consist of a Variety of Services for Tea, Coffee, Chocolate, Porringers, Dishes and Plates, of different Forms and Patterns, and of a great Variety of Pieces for Ornament in a Taste entirely new',[20] suggesting that the factory still saw itself as experimental. The style of decoration was taken up by the Worcester porcelain factory to greater success in the 1770s.

Both no. 258 and the 'Duke of Cambridge' service would have been outsourced to decorators and it is clear that the services are not decorated by the same hand. The leaves of the Royal Collection service show a greater variety of shape and freedom in the painting, and the porcelain is more densely covered overall. James Giles (1718–80) has been credited with decorating certain wares in this style and it is possible that his workshop undertook both services for Chelsea, outsourcing them in turn to different artists, although he is not known to have worked with Chelsea wares. KJ

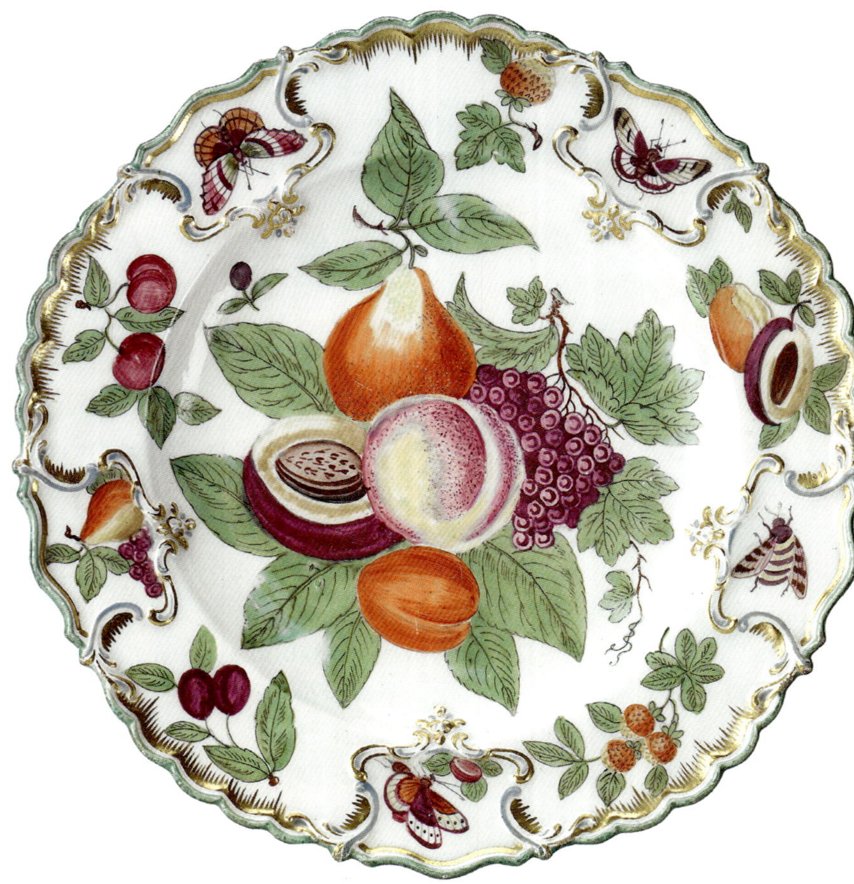

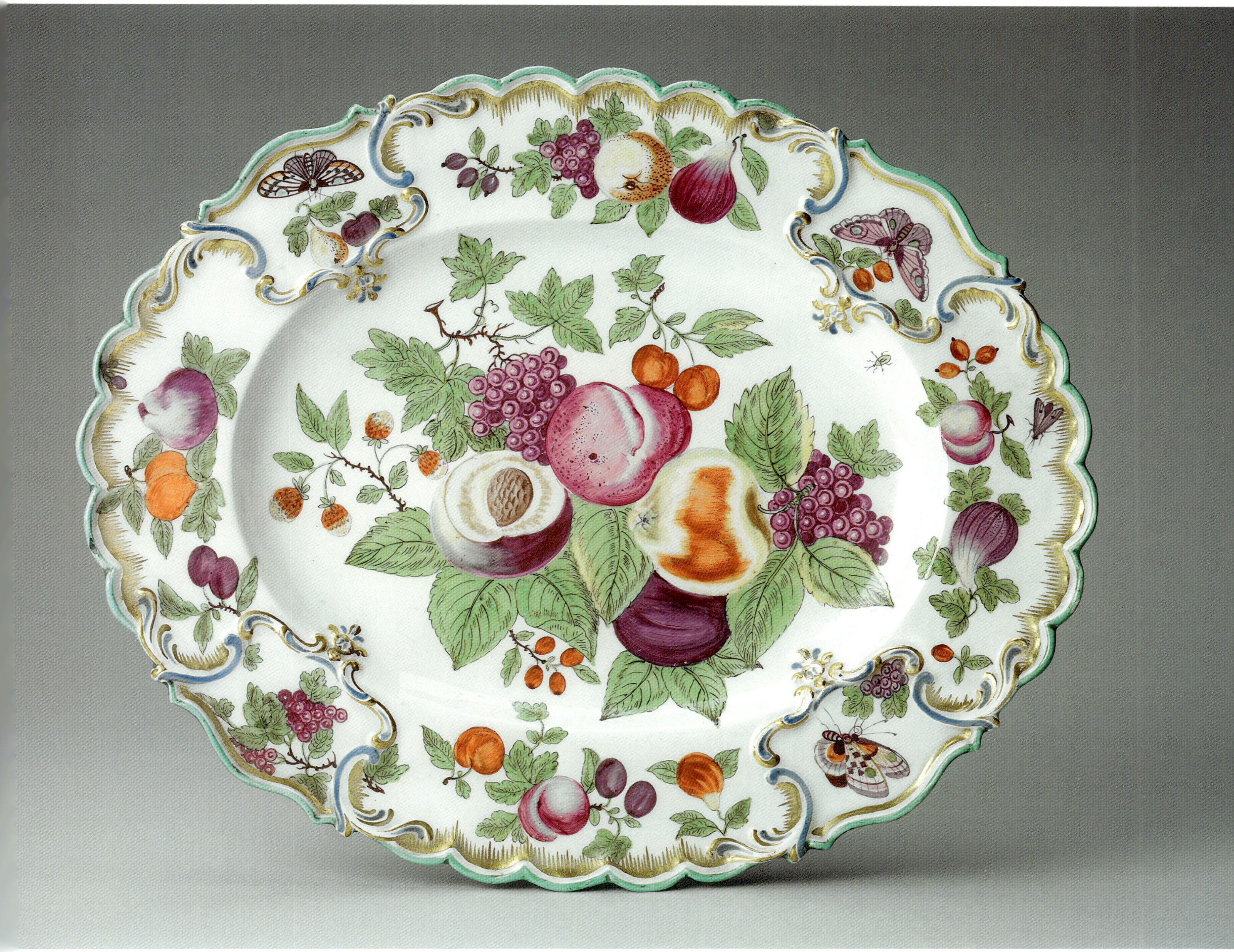

259

CHELSEA PORCELAIN MANUFACTORY (*c*.1745–69)

Hot-water jug *c*.1760

Soft-paste porcelain, 14.0 cm high
Marks: gold anchor
RCIN 33691

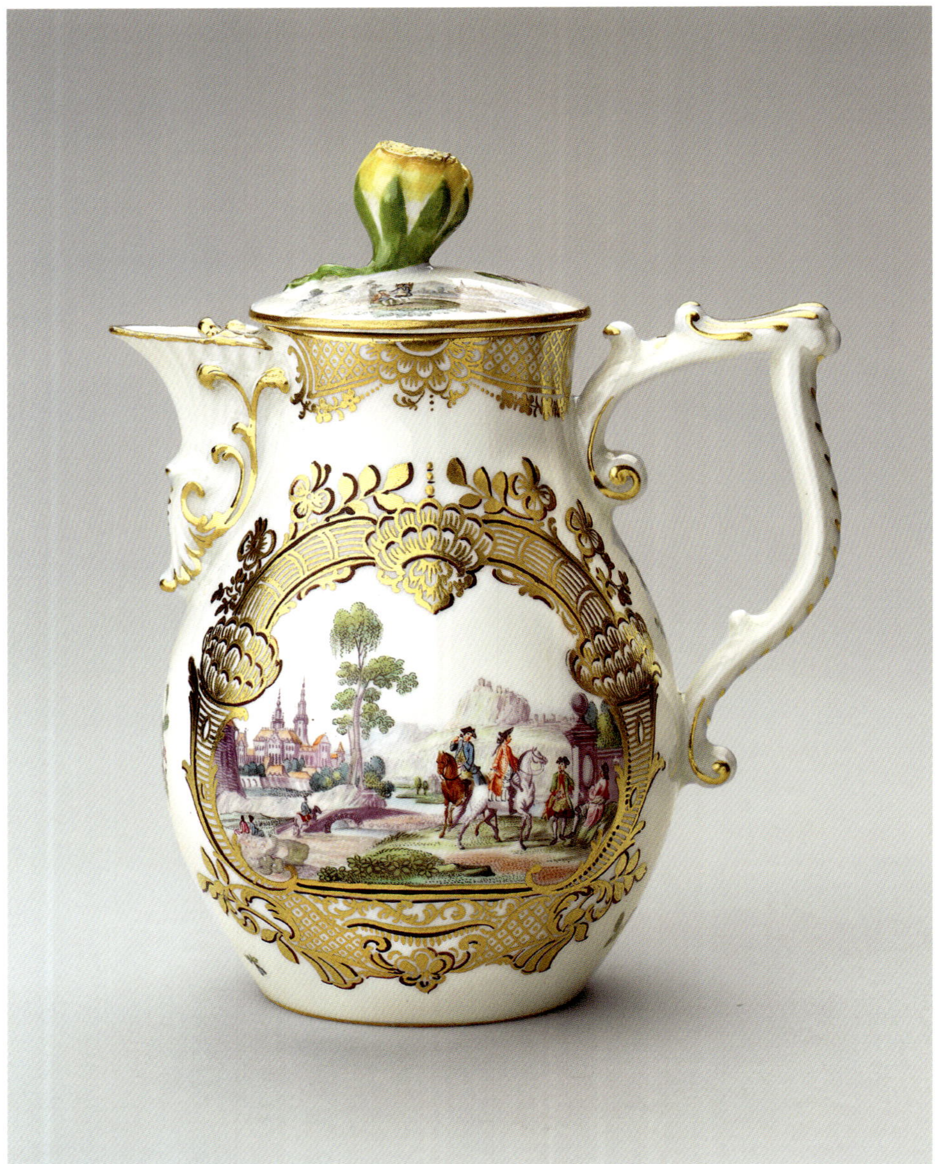

PROVENANCE First recorded in the Royal Collection in 1872

The chief financier of the Chelsea Porcelain Manufactory in the late 1740s was Sir Everard Fawkener (1695–1758), secretary to William, Duke of Cumberland, and a friend of the English ambassador to the Saxon court, Sir Charles Hanbury-Williams (1708–59). In 1742 Fawkener wrote to Hanbury-Williams in Dresden asking him to send home samples of the porcelain wares being created in Meissen so that they might be studied at the Chelsea factory. Instead Sir Charles offered the manufactory free access to his collections at Holland House.[21] Much of the output of the Chelsea factory during the 1740s seems to have been based on or inspired by Meissen, and in some cases, like that of this jug, it is almost impossible to tell the two apart. This is why Chelsea's director, Sprimont, petitioned Parliament in 1752 to protect his business from foreign imports (see above, p. 397).

The clientele for Chelsea porcelain was at the highest end of the market. In later life Mrs Papendiek, dresser to Queen Charlotte, recorded that when she first set up home she could only furnish her house with 'a tea and coffee set of Common India [Chinese] china ... there was nothing superior, Chelsea porcelain and fine India china being only for the wealthy'.[22] KJ

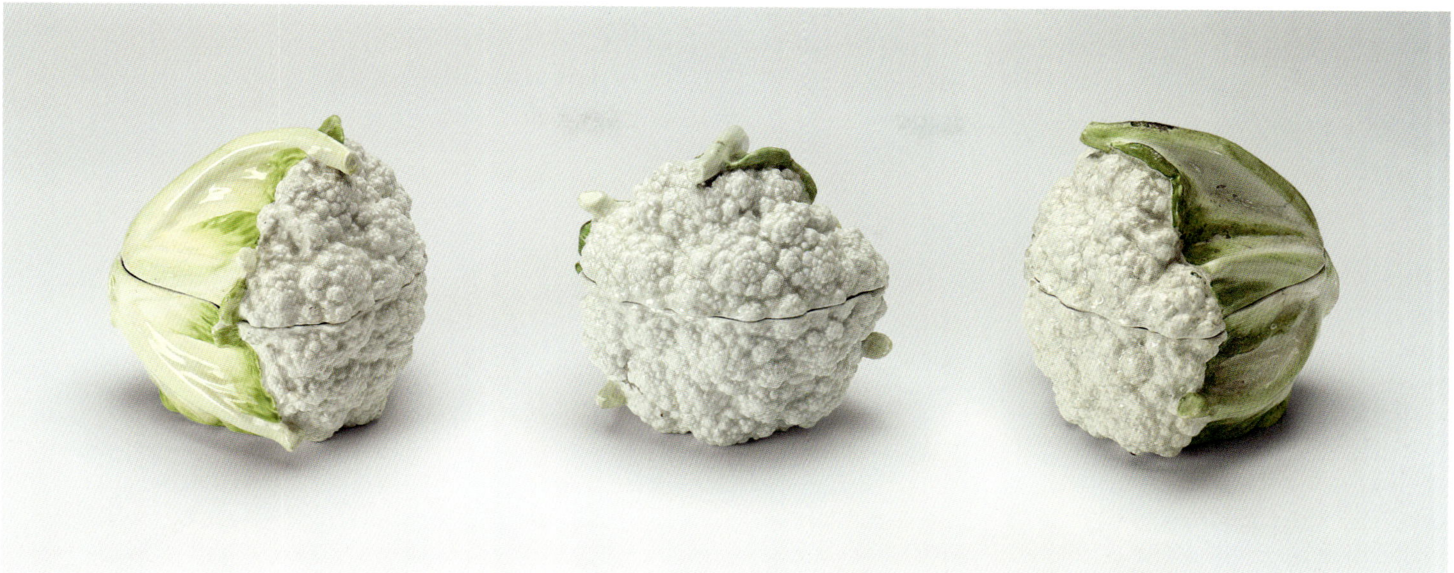

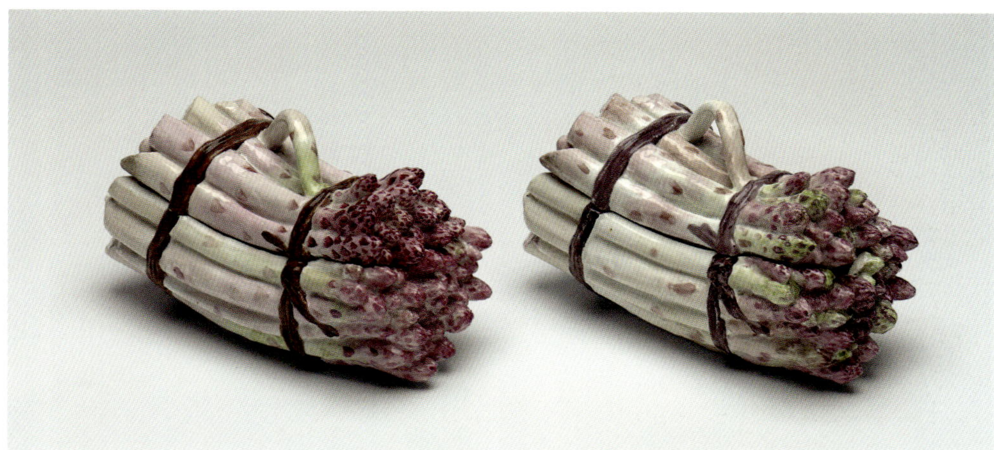

260 & 261

CHELSEA PORCELAIN MANUFACTORY

Three tureens *c.*1755

Soft-paste porcelain, 12.9 × 13 × 13 cm
Marks: all marked with a red anchor
RCIN 107366.1-3

Pair of tureens *c.*1755

Soft-paste porcelain, 10.9 × 18.5 × 9.8 cm
Marks: red anchor marks on lids
RCIN 107360.1-2

PROVENANCE Purchased by HM Queen Elizabeth The Queen Mother

The Chelsea factory seems to have delighted in creating all sorts of fruit and vegetable shapes to decorate the dining table. Although the most rococo pieces of contemporary silver similarly sought to imitate real vegetable forms, only in porcelain could the correct colours also be applied, and the factory produced everything from peapods to full-size chickens and boars' heads. In the 1755 sale of Chelsea wares, for example, the catalogue lists 'a compleat service for the desart' including a 'large cabbage leaf and bason, 2 vine leav'd dishes & four sunflower leaves'.[23] Some of these were based on Meissen prototypes but Chelsea experimented widely with the forms used. These items were not necessarily created to serve related foodstuffs. It was another rococo conceit that many of the vegetable forms were in fact used during the dessert course and may have contained sweet dishes rather than savoury ones. Ices and other desserts were moulded to resemble vegetables in the same way. Indeed the capacity of these vessels was not large and the pieces may have only acted as decorations. KJ

262

ATTRIBUTED TO CHELSEA PORCELAIN MANUFACTORY

Pair of salts *c.*1750

Soft-paste porcelain, 7.6 × 11.5 × 11.0 cm
RCIN 103913

PROVENANCE Acquired by HM Queen Elizabeth The Queen Mother in 1953

Nicholas Sprimont had worked in London as a goldsmith for only a brief period before founding the Chelsea factory and he continued to employ his skills as a designer in his new role. The early wares of the Chelsea factory drew on designs that Sprimont had used as a goldsmith – sauceboats with swags of flowers, shell-shaped dishes which closely resembled the stands for the sauceboats supplied to the Prince of Wales (no. 314), the 'goat and bee' jugs which had direct silver equivalents, and these salts which were one of the factory's most popular designs. This pair of salts relates directly in design to the silver-gilt salts he created in 1743 for Frederick, Prince of Wales (no. 315), which in turn depend upon an engraving by Juste-Aurele Meissonnier.

The choice of porcelain for salt cellars was nothing new. As early as 1727 Mary Delany (1700–88), a companion to Lady Stanley, had sent her sister a pair of ceramic salt cellars, noting in her letter, 'you may think old fashion, but it is the new mode and all saltsellers are now made in that manner'.[24] At this date they cannot have been English porcelain but her comment shows the demand for such pieces. The sale catalogues of Chelsea wares from the 1750s record dozens of pairs of crayfish salts in both white and polychrome, and Horace Walpole is known to have owned a white pair, which were sold at the Strawberry Hill sale in 1842. KJ

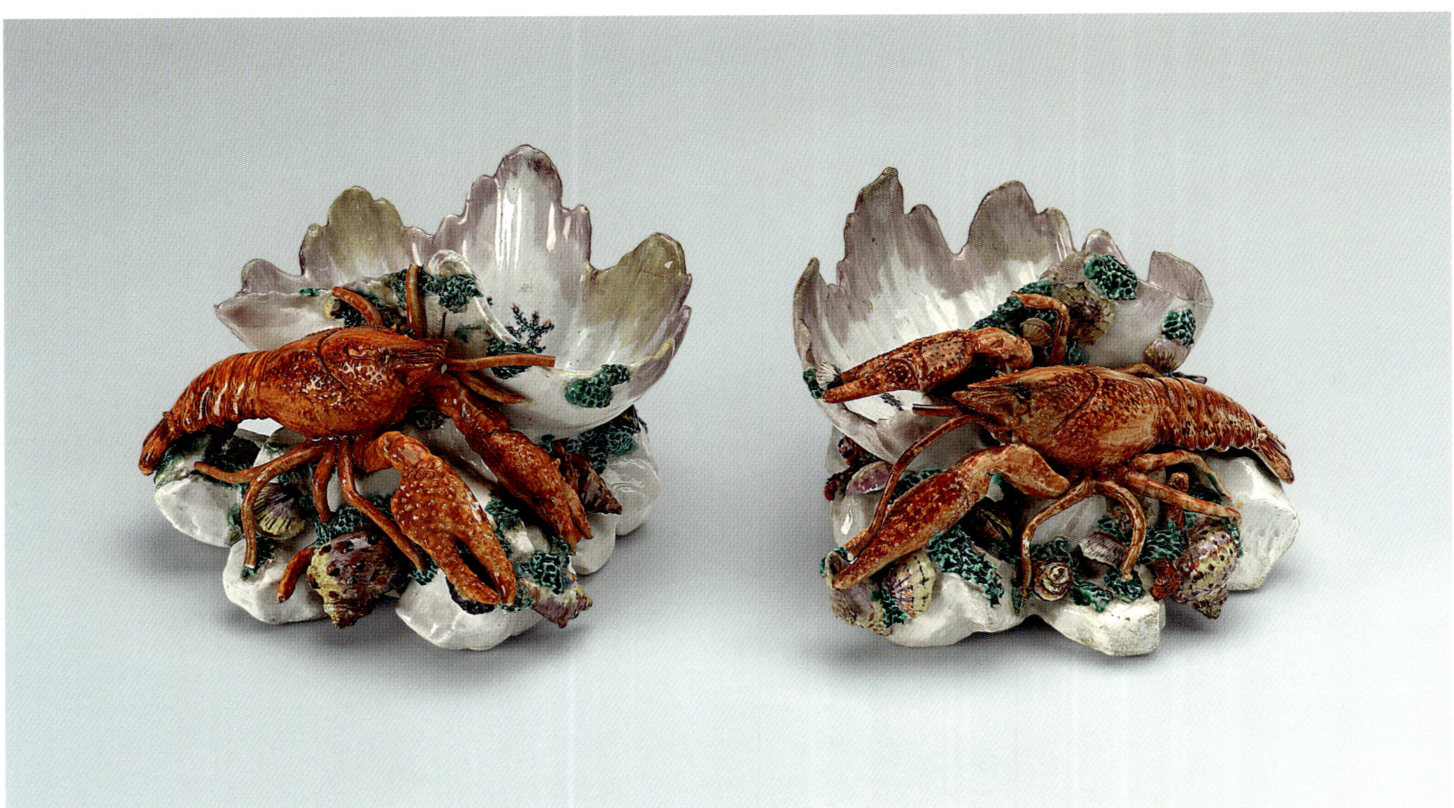

263

BOW CHINA FACTORY (*c*.1747–*c*.1776)

Pair of tea cups *c*.1755

Soft-paste porcelain, 7.0 × 9.1 × 6.9 cm
RCIN 59162.1-2

PROVENANCE First recorded in the Royal Collection in 1872

During the early years of porcelain manufacturing in England, the models and designs were drawn from a small pool of prototypes. In the 1730s and 1740s the majority of fashionable ceramics bought by consumers were either Asian porcelains or European Delftwares, although a few French and German porcelain pieces were making their way into England. The fledgling Bow factory in the East End of London specialised in items based on Chinese or Japanese models. Bow produced works that resembled white 'blanc de chine' porcelain, although they were not able to recreate the purity of colour of the originals and their products had a rather creamy body by comparison. Many of the Bow wares were simply decorated with stamped and applied prunus blossoms.

Although a short-lived venture, at its height in the 1750s the factory at Bow employed over 300 workmen. It also drew on the skills of the renowned chaser George Michael Moser (1704–83) and the sculptor John Bacon (1740–99) to create designs for some of its wares. The factory had a retail outlet in Cornhill, and for one year between 1757 and 1758 they also supported a shop in St James's, close to the royal court. KJ

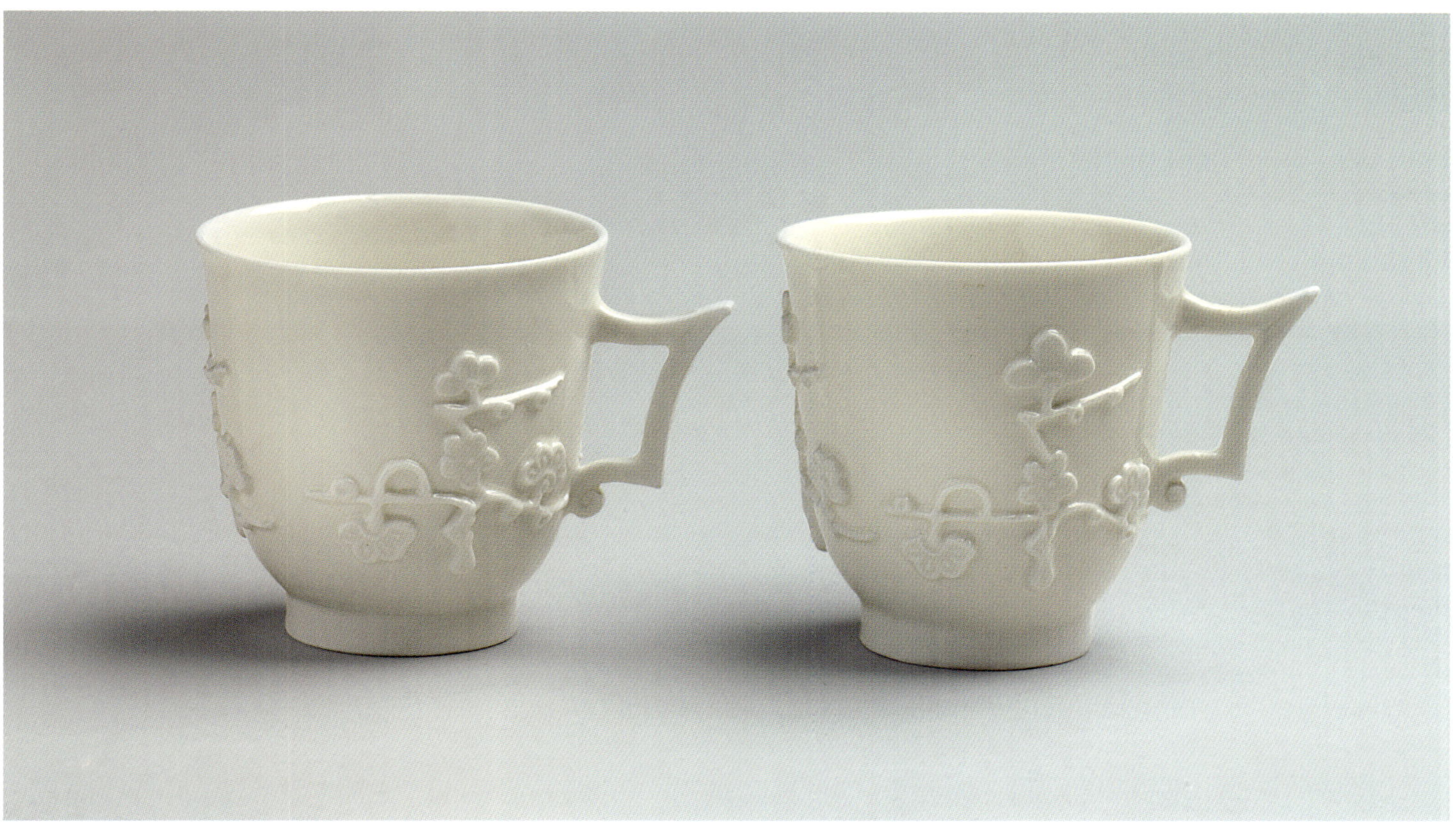

264

ATTRIBUTED TO RICHARD CHAFFERS'S MANUFACTORY, LIVERPOOL (ACTIVE 1754–65)

George II (1683–1760) 1757–9

Soft-paste porcelain, 43.0 × 32.8 × 16.2 cm
RCIN 45085

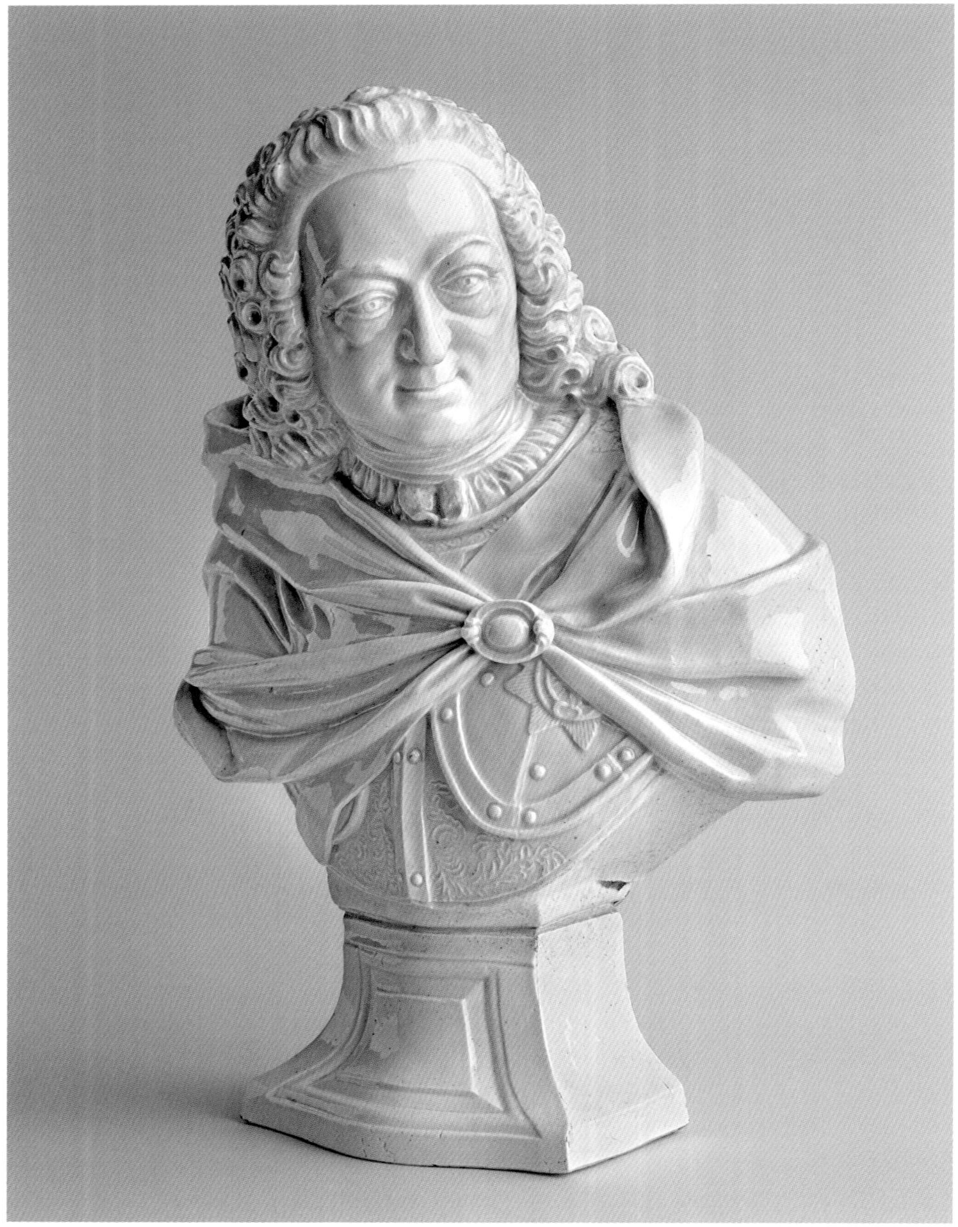

PROVENANCE Acquired by Queen Mary *c.*1950

This bust of George II is one of about twenty to survive, but it has not been possible to trace with certainty which factory created them. The most likely is the Liverpool manufactory run by Richard Chaffers. This attribution is based on the consistency of the porcelain, which contains a high percentage of soap-rock, which was mined under licence from Cornwall, and Chaffers was known to have held a licence for its use. However, the factories at Vauxhall and Bow in London and another in Plymouth have also been suggested as possible sources for the figure.

The size and thickly modelled clay show that the factory, whichever it was, was experimenting with the creation of large-scale pieces. A number of the versions of the bust have brackets modelled into the reverse to support the hollow back, and the bust is affixed to its socle with a large wooden screw. Although large pieces of this kind are rare in England, this was a time of experimentation throughout Europe. The chief modeller at Meissen, Charles Kändler, wrote in 1739 that 'everything can be made and achieved in porcelain, whatever one desires'.

At least one version of this bust was supplied with an elaborate rococo wall bracket, modelled with Britannia and St George and celebrating British military victory.[25] Certainly the martial aspect of the King, who wears both armour and a Garter star, suggests that these busts were created after the victories in America and India during the Seven Years' War (1754–63); it is possible that the bust was created posthumously. The sculptor has been named as John Michael Rysbrack (see nos. 5–6) or Louis-François Roubiliac (nos. 38–9 and 352), although the modelling is not sophisticated enough for either, and the most common attribution is John Cheere (1709–87).[26] Cheere sold plaster casts of his works from his premises on Hyde Park Corner (see no. 95) to a number of porcelain factories. KJ

265

NEWCASTLE

Wine glass *c.*1734

Lead glass, 19.0 × 8.4 × 8.4 cm
Marks: engraved underneath 2
RCIN 39766

PROVENANCE Traditionally thought to have belonged to Anne, Princess Royal; purchased by Queen Mary before 1952

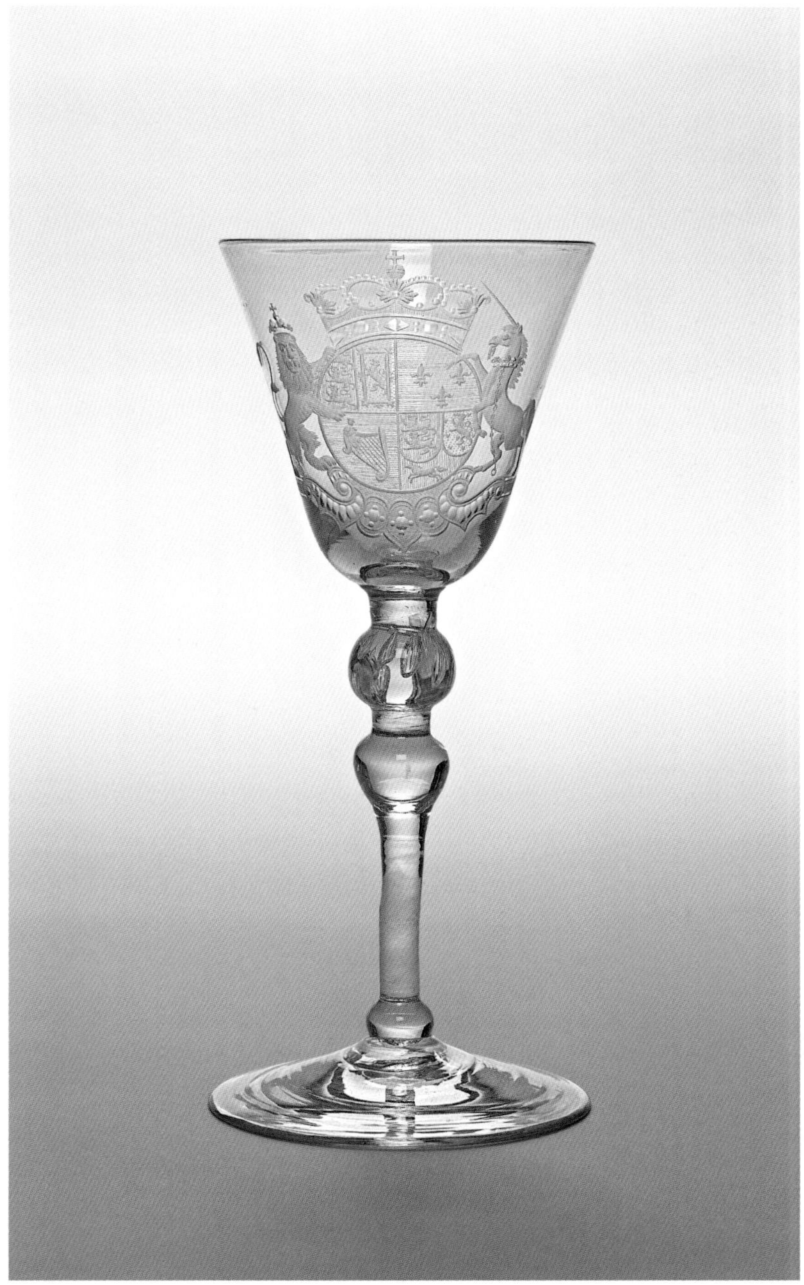

Wine glasses of this period typically had a conical bowl, a slender stem with a ball knop and a conical foot, the form being heavily influenced by German manufacturers, who dominated the markets of Europe in the early part of the century. Such glasses appear for example in Laroon's *Dinner Party* (no. 311), loaded on the full tray carried by a serving boy, and lining the buffet to the side of the room. However, the lead glass industry in England in the 1730s was still relatively young, and form and technique were subject to experimentation. English manufacturers were keen, for example, to exploit the high refractive index of lead glass by capturing air bubbles in the stems of their glasses, as in this example, to enhance the brilliance of the material (known as the metal).

Glass manufacturing had been established in Newcastle in the seventeenth century, and the glass was renowned for the softness, weight and colour of its metal, which made it highly suitable for wheel-engraving. Many Newcastle glasses were exported to the Netherlands to be engraved and it is possible that this example was one such. The glass may be a souvenir of the wedding in 1734 of Anne, Princess Royal, to William, Prince of Orange. KJ

266

JINGDEZHEN, JIANGXI PROVINCE, CHINA

***Punch bowl** c.1760*

Hard-paste porcelain, 14.5 × 36.0 cm
RCIN 26785

PROVENANCE Bought by HM The Queen in 1963

LITERATURE Howard 1974, p. 504

Chinese porcelain wares formed a part of the inherited royal collection at the accession of George I, having been amassed by William III and his co-sovereign Mary II, though the latter's collection was presented by William III to his favourite, the Duke of Albemarle, and dispersed. The demand in Britain for imported Chinese wares made specifically for export to Europe continued at least until rival European manufactories were established on native soil in the mid-eighteenth century. The royal palaces were not immune from this fever. Queen Caroline was known to be a lover of porcelain, both Chinese and German, the latter especially when from her native Ansbach.[27] On 13 August 1728 Lord Chesterfield wrote to Henrietta Howard, Countess of Suffolk, George II's mistress, regarding a Chinese dinner service he had bought in The Hague: 'As I know the Queen loves china I fancy She would like these'.[28] RB

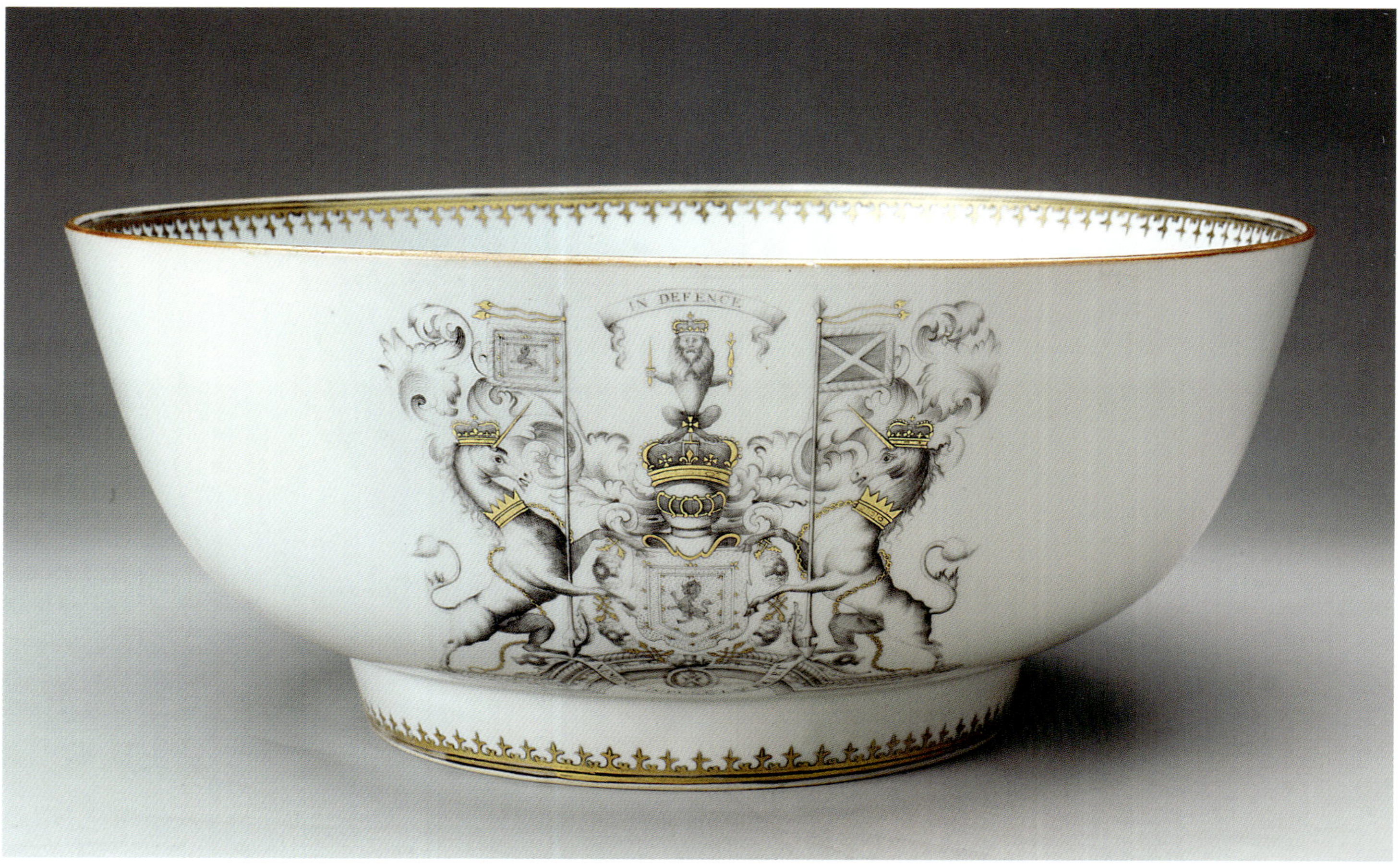

267

MEISSEN PORCELAIN FACTORY

Augustus II 'the Strong', Elector of Saxony and King of Poland (1670–1733) c.1720

Hard-paste porcelain, 12.5 × 6.5 × 5.7 cm
Marks: underglaze blue crossed sword mark
RCIN 39958

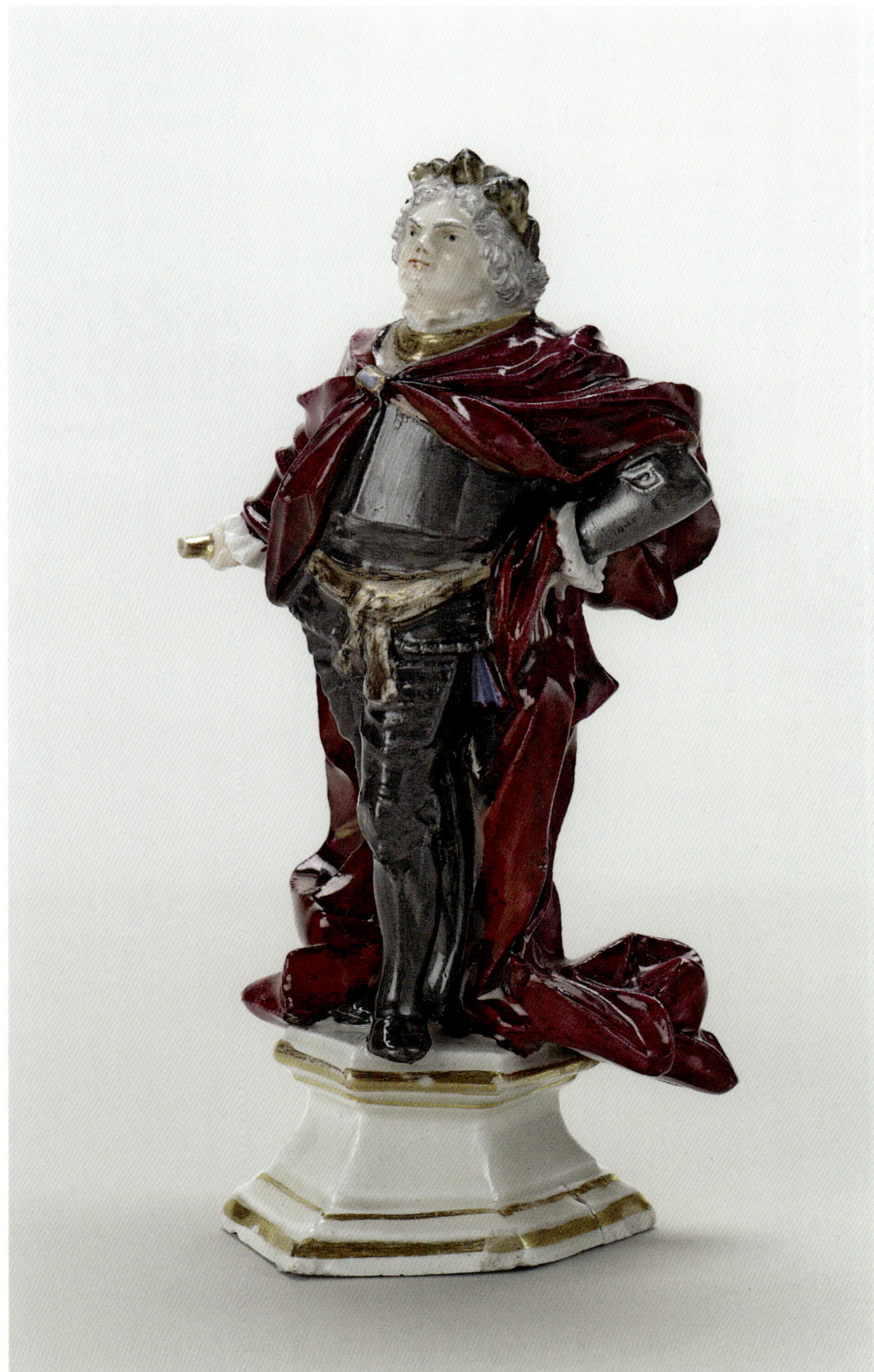

PROVENANCE Possibly acquired by Queen Alexandra

Unlike in England, the quest in Saxony to discover the secret 'alchemy' of porcelain production was driven by royal patronage. Augustus the Strong was an avid collector of Asian ceramics and it was his interest in porcelain which provided the momentum for the founding of the Meissen factory, near Dresden, in the early eighteenth century. After Augustus had encouraged the alchemist Johann Friedrich Böttger and the scientist Ehrenfried Walter von Tschirnhaus, the first successful attempts to create a viable porcelain were announced in 1709. One of the earliest models to be made by the factory was a figure of their royal patron wearing armour and a laurel wreath. The figure was reproduced many times in stoneware, white porcelain and a variety of colours.

Within a year of a patent being issued to establish the factory, Augustus was presenting Meissen porcelain as diplomatic gifts – the first example being sent to Frederick IV of Denmark in 1711. During the 1730s Augustus III (1696–1763) continued this tradition, sending gifts of Meissen to England in an attempt to gain support in the War of Polish Succession (1733–8). When George II visited Hanover in 1745, for example, his Prime Minister, Gerlach Adolf von Munchhausen, was presented with a Meissen service in gratitude, as it was under Munchhausen's direction that Hanover had been persuaded to make financial loans to Saxony, in opposition to Prussian and French interests.[29] KJ

MEISSEN PORCELAIN FACTORY

Tea and coffee service *c*.1730

Hard-paste porcelain with silver mounts
Teapot: 12.1 × 17.4 × 11.3 cm
Coffee pot: 22.5 × 14 × 11.5 cm
Hot water jug: 16 × 11.7 × 9.1 cm
Sugar bowl: 7 × 10 × 12.5 cm
3 tea bowls: 4.5 × 7.2 cm
3 saucers: 2 × 12.5 cm
Marks: each piece marked in underglaze blue with crossed sword marks; the silver hallmarked for Augsburg
RCIN 36033–7

PROVENANCE First recorded in the Royal Collection in 1927

For its tea-wares, the Meissen factory relied heavily on Chinese porcelain shapes and decorative motifs, as there was no real precedent in European ceramics. The tea bowls in particular were drawn directly from Chinese examples; a similar service, undoubtedly of Chinese porcelain, may be seen in Laroon's *Musical Tea Party* (no. 312).

George II owned a quantity of Meissen for use in Hanover. On his visit in 1743 the King acquired a 24-piece table service, comprising serving dishes, plates, tureens and smaller wares, probably used for the first time at the marriage ceremony of Princess Louise to Frederick, Crown Prince of Denmark. The inventories of Hanover also list blue and white 'Dresden porcelain', including 24 teacups with handles, which were purchased on the King's final visit to Hanover in 1755.[30]

Meissen porcelain was also traded in England, via representatives from Dresden. An armorial service created for Edward Howard, Duke of Norfolk (1686–1777), for example, now in Missouri, London, Toronto and Amsterdam, is traditionally thought to have been a gift from Frederick, Prince of Wales, in return for the loan of Norfolk House in 1737–8. Frederick is also known to have made a large purchase of Meissen porcelain through Baron Adam Adolf d'Ütterodt, who was the Saxon envoy to the British court between April 1739 and November 1742. The order was billed to the Prince in February 1742 and included a complete dinner service and tea table equipage. The latter was charged at nine guineas.[31] KJ

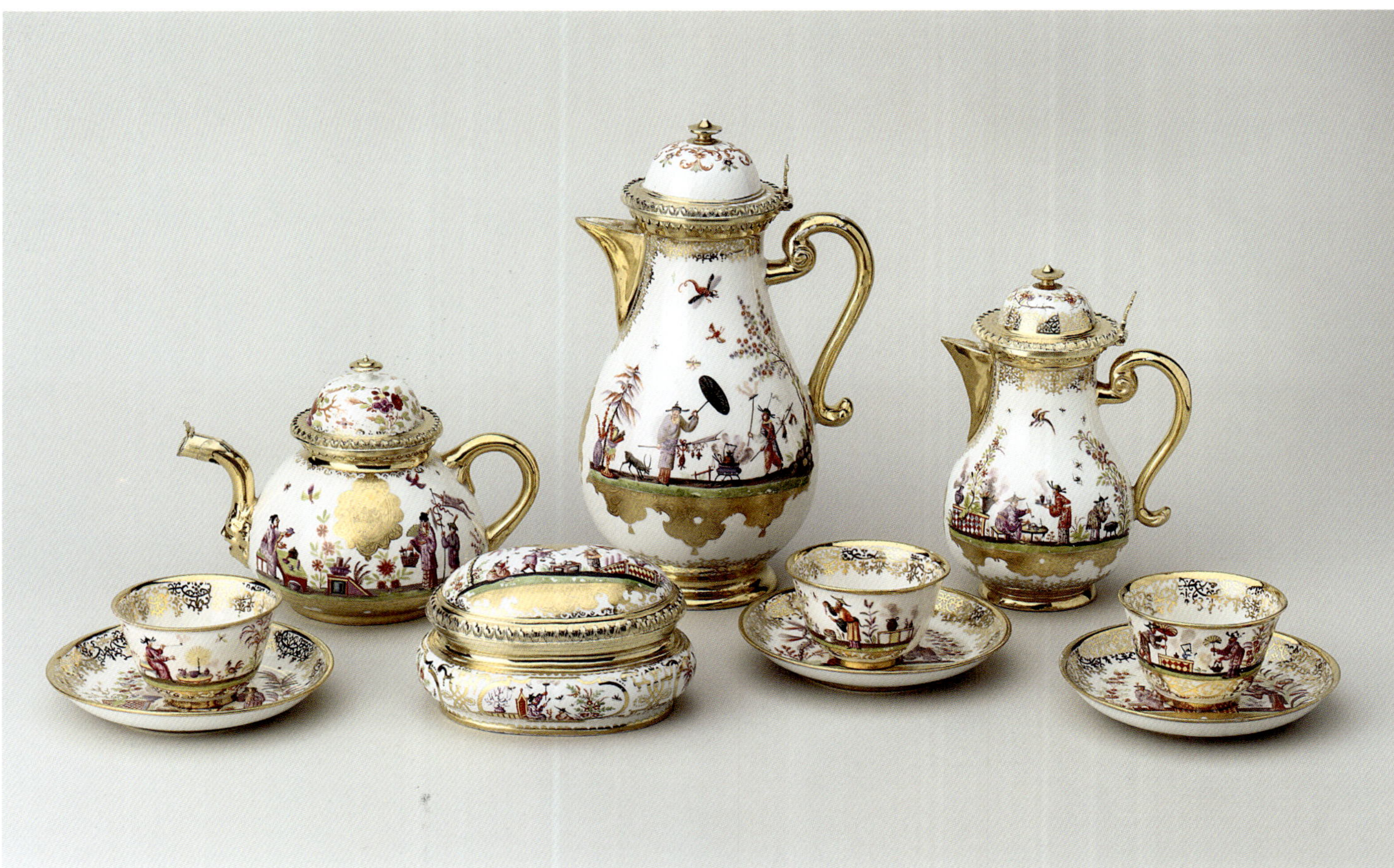

269

MEISSEN PORCELAIN FACTORY

Tea, coffee and chocolate service
*c.*1725

Hard-paste porcelain
Coffee pot: 21.4 × 14.2 × 11.2 cm
Chocolate pot: 13.0 × 13.6 × 12.5 cm
Small teapot: 7.5 × 13.5 × 7.5 cm
Teapot: 9.5 × 16.3 × 9.5 cm
2 tea caddies: 12.2 × 8.5 × 5.0 cm
3 tea bowls and saucers: 4.5 × 13.7 cm
Slop bowl: 8.2 × 16.0 × 16.0 cm
Sugar bowl: 11.5 × 11.9 × 11.9 cm
2 chocolate cups with stands: 10.2 × 10.2 cm
Pentagonal tray: 2.8 × 15.0 × 14.8 cm
Square tray: 2.7 × 11.0 × 11.0 cm
Jug and cover: 15.0 × 13.0 × 9.0 cm
Marks: each piece marked in underglaze blue with a crossed sword mark
RCIN 39810–21

PROVENANCE First recorded in the Royal Collection in 1872

As the Meissen factory grew the artists began to turn not only to Chinese precedents but to introduce European motifs of decoration: landscape and harbour scenes derived from seventeenth-century French and Dutch paintings and European flower pieces and hunting and genre scenes became more common. This service combines European scenes with a delicate turquoise-green ground which may have been intended to resemble Chinese celadon in its hue.

Queen Caroline led the way in the acquisition of German and Chinese porcelains, but Meissen porcelain was also mentioned in the accounts of Princess Augusta. In 1755, for example, a bill was charged by John Taylor, a china and glass dealer on Pall Mall, for packing and transporting Dresden china to Kew Palace.[32] KJ

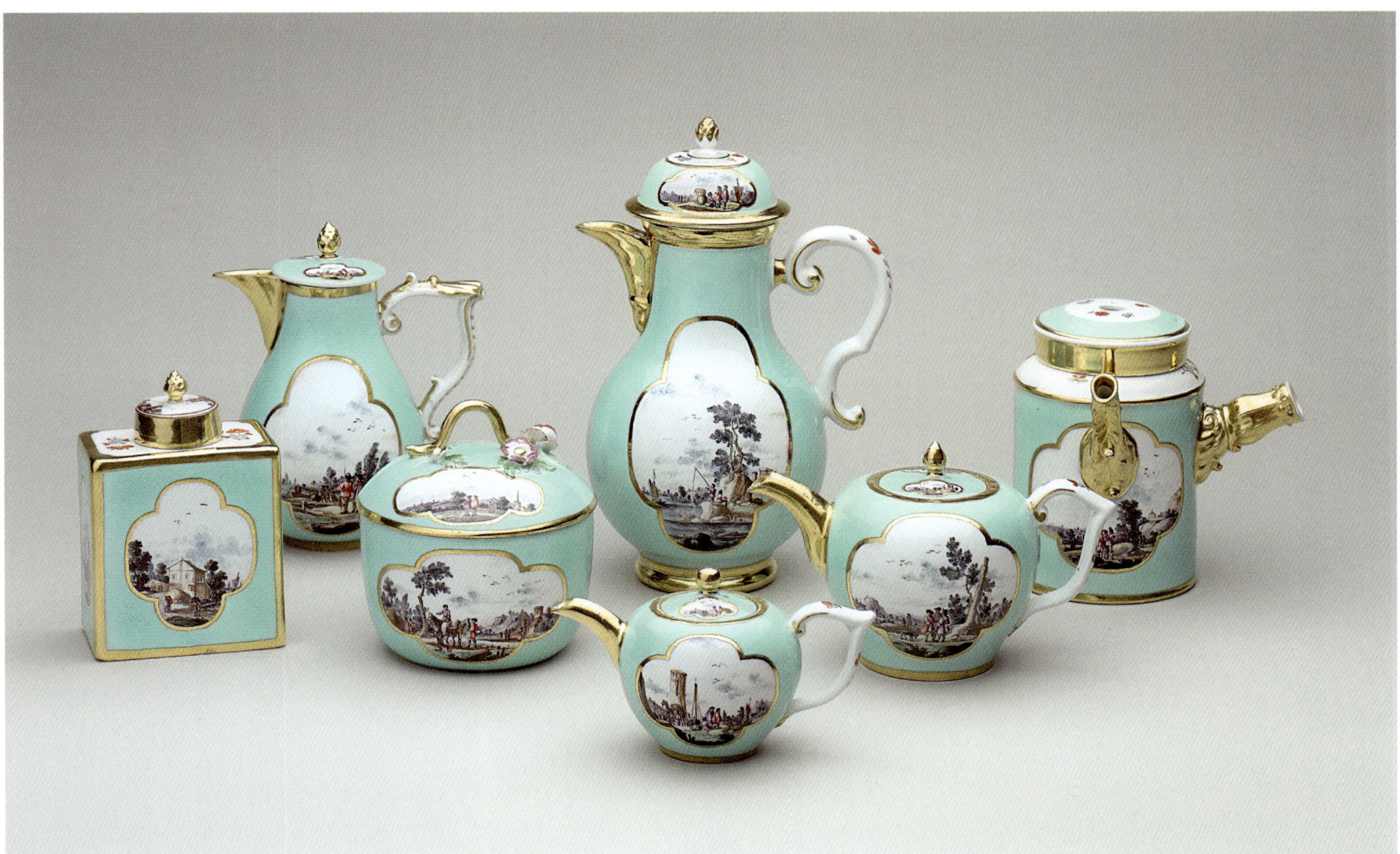

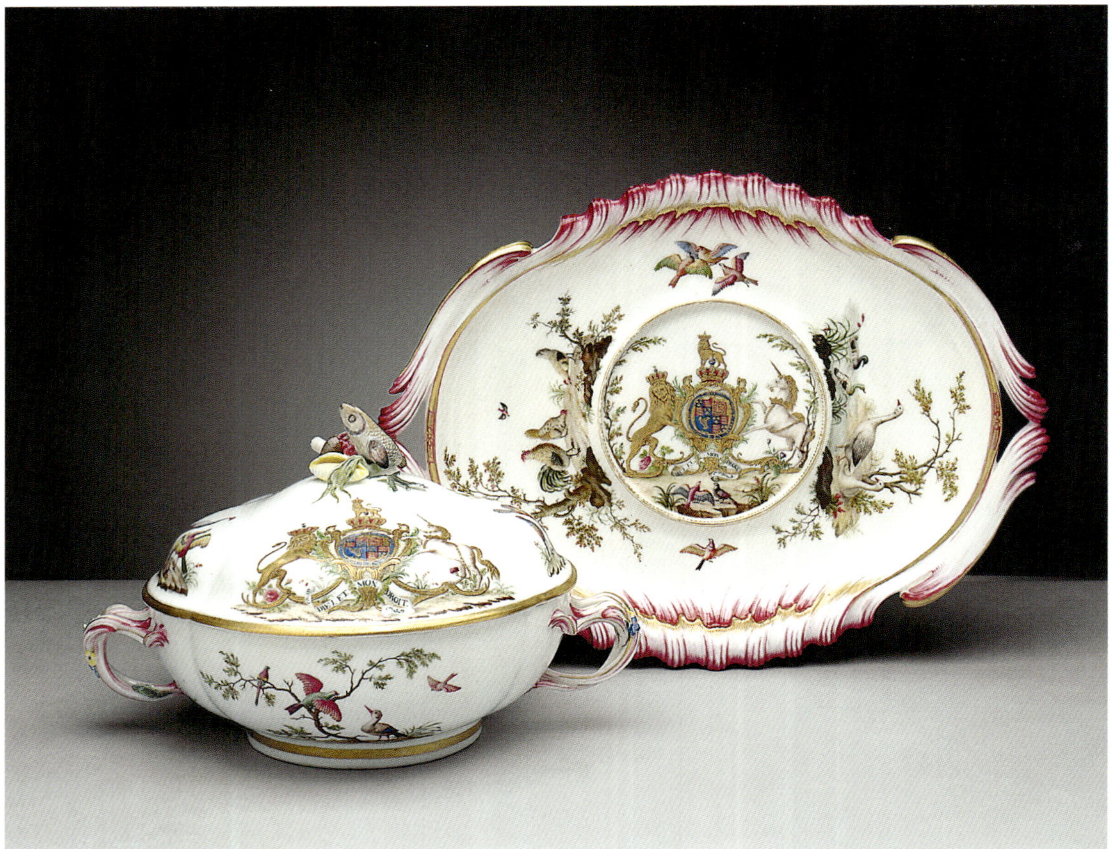

270

VINCENNES PORCELAIN FACTORY (1738–56)

Broth bowl and stand *c.*1748

Soft-paste porcelain
Bowl and cover: 12.2 × 22.2 × 21.5 cm, stand: 4.7 × 29.0 × 21.5 cm
Marks: both bowl and stand marked with interlaced LLs for the Vincennes factory
RCIN 19605

PROVENANCE Probably belonged to Charles Edward Stuart (1720–88); the bowl and cover purchased by HM The Queen, Sotheby's, London, 21 April 1964, lot 42; stand bought separately in 1997

LITERATURE de Bellaigue 2009, III, no. 262, pp. 933–6; *French Porcelain* 2009, p. 170

Experiments in the creation of porcelain first took place in France in St Cloud and Chantilly, but real success only came with the intervention of Louis XV, who in 1745 issued a 'privilege for manufacturing porcelain' and offered a large financial loan to support a new venture. The new factory was based in the château de Vincennes near Paris, and was able to produce a range of wares in a sought-after white paste and with sophisticated painted decoration.

This piece is an exceptional and rare example of the manufactory's early wares. The shape is associated not with the dining room but the boudoir or bedroom, where broth was taken by invalids for its medicinal qualities. It may be that the fish finial was an indication that the basin was to be used for the fish *bouillons* traditionally served on Fridays and holy days.

The basin and stand bear the royal coat of arms of the House of Stuart, and, although there is no label of cadency included in the heraldic painting, the pieces are thought to have been purchased by Charles Edward Stuart, the 'Young Pretender'. There is record of a payment to the manufactory of 120 *livres* from '*le prince Edouard*', and the Prince is known to have lodged briefly in the château de Vincennes in the winter of 1748.[33] KJ

271

LEWIS METTAYER (ACTIVE 1700–35)

Set of strawberry dishes 1714/15

Silver gilt
Circular dishes: 5.1 × 21.9 cm; 6.4 × 28.1 cm; Fan-shaped dishes: 3.6 × 34.4 × 19.9 cm
Marks: each piece hallmarked with Britannia standard mark, mark for London, 1714/5, and maker's mark of Lewis Mettayer
Engraved with the royal coat of arms and GR cipher
RCIN 104154–6

PROVENANCE Issued to Sir Paul Methuen (*c*.1672–1757), ambassador to Spain, in 1715; acquired by HM Queen Elizabeth The Queen Mother

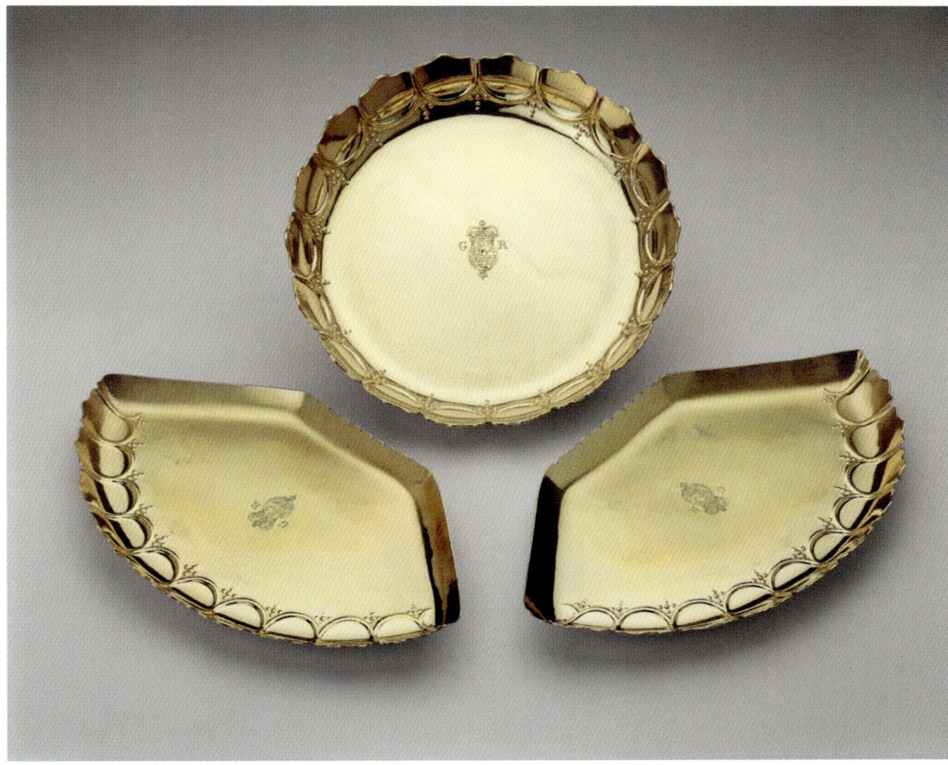

Sir Paul Methuen was appointed ambassador to Spain in 1714, and was given a particular brief to conclude a commercial treaty with that country, following the conclusion of the Treaty of Utrecht in 1713. It was one of the perquisites of the role that the ambassador was able to commission a quantity of plate from the Jewel Office for use during his embassy – the usual allowance being 5,893 troy oz of white plate and 1,077 troy oz of gilt plate. According to the warrant issued, the quantity of plate was 'to be made into such vessels and after such fashion as his Lordship shall direct', allowing the recipient almost free rein in deciding on the pieces to be commissioned.

The order for Methuen's gilt plate is listed in the records of the Jewel Office as comprising four square canisters, four butter and salt boxes, two chased cups and covers, three casters, two square boxes, two dozen sets of flatware and 'seaventeene fine scollops & ribed fruite Dishes'.[36] The dishes weighed a little more than 403 oz and cost a total of £253 16s 8d. An almost identical set of dishes is now in the Metropolitan Museum, New York,[37] and is thought to have been issued to Joseph Addison, who was appointed Secretary of State for the Southern Department in 1717. Both sets of plate were marked by Lewis Mettayer, a goldsmith of Huguenot descent, who was frequently contracted to the Jewel Office to work on ambassadorial commissions. Mettayer's work was conservative in design, perhaps suggesting a desire on the part of the British ambassadors of this period to demonstrate continuity with the previous reign. KJ

272

AYMÉ VEDEAU (ACTIVE 1733–73), MATTHEW LOFTHOUSE (ACTIVE 1697–1733) AND MARY PANTIN (MARK ENTERED 1733)

Tea service 1732–4

Silver gilt, the teapot and hot water jug with ivory handles and finials; the kettle with leather grip
Pair of tea caddies: 11.4 × 7.1 × 9.1 cm
RCIN 46994.1 hallmarked for London, 1733/4, and maker's mark of Aymé Vedeau
Tea caddy: 7.8 × 11.5 × 10.5 cm
RCIN 46995 hallmarked for London, 1733/4, and maker's mark of Aymé Vedeau
Tea kettle and stand: 39.0 × 27.2 × 27.2 cm
RCIN 49123 kettle and tripod hallmarked for London, and maker's mark of Matthew Lofthouse; stand hallmarked for London, 1732/3, and maker's mark of Matthew Lofthouse
Teapot: 11.9 × 11.2 × 20.5 cm
RCIN 49138 hallmarked London, 1733/4
Hot-water jug: 22.3 × 16.4 × 9.3 cm
RCIN 50648 hallmarked London, and maker's mark of Aymé Vedeau
Cream jug: 7.3 × 14.8 × 7.3 cm
RCIN 51437 marked several times with maker's mark of Aymé Vedeau
Sugar bowl: 9.5 × 16.7 × 16.7 cm
RCIN 51573 marked for London, 1733/4, and maker's mark of Mary Pantin

PROVENANCE Probably acquired by Frederick, Prince of Wales

Though hardly known on the Continent, tea-drinking was highly fashionable in Britain in this period. In 1734 Thomas Twining (1675–1741) imported more than 13,000 lb of tea into Britain. All teas sold at this date were imported from China or Japan, and were highly taxed. Mary Delany frequently sent parcels of tea from London to her mother and sister, although she noted the rising costs of both green and black varieties. On 5 October 1727, for example, she wrote to her sister: 'Mrs Badge ... has bought two pound of Bohea [black tea], at thirteen shilling a pound, which the man says is extraordinarily good; but everything of that kind grows very dear'.[34] By May 1728 Bohea tea had risen to 20 shillings a pound, and green tea had risen from twelve to 30 shillings. Tea was thus a highly luxurious item and the tea service consequently of particularly high value by association. This is reflected in the genre scenes of the period, which often show the tea service prominently displayed on the table. In Laroon's *Musical Tea Party* (no. 312) for example, tea is being served in porcelain tea-bowls, while the teapot is replenished with a silver kettle, its stand on the floor beside the table.

This tea service is first recorded in an inventory of 1832 as belonging to Frederick, Prince of Wales. It would have been an early purchase by the Prince, who did not spend lavishly on plate until the reconciliation with his father in 1741, and the grant of a greater allowance by Parliament. Until this point Frederick relied on plate existing in the Jewel Office for his evening parties. In August 1732, for example, the Plate Book records silver 'delivered for an Entertainment His RH the Prince of Wales gives to Her Majesty at Kew on Monday next 21 Augt. 1732'.[35] On Frederick's marriage in 1736, George II gave him second-hand plate from the Jewel Office, which he then had replaced with new pieces for himself. Neither the gift nor the replacement included any tea-wares, which suggests that, in this department at least, the Prince was already well provided.

The original service supplied to the Prince is listed in the 1832 inventory as containing a plated jug for serving hot milk or water, which no longer survives, and a further four caddies – two with flower finials and two beaded ones. This suggests that the Prince was able to offer his guests a huge variety of exotic teas. The flowered caddies may have been used to contain Pekoe tea, which was distinguished by the addition of dried white tea blossoms. KJ

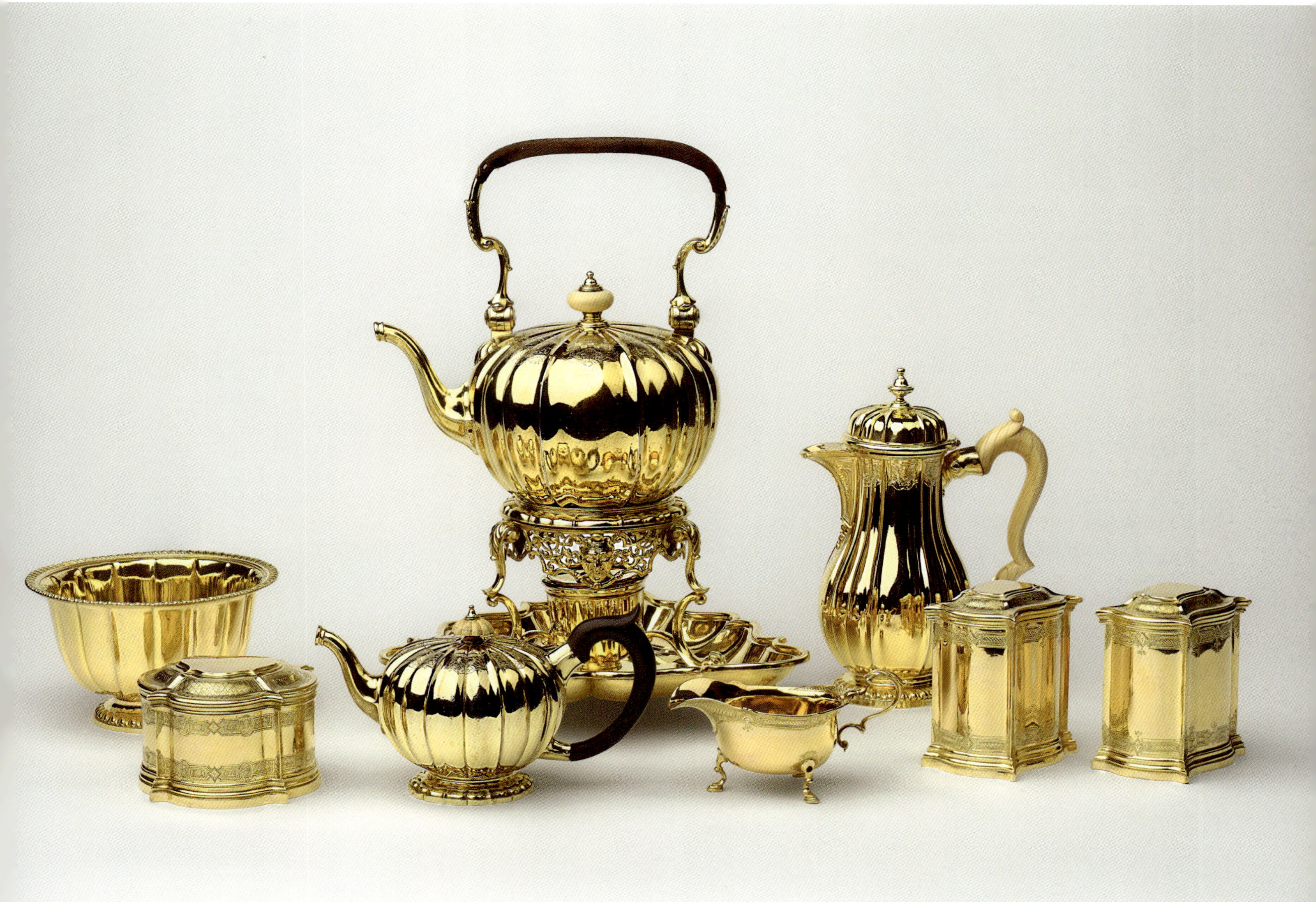

273

PAUL CRESPIN (1694–1770)

Cup and cover 1718/9

Silver, 26.5 × 24.0 × 13.6 cm
Marks: hallmarked for London, 1718/9, and maker's mark of Paul Crespin
The base scratch marked with the weight *46=09* and *AD 1718*
RCIN 46376

PROVENANCE Probably acquired by Queen Mary

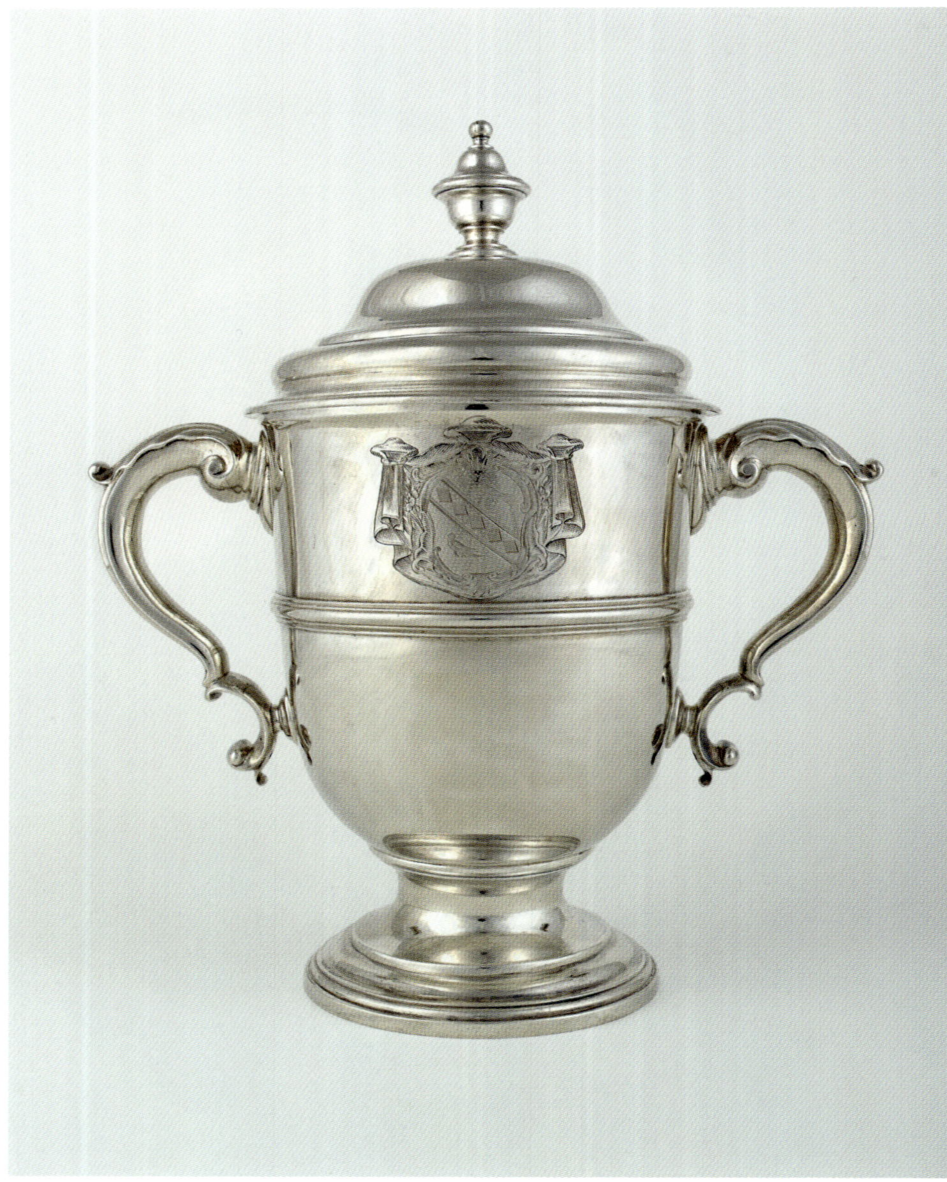

Two-handled cups of this form varied little throughout this period – the standard form being a plain ovoid body with a single rib around it and leaf-capped scroll handles. In this case no. 274 has been embellished with pierced 'spoon-handle' straps, but otherwise the decoration tended to be reserved for the engraved coat of arms with more or less elaborate mantling. Recent scholarship has suggested that this form of cup was an English innovation rather than a Huguenot import, as was once assumed;[38] Samuel Lea (no. 274) shows no obvious connections with the Huguenot community. Such cups were usually intended as gifts rather than for any practical purpose – the king traditionally presenting such pieces to his godchildren – and the Jewel Office records are littered with orders for cups of this type. It is possible that the piece by Crespin (no. 273) was indeed a christening gift, although no record of this is made on the cup itself. The cup by Lea (no. 274) was presented to John Manley, a resident in Greenwich Park, whom Frederick visited in 1738. KJ

274

SAMUEL LEA (ACTIVE 1711–24)

Cup and cover 1721/2

Silver (Britannia standard), 26.8 × 25.5 × 14.5 cm
Marks: Hallmarked on cover with maker's mark of Samuel Lea
Hallmarked on cup for London, 1721/2, and maker's mark of Samuel Lea
RCIN 47505

PROVENANCE Presented to John Manley by Frederick, Prince of Wales, in 1738; acquired by Queen Mary in 1933 .

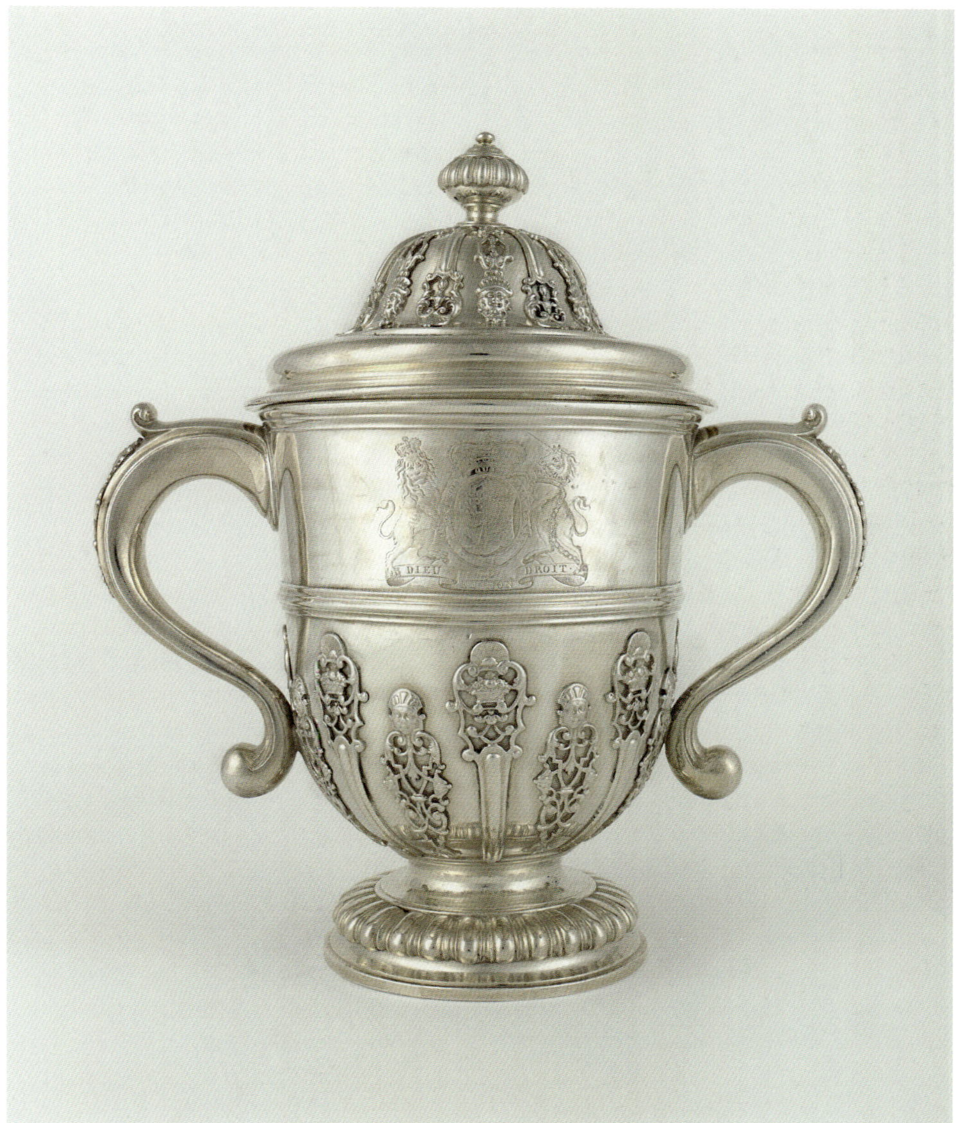

275

ATTRIBUTED TO PAUL DE LAMERIE (1688–1751)

Cup and cover *c.*1740

Silver gilt, 45.0 × 24.0 × 16.2 cm
RCIN 51016

PROVENANCE Acquired by Frederick, Prince of Wales, 24 January 1740

LITERATURE Jones 1911, pl. XXXVIII; Grimwade 1974, p. 28 ; Barr 1980, pp. 160–2

This cup appears in the ledgers of George Wickes, goldsmith to the Prince of Wales, on 24 January 1740, as a 'fine cheased gilt cup and cover', costing £61 3s.[39] Although unmarked, it bears many close similarities to a number of works by Paul de Lamerie, including the Bath Cup, presented by Frederick, Prince of Wales, to the city of Bath on his visit in 1738. Another cup, marked by de Lamerie in 1737, which has identical handles in the form of entwined serpents weaving in and out of the body of the cup, is found in the Fishmongers' Company. Many of the decorative elements of no. 275 relate to other works by de Lamerie – particularly the putto finial with its dimpled limbs and high forehead, and the exuberant asymmetric shell and scale elements decorating the cup, which are reminiscent, for example, of the coffee pot made for Sir John Lequesne in 1738.[40]

Paul de Lamerie was of Huguenot descent. He was made free of the Goldsmiths' Company in 1713 and thereafter worked in Windmill Street, St James's, and later in Gerrard Street in Soho. Despite his appointment as royal goldsmith in 1716, he does not appear at that date to have supplied the Jewel Office, and no bill for his work has been traced. No. 275 belongs to the acknowledged high point of Lamerie's output, in the late 1730s and early 1740s. This purple patch includes a group of pieces created for Grey Maynard, 5th Baron Maynard (1679–1745), including the famous Maynard sideboard dish of 1736 (now in the Cahn Collection, St Louis). In these years Lamerie also produced exceptionally inventive ewers and basins for Stephen Fox, Earl of Ilchester (*c.*1740, private collection), the Goldsmiths' Company (1741/2, Goldsmiths' Hall, London) and Algernon Coote, 6th Earl of Mountrath (1742, Gilbert Collection, London). All of these pieces show a highly developed use of rococo ornament and asymmetrical design, and display modelling of exceptional quality. It has been suggested that they relate to a particular craftsman in the Lamerie workshop, traditionally known as the 'Maynard modeller' after the Maynard sideboard dish. This modeller remains unidentified but may be related to the Kändler family – who were so instrumental in the development of the Meissen factory in Dresden.[41]

The 1832 inventory of plate records that the cup belonged to Princess Augusta. This is not mentioned in Wickes's bill, but it may have been a gift to her from her husband, or she may have claimed it after his death, to prevent it being absorbed into the Jewel Office. KJ

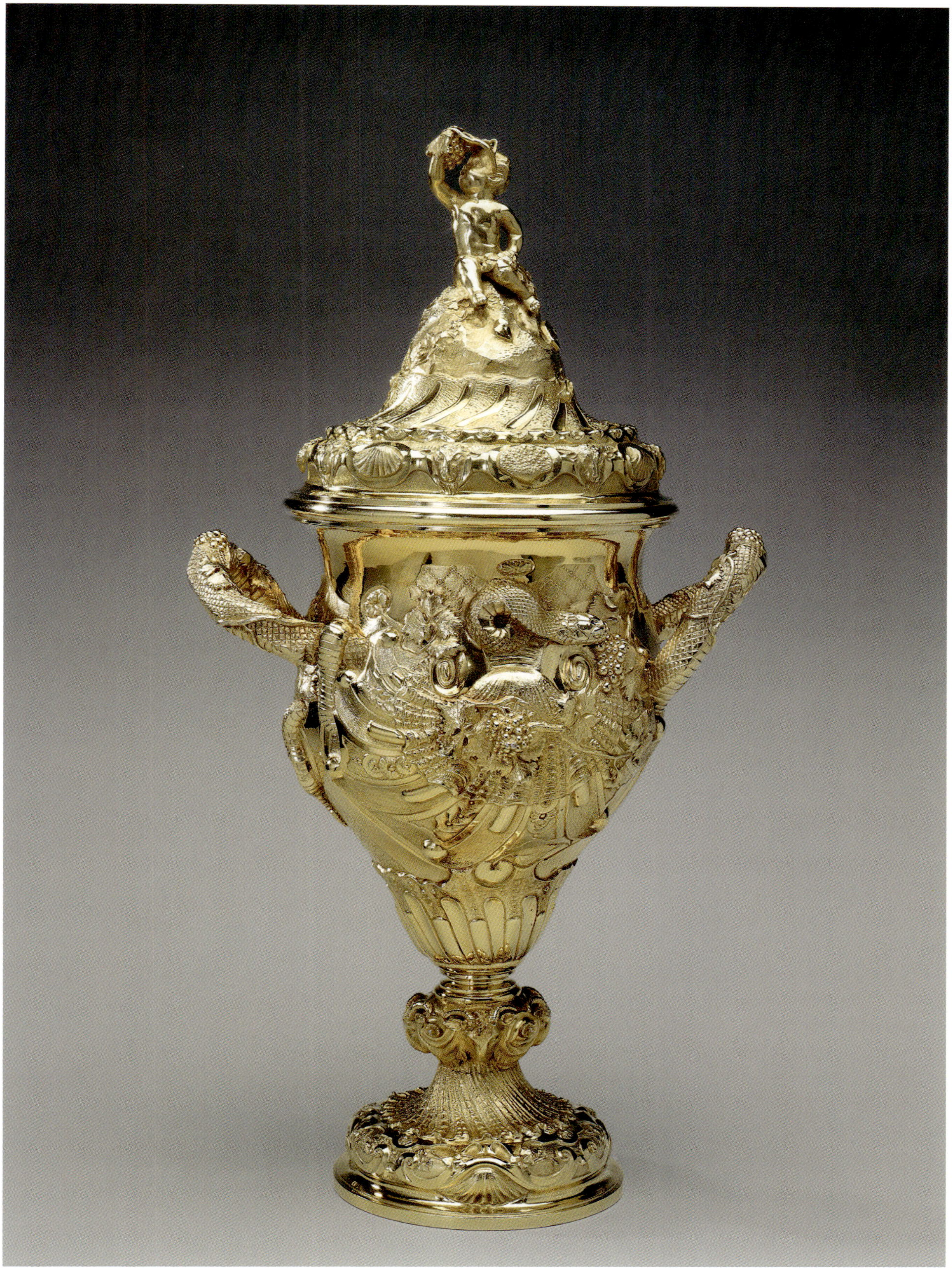

276

GEORGE WICKES (1698–1761), AFTER A DESIGN BY WILLIAM KENT (*c*.1685–1748)

Epergne 1745/6 with later additions of 1828/9

Silver gilt, 72.5 × 75.5 × 48 cm
Marks: central element and stand with hallmarks for London, 1745/6, and maker's mark of George Wickes; nozzles with hallmarks for London, 1828/9, and maker's mark of John Bridge
RCIN 50845

PROVENANCE Delivered to Frederick, Prince of Wales, in November 1745 for £695 14s 4d

LITERATURE Hayward, 1959 pp. 82–3; Oman 1972; Grimwade 1974, pp. 32–3; Barr 1980, pp. 169–72

In his *Anecdotes of Painting in England* Horace Walpole said of William Kent that his 'style however predominated authoritatively during his life; and his oracle was so much consulted by all who affected taste, that nothing was thought compleat without his assistance. He was not only consulted for furniture ... but for plate.'[42] Kent is known to have designed a number of works in silver. The most celebrated piece was undoubtedly the chandelier designed for George II for his palace at Herrenhausen, but he also worked on smaller items such as mugs and dish-covers, tureens, candlesticks and inkstands. A number of Kent's ideas for items of plate appear in John Vardy's 1744 publication, *Some Designs of Mr. Inigo Jones and Mr. Wm. Kent*, including the original design for this 'surtoute' or centrepiece (fig. 101).[43] The published design does not show the Prince of Wales's feathers that appear on the finished piece, which suggests that it was conceived with no particular client in mind.

At some stage, perhaps while Vardy's book was in production, this design was realised in silver by George Wickes, goldsmith to Frederick, Prince of Wales; the resulting centrepiece is hallmarked for the year 1744/5. Although restrained in style, the design must rank as one of the most rococo of all Kent's works. Wickes made adjustments to the design by, for example, adding candle branches, and later alterations were made to the piece in the nineteenth century. Kent also included a sauceboat in his drawing, although it seems it was never created. In spite of these changes, the essence of Kent's design survives in the finished work – in the airy central trellis, the swagged and scalloped central dish, the shaped base plate, the scrolled uprights and particularly in the winged term figures with putti heads. It is even possible that Kent was further involved in this development stage of his original design, in collaboration with Wickes. The base plate in the finished work bears an engraved coat of arms of the highest quality; the work has not been attributed to any contemporary engraver and it has been suggested that the acanthus scrolls which surround the arms may be the design of Kent.[44]

It has been proposed that this light-hearted piece, with its associations with a garden and its putti, may have been intended for use in the Prince's supper box at Vauxhall.[45] It is true that items of plate were dispatched by the Jewel Office for entertainments – George I, for example, used the royal epergne at Hampton Court during the summer period of 1717.[46] To use the Jewel Office to furnish a setting as public and ephemeral as a Vauxhall supper box would, however, have represented a departure from precedent. KJ

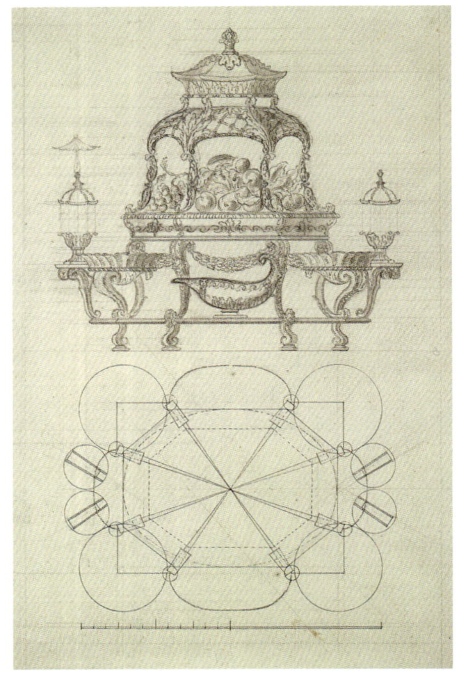

FIG. 101
John Vardy after William Kent
Design for a centrepiece, 1744
Pencil, pen and ink, wash
British Architectural Library, RIBA, London

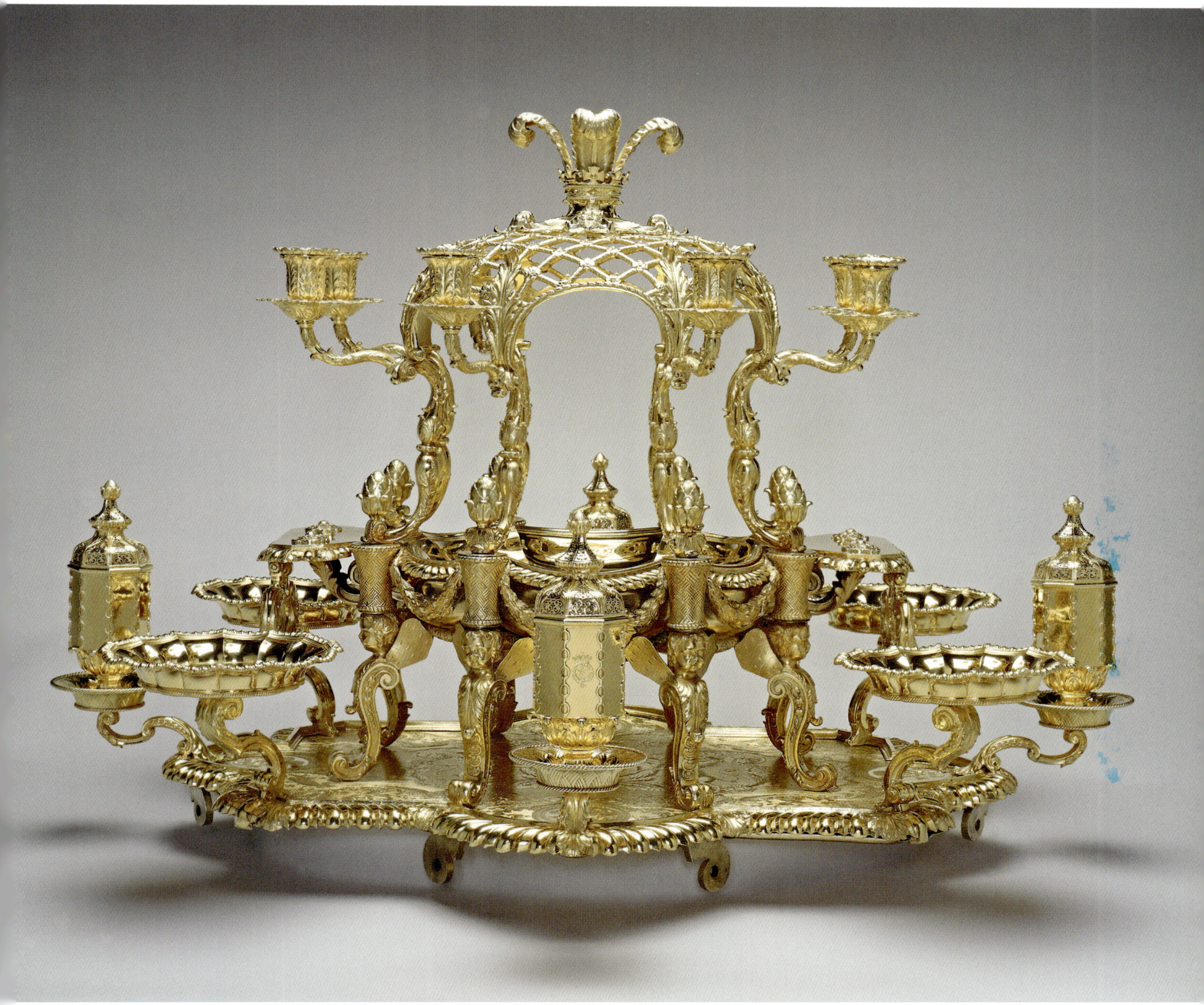

277

ATTRIBUTED TO LEWIS PANTIN (MARK ENTERED 1734)

Ewer and basin *c.*1738

Silver gilt
Ewer: 45.7 cm high; basin: 45.7 cm long
Marks: engraved on ewer and basin: *THIS EWER and BASIN was used at the Christening of George the Third at Norfolk House June the 21st in the year 1738. Was Presented on that occasion by his father Frederick Prince of Wales to THE PRINCESS OF WALES And on the 17th October 1780 was used at the christening of HRH Prince Alfred son of George the Third*
RCIN 31740

PROVENANCE Acquired by Frederick, Prince of Wales, in 1738

LITERATURE Blair 1998, II, no. 37

The *Gentleman's Magazine* of May 1738 stated that 'This morning between 6 and 7 the Princess of Wales was happily deliver'd of a Prince at Norfolk House, St James's Square, the Archbishop of Canterbury being present .... The same day the newborn Prince was very ill and at 11 at Night was privately baptiz'd by the Bp of Oxford by the Name of George; but next Day was much better and her Royal Highness in a fair Way.'[47] The engraved inscriptions on the ewer and basin themselves indicate that they were used during the ceremony at Norfolk House.

These works do not appear in the 1738 ledgers of the Prince's goldsmith, George Wickes. They may be the ewer and basin for which he was charged in 1742, though such a delay for such an important commission seems unlikely; it may be that the work was supplied through another goldsmith. There is a third possibility, which is that the ewer and basin were created with some other purpose in mind. Both parts lack any imagery associated with christenings and the figure of Hercules slaying the Hydra, which forms the handle of the ewer, seems particularly inappropriate. It has been suggested that it may represent the Church Triumphant, but this would be an unusually tenuous allegorical device.[48] Prince George was dangerously ill on the day of his birth and was baptised that evening; in the circumstances any vessel to hand might be used expeditiously. This possibility seems to be confirmed by the inscription itself, which suggests that the font was not used again until the baptism in 1780 of George III's own son, Prince Alfred. For other christenings the royal family reverted to their traditional receptacle – the font and basin created for Charles II (RCIN 31739). Moreover there is evidence that the coats of arms on the pieces, which date from the reign of George III, were engraved over another set of arms. These might have been Frederick's arms or some other's, as it is surely possible that the ewer and basin were hastily presented by a third party for the occasion of the christening.

The oval shape of the basin and its deep well are associated with French design of the period, and it is probable that it was created by one of the Huguenot goldsmiths working in London at the time. Lewis Pantin worked closely with Wickes and is known to have supplied other plate to Frederick, such as the salver which he presented to the city of Bath on his visit there in 1738. KJ

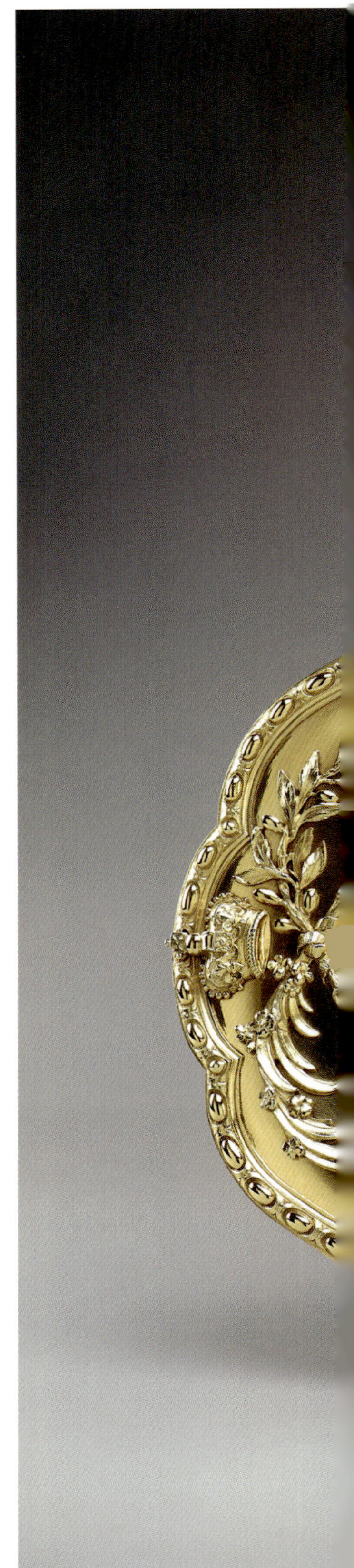

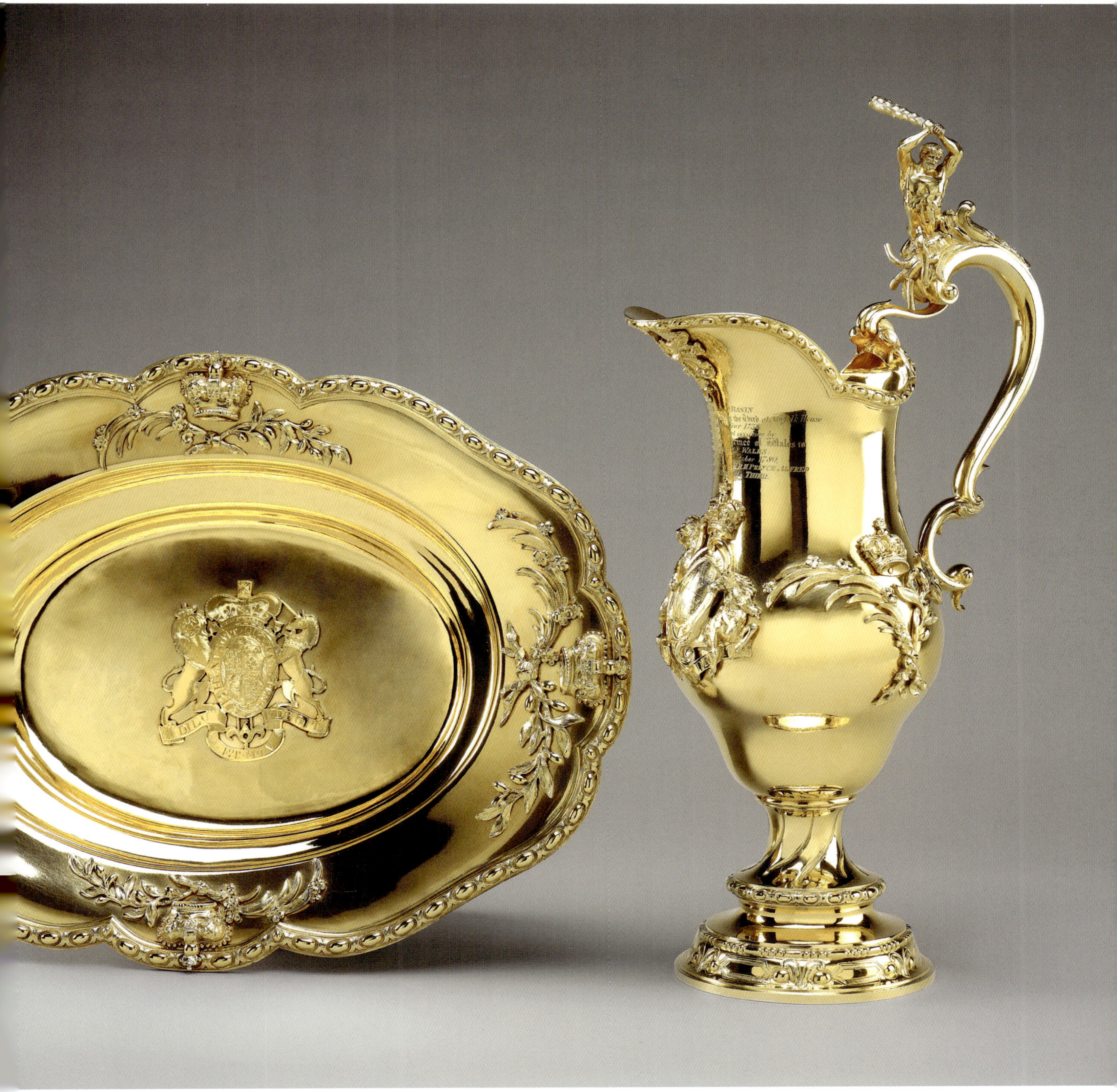

278

ROBERT ROWLAND (ACTIVE 1715–21)

Flintlock breech-loading rifle 1718

Walnut, steel, 121.0 × 8.0 × 19.0 cm; barrel 83.8 cm long; calibre 1.625 cm
Marks: lock and breech signed *R.ROWLAND LONDINI*
Butt plate engraved *6*; escutcheon engraved with the coat of arms of Tournay
Trigger guard engraved *Mr IOHN TOURNAY NEAR LONDON BRIDGE OR NEAR KINGSTON IN SURREY 1718*
London Gunmakers' Company proof marks and 'foreigner's mark' on the breech
RCIN 61095

PROVENANCE Made for John Tournay of Esher, Surrey (d. 1737); acquired by George IV when Prince of Wales, before 1806

LITERATURE Blackmore 1968, p. 37

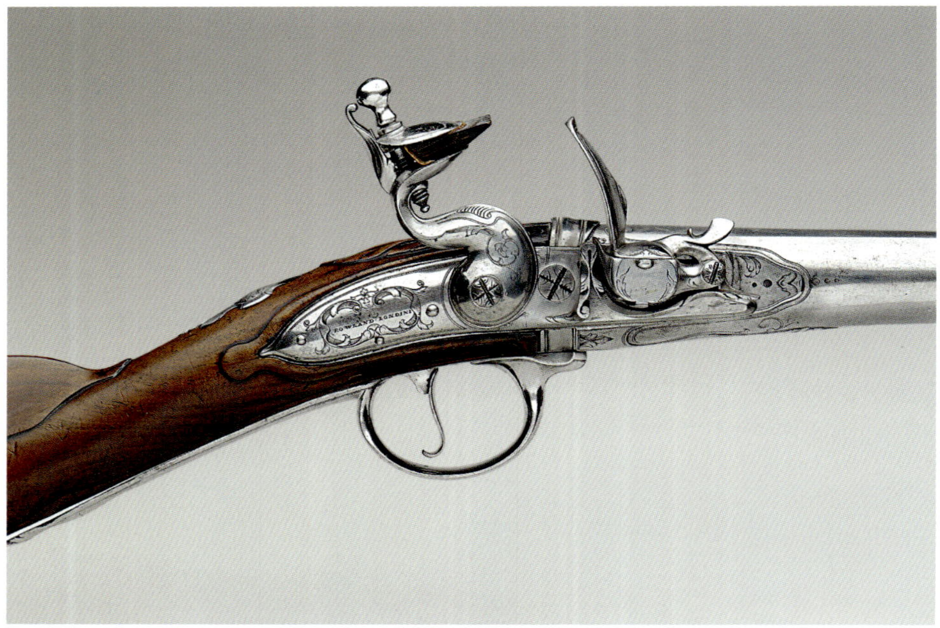

Robert Rowland was made free of the Gunmakers' Company in 1715, so it is not clear why a foreigner's mark was used on the breech of this gun, as these were usually reserved for any gunmaker who did not belong to the London Company. Rowland was a noted maker of breech-loading guns and pistols, although this mechanism is unusual. The breech contains a detachable steel cartridge which may be pre-loaded. It is one of a small group of such guns – another by Rowland and a third by the Huguenot maker Henry Delany (active 1715–46) of *c.*1720 being the only others of this type.[49] As the inscription makes clear, the gun was made for John Tournay, a London merchant, with a property in Esher, Surrey, known as Sandy Chapel. It may be that this is the residence engraved on the butt of the gun. According to Blackmore Tournay commissioned unusual guns bearing his name and address.[50]

The stock of the gun contains a hollow 'patch-box' or covered cavity in which the accoutrements for shooting could be stored. In this instance the cover is engraved with a figure firing at a target and it is possible that the rifle was made for target shooting. KJ

279

JOHN HARMAN (ACTIVE 1714–60)

Pair of flintlock guns 1729

Walnut, browned and gilt steel, silver, RCIN 61489: 130 cm; RCIN 61490: 132.0 cm;
both guns: barrel 91.4 cm long; calibre: 1.82 cm
Marks: steel lock signed *JOHN HARMAN*; barrels signed *JOHN HARMAN LONDON*
Escutcheon engraved with the coat of arms of the Prince of Wales
Barrels stamped with London Gunmakers' Company proof marks and maker's mark of John Harman
RCIN 61489 and 61490

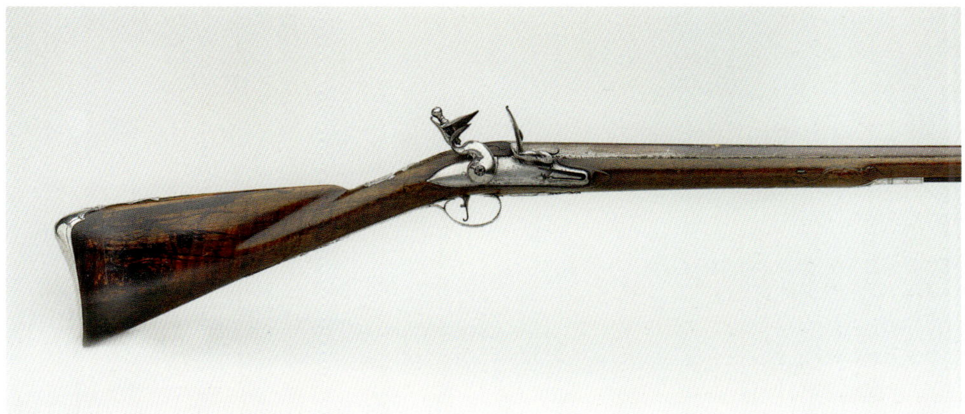

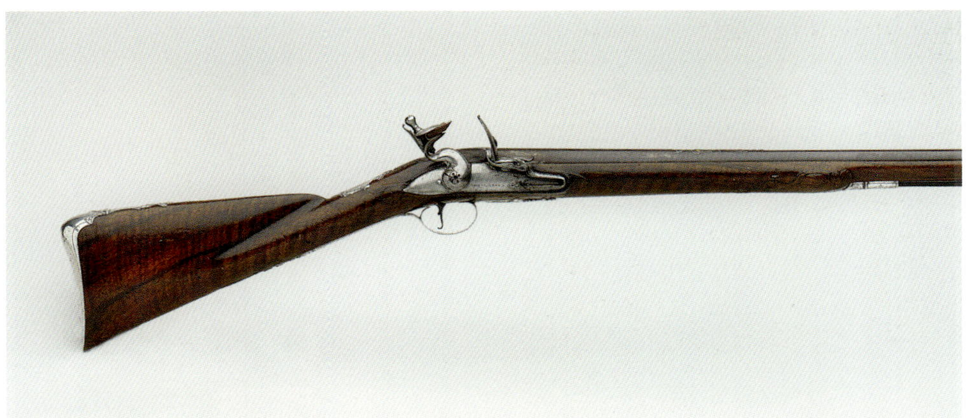

PROVENANCE Probably commissioned by Frederick, Prince of Wales, in 1729

LITERATURE Blackmore 1968, p. 47

In the *Daily Journal* of 7 November 1729, Harman claimed that he had made shotguns with barrels only 30 in. (76.2 cm) in length which 'out-shot other Guns from 6 to 12 inches longer'. Much of the debate in shooting circles of the time was about the ideal length of the barrel, weighing accuracy against balance. George Edie's guide to shooting noted that 'As to the apparent good properties of one of our modern Pieces, they may be reckoned thus: the barrel of a tolerable large bore, and very smooth, with a handsome outside, and the length from three foot to three foot six inches; the lock rather small, with good and strong springs; the stock neat, not too much bent in the butt; and on the whole, the Piece to rise light and handy to the shoulder; the mounting may be according to fancy'.[51] In this case Harman chose longer barrel lengths, and in the instance of one of the pair (RCIN 61490) the stock has also been lengthened.

John Harman was apprenticed to John Shaw (active 1673–1720), who had been Gunsmith-in-Ordinary to every monarch from Charles II to George I. In 1729 Harman became Gunmaker to Frederick, Prince of Wales. As well as the Prince's coat of arms on the escutcheons, the barrel tangs have been engraved with a thistle and two roses, and with a pair of daffodils in reference to their princely patron. A bill in the Duchy of Cornwall accounts from Harman, dated 20 March 1729, charges for 'a fine shot gun mounted in silver at 60 guineas as pr agreement'; it was sold with a tortoiseshell and silver powder-flask at a further four guineas.[52] KJ

280

GUN-MOUNTER: WILLIAM TURVEY (ACTIVE 1711–44);
BARREL-MAKER: ANDREW DOLEP (ACTIVE 1686–1713);
SILVER MOUNTS: ABRAHAM BUTEUX (ACTIVE 1721–31)

Flintlock gun barrel: *c.*1700; lock and mounts 1731/2; later stock?

Walnut, steel, silver (Britannia standard)
21.0 × 6.2 × 153.5 cm; barrel 112.4 cm long; calibre 1.5 cm
Marks: lock signed *W. TURVEY*
Silver hallmarks for London, 1731/2, and maker's mark of Abraham Buteux
Barrel signed *DOLEP LONDINI*
Breech stamped with London Gunmakers' Company proof marks and maker's mark of Andrew Dolep
RCIN 61114

PROVENANCE Acquired by George IV when Prince of Wales, before 1806

LITERATURE Blackmore 1968, p. 56

The Carlton House inventory drawn up before 1806 has a note beside the entry for this piece, saying 'this is a very handsome Gun, the Carving on the breech extremely well executed not inferior to the style of Benvenuto Cellini and probably his work'. In fact the work is that of Andrew Dolep, a Dutchman, who worked for Prince George of Denmark in the early part of the eighteenth century. Blackmore notes that his work was renowned for its high quality and inventiveness.[53] Among Dolep's other clients were the Medici family in Florence, while this gun bears a profile portrait of Empeor Leopold I, so it may originally have been intended for the imperial household. The decorative mounts, which include a figure of Mars, an eagle and a figure in chains, derive from Jean Berain's pattern book *Diverses Pieces très utiles pour les Arquebuzières*, printed in Paris in 1659; the motif of a bound prisoner was a common one on Dolep's work.

The gun was remounted in 1731–2 by William Turvey, who was contracted by the Board of Ordnance to supply guns in the 1720s; he was elected a Master of the Gunmakers' Company in 1733, and from 1741 he also supplied the East India Company. Unusually for this date the silver mounts are Britannia standard, not a legal requirement after 1719, and suggesting a commission from a patron of high standing. KJ

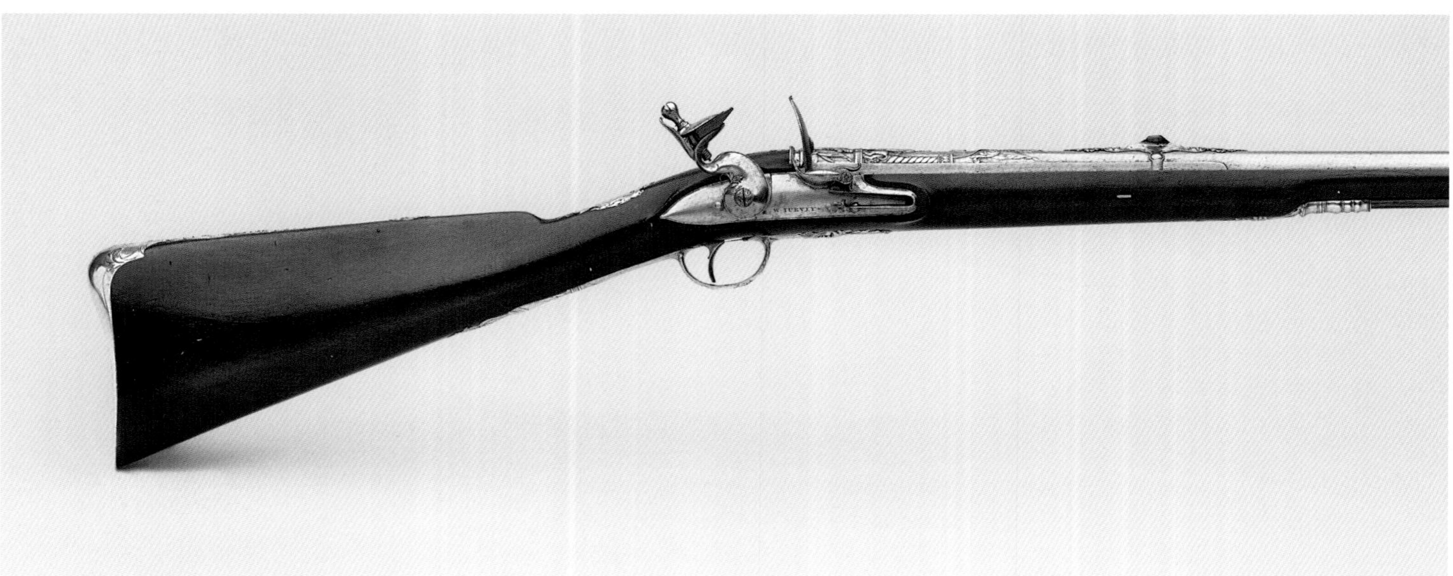

281

LEWIS BARBAR I (ACTIVE 1704–AFTER 1741)

Four-barrelled flintlock carbine *c.*1730

Walnut and steel, 124.0 cm long; barrel 55 cm; calibre 1.29 cm
Marks: lock stamped *BARBAR*
Barrels marked with London Gunmakers' Company proof marks and maker's mark of Lewis Barbar
RCIN 61458

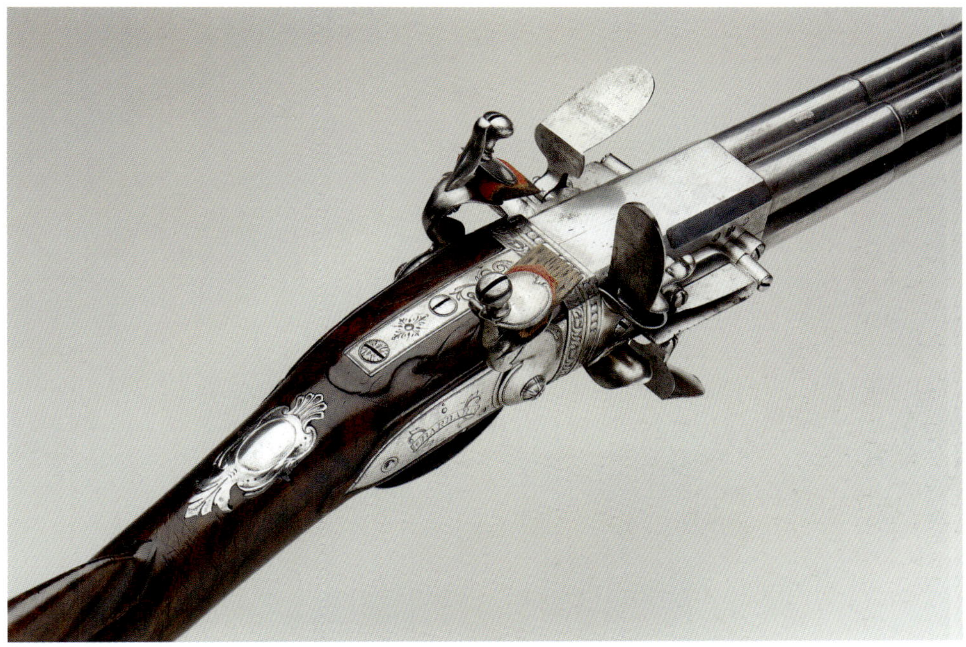

PROVENANCE Possibly made for George II; first recorded in the Royal Collection in 1822

LITERATURE Blackmore 1968, p. 47

Lewis Barbar was appointed Gentleman Armourer to George I in 1717 and continued in the post under George II; from 1718 he was also responsible for the private armoury at Kensington Palace. Although Barbar experimented with different forms of breech-loading guns, he was not known for his work with repeating arms. Here, however, he ventured into creating a four-barrelled carbine, the side-by-side barrels being released by pressing in the trigger guard so that they might be rotated. George II is known to have shown an interest in experimental guns: he also owned a unique air-gun, possibly made for him after the Battle of Dettingen by Johan Gottfried Kolbe.[54] The disadvantage of Barbar's four-barrelled carbine was the lack of a ramrod; although the stock is hollow to allow for storage of accessories, the cavity is not long enough to contain a ramrod, and there is no space on the rotating barrels to place one. The carbine is also heavy, weighing more than 8 lb (3.9 kg). It is possible that the barrels of the gun were shortened in order to reduce the weight. A similar gun in the Musée des Armes, Liège, has barrels of 78 cm long and weighs over 10 lb (4.5 kg). KJ

282

JAMES WILLMORE (1716–1764)

Flintlock breech-loading gun *c.*1745

Steel, walnut and silver, 118.0 cm long; barrel 77.7 cm; calibre: 2.225 cm
Marks: signed on barrel, lockplate and sideplate *WILLMORE LONDON*
'Foreigner's' proof marks on the barrel
RCIN 61485

PROVENANCE Possibly made for George II; first recorded in the Royal Collection in 1822

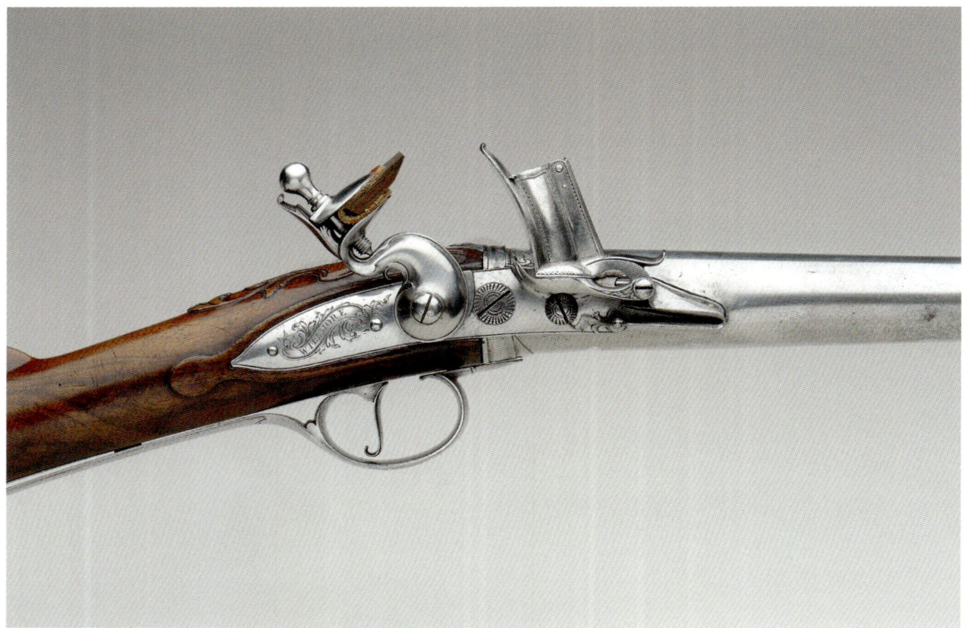

James Willmore was appointed Gunmaker in Ordinary to George II in 1740, receiving lodgings in Whitehall, although in the same post under George III he accepted an annual allowance in lieu of a residence. He was one of the earliest gunmakers to develop the rifled barrel. Here he was also experimenting with a capped and hinged priming powder reservoir, which has been incorporated into the lock behind the frizzen, and with a 'swamped' barrel to improve the velocity of the shot. No. 282 shows the most advanced rococo decoration of any shotgun in the Royal Collection, displaying an engraved trophy of game, raffle leaves, shells and rocaille scrolls.
KJ

283

DAVID COLUMBELL (ACTIVE 1730–77)

Pair of box-lock flintlock pistols *c.*1751

Walnut, silver, steel, 31.0 × 16.0 × 3.5 cm; calibre 1.58 cm
Marks: lock engraved *COLUMBELL*
Butt cap hallmarked for London, maker's mark of *JA* (not identified)
Engraved with Prince of Wales's feathers, Garter, coronet and GP monogram
RCIN 61062.1-2

284

THOMAS DAVIS (ACTIVE 1722–35)

Pair of pistols *c.*1730

Steel, brass, silver, walnut, 35.0 × 14.0 × 5.3 cm; calibre 1.5 cm
Marks: locks engraved *T.DAVIS*
Barrels engraved *DAVIS LONDON*
RCIN 61603.1-2

PROVENANCE (no. 283) probably made for George III when Prince of Wales; (no. 284) first recorded in the Royal Collection in 1822

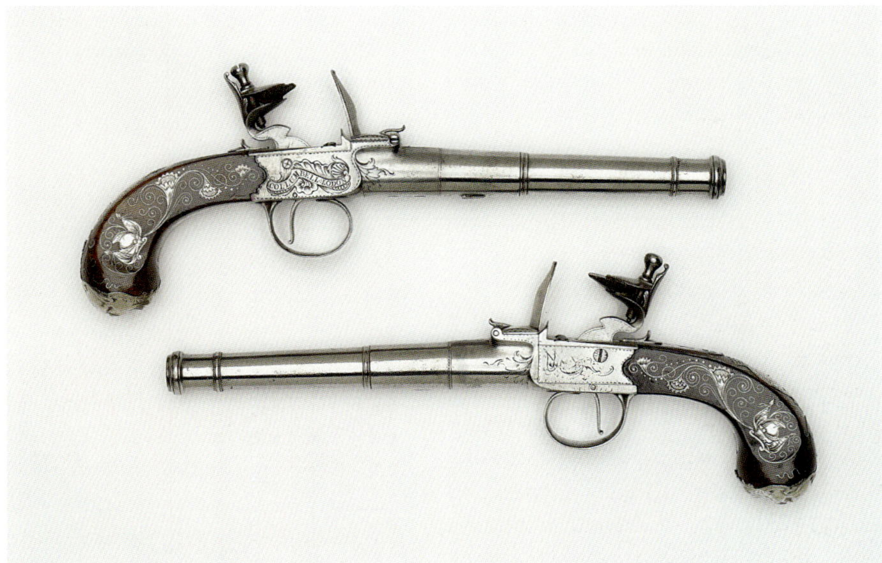

No bill for either of these pairs of pistols survives in the Duchy of Cornwall accounts, although no. 283 was probably commissioned after Frederick, Prince of Wales's death for the young Prince George. This form of pistol with a 'turn-off' barrel to allow for loading was extremely popular in the early eighteenth century, particularly for guns for personal protection which did not have to be reloaded rapidly. The locks include safety catches – another innovation of the period.

David Columbell may have been of Huguenot descent; he was apprenticed to the gunmaker Gerrett Johnson in 1712 and after obtaining his freedom worked in the area around Westminster. He was appointed Gunmaker in Ordnance in 1756. Little is known of Thomas Davis, although he was made free of the Gunmakers' Company in 1722. In employing brass barrels for his pistols, Davis was participating in one of the debates of the period over the best materials to be used in gun-making. Although brass was softer than steel, George Edie, in his *Art of English Shooting* of 1777, recommended its use 'as being less liable to be damaged by wet, and no trouble to keep clean, [it] is certainly preferable to steel'.[55] KJ

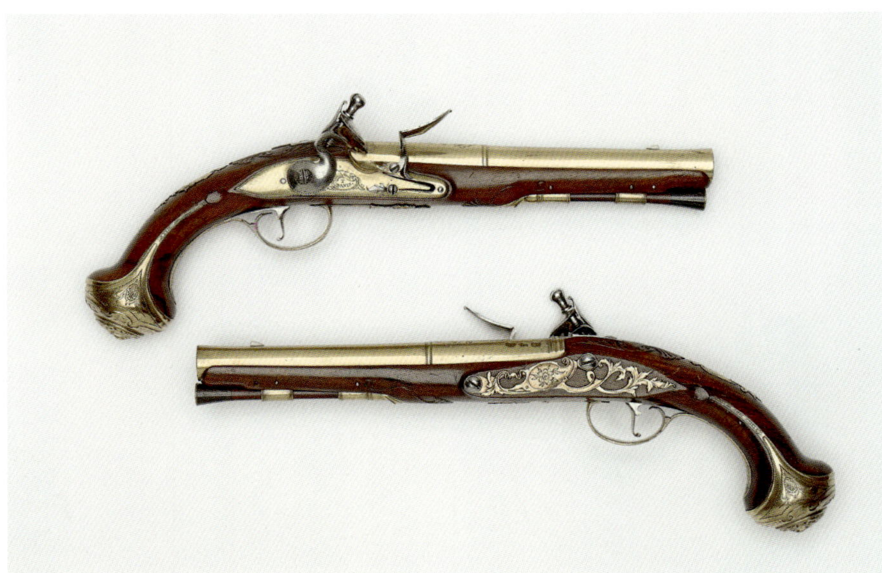

285

BOX: ENGLISH; MINIATURE: CHRISTIAN FRIEDRICH ZINCKE (1683/4–1767)

Snuff box with inset miniature of George II (1683–1760) c.1745

Tortoiseshell, gold, enamel, glass, 3.4 × 8.0 cm
Indistinct hallmark on rim of box

RCIN 4077

PROVENANCE Vuillamy & Son, 30 January 1810, 'For a Tortoiseshell Snuff Box mounted in Gold with an enamel Painting of the late King George the 2nd in the cover at 30 guineas' (WRA 25822); given to Queen Victoria by her aunts Princess Augusta and Princess Sophia (Osborne House inventory 1876)

LITERATURE Walker 1992, no. 33

286

BOX: ENGLISH; MINIATURE: CHRISTIAN FRIEDRICH ZINCKE

Snuff box with inset miniature of Frederick, Prince of Wales (1707–1751) c.1743

Tortoiseshell, gold, enamel, 2.7 × 9.5 × 6.6 cm

RCIN 3754

PROVENANCE Given to King George V on his birthday by the Earl and Countess of Derby, 3 June 1914

LITERATURE Walker 1992, no. 44

The form of these two boxes shows that they were not intended to contain snuff, as snuff boxes were invariably hinged, but were souvenirs. Mary Cowper, Lady of the Bedchamber to Queen Caroline when she was Princess of Wales, recorded in her diary on 20 February 1716 that 'The Princess told me she had sent for Amber out of Germany for Boxes for her Ladies; but as she loved and esteemed me a hundred Times more than any of the Rest, she would make a Distinction and so pulled out of a Drawer a fine gold Box, and gave it me'.[56] This comment makes clear that there was an unofficial hierarchy in the presentation of boxes from members of the royal family. Boxes were the gift of choice to ambassadors and other envoys and to members of the household, and finely chased gold examples were given to those closest to the donor, or to those of high rank. But boxes were also given to those who had rendered service in some way. In 1738, for example, Frederick, Prince of Wales, presented Richard Nash, the Master of Ceremonies at the Assembly Rooms in Bath, with an enamelled box in token of his attention during the Prince's visit to the city. In return Nash erected an obelisk in Queen's Square commemorating Frederick's visit. Although these two boxes are not of the finest quality, they do each bear a portrait by Zincke (see nos 204–20), suggesting that they were not a negligible gift. KJ

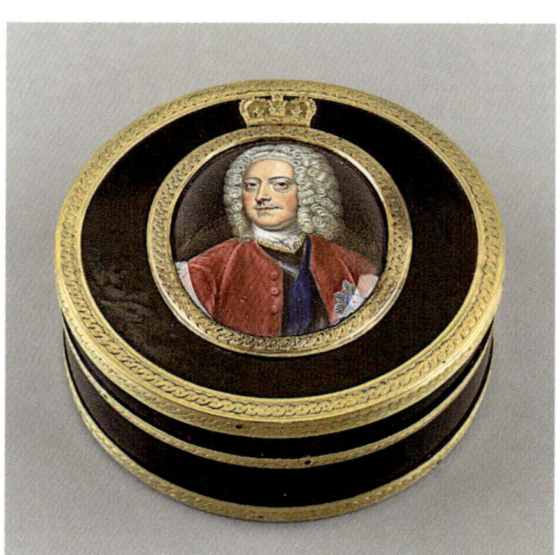

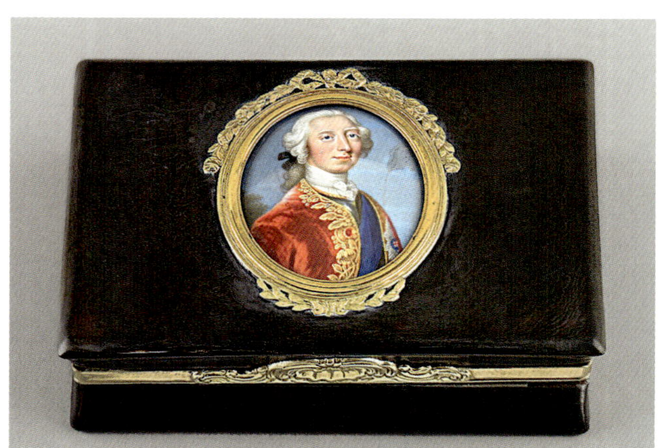

287

BOX: ENGLISH; MINIATURE: BRITISH SCHOOL, 18TH CENTURY

Snuff box with miniature of Anne, Princess Royal (1709–1759) *c.*1734

Agate, gold with enamel miniature, 3.6 × 5.0 × 6.0 cm
Marks: the inner lid is engraved with the cipher of Princess Anne
RCIN 4041

PROVENANCE Acquired from the Cumberland Collection and given to King George V by Queen Mary, Christmas 1913

LITERATURE Walker 1992, no. 74

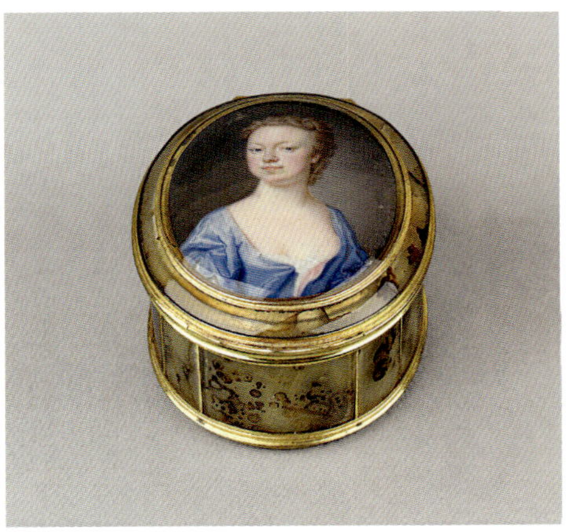

288

BOX: ENGLISH; MINIATURE: BRITISH SCHOOL, 18TH CENTURY

Glass box with miniature of a lady, perhaps Princess Amelia (1711–1786) *c.*1745

Glass, tortoiseshell, gold with enamel miniature, 2.8 × 6.1 cm
Marks: Paris charge and discharge marks for 1744–50
RCIN 4031

PROVENANCE Probably acquired by Edward VII; first recorded in the Royal Collection *c.*1910

LITERATURE Walker 1992, no. 85

289

BOX: ENGLISH; MINIATURES: ATTRIBUTED TO CLARA LEIGH (1750?–1838)

Agate snuff box with miniatures of Augusta, Princess of Wales (1719–1772), and Frederick, Prince of Wales (1707–1751) *c.*1790–1830

Agate, gold; miniature: watercolour on ivory, 3.5 × 5.0 × 5.8 cm
RCIN 4030

PROVENANCE Acquired from the Cumberland Collection; given to King George V by Queen Mary, Christmas 1924

LITERATURE Walker 1992, no. 248

These boxes are likely to have been keepsakes presented to members of the Princesses' households or their friends. The two agate and gold cagework boxes are typical of the snuff boxes produced in England in the mid-century. In each case the artist has not been identified with certainty although the portrait of Princess Anne is attributed to a follower of Zincke and those of Princess Augusta and Frederick, Prince of Wales, have been attributed to Clara Leigh, working from the pastel portraits by Jean-Etienne Liotard (see RCIN 400892–3). It has been suggested that the sitter in the miniature inset into the third box is Princess Amelia, as she was one of the only members of the royal family to have dark eyes. The artist has been tentatively identified as Gervase Spencer (active 1740–63).[57] Spencer was described by George Vertue as 'a young man ... who not long or a few years ago was in the capacity of a footman ... and now professes to liming [painting] with some succes. Which demonstrates a Genius pratizing by degrees of himself – and really is in a curious neat manner and masterly'.[58] KJ

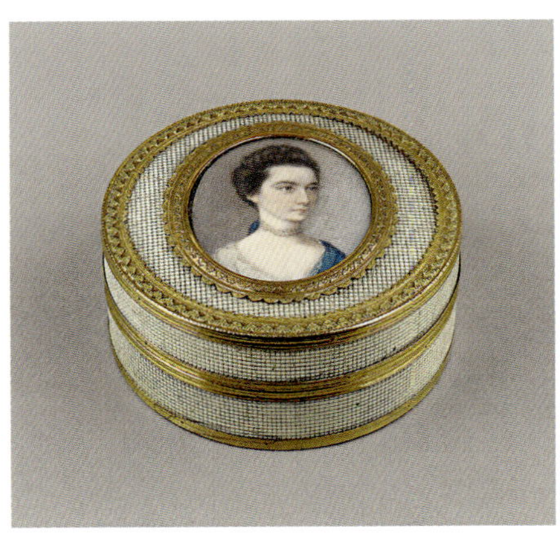

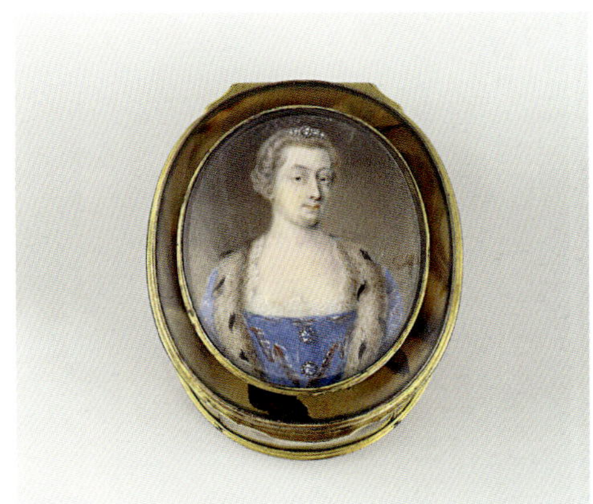

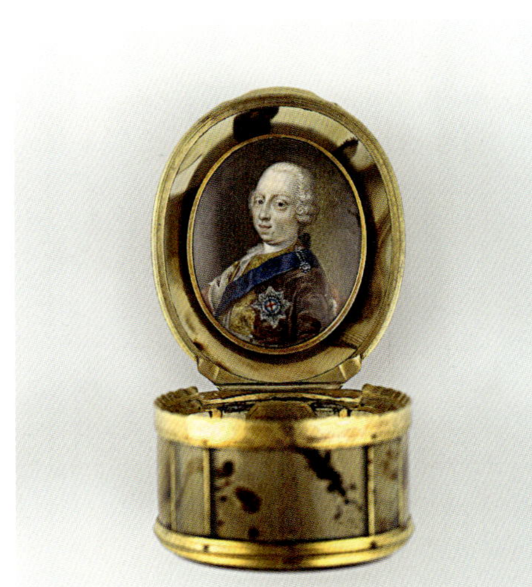

290

BOX: ENGLISH; MINIATURES: CHRISTIAN FRIEDRICH ZINCKE (1683/4–1767)

Agate snuff box with inset miniature of Robert Darcy, 4th Earl of Holdernesse (1718–1778), the interior with miniature of an unknown man, previously identified as the Duke of Schomberg *c.*1745

Agate, gold, enamel, glass, 4.1 × 5.6 × 6.3 cm
RCIN 4734

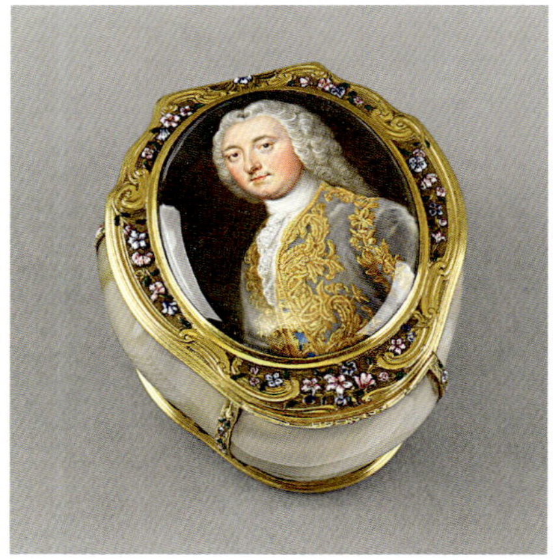

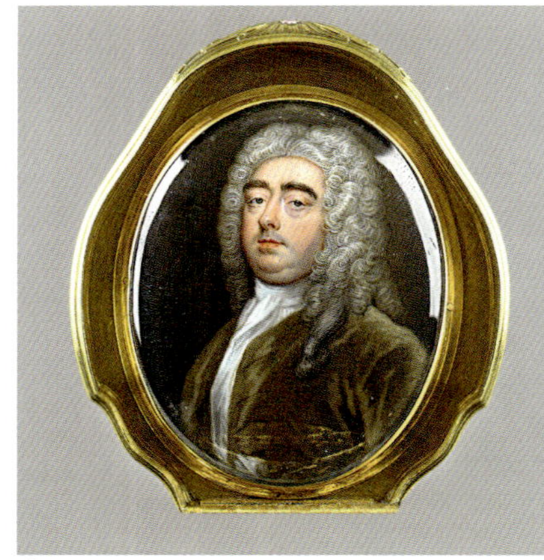

PROVENANCE Probably acquired by Edward VII

LITERATURE Walker 1992, nos 66 and 70

Robert Darcy held several prominent positions during the reign of George II. He was a Lord of the Bedchamber to the King, and present at Dettingen in 1743. From 1744 he was ambassador to Venice and from 1749–51 to The Hague, before he was appointed Secretary of State for the Southern Department and then the Northern Department. The box also contains a second miniature, formerly thought to be Darcy's grandfather, Meinhardt, Duke of Schomberg, although this attribution has now been rejected. It may therefore represent one of the envoys with whom Darcy dealt as an ambassador. According to the Duke of Newcastle, he was 'universally loved and esteemed ... diligent and exact in all his proceedings'.[59] It is possible that he acquired this box in Venice during his embassy there. Lady Mary Wortley Montagu noted in a letter to her daughter from Italy of 27 December 1756 '[I] am highly delighted with the snuff box: that manufacture is at present as much in fashion at Venice as at London. In general all the shops are full of English merchandise, and they boast of every thing as coming from London'.[60] KJ

291

BOX: ENGLISH; MINIATURE BY CHRISTIAN FRIEDRICH ZINCKE

Gold box 1749

Gold, enamel, 3.8 × 6.8 × 9.1 cm
RCIN 3926

PROVENANCE Given by Frederick, Prince of Wales, to Francis, 7th Baron North in 1749; acquired by Queen Mary and given to King George V on his 49th birthday, 3 June 1914

LITERATURE Walker 1992, no. 45

This exceptionally fine box was presented to Francis, Baron North (1704–90) on his appointment as governor to Frederick's son, the eleven-year old Prince George of Wales, in 1749. The box incorporates North's crest on the thumbpiece as well as a portrait miniature of the Prince of Wales by Zincke inside the lid.

The iconography represented on the box seems to relate to North's role as preceptor to the young Prince. The lid and base show scenes of ploughing and harvest – perhaps a reference to North's work in tilling the ground in preparation for the future harvest when his pupil becomes King. A pelican, the symbol of piety, and a peacock, symbolic of vanity, are incorporated into the design together with the motto *Non sibi sed suis* ('not for one's self but for one's own'). The chaser of this high quality work has not been identified, although it is possibly the work of an immigrant German or French workman.

Francis North was one of the Gentlemen of the Bedchamber to Frederick, Prince of Wales. As governor to the future King he was expected to 'go about with Prince George and appear with him in public', for which he received £1000 a year.[61] Walpole wryly commented to Horace Mann in a letter of November 1790 that 'Lord North is made governor to Prince George with 1000*l.* a year, and an Earl's patent in his pocket, but as the passing of the patent is in the pocket of time it would not sell for much'. However, although on Frederick's death North was removed from office as governor to the Prince, he did retain the patent, becoming Earl Guilford in 1752. KJ

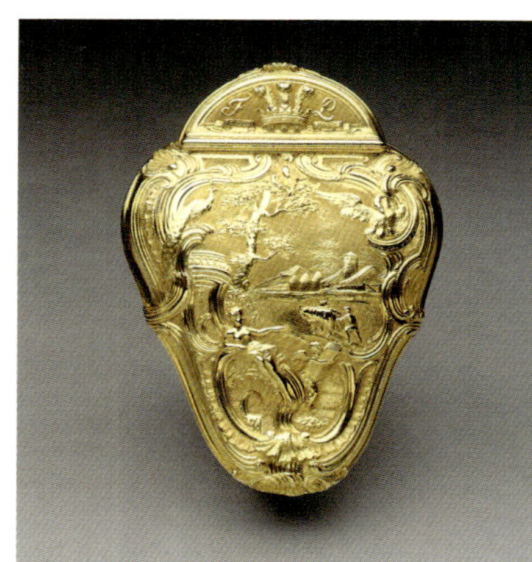

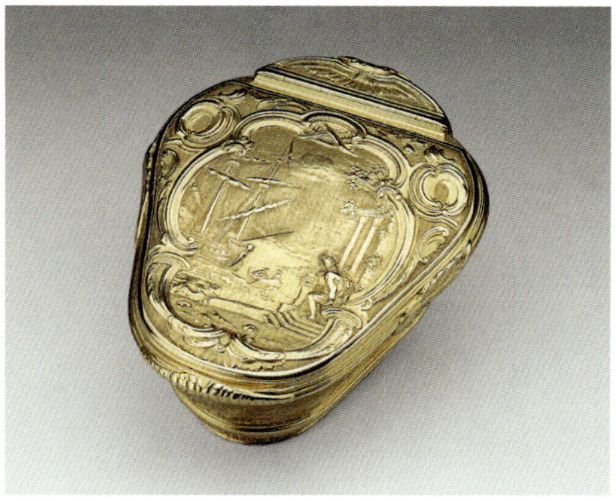

292

ENGLISH

Snuff box *c.*1750

Gold, 3.5 × 6.5 × 8.0 cm
RCIN 3932

PROVENANCE Bequeathed to George, Duke of York (later King George V) by Emily Caroline, Countess Sydney in 1893

The close similarity in shape, decoration and chasing between this box and no. 291 suggest that they were both from the same workshop. Although this example lacks any royal iconography it was also possibly a gift to a member of the household of the young Prince George. Thomas Townshend, later Viscount Sydney, was Clerk of Prince George's Household from 1756. No direct reference is made on the box to his family, but it was known to have been in the Sydney family until it was presented to King George V in 1893. KJ

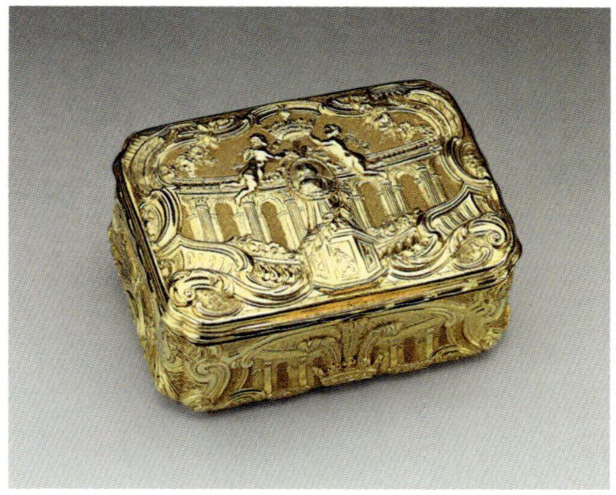

293

ENGLISH

Snuff box *c.*1745

Gold, 2.8 × 6.8 × 5.2 cm
RCIN 4047

PROVENANCE First recorded in the Hunt and Roskell collection, exhibited at the South Kensington Museum in 1862; a wedding gift from M. and Mme de Falbe to King George V and Queen Mary, 1893

This box incorporates both a small profile portrait of Frederick, Prince of Wales, and his applied heraldic badge as the thumbpiece. This commemorative iconography on the lid suggests that the box was a presentation piece. The architectural arcading and use of different textures of gold mirror the design of contemporary French boxes, and this example is the most francophilic of those associated with Frederick.

The Prince of Wales's accounts include payments for boxes supplied by Jasper Cunst (active 1725–76). In 1734, for example, Frederick purchased 'a gold snuff box with diamonds and rubies on a bloodstone' from Cunst for £46.[62] Augustin Heckel (*c.*1690–1770), one of the leading gold chasers working in London, appears to have designed and chased gold boxes supplied by Cunst. Similarities between this box and one signed by both Cunst and Heckel (private collection) have led to the suggestion that no. 293 is also Heckel's work.[63] KJ

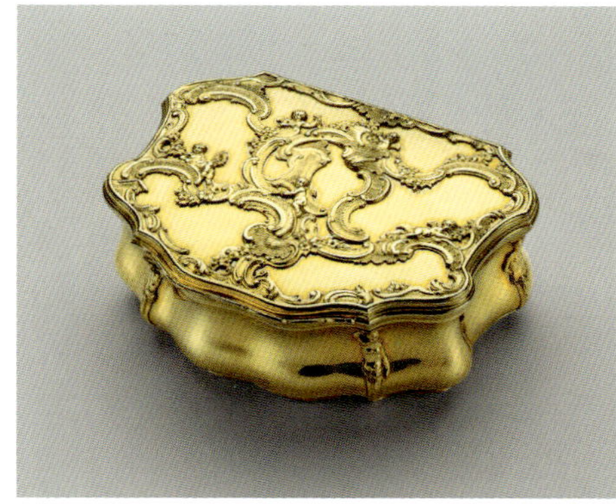

294

BOX, ENGLISH; MINIATURES AFTER CHRISTIAN FRIEDRICH ZINCKE

Snuff box *c.*1745

Gold, enamel, 2.8 × 7.5 × 6.0 cm
Marks: scratch mark on thumbpiece *John hane* (?)
RCIN 73414

PROVENANCE Presented to Queen Mary by her family, Christmas 1935

The design of this cartouche-shaped box, with architectural motifs and herm figures around the sides, is more usually found in hardstone examples, mounted with gold cagework. The most notable boxes of this type were usually made in Berlin or Dresden, although French examples are known.[64] However, this example is probably English in origin, although the marked rococo style suggests a familiarity with Continental examples. The thumbpiece bears a scratch mark on either side, possibly reading John Hane, although this name has not been traced among the box makers of the period. He may have been related to the Huguenot Hanet family of goldsmiths and watch-case makers recorded working around St Martin's Court, close to Leicester Square.[65] The box contains miniatures of Frederick and Augusta and may have been a presentation piece. KJ

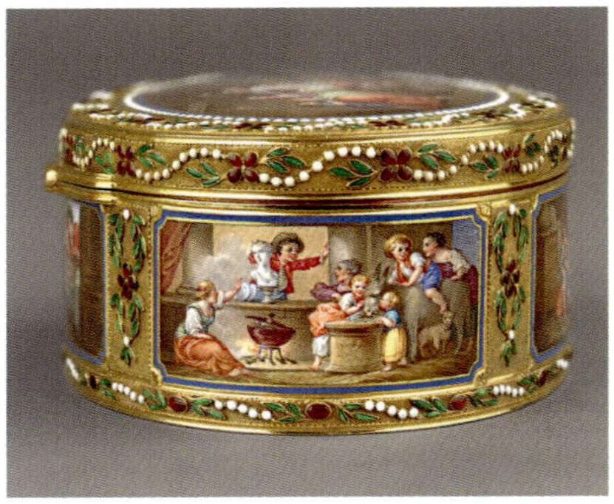

295

FRENCH

Snuff box *c.*1750–56

Gold and enamel, 3.8 × 9.6 × 7.0 cm
Hallmarks: Paris charge and discharge marks for 1750–56
RCIN 4024

PROVENANCE Presented to King George V on his Silver Jubilee, May 1935, by the Empire Societies

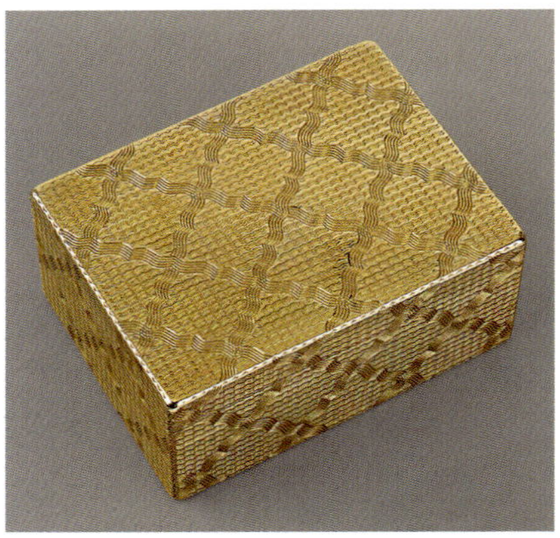

296

PHILIPPE EMANUEL GARBE (ACTIVE 1748–93)

Snuff box *c.*1754/5

Gold, 2.9 × 6.5 × 4.8 cm
RCIN 4409
Hallmarks: Paris charge and discharge marks for 1750–56; maker's mark of P.E. Garbe

PROVENANCE Collection of Adolphus Frederick, Duke of Cambridge; acquired by Queen Mary in 1904

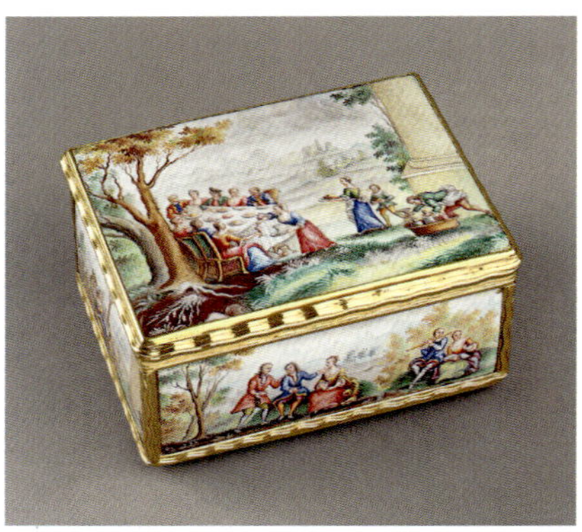

297

FRENCH

Snuff box 1744/5

Enamel, gold, 4.0 × 7.9 × 6.2 cm
Hallmarks: Paris assay mark of 1744/5
RCIN 4750

PROVENANCE Presented to King George V by Queen Mary on his birthday, 3 June 1933

The strict regulation of the goldsmiths' guild in France and the restriction of the number of specialist makers permitted to make boxes at any one time in Paris meant that French snuff boxes were highly sought after. The amount of gold used by a single snuff box-maker annually suggests that he could only create a dozen boxes each year, and specialist turners, chasers and enamellers were also involved in each work, which forced the price high. Consequently such pieces were amongst the most luxurious items on the market. Despite the efforts of the Anti-Gallican Society, founded in London in 1745 to prevent the import of French goods into England, some of the highest quality pieces did inevitably make their way across the Channel.

Whereas English boxes of the period tended towards the use of hardstones or chased gold, these three examples show the strengths of the French makers – engine-turning in elaborately interwoven designs, and enamelling. Some of the enamellers of the period were themselves members of the Parisian goldsmiths' guild (the *corporation des marchands-orfèvres-joailliers*); others, such as Philippe Parpette and Jean Coteau, worked both on boxes and at the Sèvres manufactory. The scenes on these boxes were usually taken from contemporary prints – those on no. 295 are possibly derived from the work of François-Bernard Lépicié (1698–1755), whose work was particularly popular with box designers. KJ

298

ENGLISH

Snuff box 1751

Tortoiseshell, gold, 3.1 × 6.4 × 4.8 cm
RCIN 22170

PROVENANCE Acquired by Queen Mary in 1935

Tobias Smollett's *Continuation of the complete History of England* recorded the death of the Prince of Wales in the following words: 'This excellent Prince, who now died in the forty-fifth year of his age, was possessed of every amiable quality which could engage the affection of the people, a tender and obliging husband, a fond parent, a kind master, liberal, generous, candid and humane; a munificent patron of the arts, an unwearied friend to merit; well disposed to assert the rights of mankind in general, and warmly attached to the interest of Great Britain'.[66]

On Frederick's death the King prescribed six months of official mourning at court. Dress was strictly regulated, the rules being laid down in contemporary newspapers and magazines: 'Ladies to wear black bombazines, plain muslin or long lawn, crape hoods, shamoy shoes and gloves, and crape fans .... The men to wear black cloth, without buttons on the sleeves or pockets, plain muslin or long lawn cravats and weepers, shamoy shoes and gloves, crape hat bands and black dress swords and buckles'.[67] For the court elite it would be expected that fashionable accessories such as this snuff box would complement mourning dress, and a number of these piqué boxes were created to supply this demand. KJ

299

ENGLISH

Vinaigrette with lid 1757–8

Gold, enamel, 2.9 × 5.4 × 4.6 cm
Marks: inscribed *FELL ASLEEP Dec: 28 1757*
RCIN 65777

PROVENANCE Acquired by Queen Mary before 1914

This small box intended to contain an aromatic vinegar-soaked sponge was made to commemorate the death on 28 December 1757 of Princess Caroline Elizabeth (1713–57), daughter of George II (see nos 211 and 219). Walpole claimed that she spent much of her life in seclusion at St James's Palace, pining after the death of Lord Hervey and commented, 'Though her state of health had been so dangerous for years, and her absolute confinement for many of them, her disorder was, in a manner, new and sudden, and her death unexpected by herself, though earnestly her wish. Her goodness was constant and uniform, her generosity immense, her charities most extensive; in short, I, no royalist, could be lavish in her praise'.[68]

Whether or not her death had been expected, the Princess left a brief will, making her sister, Princess Amelia, her executor, and leaving items of jewellery to her sisters and her brother, William, Duke of Cumberland. To her 'dear sister Anne' she bequeathed 'an enamelled case and two bottles of the same sort'.[69] KJ

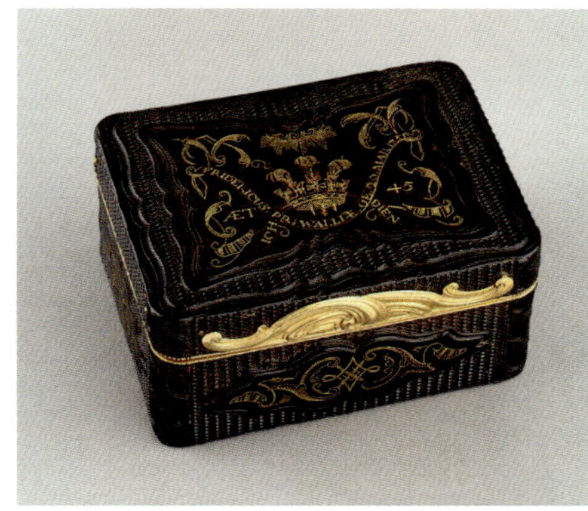

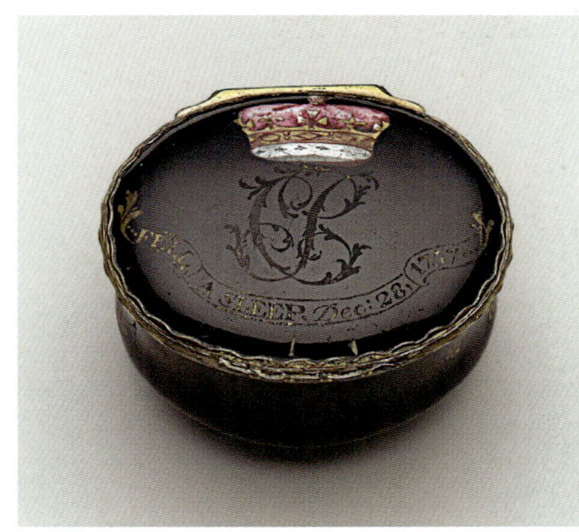

300–308

ENGLISH

Etui c.1750

Gold, containing implements of gold, ivory and steel, 10.3 × 3.6 × 2.5 cm
RCIN 9045

PROVENANCE Acquired by Queen Mary

Etui c.1740

Agate, gold, diamond, 10.1 × 3.5 × 2.7 cm
RCIN 4540

PROVENANCE First recorded in the Royal Collection in 1933

Egg-shaped box c.1750

Bloodstone, gold, enamel, 4.8 × 2.9 cm
RCIN 4568

PROVENANCE Presented to Queen Mary by Lady Northcote, 1927

Pill box c.1740

Gold, agate, 2.3 × 3.8 × 3.1 cm
RCIN 14243

PROVENANCE Probably acquired by Queen Alexandra

Scent bottle holder c.1750

Hardstone, gold, diamond, 4.2 × 2.5 × 1.8 cm
RCIN 4508

PROVENANCE Probably acquired by Queen Mary

Scent bottle holder c.1750

Gold, diamonds, 1.6 × 2.3 × 0.7 cm
RCIN 24527

PROVENANCE Probably acquired by Queen Alexandra

ENGLISH

Scent bottle holder c.1750

Agate, gold, rubies, diamond, emeralds, 7.4 × 7.1 × 3.6 cm
RCIN 4544

PROVENANCE Acquired by Queen Mary

PROBABLY CHELSEA PORCELAIN MANUFACTORY

Needlecase c.1760

Porcelain, gold, 8.7 × 2.3 cm
RCIN 4472

PROVENANCE Acquired by Queen Mary

'GIRL-IN-A-SWING' FACTORY, CHARLES GOUYN, LONDON

Needlecase 1755

Porcelain, gold, 10.5 × 2.0 cm
RCIN 107350

PROVENANCE Acquired by HM Queen Elizabeth The Queen Mother

This group of objects, all English, comprises items typically purchased in a toy-shop of the period. A bill to Frederick, Prince of Wales, from the shop of Paul Bertrand of October 1738 included not only eight snuff boxes in various materials, but also two etuis, two pocket books, a toothpick case, a gold 'smelling bottle' and an onyx egg.[70] The Prince paid £21 for a single etui, and a protective outer case for one of these items cost as much as ten guineas.

An etui was a small case to contain implements for writing, manicure or sewing, so named after the French word *estuier*, meaning to keep. The bill from Bertrand shows that the items contained within an etui were sold separately: the Prince paid £5 15s 6d for 'trincketts' for his bloodstone example, together with a set of five chains to suspend it from a belt. Several of the smaller pieces in this group (nos 300, 304 and 305) have suspension loops for such chains.

Mary Delany's letter to her sister Anne Dewes of 14–17 January 1756 suggests that these small objects were an essential element of one's fashionable costume. Describing the clothes of their cousin Mrs Spencer on her first visit to court, she notes not only her white and silver dress and her lavish diamond jewellery but also 'her watch and etuy suited to the rest'.[71] Their precious nature is emphasised by the use of gemstones as thumbpieces (nos 301, 304, 305 and 306) and the quality of the chasing on some of the cases. No. 300 in particular shows the highest-quality workmanship, combining polished rococo scrolls and scenes from Aesop's *Fables* against a sablé ground. In 1749 Vertue praised the London chasers who 'yearly produce works of Gold boxeses watch cases – tweezers &c multitudes for their excellence not only admired here but sold for abroad to many parts of the World'.[72]

Bertrand's bill makes clear that these luxury scent bottle cases and etuis came in a range of materials and decorative finishes: Frederick bought not only 'an inlay'd estwey' but also versions in bloodstone and carnelian. The use of polished hardstones was also described by Mrs Delany, who, on 22 April 1740, visited 'Faulkner's the famous lapidary, where we saw abundance of fine things, and the manner of cutting and polishing pebbles &c'.[73]

These items were also made in fashionable English porcelain. No. 307, a needle-case in the form of a stalk of asparagus, is probably the work of the Chelsea porcelain factory, but the bouquet (no. 308) is attributed to its sister company, run by the jeweller Charles Gouyn, who until 1749 was a partner of Nicholas Sprimont at Chelsea and who supplied porcelain to a dealer on St James's Street. Little is known of Gouyn's operation but the needlecase is typical of his output. KJ

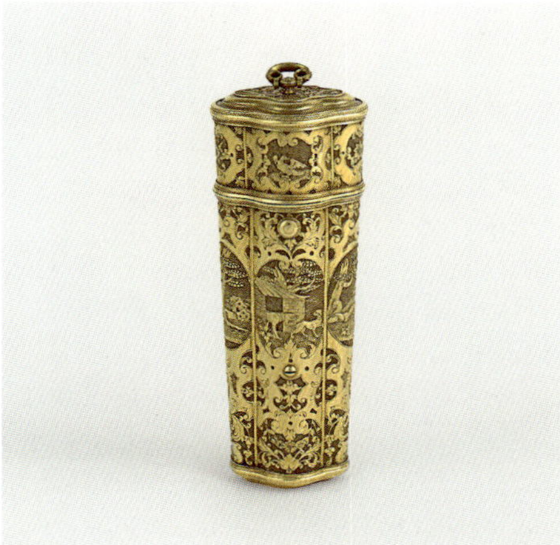

no. 300

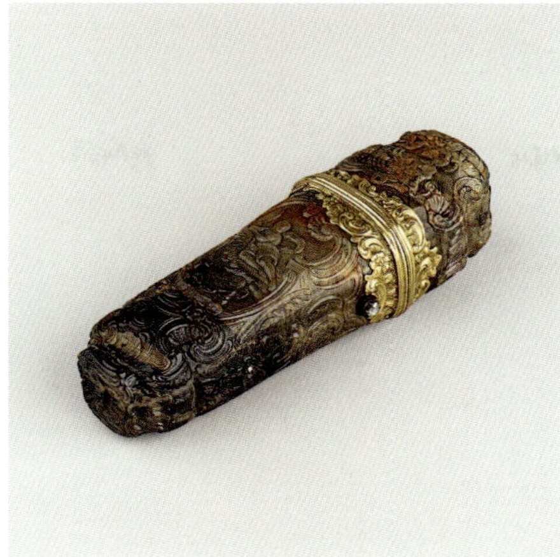

no. 301

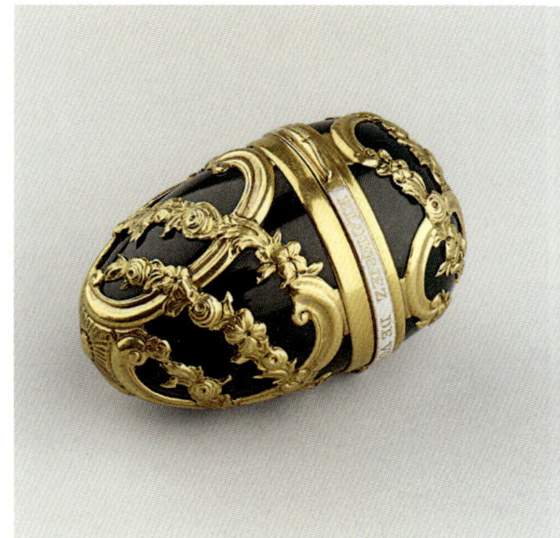

no. 302

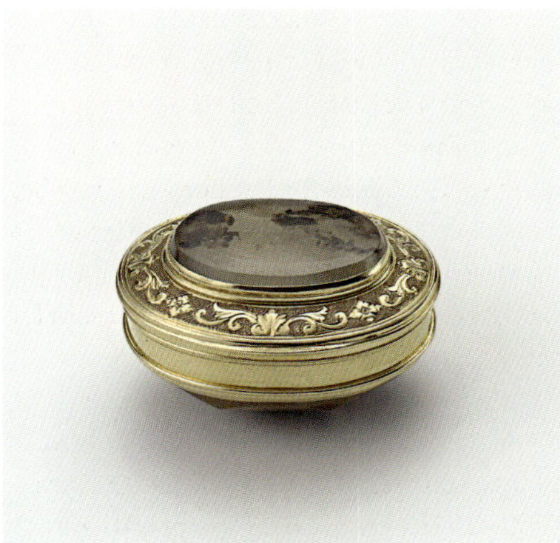

no. 303

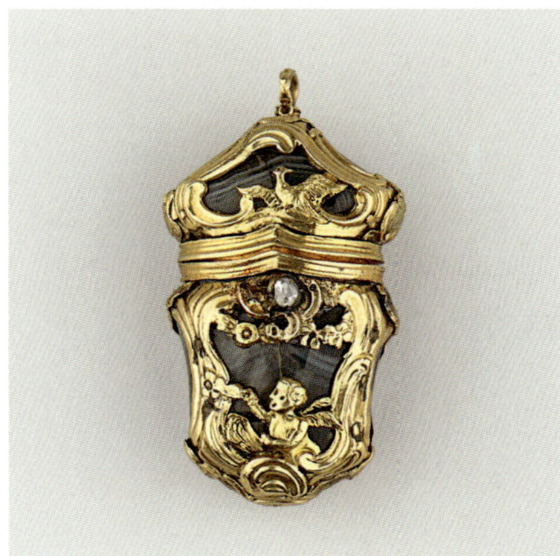

no. 304

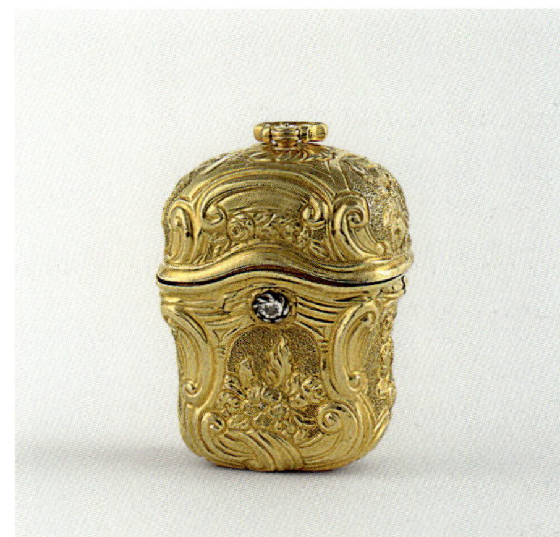

no. 305

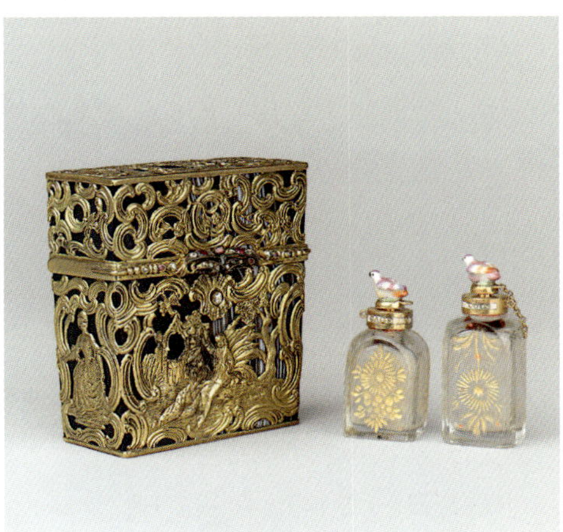

no. 306

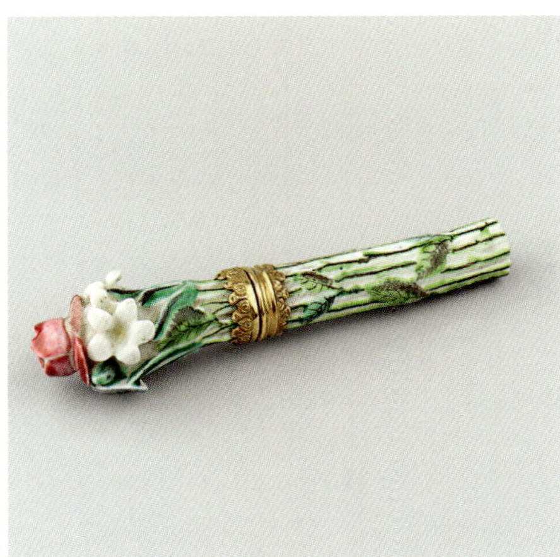

no. 307

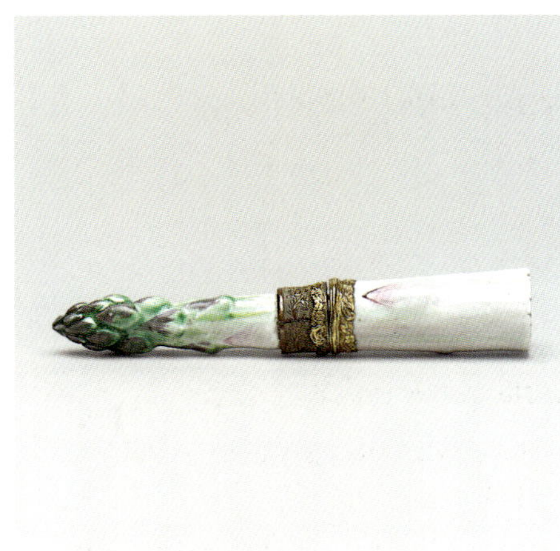

no. 308

309

ENGLISH

Ring 1736

Silver, gold, diamonds, enamel, hair, 1.5 × 2.5 × 2.3 cm
Marks: engraved *F.P.W. 1736* and *Sem H.N.Q.T.L.Q.Man*
RCIN 9020

PROVENANCE Presented to Sir John Chardin by Frederick, Prince of Wales; bequeathed to Sir Philip Musgrave; given to Queen Mary by Lord and Lady Cromer, 26 May 1934

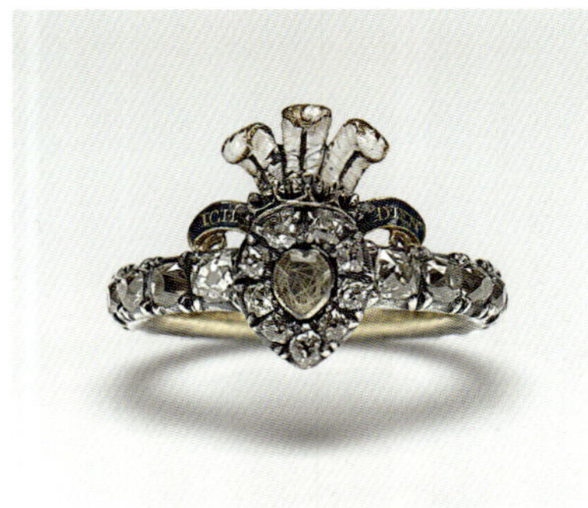

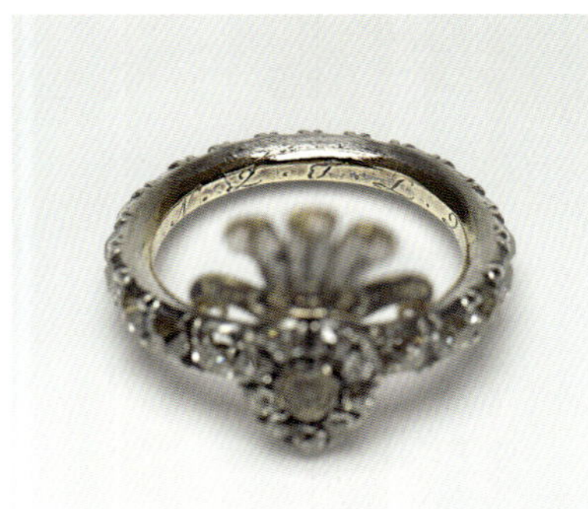

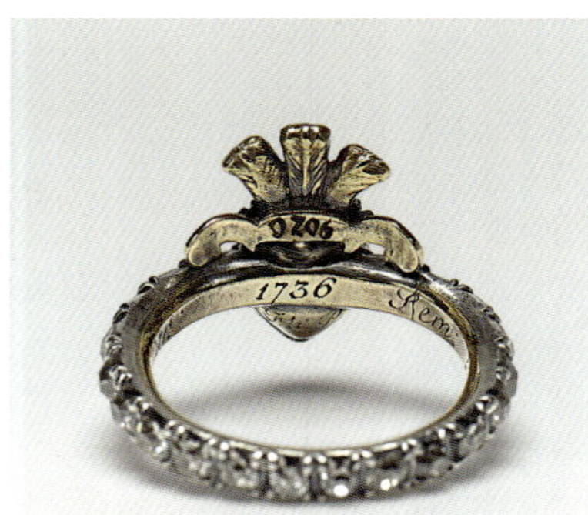

John Chardin (d. 1755) was the son of a Huguenot jeweller and famous traveller, and a close friend of Frederick, Prince of Wales. In 1720 he was created 1st Baronet of the Inner Temple by George I and according to the *English Baronetage* of 1741 'both father and son brought great riches into England'.[74] Chardin organised hunting parties for the Prince on his estates at Kempton Park in Sunbury, Middlesex, and corresponded informally with Frederick and other members of his set, including Charles Calvert, Lord Baltimore, and Henry, Marquis of Carnarvon (1708–71), seeking positions for his relations. Chardin was distantly related to the sculptor Henry Cheere, addressed in his letters as 'my dear and worthy kinsman', and it seems to have been through Chardin's persuasive correspondence that Cheere was employed at Baltimore's house, Woodcote Park, in Surrey, as well as receiving the commission for a monument to Carnarvon's wife.[75]

Frederick chose to acknowledge his friendship with Chardin with this highly personal gift, displaying not only the Prince of Wales's badge but also a lock of his hair, with an engraved inscription from the Aeneid: *Semper Honos Nomenque Tuum Laudesque Manebunt* (Your honour, name and praise will endure forever). KJ

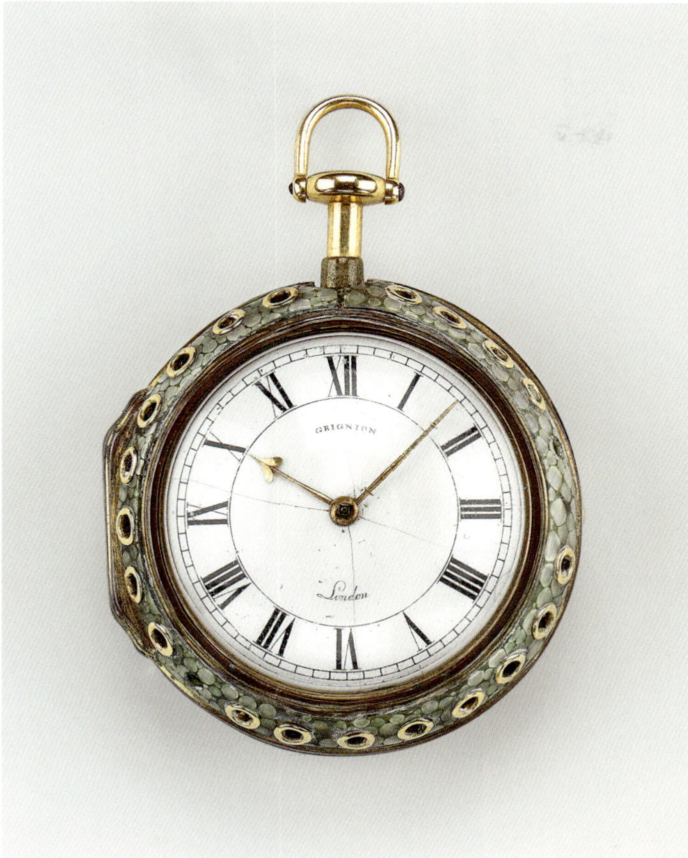

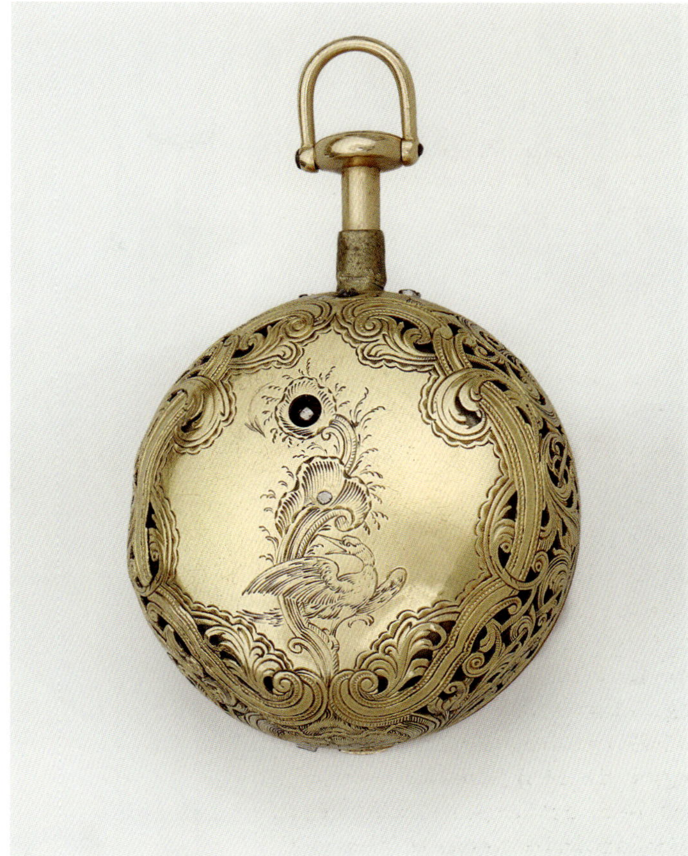

310

THOMAS GRIGNION (1713–1784)

***Case watch** c.1755*

Gold, enamel, steel, with a shagreen case,
7.0 × 5.0 × 3.0 cm
Dial inscribed *GRIGNION London* and movement numbered *No. 1573*
RCIN 14296

PROVENANCE Possibly acquired by Edward VII or Queen Alexandra

The small luxury items sold in the toy-shops of London included watches. In 1738, at Bertrand's shop, for example, the Prince of Wales purchased a bloodstone watch with chain for £33 and a repeater with chain and seal for £48.[76] Although this example is elaborately pierced and chased around its outer rim, the back is simply engraved with a ho-ho bird and rococo cartouche, rather than carrying any of the sophisticated chasing seen on other watches by Grignion. It must therefore have been for the watch movement itself that the piece was purchased.

Until Thomas Mudge's innovatory lever escapement, which seems to have first been used in a watch created for Queen Charlotte dating from 1770,[77] the cylinder escapement was the most accurate mechanism for keeping time. Thomas Grignion is credited with making improvements to this form of escapement. An engraved plaque of about 1795, found in the vestry-room of the church of St Paul, Covent Garden, where Grignion worked on the turret clock, stated that he 'brought to perfection in 1740 the horizontal principle in watches and the dead beat in clocks'.[78] ES

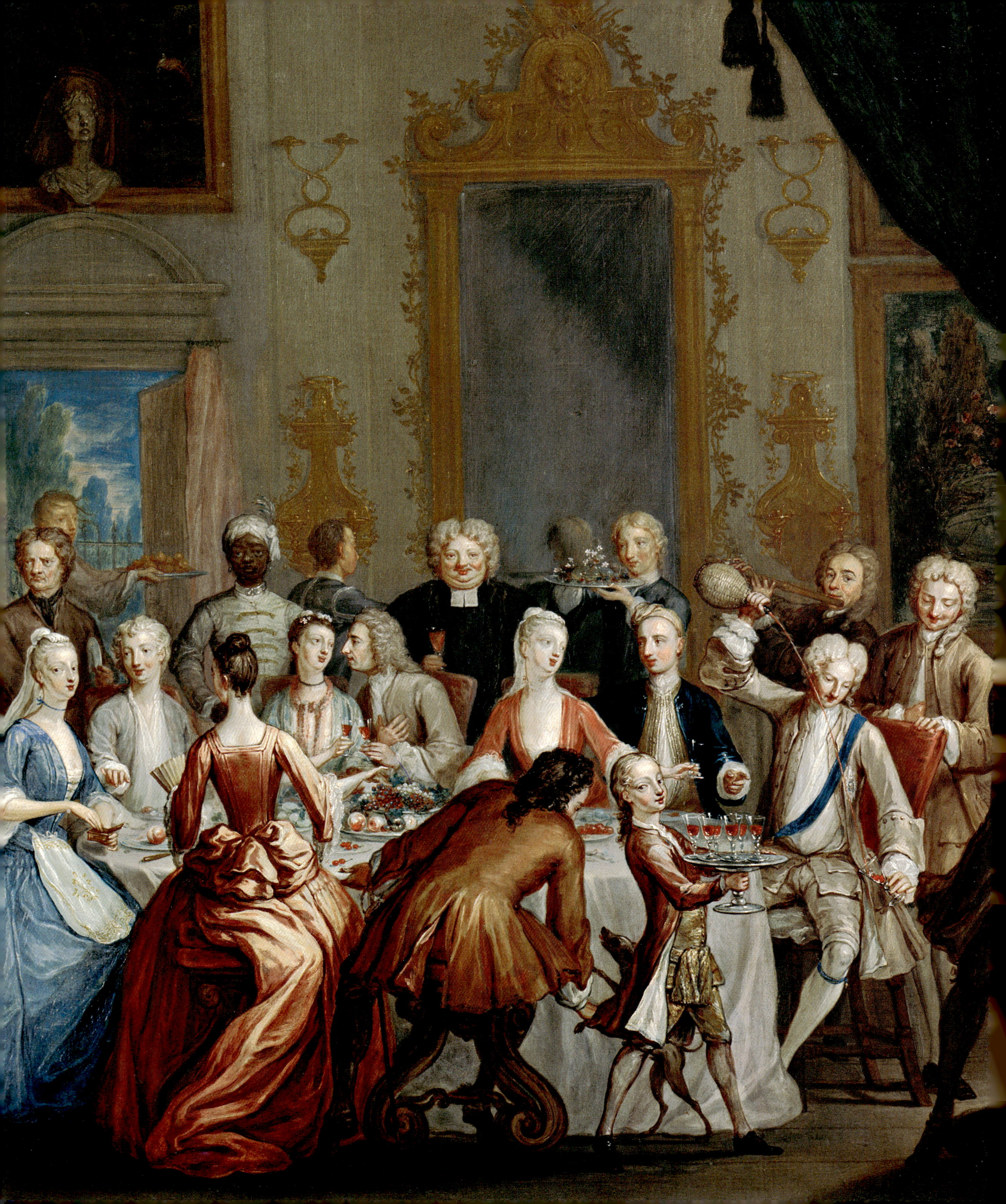

XI
Dining at Court

KATHRYN JONES

AS EARLY AS 1714 John Macky noted that:

> King George hath entirely altered that Method; he dines at St James's privately serv'd by his Domesticks and often sups abroad with his Nobility, and when he is at Hampton-Court, and keeps open Table, he generally hath a dozen of Noblemen and Gentlemen to sit at Table with him. No Prince that ever sat upon the English Throne gave better Tables to the inferior officers.[1]

The Stuart ordinances for the government of the Royal Household included strict regulations about who might approach the royal table or serve the monarch, limiting the numbers to 'none but persons of good quality'.[2] Queen Anne retained the tradition of being served only by members of the nobility, who would kneel to do so. By contrast, the Hanoverian monarchs introduced an element of informality to the court. As Macky reported in his letters, the nobility were more likely to be invited to dine alongside the King, although he was still served by members of the Household. George II went so far as to show concern on the marriage of Frederick, Prince of Wales, that he might demand to be served 'on the knee' to distinguish himself from his guests, which the King considered unsuitable.[3]

The idea of a separate 'eating room' was still, at this period, a relatively new one. At St James's Palace no official eating space existed, and public dining took place in the Ballroom, although a room at Kensington Palace was designated the King's Dining Room. George I, who disliked the tradition of eating in public, remained in his bedchamber to dine, and in the evenings he would sup in the apartment of Madame Schulenberg, or visit the theatre or the homes of political allies such as Sir Richard Onslow (d. 1760) or Henry Hyde, Earl of Rochester (1672–1753). The role of entertaining was undertaken instead by the Prince and Princess of Wales, who hosted the 'drawing rooms', evening parties and occasional balls at Somerset House or St James's, although George I would attend from time to time. It was the Prince and Princess who also undertook dining in public and they usually were to be viewed on a Sunday after chapel at St James's Palace, where the public were admitted by ticket. On such occasions, 'as many visitors as the appointed space could conveniently admit, were permitted to see their sovereign seated at his meal', and indeed, the royal family were noted for their liberal attitude.[4] A contemporary source in the summer of 1716 noted that 'The Prince and Princess dine every day in public at Hampton Court and all sorts of people have free admission to see them even of the lower sort and rank ... and the Prince and Princess are so affable and courteous to them that it gains on the people's minds extremely'.[5]

Lady Mary Wortley Montagu reported a different story from Hanover, where George I was a genial host and entertainer, having a company of French comedians play each night at court, and 'His majesty dines and sups constantly in publick. The court is very numerous and his affability and goodness makes it one of the most agreeable places in the world'.[6] When George I was feeling politically threatened during the years 1717–18 he certainly made an effort to entertain more lavishly, particularly during the summer months at Hampton Court, where he would frequently leave his own apartments to mingle with the court, and the bills of fare show a dramatic increase in the number and style of dishes served.

On high days and holidays particularly lavish meals were served. These included the birthdays of members of the royal family and the anniversaries of the accession and the coronation. On these days there were gun salutes, bonfires and illuminations in the city, and at court public tables would be erected for visiting ambassadors and other important guests. In October 1718, on the anniversary of the coronation, for example, George I was at Hampton Court, where the bills of fare show the King's Table, a second and third table, a Grand Table and a Ladies' Table.[7]

George II, more at home entertaining, seems to have continued to eat in public at least once a week until the death of Queen Caroline; thereafter the daily menus dwindle considerably. Other entertainments, such as 'drawing rooms' and levees, were held almost daily and reports of these occasions show a relaxed atmosphere. Those not in immediate attendance on the royal family talked informally or played cards or billiards, and conversations with the King and Queen were free-flowing and affable. In April 1731 Lord Egmont noted that 'I went to Court where the King and Queen spoke to me, and the latter held a long discourse with me about Dr. Couraye, Popery, Thuanus, medals, etc.'.[8]

Perhaps the most informal of the family was Frederick, Prince of Wales, who seems to have entertained freely when the funds were available. On 21 February 1736 he held a supper at St James's where larks, pigeons, partridges, truffles, veal, turkey, lamb, turbot, salmon, teal, blackbird, asparagus, broccoli, sweetbreads, coffee cream and jelly were among the items on the menu.[9] On the birth of his son, Prince Frederick William, in May 1750, Carlton House was opened with a public table 'in honour of her royal highness's accouchement, and the hospitable festivities continued for ten successive days'.[10]

German, French or English?

On his arrival in England, George I was accompanied by a Hanoverian kitchen staff, who were expected to prepare the King's own dishes, while the English domestics produced the food for the rest of the household. Many of the German cooks returned to Hanover with the King during his visit in 1716 and by 1719 only six remained in England.[11] In 1717 the Lord Chamberlain requested a new kitchen at St James's Palace for the Prince of Wales's household, as 'great inconveniences' had been experienced 'in dressing dayly great quantities of provisions for His Majesty and the Prince's family in the same kitchen' (see no. 28).[12] By the time it was complete the Prince had been banished from the court, and the kitchen was used by the King's staff.

The traditional view is that George I retained a heavily German diet, prepared by his Hanoverian staff in one kitchen, while his son dined on fashionable French fare prepared next door. In fact the bills of fare through the period show a more varied picture. Written in an eclectic mixture of English, French and German, they show that both King and Prince of Wales often ate similar dishes – much in keeping with the rest of the English aristocracy of the period. Large quantities of game, meat and fish were consumed, interspersed with seasonal vegetables and fruits. The English were particularly proud of their meat, which was usually roasted and served with the ubiquitous gravy. As César de Saussure noted in 1726: 'England is justly renowned for its meat, particularly for its beef and veal', and these were certainly served regularly at the royal table.[13] He further commented that 'The great lords ... have French cooks, who prepare their food half in the French manner, half in the English, that is to say that they combine the French pastries and first courses with the English piece of roast beef and puddings. Their meals are served with abundance, with magnificence and, above all, with great cleanliness.'[14]

There is certainly reference to sauerkraut, *Wurst*, *Spitzen* and other German dishes in the menus, but then French specialities were also on royal menus from the first – including ragouts, soups, bisques, terrines, oleos and other dishes that were dressed or cooked in rich sauces. These were mixed with the more traditional pies and pasties, puddings and tarts, although exotic items such as *ravioli* and *macaroni* do appear, as do Parmesan cheese and mangoes.

Often the source of individual items is listed in the bills of fare, such as Thames salmon or Westphalian ham. Food was also donated – items of game from courtiers litter the menus, and pineapples were a popular gift. Richard Petit, a gardener from Hertfordshire, presented the first melon of the season for ten years in succession to the King. Later reports noted that 'these presents were used to be made when their majesties dined in public; which ceremony was performed on Sundays. On these occasions a great crowd assembled to witness the royal repast'.[15]

As early as 1717 new items of plate appear in the Jewel Office records, associated with serving a sophisticated range of foodstuffs in a greater variety of ways. These include an 'epargne' or centrepiece, a French invention, complete with a central basket surrounded by salts, casters and sauceboats.[16] Ice pails and tureens, which had not been part of the Stuart inventory, also appear in the daybooks for the first time. The royal diet also started to change over the period. By the 1730s dishes such as bisque of pigeon, *potage à la reine*, turkey with India corn, capons *en beurre*, cardoon sauce, cherry sauce, 'eggs à la hugonot' [sic] and *crème brûlé* appear among the more traditional dishes of asparagus, pheasant, apple pie or rice pudding. This range is reflected in the new plate commissioned: chafing dishes, which had been traditionally used to keep food hot in the 1710s, were replaced by centrepieces or epergnes, and in the 1730s an increasing number of sauceboats appear in the ledgers. In July 1733, when George II dined at Hampton Court, the menu listed 'two dishes of five china plates', suggesting that porcelain was in use on the table by this date, for the service of the smaller side dishes such as eggs, pickles, 'peepers in jelly', 'Dutch beef' and a 'salmagundi', which were arranged in symmetrical fashion around the larger silver dishes on the table.[17]

It is noticeable that after the death of Queen Caroline George II's diet reverted to plainer fare, the menus often containing sausages or sauerkraut, and it is the young Princesses who benefited from the more sophisticated cuisine available: flower pudding, star jelly, beef 'tremblant' and venison with cherry sauce all appeared while the King was absent in Hanover in 1743.[18]

Hanover and London

The royal establishments in Hanover and England were largely kept separate, particularly during the reign of George II. Plate for the English table was supplied by the royal goldsmiths and other associates; in 1717, for example, George, Prince of Wales, commissioned a large service from Benjamin Pyne, and later pieces were supplied by the Huguenot makers Pierre Platel and David Willaume.[19] The plate used in the kitchens was repaired and resupplied almost constantly, new pieces being commissioned every season; the costs were offset by the melting down of existing worn out or damaged plate, which served as bullion. A large new service was commissioned in 1736 to replace the plate which had been presented by the King to Frederick, Prince of Wales, on his marriage.[20] Despite the evidence of the use of china on the royal table, there is no suggestion that the royal family commissioned English porcelain – with the exception of William, Duke of Cumberland, who seems to have acquired a service from the Chelsea factory sometime around 1752 (see no. 258). The china plates listed in the bills of fare were probably Chinese in origin, although Frederick and Augusta certainly owned a Meissen dinner service, which travelled with them to their various residences.

Plate in Germany was created by local goldsmiths, including Conrad Hölling of Hanover, Lewis Dedecke from Celle and Johann Wilhelm Voight I of Osnabrück. Some of these works were supplied to George I when Elector of Hanover, but the later plate inventories of Hanover make it clear that further pieces were acquired throughout the eighteenth century.[21] Much of this silver was based on English designs, although the individual works show the simplicity and austerity of German manufacture. In 1736, when George II ordered a chandelier based on a design by William Kent, he also commissioned several silver works following English models, including fish plates and pastry dishes. Two further services were commissioned in 1750 and 1752 to coincide with the King's visits to Hanover. As in England, silver was frequently melted down – in Hanover this was undertaken in the bake-ovens on site – and new works such as sauceboats and candlesticks supplied in a more contemporary style. A Japanese porcelain service was used in the court of Hanover for the first time in 1740, and during his later visits to Germany George II also acquired Meissen porcelain for his table, including a 24-piece service which was probably used to celebrate the marriage of Princess Louise.[22]

There were exceptions to this division. In July 1716 plate from the Jewel Office was shipped out of the country to the Hanoverian court. *The Shift Shifted* recorded that 'such numbers of Waggon loads are sent away from St James's as the like was never known'.[23] Among the items taken there appeared a gold couvert which had belonged to William III and flatware from Queen Anne's collection. According to Horace Walpole, George II was concerned that these items had been removed to Hanover and on his first visit there in 1729 he asked that they be returned to London, although there appears to be no evidence in the inventories that his orders were carried out.[24] Similarly George II's service by Pyne of 1717 was removed from London in 1738 and appears in the Hanover inventory that year.

The Rococo Table

Outwardly at least it appears that it fell to Frederick to celebrate the new fashion for the Rococo, commissioning works in silver from those goldsmiths who were keenly aware of developing styles in France. The marine service hallmarked by Paul Crespin and Nicholas Sprimont shows some of the most advanced rococo taste of the day (nos 313–6). This fashion seems to have spilled over into the work of George Wickes, the Prince's goldsmith, who adapted Kent's surprisingly light-hearted design for a centrepiece for Frederick (no. 276), as well as supplying rococo dishes with swirling flutes and cast shell decoration to the Prince's table (no. 321). (This does not apply, however, to all Frederick's plate and much of it was as pared down and conservative in decoration as that supplied to his father or grandfather.) Moreover it is likely that the food itself as much as the plate on which it was served showed the most developed rococo style. By the mid-century it was common to embellish the dessert table with parterres created from sugar, scattered with porcelain figurines from Meissen, or to serve food in Chelsea porcelain tureens and dishes in the form of fruit and vegetables, often themselves mirroring desserts and ices disguised as other foods. The ephemeral nature of these visual jokes makes it almost impossible to reconstruct just how rococo the royal tables were, but hints may be found in the inventories. In Hanover among the pastry chef's moulds, for example, are listed caramel forms of Hercules, Juno, Amor and a sphinx.[25]

Little of George I or George II's plate survived the reigns of their successors but Frederick's marine service provided the inspiration for his grandson's magnificent Grand Service – a vast dining service of silver gilt which incorporated rococo revival items to complement the work of Sprimont and Crespin.

311

MARCELLUS LAROON THE YOUNGER (1679–1772)

A Dinner Party *c.* 1719–25

Oil on canvas, 90.8 × 85.8 cm
A drawing for this composition is signed and dated 1719 and inscribed *Premiere Pensée / presented to King George 1st / a picture I painted in 1725'*
RCIN 403539

PROVENANCE First recorded at Kensington Palace in 1818

LITERATURE Millar 1963, p. 174, no. 520; *Conversation Piece* 2009, pp. 72–5, no. 11

Marcellus Laroon was born in London of Anglo-French parents. He travelled in Italy, France and Holland, and served for many years as a soldier, before taking up painting. He specialised in a painted equivalent of Restoration Comedy – conversation pieces in which the fashionable world saw a mirror of their lifestyles depicted with considerable fidelity in costumes, settings and *mores*.

These two examples in the Royal Collection date from either side of Hogarth's emergence as a satirical painter of modern life in the 1730s and yet seem substantially similar in comic tone, suggesting that throughout his career Laroon ploughed his own furrow. Both images contain the same stock comic characters – the pampered lap-dogs, the well-fed and worldly vicars, the flirting couples and the exotically dressed black slaves. In each individual and group it seems possible to read character traits and potential comic episodes.

These two paintings show interiors belonging in style to the reign of George I, with paintings incorporated as over-doors, arranged frame-to-frame as if part of the panelling, or, in the case of the full-length equestrian portrait in no. 312, as if a tapestry. The arch supported by Telemones above the buffet and opening on to a further space is reminiscent of the arrangement of the alcoves in the dining rooms at Houghton and Raynham.

In the *Dinner Party* (no. 311) we are to imagine that the dinner guests have left the main house during the meal and proceeded to the 'banquet-house' for sweets. Through the open door we can see glimpses of wrought iron decorated with the host's coronet, which also appears with the gilded phoenix above the mirror. At the table, members of the company are served jellies and fruit with white and red wine. The wine is poured with dexterity by the host from a wicker-covered bottle, suggesting it is an imported Italian red. Wines from Italy were not much consumed in England with the exception of Florentine reds, particularly Chiantis, which were sold in 'wanded' or wicker-covered flattened ovoid bottles of the type depicted by Laroon. The pouring of the wine from a distance was intended to aerate it. The wealth of the host is emphasised not only by his fashionably expensive wine but also by the silver fountain in the foreground for rinsing glasses, and by the large group of matching wine glasses of lead glass, scattered among the guests and carried by the serving boy on a stemmed tray (compare no. 265). Moreover the guests are indulging in fruits presumably grown in the garden hothouses – grapes and peaches being clearly shown – and the artist suggests that they were using porcelain on the table: a servant to the left is clasping a turquoise blue plate painted with fruits – all suggesting a highly fashionable host.

At this date it was uncommon for guests to be seated in an alternating male and female pattern – which was termed promiscuous if the guests were not family members. The seating arrangements are therefore perhaps another sly comment on the manners of the party by Laroon, and the artist draws further attention to this by showing the prominent flirtation between guests in the centre of the work. DS-T & KJ

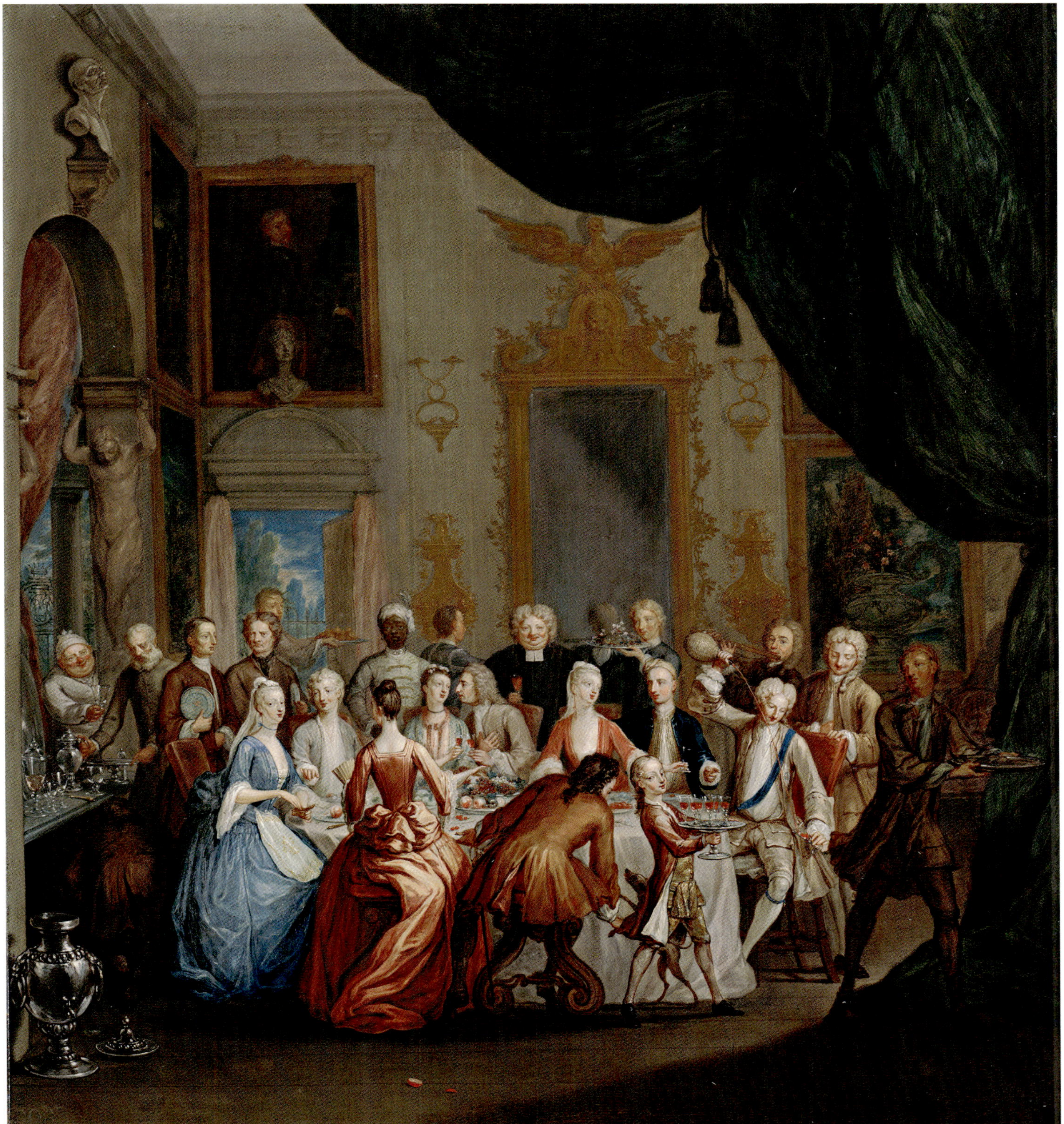

312

MARCELLUS LAROON THE YOUNGER (1679–1772)

A Musical Tea Party signed and dated 1740

Oil on canvas, 91.4 × 71.0 cm
Signed and dated: *Mar. Laroon. F. 1740*
RCIN 403544

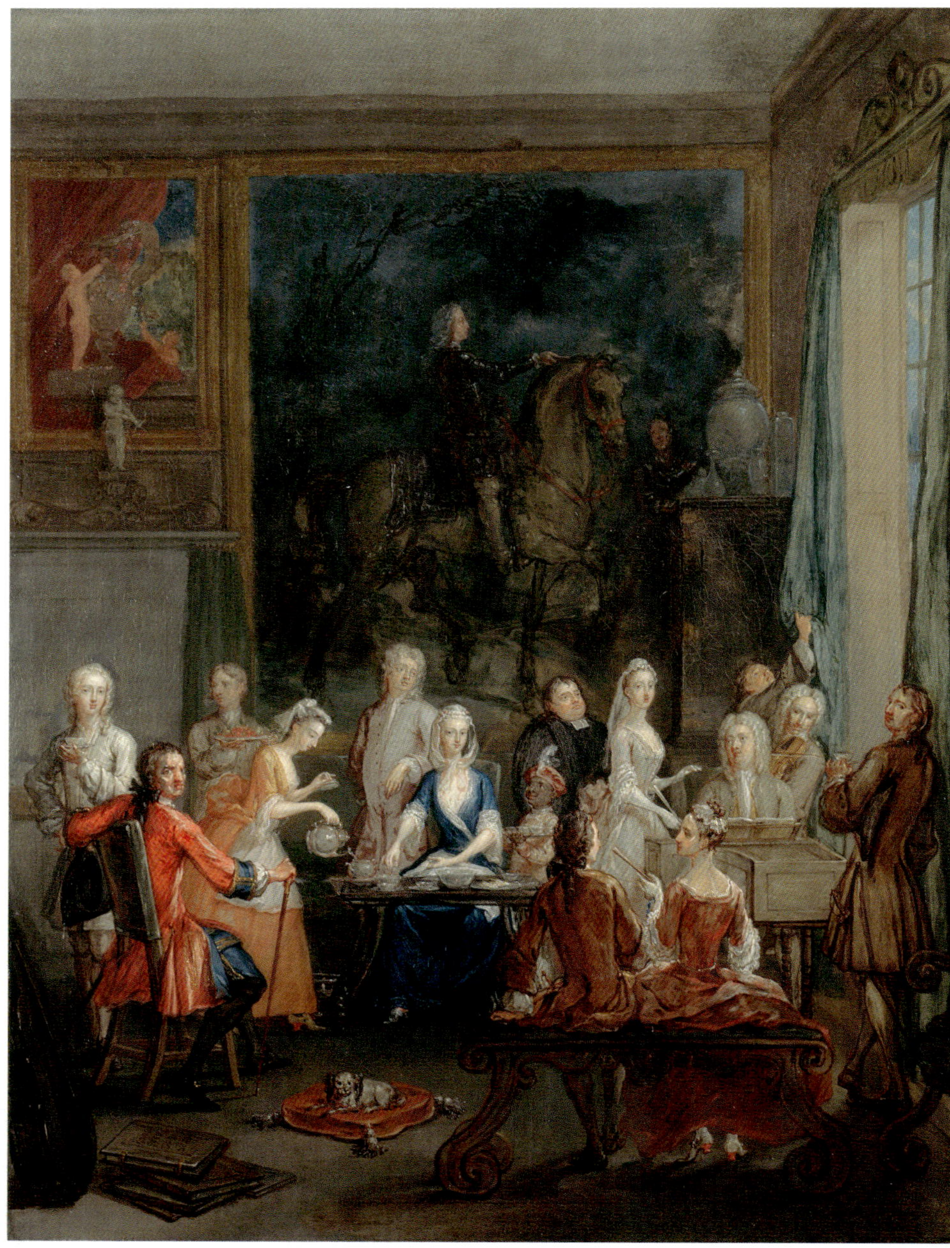

PROVENANCE First recorded in the Royal Collection in 1903

LITERATURE Millar 1963, p. 174, no. 521; *Conversation Piece* 2009, pp. 76–7, no. 12

This is a levee: a lady is attended by professionals seeking work and acquaintances seeking favours, as well as friends, while her servant opens the curtains. She wears fashionable undress, worn by ladies before getting properly dressed for dinner at two or three in the afternoon and already criticised in the *Spectator* in 1711.[26] Tea is served in Chinese porcelain, prominently displayed on the table. The price of tea in this period was high, as it was heavily taxed, and the tea-service by association therefore an item of high value (compare no. 272). According to John Macky in 1723, many hours of the day appear to have spent indulging in the drinking of tea, coffee or chocolate. In one of his letters he relates: 'We rise by nine, and those that frequent the great men's levees find entertainment at them till eleven; or, as in Holland, go to tea-tables. About twelve the beau-monde assembles in various chocolate and coffee-houses.'[27]

The name 'Corelli' on one of the scores on the floor refers to the violinist-composer Arcangelo Corelli (1653–1713), author of several sets of trio sonatas (for two violins and continuo) and some solo sonatas. The work performed here would seem to be a violin sonata, with harpsichord accompaniment (like the Opus 5 set, published in Rome in 1700). The cello to the left could easily join in the performance of such a work, by doubling the bass line. DS-T & KJ

313

ANDREA BOUCHERON (1701–1761), PAUL CRESPIN (1694–1770) AND ATTRIBUTED TO NICHOLAS SPRIMONT (1716–1771)

The Neptune Centrepiece 1741/2

Silver gilt, 49.0 × 66.0 × 47.0 cm
Marks: hallmarked on base with London marks for 1741/2 and maker's mark of Paul Crespin; the shell mount below the tureen with Turin city mark and maker's mark of Andrea Boucheron
RCIN 50282

PROVENANCE Almost certainly made for Frederick, Prince of Wales, in 1741/2; first recorded in the Royal Collection in 1801 (TNA, LC5/206)

LITERATURE Jones 1911, pp. 72 and 98; Grimwade 1969, p. 126; Clayton 1971, p. 233; Grimwade 1974, p. 22; Barr 1980, pp. 164–6; Newman 1987, p. 222; Jones and Garibaldi 2006, pp. 25–39

This object, which has been described as 'the purest rococo creation in English silver', was the centrepiece of a table service displaying the most advanced French taste of the period.[28] The marine theme of the piece, with its Neptune finial, swags of shells and pieces of coral and detachable dishes in the form of abalone shells, suggests it was used to serve fish soups and seafood. The plateau on which the tureen sits, similarly decorated with shells, coral and small sea-creatures, resembles a beach from which the sea has retreated. Even the dolphins which entwine themselves around the supports for the tureen relate to the nautical theme, although these might also be a witty reference to the Prince of Wales, patron of the piece, as the English *dauphin* or 'dolphin'.

Frederick's household accounts record large quantities of fish consumed by the Prince, including turbot, sole, cod, salmon, trout, pike, carp, flounders, lobsters and shrimps. Oysters were one of the Prince's favourites and were ordered by the barrel, either to be eaten alone or incorporated into other dishes.[29] Traditionally the items of plate used to serve fish and soup were removed from the dining table after the service of the first course. However, this elaborate piece is likely to have remained throughout the meal – the nozzles modelled as sea-foam attached to the candle branches being removed in later courses to be replaced by candles for added illumination during the dessert course.

Although it has not been possible to trace the bill for the centrepiece in either the Duchy of Cornwall account books or the ledgers of George Wickes, goldsmith to the Prince, it was certainly in the Royal Collection by 1801, when it was recorded in the Warrant books undergoing repair. In the plate inventories of 1832 it appears under the heading 'Frederick, Prince of Wales' together with its accompanying sauceboats, stands and salts (nos 314–6).

Several theories as to the complicated history of the centrepiece have been posited. The object itself bears two contrasting hallmarks – one from Turin, dating from the 1720s, with the sponsor's mark of Andrea Boucheron, the other from London, 1741/2, with the sponsor's mark of the Huguenot goldsmith Paul Crespin, who ran premises in Compton Street in Soho. The two marks make it clear that the work is an amalgam – a reusing of the Turinese silver incorporated into a later English work. This might explain the mismatched scale of the Neptune figure with regard to the other decorative elements of the tureen. Based on stylistic similarities with other hallmarked works it has long been suspected, moreover, that a third hand was involved in the design and creation of this piece – that of the Liègeois goldsmith and founder of the Chelsea porcelain factory, Nicholas Sprimont (see p. 397). Sprimont appears to have arrived in London some time in 1742 and did not enter an official mark at Goldsmiths' Hall until 1743. He would not, therefore, have been able to sponsor the centrepiece, although his mark certainly appears on the other parts of the service to which it belongs (see nos 314–6). It is possible that the two goldsmiths collaborated on the centrepiece, as fellow Huguenots, one simply sponsoring the work of the other, or dividing the work between them, or perhaps Sprimont working for his neighbour Crespin while anticipating his English hallmark.

It is possible that Charles Calvert, Lord Baltimore, was involved in the commission of the centrepiece and its accompanying wares. Baltimore's taste for the Rococo was more dramatic than Frederick's – the interiors of his Surrey residence, Woodcote Park, displayed some of the most advanced French Rococo taste of the day. Baltimore also worked on other artistic commissions for the Prince, supervising the creation of the Prince's barge in 1732 (see fig. 44), for example, and his accounts reveal that he acquired works from both Crespin and Sprimont in 1743–4.[30] In 1742, Baltimore was promoted to a Lordship of the Admiralty and it is possible that the marine service was a grateful gift to the Prince in return. KJ

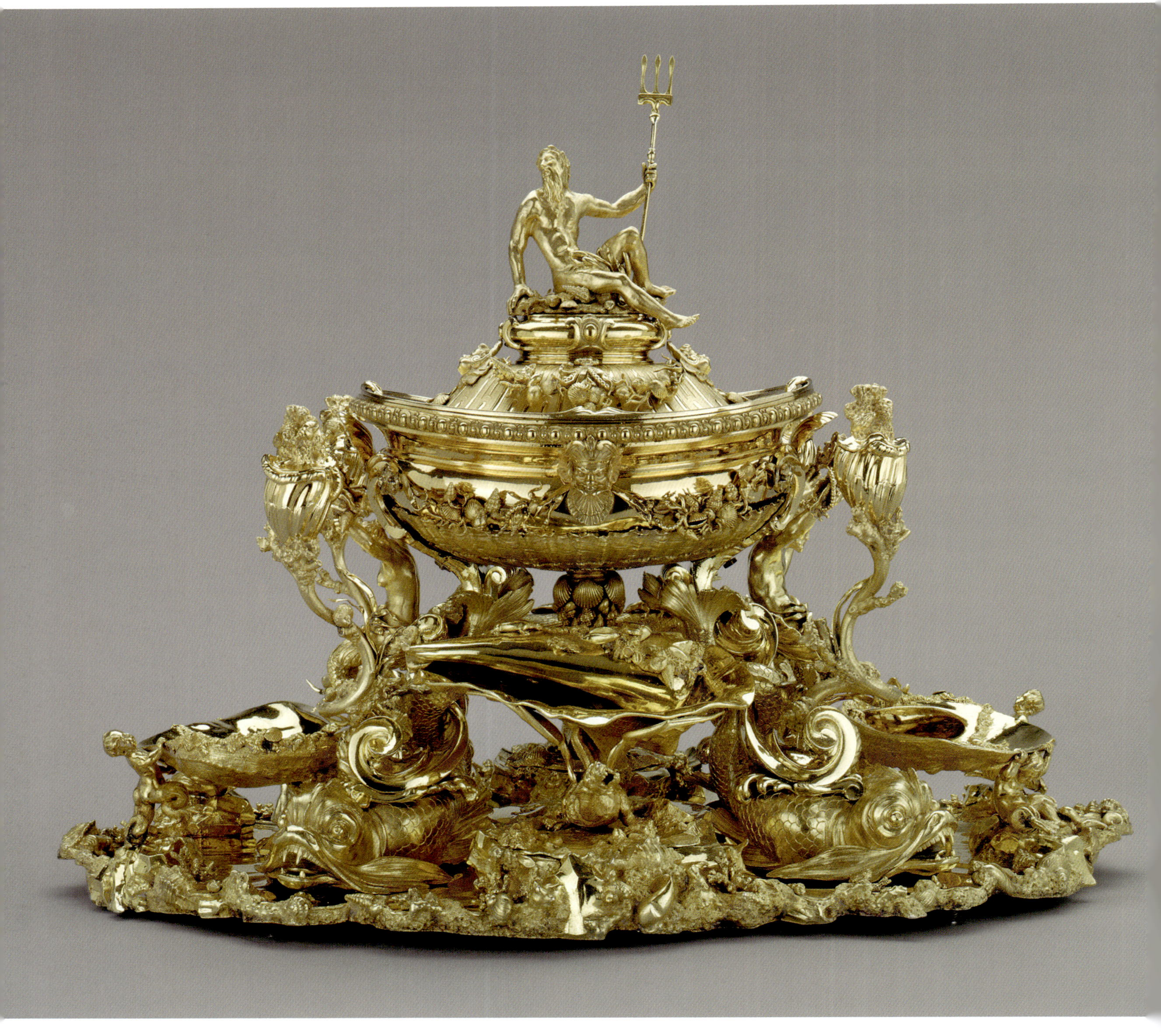

314

NICHOLAS SPRIMONT (1716–1771)

Sauceboats, stands and ladles 1743–5

Silver gilt

Sauceboats: 22.7 × 23.2 × 13 cm; stands: 28 × 22.4 × 3 cm; ladles 19.9 cm long

Marks: sauceboats marked on the underside with city marks of London, 1743/4 (.3-4) or 1744/5 (.1-2) and maker's mark of Nicholas Sprimont; stands and ladles unmarked

Sauceboats and stands: RCIN 51271.1-4; ladles RCIN 51259.1-4

PROVENANCE Almost certainly made for Frederick, Prince of Wales

LITERATURE Jones 1911, p. 100; Grimwade 1974, pp. 16, 31, 45, pl.33A; Jones and Garibaldi 2006, pp. 24–38

Despite Voltaire's rather acerbic comment that England had 42 religions but only two sauces, the royal bills of fare for this period reveal a more varied picture. Gravy was certainly made every day – the quantities of beef, mutton and veal required being recorded alongside the daily menus. Among the delicacies served to the royal family were sauces made from egg, bread, celery, parsley, orange, apple, cucumber, horseradish, mustard, mint, cherry and cardoons, as well as savoury sauce, Dutch sauce (Hollandaise), sauce douce and sauce blanc, which are also listed. The 1721 inventory of royal plate describes only a single gilt 'sawce boat' in the Jewel Office at Whitehall together with four silver versions which formed part of an 'aparn' (epergne or centrepiece). But by the 1730s and 1740s they were supplied to the Jewel Office in increasing numbers.

Sprimont's design for these sauceboats relates closely to the Neptune centrepiece – particularly the rococo dolphins which form the bases, each with a ripple of water forming whisker-like spray around its mouth. These in particular support the theory that Sprimont was involved in the creation of the centrepiece (see no. 313). It may be that Sprimont and Crespin were simply employing the same modeller to complete the service for the Prince of Wales. Roubiliac has been suggested as the most obvious candidate.[31] Sprimont stood as godfather to Roubiliac's daughter Sophie in 1744. However, Sprimont seems to have been involved in both the designing and modelling processes to an unusual degree, and one theory is that Sprimont may have earned his money by working as a modeller for fellow Huguenot craftsmen in London while waiting for his official hallmark from Goldsmiths' Hall.[32]

The importance of decking a table in a symmetrical pattern meant that sauceboats were usually, at this date, supplied in pairs – in this case two with perching sea-nymphs and two with youths, each forming an almost helical handle. The figures owe a debt to Baroque fountain sculpture, and Sprimont may have been calling on the architecture of his native Liège as inspiration.[33] The sauce ladles relate to an undated drawing, attributed to Sprimont, depicting a salt with marine elements, including dolphins, shells and pieces of coral, which shows two alternative designs for spoons, with shell bowls and coral stems.[4] KJ

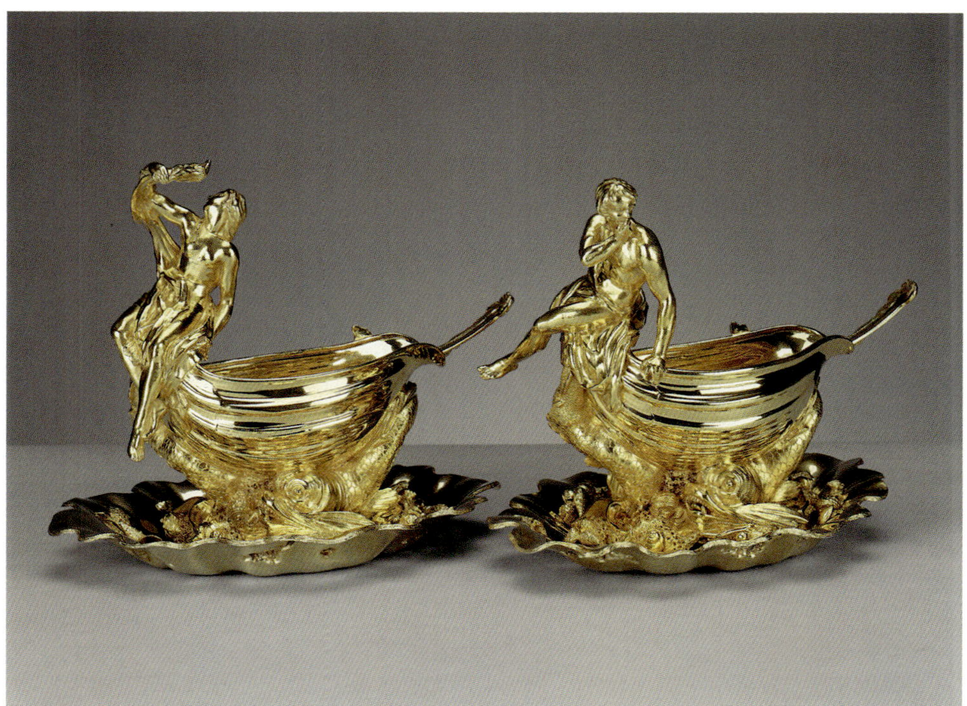

315

NICHOLAS SPRIMONT (1716–1771)

Pair of salts and salt spoons 1742/3

Silver gilt
Salts: 8.5 × 17.6 × 12.0 cm; spoons: 11 cm long
Marks: salts marked on underside with city mark of London, 1742/3, and maker's mark of Nicholas Sprimont; spoons unmarked
Salts: RCIN 51393.1-2; spoons: RCIN 51368.3-4

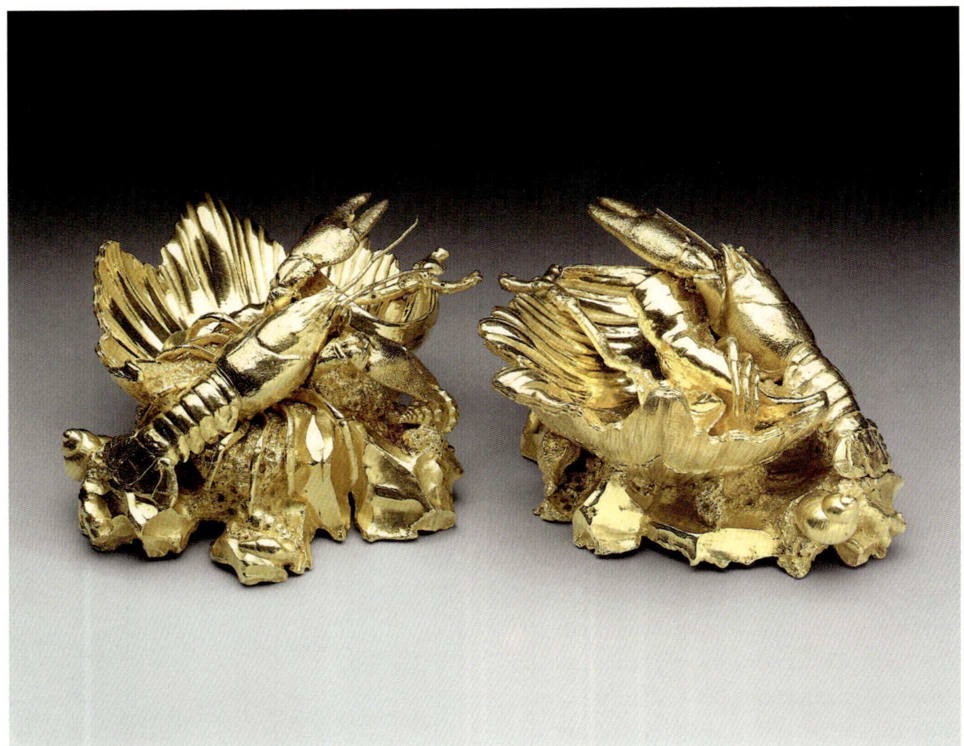

PROVENANCE Almost certainly made for Frederick, Prince of Wales

LITERATURE Jones 1911, p. 98; Grimwade 1974, pp. 4, 16, 31, 45, pl. 37B; Jones and Garibaldi 2006, pp. 37–8

The design of these pieces owes a debt to Juste-Aurèle Meissonnier (1695–1750). From 1734 Meissonnier, the *dessinateur du roi* to Louis XV, began issuing a series of engravings of work he had executed both for the King and for other private patrons in the *genre pittoresque*. Many of these engravings were published by Gabriel Huquier in a volume entitled *Œuvre de Juste Aurele Meissonier, peintre, sculpteur, architect, et dessinateur de la Chambre et Cabinet du Roy*. Among the designs was an image of a crayfish crawling over a scallop shell, surrounded by bulrushes and other aquatic plants. The designs were printed in London for the first time in 1738. Meissonnier had trained as a chaser and it is unlikely that his engravings were ever intended as a pattern book, but rather as inspiration for decorative motifs.

Certain English aristocrats in the 1730s and 1740s commissioned silver directly from French goldsmiths – the most celebrated example being Evelyn Pierrepont, 2nd Duke of Kingston (1711–73), who asked Meissonnier himself to design a set of tureens and vegetable dishes in the most exuberant rococo style, displaying an extravagant confection of vegetables and game on asymmetric bodies. Although Frederick may have purchased Meissen porcelain through the offices of Lord Baltimore, for plate he seems to have relied on English makers, albeit those most sensitive to the latest French styles. Nicholas Sprimont was one of the few goldsmiths who could translate Meissonnier's fascination with natural shapes and extreme asymmetry into concrete form. The goldsmith was described by his widow as having 'superior skill and taste in the arts of drawing and modelling and painting'.[35]

Sprimont's fondness for the form of these salts manifested itself again when, as director of the Chelsea Porcelain Factory in the 1750s, he had them produced in porcelain (see no. 262). KJ

316

NICHOLAS SPRIMONT

Pair of salts and salt spoons 1742/3

Silver gilt
Salts: 8.5 × 17.6 × 12.0 cm; spoons: 11 cm long
Marks: salts marked on underside with city mark of London, 1742/3, and maker's mark of Nicholas Sprimont; spoons unmarked
Salts: RCIN 51392.1-2; spoons: RCIN 51368.1-2

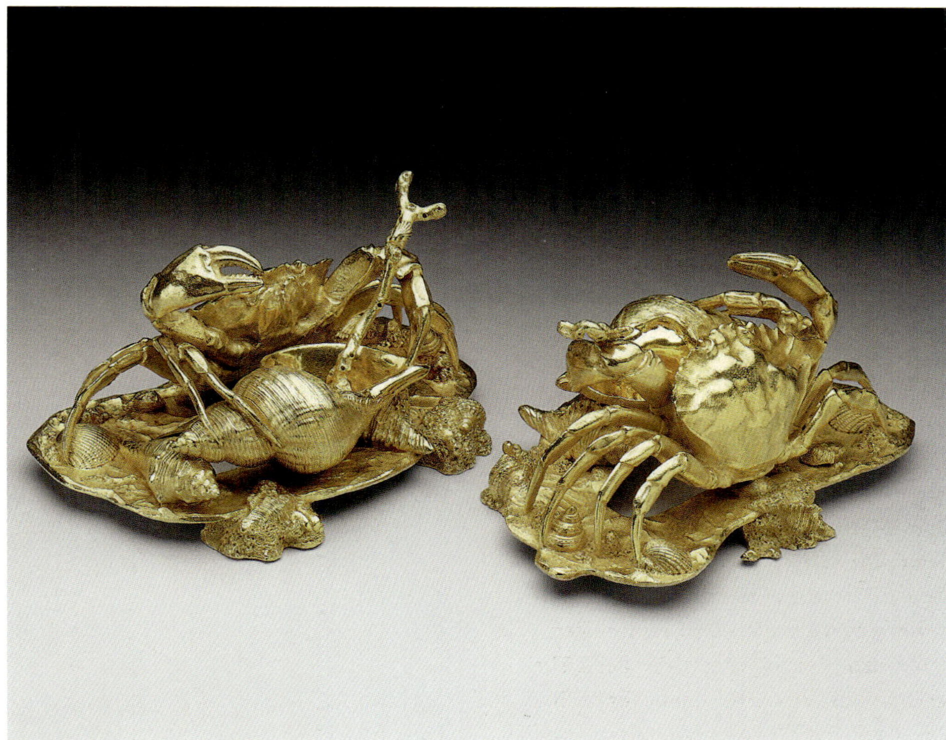

PROVENANCE Almost certainly made for Frederick, Prince of Wales

LITERATURE Jones 1911, p. 98; Grimwade 1974, pp. 4, 16, 31, 45, pl. 37B; Jones and Garibaldi 2006, pp. 37–8

The Prince of Wales's marine service contains two pairs of salts decorated with crustaceans, but while the pair ornamented with crayfish draw directly on the rococo designs of Meissonnier (see no. 315), the source of the pair with crabs is less obvious. The crabs themselves are cast from life from European shore crabs (*Carcinius Mediterraneus*); the surrounding shells are similarly cast from natural examples. In form the closest parallel, and possible source, is a sixteenth-century bronze inkwell, probably Italian in origin, which was purchased by Sir Hans Sloane in 1725 for a guinea.[36] Not only the crab itself, but the whelk shell resting between its pincers, the scattered smaller shells around it and the oval ring forming the base all relate to Sprimont's salts.

It has not been ascertained whether Sprimont ever visited Sloane's famed collection but the Prince of Wales himself did so in 1748. Cromwell Mortimer commented in the *Gentleman's Magazine* that he and Augusta 'were not wanting in expressing their satisfaction and pleasure at seeing a collection, which surpass'd all the notions or ides they had formed from even the most favourable account of it'.[37] Sloane had known Frederick before this date – in 1728, shortly after the Prince arrived in England, Sloane, as President, had welcomed him to the Royal Society. Moreover, Frederick greatly approved of the opening of Sloane's collections to the public, and in 1746 a dinner was held in his honour.[38]

The spoons, like the sauce ladles in the service, relate closely to an undated drawing attributed to Sprimont, which shows two alternative designs for spoons with shell bowls and coral stems.[39] KJ

317

THOMAS FARREN (ACTIVE 1707–42/3)

Pair of casters *c.*1725

Silver-gilt, 16.0 × 6.0 × 6.0 cm
Marks: hallmarked with maker's mark of Thomas Farren
Both engraved with royal coat of arms, Garter and GR cipher, and with inscription
From the Drapers' Company, 6th May 1935
RCIN 46991.1-2

PROVENANCE Probably made for George II; presented to King George V on 6 May 1935 by the Drapers' Company

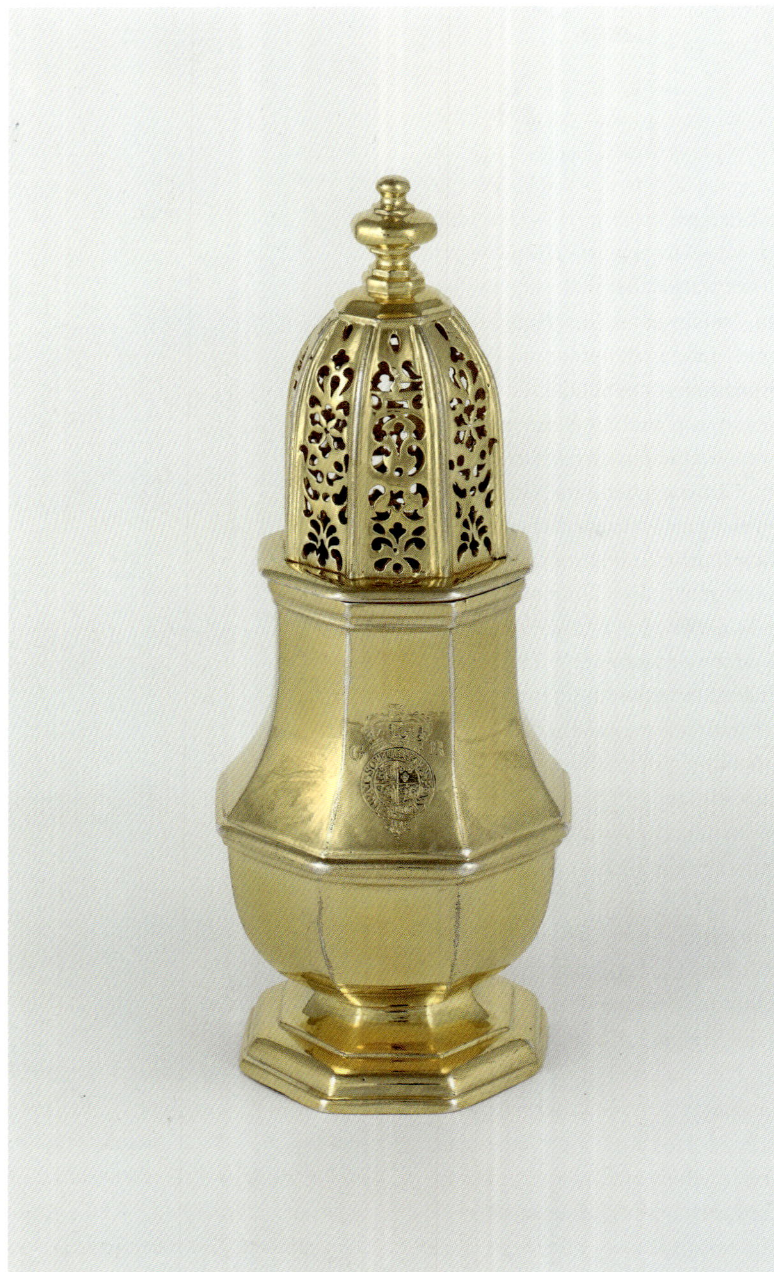

These casters (only one is shown) may have been supplied at any time during Farren's period as Subordinate Goldsmith to the King, a role he occupied between 1723 and 1742. The Plate Book of the Jewel Office shows regular requirements for new sets of casters in both gilt and white plate, often using reworked existing plate to defray the costs. Five sets were supplied in 1730, for example.[40] Casters were usually supplied in sets of three – one larger being used for sugar, and two smaller for dry mustard and pepper or other spices. Equally these examples may be part of an issue of plate to an ambassador. The designs for ambassadorial plate were typically conservative during the reigns of both Georges, often the only embellishment being the royal crest or cipher. KJ

318

GEORGE WICKES (1698–1761)

Set of plates 1737/8

Silver gilt, each (only one shown) 1.8 × 24.4 × 24.3 cm
Marks: hallmarks of London, 1737/8, and maker's mark of George Wickes
RCIN 51681

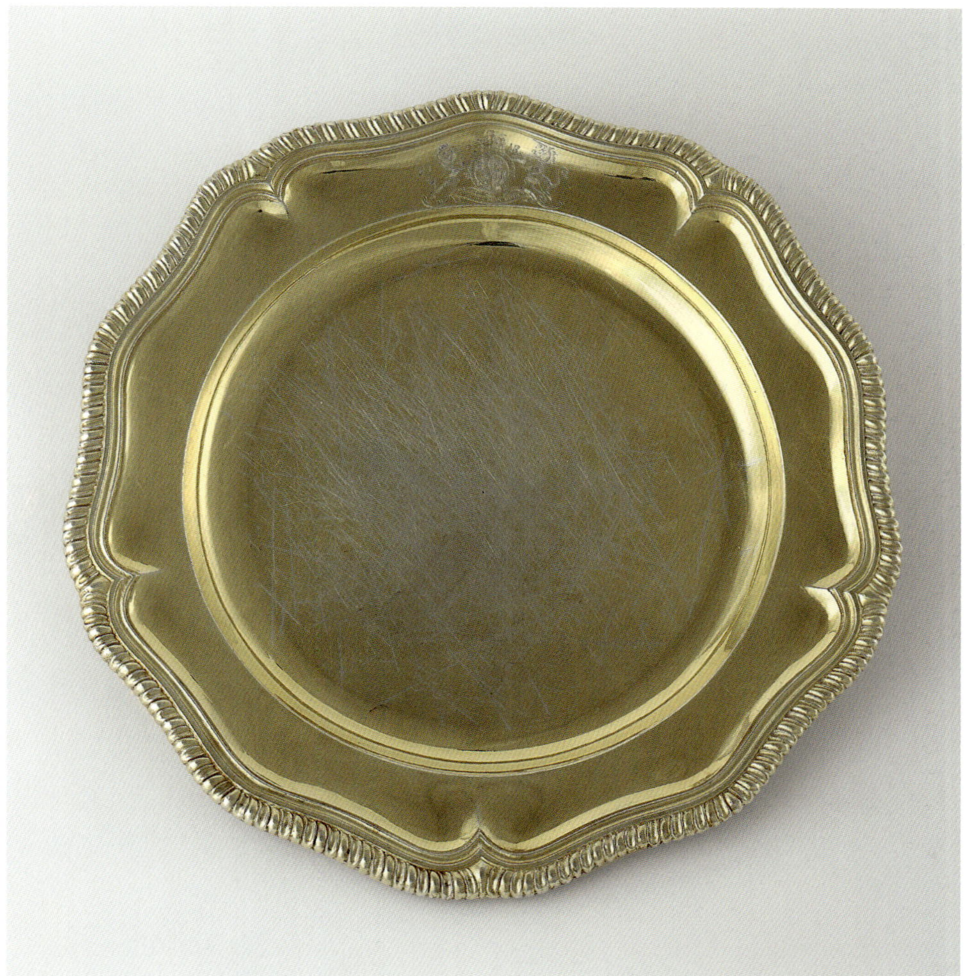

PROVENANCE Commissioned by Frederick, Prince of Wales, in 1737

George Wickes was appointed goldsmith to Frederick, Prince of Wales, in 1735, although there is evidence that he was working for the Prince's household as early as 1731.[41] At first his work mainly consisted of cleaning and repairing plate rather than supplying new wares. On Frederick's marriage in 1736, Wickes would have expected a commission for a new dinner service, but the Jewel Office records simply note that the King presented his son with existing plate from the pantries, and reserved any new items for himself.[42] The King's extreme wariness of the Prince setting himself up as a rival is clear from Lord Egmont's report of the wedding received from his cousin Moll Bering. Egmont records that on the day of the wedding itself 'The Prince had designed to eat in a public manner with the Princess in his own apartment, but in the morning the King sent an order that nobody should see him dine', and the following day 'The Prince being to dine with the Princess and the Duke and the other Princesses in his own apartment, had ordered an elbow chair only for himself, and so to dine as does the King, but that the King had sent to her to take care that there were seven elbow chairs at the table in order to preserve an equality among them all'.[43]

In the late part of 1737, however, Wickes received a large order from the Prince for a dining service, which in total weighed over 7,710 oz. Frederick's commission was poorly timed. Almost immediately after the order, he broke with his father and was banished to Kew. The Prince was forced to retrench and Wickes's ledgers record, 'To the damadge and loss to me in a large parcell of plate bespoke and ordered by the Prince which was in such forwardness when countermand as amounts to more then £500'.[44] But by July 1738 he had been ordered to proceed and a sum of £1,678 12s 5d was paid out by Frederick for what Wickes describes as a 'large parcell of plate bespoke and ordered by the Prince'. The service included 96 plates, as well as serving dishes and covers, sauceboats, salts, casters, salvers, flatware, candlesticks and sconces. KJ

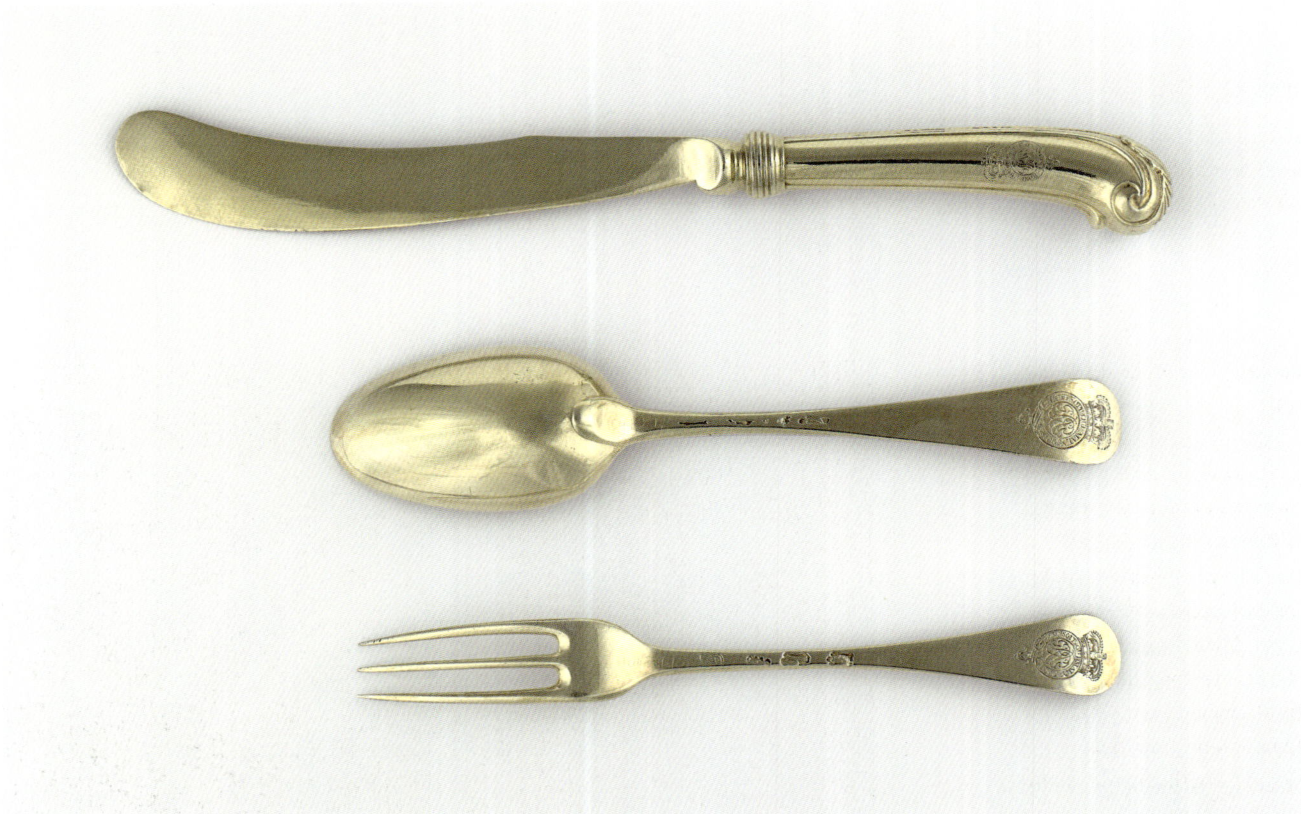

319

PAUL DE LAMERIE (1688–1751) AND PHILIP ROKER II (1693–1755?)

Dessert knives, forks and spoons *c.*1740

Silver gilt
Knives: 22.8 × 2.5 cm; forks: 16.5 × 1.9 cm; spoons: 16.8 × 3.4 cm (only one set shown)
Marks: knives marked with the maker's mark of Paul de Lamerie; forks and spoons with the maker's mark of Philip Roker II
Each piece engraved with the cipher of George II
Knives: RCIN 104757; forks: RCIN 104759; spoons RCIN 104758

PROVENANCE Probably made for George II; acquired by HM Queen Elizabeth The Queen Mother at Christie's, London, 17 July 1946, lot 74

Sets of knives, forks and spoons were supplied by the dozen to the Jewel Office almost every year between 1715 and 1760, and so it is not possible to identify with certainty in which year these pieces were created. The form of flatware and cutlery altered little in the early part of the eighteenth century and typically knives were created with a pistol-shaped handle, while forks and spoons were often, as here, in the so-called Hanoverian pattern, and until the 1750s almost no decoration other than an engraved crest was applied. Paul de Lamerie was named 'royal goldsmith' for one year in 1716, although none of his work for the royal family at that date has been traced and no bill is listed in the Jewel Office records. KJ

320

ATTRIBUTED TO GEORGE WICKES (1698–1761)

Set of candlesticks *c.*1740

Silver gilt, 21.0 × 12.7 × 12.7 cm
Each (only one shown) engraved on the foot with the Prince of Wales's feathers and FP cipher
RCIN 50177

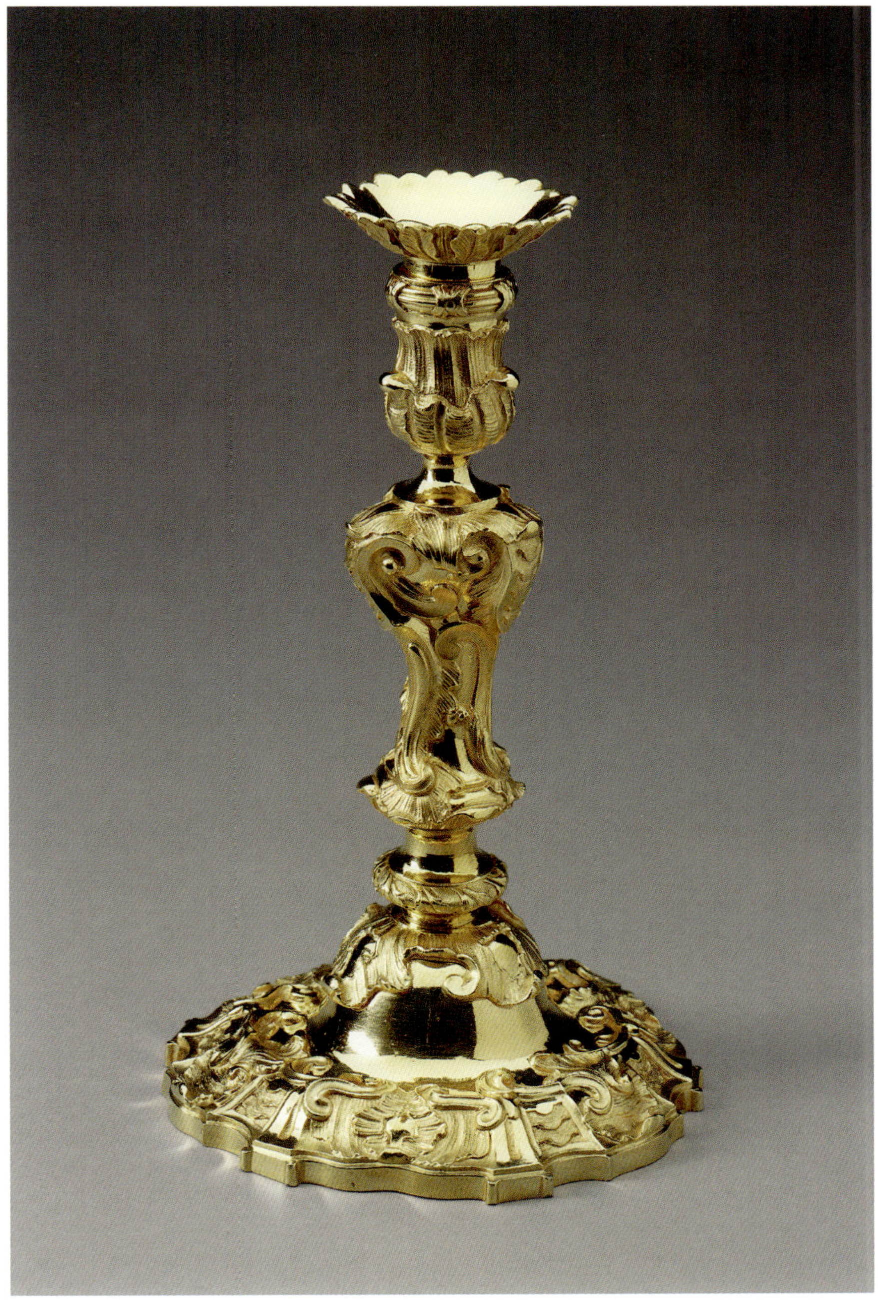

PROVENANCE Supplied to Frederick, Prince of Wales (bill untraced)

Although candlesticks are rarely depicted on the dinner table in contemporary images, they were certainly considered integral to the setting. The cost of wax lights was high – the Duchy of Cornwall accounts note that Frederick paid 7s per dozen in 1740 – and the dinner hour early, often beginning at two or three in the afternoon, so that much of the meal would be eaten by daylight. Nevertheless table plans of the period, such as Vincent La Chapelle's diagram for a dinner for 15 or 16, clearly show candlesticks placed on the table.[45] Until 1738, when the Prince was granted greater funds by his father, Frederick was forced to hire candlesticks from George Wickes: in December 1736, for example, a set of 54 were required.[46]

The inventories of plate in the Royal Collection, dating from 1832 onwards, describe these examples as 'for the card table'. Although this might explain their later role, few candlesticks of the 1740s would have had a single function. It is true, however, that Frederick was extremely fond of card playing, an activity which often went on late into the evening. In his diary of 13 November 1731, Lord Egmont described the Prince, saying 'he has no reigning passion, if it be it is to pass the evening with six or seven others over a glass of wine and hear them talk of a variety of things, but he does not drink. He loves play and plays to win, that he may supply his pleasures and generosity, which last are great'.[4] KJ

321

GEORGE WICKES (1698–1761)

***Pair of circular dishes** c.1744*

Silver gilt, 5.5 × 25.5 cm
Marks: struck four times each with the maker's mark of George Wickes
Engraved with the coat of arms of Frederick, Prince of Wales
RCIN 104158.1-2

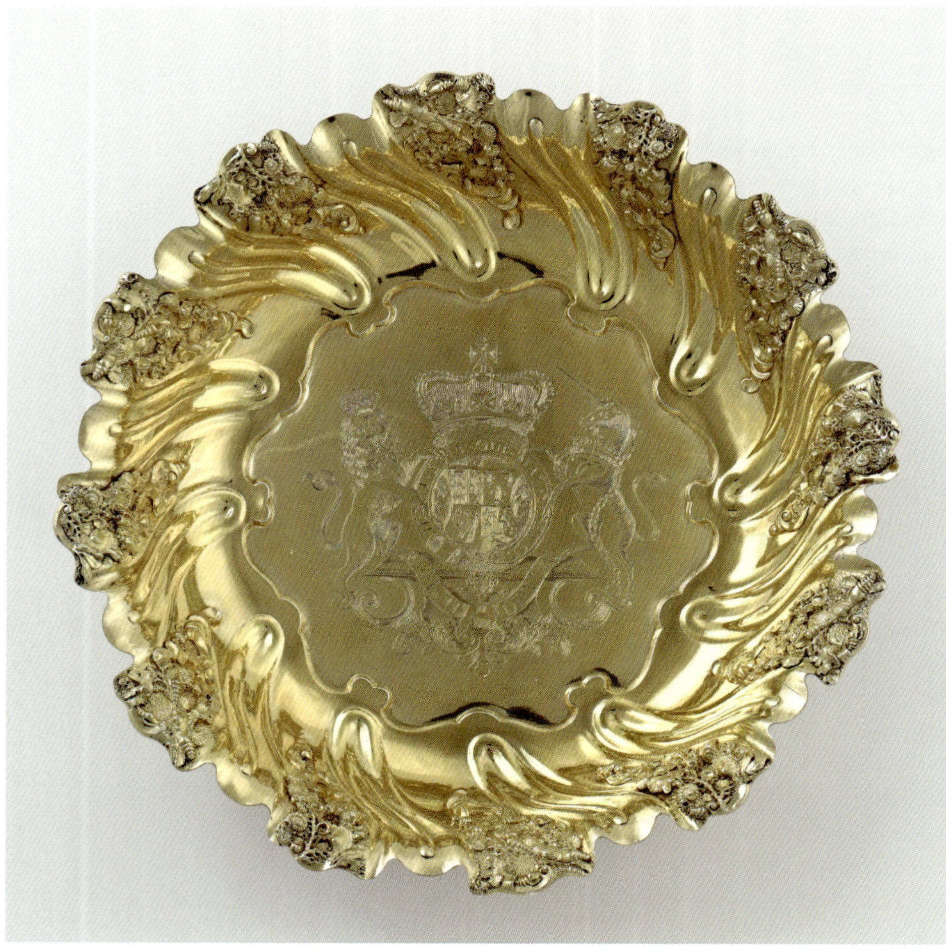

PROVENANCE Purchased by HM Queen Elizabeth The Queen Mother

The design of these dishes (only one is shown) relates closely to a silver-gilt sugar basin marked by Wickes dating from 1744/5, decorated with similar swirling flutes and panels of shells and engraved with the arms of William Capel, 4th Earl of Essex (1732–99).[48] However, it is possible that these pieces were created to complement the service marked by Crespin and Sprimont (nos 313–6), which incorporated shells cast from life and a clear rococo design. Wickes's response to contemporary French style was less marked than either of his fellow goldsmiths', and it may be that he relied more heavily on books of ornament rather than real examples. In this case it is likely that he had seen the marine service of his patron.

A bill from Wickes records the supply of two tureens and ladles, two bread baskets, and two dishes in April 1744, to supplement the plate he had delivered in 1738. The dishes weighed together 109 oz 13 dwt, and cost the Prince £44 15s 6d, exclusive of the engraving of coats of arms.[49] KJ

322

EDWARD WAKELIN (ACTIVE 1747–84)

Strawberry dish 1748/9

Silver gilt, 3.5 × 27.3 × 26.7 cm
Marks: hallmarked with city mark of London, 1748/9, and maker's mark of Edward Wakelin
Engraved with royal coat of arms
RCIN 49187

PROVENANCE Made for Frederick, Prince of Wales

In the autumn of 1748 Frederick commissioned a new set of plate to augment the silver-gilt service supplied by Wickes (see no. 318). The order included new dishes, sauceboats, salts and a dozen salad dishes, which may be these pieces (four exhibited; one shown here). Although their form is often referred to as a 'strawberry dish', the term is probably nineteenth-century in origin and these fluted or scalloped dishes were often used for the service of 'sallet' (salad), which seems to have referred to both raw and cooked vegetables.[50] The dishes are marked by Edward Wakelin, who had joined the workshop of George Wickes in 1747 and who almost immediately took over the business. Like Wickes, he incorporated the Prince of Wales's feathers into his hallmark. By 1748 Wickes was clearly wary of delays in payment, and Frederick signed an 'imprest warrant' to his 'trusty and right wellbeloved cousin Thomas, Earl of Scarbrough' asking him to pay £1,000 to Mr George Wickes 'on account in part for gilt plate to be made for our service'.[51] By this date George Wickes had earned the prefix 'Mr', suggesting a degree of respect from the Prince. KJ

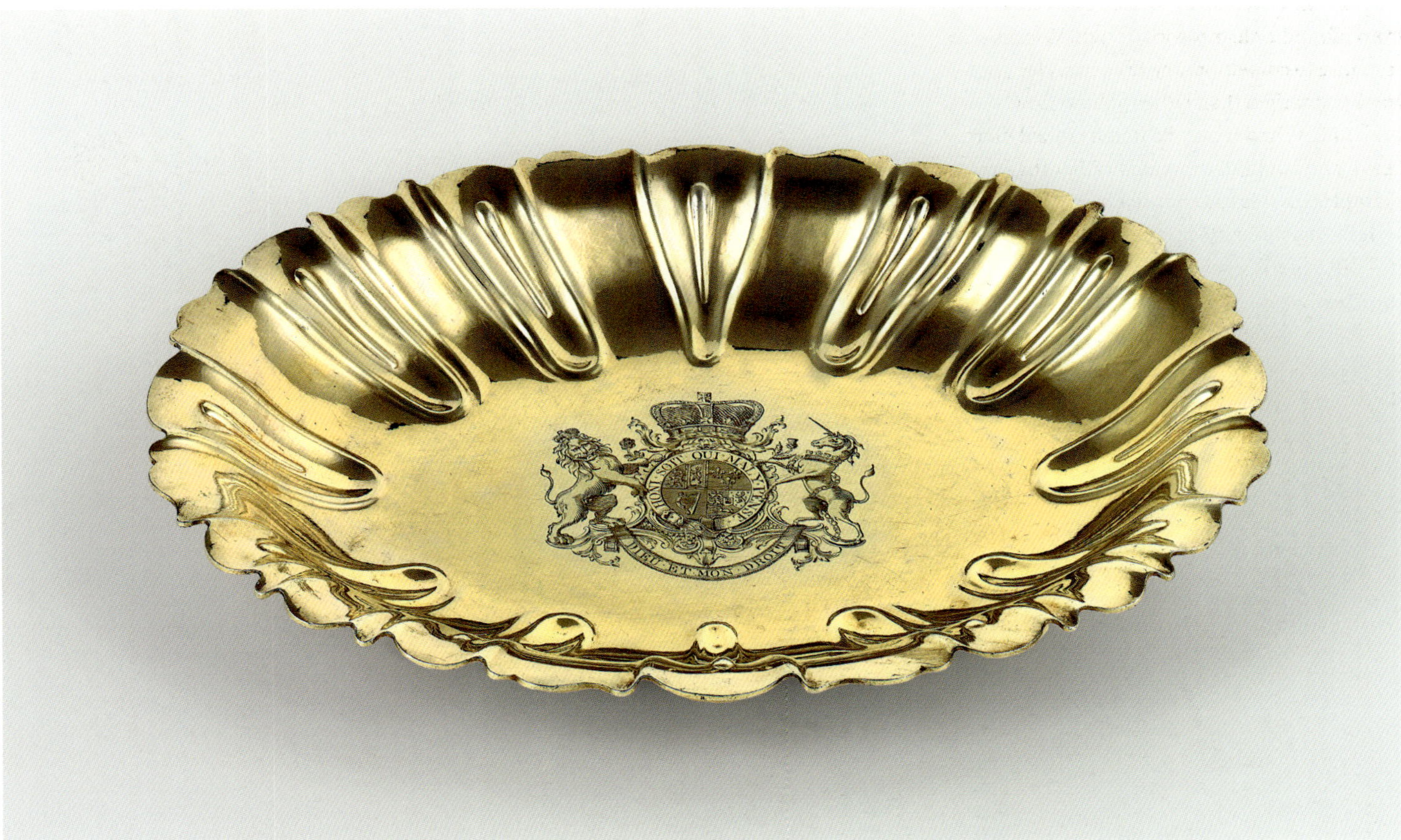

Notes

I. *Ruling a Free Nation*

1 Voltaire 1728, Dedication, quoted in White 1918, pp. 129–40 and p. 137.
2 All these figures are identified in an undated pamphlet by Sir James Thornhill, *An Explanation of the Painting in the Royal-Hospital at Greenwich*, which was sold to visitors in aid of the charity boys; see Bold 2000, pp. 145–53.
3 See Jarrett 1965, pp. 6–9.
4 Jarrett 1965, pp. 10–1, discusses the Declaration of Rights and the new Coronation oath. The idea that power should rest with the people by means of law is expressed by John Locke, who maintained that 'the Community may be said in this respect to be always the Supreme Power' (*Two Treatises of Government*, 1689, II, ch. 13, sect. 149), and David Hume, who argued, 'It may now be affirm'd of civiliz'd Monarchies, what was formerly said in Praise of republics alone, *that they are a Government of Laws, not of men*' ('Of Civil Liberty'); both quoted in Porter 2000, pp. 186 and 200.
5 For the pairing of Protestantism and Liberty in the early Georgian mind, see Porter 2000, pp. 49ff.
6 According to le Blanc (1747, II, p. 158) the English fox-hunting gentleman knew two words: 'Liberty' and 'Property'. See also Saussure 2006, p. 106, letter of 7 February 1727, and any number of other references: Porter 2000, pp. 42–3.
7 Saussure 2006, p. 207, letter of August 1729. Voltaire expresses the same idea, Voltaire 1733, p. 53, letter 8, quoted by Porter 2000, p. 6.
8 For Bolinbroke's plans to recall the exiled James III in 1714, see Jarrett 1965, pp. 146–7 and 153.
9 Voltaire calls the play 'a Master-piece both with regard to the Diction, and to the Beauty and Harmony of the Numbers': Voltaire 1733, p. 178, letter 18; for Washington's performance see Bryan 2010, pp. 124–5; 'Cato' was a *nom de plume* adopted by high-minded opponents of corruption in high places: Porter 2000, pp. 190–1.
10 Voltaire contrasts, with obvious and bitter reference to his own experience, the situation of an Addison in France and England: Voltaire 1733, pp. 224–5, letter 23. See also Colley 2012, pp. 50–1.
11 The early Georgians, though much given to boasting of their liberty, were aware of European precedents. David Hume lists some, characteristically linking liberty and trade: 'If we trace commerce in its progress, through Tyre, Athens, Syracuse, Carthage, Venice, Florence, Genoa, Antwerp, Holland, England, etc. ... we shall always find it to have fixed its seat in free governments' ('On the Origin of Commerce', 1741–2), quoted in Porter 2000, p. 198.
12 Saussure describes freedom of conscience; the number of Jews protected by law in London; and the relative prosperity of the 'common people': Saussure 2006, p. 131, letter of 29 May 1727, and p. 192, letter of 29 April 1729. The limits of the 'Toleration Act' of 1689 are discussed in Porter 2000, p. 107, and Colley 2012, p. 19. Press freedom dated from the lapsing of the Licensing Act in 1695: Porter 2000, p. 31 and 73; appropriately the first newspaper, the *Daily Courant*, began life in 1702; see Jarrett 1965, p. 36.
13 In 1731 Frederick, Prince of Wales, acquired a portrait of William the Silent (RCIN 402649) appropriately inscribed: 'WILLIAM OF NASSAW, PRINCE OF ORANGE, THE GREAT ASSERTOR OF THE BELGICK LIBERTY'S. SLAIN IN THE YEARE 1584. AND GREAT GRANDFATHER TO WILLIAM HENRY GLORIOUS INSTRUMENT IN DELIVERING ENGLAND SCOTLAND AND IRELAND FROM POPERY AND ARBITRARY POWER'.
14 In 1742 William Pitt the Elder, 1st Earl of Chatham (1708–78), told the House of Commons, 'It is now too apparent that this great, this powerful, this formidable kingdom, is considered only as a province of a despicable Electorate': Jarrett 1965, p. 224. For the historiography of the early Georgian monarchs, see Smith 2006, pp. 1–8.
15 'From the late seventeenth century, however, the cultural centre of gravity was conspicuously migrating away from Court into metropolitan spaces at large – into coffee houses, taverns, learned societies, salons, assembly rooms, debating clubs, theatres, galleries and concert rooms; formerly the minions of monarchy, the arts and letters were to become the consorts of commerce and the citizenry': Porter 2000, p. 34.
16 For London hospitals – Westminster (1720), Guy's (1724), St George's (1733), the London (1740) and the Middlesex (1745) – see Porter 2000, p. 207; for the Foundling Hospital, see Colley 2012, pp. 58–9. The Foundling Hospital was also an important exhibition and concert venue as enterprising artists and composers combined philanthropy with self-promotion; see *Manners and Morals* 1987, pp. 172ff. For the State of Georgia, founded in 1732 and transferred to the Crown in 1754, see Treasure 1992, pp. 122–3, and Jarrett 1965, p. 204, n. 2.
17 Colley 2012, pp. 44 and 49.
18 Saussure 2006, p. 30, letter of 17 September 1725; for loyalism see Colley 2012.
19 Hervey 1931, I, p. 4. David Hume, *The Parties of Great Britain*, 1742, concluded 'to determine the nature of these parties is, perhaps, one of the most difficult problems that can be met with': see Jarrett 1965, p. 212. It was generally agreed in the period, especially by foreigners, that the country as a whole became caught up in these factions and their disputes: for example, *The Craftsman*, 4 October 1729, 'We are become a Nation of Statesmen our Coffee-houses and Taverns are full of them': Porter 2000, p. 36.
20 For Frederick, Prince of Wales, as an opposition figurehead, see Jarrett 1965, pp. 234–5.
21 Hervey 1931, II, p. 625; Ridley 1999, p. 44; for the Prince's own clubs see *Conversation Piece* 2009, pp. 86–8, discussing RCIN 406101 and 405737. On the general importance of clubs see Porter 2000, pp. 36–7.
22 Bolinbroke wrote his *Idea of a Patriot King* of 1738 with Frederick in mind: see Colley 2012, p. 47.
23 William Pitt said in the Commons in 1758 that he would be 'prouder to be an Alderman than a peer of the realm': see Colley 2012, pp. 61–2.
24 The Bridgewater Canal (1759–61) was sponsored at great financial risk by the Duke of the same name and launched the career of James Brindley (1716–72), who went on to create 360 miles of canal; see Jarrett 1965, p. 331, and Treasure 1992, p. 255–7. For the significance of Plassey see Treasure 1992, p. 219.
25 Voltaire 1733, p. 72, letter 10; see also Saussure 2006, p. 129, letter of 29 May 1727.
26 Freeport is introduced in *The Spectator* no. 2, 2 March 1711; for John Bull, see Treasure 1992, p. 68. The spokesperson for this class was William Pitt the Elder, who gained power in 1757 as a result of national and Parliamentary support (and in spite of the King) and used it to engineer the British military

triumphs of 1759: see Treasure 1992, pp. 151–4.

27 See Voltaire 1728, p. 22.

28 Rose 1993; Deazley 2004, p. 32; Porter 2000, p. 83.

29 This meant the death of patronage (see p. 390 for the example of Pope): Porter 2000, pp. 84–5.

30 For 'Hogarth's Act' see Paulson 1971, I, pp. 359ff.

31 Johnson's *Life of Mr Richard Savage* of 1744 describes this struggling existence: see Porter 2000, p. 83.

32 Voltaire 1733, p. 83, letter 12.

33 For the honours bestoyed in Newton in England, see Voltaire 1733, p. 226, letter 23.

34 This generalising and popularising of Newton's method, pioneered by Samuel Clarke and others, was called 'Newtonism'. Examples of publications of this type include Henry Pemberton, *A View of Sir Isaac Newton's Philosophy*, 1728, and Francesco Algarotti, *Newtonianismo per le Dame*, 1737, translated into English in 1739; see Porter 2000, p. 134. Newtonism was even taught to children: *The Newtonian System of Philosophy*, by 'Tom Telescope', appeared in 1761; see Porter 2000, p. 351.

35 Voltaire 1733, p. 109, letter 14; see also Porter 2000, p. 140.

36 Voltaire describes 'those impertinent Terms which not only Ignorance had rendred venerable, but which had been made sacred, by their being ridiculously blended with Religion'. In this list he includes 'Horrors of the *Vacuum*': Voltaire 1733, p. 87, letter 12.

37 Locke believed that Papists should not be tolerated like other religions because their beliefs were 'absolutely destructive of all governments except the Pope's': Porter 2000, p. 106. The decree permitting the publication of heliocentric books in Rome was only approved in 1822 (by Pope Pius VII).

38 Newton, *Chronology of Ancient Kingdoms Amended*, 1728 and *Observations on the Prophecies*, 1733, tried to get sacred history tidied up with astronomical dating: Porter 2000, p. 133. Locke published *The Reasonableness of Christianity* in 1695; see Porter 2000, pp. 31, 50 and 104–5.

39 Jarrett 1965, pp. 347 and 347–8.

40 The phrase comes from Anderson, *The Constitutions of the Free-Masons*, London, 1723, quoted in Ridley 1999, p. 40.

41 Antognazza 2009, p. 102.

42 Locke, *Essay concerning Human Understanding*, 1690, and *Some Thoughts concerning Education*, 1693; see Porter 2000, pp. 60ff. and 263.

43 Joseph Tucker draws the specific parallel: see Porter 2000, p. 387; Johnson remarked, 'there are few ways in which a man can be more innocently employed than in getting money': Porter 2000, p. 388.

44 Porter 2000, p. 384.

45 Mandeville's work is discussed in Porter 2000, p. 172–3; see also Sir Dudley North, *Discourse Upon Trade*, 1691, in Porter 2000, p. 149.

46 Porter 2000, pp. 389ff.

47 See Jarrett 1965, p. 33, on the founding of the Bank of England. The first factory in England was established for silk-throwing on the river Derwent by the Lombe brothers, John (1693–1722) and Thomas (1685–1739): Treasure 1992, pp. 258–9.

48 Porter 2000, p. 176.

49 Mandeville advocated coming clean about unclean desires in *The Virgin Unmask'd* of 1709; see Porter 2000, p. 172. On the importance of Assembly Rooms in York, Exeter, Bristol, Norwich and elsewhere, see Porter 2000, p. 40.

50 Jarrett 1965, pp. 359–60; see also J.T. Desaguliers, *The Newtonian System of the World: The Best Model of Government, an Allegorical Poem*, 1728, discussed in Porter 2000, pp. 137 and 184.

51 The Regency Act of 1751 stipulated that Princess Augusta would act as Regent should George II die before her son, Prince George (George III), came of age; see Jarrett 1965, p. 236.

52 See Porter 2000, p. 7.

53 So important is this removal of false authority that John Locke, in *An Essay Concerning Human Understanding* of 1690, called philosophy 'an Under-Labourer in clearing Ground a little and removing some of the Rubbish that lies in the way of Knowledge for the Master-builders': Porter 2000, p. 60. John Hunter (1728–93) put the matter more succinctly when he told his students: 'Don't think, try': see Treasure 1992, p. 263.

54 Johnson in *Lives of the Poets* said that before the *Tatler* and *Spectator*, 'England had no masters of the common life. No writers had yet undertaken to reform either the savageness of neglect, or the impertinence of civility': Porter 2000, p. 80; Hume's *Dialogues Concerning Natural Religion* were written in 1751, though not published until 1779: Porter 2000, p. 126; George Berkeley (1685–1753) wrote his *Dialogues* in 1713.

55 See also Voltaire 1733, p. 179, letter 18.

56 Watkin 2004, and see *George III and Queen Charlotte* 2004, pp. 93–102; Ramsay (1762, p. 33) described the artist who may 'by a Palladian receipt alone, without any taste, form a very elegant Corinthian pillar; as a cook, without any palate, and by the help of the *housewife's vade mecum* only, makes an unexceptionable dish of *beef a la daube*'. On the other hand the same training in accurate draughtsmanship was an essential element in the 'Industrial Enlightenment', as Celina Fox has demonstrated: Fox 2009.

57 Richardson 1725, pp. 222–3, concludes that 'no Nation under Heaven so nearly resembles the ancient *Greeks*, and *Romans* as well as We'.

58 Dr Johnson's *Dictionary* of 1755 represents a key moment in the process of correcting the English language by analogy with Latin, so that it too might be considered a 'classical' language. It is not surprising that this process occurred at a time when literary English was more Latinate (and therefore closer to French) than at any other time in history: see Brewer 1997, p. 475, and Porter 2000, pp. 214–5.

59 Hogarth 1955 (*Analysis*), pp. 62 and 105–6, criticises by-the-book Palladianism and the adulation of antique beauty; in his *Autobiographical Notes* he gives up on those 'brought up to the old religion of pictures [who] love to deceive and delight in antiquity and the marvelous and what they do not understand, but I own I have hope of succeeding a little with such as dare think for themselves and can believe their own Eyes': Hogarth 1955, pp. 209–10 (*Autobiographical Notes*, fol. 117); his views on castrati are expressed visually in scene four of *Marriage à-la-Mode* (no. 89).

60 According to Hogarth 'the art of composing well is the art of varying well': Hogarth 1955, p. 57 (*Analysis of Beauty*); see also p. 223 (*Autobiographical Notes*, fol. 43).

61 Quoted in Smart 1992, p. 140.

62 Ramsay 1762, pp. 25–6, quoted and discussed in Smart 1992, p. 141.

63 Smart 1992, pp. 139–48.

64 Voltaire 1733, p. 166, letter 18.

65 Dr Johnson writes, 'A poet who should now make the whole action of his tragedy depend upon enchantment and produce the chief events by the assistance of supernatural agents, would be censured as transgressing the bounds of probability, be banished from the theatre to the nursery, and condemned to write fairy tales instead of tragedies': Porter 2000, p. 225.

66 Vivian 2006, p. 394, quoting from the papers of John, 2nd Earl of Egmont, *Leicester House Politics, 1750–60*, ed. Aubrey N. Newman, p. 190.

67 Vivian 2006, pp. 460–1.

68 Colley 2012, pp. 140–1, discusses widespread British support for the American Revolution.

69 This is the central thrust of Thomas Paine's *The Rights of Man* of 1791; see Treasure 1992, p. 340.

70 In 1805 the 'unprincipled and sanguinary usurper' (Napoleon) was accused in the *Times* of daring 'to imitate, by a splendid mockery, the long recognised, the consecrated and venerable institutions of the unpolluted honour of ancient states'; quoted in Colley 2012, p. 221.

71 Burke 1790, pp. 49–50; see Jarrett 1965, pp. 367–8 and 417–8; Pitt's monument in the Guildhall reads, 'he rallied the loyal, the sober-minded and the good around the venerable structure of the English monarchy': Jarrett 1965, p. 434.

72 For the celebration of June 1814 and their importance for the inception of the Waterloo Chamber at Windsor, see Shawe-Taylor 2013, pp. 251–2.

73 After the French invasion of Italy George III recognised the awkward circumstances of his rival for the throne, Henry Benedict, Cardinal York (1725–1807), and sent a pension to support him: Treasure 1992, p. 200.

74 Millar 1963, p. 144.

75 Stewart 1983, p. 61.

76 Porter 2000, p. 228; Treasure 1992, pp. 176–7.

77 Jarrett 1965, p. 70.

78 Corp 2004, pp. 76ff.

79 Boyer 1992, p. 110.

80 Boyer 1992, p. 110.

81 Toland 1705, p. 67.

82 Niedersächsische Landesbibliothek, MS XXIII 387.

83 Rohr 1981, p. 137.

84 Rohr 1981, p. 127.

85 Thieme-Becker XIX/XX, p. 208.

86 Sotheby's 2005, lot 169.

87 Hatton 1978, pp. 15ff.

88 Millar 1963, p. 148; Sotheby's 2005, lot 171; In January 1715, the Duke of Shrewsbury issued a warrant to Sir Godfrey Kneller requiring him 'to deliver to Sir Isaac Newton Master Worker of the Mint, his Majestys Picture take in Prophile, which you drew for the use of the Mint.' See TNA PRO LC 5/156 f. 66. We are grateful to Sebastian Edwards for generously providing us with this archival reference.

89 Weiß 2008, pp. 118ff.; Thompson 2011, pp. 69ff.

90 Thompson 2011, p. 22.

91 Walpole 1798, IV, p. 304.

92 Black 2007, pp. 125–7; Burchard 2011a, pp. 195–7.

93 Thompson 2011, pp. 28–31.

94 Hervey 1931, III, p. 896.

95 Freiherr von Pöllnitz cited in Marschner 2006, p. 270.

96 Vertue III, p. 84.

97 Vertue III, p. 95.

98 Sold Sotheby's, 23 March 1971, lot 125; several other versions of the bust are known.

99 Scholten 1995, p. 76.

100 Lady Mary Wortley Montagu to the Countess of Bristol, Hanover, 25 November 1716: Wortley Montagu 1837, p. 316.

101 Weiß 2008, p. 130.

102 Vivian 2006, pp. 196ff.

103 Thompson 2011, p. 113.

104 Weiß 2008, p. 136.

105 Roscoe 1999, nos 187, 201, 207; the terms survive at Kew.

106 Roscoe 1999, p. 213.

107 Jutsham Dels, p. 110.

108 Information kindly provided by Malcolm Baker.

109 DNB, s.v. Wale; DNB, s.v. Müller.

110 Risk 1972, p. 1.

111 Desmond 1995, p. 25.

II. *Houses, Palaces and Gardens: The First Georgians and Architecture*

1 Fougeroux 1728, p. 55: '[*Une*] *maison a qui l'on â donné le nom fort improprement de palais St. James*'.

2 Fougeroux 1728, p. 55: '*Il faut se depouiller icy de l'idée de Versailles et des grands palais des Rois. Il faut entrer dans l'esprit de la nation Angloise*'.

3 Mowl 2006, pp. 91–108, and *Kent* 2013.

4 Campbell 1715, Introduction to *Vitruvius Britannicus or the British Architect*, n.p.

5 Campbell 1715, Introduction.

6 Burchard 2011a, p. 178.

7 Scott 2010, pp. 27–8.

8 Scott 2010, pp. 191ff.

9 Smith 2006, p. 73; Burchard 2011a, p. 197.

10 Colvin 1976, p. 240.

11 When Fougeroux visited St James's in 1728, the tapestries were covered by black cloth as the court was mourning the recent death of George I: Fougeroux 1728, p. 56.

12 See *George I Inventory*, n.p.

13 Smith 2006, p. 199.

14 Impey 2003, p. 58, and Mowl 2006, pp. 107–8.

15 Arciszewska 2002, pp. 97–176.

16 Smith 2006, p. 200.

17 Harris 2006, p. 17.

18 Macky 1722, p. 184.

19 Harris 2006, p. 21.

20 Sir Thomas Robinson to the Earl of Carlisle, his father-in-law, 23 December 1734, quoted in Vivian 2006, p. 143.

21 Harris 2006, p. 21.

22 *Mercure Galant*, September 1682, pp. 205–6: '*La Cour de Hanover estant une des plus galantes Cours d'Allemagne*'. An earlier issue describes several celebrations taking place at the Leineschloss and Herrenhausen, such as a fireworks display as well as the visit of the Prince of Orange, later to become William III: see *Mercure Galant*, 1680, pp. 235–47.

23 Halsband 1960, p. 65; the French Theatre was kept throughout the reign of George II: Smith 2006, p. 71.

24 Smith 2006, p. 71.

25 Stieglitz 2001, pp. 68–83.

26 Schnath 1962, pp. 53–6; Arciszewska 2002, pp. 56–9.

27 '*Nous nous préparons ... aller demeurer à Hanover dans une bien sale et vilaine maison pour en quitter une belle et commode où il y a un beau jardin. On me console un peu par Herihausen*': quoted in Schnath 1962, p. 61, endnote 3.

28 Toland 1705, p. 66.

29 Schnath 1962, pp. 69–76; Arciszewska 2002, p. 44–6. The Leineschloss's Opera House, one of the largest in Europe, was built in less than a year, in competition with Duke Anton Ulrich of Brunswick-Wolfenbüttel, head of the senior line of the Guelf dynasty, who was an even greater patron of the arts and saw himself as the rightful candidate for the new Electorate.

30 Queen Caroline's library contained a copy of Steffani's opera *Enrico Leone* as well as separate excerpts of arias; see *A Catalogue of the Royal Library of Her late Majesty, Queen Caroline, distributed into faculties* (manuscript), 1743 (RCIN 1028932).

31 Litzke 2001, pp. 119–25.

32 Gädeke 2005, pp. 157ff.; Heuvel 2001, pp. 85–7.

33 Leibniz's own sketch for the hang of the now lost Rittersaal is preserved at the Niedersächsische Landesbibliothek, Hanover (Handschrift XXIII 32): see Schnath 1962, p. 65; see also Dann 2000, pp. 94–8.

34 Schnath 1976, p. 397; Alvensleben and Reuther 1966 pp. 32–39.

35 Fittschen 2006; Alvensleben and Reuther 1966, p. 39.

36 Burchard 2011a, pp. 201–2.

37 Brindle 2013, pp. 280–1; Thurley 2003, pp. 275–7.

38 Brindle 2013, p. 280.

39 Thurley 2003, p. 277.

40 Wilson 1984, p. 147.

41 Marschner 2006, pp. 259–71; Colvin 1976, pp. 242–3; Burchard 2011a, pp. 186–91.

42 Braun 1956, p. 465, and Maier 2005, pp. 176 and 532; Bayerisches Staatsarchiv Nüremberg (StAN), Fm AN, Hofbauamt, Akten, Nr. 476 I, prod. 65, 60 and 61; the designs are now preserved at the British Library.

43 Burchard 2011a, pp. 197–202; Schnath 1962, pp. 94–98.

44 Köhler 2008, pp. 316–8; Adam 2010, p. 37.

45 Alvensleben and Reuther 1966 and Meyer 1966.

46 Adam 2010, pp. 35–37.

47 Adam 2005, p. 203.

48 Vossnack 1966, pp. 19–28.

49 Schnath 1978, p. 522; Reuther 1976, pp. 133–5; Adam 2001, p. 80; Adam, 2005, p. 206.

50 Adam 2001, p. 91.

51 *Magnificent Maps* 2010, pp. 46–47; Adam 2005, pp. 209–14.

52 Adam 2005, pp. 213–4.

53 Adam 2005, p. 213.

54 Bredekamp 2013, pp. 73–7.

55 Bredekamp 2013, p. 75.

56 Adam 2005, p. 200; Bredekamp 2013, p. 65.

57 Thompson 2011, p. 86.

58 Palm 2010, pp. 46–51.

59 Palm 2010, pp. 52–3.

60 Strong 1992, p. 42.

61 Colton 1976, pp. 1–20.

62 Groom and Prosser 2006, pp. 46–9.

63 Watkin 2004, pp. 59–60.

64 Harris 1996, pp. 59–67.

65 Watkin 2004, p. 41; Wilton-Ely in *Triumph of the Baroque* 1999, p. 482, no. 175.

66 Hatton 1708, p. 625; Dangeau 1856, p. 282: '*... le palais de Whitehall est presque entièrement brûlé; c'est le palais des rois d'Angleterre, une des plus grandes, une des plus vilaines maisons du monde, et la plus habitée*.'

67 See note 2.

68 Kremeier 1999, p. 70.

69 Vossnack 1966, p. 21.

70 Wolff-Metternich 2004, pp. 144–8.

71 *The Daily Courant*, 29 November 1715, in 'The art world in Britain 1660 to 1735,' at http://artworld.york.ac.uk (accessed 25 May 2013).

72 *The Daily Courant*, 8 June 1720, in 'The art world in Britain 1660 to 1735,' at http://artworld.york.ac.uk (accessed 25 May 2013).

73 Hyde 2003, p. 4.

74 *Post Man*, 4 August 1716, in 'The art world in Britain 1660 to 1735', at http://artworld.york.ac.uk (accessed 4 July 2013).

75 Hyde 2003 gives a publication history.

76 Hyde 2003, p. 4.

77 Hyde 2003, p. 4.

78 Strong 1992, p. 33.

79 Strong 1992, pp. 38–9.

80 Bickham 1742, p. 40.

81 Strong 1992, p. 42.

82 Colvin 1976, p. 227.

83 Colvin 1976, p. 218; *George III & Queen Charlotte* 2004, p. 128.

84 DNB, s.v. Joseph Goupy.

85 Inv. 1880,1113.5556.

86 Colvin 1976, pp. 220–1; Watkin 2004, p. 41.

87 Roberts 1997, pp. 35ff.

88 Roberts 1997, p. 449.

89 DNB, s.v. Thomas Sandby.

90 *Views of Windsor* 1995–97, p. 124.

91 Watkin 2004, pp. 58–9.

92 Colvin 1976, p. 240.

93 Burchard 2011a, pp. 185–6.

94 Thurley 2003, pp. 261–2.

95 Burchard 2011a, pp. 186–91.

96 Colvin 1976, pp. 242–3; Mowl 2006, p. 220.

97 Marschner 2006, p. 253.

98 Eustace 1998, p. 57.

99 Burchard 2011a, pp. 189–90.

100 Croft-Murray 1970, pp. 27–8; Watkin 1984, p. 68.

101 Colvin 1976, pp. 198–9.

102 Clark 2009.
103 Vertue III, p. 19, quoted in Mowl 2006, p. 102.
104 Colvin 1976, p. 200; Watkin 1984, p. 70.
105 Hervey 1931, II, p. 489.
106 Colvin 1976, p. 200.
107 Watkin 1984, p. 67; they were finally altered in the early twentieth century by White, Allom & Co., who added vitrine cases for the display of medals.
108 Campbell 1993, pp. 14–15 and 17–19; *Kensington Inventory c.* 1736.
109 Colvin 1976, pp. 189–90.
110 Evelyn 1955, V, p. 237, quoted in Colvin 1976, p. 190.
111 Colvin 1976, pp. 200–1.
112 Pyne II, pp. 29–32; Colvin 1976, p. 200; Watkin 1984, p. 64; Croft-Murray 1970, p. 28.
113 Bickham 1742, p. 28.
114 Mowl 2006, p. 105.
115 For the staircase at Windsor, see Downes 1966, p. 20; for the one at Hampton Court, Thurley 2003, pp. 212–3.
116 Thurley 2003, p. 254.
117 Vittet 2008.
118 Campbell 1992, p. 29.
119 Jakob 1997, pp. 26–32.
120 Alvensleben and Reuther 1966, p. 34; Fittschen 2006.
121 Fryman 2011, pp. 84–5; Davies 2003, p. 60.
122 Brett 2013, pp. 3–8.
123 Croft-Murray 1970, pp. 69–78.
124 Bickham 1742, p. 15; Thurley 2003, p. 247.
125 *George I Inventory*, n.p.; Thompson 2011, p. 201, with reference to the 1754 inventory of pictures at Herrenhausen and the Leineschloss, NHStA, Dep. 103, XXIV, Nr. 2587.
126 Pyne 1819, II, p 63; Croft-Murray 1962, p. 269; Brett 2013, pp. 3–8.

III. *A 'Wondrous Game': The Early Georgians at War*

1 Among the many works on this period, see Colley (1992) 2012, Blanning 2002, Smith 2006, Thompson 2006, Simms 2007.
2 Quoted in Simms 2007, p. 300.
3 For the religious elements of the rivalry see, among others, Colley 2012, *passim*. France and Britain were allies between 1716 and 1731: see Simms 2007, p. 86.
4 Walpole, quoted in Simms 2007, p. 97. See also Colley 2012, p. 88 and *passim*, Simms 2007, p. 365.
5 Thompson 2006, p. 172.
6 For the debates surrounding a standing army see Speck 1977, where it is suggested that the British army numbered 8,000–17,000 in peacetime and 35,000–74,000 in times of war (p. 58).
7 Simms 2007, p. 85.
8 *A Speech Against Continuing the Army, 1717,* printed 1718, Society of Antiquaries, Dyson Perrins IV, fol. 95. See also Simms 2007, p. 104.
9 *A Letter from John Pately, in the English Cavalry in Hanover, to John Stubbs his Old Comrade in England*, 1759, Society of Antiquaries, Dyson Perrins IV, fol. 143.
10 Forbes 1815, p. 31.
11 Hartshorne 1905, p. 113.
12 Hewitt 2010.
13 Letter, David Hume to William Rouet, Friday, 6 July 1759, *Electronic Enlightenment*, ed. Robert McNamee *et al.*, Version 2.4, University of Oxford, 2013: http://www.e-enlightenment.com/item/humedaOU0010309_1key001cor/ (accessed 12 October 2013).
14 *The Monitor*, July 1756, quoted in Simms 2007, p. 417.
15 Hartshorne 1905, p. 273.
16 Churchill 1957, III, p. 123.
17 Although, as Hannah Smith points out, George I and George II had the simple advantage of gender over their predecessor, who as a woman could not gain or demonstrate military ability (Smith 2006, p. 23).
18 DNB, s.v. George I.
19 Quoted in Smith 2006, p. 23.
20 Thompson 2006, p. 153.
21 Thompson 2006, p. 106; Hayes 1957–8, *passim*, quotation on p. 335.
22 DNB, s.v. William Augustus, Duke of Cumberland.
23 Hervey 1821, p. 110.
24 Hayes 1957–8, p. 350.
25 Hughes 1747, p. 37.
26 Hodson 1988.
27 The entry in Ligonier's regimental account for £153 11s, dated 5 February 1763, may refer to these busts: see Murdoch 1983, p. 39.
28 Millar 1963, p. 183.
29 Endell 1908, p. 50.
30 Gilmour 2000, p. 102.
31 Corp 2007, p. 166.
32 DNB, s.v. Prince James Francis Edward Stuart.
33 *King over the Water* 2001, p. 49.
34 See above, p. 93.
35 Szechi 2006.
36 See above, p. 93.
37 *Post Man*, 7 January 1716, in 'The art world in Britain 1660 to 1735', http://artworld.york.ac.uk (accessed 9 October 2013).
38 BL, Maps 3230.1.
39 DNB, s.v. Sir Charles Wills.
40 Quoted in Lenman 1980, p. 194.
41 See above, p. 93.
42 Lenman 1980, p. 194.
43 Sanford Terry 1905, p. 422; Portland 1891–1931, V, pp. 584–5.
44 Pollard 2009a, p. 29.
45 Pollard 2009a, pp. 29ff.
46 Orrery 1903, I, p. 295.
47 Letter, David Hume to John Home of Ninewells, Sunday, 3 March 1748, *Electronic Enlightenment* (see note 13): http://www.e-enlightenment.com/item/humedaOU0010114_1key001cor (accessed 9 October 2013).
48 Clifton 1996, p. 124.
49 Museum of the History of Science, Oxford, inv. 34654. I am very grateful to Stephen Johnston of the Museum of the History of Science for his help with this entry.
50 Crawforth 1987, p. 1.
51 Henderson 2010, p. 389.
52 Sandby 1892, p. 14, where it is mistakenly described as a view of Kenilworth.
53 Prebble 2002, p. 15.
54 Kopperman 1996, p. 449.
55 Lloyd 1897, p. 528.
56 Harding 2007, p. 141.
57 Walpole 1937–83, XIX, p. 424.
58 DNB, s.v. Sir John Ligonier.
59 Simms 2007, p. 350; Doderer-Winkler 2013.
60 Hunter 2012.
61 Smith 2006, p. 72.
62 *King over the Water* 2001, pp. 78–80.
63 Sharp 1996, p. 112.
64 Reid 1996, p. 29.
65 Reid 1996, p. 29.
66 Reid 1996, p. 35.
67 Gardiner 1977, p. 440; *Magnificent Maps* 2010, p. 110.
68 McLynn 1983, p. 36.
69 Hughes 1747, p. 19.
70 Prebble 2002, p. 17.
71 Prebble 2002, p. 25.
72 Hughes 1747, p. 39.
73 Reid 2009.
74 Pollard 2009b, p. 37.
75 RA SP/MAIN/274/95.
76 See above, p. 93.
77 Hayes 1943, p. 252.
78 Worms and Baynton-Williams 2011, p. 78; DNB, s.v. George Bickham; Monod 1993, p. 83.
79 TNA MPF 1/2, 1.
80 Houston 2009; letter from Braddock quoted in DNB, s.v. Edward Braddock.
81 McCormack 2006, p. 982.
82 Whitworth 1992, pp. 190–2.
83 Henderson 2010, p. 249.
84 Quoted in Whitworth 1992, p. 198.
85 Barber 1997, pp. 106–7.
86 Hallett 1997.
87 Stacey 2002, p. 194.
88 DNB, s.v. Hugh Debbieg.
89 Parson Woodforde, quoted in Stacey 2002, p. 15.
90 See above, p. 93.
91 Orme 1763–77, II, p. 723.
92 Orme 1763–77, II, p. 734.

IV. *'Prints should be prized as Authors should be read': Hogarth and Graphic Art*

1 Hogarth 1955, p. 201.
2 Hogarth's career has been well studied. The following discussion benefits particularly from Uglow 1997; DNB, s.v. William Hogarth; Paulson 1989; *Hogarth* 2006.
3 Hogarth 1753, preface.
4 *Hogarth* 2006, no. 5.
5 Fielding 1965, p. 9.
6 Mitchell 1731.
7 Einberg 2004.
8 DNB, s.v. Hogarth.
9 Einberg 2004, p. 32.
10 RCIN 1151343, the binding of which bears the royal arms in a form used on other bindings owned by George II. There are stubs remaining at pp. VIII–IX and pp. 94–95 which may indicate the presence of the plates. There is, however, no indication that the King himself read or used the volume in any way.
11 James Thornhill gave George I a set of the prints after his paintings in the cupola at St Paul's and Nicholas Dorigny had presented impressions of his prints after the Raphael Cartoons to George I and the Prince and Princess of Wales (Clayton 1997, pp. 52 and 55). The Thornhill prints are probably those in the King's Topographical Collection, today in the British Library. The Prince of Wales's sumptuous copy of Dorigny's presentation volume remains in the Royal Library, RCIN 809020. Dorigny also presented a volume of his heads

after the Apostles in the Raphael Tapestries to Caroline, Princess of Wales, in 1722 (RCIN 809052). The volume appears thereafter to have entered the Royal Library and bears the binding stamp of George II. Press notices are a good source for prints presented to members of the royal family, often recording works which do not survive in the Royal Collection.

12 *Great Men's Heads*, for which regular payments are listed in the Princess's surviving accounts (RA GEO/ADD/17/65/1-2, 1736–45). This may have been the 'Heads of the most Illustrious Persons of Great Britain' published from 1737 by John and Paul Knapton (Alexander 2008, p. 219).

13 McGeary 2002; Vivian 2006, particularly pp. 421–4.

14 McGeary 2002, p. 258; Vivian 2006, p. 411.

15 Hogarth 1955, p. 213.

16 Jonathan Swift, *Travels into several remote nations of the world. In four parts, ... By Lemuel Gulliver*, 1758 p. 222.

17 Note by John Glover in RCIN 1043011.

18 Richardson 1936.

19 Letter, Jonathan Swift to Esther Vanhomrigh: Saturday, 26 October 1720, *Electronic Enlightenment*, ed. Robert McNamee *et al.*, Version 2.4, University of Oxford, 2013: http://www.e-enlightenment.com/item/swifjoOU0020359_1keyoo1cor (accessed 2 October 2013).

20 British Museum, inv. 1858,0213.86.37.

21 *Daily Post*, 19 September 1724, in 'The art world in Britain 1660 to 1735,' at http://artworld.york.ac.uk (accessed 2 October 2013); Hogarth 1955, p. 205.

22 *Hogarth* 1997, no. 51.

23 Note by John Glover in RCIN 1043011.

24 Thornbury and Walford 1873–8, III, pp. 41–2.

25 Genesis 29: 13–14; Ireland 1808.

26 Beckett 1948, p. 167.

27 Letter, John Gay to Jonathan Swift, Thursday, 26 February 1728, *Electronic Enlightenment* (see note 19): http://www.e-enlightenment.com/item/gayxjoOU0010070_1keyoo1cor (accessed 2 October 2013).

28 Letter, John Gay to Jonathan Swift, Saturday, 17 July 1728, *Electronic Enlightenment* (see note 19): http://www.e-enlightenment.com/item/gayxjoOU0010075_1keyoo1cor (accessed 2 October 2013).

29 *Hogarth* 2006, no. 37; Beckett 1948, p. 168.

30 Scouten and Hughes 1944, p. 30.

31 Stephens and George 1870–1954, no. 1987.

32 Baum 1934.

33 Paulson 1967, p. 83.

34 Paulson 1989, p. 75.

35 Note by John Glover in RCIN 1043011.

36 Paulson 1989, no. 118.

37 Paulson 1989, pp. 75–6.

38 RCIN 1155588a, fol. 88.

39 RA GEO/MAIN/27253.

40 RCIN 1043011.

41 Hogarth 1955, p. 209.

42 Paulson 1989, p. 76.

43 Paulson 1989, pp. 76–7.

44 Note by John Glover in RCIN 1043011.

45 Inv. 1960,0409.113.

46 RCIN 1155588a, fol. 88.

47 RCIN 1043011.

48 *Hogarth* 2006, nos 80–81.

49 Note by John Glover in RCIN 1043011.

50 RA GEO MAIN/28336, 16 July 1821

51 O'Connell 1997, p. 58.

52 Note by John Glover in RCIN 1043011.

53 Einberg 2004.

54 Coley 1967.

55 John Ireland, quoted in Paulson 1989, p. 142.

56 Quoted in Einberg 2004, p. 32.

57 Quoted in Einberg 2004, p. 33.

58 RCIN 1155588a, fol. 88.

59 RCIN 1043011.

60 Acts 24: 10–13.

61 Hogarth 1753, p. XI.

62 For hostile reactions see, for example, Jackson 1966; *Hogarth* 2006, p. 45; *Sandby* 2009–10. For binding stamps associated with George II, see Davenport 1896.

63 RA GEO/MAIN/27251.

64 RCIN 1043011.

65 Hogarth 1753, p. 2.

66 Paulson 1989, no. 195.

V. *Furniture and Interiors in the Royal Palaces 1714–1760*

'Wardrobe accounts' indicates a warrant or payment found in the papers of the Great Wardrobe, either as a part of the Lord Chamberlain's papers deposited at The National Archives, Kew (reference preceded by TNA LC) or from one of the leather-bound folio volumes of accounts in the Royal Archives, Windsor Castle (reference preceded by RA GEO/MAIN).

1 Wardrobe accounts, RA GEO/MAIN 81127; signed Montagu 2 June 1715.

2 By the end of William III's reign the offices of the Wardrobe had moved to Great Queen Street, St Giles-in-the-Fields, having earlier moved from Baynard's Castle, St Andrews, in the City of London to Buckingham Street in the Savoy: Beard 1997, p. 10.

3 Masters of the Great Wardrobe after the long tenure of John, 2nd Duke of Montagu were, 1750–54, Sir Thomas Robinson (later Lord Grantham); 1754–55, William Wildman, Viscount Barrington; 1755–60, Sir Thomas Robinson (again). See Haydn 1890, p. 296.

4 Haydn 1890, p. 295. The post was held by the Duke of Grafton from 1724 to 1757, when it was taken on by William, Duke of Devonshire. Prior to the Duke of Grafton, the post-holders were the Dukes of Shrewsbury (1714–15), Bolton (1715–16), and Newcastle (1717–24). The office of Lord Chamberlain remained vacant for the period 4 July 1716–14 April 1717.

5 Beard 1997, pp. 147 and 157.

6 Wardrobe accounts, RA GEO/MAIN 81588. The total cost came to £897.15s.

7 RA GEO/MAIN 81591.

8 RA GEO/MAIN 81590.

9 Edwards and Jourdain 1944, p. 2.

10 Beard and Gilbert 1986, pp. 753 and 980.

11 Beard 1997, p. 148.

12 Wood 2008, p. 12.

13 Wood 2008, p. 63, and Thurley 2003, pp. 197–8.

14 Cornforth 2004, p. 125. It is unusual at this date to find giltwood furniture in a wood-panelled room.

15 Wood 2008, pp. 71–78.

16 Wardrobe accounts, RA GEO/MAIN 81618.

17 Wilmot-Sitwell 2009, p. 82. Although created during the reign of George III, Chippendale's most expensive chairs, at £20 each, were oil-gilded. They were made for Sir Lawrence Dundas's London town house, 22 Arlington Street, to designs by Robert Adam.

18 Wardrobe accounts, TNA LC9/288-90.

19 Saussure 2006, p. 42. Saussure also noted in the Bedchamber a French-style bed rail: 'The bed stands in a sort of alcove, shut off from the rest of the room by a balustrade of gilded wood'.

20 There are numerous examples: 120 cane chairs were supplied by Richard Roberts, joiner 'For His Majesties Service at Greenwich' six dozen at 16s each; two dozen at 14s each; two dozen at 12s each (Wardrobe accounts, RA GEO/MAIN 81130, signed Montagu 2 June 1715).

21 Bickham notes what is likely to be the Andrew Moore set in the Ballroom, where they can be seen today (RCIN 35301–2).

22 Wardrobe accounts, RA GEO/MAIN 81651.

23 Tapestries featured in all rooms except the King's and Queen's Guard Chambers, the Queen's Dressing Room, Queen Elizabeth's Gallery, the King's Closet, King's Dressing Room, the King's Drawing Room, King's Audience Chamber and St George's Hall.

24 Pote 1749, p. 419.

25 Wardrobe accounts, RA GEO/MAIN 81180.

26 Kent succeeded Thomas Ripley in 1726 in the post of Master Carpenter in the Office of Works and became Deputy Surveyor in 1735 until his death in 1748. Ripley in turn succeeded Sir John Vanbrugh as Comptroller of the King's Works, a post he held until 1758.

27 Blackett-Ord 2001, p. 76.

28 Blackett-Ord 2001, p. 102.

29 In response to Burrell Massingberd's commission for a ceiling design he wrote on 15 February 1717, 'I have received your measure for ye cieling piece .... Mr Talman was here this morning & would have had me done this cieling after ye grotesk manner, but I think it will not be well unlese the whole was so – I believe you may remember this sort of painting its what ye Ancients used, *but am resolved to do a thought of my own*' [my emphasis]: Blackett-Ord 2001, p. 94.

30 On 3 April 1717 Kent wrote to Burrell Massingberd, 'here are several English, and one Mr Hewit desir'd me to give his service to you': Blackett-Ord 2001, p. 96.

31 Written, significantly, from his beloved Italy.

32 Shaftesbury, *Soliloquy: or Advice to an Author*, 1710; Wittkower 1974, p. 179 ('English Neo-Palladianism, the Landscape Garden, China and the Enlightenment').

33 However, it is interesting to note that in the 1740s George II rebuilt the Kammerflügel at the Leineschloss in Hanover to designs by J.-F. Blondel; see Burchard 2011a, p. 200.

34 See Wittkower 1974, pp. 193–204 ('Classical Theory and Eighteenth-century Sensibility').

35 See Murdoch 1997, *passim*, but especially pp. 732–3 and n. 10; Murdoch 1998, pp. 364–7.

36 Le Pautre *c.*1650–1750 and *c.*1700–15.
37 Cornforth 2004, p. 159.
38 Weber 2013, p. 449–51, fig. 17.2–3.
39 Cornforth 2004, p. 154.
40 Ince and Mayhew 1759–63.
41 Ryder 1939, entry 18 August 1716, pp. 298–9.
42 Wardobe accounts, RA GEO/MAIN 81174.
43 RA GEO/MAIN 81160, approved by Montagu 15 September 1715; RA GEO/MAIN 81163; RA GEO/MAIN 81166–69. This lengthy bill from Phill & Fletcher includes the upholstery done by them at Hampton Court in the Drawing Room, Privy Chamber, Dining Room, Dressing Room, Closet, King's Bedchamber and Privy Chamber: total £628.9.0; signed Montagu 15 September 1715.
44 A State Bedchamber was usually occupied by one person, but at Hampton Court, almost certainly owing to the King's reluctance to engage in any new major building project, the Prince and Princess of Wales 'shared' the Bedchamber planned for Mary II's use.
45 RA GEO/MAIN 81161.
46 Thornhill's ceiling painting, with its portrait roundels of George I, the Prince and Princess of Wales and Prince Frederick of Wales in the coving, represented the present dynasty and the walls represented the historic roots of that dynasty, with portraits of James I, his Queen, Anne of Denmark, their daughter Elizabeth of Bohemia and their son Henry, Prince of Wales. See Thurley 2003, pp. 246–7.
47 John Robinson: 'Line 5 pcs of Tapestry hangings called Joshua, 3 pcs of Solebay fight, and One piece of Tobias for Hampton Court. Nine pcs of the Sciences for ye Presence Chamr; 3 peices of the Seasons for the little Drawing Room; 4 pcs of the Planetts for the Privy Chamr; and 2 pcs of the Apostles for the Prince's Drawing Room at St James's'. Vanderbank's entry for restoring the tapestries also falls in RA GEO/MAIN 81164.
48 Murdoch 1998, pp. 364–5, fig. 6.
49 RA GEO/MAIN 81137.
50 RA GEO/MAIN 81138.
51 RA GEO/MAIN 81160.
52 For the Bedchamber, Richard Chamberlayne supplied 282 yards of crimson Genoa damask (at 25s per yard); John Johnson supplied 126 yards of rich broad crimson damask (at 28s per yard), and 573 yards of crimson damask (at 23s per yard): RA GEO/MAIN 81163.
53 For the Prince and Princess of Wales's apartment at Hampton Court, William Weeks, laceman, supplied '617 yds ½ of very broad rich Crim[son] in gr[ain] silk arras lace at 3/3 £100:6:10 ½.
54 Bowett 2002, p. 241, pl. 8:21, illustrates this form on the Chair of State made by Thomas Roberts for the Coronation of Queen Anne, 1702.
55 The Bedchamber mirror was 10' 7" high and that in the Privy Chamber 10' 4" in. high. Those in the Privy Chamber and Drawing Room were accompanied by 'a Table & Stands finely carved and gilt', while the table and the stands for the Bedchamber were each embellished with an 'Indian [i.e. lacquer] Top': RA GEO/MAIN 81174.
56 RA GEO/MAIN 81174.
57 Bowett 2009, pp. 290–1.
58 Wardrobe accounts, TNA LC9/286 51r.
59 Wood 2008, pp. 71–78.
60 The King and court made summer visits to Kensington in 1718, 1720, 1721, 1722, 1724 and 1726 whilst building work was carrying on.
61 Saussure 2006, p. 136.
62 Gaunt and Knight 1990, II, p. 360.
63 On 21 October 1720 John Vanderbank, Yeoman Arras Worker to the Great Wardrobe, was paid £475 for working on all the tapestries at Kensington, which included four pieces from the Caesar and Pompey series, three 'Landskip & figures' and seven pieces from the 'Dutch Boors'. Furthermore Vanderbank added '50 Ells of new fine Tapestry hangings (called the Dutch Boors) at £3:10s per Ell Fflemish £175': RA GEO/MAIN 81383.
64 Bickham 1742, pp. 3, 6, 25, and RA GEO/MAIN 81514, 'For a large Oak Bedstead £40'.
65 Colvin 1976, p. 198.
66 In a Roman house, the room leading off the atrium giving on to the garden or peristyle, normally the principal room of business.
67 Sicca 1986, pp. 142–3.
68 Vertue III, p. 19.
69 Quoted in Gaunt and Knight 1990, II, p. 42.
70 In 1724, Gumley & Moore supplied for 'His Majesties Bedchamber' in the new apartments at Kensington Palace '4 large sphynx stands for Tables at £36 each £144': RA GEO/MAIN 81525. A year later Gumley & Moore charged 'for 2 fine sphynx table frames at £36 each £72': RA GEO/MAIN 81549/ TNA LC9/287.
71 Pyne 1819, II, p. 72.
72 Blackett-Ord 2001, p. 90, letters dated 12 October 1715 and 14 January 1716 referring to Kent's copying of *Diana and Actaeon* by Dughet and Maratta in the Palazzo Pallavicini, Rome. The original is now at Chatsworth, Derbyshire.
73 See Wood 2008, pp. 9–10, for an explanation of the influence of Chinese furniture on English furniture design of the early 18th century.
74 Wardrobe accounts, TNA LC9/287 f24. Furthermore, a very similar stand for a lacquer or japanned cabinet in the Victoria and Albert Museum (W.30-1958) was, by repute, claimed by the Earl of Rochford, George II's Groom of the Stole, upon the King's death. The cabinet was at St Osyth's Priory and descended in the family until acquired by the Museum in 1958. Information kindly supplied by Lucy Wood.
75 Bowett 2005, p. 46.
76 Wardrobe accounts, TNA LC9/287, fol. 70.
77 Gilbert 1996, p. 251, fig. 458.
78 RA GEO/MAIN 81525 and TNA LC9/287; Bowett 2005, p. 45, fig. 12.
79 Marot 1703.
80 Wood 2008, p. 128, no. 5, n. 48.
81 Wardrobe accounts RA GEO/MAIN 81618; LC9/287 fol. 114; Bowett 2005.
82 RCIN 922106; Pyne 1819, I, opposite p. 152; Bowett 2005, p. 42, fig. 8.
83 Baldinucci 1975, p. 91.
84 Interestingly, they were copied in marble to support the marble busts of George II and Queen Caroline by Michael Rysbrack (nos 5 and 6).
85 The present appearance of the bronze plaques is due to the re-patination carried out for George IV in 1814.
86 Avery 1995/6, pp. 1–17.
87 Walpole 1758, p. 52.
88 Vertue I, pp. 132–3.
89 Cruickshanks 1995, p. 210.
90 Lankheit 1957, p. 8.
91 Jutsham Recs &Dels, I, p. 253, 14 April 1814.
92 Gaunt and Knight 1990, II, pp. 362–3.
93 Gaunt and Knight 1990, II, pp. 362–3
94 Gaunt and Knight 1990, II, p. 365.
95 Gaunt and Knight 1990, II, p. 366; Wardrobe accounts TNA LC5/74 pp. 146–300; TNA LC9/291, fols. 22–185; TNA LC9/292, fols. 2–118v.
96 The contents have vanished, and were probably either claimed by courtiers as perquisites after George II's death or were given away.
97 On loan to the National Maritime Museum, Greenwich. See Beard and Hardy 2013, pp. 303–12.
98 'The French have furnished us with abundance of fanciful decorations for these purposes, little less barbarous than the Gothic; and they were like that species of building (for we will not descend to call it architecture) received with great readiness: the art [of good design] seemed upon the point of being lost in England: but a better taste has now prevailed': Isaac Ware, *A Complete Body of Architecture*, 1756, quoted in Worsley 1995, p. 208.
99 Bowett 2012, p. 122.
100 For example, *Some Designs of Inigo Jones* ..., an edition of which had been edited by William Kent at Lord Burlington's request.
101 They were photographed for Guy Laking's 1905 book, *The Furniture of Windsor Castle*:
no. 108 appeared as plate 18.
102 TNA LC9/289 fol. 46: (Michaelmas 1736–Michaelmas 1737) Sarah Gilbert's account for making. Mathew Vernon supplied 457 yds of green Genoa Damask (fol. 44). Weeks's account was 'For making Hangings of Green Genoa Damask to fix between the pictures & over & under ym, trimm'd very neatly wth Lace & for sewing silk and other materials used'.
103 Thurley 2003, p. 275; see Walpole 1862, II, pp. 563–4.
104 White 1982, no. 74.
105 'For 3 large Glass Sconces in carved & gilt Frames wth 2 wrot Arms to Each £27': TNA/LC9/288. With a few exceptions, the descriptions of furnishings in the Wardrobe accounts are scanty in detail and it is difficult to associate the very few surviving objects from this period with a brief description in an account.
106 Wardrobe accounts TNA LC9/288; TNA LC9/163 fol.124; TNA LC5/147 fol.217; AO (Audit Office) 3/1168.
107 RA GEO/MAIN 82084.
108 RA GEO/MAIN 82084.
109 RA GEO/MAIN 82083.
110 Although Bickham suggests that the Alexander tapestries were acquired by Cadogan, they are not recorded in the Earl's posthumous sale: *A Catalogue of the Rich Furniture Of the*

Right Honourable the Earl of Cadogan .... As likewise and Excellent Collection of Pictures .... Which will be Sold by Auction, at his Lordships House in Piccadilly, on Thursday the 14th of February, 1726–7, and no record of the acquisition for the collection has been traced.

111 Murdoch 2003, pp. 414–5., figs. 16, 17 and 19.

112 Wood 2008, I, p. 18.

113 TNA LC9/289 fol. 47.

114 RCIN 1230.1–14 and 28062.1–9; the latter are marked with a Kensington Palace inventory brand of 1910 and a brand for the Palace of Holyroodhouse for 1911.

115 One, with the same brands as those found on the stools at the Palace of Holyroodhouse, is at Rienzi, Museum of Fine Arts, Houston; another (apparently lacking brands) was with Mallett, London, 2001; and two, also lacking brands, are in the collection of the National Trust at Hughenden Manor, Buckinghamshire, NT inv. 428620.1-2.

116 A number of X-frame armchairs dated to *c.*1605 survive at Knole, Kent (NT inv. 129463); Beard and Goodison 1987, p. 15, is a chair covered in fabric *en suite* with the Spangle Bed, 1600–10.

117 Cornforth 2004, pp. 159–60, fig. 202. It is highly probable that Kent designed the chairs for the Saloon, although no design or documentation survives.

118 TNA LC9/289 fl.44.

119 RA GEO/MAIN 82084

120 RA GEO/MAIN 82083

121 Carlisle 1897, p. 84, letter from Robinson to his father-in-law, the Earl of Carlisle, at Castle Howard.

122 Worsley 1987, II, p. 179, fig. 12, and III, p. 117.

123 Beard 1993, p. 120, fig. 1.

124 *Stowe: A Description of the Magnificent House & Garden ...*, London, 1756, p. 44: 'The Bed and Ceiling, by Signior Borra'; see Wood 2008, no. 100, where an argument is advanced for William Linnell as maker.

125 See http://www.vam.ac.uk/content/articles/n/norfolk-house-music-room (accessed 10 December 2013).

126 The Stowe papers are preserved at The Huntington Library. Although a great deal of research has been undertaken, relatively little is known about the furnishings in the house before 1750. One of the double-chair-back settees has been associated with lot 242 in the August 1848 Stowe sale and four side chairs from this set may be those listed as lots 1337 and 1338.

127 Victoria and Albert Museum, W.30-1947. The tables display the Cobham family arms surmounted by a baron's coronet. He was ennobled in 1714.

128 Rieder 1978, pp. 10–11.

129 Christie's, London, 9 July 1998, lot 100; the tables and a pair of stools were sold in 1921 by Col. W. Selby Lowndes, a direct descendant of W. Selby Lowndes of Whaddon Hall, Buckinghamshire, MP and neighbour of the Duke of Buckingham.

130 Himmelheber 1975, p. 115.

131 A longer extract from the advertisement: '... Mrs Clay therefore humbly hopes that Gentlemen and Ladies, encouragers of Art and Exquisite Workmanship, will not think a Shilling ill bestow'd for the Sight of so Extraordinary a Performance, and the Hearing of such Excellent Musick, the whole exceeding by many Degrees, any thing ever exhibited to publick View in any Nation, or by any Artist whatsoever. Remov'd over-against Cecil-Street in the Strand, where it is to be seen at One Shilling each'. See Gwynn 1997.

132 The same *London Newspaper* advertisement of 27 August 1743 explained the *Temple and Oracle of Apollo* in glowing terms: '... the whole exceeding by many Degrees, any thing ever exhibited to publick View in any Nation, or by any Artist whatsoever'.

VI. *The 'Battle of the Pictures'*

1 Hogarth's article of 7–9 June 1737 in the *St James's Evening Post*, signed 'Britophil', is his most brilliant and sustained attack (see Paulson 1971, I, pp. 372ff.); the arrangement of copies and parodies of Old Master paintings visible on the walls of *Marriage à-la-Mode* (no. 89) makes these points visually. He was not the only one to voice these opinions: Horace Walpole maintained that it was 'easier to distinguish the Hands of the Masters, than to decipher the Cant of the Virtuosi' (*Aedes Walpolianae*, 1752; Dukelskaya and Moore 2002, p. 358).

2 Dukelskaya and Moore 2002; *Houghton Revisited* 2013.

3 Hervey 1931, II, p. 502.

4 Richardson 1719, I, pp. 40–2, maintained that painting was for improvement as well as pleasure, regretting that many 'look on Pictures as they would on a Piece of Rich Hanging', whereas in fact 'one may as well say a Library is only for Ornament, and Ostentation, as a Collection of Pictures, or Drawings'.

5 Robert Walpole used many such drawings in order to create his real picture hangs at 10 Downing Street and Houghton Hall: see Dukelskaya and Moore 2002, pp. 24–30 and 419–28.

6 Harris, de Bellaigue, Millar 1968, pp. 24–9; *George III and Queen Charlotte 2004*, pp. 115–24.

7 Hervey 1931, II, p. 489.

8 According to Vitruvius, IX, VI, 1–6, a frame should actually comprise an architrave only.

9 The attribution of this and other frames is made by analogy with the frame surrounding Rubens's *Gerbier Family* for which Goodison submitted a bill on 12 October 1749: 'A very Large Picture frame for a Family peice wh side & Corner ornaments & a carved Goloss all round ye frame' (WRA GEO. 54868), quoted in White 2007, p. 262.

10 Frederick's accounts mention many names of frame makers, including George Murray, Joseph Dufour, Jacob Gossett, Waters, Benjamin Goodison, John Boson, John Bradburn and William France and Paul Petit; see Millar 1977, p. 103.

11 In a manuscript inventory in the Royal Archive, see *Leicester House* 1749, fol. 3; the room was described by Vertue in 1749 (III, p. 152).

12 Vertue I, p. 11.

13 The French Academy in Paris was founded in 1648, see Montagu 1994, pp. 68ff. Mahon 1947, pp. 183–9, discusses the foundation of the French Academy in Rome in 1666 (with the close involvement of Giovanni Pietro Bellori) and the way in which the French state colonised Italian artistic theory and institutions at the time.

14 Dryden's *The Art of Painting*, a translation of *De arte graphica* of Charles Alphonse Du Fresnoy, appeared in 1695; *L'Idée du peintre parfait* of Roger de Piles (1699) appeared in English in 1706 as *The Idea of a Perfect Painter: or; Rules for forming a right judgement on the works of the Painters*; Jonathan Richardson's written works include *An Essay on the Theory of Painting* of 1715 and *Two Discourses* of 1719, which comprise 'An Essay on the whole Art of Criticism as it relates to Painting' and 'An Argument on behalf of the Science of the Connoisseur'; see Gibson-Wood 2000, pp. 14, 143 and 253–4; Reynolds wrote three articles for the *Idler* on 29 September, 20 October and 10 November 1759, as well as delivering fifteen *Discourses* at the Royal Academy between 1769 and 1790; see Reynolds 1997.

15 Reynolds 1997, p. 32 (*Discourse* II of 1769); Shaftesbury had given substantially the same advice in his *Second Characters or the Language of Forms* of 1712: Shaftesbury 1969, p. 13.

16 Reynolds 1997, p. 102 (*Discourse* VI of 1774) discusses 'those peculiarities, or prominent parts, which at first force themselves upon view; and are the marks, or what is commonly called the manner, by which that individual artist is distinguished'. His conclusion upon this subject is the exact reverse of ours: 'Peculiar marks, I hold to be, generally, if not always, defects; however difficult it may be wholly to escape them'.

17 The generosity of Vasari's assessment of artists of all periods, as well as his layers of discrimination, is described in Rubin 1995, pp. 231ff.

18 See Enggass and Brown 1970, pp. 5–8.

19 See Enggass and Brown 1970, p. 136.

20 Millar 1969, pp. 154–7, no. 1211; he lists the works and their original locations; see also *Conversation Piece* 2009, pp. 130–7, no. 25.

21 During his Italian visit in 1750–52 Reynolds observed that painters earlier than Raphael were superior to those later than Carlo Maratta – not something which would need pointing out today; Leslie and Taylor 1865, I, p. 61.

22 Walpole, *Aedes Walpolianae*, 1752, reprinted in Dukelskaya and Moore 2002, p. 366, quoted in Pepper 1984, p. 47.

23 Walpole, *Aedes Walpolianae*; Dukelskaya and Moore 2002, pp. 362 and 379–81.

24 Bellori's life is discussed and translated in Enggass and Brown 1970, pp. 136–42.

25 Translated in Enggass and Brown 1970, p. 141. The study of antique sculpture teaches artists to find out the beauty in Nature: Dryden

annotated his translated Du Fresnoy by explaining, rather circularly, that 'the ancient Pieces are truly beautiful because they resemble the Beauties of Nature, and That Nature will ever be beautiful which resembles those Beauties of Antiquity': Du Fresnoy 1716, p. 93.

26 Pepper 1984, p. 48.

27 The designs for the refurbishment of the first floor of Leicester House, including the picture arrangement and framing, were probably all provided by William Kent: see Harris 2006, p. 21.

28 *Leicester House* 1749, fol. 3.

29 Vertue I, p. 10, discussed in Millar 1977, p. 99.

30 *Leicester House* 1749, fols. 2–3, which calls the space the Prince's 'Dressing Room' rather than Closet, and Vertue I, p. 11.

31 Hogarth 1955, p. 220 (*Autobiographical Notes*, fol. 37–8); Paulson 1971, II, pp. 270ff.

32 Vertue I, p. 10, and III, p. 152; the Prince tried to acquire the entire Schaub collection for £12,000 (Walpole, letter of 10 May 1758, quoted Vivian 2006, p. 407).

33 Walpole, *Aedes Walpolianae*, 1752; Dukelskaya and Moore 2002, p. 362; Jonathan Richardson, *On the Art of Criticism* (Richardson 1719, I, p. 33), writes that Maratta and Chiari will seem to be Raphael and Giulio Romano only to those that do not know any better.

34 Reynolds 1997, pp. 85–6 (*Discourse* V of 1772).

35 See Warner 1992.

36 Millar 1977, p. 99, a view which Horace Walpole evidently did not share, as he wrote of his surprise at the high prices paid for 'Pictures of Andrea del Sarto, whose Colouring was a mixture of mist and tawdry, whose Drawing hard and forc'd': *Aedes Walpolianae*, 1752; Dukelskaya and Moore 2002, p. 358.

37 *Leicester House* 1749, fol. 2, and Vertue I, pp. 10–11.

38 *Queen's House Inventory* 1819, nos 677–91.

39 All these judgements are contained in Shearman 1983, pp. 11–2, no. 5.

40 *Kensington Inventory* 1818, no. 439.

41 The works in the room known to have been acquired by George III came from the Consul Smith collection, which did not include this work.

42 *Art of Italy* 2007, p. 66.

43 Dosso Dossi's *St William* (RCIN 405775) is probably the 'Charles the Hardy' by Giorgione in the Passage Room at Kensington (*Kensington Inventory* 1750, p. 21); 'Her Majesties Dressing Room' at Kensington probably contained Lorenzo Costa's *Woman* (RCIN 405762) and *St Helena* (RCIN 403379), both listed without attribution, the latter as 'Woman Saint with a Cross' (*Kensington Inventory* 1750, p. 18). These attributions had not improved by 1818, when Dosso's *St William* (RCIN 405775) was still a Giorgione, hanging in the Privy Chamber (*Kensington Inventory* 1818, no. 54); his *Portrait of a Man* (RCIN 407269) carries the same attribution (*Kensington Inventory* 1818, no. 626). The two Costas (RCIN 405762 and 403379) both become attributed to Perugino (*Kensington Inventory* 1818, nos 18 and 240). The same failure to recognise Ferrarese painting occurs with the three paintings now attributed to Dosso Dossi (RCIN 405549, 402913 and 402913), which were given to Georgione, 'after Sebastiano', and Pordenone (*Kensington Inventory* 1818, nos 77, 428 and 607). Mazzolino's *Warriors* (RCIN 403008), on the other hand, was recognised as a 'Massolino da Ferrara' and described as a 'beautiful specimen of this scarce Master – in high preservation' (*Kensington Inventory* 1818, no. 203).

44 Vertue I, p. 11; *Leicester House* 1749, fol. 2; Pyne 1819, I, p. 148.

45 Vasari 1996, II, p. 447 (*Life* of Garofalo).

46 Garboli 1971, nos 90–3 and 191; *Art of Italy* 2007, p. 27; Haskell 2013, pp. 77–8.

47 Millar 1977, p. 90.

48 *Kensington Inventory* 1750, p. 2.

49 Pyne 1819, I, pp. 147–52; the room is illustrated by Charles Wild (RCIN 922105).

50 To the three already mentioned should be added (from the Reni school) a *St John in the Desert* (RCIN 406111), *Virgin and Child* (RCIN 403549), *St Catherine* (RCIN 405547), *St Sebastian* (RCIN 405562), *Judith and Holofernes* (RCIN 402817), all acquired during the reigns of George II and George III.

51 Malvasia 1971, p. 399, for circumstances of Reni's composition; see also *Art of Italy* 2007, p. 286.

52 See, for example, Burke 1757, Part III, Sect. XVI.

53 *'Con questo esempio insegnò Annibale in che cosa consista la perfettione delle opere di pittura, e quanto sopra gli altri Domenico prevalesse nell'attione, e ne gli affetti che principalmente debbono attendersi in quest'arte'*: Bellori 1672, p. 304 (*Life* of Domenichino); see also Malvasia 1971, p. 97.

54 Reynolds 1997, p. 78 (*Discourse* V of 1772).

55 Levey 1991, p. 109, no. 540; Millar 1977, p. 99, says that this was the Prince's favourite.

56 Vertue I, p. 11; *Queen's House Inventory* 1819, no. 695.

57 The subject, support and dimensions described by Vertue match this work, which is also recorded in *Kensington Inventory* 1750, p. 25.

58 Vertue (I, p. 11) saw 'several noble paintings by Cortona' in the second room at Leicester House in July 1749; two are listed in the 1749 inventory (*Leicester House* 1749, fol. 1), including the *Augustus and the Sibyl* (RCIN 405461), which can be seen in the King's Drawing Room in Windsor (fig. 52), in a French-style frame paired with no. 137 (Rubens, *Holy Family*); Levey 1991, p. 122, no. 575; Millar 1977, p. 99.

59 Pascoli 1736, II, p. 140.

60 *Rest on the Flight* (RCIN 402731); see Levey 1991, p. 104, no. 532; Millar 1977, p. 95; see also Dukelskaya and Moore 2002, p. 131, no. 38.

61 *Leicester House* 1749, fol. 1; see also Levey 1991, p. 103.

62 Pyne 1819, I, pp. 147–52; the room is illustrated by Charles Wild (RCIN 922105).

63 Pascoli 1736, II, p. 140.

64 Poussin as the new Raphael is discussed by Claire Pace in Félibien 1981, pp. 19–22; see no. 129 below for Le Sueur.

65 Reynolds 1997, pp. 62–3 (*Discourse* IV of 1771).

66 See von Erffa and Staley 1986, p. 44.

67 Roger de Piles 1708, pp. 201ff., distinguished between the 'heroic' style of landscape (*'le style Héroïque'*) and the merely 'pastoral' (*'le style Pastoral ou Champêtre'*); Reynolds sets out ideas which had been current throughout the century: 'Like the history-painter, a painter of landskips in this style and with this conduct [that of Claude and Poussin], sends the imagination back into antiquity; and, like the Poet, he makes the elements sympathise with his subject ... a landskip thus conducted, under the influence of a poetical mind, will have the same superiority over the more ordinary and common views, as Milton's *Allegro* and *Penseroso* have over a cold prosaick narrative; and such a picture would make a more forcible impression on the mind than the real scenes, were they presented before us': Reynolds 1997, pp. 238–9 (*Discourse* XIII of 1786).

68 Millar 1977, pp. 99–100, quotes Vertue I, p. 11.

69 *Leicester House* 1749, fol. 1, where the room is also called the '2nd Room'.

70 *Queen's House Inventory* 1819, nos 659–76; the assumption that the 'Landskips' mentioned in 1748 are one and the same as the works described in these inventories rests in part on the consistency of their early eighteenth-century frames.

71 *Queen's House Inventory* 1819, nos 659–76.

72 *Holbein to Hockney* 2004, pp. 15–21, provides the best overview of British Royal drawing collecting in this period.

73 *Poussin: Works on Paper* 1995, pp. 10–11.

74 *Holbein to Hockney* 2004, pp. 16–21; *George III and Queen Charlotte* 2004, pp. 208–12.

75 *Poussin: Works on Paper* 1995, pp. 171–4, no. 58.

76 Walpole, *Aedes Walpolianae*, 1752; Dukelskaya and Moore 2002, p. 365.

77 Reynolds 1997, pp. 69–70 (*Discourse* IV of 1771).

78 Guillet de Saint-Georges (edn 1990), quoted in Mérot 2000, p. 131.

79 *'Et Lesueur, notre Raphaël de la France, quand il arrive de colourer aussi bien qu'il invente ou qu'il dessine, n'est-il pas autant le divin Lesueur que l'autre est le divin Raphael?'*: de Brosses 1978, II, p. 164; see also Mariette 1741, all quoted in Mérot 2000, pp. 134–5. Horace Walpole described Le Sueur as a pupil of Poussin who, 'to the style of his Master, and the study of the Antique, join'd an imitation of Raphael, which, had his life been longer, would have raised him high above Poussin': *Aedes Walpolianae*, 1752; Dukelskaya and Moore 2002, p. 365.

80 Mérot 2000, pp. 228–31.

81 Plutarch 1823, I, pp. 374–5 (*Life* of Camillus).

82 Suetonius 1997, p. 179 (*Life* of Caligula, 15).

83 Suetonius 1997, pp. 175–6 (*Life* of Caligula, 8–9).

84 *Leicester House* 1749, fol. 1.
85 Hunterian Museum and Art Gallery, GLAHA 10972.
86 A list of possible examples of 'candle light' Bigots is provided by Wright 1985, pp. 139–4; Boyer 1988, pp. 355–7, established that the man documented in Rome under various names – 'Trofamonti', 'Bigotti' – was the Arles painter and not his son. The attachment of Bigot's name to the works remains conjectural.
87 *Kensington Inventory* 1818, no. 600.
88 See Bellori's *Life* of Caravaggio (1672, pp. 201–16) and Mahon 1947, pp. 176–83.
89 Millar 1977, p. 52.
90 What Horace Walpole wrote of Salvator Rosa's *Prodigal Son* at Houghton (now in the Hermitage) might apply to no. 130: 'In Lord ORFORD'S Prodigal is represented the extremity of Misery and low Nature; not foul and burlesque like Michael Angelo Caravaggio; nor minute, circumstantial and laborious like the Dutch Painters': *Aedes Walpolianae*, 1752; Dukelskaya and Moore 2002, p. 364, and *Houghton Revisited* 2013.
91 Baldinucci 1728, p. 357.
92 See Howard 1969, p. 9; Hayes 1965, I, pp. 82ff., documents the popularity of Claude in England even before the eighteenth century. Horace Walpole wrote of a *Seaport* at Houghton: 'There is a bright Sun playing on the Water, and the whole Shine of the Picture is in his very best Manner': *Aedes Walpolianae*, 1752; Dukelskaya and Moore 2002, p. 397.
93 *Queen's House Inventory* 1819, no. 673.
94 See British Museum, inv. 1957,1214.25 (LV 19) for a painting of 1637 in a private collection; a print after it reveals that it was in the Duke of Devonshire Collection: Roethlisberger 1961, LV19.
95 *Poussin: Works on Paper* 1995, pp. 201–2, no. R3.
96 Addison visited the cascade at Terni in 1701–3 and wrote, 'I must confess it was not one of the least entertainments that I met with in travelling to examine those several descriptions [by classical authors] as it were, upon the spot, and to compare the natural face of the country with the landscape that the poets have given us of it': Hayes 1965, III, pp. 444ff.
97 *Leicester House* 1749, fol. 1.
98 *Queen's House Inventory* 1819, no. 663.
99 Campbell 2004, I, pp. 187–95, nos 54–6.
100 The *View of the Villa of Maecenas* (Tate, N00108) was painted as a result of the occasion for the Earl of Thanet: see *Wilson* 1982, p. 192, with comments on the villa's importance as a moral lesson on the decline of Rome; see also Constable 1953, pp. 34–5.
101 Oberhuber 1988, p. 233.
102 *Dughet* 1980, pp. 38–9.
103 *Leicester House* 1749, fol. 1; for the Vivares print, see British Museum, inv. U,8.55.
104 *Queen's House Inventory* 1819, no. 670.
105 See Baglione 1649, p. 296.
106 '*... accompagnant ses païsages d'histoires, ou d'actions convenables: comme dans celui-ci, qui est un tems fâcheux, il a trouvé un sujet triste & lugubre*': Félibien 1981, p. 149 (reprinting Félibien, *Entretiens*, 1725, p. 161).
107 An endeavour considered beyond his powers by Reynolds (1997, pp. 255–6, *Discourse* XIV, 1788)
108 On the artist's popularity in England see Hayes 1965, I, pp. 82ff.; *Dughet* 1980, pp. 11ff.
109 *Queen's House Inventory* 1819, nos 660 and 662.
110 *Queen's House Inventory* 1819, no. 664.
111 In *The Landscape; a didactic poem* of 1795 (pp. 20–21) Richard Payne Knight describes the paradoxical way in which smooth elements in landscape make a 'harsh and edgy' effect on the eye when painted, while rough things in nature appear when painted to be 'all of softness and harmony'.
112 The 'Great Drawing Room', 'Lesser Closet' and 'His Majesty's Great Gallery' had especially rich displays of Venetian Renaissance painting: *Kensington Inventory* 1750, pp. 2–4 and 6.
113 *Kensington Inventory* 1750, p. 6, 'His Majesty's Great Gallery'; the 'Raphael' is a fragment of fresco which is still there though no longer with this attribution.
114 It can be assumed that Tintoretto's *Muses* gained its strips at top and bottom when Kent re-framed it for incorporation in the King's Gallery; Vertue (II, p. 88) wrote of the 'Great Piece': 'to make this picture more Suteable to the place of this new gallery. it is lengtned in the height ... the additional part is visible enough.'
115 *Kensington Inventory* 1750, pp. 2-3.
116 *Leicester House* 1749, fol. 2. No. 138 may be conjecturally identified as the work listed cryptically as 'The Battle of'; see White 2007, nos 34, 59, 66, 68 and 70; Millar 1963, no. 165.
117 White 2007, nos 67–8; *Queen's House Inventory* 1819, nos 666–7.
118 Millar 1977, p. 161.
119 Millar 1963, nos 154, 156, 158, 160 and 187; Millar 1977, p. 161.
120 Vertue V, p. 78: 'which shews that according to former observations so many parts of them Cartons of Raphael Rubens has pick't and culld. to make use of in his works – is now a publick observation & truth – that those great designs were in his possession – or use. before they came to England & bot by King Charles'.
121 '*Riportò egli in Fiandra il buon colorito Venetiano*': Bellori 1672, p. 248; '*simile in ciò al suo maestro Rubens, sequitando le medesime regole, e massime di colorire, se non che il VanDick riuscì più delicato nelle incarnationi, e si avvicinò più alle tinte di Titiano*': Bellori 1672, p. 264.
122 '*e benche egli stimasse sommamente Rafaelle, è l'antico, non però imitò mai l'uno, ò l'altro in parte alcuna*': Bellori 1672, p. 248; Jonathan Richardson (1719, pp. 79–80) describes Flemings in general as good colourists and imitators of nature and Rubens specifically as '*a Fleming* tho' he would fain have been an *Italian*'; Horace Walpole thought Rubens much too fond of flesh as Michelangelo had been of muscle: *Aedes Walpolianae*, 1752; Dukeslkaya and Moore 2002, p. 361.
123 Roger de Piles's views are summarised in his user-friendly '*Balance des Peintres*' in his *Cours de peinture par principes* of 1708 (pp. 489ff.), in which marks are awarded out of 18 for composition, drawing, colour and expression. First prize is a draw between Raphael and Rubens, both of whom score a total of 65 out of the possible 72. Rubens drops marks for drawing (scoring only 13) and Raphael for colour (a mere 12). This pattern is repeated amongst the next rank of painters, who divide into the draughtsmen who fall down in their colour – Domenichino (with a total of 58), Le Brun (56), Poussin (53) and Le Sueur (49) – and the colourists who flunk drawing – Van Dyck (55) and Rembrandt (50). The only consistent artists of this rank are 'the Carracci', who collectively score an impressive 58.
124 White 2007, p. 256, no. 70; *Leicester House* 1749, fol. 2.
125 See Martin 2005.
126 Colley 2012, p. 27, discusses the reprinting in 1732 of Foxe's *Book of Martyrs*, with its identification of Mary I, especially when married to Philip II, as the chief culprit.
127 Vertue III, p. 19; Millar 1977, p. 90.
128 White 2007, pp. 236–7, quotes references in seventeenth-century Spanish inventories to a much bigger painting, which he identifies with no. 136; in which case it was cut down as well as expanded.
129 The inventories variously give the size as 148 × 108 in. and 145 × 107 in.; see White 2007, p. 237.
130 Walpole, MS additions to Bathoe James II, quoted in White 2007, p. 237.
131 White 2007, p. 237; Pyne 1819, I, p. 90, describes it as 'Albert Duke of Saxony', though it is uncertain who he means; Smith 1830, II, no. 82, identifies it reasonably enough as 'Archduke Albert' (1559–1621), the Governor of the Spanish Netherlands when the work was executed.
132 White 2007, pp. 191–2.
133 Michel 1771, pp. 120ff.; for the importance of this Raphael to the French Academy see Montagu 1984, p. 77.
134 Vertue II, p. 89, quoted in Millar 1977, p. 92.
135 Reynolds provides a fuller account of all these qualities in his *Journey to Flanders and Holland* of 1781: see Malone 1798, II, pp. 397, 402 and 419–25.
136 Burnet 1827, p. 19, makes this comparison between the colour spectrum in a sunset and Rubens's flesh tones.
137 All information provided in White 2007, pp. 122–4.
138 British Library, MS 19027, fol. 20, quoted White 2007, p. 120; this painting is probably the unidentified battle-scene mentioned in the 1749 Leicester House inventory in the 3rd Room with other large paintings by Rubens and Van Dyck: *Leicester House* 1749, fol. 2.
139 Millar 1963, nos 551–2; Vertue (I, p. 11) saw them on the Great Stair Case at Leicester House in July 1749.
140 Duchy of Cornwall MSS, vol. XVII, fol. 547, quoted in Millar 1963, p. 109.
141 *Leicester House* 1749, fol. 2, see Millar 1963, p. 109, nos 187 and 188. Millar believed no. 139 to be a copy after Van

Dyck; it was identified as an original in 2012 by Philip Mould.

142 Barnes 2004, pp. 386–8, 396 and 415–6, nos. III.189–95, 208 and A31–2.

143 Millar 1977, pp. 100–1.

144 Vertue I, p. 11.

145 *Leicester House* 1749, fol. 2.

146 'in a play calld the Wanderer – a Song against Jealousy. written by T. Carew and a Mask. 1633. in the first design was writt at my request upon a dispute held betwixt Mrs Cecelia Crofts and my self [T. Killegrew] where he was present': Vertue V p. 79.

147 Christopher Lloyd provides an excellent analysis in *Queen's Pictures* 1991, p. 130, no. 41. The pairing of noble scholar and secretary pays tribute to one of the most famous paintings in England at the time, Sebastiano del Piombo's *Ferry Carondelet and his Secretary* (Madrid, Museo Thyssen-Bornemisza), acquired in 1619 by the Earl of Arundel and believed to be by Raphael; see Haskell 2013, p. 16, and *Van Dyck and Britain* 2009, p. 123.

148 See J.P. Vander Motten's entry in the DNB.

149 See Millar 1977, pp. 144–60.

150 Queen Caroline acquired two Dutch pictures probably for historical reasons – an English period 'Calm' by Willem van de Velde II (RCIN 405503) and a depiction of the King and Queen of Bohemia dining in public by Bartholomeus van Bassen (RCIN 402967); see Millar 1977, p. 95; Frederick, Prince of Wales, owned a 'Rembrandt Wife', seen by Vertue (British Library, MS 19027, fol. 20); probably White 1983, no. 165.

151 *Leicester House* 1749, fol. 1, which calls the space merely the '1st Room'; While 2007, pp. 242–53, nos 67 and 68; the paintings were cleaned by John Anderson in September 1747; Benjamin Goodison's account mentions frames 'ornamented with Festoons & flowers all round ditto with Mosaick work in the Ground & a canopy of Flowers at the top all in Burnished Gold' (WRA GEO 54559); White 2007, pp. 352–7, nos 117–20; Vertue I, p. 11.

152 Millar 1977, pp. 100–1; Vertue V, pp. 126–7, records this purchase, *c.*1739–40; Bagnall also sold Frederick two Van Dycks – the *St Martin* and the double portrait (no. 140).

153 *Bruegel to Rubens* 2007, pp. 26–7.

154 White 2007, p. 305.

155 Frederick also owned two small copies after Titian by Teniers (RCIN 400932-3) and his *Peasants outside a country inn* (RCIN 407274), which was recorded in his collection in June 1749 and may have been the painting acquired for him by Mercier for 15 guineas in 1735; see White 2007, nos 93, 105–6. The Walpole collection at Houghton similarly had an impressive range of Flemish low-life scenes, by Snyders and Teniers, but only a single Dutch genre scene (a lost work by Ostade); see Dukelskaya and Moore 2002, pp. 459ff.

156 British Museum, inv. 1850,0713.140.

157 Paul Petit, 1 June 1749, 'To mending ye Joints & Gilding where wanted of a Rich picture Frame' etc., to be sent to Carlton House by order of Mr. Goupy (WRA GEO. 54961).

158 British Museum, inv. R.I.a.131; Hollstein 49; van Someren 2238.

159 *Kensington Inventory* 1818, nos 5 and 421; *Queen's House Inventory* 1819, no. 760; Houghton had a Hals portrait correctly identified by Horace Walpole, though he seemed to think that 'Francis Halls' was Sir Godfrey Kneller's master: *Aedes Walpolianae*, 1752; Dukelskaya and Moore 2002, p. 374, no. 44.

160 White 1982, nos 57 and 116.

161 *Queen's House Inventory* 1819, no. 760.

162 *Queen's House Inventory* 1819, nos 751–60.

163 See De Piles 1706, p. 7; Vertue contrasted the 'valuable Manner of Dahl, Kneller, Lilly, Riley, Dobson Vandyke Rubens or Titian' with that of Allan Ramsay's early work, which is 'rather lick'd than pencilld. neither broad, grand, nor Free, has more of the finishd labourd uncertain – or modish French, German, etc. dutch way': Vertue III, p. 96; Vertue even criticised Van Dyck's 'Great Piece' for its 'heavines. & narrowness' in the face of the King, 'savouring something of the Dutch tast – which certainly is a habit he contracted in his native Country he coud not (no more than other famous painters) get rid of. for some time': Vertue II, pp. 88–9.

164 Reynolds 1997, p. 109 (*Discourse* VI of 1774).

VII. *'An Amiable Philosopher on the Throne': Queen Caroline and the Encouragement of Learning*

1 Voltaire 1733, p. 79, Letter 11.

2 Treasure 1992, pp. 63–5.

3 Hervey 1931, I, p. 261.

4 See Porter 2000, p. 8.

5 Leibniz's life and thought are brilliantly set out in Antognazza 2009; I am grateful to my brother, John Shawe-Taylor, for help in matters mathematical.

6 Anthony Collins called him the man 'whom all English freethinkers own as their head': *Discourse of Freethinking*, London 1713, p. 171, quoted Porter 2000, p. 516, n. 49. Clarke considered moral laws to be as demonstrable as matters of scientific fact; to deny them was like saying 'a square is not double to a triangle of equal base and height'. Pope considered Clarke's inclusion in Queen Caroline's Hermitage a nonsense (*Epistle to Burlington*, 1731, l. 78).

7 See Porter 2000, p. 112. Wollaston also coined the phrase 'pursuit of happiness'.

8 For eighteenth-century irreligion, see Porter 2000, pp. 96–7.

9 Leibniz was one of the models for Pangloss in Voltaire's *Candide* of 1759.

10 Marschner 2006, p. 166.

11 Clarke 1973, p. 566.

12 Jefferson 1774, p. 5.

13 Treasure 1992, pp. 80 and 193.

14 Delany 1861, II, pp. 536–7.

15 Vivian 2006, pp. 148–9.

16 Wilkins 1901, I, p. 102.

17 Wilkins 1901, I, pp. 103–4.

18 Piper 1982, pp. 78–90.

19 Delany 1861, III, p. 482.

20 Cowper 1864, p. 72.

21 Egmont 1920, II, p. 190.

22 *Strawberry Hill* 2009 provides the most comprehensive account of Walpole's career and at the same time of eighteenth-century English antiquarianism.

23 For antiquarian interest in architecture, seen for example in Samuel Buck's *Views of the most remarkable Ruins of Abbeys and Castles now remaining* of 1721, see Harris 1979; George II followed fashion by attending a masquerade in 'old-fashioned English habit': see Ribeiro 1984, pp. 28 and 38–45.

24 See Mowl 1988.

25 Treasure 1992, p. 195.

26 *Conversation Piece* 2009, p. 137.

27 Egmont 1920, II, p. 190.

28 See *Northern Renaissance* 2011, pp. 138–9, nos 60 and 61.

29 Millar 1963, p. 57, no. 26.

30 Millar 1963, pp. 58–9.

31 Millar 1963, p. 60.

32 Walpole's notes to the *The Heroic Epistle to Sir William Chambers* (ed. P. Toynbee, Oxford 1926), quoted in Hervey 1931, II, p. 501.

33 *Gentleman's Magazine*, August 1732, p. 917.

34 Vertue III, p. 51.

35 £52.2s; TNA WORK 4/4.

36 TNA AO 1/2454/166.

37 *Gentleman's Magazine*, August 1732, p. 917.

38 *Gentleman's Magazine*, August 1732, p. 917.

39 Marschner 2006, p. 46, citing *The Diary of Mary Countess Cowper, Lady of the Bedchamber to the Princess of Wales 1714–1720*, London, 1864, p. 84.

40 *Gentleman's Magazine*, August 1732, pp. 917–8.

41 Walpole 1928, p. 16.

42 RA GEO 53998, cited by Millar 1963, p. 171.

43 I am grateful to Robin Simon for drawing this to my attention.

44 Vertue III, p. 75.

45 *Gentleman's Magazine*, 10 June 1735, p. 498.

46 TNA WORK 1 /2, Letter book, p. 7.

47 This section relies heavily on the work of Joanna Marschner, who has generously shared her knowledge with the authors of the catalogue.

48 Vertue I, p. 13.

49 RCIN 1112557.

50 British Library, Add.Ms. 20101.

51 See Marschner 2006, pp. 176–245, 'Queen Caroline and the Wunderkammer'.

52 Vertue V, p. 23.

53 Granger 1825, I, p. 17.

54 *Kensington Inventory*, ff. 25–6; they were seen here by Vertue in 1734, when he went 'to Observe what pictures are most usefull to mee to work after'; quoted Millar 1963, p. 27.

55 Dendrochronology carried out for the Royal Collection Trust by Ian Tyers.

56 Canning 1688, p. 35.

57 British Library, North (Sheffield Park) papers, Add MS 61860, vol. I.

58 Aschengreen Piacenti and Boardman 2008, p. 17.

59 *Liselotte van der Pfalz* 1996, pp. 167–71.

60 RA GEO, Add. Ms. 16.

61 Evelyn 1955, III, pp. 79–80.

62 Evelyn 1755, p. 62.

63 RA GEO, Add. MS. 16.
64 MacGregor 1989, pp. 412–3.
65 Vertue III, p. 160.
66 Marschner 2002, p. 137.
67 Vertue III, p. 135.
68 Koninklijk Huisarchief, The Hague, A17/404, fol. 49v.
69 RA GEO 55539.
70 'An account of inoculation by Sir Hans Sloane Bart. Given by Mr. Ranby, to be published, Annon 1736. Communicated by Thomas Birch, D.D. Secret. R.S.' and read on 19 February 1756, is reprinted in *Journal of Epidemiology* 2011, vol. 40, pp. 8–9. In this Sloane says that without inoculation smallpox affected all but one in a thousand of the population; while only one out of 200 he had inoculated himself had died as a result. The statistical case for inoculation was put by the Newtonian mathematician James Jurin: see Porter 2000, p. 208.
71 For English science and the understanding of atmosphere, see Porter 2000, p. 56; for the best account of the design, application and publication of early steam engines see Fox 2009, pp. 91–116.
72 The Board of Longitude at Greenwich offered a prize of £20,000 in 1714; see Sobel 1995.
73 Willmoth 1997, p. 3.
74 *Gentleman's Magazine* 1735, pp. 3–4.
75 Voltaire 1733, pp. 87–8, letter 12; for similar ideas expressed in the preliminary discourse to the *Encyclopédie* see Porter 2000, p. 57.
76 For Kew see *George III and Queen Charlotte* 2004, pp. 126–33; and Harris 2005, p. 20, in which John Theophilus Desaguliers is described setting up a planetarium with mathematical instruments behind the portico of the White House at Kew in 1737.
77 McBurney 1997; *Amazing Rare Things* 2007.
78 *Amazing Rare Things* 2007, pp. 190–1.
79 Pietsch 1995, I, pp. 49–50.
80 Albin 1720, p. [10].
81 Stuart Mason 1992, p. 4.
82 Stuart Mason 1992, p. 6.
83 Edwards 1750, p. xviii.
84 Hughes 1750, p. vii.
85 Boswell 1791, I, p. 294.
86 Hill 1759, p. o.
87 Henrey 1975, II, p. 95.
88 Roberts 1987, p. 58.
89 *Compass and Rule* 2009, pp. 132–6.
90 Knight 1842, p. 87.

VIII. *'Curious Limnings': Portrait Miniatures in the Early Georgian Period*

1 George II's Will (RA GEO/MAIN/52936).
2 Leicestershire, Leicester and Rutland Record Office, 26D53/811.
3 George I inventory, 1723, fol. 7: 'Deux Caisses de Mignatures dans le Cabinet de Roy a Kensington'.
4 Vertue 1743, p. 13.
5 Vertue 1743, p. 13.
6 Vertue 1743, p. 22, no. 143.
7 Vertue 1743, pp. 21 and 24, nos. 139 and 159; see Reynolds 1999, nos. 260–5.
8 Recently re-attributed in Rutherford and Grosvenor 2013, no 67.
9 Rowell 1996, p. 22.
10 Horace Walpole to Richard Bentley, 2 March 1754, *Correspondence*, XXXV, p. 163.
11 Millar 1977, p. 99.
12 Goulding 1916, p. 41.
13 Lloyd 2013, pp. 20–4.
14 Walpole 1928, p. 79.
15 Vertue III, p. 50.
16 Vertue III, p. 40.
17 Walpole 1862, III, p. 749.
18 Baker-Smith 1995, p. 12.
19 Vertue III, p. 63.
20 Reynolds 1988, p. 102.
21 Vertue III, p. 50.
22 Aschengreen Piacenti and Boardman 2008, p. 17.
23 Hall 1871, p. 127.
24 Worsley 2010, p. 120.
25 Vertue III, p. 64.
26 Walker 1992, p. XIV.
27 Vertue IV, p. 178.
28 Vertue IV, p. 81.

IX. *'An Honour to our Nation': The Rise of a British School*

1 Richard Steel, *The Lover*, London 1715, pp. 223–31, quoted in Bold 2000, pp. 145–8; Thornhill was paid £2810 for the work in May 1724 and published his *An Explanation of the Painting in the Royal-Hospital at Greenwich* soon afterwards, in c.1726.
2 For Hampton Court see Thurley 2003, pp. 246–7; the decoration of St Paul's was executed 1716–19 and published in 1720 as a series of prints.
3 Paulson 1971, I, pp. 369–70; it is mentioned a decade later by Vertue (III, p. 127).
4 Vertue I, p. 10; a Hayman oil sketch (Royal Albert Memorial Museum, Exeter) shows artists presenting a plan for an academy to Frederick and Augusta: see *Manners and Morals* 1987, pp. 206–7, no. 193.
5 For the story of early English academies, see Lippincott 1983, pp. 15–7; *Manners and Morals* 1987, pp. 19–22; Bignamini 1988, pp. 61–82 and 83–95; Allen 2006, p. 34.
6 A full-size set of Thornhill's copies is at the Royal Academy; a smaller set is at Colombia University; a final set in Thornhill's sale (Christopher Cock, 24 February 1734/5, lot 98) cannot be traced; see Meyer 1996.
7 Vertue describes how various noblemen supported the claims of their favourite artists, perhaps filling the vacuum left by the royal family: Vertue III, p. 79.
8 Allen 1991b, pp. 265–9; the 1761 exhibition was seen by 20,000 people and 6,000 catalogues were sold: see Pears 1988, p. 127. Edward Edwards (1808, p. VIII) dated the transformation of interior decoration and the rise of British painting to the 'period when exhibitions were first established'.
9 Allen 2006, p. 30, quoting Pascoli 1736, II, p. 381.
10 Walpole called Amigoni 'a still fainter imitator of that nerveless master Sebastian Ricci': Paulson 1971, I, p. 352; see also Vertue III, p. 94, and *Canaletto in England* 2006, p. 9.
11 Vertue (I, p. 39) described Sebastiano Ricci as a 'great mimick of other antient Italian Masters', saying that several of his paintings were sold as earlier originals: a set of Ricci studies of heads after Veronese's *Supper in the House of Levi* (Accademia, Venice) came into the Royal Collection with the Consul Smith purchase: Levey 1991, nos 629–35. For international taste for Venetian art at this time see *Glory of Venice* 1994, pp. 44–59.
12 See Baird 2007, pp. 22–3, and Croft-Murray 1970, pp. 239–42; Vertue V, pp. 149–50, makes a diagram of the room and lists the heroes celebrated by the scenes: William III; George I; William Cavendish, 1st Duke of Devonshire (1640–1707); Thomas, 1st Marquis of Wharton (1648–1715); Charles Sackville, 6th Earl of Dorset (1638–1706); James Stanhope, 1st Earl Stanhope (1673–1721); William Cadogan, 1st Earl Cadogan (1675–1726); Sidney Godolphin, 1st Earl of Godolphin (1645–1712); Archbishop John Tillotson (1630–94) and Joseph Addison. He mentions other paintings from the same series honouring Newton, Boyle, Locke, Thomas Sydenham (1624–89) and Sir Cloudesley Shovell (1650–1707) – though not *in situ*.
13 Vivian 1989, p. 14.
14 Victoria and Albert Museum, W12-1944 and W. 13-1944; a preliminary study is also held there, D.756-1886; Dorchester, Art2350–1; Yale, B1977.14.97–8.
15 Levey 1991, p. 121, suggests this, though the best documented match of this kind – Norfolk House, containing works by Pellegrini painted for the Duke of Portland – was occupied by Frederick after 1733 (from 1737 to 1741). The Capel collection came to Frederick through his lease of Kew Palace; see Millar 1963, p. 30.
16 Mercury may pair off with Juno as the facilitator of Jupiter's gallantries and thus her adversary.
17 Daniels 1976, pp. 54–5, no. 165.
18 Daniels 1976, pp. 135–6, no. 464.
19 For Félibien's description of this painting (VIII, pp. 120–38), see Félibien 1981, pp. 139–43; Charles Le Brun delivered a lecture on the subject of the painting at the French Academy in 1667: see Jouin 1883, p. 52.
20 Vivian 1989, pp. 108–9.
21 Visentini's work at Mogliano occurred in 1730 and 1747, and his renovation of Smith's palace on the Grand Canal (now Palazzo Mangilli-Valmarana) was completed in 1751; see Vivian 1989, p. 14.
22 Vivian 1989, p. 22. The relationship between Palladianism and contemporary Venetian landscape is brilliantly discussed by John Harris in *Glory of Venice* 1994, pp. 247ff.
23 For the thirteen Canaletto caprices, nine of which are still in the Royal Collection, see Levey 1991, pp. 43–48, nos 408–16.
24 Levey 1991, pp. 162–66, nos 669–76.
25 See *Canaletto in England* 2006, pp. 64–6.
26 They are on a Venetian type of canvas with a russet ground rather than the light grey the artist used for most of his English paintings; Charles Beddington explains the relationship between the various drawings and versions in *Canaletto in England* 2006, pp. 60–9, nos 5–10.
27 *Canaletto in England* 2006, p. 63, figs 5.1 and 6.1.
28 *Canaletto in England* 2006, pp. 101–15, nos 23–30.

29 Described in Saussure 2006, pp. 94–5, letter of 29 October 1726. For a complete description of this part of the city see *London 1753* 2003, pp. 121–30.
30 Vertue II, pp. 119ff.; see also Stewart 1983.
31 Vertue described the stairway at Whitton painted with an allegory of the arts and the exalted company Kneller liked to welcome there: Vertue II, pp. 68 and 121.
32 See Field 2008.
33 Vertue commented that Kneller had been to Italy to study Raphael, Titian and Veronese and had formed himself a firm, true and 'Noble Manner of designing Chiefly Historical Subjects. but by the exactness & Correctness of his drawing made Portraiture easy to him mixing with it that Grace & Sweetness he observd in Guido & in the Antique Statues': Vertue II, p. 119.
34 Vertue noted that Kneller conversed so well and painted with such facility that there was 'no seeming confinement to sitting (as is usual) that People go away with more sprightliness than they came': Vertue II, p. 122.
35 This is seen most clearly in the artists who held Kneller's position as Principal Painter: after his death he was succeeded in 1723 by Charles Jervas (c.1675–1739), who was succeeded by William Kent (1685–1748) in 1739, who was succeeded by John Shackleton (d. 1767) in 1749. Kneller's reputation held up for at least a decade after his death. In 1727 Arthur Pond took over his house in Covent Garden (Lippincott 1983, p. 32); in 1732 his pupil Bartholomew Dandridge (1691–1754) did the same, thinking that it might 'give him some credit': Vertue III, p. 56.
36 Goldsmith identified the Augustan Age of literature as falling in the reign of Queen Anne: Goldsmith 1966, I, p. 498; Walpole thought that the arts had sunk to the lowest ebb at the accession of George I: Walpole 1827, IV, p. 1; Reynolds thought that the art of painting 'was at its lowest ebb' when he first arrived in Rome in 1750, 'it could not, indeed, be lower': Leslie and Taylor 1865, I, p. 43; Farington 1819, p. 15, assesses the merits of each case.
37 Le Blanc 1747, I, pp. 159–60.
38 Rouquet 1755, pp. 14–5, who also (pp. 34–6) describes the unthinking imitation of Kneller's style.
39 *The Spectator*, no. 83, 5 June 1711, describes what appear to be French-style portraits – all the faces with a 'smirking air' and 'the drapery of his figures was extremely well suited to his faces, and was made up of all the glaring colours that could be mixt together; every part of the dress was in a flutter and endeavoured to distinguish itself above the rest'; Hogarth places a parody of this style in the first scene of *Marriage à-la-Mode* (no. 89): see Nichols 1781, pp. 106–7, and Shawe-Taylor 1990, pp. 36–7.
40 Paulson 1971, I, p. 433; Vertue described his great success, which 'exceeds any other painter that is come to England in the memory of any one living', while at the same time causing English painters 'uneasines it has much blemishd their reputation – and business': Vertue III, pp. 84.
41 Vertue III, p. 82.
42 Millar 1963, pp. 178–9, no. 538; Walpole 1928, p. 39.
43 See Brian Allen's account of these years in Strong 1991, p. 159.
44 Letter of April 1740, quoted in Allen 2006, p. 31; see also Smart 1992, p. 74.
45 '... *weil man damals in Engeland keinen Geschmack an seiner Arbeit fand*': the biography of 1768 is quoted in Börsch-Supan 1986, pp. 156–7.
46 Quoted in Börsch-Supan 1986, p. 155.
47 In 1742 Vertue (III, p. 109) noted that 'crayon painting has met with so much encouragement of late years' that several artists – Knapton, Arthur Pond and William Hoare – who had been to Italy to study oil painting had returned to practise painting in crayons and 'several made great advantages of it'.
48 Ramsay 1755, pp. 56–7, quoted in Smart 1992, p. 143. Rouquet (1755, p. 36) describes the connection between Ramsay's thinking and his painting: he 'brought a rational taste of resemblance with him from Italy, he showed even in his portraits that just steady spirit, which he so agreeably displays in his conversation'.
49 See Smart 1992, pp. 110–4, for these developments and Smart 1999, p. 111, no. 191, for the 1757 portrait of the future George III.
50 Vertue III, pp. 97–8.
51 Vertue (III, p. 54) wrote in 1731 of Highmore's means of obtaining this portrait: 'The desire & affectation of being great in public reputation puts some men on designs that are false impositions – as in such a case Mr. Highmore who coud not obtain the Honour of the King or Queen setting to him for their pictures did by stealth draw them first on paper at Several Views, and afterwards by Memory in some parts & copying those pictures before Painted by Sr. G. Kneller – he made two pictures which he thought to be more like their Majestyes than others done before.' Vertue is otherwise complimentary of Highmore's 'free masterly manner' (III, p. 17), 'harmony throughout' (III, p. 131) and ability to complete a face in one sitting (III, p. 54). Vertue was even more scornful when the same trick to obtain a royal sitting was successfully employed by 'a little cringing creature', James Worsdale (*c.*1692–1767): Vertue III, p. 59.
52 Millar 1963, p. 173.
53 Frederick the Great's orders and letters are preserved at the Geheimes Staatsarchiv of the Preußischer Kulturbesitz, Berlin. We are grateful to David Oakey from Carlton Hobbs LLC for providing us with transcripts from these documents: '*J'ai été fort sensible d'apprendre que le prince de Galles a paru désirer d'avoir mon portrait; j'aurai la satisfaction de lui envoyer; en attendant, vous devez chercher l'occasion de lui faire de ma part un compliment dans des termes les plus obligeants que vous sauriez imaginer, en l'assurant combien j'étais charmé d'avoir l'occasion de lui envoyer mon portrait, puisqu'il irait passer dans les mains d'un de mes amis que j'estimais et chérissais infiniment, mais que ma satisfaction en serait complète, si à son tour il voulait bien m'envoyer le sien, qui me manquait encore. Vous accompagnerez tout cela de tout ce que vous pourrez imaginer d'expressions des plus polies*' (Frederick the Great to Conseiller Andrié in London, 13 December 1746, in *Politische Correspondenz Friedrichs des Großen*, V, fol. 265); '*Monsieur mon Frère. Je vous envoie mon portrait, comme vous l'avez désiré; je souhaiterais qu'il fût le fidèle interprète de ma pensée, il dirait sûrement à Votre Altesse Royale tout ce que mon cœur sent pour Elle; il vous ferait voir que les liens du sang résistent à l'éloignement comme au temps, que rien ne peut étouffer cette voix de la nature qui tôt ou tard se fait entendre aux parents même les plus divisés; il vous découvrirait toute l'étendue de l'estime que j'ai toujours eue et que je conserverai, autant que je vivrai, pour votre personne: enfin il vous entretiendrait de reconnaissance et de bien des choses que vous devinerez sans doute. Je vous prie de croire que ce sont les sentiments avec lesquels je suis inviolablement, Monsieur mon Frère et Cousin, de Votre Altesse Royale le bien bon et affectionné frère et cousin Federic*' (Frederick the Great to Frederick, Prince of Wales, Berlin, 28 January 1748, in *Politische Correspondenz Friedrichs des Großen*, VI, fol. 19); '*Voici la réponse que j'ai faite au prince de Galles, touchant son portrait qui vient d'arriver ici*' (Frederick the Great at the end of a letter of 9 August 1749, in *Politische Correspondenz Friedrichs des Großen*, VII, fol. 49).
54 'Kensington Palace Inventory' 1818, no. 84; Pyne calls the room Queen Caroline's Drawing Room; it is now again called the Privy Chamber.
55 Household accounts of Frederick, Prince of Wales, vol. XVII, October 1748–October 1749, entry no. 530 (Duchy of Cornwall Office). Archival references kindly provided by Carlton Hobbs LLC; see also Carlton Hobbs LLC, *Florence: Viol'Art Firenze (Catalogue IX)* 2012–13, no. 14, pp. 72–79.
56 Duchy of Cornwall MSS, vol. XVI, fol. 276; Walpole 1928, p. 39.
57 Ulster Museum, Belum.U129–30; bill submitted in October 1745 (Duchy of Cornwall MSS, vol. XV, fol. 384 and vol. XVI, fol. 276).
58 Harris 1996, p. 55.
59 See Credland 1994 for laws on tartan.
60 Shebbeare 1755, II, pp. 43–4.
61 *Wootton* 1984, pp. 72–3, no. 45.
62 He worked for George I before Frederick, Prince of Wales, for whom he produced a lost Stag hunt in 1729: Vivian 2006, p. 157.
63 Millar 1977, p. 96, refers to a payment for Wootton and Hogarth on 31 August 1734, £157 10s to Wootton for the landscape and 5 guineas a head for six heads by Hogarth.
64 Paulson 1971, I, pp. 312–7; *Conversation Piece* 2009, pp. 80–1.
65 Paulson 1971, II, pp. 249ff.
66 See *Wootton* 1984, p. 10, for his relationship with Wyck; Wootton's set of hunting prints engraved by Bernard Baron of 1726 (*Wootton* 1984, pp. 77–8, nos 53–6) represents an answer to Oudry's versatile designs, for use in print, painting or tapestry.
67 For the acquisition of the Paters, see *Paintings from Windsor Castle* 1990, pp. 84–91, nos 35–8. According to Oliver Millar, 'the Prince seemed to

have preferred to the solid English style of Richardson or Hudson (whose portraits of himself were not done for his own use) the elegance of Highmore or the essentially Frenchified court style of Vanloo': Millar 1977, pp. 96–7.

68 *Wootton* 1984, pp. 7 and 48.

69 Millar 1963, p. 183, no. 555.

70 *Wootton* 1984, pp. 20 and 27, n. 5.

71 *Wootton* 1984, p. 9, quoting Constable's lecture of 16 June 1836.

72 For the Prince's hunting uniform see *Conversation Piece* 2009, p. 88.

73 Jarrett 1965, p. 60.

74 Harris 2005, p. 21.

75 Walpole 1928, p. 79.

76 *Carlton House Inventory* 1819, no. 57, which describes the painting as a 'View of the Mall in St James's Park with a number of Figures, "Portraits"', and judges it to be 'A very interesting picture'.

77 Saussure 2006, pp. 34–5, letter of 17 September 1725.

78 Grosley 1772, I, p. 81.

79 See Porter 2000, p. 19; Du Bocage 1770, I, p. 17.

80 Hervey 1931, II, p. 628.

81 Jonathan Tyers leased New Spring Gardens in 1728 and opened them as Vauxhall Gardens in 1732: Jarrett 1965, p. 35; see also *London 1753* 2003, pp. 225–30 for Ranelagh and pp. 237–42 for Vauxhall.

82 The Countess makes an assignation at such an entertainment in Hogarth's *Marriage à-la-Mode*, scene four (no. 89).

83 Montagu 1994 describes the systematic expression of the passions in this period.

84 Admiration for Handel's music and excitement at the wealth-creating potential of the London market were important factors in the social history of music: Gluck felt that 'the highest praise is due to your country for having distinguished and cherished his gigantic genius'; Beethoven regarded Handel as the 'greatest composer that ever lived', claiming that he would 'uncover his head, and kneel before his tomb', which would have made a memorable spectacle in Westminster Abbey had Beethoven been persuaded to follow the examples of Handel and Haydn and come to London; see Treasure 1992, p. 79.

85 See Baron Biefeld, London, letter to Baron Knobelsdorff, Berlin, 10 March 1741, and Friedrich Gottlieb Klopstock's poem, 'Wir und Sie', both quoted in Deutsch 1955, pp. 513–4.

86 *Handel* 1985, pp. 11–3.

87 According to Hervey (1931, I, p. 273), Frederick and Anne fell out over Handel in 1734: 'the Prince, in the beginning of his enmity to his sister, set himself at the head of the other opera to irritate her'.

88 Frederick, Prince of Wales, supported the composer Giovanni Bononcini till 1732 and then Niccolò Porpora; he also patronized the new opera house at Lincoln's Inn Fields in 1733: see Jarrett 1965, p. 35.

89 Porter 2000, p. 270; the Prince's supper box was decorated by four Shakespearian scenes by Francis Hayman: see Edwards 1808, p. 50. Depictions of the exploits of Frederick, Prince of Wales, were planned for the Salon: see *London 1753* 2003, p. 238.

90 Vertue (III, p. 157) refers to Hudson's two-foot-high model of Roubiliac's *Handel*.

91 Vertue III, p. 82.

92 'The Picture of the prime Minister hangs over the Chimney in his own Closet, but I have seen that of Mr. Pope in Twenty Noblemens Houses': Voltaire 1733, p. 226, letter 23. Pope's iconography is comprehensively treated in Wimsatt 1965.

93 Leslie and Taylor 1865, I, p. 169.

94 On the entrepreneurial character of theatrical managers in the early part of the century – John Rich, J.J. Heidegger and Jonathan Tyers – see Porter 2000, p. 39.

95 Colley (2012, p. 32) argues that all Handel's Old Testament oratorios were patriotic hymns, with the Israelites understood to be British. In the *Dunciad*, 1742, IV, ll. 46–70, Pope describes Handel's manly reform of operatic music; see also Hogwood 1984, pp. 207ff.

96 Coxe 1799, p. 54.

97 RA GEO 55296.

98 Millar 1977, p. 96. Mercier trained with Pesne and became Principal Painter to the Prince of Wales on 17 February 1729 and in 1730 his Library Keeper.

99 Ribeiro 2000, p. 108.

100 Hogwood 1984, p. 120.

101 Hervey 1931, III, p. 868.

102 Pope's *First Epistle of the Second Book of Horace Imitated* of 1737 turns Horace's praise of Augustus into a mocking tribute to George Augustus (George II); his *First Satire of the Second Book of Horace Imitated* of 1733 expresses his ideals of independence, friendship and uncorrupted retirement.

103 The replacement of patronage by book-selling is best epitomised by the case of Robert Dodsley (1703–64), a footman turned bookseller (thanks to a £100 loan in 1735 from Pope) who encouraged Dr Johnson to undertake his *Dictionary* when Lord Chesterfield failed to do so; see Treasure 1992, p. 175.

104 Vivian 1989, p. 129.

105 Piper 1982, p. 78.

106 Vertue I, pp. 13–4, quoted in Whitley 1968, I, pp. 137–8. See also Harris 2006, p. 22.

107 Hervey 1931, I, pp. 385–8.

108 *Leicester House* 1749, fol. 3.

109 Vertue III, p. 62, describes the work (painted in distemper), as does the *St James's Evening Post* of 19 September 1732; see Malcolm 1810, II, p. 179.

110 This value is given in *Carlton House* 1819, no. 610; later annotation records that in 1829 the painting was in the 'Corridor' (Grand Corridor) of Windsor Castle.

111 See *Every Look Speaks* 2005, pp. 9–10; the status of an actor like Garrick is elegantly described by Oliver Goldsmith (1966, I, p. 348): 'styled vagabonds in law yet earning £1000 a year'.

112 The chair was placed in a pavilion at Garrick's villa at Hampton (presumably the Temple to Shakespeare); see Ireland 1794–9, II, p. 147.

113 There is also x-ray evidence of changes in the background.

114 Walpole 1827, IV, p. 133. The anonymous French author of the *Description du Tableau de M. Hogarth, qui represente la Marche des Gardes à leur rendez-vous De Finchley* of 1746 felt (p. 2) that 'every object becomes more piquant by the minor personal triumph one allows oneself in having deciphered it' ('*chaque object deviant plus piquant par la petite gloire qu'on se fait de l'avoir déchiffré*'). See also Busch 1984, p. 95.

115 *Genial Company* 1987, pp. 23–4.

116 Hogarth never executed the series depicting a happy marriage planned to complement *Marriage-à-la-Mode*, for which see *Hogarth* 2006, p. 153, nos 80–1.

X. *The 'Irresistible Tide of Luxury'*

1 Macky 1722, II, p. 133.

2 Smollett 1757–65, IV, p. 58.

3 Defoe 1748, III, p. 74.

4 Voltaire 1733, letter 10, p. 59.

5 Pyne 1819, III, pp. 56–7.

6 Macky 1722, II, p. 160.

7 Smollett 1757–65, I, p. 56.

8 Vertue II, p. 150.

9 Saussure 2006, p. 131, letter of 29 May 1727.

10 British Library, Lansdowne Ms no. 829, fol. 21.

11 Defoe and Richardson 1778, I, p. 2.

12 Duchy of Cornwall Accounts, Receipts & Vouchers, vol. VIII, fol. 332.

13 Saussure 2006, p. 129, letter of 29 May 1727.

14 Saussure 2006, p. 53, letter of 16 December 1725.

15 Brett 2004, p. 117.

16 Duchy of Cornwall Accounts, Receipts & Vouchers, vol. VIII, fol. 332.

17 Defoe 1727, II, p. 142.

18 Ilchester 1912, p. 361.

19 Now scattered but see, for example, Museum of Fine arts, Boston, inv. 1982.24.

20 *Daily Advertiser*, 9 January 1750.

21 Ilchester 1912, p. 361.

22 Papendiek 1887, I, p. 181.

23 Quoted in King 1922, p. 81.

24 Delany 1861, I, p. 135.

25 Victoria and Albert Museum, London, inv. 414:134-1885.

26 See, for example, *Rococo* 1984, p. 253, no. O26.

27 M. Krieger, *Ansbach Fayence und Porzellan*, 1963, no. 498, quoted in Jenkins 1996.

28 J. Croker (ed.), *Letters to and from Henrietta, Countess of Suffolk* ..., 1824, I, p. 304, quoted in Jenkins 1996.

29 Köhler 2007, p. 197.

30 'Inventarium Des, bey Koningl. und ChurFurstl. Silber Cammer zu Hannover vorhandenen Porcelains', 1740, Dep. 103, XXIV, no. 2616.

31 Duchy of Cornwall accounts, Vouchers XII, fol. 516, 12 February 1742.

32 British Library, North, Add MS 61860, vol. 1, fol. 77.

33 Manufacture Nationale de Sèvres, F1, dossier 4, liasse 1.

34 TNA/LC9/47, fol. 239.

35 Metropolitan Museum, New York, inv. 68.141.288-292.

36 Delany 1861, I, p. 134.
37 TNA/LC9/45, fol. 13.
38 See, for example, Hartop 1996, p. 88.
39 Victoria and Albert Museum, London, Wickes ledger, 24 January 1740.
40 Christie's, London, 4 July 2013, lot 48.
41 Paper delivered by M. Cassidy-Geiger at a symposium on rococo silver, Virginia Museum, 2004.
42 Walpole 1827, p. 226.
43 Vardy 1744, pl. 27.
44 Hayward 1959, p. 82.
45 Grimwade 1974, p. 32.
46 TNA/LC9/44, fol. 217.
47 *Gentleman's Magazine* 1738, p. 275.
48 Blair 1998, II, p. 447.
49 Blackmore 1999, p. 101.
50 Blackmore 1986, p. 191.
51 Edie 1777, p. 6.
52 Duchy of Cornwall accounts, Vouchers I, fol. 444.
53 Blackmore 1986, pp. 83–4.
54 Victoria and Albert Museum, London, inv. 494-1894.
55 Edie 1777, p. 6.
56 Cowper 1864, p. 79.
57 Walker 1992, no. 85.
58 Vertue III, p. 151.
59 Coxe 1829, II, pp. 386–7.
60 Wortley Montagu 1970, III, pp. 138–9.
61 Brooke 1972, pp. 24 and 28.
62 Duchy of Cornwall accounts, Vouchers V, fol. 239.
63 Edgcumbe 2000, p. 61.
64 Grandjean *et al.* 1975, pp. 36–7.
65 Grimwade 1976, p. 532.
66 Smollett 1760, I, p. 95.
67 *London Magazine and Monthly Chronicler*, March 1751, p. 158.
68 Walpole, *Correspondence*, II, p. 388, letter of 11 January 1758 to Sir Horace Mann.
69 Hall 1871, pp. 123–4.
70 Duchy of Cornwall accounts, Vouchers VIII, no. 332.
71 Delany 1861, III, p. 400.
72 Vertue III, p. 62.
73 Delany 1861, II, p. 82.
74 *English Baronetage* 1741, p. 192.
75 Craske 2000, p. 97.
76 Duchy of Cornwall accounts, Vouchers VIII, no. 332.
77 RCIN 63759.
78 Page 1911, II, pp. 158–65.

XI. *Dining at Court*

1 Macky 1722, p. 204.
2 *Household Ordinances* 1790, p. 336.
3 Egmont 1920, II, p. 266.
4 Pyne 1819, I, p. 161.
5 Ryder 1939, pp. 298–9.
6 Wortley Montagu 1970, letter XVII, 25 November 1716.
7 TNA/LS5/116/ 11 October 1727.
8 Egmont 1920, I, p. 179.
9 TNA/LS9/135/ 21 February 1736.
10 Pyne 1819, III, pp. 4–5.
11 Beattie 1967, p. 85.
12 Quoted in Colvin 1976, p. 240.
13 Saussure 2006, p. 102, letter of 29 October 1726.
14 Saussure 2006, p. 132, letter of 29 May 1727.
15 Pyne 1819, III, pp. 48–9.
16 TNA/LC5/114/1717.
17 TNA/LS9/130/ 22 July 1733.
18 TNA/LS9/150.
19 Lomax 1999, p. 135.
20 TNA/LC9/110/fol. 67 and TNA/LC9/48/ fol. 49.
21 Niedersächisches Hauptstadtsarchiv Hannover, Dep. 103. I am grateful to Ellenor Alcorn for this reference.
22 Niedersächisches Hauptstadtsarchiv Hannover, Dep. 103.
23 *The Shift Shifted*, no. 10, Part I, 7 July 1716, pp. 57–8.
24 Walpole 1923, p. 23.
25 Thompson 2011, p. 88.
26 Addison, *Spectator* no. 45, 21 April 1711.
27 Macky 1722, I, p. 107.
28 Grimwade 1974, p. 30.
29 Duchy of Cornwall, Household accounts, vol. VII, fol. 218.
30 See Jones and Garibaldi 2006, p. 27.
31 Murdoch 1983, pp. 65–6.
32 Barr 1980, p. 96.
33 Barr 1980, p. 95.
34 Victoria and Albert Museum, London, inv. E.2606.1917.
35 Quoted in Gardner 1942, p. 140.
36 British Museum, London, Ms. Sloane 4.c.1040.
37 *Gentleman's Magazine* 18, 1748, pp. 301–2.
38 Vivian 2006, p. 401.
39 Victoria and Albert Museum, inv. E.2606-1917.
40 TNA/LC9/48, fols. 13–14.
41 Barr 1980, p. 138.
42 TNA/LC5/113, quarter from June to October 1736.
43 Egmont 1920, II, p. 266.
44 Victoria and Albert Museum, London, Wickes Ledgers, 25 November 1737.
45 Illustrated in Glanville and Young 2002, p. 48.
46 Barr 1980, p. 140.
47 Egmont 1920, pp. 207–8.
48 Metropolitan Museum, New York, inv. 1970.131.33.
49 Duchy of Cornwall, Household accounts, vol. XIV, fol. 274.
50 Hartop 1996, p. 168.
51 Quoted in Barr 1980, p. 172.

Bibliography

ABBREVIATIONS

DNB *Oxford Dictionary of National Biography*, Oxford 2004; online edn, May 2009 (http://www.oxforddnb.com)

RA Royal Archives, Windsor Castle

RCIN Royal Collection inventory number

TNA The National Archives, Kew

MANUSCRIPT SOURCES

CARLTON HOUSE 1819
Catalogue of the Prince Regent's Pictures, in Carlton House, June 1819, manuscript in the Surveyor's Office, RCIN 1112581

BUCKINGHAM HOUSE ENGRAVINGS CATALOGUE *c.*1810
A Catalogue of Engravings at Buckingham House, 2 vols, manuscript in the Royal Library, Windsor Castle, RCIN 1155587–8

GEORGE I INVENTORY
Royal Pictures at Kensington, Hampton Court, Windsor & St James's, undated manuscript in French probably drawn up before 1723, original British Library, Stowe 567, transcript in the Surveyor's Office, RCIN 1112573

HAMPTON COURT INVENTORY 1750
The Collection of Pictures Paintings &c at Kensington, Hampton-court and in the Castle of Windsor, 1750, manuscript in the Surveyor's Office, vol. 2, RCIN 1112554

INVENTORY A
'Inventory A', *A catalogue of all the drawings and prints as they are arranged in the book cases* [at Buckingham House], *c.*1810, manuscript, RCIN 1155585

JUTSHAM DELS
An Account of furniture &c despatched from Carlton House, October 1820 – February 1830, drawn up by Benjamin Jutsham, manuscript in York House library, RCIN 1112485

JUTSHAM RECS
An Account of furniture &c received at Carlton House, June 1816 – December 1829, drawn up by Benjamin Jutsham, manuscript in York House library, RCIN 1112775

JUTSHAM RECS & DELS
An Account of furniture &c received and deliver'd by Benjamin Jutsham on account of His Royal Highness The Prince of Wales at Carlton House, 1806–1820, manuscript in York House library, RCIN 1112484

KENSINGTON INVENTORY *c.*1736
*A Catalogue taken of the Pictures, which are, in their Majesties Publick, and Private, Lodgings, in the Palace at Kensington, c.*1736, manuscript in the Surveyor's Office, vol. 1, RCIN 1112553

KENSINGTON INVENTORY 1750
The Collection of Pictures Paintings &c at Kensington, Hampton-court and in the Castle of Windsor, 1750, manuscript in the Surveyor's Office, vol. 1, RCIN 1112554

KENSINGTON INVENTORY 1818
Catalogue of the Pictures in the Palace at Kensington, 1818, manuscript in the Surveyor's Office, RCIN 11125430

LEICESTER HOUSE 1749
A Catalogue of his Royal Highness the Prince of Wales's Pictures in Leicester House, September 1749, RA/GEO/ADD 1/54

LIST 1858
List bound into the *Catalogue of Enamel Miniatures in Room 243* (RCIN 1112529b) copied from an earlier list compiled by Queen Victoria's dresser, Miss Marianne Skerrett, and corrected by John Glover (d. 1860), Royal Librarian

OLD LIST *c.*1837
MS list, unknown location. A list of enamels and miniatures, date and location unknown; known from a later copy (see 'List' 1858)

QUEEN ANNE INVENTORY *c.*1705–10
*A List of Her Majesties Pictures in Kensington, Hampton Court and Windsor Castle, c.*1705–10, manuscript in the Surveyor's Office, RCIN 1112574

QUEEN'S HOUSE INVENTORY 1819
Catalogue of the Pictures at the Late Queen's House, 1819, manuscript in the Surveyor's Office, RCIN 1115431

RL 1870
Inventory of Miniatures in the Royal Library Windsor Castle, 1870, RCIN 1112528

ST JAMES'S INVENTORY 1819
Catalogue of the Pictures at St James's Palace, 1819, manuscript in the Surveyor's Office, RCIN 1112511

VERTUE 1743
'Catalogue of the Pictures, Drawings, Limnings, Enamels, Models in Wax & the Ivory Carvings &c., at Kensington in Queen Caroline's Closet, next the State Bedchamber, Taken at Queen Caroline's Command by Mr Vertue in September 1743', included in *Inventory of His Majesty's Goods*, 1688, by William Chaffinch, printed by W. Bathoe, 1758, RCIN 1112557

WINDSOR CASTLE INVENTORY 1750
'The Collection of Pictures Paintings &c at Kensington, Hampton-court and in the Castle of Windsor 1750', manuscript in the Surveyor's Office, vol. 3, RCIN 1112554

PRINTED BOOKS AND ARTICLES

ADAM 2001
B. Adam, 'Neue Funde zum barocken Ausbau der Schlossanlage in Hannover-Herrenhausen', *Niederdeutsche Beiträge zur Kunstgeschichte* 40, pp. 59–97

ADAM 2005
B. Adam, 'Vergessene Pracht: Die Kurhannoverschen Residenzbauten Georgs I.', in Barmeyer 2005, pp. 199–231

ADAM 2010
B. Adam, 'Hardenbergs Wirken als Hofbautdirektor', in Bothmer and Köhler 2010, pp. 32–43

ADDISON AND STEELE 1979
J. Addison, R. Steele *et al.*, *The Spectator*, ed. G. Smith, 4 vols, London

ALBIN 1713
E. Albin, *Proposals for Printing by Subscription a Natural History of English insects*, London

ALBIN 1720
E. Albin, *A Natural History of Insects*, London

ALEXANDER 2008
D. Alexander, 'George Vertue as an Engraver', Walpole Society LXX, pp. 207–517

ALEXANDRE LE GRAND 2008
J. Vittet, *La tenture de l'histoire d'Alexandre le Grand* (exh. cat.), Paris

ALLEN 1991A
B. Allen, 'The Age of Hogarth 1720–1760', in R. Strong *et al.*, *The British Portrait, 1660–1960*, Woodbridge, pp. 128–83

ALLEN 1991B
B. Allen, 'The Society of Arts and the first exhibition of contemporary art in 1760', *RSA Journal* 139, no. 5416 (March), pp. 265–9

ALLEN 2006
B. Allen, 'The London Art World of the mid-Eighteenth Century', in *Canaletto in England* 2006, pp. 30–7

ALVENSLEBEN AND REUTHER 1966
U. von Alvensleben and H. Reuther, *Herrenhausen: Die Sommerresidenz des Welfen*, Hanover

AMAZING RARE THINGS 2007
D. Attenborough, S. Owens, M. Clayton and R. Alexandratos, *Amazing Rare Things: The art of natural history in the Age of Discovery* (exh. cat.), London

ANDERSON 2009
C. J. Anderson, 'State Imperatives: Military Mapping in Scotland, 1689–1770', *Scottish Geographical Journal* 125, no. 1 (March), pp. 4–24

ANTOGNAZZA 2009
M.R. Antognazza, *Leibniz: an Intellectual Biography*, Cambridge

ARCISZEWSKA 2002
B. Arciszewska, *The Hanoverian Court and the Triumph of Palladio: Palladian Revival in Hanover and England c. 1700*, Warsaw

ART OF CLAUDE LORRAIN 1969
M. Kitson *et al.*, *The Art of Claude Lorrain* (exh. cat.), London

ART OF ITALY 2007
L. Whitaker and M. Clayton, *The Art of Italy in the Royal Collection. Renaissance and Baroque* (exh. cat.), London

ASCHENGREEN PIACENTI AND BOARDMAN 2008
K. Aschengreen Piacenti and J. Boardman, *Ancient and Modern Gems and Jewels in the Collection of Her Majesty The Queen*, London

ATHERTON 1941
H.M. Atherton, *Political Prints in the Age of Hogarth*, Oxford

AVERY 1994
C. Avery, 'Medals and Bronzes for Milords: Soldani, Selvi and the English', *The Medal* 24, pp. 11–20

AVERY 1995/6
C. Avery, 'Soldani's Bronze Reliefs of "Summer" and "Autumn": New Documentation and Observations on Their Date and Patronage', *The Register of the Spencer Museum of Art* VII, nos 1 and 2, pp. 1–17

AVERY 1998
C. Avery, 'Lord Burlington and the Florentine Bronze Sculptor Soldani: New Documentation', in E. Corp (ed.), *Lord Burlington: The Man and his Politics*, Lewiston, Queenstown and Lampeter

AYRTON 1948
M. Ayrton and B. Denvir, *Hogarth's Drawings*, London

BAGLIONE 1649
Le Vite de' Pittori, Scultori et Architetti dal Pontificato di Gregorio XIII fino à tutto quello d'Urbano Ottavo, Rome

BAIRD 2007
R. Baird, *Goodwood; Art and Architecture, Sport and Family*, London

BAKER-SMITH 1995
V.P.M. Baker-Smith, 'A Life of Anne of Hanover, Princess Royal', Publications of the Sir Thomas Browne Institute 13, no. 13 (new series), Leiden

BALDINUCCI 1728
F.S. Baldinucci, *Notizie de' Professori del Disegno da Cimabue in Qua*, Florence

BALDINUCCI 1975
F.S. Baldinucci, *Vite di artisti dei secoli XVII – XVIII (c. 1725–30)*, ed. A. Matteoli, Rome

BARBER 1997
P. Barber, 'Maps and Monarchs in Europe 1550–1800', in R. Oresko, G.C. Gibbs and H.M. Scott (eds), *Royal and Republican Sovereignty in Early Modern Europe. Essays in Memory of Ragnhild Hatton*, Cambridge, pp. 75–124

BARMEYER 2005
H. Barmeyer (ed.), *Hannover und die englische Thronfolge*, Bielefeld

BARNARD AND CLARK 1995
T. Barnard and J. Clark (eds), *Lord Burlington: Architecture, Art and Life*, London

BARNES 2004
S.J. Barnes *et al.*, *Van Dyck: The Complete Catalogue of the Paintings*, New Haven and London

BARR 1980
E. Barr, *George Wickes, Royal Goldsmith*, London

BARRELL 1986
J. Barrell, *The Political Theory of Painting from Reynolds to Hazlitt*, New Haven and London

BAUM 1934
R. Baum, 'Hogarth and Fielding as Social Critics', *The Art Bulletin* 16, no. 1 (March), pp. 30–41

BEARD 1977
G. Beard, 'Three Eighteenth-Century Cabinet-makers: Moore, Goodison and Vile', *The Burlington Magazine* CXIX (July), pp. 479–86

BEARD 1993
G. Beard, 'Two Eighteenth-Century English Furniture Puzzles Reassessed', *Studies in the Decorative Arts* 1, no. 1 (Fall), pp. 119–26

BEARD 1997
G. Beard, *Upholsterers and Interior Decoration in England 1530–1840*, London

BEARD 2003
G. Beard, 'Kentian furniture by James Richards and others', *Apollo* CLVI (January), pp. 37–41

BEARD AND GOODISON 1987
G. Beard and J. Goodison, *English Furniture 1500–1840*, Oxford

BEARD AND HARDY 2013
G. Beard and J. Hardy, 'The Royal Barge', in *Kent* 2013, pp. 303–13

BEATTIE 1967
J.M. Beattie, *The English Court in the Reign of George I*, London

BECKETT 1948
R.B. Beckett, 'Hogarth's Early Painting II: 1728: The Beggar's Opera', *The Burlington Magazine* XC, no. 543, pp. 166–8

BELLORI 1672
G. Bellori, *Le Vite de' Pittori, Scultori et Architetti Moderni*, Rome

BICKHAM 1742
G. Bickham, *Deliciae Britannicae, or the Curiosities of Hampton Court and Windsor Castle delineated, with occasional reflections; and embellished with copper-plates of the two palaces &c.*, London

BIGNAMINI 1988
I. Bignamini, 'The Academy in Great Queen Street, 1711–20', and 'The First St Martin's Lane Academy', 1720–24', in *George Vertue, Art Historian, and Art Institutions in London, 1689–1768*, Walpole Society LIV

BLACK 2007
J. Black, *George II: Puppet of the Politicians?*, Exeter

BLACKETT-ORD 2001
C. Blackett-Ord, 'Letters from William Kent to Burrell Massingberd from the Continent 1712–1719', Walpole Society LXIII, pp. 75–109

BLACKMORE 1968
H. Blackmore, *Royal Sporting Guns at Windsor*, London

BLACKMORE 1986
H. Blackmore, *A Dictionary of London Gunmakers, 1350–1850*, Oxford

BLACKMORE 1999
H. Blackmore, *Gunmakers of London 1350–1850: Supplement*, Ontario and New York

BLAIR 1998
C. Blair (ed.), *The Crown Jewels*, 2 vols, London

BLANNING 2002
T.C.W. Blanning, *The Culture of Power and the Power of Culture: Old Regime Europe, 1660–1789*, Oxford

BLUNT 1958
A. Blunt, 'A neo-Palladian Programme executed by Visentini and Zuccarelli for Consul Smith', *The Burlington Magazine* C, pp. 283–4

BLUNT 1989
A. Blunt (ed.), *Nicolas Poussin: Lettres et propos sur l'art*, Paris

BOALCH 1995
D. Boalch, *Makers of the Harpsichord and Clavichord*, Oxford

BÖRSCH-SUPAN 1986
H. Börsch-Supan, *Der Maler Antoine Pesne: Franzose und Preusse*, Berlin 1986

BOISCLAIR 1986
M.-N. Boisclair, *Gaspard Dughet: sa vie et son œuvre: 1615–1675*, Paris

BOLD 2000
J. Bold, *Greenwich: An Architectural History of the Royal Hospital for Seamen and the Queen's House*, New Haven and London

BOORSCH 2000
S. Boorsch, *Fireworks! Five Centuries of Pyrotechnics in Prints and Drawings*, New York

BOSWELL 1791
James Boswell, *The Life of Samuel Johnson*, 2 vols, London

BOTHMER AND KÖHLER 2010
W. von Bothmer and M. Köhler, *Im Auftrag der Krone. Friedrich Karl von Hardenberg und das Leben in Hannover um 1750*, Hanover

BOWETT 2002
A. Bowett, *English Furniture 1660–1714: From Charles II to Queen Anne*, Woodbridge

BOWETT 2005
A. Bowett, 'George I's furniture at Kensington Palace', *Apollo* CLXII (November), pp. 37–47

BOWETT 2009
A. Bowett, *Early Georgian Furniture 1715–1740*, Woodbridge

BOWETT 2012
A. Bowett, *Woods in British Furniture Making: An Illustrated Historical Dictionary*, Wetherby

BOYER 1988
J.-C. Boyer, 'The one and only Bigot', *The Burlington Magazine* CXXX, no. 1022 (May), pp. 355–7

BOYER 1992
J.-C. Boyer, 'Pierre Mignard', in *La cour des Stuarts* 1992, pp. 109–10

BRAUN 1956
H. Braun, 'Ansbacher Spätbarock. Ein Beitrag zur Stilgeschichte der Baukunst im Fürstentum Brandenburg-Onolzbach 1695–1791', *Jahrbuch für fränkische Landesforschung* 16, pp. 455–91

BREDEKAMP 2013
H. Bredekamp, *Leibniz und die Revolution der Gartenkunst: Herrenhausen, Versailles und die Philosophie der Blätter*, Berlin

BRETT 2004
V. Brett, 'The great (and lesser) toyshops', *Silver Studies* 16, pp. 117–23

BRETT 2013
C. Brett, 'Revealing Thornhill's mythological scene at Hampton Court', *The British Art Journal* XIII, no. 3, pp. 3–8

BREWER 1997
J. Brewer, *The Pleasures of the Imagination: English Culture in the Eighteenth Century*, London

BRINDLE 2013
S. Brindle, 'The Royal Commissions', in *Kent* 2013, pp. 271–301

BRITISH MUSEUM 1909–11
British Museum, *Medallic Illustrations of the History of Great Britain and Ireland*, 2 vols, London

BROOKE 1972
J. Brooke, *King George III*, London

BROSSES 1978
Charles de Brosses, *Lettres familières écrites d'Italie*, 2 vols, Paris

BROWN 1982
C. Brown, *Van Dyck 1599–1641*, London

BROWNELL 1978
M.R. Brownell, *Alexander Pope and the Art of Georgian England*, Oxford 1978

BROWNING 1994
R. Browning, *The War of the Austrian Succession*, Stroud

BRUEGEL TO RUBENS 2007
D. Shawe-Taylor and J. Scott, *Bruegel to Rubens: Masters of Flemish Painting* (exh. cat.), London

BRYAN 2010
M.E. Bryan, '"Slideing into Monarchical extravagance": Cato at Valley Forge and the Testimony of William Bradford Jr.', *William and Mary Quarterly* 67, pp. 124–5

BURCHARD 2011A
W. Burchard, 'St James's Palace: George II's and Queen Caroline's Principal London Residence', *The Court Historian* 16, no. 2, pp. 177–203

BURCHARD 2011B
W. Burchard, 'Illusion and Involvement: The lost Baroque Decoration of St George's Hall at Windsor Castle', *Immediations: The Courtauld Institute of Art Journal of Postgraduate Research* 2, no. 4 (2011), pp. 98–119

BURKE 1757
E. Burke, *Philosophical Inquiry into the Origin of our Ideas of the Sublime and Beautiful*, London

BURKE 1790
E. Burke, *Reflections on the Revolution in France*, London 1790

BURNET 1827
J. Burnet, *Practical Hints in Colour in Painting: Illustrated by Examples from the Venetian, Flemish, and Dutch Schools*, London

BURNEY 1785
C. Burney, 'A sketch of the life of Handel', in *An Account of the Musical Performances ... in Commemoration of Handel*, London, pp. 1–38

BUSCH 1984
W. Busch, 'Hogarths und Reynolds' Porträts des Schauspielers Garrick', *Zeitschrift für Kunstgeschichte* XLVII, pp. 82–99

BUTTERY 1987
D. Buttery, 'The Picture Frames of Paul Petit and Frederick, Prince of Wales', *Apollo* CXXVI, pp. 12–15

CALMANN 1977
G. Calmann, *Ehret: Flower Painter Extraordinary*, Oxford

CAMPBELL 1715
C. Campbell, *Vitruvius Britannicus or the British Architect*, London

CAMPBELL 1849
J. Lord Campbell, *Lives of the Chief Justices*, 2 vols, London

CAMPBELL 1992
T.P. Campbell, *Report on the Tapestries hung in the Hampton Court State Apartments in the first half of the eighteenth century* (Historic Royal Palaces, unpublished document)

CAMPBELL 1993
T.P. Campbell, *Report on the Tapestries historically associated with Kensington Palace, London* (Historic Royal Palaces, unpublished document)

CAMPBELL 2004
I. Campbell, *Ancient Roman Topography and Architecture, The Paper Museum of Cassiano dal Pozzo*, 3 vols, London

CANALETTO IN ENGLAND 2006
C. Beddington (ed.), *Canaletto in England: A Venetian Artist Abroad, 1746–1755* (exh. cat.), New Haven and London

CANNING 1688
W. Canning, *Gesta Grayorum*, London

CARLISLE 1897
Historical Manuscripts Commission: The Manuscripts of the Earls of Carlisle, preserved at Castle Howard, London

CARMAN 1955
W.Y. Carman, *A History of Firearms*, London

CASSIDY GEIGER 2007
M. Cassidy Geiger (ed.), *Fragile Diplomacy, Meissen Porcelain for European Courts ca. 1710–63*, New York

CHAMBERLAYNE 1718
E. Chamberlayne, *Magnae Britanniae Notitia: or, The Present State of Great Britain*, 25th edn, 2 vols, London

CHAMBERS 1996
J. Harris and M. Snodin (eds), *Sir William Chambers Architect to George III* (exh. cat.), New Haven and London

CHESTERFIELD 1992
D. Roberts (ed.), *Lord Chesterfield's Letters*, Oxford

CHOMER 2000
G. Chomer, *Peinture française avant 1815. La collection du Musée de Grenoble*, Paris

CHURCHILL 1957
W. Churchill, *History of the English-Speaking Peoples*, 4 vols, London

CLARK 1995
J. Clark, 'Lord Burlington is Here', in Barnard and Clark 1995, pp. 251–310

CLARKE 1973
G. Clarke, 'Grecian Taste and Gothic Virtue: Lord Cobham's gardening programme and it's iconography' *Apollo* XCVII, pp. 566–71

CLAYTON 1971
M. Clayton, *The Collector's Dictionary of the Silver and Gold of Great Britain and North America*, Woodbridge

CLARK 2009
R. Clark, *Venus, Faune und Fechter: Die Goldenen Figuren im Heckentheater*, Hanover

CLAYTON 1997
T. Clayton, *The English Print, 1688–1802*, New Haven and London

CLAYTON 2007
T. Clayton, *Hogarth*, London

CLIFTON 1996
G. Clifton, *Directory of British Scientific Instrument Makers 1550–1851*, London

COCHRAN-PATRICK 1884
R.W. Cochran-Patrick, *Catalogue of the Medals of Scotland*, Edinburgh

COFFIN AND HOFSTETTER 2000
S. Coffin and B. Hofstetter, *The Gilbert Collection. Portrait Miniatures in Enamel*, London

COLEY 1967
W.B. Coley, 'Hogarth, Fielding, and the Dating of the March to Finchley', *Journal of the Warburg and Courtauld Institutes* XXX, pp. 317–26

COLLEY 2012
L. Colley, *Britons: Forging the Nation, 1707–1837*, 3rd edn, New Haven and London

COLLINS BAKER 1937
C.H. Collins Baker, *Principal Pictures in the Royal Collection at Windsor Castle*, London

COLTON 1976
J. Colton, 'Merlin's Cave and Queen Caroline: Garden Art as Political Propaganda', *Eighteenth Century Studies* X, pp. 1–20

COLVIN 1976
H. Colvin, *The History of the King's Works*, vol. 5, London

COMPASS AND RULE 2009
A. Gerbino and S. Johnston, *Compass and Rule. Architecture as Mathematical Practice in England, 1550–1750* (exh. cat.), New Haven and London

CONSTABLE 1953
W. G. Constable, *Richard Wilson*, London

CONSTABLE AND LINKS 1977
W.G. Constable and J.G. Links (eds), *Canaletto: Giovanni Antonio Canale, 1697–1768*, 2 vols, Oxford

CONVERSATION PIECE 2009
D. Shawe-Taylor, *The Conversation Piece. Scenes of Fashionable Life* (exh. cat.), London

COOMBS 1997
D. Coombs, 'The Garden at Carlton House of Frederick Prince of Wales and Augusta Princess Dowager of Wales. Bills in Their Household Accounts 1728 to 1772', *Garden History* 25, no. 2, pp. 153–77

CORNFORTH 2004
J. Cornforth, *Early Georgian Interiors*, New Haven and London

CORP 2004
E. Corp, *A Court in Exile: The Stuarts in France, 1689–1718*, Cambridge

CORP 2007
Edward Corp (ed.), *The Stuart Court in Rome. The Legacy of Exile*, Aldershot

COSTAMAGNA 1994
P. Costamagna, *Pontormo: Catalogue raisonné de l'œuvre peint*, Paris

COUNTRY LIFE 1930
'An Exhibition of Furniture at Messrs. Malletts, Bond Street', *Country Life* (21 June), pp. 898–99

COWPER 1864
M. Cowper, *Diary of Mary, Countess Cowper, Lady of the Bedchamber to the Princess of Wales 1714–1720*, London

COXE 1799
W. Coxe, *Anecdotes of George Frederick Handel, and John Christopher Smith*, London

COXE 1829
W. Coxe, *Memoirs of the Administration of Henry Pelham*, 2 vols, London

CRASKE 2000
M. Craske, 'Contacts and Contracts: Sir Henry Cheere and the formation of a new commercial world of sculpture in mid-18th century London', in Sicca and Yarrington 2000, pp. 94–113

CRAWFORTH 1987
M.A. Crawforth, 'Instrument makers in the London guilds', *Annals of Science* 44, pp. 319–37

CREDLAND 1994
A.G. Credland, 'Archery and its Art in Britain', *The British Sporting Art Trust*, essay no. 29 (January), n. p.

CROFT-MURRAY 1962
E. Croft-Murray, *Decorative Painting in England, 1537–1837*, vol. 1, London

CROFT-MURRAY 1970
E. Croft-Murray, *Decorative Painting in England, 1537-1837*, vol. 2, *The Eighteenth and Early Nineteenth Centuries*, London

CRUICKSHANKS 1995
E. Cruickshanks, 'The Political Career of the Third Earl of Burlington', in Barnard and Clark 1995, pp. 201–16

CUNNINGHAM 1829–33
A. Cunningham, *The Lives of the Most Eminent British Painters, Sculptors and Architects*, 6 vols, London

CURL 2011
J.S. Curl, *Georgian Architecture: the British Isles 1714–1830*, Swindon

CUST 1910
Lionel Cust, *Windsor Castle: Portrait Miniatures*, privately printed

DAEMS AND NELSON 2006
King Charles I (attr.), J. Daems and H. Nelson (eds), *Eikon Basilike: The Portraiture of His Sacred Majesty in his Solitudes and Sufferings. With, Selections from Eikonoklastes*, Peterborough, Ontario

DALE 1913
W. Dale, *Tschudi, The Harpsichord Maker*, London

DANGEAU 1856
E. Soulié, L. Dussieux *et al.* (eds), *Journal du Marquis de Dangeau*, vol. 6 (1696, 1697, 1698), Paris

DANIELS 1976
J. Daniels, *Sebastiano Ricci*, Hove

DANN 2000
T. Dann, *Die Königlichen Prunkappartements im hannoverschen Leineschloß: Untersuchungen zu Raumfolgen in der 1. Hälfte des 19. Jahrhunderts*, Hanover

DAVENPORT 1896
C. Davenport, *Royal English Bookbindings*, London

DAVIES 2003
V. Davies, *State Beds and Throne Canopies*, London

DEAZLEY 2004
R. Deazley, *On the Origin of the Right to Copy: Charting the Movement of Copyright Law in Eighteenth Century Britain (1695–1775)*, London

DE BELLAIGUE 2009
G. de Bellaigue, *French Porcelain in the Collection of Her Majesty The Queen*, 3 vols, London

DEFOE 1727
D. Defoe, *The Complete English Tradesman*, 2 vols, London

DEFOE 1748
D. Defoe, *A tour Thro' the Whole Island of Great Britain*, 4th edn, 4 vols, London

DEFOE AND RICHARDSON 1778
D. Defoe, *A tour Thro' the Whole Island of Great Britain*, with additions by S. Richardson, 10 vols, London

DELANY 1861
M. Delany, *The Autobiography and Correspondence of Mary Granville, Mrs Delany*, 3 vols, ed. Lady Llanover, London

DENVIR 1983
B. Denvir, *The Eighteenth Century: Art, Design and Society 1689–1789*, London and New York

DE PILES 1706
R. de Piles, *The Art of Painting*, trans. J. Savage with *An Essay towards an English School of Painting* by B. Buckeridge, London 1706

DE PILES 1708
R. de Piles, *Cours de Peinture par principes*, Paris

DESMOND 1995
R. Desmond, *The History of the Royal Botanic Gardens*, London

DEUTSCH 1955
O.E. Deutsch, *Handel: A Documentary Biography*, New York

DODERER-WINKLER 2013
M. Doderer-Winkler, *Magnificent Entertainments: Temporary Architecture for Georgian Festivals*, New Haven and London

DOUGLAS SCOTT 1983
J. Douglas Scott, *Sir Godfrey Kneller and the English Baroque Portrait*, Oxford

DOWNES 1966
K. Downes, *English Baroque Architecture*, London

DRAMATIC ART 1997
D. Shawe-Taylor, *Dramatic Art: Theatrical Paintings from the Garrick Club* (exh. cat.), London

DU BOCAGE 1770
Madame du Bocage, *Letters Concerning England, Holland and Italy*, 2 vols, London

DU FRESNOY 1716
C.A. Du Fresnoy, trans. J. Dryden, *The Art of Painting*, London

DUGHET 1980
A. French, *Gaspard Dughet: A French Landscape Painter in Seventeenth Century Rome and his Influence on British Art* (exh. cat.), London

DUKELSKAYA AND MOORE 2002
L. Dukelskaya and A. Moore, *A Capital Collection: Houghton Hall and the Hermitage*, New Haven and London

DUTCH LANDSCAPES 2010
D. Shawe-Taylor and J. Scott, *Dutch Landscapes* (exh. cat.), London

EDGCUMBE 2000
R. Edgcumbe, *The Art of the Gold Chaser*, London

EDIE 1777
G. Edie, *The Art of English Shooting*, London

EDWARDS 1750
G. Edwards, *A Natural History of Birds*, London

EDWARDS 1808
E. Edwards, *Anecdotes*, London

EDWARDS 1964
R. Edwards, *The Shorter Dictionary of English Furniture*, rev. edn, London

EDWARDS AND JOURDAIN 1944
R. Edwards and M. Jourdain, *Georgian Cabinet-Makers*, 1st edn, London

EDWARDS AND JOURDAIN 1955
R. Edwards and M. Jourdain, *Georgian Cabinet-Makers*, London, rev. edn, London

EGMONT 1920
Historical Manuscripts Commission: Manuscripts of the Earl of Egmont, Diary of Viscount Percival, afterwards First Earl of Egmont, 3 vols, London

EHRGEIZ, LUXUS UND FORTUNE 2001
S. Meschkat-Peters (ed.), *Ehrgeiz, Luxus und Fortune: Hannovers Weg zu Englands Krone* (exh. cat.), Hanover

EINBERG 2004
E. Einberg, 'Milton, St John, and the importance of "Bottom": Another look at Hogarth's "March of the Guards to Finchley"', *British Art Journal* V, no. 3 (Winter), pp. 27–34

ENCHANTING THE EYE 2004
C. Lloyd, *Enchanting the Eye: Dutch Paintings of the Golden Age* (exh. cat.), London

ENDELL 1908
M. Endell, *Dresden – History, Stage, Gallery*, Cambridge

ENGGASS 1976
R. Enggass, *Early Eighteenth-century Sculpture in Rome*, Pennsylvania

ENGGASS AND BROWN 1970
R. Enggass and J. Brown, *Italy and Spain 1600–1750 (Sources and Documents)*, Chicago

ENLIGHTENMENT 2003
K. Sloane (ed.), *Enlightenment: Discovering the World in the Eighteenth Century* (exh. cat.), London

ERFFA AND STALEY 1986
H. von Erffa and A. Staley, *The Paintings of Benjamin West*, New Haven and London

ESDAILE 1928
K.A. Esdaile, *The Life and Works of Louis-François Roubiliac*, London

ESDAILE 1932
K.A. Esdaile, *The Art of Rysbrack in Terracotta*, London

ESDAILE 1938
K.A. Esdaile, 'The Sculpture at Burlington House', *The Burlington Magazine* LXXII (March), pp. 139–41

EUSTACE 1998
K. Eustace, 'The Politics of the Past: Stowe and the Development of the Historical Portrait Bust', *Apollo* CXLVIII (July), pp. 31–40

EVELYN 1755
J. Evelyn, *Sculptura*, 2nd edn, London

EVELYN 1955
J. Evelyn, *The Diary of John Evelyn. Now first printed in full from the Manuscripts belonging to John Evelyn*, ed. E.S. de Beer, 6 vols, Oxford

EVERY LOOK SPEAKS 2003
I. McIntyre, D. Shawe-Taylor *et al.*, *Every Look Speaks: Portraits of David Garrick* (exh. cat.), Bath

FARINGTON 1819
J. Farington, 'Memoir of the life of Sir Joshua Reynolds', in E. Malone, *The Literary Works of Sir Joshua Reynolds*, 3 vols, London

FÉLIBIEN 1725
A. Félibien, *Sur les Vies et sur les Ouvrages des plus Excellens Peintres anciens et Modernes*, vol. IV, Trévoux

FÉLIBIEN 1981
C. Pace (ed.), *Félibien's Life of Poussin*, London

FFOULKES 1937
C.J. ffoulkes, *The Gun Founders of England*, Cambridge

FIELD 2008
O. Field, *The Kit-Cat Club*, London

FIELDING 1965
H. Fielding, *Joseph Andrews*, ed. M.C. Battestin, London

FITTSCHEN 2006
K. Fittschen, *Die Bildnisgalerie in Herrenhausen bei Hannover: Zur Rezeptions- und Sammlungsgeschichte antiker Porträts*, Göttigen

FITZGERALD 1973
D. FitzGerald, 'A History of the Interior of Stowe', *Apollo* XCVII (June), pp. 572–85

FLIGHT AND THE ARTISTIC IMAGINATION 2012
S. Smiles, *Flight and the Artistic Imagination* (exh. cat.), London

FORBES 1815
D.G. Forbes, *Culloden Papers*, London 1815

FORTNUM 1876
C.D.E. Fortnum, *A Descriptive Catalogue of the Bronzes of European Origin in the South Kensington Museum*, London

FOUGEROUX 1728
P.J. Fougeroux, *Voiage D'Angleterre, D'Hollande, Et de Flandre*, manuscript, National Art Library, MSL/1912/1255

FOX 1982
C. Fox, *The Arts of Industry in the Age of Enlightenment*, New Haven and London

FRANCE IN THE GOLDEN AGE 1982
P. Rosenberg *et al.*, *France in the Golden Age; Seventeenth-Century French Paintings in American Collections* (exh. cat.), New York

FRANKLAND-RUSSELL-ASTLEY 1900
Historic Manuscripts Commission: Report on the Manuscripts of Mrs Frankland-Russell-Astley of Chequers Court, Bucks, London

FRASER 1979
A. Fraser, *King Charles II*, London

FRENCH PORCELAIN 2009
J. Gwilt, *French Porcelain for English Palaces* (exh. cat.), London

FRIEDMAN 1988
T. Friedman, 'Lord Harrold in Italy', *The Burlington Magazine* CXXX, no. 1028, pp. 835–45

FRYMAN 2011
O. Fryman, 'Making the bed: the practice, role and significance of housekeeping in the royal bedchambers at Hampton Court Palace, 1689–1737', PhD thesis, Kingston University

GÄDEKE 2005
N. Gädeke, 'Die Rolle des Historikers: Gottfried Wilhelm Leibniz und der Aufstieg des Welfenhauses', in Barmeyer 2005, pp. 157–78

GARBOLI 1971
C. Garboli, *L'opera completa di Guido Reni*, Milan

GARDINER 1977
R.A. Gardiner, 'William Roy, Surveyor and Antiquary', *The Geographical Journal* 143, no. 3, pp. 439–50

GARDNER 1942
B. Gardner, 'Further history of the Chelsea Porcelain Manufactory', *Transactions of the English Ceramic Circle* 2, no. 8, pp. 136–41

GAUNT AND KNIGHT 1990
P. Gaunt and C. Knight, *Kensington Palace*, 1990, vol. 2 (Historic Royal Palaces, unpublished document)

GENIAL COMPANY 1987
D. Shawe-Taylor, *Genial Company; the Theme of Genius in Eighteenth-Century British Portraiture* (exh. cat.), Nottingham

GEORGE III AND QUEEN CHARLOTTE 2004
J. Roberts (ed.), *George III and Queen Charlotte: Patronage, Collecting and Court Taste* (exh. cat.), London

GEORGIAN PLAYHOUSE 1975
I. Mackintosh, *The Georgian Playhouse* (exh. cat.), London

GEORGIANS REVEALED 2013
M. Goff, J. Goldfinch *et al.*, *Georgians Revealed: Life, Style and the Making of Modern Britain* (exh. cat.), London

GIBSON-WOOD 2000
C. Gibson-Wood, *Jonathan Richardson, Art Theorist of the English Enlightenment*, New Haven and London

GILBERT 1996
C. Gilbert, *Pictorial Dictionary of Marked London Furniture, 1700–1840*, London

GILMOUR 2000
B. Gilmour, 'Dutch composite ordnance of the early 17th century', *Royal Armouries Yearbook* 5, pp. 85–105

GIOMETTI 1999
C. Giometti, 'Giovanni Battista Guelfi: New Discoveries', *Sculpture Journal* III, pp. 26–43

GIROUARD 1978
M. Girouard, *Life in the English Country House*, New Haven and London

GLANVILLE AND YOUNG 2002
P. Glanville and H. Young (eds), *Elegant Eating*, London

GLORY OF VENICE 1994
J. Martineau and A. Robison, *The Glory of Venice: Art in the Eighteenth Century* (exh. cat.), New Haven and London

GONZALEZ-PALACIOS 2000
A. Gonzalez-Palacios, 'Tracciato per il mobile Romano', in *idem*, *Il Tempio del Gusto*, Milan, pp. 21–92

GOULDING 1916
R. Goulding, *The Welbeck Abbey Miniatures: A Catalogue*, Oxford

GRANDJEAN ET AL. 1975
S. Grandjean, K. Piacenti, C. Truman, A. Blunt, *The James A. Rothschild Collection at Waddesdon Manor: Gold Boxes and Miniatures of the Eighteenth Century*, London and Fribourg

GRAND TOUR 1996
A. Wilton and I. Bignamini (ed.), *Grand Tour: the Lure of Italy in the Eighteenth Century* (exh. cat.), London

GRANGER 1825
J. Granger, *A Biographical History of England*, 6 vols, London

GRIMWADE 1969
A. Grimwade, 'Crespin or Sprimont? An unsolved problem of rococo silver', *Apollo* XC, pp. 126–8

GRIMWADE 1974
A. Grimwade, *Rococo Silver*, London

GRIMWADE 1976
A. Grimwade, *London Goldsmiths 1697–1837, Their Marks and Lives*, London

GROOM AND PROSSER 2006
S. Groom and L. Prosser, *Kew Palace: The Official Illustrated History*, London and New York

GROSLEY 1772
P.J. Grosley, *A Tour to London; or New Observations on England*, trans. T. Nugent, 2 vols, London

GUILLET DE SAINT-GEORGES 2008
J. Lichtentein and C. Michel (eds), *Les conférences au temps de Guillet de Saint-Georges, 1682–1699*, Paris

GWYNN 1997
D. Gwynn, 'The Charles Clay Organ Clock in The Royal Collection (Windsor Castle) and its connection with Georg Frideric Handel', *The British Institute of Organ Studies Reporter* XXI, no. 2 (January); http://npor.emma.cam.ac.uk/Reporter/apr97/e497.htm (accessed 27 January 2014)

HALL 1871
Mrs M. Hall, *The Royal Princesses of England*, London

HALLETT 1997
M. Hallett, 'The Medley Print in Eighteenth-Century London', *Art History* XX, pp. 214–37

HALSBAND 1960
R. Halsband, *The Life of Lady Mary Wortley Montagu*, Oxford

HANDEL 1985
J. Simon (ed.), *Handel: A Celebration of his Life and Times, 1685–1759* (exh. cat.), London

HARDING 2007
N. Harding, *Hanover and the British Empire, 1700–1837*, Woodbridge

HARRIS 1979
J. Harris, *The Artist and the Country House*, London

HARRIS 1990
E. Harris, *British Architectural Books and Writers, 1556–1785*, Cambridge

HARRIS 1996
J. Harris, 'Sir William Chambers and Kew Gardens', in *Chambers* 1996, pp. 55–67

HARRIS 2006
J. Harris, 'George III's Parents: Frederick and Augusta', in J. Marsden (ed.), *The Wisdom of George the Third*, London 2006, pp. 15–27

HARRIS, DE BELLAIGUE AND MILLAR 1968
J. Harris, G. de Bellaigue and O. Millar, *Buckingham Palace*, London

HARRIS AND SNODIN 1996
J. Harris and M. Snodin, *Sir William Chambers: Catalogue of Architectural Drawings in the Victoria and Albert Museum*, London

HARTOP 1996
C. Hartop, *The Huguenot Legacy, English Silver 1680–1760, from the Alan and Simone Hartman Collection*, London

HARTSHORNE 1905
A. Hartshorne (ed.), *Memoirs of a Royal Chaplain, 1729–1763. The Correspondence of Edmund Pyle, D.D. Chaplain in ordinary to George II, with Samuel Kerrich, D.D., vicar of Dersingham*, London

HASKELL 1967
F. Haskell, 'The Apotheosis of Newton in Art', *Texas Quarterly* X, no. 3 (Autumn), pp. 218–37

HASKELL 2013
F. Haskell, *The King's Pictures*, New Haven and London

HASPELS 1987
J. Haspels, *Automatic Musical Instruments, their Mechanics and their Music 1580–1820*, Koedijk

HATTON 1708
E. Hatton, *A New View of London*, 2 vols, London

HATTON 1978
R. Hatton, *George I: Elector and King*, London

HAWKINS 1885
E. Hawkins, *Medallic Illustrations of the History of Great Britain and Ireland to the Death of George II*, 2 vols, London

HAYDN 1890
J. Haydn, *The Book of Dignities*, London

HAYES 1943
R. Hayes, 'Biographical Dictionary of Irishmen in France', *Studies: An Irish Quarterly Review* 32, no. 126, pp. 235–52

HAYES 1957–8
J. Hayes, 'The Royal House of Hanover and the British Army, 1714–1760', *Bulletin of the John Rylands Library* 40, no. 2, pp. 328–50

HAYES 1965
J.T. Hayes, *British Patrons and Landscape Painting*, 4 vols, London

HAYWARD 1959
J.F. Hayward, 'A "Surtoute" designed by William Kent', *The Connoisseur* CXLIII (March), p. 82

HENDERSON 2010
A. Henderson, *The Life of William Augustus, Duke of Cumberland (1766)*, ed. R. Macpherson, London

HENREY 1975
B. Henrey, *British Botanical and Horticultural Literature before 1800*, 3 vols, London

HERRMAN 1973
L. Herrman, *English Landscape Painting of the Eighteenth Century*, London

HERVEY 1821
J.W. Croker (ed.), *Letters of Mary Lepel, Lady Hervey*, London

HERVEY 1884
John Lord Hervey, *Memoirs of the Reign of King George II*, ed. J.W. Croker, 3 vols, London

HERVEY 1931
R. Sedgwick (ed.), *John Lord Hervey, Some Materials towards Memoirs of the Reign of King George II*, 3 vols, London

HEUVEL 2001
G. van der Heuvel, 'Theorie und Praxis: Leibniz' Rolle in der Politik des Hauses Hannover', in *Ehrgeiz, Luxus und Fortune* 2001, pp. 84–97

HEWITT 2010
R. Hewitt, *Map of a Nation. A Biography of the Ordnance Survey*, London

HILL 1759
J. Hill, *Exotic Botany*, London

HILTON 1993
T. Hilton, *The Pre-Raphaelites*, London 1993

HIMMELHEBER 1975
G. Himmelheber, 'Ulrich und Melchior Baumgartner', *Pantheon* 33, pp. 113–20

HOBBS 2012–13
Carlton Hobbs LLC, Florence: *Viol'Art Firenze, catalogue IX*, New York and London

HODSON 1988
Y. Hodson, 'Prince William, Royal Map Collector'. The Map Collector 44, pp. 2–12

HODSON 1988
Y. Hodson, 'Prince William, Royal Map Collector', *The Map Collector* 44, pp. 2–12

HODSON FORTHCOMING
Y. Hodson, *Catalogue of the King's Military Map Collection*, London

HOGARTH 1753
W. Hogarth, *The Analysis of Beauty. Written with a view of fixing the fluctuating ideas of taste*, London

HOGARTH 1954
William Hogarth, 1697–1764 (exh. cat.), Manchester

HOGARTH 1955
W. Hogarth, *The Analysis of Beauty with the rejected passages from the manuscript drafts and autobiographical notes*, ed. J. Burke, Oxford

HOGARTH 1957
An Exhibition of Paintings and Drawings by Hogarth the Londoner (exh. cat.), London

HOGARTH 1971
L. Gowing and R. Paulson, *Hogarth* (exh. cat.), London

HOGARTH 1997
D. Bindman (ed.), *Hogarth and his Times: Serious comedy* (exh. cat.), London

HOGARTH 2006
M. Hallett and C. Riding (eds), *Hogarth* (exh. cat.), London

HOGWOOD 1984
C. Hogwood, *Handel*, London 1984

HOLBEIN TO HOCKNEY 2004
M. Clayton, *Holbein to Hockney: Drawings from the Royal Collection* (exh. cat.), London

HOUGHTON REVISITED 2013
T. Morel, A. Moore, J. Harris *et al.*, *Houghton Revisited* (exh. cat.), London

HOUSEHOLD ORDINANCES 1790
A collection of Ordinances and Regulations for the government of the Royal Household, made in divers reigns from Edward III to King William and Queen Mary, London

HOUSTON 2009
A. Houston, 'Benjamin Franklin and the "Wagon Affair" of 1755', *William and Mary Quarterly* 66, no. 2, pp. 235–86

HOWARD 1824
Letters to and from Henrietta, Countess of Suffolk, 2 vols, London

HOWARD 1969
D. Howard, 'Claude and English art', in *Art of Claude Lorrain* 1969, p. 9

HOWARD 1974
D.S. Howard, *Chinese Armorial Porcelain*, London

HUDSON 1979
E.G. Miles and J. Simon, *Thomas Hudson: Portrait Painter and Collector: A Bicentenary Exhibition* (exh. cat.), London

HUGHES 1747
M. Hughes, *The Natural History of Barbados*, London

HUGHES 1750
G. Hughes, *A Plain Narrative And Authentic Journal of the Late Rebellion, begun in 1745: Describing its Progress in Scotland, and England, till the full and glorious Defeat at Culloden*, 2nd edn, London

HUGHES 1996
P. Hughes, *The Wallace Collection: Catalogue of Furniture*, 3 vols, London

HUME 1832
D. Hume, *The Letters of David Hume*, ed. J.Y.T. Greig, 2 vols, Oxford

HUNTER 2012
D. Hunter, 'Rode the 12,000? Counting Coaches, People and Errors En Route to the Rehearsal of Handel's *Music for the Royal Fireworks* at Spring Gardens, Vauxhall in 1749', *The London Journal* 37, no. 1 (March), pp. 13–26

HUSSEY 1986
C. Hussey, *English Country Houses; Early Georgian, 1715–1760*, London

HYDE 2003
R. Hyde, *Jan Kip's Prospect of London, Westminster & St James's Park, 1720*, London

ILCHESTER 1912
The Earl of Ilchester, 'Old Chelsea China', *The Burlington Magazine* XX, no. 108 (March), p. 361

IMPEY 2003
E. Impey, *Kensington Palace: The Official Illustrated History*, London and New York

INCE AND MAYHEW 1759–63
W. Ince and J. Mayhew, *The Universal System of Household Furniture*, London

INGAMELLS 2009
J. Ingamells, *National Portrait Gallery: Later Stuart Portraits, 1685–1714*, London

INTIMATE PORTRAIT 2009
S. Lloyd and K. Sloane, *The Intimate Portrait; Drawings, Miniatures and Pastels from Ramsay to Lawrence* (exh. cat.), Edinburgh

IRELAND 1794–9
S. Ireland, *Graphic Illustrations of Hogarth*, 2 vols, London

IRELAND 1808
J. Ireland, *Catalogue of Hogarth's Prints, with the variations*, London

JACKSON 1966
W. Jackson, 'Hogarth's Analysis: The Fate of a Late Rococo Document', *Studies in English Literature* 6, pp. 543–50

JAGGER 1983
C. Jagger, *Royal Clocks*, London

JAKOB 1997
A. Jakob, 'Die Brüsseler Tapisserien des Herzogs Bernhard I. von Sachsen-Meiningen', *Patrimonia* 117, pp. 26–32

JARRETT 1965
D. Jarrett, *Britain 1688–1815*, London 1965

JAY 2006
E. Jay, 'Queen Caroline's Library and its European Contexts', *Book History* 9, pp. 31–55

JEFFERSON 1774
T. Jefferson, *A Summary View of the Rights of British America*, edn London 1774

JENKINS 1996
S. Jenkins, 'Queen Caroline's taste, the furnishing and functioning of the Queen's private apartments at Hampton Court', *Apollo* CXLIII (May), pp. 20–24

JOHNSON 1755
S. Johnson, *A Dictionary of the English Language*, 2 vols, London

JONES 1911
E.A. Jones, *The Gold and Silver of Windsor Castle*, Letchworth

JONES AND GARIBALDI 2006
K. Jones and C. Garibaldi, 'Crespin or Sprimont? A question revisited', *Silver Studies* 21, pp. 24–38

JOUIN 1883
Henri Jouin, *Conférences de l'Académie Royale de Peinture et de Sculpture*, Paris

KELLY 2009
J.M. Kelly, *The Society of Dilettanti: Archaeology and Identity in the British Enlightenment*, New Haven and London

KENT 2013
S. Weber (ed.), *William Kent: Designing Georgian Britain* (exh. cat.), New Haven and London

KERSLAKE 1977
J. Kerslake, *National Portrait Gallery: Early Georgian Portraits*, 2 vols, London

KEYNES 2005
M. Keynes, *The Iconography of Sir Isaac Newton to 1800*, Woodbridge

KING 1922
W. King, *Chelsea Porcelain*, London

KING OVER THE WATER 2001
E. Corp, *The King over the Water. Portraits of the Stuarts in Exile after 1689* (exh. cat.), Edinburgh

KINGS AND QUEENS 1983
G. Johnson, *Kings and Queens* (exh. cat.), London

KITSON 1978
M. Kitson, *Claude Lorrain: The Liber Veritatis*, London

KLEIN 1996
L. Klein, 'Coffeehouse Civility, 1660–1714: An Aspect of Post-Courtly Culture in England', *Huntington Library Quarterly* 59, no. 1, pp. 30–52

KLEIN 2002
L. Klein, 'Politeness and the Interpretation of the British Eighteenth Century', *The Historical Journal* 45, no. 4, pp. 869–98

KLEIN AND LAVOPA 1998
L. Klein and A. LaVopa (eds), *Enthusiasm and Enlightenment in Europe, 1650–1850*, San Marino

KNIGHT 1842
C. Knight, *London*, vol. 3, London

KÖHLER 2007
M. Köhler, 'Porcelain and diplomacy at the courts of Hanover and Cologne', in Cassidy Geiger 2007, pp. 209–56

KÖHLER 2008
M. Köhler, '"Paris est une mer pleine de Sirènes & d'écueils ...": Le voyage à Paris de Friedrich Karl von Hardenberg, 1741–1744', in Patrick Michel (ed.), *Art Français et Art Allemand au XVIIIe siècle, Rencontres de l'Ecole du Louvre*, Paris, pp. 311–25

KOPPERMAN 1996
P.E. Kopperman, '"The Cheapest Pay": Alcohol Abuse in the Eighteenth-Century British Army', *The Journal of Military History* 60, no. 3, pp. 445–70

KREMEIER 1999
J. Kremeier, 'Iburg, Osnabrück, Hannover – Sophie Charlottes Eltern und ihre Residenzen', in *Sophie Charlotte und ihr Schloss* (exh. cat.), Berlin, pp. 67–75

LA CHAPELLE 1735
V. La Chapelle, *The Modern Cook*, London

LA COUR DES STUARTS 1992
E. Corp and J. Sanson, *La cour des Stuarts à Saint-Germain-en-Laye au temps de Louis XIV* (exh. cat.), Saint-Germain-en-Laye

LAKING 1905
G.F. Laking, *The Furniture of Windsor Castle*, London

LANGDON 1989
H. Langdon, *Claude Lorrain*, Oxford

LANKHEIT 1957
K. Lankheit, 'Florentiner Bronzearbeiten für Kurfürst Johann Wilhelm von der Pfalz. Zu den künstlerischen Beziehungen der Häuser Medici und Pfalz-Neuburg im Spätbarock', *Münchner Jahrbuch der Bildenden Kunst* 7, pp. 185–210

LANKHEIT 1962
K. Lankheit, *Florentinische Barockplastik: Die Kunst am Hofe der letzten Medici 1670-1743*, Munich

LAVENDER 1962
D.S. Lavender, *The Monarchy in Portrait Miniatures from Elizabeth I to Queen Victoria*, London

LE BLANC 1747
Jean-Bernard Le Blanc, *Letters on the English and French Nations*, 2 vols, London

LENMAN 1980
B. Lenman, *The Jacobite Risings in Britain, 1689–1746*, London

LE PAUTRE *c*.1650–1750
J. Le Pautre, *Livre de miroirs, tables et gueridons*, Amsterdam

LE PAUTRE *c*.1700–15
P. Le Pautre, *Livre de Tables qui sont dans les apartements du Roy, sur lesquelles sont posés les bijoux du Cabinet des médailles*, Paris

LESLIE AND TAYLOR 1865
C.R. Leslie and T. Taylor, *The Life and Times of Sir Joshua Reynolds*, 2 vols, London

LE SUEUR 2000
S. Lemoine, A. Mérot *et al.*, *Eustache Le Sueur* (exh. cat.), Grenoble

LEVEY 1991
M. Levey, *The Later Italian Pictures in the Collection of Her Majesty The Queen*, Cambridge

LIOTARD 1781
J.E. Liotard, *Traité des Principes et des Règles de la Peinture*, Geneva

LIPPINCOTT 1983
L. Lippincott, *Selling Art in Georgian London. The Rise of Arthur Pond*, New Haven and London

LISELOTTE VON DER PFALZ 1996
S. Paas (ed), *Liselotte von der Pfalz, Madame am Hofe des Sonnenkönigs* (exh. cat.), Heidelberg

LITZKE 2001
A. Litzke, 'Instrumente der Macht: Höfische Musik in Hannover 1636–1714', in *Ehrgeiz, Luxus und Fortune* 2001, pp. 119–25

LLOYD 1897
E.M. Lloyd, 'Two Despatches Relative to the Battle of Fontenoy', *English Historical Review* 12, no. 47, pp. 523–30

LLOYD 2013
S. Lloyd, 'The Jacobites, propaganda and the portrait miniature (1688–1748)', in N. Lemoine-Bouchard (ed.), *La miniature en Europe: Des portraits de propogande aux œuvres éléphantesques*, Paris

LOMAX 1999
J. Lomax, 'Royalty and silver: the role of the Jewel House in the eighteenth century', *Silver Studies* 1, pp. 133–9

LONDON 1753 2003
S. O'Connell, *London 1753* (exh. cat.), London

MCBURNEY 1997
H. McBurney, *Mark Catesby's Natural History of America: the Watercolors from The Royal Library, Windsor Castle*, London

MCCORMACK 2006
M. McCormack, 'Citizenship, Nationhood, and Masculinity in the Affair of the Hanoverian Soldier, 1756', *The Historical Journal* 49, no. 4, pp. 971–93

MCGEARY 2002
T. McGeary, 'Frederick, Prince of Wales, as Print Collector, *Print Quarterly* 19, no. 3, pp. 254–60

MACGREGOR 1989
A. MacGregor (ed.), *The Late King's Goods. Collections, Possessions and Patronage of Charles I in the light of the Commonwealth Sale Inventories*, London and Oxford

MACKY 1722
J. Macky, *A Journey through England in familiar letters from a gentleman here to his friend abroad*, 2 vols, London

MCLYNN 1983
F.J. McLynn, *The Jacobite Army in England, 1745. The Final Campaign*, Edinburgh

MACMILLAN 1986
D. Macmillan, *Painting in Scotland: the Golden Age*, Oxford

MACQUOID 1905
P. Macquoid, *A History of English Furniture: The Age of Walnut*, London and New York

MACQUOID AND EDWARDS 1927
P. Macquoid and R. Edwards, *The Dictionary of English Furniture*, London

MADAN 1950
F. Madan, *A New Bibliography of the Eikon Basilike of King Charles the First: with a note on the authorship*, London

MAGNIFICENT MAPS 2010
P. Barber and T. Harper, *Magnificent Maps: Power, Propaganda and Art* (exh. cat.), London

MAHON 1947
D. Mahon, *Studies in Seicento Art and Theory*, London

MAIER 2005
J. Maier, 'Residenzschloß Ansbach. Gestalt und Ausstattung im Wandel der Zeit', *Jahrbuch des Historischen Vereins für Mittelfranken* 100

MALCOLM 1810
J.P. Malcolm, *Anecdotes of the Manners and Customs of London during the Eighteenth Century*, 2 vols, London

MALONE 1798
E. Malone, *The Literary Works of Sir Joshua Reynolds*, 3 vols, London

MALVASIA 1971
C.C. Malvasia, *Felsina Pittrice: Vite dei Pittori Bolognesi*, ed. M. Brascaglia, Bologna

MANFREDI 2005
M. Manfredi, 'Jacopo Amigoni: A Venetian painter in Georgian London', *The Burlington Magazine* CXLVII, no. 1231 (October), pp. 676–9

MANNERS AND MORALS 1987
E. Einberg *et al.*, *Manners and Morals: Hogarth and British Painting 1700–1760* (exh. cat.), London

MARIETTE 1741
P.-J. Mariette, *Description Sommaire des dessins des grands maistres d'Italie, des Pays-Bas et de France*, Paris

MAROT 1703
D. Marot, *Œuvres Du Sr. D. Marot*, The Hague

MARSCHNER 2002
J. Marschner, 'Queen Caroline of Anspach and the European princely museum tradition', in C. Campbell Orr (ed.), *Queenship in Britain 1660–1837*, Manchester and New York, pp. 130–42

MARSCHNER 2006
J. Marschner, 'Caroline of Ansbach: The Queen, Collection and Connoisseurship at the Early Georgian Court', PhD thesis, University College, London

MARTIN 1972
J. Martin, *The Decorations for the Pompa Introitus Ferdinandi*, London

MARTIN 2000
F. Martin, 'Camillo Rusconi in English Collections', in Sicca and Yarrington 2000, pp. 49–66

MARTIN 2005
G. Martin, *The Ceiling Decoration of the Banqueting Hall*, 2 vols, London

MASTER DRAWINGS 1986
Jane Roberts (ed.), *Master Drawings in the Royal Collection. From Leonardo to the Present Day* (exh. cat.), London

MASTERPIECES IN LITTLE 1996
C. Lloyd and V. Remington, *Masterpieces in Little; Portrait Miniatures from the Collection of Her Majesty the Queen* (exh. cat.), London

MEHR LICHT 1999
H. Beck (ed.), *Mehr Licht: Europa um 1770: die bildende Kunst der Aufklärung* (exh. cat.), Munich

MÉROT 1990
A. Mérot, *Poussin*, Paris

MÉROT 1995
A. Mérot, *French Painting in the Seventeenth Century*, New Haven and London

MÉROT 2000
A. Mérot, *Eustache Le Sueur, 1616–1655*, Paris

MEYER 1966
H. Meyer (ed.), *Herrenhausen 1666–1966: Europäische Gärten bis 1700*, Hanover

MEYER 1996
A. Meyer, *Apostles in England. Sir James Thornhill and the Legacy of Raphael's Tapestry Cartoons*, New York

MICHEL 1771
J.F.M. Michel, *Histoire de la Vie de P. P. Rubens*, Brussels

MILLAR 1882–3
A.H. Millar, 'The Battle of Glenshiel, 10th June 1719. Note upon an unpublished document in the possession of His Grace the Duke of Marlborough', *Proceedings of the Society of Antiquaries of Scotland* 5 (new series), pp. 57–69

MILLAR 1963
O. Millar, *The Tudor, Stuart and Early Georgian Pictures in the Collection of Her Majesty The Queen*, London

MILLAR 1967
O. Millar, *Zoffany and his Tribuna*, London

MILLAR 1969
O. Millar, *The Later Georgian Pictures in the Collection of Her Majesty The Queen*, London

MILLAR 1977
O. Millar, *The Queen's Pictures*, London

MITCHELL 1731
J. Mitchell, *Three Poetical Epistles to Mr. Hogarth, Mr. Dandridge, and Mr. Lambert*, London

MONOD 1993
P.K. Monod, *Jacobitism and the English People, 1688–1788*, Cambridge

MONTAGU 1994
J. Montagu, *The Expression of the Passions*, New Haven and London

MOWL 1988
T. Mowl, *John Wood: Architect of Obsession*, 1988

MOWL 2006
T. Mowl, *William Kent: Architect, Designer, Opportunist*, London

MURDOCH 1983
T. Murdoch, 'Roubiliac and his Huguenot connections', *Proceedings of the Huguenot Society* 24, pp. 26–45

MURDOCH 1997
T. Murdoch, 'Jean, René and Thomas Pelletier, a Huguenot Family of Carvers and Gilders in England 1682-1726. Part I', *The Burlington Magazine* CXXXIX, no. 1136 (November), pp. 732–42

MURDOCH 1998
T. Murdoch, 'Jean, René and Thomas Pelletier, a Huguenot Family of Carvers and Gilders in England 1682-1726. Part II', *The Burlington Magazine* CXL, no. 1143 (June), pp. 363–74

MURDOCH 2003
T. Murdoch, 'The King's Cabinet-Maker: The Giltwood Furniture of James Moore the Elder', *The Burlington Magazine* CXLV, no. 1203 (June), pp. 408–20

NEWMAN 1987
H. Newman, *An Illustrated Dictionary of Silverware*, London

NICHOLS 1781
J.Nichols, *Biographical Anecdotes of William Hogarth and a Catalogue of his Works*, London

NICHOLSON 2002
R. Nicholson, *Bonnie Prince Charlie and the Making of a Myth. A Study in Portraiture 1720–1892*, Lewisburg and London

NICOLSON 1965
B. Nicolson, 'The rehabilitation of Trophime Bigot', *Art and Literature* IV, pp. 66–105

NICOLSON 1979
B. Nicolson, *The International Caravaggesque Movement*, London

NORTHERN RENAISSANCE 2011
K. Heard, L. Whitaker *et al.*, *The Northern Renaissance: Dürer to Holbein* (exh. cat.), London

OBERHUBER 1988
K. Oberhuber, *Poussin: The Early Years in Rome*, New York

O'CONNELL 1997
S. O'Connell, 'Hogarthomania and the Collecting of Hogarth', in *Hogarth* 1997

O'DONOGHUE 1908
F. O'Donoghue, *Catalogue of Engraved British Portraits preserved in the ... British Museum*, London

OESTERREICH 1761
M. Oesterreich, *Beschreibung derjenigen Sammlung verschiedener Original-Gemälde von italienischen, holländischen, französischen und deutschen Meistern, welche das Cabinet ausmachen von Johann Georg Eimbke*, Berlin

OMAN 1972
C. Oman, 'Silver Designs by William Kent', *Apollo* XCV (January), pp. 22–4

OPPÉ 1947
A.P. Oppé, *The Drawings of Paul and Thomas Sandby in the Collection of His Majesty the King at Windsor Castle*, London

OPPÉ 1947–8
A.P. Oppé, *The Drawings of William Hogarth*, Oxford

OPPÉ 1950
A.P. Oppé, *English Drawings, Stuart and Georgian Periods, in the Collection of His Majesty The King at Windsor Castle*, London

ORME 1763–77
R. Orme, *A History of the Military Transactions of the British Nation in Indostan*, London

ORRERY 1903
The Countess of Cork and Orrery (ed.), *The Orrery Papers*, 2 vols, London

PAGE 1911
W. Page (ed), *A History of the County of Middlesex*, vol. 2, London

PAINTINGS FROM WINDSOR CASTLE 1990
C. Lloyd and M. Evans, *The Royal Collection. Paintings from Windsor Castle* (exh. cat.), London 1990

PALLADIO 1738
I. Ware (ed.), *The Four Books of Andrea Palladio's Architecture*, London

PALM 2010
H. Palm, 'Friedrich Karl von Hardenbergs Wirken als Hofgartendirektor', in Bothmer and Köhler 2010, pp. 44–53

PAPENDIEK 1887
C. Papendiek, *Court and Private Life in the Time of Queen Charlotte, being the Journals of Mrs Papendiek*, London

PASCOLI 1736
L. Pascoli, *Vite de' Pittori, Scultori ed Architetti Moderni*, 2 vols, Rome

PASSAVANT 1836
J.D. Passavant, *Tour of a German Artist in England*, 2 vols, London

PAULSON 1967
R. Paulson, 'New Light on Hogarth's Graphic Works', *Burlington Magazine* CIX, no. 770, pp. 280–6

PAULSON 1971
R. Paulson, *Hogarth: His Life, Art and Times*, New Haven and London

PAULSON 1989
R. Paulson, *Hogarth's Graphic Works*, 3rd edn, London

PEARS 1988
I. Pears, *The Discovery of Painting: The Growth of Interest in the Arts in England, 1680–1768*, New Haven and London

PEPPER 1984
D.S. Pepper, *Guido Reni*, London

PIETSCH 1995
T.W. Pietsch (ed.), *Fishes, Crayfishes, and Crabs: Louis Renard's Natural History of the Rarest Curiosities of the Seas of the Indies*, Baltimore and London

PIPER 1982
D. Piper, *The Image of the Poet: British Poets and their Portraits*, Oxford

PLUMB AND WHELDON 1977
J.H. Plumb and H. Wheldon, *Royal Heritage: the Story of Britain's Royal Builders and Collectors*, London

PLUTARCH 1823
Plutarch's Lives, ed. J and W Langhorne, 5 vols, London

POLITISCHE CORRESPONDENZ FRIEDRICHS DES GROSSEN
J.G. Droysen *et al.* (eds), *Politische Correspondenz Friedrichs des Großen*, 47 vols, Berlin and Leipzig 1879–1939; http://friedrich.uni-trier.de/de/politKorr/toc/

POLLARD 2009A
T. Pollard, 'Mapping Mayhem: Scottish Battle Maps and their Role in Archaeological Research', *Scottish Geographical Journal* 125, no. 1 (March), pp. 25–42

POLLARD 2009B
T. Pollard (ed.), *Culloden. The History and Archaeology of the Last Clan Battle*, Barnsley

POOLE 1995
R. Poole, '"Give us our eleven days!": Calendar Reform in Eighteenth-Century England', *Past & Present* 149 (November), pp. 95–139

POPE 1770
A. Pope, *The Works of Alexander Pope*, 9 vols, London

PORTER 2000
R. Porter, *Enlightenment: Britain and the Creation of the Modern World*, London

PORTLAND 1891–1931
Historical Manuscripts Commission: Manuscripts of His Grace the Duke of Portland, preserved at Welbeck Abbey, 10 vols, London

POTE 1749
J. Pote, *The History and Antiquities of Windsor Castle*, Eton

POTE 1976
W. Pote, *The Journal of Captain William Pote, Nr.* (facsimile reprint), New York and London

POUSSIN: WORKS ON PAPER 1995
M. Clayton, *Poussin: Works on Paper. Drawings from the Collection of Her Majesty Queen Elizabeth II* (exh. cat.), London

PREBBLE 2002
J. Prebble, *Culloden*, London 2002

PRINCES AS PATRONS 1998
M. Evans (ed.), *Princes as Patrons: The Art Collections of the Princes of Wales from the Renaissance to the Present Day* (exh. cat.), London

PURCELL 1929
P. Purcell, 'The Jacobite Rising of 1715 and the English Catholics', *The English Historical Review* 44, no. 175, pp. 418–32

PUTTFARKEN 1985
T. Puttfarken, *Roger de Piles' Theory of Art*, New Haven and London

PYNE 1819
W.H. Pyne, *The History of the Royal Residences of Windsor Castle, St James's Palace, Carlton House, Kensington Palace, Hampton Court, Buckingham House, and Frogmore*, 3 vols, London

QUEEN'S PICTURES 1991
C. Lloyd, *The Queen's Pictures: Royal Collectors through the Centuries* (exh. cat.), London

QUEEN'S PICTURES 1994
C. Lloyd, *The Queen's Pictures: Old Masters from the Royal Collection* (exh. cat.), London

QUEST FOR ALBION 1998
C. Lloyd, *The Quest for Albion: Painting and Patronage and the British Monarch* (exh. cat.), London

RAMSAY 1762
A. Ramsay, *A Dialogue on Taste*, 2nd edn, London

REID 1996
S. Reid, *1745. A Military History of the Last Jacobite Rising*, Staplehurst

REID 2009
S. Reid, 'The Battle of Culloden: A Narrative Account', in Pollard 2009b, pp. 103–29

REUTHER 1976
H. Reuther, 'Pläne des grossen Gartens zu Hannover-Herrenhausen im Nationalmuseum zu Stockholm', *Niederdeutsche Beiträge zur Kunstgeschichte* 15, pp. 127–38

REYNOLDS 1819
The Literary Works of Sir Joshua Reynolds, 3 vols, London

REYNOLDS 1996
H. Mount (ed.), *Sir Joshua Reynolds, A Journey to Flanders and Holland*, Cambridge

REYNOLDS 1997
J. Reynolds, *Discourses on Art*, ed. R.R. Wark, New Haven and London

REYNOLDS 1999
G. Reynolds, *The Sixteenth and Seventeenth Century Miniatures in the Collection of Her Majesty The Queen*, London

RIBEIRO 1984
A. Ribeiro, *The Dress Worn at Masquerades in England, 1730–1790, and its Relation to Fancy Dress in Portraiture*, New York and London

RIBEIRO 2000
A. Ribeiro, *The Gallery of Fashion*, London

RICHARDSON 1715
J. Richardson, *An Essay on the Theory of Painting*, London

RICHARDSON 1719
J. Richardson, *Two Discourses: An Essay on the whole Art of Criticism as it relates to Painting, II, An Argument on behalf of the Science of the Connoisseur*, London

RICHARDSON 1722
J. Richardson, *An Account of some of the Statues, Bas-reliefs, Drawings and Pictures in Italy*, London

RICHARDSON 1725
J. Richardson, *An Essay on the Theory of Painting*, 2nd edn, London

RICHARDSON 1936
Mrs Herbert Richardson, 'Early Commercial Advertising in England', *Journal of the Royal Society of Arts* 84, no. 4369 (August), pp. 1015–33

RIDLEY 1999
J. Ridley, *The Freemasons*, London

RIEDER 1978
W. Rieder, 'A gilt-gesso set of furniture traditionally from Stowe', *Furniture History* XIV, pp. 9–13

RISK 1972
J.C. Risk, *The History of the Order of the Bath and its Insignia*, London

ROBERTS 1987
J. Roberts, *Royal Artists. From Mary Queen of Scots to the Present Day*, London

ROBERTS 1995
H. Roberts, 'So beautiful a style', *Country Life* (23 November), pp. 58–59

ROBERTS 1997
J. Roberts, *Royal Landscape: The Gardens and Parks of Windsor*, New Haven and London

ROCOCO 1984
M. Snodin, *Rococo, Art and Design in Hogarth's England* (exh. cat.), London

ROETHLISBERGER 1961
M. Roethlisberger, *Claude Lorrain. The Paintings*, 2 vols, Princeton

RÖTHLISBERGER 1975
M. Röthlisberger, *Gaspard Dughet: Rome 1615–1675*, London

ROHR 1981
A. von Rohr, 'Bildnisse der Sophie von der Pfalz und des Kurfürsten Ernst August von Hannover', *Niederdeutsche Beiträge zur Kunstgeschichte* 20, pp. 127–50

ROHR 1988
A. von Rohr, 'Gottfried Boy (1701–1755) und die Bildnismalerei in Hannover', *Niederdeutsche Beiträge zur Kunstgeschichte* 27, pp. 153–68

RORSCHACH 1990
K. Rorschach, 'Frederick, Prince of Wales as Collector and Patron', Walpole Society LV, pp. 1–76

ROSCOE 1997
I. Roscoe, 'Peter Scheemakers and the Stowe Commission', *New Arcadian Journal* 43/44, pp. 40–65

ROSCOE 1999
I. Roscoe, 'Peter Scheemakers', Walpole Society LXI, pp. 163–304

ROSE 1993
M. Rose, *Authors and Owners; the Invention of Copyright*, Harvard

ROUQUET 1755
J.A. Rouquet, *The Present State of the Arts in England*, London

ROWELL 1996
C. Rowell, 'A seventeenth-century Cabinet restored. The Green Closet at Ham House', *Apollo* CXLIII (April), pp. 18–23

ROWELL 1996
C. Rowell (ed.), *Ham House: 400 Years of Collecting and Patronage*, New Haven and London

ROYAL MISCELLANY 1990
A Royal Miscellany from the Royal Library, Windsor Castle (exh. cat.), London

ROYAL RIVER 2012
D. Starkey, S. Doran and R. Blyth, *Royal River: Power, Pageantry and the Thames* (exh. cat.), London

ROYAL TREASURES 2002
J. Roberts (ed.), *Royal Treasures* (exh. cat.), London

RUBIN 1995
P.L. Rubin, *Giorgio Vasari: Art and History*, New Haven and London

RUDOLPH 1995
S. Rudolph, *Niccolò Maria Pallavicini. L'ascesa al Tempio della Virtù attraverso il Mecenatismo*, Rome

RUTHERFORD 1927
F.J. Rutherford, 'The Furnishing of Hampton Court Palace, 1715–1737', *Old Furniture* II, no. 6 (November), pp. 180–86

RUTHERFORD AND GROSVENOR 2013
E. Rutherford and B. Grosvenor, *Warts and All: The Portrait Miniatures of Samuel Cooper*, London

RYDER 1939
D. Ryder, *The Diary of Dudley Ryder 1715–16*, London

SANDBY 1892
W. Sandby, *Thomas and Paul Sandby, Royal Academicians. Some account of their lives*, London

SANDBY 2009–10
S. Daniels and J. Bonehill (eds), *Paul Sandby. Picturing Britain* (exh. cat.), Nottingham, Edinburgh and London

SANFORD TERRY 1905
C. Sanford Terry, 'The Battle of Glenshiel', *Scottish History* 2, no. 8, pp. 412–23

SAUSSURE 2006
C. de Saussure, *Letters from London, 1725–1730*, trans. P. Scott, London

SCHNATH 1962
G. Schnath, *Das Leineschloss: Kloster, Fürstensitz, Landtagsgebäude*, Hanover

SCHNATH 1976
G. Schnath, *Geschichte Hannovers im Zeitalter der neunten Kur und der englischen Sukzession 1674–1714*, vol. 2, *1693–1698*, Hildesheim

SCHNATH 1978
G. Schnath, *Geschichte Hannovers im Zeitalter der neunten Kur und der englischen Sukzession 1674–1714*, vol. 3, *1698–1714*, Hildesheim

SCHOLTEN 1995
F. Scholten, *Gebeeldhouwde Portretten/ Portrait Sculptures. Rijksmuseum, Amsterdam*, Amsterdam

SCOTT 2010
K. Scott, *St James's Palace: A History*, London

SCOUTEN AND HUGHES 1944
A.H. Scouten and L. Hughes, 'A Calendar of Performances of "1 Henry IV and 2 Henry IV" during the First Half of the Eighteenth Century', *The Journal of English and Germanic Philology* 43, no. 1 (January), pp. 23–41

SEELEY 1817
B. Seeley, *Stowe, a Description of the Magnificent House and Gardens of the Right Honourable George Grenville Nugent Temple, Earl Temple, Viscount and Baron Cobham*, London

SHAFTESBURY 1969
A., Earl of Shaftesbury, *Second Characters or, The Language of Forms*, ed. B. Rand., New York

SHAKESPEARE IN ART 2003
J. Martineau (ed.), *Shakespeare in Art* (exh. cat), London

SHARP 1996
R. Sharp, *The Engraved Record of the Jacobite Movement*, Aldershot

SHAWE-TAYLOR 1990
D. Shawe-Taylor, *The Georgians: Eighteenth-century Portraiture and Society*, London

SHAWE-TAYLOR 2013
D. Shawe-Taylor, 'The Waterloo Chamber before the Battle of Waterloo', in G. Perry, K. Retford and J. Vibert (eds), *Placing Faces: the Portrait and the Country House in the Long Eighteenth Century*, Manchester, pp. 244–63

SHEARMAN 1983
J. Shearman, *The Early Italian Paintings in the Collection of Her Majesty The Queen*, Cambridge

SHEBBEARE 1755
Shebbeare, purporting to translate 'Batista Angeloni', *Letters on the English Nation*, 2 vols, London

SICCA 1986
C.M. Sicca, 'On William Kent's Roman Sources', *Architectural History* 29, pp. 134–7

SICCA AND YARRINGTON 2000
C. Sicca and A. Yarrington (eds), *Lustrous Trade, Material Culture and the History of Sculpture in England and Italy, c.1700–c.1860*, London and New York

SIMMS 2007
B. Simms, *Three Victories and a Defeat. The Rise and Fall of the First British Empire, 1714–1785*, London

SMART 1992
A. Smart, *Allan Ramsay: Painter, Essayist and Man of the Enlightenment*, New Haven and London

SMART 1999
A. Smart, *Allan Ramsay; A Complete Catalogue of his Paintings*, New Haven and London

SMITH 1931
H. Smith, *Buckingham Palace: Its Furniture, Decoration and History*, London

SMITH 2006
H. Smith, *Georgian Monarchy: Politics and Culture, 1714–1760*, Cambridge

SMOLLETT 1757–65
T. Smollett, *A Complete History of England*, London

SMOLLETT 1760
T. Smollett, *A Continuation of the Complete History of England*, London

SNODIN AND STYLES 2001
M. Snodin and J. Styles (ed.), *Design and the Decorative Arts: Britain 1500–1900*, London

SOBEL 1995
D. Sobel, *Longitude: the Story of the Lone Genius who Solved the Greatest Scientific Problem of his Time*, London

SOLKIN 1996
D. Solkin, *Painting for Money: the Visual Arts and the Public Sphere in Eighteenth-Century England*, New Haven and London

SOPHIA, ELECTRESS OF HANOVER 1888
Memoirs of Sophia, Electress of Hanover, 1630–1680, trans. H. Forester, London

SOTHEBY'S 2005
Sotheby's, sale catalogue, *The Royal House of Hanover / Das Königshaus von Hannover, Schloss Marienburg, 5–15 October 2005*, 3 vols, London

SPEAR 1997
R.E. Spear, *The Divine Guido: Religion, Sex, Money and Art in the World of Guido Reni*, New Haven and London

SPECK 1977
W.A. Speck, *Stability and Strife: England 1714–1760*, London

SPECK 1981
W.A. Speck, *The Butcher: The Duke of Cumberland and the Suppression of the 45*, Oxford

STACEY 2002
C.P. Stacey, *Quebec, 1759. The Siege and the Battle*, ed. D.E. Graves, Toronto

STEARN 1967
W.T. Stearn, 'Hill's The British Herbal (1756–1757)', *Taxon* 16, no. 6 (December), pp. 494–8

STEARNS 1948
R.P. Stearns, 'Colonial Fellows of the Royal Society of London, 1661–1788', *Osiris* 8, pp. 98–99

STEPHENS AND GEORGE 1870–1954
F.G. Stephens and M.D. George, *Catalogue of Political and Personal Satires in the Department of Prints and Drawings in the British Museum*, 11 vols, London

STEWART 1983
J.D. Stewart, *Sir Godfrey Kneller and the English Baroque Portrait*, Oxford

STIEGLITZ 2001
A. von Stieglitz, 'Der teuerste Hut des Reiches: Hannovers Ringen um die Kurwürde', in *Ehrgeiz, Luxus und Fortune* 2001, pp. 68–83

STRAWBERRY HILL 2009
M. Snodin (ed.), *Horace Walpole's Strawberry Hill* (exh. cat.), London

STRONG 1991
R. Strong *et al.*, *British Portraits 1660–1960*, Woodbridge

STRONG 1992
R. Strong, *Royal Gardens*, London

STRONG 2000
R. Strong, *The Artist and the Garden*, New Haven and London

STUART MASON 1992
A. Stuart Mason, *George Edwards: The Bedell and his Birds*, London

SUETONIUS 1997
Suetonius, *Lives of the Twelve Caesars*, Ware

SWIFT 1758
J. Swift, *Travels into several remote nations of the world. In four parts, ... By Lemuel Gulliver* London

SWIFT 1957
J. Swift, *A Prospect of Reforming the English Tongue, Polite Conversation etc.*, ed. H Davis, Oxford

SZECHI 2006
D. Szechi, *1715. The Great Jacobite Rebellion*. New Haven and London

THIEME-BECKER
U. Thieme and F. Becker, *Allgemeines Lexikon der Bildenden Künste von der Antike bis zur Gegenwart*, 37 vols, Leipzig 1907–47

THOMPSON 2006
A.C. Thompson, *Britain, Hanover and the Protestant Interest, 1688–1756*, Woodbridge

THOMPSON 2011
A.C. Thompson, *George II, King and Elector*, New Haven and London

THORNBURY AND WALFORD 1873–8
W. Thornbury and E. Walford, *Old and New London: A Narrative of its History, its People, and its Places*, 6 vols, London

THORNTON 1978
P. Thornton, *Seventeenth-Century Interior Decoration in England, France and Holland*, New Haven and London

THORP 2010
J. Thorp, 'Anthony L'Abbé and the Court of St James's: Dances to Honour the Hanoverian Royal Family', *The Court Historian* 15, no. 2, pp. 189–206

THURLEY 2003
S. Thurley, *Hampton Court: A Social and Architectural History*, New Haven and London

TOLAND 1705
Mr Toland, *An Account of the Courts of Prussia and Hanover*, London

TREASURE 1992
G. Treasure, *Who's Who in Early Hanoverian Britain (1714–1789)*, London

TRIUMPH OF THE BAROQUE 1999
H.A. Millon (ed.), *The Triumph of the Baroque: Architecture in Europe 1600–1750* (exh. cat.), Montreal

UGLOW 1997
J. Uglow, *Hogarth. A Life and a World*, London

VAN DYCK 1999
C. Brown *et al.*, *Van Dyck 1599–1641* (exh. cat.), London

VAN DYCK AND BRITAIN 2009
K. Hearn *et al.*, *Van Dyck and Britain* (exh. cat.), London

VARDY 1744
J. Vardy, *Some Designs of Mr. Inigo Jones and Mr. Wm. Kent*, London

VASARI 1996
G. Vasari, *Lives of the Painters, Sculptors and Architects*, ed. G. du C. De Vere, 2 vols, London

VERTUE 1743
See 'Manuscript Sources' above

VERTUE I
G. Vertue, *Note Books*, vol. I, Walpole Society XVIII (1929–30)

VERTUE II
G. Vertue, *Note Books*, vol. II, Walpole Society XX (1931–2)

VERTUE III
G. Vertue, *Note Books*, vol. III, Walpole Society XXII (1933–4)

VERTUE IV
G. Vertue, *Note Books*, vol. IV, Walpole Society XXIV (1935–6)

VERTUE V
G. Vertue, *Note Books*, vol. V, Walpole Society XXVI (1937–8)

VERTUE VI
G. Vertue, *Note Books*, vol. VI, Walpole Society XXX (1951–2)

VIEWS OF WINDSOR 1995
J. Roberts, *Views of Windsor: Watercolours by Thomas and Paul Sandby* (exh. cat.), London

VIVIAN 1989
F. Vivian, *The Consul Smith Collection; Masterpieces of Italian Drawing from the Royal Library, Windsor Castle, Raphael to Canaletto*, Munich

VIVIAN 2006
F. Vivian, *A Life of Frederick, Prince of Wales 1707–1751, A Connoisseur of the Arts*, New York

VOLK 1966
P. Volk, 'Darstellungen Ludwigs XIV. auf Steigendem Pferd', *Wallfraf-Richartz Jahrbuch* XXVIII, pp. 61–89

VOLTAIRE 1728
Voltaire, *La Henriade*, London

VOLTAIRE 1733
Voltaire, *Letters Concerning the English Nation*, London

VOLTAIRE 1964
Voltaire, *Lettres Philosophiques*, ed. R. Pomeau, Paris

VOSSNACK 1966
L. Vossnack, 'Kurfürstin Sophie von Hannover: ihre Kenntnis europäischer Gärten des Barock', in Meyer 1966, pp. 19–28

WAITZMANN 2003
M.S. Waitzman, *Early English Keyboard Instruments: The Benton Fletcher Collection at Fenton House*, London

WALKER 1992
R. Walker, *The Eighteenth and Early Nineteenth Century Miniatures in the Collection of Her Majesty The Queen*, Cambridge and New York

WALPOLE 1752
H. Walpole, *Aedes Walpolianae or a Description of the Collection of Pictures at Houghton Hall in Norfolk*, London; reprinted in Dukelskaya and Moore 2000

WALPOLE 1758
H. Walpole, *A catalogue of the collection of pictures, etc. belonging to King James the Second : to which is added, a catalogue of the pictures and drawings in the closet of the late Queen Caroline, with their exact measures; and also of the principal pictures in the palace at Kensington*, London

WALPOLE 1798
H. Walpole, *The Works of Horace Walpole, Earl of Orford*, vol. IV, London

WALPOLE 1827
H. Walpole, *Anecdotes of Painting in England, with some account of the principal artists, and notes on other arts; collected by G. Vertue, digested from his MSS.; with additions by J. Dallaway*, London

WALPOLE 1862
H. Walpole, *Anecdotes of Painting in England*, 3 vols., London

WALPOLE 1923
H. Walpole, *Reminiscences written by Mr Horace Walpole in 1788 for the amusement of Miss Mary and Miss Agnes Berry*, Oxford

WALPOLE 1928
P. Toynbee (ed.), 'Horace Walpole's Journals of Visits to Country Seats &c.', Walpole Society XVI, pp. 9–80

WALPOLE, CORRESPONDENCE
W.S. Lewis (ed.), *The Correspondence and Journals of Horace Walpole*, 48 vols, Oxford 1937–83

WARNER 1992
M. Warner, 'The Pre-Raphaelites and the National Gallery', *Huntington Library Quarterly* 55 (Winter), pp. 1–11

WATKIN 1984
D. Watkin, *Royal Interiors of Regency England*, London

WATKIN 2004
D. Watkin, *The Architect King: George III and the Culture of the Enlightenment*, London

WEBB 1954
M.I. Webb, *Michael Rysbrack: Sculptor*, London

WEBER 2013
S. Weber, 'The Well of Inspiration: Sources for Kent's Furniture Designs', in *Kent* 2013, pp. 449–67

WEIHRAUCH 1956
H.R. Weihrauch, *Bayerisches Nationalmuseum München Katalog*, vol. 13, no. 5: *Die Bildwerke in Bronze und in anderen Metallen*, Munich

WEISS 2008
U. Weiß, *Dame, Herzog, Kurfürst, König: Das Haus der hannoverschen Welfen, 1636–1866*, Hanover

WEST 1999
S. West (ed.), *Italian Culture in Northern Europe in the Eighteenth Century*, Cambridge

WHINNEY 1964
M. Whinney, *Sculpture in Britain 1530–1830*, Harmondsworth

WHITE 1918
F.D. White, 'Voltaire and English Liberty', *The Open Court* XXXII, no. 3 (March), pp. 129–40

WHITE 1982
C. White, *The Dutch Pictures in the Collection of Her Majesty The Queen*, Cambridge

WHITE 2007
C. White, *The Later Flemish Pictures in the Collection of Her Majesty The Queen*, London

WHITLEY 1968
W.T. Whitley, *Artists and their Friends in England 1700–1799*, 2 vols, edn New York

WHITWORTH 1958
R. Whitworth, *Field Marshal Lord Ligonier*, Oxford

WHITWORTH 1992
R. Whitworth, *William Duke of Cumberland. A Life*, London

WILKINS 1901
W.H. Wilkins, *Caroline the Illustrious. Queen-Consort of George II. and sometime Queen-Regent. A Study of her Life and Time*, 2 vols, London, New York and Bombay

WILLMOTH 1997
F. Willmoth, ed., *Flamsteed's Stars*, Woodbridge

WILMOT-SITWELL 2009
C. Wilmot-Sitwell, 'The Inventory of 19 Arlington Street, 12 May 1768', *Furniture History*, XLV, pp. 73–99

WILSON 1982
D.H. Solkin, *Richard Wilson: The Landscape of Reaction* (exh. cat.), London

WILSON 1984
M. Wilson, *William Kent: Architect, Designer, Painter, Gardener, 1685–1748*, London

WIMSATT 1965
W.K. Wimsatt, *Alexander Pope: Selected Poetry and Prose*, New Haven and London

WIND 1986
E. Wind, *Hume and the Heroic Portrait: Studies in Eighteenth-century Imagery*, Oxford

WITTKOWER 1974
R. Wittkower, *Palladio and Palladianism*, New York

WITTKOWER 1985
R. Wittkower, *Palladio and English Palladianism*, London

WOLFF-METTERNICH 2004
B. Freifrau von Wolff-Metternich, *Die Porzellanmanufaktur Fürstenberg*, Munich

WOOD 2008
L. Wood, *The Upholstered Furniture in the Lady Lever Art Gallery*, 2 vols, New Haven and London

WOODWARD 1957
J. Woodward, 'Amigoni as a Portrait Painter in England', *The Burlington Magazine* XCIX, pp. 20–1

WOOSNAM-SAVAGE 2009
R.C. Woosnam-Savage, 'To Gather an Image Whole': Some Early Maps and Plans of the Battle of Culloden', in Pollard 2009b, pp. 163–86

WOOTTON 1984
A. Meyer, *John Wootton 1682-1764: Landscapes and sporting art in early Georgian England* (exh. cat.), London

WORDRUFF 1920
L. Loss Wordruff, 'The versatile Sir John Hill, M.D.', *The American Naturalist* 60, no. 670 (September–October), pp. 416–42

WORMS AND BAYNTON-WILLIAMS 2011
L. Worms and A. Baynton-Williams, *British Map Engravers: A Dictionary of Engravers, Lithographers and their Principal Employers to 1850*, London

WORSLEY 1987–II
G. Worsley, 'Rokeby Park, Yorkshire – II', *Country Life* (26 March), pp. 173–79

WORSLEY 1987–III
G. Worsley, 'Rokeby Park, Yorkshire – III', *Country Life* (2 April), pp. 116–17

WORSLEY 1995
G. Worsley, *Classical Architecture in Britain: the Heroic Age*, New Haven and London

WORSLEY 2010
L. Worsley, *Courtiers. The Secret History of Kensington Palace*, London

WORTLEY MONTAGU 1837
J. A. Stuart-Wortley-Mackenzie Wharncliffe (ed.), *The Letters and Works of Lady Mary Wortley Montagu*, London

WORTLEY MONTAGU 1970
R. Halsband (ed.), *Selected Letters of Lady Mary Wortley Montagu*, Harlow

WRIGHT 1985
C. Wright, *The French Painters of the Seventeenth Century*, London

ZOFFANY 2010
M. Postle (ed.), *Johan Zoffany: Society Observed* (exh. cat.), New Haven and London

Index

This is primarily an index of persons (and sources), but some places and subjects have been included.
The following are indexed under headings: *Acts of Parliament, Battles, Country Houses, Furniture, Royal Residences – England and Germany, Societies, Treaties, Wars.*
Members of the Royal Family (Stuart and Hanoverian) are indexed under their Christian names; aristocrats under their title.
Catalogue nos are given both for makers and for sitters or portraitees.

Acknowledgements

The compilation of this catalogue has relied on the help of a large number of people. The authors would like to thank them all for their time and generosity.

During a research visit to Brandenburg and Lower Saxony in the spring of 2012, we were generously welcomed by Dr Henriette Graf and Dr Franziska Windt (Stiftung Preussische Schlößer und Gärten, Potsdam), Professor Jochen Luckhardt (Herzog Anton Ulrich Museum, Braunschweig), Juliane Schmieglitz-Otten (Residenzmuseum im Celler Schloss, Celle) and Dr Hans-Henning Grote (Schloss Wolfenbüttel). In Hanover, Dr Bernd Adam very kindly enabled us to explore the building site of Schloss Herrenhausen (restoration completed in 2013); we also enjoyed the hospitality of HRH The Hereditary Prince of Hanover, HRH Prince Heinrich of Hanover, the Count and Countess Nikolaus von Kielmansegg and Dr and Mrs Claus von Jeinsen. Another research visit in February 2013 allowed us to study the work of William Kent in Norfolk, and we are a very grateful to our hosts the Marquess of Cholmondeley, the Marquess Townshend, the Earl of Leicester and Viscount Coke, to have made their collections accessible to us.

For their generous sharing of information and kind advice, we would like to thank the following: Sarah Bardwell, Dr Adam Bowett, Cécile Brett, Dr Jonathan Conlin, Dr Yolande Hodson, Dr Stephen Johnston, Sir Christopher White, Robin Simon, Professor John Shawe-Taylor, Philip Mould, Bendor Grosvenor, Sebastian Barfield, Maria Jordan, Dr Tessa Murdoch, David Oakey, Sir Hugh Roberts, the Hon. Lady Roberts, Dr Karin Schrader, Charles Sebag-Montefiore, Dr Hannah Smith, Dr Andrew C. Thompson, Annabel Westman and Dr Lucy Wood. From Historic Royal Palaces we would particularly like to single out the support of Dr Joanna Marschner, who so generously shared her research into the patronage of Queen Caroline before the eagerly awaited appearance of her book this year. We have also benefited hugely from the insights gained from Dr Lucy Worsley on the BBC television series. Deidre Murphy, Sebastian Edwards, Dr Olivia Fryman and Susanne Groom have also been exceptionally generous in sharing their research files on the displays at Kensington and Hampton Court and in making time to talk to us in situ.

We would also like to thank the many German scholars and curators who generously provided us with a wide array of information regarding the Hanoverian art collections in Lower Saxony as well as German sources, visual and archival material. These include: Dr Ronald Clarke (Herrenhäuser Gärten), Dr Melanie Doderer-Winkler, Dr Christine van der Heuvel (Niedersächsisches Landesarchiv), Dr Jarl Kremeier, Dr Heiko Laß, Count Eric von Platen, Dr Martin Pozsgai (Stiftung Bibliothek Werner Oechslin), Dr Alheidis von Rohr (formerly Historisches Museum, Hanover), Dr Michael Schaich (German Historical Institute, London), Dr Thomas Schwark (Historiches Museum, Hanover), Dr Christian Vogel (Landesmuseum, Hanover) and Countess Angela von Wallwitz.

For their work in preparation for this exhibition and for sharing their insights gained from a close technical examination of the works, we would like to thank Anna Sandén, Simon Bobak, Rupert Featherstone, Mary Kempski, Anna Cooper, Christine Patrick, Jenny Rose and Regine Page.

Finally, we would like to thank our many colleagues within Royal Collection Trust who have worked tirelessly on this project:

CURATORIAL INTERNS Cristina Alfonsin Barriero, Louise Cooling, Helen Ritchie, Adam Sammut, Thomas Smith, and Natalie Voorheis.

EXHIBITIONS Sandra Adler, Hannah Belcher, Roxanna Hacket, Theresa-Mary Morton and Stephen Weber

ROYAL ARCHIVES Pam Clark, Allison Derrett, Jill Kelsey and their colleagues in the Royal Archives.

ROYAL LIBRARY AND PRINT ROOM Irene Campden, Martin Clayton, Alan Donnithorne, Roderick Lane, Lauren Porter, Philippa Räder, Rosie Razzall, Susan Shaw, Kirsten Sierag, Rachael Smith, Kate Stone, Emma Turner, David Westwood and Rhian Wong and Bridget Wright.

PICTURES DEPARTMENT Jeannie Chapel, Lucy Whitaker, Lucy Peter, Jennifer Scott, Nicola Christie, Katelyn Reeves, Tabitha Teuma, Adelaide Izat, Claire Chorley, Karen Ashworth, Michael Field, Stephanie Carlton, Rosanna de Sancha and Al Brewer

WORKS OF ART DEPARTMENT Perry Bruce-Mitford, Jeremy Cheek, Paul Cradock, Steven Davidson, Gary Gronnestad, Simon Metcalf, William Miller, Fiona Norbury, Tim Ritson, Stephen Sheasby, Adrian Smith, Shaun Turner, Nicola Turner Inman, David Wheeler, Jane Wallis and Sophy Wills

PUBLISHING Jacky Colliss Harvey, Paul Holberton, Laura Parker and Elizabeth Simpson

IMAGE LIBRARY Karen Lawson, Daniel Partridge and Eva Zielinska-Millar

Authors

RB	Rufus Bird
WB	Wolf Burchard
EC	Elizabeth Clark
KH	Kate Heard
KJ	Kathryn Jones
JM	Jonathan Marsden
VR	Vanessa Remington
DS-T	Desmond Shawe-Taylor
ES	Emma Stuart

Photographic Credits

All works reproduced are Royal Collection Trust / © HM Queen Elizabeth II 2014 unless indicated otherwise below. Royal Collection Trust is grateful for permission to reproduce the following:

Page 9 © Herzog Anton Ulrich-museum Braunschweig, Kunstmuseum des Landes Niedersachsen Fotonachweis: Museumsfotograf

Pages 9, 33 © Bomann-Museum Celle / Residenzmuseum im Celler Schloss (Foto: Fotostudio Loeper, Celle)

Pages 10, 11 © MLDesign

Pages 14, 15, 301 © Old Royal Naval College (ORN), Greenwich

Pages 42, 55, 90, 209, 320, 380, 398, 399 © The Trustees of the British Museum

Page 54 © Yale Center for British Art, Paul Mellon Collection

Pages 58, 59, 60 © Historisches Museum Hannover

Pages 61, 172, 176, 178, 204, 256 © Historic Royal Palaces

Page 82 © Carlton Hobbs, New York

Pages 185, 208 © The British Library Board. Maps KTOP. 100.9-1, 12270.k.8, 1486.k.1 respectively

Page 87 Courtesy of the Trustees of Sir John Soane's Museum

Page 92 © National Army Museum

Page 168 © The Duke of Buccleuch & Queensberry Collection

Pages 173, 174, 325, 358 © National Portrait Gallery, London

Pages 175, 420 © RIBA Library Drawings & Archives Collections

Page 177 Courtesy of Bard Graduate Center: Decorative Arts, Design History, Material Culture; New York. Photographer: Bruce White

Page 248 By Permission of the Trustees of Dulwich Picture Gallery

Page 259 © Madrid, Museo Nacional del Prado

Page 259 Chris Titmus, Hamilton Kerr Institute, Fitzwilliam Museum, University of Cambridge

Page 260 © RMN-Grand Palais (Musée du Louvre)/Adrien Didierjean

Page 332 © Kulturstiftung des Hauses Hessen, Museum Schloss Fasanerie

Page 384 © Victoria and Albert Museum, London

Page 396 © Shropshire Museums

FRONT COVER William Hogarth (1697–1764), *David Garrick and his wife, Eva-Maria Veigel*, 1757–64, oil on canvas, 132.6 × 104.2 cm, RCIN 405682 (no. 257; detail)

BACK COVER Andrea Boucheron (1701–1761), Paul Crespin (1694–1770) and attributed to Nicholas Sprimont (1716–1771), *The Neptune Centrepiece*, 1741/2, silver gilt, 49.0 × 66.0 × 47.0 cm, RCIN 50282 (no. 313)

ENDPAPERS J.F.C. Schilling (fl. 1769), *Medley drawing with a map of the Battle of Krefeld (1758)*, 1767, pen and ink with watercolour, 50.7 × 71.7 cm (trimmed irregularly), RCIN 732063 (no. 71)

Published 2014 by Royal Collection Trust
York House
St James's Palace
London SW1A 1BQ

Find out more about the Royal Collection and Palaces at
www.royalcollection.org.uk

Subscribe to Royal Collection Trust's e-Newsletter at
www.royalcollection.org.uk/newsletter

ISBN 978 1 905686 79 7
014758

British Library Cataloguing in Publication data:
A catalogue record of this book is available from the British Library.

Designed by LAURA PARKER
Edited by PAUL HOLBERTON
Production by PAUL HOLBERTON PUBLISHING
Colour reproduction and printing in Italy by E-GRAPHIC

Typeset in Farnham
Printed on GardaMatt Art

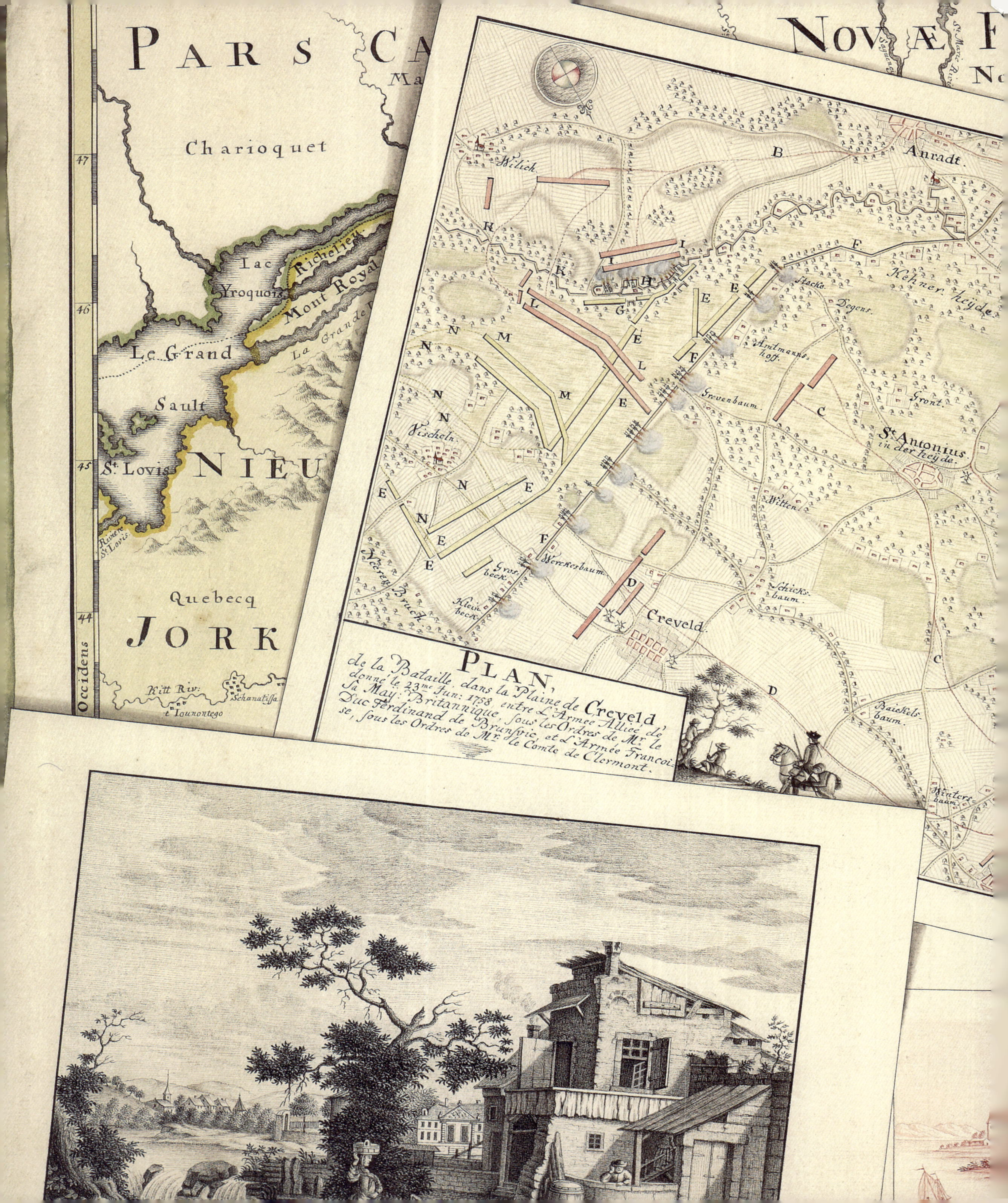

PARS CA
Charioquet
Lac Yroquois
Richelieu
Mont Royal
Le Grand Sault
NIEU
St. Lovis
Quebecq
JORK
Occidens
NOVÆ F
Wilich
Anradt
Kehner heyde
Grevenbaum
St. Antonius in der heyde
Witten
Creveld
PLAN, de la Bataille, dans la Plaine de Creveld donné le 23me Jun: 1758 entre L'Armée Alliée de Sa May.t Britannique, sous les Ordres de Mr. le Duc Ferdinand de Brunsvic, et L'Armée Françoise, sous les Ordres de Mr. le Comte de Clermont.